9th Workshop on Statistical Machine Translation 2014

AA005624

Held at ACL 2014

Baltimore, Maryland, USA
26 – 27 June 2014

ISBN: 978-1-63439-213-6

Printed from e-media with permission by:

Curran Associates, Inc.
57 Morehouse Lane
Red Hook, NY 12571

Some format issues inherent in the e-media version may also appear in this print version.

Printed by Curran Associates, Inc. (2014)

For permission requests, please contact the Association for Computational Linguistics at the address below.

Association for Computational Linguistics
209 N. Eighth Street
Stroudsburg, Pennsylvania 18360

Phone: 1-570-476-8006
Fax: 1-570-476-0860

acl@aclweb.org

Additional copies of this publication are available from:

Curran Associates, Inc.
57 Morehouse Lane
Red Hook, NY 12571 USA
Phone: 845-758-0400
Fax: 845-758-2634
Email: curran@proceedings.com
Web: www.proceedings.com

Introduction

The ACL 2014 Workshop on Statistical Machine Translation (WMT 2014) took place on Thursday and Friday, June 26–27, 2014 in Baltimore, United States, immediately following the Conference of the Association for Computational Linguistics (ACL).

This is the ninth time this workshop has been held. The first time it was held at HLT-NAACL 2006 in New York City, USA. In the following years the Workshop on Statistical Machine Translation was held at ACL 2007 in Prague, Czech Republic, ACL 2008, Columbus, Ohio, USA, EACL 2009 in Athens, Greece, ACL 2010 in Uppsala, Sweden, EMNLP 2011 in Edinburgh, Scotland, NAACL 2012 in Montreal, Canada, and ACL 2013 in Sofia, Bulgaria.

The focus of our workshop was to use parallel corpora for machine translation. Recent experimentation has shown that the performance of SMT systems varies greatly with the source language. In this workshop we encouraged researchers to investigate ways to improve the performance of SMT systems for diverse languages, including morphologically more complex languages, languages with partial free word order, and low-resource languages.

Prior to the workshop, in addition to soliciting relevant papers for review and possible presentation, we conducted four shared tasks: a general translation task, a medical translation task, a quality estimation task, and a task to test automatic evaluation metrics. The medical translation task was introduced this year to address the important issue of domain adaptation within SMT. The results of the shared tasks were announced at the workshop, and these proceedings also include an overview paper for the shared tasks that summarizes the results, as well as provides information about the data used and any procedures that were followed in conducting or scoring the task. In addition, there are short papers from each participating team that describe their underlying system in greater detail.

Like in previous years, we have received a far larger number of submission than we could accept for presentation. This year we have received 27 full paper submissions and 49 shared task submissions. In total WMT 2014 featured 12 full paper oral presentations and 49 shared task poster presentations.

The invited talk was given by Alon Lavie (Carnegie Mellon University and Safaba Translation Solutions, Inc.) entitled "Machine Translation in Academia and in the Commercial World – a Contrastive Perspective".

We would like to thank the members of the Program Committee for their timely reviews. We also would like to thank the participants of the shared task and all the other volunteers who helped with the evaluations.

Ondřej Bojar, Christian Buck, Christian Federmann, Barry Haddow, Philipp Koehn, Matouš Macháček, Christof Monz, Pavel Pecina, Matt Post, Hervé Saint-Amand, Radu Soricut, and Lucia Specia

Co-Organizers

Organizers:

Ondřej Bojar (Charles University Prague)
Christian Buck (University of Edinburgh)
Christian Federmann (Microsoft Research)
Barry Haddow (University of Edinburgh)
Philipp Koehn (University of Edinburgh / Johns Hopkins University)
Matouš Macháček (Charles University Prague)
Christof Monz (University of Amsterdam)
Pavel Pecina (Charles University Prague)
Matt Post (Johns Hopkins University)
Hervé Saint-Amand (University of Edinburgh)
Radu Soricut (Google)
Lucia Specia (University of Sheffield)

Invited Talk:

Alon Lavie (Research Professor at Carnegie Mellon University / Co-founder, President and CTO - Safaba Translation Solutions, Inc.)

Program Committee:

Lars Ahrenberg (Linköping University)
Alexander Allauzen (Université Paris-Sud / LIMSI-CNRS)
Tim Anderson (Air Force Research Laboratory)
Eleftherios Avramidis (German Research Center for Artificial Intelligence)
Wilker Aziz (University of Sheffield)
Daniel Beck (University of Sheffield)
Jose Miguel Benedi (Universitàt Politecnica de València)
Nicola Bertoldi (FBK)
Ergun Bicici (Centre for Next Generation Localisation, Dublin City University)
Alexandra Birch (University of Edinburgh)
Arianna Bisazza (University of Amsterdam)
Graeme Blackwood (IBM Research)
Phil Blunsom (University of Oxford)
Fabienne Braune (University of Stuttgart)
Chris Brockett (Microsoft Research)
Hailong Cao (Harbin Institute of Technology)
Michael Carl (Copenhagen Business School)
Marine Carpuat (National Research Council)
Francisco Casacuberta (Universitat Politécnica de Valéncia)
Daniel Cer (Google)
Boxing Chen (NRC)
Colin Cherry (NRC)
David Chiang (USC/ISI)
Vishal Chowdhary (Microsoft)

Steve DeNeefe (SDL Language Weaver)
Michael Denkowski (Carnegie Mellon University)
Jacob Devlin (Raytheon BBN Technologies)
Markus Dreyer (SDL Language Weaver)
Kevin Duh (Nara Institute of Science and Technology)
Marcello Federico (FBK)
Yang Feng (USC/ISI)
Andrew Finch (NICT)
Mark Fishel (University of Zurich)
José A. R. Fonollosa (Universitat Politècnica de Catalunya)
George Foster (NRC)
Michel Galley (Microsoft Research)
Juri Ganitkevitch (Johns Hopkins University)
Katya Garmash (University of Amsterdam)
Josef van Genabith (Dublin City University)
Ulrich Germann (University of Edinburgh)
Daniel Gildea (University of Rochester)
Kevin Gimpel (Toyota Technological Institute at Chicago)
Jesús González-Rubio (Universitat Politécnica de Valéncia)
Yvette Graham (The University of Melbourne)
Spence Green (Stanford University)
Francisco Guzmán (Qatar Computing Research Institute)
Greg Hanneman (Carnegie Mellon University)
Christian Hardmeier (Uppsala universitet)
Eva Hasler (University of Edinburgh)
Yifan He (New York University)
Kenneth Heafield (Stanford)
John Henderson (MITRE)
Felix Hieber (Heidelberg University)
Hieu Hoang (University of Edinburgh)
Stéphane Huet (UniversitÃ© d'Avignon)
Young-Sook Hwang (SKPlanet)
Gonzalo Iglesias (University of Cambridge)
Ann Irvine (Johns Hopkins University)
Abe Ittycheriah (IBM)
Laura Jehl (Heidelberg University)
Doug Jones (MIT Lincoln Laboratory)
Maxim Khalilov (BMMT)
Alexander Koller (University of Potsdam)
Roland Kuhn (National Research Council of Canada)
Shankar Kumar (Google)
Mathias Lambert (Amazon.com)
Phillippe Langlais (Université de Montréal)
Alon Lavie (Carnegie Mellon University)
Gennadi Lembersky (NICE Systems)
William Lewis (Microsoft Research)
Lemao Liu (The City University of New York)

Qun Liu (Dublin City University)
Wolfgang Macherey (Google)
Saab Mansour (RWTH Aachen University)
José B. Mariño (Universitat Politècnica de Catalunya)
Cettolo Mauro (FBK)
Arne Mauser (Google, Inc)
Jon May (SDL Language Weaver)
Wolfgang Menzel (Hamburg University)
Shachar Mirkin (Xerox Research Centre Europe)
Yusuke Miyao (National Instutite of Informatics)
Dragos Munteanu (SDL Language Technologies)
Markos Mylonakis (Lexis Research)
Lluís Màrquez (Qatar Computing Research Institute)
Preslav Nakov (Qatar Computing Research Institute)
Graham Neubig (Nara Institute of Science and Technology)
Jan Niehues (Karlsruhe Institute of Technology)
Kemal Oflazer (Carnegie Mellon University - Qatar)
Daniel Ortiz-Martínez (Copenhagen Business School)
Stephan Peitz (RWTH Aachen University)
Sergio Penkale (Lingo24)
Maja Popović (DFKI)
Stefan Riezler (Heidelberg University)
Johann Roturier (Symantec)
Raphael Rubino (Prompsit Language Engineering)
Alexander M. Rush (MIT)
Anoop Sarkar (Simon Fraser University)
Hassan Sawaf (eBay Inc.)
Lane Schwartz (Air Force Research Laboratory)
Jean Senellart (SYSTRAN)
Rico Sennrich (University of Zurich)
Kashif Shah (University of Sheffield)
Wade Shen (MIT)
Patrick Simianer (Heidelberg University)
Linfeng Song (ICT/CAS)
Sara Stymne (Uppsala University)
Katsuhito Sudoh (NTT Communication Science Laboratories / Kyoto University)
Felipe Sánchez-Martínez (Universitat d'Alacant)
Jörg Tiedemann (Uppsala University)
Christoph Tillmann (TJ Watson IBM Research)
Antonio Toral (Dublin City Unversity)
Hajime Tsukada (NTT Communication Science Laboratories)
Yulia Tsvetkov (Carnegie Mellon University)
Dan Tufiş (Research Institute for Artificial Intelligence, Romanian Academy)
Marco Turchi (Fondazione Bruno Kessler)
Ferhan Ture (University of Maryland)
Masao Utiyama (NICT)
Ashish Vaswani (University of Southern California Information Sciences Institute)

David Vilar (Pixformance GmbH)
Stephan Vogel (Qatar Computing Research Institute)
Haifeng Wang (Baidu)
Taro Watanabe (NICT)
Marion Weller (Universität Stuttgart)
Philip Williams (University of Edinburgh)
Guillaume Wisniewski (Univ. Paris Sud and LIMSI-CNRS)
Hua Wu (Baidu)
Joern Wuebker (RWTH Aachen University)
Peng Xu (Google Inc.)
Wenduan Xu (Cambridge University)
François Yvon (LIMSI/CNRS)
Richard Zens (Google)
Hao Zhang (Google)
Liu Zhanyi (Baidu)

Table of Contents

Workshop Program

Thursday, June 26, 2014

9:00–9:10 Opening Remarks

Session 1: Shared Translation Tasks

9:10–9:30 *Efficient Elicitation of Annotations for Human Evaluation of Machine Translation*
Keisuke Sakaguchi, Matt Post and Benjamin Van Durme

9:30–10:00 *Findings of the 2014 Workshop on Statistical Machine Translation*
Ondrej Bojar, Christian Buck, Christian Federmann, Barry Haddow, Philipp Koehn, Johannes Leveling, Christof Monz, Pavel Pecina, Matt Post, Herve Saint-Amand, Radu Soricut, Lucia Specia and Aleš Tamchyna

10:00-10:30 Panel Discussion

10:30–11:00 Coffee

Session 2: Poster Session

11:00-12:30 Shared Task: Translation

Parallel FDA5 for Fast Deployment of Accurate Statistical Machine Translation Systems
Ergun Bicici, Qun Liu and Andy Way

Yandex School of Data Analysis Russian-English Machine Translation System for WMT14
Alexey Borisov and Irina Galinskaya

CimS – The CIS and IMS joint submission to WMT 2014 translating from English into German
Fabienne Cap, Marion Weller, Anita Ramm and Alexander Fraser

English-to-Hindi system description for WMT 2014: Deep Source-Context Features for Moses
Marta R. Costa-jussà, Parth Gupta, Paolo Rosso and Rafael E. Banchs

The KIT-LIMSI Translation System for WMT 2014
Quoc Khanh Do, Teresa Herrmann, Jan Niehues, Alexander Allauzen, François Yvon and Alex Waibel

The IIT Bombay Hindi-English Translation System at WMT 2014
Piyush Dungarwal, Rajen Chatterjee, Abhijit Mishra, Anoop Kunchukuttan, Ritesh Shah and Pushpak Bhattacharyya

Thursday, June 26, 2014 (continued)

Thursday, June 26, 2014 (continued)

Machine Translation and Monolingual Postediting: The AFRL WMT-14 System
Lane Schwartz, Timothy Anderson, Jeremy Gwinnup and Katherine Young

CUNI in WMT14: Chimera Still Awaits Bellerophon
Aleš Tamchyna, Martin Popel, Rudolf Rosa and Ondrej Bojar

Manawi: Using Multi-Word Expressions and Named Entities to Improve Machine Translation
Liling Tan and Santanu Pal

Edinburgh's Syntax-Based Systems at WMT 2014
Philip Williams, Rico Sennrich, Maria Nadejde, Matthias Huck, Eva Hasler and Philipp Koehn

DCU-Lingo24 Participation in WMT 2014 Hindi-English Translation task
Xiaofeng Wu, Rejwanul Haque, Tsuyoshi Okita, Piyush Arora, Andy Way and Qun Liu

11:00-12:30 Shared Task: Medical Translation

Machine Translation of Medical Texts in the Khresmoi Project
Ondřej Dušek, Jan Hajič, Jaroslava Hlaváčová, Michal Novák, Pavel Pecina, Rudolf Rosa, Aleš Tamchyna, Zdeňka Urešová and Daniel Zeman

Postech's System Description for Medical Text Translation Task
Jianri Li, Se-Jong Kim, Hwidong Na and Jong-Hyeok Lee

Domain Adaptation for Medical Text Translation using Web Resources
Yi Lu, Longyue Wang, Derek F. Wong, Lidia S. Chao and Yiming Wang

DCU Terminology Translation System for Medical Query Subtask at WMT14
Tsuyoshi Okita, Ali Vahid, Andy Way and Qun Liu

LIMSI @ WMT'14 Medical Translation Task
Nicolas Pécheux, Li Gong, Quoc Khanh Do, Benjamin Marie, Yulia Ivanishcheva, Alexander Allauzen, Thomas Lavergne, Jan Niehues, Aurélien Max and François Yvon

Combining Domain Adaptation Approaches for Medical Text Translation
Longyue Wang, Yi Lu, Derek F. Wong, Lidia S. Chao, Yiming Wang and Francisco Oliveira

Experiments in Medical Translation Shared Task at WMT 2014
Jian Zhang

Thursday, June 26, 2014 (continued)

12:30–14:00 Lunch

Session 3: Invited Talk

14:00-15:30 *Machine Translation in Academia and in the Commercial World – a Contrastive Perspective.* Alon Lavie, Research Professor – Carnegie Mellon University, Co-founder, President and CTO – Safaba Translation Solutions, Inc.

15:30–16:00 Coffee

Session 4: Evaluation

16:00–16:20 *Randomized Significance Tests in Machine Translation*
Yvette Graham, Nitika Mathur and Timothy Baldwin

16:20–16:40 *Estimating Word Alignment Quality for SMT Reordering Tasks*
Sara Stymne, Jörg Tiedemann and Joakim Nivre

16:40–17:00 *Dependency-based Automatic Enumeration of Semantically Equivalent Word Orders for Evaluating Japanese Translations*
Hideki Isozaki, Natsume Kouchi and Tsutomu Hirao

Friday, June 27, 2014

Session 5: Shared Evaluation Metrics and Quality Estimation Tasks

9:00–9:30 Quality Estimation Shared Task

9:30–9:50 *Results of the WMT14 Metrics Shared Task*
Matous Machacek and Ondrej Bojar

9:50–10:30 Panel

10:30–11:00 Coffee

Friday, June 27, 2014 (continued)

Session 6: Poster Session

Friday, June 27, 2014 (continued)

VERTa participation in the WMT14 Metrics Task
Elisabet Comelles and Jordi Atserias

Meteor Universal: Language Specific Translation Evaluation for Any Target Language
Michael Denkowski and Alon Lavie

Application of Prize based on Sentence Length in Chunk-based Automatic Evaluation of Machine Translation
Hiroshi Echizen'ya, Kenji Araki and Eduard Hovy

LAYERED: Metric for Machine Translation Evaluation
Shubham Gautam and Pushpak Bhattacharyya

IPA and STOUT: Leveraging Linguistic and Source-based Features for Machine Translation Evaluation
Meritxell Gonzàlez, Alberto Barrón-Cedeño and Lluís Màrquez

DiscoTK: Using Discourse Structure for Machine Translation Evaluation
Shafiq Joty, Francisco Guzmán, Lluís Màrquez and Preslav Nakov

Tolerant BLEU: a Submission to the WMT14 Metrics Task
Jindřich Libovický and Pavel Pecina

BEER: BEtter Evaluation as Ranking
Milos Stanojevic and Khalil Sima'an

RED, The DCU-CASICT Submission of Metrics Tasks
Xiaofeng Wu, Hui Yu and Qun Liu

12:30–14:00 Lunch

Friday, June 27, 2014 (continued)

Session 7: Data and Adaptation

14:00–14:20 *Crowdsourcing High-Quality Parallel Data Extraction from Twitter*
Wang Ling, Luis Marujo, Chris Dyer, Alan W Black and Isabel Trancoso

14:20–14:40 *Using Comparable Corpora to Adapt MT Models to New Domains*
Ann Irvine and Chris Callison-Burch

14:40–15:00 *Dynamic Topic Adaptation for SMT using Distributional Profiles*
Eva Hasler, Barry Haddow and Philipp Koehn

15:00–15:20 *Unsupervised Adaptation for Statistical Machine Translation*
Saab Mansour and Hermann Ney

15:20–16:00 Coffee

Session 8: Translation Models

16:00–16:20 *An Empirical Comparison of Features and Tuning for Phrase-based Machine Translation*
Spence Green, Daniel Cer and Christopher Manning

16:20–16:40 *Bayesian Reordering Model with Feature Selection*
Abdullah Alrajeh and Mahesan Niranjan

16:40–17:00 *Augmenting String-to-Tree and Tree-to-String Translation with Non-Syntactic Phrases*
Matthias Huck, Hieu Hoang and Philipp Koehn

17:00–17:20 *Linear Mixture Models for Robust Machine Translation*
Marine Carpuat, Cyril Goutte and George Foster

Efficient Elicitation of Annotations for Human Evaluation of Machine Translation

Keisuke Sakaguchi*, **Matt Post**†, **Benjamin Van Durme**†
* Center for Language and Speech Processing
† Human Language Technology Center of Excellence
Johns Hopkins University, Baltimore, Maryland
{keisuke,post,vandurme}@cs.jhu.edu

Abstract

A main output of the annual Workshop on Statistical Machine Translation (WMT) is a ranking of the systems that participated in its shared translation tasks, produced by aggregating pairwise sentence-level comparisons collected from human judges. Over the past few years, there have been a number of tweaks to the aggregation formula in attempts to address issues arising from the inherent ambiguity and subjectivity of the task, as well as weaknesses in the proposed models and the manner of model selection.

We continue this line of work by adapting the TrueSkill™ algorithm — an online approach for modeling the relative skills of players in ongoing competitions, such as Microsoft's Xbox Live — to the human evaluation of machine translation output. Our experimental results show that TrueSkill outperforms other recently proposed models on accuracy, and also can significantly reduce the number of pairwise annotations that need to be collected by sampling non-uniformly from the space of system competitions.

1 Introduction

The Workshop on Statistical Machine Translation (WMT) has long been a central event in the machine translation (MT) community for the evaluation of MT output. It hosts an annual set of shared translation tasks focused mostly on the translation of western European languages. One of its main functions is to publish a ranking of the systems for each task, which are produced by aggregating a large number of human judgments of sentence-level pairwise rankings of system outputs. While the performance on many automatic metrics is also reported (e.g., BLEU (Papineni et al., 2002)), the human evaluation is considered primary, and is in fact used as the gold standard for its metrics task, where evaluation metrics are evaluated.

#	score	range	system
1	0.638	1	UEDIN-HEAFIELD
2	0.604	2-3	UEDIN
	0.591	2-3	ONLINE-B
4	0.571	4-5	LIMSI-SOUL
	0.562	4-5	KIT
	0.541	5-6	ONLINE-A
7	0.512	7	MES-SIMPLIFIED
8	0.486	8	DCU
9	0.439	9-10	RWTH
	0.429	9-11	CMU-T2T
	0.420	10-11	CU-ZEMAN
12	0.389	12	JHU
13	0.322	13	SHEF-WPROA

Table 1: System rankings presented as clusters (WMT13 French-English competition). The *score* column is the percentage of time each system was judged better across its comparisons (§2.1).

In machine translation, the longstanding disagreements about evaluation measures do not go away when moving from automatic metrics to human judges. This is due in no small part to the inherent ambiguity and subjectivity of the task, but also arises from the particular way that the WMT organizers produce the rankings. The system-level rankings are produced by collecting pairwise sentence-level comparisons between system outputs. These are then aggregated to produce a complete ordering of all systems, or, more recently, a partial ordering (Koehn, 2012), with systems clustered where they cannot be distinguished in a statistically significant way (Table 1, taken from Bojar et al. (2013)).

A number of problems have been noted with this approach. The first has to do with the nature of ranking itself. Over the past few years, the WMT organizers have introduced a number of minor tweaks to the ranking algorithm (§2) in reaction to largely intuitive arguments that have been

Proceedings of the Ninth Workshop on Statistical Machine Translation, pages 1–11,
Baltimore, Maryland USA, June 26–27, 2014. ©2014 Association for Computational Linguistics

raised about how the evaluation is conducted (Bojar et al., 2011; Lopez, 2012). While these tweaks have been sensible (and later corroborated), Hopkins and May (2013) point out that this is essentially a model selection task, and should properly be driven by empirical performance on held-out data according to some metric. Instead of intuition, they suggest perplexity, and show that a novel graphical model outperforms existing approaches on that metric, with less amount of data.

A second problem is the deficiency of the models used to produce the ranking, which work by computing simple ratios of wins (and, optionally, ties) to losses. Such approaches do not consider the relative difficulty of system matchups, and thus leave open the possibility that a system is ranked highly from the luck of comparisons against poorer opponents.

Third, a large number of judgments need to be collected in order to separate the systems into clusters to produce a partial ranking. The sheer size of the space of possible comparisons (all pairs of systems times the number of segments in the test set) requires sampling from this space and distributing the annotations across a number of judges. Even still, the number of judgments needed to produce statistically significant rankings like those in Table 1 grows quadratically in the number of participating systems (Koehn, 2012), often forcing the use of paid, lower-quality annotators hired on Amazon's Mechanical Turk. Part of the problem is that the sampling strategy collects data uniformly across system pairings. Intuitively, we should need many fewer annotations between systems with divergent base performance levels, instead focusing the collection effort on system pairs whose performance is more matched, in order to tease out the gaps between similarly-performing systems. Why spend precious human time on redundantly affirming predictable outcomes?

To address these issues, we developed a variation of the TrueSkill model (Herbrich et al., 2006), an adaptative model of competitions originally developed for the Xbox Live online gaming community. It assumes that each player's skill level follows a Gaussian distribution $\mathcal{N}(\mu, \sigma^2)$, in which μ represents a player's mean performance, and σ^2 the system's uncertainty about its current estimate of this mean. These values are updated after each "game" (in our case, the value of a ternary judgment) in proportion to how surprising the outcome is. TrueSkill has been adapted to a number of areas, including chess, advertising, and academic conference management.

The rest of this paper provides an empirical comparison of a number of models of human evaluation (§2). We evaluate on perplexity and also on accuracy, showing that the two are not always correlated, and arguing for the primacy of the latter (§3). We find that TrueSkill outperforms other models (§4). Moreover, TrueSkill also allows us to drastically reduce the amount of data that needs to be collected by sampling non-uniformly from the space of all competitions (§5), which also allows for greater separation of the systems into ranked clusters (§6).

2 Models

Before introducing our adaptation of the TrueSkill model for ranking translation systems with human judgments (§2.3), we describe two comparisons: the "Expected Wins" model used in recent evaluations, and the Bayesian model proposed by Hopkins and May (§2.2).

As we described briefly in the introduction, WMT produces system rankings by aggregating sentence-level ternary judgments of the form:

$$(i, S_1, S_2, \pi)$$

where i is the source segment (id), S_1 and S_2 are the system pair drawn from a set of systems $\{S\}$, and $\pi \in \{<, >, =\}$ denotes whether the first system was judged to be better than, worse than, or equivalent to the second. These ternary judgments are obtained by presenting judges with a randomly-selected input sentence and the reference, followed by *five* randomly-selected translations of that sentence. Annotators are asked to rank these systems from best (rank 1) to worst (rank 5), ties permitted, and with no meaning ascribed to the absolute values or differences between ranks. This is done to accelerate data collection, since it yields ten pairwise comparisons per ranking. Tens of thousands of judgments of this form constitute the raw data used to compute the system-level rankings. All the work described in this section is computed over these pairwise comparisons, which are treated as if they were collected independently.

2.1 Expected Wins

The "Expected Wins" model computes the percentage of times that each system wins in its pairwise comparisons. Let A be the complete set of annotations or judgments of the form $\{i, S_1, S_2, \pi_R\}$. We assume these judgments have been converted into a normal form where S_1 is either the winner or is tied with S_2, and therefore $\pi_R \in \{<, =\}$. Let $\delta(x, y)$ be the Kronecker delta function.[1] We then define the function:

$$\text{wins}(S_i, S_j) = \sum_{n=1}^{|A|} \delta(S_i, S_1^{(n)})\delta(S_j, S_2^{(n)})\delta(\pi_R^{(n)}, <)$$

which counts the number of annotations for which system S_i was ranked better than system S_j. We define a single-variable version that marginalizes over all annotations:

$$\text{wins}(S_i) = \sum_{S_j \neq S_i} \text{wins}(S_i, S_j)$$

We also define analogous functions for *loses* and *ties*. Until the WMT11 evaluation (Callison-Burch et al., 2011), the score for each system S_i was computed as follows:

$$\text{score}(S_i) = \frac{\text{wins}(S_i) + \text{ties}(S_i)}{\text{wins}(S_i) + \text{ties}(S_i) + \text{loses}(S_i)}$$

Bojar et al. (2011) suggested that the inclusion of ties biased the results, due to their large numbers, the underlying similarity of many of the models, and the fact that they are counted for both systems in the tie, and proposed the following modified scoring function:

$$\text{score}(S_i) = \frac{1}{|\{S\}|} \sum_{S_j \neq S_i} \frac{\text{wins}(S_i, S_j)}{\text{wins}(S_i, S_j) + \text{wins}(S_j, S_i)}$$

This metric computes an average relative frequency of wins, excluding ties, and was used in WMT12 and WMT13 (Callison-Burch et al., 2012; Bojar et al., 2013).

The decision to exclude ties isn't without its problems; for example, an evaluation where two systems are nearly always judged equivalent should be relevant in producing the final ranking of systems. Furthermore, as Hopkins and May (2013) point out, throwing out data to avoid biasing a model suggests a problem with the model. We now turn to a description of their model, which addresses these problems.

[1] $\delta(x, y) = \begin{cases} 1 & \text{if } x = y \\ 0 & \text{o.w.} \end{cases}$

2.2 The Hopkins and May (2013) model

Recent papers (Koehn, 2012; Hopkins and May, 2013) have proposed models focused on the *relative ability* of the competition systems. These approaches assume that each system has a mean quality represented by a Gaussian distribution with a fixed variance shared across all systems. In the graphical model formulation of Hopkins and May (2013), the pairwise judgments (i, S_1, S_2, π) are imagined to have been generated according to the following process:

- Select a source sentence i
- Select two systems S_1 and S_2. A system S_j is associated with a Gaussian distribution $\mathcal{N}(\mu_{S_j}, \sigma_a^2)$, samples from which represent the quality of translations
- Draw two "translations", adding random Gaussian noise with variance σ_{obs}^2 to simulate the subjectivity of the task and the differences among annotators:

$$q_1 \sim \mathcal{N}(\mu_{S_1}, \sigma_a^2) + \mathcal{N}(0, \sigma_{obs}^2)$$
$$q_2 \sim \mathcal{N}(\mu_{S_2}, \sigma_a^2) + \mathcal{N}(0, \sigma_{obs}^2)$$

- Let d be a nonzero real number that defines a fixed decision radius. Produce a rating π according to:[2]

$$\pi = \begin{cases} < & q_1 - q_2 > d \\ > & q_2 - q_1 > d \\ = & \text{otherwise} \end{cases}$$

The task is to then infer the posterior parameters, given the data: the system means μ_{S_j} and, by necessity, the latent values $\{q_i\}$ for each of the pairwise comparison training instances. Hopkins and May do not publish code or describe details of this algorithm beyond mentioning Gibbs sampling, so we used our own implementation,[3] and describe it here for completeness.

After initialization, we have training instances of the form $(i, S_1, S_2, \pi_R, q_1, q_2)$, where all but the q_i are observed. At a high level, the sampler iterates over the training data, inferring values of q_1 and q_2 for each annotation together in a single step of the sampler from the current values of the systems means, $\{\mu_j\}$.[4] At the end of each iteration,

[2] Note that better systems have *higher* relative abilities $\{\mu_{S_j}\}$. Better translations subsequently have on-average higher values $\{q_i\}$, which translate into a *lower* ranking π.

[3] `github.com/keisks/wmt-trueskill`

[4] This worked better than a version of the sampler that changed one at a time.

these means are then recomputed by re-averaging all values of $\{q_i\}$ associated with that system. After the burn-in period, the μs are stored as samples, which are averaged when the sampling concludes.

During each iteration, q_1 and q_2 are resampled from their corresponding system means:

$$q_1 \sim \mathcal{N}(\mu_{S_1}, \sigma_a^2)$$
$$q_2 \sim \mathcal{N}(\mu_{S_2}, \sigma_a^2)$$

We then update these values to respect the annotation π as follows. Let $t = q_1 - q_2$ (S_1 is the winner by human judgments), and ensure that the values are outside the decision radius, d:

$$q_1' = \begin{cases} q_1 & t \geq d \\ q_1 + \frac{1}{2}(d - t) & \text{otherwise} \end{cases}$$

$$q_2' = \begin{cases} q_2 & t \geq d \\ q_2 - \frac{1}{2}(d - t) & \text{otherwise} \end{cases}$$

In the case of a tie:

$$q_1' = \begin{cases} q_1 + \frac{1}{2}(d - t) & t \geq d \\ q_1 & t < d \\ q_1 + \frac{1}{2}(-d - t) & t \leq -d \end{cases}$$

$$q_2' = \begin{cases} q_2 - \frac{1}{2}(d - t) & t \geq d \\ q_2 & t < d \\ q_2 - \frac{1}{2}(-d - t) & t \leq -d \end{cases}$$

These values are stored for the current iteration and averaged at its end to produce new estimates of the system means. The quantity $d - t$ can be interpreted as a *loss function*, returning a high value when the observed outcome is unexpected and a low value otherwise (Figure 1).

2.3 TrueSkill

Prior to 2012, the WMT organizers included reference translations among the system comparisons. These were used as a control against which the evaluators could be measured for consistency, on the assumption that the reference was almost always best. They were also included as data points in computing the system ranking. Another of Bojar et al. (2011)'s suggestions was to exclude this data, because systems compared more often against the references suffered unfairly. This can be further generalized to the observation that not all competitions are equal, and a good model should incorporate some notion of "match difficulty" when evaluating system's abilities. The inference procedure above incorporates this notion implicitly in the inference procedure, but the model itself does not include a notion of match difficulty or outcome surprisal.

A model that does is TrueSkill[5] (Herbrich et al., 2006). TrueSkill is an adaptive, online system that also assumes that each system's skill level follows a Gaussian distribution, maintaining a mean μ_{S_j} for each system S_j representing its current estimate of that system's native ability. However, it also maintains a per-system variance, $\sigma_{S_j}^2$, which represents TrueSkill's uncertainty about its estimate of each mean. After an outcome is observed (a game in which the result is a win, loss, or draw), the size of the updates is proportional to how surprising the outcome was, which is computed from the current system means and variances. If a translation from a system with a high mean is judged better than a system with a greatly lower mean, the result is not surprising, and the update size for the corresponding system means will be small. On the other hand, when an upset occurs in a competition, the means will receive larger updates.

Before defining the update equations, we need to be more concrete about how this notion of surprisal is incorporated. Let $t = \mu_{S_1} - \mu_{S_2}$, the difference in system relative abilities, and let ϵ be a fixed hyper-parameter corresponding to the earlier decision radius. We then define two loss functions of this difference for wins and for ties:

$$v_{\text{win}}(t, \epsilon) = \frac{\mathcal{N}(-\epsilon + t)}{\Phi(-\epsilon + t)}$$
$$v_{\text{tie}}(t, \epsilon) = \frac{\mathcal{N}(-\epsilon - t) - \mathcal{N}(\epsilon - t)}{\Phi(\epsilon - t) - \Phi(-\epsilon - t)}$$

where $\Phi(x)$ is the cumulative distribution function and the $\mathcal{N}$s are Gaussians. Figures 1 and 2 display plots of these two functions compared to the Hopkins and May model. Note how v_{win} (Figure 1) increases exponentially as μ_{S_2} becomes greater than the (purportedly) better system, μ_{S_1}.

As noted above, TrueSkill maintains not only estimates $\{\mu_{S_j}\}$ of system abilities, but also system-specific confidences about those estimates

[5]The goal of this section is to provide an intuitive description of TrueSkill as adapted for WMT manual evaluations, with enough detail to carry the main ideas. For more details, please see Herbrich et al. (2006).

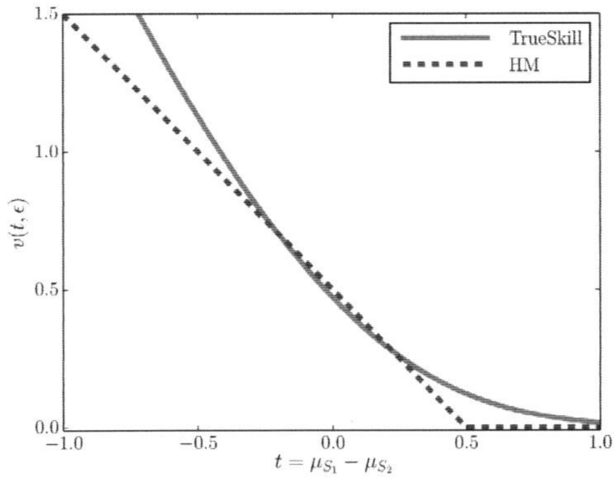

Figure 1: TrueSkill's v_{win} and the corresponding *loss function* in the Hopkins and May model as a function of the difference t of system means ($\epsilon = 0.5, c = 0.8$ for TrueSkill, and $d = 0.5$ for Hopkins and May model).

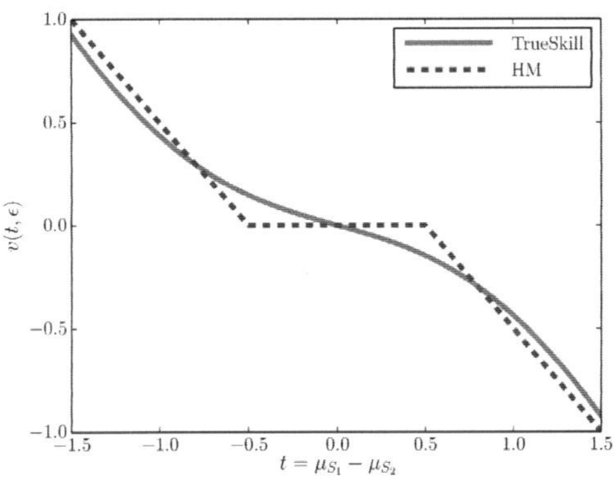

Figure 2: TrueSkills v_{tie} and the corresponding *loss function* in the Hopkins and May model as a function of the difference t of system means ($\epsilon = 0.5, c = 0.3$, and $d = 0.5$).

$\{\sigma_{S_j}\}$. These confidences also factor into the updates: while surprising outcomes result in larger updates to system means, higher confidences (represented by smaller variances) result in *smaller* updates. TrueSkill defines the following value:

$$c^2 = 2\beta^2 + \sigma_{S_1}^2 + \sigma_{S_2}^2$$

which accumulates the variances along β, another free parameter. We can now define the update equations for the system means:

$$\mu_{S_1} = \mu_{S_1} + \frac{\sigma_{S_1}^2}{c} \cdot v\left(\frac{t}{c}, \frac{\epsilon}{c}\right)$$

$$\mu_{S_2} = \mu_{S_2} - \frac{\sigma_{S_2}^2}{c} \cdot v\left(\frac{t}{c}, \frac{\epsilon}{c}\right)$$

The second term in these equations captures the idea about balancing surprisal with confidence, described above.

In order to update the system-level confidences, TrueSkill defines another set of functions, w, for the cases of wins and ties. These functions are multiplicative factors that affect the amount of change in σ^2:

$$w_{\text{win}}(t, \epsilon) = v_{\text{win}} \cdot (v_{\text{win}} + t - \epsilon)$$

$$w_{\text{tie}}(t, \epsilon) = v_{\text{tie}} + \frac{(\epsilon - t) \cdot \mathcal{N}(\epsilon - t) + (\epsilon + t) \cdot \mathcal{N}(\epsilon + t)}{\Phi(\epsilon - t) - \Phi(-\epsilon - t)}$$

The underlying idea is that these functions capture the outcome surprisal via v. This update always decreases the size of the variances σ^2, which means uncertainty of μ decreases as comparisons go on. With these defined, we can conclude by defining the updates for $\sigma_{S_1}^2$ and $\sigma_{S_2}^2$:

$$\sigma_{S_1}^2 = \sigma_{S_1}^2 \cdot \left[1 - \frac{\sigma_{S_1}^2}{c^2} \cdot w\left(\frac{t}{c}, \frac{\epsilon}{c}\right)\right]$$

$$\sigma_{S_2}^2 = \sigma_{S_2}^2 \cdot \left[1 - \frac{\sigma_{S_2}^2}{c^2} \cdot w\left(\frac{t}{c}, \frac{\epsilon}{c}\right)\right]$$

One final complication not presented here but relevant to adapting TrueSkill to the WMT setting: the parameter β and another parameter (not discussed) τ are incorporated into the update equations to give more weight to recent matches. This "latest-oriented" property is useful in the gaming setting for which TrueSkill was built, where players improve over time, but is not applicable in the WMT competition setting. To cancel this property in TrueSkill, we set $\tau = 0$ and $\beta = 0.025 \cdot |A| \cdot \sigma^2$ in order to lessen the impact of the order in which annotations are presented to the system.

2.4 Data selection with TrueSkill

A drawback of the standard WMT data collection method is that it samples uniformly from the space of pairwise system combinations. This is undesirable: systems with vastly divergent relative ability need not be compared as often as systems that are more evenly matched. Unfortunately, one cannot sample non-uniformly without knowing ahead of time which systems are better. TrueSkill provides a solution to this dilemma with its *match-selection* ability: systems with similar means and low variances can be confidently considered to be close matches. This presents a strong possibility of reducing the amount of data that needs to be collected in the WMT competitions. In fact, the TrueSkill formulation provides a way to compute the probability of a draw between two systems, which can be used to compute for a system S_i a conditional distribution over matches with other systems $\{S_{j\neq i}\}$.

Formally, in the TrueSkill model, the *match-selection* (chance to draw) between two players (systems in WMT) is computed as follows:

$$p_{\text{draw}} = \sqrt{\frac{2\beta^2}{c^2}} \cdot \exp(-\frac{(\mu_a - \mu_b)^2}{2c^2})$$

However, our setting for canceling the "latest-oriented" property affects this matching quality equation, where most systems are almost equally competitive (≈ 1). Therefore, we modify the equation in the following manner which simply depends on the difference of μ.

$$\hat{p}_{\text{draw}} = \frac{1}{\exp(|\mu_a - \mu_b|)}$$

TrueSkill selects the matches it would like to create, according to this selection criteria. We do this according to the following process:

1. Select a system S_1 (e.g., the one with the highest variance)
2. Compute a normalized distribution over matches with other systems pairs $\hat{p}_{\text{draw}}$
3. Draw a system S_2 from this distribution
4. Draw a source sentence, and present to the judge for annotation

3 Experimental setup

3.1 Datasets

We used the evaluation data released by WMT13.[6] The data contains (1) five-way system rankings made by either researchers or Turkers and (2) translation data consisting of source sentences, human reference translations, and submitted translations. Data exists for 10 language pairs. More details about the dataset can be found in the WMT 2013 overview paper (Bojar et al., 2013).

Each five-way system ranking was converted into ten pairwise judgments (§2). We trained the models using randomly selected sets of 400, 800, 1,600, 3,200, and 6,400 pairwise comparisons, each produced in two ways: selecting from all researchers, or split between researchers and Turkers. An important note is that the training data differs according to the model. For the Expected Wins and Hopkins and May model, we simply sample uniformly at random. The TrueSkill model, however, selects its own training data (with replacement) according to the description in Section 2.4.[7]

For tuning hyperparameters and reporting test results, we used development and test sets of 2,000 comparisons drawn entirely from the researcher judgments, and fixed across all experiments.

3.2 Perplexity

We first compare the Hopkins and May model and TrueSkill using perplexity on the test data T, computed as follows:

$$\text{ppl}(p|T) = 2^{-\sum_{(i,S_1,S_2,\pi)\in T} \log_2 p(\pi|S_1,S_2)}$$

where p is the model under consideration. The probability of each observed outcome π between two systems S_1 and S_2 is computed by taking a difference of the Gaussian distributions associated with those systems:

$$\begin{aligned}\mathcal{N}(\mu_\delta, \sigma_\delta^2) &= \mathcal{N}(\mu_{S_1}, \sigma_{S_1}^2) - \mathcal{N}(\mu_{S_2}, \sigma_{S_2}^2) \\ &= \mathcal{N}(\mu_{S_1} - \mu_{S_2}, \sigma_{S_1}^2 + \sigma_{S_2}^2)\end{aligned}$$

This Gaussian can then be carved into three pieces: the area where S_1 loses, the middle area representing ties (defined by a decision radius, r, whose value is fit using development data), and a third area representing where S_1 wins. By integrating over each of these regions, we have a probability distribution over these outcomes:

$$p(\pi \mid S_1, S_2) = \begin{cases} \int_{-\infty}^{0} \mathcal{N}(\mu_\delta, \sigma_\delta^2) & \text{if } \pi \text{ is } > \\ \int_{0}^{r} \mathcal{N}(\mu_\delta, \sigma_\delta^2) & \text{if } \pi \text{ is } = \\ \int_{r}^{\infty} \mathcal{N}(\mu_\delta, \sigma_\delta^2) & \text{if } \pi \text{ is } < \end{cases}$$

We do not compute perplexity for the Expected Wins model, which does not put any probability mass on ties.

[6] statmt.org/wmt13/results.html

[7] We use a Python implementation of TrueSkill (github.com/sublee/trueskill).

3.3 Accuracy

Perplexity is often viewed as a neutral metric, but without access to unbounded training data or the true model parameters, it can only be approximated. Furthermore, it does not always correlate perfectly with evaluation metrics. As such, we also present accuracy results, measuring each model's ability to predict the values of the ternary pairwise judgments made by the annotators. These are computed using the above equation, picking the highest value of $p(\pi)$ for all annotations between each system pair (S_i, S_j). As with perplexity, we emphasize that these predictions are functions of the system pair only, and not the individual sentences under consideration, so the same outcome is always predicted for all sentences between a system pair.

3.4 Parameter Tuning

We follow the settings described in Hopkins and May (2013) for their model: $\sigma_a = 0.5, \sigma_{\text{obs}} = 1.0$, and $d = 0.5$. In TrueSkill, in accordance with the Hopkins and May model, we set the initial μ and σ values for each system to 0 and 0.5 respectively, and ϵ to 0.25.

For test data, we tuned the "decision radius" parameter r by doing grid search over $\{0.001, 0.01, 0.1, 0.3, 0.5\}$, searching for the value which minimized perplexity and maximized accuracy on the development set. We do this for each model and language pair. When tuned by perplexity, r is typically either 0.3 or 0.5 for both models and language pairs, whereas, for accuracy, the best r is either 0.001, 0.01, or 0.1.

4 Results

4.1 Model Comparison

Figure 3 shows the perplexity of the two models with regard to the number of training comparisons. The perplexities in the figure are averaged over all ten language pairs in the WMT13 dataset. Overall, perplexities decrease according to the increase of training size. The Hopkins and May and TrueSkill models trained on both researcher and Turker judgments are comparable, whereas the Hopkins and May model trained on researcher judgments alone shows lower perplexity than the corresponding TrueSkill model.

In terms of accuracy, we see that the TrueSkill model has the highest accuracies, saturating at just over 3,000 training instances (Figure 4). TrueSkill

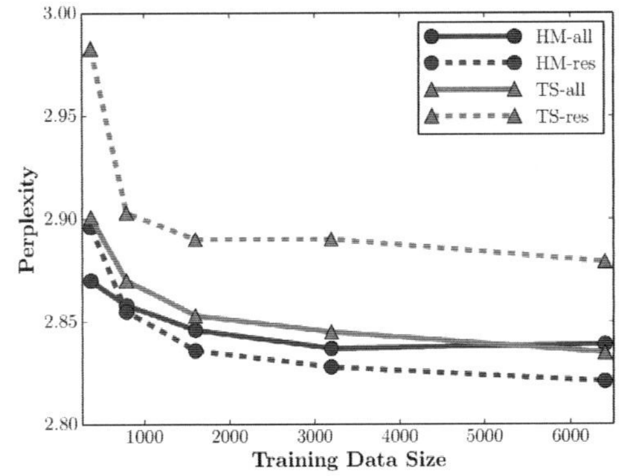

Figure 3: Model Perplexities for WMT13 dataset. 'all' indicates that models are trained on both researcher and Turker judgements, and 'res' means that models are trained on only researcher judgements.

outperforms Expected Win and the Hopkins and May, especially when the training size is small (Table 2). We also note that training on researcher judgments alone (dashed lines) results in better performance than training on both researchers and Turker judgments. This likely reflects both a better match between training and test data (recall the test data consists of researcher judgments only), as well as the higher consistency of this data, as evidenced by the annotator agreement scores published in the WMT overview paper (Bojar et al., 2013). Recall that the models only have access to the system pair (and not the sentences themselves), and thus make the same prediction for π for a particular system pair, regardless of which source sentence was selected. As an upper bound for performance on this metric, Table 2 contains an oracle score, which is computed by selecting, for each pair of systems, the highest-probability ranking.[8]

Comparing the plots, we see there is not a perfect relationship between perplexity and accuracy among the models; the low perplexity does not mean the high accuracy, and in fact the order of the systems is different.

4.2 Free-for-all matches

TrueSkill need not deal with judgments in pairs only, but was in fact designed to be used in a variety of settings, including N-way free-for-all games

[8]Note that this might not represent a consistent ranking among systems, but is itself an upper bound on the highest-scoring consistent ranking.

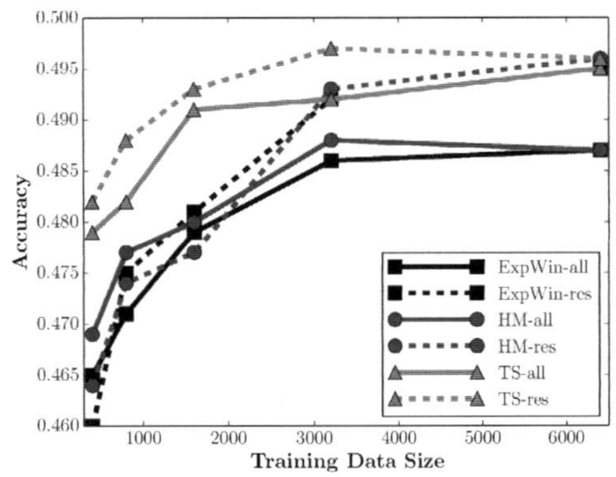

Figure 4: Model accuracies with different training domain for WMT13 dataset.

Train Size		Exp-Win	HM	TrueSkill
	400	0.465	0.471	**0.479**
	800	0.471	0.475	**0.483**
all	1600	0.479	0.477	**0.493**
	3200	0.486	0.489	**0.493**
	6400	0.487	0.490	**0.495**
	400	0.460	0.463	**0.484**
	800	0.475	0.473	**0.488**
res	1600	0.481	0.482	**0.493**
	3200	0.492	0.494	**0.497**
	6400	0.495	0.496	**0.497**
Upper Bound			0.525	

Table 2: Model accuracies: models are tuned by accuracy instead of perplexity. Upper bound is computed by selecting the most frequent choice ($<, >, =$) for each system pair.

with many players all competing for first place. This adapts nicely to WMT's actual collection setting. Recall that annotators are presented with five translations which are then ranked; we can treat this setting as a 5-way free-for-all match. While the details of these updates are beyond the scope of this paper, they are presented in the original model and are implemented in the toolkit we used. We thus also conducted experiments varying the value of N from 2 to 5.

The results are shown in Tables 3 and 4, which hold constant the number of matches and pairwise judgments, respectively. When fixing the number of matches, the 5-way setting is at an advantage, since there is much more information in each match; in contrast, when fixing the number of pairwise comparisons, the 5-way setting is at a disadvantage, since many fewer competitions constitute these comparisons. The results bear this out, but also suggest that the standard WMT setting — which extracts ten pairwise comparisons from each 5-way match and treats them independently — works well. We will not speculate further here, but provide this experiment purely to motivate potential future work. Here we will focus our conclusions to the pair-wise ranking scenario.

#	N=2	N=3	N=4	N=5
400	0.479	0.482	0.491	**0.492**
800	0.483	0.493	0.495	**0.495**
1600	0.493	0.492	**0.497**	0.495
3200	0.493	0.494	**0.498**	0.497
6400	0.495	**0.498**	0.498	0.498

Table 3: Accuracies when training with N-way free-for-all models, fixing the number of matches.

#	N=2	N=3	N=4	N=5
400	**0.479**	0.475	0.470	0.459
800	0.483	**0.488**	0.476	0.466
1600	**0.493**	0.488	0.481	0.481
3200	**0.493**	0.492	0.487	0.489
6400	0.495	**0.496**	0.494	0.495

Table 4: Accuracies when training with N-way free-for-all models, fixing the number of pairwise comparisons.

5 Reduced Data Collection with Non-uniform Match Selection

As mentioned earlier, a drawback of the selection of training data for annotation is that it is sampled uniformly from the space of system pair competitions, and an advantage of TrueSkill is its ability to instead compute a distribution over pairings and thereby focus annotation efforts on competitive matches. In this section, we report results in the form of heat maps indicating the percentage of pairwise judgments requested by TrueSkill across the full cross-product of system pairs, using the WMT13 French-English translation task.

Figure 5 depicts a system-versus-system heat map for all judgments in the dataset. Across this figure and the next two, systems are sorted along each axis by the final values of μ inferred by TrueSkill during training, and the heat of each square is proportional to the percentage of judgments obtained between those two systems. The diagonal reflects the fact that systems do not compete against themselves, and the stripe at row and column 5 reflects a system that was entered late

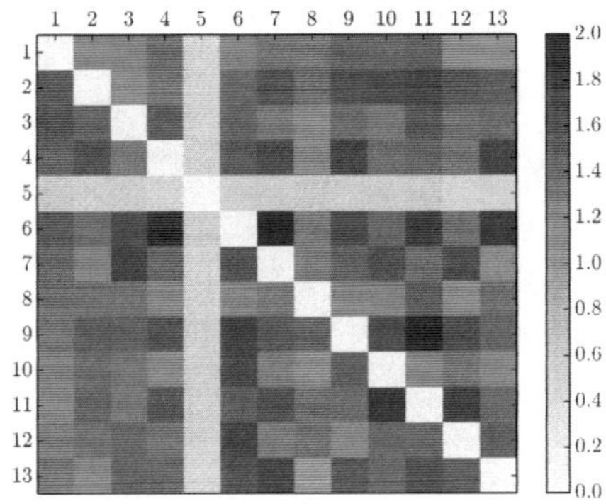

Figure 5: Heat map for the ratio of pairwise judgments across the full cross-product of systems in the WMT13 French-English translation task.

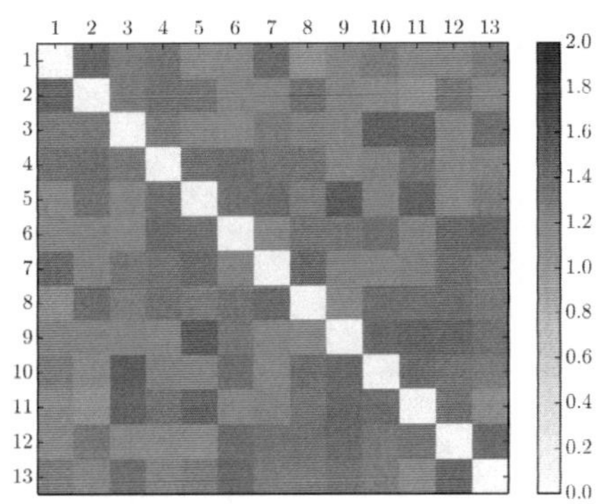

Figure 6: Heat map for the ratio of pairwise judgments across the full cross-product of systems used in the *first* 20% of TrueSkill model.

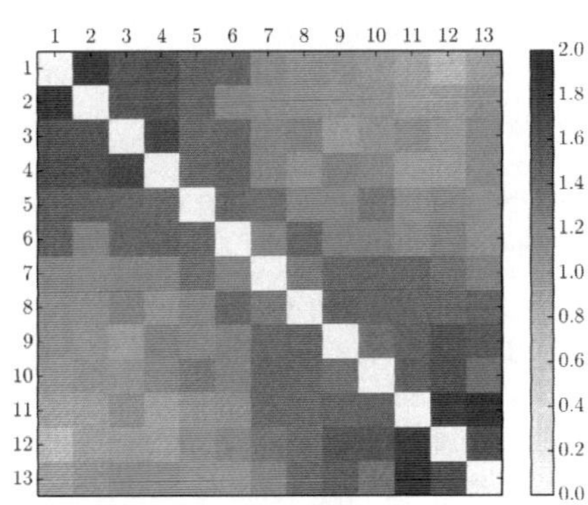

Figure 7: Heat map for the ratio of pairwise judgments across the full cross-product of systems used in the *last* 20% of TrueSkill model.

into the WMT13 competition and thus had many fewer judgments. It is clear that these values are roughly uniformly distributed. This figure serves as a sort of baseline, demonstrating the lack of patterns in the data-selection process.

The next two figures focus on the data that TrueSkill itself selected for its use from among all of the available data. Figure 6 is a second heat map presenting the set of system pairs selected by TrueSkill for the *first* 20% of its matches chosen during training, while Figure 7 presents a heat map of the *last* 20%. The contrast is striking: whereas the judgments are roughly uniformly distributed at the beginning, the bulk of the judgments obtained for the last set are clustered along the diagonal, where the most competitive matches lie.

Together with the higher accuracy of TrueSkill, this suggests that it could be used to decrease the amount of data that needs to be collected in future WMT human evaluations by focusing the annotation effort on more closely-matched systems.

6 Clustering

As pointed out by Koehn (2012), a ranking presented as a total ordering among systems conceals the closeness of comparable systems. In the WMT13 competition, systems are grouped into clusters, which is equivalent to presenting only a *partial* ordering among the systems. Clusters are constructed using bootstrap resampling to infer many system rankings. From these rankings, *rank ranges* are then collected, which can be used to construct 95% confidence intervals, and, in turn, to cluster systems whose ranges overlap. We use a similar approach for clustering in the TrueSkill model. We obtain rank ranges for each system by running the TrueSkill model 100 times,[9] throwing out the top and bottom 2 rankings for each system, and clustering where rank ranges overlap. For comparison, we also do this for the other two models, altering the amount of training data from 1k to 25k in increments of 1,000, and plotting the number of clusters that can be obtained from each technique on each amount of training data.

Figure 8 show the number of clusters according to the increase of training data for three models. TrueSkill efficiently split the systems into clusters compared to other two methods. Figure 9 and 10 present the result of clustering two different size of

[9]We also tried the sampling 1,000 times and the clustering granularities were the same.

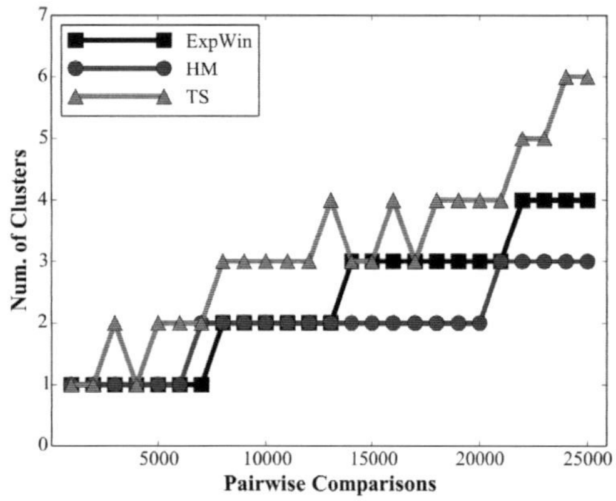

Figure 8: The number of clusters according to the increase of training data for WMT13 French-English (13 systems in total).

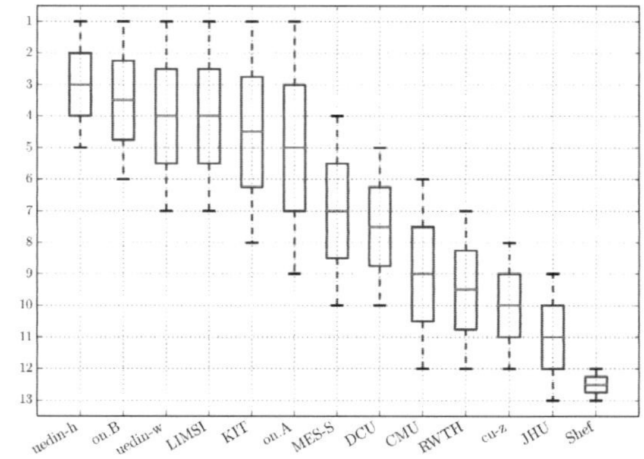

Figure 9: The result of clustering by TrueSkill model with 1K training data from WMT13 French-English. The boxes range from the lower to upper quartile values, with means in the middle. The whiskers show the full range of each system's rank after the bootstrap resampling.

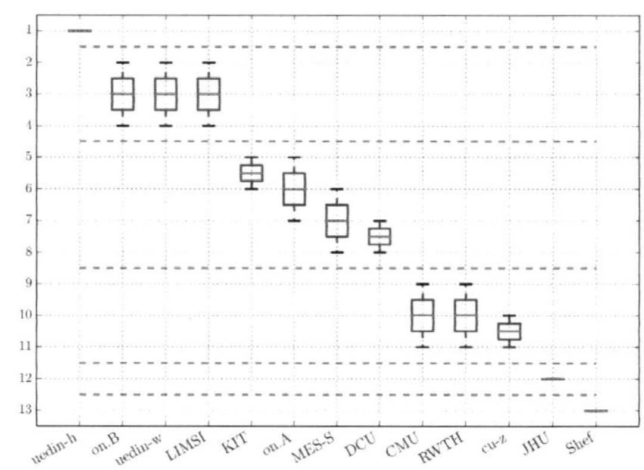

Figure 10: The result of clustering by TrueSkill model with 25K training data. Dashed lines separate systems with non-overlapping rank ranges, splitting the data into clusters.

training data (1K and 25K pairwise comparisons) on the TrueSkill model, which indicates that the rank ranges become narrow and generate clusters reasonably as the number of training samples increases. The ranking and clusters are slightly different from the official result (Table 1) mainly because the official result is based on Expected Wins.

One noteworthy observation is that the ranking of systems between Figure 9 and Figure 10 is the same, further corroborating the stability and accuracy of the TrueSkill model even with a small amount of data. Furthermore, while the need to cluster systems forces the collection of significantly more data than if we wanted only to report a total ordering, TrueSkill here produces nicely-sized clusters with only 25K pairwise comparisons, which is nearly one-third large of that used in the WMT13 campaign (80K for French-English, yielding 8 clusters).

7 Conclusion

Models of "relative ability" (Koehn, 2012; Hopkins and May, 2013) are a welcome addition to methods for inferring system rankings from human judgments. The TrueSkill variant presented in this paper is a promising further development, both in its ability to achieve higher accuracy levels than alternatives, and in its ability to sample non-uniformly from the space of system pair matchings. It's possible that future WMT evaluations could significantly reduce the amount of data they need to collect, also potentially allowing them to draw from expert annotators alone (the developers of the participating systems), without the need to hire non-experts on Mechanical Turk.

One piece missing from the methods explored and proposed in this paper is models of the actual translations being compared by judges. Clearly, it is properties of the sentences themselves that judges use to make their judgments, a fact which is captured only indirectly by modeling translation qualities sampled from system abilities. This observation has been used in the development of automatic evaluation metrics (Song and Cohn, 2011), and is something we hope to explore in future work for system ranking.

References

Ondřej Bojar, Miloš Ercegovčević, Martin Popel, and Omar Zaidan. 2011. A Grain of Salt for the WMT Manual Evaluation. In *Proceedings of the Sixth Workshop on Statistical Machine Translation*, pages 1–11, Edinburgh, Scotland, July. Association for Computational Linguistics.

Ondřej Bojar, Christian Buck, Chris Callison-Burch, Christian Federmann, Barry Haddow, Philipp Koehn, Christof Monz, Matt Post, Radu Soricut, and Lucia Specia. 2013. Findings of the 2013 Workshop on Statistical Machine Translation. In *Proceedings of the Eighth Workshop on Statistical Machine Translation*, pages 1–44, Sofia, Bulgaria, August. Association for Computational Linguistics.

Chris Callison-Burch, Philipp Koehn, Christof Monz, and Omar Zaidan. 2011. Findings of the 2011 Workshop on Statistical Machine Translation. In *Proceedings of the Sixth Workshop on Statistical Machine Translation*, pages 22–64, Edinburgh, Scotland, July. Association for Computational Linguistics.

Chris Callison-Burch, Philipp Koehn, Christof Monz, Matt Post, Radu Soricut, and Lucia Specia. 2012. Findings of the 2012 Workshop on Statistical Machine Translation. In *Proceedings of the Seventh Workshop on Statistical Machine Translation*, pages 10–51, Montréal, Canada, June. Association for Computational Linguistics.

Ralf Herbrich, Tom Minka, and Thore Graepel. 2006. TrueSkill™: A Bayesian Skill Rating System. In *Proceedings of the Twentieth Annual Conference on Neural Information Processing Systems*, pages 569–576, Vancouver, British Columbia, Canada, December. MIT Press.

Mark Hopkins and Jonathan May. 2013. Models of translation competitions. In *Proceedings of the 51st Annual Meeting of the Association for Computational Linguistics (Volume 1: Long Papers)*, pages 1416–1424, Sofia, Bulgaria, August. Association for Computational Linguistics.

Philipp Koehn. 2012. Simulating Human Judgment in Machine Translation Evaluation Campaigns. In *Proceedings of the 9th International Workshop on Spoken Language Translation (IWSLT)*, pages 179–184, Hong Kong, China, December. International Speech Communication Association.

Adam Lopez. 2012. Putting Human Assessments of Machine Translation Systems in Order. In *Proceedings of the Seventh Workshop on Statistical Machine Translation*, pages 1–9, Montréal, Canada, June. Association for Computational Linguistics.

Kishore Papineni, Salim Roukos, Todd Ward, and Wei-Jing Zhu. 2002. BLEU: a Method for Automatic Evaluation of Machine Translation. In *Proceedings of 40th Annual Meeting of the Association for Computational Linguistics*, pages 311–318, Philadelphia, Pennsylvania, July. Association for Computational Linguistics.

Xingyi Song and Trevor Cohn. 2011. Regression and Ranking based Optimisation for Sentence Level MT Evaluation. In *Proceedings of the Sixth Workshop on Statistical Machine Translation*, pages 123–129, Edinburgh, Scotland, July. Association for Computational Linguistics.

Findings of the 2014 Workshop on Statistical Machine Translation

Ondřej Bojar
Charles University in Prague

Christian Buck
University of Edinburgh

Christian Federmann
Microsoft Research

Barry Haddow
University of Edinburgh

Philipp Koehn
JHU / Edinburgh

Johannes Leveling
Dublin City University

Christof Monz
University of Amsterdam

Pavel Pecina
Charles University in Prague

Matt Post
Johns Hopkins University

Herve Saint-Amand
University of Edinburgh

Radu Soricut
Google

Lucia Specia
University of Sheffield

Aleš Tamchyna
Charles University in Prague

Abstract

This paper presents the results of the WMT14 shared tasks, which included a standard news translation task, a separate medical translation task, a task for run-time estimation of machine translation quality, and a metrics task. This year, 143 machine translation systems from 23 institutions were submitted to the ten translation directions in the standard translation task. An additional 6 anonymized systems were included, and were then evaluated both automatically and manually. The quality estimation task had four subtasks, with a total of 10 teams, submitting 57 entries.

1 Introduction

We present the results of the shared tasks of the Workshop on Statistical Machine Translation (WMT) held at ACL 2014. This workshop builds on eight previous WMT workshops (Koehn and Monz, 2006; Callison-Burch et al., 2007, 2008, 2009, 2010, 2011, 2012; Bojar et al., 2013).

This year we conducted four official tasks: a translation task, a quality estimation task, a metrics task[1] and a medical translation task. In the translation task (§2), participants were asked to translate a shared test set, optionally restricting themselves to the provided training data. We held ten translation tasks this year, between English and each of Czech, French, German, Hindi, and Russian. The Hindi translation tasks were new this year, providing a lesser resourced data condition on a challenging language pair. The system outputs for each task were evaluated both automatically and manually.

The human evaluation (§3) involves asking human judges to rank sentences output by anonymized systems. We obtained large numbers of rankings from researchers who contributed evaluations proportional to the number of tasks they entered. Last year, we dramatically increased the number of judgments, achieving much more meaningful rankings. This year, we developed a new ranking method that allows us to achieve the same with fewer judgments.

The quality estimation task (§4) this year included sentence- and word-level subtasks: sentence-level prediction of 1-3 likert scores, sentence-level prediction of percentage of word edits necessary to fix a sentence, sentence-level prediction of post-editing time, and word-level prediction of scores at different levels of granularity (correct/incorrect, accuracy/fluency errors, and specific types of errors). Datasets were released with English-Spanish, English-German, Spanish-English and German-English news translations produced by 2-3 machine translation systems and, for some subtasks, a human translation.

The medical translation task (§5) was introduced this year. Unlike the "standard" translation task, the test sets come from the very specialized domain of medical texts. The aim of this task was not only domain adaptation but also the utilization of translation systems in a larger scenario, namely cross-lingual information retrieval (IR). Extrinsic evaluation in an IR setting was a part of this task (on the other hand, manual evaluation of translation quality was not carried out).

The primary objectives of WMT are to evaluate the state of the art in machine translation, to disseminate common test sets and public training data with published performance numbers, and to refine evaluation and estimation methodologies for machine translation. As before, all of the data,

[1]The metrics task is reported in a separate paper (Macháček and Bojar, 2014).

Proceedings of the Ninth Workshop on Statistical Machine Translation, pages 12–58,
Baltimore, Maryland USA, June 26–27, 2014. ©2014 Association for Computational Linguistics

translations, and collected human judgments are publicly available.[2] We hope these datasets serve as a valuable resource for research into statistical machine translation and automatic evaluation or prediction of translation quality.

2 Overview of the Translation Task

The recurring task of the workshop examines translation between English and other languages. As in the previous years, the other languages include German, French, Czech and Russian.

We dropped Spanish and added Hindi this year. From a linguistic point of view, Spanish poses similar problems as French, making its prior inclusion less valuable. Hindi is not only interesting since it is a more distant language than the European languages we include, but also because we have much less training data, thus forcing researchers to deal with low resource conditions, but also providing them with a language pair that does not suffer from the computational complexities of having to deal with massive amounts of training data.

We created a test set for each language pair by translating newspaper articles and provided training data.

2.1 Test data

The test data for this year's task was selected from news stories from online sources, as before. However, we changed our method to create the test sets.

In previous years, we took equal amounts of source sentences from all six languages involved (around 500 sentences each), and translated them into all other languages. While this produced a multi-parallel test corpus that could be also used for language pairs (such as Czech-Russian) that we did not include in the evaluation, it did suffer from artifacts from the larger distance between source and target sentences. Most test sentences involved the translation a source sentence that was translated from a their language into a target sentence (which was compared against a translation from that third language as well). Questions have been raised, if the evaluation of, say, French-English translation is best served when testing on sentences that have been originally written in, say, Czech. For discussions about *translationese* please for instance refer to Koppel and Ordan (2011).

This year, we took about 1500 English sentences and translated them into the other 5 languages, and then additional 1500 sentences from each of the other languages and translated them into English. This gave us test sets of about 3000 sentences for our English-X language pairs, which have been either written originally written in English and translated into X, or vice versa.

The composition of the test documents is shown in Table 1. The stories were translated by the professional translation agency Capita, funded by the EU Framework Programme 7 project MosesCore, and by Yandex, a Russian search engine company.[3] All of the translations were done directly, and not via an intermediate language.

2.2 Training data

As in past years we provided parallel corpora to train translation models, monolingual corpora to train language models, and development sets to tune system parameters. Some training corpora were identical from last year (Europarl[4], United Nations, French-English 10^9 corpus, CzEng, Common Crawl, Russian-English Wikipedia Headlines provided by CMU), some were updated (Russian-English parallel data provided by Yandex, News Commentary, monolingual data), and a new corpus was added (Hindi-English corpus, Bojar et al. (2014)), Hindi-English Wikipedia Headline corpus).

Some statistics about the training materials are given in Figure 1.

2.3 Submitted systems

We received 143 submissions from 23 institutions. The participating institutions and their entry names are listed in Table 2; each system did not necessarily appear in all translation tasks. We also included four commercial off-the-shelf MT systems and four online statistical MT systems, which we anonymized.

For presentation of the results, systems are treated as either *constrained* or *unconstrained*, depending on whether their models were trained only on the provided data. Since we do not know how they were built, these online and commercial systems are treated as unconstrained during the automatic and human evaluations.

[2] `http://statmt.org/wmt14/results.html`

[3] `http://www.yandex.com/`

[4] As of Fall 2011, the proceedings of the European Parliament are no longer translated into all official languages.

Europarl Parallel Corpus

	French ↔ English		German ↔ English		Czech ↔ English	
Sentences	2,007,723		1,920,209		646,605	
Words	60,125,563	55,642,101	50,486,398	53,008,851	14,946,399	17,376,433
Distinct words	140,915	118,404	381,583	115,966	172,461	63,039

News Commentary Parallel Corpus

	French ↔ English		German ↔ English		Czech ↔ English		Russian ↔ English	
Sentences	183,251		201,288		146,549		165,602	
Words	5,688,656	4,659,619	5,105,101	5,046,157	3,288,645	3,590,287	4,153,847	4,339,974
Distinct words	72,863	62,673	150,760	65,520	139,477	55,547	151,101	60,801

Common Crawl Parallel Corpus

	French ↔ English		German ↔ English		Czech ↔ English		Russian ↔ English	
Sentences	3,244,152		2,399,123		161,838		878,386	
Words	91,328,790	81,096,306	54,575,405	58,870,638	3,529,783	3,927,378	21,018,793	21,535,122
Distinct words	889,291	859,017	1,640,835	823,480	210,170	128,212	764,203	432,062

United Nations Parallel Corpus

	French ↔ English	
Sentences	12,886,831	
Words	411,916,781	360,341,450
Distinct words	565,553	666,077

Hindi-English Parallel Corpus

	Hindi ↔ English	
Sentences	287,202	
Words	6,002,418	3,953,851
Distinct words	121,236	105,330

10^9 Word Parallel Corpus

	French ↔ English	
Sentences	22,520,400	
Words	811,203,407	668,412,817
Distinct words	2,738,882	2,861,836

Yandex 1M Parallel Corpus

	Russian ↔ English	
Sentences	1,000,000	
Words	24,121,459	26,107,293
Distinct words	701,809	387,646

CzEng Parallel Corpus

	Czech ↔ English	
Sentences	14,833,358	
Words	200,658,857	228,040,794
Distinct words	1,389,803	920,824

Wiki Headlines Parallel Corpus

	Russian ↔ English		Hindi ↔ English	
Sentences	514,859		32,863	
Words	1,191,474	1,230,644	141,042	70,075
Distinct words	282,989	251,328	25,678	26,989

Europarl Language Model Data

	English	French	German	Czech
Sentence	2,218,201	2,190,579	2,176,537	668,595
Words	59,848,044	63,439,791	53,534,167	14,946,399
Distinct words	123,059	145,496	394,781	172,461

News Language Model Data

	English	French	German	Czech	Russian	Hindi
Sentence	90,209,983	30,451,749	89,634,193	36,426,900	32,245,651	1,275,921
Words	2,109,603,244	748,852,739	1,606,506,785	602,950,410	575,423,682	36,297,394
Distinct words	4,089,792	1,906,470	10,248,707	3,101,846	2,860,837	258,759

News Test Set

	French ↔ English		German ↔ English		Czech ↔ English		Russian ↔ English		Hindi ↔ English	
Sentences	3003		3003		3003		3003		2507	
Words	81,194	71,147	63,078	67,624	60,240	68,866	62,107	69,329	86,974	55,822
Distinct words	11,715	10,610	13,930	10,458	16,774	9,893	17,009	9,938	8,292	9,217

Figure 1: Statistics for the training and test sets used in the translation task. The number of words and the number of distinct words (case-insensitive) is based on the provided tokenizer.

Language	Sources (Number of Documents)
Czech	aktuálně.cz (2), blesk.cz (3), blisty.cz (1), deník.cz (9), e15.cz (1), iDNES.cz (17), ihned.cz (14), lidovky.cz (8), medi-afax.cz (2), metro.cz (1), Novinky.cz (5), pravo.novinky.cz (6), reflex.cz (2), tyden.cz (1), zdn.cz (1).
French	BBC French Africa (1), Canoe (9), Croix (4), Cyber Presse (12), Dernieres Nouvelles (1), dhnet.be (5), Equipe (1), Euronews (6), Journal Metro.com (1), La Libre.be (2), La Meuse.be (2), Le Devoir (3), Le Figaro (8), Le Monde (3), Les Echos (15), Lexpress.fr (3), Liberation (1), L'independant (2), Metro France (1), Nice-Matin (6), Le Nouvel Observateur (3), Radio Canada (6), Reuters (7).
English	ABC News (5), BBC (5), CBS News (5), CNN (5), Daily Mail (5), Financial Times (5), Fox News (2), Globe and Mail (1), Independent (1), Los Angeles Times (1), New Yorker (1), News.com Australia (16), Reuters (3), Scotsman (2), smh.com.au (2), stv.tv (1), Telegraph (6), UPI (2).
German	Abendzeitung Nürnberg (1), all-in.de (2), Augsburger Allgemeine (1), AZ Online (1), Börsenzeitung (1), come-on.de (1), Der Westen (2), DZ Online (1), Reutlinger General-Anzeiger (1), Generalanzeiger Bonn (1), Giessener Anzeiger (1), Goslarsche Zeitung (1), Hersfelder Zeitung (1), Jüdische Allgemeine (1), Kreisanzeiger (2), Kreiszeitung (2), Krone (1), Lampertheimer Zeitung (2), Lausitzer Rundschau (1), Mittelbayerische (1), Morgenpost (1), nachrichten.at (1), Neue Presse (1), OP Online (1), Potsdamer Neueste Nachrichten (1), Passauer Neue Presse (1), Recklinghäuser Zeitung (1), Rhein Zeitung (1), salzburg.com (1), Schwarzwälder Bote (29), Segeberger Zeitung (1), Soester Anzeiger (1), Südkurier (17), svz.de (1), Tagesspiegel (1), Usinger Anzeiger (3), Volksblatt.li (1), Westfälischen Anzeiger (3), Wiener Zeitung (1), Wiesbadener Kurier (1), Westdeutsche Zeitung (1), Wilhelmshavener Zeitung (1), Yahoo Deutschland (1).
Hindi	Bhaskar (24), Jagran (61), Navbharat Times / India Times (4), ndtv (2).
Russian	168.ru (1), aif (3), altapress.ru (2), argumenti.ru (2), BBC Russian (3), belta.by (2), communa.ru (1), dp.ru (1), eg-online.ru (1), Euronews (2), fakty.ua (2), gazeta.ru (1), inotv.rt.com (1), interfax (1), Izvestiya (1), Kommersant (7), kp (2), lenta.ru (4), lgng (1), litrossia.ru (1), mirnov.ru (5), mk (8), mn.ru (2), newizv (2), nov-pravda.ru (1), novayagazeta (1), nr2.ru (8), pnp.ru (1), rbc.ru (3), ria.ru (4), rosbalt.ru (1), sovsport.ru (6), Sport Express (10), trud.ru (4), tumentoday.ru (1), vesti.ru (10), zr.ru (1).

Table 1: Composition of the test set. For more details see the XML test files. The `docid` tag gives the source and the date for each document in the test set, and the `origlang` tag indicates the original source language.

3 Human Evaluation

As with past workshops, we contend that automatic measures of machine translation quality are an imperfect substitute for human assessments. We therefore conduct a manual evaluation of the system outputs and define its results to be the principal ranking of the workshop. In this section, we describe how we collected this data and compute the results, and then present the official results of the ranking.

This year's evaluation was conducted a bit differently. The main differences are:

- In contrast to the past two years, we collected judgments entirely from researchers participating in the shared tasks and trusted friends of the community. Last year, about two thirds of the data were solicited from random volunteers on the Amazon Mechanical Turk. For some language pairs, the Turkers data had much lower inter-annotator agreement compared to the researchers.
- As a result, we collected about seventy-five percent less data, but were able to obtain good confidence intervals on the clusters with the use of new approaches to ranking.
- We compared three different ranking methodologies, selecting the one with the highest accuracy on held-out data.

We also maintain many of our customs from prior years, including the presentation of the results in terms of a *partial ordering* (clustering) of the systems. Systems in the same cluster could not be meaningfully distinguished and should be considered ties.

3.1 Data collection

The system ranking is produced from a large set of pairwise annotations between system pairs. These pairwise annotations are collected in an evaluation campaign that enlists participants in the shared task to contribute one hundred "Human Intelligence Tasks" (HITs) per system submitted. Each HIT consists of three *ranking tasks*. In a ranking task, an annotator is presented with a source segment, a human reference translation, and the outputs of five anonymized systems, randomly selected from the set of participating systems, and randomly ordered.

To run the evaluation, we use Appraise[5] (Federmann, 2012), an open-source tool built on Python's Django framework. At the top of each HIT, the following instructions are provided:

> *You are shown a source sentence followed by several candidate translations. Your task is to rank the translations from best to worst (ties are allowed).*

[5] `https://github.com/cfedermann/Appraise`

ID	Institution
AFRL, AFRL-PE	Air Force Research Lab (Schwartz et al., 2014)
CIMS	University of Stuttgart / University of Munich (Cap et al., 2014)
CMU	Carnegie Mellon University (Matthews et al., 2014)
CU-*	Charles University, Prague (Tamchyna et al., 2014)
DCU-FDA	Dublin City University (Bicici et al., 2014)
DCU-ICTCAS	Dublin City University (Li et al., 2014b)
DCU-LINGO24	Dublin City University / Lingo24 (wu et al., 2014)
EU-BRIDGE	EU-BRIDGE Project (Freitag et al., 2014)
KIT	Karlsruhe Institute of Technology (Herrmann et al., 2014)
IIT-BOMBAY	IIT Bombay (Dungarwal et al., 2014)
IIIT-HYDERABAD	IIIT Hyderabad
IMS-TTT	University of Stuttgart / University of Munich (Quernheim and Cap, 2014)
IPN-UPV-*	IPN-UPV (Costa-jussà et al., 2014)
KAZNU	Amandyk Kartbayev, FBK
LIMSI-KIT	LIMSI / Karlsruhe Instutute of Technology (Do et al., 2014)
MANAWI-*	Universität des Saarlandes (Tan and Pal, 2014)
MATRAN	Abu-MaTran Project: Promsit / DCU / UA (Rubino et al., 2014)
PROMT-RULE, PROMT-HYBRID	PROMT
RWTH	RWTH Aachen (Peitz et al., 2014)
STANFORD	Stanford University (Neidert et al., 2014; Green et al., 2014)
UA-*	University of Alicante (Sánchez-Cartagena et al., 2014)
UEDIN-PHRASE, UEDIN-UNCNSTR	University of Edinburgh (Durrani et al., 2014b)
UEDIN-SYNTAX	University of Edinburgh (Williams et al., 2014)
UU, UU-DOCENT	Uppsala University (Hardmeier et al., 2014)
YANDEX	Yandex School of Data Analysis (Borisov and Galinskaya, 2014)
COMMERCIAL-[1,2]	Two commercial machine translation systems
ONLINE-[A,B,C,G]	Four online statistical machine translation systems
RBMT-[1,4]	Two rule-based statistical machine translation systems

Table 2: Participants in the shared translation task. Not all teams participated in all language pairs. The translations from the commercial and online systems were not submitted by their respective companies but were obtained by us, and are therefore anonymized in a fashion consistent with previous years of the workshop.

Figure 2: Screenshot of the Appraise interface used in the human evaluation campaign. The annotator is presented with a source segment, a reference translation, and the outputs of five systems (anonymized and randomly ordered), and is asked to rank these according to their translation quality, with ties allowed.

A screenshot of the ranking interface is shown in Figure 2. Annotators are asked to rank the systems from 1 (best) to 5 (worst), with ties permitted. Note that a *lower* rank is better. The rankings provided by a ranking task are then reduced to a set of ten *pairwise rankings* produced by considering all $\binom{5}{2}$ combinations of systems in the ranking task. For example, consider the following annotation provided among systems A, B, F, H, and J:

	1	2	3	4	5
F				•	
A				•	
B		•			
J					•
H			•		

This is reduced to the following set of pairwise judgments:

$$A > B, A = F, A > H, A < J$$
$$B < F, B < H, B < J$$
$$F > H, F < J$$
$$H < J$$

Here, $A > B$ should be read is "A is ranked higher than (worse than) B". Note that by this procedure, the absolute value of ranks and the magnitude of their differences are discarded.

For WMT13, nearly a million pairwise annotations were collected from both researchers and paid workers on Amazon's Mechanical Turk, in a roughly 1:2 ratio. This year, we collected data from researchers only, an ability that was enabled by the use of a new technique for producing the partial ranking for each task (§3.3.3). Table 3 contains more detail.

3.2 Annotator agreement

Each year we calculate annotator agreement scores for the human evaluation as a measure of the reliability of the rankings. We measured pairwise agreement among annotators using Cohen's kappa coefficient (κ) (Cohen, 1960). If $P(A)$ be the proportion of times that the annotators agree, and $P(E)$ is the proportion of time that they would

LANGUAGE PAIR	Systems	Rankings	Average
Czech–English	5	21,130	4,226.0
English–Czech	10	55,900	5,590.0
German–English	13	25,260	1,943.0
English–German	18	54,660	3,036.6
French–English	8	26,090	3,261.2
English–French	13	33,350	2,565.3
Russian–English	13	34,460	2,650.7
English–Russian	9	28,960	3,217.7
Hindi–English	9	20,900	2,322.2
English–Hindi	12	28,120	2,343.3
TOTAL WMT 14	110	328,830	2,989.3
WMT13	148	942,840	6,370.5
WMT12	103	101,969	999.6
WMT11	133	63,045	474.0

Table 3: Amount of data collected in the WMT14 manual evaluation. The final three rows report summary information from the previous two workshops.

agree by chance, then Cohen's kappa is:

$$\kappa = \frac{P(A) - P(E)}{1 - P(E)}$$

Note that κ is basically a normalized version of $P(A)$, one which takes into account how meaningful it is for annotators to agree with each other by incorporating $P(E)$. The values for κ range from 0 to 1, with zero indicating no agreement and 1 perfect agreement.

We calculate $P(A)$ by examining all pairs of systems which had been judged by two or more judges, and calculating the proportion of time that they agreed that $A < B$, $A = B$, or $A > B$. In other words, $P(A)$ is the empirical, observed rate at which annotators agree, in the context of pairwise comparisons.

As for $P(E)$, it captures the probability that two annotators would agree randomly. Therefore:

$$P(E) = P(\text{A<B})^2 + P(\text{A=B})^2 + P(\text{A>B})^2$$

Note that each of the three probabilities in $P(E)$'s definition are squared to reflect the fact that we are considering the chance that *two* annotators would agree by chance. Each of these probabilities is computed empirically, by observing how often annotators actually rank two systems as being tied.

Table 4 gives κ values for inter-annotator agreement for WMT11–WMT14 while Table 5 details intra-annotator agreement scores, including the division of researchers (WMT13$_r$) and MTurk (WMT13$_m$) data. The exact interpretation of the kappa coefficient is difficult, but according to Landis and Koch (1977), 0–0.2 is slight, 0.2–0.4 is fair, 0.4–0.6 is moderate, 0.6–0.8 is substantial, and 0.8–1.0 is almost perfect. The agreement rates are more or less in line with prior years: worse for some tasks, better for others, and on average, the best since WMT11 (where agreement scores were likely inflated due to inclusion of reference translations in the comparisons).

3.3 Models of System Rankings

The collected pairwise rankings are used to produce a ranking of the systems. Machine translation evaluation has always been a subject of contention, and no exception to this rule exists for the WMT manual evaluation. While the precise metric has varied over the years, it has always shared a common idea of computing the average number of times each system was judged better than other systems, and ranking from highest to lowest. For example, in WMT11 Callison-Burch et al. (2011), the metric computed the percentage of the time each system was ranked better than or equal to other systems, and included comparisons to human references. In WMT12 Callison-Burch et al. (2012), comparisons to references were dropped. In WMT13, rankings were produced over 1,000 bootstrap-resampled sets of the training data. A *rank range* was collected for each system across these folds; the average value was used to order the systems, and a 95% confidence interval across these ranks was used to organize the systems into equivalence classes containing systems with over-

LANGUAGE PAIR	WMT11	WMT12	WMT13	WMT13$_r$	WMT13$_m$	WMT14
Czech–English	0.400	0.311	0.244	0.342	0.279	0.305
English–Czech	0.460	0.359	0.168	0.408	0.075	0.360
German–English	0.324	0.385	0.299	0.443	0.324	0.368
English–German	0.378	0.356	0.267	0.457	0.239	0.427
French–English	0.402	0.272	0.275	0.405	0.321	0.357
English–French	0.406	0.296	0.231	0.434	0.237	0.302
Hindi–English	—	—	—	—	—	0.400
English–Hindi	—	—	—	—	—	0.413
Russian–English	—	—	0.278	0.315	0.324	0.324
English–Russian	—	—	0.243	0.416	0.207	0.418
MEAN	0.395	0.330	0.260			0.367

Table 4: κ scores measuring inter-annotator agreement. See Table 5 for corresponding intra-annotator agreement scores.

LANGUAGE PAIR	WMT11	WMT12	WMT13	WMT13$_r$	WMT13$_m$	WMT14
Czech–English	0.597	0.454	0.479	0.483	0.478	0.382
English–Czech	0.601	0.390	0.290	0.547	0.242	0.448
German–English	0.576	0.392	0.535	0.643	0.515	0.344
English–German	0.528	0.433	0.498	0.649	0.452	0.576
French–English	0.673	0.360	0.578	0.585	0.565	0.629
English–French	0.524	0.414	0.495	0.630	0.486	0.507
Hindi–English	—	—	—	—	—	0.605
English–Hindi	—	—	—	—	—	0.535
Russian–English	—	—	0.450	0.363	0.477	0.629
English–Russian	—	—	0.513	0.582	0.500	0.570
MEAN	0.583	0.407	0.479			0.522

Table 5: κ scores measuring intra-annotator agreement, i.e., self-consistency of judges, across for the past few years of the human evaluation.

lapping ranges.

This year, we introduce two new changes. First, we pit the WMT13 method against two new approaches: that of Hopkins and May (2013, §3.3.2), and another based on TrueSkill (Sakaguchi et al., 2014, §3.3.3). Second, we compare these two methods against WMT13's "Expected Wins" approach, and then select among them by determining which of them has the highest accuracy in terms of predicting annotations on a held-out set of pairwise judgments.

3.3.1 Method 1: Expected Wins (EW)

Introduced for WMT13, the EXPECTED WINS has an intuitive score demonstrated to be accurate in ranking systems according to an underlying model of "relative ability" (Koehn, 2012a). The idea is to gauge the probability that a system S_i will be ranked better than another system randomly chosen from a pool of opponents $\{S_j : j \neq i\}$. If we define the function $\text{win}(A, B)$ as the number of times system A is ranked better than system B, then we can define this as follows:

$$\text{score}_{EW}(S_i) = \frac{1}{|\{S_j\}|} \sum_{j, j \neq i} \frac{\text{win}(S_i, S_j)}{\text{win}(S_i, S_j) + \text{win}(S_j, S_i)}$$

Note that this score ignores ties.

3.3.2 Method 2: Hopkins and May (HM)

Hopkins and May (2013) introduced a graphical model formulation of the task, which makes the notion of underlying system ability even more explicit. Each system S_J in the pool $\{S_j\}$ is represented by an associated relative ability μ_j and a variance σ_a^2 (fixed across all systems) which serve as the parameters of a Gaussian distribution. Samples from this distribution represent the quality of sentence translations, with higher quality samples having higher values. Pairwise annotations (S_1, S_2, π) are generated according to the following process:

1. Select two systems S_1 and S_2 from the pool of systems $\{S_j\}$

2. Draw two "translations", adding random Gaussian noise with variance σ^2_{obs} to simulate the subjectivity of the task and the differences among annotators:

$$q_1 \sim \mathcal{N}(\mu_{S_1}, \sigma_a^2) + \mathcal{N}(0, \sigma_{obs}^2)$$
$$q_2 \sim \mathcal{N}(\mu_{S_2}, \sigma_a^2) + \mathcal{N}(0, \sigma_{obs}^2)$$

3. Let d be a nonzero real number that defines a fixed decision radius. Produce a rating π according to:

$$\pi = \begin{cases} < & q_1 - q_2 > d \\ > & q_2 - q_1 > d \\ = & \text{otherwise} \end{cases}$$

Hopkins and May use Gibbs sampling to infer the set of system means from an annotated dataset. Details of this inference procedure can be found in Sakaguchi et al. (2014). The score used to produce the rankings is simply the system mean associated with each system:

$$\text{score}_{HM}(S_i) = \mu_{S_i}$$

3.3.3 Method 3: TrueSkill (TS)

TrueSkill is an adaptive, online system that employs a similar model of relative ability Herbrich et al. (2006). It was initially developed for Xbox Live's online player community, where it is used to model player ability, assign levels, and select competitive matches. Each player S_j is modeled by two parameters: TrueSkill's current estimate of each system's relative ability, μ_{S_j}, and a per-system measure of TrueSkill's uncertainty of those estimates, $\sigma^2_{S_j}$. When the outcome of a match is observed, TrueSkill uses the relative status of the two systems to update these estimates. If a translation from a system with a high mean is judged better than a system with a greatly lower mean, the result is not surprising, and the update size for the corresponding system means will be small. On the other hand, when an upset occurs in a competition, the means will receive larger updates. Sakaguchi et al. (2014) provide an adaptation of this approach to the WMT manual evaluation, and showed that it performed well on WMT13 data.

Similar to the Hopkins and May model, TrueSkill scores systems by their inferred means:

$$\text{score}_{TS}(S_i) = \mu_{S_i}$$

This score is then used to sort the systems and produce the ranking.

3.4 Method Selection

We have three methods which, provided with the collected data, produce different rankings of the systems. Which of them is correct? More immediately, which one of them should we publish as the official ranking for the WMT14 manual evaluation? As discussed, the method used to compute the ranking has been tweaked a bit each year over the past few years in response to criticisms (e.g., Lopez (2012); Bojar et al. (2011)). While the changes were reasonable (and later corroborated), Hopkins and May (2013) pointed out that this task of model selection should be driven by empirical evaluation on held-out data, and suggested perplexity as the metric of choice.

We choose instead a more direct gold-standard evaluation metric: the accuracy of the rankings produced by each method in predicting pairwise judgments. We use each method to produce a partial ordering of the systems, grouping them into equivalence classes. This partial ordering unambiguously assigns a prediction π_P between any pair of systems (S_i, S_j). By comparing the predicted relationship π_P to the actual annotation for each pairwise judgment in the test data (by token), we can compute an accuracy score for each model.

We predict accuracy in this manner using 100-fold cross-validation. For each task, we split the data into a fixed set of 100 randomly-selected folds. Each fold serves as a test set, with the remaining ninety-nine folds available as training data for each method. Note that the total ordering over systems provided by the score$_*$ functions defined do not predict ties. In order to do enable the models to predict ties, we produce equivalence classes using the following procedure:

- Assign S_1 to a cluster
- For each system S_i, assign it to the current cluster if $\text{score}(S_{i-1}) - \text{score}(S_i) \leq r$; otherwise, assign it to a new cluster

The value of r (the *decision radius* for ties) is tuned using accuracy on the entire training data using grid search over the values $r \in 0, 0.01, 0.02, \ldots, .25$ (26 values in total). This value is tuned separately for each method on each fold. Table 6 contains an example partial ordering.

System	Score	Rank
B	0.60	1
D	0.44	2
E	0.39	2
A	0.25	2
F	-0.09	3
C	-0.22	3

Table 6: The partial ordering computed with the provided scores when $r = 0.15$.

Task	EW	HM	TS	Oracle
Czech–English	40.4	**41.1**	**41.1**	41.2
English–Czech	45.3	45.6	**45.9**	46.8
French–English	49.0	**49.4**	49.3	50.3
English–French	44.6	44.4	**44.7**	46.0
German–English	43.5	**43.7**	**43.7**	45.2
English–German	47.3	**47.4**	47.2	48.2
Hindi–English	**62.5**	62.2	**62.5**	62.6
English–Hindi	53.3	**53.7**	53.5	55.7
Russian–English	47.6	**47.7**	**47.7**	50.6
English–Russian	**46.5**	46.1	46.4	48.2
MEAN	48.0	48.1	**48.2**	49.2

Table 7: Accuracies for each method across 100 folds, for each translation task. The oracle uses the most frequent outcome between each pair of systems, and therefore might not constitute a feasible ranking.

After training, each model has defined a partial ordering over systems.[6] This is then used to compute accuracy on all the pairwise judgments in the test fold. This process yields 100 accuracies for each method; the average accuracy across all the folds can then be used to compute the best method.

Table 7 contains accuracy results for the three methods on the WMT14 tasks. On average, there is a small improvement in accuracy moving from Expected Wins to the H&M model, and then again to the TrueSkill model; however, there is no pattern to the best model for each class. The Oracle column is computed by selecting the most probable outcome ($\pi \in \{<, =, >\}$) for each system pair, and provides an upper bound on accuracy when predicting outcomes using only system-level information. Furthermore, this method of oracle computation might not represent a feasible ranking or clustering,[7].

The TrueSkill approach was best overall, so we used it to produce the official rankings for all language pairs.

3.5 Rank Ranges and Clusters

Above we saw how to produce system scores for each method, which provides a total ordering of the systems. But we would also like to know if the obtained system ranking is statistically significant. Given the large number of systems that participate, and the similarity of the underlying systems resulting from the common training data condition and (often) toolsets, there will be some systems that will be very close in quality. These systems should be grouped together in equivalence classes.

To establish the reliability of the obtained system ranking, we use bootstrap resampling. We sample from the set of pairwise rankings an equal sized set of pairwise rankings (allowing for multiple drawings of the same pairwise ranking), compute a TrueSkill model score for each system based on this sample, and then rank the systems from $1..|\{S_j\}|$. By repeating this procedure 1,000 times, we can determine a range of ranks, into which system falls at least 95% of the time (i.e., at least 950 times) — corresponding to a p-level of $p \leq 0.05$. Furthermore, given the rank ranges for each system, we can cluster systems with overlapping rank ranges.[8]

Table 8 reports all system scores, rank ranges, and clusters for all language pairs and all systems. The official interpretation of these results is that systems in the same cluster are considered tied. Given the large number of judgments that we collected, it was possible to group on average about two systems in a cluster, even though the systems in the middle are typically in larger clusters.

3.6 Cluster analysis

The official ranking results for English-German produced clusters compute at the 90% confidence level due to the presence of a very large cluster (of nine systems). While there is always the possibility that this cluster reflects a true ambiguity, it is more likely due to the fact that we didn't have enough data: English–German had the most sys-

[6]It is a total ordering when $r = 0$, or when all the system scores are outside the decision radius.

[7]For example, if there were a cycle of "better than" judgments among a set of systems.

[8]Formally, given ranges defined by start(S_i) and end(S_i), we seek the largest set of clusters $\{C_c\}$ that satisfies:

$$\forall S\ \exists C : S \in C$$
$$S \in C_a, S \in C_b \rightarrow C_a = C_b$$
$$C_a \neq C_b \rightarrow \forall S_i \in C_a, S_j \in C_b :$$
$$\text{start}(S_i) > \text{end}(S_j) \text{ or start}(S_j) > \text{end}(S_i)$$

Czech–English

#	score	range	system
1	0.591	1	ONLINE-B
2	0.290	2	UEDIN-PHRASE
3	-0.171	3-4	UEDIN-SYNTAX
	-0.243	3-4	ONLINE-A
4	-0.468	5	CU-MOSES

English–Czech

#	score	range	system
1	0.371	1-3	CU-DEPFIX
	0.356	1-3	UEDIN-UNCNSTR
	0.333	1-4	CU-BOJAR
	0.287	3-4	CU-FUNKY
2	0.169	5-6	ONLINE-B
	0.113	5-6	UEDIN-PHRASE
3	0.030	7	ONLINE-A
4	-0.175	8	CU-TECTO
5	-0.534	9	COMMERCIAL1
6	-0.950	10	COMMERCIAL2

German–English

#	score	range	system
1	0.451	1	ONLINE-B
2	0.267	2-3	UEDIN-SYNTAX
	0.258	2-3	ONLINE-A
3	0.147	4-6	LIMSI-KIT
	0.146	4-6	UEDIN-PHRASE
	0.138	4-6	EU-BRIDGE
4	0.026	7-8	KIT
	-0.049	7-8	RWTH
5	-0.125	9-11	DCU-ICTCAS
	-0.157	9-11	CMU
	-0.192	9-11	RBMT4
6	-0.306	12	RBMT1
7	-0.604	13	ONLINE-C

English–German

#	score	range	system
1	0.264	1-2	UEDIN-SYNTAX
	0.242	1-2	ONLINE-B
2	0.167	3-6	ONLINE-A
	0.156	3-6	PROMT-HYBRID
	0.155	3-6	PROMT-RULE
	0.155	3-6	UEDIN-STANFORD
3	0.094	7	EU-BRIDGE
4	0.033	8-10	RBMT4
	0.031	8-10	UEDIN-PHRASE
	0.012	8-10	RBMT1
5	-0.032	11-12	KIT
	-0.069	11-13	STANFORD-UNC
	-0.100	12-14	CIMS
	-0.126	13-15	STANFORD
	-0.158	14-16	UU
	-0.191	15-16	ONLINE-C
6	-0.307	17-18	IMS-TTT
	-0.325	17-18	UU-DOCENT

Russian–English

#	score	range	system
1	0.583	1	AFRL-PE
2	0.299	2	ONLINE-B
3	0.190	3-5	ONLINE-A
	0.178	3-5	PROMT-HYBRID
	0.123	4-7	PROMT-RULE
	0.104	5-8	UEDIN-PHRASE
	0.069	5-8	YANDEX
	0.066	5-8	ONLINE-G
4	-0.017	9	AFRL
5	-0.159	10	UEDIN-SYNTAX
6	-0.306	11	KAZNU
7	-0.487	12	RBMT1
8	-0.642	13	RBMT4

French–English

#	score	range	system
1	0.608	1	UEDIN-PHRASE
2	0.479	2-4	KIT
	0.475	2-4	ONLINE-B
	0.428	2-4	STANFORD
3	0.331	5	ONLINE-A
4	-0.389	6	RBMT1
5	-0.648	7	RBMT4
6	-1.284	8	ONLINE-C

Hindi–English

#	score	range	system
1	1.326	1	ONLINE-B
2	0.559	2-3	ONLINE-A
	0.476	2-4	UEDIN-SYNTAX
	0.434	3-4	CMU
3	0.323	5	UEDIN-PHRASE
4	-0.198	6-7	AFRL
	-0.280	6-7	IIT-BOMBAY
5	-0.549	8	DCU-LINGO24
6	-2.092	9	IIIT-HYDERABAD

English–Russian

#	score	range	system
1	0.575	1-2	PROMT-RULE
	0.547	1-2	ONLINE-B
2	0.426	3	PROMT-HYBRID
3	0.305	4-5	UEDIN-UNCNSTR
	0.231	4-5	ONLINE-G
4	0.089	6-7	ONLINE-A
	0.031	6-7	UEDIN-PHRASE
5	-0.920	8	RBMT4
6	-1.284	9	RBMT1

English–French

#	score	range	system
1	0.327	1	ONLINE-B
2	0.232	2-4	UEDIN-PHRASE
	0.194	2-5	KIT
	0.185	2-5	MATRAN
	0.142	4-6	MATRAN-RULES
	0.120	4-6	ONLINE-A
3	0.003	7-9	UU-DOCENT
	-0.019	7-10	PROMT-HYBRID
	-0.033	7-10	UA
	-0.069	8-10	PROMT-RULE
4	-0.215	11	RBMT1
5	-0.328	12	RBMT4
6	-0.540	13	ONLINE-C

English–Hindi

#	score	range	system
1	1.008	1	ONLINE-B
2	0.915	2	ONLINE-A
3	0.214	3	UEDIN-UNCNSTR
4	0.120	4-5	UEDIN-PHRASE
	0.054	4-5	CU-MOSES
5	-0.111	6-7	IIT-BOMBAY
	-0.142	6-7	IPN-UPV-CNTXT
6	-0.233	8-9	DCU-LINGO24
	-0.261	8-9	IPN-UPV-NODEV
7	-0.449	10-11	MANAWI-H1
	-0.494	10-11	MANAWI
8	-0.622	12	MANAWI-RMOOV

Table 8: Official results for the WMT14 translation task. Systems are ordered by their inferred system means. Lines between systems indicate clusters according to bootstrap resampling at p-level $p \leq .05$, except for English–German, where $p \leq 0.1$. This method is also used to determine the range of ranks into which system falls. Systems with grey background indicate use of resources that fall outside the constraints provided for the shared task.

tems (18, compared to 13 for the next languages), yet only an average amount of per-system data. Here, we look at this language pair in more detail, in order to justify this decision, and to shed light on the differences between the ranking methods.

Table 9 presents the 95% confidence-level clusterings for English–German computed with each of the three methods, along with lines that show the reorderings of the systems between them. Reorderings of this type have been used to argue against the reliability of the official WMT ranking (Lopez, 2012; Hopkins and May, 2013). This table shows that these reorderings are captured entirely by the clustering approach we used. This relative *consensus* of these independently-computed and somewhat different models suggests that the published ranking is approaching the true ambiguity underlying systems within the same cluster.

Looking across all language pairs, we find that the total ordering predicted by EW and TS is exactly the same for eight of the ten language pair tasks, and is constrained to reorderings within the official cluster for the other two (German–English — just one adjacent swap — and English–German, depicted in Table 9).

3.7 Conclusions

The official ranking method employed by WMT over the past few years has changed a few times as a result of error analysis and introspection. Until this year, these results were largely based on the intuitions of the community and organizers about deficiencies in the models. In addition to their intuitive appeal, many of these changes (such as the decision to throw out comparisons against references) have been empirically validated Hopkins and May (2013). The actual effect of the refinements in the ranking metric has been minor perturbations in the permutation of systems. The clustering method of Koehn (2012b), in which the official rankings are presented as a partial (instead of total) ordering, alleviated many of the problems observed by Lopez (2012), and also capture all the variance across the new systems introduced this year. In addition, presenting systems as clusters appeals to intuition. As such, we disagree with claims that there is a problem with irreproducibility of the results of the workshop evaluation task, and especially disagree that there is anything approaching a "crisis of confidence" (Hopkins and May, 2013). These claims seem to us to be overstated.

Conducting proper model selection by comparison on held-out data, however, is a welcome suggestion, and our inclusion of this process supports improved confidence in the ranking results. That said, it is notable that the different methods compute very similar orderings. This avoids hallucinating distinctions among systems that are not really there, and captures the intuition that some systems are basically equivalent. The chief benefit of the TrueSkill model is not in outputting a better complete ranking of the systems, but lies in its reduced variance, which allow us to cluster the systems with less data. There is also the unexplored avenue of using TrueSkill to drive the data collection, steering the annotations of judges towards evenly matched systems during the collection phase, potentially allowing confident results to be presented while collecting even less data.

There is, of course, more work to be done. We have produced this year statistically significant clusters with a third of the data required last year, which is an improvement. Models of relative ability are a natural fit for the manual evaluation, and the introduction of an online Bayesian approach to data collection present further opportunities to reduce the amount of data needed. These methods also provide a framework for extending the models in a variety of potentially useful ways, including modeling annotator bias, incorporating sentence metadata (such as length, difficulty, or subtopic), and adding features of the sentence pairs.

4 Quality Estimation Task

Machine translation quality estimation is the task of predicting a quality score for a machine translated text without access to reference translations. The most common approach is to treat the problem as a supervised machine learning task, using standard regression or classification algorithms. The third edition of the WMT shared task on quality estimation builds on the previous editions of the task (Callison-Burch et al., 2012; Bojar et al., 2013), with tasks including both sentence-level and word-level estimation, with new training and test datasets.

The goals of this year's shared task were:

- To investigate the effectiveness of different quality labels.
- To explore word-level quality prediction at

Expected Wins	Hopkins & May	TrueSkill
UEDIN-SYNTAX	UEDIN-SYNTAX	UEDIN-SYNTAX
ONLINE-B	ONLINE-B	ONLINE-B
ONLINE-A	UEDIN-STANFORD	**ONLINE-A**
UEDIN-STANFORD	PROMT-HYBRID	PROMT-HYBRID
PROMT-RULE	ONLINE-A	PROMT-RULE
PROMT-HYBRID	PROMT-RULE	UEDIN-STANFORD
EU-BRIDGE	EU-BRIDGE	**EU-BRIDGE**
RBMT4	UEDIN-PHRASE	**RBMT4**
UEDIN-PHRASE	RBMT4	UEDIN-PHRASE
RBMT1	RBMT1	RBMT1
KIT	KIT	KIT
STANFORD-UNC	STANFORD-UNC	STANFORD-UNC
CIMS	CIMS	CIMS
STANFORD	STANFORD	STANFORD
UU	UU	UU
ONLINE-C	ONLINE-C	ONLINE-C
IMS-TTT	**UU-DOCENT**	**IMS-TTT**
UU-DOCENT	IMS-TTT	UU-DOCENT

Table 9: A comparison of the rankings produced by Expected Wins, Hopkins & May, and TrueSkill for English–German (the task with the most systems and the largest cluster). The lines extending all the way across mark the official English–German clustering (computed from TrueSkill with 90% confidence intervals), while **bold** entries mark the start of new clusters within each method or column (computed at the 95% confidence level). The TrueSkill clusterings contain all the system reorderings across the other two ranking methods.

different levels of granularity.

- To study the effects of training and test datasets with mixed domains, language pairs and MT systems.

- To examine the effectiveness of quality prediction methods on human translations.

Four tasks were proposed: Tasks 1.1, 1.2, 1.3 are defined at the sentence-level (Sections 4.1), while Task 2, at the word-level (Section 4.2). Each task provides one or more datasets with up to four language pairs each: English-Spanish, English-German, German-English, Spanish-English, and up to four alternative translations generated by: a statistical MT system (SMT), a rule-based MT system (RBMT), a hybrid MT system, and a human. These datasets were annotated with different labels for quality by professional translators as part of the QTLaunchPad[9] project. External resources (e.g. parallel corpora) were provided to participants. Any additional resources, including additional quality estimation training data, could be used by participants (no distinction between *open* and *close* tracks is made). Participants were also provided with a software package to extract quality estimation features and perform model learning, with a suggested list of *baseline* features and learning method for sentence-level prediction. Participants, described in Section 4.3, could submit up to two systems for each task.

[9] http://www.qt21.eu/launchpad/

Data used for building specific MT systems or internal system information (such as n-best lists) were not made available this year as multiple MT systems were used to produced the datasets, including rule-based systems. In addition, part of the translations were produced by humans. Information on the sources of translations was not provided either. Therefore, as a general rule, participants were only allowed to use black-box features.

4.1 Sentence-level Quality Estimation

For the sentence-level tasks, two variants of the results could be submitted for each task and language pair:

- **Scoring**: An absolute quality score for each sentence translation according to the type of prediction, to be interpreted as an error metric: lower scores mean better translations.

- **Ranking**: A ranking of sentence translations for all source test sentences from best to worst. For this variant, it does not matter how the ranking is produced (from HTER predictions, likert predictions, or even without machine learning).

Evaluation was performed against the true label and/or HTER ranking using the same metrics as in previous years:

- **Scoring**: Mean Average Error (MAE) (primary metric), Root Mean Squared Error (RMSE).

- **Ranking**: DeltaAvg (primary metric) (Bojar et al., 2013) and Spearman's rank correlation.

For all sentence-level these tasks, the same 17 features as in WMT12-13 were used to build baseline systems. The SVM regression algorithm within QuEst (Specia et al., 2013)[10] was applied for that with RBF kernel and grid search for parameter optimisation.

Task 1.1 Predicting post-editing effort

Data in this task is labelled with discrete and absolute scores for perceived post-editing effort, where:

- **1** = Perfect translation, no post-editing needed at all.

- **2** = Near miss translation: translation contains maximum of 2-3 errors, and possibly additional errors that can be easily fixed (capitalisation, punctuation, etc.).

- **3** = Very low quality translation, cannot be easily fixed.

The datasets were annotated in a "triage" phase aimed at selecting translations of type "2" (near miss) that could be annotated for errors at the word-level using the MQM metric (see Task 2, below) for a more fine-grained and systematic translation quality analysis. Word-level errors in translations of type "3" are too difficult if not impossible to annotate and classify, particularly as they often contain inter-related errors in contiguous or overlapping word spans.

[10]`http://www.quest.dcs.shef.ac.uk/`

For the *training* of prediction models, we provide a new dataset consisting of source sentences and their human translations, as well as two-three versions of machine translations (by an SMT system, an RBMT system and, for English-Spanish/German only, a hybrid system), all in the news domain, extracted from tests sets of various WMT years and MT systems that participated in the translation shared task:

# Source sentences	# Target sentences
954 English	3,816 Spanish
350 English	1,400 German
350 German	1,050 English
350 Spanish	1,050 English

As *test* data, for each language pair and MT system (or human translation) we provide a new set of translations produced by the same MT systems (and humans) as those used for the training data:

# Source sentences	# Target sentences
150 English	600 Spanish
150 English	600 German
150 German	450 English
150 Spanish	450 English

The distribution of true scores in both training and test sets for each language pair is given in Figures 3.

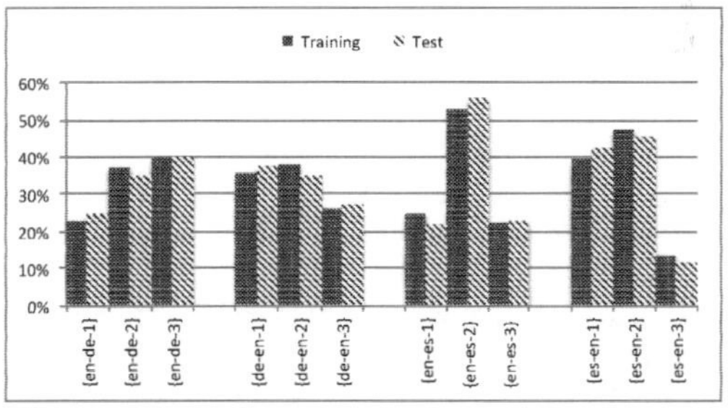

Figure 3: Distribution of true 1-3 scores by langauge pair.

Additionally, we provide some out of domain test data. These translations were annotated in the same way as above, each dataset by one Language Service Provider (LSP), i.e, one professional translator, with two LPSs producing data independently for English-Spanish. They were generated using the LSPs' own source data (a different domain from news), and own MT system (different from the three used for the official datasets). The results on these datasets were not considered for the official ranking of the participating systems:

# Source sentences	# Target sentences
971 English	971 Spanish
297 English	297 German
388 Spanish	388 English

Task 1.2 Predicting percentage of edits

In this task we use HTER (Snover et al., 2006) as quality score. This score is to be interpreted as the minimum edit distance between the machine translation and its manually post-edited version, and its range is [0, 1] (0 when no edit needs to be made, and 1 when all words need to be edited). We used TERp (default settings: tokenised, case insensitive, etc., but capped to 1)[11] to compute the HTER scores.

For practical reasons, the data is a subset of Task 1.1's dataset: only translations produced by the SMT system English-Spanish. As *training data*, we provide 896 English-Spanish translation suggestions and their post-editions. As *test* data, we provide a new set of 208 English-Spanish translations produced by the same SMT system. Each of the training and test translations was post-edited by a professional translator using the CASMACAT[12] web-based tool, which also collects post-editing time on a sentence-basis.

Task 1.3 Predicting post-editing time

For this task systems are required to produce, for each translation, a real valued estimate of the time (in milliseconds) it takes a translator to post-edit the translation. The training and test sets are a subset of that uses in Task 1.2 (subject to filtering of outliers). The difference is that the labels are now the number of milliseconds that were necessary to post-edit each translation.

As *training data*, we provide 650 English-Spanish translation suggestions and their post-editions. As *test* data, we provide a new set of 208 English-Spanish translations (same test data as for Task 1.2).

4.2 Word-level Quality Estimation

The data for this task is based on a subset of the datasets used for Task 1.1, for all language pairs, human and machine translations: those translations labelled "2" (near misses), plus additional data provided by industry (either on the news domain or on other domains, such as technical documentation, produced using their own MT systems, and also pre-labelled as "2"). All segments were annotated with word-level labels by professional translators using the core categories in MQM (Multidimensional Quality Metrics)[13] as error typology (see Figure 4). Each word or sequence of words was annotated with a single error. For (supposedly rare) cases where a decision between multiple fine-grained error types could not be made, annotators were requested to choose a coarser error category in the hierarchy.

Participants are asked to produce a label for each token that indicates quality at different levels of granularity:

- **Binary classification**: an OK / bad label, where bad indicates the need for editing the token.
- **Level 1 classification**: an OK / accuracy / fluency label, specifying coarser level categories of errors for each token, or "OK" for tokens with no error.
- **Multi-class classification**: one of the labels specifying the error type for the token (terminology, mistranslation, missing word, etc.) in Figure 4, or "OK" for tokens with no error.

As *training* data, we provide tokenised translation output for all language pairs, human and machine translations, with tokens annotated with all issue types listed above, or "OK". The annotation was performed manually by professional translators as part of the QTLaunchPad project. For the coarser variants, fine-grained errors are generalised to Accuracy or Fluency, or "bad" for the binary variant. The amount of available training data varies by language pair:

# Source sentences	# Target sentences
1,957 English	1,957 Spanish
715 English	715 German
350 German	350 English
900 Spanish	900 English

[11]http://www.umiacs.umd.edu/~snover/terp/

[12]http://casmacat.eu/

[13]http://www.qt21.eu/launchpad/content/training

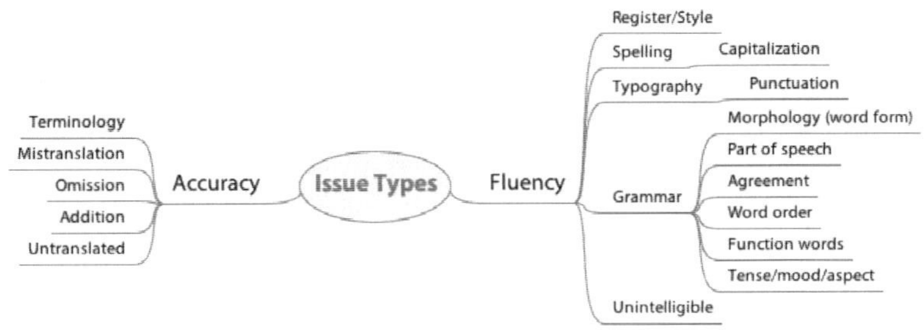

Figure 4: MQM metric as error typology.

As *test* data, we provide additional data points for all language pairs, human and machine translations:

# Source sentences	# Target sentences
382 English	382 Spanish
150 English	150 German
100 German	100 English
150 Spanish	150 English

In contrast to Tasks 1.1–1.3, no baseline feature set is provided to the participants.

Similar to last year (Bojar et al., 2013), the word-level task is primarily evaluated by macro-averaged F-measure (in %). Because the class distribution is skewed – in the test data about 78% of the tokens are marked as "OK" – we compute precision, recall, and F_1 for each class individually, weighting F_1 scores by the frequency of the class in the test data. This avoids giving undue importance to less frequent classes. Consider the following confusion matrix for Level 1 annotation, i.e. the three classes *(O)K*, *(F)luency*, and *(A)ccuracy*:

		reference O	reference F	reference A
predicted	O	4172	1482	193
predicted	F	1819	1333	214
predicted	A	198	133	69

For each of the three classes we assume a binary setting (one-vs-all) and derive true-positive (tp), false-positive (fp), and false-negative (fn) counts from the rows and columns of the confusion matrix as follows:

$$
\begin{aligned}
tp_O &= 4172\\
fp_O &= 1482 + 193 = 1675\\
fn_O &= 1819 + 198 = 2017\\
tp_F &= 1333\\
fp_F &= 1819 + 214 = 2033\\
fn_F &= 1482 + 133 = 1615\\
tp_A &= 69\\
fp_A &= 198 + 133 = 331\\
fn_A &= 193 + 214 = 407
\end{aligned}
$$

We continue to compute F_1 scores for each class $c \in \{O, F, A\}$:

$$
\begin{aligned}
\text{precision}_c &= tp_c/(tp_c + fp_c)\\
\text{recall}_c &= tp_c/(tp_c + fn_c)\\
F_{1,c} &= \frac{2 \cdot \text{precision}_c \cdot \text{recall}_c}{\text{precision}_c + \text{recall}_c}
\end{aligned}
$$

yielding:

$$
\begin{aligned}
\text{precision}_O &= 4172/(4172 + 1675) = 0.7135\\
\text{recall}_O &= 4172/(4172 + 2017) = 0.6741\\
F_{1,O} &= \frac{2 \cdot 0.7135 \cdot 0.6741}{0.7135 + 0.6741} = 0.6932\\
&\dots\\
F_{1,F} &= 0.4222\\
F_{1,A} &= 0.1575
\end{aligned}
$$

Finally, we compute the average of $F_{1,c}$ scores weighted by the occurrence count $N(c)$ of c:

$$\text{weighted } F_{1,\text{ALL}} = \frac{1}{\sum_c N(c)} \sum_c N_c \cdot F_{1,c}$$

$$\text{weighted } F_{1,\text{ERR}} = \frac{1}{\sum_{c:c \neq O} N(c)} \sum_{c:c \neq O} N_c \cdot F_{1,c}$$

which for the above example gives:

$$\text{weighted } F_{1,\text{ALL}} = \frac{1}{6189 + 2948 + 476} \cdot (6189 \cdot 0.6932 + 2948 \cdot 0.4222 + 476 \cdot 0.1575) = 0.5836$$

$$\text{weighted } F_{1,\text{ERR}} = \frac{1}{2948 + 476} \cdot (2948 \cdot 0.4222 + 476 \cdot 0.1575) = 0.3854$$

We choose $F_{1,ERR}$ as our primary evaluation measure because it most closely mimics the common application of F_1 scores in binary classification: one is interested in the performance in detecting a *positive class*, which in this case would be erroneous words. This does, however, ignore the number of correctly classified words of the *OK* class, which is why we also report $F_{1,ALL}$. In addition, we follow Powers (2011) and report Matthews Correlation Coefficient (MCC), averaged in the same way as F_1, as our secondary metric. Finally, for contrast we also report Accuracy (ACC).

4.3 Participants

Table 10 lists all participating teams. Each team was allowed up to two submissions for each task and language pair. In the descriptions below, participation in specific tasks is denoted by a task identifier: T1.1, T1.2, T1.3, and T2.

Sentence-level baseline system (T1.1, T1.2, T1.3): QUEST is used to extract 17 system-independent features from source and translation sentences and parallel corpora (same features as in the WMT12 shared task):

- number of tokens in the source and target sentences.
- average source token length.
- average number of occurrences of the target word within the target sentence.
- number of punctuation marks in source and target sentences.
- language model (LM) probability of source and target sentences based on models for the WMT News Commentary corpus.
- average number of translations per source word in the sentence as given by IBM Model 1 extracted from the WMT News Commentary parallel corpus, and thresholded so that $P(t|s) > 0.2$, or so that $P(t|s) > 0.01$ weighted by the inverse frequency of each word in the source side of the parallel corpus.
- percentage of unigrams, bigrams and trigrams in frequency quartiles 1 (lower frequency words) and 4 (higher frequency words) in the source language extracted from the WMT News Commentary corpus.
- percentage of unigrams in the source sentence seen in the source side of the WMT News Commentary corpus.

These features are used to train a Support Vector Machine (SVM) regression algorithm using a radial basis function kernel within the SCIKIT-LEARN toolkit. The γ, ϵ and C parameters were optimised via grid search with 5-fold cross validation on the training set. We note that although the system is referred to as "baseline", it is in fact a strong system. It has proved robust across a range of language pairs, MT systems, and text domains for predicting various forms of post-editing effort (Callison-Burch et al., 2012; Bojar et al., 2013).

DCU (T1.1): DCU-MIXED and DCU-SVR use a selection of features available in QUEST, such as punctuation statistics, LM perplexity, n-gram frequency quartile statistics and coarse-grained POS frequency ratios, and four additional feature types: combined POS and stop word LM features, source-side pseudo-reference features, inverse glass-box features for translating the translation and error grammar parsing features. For machine learning, the QUEST framework is expanded to combine logistic regression and support vector regression and to handle cross- validation and randomisation in a way that training items with the same source side are kept together. External resources are monolingual corpora taken from the WMT 2014 translation task for LMs, the MT system used for the inverse glass-box features (Li et al., 2014b) and, for error grammar parsing, the Penn-Treebank and an error grammar derived from it (Foster, 2007).

ID	Participating team
DCU	Dublin City University Team 1, Ireland (Hokamp et al., 2014)
DFKI	German Research Centre for Artificial Intelligence, Germany (Avramidis, 2014)
FBK-UPV-UEDIN	Fondazione Bruno Kessler, Italy, UPV Universitat Politècnica de València, Spain & University of Edinburgh, UK (Camargo de Souza et al., 2014)
LIG	Laboratoire d'Informatique Grenoble, France (Luong et al., 2014)
LIMSI	Laboratoire d'Informatique pour la Mécanique et les Sciences de l'Ingénieur, France (Wisniewski et al., 2014)
MULTILIZER	Multilizer, Finland
RTM-DCU	Dublin City University Team 2, Ireland (Bicici and Way, 2014)
SHEF-lite	University of Sheffield Team 1, UK (Beck et al., 2014)
USHEFF	University of Sheffield Team 2, UK (Scarton and Specia, 2014)
YANDEX	Yandex, Russia

Table 10: Participants in the WMT14 Quality Estimation shared task.

DFKI (T1.2): DFKI/SVR builds upon the baseline system (above) by adding non-redundant data from the WMT13 task for predicting the same label (HTER) and additional features such as (a) rule-based language corrections (language tool) (b), PCFG parsing statistics and counts of tree labels, (c) position statistics of parsing labels, (d) position statistics of trigrams with low probability. DFKI/SVRxdata uses a similar setting, with the addition of more training data from non-minimally post-edited translation outputs (references), filtered based on a threshold on the edit distance between the MT output and the freely-translated reference.

FBK-UPV-UEDIN (T1.2, T1.3, T2): The submissions for the word-level task (T2) use features extracted from word posterior probabilities and confusion network descriptors computed over the 100k-best hypothesis translations generated by a phrase-based SMT system. They also use features from word lexicons, and POS tags of each word for source and translation sentences. The predictions of the Binary model are used as a feature for the Level 1 and Multi-class settings. Both conditional random fields (CRF) and bidirectional long short-term memory recurrent neural networks (BLSTM-RNNs) are used for the Binary setting, and BLSTM-RNNs only for the Level 1 and Multi-class settings.

The sentence-level QE submissions (T1.2 and T1.3) are trained on black-box features extracted using QuEst in addition to features based on word alignments, word posterior probabilities and diversity scores (Souza et al., 2013). These features are computed over 100k-best hypothesis translations also used for task 2. In addition, a set of ratios computed from the word-level predictions of the model trained on the binary setting of task 2 is used. A total of 221 features and the extremely randomised trees (Geurts et al., 2006) learning algorithm are used to train regression models.

LIG (T2): Conditional Random Fields classifiers are trained with features used in LIG's WMT13 systems (Luong et al., 2013): target and source words, alignment information, source and target alignment context, LM scores, target and source POS tags, lexical categorisations (stopword, punctuation, proper name, numerical), constituent label, depth in the constituent tree, target polysemy count, pseudo reference. These are combined with novel features: word occurrence in multiple translation systems and POS tag-based LM scores (longest target/source n-gram length and backoff score for POS tag). These features require external NLP tools and resources such as: TreeTagger, GIZA++, Bekerley parser, Link Grammar parser, WordNet and BabelNet, Google Translate (pseudo-reference). For the binary task, the optimal classification threshold is tuned based on a development set split from the original training set. Feature selection is employed over the all features (for the binary task only), with the Sequential Backward Selection algorithm. The best performing feature set is then also used for the Level 1 and Multi-class variants.

LIMSI (T2): The submission relies on a random forest classifier and considers only 16 dense and continuous features. To prevent sparsity issues, lexicalised information such as the word or the previous word identities is not included. The features considered are mostly classic MT features and can be categorised into two classes: *association features*, which describe the quality of the association between the source sentence and each target word, and *fluency features*, which describe the 'quality' of the translation hypotheses. The latter rely on different language models (either on POS or on words) and the former on IBM Model 1 translation probabilities and on pseudo- references, i.e. translation produced by an independent MT system. Random forests are known to perform well in tasks like this one, in which only a few dense and continuous features are available, possibly because of their ability to take into account complex interactions between features and to automatically partition the continuous feature values into a discrete set of intervals that achieves the best classification performance. Since they predict the class probabilities, it is possible to directly optimize the F_1 score during training by finding, with a grid search method, the decision threshold that achieved the best F_1 score on the training set.

MULTILIZER (T1.2, T1.3): The 80 black-box features from QuEst are used in addition to new features based on using other MT engines for forward and backward translations. In forward translations, the idea is that different MT engines make different mistakes. Therefore, when several forward translations are similar to each other, these translations are more likely to be correct. This is confirmed by the Pearson correlation of similarities between the forward translations against the true scores (above 0.5). A backward translation is very error-prone and therefore it has to be used in combination with forward translations. A single back-translation similar to original source segment does not bring much information. Instead, when several MT engines give back-translations similar to this source segment, one can conclude that the translation is reliable. Those translations where similarities both in forward translation and backward translation are high are intuitively more likely to be good. A simple feature selection method that omits all features with Pearson correlation against the true scores below 0.2 is used. The systems submitted are obtained using linear regression models.

RTM-DCU (T1.1, T1.2, T1.3, T2): RTM-DCU systems are based on referential translation machines (RTM) (Biçici, 2013) and parallel feature decay algorithms (ParFDA5) (Biçici et al., 2014), which allow language and MT system-independent predictions. For each task, individual RTM models are developed using the parallel corpora and the language model corpora distributed by the WMT14 translation task and the language model corpora provided by LDC for English and Spanish. RTMs use 337 to 437 sentence-level features for coverage and diversity, IBM1 and sentence translation performance, retrieval closeness and minimum Bayes retrieval risk, distributional similarity and entropy, IBM2 alignment, character n-grams, sentence readability, and parse output tree structures. The features use ngrams defined over text or common cover link (CCL) (Seginer, 2007) structures as the basic units of information over which similarity calculations are performed. Learning models include ridge regression (RR), support vector machines (SVR), and regression trees (TREE), which are applied after partial least squares (PLS) or feature selection (FS). For word-level prediction, generalised linear models (GLM) (Collins, 2002) and GLM with dynamic learning (GLMd) (Biçici, 2013) are used with word-level features including CCL links, word length, location, prefix, suffix, form, context, and alignment, totalling up to a couple of million features.

SHEF-lite (T1.1, T1.2, T1.3): These submissions use the framework of Multi-task Gaussian Processes, where multiple datasets are combined in a multi-task setting similar to the one used by Cohn and Specia (2013). For T1.1, data for all language pairs is put together, and each language is considered a task. For T1.2 and T1.3, additional datasets from previous shared task years are used, each encoded as a different task. For all tasks, the QUEST framework is used to extract a set of 80 black-box features (a superset of the 17 baseline features). To cope with the large size of the datasets, the SHEF-lite-sparse submission uses Sparse Gaussian Processes, which provide sensible sparse approximations using only a subset of instances (inducing inputs) to speed up training and prediction. For this "sparse" submission, feature selection is performed following the approach of Shah et al. (2013) by ranking features according to their learned length-scales and selecting the top 40 features.

USHEFF (T1.1, T1.2, T1.3): USHEFF submissions exploit the use of consensus among MT systems by comparing the MT system output to several alternative translations generated by other MT systems (pseudo-references). The comparison is done using standard evaluation metrics (BLEU, TER, METEOR, ROUGE for all tasks, and two metrics based on syntactic similarities from shallow and dependency parser information for T1.2 and T1.3). Figures extracted from such metrics are used as features to complement prediction models trained on the 17 baseline features. Different from the standard use of pseudo-reference features, these features do not assume that the alternative MT systems are better than the system of interest. A more realistic scenario is considered where the quality of the pseudo-references is not known. For T1, no external systems in addition to those provided for the shared task are used: for a given translation, all alternative translations for the same source segment (two or three, depending on the language pair) are used as pseudo-references. For T1.2 and T1.3, for each source sentence, all alternative translations produced by MT systems on the same data (WMT12/13) are used as pseudo-references. The hypothesis is that by using translations from several MT systems one can find consensual information and this can smooth out the effect of "coincidences" in the similarities between systems' translations. SVM regression with radial basis function kernel and hyper-parameters optimised via grid search is used to build the models.

YANDEX (T1.1): Both submissions are based on the the 80 black-box features, plus an LM score from a larger language model, a pseudo-reference, and several additional features based on POS tags and syntactic parsers. The first attempt uses an extract of the top 5 features selected with a greedy search from the set of all features. SVM regression is used as machine learning algorithm. The second attempt uses the same features processed with Yandex' implementation of the gradient tree boosting (MatrixNet).

4.4 Results

In what follows we give the official results for all tasks followed by a discussion that highlights the main findings for each of the tasks.

Task 1.1 Predicting post-editing effort

Table 11 summarises the results for the ranking variant of Task 1.1. They are sorted from best to worst using the DeltaAvg metric scores as primary key and the Spearman's rank correlation scores as secondary key.

The winning submissions for the ranking variant of Task 1.1 are as follows: for English-Spanish it is RTM-DCU/RTM-TREE, with a DeltaAvg score of 0.26; for Spanish-English it is USHEFF, with a DeltaAvg score of 0.23; for English-German it is again RTM-DCU/RTM-TREE, with a DeltaAvg score of 0.39; and for German-English it is RTM-DCU/RTM-RR, with a DeltaAvg score of 0.38. These winning submissions are better than the baseline system by a large margin, which indicates that current best performance in MT quality estimation has reached levels that are clearly beyond what the baseline system can produce. As for the other systems, according to DeltaAvg, compared to the previous year results a smaller percentage of systems is able to beat the baseline. This might be a consequence of the use of the metric for the prediction of only three discrete labels.

The results for the scoring task are presented in Table 12, sorted from best to worst using the MAE

System ID	DeltaAvg	Spearman Corr
English-Spanish		
• RTM-DCU/RTM-PLS-TREE	0.26	0.38
• RTM-DCU/RTM-TREE	0.26	0.41
• YANDEX/SHAD_BOOSTEDTREES2	0.23	0.35
USHEFF	0.21	0.33
SHEFF-lite	0.21	0.33
YANDEX/SHAD_SVR1	0.18	0.29
SHEFF-lite-sparse	0.17	0.27
Baseline SVM	0.14	0.22
Spanish-English		
• USHEFF	0.23	0.30
• RTM-DCU/RTM-PLS-RR	0.20	0.35
• RTM-DCU/RTM-FS-RR	0.19	0.36
Baseline SVM	0.12	0.21
SHEFF-lite-sparse	0.12	0.17
SHEFF-lite	0.11	0.15
English-German		
• RTM-DCU/RTM-TREE	0.39	0.54
RTM-DCU/RTM-PLS-TREE	0.33	0.42
USHEFF	0.26	0.41
SHEFF-lite	0.26	0.36
Baseline SVM	0.23	0.34
SHEFF-lite-sparse	0.23	0.33
German-English		
• RTM-DCU/RTM-RR	0.38	0.51
• RTM-DCU/RTM-PLS-RR	0.35	0.45
USHEFF	0.28	0.30
SHEFF-lite	0.24	0.27
Baseline SVM	0.21	0.25
SHEFF-lite-sparse	0.14	0.17

Table 11: Official results for the ranking variant of the WMT14 Quality Evaluation Task 1.1. The winning submissions are indicated by a •. These are the top-scoring submission and those that are not significantly worse according to bootstrap resampling (1M times) with 95% confidence intervals. The systems in the gray area are not different from the baseline system at a statistically significant level according to the same test.

System ID	MAE	RMSE
English-Spanish		
• RTM-DCU/RTM-PLS-TREE	0.49	0.61
• SHEFF-lite	0.49	0.63
• USHEFF	0.49	0.63
• SHEFF-lite/sparse	0.49	0.69
• RTM-DCU/RTM-TREE	0.49	0.61
Baseline SVM	0.52	0.66
YANDEX/SHAD_BOOSTEDTREES2	0.56	0.68
YANDEX/SHAD_SVR1	0.64	0.81
DCU-Chris/SVR	0.66	0.88
DCU-Chris/MIXED	0.94	1.14
Spanish-English		
• RTM-DCU/RTM-FS-RR	0.53	0.64
• SHEFF-lite/sparse	0.54	0.69
• RTM-DCU/RTM-PLS-RR	0.55	0.71
USHEFF	0.57	0.67
Baseline SVM	0.57	0.68
SHEFF-lite	0.62	0.77
DCU-Chris/MIXED	0.65	0.91
English-German		
• RTM-DCU/RTM-TREE	0.58	0.68
RTM-DCU/RTM-PLS-TREE	0.60	0.71
SHEFF-lite	0.63	0.74
USHEFF	0.64	0.75
SHEFF-lite/sparse	0.64	0.75
Baseline SVM	0.64	0.76
DCU-Chris/MIXED	0.69	0.98
German-English		
• RTM-DCU/RTM-RR	0.55	0.67
• RTM-DCU/RTM-PLS-RR	0.57	0.74
USHEFF	0.63	0.76
SHEFF-lite	0.65	0.77
Baseline SVM	0.65	0.78

Table 12: Official results for the scoring variant of the WMT14 Quality Evaluation Task 1.1. The winning submissions are indicated by a •. These are the top-scoring submission and those that are not significantly worse according to bootstrap resampling (1M times) with 95% confidence intervals. The systems in the gray area are not different from the baseline system at a statistically significant level according to the same test.

metric scores as primary key and the RMSE metric scores as secondary key.

The winning submissions for the scoring variant of Task 1.1 are as follows: for English-Spanish it is RTM-DCU/RTM-TREE with a MAE of 0.49; for Spanish-English it is RTM-DCU/RTM-FS-RR with a MAE of 0.53; for English-German it is again RTM-DCU/RTM-TREE, with a MAE of 0.58; and for German-English it is RTM-DCU/RTM-RR with a MAE of 0.55. These submissions are again much better than the baseline system, which under the scoring variant seems to perform at a middle-of-the-pack level or lower compared to the overall pool of submissions. Overall, more systems are able to outperform the baseline according to the scoring metric.

The top system for most language pairs are essentially based on the same core techniques (RTM-DCU) according to both the DeltaAvg and MAE metrics. The ranking of other systems, however, can be substantially different according to the two metrics.

Task 1.2 Predicting percentage of edits

Table 13 summarises the results for the ranking variant of Task 1.2. For readability purposes we have used a multiplication-factor of 100 in the scoring script, which makes the HTER numbers (both predicted and gold) to be in the [0, 100] range. They are sorted from best to worst using the DeltaAvg metric scores as primary key and the Spearman's rank correlation scores as secondary key.

The winning submission for the ranking variant of Task 1.2 is RTM-DCU/RTM-SVR, with a DeltaAvg score of 9.31. There is a large margin between this score and the baseline score of DeltaAvg 5.08, which indicates again that current best performance has reached levels that are much beyond what this baseline system can produce. The vast majority of the submissions perform better than the baseline (the only exception is the submission from SHEFF-lite, for which the authors report a major issue with the learning algorithm).

The results for the scoring variant are presented in Table 14, sorted from best to worst by using the MAE metric scores as primary key and the RMSE metric scores as secondary key.

The winning submission for the scoring variant of Task 1.2 is FBK-UPV-UEDIN/WP with a MAE of 12.89, while the baseline system has a MAE of 15.23. Most of the submissions perform better than the baseline.

Task 1.3 Predicting post-editing time

Table 15 summarises the results for the ranking variant of Task 1.3. For readability purposes, we have used a multiplication-factor of 0.001 in the scoring script, which makes the time (both predicted and gold) to be measured in seconds. They are sorted from best to worst using the DeltaAvg metric scores as primary key and the Spearman's rank correlation scores as secondary key.

The winning submission for the ranking variant of Task 1.3 is RTM-DCU/RTM-RR, with a DeltaAvg score of 17.02 (when predicting seconds). The interesting aspect of these results is that the DeltaAvg numbers have a direct real-world interpretation, in terms of time spent (or saved, depending on one's view-point) for post-editing machine-produced translations. A more elaborate discussion on this point can be found in Section 4.5.

The winning submission for the scoring variant of Task 1.3 is RTM-DCU/RTM-SVR, with a MAE of 16.77. Note that all of the submissions perform significantly better than the baseline, which has a MAE of 21.49, and that the majority is not significantly worse than the top scoring submission.

Task 2 Predicting word-level edits

The results for Task 2 are summarised in Tables 17–19. The results are ordered by F_1 score for the Error (BAD) class. For comparison, two trivial baselines are included, one that marks every word as correct and that marks every word with the most common error class found in the training data. Both baselines are clearly useless for any application, but help put the results in perspective. Most teams submitted systems for a single language pair: English-Spanish; only a single team produced predictions for all four pairs.

Table 17 gives the results of the binary (OK vs. BAD) classification variant of Task 2. The winning submissions for this variant are as follows: for English-Spanish it is FBK-UPV-UEDIN/RNN with a weighted F_1 of 48.73; for Spanish-English it is RTM-DCU/RTM-GLMd with a weighted F_1 of 29.14; for English-German it is RTM-DCU/RTM-GLM with a weighted F_1 of 45.30; and for German-English it is again RTM-DCU/RTM-GLM with a weighted F_1 of 26.13.

Remarkably, for three out of four language pairs, the systems fail to beat our trivial baseline of

System ID	DeltaAvg	Spearman Corr
English-Spanish		
• RTM-DCU/RTM-SVR	9.31	0.53
• RTM-DCU/RTM-TREE	8.57	0.48
• USHEFF	7.93	0.45
SHEFF-lite/sparse	7.69	0.43
Baseline	5.08	0.31
SHEFF-lite	0.72	0.09

Table 13: Official results for the ranking variant of the WMT14 Quality Evaluation Task 1.2. The winning submissions are indicated by a •. These are the top-scoring submission and those that are not significantly worse according to bootstrap resampling (100k times) with 95% confidence intervals. The systems in the gray area are not different from the baseline system at a statistically significant level according to the same test.

System ID	MAE	RMSE
English-Spanish		
• FBK-UPV-UEDIN/WP	12.89	16.74
• RTM-DCU/RTM-SVR	13.40	16.69
• USHEFF	13.61	17.84
RTM-DCU/RTM-TREE	14.03	17.48
DFKI/SVR	14.32	17.74
FBK-UPV-UEDIN/NOWP	14.38	18.10
SHEFF-lite/sparse	15.04	18.38
MULTILIZER	15.04	20.86
Baseline	15.23	19.48
DFKI/SVRxdata	16.01	19.52
SHEFF-lite	18.15	23.41

Table 14: Official results for the scoring variant of the WMT14 Quality Evaluation Task 1.2. The winning submissions are indicated by a •. They are statistically indistinguishable from the top submission according to bootstrap resampling (1M times) with 95% confidence intervals. The systems in the gray area are not different from the baseline system at a statistically significant level according to the same test.

System ID	DeltaAvg	Spearman Corr
English-Spanish		
• RTM-DCU/RTM-RR	17.02	0.68
• RTM-DCU/RTM-SVR	16.60	0.67
SHEFF-lite/sparse	16.33	0.63
SHEFF-lite	16.08	0.64
USHEFF	14.98	0.59
Baseline	14.71	0.57

Table 15: Official results for the ranking variant of the WMT14 Quality Evaluation Task 1.3. The winning submissions are indicated by a •. They are statistically indistinguishable from the top submission according to bootstrap resampling (1M times) with a 95% confidence interval. The systems in the gray area are not different from the baseline system at a statistically significant level according to the same test.

System ID	MAE	RMSE
English-Spanish		
• RTM-DCU/RTM-SVR	16.77	26.17
• MULTILIZER/MLZ2	17.07	25.83
• SHEFF-lite	17.13	27.33
• MULTILIZER/MLZ1	17.31	25.51
• SHEFF-lite/sparse	17.42	27.35
• FBK-UPV-UEDIN/WP	17.48	25.31
RTM-DCU/RTM-RR	17.50	25.97
FBK-UPV-UEDIN/NOWP	18.69	26.58
USHEFF	21.48	34.28
Baseline	21.49	34.28

Table 16: Official results for the scoring variant of the WMT14 Quality Evaluation Task 1.3. The winning submissions are indicated by a •. They are statistically indistinguishable from the top submission according to bootstrap resampling (1M times) with a 95% confidence interval. The systems in the gray area are not different from the baseline system at a statistically significant level according to the same test.

System ID	weighted F_1 All	F_1 Bad ↑	MCC	ACC
English-Spanish				
Baseline (always OK)	50.43	0.00	0.00	64.38
Baseline (always Bad)	18.71	52.53	0.00	35.62
• FBK-UPV-UEDIN/RNN	62.00	48.73	18.23	61.62
LIMSI/RF	60.55	47.32	15.44	60.09
LIG/FS	63.55	44.47	19.41	64.67
LIG/BL ALL	63.77	44.11	19.91	65.12
FBK-UPV-UEDIN/RNN+tandem+crf	62.17	42.63	16.32	63.26
RTM-DCU/RTM-GLM	60.68	35.08	13.45	63.74
RTM-DCU/RTM-GLMd	60.24	32.89	12.98	63.97
Spanish-English				
Baseline (always OK)	74.41	0.00	0.00	82.37
Baseline (always Bad)	5.28	29.98	0.00	17.63
• RTM-DCU/RTM-GLMd	79.54	29.14	25.47	82.98
RTM-DCU/RTM-GLM	79.42	26.91	25.93	83.43
English-German				
Baseline (always OK)	59.39	0.00	0.00	71.33
Baseline (always Bad)	12.78	44.57	0.00	28.67
• RTM-DCU/RTM-GLM	71.51	45.30	28.61	72.97
RTM-DCU/RTM-GLMd	68.73	36.91	21.32	71.41
German-English				
Baseline (always OK)	67.82	0.00	0.00	77.60
Baseline (always Bad)	8.20	36.60	0.00	22.40
• RTM-DCU/RTM-GLM	72.41	26.13	16.08	76.14
RTM-DCU/RTM-GLMd	71.42	22.97	12.63	75.46

Table 17: Official results for the binary part of the WMT14 Quality Evaluation Task 2. The winning submissions are indicated by a •. All values are given as percentages.

marking all the words as wrong. This may either indicate that the predictions themselves are of low quality or the chosen evaluation approach is misleading. On the other hand F_1 scores are a common measure of binary classification performance and no averaging is performed here.

Table 18 gives the results of the Level 1 classification (OK, Fluency, Accuracy) variant of Task 2. Here the second baseline is to always predict Fluency errors, as this is the most common error category in the training data. The winning submissions of this variant are as follows: for English-Spanish it is FBK-UPV-UEDIN/RNN+tandem+crf with a weighted F_1 of 23.94 and for Spanish-English, English-German, and German-English it is RTM-DCU/RTM-GLMd with weighted F_1 scores of 23.94, 21.94, and 8.57 respectively.

As before, all systems fail to outperform the single-class baseline for the Spanish-English language pair according to our primary metric. However, for Spanish-English and English-German both submissions are able to beat the baseline by large margin. We also observe that the absolute numbers vary greatly between language pairs.

Table 19 gives the results of the Multi-class classification variant of Task 2. Again, the second baseline is to always predict the most common error category in the training data, which varies depending on language pair and produces and increasingly weak baseline as the number of classes rises.

The winning submissions of this variant are as follows: for English-Spanish, Spanish-English, and English-German it is RTM-DCU/RTM-GLM with weighted F_1 scores of 26.84, 8.75, and 15.02 respectively and and for German-English it is RTM-DCU/RTM-GLMd with a weighted F_1 of 3.08. Not only do these systems perform above our baselines for all but the German-English language pair, they also outperform all other submissions for English-Spanish. Remarkably, RTM-DCU/RTM-GLM wins English-Spanish for all of the proposed metrics by a sizeable margin.

4.5 Discussion

In what follows, we discuss the main accomplishments of this year's shared task starting from the goals we had previously identified for it.

Investigating the effectiveness of different quality labels

For the sentence-level tasks, the results of this year's shared task allow us to investigate the effectiveness of predicting translation quality using three very different quality labels: perceived post-editing effort on a scale of [1-3] (Task 1.1); HTER scores (Task 1.2); and the time that a translator takes to post-edit the translation (Task 1.3). One of the ways one can compare the effectiveness across all these different labels is to look at how well the models can produce predictions that correlate with the gold label that we have at our disposal. A measure of correlation that does not depend on the value of the labels is Spearman's ranking correlation. From this perspective, the label that seems the most effective appears to be post-editing time (Task 1.3), with the best system (RTM-DCU/RTM-RR) producing a Spearman's ρ of 0.68 (English-Spanish translations, see Table 15). In comparison, when perceived post-editing effort labels are used (Task 1.1), the best systems achieve a Spearman's ρ of 0.38 and 0.30 for English-Spanish and Spanish-English translations, respectively, and ρ of 0.54 and 0.51 for English-German and German-English, respectively (Table 11); for HTER scores (Task 1.2) the best systems achieve a Spearman's ρ of 0.53 for English-Spanish translations (Table 13).

This comparison across tasks seems to indicate that, among the three labels we have proposed, post-editing time seems to be the most *learnable*, in the sense that automatic predictions can vest match the gold labels (in this case, with respect to the rankings they induce). A possible reason for this is that post-editing time correlates with the length of the source sentence whereas HTER is a normalised measure.

Compared to the results regarding time prediction in the Quality Evaluation shared task from 2013 (Bojar et al., 2013), we note that this time all submissions were able to beat the baseline system (compared to only 1/3 of the submissions in 2013). In addition, better handling of the data acquisition reduced the number of outliers in this year's dataset allowing for numbers that are more reliably *interpretable*. As an example of its interpretability, consider the following: the winning submission for the ranking variant of Task 1.3 is RTM-DCU/RTM-RR, with a a Spearman's ρ of 0.68 and a DeltaAvg score of 17.02 (when predict-

System ID	weighted F_1 All	weighted F_1 Errors ↑	weighted MCC All	weighted MCC Errors	ACC
English-Spanish					
Baseline (always OK)	50.43	0.00	0.00	0.00	64.38
Baseline (always fluency)	14.39	40.41	0.00	0.00	30.67
• FBK-UPV-UEDIN/RNN+tandem+crf	58.36	38.54	16.63	13.89	57.98
FBK-UPV-UEDIN/RNN	60.32	37.25	18.22	15.51	61.75
LIG/BL ALL	58.97	31.79	14.95	11.48	61.13
LIG/FS	58.95	31.78	14.92	11.46	61.10
RTM-DCU/RTM-GLMd	58.23	26.62	12.60	12.76	62.94
RTM-DCU/RTM-GLM	56.47	29.91	8.11	7.96	58.56
Spanish-English					
Baseline (always OK)	74.41	0.00	0.00	0.00	82.37
Baseline (always fluency)	2.67	15.13	0.00	0.00	12.24
• RTM-DCU/RTM-GLMd	78.89	23.94	25.41	25.45	83.17
RTM-DCU/RTM-GLM	78.78	21.96	26.31	26.99	83.69
English-German					
Baseline (always OK)	59.39	0.00	0.00	0.00	71.33
Baseline (always fluency)	3.83	13.35	0.00	0.00	14.82
• RTM-DCU/RTM-GLMd	64.58	21.94	17.69	15.92	69.26
RTM-DCU/RTM-GLM	64.43	21.10	16.99	14.93	69.34
German-English					
Baseline (always OK)	67.82	0.00	0.00	0.00	77.60
Baseline (always fluency)	3.34	14.92	0.00	0.00	13.79
• RTM-DCU/RTM-GLMd	69.17	8.57	10.61	5.76	75.91
RTM-DCU/RTM-GLM	69.09	8.26	9.95	5.76	75.97

Table 18: Official results for the Level 1 classification part of the WMT14 Quality Evaluation Task 2. The winning submissions are indicated by a •. All values are given as percentages.

System ID	weighted F_1 All	weighted F_1 Errors ↑	weighted MCC All	weighted MCC Errors	ACC
English-Spanish					
Baseline (always OK)	50.43	0.00	0.00	0.00	64.38
Baseline (always unintelligible)	7.93	22.26	0.00	0.00	21.99
• RTM-DCU/RTM-GLM	60.52	26.84	23.77	21.45	66.83
FBK-UPV-UEDIN/RNN+tandem+crf	52.96	23.07	15.17	10.74	52.13
LIG/BL ALL	56.66	20.50	18.56	13.39	60.39
LIG/FS	56.66	20.50	18.56	13.39	60.39
FBK-UPV-UEDIN/RNN	52.84	17.09	7.66	4.24	57.18
RTM-DCU/RTM-GLMd	51.87	3.22	10.16	4.04	64.42
Spanish-English					
Baseline (always OK)	74.41	0.00	0.00	0.00	82.37
Baseline (always word order)	0.34	1.96	0.00	0.00	4.24
• RTM-DCU/RTM-GLM	76.34	8.75	19.82	13.43	83.27
RTM-DCU/RTM-GLMd	76.21	8.19	19.35	15.32	83.17
English-German					
Baseline (always OK)	59.39	0.00	0.00	0.00	71.33
Baseline (always mistranslation)	2.48	8.66	0.00	0.00	11.78
• RTM-DCU/RTM-GLM	63.57	15.02	17.57	15.08	70.82
RTM-DCU/RTM-GLMd	63.33	12.48	18.70	13.20	71.45
German-English					
Baseline (always OK)	67.82	0.00	0.00	0.00	77.60
Baseline (always word order)	1.56	6.96	0.00	0.00	9.23
• RTM-DCU/RTM-GLMd	67.62	3.08	7.19	1.48	74.73
RTM-DCU/RTM-GLM	67.86	2.36	7.55	1.79	75.75

Table 19: Official results for the Multi-class classification part of the WMT14 Quality Evaluation Task 2. The winning submissions are indicated by a •. All values are given as percentages.

ing seconds). This number has a direct real-world interpretation: using the order proposed by this system, a human translator would spend, on average, about 17 seconds less on a sentence taken from the top of the ranking compared to a sentence picked randomly from the set.[14] To put this number into perspective, for this dataset the average time to complete a sentence post-editing is 39 seconds. As such, one has an immediate interpretation for the usefulness of using such a ranking: translating around 100 sentences taken from the top of the rankings would take around 36min (at about 22 seconds/sentence), while translating the same number of sentences extracted randomly from the same dataset would take around 1h5min (at about 39 seconds/sentence). It is in this sense that we consider post-editing time an interpretable label.

Another desirable property of label predictions is *usefulness*; this property, however, it highly task-dependent and therefore cannot be judged in the absence of a specific task. For instance, an interpretable label like post-editing time may not be that useful in a task the requires one to place the machine translations into "ready to publish" and "not ready to publish" bins. For such an application, labels such as the ones used by Task 1.1 are clearly more useful, and also very much interpretable within the scope of the task. Our attempt at presenting the Quality Prediction task with a variety of prediction labels illustrates a good range of properties for the proposed labels and enables one to draw certain conclusions depending on the needs of the specific task at hand.

For the word-level tasks, different quality labels equate with using different levels of granularity for the predictions, which we discuss next.

Exploring word-level quality prediction at different levels of granularity

Previous work on word-level predictions, e.g. (Bojar et al., 2013) has focused on prediction of automatically derived labels, generally due to practical considerations as the manual annotation is labour intensive. While easily applicable, automatic annotations, using for example TER alignment between the machine translation and reference (or post-edition), face the same problems as automatic MT evaluation metrics as they fail to account for different word choices and lack the ability to reliably distinguish meaning preserving reorderings from those that change the semantics of the output. Furthermore, previous automatic annotation for word-level quality estimation has focused on binary labels: correct / incorrect, or at most, the main edit operations that can be captured by alignment metrics like TER: correct, insertion, deletion, substitution.

In this year's task we were able to provide manual fine-grained annotations at the word-level produced by humans irrespective of references or post-editions. Error categories range from frequent ones, such as *unintelligible*, *mistranslation*, and *terminology*, to rare ones such as *additions* or *omissions*. For example, only 10 out of more than 3,400 errors in the English-Spanish test set fall into the latter categories, while over 2,000 words are marked as *unintelligible*. By hierarchically grouping errors into coarser categories we aimed to find a compromise between data sparsity and the expressiveness of the labels. What marks a good compromise depends on the use case, which we do not specify here, and the quality of the finer grained predictions: if a system is able to predict even rare errors these may be grouped later if necessary.

Overall, word-level error prediction seems to remain a challenging task as evidenced by the fact that many submissions were unable to beat a trivial baseline. We hypothesise that this is at least partially due to a mismatch in loss-functions used in training and testing. We know from the system descriptions that some systems were tuned to optimise squared error or accuracy, while evaluation was performed using weighted F_1 scores. On the other hand, even a comparison of just accuracy shows that systems struggle to obtain a lower error rates than the "all-OK" baseline.

Such performance problems are consistent over the three levels of granularity, contrary to the intuition that binary classification would be easier. A notable exception is the RTM-DCU/RTM-GLM system, which is able to beat both the baseline and all other systems on the Multi-Class variant of the English-Spanish task – cf. Table 19 – with regard to all metrics. For this and most other submissions we observe that labels are not consistent for different granularities, i.e. at token marked with a specific error in the multi-class variant may still

[14] Note that the 17.02 seconds figure is a difference in real-time, not predicted time; what is considered in this variant of Task 1.3 is only the predicted ranking of data points, not the absolute values of the predictions.

carry an "OK" label in binary annotation. Thus, additional coarse grained annotations may be derived by automatic means. For example, mapping the multi-class predictions of the above system to coarser categories improves the $F_{1,ERR}$ score in Table 17 from 35.08 to 37.02 but does not change the rank with respect to the other entries.

The fact that coarse grained predictions seem not to be derived from the fine-grained ones leads us to believe that most participants treated the different granularities as independent classification tasks. The FBK-UPV-UEDIN team transfers information in the opposite direction by using their binary predictions as features for Level-1 and multi-class.

Given the current quality of word-level prediction it remains unclear if these systems can already be employed in a practical setting, e.g. to focus the attention of post-editors.

Studying the effects of training and test datasets with mixed domains, language pairs and MT systems

This year's shared task made available datasets for more than one language pair with the same or different types of annotation, 2-3 multiple MT systems (plus a human translation) per language pair, and out-of-domain test data (Tasks 1.1 and 2). Instances for each language pair were kept in separate datasets and thus the "language pair" variable can be analysed independently. However, for a given language pair, datasets mix translation systems (and humans) in Task 1.1, and also text domains in Task 2.

Directly comparing the performance across language pairs is not possible, given that their datasets have different numbers of instances (produced by 3 or 4 systems) and/or different true score distributions (see Figure 3). For a relative comparison (although not all systems submitted results for all language pairs, which is especially true in Task 2), we observe in Task 1.1 that for all language pairs generally at least half of the systems did better than the baseline. To our surprise, only one submission combined data for multiple languages together for Task 1.1: SHEF-lite, treating each language pair data as a different task in a multi-task learning setting. However, only for the 'sparse' variant of the submission significant gains were reported over modelling each task independently (with the tasks still sharing the same data kernel and the same hyperparameters).

The interpretation of the results for Task 2 is very dependent on the evaluation metric used, but generally speaking a large variation in performance was found between different languages, with English-Spanish performing the best, possibly given the much larger number of training instances. Data for Task 2 also presented varied true score distributions (as shown by the performance of the baseline (e.g. always "OK") in Tables 17-19.

One of the main goals with Task 1.1 (and Task 2 to some extent) was to test the robustness of models in a blind setting where multiple MT systems (and human translations) are put together and their identifiers are now known. All submissions for these tasks were therefore translation system agnostic, with no submission attempting to perform meta-identification of the origins of the translations. For Task 1.1, data from multiple MT systems was explicitly used by USHEFF though the idea of consensus translations. Translations from all but the system of interest for the same source segment were used as pseudo-references. The submission significantly outperformed the baseline for all language pairs and did particularly well for Spanish-English and English-Spanish.

An in depth analysis of Task 1.1's datasets on the difference in prediction performance between models built and applied for individual translation systems and models built and tested for all translations pooled together is presented in (Shah and Specia, 2014). Not surprisingly, the former models perform significantly better, with MAE scores ranging between 0.35 and 0.5 for different language pairs and MT systems, and significantly lower scores for models trained and tested on human translations only (MAE scores between 0.2 and 0.35 for different language pairs), against MAE scores ranging between 0.5 and 0.65 for models with pooled data.

For Tasks 1.2 and 1.3, two submissions included English-Spanish data which had been produced by yet different MT systems (SHEF-lite and DFKI). While using these additional instances seemed attractive given the small number of instances available for these tasks, it is not clear what their contribution was. For example, with a reduced set of instances (only 400) from the combined sets, SHEF-lite/sparse performed significantly better than its variant SHEF-lite.

Finally, with respect to out-of-domain (different

text domain and MT system) test data, for Task 1.1, none of the papers submitted included experiments. (Shah and Specia, 2014) applied the models trained on pooled datasets (as explained above) for each language pair to the out-of-domain test sets. The results were surprisingly positive, with average MAE score of 0.5, compared to the 0.5-0.65 range for in-domain data (see above). Further analysis is necessary to understand the reasons for that.

In Task 2, the official training and test sets already include out-of-domain data because of the very small amount of in-domain data available, and thus is is hard to isolate the effect of this data on the results.

Examining the effectiveness of quality prediction methods on human translations

Datasets for Tasks 1.1 and 2 contain human translations, in addition to the automatic translations from various MT systems. Predicting human translation quality is an area that has been largely unexplored. Previous work has looked into distinguishing human from machine translations (e.g. (Gamon et al., 2005)), but this problem setting is somehow artificial, and moreover arguably harder to solve nowadays given the higher general quality of current MT systems (Shah and Specia, 2014). Although human translations are obviously of higher quality in general, many segments are translated by MT systems with the same or similar levels of quality as human translation. This is particularly true for Task 2, since data had been previously categorised and only "near misses" were selected for the word-level annotation, i.e., human and machine translations that were both nearly perfect in this case.

While no distinction was made between human and machine translations in our tasks, we believe the mix of these two types of translations has had a negative impact in prediction performance. Intuitively, one can expect errors in human translation to be more subtle, and hence more difficult to capture via standard quality estimation features. For example, an incorrect lexical choice (due to, e.g., ambiguity) which still fits the context and does not make the translation ungrammatical is unlikely to be captured. We hoped that participants would design features for this particular type of translation, but although linguistically motivated features have been exploited, they did not seem appropriate for human translations.

It is interesting to mention the indirect use of human translations by USHEFF for Tasks 1.1-1.3: given a translation for a source segment, all other translations for the same segment were used as pseudo-references. Apart from when this translation was actually the human translation, the human translation was effectively used as a reference. While this reference was mixed with 2-3 other pseudo-references (other machine translations) for the feature computations, these features led to significant gains in performance over the baseline features Scarton and Specia (2014).

We believe that more investigation is needed for human translation quality prediction. Tasks dedicated to this type of data at both sentence- and word-level in the next editions of this shared task would be a possible starting point. The acquisition of such data is however much more costly, as it is arguably hard to find examples of low quality human translation, unless specific settings, such as translation learner corpora, are considered.

5 Medical Translation Task

The Medical Translation Task addresses the problem of domain-specific and genre-specific machine translation. The task is split into two subtasks: **summary translation**, focused on translation of sentences from summaries of medical articles, and **query translation**, focused on translation of queries entered by users into medical information search engines.

In general, texts of specific domains and genres are characterized by the occurrence of special vocabulary and syntactic constructions which are rare or even absent in traditional (general-domain) training data and therefore difficult for MT. Specific training data (containing such vocabulary and syntactic constructions) is usually scarce or not available at all. Medicine, however, is an example of a domain for which in-domain training data (both parallel and monolingual) is publicly available in amounts which allow to train a complete SMT system or to adapt an existing one.

5.1 Task Description

In the Medical Translation Task, we provided links to various medical-domain training resources and asked participants to use the data to train or adapt their systems to translate unseen test sets for both subtasks between English and Czech (CS), German (DE), and French (FR), in both directions.

The summary translation test data is domain-specific, but otherwise can be considered as ordinary sentences. On the other hand, the query translation test data is also specific for its genre (general style) – it contains short sequences of (more or less) of independent terms rather than complete and grammatical sentences, the usual target of current MT systems.

Similarly to the standard Translation Task, the participants of the Medical Translation Task were allowed to use only the provided resources in the *constrained task* (in addition to data allowed in the constrained standard Translation Task), but could exploit any additional resources in the *unconstrained task*. The submissions were expected with true letter casing and detokenized. The translation quality was measured using automatic evaluation metrics, manual evaluation was not performed.

5.2 Test and Development Data

The test and development data sets for this task were provided by the EU FP7 project Khresmoi.[15] This projects develops a multi-lingual multi-modal search and access system for biomedical information and documents and its MT component allows users to use non-English queries to search in English documents and see summaries of retrieved documents in their preferred language (Czech, German, or French). The statistics of the data sets are presented in Tables 20 and 21.

For the summary translation subtask, 1,000 and 500 sentences were provided for test development purposes, respectively. The sentences were randomly sampled from *automatically* generated summaries (extracts) of English documents (web pages) containing medical information relevant to 50 topics provided for the CLEF 2013 eHealth Task 3.[16] Out-of-domain and ungrammatical sentences were manually removed. The sentences were then translated by medical experts into Czech, German and French, and the translations were reviewed. Each sentence was provided with the corresponding document ID and topic ID. The set also included a description for each of the 50 topics. The data package (Khresmoi Summary Translation Test Data 1.1) is now available from the LINDAT/CLARIN repository[17] and more details can be found in Zdeňka Urešová and Pecina (2014).

For the query translation subtask, the main test set contains 1,000 queries for test and 508 queries for development purposes. The original English queries were extracted at random from real user query logs provided by the Health on the Net foundation[18] (queries by general public) and the Trip database[19] (queries by medical experts). Each query was translated into Czech, German, and French by medical experts and the translations were reviewed. The data package (Khresmoi Query Translation Test Data 1.0) is available from the LINDAT/CLARIN repository.[20]

An additional test set for the query translation subtask was adopted from the CLEF 2013 eHealth Task 3 (Pecina et al., 2014). It contains 50 queries constructed from titles of the test topics (originally in English) translated into Czech, German, and French by medical experts. The participants were asked to translate the queries back to English and the resulting translations were used in an information retrieval (IR) experiment for extrinsic evaluation.

5.3 Training Data

This section reviews the in-domain resources which were allowed for the constrained Medical Translation Task in addition to resources for the constrained standard Translation Task (see Section 2). Most of the corpora are available for direct download, others can be obtained upon registration. The corpora usually employ their own, more or less complex data format. To lower the entry barrier, we provided a set of easy-to-use scripts to convert the data to a plain text format suitable for MT training.

5.3.1 Parallel Training Data

The medical-domain parallel data includes the following corpora (see Table 22 for statistics): The *EMEA* corpus (Tiedemann, 2009) contains documents from the European Medicines Agency, automatically processed and aligned on sentence level. It is available for many language pairs, including those relevant to this task. *UMLS* is a multilingual metathesaurus of health and biomed-

[15] `http://khresmoi.eu/`

[16] `https://sites.google.com/site/shareclefehealth/`

[17] `http://hdl.handle.net/11858/00-097C-0000-0023-866E-1`

[18] `http://www.hon.ch/`

[19] `http://www.tripdatabase.com/`

[20] `http://hdl.handle.net/11858/00-097C-0000-0022-D9BF-5`

	sents	tokens			
	total	Czech	German	French	English
dev	500	9,209	9,924	12,369	10,350
test	1,000	19,191	20,831	26,183	21,423

Table 20: Statistics of summary test data.

	queries			tokens			
	total	general	expert	Czech	German	French	English
dev	508	249	259	1,128	1,041	1,335	1,084
test	1,000	500	500	2,121	1,951	2,490	2,067

Table 21: Statistics of query test data.

L1–L2	**Czech–English**			**DE–EN**			**FR–EN**		
data set	**sents**	**L1 tokens**	**L2 tokens**	**sents**	**L1 tokens**	**L2 tokens**	**sents**	**L1 tokens**	**L2 tokens**
EMEA	1,053	13,872	14,378	1,108	13,946	14,953	1,092	17,605	14,786
UMLS	1,441	4,248	5,579	2,001	6,613	8,153	2,171	8,505	8,524
Wiki	3	5	6	10	19	22	8	19	17
MuchMore				29	688	740			
PatTr				1,848	102,418	106,727	2,201	127,098	108,665
COPPA							664	49,016	39,933

Table 22: Statistics of the in-domain parallel training data allowed for the constrained task (in thousands).

data set	**English**	**Czech**	**German**	**French**
PatTR	121,592		53,242	54,608
UMLS	7,991	63	24	37
Wiki	26,945	1,784	10,232	8,376
AACT	13,341			
DrugBank	953			
FMA	884			
GENIA	557			
GREC	62			
PIL	662			

Table 23: Sizes of monolingual training data allowed for the constrained tasks (in thousands of tokens).

ical vocabularies and standards (U.S. National Library of Medicine, 2009). The UMLS dataset was constructed by selecting the concepts which have translations in the respective languages. The *Wiki* dataset contains bilingual pairs of titles of Wikipedia articles belonging to the categories identified to be medical-domain within the Khresmoi project. It is available for all three language pairs. The *MuchMore Springer Corpus* is a German–English parallel corpus of medical journals abstracts published by Springer (Buitelaar et al., 2003). *PatTR* is a parallel corpus extracted from the MAREC patent collection (Wäschle and Riezler, 2012). It is available for German–English and French–English. For the medical domain, we only consider text from patents indicated to be from the medicine-related categories (A61, C12N, C12P). *COPPA* (Corpus of Parallel Patent Applications (Pouliquen and Mazenc, 2011) is a French–English parallel corpus extracted from the MAREC patent collection (Wäschle and Riezler, 2012). The medical-domain subset is identified by the same categories as in PatTR.

5.3.2 Monolingual Training Data

The medical-domain monolingual data consists of the following corpora (statistics are presented in Table 23): The monolingual *UMLS* dataset contains concept descriptions in CS, DE, and FR extracted from the UMLS Metathesaurus (see Section 5.3.1). The monolingual *Wiki* dataset consists of articles belonging to the categories identified to be medical-domain within the Khresmoi project. The *PatTR* dataset contains non-parallel data extracted from the medical patents included in the PatTR corpus (see Section 5.3.1). *AACT* is a collection of restructured and reformatted English texts publicly available and downloadable from ClinicalTrials.gov, containing clinical studies conducted around the world. *DrugBank* is a bioinformatics and cheminformatics resource containing drug descriptions (Knox et al., 2011). *GENIA* is a corpus of biomedical literature compiled and annotated within the GENIA project (Kim et al., 2003). *FMA* stands for the Foundational Model of Anatomy Ontology, a knowledge source for biomedical informatics concerned with symbolic representation of the phenotypic structure of the human body (Rosse and Mejino Jr., 2008). *GREC* (Gene Regulation Event Corpus) is a semantically annotated English corpus of abstracts of biomedical papers (Thompson et al., 2009). The *PIL* corpus is a collection of documents giving instructions to patients about their medication (Bouayad-Agha et al., 2000).

5.4 Participants

A total of eight teams participated in the Medical Translation Task by submitting their systems to at least one subtask for one or more translation directions. A list of the participants is given in Table 24; we provide short descriptions of their systems in the following.

CUNI was involved in the organization of the task, and their primary goal was to set up a baseline for both the subtasks and for all translation directions.

ID	Participating team
CUNI	Charles University in Prague (Dušek et al., 2014)
DCU-Q	Dublin City University (Okita et al., 2014)
DCU-S	Dublin City University (Zhang et al., 2014)
LIMSI	Laboratoire dInformatique pour la Mecanique et les Sciences de lIngénieur (Pécheux et al., 2014)
POSTECH	Pohang University of Science and Technology (Li et al., 2014a)
UEDIN	University of Edinburgh (Durrani et al., 2014a)
UM-DA	University of Macau (Wang et al., 2014)
UM-WDA	University of Macau (Lu et al., 2014)

Table 24: Participants in the WMT14 Medical Translation Task.

Their systems are based on the Moses phrase-based toolkit and linear interpolation of in-domain and out-of-domain language models and phrase tables. The constrained/unconstrained systems differ in the training data only. The constrained ones are built using all allowed training data; the unconstrained ones take advantage of additional web-crawled monolingual data used for training of the language models, and additional parallel non-medical data from the PatTr and COPPA patent collections.

DCU-Q submitted a system designed specifically for terminology translation in the query translation task for EN–FR and FR–EN. This system supports six terminology extraction methods and is able to detect rare word pairs including zero-appearance word pairs. It uses monotonic decoding with lattice inputs, avoiding unnecessary hypothesis expansions by the reordering model.

DCU-S submitted a system to the FR–EN summary translation subtask only. The system is similar to DCU's system for patent translation (phrased-based using Moses) but adapted to translate medical summaries and reports.

LIMSI took part in the summary translation subtask for English to French.Their primary submission uses a combination of two translation systems: NCODE, based on bilingual n-gram translation models; and an on-the-fly estimation of the parameters of Moses along with a vector space model to perform domain adaptation. A continuous-space language model is also used in a post-processing step for each system.

POSTECH submitted a phrase-based SMT system and query translation system for the DE–EN language pair in both subtasks. They analysed three types of query formation, generated query translation candidates using term-to-term dictionaries and a phrase-based system, and then scored them using a co-occurrence word frequency measure to select the best candidate.

UEDIN applied the Moses phrase-based system to all language pairs and both subtasks. They used the hierarchical reordering model and the OSM feature, same as in UEDIN's news translation system, and applied compound splitting to German input. They used separate language models built on in-domain and out-of-domain data with linear interpolation. For all language pairs except CS-EN and DE-EN, they selected data for the translation model using modified Moore-Lewis filtering. For DE-EN and CS-EN, they concatenated all the supplied parallel training data.

UM-DA submitted systems for all language pairs in the summary translation subtask based on a combination of different adaptation steps, namely domain-specific pre-processing, language model adaptation, translation model adaptation, numeric adaptation, and hyphenated word adaptation. Data for the domain-adapted language and translation models were selected using various data selection techniques.

UM-WDA submitted systems for all language pairs in the summary translation subtask. Their systems are domain-adapted using web-crawled in-domain resources: bilingual dictionaries and monolingual data. The translation model and language model trained on the crawled data were interpolated with the best-performing language and translation model employed in the UM-DA systems.

5.5 Results

MT quality in the Medical Translation Task is evaluated using automatic evaluation metrics: BLEU (Papineni et al., 2002), TER (Snover et al., 2006), PER (Tillmann et al., 1997), and CDER (Leusch et al., 2006). BLEU scores are reported as percentage and all error rates are reported as one minus the original value, also as percentage, so that all metrics are in the 0-100 range, and higher scores indicate better translations.

The main reason for not conducting human evaluation, as it happens in the standard Trans-

	original	normalized truecased				normalized lowercased			
ID	BLEU	BLEU	1-TER	1-PER	1-CDER	BLEU	1-TER	1-PER	1-CDER
				Czech→English					
CUNI	29.64	29.79±1.07	47.45±1.15	61.64±1.06	52.18±0.98	31.68±1.14	49.84±1.10	64.38±1.06	54.10±0.96
CUNI	22.44	22.57±0.95	41.43±1.16	55.46±1.09	46.42±0.96	32.34±1.12	50.24±1.20	65.07±1.10	54.42±0.96
UEDIN	36.65	36.87±1.23	54.35±1.19	67.16±1.00	**57.61±1.01**	38.02±1.24	**56.14±1.17**	69.24±1.01	**58.96±0.96**
UM-DA	**37.62**	**37.79±1.26**	**54.55±1.20**	**68.29±0.88**	57.28±1.03	**38.81±1.28**	56.04±1.20	**70.06±0.82**	58.45±1.05
CUNI	22.92	23.06±0.97	42.49±1.10	56.10±1.12	47.13±0.95	33.18±1.15	51.48±1.15	66.00±1.03	55.30±0.96
CUNI	22.69	22.84±0.98	42.21±1.14	56.01±1.11	46.79±0.94	32.84±1.13	51.10±1.11	65.79±1.07	54.81±0.96
UM-WDA	37.35	37.53±1.26	54.39±1.19	68.21±0.83	57.16±1.07	38.61±1.27	55.92±1.17	70.02±0.81	58.36±1.07
ONLINE		39.57±1.21	58.24±1.14	70.16±0.78	60.04±1.02	40.62±1.23	59.72±1.11	71.94±0.74	61.26±1.01
				German→English					
CUNI	28.20	28.34±1.12	46.66±1.13	61.53±1.03	50.57±0.93	30.69±1.19	48.91±1.16	64.12±1.04	52.52±0.95
CUNI	28.85	28.99±1.15	47.12±1.15	61.98±1.07	50.72±0.98	31.37±1.21	49.29±1.13	64.53±1.05	52.64±0.98
POSTECH	25.92	25.99±1.06	43.66±1.14	59.62±0.92	47.13±0.90	26.97±1.06	45.13±1.12	61.53±0.89	48.37±0.88
UEDIN	**37.31**	**37.53±1.19**	**55.72±1.14**	**68.82±0.99**	**58.35±0.95**	**38.60±1.25**	**57.18±1.12**	**70.46±0.98**	**59.53±0.94**
UM-DA	35.71	35.81±1.23	53.08±1.16	66.82±0.98	55.91±0.96	36.55±1.27	54.01±1.13	68.05±0.97	56.78±0.95
CUNI	30.58	30.71±1.10	48.68±1.09	63.19±1.08	52.72±0.94	33.14±1.19	50.98±1.06	65.88±1.04	54.74±0.94
CUNI	30.22	30.32±1.12	47.71±1.18	62.20±1.10	52.17±0.91	32.75±1.20	50.00±1.14	64.87±1.06	54.19±0.92
UM-WDA	32.70	32.88±1.19	49.60±1.18	63.74±1.01	53.50±0.96	33.95±1.23	51.05±1.19	65.54±0.98	54.73±0.96
ONLINE		41.18±1.24	59.33±1.09	70.95±0.92	61.92±1.01	42.29±1.23	60.76±1.08	72.51±0.88	63.06±0.96
				French→English					
CUNI	34.42	34.55±1.20	52.24±1.17	64.52±1.03	56.48±0.91	36.52±1.23	54.35±1.12	67.07±1.00	58.34±0.91
CUNI	33.67	33.59±1.16	50.39±1.23	61.75±1.16	56.74±0.97	35.55±1.21	52.55±1.26	64.45±1.13	58.63±0.91
DCU-B	44.85	45.01±1.24	62.57±1.12	74.11±0.78	64.33±0.99	46.12±1.26	64.04±1.06	75.84±0.74	65.55±0.94
UEDIN	46.44	46.68±1.26	**64.12±1.16**	74.47±0.87	**66.40±0.96**	48.01±1.29	**65.70±1.15**	76.30±0.86	**67.76±0.91**
UM-DA	**47.08**	**47.22±1.33**	64.08±1.16	**75.41±0.88**	66.15±0.96	**48.23±1.31**	65.36±1.10	**76.95±0.89**	67.18±0.93
CUNI	34.74	34.89±1.12	52.39±1.16	63.76±1.09	57.29±0.94	36.84±1.17	54.56±1.13	66.43±1.07	59.14±0.90
CUNI	35.04	34.99±1.18	52.11±1.24	63.24±1.09	57.51±0.97	37.04±1.18	54.38±1.17	66.02±1.05	59.55±0.93
UM-WDA	43.84	44.06±1.32	61.14±1.18	73.13±0.87	63.09±1.00	45.17±1.36	62.63±1.15	74.94±0.84	64.37±0.99
ONLINE		46.99±1.35	64.31±1.12	76.07±0.78	66.09±1.00	47.99±1.33	65.65±1.07	77.65±0.75	67.20±0.96
				English→Czech					
CUNI	17.36	17.65±0.96	37.17±1.02	49.13±0.98	40.31±0.95	18.75±0.96	38.32±1.02	50.82±0.91	41.39±0.94
CUNI	16.64	16.89±0.93	36.57±1.05	48.79±0.98	39.46±0.90	17.94±0.96	37.74±1.03	50.50±0.97	40.59±0.91
UEDIN	**23.45**	**23.74±1.00**	**44.20±1.10**	**55.38±0.88**	**46.23±0.99**	**24.20±1.00**	**44.92±1.08**	**56.38±0.90**	**46.78±1.00**
UM-DA	22.61	22.72±0.98	42.73±1.16	54.12±0.93	44.73±1.01	23.12±1.01	43.41±1.14	55.11±0.93	45.32±1.02
CUNI	20.56	20.84±1.01	39.98±1.09	51.98±0.99	42.86±1.00	22.03±1.05	41.19±1.08	53.66±0.97	43.93±1.01
CUNI	19.50	19.72±0.97	38.09±1.10	50.12±1.06	41.50±0.96	20.91±1.02	39.26±1.12	51.79±1.04	42.59±0.96
UM-WDA	22.14	22.33±0.96	42.30±1.11	53.89±0.92	44.48±1.01	22.72±0.97	43.02±1.09	54.89±0.95	45.08±0.99
ONLINE		33.45±1.28	51.64±1.28	61.82±1.10	53.97±1.18	34.02±1.31	52.35±1.22	62.84±1.08	54.52±1.18
				English→German					
CUNI	12.52	12.64±0.77	29.84±0.99	45.38±1.14	34.69±0.81	16.63±0.91	33.63±1.07	50.03±1.24	38.43±0.87
CUNI	12.42	12.53±0.77	29.02±1.05	44.27±1.16	34.62±0.78	16.41±0.91	32.87±1.08	48.99±1.21	38.37±0.86
POSTECH	15.46	15.59±0.91	34.41±1.01	49.00±0.83	37.11±0.90	15.98±0.92	34.98±1.00	49.94±0.81	37.60±0.87
UEDIN	20.88	21.01±1.03	40.03±1.08	**55.54±0.91**	42.95±0.90	21.40±1.03	40.55±1.08	56.33±0.92	43.41±0.90
UM-DA	**20.89**	**21.09±1.07**	**40.76±1.03**	55.45±0.89	**43.02±0.93**	**21.52±1.08**	**41.31±1.01**	**56.38±0.90**	**43.58±0.91**
CUNI	14.29	14.42±0.81	31.82±1.03	47.01±1.13	36.81±0.79	18.87±0.90	35.76±1.11	51.76±1.17	40.65±0.87
CUNI	13.44	13.58±0.75	30.37±1.03	45.80±1.14	35.80±0.76	17.84±0.89	34.41±1.13	50.75±1.18	39.85±0.78
UM-WDA	18.77	18.91±1.00	37.92±1.02	53.59±0.85	40.90±0.86	19.30±1.02	38.42±1.01	54.40±0.85	41.34±0.86
ONLINE		23.92±1.06	44.33±0.97	57.47±0.80	46.35±0.91	24.29±1.07	44.83±0.98	58.20±0.80	46.71±0.92
				English→French					
CUNI	30.30	30.67±1.11	46.59±1.09	59.83±1.04	50.51±0.93	32.06±1.12	48.01±1.09	61.66±1.00	51.83±0.94
CUNI	29.35	29.71±1.10	45.84±1.07	58.81±1.04	50.00±0.96	31.02±1.10	47.24±1.09	60.57±1.02	51.31±0.94
LIMSI	40.14	43.54±1.22	59.70±1.04	69.45±0.86	61.35±0.96	44.04±1.22	60.32±1.03	70.20±0.85	61.90±0.94
LIMSI	38.83	42.21±1.13	58.88±1.01	68.70±0.81	60.59±0.93	42.69±1.12	59.53±0.98	69.50±0.80	61.17±0.91
UEDIN	40.74	**44.24±1.16**	**60.66±1.07**	**70.35±0.82**	**62.28±0.95**	**44.85±1.17**	**61.43±1.05**	**71.27±0.81**	**62.94±0.91**
UM-DA	**41.24**	41.68±1.12	58.72±1.06	69.37±0.78	60.12±0.95	42.16±1.11	59.39±1.05	70.21±0.77	60.71±0.92
CUNI	32.23	32.61±1.09	48.48±1.08	61.13±1.01	52.24±0.93	34.08±1.10	49.93±1.11	62.92±0.99	53.65±0.92
CUNI	32.45	32.84±1.06	48.68±1.06	61.32±0.98	52.35±0.94	34.22±1.07	50.09±1.04	63.04±0.96	53.67±0.91
UM-WDA	40.78	41.16±1.13	58.20±0.99	68.93±0.84	59.64±0.94	41.79±1.12	59.10±0.96	70.01±0.84	60.39±0.91
ONLINE		58.63±1.26	70.70±1.12	78.22±0.81	71.89±0.96	59.27±1.26	71.50±1.10	79.16±0.81	72.63±0.94

Table 25: Official results of translation quality evaluation in the medical **summary translation** subtask.

	original	normalized truecased				normalized lowercased			
ID	**BLEU**	**BLEU**	**1-TER**	**1-PER**	**1-CDER**	**BLEU**	**1-TER**	**1-PER**	**1-CDER**
				Czech→English					
CUNI	10.71	10.57±3.42	15.72±2.77	23.37±3.03	18.68±2.42	**30.13±4.85**	53.38±3.01	62.53±2.84	55.44±2.87
CUNI	9.92	9.78±3.04	16.84±2.84	23.80±3.08	19.85±2.40	28.21±4.56	**54.15±3.04**	**62.56±2.99**	**55.91±2.79**
UEDIN	**24.66**	**24.68±4.52**	**39.88±3.05**	**49.97±3.29**	**41.81±2.80**	28.25±4.94	45.31±3.14	55.66±3.06	46.67±2.77
CUNI	12.00	11.86±3.42	18.49±2.74	24.67±2.85	21.08±2.29	31.91±4.81	**57.61±3.13**	65.02±2.99	**59.24±2.69**
CUNI	10.54	10.39±3.48	18.86±2.48	26.65±2.05	20.53±2.08	**32.39±5.45**	56.79±3.02	**65.52±2.26**	57.96±2.56
ONLINE		28.88±4.96	47.31±3.35	55.19±3.21	49.88±2.89	35.33±5.20	55.80±3.20	64.05±2.97	57.94±2.85
				German→English					
CUNI	10.90	10.74±3.41	18.89±2.39	26.09±2.00	20.29±2.07	**32.15±5.23**	**55.56±2.90**	**63.68±2.34**	**56.45±2.62**
CUNI	10.71	10.55±3.47	18.40±2.35	25.45±2.04	19.84±2.07	32.06±5.19	54.85±2.91	62.87±2.39	55.52±2.61
POSTECH	18.06	17.97±4.38	28.57±3.30	40.38±2.77	31.79±2.80	21.99±4.65	35.76±3.35	47.84±2.82	38.84±2.92
POSTECH	17.99	17.88±4.72	29.79±3.04	41.15±2.48	32.49±2.63	24.41±4.83	41.72±3.19	53.33±2.55	44.06±2.88
UEDIN	**23.33**	**23.39±4.37**	**38.55±3.65**	**48.21±3.43**	**40.75±3.05**	27.17±4.63	43.87±3.52	53.76±3.48	45.72±3.03
CUNI	10.54	10.39±3.48	18.86±2.48	26.65±2.05	20.53±2.08	**32.39±5.45**	**56.79±3.02**	**65.52±2.26**	**57.96±2.56**
CUNI	8.75	8.49±3.60	19.10±2.27	24.98±1.95	19.95±2.02	30.00±5.59	56.07±2.92	62.92±2.32	56.27±2.56
ONLINE		19.97±4.46	37.03±3.26	43.91±3.22	40.95±2.93	33.86±4.87	53.28±3.28	60.86±3.22	56.33±2.98
				French→English					
CUNI	13.90	13.79±3.61	18.49±2.55	28.35±2.81	20.36±2.20	34.97±5.34	59.54±2.94	72.30±2.63	58.86±2.76
CUNI	12.10	11.95±3.41	17.23±2.57	27.12±2.88	19.15±2.28	33.74±5.01	58.95±2.96	71.25±2.76	58.20±2.81
DCU-Q	**30.85**	**31.24±5.08**	**58.88±2.97**	**67.94±2.62**	**59.19±2.62**	**36.88±5.07**	**66.38±2.85**	**75.86±2.37**	**66.29±2.55**
DCU-Q	26.51	26.16±4.40	48.02±3.72	57.34±3.24	53.56±2.79	28.61±4.52	53.65±3.73	63.51±3.21	59.07±2.79
UEDIN	27.20	27.60±3.98	38.54±3.22	48.81±3.26	39.77±2.95	32.23±4.27	43.66±3.20	54.31±3.17	44.53±2.79
CUNI	14.03	14.00±3.30	20.11±2.38	29.00±2.71	21.62±2.22	**38.98±5.08**	62.90±2.87	74.49±2.45	62.12±2.64
CUNI	13.38	13.16±3.52	17.79±2.56	28.84±2.81	19.17±2.23	35.00±5.20	59.52±2.98	73.08±2.57	58.41±2.68
ONLINE		32.96±5.04	53.68±3.21	64.27±2.80	54.40±2.66	38.09±5.52	61.44±3.08	72.59±2.61	61.60±2.78
				English→Czech					
CUNI	8.37	8.00±3.65	17.74±2.23	26.46±1.96	19.48±2.10	19.49±4.60	41.53±2.94	51.34±2.51	42.54±2.74
CUNI	9.04	8.75±3.64	18.25±2.27	26.97±1.92	19.69±2.11	**21.46±5.05**	**42.36±3.09**	**51.99±2.40**	**43.18±2.68**
UEDIN	**12.57**	**12.40±3.61**	**21.15±2.96**	**33.56±2.80**	**22.30±2.67**	14.06±3.80	24.92±2.90	37.85±2.72	25.58±2.70
UEDIN	6.64	6.21±4.73	-2.35±3.06	5.95±3.48	-0.97±3.12	14.35±3.52	14.51±3.19	24.96±3.50	15.11±3.10
CUNI	9.06	8.64±3.82	19.92±2.24	26.97±1.94	20.82±2.06	**22.42±5.24**	**44.89±2.94**	**52.89±2.40**	**45.36±2.78**
CUNI	8.49	8.01±6.05	18.13±2.28	25.19±1.86	19.19±2.01	21.04±4.80	42.66±2.87	50.34±2.47	43.30±2.74
ONLINE		21.09±4.60	48.56±2.82	54.72±2.51	48.30±2.83	24.37±4.80	51.93±2.74	58.10±2.50	51.62±2.80
				English→German					
CUNI	10.17	10.01±3.92	**26.48±3.24**	**36.71±3.37**	**29.26±2.96**	13.02±4.17	**31.96±3.41**	**42.39±3.21**	**34.61±2.95**
CUNI	9.98	9.69±3.94	26.16±3.19	35.50±3.23	28.86±2.94	12.90±4.28	31.75±3.33	41.24±3.21	34.38±3.05
POSTECH	**13.43**	13.01±5.91	26.38±3.09	35.75±3.16	27.86±2.82	**15.05±5.71**	30.45±3.10	39.89±3.14	31.79±3.00
POSTECH	13.41	**13.15±5.21**	22.18±3.09	30.89±3.31	24.17±3.06	14.96±5.15	26.13±3.19	34.92±3.40	27.98±3.12
UEDIN	10.45	10.14±3.86	23.44±3.43	34.55±3.34	25.46±3.17	11.91±4.42	27.91±3.45	39.08±3.42	29.63±3.31
CUNI	8.91	7.72±6.48	**30.05±3.22**	**40.65±2.71**	**31.91±2.88**	13.66±5.37	**35.51±3.28**	**46.12±2.74**	**37.27±3.01**
CUNI	9.14	8.69±6.44	27.66±3.31	37.95±3.45	31.00±2.82	14.03±5.92	33.53±3.45	44.03±3.53	36.73±3.00
ONLINE		20.07±6.06	41.07±3.23	47.41±2.86	41.61±3.02	21.67±6.23	43.78±3.23	50.18±2.95	44.26±3.06
				English→French					
CUNI	13.12	12.92±2.84	21.95±2.41	33.19±2.09	23.70±2.24	**28.42±3.98**	51.43±2.90	63.74±2.35	52.64±2.58
CUNI	12.80	12.65±2.81	19.16±2.61	31.61±2.21	21.91±2.32	27.52±4.05	47.47±3.08	61.43±2.37	49.82±2.72
DCU-Q	**27.69**	**27.84±4.11**	**48.97±3.06**	**60.90±2.55**	**51.84±2.83**	28.98±4.16	**51.73±3.10**	**63.84±2.47**	**54.43±2.76**
UEDIN	20.16	21.76±3.42	31.66±4.23	44.37±4.13	44.29±2.73	23.25±3.49	35.38±4.19	48.52±4.07	47.94±2.75
CUNI	13.78	13.57±3.00	21.92±2.51	33.47±2.03	24.16±2.32	30.07±4.10	51.12±3.08	63.61±2.45	52.96±2.67
CUNI	15.27	15.24±3.12	23.58±2.54	34.39±2.54	25.79±2.32	**31.40±4.15**	**53.60±2.96**	**65.39±2.57**	**55.47±2.69**
ONLINE		28.93±3.66	49.20±3.08	60.85±2.69	51.68±2.78	30.88±3.66	52.25±3.08	64.06±2.62	54.59±2.68

Table 26: Official results of translation quality evaluation in the medical **query translation** subtask.

source lang.	**ID**	**P@5**	**P@10**	**NDCG@5**	**NDCG@10**	**MAP**	**Rprec**	**bpref**	**rel**
Czech→English	CUNI	0.3280	0.3340	0.2873	0.2936	0.2217	0.2362	0.3473	1461
German→English	CUNI	0.2800	0.3000	0.2467	0.2630	0.2057	0.2077	0.3310	1426
French→English	CUNI	0.3280	0.3380	0.2811	0.2882	0.2206	0.2284	0.3504	1481
	DCU-Q	0.3480	0.3460	0.3060	0.3072	0.2252	0.2358	0.3659	1524
	UEDIN	**0.4440**	**0.4300**	**0.3793**	**0.3826**	**0.2843**	**0.2935**	**0.3936**	**1544**
English (monolingual)		0.4600	0.4700	0.4091	0.4205	0.3035	0.3198	0.3858	1638

Table 27: Official results of retrieval evaluation in the **query translation** subtask.

lation Task, was the lack of domain expertise of prospective raters. While in the standard task, the only requirement for the raters was to be a native speaker of the target language, in the Medical Translation Task, a very good knowledge of the domain would be necessary to provide reliable judgements and the raters with such an expertise (medical doctors and native speakers) were not available.

The complete results of the task are presented in Table 25 (for summary translation) and Tables 26 and 27 (for query translation). Participant IDs given in bold indicate primary submissions, IDs in normal font refer to contrastive submissions. The first section for each translation direction (white background) refers to constrained submissions and the second one (light-gray background) to unconstrained submissions. The column denoted as "original" contains BLEU scores as reported by the Matrix submission system obtained on the original submitted translations. Due to punctuation inconsistency in the original reference translations, we decided to perform punctuation normalization before calculating the official scores. The columns denoted as "normalized truecased" contain scores obtained on the submitted translations after punctuation normalization and the columns denoted as "normalized lowercased" contain scores obtained after punctuation normalization and lowercasing. The normalization script is available in the package with summary translation test data. The confidence intervals were obtained by bootstrap resampling with a confidence level of 95%. Figures in bold denote the best constrained system and, if its score is higher, the best unconstrained system for each translation direction and each metric. For comparison, we also present results of a major on-line translation system (denoted as ONLINE).

The results of the extrinsic evaluation of query translation submissions are given in 27. We used the CLEF 2013 eHealth Task 3 test collection containing about 1 million web pages (in English), 50 test queries (originally in English and translated to Czech, German, and French), and their relevance assessments. Some of the participants of the WMT Medical Task (three teams with five submissions in total) submitted translations of the queries (from Czech, German, and French) into English and these translations were used to query the CLEF 2013 eHealth Task 3 test collection using a state-of-the-art system based on a BM25 model, described in Pecina et al. (2014). Originally, we asked for 10 best translations for each query, but only the best one were used for the evaluation. The results are provided in terms of standard IR evaluation measures: precision at a cut-off of 5 and 10 documents (P@5, P@10), normalized discounted cumulative gain (Järvelin and Kekäläinen, 2002) at 5 and 10 documents (NDCG@5, NDCG@10), mean average precision (MAP) (Voorhees and Harman, 2005), precision reached after R documents retrieved, where R indicates the number of the relevant documents for each query in the entire collection (Rprec), binary preference (bpref) (Buckley and Voorhees, 2004), and number or relevant documents retrieved (rel). The cross-lingual results are also compared with the monolingual one (obtained by using the reference (English) translations of the test topics) to see how the system would perform if the queries were translated perfectly.

5.6 Discussion and Conclusion

Both the subtasks turned out to be quite challenging not only because of the specific domain – in summary sentences, we can observe much higher density of terminology than in ordinary sentences; the queries, which are also rich in terminology, do not form sentences at all.

Most submissions were based on systems participating in the standard Translation Task and trained on the provided data or its subsets CUNI provided baseline systems for all language pairs in both subtasks, which turned to be relatively strong for the query translation task, especially in translation to English, but only in terms of scores obtained on normalized and lowercased translations since their truecasing component did not perform well.

In the summary translation subtask, the best overall results were achieved by the UEDIN team which won for DE–EN, EN–CS, and EN–FR, followed by the UM-DA team, which performed on par with UEDIN in all other translation.

The unconstrained submissions in almost all cases did not outperform the results of the constrained submissions. Some improvements were observed in the query translations subtasks by the CUNI's unconstrained system with language models trained on larger in-domain data.

The ONLINE system outperforms all other submissions with only two exceptions – the UM-DA's and UEDIN's systems for the summary translation in the FR–EN direction, though the score differences are within the 95% confidence interval.

In the query translation subtask, DCU-Q built a system designed specifically for terminology translation between French and English and outperformed all other participants in translation into English; however, the confidence intervals in the query translation task are much wider and most of the differences in scores of the automatic metrics are not statistically significant.

The extrinsic evaluation in the cross-lingual information retrieval was conducted for translations into English only. CUNI provided the baselines for all directions, but other submissions were done for FR–EN only. Here, the winner is UEDIN, who outperformed both CUNI and DCU-Q, and their scores are very close to those obtained using the reference English translations.

Acknowledgments

This work was supported in parts by the MosesCore, Casmacat, Khresmoi, Matecat and QTLaunchPad projects funded by the European Commission (7th Framework Programme), and by gifts from Yandex.

We would also like to thank our colleagues Matouš Macháček and Martin Popel for detailed discussions.

References

Avramidis, E. (2014). Efforts on machine learning over human-mediated translation edit rate. In *Proceedings of the Ninth Workshop on Statistical Machine Translation*, Baltimore, Maryland, USA. Association for Computational Linguistics.

Beck, D., Shah, K., and Specia, L. (2014). Sheflite 2.0: Sparse multi-task gaussian processes for translation quality estimation. In *Proceedings of the Ninth Workshop on Statistical Machine Translation*, Baltimore, Maryland, USA. Association for Computational Linguistics.

Biçici, E. (2013). Referential translation machines for quality estimation. In *Proceedings of the Eighth Workshop on Statistical Machine Translation*, Sofia, Bulgaria.

Biçici, E., Liu, Q., and Way, A. (2014). Parallel FDA5 for fast deployment of accurate statistical machine translation systems. In *Proceedings of the Ninth Workshop on Statistical Machine Translation*, Baltimore, USA. Association for Computational Linguistics.

Bicici, E., Liu, Q., and Way, A. (2014). Parallel fda5 for fast deployment of accurate statistical machine translation systems. In *Proceedings of the Ninth Workshop on Statistical Machine Translation*, Baltimore, Maryland, USA. Association for Computational Linguistics.

Bicici, E. and Way, A. (2014). Referential translation machines for predicting translation quality. In *Proceedings of the Ninth Workshop on Statistical Machine Translation*, Baltimore, Maryland, USA. Association for Computational Linguistics.

Bojar, O., Buck, C., Callison-Burch, C., Federmann, C., Haddow, B., Koehn, P., Monz, C., Post, M., Soricut, R., and Specia, L. (2013). Findings of the 2013 Workshop on Statistical Machine Translation. In *Proceedings of the Eighth Workshop on Statistical Machine Translation*, pages 1–42, Sofia, Bulgaria. Association for Computational Linguistics.

Bojar, O., Diatka, V., Rychlý, P., Straňák, P., Tamchyna, A., and Zeman, D. (2014). Hindi-English and Hindi-only Corpus for Machine Translation. In *Proceedings of the Ninth International Language Resources and Evaluation Conference*, Reykjavik, Iceland. ELRA.

Bojar, O., Ercegovčević, M., Popel, M., and Zaidan, O. (2011). A grain of salt for the WMT manual evaluation. In *Proceedings of the Sixth Workshop on Statistical Machine Translation*, pages 1–11, Edinburgh, Scotland. Association for Computational Linguistics.

Borisov, A. and Galinskaya, I. (2014). Yandex school of data analysis russian-english machine translation system for wmt14. In *Proceedings of the Ninth Workshop on Statistical Machine Translation*, Baltimore, Maryland, USA. Association for Computational Linguistics.

Bouayad-Agha, N., Scott, D. R., and Power, R. (2000). Integrating content and style in documents: A case study of patient information leaflets. *Information Design Journal*, 9(2–3):161–176.

Buckley, C. and Voorhees, E. M. (2004). Retrieval evaluation with incomplete information.

In *Proceedings of the 27th Annual International ACM SIGIR Conference on Research and Development in Information Retrieval*, pages 25–32, Sheffield, United Kingdom.

Buitelaar, P., Sacaleanu, B., Špela Vintar, Steffen, D., Volk, M., Dejean, H., Gaussier, E., Widdows, D., Weiser, O., and Frederking, R. (2003). Multilingual concept hierarchies for medical information organization and retrieval. Public deliverable, MuchMore project.

Callison-Burch, C., Fordyce, C., Koehn, P., Monz, C., and Schroeder, J. (2007). (Meta-) evaluation of machine translation. In *Proceedings of the Second Workshop on Statistical Machine Translation (WMT07)*, Prague, Czech Republic.

Callison-Burch, C., Fordyce, C., Koehn, P., Monz, C., and Schroeder, J. (2008). Further meta-evaluation of machine translation. In *Proceedings of the Third Workshop on Statistical Machine Translation (WMT08)*, Colmbus, Ohio.

Callison-Burch, C., Koehn, P., Monz, C., Peterson, K., Przybocki, M., and Zaidan, O. F. (2010). Findings of the 2010 joint workshop on statistical machine translation and metrics for machine translation. In *Proceedings of the Fourth Workshop on Statistical Machine Translation (WMT10)*, Uppsala, Sweden.

Callison-Burch, C., Koehn, P., Monz, C., Post, M., Soricut, R., and Specia, L. (2012). Findings of the 2012 workshop on statistical machine translation. In *Proceedings of the Seventh Workshop on Statistical Machine Translation*, pages 10–51, Montréal, Canada. Association for Computational Linguistics.

Callison-Burch, C., Koehn, P., Monz, C., and Schroeder, J. (2009). Findings of the 2009 workshop on statistical machine translation. In *Proceedings of the Fourth Workshop on Statistical Machine Translation (WMT09)*, Athens, Greece.

Callison-Burch, C., Koehn, P., Monz, C., and Zaidan, O. (2011). Findings of the 2011 workshop on statistical machine translation. In *Proceedings of the Sixth Workshop on Statistical Machine Translation*, pages 22–64, Edinburgh, Scotland.

Camargo de Souza, J. G., González-Rubio, J., Buck, C., Turchi, M., and Negri, M. (2014). Fbk-upv-uedin participation in the wmt14 quality estimation shared-task. In *Proceedings of the Ninth Workshop on Statistical Machine Translation*, Baltimore, Maryland, USA. Association for Computational Linguistics.

Cap, F., Weller, M., Ramm, A., and Fraser, A. (2014). Cims – the cis and ims joint submission to wmt 2014 translating from english into german. In *Proceedings of the Ninth Workshop on Statistical Machine Translation*, Baltimore, Maryland, USA. Association for Computational Linguistics.

Cohen, J. (1960). A coefficient of agreement for nominal scales. *Educational and Psychological Measurment*, 20(1):37–46.

Cohn, T. and Specia, L. (2013). Modelling annotator bias with multi-task gaussian processes: An application to machine translation quality estimation. In *Proceedings of the 51st Annual Meeting of the Association for Computational Linguistics*, ACL-2013, pages 32–42, Sofia, Bulgaria.

Collins, M. (2002). Discriminative training methods for hidden markov models: theory and experiments with perceptron algorithms. In *Proceedings of the ACL-02 conference on Empirical methods in natural language processing - Volume 10*, EMNLP '02, pages 1–8, Stroudsburg, PA, USA. Association for Computational Linguistics.

Costa-jussà, M. R., Gupta, P., Rosso, P., and Banchs, R. E. (2014). English-to-hindi system description for wmt 2014: Deep source-context features for moses. In *Proceedings of the Ninth Workshop on Statistical Machine Translation*, Baltimore, Maryland, USA. Association for Computational Linguistics.

Do, Q. K., Herrmann, T., Niehues, J., Allauzen, A., Yvon, F., and Waibel, A. (2014). The kit-limsi translation system for wmt 2014. In *Proceedings of the Ninth Workshop on Statistical Machine Translation*, Baltimore, Maryland, USA. Association for Computational Linguistics.

Dungarwal, P., Chatterjee, R., Mishra, A., Kunchukuttan, A., Shah, R., and Bhattacharyya, P. (2014). The iit bombay hindi-english translation system at wmt 2014. In *Proceedings of the Ninth Workshop on Statistical Machine Translation*, Baltimore, Maryland, USA. Association for Computational Linguistics.

Durrani, N., Haddow, B., Koehn, P., and Heafield, K. (2014a). Edinburgh's phrase-based machine translation systems for wmt-14. In *Proceedings of the ACL 2014 Ninth Workshop of Statistical Machine Translation*, Baltimore, USA.

Durrani, N., Haddow, B., Koehn, P., and Heafield, K. (2014b). Edinburghs phrase-based machine translation systems for wmt-14. In *Proceedings of the Ninth Workshop on Statistical Machine Translation*, Baltimore, Maryland, USA. Association for Computational Linguistics.

Dušek, O., Hajič, J., Hlaváčová, J., Novák, M., Pecina, P., Rosa, R., Tamchyna, A., Urešová, Z., and Zeman, D. (2014). Machine translation of medical texts in the khresmoi project. In *Proceedings of the ACL 2014 Ninth Workshop of Statistical Machine Translation*, Baltimore, USA.

Federmann, C. (2012). Appraise: An Open-Source Toolkit for Manual Evaluation of Machine Translation Output. *The Prague Bulletin of Mathematical Linguistics (PBML)*, 98:25–35.

Foster, J. (2007). Treebanks gone bad: Parser evaluation and retraining using a treebank of ungrammatical sentences. *International Journal on Document Analysis and Recognition*, 10(3-4):129–145.

Freitag, M., Peitz, S., Wuebker, J., Ney, H., Huck, M., Sennrich, R., Durrani, N., Nadejde, M., Williams, P., Koehn, P., Herrmann, T., Cho, E., and Waibel, A. (2014). Eu-bridge mt: Combined machine translation. In *Proceedings of the Ninth Workshop on Statistical Machine Translation*, Baltimore, Maryland, USA. Association for Computational Linguistics.

Gamon, M., Aue, A., and Smets, M. (2005). Sentence-level MT evaluation without reference translations: beyond language modeling. In *Proceedings of the Annual Conference of the European Association for Machine Translation*, Budapest.

Geurts, P., Ernst, D., and Wehenkel, L. (2006). Extremely randomized trees. *Machine Learning*, 63(1):3–42.

Green, S., Cer, D., and Manning, C. (2014). Phrasal: A toolkit for new directions in statistical machine translation. In *Proceedings of the Ninth Workshop on Statistical Machine Translation*, Baltimore, Maryland, USA. Association for Computational Linguistics.

Hardmeier, C., Stymne, S., Tiedemann, J., Smith, A., and Nivre, J. (2014). Anaphora models and reordering for phrase-based smt. In *Proceedings of the Ninth Workshop on Statistical Machine Translation*, Baltimore, Maryland, USA. Association for Computational Linguistics.

Herbrich, R., Minka, T., and Graepel, T. (2006). TrueSkill^{TM}: A Bayesian Skill Rating System. In *Proceedings of the Twentieth Annual Conference on Neural Information Processing Systems*, pages 569–576, Vancouver, British Columbia, Canada. MIT Press.

Herrmann, T., Mediani, M., Cho, E., Ha, T.-L., Niehues, J., Slawik, I., Zhang, Y., and Waibel, A. (2014). The karlsruhe institute of technology translation systems for the wmt 2014. In *Proceedings of the Ninth Workshop on Statistical Machine Translation*, Baltimore, Maryland, USA. Association for Computational Linguistics.

Hokamp, C., Calixto, I., Wagner, J., and Zhang, J. (2014). Target-centric features for translation quality estimation. In *Proceedings of the Ninth Workshop on Statistical Machine Translation*, Baltimore, Maryland, USA. Association for Computational Linguistics.

Hopkins, M. and May, J. (2013). Models of translation competitions. In *Proceedings of the 51st Annual Meeting of the Association for Computational Linguistics (Volume 1: Long Papers)*, pages 1416–1424, Sofia, Bulgaria.

Järvelin, K. and Kekäläinen, J. (2002). Cumulated gain-based evaluation of ir techniques. *ACM Transactions on Information Systems*, 20(4):422–446.

Kim, J.-D., Ohta, T., Tateisi, Y., and Tsujii, J. (2003). GENIA corpus – a semantically annotated corpus for bio-textmining. *Bioinformatics*, 19(suppl 1):i180–i182.

Knox, C., Law, V., Jewison, T., Liu, P., Ly, S., Frolkis, A., Pon, A., Banco, K., Mak, C., Neveu, V., Djoumbou, Y., Eisner, R., Guo, A. C., and Wishart, D. S. (2011). DrugBank 3.0: a comprehensive resource for Omics research on drugs. *Nucleic acids research*, 39(suppl 1):D1035–D1041.

Koehn, P. (2012a). Simulating human judgment in

machine translation evaluation campaigns. In *International Workshop on Spoken Language Translation (IWSLT)*.

Koehn, P. (2012b). Simulating Human Judgment in Machine Translation Evaluation Campaigns. In *Proceedings of the Ninth International Workshop on Spoken Language Translation*, pages 179–184, Hong Kong, China.

Koehn, P. and Monz, C. (2006). Manual and automatic evaluation of machine translation between European languages. In *Proceedings of NAACL 2006 Workshop on Statistical Machine Translation*, New York, New York.

Koppel, M. and Ordan, N. (2011). Translationese and its dialects. In *Proceedings of the 49th Annual Meeting of the Association for Computational Linguistics: Human Language Techologies*, pages 1318–1326, Portland, Oregon.

Landis, J. R. and Koch, G. G. (1977). The measurement of observer agreement for categorical data. *Biometrics*, 33:159–174.

Leusch, G., Ueffing, N., and Ney, H. (2006). Cder: Efficient mt evaluation using block movements. In *Proceedings of the 11th Conference of the European Chapter of the Association for Computational Linguistics*, pages 241–248, Trento, Italy.

Li, J., Kim, S.-J., Na, H., and Lee, J.-H. (2014a). Postech's system description for medical text translation task. In *Proceedings of the ACL 2014 Ninth Workshop of Statistical Machine Translation*, Baltimore, USA.

Li, L., Wu, X., Vaillo, S. C., Xie, J., Way, A., and Liu, Q. (2014b). The dcu-ictcas mt system at wmt 2014 on german-english translation task. In *Proceedings of the Ninth Workshop on Statistical Machine Translation*, Baltimore, Maryland, USA. Association for Computational Linguistics.

Lopez, A. (2012). Putting Human Assessments of Machine Translation Systems in Order. In *Proceedings of the Seventh Workshop on Statistical Machine Translation*, pages 1–9, Montréal, Canada. Association for Computational Linguistics.

Lu, Y., Wang, L., Wong, D. F., Chao, L. S., Wang, Y., and Oliveira, F. (2014). Domain adaptation for medical text translation using web resources. In *Proceedings of the ACL 2014 Ninth Workshop of Statistical Machine Translation*, Baltimore, USA.

Luong, N. Q., Besacier, L., and Lecouteux, B. (2014). Lig system for word level qe task at wmt14. In *Proceedings of the Ninth Workshop on Statistical Machine Translation*, Baltimore, Maryland, USA. Association for Computational Linguistics.

Luong, N. Q., Lecouteux, B., and Besacier, L. (2013). LIG system for WMT13 QE task: Investigating the usefulness of features in word confidence estimation for MT. In *Proceedings of the Eighth Workshop on Statistical Machine Translation*, pages 384–389, Sofia, Bulgaria. Association for Computational Linguistics.

Macháček, M. and Bojar, O. (2014). Results of the wmt14 metrics shared task. In *Proceedings of the Ninth Workshop on Statistical Machine Translation*, Baltimore, Maryland, USA. Association for Computational Linguistics.

Matthews, A., Ammar, W., Bhatia, A., Feely, W., Hanneman, G., Schlinger, E., Swayamdipta, S., Tsvetkov, Y., Lavie, A., and Dyer, C. (2014). The cmu machine translation systems at wmt 2014. In *Proceedings of the Ninth Workshop on Statistical Machine Translation*, Baltimore, Maryland, USA. Association for Computational Linguistics.

Neidert, J., Schuster, S., Green, S., Heafield, K., and Manning, C. (2014). Stanford universitys submissions to the wmt 2014 translation task. In *Proceedings of the Ninth Workshop on Statistical Machine Translation*, Baltimore, Maryland, USA. Association for Computational Linguistics.

Okita, T., Vahid, A. H., Way, A., and Liu, Q. (2014). Dcu terminology translation system for medical query subtask at wmt14. In *Proceedings of the ACL 2014 Ninth Workshop of Statistical Machine Translation*, Baltimore, USA.

Papineni, K., Roukos, S., Ward, T., and Zhu, W.-J. (2002). BLEU: a method for automatic evaluation of machine translation. In *Proceedings of the 40th Annual Meeting of the Association for Computational Linguistics*, pages 311–318, Philadelphia, PA, USA. Association for Computational Linguistics.

Pécheux, N., Gong, L., Do, Q. K., Marie, B., Ivanishcheva, Y., Allauzen, A., Lavergne, T.,

Niehues, J., Max, A., and Yvon, Y. (2014). LIMSI @ WMT'14 Medical Translation Task. In *Proceedings of the Ninth Workshop on Statistical Machine Translation*, Baltimore, USA.

Pecina, P., Dušek, O., Goeuriot, L., Hajič, J., Hlaváčová, J., Jones, G., Kelly, L., Leveling, J., Mareček, D., Novák, M., Popel, M., Rosa, R., Tamchyna, A., and Urešová, Z. (2014). Adaptation of machine translation for multilingual information retrieval in the medical domain. *Artificial Intelligence in Medicine*, (0):–.

Peitz, S., Wuebker, J., Freitag, M., and Ney, H. (2014). The rwth aachen german-english machine translation system for wmt 2014. In *Proceedings of the Ninth Workshop on Statistical Machine Translation*, Baltimore, Maryland, USA. Association for Computational Linguistics.

Pouliquen, B. and Mazenc, C. (2011). COPPA, CLIR and TAPTA: three tools to assist in overcoming the patent barrier at WIPO. In *Proceedings of the Thirteenth Machine Translation Summit*, pages 24–30, Xiamen, China. Asia-Pacific Association for Machine Translation.

Powers, D. M. W. (2011). Evaluation: from precision, recall and f-measure to roc, informedness, markedness & correlation. *Journal of Machine Learning Technologies*.

Quernheim, D. and Cap, F. (2014). Large-scale exact decoding: The ims-ttt submission to wmt14. In *Proceedings of the Ninth Workshop on Statistical Machine Translation*, Baltimore, Maryland, USA. Association for Computational Linguistics.

Rosse, C. and Mejino Jr., J. L. V. (2008). The foundational model of anatomy ontology. In Burger, A., Davidson, D., and Baldock, R., editors, *Anatomy Ontologies for Bioinformatics*, volume 6 of *Computational Biology*, pages 59–117. Springer London.

Rubino, R., Toral, A., Sánchez-Cartagena, V. M., Ferrández-Tordera, J., Ortiz Rojas, S., Ramírez-Sánchez, G., Sánchez-Martínez, F., and Way, A. (2014). Abu-matran at wmt 2014 translation task: Two-step data selection and rbmt-style synthetic rules. In *Proceedings of the Ninth Workshop on Statistical Machine Translation*, Baltimore, Maryland, USA. Association for Computational Linguistics.

Sakaguchi, K., Post, M., and Van Durme, B. (2014). Efficient elicitation of annotations for human evaluation of machine translation. In *Proceedings of the Ninth Workshop on Statistical Machine Translation*, Baltimore, Maryland.

Sánchez-Cartagena, V. M., Pérez-Ortiz, J. A., and Sánchez-Martínez, F. (2014). The ua-prompsit hybrid machine translation system for the 2014 workshop on statistical machine translation. In *Proceedings of the Ninth Workshop on Statistical Machine Translation*, Baltimore, Maryland, USA. Association for Computational Linguistics.

Scarton, C. and Specia, L. (2014). Exploring consensus in machine translation for quality estimation. In *Proceedings of the Ninth Workshop on Statistical Machine Translation*, Baltimore, Maryland, USA. Association for Computational Linguistics.

Schwartz, L., Anderson, T., Gwinnup, J., and Young, K. (2014). Machine translation and monolingual postediting: The afrl wmt-14 system. In *Proceedings of the Ninth Workshop on Statistical Machine Translation*, Baltimore, Maryland, USA. Association for Computational Linguistics.

Seginer, Y. (2007). *Learning Syntactic Structure*. PhD thesis, University of Amsterdam.

Shah, K., Cohn, T., and Specia, L. (2013). An investigation on the effectiveness of features for translation quality estimation. In *Proceedings of the Machine Translation Summit XIV*, pages 167–174, Nice, France.

Shah, K. and Specia, L. (2014). Quality estimation for translation selection. In *Proceedings of the 17th Annual Conference of the European Association for Machine Translation*, Dubrovnik, Croatia.

Snover, M., Dorr, B., Schwartz, R., Micciulla, L., and Makhoul, J. (2006). A study of translation edit rate with targeted human annotation. In *Proceedings of the 7th Biennial Conference of the Association for Machine Translation in the Americas (AMTA-2006)*, Cambridge, Massachusetts.

Souza, J. G. C. d., Espl-Gomis, M., Turchi, M., and Negri, M. (2013). Exploiting qualitative information from automatic word alignment for cross-lingual nlp tasks. In *The 51st Annual*

Meeting of the Association for Computational Linguistics - Short Papers (ACL Short Papers 2013).

Specia, L., Shah, K., de Souza, J. G. C., and Cohn, T. (2013). QuEst - A Translation Quality Estimation Framework. In *Proceedings of the 51th Conference of the Association for Computational Linguistics (ACL), Demo Session*, Sofia, Bulgaria.

Tamchyna, A., Popel, M., Rosa, R., and Bojar, O. (2014). Cuni in wmt14: Chimera still awaits bellerophon. In *Proceedings of the Ninth Workshop on Statistical Machine Translation*, Baltimore, Maryland, USA. Association for Computational Linguistics.

Tan, L. and Pal, S. (2014). Manawi: Using multi-word expressions and named entities to improve machine translation. In *Proceedings of the Ninth Workshop on Statistical Machine Translation*, Baltimore, Maryland, USA. Association for Computational Linguistics.

Thompson, P., Iqbal, S., McNaught, J., and Ananiadou, S. (2009). Construction of an annotated corpus to support biomedical information extraction. *BMC bioinformatics*, 10(1):349.

Tiedemann, J. (2009). News from OPUS – a collection of multilingual parallel corpora with tools and interfaces. In *Recent Advances in Natural Language Processing*, volume 5, pages 237–248, Borovets, Bulgaria. John Benjamins.

Tillmann, C., Vogel, S., Ney, H., Zubiaga, A., and Sawaf, H. (1997). Accelerated DP based search for statistical translation. In Kokkinakis, G., Fakotakis, N., and Dermatas, E., editors, *Proceedings of the Fifth European Conference on Speech Communication and Technology*, pages 2667–2670, Rhodes, Greece. International Speech Communication Association.

U.S. National Library of Medicine (2009). UMLS reference manual. Metathesaurus. Bethesda, MD, USA.

Voorhees, E. M. and Harman, D. K., editors (2005). *TREC: Experiment and evaluation in information retrieval*, volume 63 of *Digital libraries and electronic publishing series*. MIT press Cambridge, Cambridge, MA, USA.

Wang, L., Lu, Y., Wong, D. F., Chao, L. S., Wang, Y., and Oliveira., F. (2014). Combining domain adaptation approaches for medical text translation. In *Proceedings of the ACL 2014 Ninth Workshop of Statistical Machine Translation*, Baltimore, USA.

Wäschle, K. and Riezler, S. (2012). Analyzing parallelism and domain similarities in the MAREC patent corpus. In Salampasis, M. and Larsen, B., editors, *Multidisciplinary Information Retrieval*, volume 7356 of *Lecture Notes in Computer Science*, pages 12–27. Springer Berlin Heidelberg.

Williams, P., Sennrich, R., Nadejde, M., Huck, M., Hasler, E., and Koehn, P. (2014). Edinburghs syntax-based systems at wmt 2014. In *Proceedings of the Ninth Workshop on Statistical Machine Translation*, Baltimore, Maryland, USA. Association for Computational Linguistics.

Wisniewski, G., Pécheux, N., Allauzen, A., and Yvon, F. (2014). Limsi submission for wmt'14 qe task. In *Proceedings of the Ninth Workshop on Statistical Machine Translation*, Baltimore, Maryland, USA. Association for Computational Linguistics.

wu, x., Haque, R., Okita, T., Arora, P., Way, A., and Liu, Q. (2014). Dcu-lingo24 participation in wmt 2014 hindi-english translation task. In *Proceedings of the Ninth Workshop on Statistical Machine Translation*, Baltimore, Maryland, USA. Association for Computational Linguistics.

Zdeňka Urešová, Ondřej Dušek, J. H. and Pecina, P. (2014). Multilingual test sets for machine translation of search queries for cross-lingual information retrieval in the medical domain. In *To appear in Proceedings of the Ninth International Conference on Language Resources and Evaluation*, Reykjavik, Iceland.

Zhang, J., Wu, X., Calixto, I., Vahid, A. H., Zhang, X., Way, A., and Liu, Q. (2014). Experiments in medical translation shared task at wmt 2014. In *Proceedings of the ACL 2014 Ninth Workshop of Statistical Machine Translation*, Baltimore, USA.

A Pairwise System Comparisons by Human Judges

Tables 28–37 show pairwise comparisons between systems for each language pair. The numbers in each of the tables' cells indicate the percentage of times that the system in that column was judged to be better than the system in that row, ignoring ties. Bolding indicates the winner of the two systems.

Because there were so many systems and data conditions the significance of each pairwise comparison needs to be quantified. We applied the Sign Test to measure which comparisons indicate genuine differences (rather than differences that are attributable to chance). In the following tables ⋆ indicates statistical significance at $p \leq 0.10$, † indicates statistical significance at $p \leq 0.05$, and ‡ indicates statistical significance at $p \leq 0.01$, according to the Sign Test.

Each table contains final rows showing how likely a system would win when paired against a randomly selected system (the expected win ratio score) and the rank range according the official method used in Table 8. Gray lines separate clusters based on non-overlapping rank ranges.

	ONLINE-B	UEDIN-PHRASE	UEDIN-SYNTAX	ONLINE-A	CU-MOSES
ONLINE-B	–	.47‡	.43‡	.42‡	.39‡
UEDIN-PHRASE	**.53‡**	–	.44‡	.44‡	.41‡
UEDIN-SYNTAX	**.57‡**	**.56‡**	–	.49	.48†
ONLINE-A	**.58‡**	**.56‡**	**.51**	–	.48⋆
CU-MOSES	**.61‡**	**.59‡**	**.52†**	**.52⋆**	–
score	.57	.54	.47	.46	.44
rank	1	2	3-4	3-4	5

Table 28: Head to head comparison, ignoring ties, for Czech-English systems

	CU-DEPFIX	UEDIN-UNCNSTR	CU-BOJAR	CU-FUNKY	ONLINE-B	UEDIN-PHRASE	ONLINE-A	CU-TECTO	COMMERCIAL1	COMMERCIAL2
CU-DEPFIX	–	.50	.42‡	.48	.44‡	.43‡	.41‡	.35‡	.30‡	.24‡
UEDIN-UNCNSTR	.50	–	**.51**	.48	.42‡	.37‡	.42‡	.39‡	.31‡	.26‡
CU-BOJAR	**.58‡**	.49	–	.49	.45‡	.44‡	.40‡	.36‡	.32‡	.24‡
CU-FUNKY	**.52**	**.52**	**.51**	–	.48	.47†	.44‡	.34‡	.33‡	.26‡
ONLINE-B	**.56‡**	**.58‡**	**.55‡**	**.52**	–	.48	.47†	.41‡	.31‡	.26‡
UEDIN-PHRASE	**.57‡**	**.63‡**	**.56‡**	**.53†**	**.52**	–	.48	.44‡	.32‡	.27‡
ONLINE-A	**.59‡**	**.58‡**	**.60‡**	**.56‡**	**.53†**	**.52**	–	.45‡	.37‡	.30‡
CU-TECTO	**.65‡**	**.61‡**	**.64‡**	**.66‡**	**.59‡**	**.56‡**	**.55‡**	–	.42‡	.30‡
COMMERCIAL1	**.70‡**	**.69‡**	**.68‡**	**.67‡**	**.69‡**	**.68‡**	**.63‡**	**.58‡**	–	.40‡
COMMERCIAL2	**.76‡**	**.74‡**	**.76‡**	**.74‡**	**.74‡**	**.73‡**	**.70‡**	**.70‡**	**.60‡**	–
score	.60	.59	.58	.57	.54	.52	.50	.44	.36	.28
rank	1-3	1-3	1-4	3-4	5-6	5-6	7	8	9	10

Table 29: Head to head comparison, ignoring ties, for English-Czech systems

	ONLINE-B	UEDIN-SYNTAX	ONLINE-A	LIMSI-KIT	EU-BRIDGE	UEDIN-PHRASE	KIT	RWTH	DCU-ICTCAS	CMU	RBMT4	RBMT1	ONLINE-C
ONLINE-B	–	.46	.40‡	.41‡	.35‡	.42‡	.38‡	.35‡	.40‡	.31‡	.33‡	.32‡	.22‡
UEDIN-SYNTAX	**.54**	–	**.51**	.47	.47	.45	.45⋆	.39‡	.36‡	.38‡	.35‡	.34‡	.27‡
ONLINE-A	**.60‡**	.49	–	.42†	.44†	**.51**	.41‡	.38‡	.44⋆	.42‡	.38‡	.31‡	.20‡
LIMSI-KIT	**.59‡**	**.53**	**.58†**	–	**.55**	**.53**	.31‡	.45⋆	.39‡	.41‡	.37‡	.35‡	.29‡
EU-BRIDGE	**.65‡**	**.53**	**.56†**	.45	–	.45	.44⋆	.48	.40‡	.37‡	.39‡	.37‡	.30‡
UEDIN-PHRASE	**.58‡**	**.55**	.49	.47	**.55**	–	.48	.39‡	.34‡	.45⋆	.40‡	.40‡	.34‡
KIT	**.62‡**	**.55⋆**	**.59‡**	**.69‡**	**.56⋆**	**.52**	–	.45⋆	.41‡	.45⋆	.47	.40‡	.31‡
RWTH	**.65‡**	**.61‡**	**.62‡**	**.55⋆**	**.52**	**.61‡**	**.55⋆**	–	**.54**	.44†	.44†	.38‡	.37‡
DCU-ICTCAS	**.60‡**	**.64‡**	**.56⋆**	**.61‡**	**.60‡**	**.66‡**	**.59‡**	.46	–	**.51**	.49	.46⋆	.40‡
CMU	**.69‡**	**.62‡**	**.58‡**	**.59‡**	**.63‡**	**.55⋆**	**.55⋆**	**.56†**	.49	–	**.53**	.42‡	.43†
RBMT4	**.67‡**	**.65‡**	**.62‡**	**.63‡**	**.61‡**	**.60‡**	**.53**	**.56†**	**.51**	.47	–	**.51**	.37‡
RBMT1	**.68‡**	**.66‡**	**.69‡**	**.65‡**	**.63‡**	**.60‡**	**.60‡**	**.62‡**	**.54⋆**	**.58‡**	.49	–	.38‡
ONLINE-C	**.78‡**	**.73‡**	**.80‡**	**.71‡**	**.70‡**	**.66‡**	**.69‡**	**.63‡**	**.60‡**	**.57†**	**.63‡**	**.62‡**	–
score	.63	.58	.58	.55	.55	.54	.49	.47	.45	.44	.44	.40	.32
rank	1	2-3	2-3	4-6	4-6	4-6	7-8	7-8	9-11	9-11	9-11	12	13

Table 30: Head to head comparison, ignoring ties, for German-English systems

	UEDIN-SYNTAX	ONLINE-B	ONLINE-A	PROMT-HYBRID	PROMT-RULE	UEDIN-STANFORD	EU-BRIDGE	RBMT4	UEDIN-PHRASE	RBMT1	KIT	STANFORD-UNC	CIMS	STANFORD	UU	ONLINE-C	IMS-TTT	UU-DOCENT
UEDIN-SYNTAX	–	**.55⋆**	.46⋆	.45⋆	.46⋆	.44†	.41‡	.45†	.43‡	.41‡	.38‡	.38‡	.36‡	.33‡	.38‡	.30‡	.30‡	.25‡
ONLINE-B	.45⋆	–	.50	.48	.50	.47	.43†	.46⋆	.41‡	.45†	.39‡	.39‡	.37‡	.32‡	.35‡	.34‡	.30‡	.29‡
ONLINE-A	**.54⋆**	.50	–	.44†	**.52**	.50	.45⋆	.43‡	.43†	.42‡	.39‡	.41‡	.42‡	.42‡	.37‡	.44†	.38‡	.33‡
PROMT-HYBRID	**.55⋆**	**.52**	**.56†**	–	.45⋆	.47	.47	.46⋆	.50	.44†	.42‡	.40‡	.41‡	.38‡	.39‡	.39‡	.33‡	.34‡
PROMT-RULE	**.54⋆**	.50	.48	**.55⋆**	–	**.51**	.47	.47	.45⋆	.38‡	.42‡	.40‡	.43†	.41‡	.43†	.38‡	.35‡	.29‡
UEDIN-STANFORD	**.56†**	**.53**	.50	**.53**	.49	–	.48	.50	.47	.44†	.46	.36‡	.36‡	.36‡	.36‡	.35‡	.30‡	.32‡
EU-BRIDGE	**.59‡**	**.57†**	**.55⋆**	**.53**	**.53**	**.52**	–	.46⋆	.43†	**.52**	.42‡	.42‡	.45⋆	.35‡	.36‡	.41‡	.38‡	.30‡
RBMT4	**.55†**	**.54⋆**	**.57‡**	**.54⋆**	**.53**	.50	**.54⋆**	–	**.53**	.49	.44†	.49	.50	.47	.40‡	.42‡	.38‡	.40‡
UEDIN-PHRASE	**.57‡**	**.59‡**	**.57†**	.50	**.55⋆**	**.53**	**.57†**	.47	–	.50	**.55⋆**	.47	.45⋆	.44†	.43†	.42‡	.37‡	.34‡
RBMT1	**.59‡**	**.55†**	**.58‡**	**.56†**	**.62‡**	**.56†**	.48	**.51**	.50	–	.47	.47	.45†	.47	.43‡	.42‡	.38‡	.41‡
KIT	**.62‡**	**.61‡**	**.61‡**	**.58‡**	**.58‡**	**.54**	**.58‡**	**.56†**	.45⋆	**.53**	–	.47	.49	.46	.43‡	.48	.34‡	.37‡
STANFORD-UNC	**.62‡**	**.61‡**	**.59‡**	**.60‡**	**.60‡**	**.64‡**	**.58‡**	**.51**	**.53**	**.53**	**.53**	–	.48	.47	.45†	.45⋆	.39‡	.41‡
CIMS	**.64‡**	**.63‡**	**.58‡**	**.59‡**	**.57†**	**.64‡**	**.55⋆**	.50	**.55⋆**	**.55†**	**.51**	**.52**	–	**.53**	.42‡	**.52**	.47	.42‡
STANFORD	**.67‡**	**.68‡**	**.58‡**	**.62‡**	**.59‡**	**.64‡**	**.65‡**	**.53**	**.56†**	**.53**	**.54**	**.53**	.47	–	**.53**	.42‡	.39‡	.48
UU	**.62‡**	**.65‡**	**.62‡**	**.61‡**	**.57†**	**.64‡**	**.64‡**	**.60‡**	**.57†**	**.57‡**	**.57‡**	**.55†**	**.58‡**	.47	–	.46⋆	.45†	.38‡
ONLINE-C	**.70‡**	**.66‡**	**.56†**	**.61‡**	**.62‡**	**.65‡**	**.59‡**	**.58‡**	**.58‡**	**.58‡**	**.52**	**.55⋆**	.48	**.58‡**	**.54⋆**	–	.48	.47
IMS-TTT	**.70‡**	**.70‡**	**.62‡**	**.67‡**	**.65‡**	**.70‡**	**.62‡**	**.62‡**	**.63‡**	**.62‡**	**.66‡**	**.61‡**	**.53**	**.61‡**	**.55†**	**.52**	–	.49
UU-DOCENT	**.75‡**	**.71‡**	**.67‡**	**.66‡**	**.71‡**	**.68‡**	**.70‡**	**.60‡**	**.66‡**	**.59‡**	**.63‡**	**.59‡**	**.58‡**	**.52**	**.62‡**	**.53**	**.51**	–
score	.60	.59	.56	.56	.56	.56	.54	.51	.51	.50	.48	.47	.46	.44	.43	.42	.38	.37
rank	1-2	1-2	3-6	3-6	3-6	3-6	7	8-10	8-10	8-10	11-12	11-13	12-14	13-15	14-16	15-16	17-18	17-18

Table 31: Head to head comparison, ignoring ties, for English-German systems

	UEDIN-PHRASE	KIT	ONLINE-B	STANFORD	ONLINE-A	RBMT1	RBMT4	ONLINE-C
UEDIN-PHRASE	–	.48	.48	.45‡	.43‡	.28‡	.28‡	.19‡
KIT	**.52**	–	**.54**†	.48	.44‡	.31‡	.29‡	.21‡
ONLINE-B	**.52**	.46†	–	**.51**	.47	.31‡	.30‡	.24‡
STANFORD	**.55**‡	**.52**	.49	–	.46†	.34‡	.30‡	.23‡
ONLINE-A	**.57**‡	**.56**‡	**.53**	**.54**†	–	.32‡	.29‡	.21‡
RBMT1	**.72**‡	**.69**‡	**.69**‡	**.66**‡	**.68**‡	–	.42‡	.33‡
RBMT4	**.72**‡	**.71**‡	**.70**‡	**.70**‡	**.71**‡	**.58**‡	–	.39‡
ONLINE-C	**.81**‡	**.79**‡	**.76**‡	**.77**‡	**.79**‡	**.67**‡	**.61**‡	–
score	.63	.60	.59	.58	.57	.40	.35	.25
rank	1	2-4	2-4	2-4	5	6	7	8

Table 32: Head to head comparison, ignoring ties, for French-English systems

	ONLINE-B	UEDIN-PHRASE	KIT	MATRAN	MATRAN-RULES	ONLINE-A	UU-DOCENT	PROMT-HYBRID	UA	PROMT-RULE	RBMT1	RBMT4	ONLINE-C
ONLINE-B	–	.46⋆	.48	.46⋆	.50	.41‡	.39‡	.39‡	.37‡	.38‡	.37‡	.35‡	.27‡
UEDIN-PHRASE	**.54**⋆	–	.50	.47	.46	.46⋆	.42‡	.41‡	.46⋆	.42‡	.35‡	.34‡	.33‡
KIT	**.52**	.50	–	**.53**	**.51**	.50	.43‡	.49	.41‡	.42‡	.35‡	.37‡	.29‡
MATRAN	**.54**⋆	**.53**	.47	–	.49	.50	.43‡	.43‡	.38‡	.48	.40‡	.34‡	.32‡
MATRAN-RULES	.50	**.54**	.49	**.51**	–	**.53**	.40‡	.45†	.46⋆	.42‡	.44†	.40‡	.34‡
ONLINE-A	**.59**‡	**.54**⋆	.50	.50	.47	–	.44†	.49	.47	.45⋆	.42‡	.37‡	.34‡
UU-DOCENT	**.61**‡	**.58**‡	**.57**‡	**.57**‡	**.60**‡	**.56**†	–	.43‡	**.52**	.46⋆	.39‡	.44†	.33‡
PROMT-HYBRID	**.61**‡	**.59**‡	**.51**	**.57**‡	**.55**†	**.51**	**.57**‡	–	.50	.41‡	.46⋆	.44†	.35‡
UA	**.63**‡	**.54**⋆	**.59**‡	**.62**‡	**.54**⋆	**.53**	.48	.50	–	.49	.46⋆	.43‡	.34‡
PROMT-RULE	**.62**‡	**.58**‡	**.58**‡	**.52**	**.58**‡	**.55**⋆	**.54**⋆	**.59**‡	**.51**	–	.47	.39‡	.37‡
RBMT1	**.63**‡	**.65**‡	**.65**‡	**.60**‡	**.56**†	**.58**‡	**.61**‡	**.54**⋆	**.54**⋆	**.53**	–	.46⋆	.45†
RBMT4	**.65**‡	**.66**‡	**.63**‡	**.66**‡	**.60**‡	**.63**‡	**.56**†	**.56**†	**.57**‡	**.61**‡	**.54**⋆	–	.45⋆
ONLINE-C	**.73**‡	**.67**‡	**.71**‡	**.67**‡	**.66**‡	**.66**‡	**.67**‡	**.65**‡	**.66**‡	**.63**‡	**.55**†	**.55**⋆	–
score	.59	.57	.55	.55	.54	.53	.49	.49	.48	.47	.43	.40	.34
rank	1	2-4	2-5	2-5	4-6	4-6	7-9	7-10	7-10	8-10	11	12	13

Table 33: Head to head comparison, ignoring ties, for English-French systems

	ONLINE-B	ONLINE-A	UEDIN-SYNTAX	CMU	UEDIN-PHRASE	AFRL	IIT-BOMBAY	DCU-LINGO24	IIIT-HYDERABAD
ONLINE-B	–	.36‡	.33‡	.37‡	.31‡	.21‡	.20‡	.14‡	.00
ONLINE-A	**.64**‡	–	.48	.47⋆	.44‡	.31‡	.30‡	.24‡	.12‡
UEDIN-SYNTAX	**.67**‡	**.52**	–	.47	.46†	.33‡	.29‡	.24‡	.12‡
CMU	**.63**‡	**.53**⋆	**.53**	–	.47	.37‡	.31‡	.26‡	.11‡
UEDIN-PHRASE	**.69**‡	**.56**‡	**.54**†	**.53**	–	.40‡	.33‡	.25‡	.11‡
AFRL	**.79**‡	**.69**‡	**.67**‡	**.63**‡	**.60**‡	–	**.53**	.40‡	.16‡
IIT-BOMBAY	**.80**‡	**.70**‡	**.71**‡	**.69**‡	**.67**‡	.47	–	.44‡	.19‡
DCU-LINGO24	**.86**‡	**.76**‡	**.76**‡	**.74**‡	**.75**‡	**.60**‡	**.56**‡	–	.19‡
IIIT-HYDERABAD	**.94**‡	**.88**‡	**.88**‡	**.89**‡	**.89**‡	**.84**‡	**.81**‡	**.81**‡	–
score	.75	.62	.61	.60	.57	.44	.41	.34	.13
rank	1	2-3	2-4	3-4	5	6-7	6-7	8	9

Table 34: Head to head comparison, ignoring ties, for Hindi-English systems

	ONLINE-B	ONLINE-A	UEDIN-UNCNSTR	UEDIN-PHRASE	CU-MOSES	IIT-BOMBAY	IPN-UPV-CNTXT	DCU-LINGO24	IPN-UPV-NODEV	MANAWI-H1	MANAWI	MANAWI-RMOOV
ONLINE-B	–	.49	.28‡	.29‡	.27‡	.23‡	.22‡	.20‡	.17‡	.12‡	.13‡	.13‡
ONLINE-A	**.51**	–	.31‡	.29‡	.27‡	.25‡	.20‡	.20‡	.21‡	.19‡	.16‡	.15‡
UEDIN-UNCNSTR	**.72‡**	**.69‡**	–	.44†	.49	.39‡	.40‡	.34‡	.39‡	.29‡	.30‡	.27‡
UEDIN-PHRASE	**.71‡**	**.71‡**	**.56†**	–	.48	.45†	.44†	.39‡	.37‡	.31‡	.31‡	.32‡
CU-MOSES	**.73‡**	**.73‡**	**.51**	**.52**	–	.47	.42‡	.40‡	.45⋆	.36‡	.35‡	.33‡
IIT-BOMBAY	**.77‡**	**.75‡**	**.61‡**	**.55†**	**.53**	–	.50	.47	.45†	.41‡	.40‡	.36‡
IPN-UPV-CNTXT	**.78‡**	**.80‡**	**.60‡**	**.56†**	**.58‡**	.50	–	**.51**	.41‡	.40‡	.40‡	.37‡
DCU-LINGO24	**.80‡**	**.80‡**	**.66‡**	**.61‡**	**.60‡**	**.53**	.49	–	**.52**	.41‡	.41‡	.39‡
IPN-UPV-NODEV	**.83‡**	**.79‡**	**.61‡**	**.63‡**	**.55⋆**	**.55†**	**.59‡**	.48	–	.46⋆	.44†	.38‡
MANAWI-H1	**.88‡**	**.81‡**	**.71‡**	**.69‡**	**.64‡**	**.59‡**	**.60‡**	**.59‡**	**.54⋆**	–	.35‡	.34‡
MANAWI	**.87‡**	**.84‡**	**.70‡**	**.69‡**	**.65‡**	**.60‡**	**.60‡**	**.59‡**	**.56†**	**.65‡**	–	.39‡
MANAWI-RMOOV	**.87‡**	**.85‡**	**.73‡**	**.68‡**	**.67‡**	**.64‡**	**.63‡**	**.61‡**	**.62‡**	**.66‡**	**.61‡**	–
score	.77	.75	.57	.54	.52	.47	.46	.43	.42	.38	.35	.31
rank	1	2	3	4-5	4-5	6-7	6-7	8-9	8-9	10-11	10-11	12

Table 35: Head to head comparison, ignoring ties, for English-Hindi systems

	AFRL-PE	ONLINE-B	ONLINE-A	PROMT-HYBRID	PROMT-RULE	UEDIN-PHRASE	YANDEX	ONLINE-G	AFRL	UEDIN-SYNTAX	KAZNU	RBMT1	RBMT4
AFRL-PE	–	.42‡	.40‡	.39‡	.39‡	.41‡	.35‡	.39‡	.28‡	.26‡	.26‡	.29‡	.21‡
ONLINE-B	**.58‡**	–	.42‡	.43‡	.45†	.45†	.42‡	.43‡	.46⋆	.37‡	.33‡	.29‡	.31‡
ONLINE-A	**.60‡**	**.58‡**	–	.50	.45†	**.51**	.47	.45†	.42‡	.40‡	.33‡	.32‡	.30‡
PROMT-HYBRID	**.61‡**	**.57‡**	.50	–	.47	.45⋆	.49	.44†	.43‡	.44†	.39‡	.31‡	.27‡
PROMT-RULE	**.61‡**	**.55†**	**.55†**	**.53**	–	.46⋆	.47	.49	.48	.42‡	.36‡	.34‡	.30‡
UEDIN-PHRASE	**.59‡**	**.55†**	.49	**.55⋆**	**.54⋆**	–	.49	.50	.47	.44†	.32‡	.37‡	.29‡
YANDEX	**.65‡**	**.58‡**	**.53**	**.51**	**.53**	**.51**	–	.48	.50	.43‡	.34‡	.36‡	.34‡
ONLINE-G	**.61‡**	**.57‡**	**.55†**	**.56†**	**.51**	.50	**.52**	–	.48	.43‡	.39‡	.35‡	.30‡
AFRL	**.72‡**	**.54⋆**	**.58‡**	**.57‡**	**.52**	**.53**	.50	**.52**	–	.44†	.41‡	.41‡	.37‡
UEDIN-SYNTAX	**.74‡**	**.63‡**	**.60‡**	**.56†**	**.58‡**	**.56†**	**.57‡**	**.57‡**	**.56†**	–	**.51**	.36‡	.37‡
KAZNU	**.74‡**	**.67‡**	**.67‡**	**.61‡**	**.64‡**	**.68‡**	**.66‡**	**.61‡**	**.59‡**	.49	–	.44†	.38‡
RBMT1	**.71‡**	**.71‡**	**.68‡**	**.69‡**	**.66‡**	**.63‡**	**.64‡**	**.65‡**	**.59‡**	**.64‡**	**.56†**	–	.47
RBMT4	**.79‡**	**.69‡**	**.70‡**	**.73‡**	**.70‡**	**.71‡**	**.66‡**	**.70‡**	**.63‡**	**.63‡**	**.62‡**	**.53**	–
score	.66	.58	.55	.55	.53	.53	.52	.51	.49	.45	.40	.36	.32
rank	1	2	3-5	3-5	4-7	5-8	5-8	5-8	9	10	11	12	13

Table 36: Head to head comparison, ignoring ties, for Russian-English systems

	PROMT-RULE	ONLINE-B	PROMT-HYBRID	UEDIN-UNCNSTR	ONLINE-G	ONLINE-A	UEDIN-PHRASE	RBMT4	RBMT1
PROMT-RULE	–	**.51**	.45†	.43‡	.43‡	.39‡	.38‡	.15‡	.00
ONLINE-B	.49	–	.50	.47⋆	.38‡	.36‡	.38‡	.16‡	.13‡
PROMT-HYBRID	**.55†**	.50	–	.49	.47	.39‡	.40‡	.18‡	.15‡
UEDIN-UNCNSTR	**.57‡**	**.53⋆**	**.51**	–	.50	.44‡	.36‡	.25‡	.18‡
ONLINE-G	**.57‡**	**.62‡**	**.53**	.50	–	.46⋆	.44‡	.23‡	.18‡
ONLINE-A	**.61‡**	**.64‡**	**.61‡**	**.56‡**	**.54⋆**	–	.49	.24‡	.18‡
UEDIN-PHRASE	**.62‡**	**.62‡**	**.60‡**	**.64‡**	**.56‡**	**.51**	–	.30‡	.21‡
RBMT4	**.85‡**	**.84‡**	**.82‡**	**.75‡**	**.77‡**	**.76‡**	**.70‡**	–	.42‡
RBMT1	**.91‡**	**.87‡**	**.85‡**	**.82‡**	**.82‡**	**.82‡**	**.79‡**	**.58‡**	–
score	.64	.64	.61	.58	.55	.51	.49	.26	.19
rank	1-2	1-2	3	4-5	4-5	6-7	6-7	8	9

Table 37: Head to head comparison, ignoring ties, for English-Russian systems

Parallel FDA5 for Fast Deployment of Accurate Statistical Machine Translation Systems

Ergun Biçici
Centre for Next Generation Localisation
School of Computing
Dublin City University
ergun.bicici@computing.dcu.ie

Qun Liu
Centre for Next Generation Localisation
School of Computing
Dublin City University
qliu@computing.dcu.ie

Andy Way
Centre for Next Generation Localisation
School of Computing
Dublin City University
away@computing.dcu.ie

Abstract

We use parallel FDA5, an efficiently parameterized and optimized parallel implementation of feature decay algorithms for fast deployment of accurate statistical machine translation systems, taking only about half a day for each translation direction. We build Parallel FDA5 Moses SMT systems for all language pairs in the WMT14 translation task and obtain SMT performance close to the top Moses systems with an average of 3.49 BLEU points difference using significantly less resources for training and development.

1 Introduction

Parallel FDA5 is developed for fast deployment of accurate statistical machine translation systems using an efficiently parameterized and optimized parallel implementation of feature decay algorithms (Biçici and Yuret, 2014). Parallel FDA5 takes about half a day for each translation direction. We achieve SMT performance that is on par with the top constrained Moses SMT systems.

Statistical machine translation (SMT) is a data intensive problem. If you have the translations for the source sentences you are translating in your training set or even portions of it, then the translation task becomes easier. If some tokens are not found in the training data then you cannot translate them and if some translated word do not appear in your language model (LM) corpus, then it becomes harder for the SMT engine to find its correct position in the translation. The importance of parallel FDA5 increases with the proliferation of training material available for building SMT systems. Table 2 presents the statistics of the available training and LM corpora for the constrained (C) systems as well as the statistics of the Parallel FDA5 selected training and LM corpora.

Parallel FDA5 runs separate FDA5 models on randomized subsets of the training data and combines the selections afterwards. We run parallel FDA5 SMT experiments using Moses (Koehn et al., 2007) in all language pairs in WMT14 (Bojar et al., 2014) and obtain SMT performance close to the top constrained Moses systems training using all of the training material. Parallel FDA5 allows rapid prototyping of SMT systems for a given target domain or task and can be very useful for MT in target domains with limited resources or in disaster and crisis situations (Lewis et al., 2011).

2 Parallel FDA5 for Instance Selection

2.1 FDA5

FDA is developed mainly for building high performance SMT systems using fewer yet relevant data that is selected for increasing the coverage of the test set features while maximizing their diversity (Biçici and Yuret, 2011; Biçici, 2011). Parallel FDA parallelize instance selection and significantly reduces the time to deploy accurate MT systems in the presence of large training data from weeks to half a day and still achieve state-of-the-art SMT performance (Biçici, 2013). FDA5 is developed for efficient parameterization, optimization, and implementation of FDA (Biçici and Yuret, 2014). FDA5 can be used in both transductive learning scenarios where test set is used to select the training data or in active learning scenarios where training set itself is used to obtain a sorting of the training data and select.

We run transductive learning experiments in this work such that the instance selection is performed for the given test set. According to SMT experiments performed on the 2 million sentence English-German section of the Europarl corpus (Biçici and Yuret, 2014), FDA5 can increase the performance by 0.41 BLEU points compared to using all of the available training data and by

Proceedings of the Ninth Workshop on Statistical Machine Translation, pages 59–65,
Baltimore, Maryland USA, June 26–27, 2014.

Algorithm 1: Parallel FDA5

Input: Parallel training sentences $\mathcal{U}$, test set features $\mathcal{F}$, and desired number of training instances N.

Output: Subset of the parallel sentences to be used as the training data $\mathcal{L} \subseteq \mathcal{U}$.

$\mathcal{U} \leftarrow \texttt{shuffle}(\mathcal{U})$

$\boldsymbol{\mathcal{U}}, M \leftarrow \texttt{split}(\mathcal{U}, N)$

$\mathbf{L} \leftarrow \{\}$

foreach $\mathcal{U}_i \in \boldsymbol{\mathcal{U}}$ **do**

  $\langle \mathcal{L}_i, \mathbf{s}_i \rangle \leftarrow \texttt{FDA5}(\mathcal{U}_i, \mathcal{F}, M)$

  $\mathbf{L} \leftarrow \mathbf{L} \cup \langle \mathcal{L}_i, \mathbf{s}_i \rangle$

$\mathcal{L} \leftarrow \texttt{merge}(\mathbf{L})$

3.22 BLEU points compared to random selection. FDA5 is also used for selecting the training set in the WMT14 medical translation task (Calixto et al., 2014) and the tuning set in the WMT14 German-English translation task (Li et al., 2014).

FDA5 has 5 parameters that effect the instance scores based on the three formulas used:

- Initialization:

$$\texttt{init}(f) = \log(|\mathcal{U}|/C_{\mathcal{U}}(f))^{i}\,|f|^{l} \quad (1)$$

- Decay:

$$\texttt{decay}(f) = \texttt{init}(f)(1+C_{\mathcal{L}}(f))^{-c} d^{C_{\mathcal{L}}(f)} \quad (2)$$

- Sentence score:

$$\texttt{sentScore}(S) = \frac{1}{|S|^{s}} \sum_{f \in F(S)} \mathit{fvalue}(f) \quad (3)$$

$C_{\mathcal{L}}(f)$ returns the count of feature f in $\mathcal{L}$. `d` is the feature score polynomial decay factor, `c` is the feature score exponential decay factor, `s` is the sentence score length exponent, `i` is the initial feature score idf exponent, and `l` is the initial feature score n-gram length exponent. FDA5 is available at `http://github.com/bicici/FDA` and the FDA5 optimizer is available at `http://github.com/bicici/FDAOptimization`.

2.2 Parallel FDA5

Parallel FDA5 (ParFDA5) is presented in Algorithm 1, which first shuffles the training sentences, $\mathcal{U}$ and runs individual FDA5 models on the multiple splits from which equal number of sentences, M, are selected. We use ParFDA5 for selecting parallel training data and LM data for building SMT systems. `merge` combines k sorted arrays, $\mathcal{L}_i$, into one sorted array in $O(Mk \log k)$ using their scores, $\mathbf{s}_i$, where Mk is the total number of elements in all of the input arrays. [1] ParFDA5 makes FDA5 more scalable to domains with large training corpora and allows rapid deployment of SMT systems. By selecting from random splits of the original corpus, we work with different n-gram feature distributions in each split and prevent feature values from becoming negligible, which can enhance the diversity.

2.3 Language Model Data Selection

We select the LM training data with ParFDA5 based on the following observation (Biçici, 2013):

> No word not appearing in the training set can appear in the translation.

It is impossible for an SMT system to translate a word unseen in the training corpus nor can it translate it with a word not found in the target side of the training set [2]. Thus we are only interested in correctly ordering the words appearing in the training corpus and collecting the sentences that contain them for building the LM. At the same time, a compact and more relevant LM corpus is also useful for modeling longer range dependencies with higher order n-gram models. We use 1-gram features for LM corpus selection since we don't know which phrases will be generated by the translation model. After the LM corpus selection, the target side of the parallel training data is added to the LM corpus.

3 Results

We run ParFDA5 SMT experiments for all language pairs in both directions in the WMT14 translation task (Bojar et al., 2014), which include English-Czech (en-cs), English-German (en-de), English-French (en-fr), English-Hindi (en-hi), and English-Russian (en-ru). We true-case all of the corpora, use 150-best lists during tuning, set the LM order to a value between 7 and 10 for all language pairs, and train the LM using SRILM (Stolcke, 2002). We set the maximum sentence length filter to 126 and for GIZA++ (Och and Ney, 2003),

[1] (Cormen et al., 2009), question 6.5-9. Merging k sorted lists into one sorted list using a min-heap for k-way merging.

[2] Unless the translation is a verbatim copy of the source.

$S \rightarrow T$	Data	Training Data #word S (M)	#word T (M)	#sent (K)	SCOV	TCOV	LM Data #word (M)	TCOV
en-cs	C	253.5	223.4	16068	0.8282	0.7046	717.0	0.8539
en-cs	ParFDA5	22.0	19.6	1205	0.8161	0.6062	325.8	0.8238
cs-en	C	223.4	253.5	16068	0.7046	0.8282	5541.9	0.9552
cs-en	ParFDA5	19.3	22.0	1205	0.7046	0.7581	351.0	0.9132
en-de	C	116.0	109.5	4511	0.812	0.7101	1573.8	0.8921
en-de	ParFDA5	16.7	16.8	845	0.8033	0.6316	206.9	0.8184
de-en	C	109.5	116.0	4511	0.7101	0.812	5446.8	0.9525
de-en	ParFDA5	17.8	19.6	845	0.7087	0.753	339.5	0.9082
en-fr	C	1096.1	1287.8	40344	0.8885	0.9163	2534.5	0.9611
en-fr	ParFDA5	22.6	26.6	1008	0.8735	0.8412	737.4	0.9491
fr-en	C	1287.8	1096.1	40344	0.9163	0.8885	6255.8	0.9675
fr-en	ParFDA5	20.9	19.3	1008	0.8963	0.7845	463.4	0.9282
en-hi	C	3.4	5.0	306	0.5467	0.5986	36.3	0.7972
en-hi	ParFDA5	3.3	4.9	254	0.5467	0.5976	41.2	0.8115
hi-en	C	5.0	3.4	306	0.5986	0.5467	5350.4	0.9473
hi-en	ParFDA5	5.0	3.3	284	0.5985	0.5466	966.8	0.9209
en-ru	C	49.6	46.1	2531	0.7992	0.6823	590.8	0.8679
en-ru	ParFDA5	19.6	18.6	1107	0.7991	0.6388	282.1	0.8447
ru-en	C	46.1	49.6	2531	0.6823	0.7992	5380.6	0.9567
ru-en	ParFDA5	16.6	19.4	1107	0.6821	0.7586	225.1	0.9009

Table 2: The data statistics for the available training and LM corpora for the constrained (C) submissions compared with the ParFDA5 selected training and LM corpora statistics. #words is in millions (M) and #sents is in thousands (K).

	$S \rightarrow T$	d	c	s	i	l
Training, $n = 2$	en-de	1.0	0.5817	1.4176	5.0001	-3.154
	de-en	1.0	1.0924	1.3604	5.0001	-4.341
	en-cs	1.0	0.0676	0.8299	5.0001	-0.8788
	cs-en	1.0	1.5063	0.7777	3.223	-2.3824
	en-ru	1.0	0.6519	1.6877	5.0001	-1.1888
	ru-en	1.0	1.607	3.0001	0.0	-1.8247
	en-hi	1.0	3.0001	3.0001	1.5701	-1.5699
	hi-en	1.0	0.0	1.1001	5.0001	-0.8264
	en-fr	1.0	0.8143	0.801	3.5996	-1.3394
	fr-en	1.0	0.19	1.0106	5.0001	1.238
LM, $n = 1$	en-de	1.0	0.1924	1.0487	5.0001	4.9404
	de-en	1.0	1.7877	3.0001	3.1213	-0.4147
	en-cs	1.0	0.4988	1.1586	5.0001	-5.0001
	cs-en	0.9255	0.2787	0.7439	3.7264	-2.0564
	en-ru	1.0	1.4419	2.239	1.5543	-0.5097
	ru-en	1.0	2.4844	3.0001	4.6669	3.7978
	en-hi	1.0	0.0	0.0	5.0001	-4.944
	hi-en	1.0	0.3053	3.0001	5.0001	4.1216
	en-fr	1.0	3.0001	2.0452	3.0229	3.4364
	fr-en	1.0	0.7467	0.7641	5.0001	5.0001

Table 1: Optimized ParFDA5 parameters for selecting the training set using 2-grams or the LM corpus using 1-grams.

max-fertility is set to 10, with the number of iterations set to 7,3,5,5,7 for IBM models 1,2,3,4, and the HMM model and 70 word classes are learned over 3 iterations with the mkcls tool during training. The development set contains 5000 sentences, 2000 of which are randomly sampled from previous years' development sets (2008-2012) and 3000 come from the development set for WMT14.

3.1 Optimized ParFDA5 Parameters

Table 1 presents the optimized ParFDA5 parameters obtained using the development set. Translation direction specific differences are visible. A negative value for `l` shows that FDA5 prefers shorter features, which we observe mainly when the target language is English. We also observe higher exponential decay rates when the target language is mainly English. For optimizing the parameters for selecting LM corpus instances, we still use a parallel corpus and instead of optimizing for TCOV, we optimize for SCOV such that we select instances that are relevant for the target training corpus but still maximize the coverage of source features and be able to represent the source sentences within a translation task. The selected LM corpus is prepared for a translation task.

3.2 Data Selection

We select the same number of sentences with Parallel FDA (Biçici, 2013), which is roughly 15% of the training corpus for en-de, 35% for ru-en, 6% for cs-en, and 2% for en-fr. After the training set selection, we select the LM data using the target side of the training set as the target domain to select LM instances for. For en and fr, we have access to the LDC Gigaword corpora (Parker et al., 2011; Graff et al., 2011), from which we extract only the story type news. We select 15 million sentences for each LM not including the se-

$S \rightarrow T$	Time (Min)							Space (MB)		
	ParFDA5			Moses			Overall	Moses		
	Train	LM	Total	Train	Tune	Total		PT	LM	ALL
en-cs	5	28	34	375	702	1162	1196	1871	5865	19746
cs-en	7	65	72	358	448	867	939	1808	4906	18650
en-de	8	29	38	302	1059	1459	1497	1676	2923	18313
de-en	8	85	93	358	474	924	1017	1854	5219	19247
en-fr	23	60	84	488	781	1372	1456	2309	9577	24362
fr-en	21	99	120	315	490	897	1017	1845	4888	17466
en-hi	2	9	11	91	366	511	522	269	817	4292
hi-en	1	36	37	91	330	467	504	285	9697	3845
en-ru	11	25	35	358	369	837	872	2174	4770	21283
ru-en	10	62	71	309	510	895	966	1939	2735	19537

Table 3: The space and time required for building the ParFDA5 Moses SMT systems. The sizes are in MB and time in minutes. PT stands for the phrase table. ALL does not contain the size of the LM.

BLEUc	$S \rightarrow en$					$en \rightarrow T$				
	cs-en	de-en	fr-en	hi-en	ru-en	en-cs	en-de	en-fr	en-hi	en-ru
WMT14C	0.288	0.28	0.35	0.139	0.318	0.21	0.201	0.358	0.111	0.287
ParFDA5	0.256	0.239	0.319	0.105	0.282	0.172	0.168	0.325	0.07	0.257
diff	0.032	0.041	0.031	0.034	0.036	0.038	0.033	0.033	0.041	0.03
LM order	9	9	9	9	9	9	9	7	10	9

Table 4: BLEUc for the top constrained result in WMT14 (WMT14C) and for ParFDA5 results, their difference to WMT14C, and the LM order used are presented. Average difference is 3.49 BLEU points.

lected training set, which is added later. The statistics of the ParFDA5 selected training data and the available training data for the constrained translation task is given in Table 2. The size of the LM corpora includes both the LDC and the monolingual LM corpora provided by WMT14. Table 2 shows the significant size differences between the constrained dataset (C) and the ParFDA5 selected data. Table 2 also present the source and target coverage (SCOV and TCOV) in terms of the 2-grams of the test set observed in the training data or the LM data. The quality of the training corpus can be measured by TCOV, which is found to correlate well with the BLEU performance achievable (Biçici and Yuret, 2011; Biçici, 2011).

3.3 Computing Statistics

We quantify the time and space requirements for running ParFDA5 SMT systems for each translation direction. The space and time required for building the ParFDA5 Moses SMT systems are given in Table 3 where the sizes are in MB and the time in minutes. PT stands for the phrase table. We used Moses version 2.1.1, from `www.statmt.org/moses`. Building a ParFDA5 Moses SMT system takes about half a day.

3.4 Translation Results

The results of our two ParFDA5 SMT experiments for each language pair and their tokenized BLEU performance, BLEUc, together with the LM order used and the top constrained submissions to the WMT14 are given in Table 4 [3], which use phrase-based Moses for comparison [4]. We observed significant gains (+0.23 BLEU points) using higher order LMs last year (Biçici, 2013) and therefore we use LMs of order 7 to 10. The test set contains 10,000 sentences and only 3000 of which are used for evaluation, which can make the transductive learning application of ParFDA5 harder. In the transductive learning setting, ParFDA5 is selecting target test task specific SMT resources and therefore, having irrelevant instances in the test set may decrease the performance by causing FDA5 to select more domain specific data and less task specific. ParFDA5 significantly reduces the time required for training, development, and deployment of an SMT system for a given translation

[3] We use the results from matrix.statmt.org.

[4] Phrase-based Moses systems usually rank in the top 3.

			OOV				ppl							
							log OOV = -19				log OOV = -11			
Translation	T	order	train	FDA5	FDA5 LM	% red.	train	FDA5	FDA5 LM	% red.	train	FDA5	FDA5 LM	% red.
en-cs	en	3	866	1205	525	0.39	1764	1731	938	0.47	1370	1218	805	0.41
		4					1788	1746	877	0.51	1389	1229	753	0.46
		5					1799	1752	868	0.52	1398	1233	745	0.47
		6					1802	1753	867	0.52	1400	1234	744	0.47
cs-en	cs	3	557	706	276	0.5	480	419	333	0.31	408	342	307	0.25
		4					487	422	292	0.4	415	344	269	0.35
		5					495	424	285	0.42	421	346	263	0.38
		6					497	425	284	0.43	423	346	262	0.38
en-de	en	3	1666	2116	744	0.55	1323	1605	747	0.44	831	890	607	0.27
		4					1307	1596	689	0.47	821	885	560	0.32
		5					1307	1596	680	0.48	822	885	553	0.33
		6					1308	1596	679	0.48	822	885	552	0.33
de-en	de	3	691	849	417	0.4	482	498	394	0.18	386	379	345	0.11
		4					470	490	344	0.27	376	373	301	0.2
		5					470	490	336	0.29	377	373	293	0.22
		6					471	490	334	0.29	377	373	292	0.23
en-fr	en	3	270	411	153	0.43	185	167	173	0.07	173	151	166	0.04
		4					170	160	135	0.21	159	144	130	0.19
		5					171	160	126	0.27	160	145	121	0.24
fr-en	fr	3	306	604	179	0.42	349	325	275	0.21	320	275	261	0.19
		4					338	321	235	0.3	310	271	224	0.28
		5					342	322	228	0.33	314	272	217	0.31
en-hi	en	3	2035	2123	950	0.53	242	246	114	0.53	168	168	96	0.43
		4					237	241	87	0.63	164	165	73	0.55
		5					238	242	78	0.67	165	165	66	0.6
		6					239	242	75	0.68	165	165	64	0.62
hi-en	hi	3	1842	1860	623	**0.66**	1894	1898	482	0.75	915	911	377	0.59
		4					1910	1914	398	0.79	923	919	312	0.66
		5					1915	1919	378	**0.8**	925	921	296	0.68
		6					1915	1919	378	**0.8**	926	921	296	0.68
en-ru	en	3	959	1176	585	0.39	1067	1171	668	0.37	814	840	566	0.3
		4					1053	1159	603	0.43	803	831	511	0.36
		5					1052	1159	591	0.44	802	831	501	0.38
		6					1052	1159	588	0.44	802	831	498	0.38
ru-en	ru	3	558	689	340	0.39	385	398	363	0.06	334	334	333	0.0
		4					377	391	325	0.14	327	328	298	0.09
		5					378	392	318	0.16	328	329	292	0.11
		6					378	392	318	0.16	328	329	291	0.11

Table 5: Perplexity comparison of the LM built from the training corpus (train), ParFDA5 selected training corpus (FDA5), and the ParFDA5 selected LM corpus (FDA5 LM). % red. column lists the percentage of reduction.

task. The average difference to the top constrained submission in WMT14 is 3.49 BLEU points. For en-ru and en-cs, true-casing the LM using a true-caser trained on all of the available training data decreased the performance by 0.5 and 0.9 BLEU points respectively and for cs-en and fr-en, increased the performance by 0.2 and 0.5 BLEU points. We use the true-cased LM results using a true-caser trained on all of the available training data for all language pairs where for hi-en, the true-caser is trained on the ParFDA5 selected training data.

3.5 LM Data Quality

A LM training data selected for a given translation task allows us to train higher order language models, model longer range dependencies better, and at the same time, achieve lower perplexity as given in Table 5. We compare the perplexity of the ParFDA5 selected LM with a LM trained on the ParFDA5 selected training data and a LM trained using all of the available training corpora. To be able to compare the perplexities, we take the OOV tokens into consideration during calculations (Biçici, 2013). We present results for the cases when we handle OOV words with a cost of -19 or -11 each in Table 5. We are able to achieve significant reductions in the number of OOV tokens and the perplexity, reaching up to 66% reduction in the number of OOV tokens and up to 80% reduction in the perplexity.

BLEUc	$S \to en$				$en \to T$			
	cs-en	de-en	fr-en	ru-en	en-cs	en-de	en-fr	en-ru
ParFDA5	0.256	0.239	0.319	0.282	0.172	0.168	0.325	0.257
ParFDA	0.243	0.241	0.254	0.223	0.171	0.179	0.238	0.173
diff	0.013	-0.002	0.065	0.059	0.001	-0.011	0.087	0.084

Table 7: Parallel FDA5 WMT14 results compared with parallel FDA WMT13 results. Training set sizes are given in millions (M) of words on the target side. Average difference is 3.7 BLEU points.

BLEUc	$S \to en$		$en \to T$	
	cs-en	fr-en	en-cs	en-fr
ParFDA5	0.256	0.319	0.172	0.325
ParFDA5 15%	0.248	0.321	0.178	0.333
diff	-0.008	0.002	0.006	0.008

Table 6: ParFDA5 results, ParFDA5 results using 15% of the training set, and their difference.

3.6 Using 15% of the Available Training Set

In the FDA5 results (Biçici and Yuret, 2014), we found that selecting 15% of the best training set size maximizes the performance for the English-German out-of-domain translation task and achieves 0.41 BLEU points improvement over a baseline system using all of the available training data. We run additional experiments selecting 15% of the training data for fr-en and cs-en language pairs to see the effect of increased training sets selected with ParFDA5. The results are given in Table 6 where most of the results improve. The slight performance decrease for cs-en may be due to using a true-caser trained on only the selected training data. We observe larger gains in the $en \to T$ translations.

3.7 ParFDA5 versus Parallel FDA

We compare this year's results with the results we obtained last year (Biçici, 2013) in Table 7. The task setting is different in WMT14 since the test set contains 10,000 sentences but only 3000 of these are used as the actual test set, which can make the transductive learning application of ParFDA5 harder. We select the same number of instances for the training sets but 5 million more instances for the LM corpus this year. The average difference to the top constrained submission in WMT13 was 2.88 BLEU points (Biçici, 2013) and this has increased to 3.49 BLEU points in WMT14. On average, the performance improved 3.7 BLEU points when compared with ParFDA results last year. For the fr-en, en-fr, and en-ru translation directions, we observe increases in the performance. This may be due to better modeling of the target domain by better parameterization and optimization that FDA5 is providing. We observe some decrease in the performance in en-de and de-en results. Since the training material remained the same for WMT13 and WMT14 and the modeling power of FDA5 increased, building a domain specific rather than a task specific ParFDA5 model may be the reason for the decrease.

4 Conclusion

We use parallel FDA5 for solving computational scalability problems caused by the abundance of training data for SMT models and LMs and still achieve SMT performance that is on par with the top performing SMT systems. Parallel FDA5 raises the bar of expectations from SMT with highly accurate translations and lower the bar to entry for SMT into new domains and tasks by allowing fast deployment of SMT systems in about half a day. Parallel FDA5 enables a shift from general purpose SMT systems towards task adaptive SMT solutions.

Acknowledgments

This work is supported in part by SFI (07/CE/I1142) as part of the CNGL Centre for Global Intelligent Content (www.cngl.org) at Dublin City University and in part by the European Commission through the QTLaunchPad FP7 project (No: 296347). We also thank the SFI/HEA Irish Centre for High-End Computing (ICHEC) for the provision of computational facilities and support.

References

Ergun Biçici and Deniz Yuret. 2011. Instance selection for machine translation using feature decay algorithms. In *Proceedings of the Sixth Workshop on Statistical Machine Translation*, pages 272–283, Edinburgh, Scotland, July. Association for Computational Linguistics.

Ergun Biçici and Deniz Yuret. 2014. Optimizing instance selection for statistical machine translation with feature decay algorithms. *IEEE/ACM Transactions On Audio, Speech, and Language Processing (TASLP)*.

Ergun Biçici. 2011. *The Regression Model of Machine Translation*. Ph.D. thesis, Koç University. Supervisor: Deniz Yuret.

Ergun Biçici. 2013. Feature decay algorithms for fast deployment of accurate statistical machine translation systems. In *Proceedings of the Eighth Workshop on Statistical Machine Translation*, Sofia, Bulgaria, August. Association for Computational Linguistics.

Ondřej Bojar, Christian Buck, Christian Federmann, Barry Haddow, Philipp Koehn, Matouš Macháček, Christof Monz, Pavel Pecina, Matt Post, Herve Saint-Amand, Radu Soricut, and Lucia Specia. 2014. Findings of the 2014 workshop on statistical machine translation. In *Proc. of the Ninth Workshop on Statistical Machine Translation*, Balrimore, USA, June. Association for Computational Linguistics.

Iacer Calixto, Ali Hosseinzadeh Vahid, Xiaojun Zhang, Jian Zhang, Xiaofeng Wu, Andy Way, and Qun Liu. 2014. Experiments in medical translation shared task at wmt 2014. In *Proceedings of the Ninth Workshop on Statistical Machine Translation*, Baltimore, USA, June. Association for Computational Linguistics.

Thomas H. Cormen, Charles E. Leiserson, Ronald L. Rivest, and Clifford Stein. 2009. *Introduction to Algorithms (3. ed.)*. MIT Press.

David Graff, Ângelo Mendonça, and Denise DiPersio. 2011. French Gigaword third edition, Linguistic Data Consortium.

Philipp Koehn, Hieu Hoang, Alexandra Birch, Chris Callison-Burch, Marcello Federico, Nicola Bertoldi, Brooke Cowan, Wade Shen, Christine Moran, Richard Zens, Chris Dyer, Ondrej Bojar, Alexandra Constantin, and Evan Herbst. 2007. Moses: Open source toolkit for statistical machine translation. In *ACL*, pages 177–180, Prague, Czech Republic, June.

William Lewis, Robert Munro, and Stephan Vogel. 2011. Crisis mt: Developing a cookbook for mt in crisis situations. In *Proceedings of the Sixth Workshop on Statistical Machine Translation*, pages 501–511, Edinburgh, Scotland, July. Association for Computational Linguistics.

Liangyou Li, Xiaofeng Wu, Santiago Cortes Vaillo, Jun Xie, Jia Xu, Andy Way, and Qun Liu. 2014. The dcu-ictcas-tsinghua mt system at wmt 2014 on german-english translation task. In *Proceedings of the Ninth Workshop on Statistical Machine Translation*, Baltimore, USA, June. Association for Computational Linguistics.

Franz Josef Och and Hermann Ney. 2003. A systematic comparison of various statistical alignment models. *Computational Linguistics*, 29(1):19–51.

Robert Parker, David Graff, Junbo Kong, Ke Chen, and Kazuaki Maeda. 2011. English Gigaword fifth edition, Linguistic Data Consortium.

Andreas Stolcke. 2002. Srilm - an extensible language modeling toolkit. In *Proc. Intl. Conf. on Spoken Language Processing*, pages 901–904.

Yandex School of Data Analysis Russian-English Machine Translation System for WMT14

Alexey Borisov and Irina Galinskaya
Yandex School of Data Analysis
16, Leo Tolstoy street, Moscow, Russia
{alborisov, galinskaya}@yandex-team.ru

Abstract

This paper describes the Yandex School of Data Analysis Russian-English system submitted to the ACL 2014 Ninth Workshop on Statistical Machine Translation shared translation task. We start with the system that we developed last year and investigate a few methods that were successful at the previous translation task including unpruned language model, operation sequence model and the new reparameterization of IBM Model 2. Next we propose a {simple yet practical} algorithm to transform Russian sentence into a more easily translatable form before decoding. The algorithm is based on the linguistic intuition of native Russian speakers, also fluent in English.

1 Introduction

The annual shared translation task organized within the ACL Workshop on Statistical Machine Translation (WMT) aims to evaluate the state of the art in machine translation for a variety of languages. We participate in the Russian to English translation direction.

The rest of the paper is organized as follows. Our baseline system as well as the experiments concerning the methods already discussed in literature are described in Section 2. In Section 3 we present an algorithm we use to transform the Russian sentence before translation. In Section 4 we discuss the results and conclude.

2 Initial System Development

We use all the Russian-English parallel data available in the constraint track and the Common Crawl English monolingual corpus.

2.1 Baseline

We use the phrase-based Moses statistical machine translation system (Koehn et al., 2007) with mostly default settings and a few changes (Borisov et al., 2013) made in the following steps.

Data Preprocessing includes filtering out non Russian-English sentence pairs and correction of spelling errors.

Phrase Table Smoothing uses Good-Turing scheme (Foster et al., 2006).

Consensus Decoding selects the translation with minimum Bayes risk (Kumar and Byrne, 2004).

Handling of Unknown Words comprises incorporation of proper names from Wiki Headlines parallel data provided by CMU[1] and transliteration. We improve the transliteration algorithm in Section 2.4.

Note that unlike last year we do not use word alignments computed for the lemmatized word forms.

2.2 Language Model

We use 5-gram unpruned language model with modified Kneser-Ney discount estimated with KenLM toolkit (Heafield et al., 2013).

2.3 Word alignment

Word alignments are generated using the fast_align tool (Dyer et al., 2013), which is much faster than IBM Model 4 from MGIZA++ (Gao and Vogel, 2008) and outperforms the latter in terms of BLEU. Results are given in Table 1.

2.4 Transliteration

We employ machine transliteration to generate additional translation options for out-of-vocabulary

[1] http://www.statmt.org/wmt14/wiki-titles.tgz

Proceedings of the Ninth Workshop on Statistical Machine Translation, pages 66–70,
Baltimore, Maryland USA, June 26–27, 2014.

	MGIZA++	fast_align
Run Time	22 h 14 m	2h 49 m
Perplexity		
– **ru→en**	97.00	90.37
– **en→ru**	209.36	216.71
BLEU		
– **WMT13**	25.27	25.49
– **WMT14**	31.76	31.92

Table 1: Comparison of word alignment tools: MGIZA++ vs. fast_align. fast_align runs ten times as fast and outperforms the IBM Model 4 from MGIZA++ in terms of BLEU scores.

words. The transformation model we use is a transfeme based model (Duan and Hsu, 2011), which is analogous to translation model in phrase-based machine translation. Transformation units, or transfemes, are trained with Moses using the default settings. Decoding is very similar to beam search. We build a trie from the words in English monolingual corpus, and search in it, based on the transformation model.

2.5 Operation Sequence Model

The Operation Sequence N-gram Model (OSM) (Durrani et al., 2011) integrates reordering operations and lexical translations into a heterogeneous sequence of minimal translation units (MTUs) and learns a Markov model over it. Reordering decisions influence lexical selections and vice versa thus improving the translation model. We use OSM as a feature function in phrase-based SMT. Please, refer to (Durrani et al., 2013) for implementation details.

3 Morphological Transformations

Russian is a fusional synthetic language, meaning that the relations between words are redundant and encoded inside the words. Adjectives alter their form to reflect the gender, case, number and in some cases, animacy of the nouns, resulting in dozens of different word forms matching a single English word. An example is given in Table 2. Verbs in Russian are typically constructed from the morphemes corresponding to functional words in English (to, shall, will, was, were, has, have, had, been, etc.). This Russian phenomenon leads to two problems: data sparsity and high number of one-to-many alignments, which both may result in translation quality degradation.

		Number	
		SG	PL
Case	**Gender**		
NOM	MASC	летний	летние
NOM	FEM	летняя	
NOM	NEUT	летнее	
GEN	MASC	летнего	летних
GEN	FEM	летней	
GEN	NEUT	летнего	
DAT	MASC	летнему	летним
DAT	FEM	летней	
DAT	NEUT	летнему	
ACC	MASC, AN	летнего	летним
ACC	MASC, INAN	летний	
ACC	FEM	летнюю	
ACC	NEUT	летнее	
INS	MASC	летним	летним
INS	FEM	летней	
INS	FEM	летнею	
INS	NEUT	летним	
ABL	MASC	летнем	летних
ABL	FEM	летней	
ABL	NEUT	летнем	

Table 2: Russian word forms corresponding to the English word "summer" (adj.).

Hereafter, we propose an algorithm to transform the original Russian sentence into a more easily translatable form. The algorithm is based on the linguistic intuition of native Russian speakers, also fluent in English.

3.1 Approach

Based on the output from Russian morphological analyzer we rewrite the input sentence based on the following principles:

1. the original sentence is restorable (by a Russian native speaker)
2. redundant information is omitted
3. word alignment is less ambiguous

3.2 Algorithm

The algorithm consists of two steps.

On the first step we employ in-house Russian morphological analyzer similar to Mystem (Segalovich, 2003) to convert each word (WORD) into a tuple containing its canonical form (LEMMA), part of speech tag (POS) and a set

Category	Abbr.	Values
Animacy	ANIM	AN, INAN
Aspect	ASP	IMPERF, PERF
Case	CASE	NOM, GEN, DAT, ACC, INS, ABL
Comparison Type	COMP	COMP, SURP
Gender	GEND	MASC, FEM, NEUT
Mood	MOOD	IND, IMP, COND, SBJV
Number	NUM	SG, PL
Participle Type	PART	ACT, PASS
Person	PERS	PERS1, PERS2, PERS3
Tense	TNS	PRES, NPST, PST

Table 3: Morphological Categories

of other grammemes associated with the word (GRAMMEMES). The tuple is later referred to as LPG. If the canonical form or part of speech are ambiguous, we set LEMMA to WORD; POS to "undefined"; and GRAMMEMES to ∅. Grammemes are grouped into grammatical categories listed in Table 3.

WORD ⟶ LEMMA + POS + GRAMMEMES

On the second step, the LPGs are converted into tokens that, we hope, will better match English structure. Some grammemes result in separate tokens, others stay with the lemma, and the rest get dropped. The full set of morphological transformations we use is given in Table 4.

An example of applying the algorithm to a Russian sentence is given in Figure 1.

3.3 Results

The translation has been improved in several ways:

Incorrect Use of Tenses happens quite often in statistical machine translation, which is especially vexing in simple cases such as *asks* instead of *asked*, *explains* instead of *explain* along with more difficult ones e.g. *has increased* instead of *would increase*. The proposed algorithm achieves considerable improvement, since it explicitly models tenses and all its relevant properties.

Missing Articles is a common problem of most Russian-English translation systems, because there are no articles in Russian. Our model creates an auxiliary token for each noun, which reflects its case and motivates an article.

Use of Simple Vocabulary is not desirable when the source text is a vocabulary-flourished one. News are full of academic, bookish, inkhorn, and other rare words. Phrase Table smoothing methods discount the translation probabilities for rare phrase pairs, preventing them from appearing in English translation, while many of these rare phrase pairs are correct. The good thing is that the phrase pairs containing the transformed Russian words may not be rare themselves, and thereby are not discounted so heavily. A more effective use of English vocabulary has been observed on WMT13 test dataset (see Table 5).

We have demonstrated the improvements on a qualitative level. The quantitative results are summarized in Table 6 (baseline – without morphological transformations; proposed – with morphological transformations).

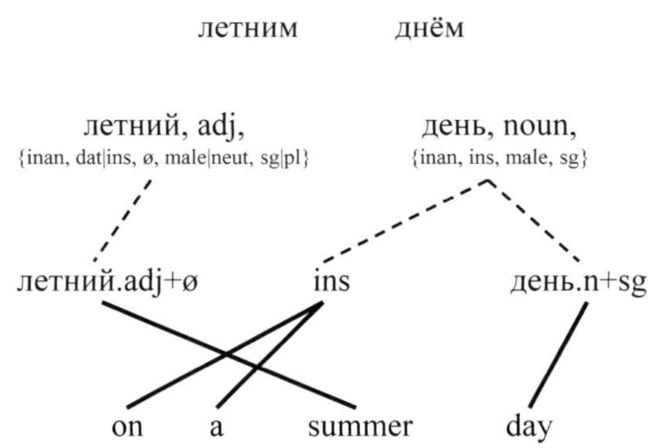

Figure 1: An illustration of the proposed algorithm to transform Russian sentence летним днём *(letnim dnem)*, meaning *on a summer day*, into a more easily translatable form. First, for each word we extract its canonical form, part of speech tag and a set of associated morphological properties (grammemes). Then we apply hand-crafted rules (Table 4) to transform them into separate tokens.

LPG ⇒ tokens
LEMMA, adj, {ANIM, CASE, COMP, GEND, NUM} ⇓ LEMMA.adj+COMP
LEMMA, noun, {ANIM, CASE, GEND, NUM} ⇓ CASE LEMMA.n+NUM
LEMMA, verb (ger), {ASP, TNS} ⇓ LEMMA.vg+ASP+TNS
LEMMA, verb (inf), {ASP} ⇓ LEMMA.vi+ASP
LEMMA, verb (part), {PART, ASP, TNS} ⇓ LEMMA.vp+PART+ASP+TNS
LEMMA, verb (–), {PART, ASP, MOOD, TENSE, NUM, PERS} ⇓ 1. TNS={PRES} | TNS={NPST} & ASP={IMPERF} a. PERS3 ∈ PERS & SG ∈ NUM LEMMA.v+pres+MOOD+PERS+NUM b. otherwise LEMMA.v+pres+MOOD 2. TNS={PST} ASP LEMMA.v+pst+MOOD 3. TNS={NPST} & ASP={IMPERF} fut LEMMA.v+MOOD 4. if ambiguous LEMMA.v+PART+ASP+MOOD +TNS+NUM+PERS
LEMMA, OTHER, GRAMMEMES ⇓ LEMMA.POS+GRAMMEMES

Table 4: A set of rules we use to transform the LPGs (LEMMA, POS, GRAMMEMES), extracted on the first step, into individual tokens.

4 Discussion and Conclusion

We described the Yandex School of Data Analysis Russian-English system submitted to the ACL 2014 Ninth Workshop on Statistical Machine Translation shared translation task. The main contribution of this work is an algorithm to transform the Russian sentence into a more easily translatable form before decoding. Significant improvements in human satisfaction and BLEU scores have been demonstrated from applying this algorithm.

Input	Translation
разногласия (raznoglasiya)	(a) differences (b) disputes
пропагандистом (propagandistom)	(a) promoter (b) propagandist
преимущественно (preimuschestvenno)	(a) mainly (b) predominantly

Table 5: Morphological Transformations lead to more effective use of English vocabulary. Translations marked with *"a"* were produced using the baseline system; with *"b"* also use Morphological Transformations.

	Baseline	Proposed
Distinct Words	899,992	564,354
OOV Words		
– **WMT13**	829	590
– **WMT14**	884	660
Perplexity		
– **ru→en**	90.37	99.81
– **en→ru**	216.71	128.15
BLEU		
– **WMT13**	25.49	25.63
– **WMT14**	31.92	32.56

Table 6: Results of Morphological Transformations. We improved the statistical characteristics of our models by reducing the number of distinct words by 37% and managed to translate 25% of previously untranslated words. BLEU scores were improved by 0.14 and 0.64 points for WMT13 and WMT14 test sets respectively.

One limitation of the proposed algorithm is that it does not take into account the relations between words sharing the same root. E.g. the word аистиных *(aistinyh)* meaning stork (adj.) is handled independently from the word аист *(aist)* meaning stork (n.). Our system as well as the major online services (Bing, Google, Yandex) transliterated this word, but the word *aistinyh* does not make much sense to a non-Russian reader. It might be worthwhile to study this problem in more detail.

Another direction for future work is to apply the proposed algorithm in reverse direction. We suggest the following two-step procedure. English sentence is first translated into Russian* (Russian after applying the morphological transformations), and at the next step it is translated again with an auxiliary SMT system trained on the (Russian*, Russian) parallel corpus created from the Russian monolingual corpus.

References

Alexey Borisov, Jacob Dlougach, and Irina Galinskaya. 2013. Yandex school of data analysis machine translation systems for wmt13. In *Proceedings of the Eighth Workshop on Statistical Machine Translation (WMT)*, pages 97–101. Association for Computational Linguistics.

Huizhong Duan and Bo-June Paul Hsu. 2011. Online spelling correction for query completion. In *Proceedings of the 20th international conference on World Wide Web (WWW)*, pages 117–126. ACM.

Nadir Durrani, Helmut Schmid, and Alexander Fraser. 2011. A joint sequence translation model with integrated reordering. In *Proceedings of the 49th Annual Meeting of the Association for Computational Linguistics (ACL)*, pages 1045–1054. Association for Computational Linguistics.

Nadir Durrani, Barry Haddow, Kenneth Heafield, and Philipp Koehn. 2013. Edinburgh's machine translation systems for european language pairs. In *Proceedings of the Eighth Workshop on Statistical Machine Translation (WMT)*, pages 112–119. Association for Computational Linguistics.

Chris Dyer, Victor Chahuneau, and Noah A Smith. 2013. A simple, fast, and effective reparameterization of IBM model 2. In *Proceedings of the Human Language Technology Conference of the North American Chapter of the Association for Computational Linguistics (HLT-NAACL)*, pages 644–648. Association for Computational Linguistics.

George Foster, Roland Kuhn, and John Howard Johnson. 2006. Phrasetable smoothing for statistical machine translation. In *Proceedings of the 44th Annual Meeting of the Association for Computational Linguistics (ACL)*, pages 53–61. Association for Computational Linguistics.

Qin Gao and Stephan Vogel. 2008. Parallel implementations of word alignment tool. In *Proceedings of the 46th Annual Meeting of the Association for Computational Linguistics (ACL)*, pages 49–57. Association for Computational Linguistics.

Kenneth Heafield, Ivan Pouzyrevsky, Jonathan H. Clark, and Philipp Koehn. 2013. Scalable modified Kneser-Ney language model estimation. In *Proceedings of the 51st Annual Meeting of the Association for Computational Linguistics (ACL)*, pages 690–696, Sofia, Bulgaria, August. Association for Computational Linguistics.

Philipp Koehn, Hieu Hoang, Alexandra Birch, Chris Callison-burch, Richard Zens, Rwth Aachen, Alexandra Constantin, Marcello Federico, Nicola Bertoldi, Chris Dyer, Brooke Cowan, Wade Shen, Christine Moran, and Ondřej Bojar. 2007. Moses: Open source toolkit for statistical machine translation. In *Proceedings of the 45th Annual Meeting of the Association for Computational Linguistics (ACL)*, pages 177–180. Association for Computational Linguistics.

Shankar Kumar and William Byrne. 2004. Minimum bayes-risk decoding for statistical machine translation. In *Proceedings of the Human Language Technology Conference of the North American Chapter of the Association for Computational Linguistics (HLT-NAACL)*, pages 163–171. Association for Computational Linguistics.

Ilya Segalovich. 2003. A fast morphological algorithm with unknown word guessing induced by a dictionary for a web search engine. In Hamid R. Arabnia and Elena B. Kozerenko, editors, *Proceedings of the International Conference on Machine Learning; Models, Technologies and Applications (MLMTA)*, pages 273–280, Las Vegas, NV, USA, June. CSREA Press.

CimS – The CIS and IMS joint submission to WMT 2014 translating from English into German

Fabienne Cap[✿], Marion Weller[✿✐], Anita Ramm[✐], Alexander Fraser[✿]

[✿] CIS, Ludwig-Maximilian University of Munich – (cap|fraser)@cis.uni-muenchen.de

[✐] IMS, University of Stuttgart – (wellermn|ramm)@ims.uni-stuttgart.de

Abstract

We present the CimS submissions to the 2014 Shared Task for the language pair EN→DE. We address the major problems that arise when translating into German: complex nominal and verbal morphology, productive compounding and flexible word ordering. Our morphology-aware translation systems handle word formation issues on different levels of morpho-syntactic modeling.

1 Introduction

In our shared task submissions, we focus on the English to German translation direction: we address different levels of productivity of the German language, i.e., nominal and verbal inflection and productive word formation, which lead to data sparsity and thus confuse classical SMT systems.

Our basic goal is to make the two languages as morphosyntactically similar as possible. We use a parser and a morphological analyser to remove linguistic features from German that are not present in English and reorder the English input to make it more similar to the German sentence structure. Prior to training, all words are lemmatised and compounds are split into single words. This is not only beneficial for word alignment, but it also allows us to generalise over inflectional variants of the same lexemes and over single words which could occur in one place as a standalone word and in another place as part of a compound. Translation happens in two steps: first, we translate from English into split, lemmatised German and then, we perform compound merging and generation of inflection as a post-processing step. This way, we are able to create German compounds and inflectional variants that have not been seen in the parallel training data.

In this paper, we investigate the performance of well-established source-side reordering, nominal re-inflection and compound processing systems on an up-to-date shared task. In addition, we present experimental results on a verbal inflection component and a syntax-based variant including source-side reordering.

2 Related Work

Re-Inflection The two-step translation approach we use was described by e.g. Toutanova et al. (2008) and Jeong et al. (2010), who use a number of morphological and syntactic features derived from both source and target language. More recently, Fraser et al. (2012) describe a similar approach for German using different CRF-based feature prediction models, one for each of the four grammatical features to be predicted for German words in noun phrases, namely *number*, *gender*, *case* and *definiteness*. This approach also handles word-formation issues such as portmanteau splitting and compounding. Weller et al. (2013) added subcategorization information in combination with source-side syntactic features in order to improve the prediction of *case*.

De Gispert and Mariño (2008) generate verbal inflection for translation from English into Spanish. They use classifiers trained not only on target language but also on source language features, which is even more crucial for the prediction of verbs than it is for nominal inflection.

More recently, Williams and Koehn (2011) translate directly into target language surface forms. Agreement within NPs and PPs, and also between subject and verb is considered during the decoding process: they use string-to-tree translation, where the target language (German) morphology is expressed as a set of unification constraints automatically learned from a morphologically annotated German corpus.

Proceedings of the Ninth Workshop on Statistical Machine Translation, pages 71–78,
Baltimore, Maryland USA, June 26–27, 2014. ©2014 Association for Computational Linguistics

Compound Processing Compound splitting for SMT has been addressed by numerous different groups, for translation from German to English, e.g. using corpus-based frequencies (Koehn and Knight, 2003), using POS-constraints (Stymne et al., 2008), a lattice-based approach propagating the splitting decision to the decoder (Dyer, 2009), a rule-based morphological analyser (Fritzinger and Fraser, 2010) or unsupervised, language-independent segmentation (Macherey et al., 2011).

Compound processing in the other translation direction, however, has been much less investigated. Popović et al. (2006) describe a list-based approach, in which words are only re-combined if they have been seen as compounds in a huge corpus. However this approach is limited to the list's coverage. The approach of Stymne (2009) overcomes this coverage issue by making use of a POS-markup which distinguishes former compound modifiers from former heads and thus allows for their adequate recombination after translation. An extension of this approach is reported in Stymne and Cancedda (2011) where a CRF-model is used for compound prediction. In Cap et al. (2014) their approach is extended through using source-language features and lemmatisation, allowing for maximal generalisation over compound parts.

Source-side Reordering One major problem in English to German translation is the divergent clausal ordering: in particular, German verbs tend to occur at the very end of clauses, whereas English sticks to a rigid SVO order in most cases. Collins et al. (2005), Fraser (2009) and Gojun and Fraser (2012) showed that restructuring the source language so that it corresponds to the expected structure of the target language is helpful for SMT.

3 Inflection Prediction

German has a rich morphology, both for nominal and verbal inflection. It requires different forms of agreement, e.g., for adjectives and nouns or verbs and their subjects. Traditional phrase-based SMT systems often get such agreements wrong. In our systems, we explicitly model agreement using a two-step approach: first we translate from English into lemmatised German and then generate fully inflected forms in a second step. In this section, we describe our nominal inflection component and first experimental steps towards verbal re-inflection.

3.1 Noun Phrase Inflection

Prior to training, the German data is reduced to a lemmatised representation containing translation-relevant morphological features. For nominal inflection, the lemmas are marked with *number* and *gender*: *gender* is considered as part of the lemma, whereas *number* is indirectly determined by the source-side, as we expect nouns to be translated with their appropriate *number* value. We use a linear chain CRF (Lafferty et al., 2001) to predict the morphological features (*number*, *gender*, *case* and *strong/weak*). The features that are part of the lemma of nouns (*number*, *gender*) are propagated over the rest of the linguistic phrase. In contrast, *case* depends on the role of the NP in the sentence (e.g. subject or direct/indirect object) and is thus to be determined entirely from the respective context in the sentence. The value for *strong/weak* depends on the combination of the other features. Based on the lemma and the predicted features, inflected forms are then generated using the rule-based morphological analyser SMOR (Schmid et al., 2004). This system is described in more detail in Fraser et al. (2012).

3.2 Verbal Inflection

German verbs agree in number and person with their subjects. We thus have to derive this information from a noun phrase in nominative case (= the subject) near the verb. This information comes from the nominal inflection prediction described in section 3.1. We predict tense and mode of the verb using a maximum-entropy classifier which is trained on English and German contextual information. After deriving all information needed for the generation of the verbs, the inflected forms are generated with SMOR.

4 Compound Processing

In English to German translation, compound processing is more difficult than in the opposite direction. Not only do compounds have to be split accurately, but they also have to be put together correctly after decoding. The disfluency of MT output and the difficulty of deciding which single words should be merged into compounds make this task even more challenging.

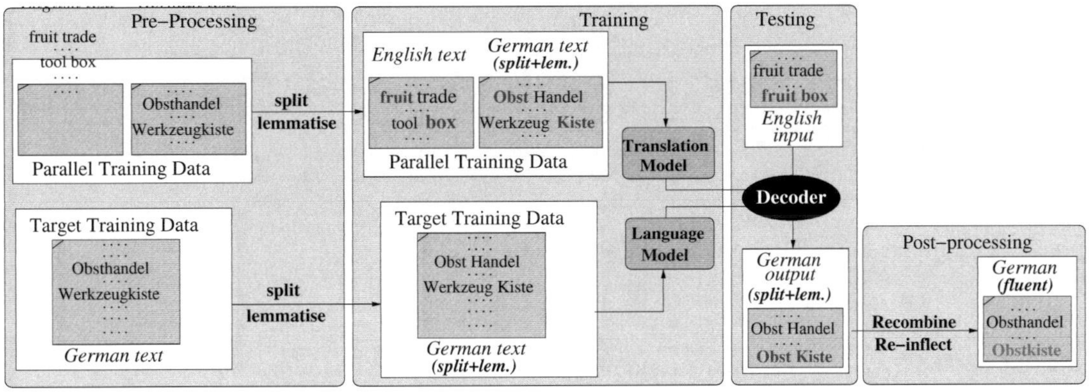

Figure 1: Pipeline overview of our primary CimS-CoRI system.

We combine compound processing with inflection prediction (see Section 3) and thus extend the two-step approach respectively: compounds are split and lemmatised simultaneously, again using SMOR. This allows for maximal generalisation over former compound parts and independently occurring simple words. We use this split representation for training. After decoding, we re-combine words into compounds again, using our extended CRF-based approach, which is based on Stymne and Cancedda (2011), but includes source-language features and allows for maximal generalisation through lemmatisation. More details can be found in Cap et al. (2014). We then use SMOR to generate sound German compounds (including morphological transformations such as introduction or deletion of filler letters). Finally, the whole text including the newly-created compounds, is re-inflected using the nominal inflection prediction models as described in Section 3.1 above. This procedure allows us to create compounds that have not been seen in the parallel training data, and also inflectional variants of seen compounds. See Figure 1 for an overview of our compound processing pipeline.

4.1 Portmanteaus

Portmanteaus are a special kind of compound. They are a fusion of a preposition and a definite article (thus not productive) and their *case* must agree with the *case* of the noun. For example, *"zum"* can be split into *"zu"* + *"dem"* = to+the_{Dative}. They introduce additional sparsity to the training data: imagine a noun occurred with its definite article in the training data, but not with the portemanteau required at testing time. Splitting portemanteaus allows a phrase-based SMT system to access phrases covering nouns and their corresponding definite articles. In a post-processing step, definite articles are then re-merged with their preceding prepositions to restore the original portmanteau, see (Fraser et al., 2012) for details. This generalisation effect is even larger as we not only split portmanteaus, but also lemmatise the articles.

5 System descriptions

Our shared task submissions include different combinations of the inflection and compound processing procedures as described in the previous two sections. We give an overview of all our systems in Table 1. Note that we did not re-train the compound processing CRFs on the new dataset, but used our models trained on the 2009 training data instead. However, this does not hurt performance, as the CRF we use is not trained on surface forms, but only frequencies and source-side features instead. See (Fraser et al., 2012) and (Cap et al., 2014) for more details on how we trained the respective CRFs. In contrast, the verbal classifier has been trained on WMT 2014 data.

6 Experimental Settings

In all our systems, we only used data distributed for the shared task. All available German data was morphologically analysed with SMOR. For lemmatisation of the German training data, we disambiguated SMOR using POS tags we obtained through parsing the German section of the parallel training data with BitPar (Schmid,

No.	apprart splitting	nominal inflection	compound processing	verbal inflection	source-side reordering
CimS-RI	X	X			
CimS-CoRI^P	X	X	X		
CimS-RIVe	X	X		X	
CimS-CoRIVe	X	X	X	X	
CimS-Syntax-RORI	X	X			X

Table 1: Overview of our submission systems.RI = nominal **Re-In**flection, Co = **Co**mpound processing, Ve = **Ve**rbal inflection, RO = source-side **Re-O**rdering. Syntax = syntax-based SMT ^{P} = primary submission.

2004) and tagging the big monolingual training data using RFTagger (Schmid and Laws, 2008)[1]. Note that we did not normalise German language e.g. with respect to old vs. new writing convention etc. as we did in previous submissions (e.g. (Fraser, 2009)).

For the compound prediction CRFs using syntactic features derived from the source language, we parsed the English section of the parallel data using EGRET, a re-implementation of the Berkeley-Parser by Hui Zhang[2]. Before training our models on the English data, we normalised all occurrences of British vs. American English variants to British English. We did so for training, tuning and testing input.

Language Model We trained 5-gram language models based on all available German monolingual training data from the shared task (roughly 1.5 billion words) using the SRILM toolkit (Stolcke, 2002) with Kneser-Ney smoothing. We then used KenLM (Heafield, 2011) for faster processing. For each of our experiments, we trained a separate language model on the whole data set, corresponding to the different underspecified representations of German used in our experiments, e.g. lemmatised for *CimS-RI*, lemmatised with split compounds for *CimS-CoRI*, etc.

Phrase-based Translation model We performed word alignment using the multithreaded GIZA++ toolkit (Och and Ney, 2003; Gao and Vogel, 2008). For translation model training and decoding, we used the Moses toolkit (Koehn et al., 2007) to build phrase-based statistical machine translation systems, following the instructions for the baseline system for the shared task, using only default settings.

[1]We could not parse the whole monolingual dataset due to time-constraints and thus used RFTagger as a substitute.

[2]available from https://sites.google.com/site/zhangh1982/egret.

Syntax-based Translation model As a variant to the phrase-based systems, we applied the inflection prediction system to a string-to-tree system with GHKM extraction (Galley et al. (2004), Williams and Koehn (2012)). We used the same data-sets as for the phrase-based systems, and applied BitPar (Schmid, 2004) to obtain target-side trees. For this system, we used source-side reordering according to Gojun and Fraser (2012) relying on parses obtained with EGRET[3].

Tuning For tuning of feature weights, we used *batch-mira* with *'–safe-hope'* (Cherry and Foster, 2012) until convergence (or maximal 25 runs). We used the 3,000 sentences of *newstest2012* for tuning. Each experiment was tuned separately, optimising Bleu scores (Papineni et al., 2002) against a lemmatised version of the tuning reference. In the compound processing systems we integrated the CRF-based prediction and merging procedure into each tuning iteration and scored each output against the same unsplit and lemmatised reference as the other systems.

Testing After decoding, the underspecified representation has to be retransformed into fluent German text, i.e., compounds need to be re-combined and all words have to be re-inflected. The whole procedure can be divided into the following steps:

1a) translation into lemmatised German representation (RI, RIVe)
1b) translation into split and lemmatised German (CoRi, CoRIVe)
2) compound merging (CoRI, CoRIVe):
3) nominal inflection prediction and generation of full forms using SMOR (all)
4) verbal re-inflection (RIVe, CoRIVe)
5) merging of portmanteaus (all)

[3]Note that we observed some data-related issues on the Syntax-RORI experiments that we hope to resolve in the near future.

Experiment	mert.log news2012	Bleu ci news2013	Bleu cs news2013	Bleu ci news2014	Bleu cs news2014
raw	16.52	18.62	17.61	17.80	17.25
CimS-RI	18.51	19.23	18.38	18.33	17.75
CimS-CoRI^P	18.36	19.13	18.25	18.51	17.87
CimS-RIVe	19.08	18.89	18.06	17.86	17.31
CimS-CoRIVe	18.69	18.60	17.77	17.38	16.78
CimS-Syntax-RORI	18.26	19.04	18.17	18.15	17.59

Table 2: Bleu scores for all CimS-submissions of the 2014 shared task. ci = case-insensitive, cs = case-sensitive; ^{P} = primary submission.

After these post-processing steps, the text was automatically recapitalised and detokenised, using the tools provided by the shared task, which we trained on the whole German dataset. We calculated Bleu (Papineni et al., 2002) scores using the NIST script version 13a.

7 Results

We evaluated our systems with the 3,000 sentences of last year's *newstest2013* and also the 2,737 sentences of the 2014 blind test set for the German-English language pair. The Bleu scores of our systems are given in Table 2, where *raw* denotes our baseline system which we ran without any pre- or postprocessing whatsoever. Note that the big gap in mert.log scores between *raw* and the CimS-systems comes from the fact that *raw* is scored against the original (i.e. fully inflected) version of the tuning reference, while the CimS-systems are scored against the stemmed tuning reference.

As for the Bleu scores of the test sets, we observe similar improvements for the CimS-RI and CimS-CoRI systems of +0.5/0.6 with respect to the *raw* baseline as we did in previous experiments (Cap et al., 2014)[4]. In contrast, our systems incorporating verbal prediction inflection (CimS-RIVe/CoRIVe) cannot yet catch up with the performance of the well-investigated nominal inflection and compound processing systems (CimS-RI/CoRI). We attribute this partly to the positive influence we assume fully inflected verbs to have in nominal inflection prediction models, but as the verb processing systems are still under development, there might be other issues we have not discovered yet. We plan to revisit these systems and improve them.

Finally, the syntax-based reordering system yields scores that are competitive to those of CimS-RI/CoRI. While Syntax-RORI so far only incorporates source-side reordering and nominal re-inflection, we plan to investigate further extensions of this approach in the future.

7.1 Additional Evaluation

We manually screened the filtered 2014 test set and identified 3,456 German compound tokens, whereof 862 did not occur in the parallel training data and thereof, 244 did not even occur in the monolingual training data. For each of our systems, we calculated the number of compound reference matches they produced. The results are given in Table 3.

system	ref	new
raw	827	0
CimS-RI .	864	5
CimS-CoRI^P	1,064	109
CimS-RIVe	853	5
CimS-CoRIVe	1,070	122
CimS-Syntax-RORI	900	20

Table 3: Numbers of compounds produced by the systems that matched the reference (*ref*) and did not occur in the parallel training data (*new*).

The compound processing systems (with Co in the name) generate many more correct compounds than comparable systems without compound handling. Compared to the raw baseline, CoRI/CoRIVe did not only produce 237/243 more reference matches, but also 109/122 compounds that matched the reference but did not occur in the parallel training data. A lookup of those 109/122 compounds in the monolingual training data (consisting of roughly 1.5 billion words) revealed, that 8/6 of them did not oc-

[4]We will have a closer look at the data from a compound processing view in Section 7.1 below.

cur there either[5]. These were thus not accessible to a list-based compound merging approach either. This result also shows that despite the fact that CoRIVe does not yield a competitive translation quality performance yet, the compound processing component seems to benefit from the verbal inflection and it is definitely worth more investigation in the future.

Moreover, it can be seen from Table 3 that the re-inflection systems (*RI*) produce more reference matches than the raw baseline. Interestingly, they even produce some reference matches that have not been seen in the parallel training data due to inflectional variation, and in the case of the syntax-based system due to a naive list-based compound merging: even though it has not been trained on a split representation of German text, it might occasionally occur that two German nouns occur next to each other in the MT output. If so, these two words are merged into a compound, using a list-based approach, similar to Popović et al. (2006).

8 Reordering

For the system CimS-Syntax-RORI, English data parsed with EGRET was reordered using scripts written for parse trees produced by the constituent parser (Charniak and Johnson, 2005), using a model we trained on the standard Penn Treebank sections. Unfortunately, the reordering scripts could not be straightforwardly applied to EGRET parses and require more significant modifications than we first expected.

We thus decided to parse the Europarl data (v7) with (Charniak and Johnson, 2005) instead and run our reordering scripts on it (CimS-RO). For evaluation purposes, we build a baseline system *raw'* which has been trained only on Europarl. Tuning and testing setup is the same as for the systems described in Section 6 with the difference that the weights have been tuned on newstest2013. The evaluation results are shown in Table 4. Similarly to previous results reported in (Gojun and Fraser, 2012), the CimS-RO system shows an improvement of 0.5 Bleu points when compared to the *raw'* baseline .

[5]Namely: *Testflugzeugen (test airplanes), Medientribunal (media tribunal), RBS-Mitarbeiter (RBS worker), Schulmauersanierung (school wall renovation), Anti-Terror-Organisationen (anti-terror organisations), and Tabakimpfstoffe (tobacco-plant-created vaccines)* in both and in CoRI also *Hand-gepäckgebühr (hand luggage fee)* and *Haftungsstreitigkeiten (liability litigation).*

Experiment	**mert.log** news2013	**Bleu ci** news2014	**Bleu cs** news2014
raw'	16.87	16.25	15.31
CimS-RO	17.76	16.81	15.81

Table 4: Evaluation of the reordering system trained on Europarl v7.

9 Summary

We presented the CimS systems, a set of morphology-aware translation systems customised for translation from English to German. Each system operates on a different level of morphological description, be it nominal inflection, verbal inflection, compound processing or source-side reordering. Some of the systems are well-established (RI, CoRI and RO), others are still under developement (RIVe, CoRIVe and Syntax-RORI). However, all of them, with the exception of CoRIVe, lead to improved translation quality when evaluated against a contrastive baseline without linguistic processing. In an additional evaluation, we could show that the compound processing systems are able to create a considerable number of compounds unseen in the parallel training data.

In the future, we will investigate further combinations and extensions of our morphological components, including reordering, compound processing and verbal inflection. There are still many many interesting challenges to be solved in all of these areas, and this is especially true for verbal inflection.

Acknowledgments

This work was supported by Deutsche Forschungsgemeinschaft grants Models of Morphosyntax for Statistical Machine Translation (Phase 2) and Distributional Approaches to Semantic Relatedness. We would like to thank Daniel Quernheim for sharing the workload of preprocessing the data with us.

Moreover, we thank Edgar Hoch from the IMS system administration for generously providing us with disk space and all our colleagues at IMS, especially Fabienne Braune, Junfei Guo, Nina Seemann and Jason Utt for postponing their experiments to let us use most of IMS' computing facilities for a whole week. Thank you each beaucoup!

References

Fabienne Cap, Alexander Fraser, Marion Weller, and Aoife Cahill. 2014. How to Produce Unseen Teddy Bears: Improved Morphological Processing of Compounds in SMT. In *Proceedings of EACL 2014*.

Eugene Charniak and Mark Johnson. 2005. Coarse-to-fine n-best parsing and MaxEnt discriminative reranking. In *Proceedings of the 43rd Annual Meeting on Association for Computational Linguistics (ACL)*, Ann Arbor, Michigan.

Colin Cherry and George Foster. 2012. Batch Tuning Strategies for Statistical Machine Translation. In *Proceedings of HLT-NAACL 2012*.

Michael Collins, Philipp Koehn, and Ivona Kučerová. 2005. Clause restructuring for statistical machine translation. In *Proceedings ACL 2005*.

Chris Dyer. 2009. Using a maximum entropy model to build segmentation lattices for MT. In *Proceedings of HLT-NAACL 2009*.

Alexander Fraser, Marion Weller, Aoife Cahill, and Fabienne Cap. 2012. Modeling Inflection and Word Formation in SMT. In *Proceedings of EACL 2012*.

Alexander Fraser. 2009. Experiments in Morphosyntactic Processing for Translation to and from German. In *Proceedings of WMT 2009*.

Fabienne Fritzinger and Alexander Fraser. 2010. How to Avoid Burning Ducks: Combining Linguistic Analysis and Corpus Statistics for German Compound Processing. In *Proceedings of WMT@ACL2010*.

Michel Galley, Mark Hopkins, Kevin Knight, and Daniel Marcu. 2004. What's in a Translation Rule? In *Proceedings of HLT-NAACL 2004*.

Qin Gao and Stephan Vogel. 2008. Parallel implementations of word alignment tool. In *ACL 2008: Proceedings of the Workshop on Software Engineering, Testing, and Quality Assurance for Natural Language Processing*.

Adrià De Gispert and José B. Mariño. 2008. On the impact of morphology in English to Spanish statistical MT. *Speech Communication*.

Anita Gojun and Alexander Fraser. 2012. Determining the placement of German verbs in English-to-German SMT. In *Proceedings of EACL 2012*.

Kenneth Heafield. 2011. KenLM: Faster and Smaller Language Model Queries. In *Proceedings of WMT 2011*.

Minwoo Jeong, Kristina Toutanova, Hisami Suzuki, and Chris Quirk. 2010. A discriminative lexicon model for complex morphology. In *Proceedings of AMTA 2010*.

Philipp Koehn and Kevin Knight. 2003. Empirical Methods for Compound Splitting. In *Proceedings of EACL 2003*.

Philipp Koehn, Hieu Hoang, Alexandra Birch, Chris Callison-Burch, Marcello Federico, Nicola Bertoldi, Brooke Cowan, Wade Shen, Christine Moran, Richard Zens, Chris Dyer, Ondrej Bojar, Alexandra Constantin, and Evan Herbst. 2007. Moses: Open Source Toolkit for Statistical Machine Translation. In *Proceedings of ACL 2007 (Demo Session)*.

John Lafferty, Andrew McCallum, and Fernando Pereira. 2001. Conditional Random Fields: Probabilistic Models for Segmenting and Labeling Sequence Data. In *ICML'01*.

Klaus Macherey, Andrew M. Dai, David Talbot, Ashok C. Popat, and Franz Och. 2011. Language-independent Compound Splitting with Morphological Operations. In *Proceedings of ACL 2011*.

Franz Josef Och and Hermann Ney. 2003. A systematic comparison of various statistical alignment models. *Computational Linguistics*, 29(1):19–51,.

Kishore Papineni, Salim Roukos, Todd Ward, and Wei-Jing Zhu. 2002. Bleu: A Method for Automatic Evaluation of Machine Translation. In *Proceedings of ACL 2002*.

Maja Popović, Daniel Stein, and Hermann Ney. 2006. Statistical Machine Translation of German Compound Words. In *Proceedings of FinTAL 2006*.

Helmut Schmid and Florian Laws. 2008. Estimation of conditional probabilities with decision trees and an application to fine-grained pos tagging. In *Proceedings of COLING 2008*.

Helmut Schmid, Arne Fitschen, and Ulrich Heid. 2004. SMOR: A German Computational Morphology Covering Derivation, Composition and Inflection. In *Proceedings of LREC 2004*.

Helmut Schmid. 2004. Efficient Parsing of Highly Ambiguous Context-Free Grammars with Bit Vectors. In *Proceedings of Coling 2004*.

Andreas Stolcke. 2002. SRILM – an Extensible Language Modelling Toolkit. In *Proceedings of ICSLN 2002*.

Sara Stymne and Nicola Cancedda. 2011. Productive Generation of Compound Words in Statistical Machine Translation. In *Proceedings of WMT@EMNLP'11*.

Sara Stymne, Maria Holmqvist, and Lars Ahrenberg. 2008. Effects of Morphological Analysis in Translation between German and English. In *Proceedings of WMT 2008*.

Sara Stymne. 2009. A Comparison of Merging Strategies for Translation of German Compounds. In *Proceedings of EACL 2009 (Student Workshop)*.

Kristina Toutanova, Hisami Suzuki, and Achim Ruopp. 2008. Applying Morphology Generation Models to Machine Translation. In *Proceedings of HLT-ACL 2008.*

Marion Weller, Alexander Fraser, and Sabine Schulte im Walde. 2013. Using Subcategorization Knowledge to Improve Case Prediction for Translation to German. In *Proceedings of ACL'13.*

Philip Williams and Philipp Koehn. 2011. Agreement constraints for statistical machine translation into German. In *Proceedings of WMT 2011.*

Philip Williams and Phillipp Koehn. 2012. GHKM-Rule Extraction and Scope-3 Parsing in Moses. In *Proceedings of WMT 2007.*

English-to-Hindi system description for WMT 2014: Deep Source-Context Features for Moses

Marta R. Costa-jussà[1], Parth Gupta[2], Rafael E. Banchs[3] and Paolo Rosso[2]
[1]Centro de Investigación en Computación, Instituto Politécnico Nacional, Mexico
[2]NLE Lab, PRHLT Research Center, Universitat Politècnica de València
[3]Human Language Technology, Institute for Infocomm Research, Singapore
[1]marta@nlp.cic.ipn.mx, [2]{pgupta,prosso}@dsic.upv.es,
[3]rembanchs@i2r.a-star.edu.sg

Abstract

This paper describes the IPN-UPV participation on the English-to-Hindi translation task from WMT 2014 International Evaluation Campaign. The system presented is based on Moses and enhanced with deep learning by means of a source-context feature function. This feature depends on the input sentence to translate, which makes it more challenging to adapt it into the Moses framework. This work reports the experimental details of the system putting special emphasis on: how the feature function is integrated in Moses and how the deep learning representations are trained and used.

1 Introduction

This paper describes the joint participation of the Instituto Politécnico Nacional (IPN) and the Universitat Politècnica de Valencia (UPV) in cooperation with Institute for Infocomm Research (I2R) on the 9th Workshop on Statistical Machine Translation (WMT 2014). In particular, our participation was in the English-to-Hindi translation task.

Our baseline system is an standard phrase-based SMT system built with Moses (Koehn et al., 2007). Starting from this system we propose to introduce a source-context feature function inspired by previous works (R. Costa-jussà and Banchs, 2011; Banchs and Costa-jussà, 2011). The main novelty of this work is that the source-context feature is computed in a new deep representation.

The rest of the paper is organized as follows. Section 2 presents the motivation of this semantic feature and the description of how the source context feature function is added to Moses. Section 3 explains how both the latent semantic indexing and deep representation of sentences are used to better compute similarities among source contexts. Section 4 details the WMT experimental framework and results, which proves the relevance of the technique proposed. Finally, section 5 reports the main conclusions of this system description paper.

2 Integration of a deep source-context feature function in Moses

This section reports the motivation and description of the source-context feature function, together with the explanation of how it is integrated in Moses.

2.1 Motivation and description

Source context information in the phrase-based system is limited to the length of the translation units (phrases). Also, all training sentences contribute equally to the final translation.

We propose a source-context feature function which measures the similarity between the input sentence and all training sentences. In this way, the translation unit should be extended from $source|||target$ to $source|||target|||trainingsentence$, with the $trainingsentence$ the sentence from which the $source$ and $target$ phrases were extracted. The measured similarity is used to favour those translation units that have been extracted from training sentences that are similar to the current sentence to be translated and to penalize those translation units that have been extracted from unrelated or dissimilar training sentences as shown in Figure 2.1.

In the proposed feature, sentence similarity is measured by means of the cosine distance in a reduced dimension vector-space model, which is constructed either by means of standard latent semantic analysis or using deep representation as decribed in section 3.

Proceedings of the Ninth Workshop on Statistical Machine Translation, pages 79–83,
Baltimore, Maryland USA, June 26–27, 2014.

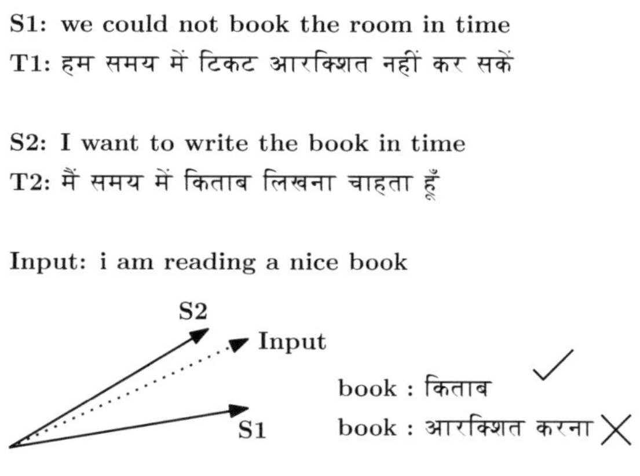

Figure 1: Illustration of the method

2.2 Integration in Moses

As defined in the section above and, previously, in (R. Costa-jussà and Banchs, 2011; Banchs and Costa-jussà, 2011), the value of the proposed source context similarity feature depends on each individual input sentence to be translated by the system. We are computing the similarity between the source input sentence and all the source training sentences.

This definition implies the feature function depends on the input sentence to be translated. To implement this requirement, we followed our previous implementation of an off-line version of the proposed methodology, which, although very inefficient in the practice, allows us to evaluate the impact of the source-context feature on a state-of-the-art phrase-based translation system. This practical implementation follows the next procedure:

1. Two sentence similarity matrices are computed: one between sentences in the development and training sets, and the other between sentences in the test and training datasets.

2. Each matrix entry m_{ij} should contain the similarity score between the ith sentence in the training set and the jth sentence in the development (or test) set.

3. For each sentence s in the test and development sets, a phrase pair list L_S of all potential phrases that can be used during decoding is extracted from the aligned training set.

4. The corresponding source-context similarity values are assigned to each phrase in lists L_S according to values in the corresponding similarity matrices.

5. Each phrase list L_S is collapsed into a phrase table T_S by removing repetitions (when removing repeated entries in the list, the largest value of the source-context similarity feature is retained).

6. Each phrase table is completed by adding standard feature values (which are computed in the standard manner).

7. Moses is used on a sentence-per-sentence basis, using a different translation table for each development (or test) sentence.

3 Representation of Sentences

We represent the sentences of the source language in the latent space by means of linear and non-linear dimensionality reduction techniques. Such models can be seen as topic models where the low-dimensional embedding of the sentences represent conditional latent topics.

3.1 Deep Autoencoders

The non-linear dimensionality reduction technique we employ is based on the concept of deep learning, specifically deep autoencoders. Autoencoders are three-layer networks (input layer, hidden layer and output layer) which try to learn an identity function. In the neural network representation of autoencoder (Rumelhart et al., 1986), the visible layer corresponds to the input layer and hidden layer corresponds to the latent features. The autoencoder tries to learn an abstract representation of the data in the hidden layer in such a way that minimizes reconstruction error. When the dimension of the hidden layer is sufficiently small, autoencoder is able to generalise and derive powerful low-dimensional representation of data. We consider bag-of-words representation of text sentences where the visible layer is binary feature vector ($\mathbf{v}$) where v_i corresponds to the presence or absence of ith word. We use binary restricted Boltzmann machines to construct an autoencoder as shown in (Hinton et al., 2006). Latent representation of the input sentence can be obtained as shown below:

$$p(\mathbf{h}|\mathbf{v}) = \sigma(W * \mathbf{v} + \mathbf{b}) \quad (1)$$

where W is the symmetric weight matrix between visible and hidden layer and $\mathbf{b}$ is hidden layer bias vector and $\sigma(x)$ is sigmoid logistic function $1/(1+\exp(-x))$.

Autoencoders with single hidden layer do not have any advantage over linear methods like PCA (Bourlard and Kamp, 1988), hence we consider deep autoencoder by stacking multiple RBMs on top of each other (Hinton and Salakhutdinov, 2006). The autoencoders have always been difficult to train through back-propagation until greedy layerwise pre-training was found (Hinton and Salakhutdinov, 2006; Hinton et al., 2006; Bengio et al., 2006). The pre-training initialises the network parameters in such a way that fine-tuning them through back-propagation becomes very effective and efficient (Erhan et al., 2010).

3.2 Latent Semantic Indexing

Linear dimensionality reduction technique, latent semantic indexing (LSI) is used to represent sentences in abstract space (Deerwester et al., 1990). The term-sentence matrix ($\mathbf{X}$) is created where x_{ij} denotes the occurrence of ith term in j^{th} sentence. Matrix $\mathbf{X}$ is factorized using singular value decomposition (SVD) method to obtain top m principle components and the sentences are represented in this m dimensional latent space.

4 Experiments

This section describes the experiments carried out in the context of WMT 2014. For English-Hindi the parallel training data was collected by Charles University and consisted of 3.6M English words and 3.97M Hindi words. There was a monolingual corpus for Hindi comming from different sources which consisted of 790.8M Hindi words. In addition, there was a development corpus of news data translated specifically for the task which consisted of 10.3m English words and 10.1m Hindi words. For internal experimentation we built a test set extracted from the training set. We selected randomly 429 sentences from the training corpus which appeared only once, removed them from training and used them as internal test set. Monolingual Hindi corpus was used to build a larger language model. The language model was computed doing an interpolation of the language model trained on the Hindi part of the bilingual corpus (3.97M words) and the language model trained on the monolingual Hindi corpus (790.8M words). Interpolation was optimised in the development set provided by the organizers. Both language models interpolated were 5-grams using Kneser-Ney smoothing.

The preprocessing of the corpus was done with the standard tools from Moses. English was lowercased and tokenized. Hindi was tokenized with the simple tokenizer provided by the organizers. We cleaned the corpus using standard parameters (i.e. we keep sentences between 1 and 80 words of length).

For training, we used the default Moses options, which include: the *grow-diag-final and* word alignment symmetrization, the lexicalized reordering, relative frequencies (conditional and posterior probabilities) with phrase discounting, lexical weights and phrase bonus for the translation model (with phrases up to length 10), a language model (see details below) and a word bonus model. Optimisation was done using the MERT algorithm available in Moses. Optimisation is slow because of the way integration of the feature function is done that it requires one phrase table for each input sentence.

During translation, we dropped unknown words and used the option of minimum bayes risk decoding. Postprocessing consisted in de-tokenizing Hindi using the standard detokenizer of Moses (the English version).

4.1 Autoencoder training

The architecture of autoencoder we consider was n-500-128-500-n where n is the vocabulary size. The training sentences were stemmed, stopwords were removed and also the terms with sentences frequency[1] less than 20 were also removed. This resulted in vocabulary size n=7299.

The RBMs were pretrained using Contrastive Divergence (CD) with step size 1 (Hinton, 2002). After pretraining, the RBMs were stacked on top of each other and unrolled to create deep autoencoder (Hinton and Salakhutdinov, 2006). During the fine-tuning stage, we backpropagated the reconstruction error to update network parameters. The size of mini-batches during pretraining and fine-tuning were 25 and 100 respectively. Weight decay was used to prevent overfitting. Additionally, in order to encourage sparsity in the hidden units, Kullback-Leibler sparsity regularization was used. We used GPU[2] based implementation of autoencoder to train the models which took around 4.5 hours for full training.

[1] total number of training sentences in which the term appears

[2] NVIDIA GeForce GTX Titan with Memory 5 GiB and 2688 CUDA cores

4.2 Results

Table 1 shows the improvements in terms of BLEU of adding deep context over the baseline system for English-to-Hindi (En2Hi) over development and test sets. Adding source-context information using deep learning outperforms the latent semantic analysis methodology.

	En2Hi	
	Dev	Test
baseline	9.42	14.99
+lsi	**9.83**	**15.12**
+deep context	**10.40**†	**15.43**†

Table 1: BLEU scores for En2Hi translation task.. † depicts statistical significance (p-value<0.05).

Our source-context feature function may be more discriminative in a task like English-to-Hindi where the target language has a larger vocabulary than the source one.

Table 2 shows an example of how the translation is improving in terms of lexical semantics which is the goal of the methodology presented in the paper. The most frequent sense of word *cry* is रोना, which literally means "to cry" while the example in Table 2 refers to the sense of *cry* as चीख, which means to *scream*. Our method could identify the context and hence the source context feature (scf) of the unit cry|||चीख is higher than for the unit scf(cry|||रोना) as shown in Table 3 and for this particular input sentence.

5 Conclusion

This paper reports the IPN-UPV participation in the WMT 2014 Evaluation Campaign. The system is Moses-based with an additional feature function based on deep learning. This feature function introduces source-context information in the standard Moses system by adding the information of how similar is the input sentence to the different training sentences. Significant improvements over the baseline system are reported in the task from English to Hindi.

System	**Translation**
Source	soft cry from the depth
Baseline	गहराइयों से मूलायम रोने लगते
+deep context	गहराइयों से मूलायम **चीख**
Reference	गहराइयों से कोमल **चीख**

Table 2: Manual analysis of a translation output.

	cp	*pp*	*scf*
cry|||रोना	0.23	0.06	0.85
cry|||चीख	0.15	0.04	0.90

Table 3: Probability values (conditional, cp, and posterior, pp, as standard features in a phrase-based system) for the word *cry* and two Hindi translations.

As further work, we will implement our feature function in Moses using suffix arrays in order to make it more efficient.

Acknowledgements

This work has been supported in part by Spanish Ministerio de Economía y Competitividad, contract TEC2012-38939-C03-02 as well as from the European Regional Development Fund (ERDF/FEDER). The work of the second and fourth authors is also supported by WIQ-EI (IRSES grant n. 269180) and DIANA-APPLICATIONS (TIN2012-38603-C02-01) project and VLC/CAMPUS Microcluster on Multimodal Interaction in Intelligent Systems.

References

Rafael E. Banchs and Marta R. Costa-jussà. 2011. A semantic feature for statistical machine translation. In *Proceedings of the Fifth Workshop on Syntax, Semantics and Structure in Statistical Translation*, SSST-5, pages 126–134.

Yoshua Bengio, Pascal Lamblin, Dan Popovici, and Hugo Larochelle. 2006. Greedy layer-wise training of deep networks. In *NIPS*, pages 153–160.

Hervé Bourlard and Yves Kamp. 1988. Auto-association by multilayer perceptrons and singular value decomposition. *Biological Cybernetics*, 59(4):291–294, September.

Scott Deerwester, Susan T. Dumais, George W. Furnas, Thomas K. Landauer, and Richard Harshman. 1990. Indexing by latent semantic analysis. *Journal of the American Society for Information Science*, 41(6):391–407.

Dumitru Erhan, Yoshua Bengio, Aaron C. Courville, Pierre-Antoine Manzagol, Pascal Vincent, and Samy Bengio. 2010. Why does unsupervised pre-training help deep learning? *Journal of Machine Learning Research*, 11:625–660.

Geoffrey Hinton and Ruslan Salakhutdinov. 2006. Reducing the dimensionality of data with neural networks. *Science*, 313(5786):504 – 507.

Geoffrey E. Hinton, Simon Osindero, and Yee Whye Teh. 2006. A fast learning algorithm for deep belief nets. *Neural Computation*, 18(7):1527–1554.

Geoffrey E. Hinton. 2002. Training products of experts by minimizing contrastive divergence. *Neural Computation*, 14(8):1771–1800.

Philipp Koehn, Hieu Hoang, Alexandra Birch, Chris Callison-Burch, Marcello Federico, Nicola Bertoldi, Brooke Cowan, Wade Shen, Christine Moran, Richard Zens, Chris Dyer, Ondřej Bojar, Alexandra Constantin, and Evan Herbst. 2007. Moses: Open source toolkit for statistical machine translation. In *Proceedings of the 45th Annual Meeting of the ACL on Interactive Poster and Demonstration Sessions*, ACL '07, pages 177–180.

Marta R. Costa-jussà and Rafael E. Banchs. 2011. The bm-i2r haitian-créole-to-english translation system description for the wmt 2011 evaluation campaign. In *Proceedings of the Sixth Workshop on Statistical Machine Translation*, pages 452–456, Edinburgh, Scotland, July. Association for Computational Linguistics.

David E. Rumelhart, Geoffrey E. Hinton, and Ronald J. Williams. 1986. Learning representations by back-propagating errors. *Nature*, 323(6088):533–536.

The KIT-LIMSI Translation System for WMT 2014

*Quoc Khanh Do, †Teresa Herrmann, *†Jan Niehues,
*Alexandre Allauzen, *François Yvon and †Alex Waibel
*LIMSI-CNRS, Orsay, France
†Karlsruhe Institute of Technology, Karlsruhe, Germany
*surname@limsi.fr †firstname.surname@kit.edu

Abstract

This paper describes the joined submission of LIMSI and KIT to the Shared Translation Task for the German-to-English direction. The system consists of a phrase-based translation system using a pre-reordering approach. The baseline system already includes several models like conventional language models on different word factors and a discriminative word lexicon. This system is used to generate a k-best list. In a second step, the list is reranked using *SOUL* language and translation models (Le et al., 2011).

Originally, *SOUL* translation models were applied to n-gram-based translation systems that use tuples as translation units instead of phrase pairs. In this article, we describe their integration into the KIT phrase-based system. Experimental results show that their use can yield significant improvements in terms of BLEU score.

1 Introduction

This paper describes the KIT-LIMSI system for the Shared Task of the ACL 2014 Ninth Workshop on Statistical Machine Translation. The system participates in the German-to-English translation task. It consists of two main components. First, a k-best list is generated using a phrase-based machine translation system. This system will be described in Section 2. Afterwards, the k-best list is reranked using *SOUL* (*Structured OUtput Layer*) models. Thereby, a neural network language model (Le et al., 2011), as well as several translation models (Le et al., 2012a) are used. A detailed description of these models can be found in Section 3. While the translation system uses phrase pairs, the *SOUL* translation model uses tuples as described in the n-gram approach (Mariño et al., 2006). We describe the integration of the *SOUL* models into the translation system in Section 3.2. Section 4 summarizes the experimental results and compares two different tuning algorithms: Minimum Error Rate Training (Och, 2003) and k-best Batch Margin Infused Relaxed Algorithm (Cherry and Foster, 2012).

2 Baseline system

The KIT translation system is an in-house implementation of the phrase-based approach and includes a pre-ordering step. This system is fully described in Vogel (2003).

To train translation models, the provided Europarl, NC and Common Crawl parallel corpora are used. The target side of those parallel corpora, the News Shuffle corpus and the GigaWord corpus are used as monolingual training data for the different language models. Optimization is done with Minimum Error Rate Training as described in Venugopal et al. (2005), using newstest2012 and newstest2013 as development and test data, respectively.

Compound splitting (Koehn and Knight, 2003) is performed on the source side (German) of the corpus before training. Since the web-crawled Common Crawl corpus is noisy, this corpus is first filtered using an SVM classifier as described in Mediani et al. (2011).

The word alignment is generated using the GIZA++ Toolkit (Och and Ney, 2003). Phrase extraction and scoring is done using the Moses toolkit (Koehn et al., 2007). Phrase pair probabilities are computed using modified Kneser-Ney smoothing (Foster et al., 2006).

We apply short-range reorderings (Rottmann and Vogel, 2007) and long-range reorderings (Niehues and Kolss, 2009) based on part-of-speech tags. The POS tags are generated using the TreeTagger (Schmid, 1994). Rewriting rules

Proceedings of the Ninth Workshop on Statistical Machine Translation, pages 84–89,
Baltimore, Maryland USA, June 26–27, 2014.

based on POS sequences are learnt automatically to perform source sentence reordering according to the target language word order. The long-range reordering rules are further applied to the training corpus to create reordering lattices to extract the phrases for the translation model. In addition, a tree-based reordering model (Herrmann et al., 2013) trained on syntactic parse trees (Rafferty and Manning, 2008; Klein and Manning, 2003) is applied to the source sentence. In addition to these pre-reordering models, a lexicalized reordering model (Koehn et al., 2005) is applied during decoding.

Language models are trained with the SRILM toolkit (Stolcke, 2002) using modified Kneser-Ney smoothing (Chen and Goodman, 1996). The system uses a 4-gram word-based language model trained on all monolingual data and an additional language model trained on automatically selected data (Moore and Lewis, 2010). The system further applies a language model based on 1000 automatically learned word classes using the MKCLS algorithm (Och, 1999). In addition, a bilingual language model (Niehues et al., 2011) is used as well as a discriminative word lexicon (DWL) using source context to guide the word choices in the target sentence.

3 *SOUL* models for statistical machine translation

Neural networks, working on top of conventional n-gram back-off language models (BOLMs), have been introduced in (Bengio et al., 2003; Schwenk, 2007) as a potential means to improve discrete language models. The *SOUL* model (Le et al., 2011) is a specific neural network architecture that allows us to estimate n-gram models using large vocabularies, thereby making the training of large neural network models feasible both for target language models and translation models (Le et al., 2012a).

3.1 *SOUL* translation models

While the integration of *SOUL* target language models is straightforward, *SOUL* translation models rely on a specific decomposition of the joint probability $P(\mathbf{s}, \mathbf{t})$ of a sentence pair, where $\mathbf{s}$ is a sequence of I *reordered* source words $(s_1, ..., s_I)$[1] and $\mathbf{t}$ contains J target words $(t_1, ..., t_J)$. In the n-gram approach (Mariño et al., 2006; Crego et al., 2011), this segmentation is a by-product of source reordering, and ultimately derives from initial word and phrase alignments. In this framework, the basic translation units are *tuples*, which are analogous to phrase pairs, and represent a matching $\mathrm{u} = (\overline{s}, \overline{t})$ between a source phrase $\overline{s}$ and a target phrase $\overline{t}$.

Using the n-gram assumption, the joint probability of a segmented sentence pair using L tupels decomposes as:

$$P(\mathbf{s}, \mathbf{t}) = \prod_{i=1}^{L} P(\mathrm{u}_i | \mathrm{u}_{i-1}, ..., \mathrm{u}_{i-n+1}) \qquad (1)$$

A first issue with this decomposition is that the elementary units are bilingual pairs. Therefore, the underlying vocabulary and hence the number of parameters can be quite large, even for small translation tasks. Due to data sparsity issues, such models are bound to face severe estimation problems. Another problem with Equation (1) is that the source and target sides play symmetric roles, whereas the source side is known, and the target side must be predicted. To overcome some of these issues, the n-gram probability in Equation (1) can be factored by first decomposing tuples in two (source and target) parts, and then decomposing the source and target parts at the word level.

Let s_i^k denote the kth word of source part of the tuple $\overline{s}_i$. Let us consider the example of Figure 1, s_{11}^1 corresponds to the source word *nobel*, s_{11}^4 to the source word *paix*, and similarly t_{11}^2 is the target word *peace*. We finally define $h^{n-1}(t_i^k)$ as the sequence of the $n-1$ words preceding t_i^k in the target sentence, and $h^{n-1}(s_i^k)$ as the $n-1$ words preceding s_i^k in the reordered source sentence: in Figure 1, $h^3(t_{11}^2)$ thus refers to the three word context *receive the nobel* associated with the target word *peace*. Using these notations, Equation 1 can be rewritten as:

$$P(\mathbf{s}, \mathbf{t}) = \prod_{i=1}^{L} \Big[\prod_{k=1}^{|\overline{t}_i|} P\big(t_i^k | h^{n-1}(t_i^k), h^{n-1}(s_{i+1}^1)\big) \times \prod_{k=1}^{|\overline{s}_i|} P\big(s_i^k | h^{n-1}(t_i^1), h^{n-1}(s_i^k)\big)\Big] \qquad (2)$$

This decomposition relies on the n-gram assumption, this time at the word level. Therefore, this

[1] In the context of the n-gram translation model, $(\mathbf{s}, \mathbf{t})$ thus denotes an *aligned* sentence pair, where the source words are reordered.

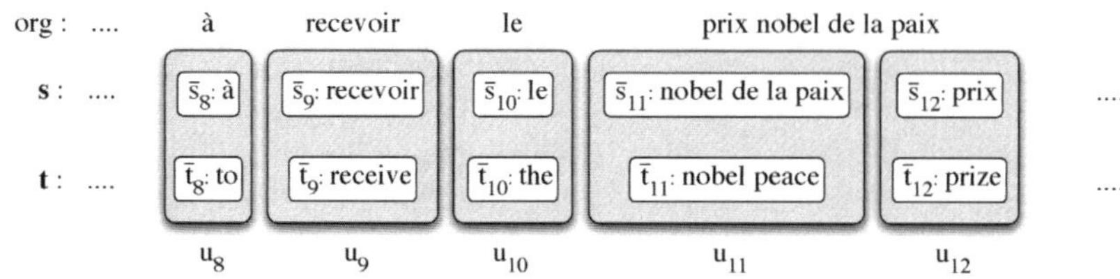

Figure 1: Extract of a French-English sentence pair segmented into bilingual units. The original (*org*) French sentence appears at the top of the figure, just above the reordered source $\mathbf{s}$ and the target $\mathbf{t}$. The pair $(\mathbf{s}, \mathbf{t})$ decomposes into a sequence of L bilingual units (*tuples*) $u_1, ..., u_L$. Each tuple u_i contains a source and a target phrase: $\bar{s}_i$ and $\bar{t}_i$.

model estimates the joint probability of a sentence pair using two sliding windows of length n, one for each language; however, the moves of these windows remain synchronized by the tuple segmentation. Moreover, the context is not limited to the current phrase, and continues to include words in adjacent phrases. Equation (2) involves two terms that will be further denoted as *TrgSrc* and *Src*, respectively $P\big(t_i^k|h^{n-1}(t_i^k), h^{n-1}(s_{i+1}^1)\big)$ and $P\big(s_i^k|h^{n-1}(t_i^1), h^{n-1}(s_i^k)\big)$. It is worth noticing that the joint probability of a sentence pair can also be decomposed by considering the following two terms: $P\big(s_i^k|h^{n-1}(s_i^k), h^{n-1}(t_{i+1}^1)\big)$ and $P\big(t_i^k|h^{n-1}(s_i^1), h^{n-1}(t_i^k)\big)$. These two terms will be further denoted by *SrcTrg* and *Trg*. Therefore, adding *SOUL* translation models means that 4 scores are added to the phrase-based systems.

3.2 Integration

During the training step, the *SOUL* translation models are trained as described in (Le et al., 2012a). The main changes concern the inference step. Given the computational cost of computing n-gram probabilities with neural network models, a solution is to resort to a two-pass approach: the first pass uses a conventional system to produce a k-best list (the k most likely hypotheses); in the second pass, probabilities are computed by the *SOUL* models for each hypothesis and added as new features. Then the k-best list is reordered according to a combination of all features including these new features. In the following experiments, we use 10-gram *SOUL* models to rescore 300-best lists. Since the phrase-based system described in Section 2 uses source reordering, the decoder was modified in order to generate k-best lists that contain necessary word alignment information between the reordered source sentence and its associated target hypothesis. The goal is to recover the information that is illustrated in Figure 1 and to apply the n-gram decomposition of a sentence pair.

These (target and bilingual) neural network models produce scores for each hypothesis in the k-best list; these new features, along with the features from the baseline system, are then provided to a new phase which runs the traditional Minimum Error Rate Training (*MERT*) (Och, 2003), or a recently proposed k-best Batch Margin Infused Relaxed Algorithm (*KBMIRA*) (Cherry and Foster, 2012) for tuning purpose. The *SOUL* models used for this year's evaluation are similar to those described in Allauzen et al. (2013) and Le et al. (2012b). However, since compared to these evaluations less parallel data is available for the German-to-English task, we use smaller vocabularies of about $100K$ words.

4 Results

We evaluated the SOUL models on the German-to-English translation task using two systems to generate the k-best lists. The first system used all models of the baseline system except the DWL model and the other one used all models.

Table 1 summarizes experimental results in terms of BLEU scores when the tuning is performed using *KBMIRA*. As described in Section 3, the probability of a phrase pair can be decomposed into products of words' probabilities in 2 different ways: we can first estimate the probability of words in the source phrase given the context, and then the probability of the target phrase given its associated source phrase and context words (see Equation (2)); or inversely we can generate the target side before the source side. The former proceeds by adding *Src* and *TrgSrc* scores as

	No DWL		DWL	
Soul models	Dev	Test	Dev	Test
No	26.02	27.02	26.27	27.46
Target	26.30	27.42	26.43	27.85
Translation st	26.46	27.70	26.66	28.04
Translation ts	26.48	27.41	26.61	28.00
All Translation	26.50	27.86	26.70	28.08
All *SOUL* models	26.62	27.84	26.75	28.10

Table 1: Results using *KBMIRA*

	No DWL		DWL	
Soul models	Dev	Test	Dev	Test
No	26.02	27.02	26.27	27.46
Target	26.18	27.09	26.44	27.54
Translation st	26.36	27.59	26.66	27.80
Translation ts	26.44	27.69	26.63	27.94
All Translation	26.53	27.65	26.69	27.99
All *SOUL* models	26.47	27.68	**26.66**	**28.01**

Table 2: Results using *MERT*. Results in bold correpond to the submitted system.

2 new features into the k-best list, and the latter by adding *Trg* and *SrcTrg* scores. These 2 methods correspond respectively to the *Translation ts* and *Translation st* lines in the Table 1. The 4 translation models may also be added simultaneously (*All Translations*). The first line gives baseline results without *SOUL* models, while the *Target* line shows results in adding only *SOUL* language model. The last line (*All SOUL models*) shows the results for adding all neural network models into the baseline systems.

As evident in Table 1, using the *SOUL* translation models yields generally better results than using the *SOUL* target language model, yielding about 0.2 BLEU point differences on dev and test sets. We can therefore assume that the *SOUL* translation models provide richer information that, to some extent, covers that contained in the neural network language model. Indeed, these 4 translation models take into account not only lexical probabilities of translating target words given source words (or in the inverse order), but also the probabilities of generating words in the target side (*Trg* model) as does a language model, with the same context length over both source and target sides. It is therefore not surprising that adding the *SOUL* language model along with all translation models (the last line in the table) does not give significant improvement compared to the other configurations. The different ways of using the *SOUL* translation models perform very similarly.

Table 2 summarizes the results using *MERT* instead of *KBMIRA*. We can observe that using *KBMIRA* results in 0.1 to 0.2 BLEU point improvements compared to *MERT*. Moreover, this impact becomes more important when more features are considered (the last line when all 5 neural network models are added into the baseline systems). In short, the use of neural network models yields up to 0.6 BLEU improvement on the DWL system, and a 0.8 BLEU gain on the system without DWL. Unfortunately, the experiments with *KBMIRA* were carried out after the the submission date. Therefore the submitted system corresponds to the last line of table 2 indicated in bold.

5 Conclusion

We presented a system with two main features: a phrase-based translation system which uses prereordering and the integration of *SOUL* target language and translation models. Although the translation performance of the baseline system is already very competitive, the rescoring by *SOUL* models improve the performance significantly. In the rescoring step, we used a continuous language model as well as four continuous translation models. When combining the different *SOUL* models, the translation models are observed to be more important in increasing the translation performance than the language model. Moreover, we observe a slight benefit to use KBMIRA instead of the standard MERT tuning algorithm. It is worth noticing that using KBMIRA improves the performance but also reduces the variance of the final results.

As future work, the integration of the *SOUL* translation models could be improved in different ways. For *SOUL* translation models, there is a mismatch between translation units used during the training step and those used by the decoder. The former are derived using the n-gram-based approach, while the latter use the conventional phrase extraction heuristic. We assume that reducing this mismatch could improve the overall performance. This can be achieved for instance using forced decoding to infer a segmentation of the training data into translation units. Then the *SOUL* translation models can be trained using this segmentation. For the *SOUL* target language model, in these experiments we only used the English part of the parallel data for training. Results may be improved by including all the monolingual data.

Acknowledgments

The research leading to these results has received funding from the European Union Seventh Framework Programme (FP7/2007-2013) under grant agreement n° 287658 as well as the French Armaments Procurement Agency (DGA) under the RAPID Rapmat project.

References

Alexandre Allauzen, Nicolas Pécheux, Quoc Khanh Do, Marco Dinarelli, Thomas Lavergne, Aurélien Max, Hai-Son Le, and François Yvon. 2013. Limsi@ wmt13. In *Proceedings of the Eighth Workshop on Statistical Machine Translation*, pages 60–67.

Yoshua Bengio, Réjean Ducharme, Pascal Vincent, and Christian Janvin. 2003. A neural probabilistic language model. *Journal of Machine Learning Research*, 3:1137–1155.

S.F. Chen and J. Goodman. 1996. An empirical study of smoothing techniques for language modeling. In *Proceedings of the 34th Annual Meeting on Association for Computational Linguistics (ACL '96)*, pages 310–318, Santa Cruz, California, USA.

Colin Cherry and George Foster. 2012. Batch tuning strategies for statistical machine translation. In *Proceedings of the 2012 Conference of the North American Chapter of the Association for Computational Linguistics: Human Language Technologies*, pages 427–436. Association for Computational Linguistics.

Josep M. Crego, Franois Yvon, and Jos B. Mariño. 2011. N-code: an open-source Bilingual N-gram SMT Toolkit. *Prague Bulletin of Mathematical Linguistics*, 96:49–58.

George F. Foster, Roland Kuhn, and Howard Johnson. 2006. Phrasetable smoothing for statistical machine translation. In *EMNLP*, pages 53–61.

Teresa Herrmann, Jan Niehues, and Alex Waibel. 2013. Combining Word Reordering Methods on different Linguistic Abstraction Levels for Statistical Machine Translation. In *Proceedings of the Seventh Workshop on Syntax, Semantics and Structure in Statistical Translation*, Altanta, Georgia, USA, June. Association for Computational Linguistics.

Dan Klein and Christopher D. Manning. 2003. Accurate Unlexicalized Parsing. In *Proceedings of ACL 2003*.

Philipp Koehn and Kevin Knight. 2003. Empirical Methods for Compound Splitting. In *EACL*, Budapest, Hungary.

Philipp Koehn, Amittai Axelrod, Alexandra B. Mayne, Chris Callison-Burch, Miles Osborne, and David Talbot. 2005. Edinburgh System Description for the 2005 IWSLT Speech Translation Evaluation. In *Proceedings of the International Workshop on Spoken Language Translation (IWSLT)*, Pittsburgh, PA, USA.

Philipp Koehn, Hieu Hoang, Alexandra Birch, Chris Callison-Burch, Marcello Federico, Nicola Bertoldi, Brooke Cowan, Wade Shen, Christine Moran, Richard Zens, Chris Dyer, Ondrej Bojar, Alexandra Constantin, and Evan Herbst. 2007. Moses: Open Source Toolkit for Statistical Machine Translation. In *Proceedings of ACL 2007, Demonstration Session*, Prague, Czech Republic.

Hai-Son Le, Ilya Oparin, Alexandre Allauzen, Jean-Luc Gauvain, and François Yvon. 2011. Structured output layer neural network language model. In *Proceedings of ICASSP*, pages 5524–5527.

Hai-Son Le, Alexandre Allauzen, and François Yvon. 2012a. Continuous space translation models with neural networks. pages 39–48, Montréal, Canada, June. Association for Computational Linguistics.

Hai-Son Le, Thomas Lavergne, Alexandre Allauzen, Marianna Apidianaki, Li Gong, Aurélien Max, Artem Sokolov, Guillaume Wisniewski, and François Yvon. 2012b. Limsi@ wmt'12. In *Proceedings of the Seventh Workshop on Statistical Machine Translation*, pages 330–337. Association for Computational Linguistics.

José B. Mariño, Rafael E. Banchs, Josep M. Crego, Adrià de Gispert, Patrick Lambert, José A.R. Fonollosa, and Marta R. Costa-Jussà. 2006. N-gram-based machine translation. *Computational Linguistics*, 32(4):527–549.

Mohammed Mediani, Eunah Cho, Jan Niehues, Teresa Herrmann, and Alex Waibel. 2011. The KIT English-French Translation systems for IWSLT 2011. In *Proceedings of the Eight International Workshop on Spoken Language Translation (IWSLT)*.

R.C. Moore and W. Lewis. 2010. Intelligent selection of language model training data. In *Proceedings of the ACL 2010 Conference Short Papers*, pages 220–224, Stroudsburg, PA, USA. Association for Computational Linguistics.

Jan Niehues and Muntsin Kolss. 2009. A POS-Based Model for Long-Range Reorderings in SMT. In *Fourth Workshop on Statistical Machine Translation (WMT 2009)*, Athens, Greece.

Jan Niehues, Teresa Herrmann, Stephan Vogel, and Alex Waibel. 2011. Wider Context by Using Bilingual Language Models in Machine Translation. In *Sixth Workshop on Statistical Machine Translation (WMT 2011)*, Edinburgh, UK.

Franz Josef Och and Hermann Ney. 2003. A Systematic Comparison of Various Statistical Alignment Models. *Computational Linguistics*, 29(1):19–51.

Franz Josef Och. 1999. An Efficient Method for Determining Bilingual Word Classes. In *EACL'99*.

Franz Josef Och. 2003. Minimum error rate training in statistical machine translation. In *Proceedings of the 41st Annual Meeting on Association for Computational Linguistics-Volume 1*, pages 160–167. Association for Computational Linguistics.

Anna N. Rafferty and Christopher D. Manning. 2008. Parsing Three German Treebanks: Lexicalized and Unlexicalized Baselines. In *Proceedings of the Workshop on Parsing German*.

Kay Rottmann and Stephan Vogel. 2007. Word Reordering in Statistical Machine Translation with a POS-Based Distortion Model. In *Proceedings of the 11th International Conference on Theoretical and Methodological Issues in Machine Translation (TMI)*, Skövde, Sweden.

Helmut Schmid. 1994. Probabilistic Part-of-Speech Tagging Using Decision Trees. In *International Conference on New Methods in Language Processing*, Manchester, United Kingdom.

Holger Schwenk. 2007. Continuous space language models. *Computer Speech and Language*, 21(3):492–518, July.

Andreas Stolcke. 2002. SRILM – An Extensible Language Modeling Toolkit. In *International Conference on Spoken Language Processing*, Denver, Colorado, USA.

Ashish Venugopal, Andreas Zollman, and Alex Waibel. 2005. Training and Evaluating Error Minimization Rules for Statistical Machine Translation. In *Workshop on Data-drive Machine Translation and Beyond (WPT-05)*, Ann Arbor, Michigan, USA.

Stephan Vogel. 2003. SMT Decoder Dissected: Word Reordering. In *International Conference on Natural Language Processing and Knowledge Engineering*, Beijing, China.

The IIT Bombay Hindi⇔English Translation System at WMT 2014

Piyush Dungarwal, Rajen Chatterjee, Abhijit Mishra, Anoop Kunchukuttan,
Ritesh Shah, Pushpak Bhattacharyya
Department of Computer Science and Engineering
Indian Institute of Technology, Bombay
{piyushdd,rajen,abhijitmishra,anoopk,ritesh,pb}@cse.iitb.ac.in

Abstract

In this paper, we describe our English-Hindi and Hindi-English statistical systems submitted to the WMT14 shared task. The core components of our translation systems are phrase based (Hindi-English) and factored (English-Hindi) SMT systems. We show that the use of number, case and Tree Adjoining Grammar information as factors helps to improve English-Hindi translation, primarily by generating morphological inflections correctly. We show improvements to the translation systems using pre-procesing and post-processing components. To overcome the structural divergence between English and Hindi, we preorder the source side sentence to conform to the target language word order. Since parallel corpus is limited, many words are not translated. We translate out-of-vocabulary words and transliterate named entities in a post-processing stage. We also investigate ranking of translations from multiple systems to select the best translation.

1 Introduction

India is a multilingual country with Hindi being the most widely spoken language. Hindi and English act as *link languages* across the country and languages of official communication for the Union Government. Thus, the importance of English⇔Hindi translation is obvious. Over the last decade, several rule based (Sinha, 1995) , interlingua based (Dave et. al., 2001) and statistical methods (Ramanathan et. al., 2008) have been explored for English-Hindi translation.

In the WMT 2014 shared task, we undertake the challenge of improving translation between the English and Hindi language pair using Statistical Machine Translation (SMT) techniques. The WMT 2014 shared task has provided a standardized test set to evaluate multiple approaches and avails the largest publicly downloadable English-Hindi parallel corpus. Using these resources, we have developed a phrase-based and a factored based system for Hindi-English and English-Hindi translation respectively, with pre-processing and post-processing components to handle structural divergence and morphlogical richness of Hindi. Section 2 describes the issues in Hindi↔English translation.

The rest of the paper is organized as follows. Section 3 describes corpus preparation and experimental setup. Section 4 and Section 5 describe our English-Hindi and Hindi-English translation systems respectively. Section 6 describes the post-processing operations on the output from the core translation system for handling OOV and named entities, and for reranking outputs from multiple systems. Section 7 mentions the details regarding our systems submitted to WMT shared task. Section 8 concludes the paper.

2 Problems in Hindi⇔English Translation

Languages can be differentiated in terms of structural divergences and morphological manifestations. English is structurally classified as a Subject-Verb-Object (SVO) language with a poor morphology whereas Hindi is a morphologically rich, Subject-Object-Verb (SOV) language. Largely, these divergences are responsible for the difficulties in translation using a phrase based/factored model, which we summarize in this section.

2.1 English-to-Hindi

The fundamental structural differences described earlier result in large distance verb and modifier movements across English-Hindi. Local reordering models prove to be inadequate to over-

Proceedings of the Ninth Workshop on Statistical Machine Translation, pages 90–96,
Baltimore, Maryland USA, June 26–27, 2014.

come the problem; hence, we transformed the source side sentence using pre-ordering rules to conform to the target word order. Availability of robust parsers for English makes this approach for English-Hindi translation effective.

As far as morphology is concerned, Hindi is more richer in terms of case-markers, inflection-rich surface forms including verb forms etc. Hindi exhibits gender agreement and syncretism in inflections, which are not observed in English. We attempt to enrich the source side English corpus with linguistic factors in order to overcome the morphological disparity.

2.2 Hindi-to-English

The lack of accurate linguistic parsers makes it difficult to overcome the structural divergence using preordering rules. In order to preorder Hindi sentences, we build rules using shallow parsing information. The source side reordering helps to reduce the decoder's search complexity and learn better phrase tables. Some of the other challenges in generation of English output are: (1) generation of articles, which Hindi lacks, (2) heavy overloading of English prepositions, making it difficult to predict them.

3 Experimental Setup

We process the corpus through appropriate filters for normalization and then create a train-test split.

3.1 English Corpus Normalization

To begin with, the English data was tokenized using the Stanford tokenizer (Klein and Manning, 2003) and then true-cased using *truecase.perl* provided in MOSES toolkit.

3.2 Hindi Corpus Normalization

For Hindi data, we first normalize the corpus using NLP Indic Library (Kunchukuttan et. al., 2014)[1]. Normalization is followed by tokenization, wherein we make use of the *trivtokenizer.pl*[2] provided with WMT14 shared task. In Table 1, we highlight some of the post normalization statistics for en-hi parallel corpora.

[1] https://bitbucket.org/anoopk/indic_nlp_library

[2] http://ufallab.ms.mff.cuni.cz/~bojar/hindencorp/

	English	**Hindi**
Token	2,898,810	3,092,555
Types	95,551	118,285
Total Characters	18,513,761	17,961,357
Total sentences	289,832	289,832
Sentences (word count ≤ 10)	188,993	182,777
Sentences (word count > 10)	100,839	107,055

Table 1: en-hi corpora statistics, post normalisation.

3.3 Data Split

Before splitting the data, we first randomize the parallel corpus. We filter out English sentences longer than 50 words along with their parallel Hindi translations. After filtering, we select 5000 sentences which are 10 to 20 words long as the test data, while remaining 284,832 sentences are used for training.

4 English-to-Hindi (en-hi) translation

We use the MOSES toolkit (Koehn et. al., 2007a) for carrying out various experiments. Starting with Phrase Based Statistical Machine Translation (PB-SMT)(Koehn et. al., 2003) as baseline system we go ahead with pre-order PBSMT described in Section 4.1. After pre-ordering, we train a Factor Based SMT(Koehn, 2007b) model, where we add factors on the pre-ordered source corpus. In Factor Based SMT we have two variations- (a) using *Supertag* as factor described in Section 4.2 and (b) using *number, case* as factors described in Section 4.3.

4.1 Pre-ordering source corpus

Research has shown that pre-ordering source language to conform to target language word order significantly improves translation quality (Collins et. al, 2005). There are many variations of pre-ordering systems primarily emerging from either rule based or statistical methods. We use rule based pre-ordering approach developed by (Patel et. al., 2013), which uses the Stanford parser (Klein and Manning, 2003) for parsing English sentences. This approach is an extension to an earlier approach developed by (Ramanathan et. al., 2008). The existing source reordering system requires the input text to contain only surface form, however, we extended it to support surface form

along with its factors like POS, lemma etc.. An example of improvement in translation after pre-ordering is shown below:
Example: trying to replace bad ideas with good ideas .
Phr: replace बुरे विचारों को अच्छे विचारों के साथ
(*replace bure vichaaron ko acche vichaaron ke saath*)
Gloss: replace bad ideas good ideas with
Pre-order PBSMT: अच्छे विचारों से बुरे विचारों को बदलने की कोशिश कर रहे हैं
(*acche vichaaron se bure vichaaron ko badalane ki koshish kara rahe hain*)
Gloss: good ideas with bad ideas to replace trying

4.2 Supertag as Factor

The notion of *Supertag* was first proposed by Joshi and Srinivas (1994). Supertags are elementary trees of Lexicalized Tree Adjoining Grammar (LTAG) (Joshi and Schabes, 1991). They provide syntactic as well as dependency information at the word level by imposing complex constraints in a local context. These elementary trees are combined in some manner to form a parse tree, due to which, supertagging is also known as "An approach to almost parsing"(Bangalore and Joshi, 1999). A supertag can also be viewed as fragments of parse trees associated with each lexical item. Figure 1 shows an example of supertagged sentence "The purchase price includes taxes"described in (Hassan et. al., 2007). It clearly shows the sub-categorization information available in the verb *include*, which takes subject NP to its left and an object NP to its right.

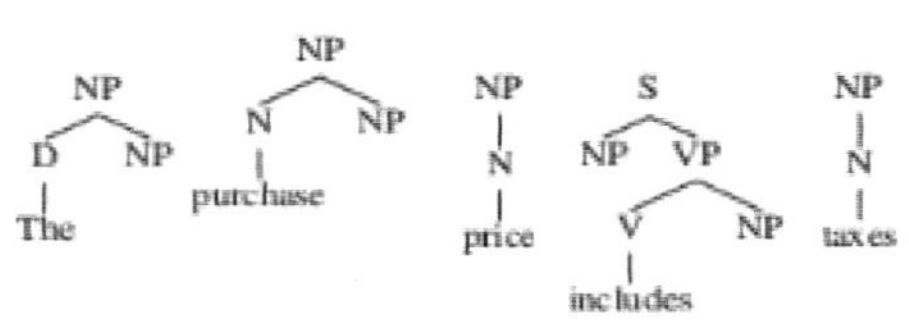

Figure 1: LTAG supertag sequence obtained using MICA Parser.

Use of supertags as factors has already been studied by Hassan (2007) in context of Arabic-English SMT. They use supertag language model along with supertagged English corpus. Ours is the first study in using supertag as factor for English-to-Hindi translation on a pre-ordered source corpus.

We use MICA Parser (Bangalore et. al., 2009) for obtaining supertags. After supertagging we run pre-ordering system preserving the supertags in it. For translation, we create mapping from *source-word|supertag* to *target-word*. An example of improvement in translation by using supertag as factor is shown below:
Example: trying to understand what your child is saying to you
Phr: आपका बच्चा आपसे क्या कह रहा है यह
(*aapkaa bacchaa aapse kya kaha rahaa hai yaha*)
Gloss: your child you what saying is this
Supertag Fact: आपका बच्चा आपसे क्या कह रहा है , उसे समझने की कोशिश करना
(*aapkaa bacchaa aapse kya kaha rahaa hai, use samajhane kii koshish karnaa*)
Gloss: your child to you what saying is , that understand try

4.3 Number, Case as Factor

In this section, we discuss how to generate correct noun inflections while translating from English to Hindi. There has been previous work done in order to solve the problem of *data sparsity* due to complex *verb morphology* for English to Hindi translation (Gandhe, 2011). Noun inflections in Hindi are affected by the number and case of the noun only. *Number* can be singular or plural, whereas, *case* can be direct or oblique. We use the factored SMT model to incorporate this linguistic information during training of the translation models. We attach *root-word*, *number* and *case* as factors to English nouns. On the other hand, to Hindi nouns we attach *root-word* and *suffix* as factors. We define the translation and generation step as follows:

- Translation step (T0): Translates English $root|number|case$ to Hindi $root|suffix$
- Generation step (G0): Generates Hindi surface word from Hindi $root|suffix$

An example of improvement in translation by using number and case as factors is shown below:
Example: Two sets of statistics
Phr: दो के आँकड़े
(*do ke aankade*)
Gloss: two of statistics
Num-Case Fact: आँकड़ों के दो सेट
(*aankadon ke do set*)
Gloss: statistics of two sets

4.3.1 Generating number and case factors

With the help of syntactic and morphological tools, we extract the number and case of the English nouns as follows:

- **Number factor:** We use *Stanford POS tagger*[3] to identify the English noun entities (Toutanova, 2003). The POS tagger itself differentiates between singular and plural nouns by using different tags.

- **Case factor:** It is difficult to find the direct/oblique case of the nouns as English nouns do not contain this information. Hence, to get the case information, we need to find out features of an English sentence that correspond to direct/oblique case of the parallel nouns in Hindi sentence. We use object of preposition, subject, direct object, tense as our features. These features are extracted using semantic relations provided by Stanford's typed dependencies (Marneffe, 2008).

4.4 Results

Listed below are different statistical systems trained using *Moses*:

- Phrase Based model (*Phr*)
- Phrase Based model with pre-ordered source corpus (*PhrReord*)
- Factor Based Model with factors on pre-ordered source corpus
  - Supertag as factor (*PhrReord+STag*)
  - Number, Case as factor (*PhrReord+NC*)

We evaluated translation systems with BLEU and TER as shown in Table 2. Evaluation on the development set shows that factor based models achieve competitive scores as compared to the baseline system, whereas, evaluation on the WMT14 test set shows significant improvement in the performance of factor based models.

	Development		WMT14	
Model	**BLEU**	**TER**	**BLEU**	**TER**
Phr	27.62	0.63	8.0	0.84
PhrReord	28.64	0.62	8.6	0.86
PhrReord+STag	27.05	0.64	9.8	0.83
PhrReord+NC	27.50	0.64	10.1	0.83

Table 2: English-to-Hindi automatic evaluation on development set and on WMT14 test set.

5 Hindi-to-English (hi-en) translation

As English follows SVO word order and Hindi follows SOV word order, simple distortion penalty in phrase-based models can not handle the reordering well. For the shared task, we follow the approach that pre-orders the source sentence to conform to target word order.

A substantial volume of work has been done in the field of source-side reordering for machine translation. Most of the experiments are based on applying reordering rules at the nodes of the parse tree of the source sentence. These reordering rules can be automatically learnt (Genzel, 2010). But, many source languages do not have a good robust parser. Hence, instead we can use shallow parsing techniques to get chunks of words and then reorder them. Reordering rules can be learned automatically from chunked data (Zhang, 2007).

Hindi does not have a functional constituency or dependency parser available, as of now. But, a shallow parser[4] is available for Hindi. Hence, we follow a chunk-based pre-ordering approach, wherein, we develop a set of rules to reorder the chunks in a source sentence. The following are the chunks tags generated by this shallow parser: Noun chunks (NP), Verb chunks (VGF, VGNF, VGNN), Adjectival chunks (JJP), Adverb chunks (RBP), Negatives (NEGP), Conjuncts (CCP), Chunk fragments (FRAGP), and miscellaneous entities (BLK) (Bharati, 2006).

5.1 Development of rules

After chunking an input sentence, we apply handcrafted reordering rules on these chunks. Following sections describe these rules. Note that we apply rules in the same order they are listed below.

5.1.1 Merging of chunks

After chunking, we merge the adjacent chunks, if they follow same order in target language.

1. Merge {JJP VGF} chunks (Consider this chunk as a single VGF chunk)
   e.g., वर्णित है (*varnit hai*), स्थित है (*sthit hai*)

[3]http://nlp.stanford.edu/software/tagger.shtml

[4]`http://ltrc.iiit.ac.in/showfile.php?filename=downloads/shallow_parser.php`

2. Merge adjacent verb chunks (Consider this chunk as a single verb chunk)
   e.g., गिरता है (*girataa hai*), लुभाता है (*lubhaataa hai*)

3. Merge NP and JJP chunks separated by commas and CCP (Consider this chunk as a single NP chunk)
   e.g., बड़ा और अहम (*badaa aur aham*)

5.1.2 Preposition chunk reordering

Next we find sequence of contiguous chunks separated by prepositions (Can end in verb chunks). We apply following reordering rules on these contiguous chunks:

1. Reorder multi-word preposition locally by reversing the order of words in that chunk
   e.g., के अलावा (*ke alaawaa*) → अलावा के, के सामने (*ke saamane*) → सामने के

2. Reorder contiguous preposition chunk by reversing the order of chunks (Consider this chunk as a single noun chunk)
   e.g., हिंदू धर्म में तीर्थ का बड़ा महत्व (*hinduu dharma me tirtha ka badaa mahatva*) → बड़ा महत्व का तीर्थ में हिंदू धर्म

5.1.3 Verb chunk reordering

We find contiguous verb chunks and apply following reordering rules:

1. Reorder chunks locally by reversing the order of the chunks
   e.g., वर्णित है (*varnit hai*) → है वर्णित

2. Verb chunk placement: We place the new verb chunk after first NP chunk. Same rule applies for all verb chunks in a sentence, i.e., we place each verb chunk after first NP chunk of the clause to which the verb belongs.

   Note that, even though placing verb chunk after first NP chunk may be wrong reordering. But we also use distortion window of 6 to 20 while using phrase-based model. Hence, further reordering of verb chunks can be somewhat handled by phrase-based model itself.

Thus, using chunker and reordering rules, we get a source-reordered Hindi sentence.

5.2 Results

We trained two different translation models:

- Phrase-based model without source reordering (*Phr*)
- Phrase-based model with chunk-based source reordering (*PhrReord*)

	Development		WMT14	
Model	**BLEU**	**TER**	**BLEU**	**TER**
Phr	27.53	0.59	13.5	0.87
PhrReord	25.06	0.62	13.7	0.90

Table 3: Hindi-to-English automatic evaluation on development set and on WMT14 test set.

Table 3 shows evaluation scores for development set and WMT14 test set. Even though we do not see significant improvement in automatic evaluation of *PhrReord*, but this model contributes in improving translation quality after ranking, as discussed in Section 5. In subjective evaluation we found many translation to be better in *PhrReord* model as shown in the following examples:

Example 1: सन 2004 से वे कई बार चोटग्रस्त रहे हैं।
(*sana 2004 se ve kaii baar chotagrasta rahe hain.*)
Phr: *since 2004 he is injured sometimes .*
PhrReord: *he was injured many times since 2004 .*

Example 2: ओबामा का राष्ट्रपति पद के चुनाव प्रचार हेतु बनाया आधिकारिक जालस्थल
(*obama ka rashtrapti pad ke chunaav prachaar hetu banaayaa aadhikarik jaalsthal*)
Phr: of Obama for election campaign
PhrReord: official website of Obama created for President campaign

6 Post processing

All experimental results reported in this paper are after post processing the translation output. In post processing, we remove some Out-of-Vocabulary (OOV) words as described in subsection 6.1, after which we transliterate the remaining OOV words.

6.1 Removing OOV

We noticed, there are many words in the training corpus which were not present in the phrase table, but, were present in the lexical tranlsation table. So we used the lexical table as a dictionary to lookup bilingual translations. Table 4 gives the statistics of number of OOV reduced.

Model	Before	After
Phrased Based	2313	1354
Phrase Based (pre-order)	2256	1334
Supertag as factor	4361	1611
Num-Case as factor	2628	1341

Table 4: Statistics showing number of OOV before and after post processing the English-to-Hindi translation output of Development set.

6.2 Transliteration of Untranslated Words

OOV words which were not present in the lexical translation table were then transliterated using a naive transliteration system. The transliteration step was applied on Hindi-to-English translation outputs only. After transliteration we noticed fractional improvements in BLEU score varying from 0.1 to 0.5.

6.3 Ranking of Ensemble MT Output

We propose a ranking framework to select the best translation output from an ensemble of multiple MT systems. In order to exploit the strength of each system, we augment the translation pipeline with a ranking module as a post processing step. For English-to-Hindi ranking we combine the output of both factor based models, whereas, for Hindi-to-English ranking we combine *phrase based* and *phrase based with pre-ordering* outputs.

For most of the systems, the output translations are adequate but not fluent enough. So, based on their fluency scores, we decided to rank the candidate translations. Fluency is well quantified by *LM log probability score* and *Perplexity*. For a given translation , we compute these scores by querying the 5-gram language model built using SRILM. Table 5 shows more than 4% relative improvement in BLEU score for en-hi as well as hi-en translation system after applying ranking module.

Model	BLEU	METEOR	TER
Phr(en-hi)	27.62	0.41	0.63
After Ranking (en-hi)	28.82	0.42	0.63
Phr(hi-en)	27.53	0.27	0.59
After Ranking (hi-en)	28.69	0.27	0.59

Table 5: Comparision of ranking score with baseline

7 Primary Systems in WMT14

For English-to-Hindi, we submitted the ranked output of factored models trained on pre-ordered source corpus. For Hindi-to-English, we submitted the ranked output of phrase based and pre-ordered phrase based models. Table 6 shows evaluation scores of these systems on WMT14 test set.

Lang. pair	BLEU	TER
en-hi	10.4	0.83
hi-en	14.5	0.89

Table 6: WMT14 evaluation for *en-hi* and *hi-en*.

8 Conclusion

We conclude that the difficulties in English-Hindi MT can be tackled by the use of factor based SMT and various pre-processing and post processing techniques. Following are our primary contributions towards English-Hindi machine translation:

- Use of supertag factors for better translation of structurally complex sentences
- Use of number-case factors for accurately generating noun inflections in Hindi
- Use of shallow parsing for pre-ordering Hindi source corpus

We also observed that simple ranking strategy benefits in getting the best translation from an ensemble of translation systems.

References

Avramidis, Eleftherios, and Philipp Koehn. 2008. *Enriching Morphologically Poor Languages for Statistical Machine Translation.* ACL.

Banerjee, Satanjeev, and Alon Lavie. 2005. *METEOR: An automatic metric for MT evaluation with improved correlation with human judgments.* Proceedings of the ACL Workshop on Intrinsic and Extrinsic Evaluation Measures for Machine Translation and/or Summarization.

Srinivas Bangalore and Aravind K. Joshi. 1999. *Supertagging: An approach to almost parsing.* Computational linguistics.

Srinivas Bangalore, Pierre Boulllier, Alexis Nasr, Owen Rambow, and BenoÃőt Sagot. 2009. *MICA: a probabilistic dependency parser based on tree insertion grammars application note.* Proceedings of

Human Language Technologies The 2009 Annual Conference of the North American Chapter of the Association for Computational Linguistics, Association for Computational Linguistics.

A. Bharati, R. Sangal, D. M. Sharma and L. Bai. 2006. *AnnCorra: Annotating Corpora Guidelines for POS and Chunk Annotation for Indian Languages.* Technical Report (TR-LTRC-31), LTRC, IIIT-Hyderabad.

Dave, Shachi and Parikh, Jignashu and Bhattacharyya, Pushpak. 2001. *Interlingua-based English–Hindi Machine Translation and Language Divergence* Journal Machine Translation

Gandhe, Ankur, Rashmi Gangadharaiah, Karthik Visweswariah, and Ananthakrishnan Ramanathan. 2011. *Handling verb phrase morphology in highly inflected Indian languages for Machine Translation.* IJCNLP.

Genzel, Dmitriy. 2010. *Automatically learning source-side reordering rules for large scale machine translation* Proceedings of the 23rd international conference on computational linguistics. Association for Computational Linguistics

Hany Hassan, Khalil Sima'an, and Andy Way 2007. *Supertagged phrase-based statistical machine translation.* Proceedings of the Association for Computational Linguistics Association for Computational Linguistics.

Aravind K. Joshi and Yves Schabes 1991. *Tree-adjoining grammars and lexicalized grammars.* Technical Report No. MS-CIS-91-22

Dan Klein and Christopher D. Manning. 2003. *Accurate Unlexicalized Parsing.* Proceedings of the 41st Meeting of the Association for Computational Linguistics. Association for Computational Linguistics.

Koehn, Philipp, Franz Josef Och, and Daniel Marcu. 2003. *Statistical phrase-based translation.* Proceedings of the 2003 Conference of the North American Chapter of the Association for Computational Linguistics on Human Language Technology-Volume 1. Association for Computational Linguistics

Philipp Koehn, Hieu Hoang, Alexandra Birch, Chris Callison-Burch, Marcello Federico, Nicola Bertoldi, Brooke Cowan, Wade Shen, Christine Moran, Richard Zens, Chris Dyer, OndÅŹej Bojar, Alexandra Constantin and Evan Herbst. 2007. *Moses: open source toolkit for statistical machine translation.* Proceedings of the Second Workshop on Hybrid Approaches to Translation. Association for Computational Linguistics.

Philipp Koehn and Hieu Hoang 2007. *Factored Translation Models* Conference on Empirical Methods in Natural Language Processing.

Anoop Kunchukuttan, Abhijit Mishra, Rajen Chatterjee,Ritesh Shah, and Pushpak Bhattacharyya. 2014. *Sata-Anuvadak: Tackling Multiway Translation of Indian Languages.* Proceedings of the Ninth International Conference on Language Resources and Evaluation Conference

De Marneffe, Marie-Catherine, and Christopher D. Manning. 2008. *Stanford typed dependencies manual.* URL http://nlp. stanford. edu/software/dependencies manual. pdf (2008).

Papineni, Kishore, Salim Roukos, Todd Ward, and Wei-Jing Zhu. 2002. *BLEU: a method for automatic evaluation of machine translation.* Proceedings of the 40th annual meeting on association for computational linguistics. Association for Computational Linguistics.

Raj Nath Patel, Rohit Gupta, Prakash B. Pimpale and Sasikumar M. 2013. *Reordering rules for English-Hindi SMT.* Proceedings of the Second Workshop on Hybrid Approaches to Translation. Association for Computational Linguistics.

Ananthakrishnan Ramanathan, Pushpak Bhattacharyya, Jayprasad Hegde, Ritesh M. Shah, and M. Sasikumar. 2008. *Simple syntactic and morphological processing can help English-Hindi statistical machine translation.* In International Joint Conference on NLP.

Sinha, RMK and Sivaraman, K and Agrawal, A and Jain, R and Srivastava, R and Jain, A. 1995. *ANGLABHARTI: a multilingual machine aided translation project on translation from English to Indian languages* IEEE International Conference on Systems, Man and Cybernetics

Toutanova, Kristina, Dan Klein, Christopher D. Manning, and Yoram Singer 2003. *Feature-rich part-of-speech tagging with a cyclic dependency network.* Proceedings of the 2003 Conference of the North American Chapter of the Association for Computational Linguistics on Human Language Technology-Volume 1. Association for Computational Linguistics.

Zhang, Yuqi, Richard Zens, and Hermann Ney. 2007. *Chunk-level reordering of source language sentences with automatically learned rules for statistical machine translation* Proceedings of the NAACL-HLT 2007/AMTA Workshop on Syntax and Structure in Statistical Translation. Association for Computational Linguistics

Collins, Michael, Philipp Koehn, and Ivona Kučerova 2005 *Clause restructuring for statistical machine translation.* Proceedings of the 43rd annual meeting on association for computational linguistics. Association for Computational Linguistics

Edinburgh's Phrase-based Machine Translation Systems for WMT-14

Nadir Durrani **Barry Haddow** **Philipp Koehn**
School of Informatics
University of Edinburgh
{dnadir,bhaddow,pkoehn}@inf.ed.ac.uk

Kenneth Heafield
Computer Science Department
Stanford University
heafield@cs.stanford.edu

Abstract

This paper describes the University of Edinburgh's (UEDIN) phrase-based submissions to the translation and medical translation shared tasks of the 2014 Workshop on Statistical Machine Translation (WMT). We participated in all language pairs. We have improved upon our 2013 system by i) using generalized representations, specifically automatic word clusters for translations out of English, ii) using unsupervised character-based models to translate unknown words in Russian-English and Hindi-English pairs, iii) synthesizing Hindi data from closely-related Urdu data, and iv) building huge language on the common crawl corpus.

1 Translation Task

Our baseline systems are based on the setup described in (Durrani et al., 2013b) that we used for the Eighth Workshop on Statistical Machine Translation (Bojar et al., 2013). The notable features of these systems are described in the following section. The experiments that we carried out for this year's translation task are described in the following sections.

1.1 Baseline

We trained our systems with the following settings: a maximum sentence length of 80, grow-diag-final-and symmetrization of GIZA++ alignments, an interpolated Kneser-Ney smoothed 5-gram language model with KenLM (Heafield, 2011) used at runtime, hierarchical lexicalized reordering (Galley and Manning, 2008), a lexically-driven 5-gram operation sequence model (OSM) (Durrani et al., 2013a) with 4 count-based supportive features, sparse domain indicator, phrase length, and count bin features (Blunsom and Osborne, 2008; Chiang et al., 2009), a distortion limit of 6, maximum phrase-length of 5, 100-best translation options, Minimum Bayes Risk decoding (Kumar and Byrne, 2004), Cube Pruning (Huang and Chiang, 2007), with a stack-size of 1000 during tuning and 5000 during test and the no-reordering-over-punctuation heuristic (Koehn and Haddow, 2009). We used POS and morphological tags as additional factors in phrase translation models (Koehn and Hoang, 2007) for German-English language pairs. We also trained target sequence models on the in-domain subset of the parallel corpus using Kneser-Ney smoothed 7-gram models. We used syntactic-preordering (Collins et al., 2005) and compound splitting (Koehn and Knight, 2003) for German-to-English systems. We used trivia tokenizer for tokenizing Hindi.

The systems were tuned on a very large tuning set consisting of the test sets from 2008-2012, with a total of 13,071 sentences. We used news-test 2013 for the dev experiments. For Russian-English pairs news-test 2012 was used for tuning and for Hindi-English pairs, we divided the news-dev 2014 into two halves, used the first half for tuning and second for dev experiments.

1.2 Using Generalized Word Representations

We explored the use of automatic word clusters in phrase-based models (Durrani et al., 2014a). We computed the clusters with GIZA++'s `mkcls` (Och, 1999) on the source and target side of the parallel training corpus. Clusters are word classes that are optimized to reduce n-gram perplexity. By generating a cluster identifier for each output word, we are able to add an n-gram model

Proceedings of the Ninth Workshop on Statistical Machine Translation, pages 97–104,
Baltimore, Maryland USA, June 26–27, 2014.

over these identifiers as an additional scoring function. The inclusion of such an additional factor is trivial given the factored model implementation (Koehn and Hoang, 2007) of Moses (Koehn et al., 2007). The n-gram model is trained in the similar way as the regular language model. We trained domain-specific language models separately and then linearly interpolated them using SRILM with weights optimized on the tuning set (Schwenk and Koehn, 2008).

We also trained OSM models over cluster-ids (**?**). The lexically driven OSM model falls back to very small context sizes of two to three operations due to data sparsity. Learning operation sequences over cluster-ids enables us to learn richer translation and reordering patterns that can generalize better in sparse data conditions. Table 1 shows gains from adding target LM and OSM models over cluster-ids. Using word clusters was found more useful translating from English-to-*.

	from English			into English		
Lang	$\mathbf{B_0}$	**+Cid**	Δ	$\mathbf{B_0}$	**+Cid**	Δ
de	20.60	20.85	+0.25	27.44	27.34	-0.10
cs	18.84	19.39	+0.55	26.42	26.42	±0.00
fr	30.73	30.82	+0.09	31.64	31.76	+0.12
ru	18.78	19.67	+0.89	24.45	24.63	+0.18
hi	10.39	10.52	+0.13	15.48	15.26	-0.22

Table 1: Using Word Clusters in Phrase-based and OSM models – $\mathbf{B_0}$ = System without Clusters, **+Cid** = with Cluster

We also trained OSM models over POS and morph tags. For the English-to-German system we added an OSM model over [pos, morph] (source:pos, target:morph) and for the German-to-English system we added an OSM model over [morph,pos] (source:morph, target:pos), a configuration that was found to work best in our previous experiments (Birch et al., 2013). Table 2 shows gains from additionally using OSM models over POS/morph tags.

Lang	$\mathbf{B_0}$	$+\mathbf{OSM_{p,m}}$	Δ
en-de	20.44	20.60	+0.16
de-en	27.24	27.44	+0.20

Table 2: Using POS and Morph Tags in OSM models – $\mathbf{B_0}$ = Baseline, $+\mathbf{OSM_{p,m}}$ = POS/Morph-based OSM

1.3 Unsupervised Transliteration Model

Last year, our Russian-English systems performed badly on the human evaluation. In comparison other participants that used transliteration did well. We could not train a transliteration system due to unavailability of a transliteration training data. This year we used an EM-based method to induce unsupervised transliteration models (Durrani et al., 2014b). We extracted transliteration pairs automatically from the word-aligned parallel data and used it to learn a transliteration system. We then built transliteration phrase-tables for translating OOV words and used the post-decoding method (Method 2 as described in the paper) to translate these.

Pair	Training	OOV	$\mathbf{B_0}$	$+\mathbf{T_r}$	Δ
ru-en	232K	1356	24.63	25.06	+0.41
en-ru	232K	681	19.67	19.91	+0.24
hi-en	38K	503	14.67	15.48	+0.81
en-hi	38K	394	11.76	12.83	+1.07

Table 3: Using Unsupervised Transliteration Model – Training = Extracted Transliteration Corpus (types), OOV = Out-of-vocabulary words (tokens) $\mathbf{B_0}$ = System without Transliteration, $+\mathbf{T_r}$ = Transliterating OOVs

Table 3 shows the number (types) of transliteration pairs extracted using unsupervised mining, number of OOV words (tokens) in each pair and the gains achieved by transliterating unknown words.

1.4 Synthesizing Hindi Data from Urdu

Hindi and Urdu are closely related language pairs that share grammatical structure and have a large overlap in vocabulary. This provides a strong motivation to transform any Urdu-English parallel data into Hindi-English by translating the Urdu part into Hindi. We made use of the Urdu-English segment of the Indic multi-parallel corpus (Post et al., 2012) which contains roughly 87K sentence pairs. The Hindi-English segment of this corpus is a subset of parallel data made available for the translation task but is completely disjoint from the Urdu-English segment.

We initially trained a Urdu-to-Hindi SMT system using a very tiny EMILLE[1] corpus (Baker

[1]EMILLE corpus contains roughly 12000 sentences of Hindi and Urdu comparable data. From these we were able to sentence align 7000 sentences to build an Urdu-to-Hindi system.

et al., 2002). But we found this system to be useless for translating the Urdu part of Indic data due to domain mismatch and huge number of OOV words (approximately 310K tokens). To reduce sparsity we synthesized additional phrase-tables using interpolation and transliteration.

Interpolation: We trained two phrase translation tables $p(\bar{u}_i|\bar{e}_i)$ and $p(\bar{e}_i|\bar{h}_i)$, from Urdu-English (Indic corpus) and Hindi-English (HindEnCorp (Bojar et al., 2014)) bilingual corpora. Given the phrase-table for Urdu-English $p(\bar{u}_i|\bar{e}_i)$ and the phrase-table for English-Hindi $p(\bar{e}_i|\bar{h}_i)$, we estimated a Urdu-Hindi phrase-table $p(\bar{u}_i|\bar{h}_i)$ using the well-known convolution model (Utiyama and Isahara, 2007; Wu and Wang, 2007):

$$p(\bar{u}_i|\bar{h}_i) = \sum_{\bar{e}_i} p(\bar{u}_i|\bar{e}_i)p(\bar{e}_i|\bar{h}_i)$$

The number of entries in the baseline Urdu-to-Hindi phrase-table were approximately 254K. Using interpolation we were able to build a phrase-table containing roughly 10M phrases. This reduced the number of OOV tokens from 310K to approximately 50K.

Transliteration: Urdu and Hindi are written in different scripts (Arabic and Devanagri respectively). We added a transliteration component to our Urdu-to-Hindi system. An unsupervised transliteration model is learned from the word-alignments of Urdu-Hindi parallel data. We were able to extract around 2800 transliteration pairs. To learn a richer transliteration model, we additionally fed the interpolated phrase-table, as described above, to the transliteration miner. We were able to mine additional 21000 transliteration pairs and built a Urdu-Hindi character-based model from it. The transliteration module can be used to translate the 50K OOV words but previous research (Durrani et al., 2010; Nakov and Tiedemann, 2012) has shown that transliteration is useful for more than just translating OOV words when translating closely related language pairs. To fully capitalize on the large overlap in Hindi–Urdu vocabulary, we transliterated each word in the Urdu test-data into Hindi and produced a phrase-table with 100-best transliterations. The two synthesized (triangulated and transliterated) phrase-tables are then used along with the baseline Urdu-to-Hindi phrase-table in a log-linear model. Detailed results on Urdu-to-Hindi baseline and improvements obtained from using transliteration and triangulated phrase-tables are presented in Durrani and Koehn (2014). Using our best Urdu-to-Hindi system, we translated the Urdu part of the multi-indic corpus to form Hindi-English parallel data. Table 4 shows results from using the synthesized Hindi-English corpus in isolation (**Syn**) and on top of the baseline system (**B**$_0$ + **Syn**).

Pair	$\mathbf{B_0}$	**Syn**	Δ	$\mathbf{B_0} + \mathbf{Syn}$	Δ
hi-en	14.28	10.49	-3.79	14.72	+0.44
en-hi	10.59	9.01	-1.58	11.76	+1.17

Table 4: Evaluating Synthesized (Syn) Hindi-English Parallel Data, $\mathbf{B_0}$ = System without Synthesized Data

1.5 Huge Language Models

Our unconstrained submissions use an additional language model trained on web pages from the 2012, 2013, and winter 2013 CommonCrawl.[2] The additional language model is the only difference between the constrained and unconstrained submissions; we did not use additional parallel data. These language models were trained on text provided by the CommonCrawl foundation, which they converted to UTF-8 after stripping HTML. Languages were detected using the Compact Language Detection 2[3] and, except for Hindi where we lack tools, sentences were split with the Europarl sentence splitter (Koehn, 2005). All text was then deduplicated, minimizing the impact of boilerplate, such as social media sharing buttons. We then tokenized and truecased the text as usual. Statistics are shown in Table 5. A full description of the pipeline, including a public data release, appears in Buck et al. (2014).

Lang	Lines (B)	Tokens (B)	Bytes
en	59.13	975.63	5.14 TiB
de	3.87	51.93	317.46 GiB
fr	3.04	49.31	273.96 GiB
ru	1.79	21.41	220.62 GiB
cs	0.47	5.79	34.67 GiB
hi	0.01	0.28	3.39 GiB

Table 5: Size of huge language model training data

We built unpruned modified Kneser-Ney language models using lmplz (Heafield et al., 2013).

[2]http://commoncrawl.org
[3]https://code.google.com/p/cld2/

Pair	B_0		+L	
newstest	2013	2014	2013	2014
en-de	20.85	20.10	–	20.61 +0.51
en-cs	19.39	21.00	20.03 +0.64	21.60 +0.60
en-ru	19.90	28.70	20.80 +0.90	29.90 +1.20
en-hi	11.43	11.10	12.83 +1.40	12.50 +1.40
hi-en	15.48	13.90	–	14.80 +0.90

Table 6: Gains obtained by using huge language models – $\mathbf{B_0}$ = Baseline, $+\mathbf{L}$ = Adding Huge LM

While the Hindi and Czech models are small enough to run directly, models for other languages are quite large.We therefore created a filter that operates directly on files in KenLM trie binary format, preserving only n-grams whose words all appear in the target side vocabulary of at least one source sentence. For example, an English language model trained on just the 2012 and 2013 crawls takes 3.5 TB without any quantization. After filtering to the Hindi-English tuning set, the model fit in 908 GB, again without quantization. We were then able to tune the system on a machine with 1 TB RAM. Results are shown in Table 6; we did not submit to English-French because the system takes too long to tune.

1.6 Miscellaneous

Hindi-English: 1) A large number of Hindi sentences in the Hindi-English parallel corpus were ending with a full-stop ".", although the end-of-the-sentence marker in Hindi is "Danda" (|). Replacing full-stops with Danda gave improvement of +0.20 for hi-en and +0.40 in en-hi. 2) Using Wiki subtitles did not give any improvement in BLEU and were in fact harmful for the en-hi direction.

Russian-English: We tried to improve word-alignments by integrating a transliteration submodel into GIZA++ word aligner. The probability of a word pair is calculated as an interpolation of the transliteration probability and translation probability stored in the t-table of the different alignment models used by the GIZA++ aligner. This interpolation is done for all iterations of all alignment models (See Sajjad et al. (2013) for details). Due to shortage of time we could only run it for Russian-to-English. The improved alignments gave a gain of +0.21 on news-test 2013 and +0.40 on news-test 2014.

Pair	GIZA++	Fast Align	Δ
de-en	24.02	23.89	–.13
fr-en	30.78	30.66	–.12
es-en	34.07	34.24	+.17
cs-en	22.63	22.44	–.19
ru-en	31.68	32.03	+.35
en-de	18.04	17.88	–.16
en-fr	28.96	28.83	–.13
en-es	34.15	34.32	+.17
en-cs	15.70	16.02	+.32
avg			+.03

Table 7: Comparison of fast word alignment method (Dyer et al., 2013) against GIZA++ (WMT 2013 data condition, test on newstest2012). The method was not used in the official submission.

Pair	Baseline MSD	Hier. MSD	Hier. MSLR
de-en	27.04	27.10 +.06	27.17 +.13
fr-en	31.63	-	31.65 +.02
es-en	31.20	31.14 –.06	31.25 +.05
cs-en	26.11	26.32 +.21	26.26 +.15
ru-en	24.09	24.01 –.08	24.19 +.11
en-de	20.43	20.34 –.09	20.32 -.11
en-fr	30.54	-	30.52 –.02
en-es	30.36	30.44 +.08	30.51 +.15
en-cs	18.53	18.59 +.06	18.66 +.13
en-ru	18.37	18.47 +.10	18.19 –.18
avg		+ .035	+.045

Table 8: Hierarchical lexicalized reordering model (Galley and Manning, 2008).

Fast align: In preliminary experiments, we compared the fast word alignment method by Dyer et al. (2013) against our traditional use of GIZA++. Results are quite mixed (Table 7), ranging from a gain of +.35 for Russian-English to a loss of –.19 for Czech-English. We stayed with GIZA++ for all of our other experiments.

Hierarchical lexicalized reordering model: We explored the use of the hierarchical lexicalized reordering model (Galley and Manning, 2008) in two variants: using the same orientations as our traditional model (*monotone, discontinuous, swap*), and one that distinguishes the *discontinuous* orientations to the *left* and *right*. Table 8 shows slight improvements with these models, so we used them in our baseline.

Threshold filtering of phrase table: We experimented with discarding some phrase table entry due to their low probability. We found that phrase translations with the phrase translation probability

$\phi(f|e)<10^{-4}$ can be safely discarded with almost no change in translations. However, discarding phrase translations with the inverse phrase translation probability $\phi(e|f)<10^{-4}$ is more risky, especially with morphologically rich target languages, so we kept those.

1.7 Summary

Table 9 shows cumulative gains obtained from using word classes, transliteration and big language models[4] over the baseline system. Our German-English constrained systems were used for EU-Bridge system combination, a collaborative effort to improve the state-of-the-art in machine translation (See Freitag et al. (2014) for details).

	from English			into English		
Lang	B_0	B_1	Δ	B_0	B_1	Δ
de	20.44	20.85	+0.41	27.24	27.44	+0.20
cs	18.84	20.03	+1.19	26.42	26.42	±0.00
fr	30.73	30.82	+0.09	31.64	31.76	+0.12
ru	18.78	20.81	+2.03	24.45	25.21	+0.76
hi	9.27	12.83	+3.56	14.08	15.48	+1.40

Table 9: Cumulative gains obtained for each language – $\mathbf{B_0}$ = Baseline, $\mathbf{B_1}$ = Best System

2 Medical Translation Task

For the medical translation task, the organisers supplied several medical domain corpora (detailed on the task website), as well some out-of-domain patent data, and also all the data available for the constrained track of the news translation task was permitted. In general, we attempted to use all of this data, except for the LDC Gigaword language model data (for reasons of time) and we divided the data into "in-domain" and "out-of-domain" corpora. The data sets are summarised in Tables 10 and 11.

In order to create systems for the medical translation tasks, we used phrase-based Moses with exactly the same settings as for the news translation task, including the OSM (Durrani et al., 2011), and compound splitting Koehn and Knight (2003) for German source. We did not use word clusters (Section 1.2), as they did not give good results on this task, but we have yet to find a reason for this. For language model training, we decided not to build separate models on each corpus as there was

[4]Cumulative gains do not include gains obtain from big language models for hi-en and en-de.

Data Set	cs-en	de-en	fr-en
coppa-in	n	n	y
PatTR-in-claims	n	y	y
PatTR-in-abstract	n	y	y
PatTR-in-titles	n	y	y
UMLS	y	y	y
MuchMore	n	y	n
EMEA	y	y	y
WikiTitles	y	y	y
PatTR-out	n	y	y
coppa-out	n	n	y
MultiUN	n	n	y
czeng	y	n	n
europarl	y	y	y
news-comm	y	y	y
commoncrawl	y	y	y
FrEnGiga	n	n	y

Table 10: Parallel data sets used in the medical translation task. The sets above the line were classified as "in-domain" and those below as "out-of-domain".

Data Set	cs	de	en	fr
PIL	n	n	y	n
DrugBank	n	n	y	n
WikiArticles	y	y	y	y
PatTR-in-description	n	y	y	y
GENIA	n	n	y	n
FMA	n	n	y	n
AACT	n	n	y	n
PatTR-out-description	n	y	y	y

Table 11: Additional monolingual data used in the medical translation task. Those above the line were classified as "in-domain" and the one below as "out-of-domain". We also used the target sides of all the parallel corpora for language modelling.

a large variation in corpus sizes. Instead we concatenated the in-domain target sides with the in-domain extra monolingual data to create training data for an in-domain language model, and similarly for the out-of-domain data. The two language models were interpolated using SRILM, minimising perplexity on the Khresmoi summary development data.

During system development, we only had 500 sentences of development data (SUMMARY-DEV) from the Khresmoi project, so we decided to select further development and devtest data from the EMEA corpus, reasoning that it was fairly close in domain to SUMMARY-DEV. We selected a tuning set (5000 sentence pairs, which were added to SUMMARY-DEV) and a devtest set (3000 sentence pairs) from EMEA after first de-duplicating it, and ignoring sentence pairs which were too short, or contained too many capital letters or numbers. The EMEA contains many duplicated sentences, and we removed all sentence pairs where either side was a duplicate, reducing the size of the corpus to about 25% of the original. We also removed EMEA from Czeng, since otherwise it would overlap with our selected development sets.

We also experimented with modified Moore-Lewis (Moore and Lewis, 2010; Axelrod et al., 2011) data selection, using the EMEA corpus as the in-domain corpus (for the language model required in MML) and selecting from all the out-of-domain data.

When running on the final test set (SUMMARY-TEST) we found that it was better to tune just on SUMMARY-DEV, even though it was much smaller than the EMEA dev set we had selected. All but two (cs-en, de-en) of our submitted systems used the MML selection, because it worked better on our EMEA devtest set. However, as can be seen from Table 12, systems built with all the data generally perform better. We concluded that EMEA was not a good representative of the Khresmoi data, perhaps because of domain differences, or perhaps just because of the alignment noise that appears (from informal inspection) to be present in EMEA.

	from English			**into English**		
	in	in+20	in+out	in	in+20	in+out
de	18.59	*20.88*	–	36.17	–	38.57
cs	18.78	*23.45*	23.77	30.12	–	36.32
fr	35.24	*40.74*	41.04	45.15	*46.44*	46.58

Table 12: Results (cased BLEU) on the khresmoi summary test set. The "in" systems include all in-domain data, the "in+20" systems also include 20% of the out-of-domain data and the "out" systems include all data. The submitted systems are shown in italics, except for de-en and cs-en where we submitted a "in+out" systems. For de-en, this was tuned on SUMMARY-DEV plus the EMEA dev set and scored 37.31, whilst for cs-en we included LDC Giga in the LM, and scored 36.65.

For translating the Khresmoi queries, we used the same systems as for the summaries, except that generally we did not retune on the SUMMARY-DEV data. We added a post-processing script to strip out extraneous stop words, which improved BLEU, but we would not expect it to matter in a real CLIR system as it would do its own stop-word removal.

Acknowledgments

The research leading to these results has received funding from the European Union Seventh Framework Programme (FP7/2007-2013) under grant agreements n ° 287658 (EU-BRIDGE), n ° 287688 (MateCat) and n ° 288769 (ACCEPT). Huge language model experiments made use of the Stampede supercomputer provided by the Texas Advanced Computing Center (TACC) at The University of Texas at Austin under NSF XSEDE allocation TG-CCR140009. We also acknowledge the support of the Defense Advanced Research Projects Agency (DARPA) Broad Operational Language Translation (BOLT) program through IBM. This publication only reflects the authors' views.

References

Axelrod, A., He, X., and Gao, J. (2011). Domain adaptation via pseudo in-domain data selection. In *Proceedings of the 2011 Conference on Empirical Methods in Natural Language Processing*, pages 355–362, Edinburgh, Scotland, UK. Association for Computational Linguistics.

Baker, P., Hardie, A., McEnery, T., Cunningham, H., and Gaizauskas, R. J. (2002). EMILLE, a 67-million word corpus of indic languages: Data collection, mark-up and harmonisation. In *LREC*.

Birch, A., Durrani, N., and Koehn, P. (2013). Edinburgh SLT and MT system description for the IWSLT 2013 evaluation. In *Proceedings of the 10th International Workshop on Spoken Language Translation*, pages 40–48, Heidelberg, Germany.

Blunsom, P. and Osborne, M. (2008). Probabilistic inference for machine translation. In *Proceedings of the 2008 Conference on Empirical Methods in Natural Language Processing*, pages 215–223, Honolulu, Hawaii. Association for Computational Linguistics.

Bojar, O., Buck, C., Callison-Burch, C., Federmann, C., Haddow, B., Koehn, P., Monz, C., Post, M., Soricut, R., and Specia, L. (2013). Findings of the 2013 workshop on statistical machine translation. In *Eighth Workshop on Statistical Machine Translation*, WMT-2013, pages 1–44, Sofia, Bulgaria.

Bojar, O., Diatka, V., Rychlý, P., Straňák, P., Tamchyna, A., and Zeman, D. (2014). Hindi-

English and Hindi-only Corpus for Machine Translation. In *Proceedings of the Ninth International Language Resources and Evaluation Conference (LREC'14)*, Reykjavik, Iceland. ELRA, European Language Resources Association. in prep.

Buck, C., Heafield, K., and van Ooyen, B. (2014). N-gram counts and language models from the common crawl. In *Proceedings of the Language Resources and Evaluation Conference*, Reykjavík, Iceland.

Chiang, D., Knight, K., and Wang, W. (2009). 11,001 New Features for Statistical Machine Translation. In *Proceedings of Human Language Technologies: The 2009 Annual Conference of the North American Chapter of the Association for Computational Linguistics*, pages 218–226, Boulder, Colorado. Association for Computational Linguistics.

Collins, M., Koehn, P., and Kucerova, I. (2005). Clause restructuring for statistical machine translation. In *Proceedings of the 43rd Annual Meeting of the Association for Computational Linguistics (ACL'05)*, pages 531–540, Ann Arbor, Michigan. Association for Computational Linguistics.

Durrani, N., Fraser, A., Schmid, H., Hoang, H., and Koehn, P. (2013a). Can markov models over minimal translation units help phrase-based SMT? In *Proceedings of the 51st Annual Meeting of the Association for Computational Linguistics*, Sofia, Bulgaria. Association for Computational Linguistics.

Durrani, N., Haddow, B., Heafield, K., and Koehn, P. (2013b). Edinburgh's machine translation systems for european language pairs. In *Proceedings of the Eighth Workshop on Statistical Machine Translation*, Sofia, Bulgaria. Association for Computational Linguistics.

Durrani, N. and Koehn, P. (2014). Improving machine translation via triangulation and transliteration. In *Proceedings of the 17th Annual Conference of the European Association for Machine Translation (EAMT)*, Dubrovnik, Croatia.

Durrani, N., Koehn, P., Schmid, H., and Fraser, A. (2014a). Investigating the usefulness of generalized word representations in SMT. In *Proceedings of the 25th Annual Conference on Computational Linguistics (COLING)*, Dublin, Ireland. To Appear.

Durrani, N., Sajjad, H., Fraser, A., and Schmid, H. (2010). Hindi-to-urdu machine translation through transliteration. In *Proceedings of the 48th Annual Meeting of the Association for Computational Linguistics*, pages 465–474, Uppsala, Sweden. Association for Computational Linguistics.

Durrani, N., Sajjad, H., Hoang, H., and Koehn, P. (2014b). Integrating an unsupervised transliteration model into statistical machine translation. In *Proceedings of the 15th Conference of the European Chapter of the ACL (EACL 2014)*, Gothenburg, Sweden. Association for Computational Linguistics.

Durrani, N., Schmid, H., and Fraser, A. (2011). A joint sequence translation model with integrated reordering. In *Proceedings of the 49th Annual Meeting of the Association for Computational Linguistics: Human Language Technologies*, pages 1045–1054, Portland, Oregon, USA.

Dyer, C., Chahuneau, V., and Smith, N. A. (2013). A simple, fast, and effective reparameterization of ibm model 2. In *Proceedings of the 2013 Conference of the North American Chapter of the Association for Computational Linguistics: Human Language Technologies*, pages 644–648, Atlanta, Georgia. Association for Computational Linguistics.

Freitag, M., Peitz, S., Wuebker, J., Ney, H., Huck, M., Sennrich, R., Durrani, N., Nadejde, M., Williams, P., Koehn, P., Herrmann, T., Cho, E., and Waibel, A. (2014). EU-BRIDGE MT: combined machine translation. In *Proceedings of the ACL 2014 Ninth Workshop on Statistical Machine Translation*, Baltimore, MD, USA.

Galley, M. and Manning, C. D. (2008). A simple and effective hierarchical phrase reordering model. In *Proceedings of the 2008 Conference on Empirical Methods in Natural Language Processing*, pages 848–856, Honolulu, Hawaii.

Heafield, K. (2011). Kenlm: Faster and smaller language model queries. In *Proceedings of the Sixth Workshop on Statistical Machine Translation*, pages 187–197, Edinburgh, Scotland, United Kingdom.

Heafield, K., Pouzyrevsky, I., Clark, J. H., and Koehn, P. (2013). Scalable modified Kneser-Ney language model estimation. In *Proceedings of the 51st Annual Meeting of the Association for Computational Linguistics*, Sofia, Bulgaria.

Huang, L. and Chiang, D. (2007). Forest rescoring: Faster decoding with integrated language models. In *Proceedings of the 45th Annual Meeting of the Association of Computational Linguistics*, pages 144–151, Prague, Czech Republic. Association for Computational Linguistics.

Koehn, P. (2005). Europarl: A parallel corpus for statistical machine translation. In *Proceedings of MT Summit*.

Koehn, P. and Haddow, B. (2009). Edinburgh's Submission to all Tracks of the WMT 2009 Shared Task with Reordering and Speed Improvements to Moses. In *Proceedings of the Fourth Workshop on Statistical Machine Translation*, pages 160–164, Athens, Greece. Association for Computational Linguistics.

Koehn, P. and Hoang, H. (2007). Factored translation models. In *Proceedings of the 2007 Joint Conference on Empirical Methods in Natural Language Processing and Computational Natural Language Learning (EMNLP-CoNLL)*, pages 868–876, Prague, Czech Republic. Association for Computational Linguistics.

Koehn, P., Hoang, H., Birch, A., Callison-Burch, C., Federico, M., Bertoldi, N., Cowan, B., Shen, W., Moran, C., Zens, R., Dyer, C., Bojar, O., Constantin, A., and Herbst, E. (2007). Moses: Open source toolkit for statistical machine translation. In *ACL 2007 Demonstrations*, Prague, Czech Republic.

Koehn, P. and Knight, K. (2003). Empirical methods for compound splitting. In *Proceedings of Meeting of the European Chapter of the Association of Computational Linguistics (EACL)*.

Kumar, S. and Byrne, W. J. (2004). Minimum bayes-risk decoding for statistical machine translation. In *HLT-NAACL*, pages 169–176.

Moore, R. C. and Lewis, W. (2010). Intelligent selection of language model training data. In *Proceedings of the ACL 2010 Conference Short Papers*, pages 220–224, Uppsala, Sweden. Association for Computational Linguistics.

Nakov, P. and Tiedemann, J. (2012). Combining word-level and character-level models for machine translation between closely-related languages. In *Proceedings of the 50th Annual Meeting of the Association for Computational Linguistics (Volume 2: Short Papers)*, pages 301–305, Jeju Island, Korea. Association for Computational Linguistics.

Och, F. J. (1999). An efficient method for determining bilingual word classes. In *Ninth Conference the European Chapter of the Association for Computational Linguistics (EACL)*, pages 71–76.

Post, M., Callison-Burch, C., and Osborne, M. (2012). Constructing parallel corpora for six indian languages via crowdsourcing. In *Proceedings of the Seventh Workshop on Statistical Machine Translation*, pages 401–409, Montréal, Canada. Association for Computational Linguistics.

Sajjad, H., Smekalova, S., Durrani, N., Fraser, A., and Schmid, H. (2013). QCRI-MES submission at wmt13: Using transliteration mining to improve statistical machine translation. In *Proceedings of the Eighth Workshop on Statistical Machine Translation*, Sofia, Bulgaria. Association for Computational Linguistics.

Schwenk, H. and Koehn, P. (2008). Large and diverse language models for statistical machine translation. In *International Joint Conference on Natural Language Processing*, pages 661–666.

Utiyama, M. and Isahara, H. (2007). A comparison of pivot methods for phrase-based statistical machine translation. In *2007 Meeting of the North American Chapter of the Association for Computational Linguistics (NAACL)*, pages 484–491.

Wu, H. and Wang, H. (2007). Pivot language approach for phrase-based statistical machine translation. In *Proceedings of the 45th Annual Meeting of the Association of Computational Linguistics*, pages 856–863, Prague, Czech Republic. Association for Computational Linguistics.

EU-BRIDGE MT: Combined Machine Translation

*Markus Freitag, *Stephan Peitz, *Joern Wuebker, *Hermann Ney,
‡Matthias Huck, ‡Rico Sennrich, ‡Nadir Durrani,
‡Maria Nadejde, ‡Philip Williams, ‡Philipp Koehn,
†Teresa Herrmann, †Eunah Cho, †Alex Waibel
*RWTH Aachen University, Aachen, Germany
‡University of Edinburgh, Edinburgh, Scotland
†Karlsruhe Institute of Technology, Karlsruhe, Germany
*{freitag,peitz,wuebker,ney}@cs.rwth-aachen.de
‡{mhuck,ndurrani,pkoehn}@inf.ed.ac.uk
‡v1rsennr@staffmail.ed.ac.uk
‡maria.nadejde@gmail.com,p.j.williams-2@sms.ed.ac.uk
†{teresa.herrmann,eunah.cho,alex.waibel}@kit.edu

Abstract

This paper describes one of the collaborative efforts within EU-BRIDGE to further advance the state of the art in machine translation between two European language pairs, German→English and English→German. Three research institutes involved in the EU-BRIDGE project combined their individual machine translation systems and participated with a joint setup in the shared translation task of the evaluation campaign at the *ACL 2014 Eighth Workshop on Statistical Machine Translation* (WMT 2014).

We combined up to nine different machine translation engines via system combination. RWTH Aachen University, the University of Edinburgh, and Karlsruhe Institute of Technology developed several individual systems which serve as system combination input. We devoted special attention to building syntax-based systems and combining them with the phrase-based ones. The joint setups yield empirical gains of up to 1.6 points in BLEU and 1.0 points in TER on the WMT newstest2013 test set compared to the best single systems.

1 Introduction

EU-BRIDGE[1] is a European research project which is aimed at developing innovative speech translation technology. This paper describes a joint WMT submission of three EU-BRIDGE project partners. RWTH Aachen University (RWTH), the University of Edinburgh (UEDIN) and Karlsruhe Institute of Technology (KIT) all provided several individual systems which were combined by means of the RWTH Aachen system combination approach (Freitag et al., 2014). As distinguished from our EU-BRIDGE joint submission to the IWSLT 2013 evaluation campaign (Freitag et al., 2013), we particularly focused on translation of news text (instead of talks) for WMT. Besides, we put an emphasis on engineering syntax-based systems in order to combine them with our more established phrase-based engines. We built combined system setups for translation from German to English as well as from English to German. This paper gives some insight into the technology behind the system combination framework and the combined engines which have been used to produce the joint EU-BRIDGE submission to the WMT 2014 translation task.

The remainder of the paper is structured as follows: We first describe the individual systems by RWTH Aachen University (Section 2), the University of Edinburgh (Section 3), and Karlsruhe Institute of Technology (Section 4). We then present the techniques for machine translation system combination in Section 5. Experimental results are given in Section 6. We finally conclude the paper with Section 7.

2 RWTH Aachen University

RWTH (Peitz et al., 2014) employs both the phrase-based (*RWTH scss*) and the hierarchical (*RWTH hiero*) decoder implemented in RWTH's publicly available translation toolkit Jane (Vilar

[1] http://www.eu-bridge.eu

Proceedings of the Ninth Workshop on Statistical Machine Translation, pages 105–113,
Baltimore, Maryland USA, June 26–27, 2014.

et al., 2010; Wuebker et al., 2012). The model weights of all systems have been tuned with standard Minimum Error Rate Training (Och, 2003) on a concatenation of the newstest2011 and newstest2012 sets. RWTH used BLEU as optimization objective. Both for language model estimation and querying at decoding, the KenLM toolkit (Heafield et al., 2013) is used. All RWTH systems include the standard set of models provided by Jane. Both systems have been augmented with a hierarchical orientation model (Galley and Manning, 2008; Huck et al., 2013) and a cluster language model (Wuebker et al., 2013). The phrase-based system (*RWTH scss*) has been further improved by maximum expected BLEU training similar to (He and Deng, 2012). The latter has been performed on a selection from the News Commentary, Europarl and Common Crawl corpora based on language and translation model cross-entropies (Mansour et al., 2011).

3 University of Edinburgh

UEDIN contributed phrase-based and syntax-based systems to both the German→English and the English→German joint submission.

3.1 Phrase-based Systems

UEDIN's phrase-based systems (Durrani et al., 2014) have been trained using the Moses toolkit (Koehn et al., 2007), replicating the settings described in (Durrani et al., 2013b). The features include: a maximum sentence length of 80, grow-diag-final-and symmetrization of GIZA++ alignments, an interpolated Kneser-Ney smoothed 5-gram language model with KenLM (Heafield, 2011) used at runtime, a lexically-driven 5-gram operation sequence model (OSM) (Durrani et al., 2013a), msd-bidirectional-fe lexicalized reordering, sparse lexical and domain features (Hasler et al., 2012), a distortion limit of 6, a maximum phrase length of 5, 100-best translation options, Minimum Bayes Risk decoding (Kumar and Byrne, 2004), cube pruning (Huang and Chiang, 2007), with a stack size of 1000 during tuning and 5000 during testing and the no-reordering-over-punctuation heuristic. UEDIN uses POS and morphological target sequence models built on the in-domain subset of the parallel corpus using Kneser-Ney smoothed 7-gram models as additional factors in phrase translation models (Koehn and Hoang, 2007). UEDIN has furthermore built OSM models over POS and morph sequences following Durrani et al. (2013c). The English→German system additionally comprises a target-side LM over automatically built word classes (Birch et al., 2013). UEDIN has applied syntactic pre-reordering (Collins et al., 2005) and compound splitting (Koehn and Knight, 2003) of the source side for the German→English system. The systems have been tuned on a very large tuning set consisting of the test sets from 2008-2012, with a total of 13,071 sentences. UEDIN used newstest2013 as held-out test set. On top of *UEDIN phrase-based 1* system, *UEDIN phrase-based 2* augments word classes as additional factor and learns an interpolated target sequence model over cluster IDs. Furthermore, it learns OSM models over POS, morph and word classes.

3.2 Syntax-based Systems

UEDIN's syntax-based systems (Williams et al., 2014) follow the GHKM syntax approach as proposed by **G**alley, **H**opkins, **K**night, and **M**arcu (Galley et al., 2004). The open source *Moses* implementation has been employed to extract GHKM rules (Williams and Koehn, 2012). Composed rules (Galley et al., 2006) are extracted in addition to minimal rules, but only up to the following limits: at most twenty tree nodes per rule, a maximum depth of five, and a maximum size of five. Singleton hierarchical rules are dropped.

The features for the syntax-based systems comprise Good-Turing-smoothed phrase translation probabilities, lexical translation probabilities in both directions, word and phrase penalty, a rule rareness penalty, a monolingual PCFG probability, and a 5-gram language model. UEDIN has used the SRILM toolkit (Stolcke, 2002) to train the language model and relies on KenLM for language model scoring during decoding. Model weights are optimized to maximize BLEU. 2000 sentences from the newstest2008-2012 sets have been selected as a development set. The selected sentences obtained high sentence-level BLEU scores when being translated with a baseline phrase-based system, and each contain less than 30 words for more rapid tuning. Decoding for the syntax-based systems is carried out with cube pruning using Moses' hierarchical decoder (Hoang et al., 2009).

UEDIN's German→English syntax-based setup is a string-to-tree system with compound splitting on the German source-language side and syntactic annotation from the Berkeley Parser (Petrov et al., 2006) on the English target-language side.

For English→German, UEDIN has trained various string-to-tree GHKM syntax systems which differ with respect to the syntactic annotation. A tree-to-string system and a string-to-string system (with rules that are not syntactically decorated) have been trained as well. The English→German UEDIN GHKM system names in Table 3 denote:

UEDIN GHKM S2T (ParZu): A string-to-tree system trained with target-side syntactic annotation obtained with ParZu (Sennrich et al., 2013). It uses a modified syntactic label set, target-side compound splitting, and additional syntactic constraints.

UEDIN GHKM S2T (BitPar): A string-to-tree system trained with target-side syntactic annotation obtained with BitPar (Schmid, 2004).

UEDIN GHKM S2T (Stanford): A string-to-tree system trained with target-side syntactic annotation obtained with the German Stanford Parser (Rafferty and Manning, 2008a).

UEDIN GHKM S2T (Berkeley): A string-to-tree system trained with target-side syntactic annotation obtained with the German Berkeley Parser (Petrov and Klein, 2007; Petrov and Klein, 2008).

UEDIN GHKM T2S (Berkeley): A tree-to-string system trained with source-side syntactic annotation obtained with the English Berkeley Parser (Petrov et al., 2006).

UEDIN GHKM S2S (Berkeley): A string-to-string system. The extraction is GHKM-based with syntactic target-side annotation from the German Berkeley Parser, but we strip off the syntactic labels. The final grammar contains rules with a single generic non-terminal instead of syntactic ones, plus rules that have been added from plain phrase-based extraction (Huck et al., 2014).

4 Karlsruhe Institute of Technology

The KIT translations (Herrmann et al., 2014) are generated by an in-house phrase-based translations system (Vogel, 2003). The provided News Commentary, Europarl, and Common Crawl parallel corpora are used for training the translation model. The monolingual part of those parallel corpora, the News Shuffle corpus for both directions and additionally the Gigaword corpus for German→English are used as monolingual training data for the different language models. Optimization is done with Minimum Error Rate Training as described in (Venugopal et al., 2005), using newstest2012 and newstest2013 as development and test data respectively.

Compound splitting (Koehn and Knight, 2003) is performed on the source side of the corpus for German→English translation before training. In order to improve the quality of the web-crawled Common Crawl corpus, noisy sentence pairs are filtered out using an SVM classifier as described by Mediani et al. (2011).

The word alignment for German→English is generated using the GIZA++ toolkit (Och and Ney, 2003). For English→German, KIT uses discriminative word alignment (Niehues and Vogel, 2008). Phrase extraction and scoring is done using the Moses toolkit (Koehn et al., 2007). Phrase pair probabilities are computed using modified Kneser-Ney smoothing as in (Foster et al., 2006).

In both systems KIT applies short-range reorderings (Rottmann and Vogel, 2007) and long-range reorderings (Niehues and Kolss, 2009) based on POS tags (Schmid, 1994) to perform source sentence reordering according to the target language word order. The long-range reordering rules are applied to the training corpus to create reordering lattices to extract the phrases for the translation model. In addition, a tree-based reordering model (Herrmann et al., 2013) trained on syntactic parse trees (Rafferty and Manning, 2008b; Klein and Manning, 2003) as well as a lexicalized reordering model (Koehn et al., 2005) are applied.

Language models are trained with the SRILM toolkit (Stolcke, 2002) and use modified Kneser-Ney smoothing. Both systems utilize a language model based on automatically learned word classes using the MKCLS algorithm (Och, 1999). The English→German system comprises language models based on fine-grained part-of-speech tags (Schmid and Laws, 2008). In addition, a bilingual language model (Niehues et al., 2011) is used as well as a discriminative word lexicon (Mauser et al., 2009) using source context to guide the word choices in the target sentence.

In total, the English→German system uses the following language models: two 4-gram word-based language models trained on the parallel data and the filtered Common Crawl data separately, two 5-gram POS-based language models trained on the same data as the word-based language models, and a 4-gram cluster-based language model trained on 1,000 MKCLS word classes.

The German→English system uses a 4-gram word-based language model trained on all monolingual data and an additional language model trained on automatically selected data (Moore and Lewis, 2010). Again, a 4-gram cluster-based language model trained on 1000 MKCLS word classes is applied.

5 System Combination

System combination is used to produce consensus translations from multiple hypotheses which are outputs of different translation engines. The consensus translations can be better in terms of translation quality than any of the individual hypotheses. To combine the engines of the project partners for the EU-BRIDGE joint setups, we apply a system combination implementation that has been developed at RWTH Aachen University.

The implementation of RWTH's approach to machine translation system combination is described in (Freitag et al., 2014). This approach includes an enhanced alignment and reordering framework. Alignments between the system outputs are learned using METEOR (Banerjee and Lavie, 2005). A confusion network is then built using one of the hypotheses as "primary" hypothesis. We do not make a hard decision on which of the hypotheses to use for that, but instead combine all possible confusion networks into a single lattice. Majority voting on the generated lattice is performed using the prior probabilities for each system as well as other statistical models, e.g. a special n-gram language model which is learned on the input hypotheses. Scaling factors of the models are optimized using the Minimum Error Rate Training algorithm. The translation with the best total score within the lattice is selected as consensus translation.

6 Results

In this section, we present our experimental results on the two translation tasks, German→English and English→German. The weights of the individual system engines have been optimized on different test sets which partially or fully include newstest2011 or newstest2012. System combination weights are either optimized on newstest2011 or newstest2012. We kept newstest2013 as an unseen test set which has not been used for tuning the system combination or any of the individual systems.

6.1 German→English

The automatic scores of all individual systems as well as of our final system combination submission are given in Table 1. KIT, UEDIN and RWTH are each providing one individual phrase-based system output. RWTH (*hiero*) and UEDIN (*GHKM*) are providing additional systems based on the hierarchical translation model and a string-to-tree syntax model. The pairwise difference of the single system performances is up to 1.3 points in BLEU and 2.5 points in TER. For German→English, our system combination parameters are optimized on newstest2012. System combination gives us a gain of 1.6 points in BLEU and 1.0 points in TER for newstest2013 compared to the best single system.

In Table 2 the pairwise BLEU scores for all individual systems as well as for the system combination output are given. The pairwise BLEU score of both RWTH systems (taking one as hypothesis and the other one as reference) is the highest for all pairs of individual system outputs. A high BLEU score means similar hypotheses. The syntax-based system of UEDIN and *RWTH scss* differ mostly, which can be observed from the fact of the lowest pairwise BLEU score. Furthermore, we can see that better performing individual systems have higher BLEU scores when evaluating against the system combination output.

In Figure 1 system combination output is compared to the best single system *KIT*. We distribute the sentence-level BLEU scores of all sentences of newstest2013. To allow for sentence-wise evaluation, all bi-, tri-, and four-gram counts are initialized with 1 instead of 0. Many sentences have been improved by system combination. Nevertheless, some sentences fall off in quality compared to the individual system output of *KIT*.

6.2 English→German

The results of all English→German system setups are given in Table 3. For the English→German translation task, only UEDIN and KIT are con-

system	newstest2011		newstest2012		newstest2013	
	BLEU	TER	BLEU	TER	BLEU	TER
KIT	25.0	57.6	25.2	57.4	27.5	54.4
UEDIN	23.9	59.2	24.7	58.3	27.4	55.0
RWTH scss	23.6	59.5	24.2	58.5	27.0	55.0
RWTH hiero	23.3	59.9	24.1	59.0	26.7	55.9
UEDIN GHKM S2T (Berkeley)	23.0	60.1	23.2	60.8	26.2	56.9
syscom	25.6	57.1	**26.4**	**56.5**	**29.1**	**53.4**

Table 1: Results for the German→English translation task. The system combination is tuned on newstest2012, newstest2013 is used as held-out test set for all individual systems and system combination. Bold font indicates system combination results that are significantly better than the best single system with $p < 0.05$.

	KIT	UEDIN	RWTH scss	RWTH hiero	UEDIN S2T	syscom
KIT		59.07	57.60	57.91	55.62	77.68
UEDIN	59.17		56.96	57.84	59.89	72.89
RWTH scss	57.64	56.90		64.94	53.10	71.16
RWTH hiero	57.98	57.80	64.97		55.73	70.87
UEDIN S2T	55.75	59.95	53.19	55.82		65.35
syscom	77.76	72.83	71.17	70.85	65.24	

Table 2: Cross BLEU scores for the German→English newstest2013 test set. (Pairwise BLEU scores: each entry is taking the horizontal system as hypothesis and the other one as reference.)

system	newstest2011		newstest2012		newstest2013	
	BLEU	TER	BLEU	TER	BLEU	TER
UEDIN phrase-based 1	17.5	67.3	18.2	65.0	20.5	62.7
UEDIN phrase-based 2	17.8	66.9	18.5	64.6	20.8	62.3
UEDIN GHKM S2T (ParZu)	17.2	67.6	18.0	65.5	20.2	62.8
UEDIN GHKM S2T (BitPar)	16.3	69.0	17.3	66.6	19.5	63.9
UEDIN GHKM S2T (Stanford)	16.1	69.2	17.2	67.0	19.0	64.2
UEDIN GHKM S2T (Berkeley)	16.3	68.9	17.2	66.7	19.3	63.8
UEDIN GHKM T2S (Berkeley)	16.7	68.9	17.5	66.9	19.5	63.8
UEDIN GHKM S2S (Berkeley)	16.3	69.2	17.3	66.8	19.1	64.3
KIT	17.1	67.0	17.8	64.8	20.2	62.2
syscom	**18.4**	**65.0**	18.7	**63.4**	*21.3*	**60.6**

Table 3: Results for the English→German translation task. The system combination is tuned on newstest2011, newstest2013 is used as held-out test set for all individual systems and system combination. Bold font indicates system combination results that are significantly (Bisani and Ney, 2004) better than the best single system with $p < 0.05$. Italic font indicates system combination results that are significantly better than the best single system with $p < 0.1$.

tributing individual systems. KIT is providing a phrase-based system output, UEDIN is providing two phrase-based system outputs and six syntax-based ones (*GHKM*). For English→German, our system combination parameters are optimized on newstest2011. Combining all nine different system outputs yields an improvement of 0.5 points in BLEU and 1.7 points in TER over the best single system performance.

In Table 4 the cross BLEU scores for all English→German systems are given. The individual system of *KIT* and the syntax-based *ParZu* system of UEDIN have the lowest BLEU score when scored against each other. Both approaches are quite different and both are coming from different institutes. In contrast, both phrase-based systems *pbt 1* and *pbt 2* from UEDIN are very similar and hence have a high pairwise BLEU score.

	pbt 1	pbt 2	ParZu	BitPar	Stanford	S2T	T2S	S2S	KIT	syscom
pbt 1		75.84	51.61	53.93	55.32	54.79	54.52	60.92	54.80	70.12
pbt 2	75.84		51.96	53.39	53.93	53.97	53.10	57.32	54.04	73.75
ParZu	51.57	51.91		56.67	55.11	56.05	52.13	51.22	48.14	68.39
BitPar	54.00	53.45	56.78		64.59	65.67	56.33	56.62	49.23	62.08
Stanford	55.37	53.98	55.19	64.56		69.22	58.81	61.19	50.50	61.51
S2T	54.83	54.02	56.14	65.64	69.21		59.32	60.16	50.07	62.81
T2S	54.57	53.15	52.21	56.30	58.81	59.32		59.34	50.01	63.13
S2S	60.96	57.36	51.29	56.59	61.18	60.15	59.33		53.68	60.46
KIT	54.75	53.98	48.13	49.13	50.41	49.98	49.93	53.59		63.33
syscom	70.01	73.63	68.32	61.92	61.37	62.67	62.99	60.32	63.27	

Table 4: Cross BLEU scores for the German→English newstest2013 test set. (Pairwise BLEU scores: each entry is taking the horizontal system as reference and the other one as hypothesis.)

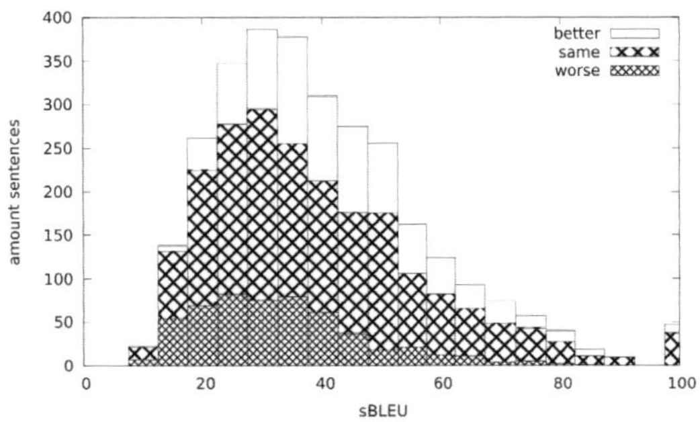

Figure 1: Sentence distribution for the German→English newstest2013 test set comparing system combination output against the best individual system.

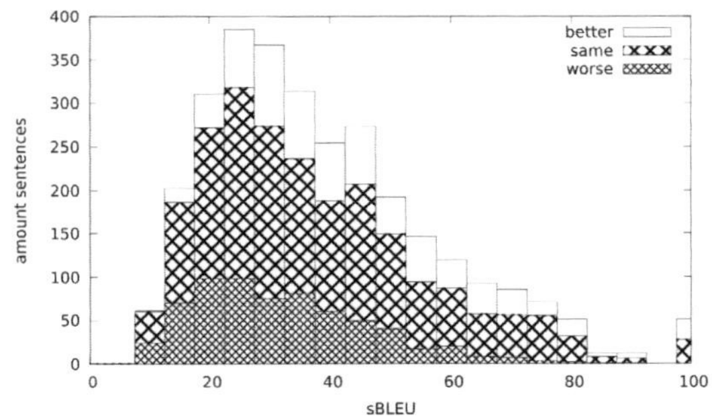

Figure 2: Sentence distribution for the English→German newstest2013 test set comparing system combination output against the best individual system.

As for the German→English translation direction, the best performing individual system outputs are also having the highest BLEU scores when evaluated against the final system combination output.

In Figure 2 system combination output is compared to the best single system *pbt 2*. We distribute the sentence-level BLEU scores of all sentences of newstest2013. Many sentences have been improved by system combination. But there is still room for improvement as some sentences are still better in terms of sentence-level BLEU in the individual best system *pbt 2*.

7 Conclusion

We achieved significantly better translation performance with gains of up to +1.6 points in BLEU and -1.0 points in TER by combining up to nine different machine translation systems. Three different research institutes (RWTH Aachen University, University of Edinburgh, Karlsruhe Institute of Technology) provided machine translation engines based on different approaches like phrase-based, hierarchical phrase-based, and syntax-based. For English→German, we included six different syntax-based systems, which were combined to our final combined translation. The automatic scores of all submitted system outputs for the actual 2014 evaluation set are presented on the WMT submission page.[2] Our joint submission is the best submission in terms of BLEU and TER for both translation directions German→English and English→German without adding any new data.

Acknowledgements

The research leading to these results has received funding from the European Union Seventh Framework Programme (FP7/2007-2013) under grant agreement n° 287658.

Rico Sennrich has received funding from the Swiss National Science Foundation under grant P2ZHP1_148717.

[2] http://matrix.statmt.org/

References

Satanjeev Banerjee and Alon Lavie. 2005. METEOR: An Automatic Metric for MT Evaluation with Improved Correlation with Human Judgments. In *43rd Annual Meeting of the Assoc. for Computational Linguistics: Proc. Workshop on Intrinsic and Extrinsic Evaluation Measures for MT and/or Summarization*, pages 65–72, Ann Arbor, MI, USA, June.

Alexandra Birch, Nadir Durrani, and Philipp Koehn. 2013. Edinburgh SLT and MT System Description for the IWSLT 2013 Evaluation. In *Proceedings of the 10th International Workshop on Spoken Language Translation*, pages 40–48, Heidelberg, Germany, December.

Maximilian Bisani and Hermann Ney. 2004. Bootstrap Estimates for Confidence Intervals in ASR Performance Evaluation. In *IEEE International Conference on Acoustics, Speech, and Signal Processing*, volume 1, pages 409–412, Montréal, Canada, May.

Michael Collins, Philipp Koehn, and Ivona Kucerova. 2005. Clause Restructuring for Statistical Machine Translation. In *Proceedings of the 43rd Annual Meeting of the Association for Computational Linguistics (ACL'05)*, pages 531–540, Ann Arbor, Michigan, June.

Nadir Durrani, Alexander Fraser, Helmut Schmid, Hieu Hoang, and Philipp Koehn. 2013a. Can Markov Models Over Minimal Translation Units Help Phrase-Based SMT? In *Proceedings of the 51st Annual Meeting of the Association for Computational Linguistics*, Sofia, Bulgaria, August.

Nadir Durrani, Barry Haddow, Kenneth Heafield, and Philipp Koehn. 2013b. Edinburgh's Machine Translation Systems for European Language Pairs. In *Proceedings of the Eighth Workshop on Statistical Machine Translation*, Sofia, Bulgaria, August.

Nadir Durrani, Helmut Schmid, Alexander Fraser, Hassan Sajjad, and Richard Farkas. 2013c. Munich-Edinburgh-Stuttgart Submissions of OSM Systems at WMT13. In *Proceedings of the Eighth Workshop on Statistical Machine Translation*, Sofia, Bulgaria.

Nadir Durrani, Barry Haddow, Philipp Koehn, and Kenneth Heafield. 2014. Edinburgh's Phrase-based Machine Translation Systems for WMT-14. In *Proceedings of the ACL 2014 Ninth Workshop on Statistical Machine Translation*, Baltimore, MD, USA, June.

George Foster, Roland Kuhn, and Howard Johnson. 2006. Phrasetable Smoothing for Statistical Machine Translation. In *EMNLP*, pages 53–61.

M. Freitag, S. Peitz, J. Wuebker, H. Ney, N. Durrani, M. Huck, P. Koehn, T.-L. Ha, J. Niehues, M. Mediani, T. Herrmann, A. Waibel, N. Bertoldi, M. Cettolo, and M. Federico. 2013. EU-BRIDGE MT: Text Translation of Talks in the EU-BRIDGE Project. In *International Workshop on Spoken Language Translation*, Heidelberg, Germany, December.

Markus Freitag, Matthias Huck, and Hermann Ney. 2014. Jane: Open Source Machine Translation System Combination. In *Conference of the European Chapter of the Association for Computational Linguistics*, Gothenburg, Sweden, April.

Michel Galley and Christopher D. Manning. 2008. A Simple and Effective Hierarchical Phrase Reordering Model. In *Proceedings of the 2008 Conference on Empirical Methods in Natural Language Processing*, pages 847–855, Honolulu, HI, USA, October.

Michel Galley, Mark Hopkins, Kevin Knight, and Daniel Marcu. 2004. What's in a translation rule? In *Proc. of the Human Language Technology Conf. / North American Chapter of the Assoc. for Computational Linguistics (HLT-NAACL)*, pages 273–280, Boston, MA, USA, May.

Michel Galley, Jonathan Graehl, Kevin Knight, Daniel Marcu, Steve DeNeefe, Wei Wang, and Ignacio Thayer. 2006. Scalable Inference and Training of Context-Rich Syntactic Translation Models. In *Proc. of the 21st International Conf. on Computational Linguistics and 44th Annual Meeting of the Assoc. for Computational Linguistics*, pages 961–968, Sydney, Australia, July.

Eva Hasler, Barry Haddow, and Philipp Koehn. 2012. Sparse Lexicalised features and Topic Adaptation for SMT. In *Proceedings of the seventh International Workshop on Spoken Language Translation (IWSLT)*, pages 268–275.

Xiaodong He and Li Deng. 2012. Maximum Expected BLEU Training of Phrase and Lexicon Translation Models. In *Proceedings of the 50th Annual Meeting of the Association for Computational Linguistics (ACL)*, pages 292–301, Jeju, Republic of Korea, July.

Kenneth Heafield, Ivan Pouzyrevsky, Jonathan H. Clark, and Philipp Koehn. 2013. Scalable modified Kneser-Ney language model estimation. In *Proceedings of the 51st Annual Meeting of the Association for Computational Linguistics*, pages 690–696, Sofia, Bulgaria, August.

Kenneth Heafield. 2011. KenLM: Faster and Smaller Language Model Queries. In *Proceedings of the Sixth Workshop on Statistical Machine Translation*, pages 187–197, Edinburgh, Scotland, UK, July.

Teresa Herrmann, Jan Niehues, and Alex Waibel. 2013. Combining Word Reordering Methods on different Linguistic Abstraction Levels for Statistical Machine Translation. In *Proceedings of the Seventh Workshop on Syntax, Semantics and Structure in Statistical Translation*, Atlanta, GA, USA, June.

Teresa Herrmann, Mohammed Mediani, Eunah Cho, Thanh-Le Ha, Jan Niehues, Isabel Slawik, Yuqi Zhang, and Alex Waibel. 2014. The Karlsruhe Institute of Technology Translation Systems for the WMT 2014. In *Proceedings of the ACL 2014 Ninth Workshop on Statistical Machine Translation*, Baltimore, MD, USA, June.

Hieu Hoang, Philipp Koehn, and Adam Lopez. 2009. A Unified Framework for Phrase-Based, Hierarchical, and Syntax-Based Statistical Machine Translation. pages 152–159, Tokyo, Japan, December.

Liang Huang and David Chiang. 2007. Forest Rescoring: Faster Decoding with Integrated Language Models. In *Proceedings of the 45th Annual Meeting of the Association of Computational Linguistics*, pages 144–151, Prague, Czech Republic, June.

Matthias Huck, Joern Wuebker, Felix Rietig, and Hermann Ney. 2013. A Phrase Orientation Model for Hierarchical Machine Translation. In *ACL 2013 Eighth Workshop on Statistical Machine Translation*, pages 452–463, Sofia, Bulgaria, August.

Matthias Huck, Hieu Hoang, and Philipp Koehn. 2014. Augmenting String-to-Tree and Tree-to-String Translation with Non-Syntactic Phrases. In *Proceedings of the ACL 2014 Ninth Workshop on Statistical Machine Translation*, Baltimore, MD, USA, June.

Dan Klein and Christopher D. Manning. 2003. Accurate Unlexicalized Parsing. In *Proceedings of ACL 2003*.

Philipp Koehn and Hieu Hoang. 2007. Factored Translation Models. In *EMNLP-CoNLL*, pages 868–876, Prague, Czech Republic, June.

Philipp Koehn and Kevin Knight. 2003. Empirical Methods for Compound Splitting. In *EACL*, Budapest, Hungary.

Philipp Koehn, Amittai Axelrod, Alexandra B. Mayne, Chris Callison-Burch, Miles Osborne, and David Talbot. 2005. Edinburgh System Description for the 2005 IWSLT Speech Translation Evaluation. In *Proceedings of the International Workshop on Spoken Language Translation (IWSLT)*, Pittsburgh, PA, USA.

P. Koehn, H. Hoang, A. Birch, C. Callison-Burch, M. Federico, N. Bertoldi, B. Cowan, W. Shen, C. Moran, R. Zens, C. Dyer, O. Bojar, A. Constantin, and E. Herbst. 2007. Moses: Open Source Toolkit for Statistical Machine Translation. In *Proceedings of the 45th Annual Meeting of the ACL on Interactive Poster and Demonstration Sessions*, pages 177–180, Prague, Czech Republic, June.

Shankar Kumar and William Byrne. 2004. Minimum Bayes-Risk Decoding for Statistical Machine Translation. In *Proc. Human Language Technology Conf. / North American Chapter of the Association for Computational Linguistics Annual Meeting (HLT-NAACL)*, pages 169–176, Boston, MA, USA, May.

Saab Mansour, Joern Wuebker, and Hermann Ney. 2011. Combining Translation and Language Model Scoring for Domain-Specific Data Filtering. In *Proceedings of the International Workshop on Spoken Language Translation (IWSLT)*, pages 222–229, San Francisco, CA, USA, December.

Arne Mauser, Saša Hasan, and Hermann Ney. 2009. Extending Statistical Machine Translation with Discriminative and Trigger-Based Lexicon Models. In *Conference on Empirical Methods in Natural Language Processing*, pages 210–217, Singapore, August.

Mohammed Mediani, Eunah Cho, Jan Niehues, Teresa Herrmann, and Alex Waibel. 2011. The KIT English-French Translation systems for IWSLT 2011. In *Proceedings of the Eight International Workshop on Spoken Language Translation (IWSLT)*, San Francisco, CA, USA.

Robert C. Moore and William Lewis. 2010. Intelligent selection of language model training data. In *Proceedings of the ACL 2010 Conference Short Papers*, pages 220–224, Uppsala, Sweden, July.

Jan Niehues and Muntsin Kolss. 2009. A POS-Based Model for Long-Range Reorderings in SMT. In *Fourth Workshop on Statistical Machine Translation (WMT 2009)*, Athens, Greece.

Jan Niehues and Stephan Vogel. 2008. Discriminative Word Alignment via Alignment Matrix Modeling. In *Proceedings of Third ACL Workshop on Statistical Machine Translation*, Columbus, USA.

Jan Niehues, Teresa Herrmann, Stephan Vogel, and Alex Waibel. 2011. Wider Context by Using Bilingual Language Models in Machine Translation. In *Sixth Workshop on Statistical Machine Translation (WMT 2011)*, Edinburgh, UK.

Franz Josef Och and Hermann Ney. 2003. A Systematic Comparison of Various Statistical Alignment Models. *Computational Linguistics*, 29(1):19–51.

Franz Josef Och. 1999. An Efficient Method for Determining Bilingual Word Classes. In *EACL'99*.

Franz Josef Och. 2003. Minimum Error Rate Training in Statistical Machine Translation. In *Proc. of the 41th Annual Meeting of the Association for Computational Linguistics (ACL)*, pages 160–167, Sapporo, Japan, July.

Stephan Peitz, Joern Wuebker, Markus Freitag, and Hermann Ney. 2014. The RWTH Aachen German-English Machine Translation System for WMT 2014. In *Proceedings of the ACL 2014 Ninth Workshop on Statistical Machine Translation*, Baltimore, MD, USA, June.

Slav Petrov and Dan Klein. 2007. Improved Inference for Unlexicalized Parsing. In *Human Language Technologies 2007: The Conference of the North American Chapter of the Association for Computational Linguistics; Proceedings of the Main Conference*, pages 404–411, Rochester, New York, April.

Slav Petrov and Dan Klein. 2008. Parsing German with Latent Variable Grammars. In *Proceedings of the Workshop on Parsing German at ACL '08*, pages 33–39, Columbus, OH, USA, June.

Slav Petrov, Leon Barrett, Romain Thibaux, and Dan Klein. 2006. Learning Accurate, Compact, and Interpretable Tree Annotation. In *Proc. of the 21st International Conference on Computational Linguistics and 44th Annual Meeting of the Assoc. for Computational Linguistics*, pages 433–440, Sydney, Australia, July.

Anna N. Rafferty and Christopher D. Manning. 2008a. Parsing Three German Treebanks: Lexicalized and Unlexicalized Baselines. In *Proceedings of the Workshop on Parsing German at ACL '08*, pages 40–46, Columbus, OH, USA, June.

Anna N. Rafferty and Christopher D. Manning. 2008b. Parsing Three German Treebanks: Lexicalized and Unlexicalized Baselines. In *Proceedings of the Workshop on Parsing German*.

Kay Rottmann and Stephan Vogel. 2007. Word Reordering in Statistical Machine Translation with a POS-Based Distortion Model. In *Proceedings of the 11th International Conference on Theoretical and Methodological Issues in Machine Translation (TMI)*, Skövde, Sweden.

Helmut Schmid and Florian Laws. 2008. Estimation of Conditional Probabilities with Decision Trees and an Application to Fine-Grained POS Tagging. In *COLING 2008*, Manchester, UK.

Helmut Schmid. 1994. Probabilistic Part-of-Speech Tagging Using Decision Trees. In *International Conference on New Methods in Language Processing*, Manchester, UK.

Helmut Schmid. 2004. Efficient Parsing of Highly Ambiguous Context-Free Grammars with Bit Vectors. In *Proc. of the Int. Conf. on Computational Linguistics (COLING)*, Geneva, Switzerland, August.

Rico Sennrich, Martin Volk, and Gerold Schneider. 2013. Exploiting Synergies Between Open Resources for German Dependency Parsing, POS-tagging, and Morphological Analysis. In *Proceedings of the International Conference Recent Advances in Natural Language Processing 2013*, pages 601–609, Hissar, Bulgaria.

Andreas Stolcke. 2002. SRILM – An Extensible Language Modeling Toolkit. In *Proc. of the Int. Conf. on Speech and Language Processing (ICSLP)*, volume 2, pages 901–904, Denver, CO, USA, September.

Ashish Venugopal, Andreas Zollman, and Alex Waibel. 2005. Training and Evaluation Error Minimization Rules for Statistical Machine Translation. In *Workshop on Data-drive Machine Translation and Beyond (WPT-05)*, Ann Arbor, Michigan, USA.

David Vilar, Daniel Stein, Matthias Huck, and Hermann Ney. 2010. Jane: Open Source Hierarchical Translation, Extended with Reordering and Lexicon Models. In *ACL 2010 Joint Fifth Workshop on Statistical Machine Translation and Metrics MATR*, pages 262–270, Uppsala, Sweden, July.

Stephan Vogel. 2003. SMT Decoder Dissected: Word Reordering. In *International Conference on Natural Language Processing and Knowledge Engineering*, Beijing, China.

Philip Williams and Philipp Koehn. 2012. GHKM Rule Extraction and Scope-3 Parsing in Moses. In *Proceedings of the Seventh Workshop on Statistical Machine Translation (WMT)*, pages 388–394, Montréal, Canada, June.

Philip Williams, Rico Sennrich, Maria Nadejde, Matthias Huck, Eva Hasler, and Philipp Koehn. 2014. Edinburgh's Syntax-Based Systems at WMT 2014. In *Proceedings of the ACL 2014 Ninth Workshop on Statistical Machine Translation*, Baltimore, MD, USA, June.

Joern Wuebker, Matthias Huck, Stephan Peitz, Malte Nuhn, Markus Freitag, Jan-Thorsten Peter, Saab Mansour, and Hermann Ney. 2012. Jane 2: Open Source Phrase-based and Hierarchical Statistical Machine Translation. In *COLING '12: The 24th Int. Conf. on Computational Linguistics*, pages 483–491, Mumbai, India, December.

Joern Wuebker, Stephan Peitz, Felix Rietig, and Hermann Ney. 2013. Improving Statistical Machine Translation with Word Class Models. In *Conference on Empirical Methods in Natural Language Processing*, pages 1377–1381, Seattle, WA, USA, October.

Phrasal: A Toolkit for New Directions in Statistical Machine Translation

Spence Green, Daniel Cer, and **Christopher D. Manning**
Computer Science Department, Stanford University
{spenceg,danielcer,manning}@stanford.edu

Abstract

We present a new version of Phrasal, an open-source toolkit for statistical phrase-based machine translation. This revision includes features that support emerging research trends such as (a) tuning with large feature sets, (b) tuning on large datasets like the bitext, and (c) web-based interactive machine translation. A direct comparison with Moses shows favorable results in terms of decoding speed and tuning time.

1 Introduction

In the early part of the last decade, phrase-based machine translation (MT) (Koehn et al., 2003) emerged as the preeminent design of statistical MT systems. However, most systems were proprietary or closed-source, so progress was initially constrained by the high engineering barrier to entry into the field. Then Moses (Koehn et al., 2007) was released. What followed was a flowering of work on all aspects of the translation problem, from rule extraction to deployment issues. Other toolkits appeared including Joshua (Post et al., 2013), Jane (Wuebker et al., 2012), cdec (Dyer et al., 2010) and the first version of our package, Phrasal (Cer et al., 2010), a Java-based, open source package.

This paper presents a completely re-designed release of Phrasal that lowers the barrier to entry into several exciting areas of MT research. First, Phrasal exposes a simple yet flexible feature API for building large-scale, feature-rich systems. Second, Phrasal provides multi-threaded decoding and online tuning for learning feature-rich models on very large datasets, including the bitext. Third, Phrasal supplies the key ingredients for web-based, interactive MT: an asynchronous RESTful JSON web service implemented as a J2EE servlet, integrated pre- and post-processing, and fast search.

Revisions to Phrasal were guided by several design choices. First, we optimized the system for multi-core architectures, eschewing distributed infrastructure like Hadoop and MapReduce. While "scaling-out" with distributed infrastructure is the conventional industry and academic choice, we find that "scaling-up" on a single large-node is an attractive yet overlooked alternative (Appuswamy et al., 2013). A single "scale-up" node is usually competitive in terms of cost and performance, and multi-core code has fewer dependencies in terms of software and expertise. Second, Phrasal makes extensive use of Java interfaces and reflection. This is especially helpful in the feature API. A feature function can be added to the system by simply implementing an interface and specifying the class name on the decoder command line. There is no need to modify or recompile anything other than the new feature function.

This paper presents a direct comparison of Phrasal and Moses that shows favorable results in terms of decoding speed and tuning time. An indirect comparison via the WMT2014 shared task (Neidert et al., 2014) showed that Phrasal compares favorably to Moses in an evaluation setting. The source code is freely available at: `http://nlp.stanford.edu/software/phrasal/`

2 Standard System Pipeline

This section describes the steps required to build a phrase-based MT system from raw text. Each step is implemented as a stand-alone executable. For convenience, the Phrasal distribution includes a script that coordinates the steps.

2.1 Prerequisites

Phrasal assumes offline preparation of word alignments and at least one target-side language model.

Word Alignment The rule extractor can accommodate either unsymmetrized or symmetrized alignments. Unsymmetrized alignments can be produced with either GIZA++ or the Berkeley Aligner (Liang et al., 2006). Phrasal then applies symmetrization on-the-fly using heuristics such as grow-diag or grow-diag-final. If the alignments are symmetrized separately, then Phrasal accepts align-

Proceedings of the Ninth Workshop on Statistical Machine Translation, pages 114–121,
Baltimore, Maryland USA, June 26–27, 2014.

ments in the i-j Pharaoh format, which indicates that source token i is aligned to target token j.

Language Modeling Phrasal can load any n-gram language model saved in the ARPA format. There are two LM loaders. The Java-based loader is used by default and is appropriate for small-scale experiments and pure-Java environments. The C++ KenLM (Heafield, 2011) loader[1] is best for large-scale LMs such as the unfiltered models produced by lmplz (Heafield et al., 2013). Profiling shows that LM queries often account for more than 50% of the CPU time in a Phrasal decoding run, so we designed the Phrasal KenLM loader to execute queries mostly in C++ for efficiency. The KenLM binding efficiently passes full strings to C++ via JNI. KenLM then iterates over the string, returning a score and a state length. Phrasal can load multiple language models, and includes native support for the class-based language models that have become popular in recent evaluations (Wuebker et al., 2012; Ammar et al., 2013; Durrani et al., 2013).

2.2 Rule Extraction

The next step in the pipeline is extraction of a phrase table. Phrasal includes a multi-threaded version of the rule extraction algorithm of Och and Ney (2004). Phrase tables can be filtered to a specific data set—as is common in research environments. When filtering, the rule extractor lowers memory utilization by splitting the data into arbitrary-sized chunks and extracting rules from each chunk.

The rule extractor includes a feature API that is independent of the decoder feature API. This allows for storage of **static rule feature** values in the phrase table. Static rule features are useful in two cases. First, if a feature value depends on bitext statistics, which are not accessible during tuning or decoding, then that feature should be stored in the phrase table. Examples are the standard phrase translation probabilities, and the dense rule count and rule uniqueness indicators described by Green et al. (2013). Second, if a feature depends only on the rule and is unlikely to change, then it may be more efficient to store that feature value in the phrase table. An example is a feature template that indicates inclusion in a specific data domain (Durrani et al., 2013). Rule extractor feature templates must implement the `FeatureExtractor` interface and are loaded via reflection.

[1]Invoked by prefixing the LM path with the "kenlm:".

The rule extractor can also create lexicalized reordering tables. The standard phrase orientation model (Tillmann, 2004) and the hierarchical model of Galley and Manning (2008) are available.

2.3 Tuning

Once a language model has been estimated and a phrase table has been extracted, the next step is to estimate model weights. Phrasal supports tuning over n-best lists, which permits rapid experimentation with different error metrics and loss functions. Lattice-based tuning, while in principle more powerful, requires metrics and losses that factor over lattices, and in practice works no better than n-best tuning (Cherry and Foster, 2012).

Tuning requires a parallel set $\{(f_t, e_t)\}_{t=1}^{T}$ of source sentences f_t and target references e_t.[2] Phrasal follows the log-linear approach to phrase-based translation (Och and Ney, 2004) in which the predictive translation distribution $p(e|f;w)$ is modeled directly as

$$p(e|f;w) = \frac{1}{Z(f)} \exp\left[w^{\top}\phi(e,f)\right] \quad (1)$$

where $w \in \mathbb{R}^d$ is the vector of model parameters, $\phi(\cdot) \in \mathbb{R}^d$ is a feature map, and $Z(f)$ is an appropriate normalizing constant.

MT differs from other machine learning settings in that it is not common to tune to log-likelihood under (1). Instead, a gold error metric $G(e', e)$ is chosen that specifies the similarity between a hypothesis e' and a reference e, and that error is minimized over the tuning set. Phrasal includes Java implementations of BLEU (Papineni et al., 2002), NIST, and WER, and bindings for TER (Snover et al., 2006) and METEOR (Denkowski and Lavie, 2011). The error metric is incorporated into a loss function ℓ that returns the loss at either the sentence- or corpus- level.

For conventional corpus-level (batch) tuning, Phrasal includes multi-threaded implementations of MERT (Och, 2003) and PRO (Hopkins and May, 2011). The MERT implementation uses the line search of Cer et al. (2008) to directly minimize corpus-level error. The PRO implementation uses a pairwise logistic loss to minimize the number of inversions in the ranked n-best lists. These batch implementations accumulate n-best lists across epochs.

[2]For simplicity, we assume one reference, but the multi-reference case is analogous.

Online tuning is faster and more scalable than batch tuning, and sometimes leads to better solutions for non-convex settings like MT (Bottou and Bousquet, 2011). Weight updates are performed after each tuning example is decoded, and n-best lists are not accumulated. Consequently, online tuning is preferable for large tuning sets, or for rapid iteration during development. Phrasal includes the AdaGrad-based (Duchi et al., 2011) tuner of Green et al. (2013). The regularization options are L_2, efficient L_1 for feature selection (Duchi and Singer, 2009), or $L_1 + L_2$ (elastic net). There are two online loss functions: a pairwise (PRO) objective and a listwise minimum expected error objective (Och, 2003). These online loss functions require sentence-level error metrics, several of which are available in the toolkit: BLEU+1 (Lin and Och, 2004), Nakov BLEU (Nakov et al., 2012), and TER.

2.4 Decoding

The Phrasal decoder can be invoked either programmatically as a Java object or as a standalone application. In both cases the decoder is configured via options that specify the language model, phrase table, weight vector w, etc. The decoder is multithreaded, with one decoding instance per thread. Each decoding instance has its own weight vector, so in the programmatic case, it is possible to decode simultaneously under different weight vectors.

Two search procedures are included. The default is the phrase-based variant of cube pruning (Huang and Chiang, 2007). The standard multi-stack beam search (Och and Ney, 2004) is also an option. Either procedure can be configured in one of several recombination modes. The "Pharaoh" mode only considers linear distortion, source coverage, and target LM history. The "Exact" mode considers these states in addition to any feature that declares recombination state (see section 3.3).

The decoder includes several options for deployment environments such as an unknown word API, pre-/post-processing APIs, and both full and prefix-based force decoding.

2.5 Evaluation and Post-processing

All of the error metrics available for tuning can also be invoked for evaluation. For significance testing, the toolkit includes an implementation of the permutation test of Riezler and Maxwell (2005), which was shown to be less susceptible to Type-I error than bootstrap re-sampling (Koehn, 2004).

$\dfrac{}{r : s(r,w)} \; r \in R$	axiom
$\dfrac{d : w(d) \quad r : s(r,w)}{d' : s(d',w)} \; r \notin cov(d)$	item
$\lvert cov(d)\rvert = \lvert s\rvert$	goal

Table 1: Phrase-based MT as deductive inference. This notation can be read as follows: if the antecedents on the top are true, then the consequent on the bottom is true subject to the conditions on the right. The new item d' is creating by appending r to the ordered sequence of rules that define d.

Phrasal also includes two truecasing packages. The LM-based truecaser (Lita et al., 2003) requires an LM estimated from cased, tokenized text. A subsequent detokenization step is thus necessary. A more convenient alternative is the CRF-based post-processor that can be trained to invert an arbitrary pre-processor. This post-processor can perform truecasing and detokenization in one pass.

3 Feature API

Phrasal supports dynamic feature extraction during tuning and decoding. In the API, feature templates are called **featurizers**. There are two types with associated interfaces: `RuleFeaturizer` and `DerivationFeaturizer`. One way to illustrate these two featurizers is to consider phrase-based decoding as a deductive system. Let $r = \langle f, e\rangle$ be a rule in a set R, which is conventionally called the phrase table. Let $d = \{r_i\}_{i=1}^N$ be an ordered sequence of derivation N rules called a derivation, which specifies a translation for some source input sequence s (which, by some abuse of notation, is equivalent to f in Eq. (1)). Finally, define functions $cov(d)$ as the source coverage set of d as a bit vector and $s(\cdot, w)$ as the score of a rule or derivation under w.[3] The expression $r \notin cov(d)$ means that r maps to an empty/uncovered span in $cov(d)$. Table 1 shows the deductive system.

3.1 Dynamic Rule Features

RuleFeaturizers are invoked when scoring axioms, which do not require any derivation context. The static rule features described in section 2.2 also contribute to axiom scoring, and differ only from RuleFeaturizers in that they are stored permanently in the phrase table. In contrast, RuleFeaturizers

[3]Note that $s(d, w) = w^\top \phi(d)$ in the log-linear formulation of MT (see Eq. (1)).

Listing 1: A `RuleFeaturizer`, which depends only on a translation rule.

```
public class WordPenaltyFeaturizer
 implements RuleFeaturizer {

 @Override
 public List<FeatureValue>
  ruleFeaturize(Featurizable f) {

  List<FeatureValue> features =
   Generics.newLinkedList();

  // Extract single feature
  features.add(new FeatureValue(
   "WordPenalty", f.targetPhrase.size()));

  return features;
 }
}
```

are extracted during decoding. An example feature template is the word penalty, which is simply the dimension of the target side of r (Listing 1).

`Featurizable` wraps decoder state from which features can be extracted. RuleFeaturizers are extracted during each phrase table query and cached, so they can be simply efficiently retrieved during decoding.

Once the feature is compiled, it is simply specified on the command-line when the decoder is executed. No other configuration is required.

3.2 Derivation Features

DerivationFeaturizers are invoked when scoring items, and thus depend on some derivation context. An example is the LM, which requires the n-gram context from d to score r when creating the new hypothesis d' (Listing 2).

The LM featurizer first looks up the recombination state of the derivation, which contains the n-gram context. Then it queries the LM by passing the rule and context, and sets the new state as the result of the LM query. Finally, it returns a feature "LM" with the value of the LM query.

3.3 Recombination State

Listing 2 shows a state lookup during feature extraction. Phrase-based MT feature design differs significantly from that of convex classifiers in terms of the interaction with inference. For example, in a maximum entropy classifier inference is exact, so a good optimizer can simply nullify bad features to retain baseline accuracy. In contrast, MT feature templates affect search through both future cost heuristics and recombination state. Bad features can introduce search errors and thus decrease

Listing 2: A `DerivationFeaturizer`, which must lookup and save recombination state for extraction.

```
public class NGramLanguageModelFeaturizer
 extends DerivationFeaturizer {

 @Override
 public List<FeatureValue> featurize(
  Featurizable f) {

  // Get recombination state
  LMState priorState = f.prior.getState(this);

  // LM query
  LMState state = lm.score(f.targetPhrase, priorState);

  List<FeatureValue> features =
   Generics.newLinkedList();

  // Extract single feature
  features.add(
   new FeatureValue("LM", state.getScore()));

  // Set new recombination state
  f.setState(this, state);

  return features;
 }
}
```

accuracy, sometimes catastrophically.

The feature API allows DerivationFeaturizers to explicitly declare recombination state via the `FeaturizerState` interface.[4] The interface requires a state equality operator and a hash code function. Then the search procedure will only recombine derivations with equal states. For example, the state of the n-gram LM DerivationFeaturizer (Listing 2) is the n-1 gram context, and the hashcode is a hash of that context string. Only derivations for which the equality operator of LMState returns true can be recombined.

4 Web Service

Machine translation output is increasingly utilized in computer-assisted translation (CAT) workbenches. To support deployment, Phrasal includes a lightweight J2EE servlet that exposes a RESTful JSON API for querying a trained system. The toolkit includes a standalone servlet container, but the servlet may also be incorporated into a J2EE server. The servlet requires just one input parameter: the Phrasal configuration file, which is also used for tuning and decoding. Consequently, after running the standard pipeline, the trained system can be deployed with one command.

[4] To control future cost estimation, the designer would need to write a new heuristic that considers perhaps a subset of the full feature map. There is a separate API for future cost heuristics.

4.1 Standard Web Service

The standard web service supports two types of requests. The first is `TranslationRequest`, which performs full decoding on a source input. The JSON message structure is:

Listing 3: `TranslationRequest` message.

```
TranslationRequest {
  srcLang :(string),
  tgtLang :(string),
  srcText :(string),
  tgtText :(string),
  limit :(integer),
  properties :(object)
}
```

The `srcLang` and `tgtLang` fields are ignored by the servlet, but can be used by a middleware proxy to route requests to Phrasal servlet instances, one per language pair. The `srcText` field is the source input, and `properties` is a Javascript associative array that can contain key/value pairs to pass to the feature API. For example, we often use the `properties` field to pass domain information with each request.

Phrasal will perform full decoding and respond with the message:

Listing 4: `TranslationReply` message, which is returned upon successful processing of `TranslationRequest`.

```
TranslationReply {
  resultList :[
   {tgtText :(string),
     align :(string),
     score :(float)
   },...]
}
```

`resultList` is a ranked n-best list of translations, each with target tokens, word alignments, and a score.

The second request type is `RuleRequest`, which enables phrase table queries. These requests are processed very quickly since decoding is not required. The JSON message structure is:

Listing 5: `RuleRequest` message, which prompts a direct lookup into the phrase table.

```
RuleRequest {
  srcLang :(string),
  tgtLang :(string),
  srcText :(string),
  limit :(integer),
  properties :(object)
}
```

`limit` is the maximum number of translations to return. The response message is analogous to that for TranslationRequest, so we omit it.

4.2 Interactive Machine Translation

Interactive machine translation (Bisbey and Kay, 1972) pairs human and machine translators in hopes of increasing the throughput of high quality translation. It is an old idea that is again in focus. One challenge is to present relevant machine suggestions to humans. To that end, Phrasal supports context-sensitive translation queries via prefix decoding. Consider again the `TranslationRequest` message. When the `tgtText` field is empty, the source input is decoded from scratch. But when this field contains a prefix, Phrasal returns translations that begin with the prefix. The search procedure force decodes the prefix, and then completes the translation via conventional decoding. Consequently, if the user has typed a partial translation, Phrasal can suggest completions conditioned on that prefix. The longer the prefix, the faster the decoding, since the user prefix constrains the search space. This feature allows Phrasal to produce increasingly precise suggestions as the user works.

5 Experiments

We compare Phrasal and Moses by restricting an existing large-scale system to a set of common features. We start with the Arabic–English system of Green et al. (2014), which is built from 6.6M parallel segments. The system includes a 5-gram English LM estimated from the target-side of the bitext and 990M English monolingual tokens. The feature set is their dense baseline, but without lexicalized reordering and the two extended phrase table features. This leaves the nine baseline features also implemented by Moses. We use the same phrase table, phrase table query limit (20), and distortion limit (5) for both decoders. The tuning set (mt023568) contains 5,604 segments, and the development set (mt04) contains 1,075 segments.

We ran all experiments on a dedicated server with 16 physical cores and 128GB of memory.

Figure 1 shows single-threaded decoding time of the dev set as a function of the cube pruning pop limit. At very low limits Moses is faster than Phrasal, but then slows sharply. In contrast, Phrasal scales linearly and is thus faster at higher pop limits.

Figure 2 shows multi-threaded decoding time of the dev set with the cube pruning pop limit fixed at 1,200. Here Phrasal is initially faster, but Moses becomes more efficient at four threads. There are two possible explanations. First, profiling shows that LM queries account for approximately 75%

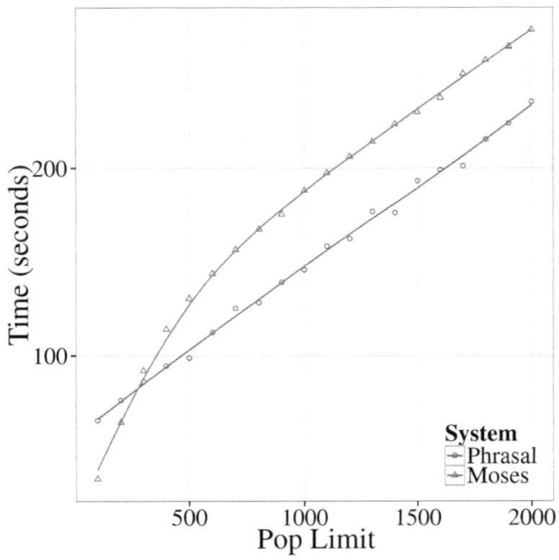

Figure 1: Development set decoding time as a function of the cube pruning pop limit.

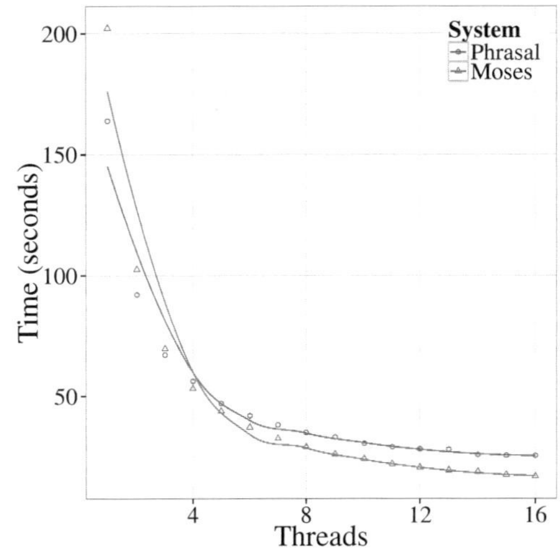

Figure 2: Development set decoding time as a function of the threadpool size.

of the Phrasal CPU-time. KenLM is written in C++, and Phrasal queries it via JNI. It appears as though multi-threading across this boundary is a source of inefficiency. Second, we observe that the Java parallel garbage collector (GC) runs up to seven threads, which become increasingly active as the number of decoder threads increases. These and other Java overhead threads must be scheduled, limiting gains as the number of decoding threads approaches the number of physical cores.

Finally, Figure 3 shows tuning BLEU as a function of wallclock time. For Moses we chose the batch MIRA implementation of Cherry and Foster (2012), which is popular for tuning feature-rich systems. Phrasal uses the online tuner with the expected BLEU objective (Green et al., 2014). Moses achieves a maximum BLEU score of 47.63 after 143 minutes of tuning, while Phrasal reaches this level after just 17 minutes, later reaching a maximum BLEU of 47.75 after 42 minutes. Much of the speedup can be attributed to phrase table and LM loading time: the Phrasal tuner loads these data structures just once, while the Moses tuner loads them every epoch. Of course, this loading time becomes more significant with larger-scale systems.

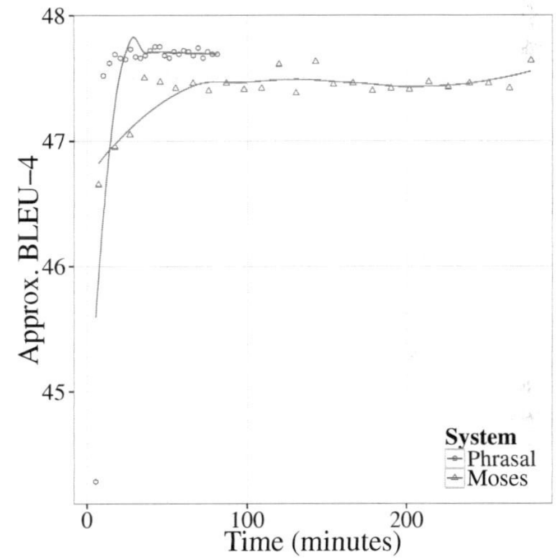

Figure 3: Approximate BLEU-4 during tuning as a function of time over 25 tuning epochs. The horizontal axis is accumulated time, while each point indicates BLEU at the end of an epoch.

6 Conclusion

We presented a revised version of Phrasal, an open-source, phrase-based MT toolkit. The revisions support new directions in MT research including feature-rich models, large-scale tuning, and web-based interactive MT. A direct comparison with Moses showed favorable performance on a large-scale translation system.

Acknowledgments We thank Michel Galley for previous contributions to Phrasal. The first author is supported by a National Science Foundation Graduate Research Fellowship. This work was supported by the Defense Advanced Research Projects Agency (DARPA) Broad Operational Language Translation (BOLT) program through IBM. Any opinions, findings, and conclusions or recommendations expressed in this material are those of the author(s) and do not necessarily reflect the view of DARPA or the US government.

References

W. Ammar, V. Chahuneau, M. Denkowski, G. Hanneman, W. Ling, A. Matthews, et al. 2013. The CMU machine translation systems at WMT 2013: Syntax, synthetic translation options, and pseudo-references. In *WMT*.

R. Appuswamy, C. Gkantsidis, D. Narayanan, O. Hodson, and A. Rowstron. 2013. Nobody ever got fired for buying a cluster. Technical report, Microsoft Corporation, MSR-TR-2013-2.

R. Bisbey and Kay. 1972. The MIND translation system: a study in man-machine collaboration. Technical Report P-4786, Rand Corp., March.

L. Bottou and O. Bousquet. 2011. The tradeoffs of large scale learning. In *Optimization for Machine Learning*, pages 351–368. MIT Press.

D. Cer, D. Jurafsky, and C. D. Manning. 2008. Regularization and search for minimum error rate training. In *WMT*.

D. Cer, M. Galley, D. Jurafsky, and C. D. Manning. 2010. Phrasal: A statistical machine translation toolkit for exploring new model features. In *HLT-NAACL, Demonstration Session*.

C. Cherry and G. Foster. 2012. Batch tuning strategies for statistical machine translation. In *HLT-NAACL*.

M. Denkowski and A. Lavie. 2011. Meteor 1.3: Automatic metric for reliable optimization and evaluation of machine translation systems. In *WMT*.

J. Duchi and Y. Singer. 2009. Efficient online and batch learning using forward backward splitting. *JMLR*, 10:2899–2934.

J. Duchi, E. Hazan, and Y. Singer. 2011. Adaptive subgradient methods for online learning and stochastic optimization. *JMLR*, 12:2121–2159.

N. Durrani, B. Haddow, K. Heafield, and P. Koehn. 2013. Edinburgh's machine translation systems for European language pairs. In *WMT*.

C. Dyer, A. Lopez, J. Ganitkevitch, J. Weese, F. Ture, et al. 2010. cdec: A decoder, alignment, and learning framework for finite-state and context-free translation models. In *ACL System Demonstrations*.

M. Galley and C. D. Manning. 2008. A simple and effective hierarchical phrase reordering model. In *EMNLP*.

S. Green, S. Wang, D. Cer, and C. D. Manning. 2013. Fast and adaptive online training of feature-rich translation models. In *ACL*.

S. Green, D. Cer, and C. D. Manning. 2014. An empirical comparison of features and tuning for phrase-based machine translation. In *WMT*.

K. Heafield, I. Pouzyrevsky, J. H. Clark, and P. Koehn. 2013. Scalable modified Kneser-Ney language model estimation. In *ACL, Short Papers*.

K. Heafield. 2011. KenLM: Faster and smaller language model queries. In *WMT*.

M. Hopkins and J. May. 2011. Tuning as ranking. In *EMNLP*.

L. Huang and D. Chiang. 2007. Forest rescoring: Faster decoding with integrated language models. In *ACL*.

P. Koehn, F. J. Och, and D. Marcu. 2003. Statistical phrase-based translation. In *NAACL*.

P. Koehn, H. Hoang, A. Birch, C. Callison-Burch, M. Federico, N. Bertoldi, et al. 2007. Moses: Open source toolkit for statistical machine translation. In *ACL, Demonstration Session*.

P. Koehn. 2004. Statistical significance tests for machine translation evaluation. In *EMNLP*.

P. Liang, B. Taskar, and D. Klein. 2006. Alignment by agreement. In *NAACL*.

C.-Y. Lin and F. J. Och. 2004. ORANGE: a method for evaluating automatic evaluation metrics for machine translation. In *COLING*.

L. V. Lita, A. Ittycheriah, S. Roukos, and N. Kambhatla. 2003. tRuEcasIng. In *ACL*.

P. Nakov, F. Guzman, and S. Vogel. 2012. Optimizing for sentence-level BLEU+1 yields short translations. In *COLING*.

J. Neidert, S. Schuster, S. Green, K. Heafield, and C. D. Manning. 2014. Stanford University's submissions to the WMT 2014 translation task. In *WMT*.

F. J. Och and H. Ney. 2004. The alignment template approach to statistical machine translation. *Computational Linguistics*, 30(4):417–449.

F. J. Och. 2003. Minimum error rate training for statistical machine translation. In *ACL*.

K. Papineni, S. Roukos, T. Ward, and W. Zhu. 2002. BLEU: a method for automatic evaluation of machine translation. In *ACL*.

M. Post, J. Ganitkevitch, L. Orland, J. Weese, Y. Cao, and C. Callison-Burch. 2013. Joshua 5.0: Sparser, better, faster, server. In *WMT*.

S. Riezler and J. T. Maxwell. 2005. On some pitfalls in automatic evaluation and significance testing in MT. In *ACL Workshop on Intrinsic and Extrinsic Evaluation Measures for Machine Translation and/or Summarization*.

M. Snover, B. Dorr, R. Schwartz, L. Micciulla, and J. Makhoul. 2006. A study of translation edit rate with targeted human annotation. In *AMTA*.

C. Tillmann. 2004. A unigram orientation model for statistical machine translation. In *NAACL*.

J. Wuebker, M. Huck, S. Peitz, M. Nuhn, M. Freitag, J. T. Peter, S. Mansour, and H. Ney. 2012. Jane 2: Open source phrase-based and hierarchical statistical machine translation. In *COLING: Demonstration Papers*.

Anaphora Models and Reordering for Phrase-Based SMT

Christian Hardmeier Sara Stymne Jörg Tiedemann Aaron Smith Joakim Nivre
Uppsala University
Department of Linguistics and Philology
firstname.lastname@lingfil.uu.se

Abstract

We describe the Uppsala University systems for WMT14. We look at the integration of a model for translating pronominal anaphora and a syntactic dependency projection model for English–French. Furthermore, we investigate post-ordering and tunable POS distortion models for English–German.

1 Introduction

In this paper we describe the Uppsala University systems for WMT14. We present three different systems. Two of them are based on the document-level decoder Docent (Hardmeier et al., 2012; Hardmeier et al., 2013a). In our English–French system we extend Docent to handle pronoun anaphora, and in our English–German system we add part-of-speech phrase-distortion models to Docent. For German–English we also have a system based on Moses (Koehn et al., 2007). Again the focus is on word order, this time by using pre- and post-reordering.

2 Document-Level Decoding

Traditional SMT decoders translate texts as bags of sentences, assuming independence between sentences. This assumption allows efficient algorithms for exploring a large search space based on dynamic programming (Och et al., 2001). Because of the dynamic programming assumptions it is hard to directly include discourse-level and long-distance features into a traditional SMT decoder.

In contrast to this very popular stack decoding approach, our decoder Docent (Hardmeier et al., 2012; Hardmeier et al., 2013a) implements a search procedure based on local search. At any stage of the search process, its search state consists of a complete document translation, making it easy for feature models to access the complete document with its current translation at any point in time. The search algorithm is a stochastic variant of standard hill climbing. At each step, it generates a successor of the current search state by randomly applying one of a set of state changing operations to a random location in the document, and accepts the new state if it has a better score than the previous state. The operations are to change the translation of a phrase, to change the word order by swapping the positions of two phrases or moving a sequence of phrases, and to resegment phrases. The initial state can either be initialized randomly, or be based on an initial run from Moses. This setup is not limited by dynamic programming constraints, and enables the use of the full translated target document to extract features.

3 English–French

Our English–French system is a phrase-based SMT system with a combination of two decoders, Moses (Koehn et al., 2007) and Docent (Hardmeier et al., 2013a). The fundamental setup is loosely based on the system submitted by Cho et al. (2013) to the WMT 2013 shared task. Our phrase table is trained on data taken from the News commentary, Europarl, UN, Common crawl and 10^9 corpora. The first three of these corpora were included integrally into the training set after filtering out sentences of more than 80 words. The Common crawl and 10^9 data sets were run through an additional filtering step with an SVM classifier, closely following Mediani et al. (2011). The system includes three language models, a regular 6-gram model with modified Kneser-Ney smoothing (Chen and Goodman, 1998) trained with KenLM (Heafield, 2011), a 4-gram bilingual language model (Niehues et al., 2011) with Kneser-Ney smoothing trained with KenLM and a 9-gram model over Brown clusters (Brown et al., 1992) with Witten-Bell smoothing (Witten and Bell, 1991) trained with SRILM (Stolcke, 2002).

Proceedings of the Ninth Workshop on Statistical Machine Translation, pages 122–129,
Baltimore, Maryland USA, June 26–27, 2014.

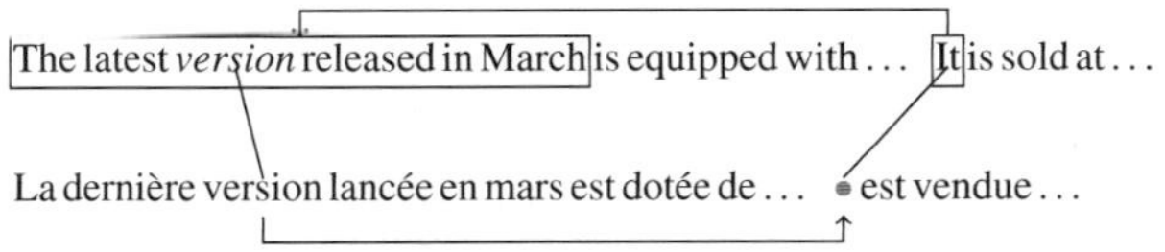

Figure 1: Pronominal Anaphora Model

Our baseline system achieved a cased BLEU score of 33.2 points on the newstest2014 data set. Since the anaphora model used in our submission suffered from a serious bug, we do not discuss the results of the primary submission in more detail.

3.1 Pronominal Anaphora Model

Our pronominal anaphora model is an adaptation of the pronoun prediction model described by Hardmeier et al. (2013b) to SMT. The model consists of a neural network that discriminatively predicts the translation of a source language pronoun from a short list of possible target language pronouns using features from the context of the source language pronouns and from the translations of possibly remote antecedents. The objective of this model is to handle situations like the one depicted in Figure 1, where the correct choice of a target-language pronoun is subject to morphosyntactic agreement with its antecedent. This problem consists of several steps. To score a pronoun, the system must decide if a pronoun is anaphoric and, if so, find potential antecedents. Then, it can predict what pronouns are likely to occur in the translation. Our pronoun prediction model is trained on both tasks jointly, including anaphora resolution as a set of latent variables. At test time, we split the network in two parts. The anaphora resolution part is run separately as a preprocessing step, whereas the pronoun prediction part is integrated into the document-level decoder with two additional feature models.

The features correspond to two copies of the neural network, one to handle the singular pronoun *it* and one to handle the plural pronoun *they*. Each network just predicts a binary distinction between two cases, *il* and *elle* for the singular network and *ils* and *elles* for the plural network. Unlike Hardmeier et al. (2013b), we do not use an OTHER category to capture cases that should not be translated with any of these options. Instead, we treat all other cases in the phrase table and activate the anaphora models only if one of their target pronouns actually occurs in the output.

To achieve this, we generate pronouns in two steps. In the phrase table training corpus, we replace all pronouns that should be handled by the classifier, i.e. instances of *il* and *elle* aligned to *it* and instances of *ils* and *elles* aligned to *they*, with special placeholders. At decoding time, if a placeholder is encountered in a target language phrase, the applicable pronouns are generated with equal translation model probability, and the anaphora model adds a score to discriminate between them.

To reduce the influence of the language model on pronoun choice and give full control to the anaphora model, our primary language model is trained on text containing placeholders instead of pronouns. Since all output pronouns can also be generated without the interaction of the anaphora model if they are not aligned to a source language pronoun, we must make sure that the language model sees training data for both placeholders and actual pronouns. However, for the monolingual training corpora we have no word alignments to decide whether or not to replace a pronoun by a placeholder. To get around this problem, we train a 6-gram placeholder language model on the target language side of the Europarl and News commentary corpora. Then, we use the Viterbi n-gram model decoder of SRILM (Stolcke, 2002) to map pronouns in the entire language model training set to placeholders where appropriate. No substitutions are made in the bilingual language model or the Brown cluster language model.

3.2 Dependency Projection Model

Our English–French system also includes a dependency projection model, which uses source-side dependency structure to model target-side relations between words. This model assigns a score to each dependency arc in the source language by considering the target words aligned to the head and the dependent. In Figure 2, for instance, there is an *nsubjpass* arc connecting *dominated* to *production*. The head is aligned to the target word *dominée*, while the dependent is aligned to the set $\{production, de\}$. The score is computed by a neural network taking as features the head and dependent words and their part-of-speech tags in the source language, the target word sets aligned to the head and dependent, the label of the dependency arc, the distance between the head and dependent word in the source language as well as the shortest distance between any pair of words in the aligned sets. The network is a binary classifier trained to discriminate positive examples extracted from human-made reference

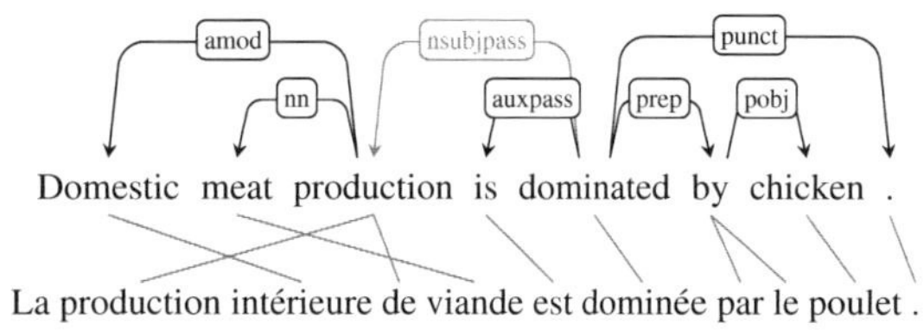

Figure 2: Dependency projection model

translations from negative examples extracted from n-best lists generated by a baseline SMT system.

4 English–German

For English–German we have two systems, one based on Moses, and one based on Docent. In both cases we have focused on word order, particularly for verbs and particles.

Both our systems are trained on the same data made available by WMT. The Common crawl data was filtered using the method of Stymne et al. (2013). We use factored models with POS tags as a second output factor for German. The possibility to use language models for different factors has been added to our Docent decoder. Language models include an in-domain news language model, an out-of-domain model trained on the target side of the parallel training data and a POS language model trained on tagged news data. The LMs are trained in the same way as for English–French. All systems are tuned using MERT (Och, 2003). Phrase-tables are filtered using entropy-based pruning (Johnson et al., 2007) as implemented in Moses. All BLEU scores are given for uncased data.

4.1 Pre-Ordered Alignment and Post-Ordered Translation

The use of syntactic reordering as a separate preprocessing step has already a long tradition in statistical MT. Handcrafted rules (Collins et al., 2005; Popović and Ney, 2006) or data-driven models (Xia and McCord, 2004; Genzel, 2010; Rottmann and Vogel, 2007; Niehues and Kolss, 2009) for *preordering* training data and system input have been explored in numerous publications. For certain language pairs, such as German and English, this method can be very effective and often improves the quality of standard SMT systems significantly. Typically, the source language is reordered to better match the syntax of the target language when translating between languages that exhibit consistent word order differences, which are difficult to handle by SMT systems with limited reordering capabilities such as phrase-based models. Preordering is often done on the entire training data as well to optimize translation models for the pre-ordered input. Less common is the idea of *post-ordering*, which refers to a separate step after translating source language input to an intermediate target language with corrupted (source-language like) word order (Na et al., 2009; Sudoh et al., 2011).

In our experiments, we focus on the translation from English to German. Post-ordering becomes attractive for several reasons: One reason is the common split of verb-particle constructions that can lead to long distance dependencies in German clauses. Phrase-based systems and n-gram language models are not able to handle such relations beyond a certain distance and it is desirable to keep them as connected units in the phrase translation tables. Another reason is the possible distance of finite and infinitival verbs in German verb phrases that can lead to the same problems described above with verb-particle constructions. The auxiliary or modal verb is placed at the second position but the main verb appears at the end of the associated verb phrase. The distances can be arbitrarily long and long-range dependencies are quite frequent. Similarly, negation particles and adverbials move away from the inflected verb forms in certain constructions. For more details on specific phenomena in German, we refer to (Collins et al., 2005; Gojun and Fraser, 2012). Pre-ordering, i.e. moving English words into German word order does not seem to be a good option as we loose the connection between related items when moving particles and main verbs away from their associated elements. Hence, we are interested in reordering the target language German into English word order which can be beneficial in two ways: (i) Reordering the German part of the parallel training data makes it possible to improve word alignment (which tends to prefer monotonic mappings) and subsequent phrase extraction which leads to better translation models. (ii) We can explore a two-step procedure in which we train a phrase-based SMT model for translating English into German with English word order first (which covers many long-distance relations locally) and then apply a second system that moves words into place according to correct German syntax (which may involve long-range distortion).

For simplicity, we base our experiments on handcrafted rules for some of the special cases discussed above. For efficiency reasons, we define our rules over POS tag patterns rather than on full syntactic parse trees. We rely on TreeTagger and apply rules to join verbs in discontinuous verb phrases and to move verb-finals in subordinate clauses, to move verb particles, adverbials and negation particles. Table 1 shows two examples of reordered sentences together with the original sentences in English and German. Our rules implement rough heuristics to identify clause boundaries and word positions. We do not properly evaluate these rules but focus on the down-stream evaluation of the MT system instead.

It is therefore dangerous to extrapolate from short-term trends.
Daher ist es gefährlich, aus kurzfristigen Trends Prognosen abzuleiten.
Daher ist gefährlich es, abzuleiten aus kurzfristigen Trends Prognosen.

The fall of Saddam ushers in the right circumstances.
Der Sturz von Saddam leitet solche richtigen Umstände ein.
Der Sturz von Saddam ein leitet solche richtigen Umstände.

Table 1: Two examples of pre-ordering outputs. The first two lines are the original English and German sentences and the third line shows the reordered sentence.

We use three systems based on Moses to compare the effect of reordering on alignment and translation. All systems are case-sensitive phrase-based systems with lexicalized reordering trained on data provided by WMT. Word alignment is performed using fast_align (Dyer et al., 2013). For tuning we use newstest2011. Additionally, we also test parallel data from OPUS (Tiedemann, 2012) filtered by a method adopted from Mediani et al. (2011).

To contrast our baseline system, we trained a phrase-based model on parallel data that has been aligned on data pre-ordered using the reordering rules for German, which has been restored to the original word order after word alignment and before phrase extraction (similar to (Carpuat et al., 2010; Stymne et al., 2010)). We expect that the word alignment is improved by reducing crossings and long-distance links. However, the translation model as such has the same limitations as the baseline system in terms of long-range distortions. The final system is a two-step model in which we apply translation and language models trained on pre-ordered target language data to perform the first step, which also includes a reordered POS language model. The second step is also treated as a translation problem as in Sudoh et al. (2011), and in our case we use a phrase-based model here with lexicalized reordering and a rather large distortion limit of 12 words. Another possibility would be to apply another rule set that reverts the misplaced words to the grammatically correct positions. This, however, would require deeper syntactic information about the target language to, for example, distinguish main from subordinate clauses. Instead, our model is trained on parallel target language data with the pre-ordered version as input and the original version as output language. For this model, both sides are tagged and a POS language model is used again as one of the target language factors in decoding. Table 2 shows the results in terms of BLEU scores on the newstest sets from 2013 and 2014.

	newstest2013	newstest2014
baseline	19.3	19.1
pre	19.4	19.3
post	18.6	18.7
baseline+OPUS	19.5	19.3
pre+OPUS	19.5	19.3
post+OPUS	19.7	18.8

Table 2: BLEU4 scores for English-German systems (w/o OPUS): Standard phrase-based (*baseline*); phrase-based with pre-ordered parallel corpus used for word alignment (*pre*); two-step phrase-based with post-reordering (*post*)

The results show that pre-ordering has some effect on word alignment quality in terms of supporting better phrase extractions in subsequent steps. Our experiments show a consistent but small improvement for models trained on data that have been prepared in this way. In contrast, the two-step procedure is more difficult to judge in terms of automatic metrics. On the 2013 newstest data we can see another small improvement in the setup that includes OPUS data but in most cases the BLEU scores go down, even below the baseline. The short-comings of the two-step procedure are obvious. Separating translation and reordering in a pipeline adds the risk of error propagation. Furthermore, reducing the second step to single-best translations is a strong limitation and using phrase-based models for the final reordering procedure is probably not the wisest decision. However, manual inspections reveals that many interesting phenomena can be handled even with this simplistic setup.

Table 3 illustrates this with a few selected outcomes of our three systems. They show how verb-particle constructions with long-range distortion

reference	Schauspieler Orlando Bloom **hat sich** zur Trennung von seiner Frau , Topmodel Miranda Kerr , **geäußert** .
baseline	Schauspieler Orlando Bloom **hat** die Trennung von seiner Frau , Supermodel Miranda Kerr .
pre-ordering	Schauspieler Orlando Bloom **hat angekündigt** , die Trennung von seiner Frau , Supermodel Miranda Kerr .
post-ordering	Schauspieler Orlando Bloom **hat** seine Trennung von seiner Frau **angekündigt** , Supermodel Miranda Kerr .
reference	Er **gab** bei einer früheren Befragung den Kokainbesitz **zu** .
baseline	Er **gab** den Besitz von Kokain in einer früheren Anhörung .
pre-ordering	Er **räumte** den Besitz von Kokain in einer früheren Anhörung .
post-ordering	Er **räumte** den Besitz von Kokain in einer früheren Anhörung **ein** .
reference	Borussia Dortmund **kündigte** daraufhin harte Konsequenzen **an** .
baseline	Borussia Dortmund **kündigte an** , es werde schwere Folgen .
pre-ordering	Borussia Dortmund **hat angekündigt** , dass es schwerwiegende Konsequenzen .
post-ordering	Borussia Dortmund **kündigte an** , dass es schwere Folgen **geben werde** .

Table 3: Selected translation examples from the newstest 2014 data; the human *reference* translation; the *baseline* system, *pre-ordering* for word alignment and two-step translation with *post-ordering*.

such as "räumte ... ein" can be created and how discontinuous verb phrases can be handled ("hat ... angekündigt") with the two-step procedure. The model is also often better in producing verb finals in subordinate clauses (see the final example with "geben werde"). Note that many of these improvements do not get any credit by metrics like BLEU. For example the acceptable expression "räumte ein" which is synonymous to "gab zu" obtains less credit then the incomplete baseline translation. Interesting is also to see the effect of pre-ordering when used for alignment only in the second system. The first example in Table 3, for example, includes a correct main verb which is omitted in the baseline translation, probably because it is not extracted as a valid translation option.

4.2 Part-of-Speech Phrase-Distortion Models

Traditional SMT distortion models consist of two parts. A distance-based distortion cost is based on the position of the last word in a phrase, compared to the first word in the next phrase, given the source phrase order. A hard distortion limit blocks translations where the distortion is too large. The distortion limit serves to decrease the complexity of the decoder, thus increasing its speed.

In the Docent decoder, the distortion limit is not implemented as a hard limit, but as a feature, which could be seen as a soft constraint. We showed in previous work (Stymne et al., 2013) that it was useful to relax the hard distortion limit by either using a soft constraint, which could be tuned, or removing the limit completely. In that work we still used the standard parametrization of distortion, based on the positions of the first and last words in phrases.

Our Docent decoder, however, always provides us with a full target translation that is step-wise improved, which means that we can apply distortion measures on the phrase-level without resorting to heuristics, which, for instance, are needed in the case of the lexicalized reordering models in Moses (Koehn et al., 2005). Because of this it is possible to use phrase-based distortion, where we calculate distortion based on the order of phrases, not on the order of some words. It is possible to parametrize phrase-distortion in different ways. In this work we use the phrase-distortion distance and a soft limit on the distortion distance, to mimic the word-based distortion. In our experiments we always set the soft limit to a distance of four phrases. In addition we use a measure based on how many crossings a phrase order gives rise to. We thus have three phrase-distortion features.

As captured by lexicalized reordering models, different phrases have different tendencies to move. To capture this to some extent, we also decided to add part-of-speech (POS) classes to our models. POS has previously successfully been used in pre-reordering approaches (Popović and Ney, 2006; Niehues and Kolss, 2009). The word types that are most likely to move long distances in English–German translation are verbs and particles. Based on this observation we split phrases into two classes, phrases that only contains verbs and particles, and all other phrases. For these two groups we use separate phrase-distortion features, thus having a total of six part-of-speech phrase-distortion features. All of these features are soft, and are optimized during tuning.

In our system we initialize Docent by running Moses with a standard distortion model and lexicalized reordering, and then continuing the search with Docent including our part-of-speech phrase-distortion features. Tuning was done separately for the two components, first for the Moses component, and then for the Docent component initialized by

reference	Laut Dmitrij Kislow von der Organisation "Pravo na oryzhie" **kann** man eine Pistole vom Typ Makarow für 100 bis 300 Dollar **kaufen**.
baseline	Laut Dmitry Kislov aus der Rechten zu Waffen, eine Makarov Gun-spiele **erworben werden können** für 100-300 Dollar.
POS+phrase	Laut Dmitry Kislov von die Rechte an Waffen, eine Pistole Makarov für 100-300 Dollar **erworben werden können**.
reference	Die Waffen **gelangen** über mehrere Kanäle auf den Schwarzmarkt.
baseline	Der "Schwarze" Markt der Waffen ist wieder **aufgefüllt** über mehrere Kanäle.
POS+phrase	Der "Schwarze" Markt der Waffen durch mehrere Kanäle wieder **aufgefüllt ist**.
reference	Mehr Kameras **könnten** möglicherweise das Problem **lösen**...
baseline	Möglicherweise **könnte** das Problem **lösen**, eine große Anzahl von Kameras...
POS+phrase	Möglicherweise, eine große Anzahl von Kameras **könnte** das Problem **lösen**...

Table 4: Selected translation examples from the newstest2013 data; the human *reference* translation; the *baseline* system (Moses with lexicalized reordering) and the system with a *POS+phrase* distortion model.

Moses with lexicalized reordering with its tuned weights. We used newstest2009 for tuning. The training data was lowercased for training and decoding, and recasing was performed using a second Moses run trained on News data. As baselines we present two Moses systems, without and with lexicalized reordering, in addition to standard distortion features.

Table 5 shows results with our different distortion models. Overall the differences are quite small. The clearest difference is between the two Moses baselines, where the lexicalized reordering model leads to an improvement. With Docent, both the word distortion and phrase distortion without POS do not help to improve on Moses, with a small decrease in scores on one dataset. This is not very surprising, since lexical distortion is currently not supported by Docent, and the distortion models are thus weaker than the ones implemented in Moses. For our POS phrase distortion, however, we see a small improvement compared to Moses, despite the lack of lexicalized distortion. This shows that this distortion model is actually useful, and can even successfully replace lexicalized reordering. In future work, we plan to combine this method with a lexicalized reordering model, to see if the two models have complementary strengths. Our submitted system uses the POS phrase-distortion model.

System	Distortion	newstest2013	newstest2014
Moses	word	19.4	19.3
Moses	word+LexReo	19.6	19.6
Docent	word	19.5	19.6
Docent	phrase	19.5	19.6
Docent	POS+phrase	19.7	19.7

Table 5: BLEU4 scores for English–German systems with different distortion models.

If we inspect the translations, most of the differences between the Moses baseline and the system with POS+phrase distortion are actually due to lexical choice. Table 4 shows some examples where there are word order differences. The result is quite mixed with respect to the placement of verbs. In the first example, both systems put the verbs together but in different positions, instead of splitting them like the reference suggests. In the second example, our system erroneously put the verbs at the end, which would be fine if the sentence had been a subordinate clause. In the third example, the baseline system has the correct placement of the auxiliary "könnte", while our system is better at placing the main verb "lösen". In general, this indicates that our system is able to support long-distance distortion as it is needed in certain cases but sometimes overuses this flexibility. A better model would certainly need to incorporate syntactic information to distinguish main from subordinate clauses. However, this would add a lot of complexity to the model.

5 Conclusion

We have described the three Uppsala University systems for WMT14. In the English–French system we extend our document-level decoder Docent (Hardmeier et al., 2013a) to handle pronoun anaphora and introduced a dependency projection model. In our two English–German system we explore different methods for handling reordering, based on Docent and Moses. In particular, we look at post-ordering as a separate step and tunable POS phrase distortion.

Acknowledgements

This work forms part of the Swedish strategic research programme eSSENCE. We also acknowledge the use of the Abel cluster, owned by the University of Oslo and the Norwegian metacenter for High Performance Computing (NOTUR) and operated by the Department for Research Computing at USIT, under project `nn9106k`. Finally, we would also like to thank Eva Pettersson, Ali Basirat, and Eva Martinez for help with human evaluation.

References

Peter F. Brown, Peter V. deSouza, Robert L. Mercer, Vincent J. Della Pietra, and Jenifer C. Lai. 1992. Class-based n-gram models of natural language. *Computational linguistics*, 18(4):467–479.

Marine Carpuat, Yuval Marton, and Nizar Habash. 2010. Improving Arabic-to-English statistical machine translation by reordering post-verbal subjects for alignment. In *Proceedings of the ACL 2010 Conference Short Papers*, pages 178–183, Uppsala, Sweden.

Stanley F. Chen and Joshua Goodman. 1998. An empirical study of smoothing techniques for language modeling. Technical report, Computer Science Group, Harvard University, Cambridge, Massachusetts, USA.

Eunah Cho, Thanh-Le Ha, Mohammed Mediani, Jan Niehues, Teresa Herrmann, Isabel Slawik, and Alex Waibel. 2013. The Karlsruhe Institute of Technology translation systems for the WMT 2013. In *Proceedings of the Eighth Workshop on Statistical Machine Translation*, pages 104–108, Sofia, Bulgaria. Association for Computational Linguistics.

Michael Collins, Philipp Koehn, and Ivona Kučerová. 2005. Clause restructuring for statistical machine translation. In *Proceedings of the 43rd Annual Meeting of the ACL*, pages 531–540, Ann Arbor, Michigan, USA.

Chris Dyer, Victor Chahuneau, and Noah A. Smith. 2013. A simple, fast, and effective reparameterization of IBM model 2. In *Proceedings of the 2013 Conference of the NAACL: Human Language Technologies*, pages 644–648, Atlanta, Georgia, USA.

Dmitriy Genzel. 2010. Automatically learning source-side reordering rules for large scale machine translation. In *Proceedings of the 23rd International Conference on Computational Linguistics*, pages 376–384, Beijing, China.

Anita Gojun and Alexander Fraser. 2012. Determining the placement of German verbs in English–to–German SMT. In *Proceedings of the 13th Conference of the EACL*, pages 726–735, Avignon, France.

Christian Hardmeier, Joakim Nivre, and Jörg Tiedemann. 2012. Document-wide decoding for phrase-based statistical machine translation. In *Proceedings of the 2012 Joint Conference on Empirical Methods in Natural Language Processing and Computational Natural Language Learning*, pages 1179–1190, Jeju Island, Korea.

Christian Hardmeier, Sara Stymne, Jörg Tiedemann, and Joakim Nivre. 2013a. Docent: A document-level decoder for phrase-based statistical machine translation. In *Proceedings of the 51st Annual Meeting of the ACL, Demonstration session*, pages 193–198, Sofia, Bulgaria.

Christian Hardmeier, Jörg Tiedemann, and Joakim Nivre. 2013b. Latent anaphora resolution for cross-lingual pronoun prediction. In *Proceedings of the 2013 Conference on Empirical Methods in Natural Language Processing*, pages 380–391, Seattle, Washington, USA. Association for Computational Linguistics.

Kenneth Heafield. 2011. KenLM: faster and smaller language model queries. In *Proceedings of the Sixth Workshop on Statistical Machine Translation*, pages 187–197, Edinburgh, Scotland. Association for Computational Linguistics.

Howard Johnson, Joel Martin, George Foster, and Roland Kuhn. 2007. Improving translation quality by discarding most of the phrasetable. In *Proceedings of the 2007 Joint Conference on Empirical Methods in Natural Language Processing and Computational Natural Language Learning*, pages 967–975, Prague, Czech Republic.

Philipp Koehn, Amittai Axelrod, Alexandra Birch Mayne, Chris Callison-Burch, Miles Osborne, and David Talbot. 2005. Edinburgh system description for the 2005 IWSLT speech translation evaluation. In *Proceedings of the International Workshop on Spoken Language Translation*, Pittsburgh, Pennsylvania, USA.

Philipp Koehn, Hieu Hoang, Alexandra Birch, Chris Callison-Burch, Marcello Federico, Nicola Bertoldi, Brooke Cowan, Wade Shen, Christine Moran, Richard Zens, Chris Dyer, Ondrej Bojar, Alexandra Constantin, and Evan Herbst. 2007. Moses: Open source toolkit for statistical machine translation. In *Proceedings of the 45th Annual Meeting of the ACL, Demo and Poster Sessions*, pages 177–180, Prague, Czech Republic.

Mohammed Mediani, Eunah Cho, Jan Niehues, Teresa Herrmann, and Alex Waibel. 2011. The KIT English–French translation systems for IWSLT 2011. In *Proceedings of the International Workshop on Spoken Language Translation*, pages 73–78, San Francisco, California, USA.

Hwidong Na, Jin-Ji Li, Jungi Kim, and Jong-Hyeok Lee. 2009. Improving fluency by reordering target constituents using MST parser in English-to-Japanese phrase-based SMT. In *Proceedings of MT Summit XII*, pages 276–283, Ottawa, Ontario, Canada.

Jan Niehues and Muntsin Kolss. 2009. A POS-based model for long-range reorderings in SMT. In *Proceedings of the Fourth Workshop on Statistical Machine Translation*, pages 206–214, Athens, Greece.

Jan Niehues, Teresa Herrmann, Stephan Vogel, and Alex Waibel. 2011. Wider context by using bilingual language models in machine translation. In *Proceedings of the Sixth Workshop on Statistical Machine Translation*, pages 198–206, Edinburgh, Scotland. Association for Computational Linguistics.

Franz Josef Och, Nicola Ueffing, and Hermann Ney. 2001. An efficient A* search algorithm for Statistical Machine Translation. In *Proceedings of the ACL 2001 Workshop on Data-Driven Machine Translation*, pages 55–62, Toulouse, France.

Franz Josef Och. 2003. Minimum error rate training in statistical machine translation. In *Proceedings of the 42nd Annual Meeting of the ACL*, pages 160–167, Sapporo, Japan.

Maja Popović and Hermann Ney. 2006. POS-based reorderings for statistical machine translation. In *Proceedings of the 5th International Conference on Language Resources and Evaluation (LREC'06)*, pages 1278–1283, Genoa, Italy.

Kay Rottmann and Stephan Vogel. 2007. Word reordering in statistical machine translation with a POS-based distortion model. In *Proceedings of the 11th International Conference on Theoretical and Methodological Issues in Machine Translation*, pages 171–180, Skövde, Sweden.

Andreas Stolcke. 2002. SRILM – an extensible language modeling toolkit. In *Proceedings of the Seventh International Conference on Spoken Language Processing*, pages 901–904, Denver, Colorado, USA.

Sara Stymne, Maria Holmqvist, and Lars Ahrenberg. 2010. Vs and OOVs: Two problems for translation between German and English. In *Proceedings of the Joint Fifth Workshop on Statistical Machine Translation and MetricsMATR*, pages 183–188, Uppsala, Sweden.

Sara Stymne, Christian Hardmeier, Jörg Tiedemann, and Joakim Nivre. 2013. Tunable distortion limits and corpus cleaning for SMT. In *Proceedings of the Eighth Workshop on Statistical Machine Translation*, pages 225–231, Sofia, Bulgaria.

Katsuhito Sudoh, Xianchao Wu, Kevin Duh, Hajime Tsukada, and Masaaki Nagata. 2011. Post-ordering in statistical machine translation. In *Proceedings of MT Summit XIII*, pages 316–323, Xiamen. China.

Jörg Tiedemann. 2012. Parallel data, tools and interfaces in OPUS. In *Proceedings of the 8th International Conference on Language Resources and Evaluation (LREC'12)*, pages 2214–2218, Istanbul, Turkey.

Ian H. Witten and Timothy C. Bell. 1991. The zero-frequency problem: Estimating the probabilities of novel events in adaptive text compression. *IEEE Transactions on Information Theory*, 37(4):1085–1094.

Fei Xia and Michael McCord. 2004. Improving a statistical MT system with automatically learned rewrite patterns. In *Proceedings of the 20th International Conference on Computational Linguistics*, pages 508–514, Geneva, Switzerland.

The Karlsruhe Institute of Technology Translation Systems for the WMT 2014

Teresa Herrmann, Mohammed Mediani, Eunah Cho, Thanh-Le Ha, Jan Niehues, Isabel Slawik, Yuqi Zhang and Alex Waibel
Institute for Anthropomatics and Robotics
KIT - Karlsruhe Institute of Technology
firstname.lastname@kit.edu

Abstract

In this paper, we present the KIT systems participating in the Shared Translation Task translating between English↔German and English↔French. All translations are generated using phrase-based translation systems, using different kinds of word-based, part-of-speech-based and cluster-based language models trained on the provided data. Additional models include bilingual language models, reordering models based on part-of-speech tags and syntactic parse trees, as well as a lexicalized reordering model. In order to make use of noisy web-crawled data, we apply filtering and data selection methods for language modeling. A discriminative word lexicon using source context information proved beneficial for all translation directions.

1 Introduction

We describe the KIT systems for the Shared Translation Task of the ACL 2014 Ninth Workshop on Statistical Machine Translation. We participated in the English↔German and English↔French translation directions, using a phrase-based decoder with lattice input.

The paper is organized as follows: the next section describes the data used for each translation direction. Section 3 gives a detailed description of our systems including all the models. The translation results for all directions are presented afterwards and we close with a conclusion.

2 Data

We utilize the provided EPPS, NC and Common Crawl parallel corpora for English→German and German→English, plus Giga for English→French and French→English. The monolingual part of those parallel corpora, the News Shuffle corpus for all four directions and additionally the Gigaword corpus for English→French and German→English are used as monolingual training data for the different language models. For optimizing the system parameters, newstest2012 and newstest2013 are used as development and test data respectively.

3 System Description

Before training we perform a common preprocessing of the raw data, which includes removing long sentences and sentences with a length mismatch exceeding a certain threshold. Afterwards, we normalize special symbols, dates, and numbers. Then we perform smart-casing of the first letter of every sentence. Compound splitting (Koehn and Knight, 2003) is performed on the source side of the corpus for German→English translation. In order to improve the quality of the web-crawled Common Crawl corpus, we filter out noisy sentence pairs using an SVM classifier for all four translation tasks as described in Mediani et al. (2011).

Unless stated otherwise, we use 4-gram language models (LM) with modified Kneser-Ney smoothing, trained with the SRILM toolkit (Stolcke, 2002). All translations are generated by an in-house phrase-based translation system (Vogel, 2003), and we use Minimum Error Rate Training (MERT) as described in Venugopal et al. (2005) for optimization. The word alignment of the parallel corpora is generated using the GIZA++ Toolkit (Och and Ney, 2003) for both directions. Afterwards, the alignments are combined using the grow-diag-final-and heuristic. For English→German, we use discriminative word alignment trained on hand-aligned data as described in Niehues and Vogel (2008). The phrase table (PT) is built using the Moses toolkit (Koehn et al., 2007). The phrase scoring for the small data sets (German↔English) is also

Proceedings of the Ninth Workshop on Statistical Machine Translation, pages 130–135,
Baltimore, Maryland USA, June 26–27, 2014.

done by the Moses toolkit, whereas the bigger sets (French↔English) are scored by our in-house parallel phrase scorer (Mediani et al., 2012a). The phrase pair probabilities are computed using modified Kneser-Ney smoothing as described in Foster et al. (2006).

Since German is a highly inflected language, we try to alleviate the out-of-vocabulary problem through quasi-morphological operations that change the lexical entry of a known word form to an unknown word form as described in Niehues and Waibel (2011).

3.1 Word Reordering Models

We apply automatically learned reordering rules based on part-of-speech (POS) sequences and syntactic parse tree constituents to perform source sentence reordering according to the target language word order. The rules are learned from a parallel corpus with POS tags (Schmid, 1994) for the source side and a word alignment to learn reordering rules that cover short range (Rottmann and Vogel, 2007) and long range reorderings (Niehues and Kolss, 2009). In addition, we apply a tree-based reordering model (Herrmann et al., 2013) to better address the differences in word order between German and English. Here, a word alignment and syntactic parse trees (Rafferty and Manning, 2008; Klein and Manning, 2003) for the source side of the training corpus are required to learn rules on how to reorder the constituents in the source sentence. The POS-based and tree-based reordering rules are applied to each input sentence before translation. The resulting reordered sentence variants as well as the original sentence are encoded in a reordering lattice. The lattice, which also includes the original position of each word, is used as input to the decoder.

In order to acquire phrase pairs matching the reordered sentence variants, we perform lattice phrase extraction (LPE) on the training corpus where phrase are extracted from the reordered word lattices instead of the original sentences.

In addition, we use a lexicalized reordering model (Koehn et al., 2005) which stores reordering probabilities for each phrase pair. During decoding the lexicalized reordering model determines the reordering orientation of each phrase pair at the phrase boundaries. The probability for the respective orientation with respect to the original position of the words is included as an additional score in the log-linear model of the translation system.

3.2 Adaptation

In the French→English and English→French systems, we perform adaptation for translation models as well as for language models. The EPPS and NC corpora are used as in-domain data for the direction English→French, while NC corpus is the in-domain data for French→English.

Two phrase tables are built: one is the out-of-domain phrase table, which is trained on all corpora; the other is the in-domain phrase table, which is trained on in-domain data. We adapt the translation model by using the scores from the two phrase tables with the backoff approach described in Niehues and Waibel (2012). This results in a phrase table with six scores, the four scores from the general phrase table as well as the two conditional probabilities from the in-domain phrase table. In addition, we take the union of the candidate phrase pairs collected from both phrase tables A detailed description of the union method can be found in Mediani et al. (2012b).

The language model is adapted by log-linearly combining the general language model and an in-domain language model. We train a separate language model using only the in-domain data. Then it is used as an additional language model during decoding. Optimal weights are set during tuning by MERT.

3.3 Special Language Models

In addition to word-based language models, we use different types of non-word language models for each of the systems. With the help of a bilingual language model (Niehues et al., 2011) we are able to increase the bilingual context between source and target words beyond phrase boundaries. This language model is trained on bilingual tokens created from a target word and all its aligned source words. The tokens are ordered according to the target language word order.

Furthermore, we use language models based on fine-grained part-of-speech tags (Schmid and Laws, 2008) as well as word classes to alleviate the sparsity problem for surface words. The word classes are automatically learned by clustering the words of the corpus using the MKCLS algorithm (Och, 1999). These n-gram language models are trained on the target language corpus, where the words have been replaced either by their corresponding POS tag or cluster ID. During decoding, these language models are used as additional models in the log-linear combination.

The data selection language model is trained on data automatically selected using cross-entropy differences between development sets from previous WMT workshops and the noisy crawled data (Moore and Lewis, 2010). We selected the top 10M sentences to train this language model.

3.4 Discriminative Word Lexicon

A discriminative word lexicon (DWL) models the probability of a target word appearing in the translation given the words of the source sentence. DWLs were first introduced by Mauser et al. (2009). For every target word, they train a maximum entropy model to determine whether this target word should be in the translated sentence or not using one feature per source word.

We use two simplifications of this model that have shown beneficial to translation quality and training time in the past (Mediani et al., 2011). Firstly, we calculate the score for every phrase pair before translating. Secondly, we restrict the negative training examples to words that occur within matching phrase pairs.

In this evaluation, we extended the DWL with n-gram source context features proposed by Niehues and Waibel (2013). Instead of representing the source sentence as a bag-of-words, we model it as a bag-of-n-grams. This allows us to include information about source word order in the model. We used one feature per n-gram up to the order of three and applied count filtering for bigrams and trigrams.

4 Results

This section presents the participating systems used for the submissions in the four translation directions of the evaluation. We describe the individual components that form part of each of the systems and report the translation qualities achieved during system development. The scores are reported in case-sensitive BLEU (Papineni et al., 2002).

4.1 English-French

The development of our English→French system is shown in Table 1.

It is noteworthy that, for this direction, we chose to tune on a subset of 1,000 pairs from newstest2012, due to the long time the whole set takes to be decoded. In a preliminary set of experiments (not reported here), we found no significant differences between tuning on the small or the big development sets. The translation model of the baseline system is trained on the whole parallel data after filtering (EPPS, NC, Common Crawl, Giga). The same data was also used for language modeling. We also use POS-based reordering.

The biggest improvement was due to using two additional language models. One consists of a log-linear interpolation of individual language models trained on the target side of the parallel data, the News shuffle, Gigaword and NC corpora. In addition, an in-domain language model trained only on NC data is used. This improves the score by more than 1.4 points. Adaptation of the translation model towards a smaller model trained on EPPS and NC brings an additional 0.3 points.

Another 0.3 BLEU points could be gained by using other special language models: a bilingual language model together with a 4-gram cluster language model (trained on all monolingual data using the MKCLS tool and 500 clusters). Incorporating a lexicalized reordering model into the system had a very noticeable effect on test namely more than half a BLEU point.

Finally, using a discriminative word lexicon with source context has a very small positive effect on the test score, however more than 0.3 on dev. This final configuration was the basis of our submitted official translation.

System	Dev	Test
Baseline	15.63	27.61
+ Big LMs	16.56	29.02
+ PT Adaptation	16.77	29.32
+ Bilingual + Cluster LM	16.87	29.64
+ Lexicalized Reordering	16.92	30.17
+ Source DWL	17.28	**30.19**

Table 1: Experiments for English→French

4.2 French-English

Several experiments were conducted for the French→English translation system. They are summarized in Table 2.

The baseline system is essentially a phrase-based translation system with some preprocessing steps on the source side and utilizing the short-range POS-based reordering on all parallel data and fine-grained monolingual corpora such as EPPS and NC.

Adapting the translation model using a small in-domain phrase table trained on NC data only helps us gain more than 0.4 BLEU points.

Using non-word language models including a bilingual language model and a 4-gram 50-cluster language model trained on the whole parallel data attains 0.24 BLEU points on the test set.

Lexicalized reordering improves our system on the development set by 0.3 BLEU points but has less effect on the test set with a minor improvement of around 0.1 BLEU points.

We achieve our best system, which is used for the evaluation, by adding a DWL with source context yielding 31.54 BLEU points on the test set.

System	Dev	Test
Baseline	30.16	30.70
+ LM Adaptation	30.58	30.94
+ PT Adaptation	30.69	31.14
+ Bilingual + Cluster LM	30.85	31.38
+ Lexicalized Reordering	31.14	31.46
+ Source DWL	31.19	**31.54**

Table 2: Experiments for French→English

4.3 English-German

Table 3 presents how the English-German translation system is improved step by step.

In the baseline system, we used parallel data which consists of the EPPS and NC corpora. The phrase table is built using discriminative word alignment. For word reordering, we use word lattices with long range reordering rules. Five language models are used in the baseline system; two word-based language models, a bilingual language model, and two 9-gram POS-based language models. The two word-based language models use 4-gram context and are trained on the parallel data and the filtered Common Crawl data separately, while the bilingual language model is built only on the Common Crawl corpus. The two POS-based language models are also based on the parallel data and the filtered crawled data, respectively.

When using a 9-gram cluster language model, we get a slight improvement. The cluster is trained with 1,000 classes using EPPS, NC, and Common Crawl data.

We use the filtered crawled data in addition to the parallel data in order to build the phrase table; this gave us 1 BLEU point of improvement.

The system is improved by 0.1 BLEU points when we use lattice phrase extraction along with lexicalized reordering rules.

Tree-based reordering rules improved the system performance further by another 0.1 BLEU points.

By reducing the context of the two POS-based language models from 9-grams to 5-grams and shortening the context of the language model trained on word classes to 4-grams, the score on the development set hardly changes but we can see a slightly improvement for the test case.

Finally, we use the DWL with source context and build a big bilingual language model using both the crawled and parallel data. By doing so, we improved the translation performance by another 0.3 BLEU points. This system was used for the translation of the official test set.

System	Dev	Test
Baseline	16.64	18.60
+ Cluster LM	16.76	18.66
+ Common Crawl Data	17.27	19.66
+ LPE + Lexicalized Reordering	17.45	19.75
+ Tree Rules	17.53	19.85
+ Shorter n-grams	17.55	19.92
+ Source DWL + Big BiLM	17.82	**20.21**

Table 3: Experiments for English→German

4.4 German-English

Table 4 shows the development steps of the German-English translation system.

For the baseline system, the training data of the translation model consists of EPPS, NC and the filtered parallel crawled data. The phrase table is built using GIZA++ word alignment and lattice phrase extraction. All language models are trained with SRILM and scored in the decoding process with KenLM (Heafield, 2011). We use word lattices generated by short and long range reordering rules as input to the decoder. In addition, a bilingual language model and a target language model trained on word clusters with 1,000 classes are included in the system.

Enhancing the word reordering with tree-based reordering rules and a lexicalized reordering model improved the system performance by 0.6 BLEU points.

Adding a language model trained on selected data from the monolingual corpora gave another small improvement.

The DWL with source context increased the score on the test set by another 0.5 BLEU points and applying morphological operations to unknown words reduced the out-of-vocabulary rate, even though no improvement in BLEU can be observed. This system was used to generate the translation submitted to the evaluation.

System	Dev	Test
Baseline	24.40	26.34
+ Tree Rules	24.71	26.86
+ Lexicalized Reordering	24.89	26.93
+ LM Data Selection	24.96	27.03
+ Source DWL	25.32	27.53
+ Morphological Operations	-	**27.53**

Table 4: Experiments for German→English

5 Conclusion

In this paper, we have described the systems developed for our participation in the Shared Translation Task of the WMT 2014 evaluation for English↔German and English↔French. All translations were generated using a phrase-based translation system which was extended by additional models such as bilingual and fine-grained part-of-speech language models. Discriminative word lexica with source context proved beneficial in all four language directions.

For English-French translation using a smaller development set performed reasonably well and reduced development time. The most noticeable gain comes from log-linear interpolation of multiple language models.

Due to the large amounts and diversity of the data available for French-English, adaptation methods and non-word language models contribute the major improvements to the system.

For English-German translation, the crawled data and a DWL using source context to guide word choice brought most of the improvements.

Enhanced word reordering models, namely tree-based reordering rules and a lexicalized reordering model as well as the source-side features for the discriminative word lexicon helped improve the system performance for German-English translation.

In average we achieved an improvement of over 1.5 BLEU over the respective baselines for all our systems.

Acknowledgments

The research leading to these results has received funding from the European Union Seventh Framework Programme (FP7/2007-2013) under grant agreement n° 287658.

References

George F. Foster, Roland Kuhn, and Howard Johnson. 2006. Phrasetable Smoothing for Statistical Machine Translation. In *Proceedings of the 2006 Conference on Empirical Methods on Natural Language Processing (EMNLP)*, Sydney, Australia.

Kenneth Heafield. 2011. KenLM: Faster and Smaller Language Model Queries. In *Proceedings of the Sixth Workshop on Statistical Machine Translation*, Edinburgh, Scotland, United Kingdom.

Teresa Herrmann, Jan Niehues, and Alex Waibel. 2013. Combining Word Reordering Methods on different Linguistic Abstraction Levels for Statistical Machine Translation. In *Proceedings of the Seventh Workshop on Syntax, Semantics and Structure in Statistical Translation*, Altanta, Georgia, USA.

Dan Klein and Christopher D. Manning. 2003. Accurate Unlexicalized Parsing. In *Proceedings of the 41st Annual Meeting on Association for Computational Linguistics (ACL 2003)*, Sapporo, Japan.

Philipp Koehn and Kevin Knight. 2003. Empirical Methods for Compound Splitting. In *Proceedings of the Eleventh Conference of the European Chapter of the Association for Computational Linguistics (EACL 2003)*, Budapest, Hungary.

Philipp Koehn, Amittai Axelrod, Alexandra B. Mayne, Chris Callison-Burch, Miles Osborne, and David Talbot. 2005. Edinburgh System Description for the 2005 IWSLT Speech Translation Evaluation. In *Proceedings of the Second International Workshop on Spoken Language Translation (IWSLT 2005)*, Pittsburgh, PA, USA.

Philipp Koehn, Hieu Hoang, Alexandra Birch, Chris Callison-Burch, Marcello Federico, Nicola Bertoldi, Brooke Cowan, Wade Shen, Christine Moran, Richard Zens, Chris Dyer, Ondrej Bojar, Alexandra Constantin, and Evan Herbst. 2007. Moses: Open Source Toolkit for Statistical Machine Translation. In *Proceedings of the 45th Annual Meeting of the Association for Computational Linguistics (ACL 2007), Demonstration Session*, Prague, Czech Republic.

Arne Mauser, Saša Hasan, and Hermann Ney. 2009. Extending Statistical Machine Translation with Discriminative and Trigger-based Lexicon Models. In *Proceedings of the 2009 Conference on Empirical Methods in Natural Language Processing (EMNLP)*, Suntec, Singapore.

Mohammed Mediani, Eunah Cho, Jan Niehues, Teresa Herrmann, and Alex Waibel. 2011. The KIT English-French Translation systems for IWSLT 2011. In *Proceedings of the Eight International Workshop on Spoken Language Translation (IWSLT 2011)*, San Francisco, CA, USA.

Mohammed Mediani, Jan Niehues, and Alex Waibel. 2012a. Parallel Phrase Scoring for Extra-large Corpora. In *The Prague Bulletin of Mathematical Linguistics*, number 98.

Mohammed Mediani, Yuqi Zhang, Thanh-Le Ha, Jan Niehues, Eunach Cho, Teresa Herrmann, Rainer Kärgel, and Alexander Waibel. 2012b. The KIT Translation Systems for IWSLT 2012. In *Proceedings of the Ninth International Workshop on Spoken Language Translation (IWSLT 2012)*, Hong Kong, HK.

R.C. Moore and W. Lewis. 2010. Intelligent Selection of Language Model Training Data. In *Proceedings of the ACL 2010 Conference Short Papers*, Uppsala, Sweden.

Jan Niehues and Muntsin Kolss. 2009. A POS-Based Model for Long-Range Reorderings in SMT. In *Proceedings of the Fourth Workshop on Statistical Machine Translation (WMT 2009)*, Athens, Greece.

Jan Niehues and Stephan Vogel. 2008. Discriminative Word Alignment via Alignment Matrix Modeling. In *Proceedings of the Third Workshop on Statistical Machine Translation (WMT 2008)*, Columbus, OH, USA.

Jan Niehues and Alex Waibel. 2011. Using Wikipedia to Translate Domain-specific Terms in SMT. In *Proceedings of the Eight International Workshop on Spoken Language Translation (IWSLT 2008)*, San Francisco, CA, USA.

J. Niehues and A. Waibel. 2012. Detailed Analysis of Different Strategies for Phrase Table Adaptation in SMT. In *Proceedings of the Tenth Conference of the Association for Machine Translation in the Americas (AMTA 2012)*, San Diego, CA, USA.

J. Niehues and A. Waibel. 2013. An MT Error-Driven Discriminative Word Lexicon using Sentence Structure Features. In *Proceedings of the Eighth Workshop on Statistical Machine Translation*, Sofia, Bulgaria.

Jan Niehues, Teresa Herrmann, Stephan Vogel, and Alex Waibel. 2011. Wider Context by Using Bilingual Language Models in Machine Translation. In *Sixth Workshop on Statistical Machine Translation (WMT 2011)*, Edinburgh, Scotland, United Kingdom.

Franz Josef Och and Hermann Ney. 2003. A Systematic Comparison of Various Statistical Alignment Models. *Computational Linguistics*, 29(1):19–51.

Franz Josef Och. 1999. An Efficient Method for Determining Bilingual Word Classes. In *Proceedings of the Ninth Conference of the European Chapter of the Association for Computational Linguistics (EACL 1999)*, Bergen, Norway.

Kishore Papineni, Salim Roukos, Todd Ward, and Wei-Jing Zhu. 2002. Bleu: a Method for Automatic Evaluation of Machine Translation. Technical Report RC22176 (W0109-022), IBM Research Division, T. J. Watson Research Center.

Anna N. Rafferty and Christopher D. Manning. 2008. Parsing Three German Treebanks: Lexicalized and Unlexicalized Baselines. In *Proceedings of the Workshop on Parsing German*, Columbus, OH, USA.

Kay Rottmann and Stephan Vogel. 2007. Word Reordering in Statistical Machine Translation with a POS-Based Distortion Model. In *Proceedings of the 11th International Conference on Theoretical and Methodological Issues in Machine Translation (TMI 2007)*, Skövde, Sweden.

Helmut Schmid and Florian Laws. 2008. Estimation of Conditional Probabilities with Decision Trees and an Application to Fine-Grained POS Tagging. In *International Conference on Computational Linguistics (COLING 2008)*, Manchester, Great Britain.

Helmut Schmid. 1994. Probabilistic Part-of-Speech Tagging Using Decision Trees. In *International Conference on New Methods in Language Processing*, Manchester, United Kingdom.

Andreas Stolcke. 2002. SRILM – An Extensible Language Modeling Toolkit. In *International Conference on Spoken Language Processing*, Denver, Colorado, USA.

Ashish Venugopal, Andreas Zollman, and Alex Waibel. 2005. Training and Evaluation Error Minimization Rules for Statistical Machine Translation. In *Proceedings of the ACL Workshop on Building and Using Parallel Texts*, Ann Arbor, Michigan, USA.

Stephan Vogel. 2003. SMT Decoder Dissected: Word Reordering. In *International Conference on Natural Language Processing and Knowledge Engineering*, Beijing, China.

The DCU-ICTCAS MT system at WMT 2014 on German-English Translation Task

Liangyou Li*, **Xiaofeng Wu***, **Santiago Cortés Vaíllo***
Jun Xie†, **Andy Way***, **Qun Liu***†
* CNGL Centre for Global Intelligent Content, School of Computing
Dublin City University, Dublin 9, Ireland
† Key Laboratory of Intelligent Information Processing, Institute of Computing Technology
Chinese Academy of Sciences, Beijing, China
{liangyouli,xiaofengwu,scortes,away,qliu}@computing.dcu.ie
xiejun@ict.ac.cn

Abstract

This paper describes the DCU submission to WMT 2014 on German-English translation task. Our system uses phrase-based translation model with several popular techniques, including Lexicalized Reordering Model, Operation Sequence Model and Language Model interpolation. Our final submission is the result of system combination on several systems which have different pre-processing and alignments.

1 Introduction

On the German-English translation task of WMT 2014, we submitted a system which is built with Moses phrase-based model (Koehn et al., 2007).

For system training, we use all provided German-English parallel data, and conducted several pre-processing steps to clean the data. In addition, in order to improve the translation quality, we adopted some popular techniques, including three Lexicalized Reordering Models (Axelrod et al., 2005; Galley and Manning, 2008), a 9-gram Operation Sequence Model (Durrani et al., 2011) and Language Model interpolation on several datasets. And then we use system combination on several systems with different settings to produce the final outputs.

Our phrase-based systems are tuned with k-best MIRA (Cherry and Foster, 2012) on development set. We set the maximum iteration to be 25.

The Language Models in our systems are trained with SRILM (Stolcke, 2002). We trained a 5-gram model with Kneser-Ney discounting (Chen and Goodman, 1996).

In the next sections, we will describe our system in detail. In section 2, we will explain our pre-processing steps on corpus. Then in section 3, we will describe some techniques we have tried for this task and the experiment results. In section 4, our final configuration for submitted system will be presented. And we conclude in the last section.

Corpus	Filtered Out (%)
Bilingual	7.17
Monolingual (English)	1.05

Table 1: Results of language detection: percentage of filtered out sentences

2 Pre-processing

We use all the training data for German-English translation, including Europarl, News Commentary and Common Crawl. The first thing we noticed is that some Non-German and Non-English sentences are included in our training data. So we apply Language Detection (Shuyo, 2010) for both monolingual and bilingual corpora. For monolingual data (only including English sentences in our task), we filter out sentences which are detected as other language with probability more than 0.999995. And for bilingual data, A sentence pair is filtered out if the language detector detects a different language with probability more than 0.999995 on either the source or the target. The filtering results are given in Table 1.

In our experiment, German compound words are splitted based on frequency (Koehn and

Proceedings of the Ninth Workshop on Statistical Machine Translation, pages 136–141,
Baltimore, Maryland USA, June 26–27, 2014.

Knight, 2003). In addition, for both monolingual and bilingual data, we apply tokenization, normalizing punctuation and truecasing using Moses scripts. For parallel training data, we also filter out sentence pairs containing more than 80 tokens on either side and sentence pairs whose length ratio between source and target side is larger than 3.

3 Techniques

In our preliminary experiments, we take newstest 2013 as our test data and newstest 2008-2012 as our development data. In total, we have more than 10,000 sentences for tuning. The tuning step would be very time-consuming if we use them all. So in this section, we use Feature Decay Algorithm (FDA) (Biçici and Yuret, 2014) to select 2000 sentences as our development set. Table 2 shows that system performance does not increase with larger tuning set and the system using only 2K sentences selected by FDA is better than the baseline tuned with all the development data.

In this section, alignment model is trained by MGIZA++ (Gao and Vogel, 2008) with `grow-diag-final-and` heuristic function. And other settings are mostly default values in Moses.

3.1 Lexicalized Reordering Model

German and English have different word order which brings a challenge in German-English machine translation. In our system, we adopt three Lexicalized Reordering Models (LRMs) for addressing this problem. They are word-based LRM (wLRM), phrase-based LRM (pLRM) and hierarchal LRM (hLRM).

These three models have different effect on the translation. Word-based and phrase-based LRMs are focus on local reordering phenomenon, while hierarchical LRM could be applied into longer reordering problem. Figure 1 shows the differences (Galley and Manning, 2008). And Table 3 shows effectiveness of different LRMs.

In our system based on Moses, we use `wbe-msd-bidirectional-fe`, `phrase-msd-bidirectional-fe` and `hier-mslr-bidirectional-fe` to specify these three LRMs. From Table 2, we could see that LRMs significantly improves the translation.

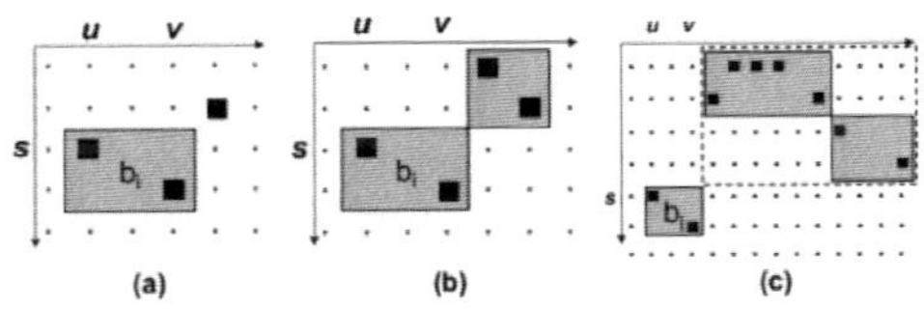

Figure 1: Occurrence of a swap according to the three orientation models: word-based, phrase-based, and hierarchical. Black squares represent word alignments, and gray squares represent blocks identified by phrase-extract. In (a), block $b_i = (e_i, f_{a_i})$ is recognized as a swap according to all three models. In (b), b_i is not recognized as a swap by the word-based model. In (c), b_i is recognized as a swap only by the hierarchical model. (Galley and Manning, 2008)

3.2 Operation Sequence Model

The Operation Sequence Model (OSM) (Durrani et al., 2011) explains the translation procedure as a linear sequence of operations which generates source and target sentences in parallel. Durrani et al. (2011) defined four translation operations: Generate(X,Y), Continue Source Concept, Generate Source Only (X) and Generate Identical, as well as three reordering operations: Insert Gap, Jump Back(W) and Jump Forward. These operations are described as follows.

- *Generate(X,Y)* make the words in Y and the first word in X added to target and source string respectively.
- *Continue Source Concept* adds the word in the queue from Generate(X,Y) to the source string.
- *Generate Source Only (X)* puts X in the source string at the current position.
- *Generate Identical* generates the same word for both sides.
- *Insert Gap* inserts a gap in the source side for future use.
- *Jump Back (W)* makes the position for translation be the Wth closest gap to the current position.
- *Jump Forward* moves the position to the index after the right-most source word.

Systems	Tuning Set	newstest 2013
Baseline	–	24.1
+FDA	–	24.2
+LRMs	24.0	25.4
+OSM	24.4	26.2
+LM Interpolation	24.6	26.4
+Factored Model	–	25.9
+Sparse Feature	25.6	25.9
+TM Combination	24.1	25.4
+OSM Interpolation	24.4	26.0

Table 2: Preliminary results on tuning set and test set (newstest 2013). All scores on test set are case-sensitive BLEU[%] scores. And scores on tuning set are case-insensitive BLEU[%] directly from tuning result. Baseline uses all the data from newstest 2008-2012 for tuning.

Systems	Tuning Set (uncased)	newstest 2013
Baseline+FDA	–	24.2
+wLRM	23.8	25.1
+pLRM	23.9	25.2
+hLRM	24.0	25.4
+pLRM	23.8	25.1
+hLRM	23.7	25.2

Table 3: System BLEU[%] scores when different LRMs are adopted.

The probability of an operation sequence $O = (o_1 o_2 \cdots o_J)$ is:

$$p(O) = \prod_{j=1}^{J} p(o_j | o_{j-n+1} \cdots o_{j-1}) \quad (1)$$

where n indicates the number of previous operations used.

In this paper we train a 9-gram OSM on training data and integrate this model directly into log-linear framework (OSM is now available to use in Moses). Our experiment shows OSM improves our system by about 0.8 BLEU (see Table 2).

3.3 Language Model Interpolation

In our baseline, Language Model (LM) is trained on all the monolingual data provided. In this section, we try to build a large language model by including data from English Gigaword fifth edition (only taking partial data with size of 1.6G), English side of UN corpus and English side of 10^9 French-English corpus. Instead of training a single model on all data, we interpolate language models trained on each subset (monolingual data provided is splitted into three parts: News 2007-2013, Europarl and News Commentary) by tuning weights to minimize perplexity of language model measured on the target side of development set.

In our experiment, after interpolation, the language model doesn't get a much lower perplexity, but it slightly improves the system, as shown in Table 2.

3.4 Other Tries

In addition to the techniques mentioned above, we also try some other approaches. Unfortunately all of these methods described in this section are non-effective in our experiments. The results are shown in Table 2.

- *Factored Model* (Koehn and Hoang, 2007): We tried to integrate a target POS factored model into our system with a 9-gram POS language model to address the problem of word selection and word order. But experiment doesn't show improvement. The English POS is from Stanford POS Tagger (Toutanova et al., 2003).

- *Translation Model Combination*: In this experiment, we try to use the method of (Sennrich, 2012) to combine phrase tables or reordering tables from different subsets of data to minimize perplexity measured on development set. We try to split the training data in two ways. One is according to data source, resulting in three subsets: Europarl, News Commentary and Common Crawl. Another one is to use data selection. We use FDA to select 200K sentence pairs as in-domain data and the rest as out-domain data. Unfortunately both experiments failed. In Table 2, we only report results of phrase table combination on FDA-based data sets.

- *OSM Interpolation*: Since OSM in our system could be taken as a special language model, we try to use the idea of interpolation similar with language model to make OSM adapted to some data. Training data are splitted into two subsets with FDA. We train 9-gram OSM on each subsets and interpolate them according to OSM trained on the development set.

- *Sparse Features*: For each source phrase, there is usually more than one corresponding translation option. Each different translation may be optimal in different contexts. Thus in our systems, similar to (He et al., 2008) which proposed a Maximum Entropy-based rule selection for the hierarchical phrase-based model, features which describe the context of phrases, are designed to select the right translation. But different with (He et al., 2008), we use sparse features to model the context. And instead of using syntactic POS, we adopt independent POS-like features: cluster ID of word. In our experiment *mkcls* was used to cluster words into 50 groups. And all features are generalized to cluster ID.

4 Submission

Based on our preliminary experiments in the section above, we use LRMs, OSM and LM interpolation in our final system for newstest 2014. But as we find that Language Models trained on UN corpus and 10^9 French-English corpus have a very high perplexity and in order to speed up the translation by reducing the model size, in this section, we interpolate only three language models from monolingual data provided, English Gigaword fifth edition and target side of training data. In addition, we also try some different methods for final submission. And the results are shown in Table 4.

- *Development Set Selection*: Instead of using FDA which is dependent on test set, we use the method of (Nadejde et al., 2013) to select tuning set from newstest 2008-2013 for the final system. We only keep 2K sentences which have more than 30 words and higher BLEU score. The experiment result is shown in Table 4 (The system is indicated as Baseline).

- *Pre-processing*: In our preliminary experiments, sentences are tokenized without changing hyphen. Thus we build another system where all the hyphens are tokenized aggressively.

- *SyMGIZA++*: Better alignment could lead to better translation. So we carry out some experiments on SyMGIZA++ aligner (Junczys-Dowmunt and Sza, 2012), which modifies the original IBM/GIZA++ word alignment models to allow to update the symmetrized models between chosen iterations of the original training algorithms. Experiment shows this new alignment improves translation quality.

- *Multi-alignment Selection*: We also try to use multi-alignment selection (Tu et al., 2012) to generate a "better" alignment from three alignmens: MGIZA++ with function *grow-diag-final-and*, SyMGIZA++ with function *grow-diag-final-and* and fast alignment (Dyer et al., 2013). Although this method show comparable or better result on development set, it fails on test set.

Since we build a few systems with different setting on Moses phrase-based model, a straightforward thinking is to obtain the better translation from several different translation systems. So we use system combination (Heafield and Lavie, 2010) on the 1-best outputs of three systems (indicated with * in table 4). And this results in our best system so far, as shown in Table 4. In our final submission, this result is taken as primary.

5 Conclusion

This paper describes our submitted system to WMT 2014 in detail. This system is based on

Systems	Tuning Set	newstest 2014
Baseline*	34.2	25.6
+SyMGIZA++*	34.3	26.0
+Multi-Alignment Selection	34.4	25.6
+Hyphen-Splitted	33.9	25.9
+SyMGIZA++*	34.0	26.0
+Multi-Alignment Selection	34.0	25.7
System Combination	–	26.5

Table 4: Experiment results on newstest 2014. We report case-sensitive BLEU[%] score on test set and case-insensitive BLEU[%] on tuning set which is directly from tuning result. Baseline is the phrase-based system with LRMs, OSM and LM interpolation on smaller datasets, tuned with selected development set. Systems indicated with * are used for system combination.

Moses phrase-based model, and integrates Lexicalized Reordering Models, Operation Sequence Model and Language Model interpolation. Also system combination is used on several systems which have different pre-processing and alignment.

Acknowledgments

This work is supported by EC Marie-Curie initial training Network EXPERT (EXPloiting Empirical appRoaches to Translation) project (`http://expert-itn.eu`). Thanks to Johannes Leveling for his help on German compound splitting. And thanks to Jia Xu and Jian Zhang for their advice and help on this paper and experiments.

References

Amittai Axelrod, Ra Birch Mayne, Chris Callison-burch, Miles Osborne, and David Talbot. 2005. Edinburgh system description for the 2005 iwslt speech translation evaluation. In *Proceedings of the International Workshop on Spoken Language Translation (IWSLT)*.

Ergun Biçici and Deniz Yuret. 2014. Optimizing instance selection for statistical machine translation with feature decay algorithms. *IEEE/ACM Transactions On Audio, Speech, and Language Processing (TASLP)*.

Stanley F. Chen and Joshua Goodman. 1996. An empirical study of smoothing techniques for language modeling. In *Proceedings of the 34th Annual Meeting on Association for Computational Linguistics*, ACL '96, pages 310–318, Stroudsburg, PA, USA. Association for Computational Linguistics.

Colin Cherry and George Foster. 2012. Batch tuning strategies for statistical machine translation. In *Proceedings of the 2012 Conference of the North American Chapter of the Association for Computational Linguistics: Human Language Technologies*, NAACL HLT '12, pages 427–436, Stroudsburg, PA, USA. Association for Computational Linguistics.

Nadir Durrani, Helmut Schmid, and Alexander Fraser. 2011. A joint sequence translation model with integrated reordering. In *Proceedings of the 49th Annual Meeting of the Association for Computational Linguistics: Human Language Technologies - Volume 1*, HLT '11, pages 1045–1054, Stroudsburg, PA, USA. Association for Computational Linguistics.

Chris Dyer, Victor Chahuneau, and Noah A. Smith. 2013. A simple, fast, and effective reparameterization of ibm model 2. In *Proceedings of NAACL*.

Michel Galley and Christopher D. Manning. 2008. A simple and effective hierarchical phrase reordering model. In *Proceedings of the 2008 Conference on Empirical Methods in Natural Language Processing*, pages 848–856, Honolulu, Hawaii, October. Association for Computational Linguistics.

Qin Gao and Stephan Vogel. 2008. Parallel implementations of word alignment tool. In *Software Engineering, Testing, and Quality Assurance for Natural Language Processing*, SETQA-NLP '08, pages 49–57, Stroudsburg, PA, USA. Association for Computational Linguistics.

Zhongjun He, Qun Liu, and Shouxun Lin. 2008. Improving statistical machine translation using lexicalized rule selection. In *Proceedings of the 22nd International Conference on Computational Linguistics (Coling 2008)*, pages 321–328, Manchester, UK, August. Coling 2008 Organizing Committee.

Kenneth Heafield and Alon Lavie. 2010. Combining machine translation output with open source: The Carnegie Mellon multi-engine machine translation scheme. *The Prague Bulletin of Mathematical Linguistics*, 93:27–36, January.

Marcin Junczys-Dowmunt and Arkadiusz Sza. 2012. Symgiza++: Symmetrized word alignment models for statistical machine translation. In Pascal Bouvry, MieczysawA. Kopotek, Franck Leprvost, Magorzata Marciniak, Agnieszka Mykowiecka, and Henryk

Rybiski, editors, *Security and Intelligent Information Systems*, volume 7053 of *Lecture Notes in Computer Science*, pages 379–390. Springer Berlin Heidelberg.

Philipp Koehn and Hieu Hoang. 2007. Factored translation models. In *Proceedings of the 2007 Joint Conference on Empirical Methods in Natural Language Processing and Computational Natural Language Learning (EMNLP-CoNLL)*, pages 868–876.

Philipp Koehn and Kevin Knight. 2003. Empirical methods for compound splitting. In *Proceedings of the Tenth Conference on European Chapter of the Association for Computational Linguistics - Volume 1*, EACL '03, pages 187–193, Stroudsburg, PA, USA. Association for Computational Linguistics.

Philipp Koehn, Hieu Hoang, Alexandra Birch, Chris Callison-Burch, Marcello Federico, Nicola Bertoldi, Brooke Cowan, Wade Shen, Christine Moran, Richard Zens, Chris Dyer, Ondřej Bojar, Alexandra Constantin, and Evan Herbst. 2007. Moses: Open source toolkit for statistical machine translation. In *Proceedings of the 45th Annual Meeting of the ACL on Interactive Poster and Demonstration Sessions*, ACL '07, pages 177–180, Stroudsburg, PA, USA. Association for Computational Linguistics.

Maria Nadejde, Philip Williams, and Philipp Koehn. 2013. Edinburgh's syntax-based machine translation systems. In *Proceedings of the Eighth Workshop on Statistical Machine Translation*, pages 170–176, Sofia, Bulgaria, August. Association for Computational Linguistics.

Rico Sennrich. 2012. Perplexity minimization for translation model domain adaptation in statistical machine translation. In *Proceedings of the 13th Conference of the European Chapter of the Association for Computational Linguistics*, pages 539–549, Avignon, France, April. Association for Computational Linguistics.

Nakatani Shuyo. 2010. Language detection library for java.

Andreas Stolcke. 2002. Srilm – an extensible language modeling toolkit. In *Proceedings of the International Conference Spoken Language Processing*, pages 901–904, Denver, CO.

Kristina Toutanova, Dan Klein, Christopher D. Manning, and Yoram Singer. 2003. Feature-rich part-of-speech tagging with a cyclic dependency network. In *Proceedings of the 2003 Conference of the North American Chapter of the Association for Computational Linguistics on Human Language Technology - Volume 1*, NAACL '03, pages 173–180, Stroudsburg, PA, USA. Association for Computational Linguistics.

Zhaopeng Tu, Yang Liu, Yifan He, Josef van Genabith, Qun Liu, and Shouxun Lin. 2012. Combining multiple alignments to improve machine translation. In *COLING (Posters)*, pages 1249–1260.

The CMU Machine Translation Systems at WMT 2014

Austin Matthews Waleed Ammar Archna Bhatia Weston Feely
Greg Hanneman Eva Schlinger Swabha Swayamdipta Yulia Tsvetkov
Alon Lavie Chris Dyer*
Language Technologies Institute
Carnegie Mellon University
Pittsburgh, PA 15213 USA
*Corresponding author: cdyer@cs.cmu.edu

Abstract

We describe the CMU systems submitted to the 2014 WMT shared translation task. We participated in two language pairs, German–English and Hindi–English. Our innovations include: a label coarsening scheme for syntactic tree-to-tree translation, a host of new discriminative features, several modules to create "synthetic translation options" that can generalize beyond what is directly observed in the training data, and a method of combining the output of multiple word aligners to uncover extra phrase pairs and grammar rules.

1 Introduction

The MT research group at Carnegie Mellon University's Language Technologies Institute participated in two language pairs for the 2014 Workshop on Machine Translation shared translation task: German–English and Hindi–English. Our systems showcase our multi-phase approach to translation, in which **synthetic translation options** supplement the default translation rule inventory that is extracted from word-aligned training data.

In the German–English system, we used our compound splitter (Dyer, 2009) to reduce data sparsity, and we allowed the translator to back off to translating lemmas when it detected case-inflected OOVs. We also demonstrate our group's syntactic system with coarsened nonterminal types (Hanneman and Lavie, 2011) as a contrastive German–English submission.

In both the German–English and Hindi–English systems, we used an array of supplemental ideas to enhance translation quality, ranging from lemmatization and synthesis of inflected phrase pairs to novel reordering and rule preference features.

2 Core System Components

The decoder infrastructure we used was cdec (Dyer et al., 2010). For our primary systems, all data was tokenized using cdec's tokenization tool. Only the constrained data resources provided for the shared task were used for training both the translation and language models. Word alignments were generated using both FastAlign (Dyer et al., 2013) and GIZA++ (Och and Ney, 2003). All our language models were estimated using KenLM (Heafield, 2011). Translation model parameters were chosen using MIRA (Eidelman, 2012) to optimize BLEU (Papineni et al., 2002) on a held-out development set.

Our data was filtered using qe-clean (Denkowski et al., 2012), with a cutoff of two standard deviations from the mean. All data was left in fully cased form, save the first letter of each segment, which was changed to whichever form the first token more commonly used throughout the data. As such, words like *The* were lowercased at the beginning of segments, while words like *Obama* remained capitalized.

Our primary German–English and Hindi–English systems were Hiero-based (Chiang, 2007), while our contrastive German–English system used cdec's tree-to-tree SCFG formalism.

Before submitting, we ran cdec's implementation of MBR on 500-best lists from each of our systems. For both language pairs, we used the Nelder–Mead method to optimize the MBR parameters. In the German–English system, we ran MBR on 500 hypotheses, combining the output of the Hiero and tree-to-tree systems.

The remainder of the paper will focus on our primary innovations in the two language pairs.

Proceedings of the Ninth Workshop on Statistical Machine Translation, pages 142–149,
Baltimore, Maryland USA, June 26–27, 2014.

3 Common System Improvements

A number of our techniques were used for both our German–English and Hindi–English primary submissions. These techniques each fall into one of three categories: those that create translation rules, those involving language models, or those that add translation features. A comparison of these techniques and their performance across the two language pairs can be found in Section 6.

3.1 Rule-Centric Enhancements

While many of our methods of enhancing the translation model with extra rules are language-specific, three were shared between language pairs.

First, we added sentence-boundary tokens <*s*> and </*s*> to the beginning and end of each line in the data, on both the source and target sides.

Second, we aligned all of our training data using both FastAlign and GIZA++ and simply concatenated two copies of the training corpus, one aligned with each aligner, and extracted rules from the resulting double corpus.

Third, we hand-wrote a list of rules that transform numbers, dates, times, and currencies into well-formed English equivalents, handling differences such as the month and day reversal in dates or conversion from 24-hour time to 12-hour time.

3.2 Employed Language Models

Each of our primary systems uses a total of three language models.

The first is a traditional 4-gram model generated by interoplating LMs built from each of the available monolingual corpora. Interpolation weights were calculated used the SRILM toolkit (Stolcke, 2002) and 1000 dev sentences from the Hindi–English system.

The second is a model trained on word clusters instead of surface forms. For this we mapped the LM vocabulary into 600 clusters based on the algorithm of Brown et al. (1992) and then constructed a 7-gram LM over the resulting clusters, allowing us to capture more context than our traditional surface-form language model.

The third is a bigram model over the *source* side of each language's respective bitext. However, at run time this LM operates on the target-side output of the translator, just like the other two. The intuition here is that if a source-side LM likes our output, then we are probably passing through more than we ought to.

Both source and target surface-form LM used modified Kneser-Ney smoothing (Kneser and Ney, 1995), while the model over Brown clusters (Brown et al., 1992) used subtract-0.5 smoothing.

3.3 New Translation Features

In addition to the standard array of features, we added four new indicator feature templates, leading to a total of nearly 150,000 total features.

The first set consists of target-side n-gram features. For each bigram of Brown clusters in the output string generated by our translator, we fire an indicator feature. For example, if we have the sentence, *Nato will ihren Einfluss im Osten stärken* translating as *NATO intends to strengthen its influence in the East*, we will fire an indicator features NGF_C367_C128=1, NGF_C128_C31=1, etc.

The second set is source-language n-gram features. Similar to the previous feature set, we fire an indicator feature for each $n$gram of Brown clusters in the output. Here, however, we use $n = 1$, and we use the map of *source* language words to Brown clusters, rather than the target language's, despite the fact that this is examining target language output. The intuition here is to allow this feature to penalize passthroughs differently depending on their source language Brown cluster. For example, passing through the German word *zeitung* ("newspaper") is probably a bad idea, but passing through the German word *Obama* probably should not be punished as severely.

The third type of feature is source path features. We can imagine translation as a two-step process in which we first permute the source words into some order, then translate them phrase by phrase. This set of features examines that intermediate string in which the source words have been permuted. Again, we fire an indicator feature for each bigram in this intermediate string, this time using surface lexical forms directly instead of first mapping them to Brown clusters.

Lastly, we create a new type of rule shape feature. Traditionally, rule shape features have indicated, for each rule, the sequence of terminal and non-terminal items on the right-hand side. For example, the rule [X] $\rightarrow$ der [X] :: the [X] might have an indicator feature Shape_TN_TN, where T represents a terminal and N represents a non-terminal. One can also imagine lexicalizing such rules by replacing each T with its surface form. We believe such features would be too sparse, so instead of replacing each terminal by its surface form, we instead replace it with its Brown cluster, creating a feature like Shape_C37_N_C271_N.

4 Hindi–English Specific Improvements

In addition to the enhancements common to the two primary systems, our Hindi–English system includes improved data cleaning of development data, a sophisticated linguistically-informed tokenization scheme, a transliteration module, a synthetic phrase generator that improves handling of function words, and a synthetic phrase generator that leverages source-side paraphrases. We will discuss each of these five in turn.

4.1 Development Data Cleaning

Due to a scarcity of clean development data, we augmented the 520 segments provided with 480 segments randomly drawn from the training data to form our development set, and drew another random 1000 segments to serve as a dev test set.

After observing large discrepencies between the types of segments in our development data and the well-formed news domain sentences we expected to be tested on, we made the decision to prune our tuning set by removing any segment that did not appear to be a full sentence on both the Hindi and English sides. While this reduced our tuning set from 1000 segments back down to 572 segments, we believe it to be the single largest contributor to our success on the Hindi–English translation task.

4.2 Nominal Normalization

Another facet of our system was normalization of Hindi nominals. The Hindi nominal system shows much more morphological variation than English. There are two genders (masculine and feminine) and at least six noun stem endings in pronunciation and 10 in writing.

The pronominal system also is much richer than English with many variants depending on whether pronouns appear with case markers or other postpositions.

Before normalizing the nouns and pronouns, we first split these case markers / postpositions from the nouns / pronouns to result in two words instead of the original combined form. If the case marker was ने (*ne*), the ergative case marker in Hindi, we deleted it as it did not have any translation in English. All the other postpositions were left intact while splitting from and normalizing the nouns and pronouns.

These changes in stem forms contribute to the sparsity in data; hence, to reduce this sparsity, we construct for each input segment an input lattice that allows the decoder to use the split or original forms of all nouns or pronouns, as well as allowing it to keep or delete the case marker *ne*.

4.3 Transliteration

We used the 12,000 Hindi–English transliteration pairs from the ACL 2012 NEWS workshop on transliteration to train a linear-chained CRF tagger[1] that labels each character in the Hindi token with a sequence of zero or more English characters (Ammar et al., 2012). At decoding, unseen Hindi tokens are fed to the transliterator, which produces the 100 most probable transliterations. We add a synthetic translation option for each candidate transliteration.

In addition to this sophisticated transliteration scheme, we also employ a rule-based transliterator that specifically targets acronyms. In Hindi, many acronyms are spelled out phonetically, such as *NSA* being rendered as एनएसए (*en.es.e*). We detected such words in the input segments and generated synthetic translation options both with and without periods (e.g. *N.S.A.* and *NSA*).

4.4 Synthetic Handling of Function Words

In different language pairs, individual source words may have many different possible translations, e.g., when the target language word has many different morphological inflections or is surrounded by different function words that have no direct counterpart in the source language. Therefore, when very large quantities of parallel data are not available, we can expect our phrasal inventory to be incomplete. Synthetic translation option generation seeks to fill these gaps using secondary generation processes that exploit existing phrase pairs to produce plausible phrase translation alternatives that are not directly extractable from the training data (Tsvetkov et al., 2013; Chahuneau et al., 2013).

To generate synthetic phrases, we first remove function words from the source and target sides of existing non-gappy phrase pairs. We manually constructed English and Hindi lists of common function words, including articles, auxiliaries, pronouns, and adpositions. We then employ the SRILM hidden-ngram utility (Stolcke, 2002) to restore missing function words according to an n-gram language model probability, and add the resulting synthetic phrases to our phrase table.

[1] https://github.com/wammar/transliterator

4.5 Paraphrase-Based Synthetic Phrases

We used a graph-based method to obtain translation distributions for source phrases that are not present in the phrase table extracted from the parallel corpus. Monolingual data is used to construct separate similarity graphs over phrases (word sequences or n-grams), using distributional features extracted from the corpora. The source similarity graph consists of phrase nodes representing sequences of words in the source language. In our instance, we restricted the phrases to bigrams, and the bigrams come from both the phrase table (the *labeled* phrases) and from the evaluation set but not present in the phrase table (unlabeled phrases).

The labels for these source phrases, namely the target phrasal inventory, can also be represented in a graph form, where the distributional features can also be computed from the target monolingual data. Translation information is then propagated from the labeled phrases to the unlabeled phrases in the source graph, proportional to how similar the phrases are to each other on the source side, as well as how similar the translation candidates are to each other on the target side. The newly acquired translation distributions for the unlabeled phrases are written out to a secondary phrase table. For more information, see Saluja et al. (2014).

5 German–English Specific Improvements

Our German–English system also had its own suite of tricks, including the use of "pseudo-references" and special handling of morphologically inflected OOVs.

5.1 Pseudo-References

The development sets provided have only a single reference, which is known to be sub-optimal for tuning of discriminative models. As such, we use the output of one or more of last year's top performing systems as pseudo-references during tuning. We experimented with using just one pseudo-reference, taken from last year's Spanish–English winner (Durrani et al., 2013), and with using four pseudo-references, including the output of last year's winning Czech–English, French–English, and Russian–English systems (Pino et al., 2013).

5.2 Morphological OOVs

Examination of the output of our baseline systems lead us to conclude that the majority of our system's OOVs were due to morphologically inflected nouns in the input data, particularly those in genitive case. As such, for each OOV in the input, we attempt to remove the German genitive case marker *-s* or *-es*. We then run the resulting form f through our baseline translator to obtain a translation e of the lemma. Finally, we add two translation rules to our translation table: $f \rightarrow e$, and $f \rightarrow e$'s.

6 Results

As we added each feature to our systems, we first ran a one-off experiment comparing our baseline system with and without each individual feature. The results of that set of experiments are shown in Table 1 for Hindi–English and Table 2 for German–English. Features marked with a * were not included in our final system submission.

The most surprising result is the strength of our Hindi–English baseline system. With no extra bells or whistles, it is already half a BLEU point ahead of the second best system submitted to this shared task. We believe this is due to our filtering of the tuning set, which allowed our system to generate translations more similar in length to the final test set.

Another interesting result is that only one feature set, namely our rule shape features based on Brown clusters, helped on the test set in both language pairs. No feature hurt the BLEU score on the test set in both language pairs, meaning the majority of features helped in one language and hurt in the other.

If we compare results on the tuning sets, however, some clearer patterns arise. Brown cluster language models, n-gram features, and our new rule shape features all helped.

Furthermore, there were a few features, such as the Brown cluster language model and tuning to Meteor (Denkowski and Lavie, 2011), that helped substantially in one language pair while just barely hurting the other. In particular, the fact that tuning to Meteor instead of BLEU can actually help both BLEU and Meteor scores was rather unexpected.

7 German–English Syntax System

In addition to our primary German–English system, we also submitted a contrastive German–English system showcasing our group's tree-to-tree syntax-based translation formalism.

System	Test (2014) BLEU	Met	TER	Dev Test (2012) BLEU	Met	TER
Baseline	15.7	25.3	68.0	11.4	22.9	70.3
*Meteor Tuning	15.2	25.8	71.3	12.8	23.7	71.3
Sentence Boundaries	15.2	25.4	69.1	12.1	23.4	70.0
Double Aligners	16.1	25.5	66.6	11.9	23.1	69.2
Manual Number Rules	15.7	25.4	68.5	11.6	23.0	70.3
Brown Cluster LM	15.6	25.1	67.3	11.5	22.7	69.8
*Source LM	14.2	25.1	72.1	11.3	23.0	72.3
N-Gram Features	15.6	25.2	67.9	12.2	23.2	69.2
Src N-Gram Features	15.3	25.2	68.9	12.0	23.4	69.5
Src Path Features	15.8	25.6	68.8	11.9	23.3	70.4
Brown Rule Shape	15.9	25.4	67.2	11.8	22.9	69.6
Lattice Input	15.2	25.8	71.3	11.4	22.9	70.3
CRF Transliterator	15.7	25.7	69.4	12.1	23.5	70.1
Acronym Translit.	15.8	25.8	68.8	12.4	23.4	70.2
Synth. Func. Words	15.7	25.3	67.8	11.4	22.8	70.4
Source Paraphrases	15.6	25.2	67.7	11.5	22.7	69.9
Final Submission	16.7					

Table 1: BLEU, Meteor, and TER results for one-off experiments conducted on the primary Hiero Hindi–English system. Each line is the baseline plus that one feature, non-cumulatively. Lines marked with a * were not included in our final WMT submission.

System	Test (2014) BLEU	Met	TER	Dev Test (2012) BLEU	Met	TER
Baseline	25.3	30.4	52.6	26.2	31.3	53.6
*Meteor Tuning	26.2	31.3	53.1	26.9	32.2	54.4
Sentence Boundaries	25.4	30.5	52.2	26.1	31.4	53.3
Double Aligners	25.2	30.4	52.5	26.0	31.3	53.6
Manual Number Rules	25.3	30.3	52.5	26.1	31.4	53.4
Brown Cluster LM	26.4	31.0	51.9	27.0	31.8	53.2
*Source LM	25.8	30.6	52.4	26.4	31.5	53.4
N-Gram Features	25.4	30.4	52.6	26.7	31.6	53.0
Src N-Gram Features	25.3	30.5	52.5	26.2	31.5	53.4
Src Path Features	25.0	30.1	52.6	26.0	31.2	53.3
Brown Rule Shape	25.5	30.5	52.4	26.3	31.5	53.2
One Pseudo Ref	25.5	30.4	52.6	34.4	32.7	49.3
*Four Psuedo Refs	22.6	29.2	52.6	49.8	35.0	46.1
OOV Morphology	25.5	30.5	52.4	26.3	31.5	53.3
Final Submission	27.1					

Table 2: BLEU, Meteor, and TER results for one-off experiments conducted on the primary Hiero German–English system. Each line is the baseline plus that one feature, non-cumulatively.

System	Dev (2013) BLEU	Met	TER	Dev Test (2012) BLEU	Met	TER
Baseline	20.98	29.81	58.47	18.65	28.72	61.80
+ Label coarsening	23.07	30.71	56.46	20.43	29.34	60.16
+ Meteor tuning	23.48	30.90	56.18	20.96	29.60	59.87
+ Brown LM + Lattice + Synthetic	24.46	31.41	56.66	21.50	30.28	60.51
+ Span limit 15	24.20	31.25	55.48	21.75	29.97	59.18
+ Pseudo-references	24.55	31.30	56.22	22.10	30.12	59.73

Table 3: BLEU, Meteor, and TER results for experiments conducted in the tree-to-tree German–English system. The system in the bottom line was submitted to WMT as a contrastive entry.

7.1 Basic System Construction

Since all training data for the tree-to-tree system must be parsed in addition to being word-aligned, we prepared separate copies of the training, tuning, and testing data that are more suitable for input into constituency parsing. Importantly, we left the data in its original mixed-case format. We used the Stanford tokenizer to replicate Penn Treebank tokenization on the English side. On the German side, we developed new in-house normalization and tokenization script.

We filtered tokenized training sentences by sentence length, token length, and sentence length ratio. The final corpus for parsing and word alignment contained 3,897,805 lines, or approximately 86 percent of the total training resources released under the WMT constrained track. Word alignment was carried out using FastAlign (Dyer et al., 2013), while for parsing we used the Berkeley parser (Petrov et al., 2006).

Given the parsed and aligned corpus, we extracted synchronous context-free grammar rules using the method of Hanneman et al. (2011).

In addition to aligning subtrees that natively exist in the input trees, our grammar extractor also introduces "virtual nodes." These are new and possibly overlapping constituents that subdivide regions of flat structure by combining two adjacent sibling nodes into a single nonterminal for the purposes of rule extraction. Virtual nodes are similar in spirit to the "A+B" extended categories of SAMT (Zollmann and Venugopal, 2006), and their nonterminal labels are constructed in the same way, but with the added restriction that they do not violate any existing syntactic structure in the parse tree.

7.2 Improvements

Nonterminals in our tree-to-tree grammar are made up of pairs of symbols: one from the source side and one from the target side. With virtual nodes included, this led to an initial German–English grammar containing 153,219 distinct nonterminals — a far larger set than is used in SAMT, tree-to-string, string-to-tree, or Hiero systems. To combat the sparsity introduce by this large nonterminal set, we coarsened the label set with an agglomerative label-clustering technique(Hanneman and Lavie, 2011; Hanneman and Lavie, 2013). The stopping point was somewhat arbitrarily chosen to be a grammar of 916 labels.

Table 3 shows a significant improvement in translation quality due to coarsening the label set: approximately +1.8 BLEU, +0.6 Meteor, and –1.6 TER on our dev test set, newtest2012.[2]

In the MERT runs, however, we noticed that the length of the MT output can be highly variable, ranging on the tuning set from a low of 92.8% of the reference length to a high of 99.1% in another. We were able to limit this instability by tuning to Meteor instead of BLEU. Aside from a modest score improvement, we note that the variability in length ratio is reduced from 6.3% to 2.8%.

Specific difficulties of the German–English language pair led to three additional system components to try to combat them.

First, we introduced a second language model trained on Brown clusters instead of surface forms.

Next we attempted to overcome the sparsity of German input by making use of cdec's lattice input functionality introduce compound-split versions of dev and test sentences.

Finally, we attempted to improve our grammar's coverage of new German words by introducing synthetic rules for otherwise out-of-vocabulary items. Each token in a test sentence that the grammar cannot translate generates a synthetic rule allowing the token to be translated as itself. The left-hand-side label is decided heuristically: a (coarsened) "noun" label if the German OOV starts with a capital letter, a "number" label if the OOV contains only digits and select punctuation characters, an "adjective" label if the OOV otherwise starts with a lowercase letter or a number, or a "symbol" label for anything left over.

The effect of all three of these improvements combined is shown in the fourth row of Table 3.

By default our previous experiments were performed with a span limit of 12 tokens. Increasing this limit to 15 has a mixed effect on metric scores, as shown in the fifth row of Table 3. Since two out of three metrics report improvement, we left the longer span limit in effect in our final system.

Our final improvement was to augment our tuning set with the same set of pseudo-references as our Hiero systems. We found that using one pseudo-reference versus four pseudo-references had negligible effect on the (single-reference) tuning scores, but four produced a better improvement on the test set.

The best MERT run of this final system (bottom line of Table 3) was submitted to the WMT 2014 evaluation as a contrastive entry.

Acknowledgments

We sincerely thank the organizers of the workshop for their hard work, year after year, and the reviewers for their careful reading of the submitted draft of this paper. This research work was supported in part by the U. S. Army Research Laboratory and the U. S. Army Research Office under contract/grant number W911NF-10-1-0533, by the National Science Foundation under grant

[2]We follow the advice of Clark et al. (2011) and evaluate our tree-to-tree experiments over multiple independent MERT runs. All scores in Table 3 are averages of two or three runs, depending on the row.

IIS-0915327, by a NPRP grant (NPRP 09-1140-1-177) from the Qatar National Research Fund (a member of the Qatar Foundation), and by computing resources provided by the NSF-sponsored XSEDE program under grant TG-CCR110017. The statements made herein are solely the responsibility of the authors.

References

Waleed Ammar, Chris Dyer, and Noah A. Smith. 2012. Transliteration by sequence labeling with lattice encodings and reranking. In *NEWS workshop at ACL*.

Peter F Brown, Peter V Desouza, Robert L Mercer, Vincent J Della Pietra, and Jenifer C Lai. 1992. Class-based n-gram models of natural language. *Computational linguistics*, 18(4):467–479.

Victor Chahuneau, Eva Schlinger, Noah A. Smith, and Chris Dyer. 2013. Translating into morphologically rich languages with synthetic phrases. In *Proceedings of EMNLP*.

David Chiang. 2007. Hierarchical phrase-based translation. *Computational Linguistics*, 33(2):201–228.

Jonathan H. Clark, Chris Dyer, Alon Lavie, and Noah A. Smith. 2011. Better hypothesis testing for statistical machine translation: Crontrolling for optimizer instability. In *Proceedings of the 49th Annual Meeting of the Association for Computational Linguistics: Short Papers*, pages 176–181, Portland, Oregon, USA, June.

Michael Denkowski and Alon Lavie. 2011. Meteor 1.3: Automatic metric for reliable optimization and evaluation of machine translation systems. In *Proceedings of the Sixth Workshop on Statistical Machine Translation*, pages 85–91, Edinburgh, Scotland, UK, July.

Michael Denkowski, Greg Hanneman, and Alon Lavie. 2012. The cmu-avenue french-english translation system. In *Proceedings of the NAACL 2012 Workshop on Statistical Machine Translation*.

Nadir Durrani, Barry Haddow, Kenneth Heafield, and Philipp Koehn. 2013. Edinburgh's machine translation systems for european language pairs.

Chris Dyer, Adam Lopez, Juri Ganitkevitch, Johnathan Weese, Ferhan Ture, Phil Blunsom, Hendra Setiawan, Vladimir Eidelman, and Philip Resnik. 2010. cdec: A decoder, alignment, and learning framework for finite-state and context-free translation models. In *Proc. of ACL*.

Chris Dyer, Victor Chahuneau, and Noah A. Smith. 2013. A simple, fast, and effective reparameterization of IBM Model 2. In *Proc. of NAACL*.

Chris Dyer. 2009. Using a maximum entropy model to build segmentation lattices for mt. In *Proceedings of Human Language Technologies: The 2009 Annual Conference of the North American Chapter of the Association for Computational Linguistics*, pages 406–414. Association for Computational Linguistics.

Vladimir Eidelman. 2012. Optimization strategies for online large-margin learning in machine translation. In *Proceedings of the Seventh Workshop on Statistical Machine Translation*.

Greg Hanneman and Alon Lavie. 2011. Automatic category label coarsening for syntax-based machine translation. In *Proceedings of SSST-5: Fifth Workshop on Syntax, Semantics, and Structure in Statistical Translation*, pages 98–106, Portland, Oregon, USA, June.

Greg Hanneman and Alon Lavie. 2013. Improving syntax-augmented machine translation by coarsening the label set. In *Proceedings of NAACL-HLT 2013*, pages 288–297, Atlanta, Georgia, USA, June.

Greg Hanneman, Michelle Burroughs, and Alon Lavie. 2011. A general-purpose rule extractor for SCFG-based machine translation. In *Proceedings of SSST-5: Fifth Workshop on Syntax, Semantics, and Structure in Statistical Translation*, pages 135–144, Portland, Oregon, USA, June.

Kenneth Heafield. 2011. KenLM: Faster and smaller language model queries. In *Proceedings of the Sixth Workshop on Statistical Machine Translation*, Edinburgh, Scotland, UK, July.

R. Kneser and H. Ney. 1995. Improved backing-off for m-gram language modeling. In *Proceedings of IEEE Internation Conference on Acoustics, Speech, and Signal Processing*, pages 181–184.

Franz Josef Och and Hermann Ney. 2003. A systematic comparison of various statistical alignment models. *Computational linguistics*, 29(1):19–51.

Kishore Papineni, Salim Roukos, Todd Ward, and Wei-Jing Zhu. 2002. BLEU: A method for automatic evalution of machine translation. In *Proceedings of the 40th Annual Meeting of the Association for Computational Linguistics*, pages 311–318, Philadelphia, Pennsylvania, USA, July.

Slav Petrov, Leon Barrett, Romain Thibaux, and Dan Klein. 2006. Learning accurate, compact, and interpretable tree annotation. In *Proceedings of the 21st International Conference on Computational Linguistics and the 44th annual meeting of the Association for Computational Linguistics*, pages 433–440. Association for Computational Linguistics.

Juan Pino, Aurelien Waite, Tong Xiao, Adrià de Gispert, Federico Flego, and William Byrne. 2013. The university of cambridge russian-english system at wmt13.

Avneesh Saluja, Hany Hassan, Kristina Toutanova, and Chris Quirk. 2014. Graph-based semi-supervised learning of translation models from monolingual data. In *Proceedings of the 52nd Annual Meeting of the Association for Computational Linguistics (ACL)*, Baltimore, Maryland, June.

Andreas Stolcke. 2002. Srilm-an extensible language modeling toolkit. In *INTERSPEECH*.

Yulia Tsvetkov, Chris Dyer, Lori Levin, and Archna Batia. 2013. Generating English determiners in phrase-based translation with synthetic translation options. In *Proceedings of the Eighth Workshop on Statistical Machine Translation*.

Andreas Zollmann and Ashish Venugopal. 2006. Syntax augmented machine translation via chart parsing. In *Proceedings of the Workshop on Statistical Machine Translation*, pages 138–141, New York, New York, USA, June.

Stanford University's Submissions to the WMT 2014 Translation Task

Julia Neidert,[*] Sebastian Schuster,[*] Spence Green,
Kenneth Heafield, and **Christopher D. Manning**
Computer Science Department, Stanford University
{jneid, sebschu, spenceg, heafield, manning}@cs.stanford.edu

Abstract

We describe Stanford's participation in the French-English and English-German tracks of the 2014 Workshop on Statistical Machine Translation (WMT). Our systems used large feature sets, word classes, and an optional unconstrained language model. Among constrained systems, ours performed the best according to uncased BLEU: 36.0% for French-English and 20.9% for English-German.

1 Introduction

Phrasal (Green et al., 2014b) is a phrase-based machine translation system (Och and Ney, 2004) with an online, adaptive tuning algorithm (Green et al., 2013c) which allows efficient tuning of feature-rich translation models. We improved upon the basic Phrasal system with sparse features over word classes, class-based language models, and a web-scale language model.

We submitted one constrained French-English (Fr-En) system, one unconstrained English-German (En-De) system with a huge language model, and one constrained English-German system without it. Each system was built using over 100,000 features and was tuned on over 10,000 sentences. This paper describes our submitted systems and discusses how the improvements affect translation quality.

2 Data Preparation & Post-Processing

We used all relevant data allowed by the constrained condition, with the exception of HindEnCorp and Wiki Headlines, which we deemed too noisy. Specifically, our parallel data consists of the Europarl version 7 (Koehn, 2005), parallel CommonCrawl (Smith et al., 2013), French-English UN, Giga-FrEn, and News Commentary corpora provided by the evaluation. For monolingual data, we used the provided news crawl data from all years, English Gigaword version 5 (Parker et al., 2011), and target sides of the parallel data. This includes English from the Yandex, CzEng, and parallel CommonCrawl corpora. For parallel CommonCrawl, we concatenated the English halves for various language pairs and then deduplicated at the sentence level.

	Sentences	Tokens
En-De	4.5M	222M
Fr-En	36.3M	2.1B

Table 1: Gross parallel corpus statistics after pre-processing.

	Constrained LM	Unconstrained LM
German	1.7B	38.9 B
English	7.2B	-

Table 2: Number of tokens in pre-processed monolingual corpora used to estimate the language models. We split the constrained English data into two models: 3.7 billion tokens from Gigaword and 3.5 billion tokens from all other sources.

In addition, our unconstrained English-German system used German text extracted from the entire 2012, 2013, and winter 2013 CommonCrawl[1] corpora by Buck et al. (2014).

Tables 1 and 2 show the sizes of the pre-processed corpora of parallel text and monolingual text from which our systems were built.

2.1 Pre-Processing

We used Stanford CoreNLP to tokenize the English and German data according to the Penn Treebank standard (Marcus et al., 1993). The French source data was tokenized similarly to the French Treebank

[*]These authors contributed equally.

[1]http://commoncrawl.org

Proceedings of the Ninth Workshop on Statistical Machine Translation, pages 150–156,
Baltimore, Maryland USA, June 26–27, 2014.

(Abeillé et al., 2003) using the Stanford French tokenizer (Green et al., 2013b).

We also lowercased the data and removed any control characters. Further, we filtered out all lines that consisted mainly of punctuation marks, removed characters that are frequently used as bullet points and standardized white spaces and newlines. We additionally filtered out sentences longer than 100 tokens from the parallel corpora in order to speed up model learning.

2.2 Alignment

For both systems, we used the Berkeley Aligner (Liang et al., 2006) with default settings to align the parallel data. We symmetrized the alignments using the grow-diag heuristic.

2.3 Language Models

Our systems used up to three language models.

2.3.1 Constrained Language Models

For En-De, we used lmplz (Heafield et al., 2013) to estimate a 5-gram language model on all WMT German monolingual data and the German side of the parallel Common Crawl corpus. To query the model, we used KenLM (Heafield, 2011).

For the Fr-En system, we also estimated a 5-gram language model from all the monolingual English data and the English side of the parallel Common Crawl, UN, Giga-FrEn, CzEng and Yandex corpora using the same procedure as above. Additionally, we estimated a second language model from the English Gigaword corpus.

All of these language models used interpolated modified Kneser-Ney smoothing (Kneser and Ney, 1995; Chen and Goodman, 1998).

2.3.2 Unconstrained Language Model

Our unconstrained En-De submission used an additional language model trained on German web text gathered by the Common Crawl Foundation and processed by Buck et al. (2014). This corpus was formed from the 2012, 2013, and winter 2013 Common Crawl releases, which consist of web pages converted to UTF-8 encoding with HTML stripped. Applying the Compact Language Detector 2,[2] 2.89% of the data was identified as German, amounting to 1 TB of uncompressed text. After splitting sentences with the Europarl sentence splitter (Koehn, 2005), the text was deduplicated at the sentence level to reduce the impact of boilerplate and pages that appeared in multiple crawls, discarding 78% of the data. We treated the resulting data as normal text, pre-processing it as described in Section 2.1 to yield 38.9 billion tokens. We built an unpruned interpolated modified Kneser-Ney language model with this corpus (Table 3) and added it as an additional feature alongside the constrained language models. At 38.9 billion tokens after deduplication, this monolingual data is almost 23 times as large as the rest of the German monolingual corpus. Since the test data was also collected from the web, we cannot be sure that the test sentences were not in the language model. However, substantial portions of the test set are translations from other languages, which were not posted online until after 2013.

Order	1	2	3	4	5
Count	226	1,916	6,883	13,292	17,576

Table 3: Number of unique n-grams, in millions, appearing in the Common Crawl German language model.

2.3.3 Word-Class Language Model

We also built a word-class language model for the En-De system. We trained 512 word classes on the constrained German data using the predictive one-sided class model of Whittaker and Woodland (2001) with the parallelized clustering algorithm of Uszkoreit and Brants (2008) by Green et al. (2014a). All tokens were mapped to their word class; infrequent tokens appearing fewer than 5 times were mapped to a special cluster for unknown tokens. Finally, we estimated a 7-gram language model on the mapped corpus with SRILM (Stolcke, 2002) using Witten-Bell smoothing (Bell et al., 1990).

2.4 Tuning and Test Data

For development, we tuned our systems on all 13,573 sentences contained in the newstest2008-2012 data sets and tested on the 3,000 sentences of the newstest2013 data set. The final system weights were chosen among all tuning iterations using performance on the newstest2013 data set.

2.5 Post-Processing

Our post-processor recases and detokenizes system output. For the English-German system, we combined both tasks by using a Conditional Random Field (CRF) model (Lafferty et al., 2001) to

[2] https://code.google.com/p/cld2/

learn transformations between the raw output characters and the post-processed versions. For each test dataset, we trained a separate model on 500,000 sentences selected using the Feature Decay Algorithm for bitext selection (Biçici and Yuret, 2011). Features used include the character type of the current and surrounding characters, the token type of the current and surrounding tokens, and the position of the character within its token.

The English output was recased using a language model based recaser (Lita et al., 2003). The language model was trained on the English side of the Fr-En parallel data using lmplz.

3 Translation System

We built our translation systems using Phrasal.

3.1 Features

Our translation model has 19 dense features that were computed for all translation hypotheses: the nine Moses (Koehn et al., 2007) baseline features, the eight hierarchical lexicalized reordering model features by Galley and Manning (2008), the log count of each rule, and an indicator for unique rules. On top of that, the model uses the following additional features of Green et al. (2014a).

Rule indicator features: An indicator feature for each translation rule. To combat overfitting, this feature fires only for rules that occur more than 50 times in the parallel data. Additional indicator features were constructed by mapping the words in each rule to their corresponding word classes.

Target unigram class: An indicator feature for the class of each target word.

Alignments: An indicator feature for each alignment in a translation rule, including multi-word alignments. Again, class-based translation rules were used to extract additional indicator features.

Source class deletion: An indicator feature for the class of each unaligned source word in a translation rule.

Punctuation count ratio: The ratio of target punctuation tokens to source punctuation tokens for each derivation.

Function word ratio: The ratio of target function words to source function words. The function words for each language are the 35 most frequent words on each side of the parallel data. Numbers and punctuation marks are not included in this list.

Target-class bigram boundary: An indicator feature for the concatenation of the word class of the rightmost word in the left rule and the word class of the leftmost word in the right rule in each adjacent rule pair in a derivation.

Length features: Indicator features for the length of the source side and for the length of the target side of the translation rule and an indicator feature for the concatenation of the two lengths.

Rule orientation features: An indicator feature for each translation rule combined with its orientation class (monotone, swap, or discontinuous). This feature also fires only for rules that occur more than 50 times in the parallel data. Again, class-based translation rules were used to extract additional features.

Signed linear distortion: The signed linear distortion δ for two rules a and b is $\delta = r(a) - l(b) + 1$, where $r(x)$ is the rightmost source index of rule x and $l(x)$ is the leftmost source index of rule x. Each adjacent rule pair in a derivation has an indicator feature for the signed linear distortion of this pair.

Many of these features consider word classes instead of the actual tokens. For the target side, we used the same word classes as we used to train the class-based language model. For the source side, we trained word classes on all available data using the same method.

3.2 Tuning

We used an online, adaptive tuning algorithm (Green et al., 2013c) to learn the feature weights. The loss function is an online variant of expected BLEU (Green et al., 2014a). As a sentence-level metric, we used the extended BLEU+1 metric that smooths the unigram precision as well as the reference length (Nakov et al., 2012). For feature selection, we used L_1 regularization. Each tuning epoch produces a different set of weights; we tried all of them on newstest2013, which was held out from the tuning set, then picked the weights that produced the best uncased BLEU score.

3.3 System Parameters

We started off with the parameters of our systems for the WMT 2013 Translation Task (Green et al., 2013a) and optimized the L_1-regularization strength. Both systems used the following tuning parameters: a 200-best list, a learning rate of 0.02 and a mini-batch size of 20. The En-De system

Track	Stanford	Best	Rank
En-De constrained	19.9	20.1	3
En-De unconstrained	20.0	20.6	5
Fr-En constrained	34.5	35.0	3

(a) cased BLEU (%)

Track	Stanford	Best	Rank
En-De constrained	20.7	20.7	1
En-De unconstrained	20.9	21.0	3
Fr-En constrained	36.0	36.0	1

(b) uncased BLEU (%)

Table 4: Official results in terms of cased and uncased BLEU of our submitted systems compared to the best systems for each track. The ranks for the unconstrained system are calculated relative to all primary submissions for the language pair, whereas the ranks for the constrained systems are relative to only the constrained systems submitted.

used a phrase length limit of 8, a distortion limit of 6 and a L_1-regularization strength of 0.0002. The Fr-En system used a phrase length limit of 9, a distortion limit of 5 and a L_1-regularization strength of 0.0001.

During tuning, we set the stack size for cube pruning to Phrasal's default value of 1200. To decode the test set, we increased the stack size to 3000.

4 Results

Table 4 shows the official results of our systems compared to other submissions to the WMT shared task. Both our En-De and Fr-En systems achieved the highest uncased BLEU scores among all constrained submissions. However, our recaser evidently performed quite poorly compared to other systems, so our constrained systems ranked third by cased BLEU score. Our unconstrained En-De submission ranked third among all systems by uncased BLEU and fifth by cased BLEU.

To demonstrate the effectiveness of the individual improvements, we show results for four different En-De systems: (1) A baseline that contains only the 19 dense features, (2) a feature-rich translation system with the additional rich features, (3) a feature-rich translation system with an additional word class LM, and (4) a feature-rich translation system with an additional wordclass LM and a huge language model. For Fr-En we only built systems (1)-(3). Results for all systems can be seen in Table 5 and Table 6. From these results, we can see that both language pairs benefitted from adding rich features (+0.4 BLEU for En-De and +0.5 BLEU for Fr-En). However, we only see improvements from the class-based language model in the case of the En-De system (+0.4 BLEU). For this reason our Fr-En submission did not use a class-based language model. Using additional data in the form of a huge language model further improved our En-De system by almost 1% BLEU on the newstest2013 data set. However, we only saw 0.2 BLEU improvement on the newstest2014 data set.

4.1 Analysis

Gains from rich features are in line with the gains we saw in the WMT 2013 translation task (Green et al., 2013a). We suspect that rich features would improve the translation quality a lot more if we had several reference translations to tune on.

The word class language model seemed to improve only translations in our En-De system while it had no effect on BLEU in our Fr-En system. One of the main reasons seems to be that the 7-gram word class language model helped particularly with long range reordering, which happens far more frequently in the En-De language pair compared to the Fr-En pair. For example, in the following translation, we can see that the system with the class-based language model successfully translated the verb in the second clause (set in *italic*) while the system without the class-based language model did not translate the verb.

Source: It became clear to me that this *is* my path.

Feature-rich: Es wurde mir klar, dass das mein Weg.

Word class LM: Es wurde mir klar, dass das mein Weg *ist*.

We can also see that the long range of the word class language model improved grammaticality as shown in the following example:

Source: Meanwhile, more than 40 percent of the population *are* HIV positive.

Feature-rich: Inzwischen *sind* mehr als 40 Prozent der Bevölkerung *sind* HIV positiv.

	#iterations	tune	2013	2013 cased	2014	2014 cased
Dense	8	16.9	19.6	18.7	20.0	19.2
Feature-rich	10	20.1	20.0	19.0	20.0	19.2
+ Word class LM	15	21.1	20.4	19.5	20.7	19.9
+ Huge LM	9	21.0	21.3	20.3	20.9	20.1

Table 5: En-De BLEU results. The tuning set is newstest2008–2012. Scores on newstest2014 were computed after the system submission deadline using the released references.

	#iterations	tune	2013	2013 cased	2014	2014 cased
Dense	1	29.1	32.0	30.4	35.6	34.0
Feature-rich	12	37.2	32.5	30.9	36.0	34.5
+ Word class LM	14	35.7	32.3	30.7	–	–

Table 6: Fr-En BLEU results. The tuning set is newstest2008–2012. Scores on newstest2014 were computed after the system submission deadline using the released references.

Word class LM: Unterdessen mehr als 40 Prozent der Bevölkerung *sind* HIV positiv.

In this example, the system without the class-based language model translated the verb twice. In the second translation, the class-based language model prevented this long range disagreement. An analysis of the differences in the translation output of our Fr-En systems showed that the word class language model mainly led to different word choices but does not seem to help grammatically.

4.2 Casing

Our system performed comparatively poorly at casing, as shown in Table 4. In analysis after the evaluation, we found many of these errors related to words with internal capitals, such as "McCaskill", because the limited recaser we used, which is based on a language model, considered only all lowercase, an initial capital, or all uppercase words. We addressed this issue by allowing any casing seen in the monolingual data. Some words were not seen at all in the monolingual data but, since the target side of the parallel data was included in monolingual data, these words must have come from the source sentence. In such situations, we preserved the word's original case. Table 7 shows the results with the revised casing model. We gained about 0.24% BLEU for German recasing and 0.15% BLEU for English recasing over our submitted systems. In future work, we plan to compare with a truecased system.

	En-De	Fr-En
Uncased Oracle	20.71	36.05
Conditional Random Field	*19.85*	–
Limited Recaser	19.82	*34.51*
Revised Recaser	20.09	34.66

Table 7: Casing results on newstest2014 performed after the evaluation. The oracle scores are uncased BLEU (%) while all other scores are cased. Submitted systems are shown in *italic*.

5 Negative Results

We experimented with several additions that did not make it into the final submissions.

5.1 Preordering

One of the key challenges when translating from English to German is the long-range reordering of verbs. For this reason, we implemented a dependency tree based reordering system (Lerner and Petrov, 2013). We parsed all source side sentences using the Stanford Dependency Parser (De Marneffe et al., 2006) and trained the preordering system on the entire bitext. Then we preordered the source side of the bitext and the tuning and development data sets using our preordering system, realigned the bitext and tuned a machine translation system using the preordered data. While preordering improved verb reordering in many cases, many other parts of the sentences were often also reordered which led to an overall decrease in translation quality. Therefore, we concluded that this system will require further development before it is useful within our translation system.

5.2 Minimum Bayes Risk Decoding

We further attempted to improve our output by reordering the best 1000 translations for each sentence using Minimum Bayes Risk decoding (Kumar and Byrne, 2004) with BLEU as the distance measure. This in effect increases the score of candidates that are "closer" to the other likely translations, where "closeness" is measured by the BLEU score for the candidate when the other translations are used as the reference. Choosing the best translation following this reordering improved overall performance when tuned on the first half of the newstest2013 test set by only 0.03 BLEU points for the English-German system and 0.005 BLEU points for the French-English system, so we abandoned this approach.

6 Conclusion

We submitted three systems: one constrained Fr-En system, one constrained En-De system, and one unconstrained En-De system. Among all constrained systems, ours performed the best according to uncased BLEU. The key differentiating components of our systems are class-based features, word class language models, and a huge web-scale language model. In ongoing work, we are investigating preordering for En-De translation as well as improved recasing.

Acknowledgements

We thank Michael Kayser and Thang Luong for help with experiments. This work was supported by the Defense Advanced Research Projects Agency (DARPA) Broad Operational Language Translation (BOLT) program through IBM. This work used the Extreme Science and Engineering Discovery Environment (XSEDE), which is supported by National Science Foundation grant number OCI-1053575. The authors acknowledge the Texas Advanced Computing Center (TACC) at The University of Texas at Austin for providing HPC resources that have contributed to the research results reported within this paper. Any opinions, findings, and conclusions or recommendations expressed in this material are those of the author(s) and do not necessarily reflect the view of DARPA or the US government.

References

Anne Abeillé, Lionel Clément, and Alexandra Kinyon, 2003. *Building a treebank for French*, chapter 10. Kluwer.

Timothy C. Bell, John G. Cleary, and Ian H. Witten. 1990. *Text compression*. Prentice-Hall.

Ergun Biçici and Deniz Yuret. 2011. Instance selection for machine translation using feature decay algorithms. In *WMT*.

Christian Buck, Kenneth Heafield, and Bas van Ooyen. 2014. N-gram counts and language models from the common crawl. In *LREC*.

Stanley Chen and Joshua Goodman. 1998. An empirical study of smoothing techniques for language modeling. Technical Report TR-10-98, Harvard University, August.

Marie-Catherine De Marneffe, Bill MacCartney, Christopher D Manning, et al. 2006. Generating typed dependency parses from phrase structure parses. In *LREC*.

Michel Galley and Christopher D. Manning. 2008. A simple and effective hierarchical phrase reordering model. In *EMNLP*.

Spence Green, Daniel Cer, Kevin Reschke, Rob Voigt, John Bauer, Sida Wang, et al. 2013a. Feature-rich phrase-based translation: Stanford University's submission to the WMT 2013 translation task. In *WMT*.

Spence Green, Marie-Catherine de Marneffe, and Christopher D. Manning. 2013b. Parsing models for identifying multiword expressions. *Computational Linguistics*, 39(1):195–227.

Spence Green, Sida Wang, Daniel Cer, and Christopher D. Manning. 2013c. Fast and adaptive online training of feature-rich translation models. In *ACL*.

Spence Green, Daniel Cer, and Christopher D. Manning. 2014a. An empirical comparison of features and tuning for phrase-based machine translation. In *WMT*.

Spence Green, Daniel Cer, and Christopher D. Manning. 2014b. Phrasal: A toolkit for new directions in statistical machine translation. In *WMT*.

Kenneth Heafield, Ivan Pouzyrevsky, Jonathan H. Clark, and Philipp Koehn. 2013. Scalable modified Kneser-Ney language model estimation. In *ACL*.

Kenneth Heafield. 2011. KenLM: Faster and smaller language model queries. In *WMT*.

Reinhard Kneser and Hermann Ney. 1995. Improved backing-off for m-gram language modeling. In *ICASSP*.

Philipp Koehn, Hieu Hoang, Alexandra Birch, Chris Callison-Burch, Marcello Federico, Nicola Bertoldi, et al. 2007. Moses: Open source toolkit for statistical machine translation. In *ACL, Demonstration Session*.

Philipp Koehn. 2005. Europarl: A parallel corpus for statistical machine translation. In *Proceedings of MT Summit*.

Shankar Kumar and William Byrne. 2004. Minimum bayes-risk decoding for statistical machine translation. In *HLT-NAACL*.

John D. Lafferty, Andrew McCallum, and Fernando C. N. Pereira. 2001. Conditional random fields: Probabilistic models for segmenting and labeling sequence data. In *ICML*.

Uri Lerner and Slav Petrov. 2013. Source-side classifier preordering for machine translation. In *EMNLP*.

Percy Liang, Ben Taskar, and Dan Klein. 2006. Alignment by agreement. In *NAACL*.

Lucian Vlad Lita, Abe Ittycheriah, Salim Roukos, and Nanda Kambhatla. 2003. tRuEcasIng. In *ACL*.

Mitchell P Marcus, Mary Ann Marcinkiewicz, and Beatrice Santorini. 1993. Building a large annotated corpus of English: The Penn Treebank. *Computational Linguistics*, 19:313–330.

Preslav Nakov, Francisco Guzman, and Stephan Vogel. 2012. Optimizing for sentence-level BLEU+1 yields short translations. In *COLING*.

Franz Josef Och and Hermann Ney. 2004. The alignment template approach to statistical machine translation. *Computational Linguistics*, 30(4):417–449.

Robert Parker, David Graff, Junbo Kong, Ke Chen, and Kazuaki Maeda. 2011. English gigaword fifth edition, june. *Linguistic Data Consortium, LDC2011T07*.

Jason Smith, Hervé Saint-Amand, Magdalena Plamada, Philipp Koehn, Chris Callison-Burch, and Adam Lopez. 2013. Dirt cheap web-scale parallel text from the common crawl. In *ACL*. Association for Computational Linguistics, August.

Andreas Stolcke. 2002. SRILM—an extensible language modeling toolkit. In *ICLSP*.

Jakob Uszkoreit and Thorsten Brants. 2008. Distributed word clustering for large scale class-based language modeling in machine translation. In *ACL*.

Ed W. D. Whittaker and Philip C. Woodland. 2001. Efficient class-based language modelling for very large vocabularies. In *ICASSP*.

The RWTH Aachen German-English Machine Translation System for WMT 2014

Stephan Peitz, Joern Wuebker, Markus Freitag and Hermann Ney
Human Language Technology and Pattern Recognition Group
Computer Science Department
RWTH Aachen University
D-52056 Aachen, Germany
<surname>@cs.rwth-aachen.de

Abstract

This paper describes the statistical machine translation (SMT) systems developed at RWTH Aachen University for the German→English translation task of the *ACL 2014 Eighth Workshop on Statistical Machine Translation* (WMT 2014). Both hierarchical and phrase-based SMT systems are applied employing hierarchical phrase reordering and word class language models. For the phrase-based system, we run discriminative phrase training. In addition, we describe our preprocessing pipeline for German→English.

1 Introduction

For the WMT 2014 shared translation task[1] RWTH utilized state-of-the-art phrase-based and hierarchical translation systems. First, we describe our preprocessing pipeline for the language pair German→English in Section 2. Furthermore, we utilize morpho-syntactic analysis to preprocess the data (Section 2.3). In Section 3, we give a survey of the employed systems and the basic methods they implement. More details are given about the discriminative phrase training (Section 3.4) and the hierarchical reordering model for hierarchical machine translation (Section 3.5). Experimental results are discussed in Section 4.

2 Preprocessing

In this section we will describe the modification of our preprocessing pipeline compared to our 2013 WMT German→English setup.

2.1 Categorization

We put some effort in building better categories for digits and written numbers. All written numbers were categorized. In 2013 they were just handled as normal words which leads to a higher number of out-of-vocabulary words. For German→English, in most cases for numbers like '3,000' or '2.34' the decimal mark ',' and the thousands separator '.' has to be inverted. As the training data and also the test sets contain several errors for numbers in the source as well as in the target part, we put more effort into producing correct English numbers.

2.2 Remove Foreign Languages

The WMT German→English corpus contains some bilingual sentence pairs with non-German source or/and non-English target sentences. For this WMT translation task, we filtered all non-matching language pairs (in terms of source language German and target language English) from our bilingual training set.

First, we filtered languages which contain non-ascii characters. For example Chinese, Arabic or Russian can be easily filtered when deleting sentences which contain more than 70 percent non-ascii words. The first examples of Table 1 was filtered due to the fact, that the source sentence contains too many non-ascii characters.

In a second step, we filtered European languages containing ascii characters. We used the WMT monolingual corpora in Czech, French, Spanish, English and German to filter these languages from our bilingual data. We could both delete a sentence pair if it contains a wrong source language or a wrong target language. That is the reason why we even search for English sentences in the source part and for German sentences in the target part. For each language, we built a word count of all words in the monolingual data for each language separately. We removed punctuation which are no indicator of a language. In our experiments, we only considered words with frequency higher than 20 (e.g. to ignore names). Given the word frequency, we removed a bilingual

[1] http://www.statmt.org/wmt14/translation-task.html

Proceedings of the Ninth Workshop on Statistical Machine Translation, pages 157–162,
Baltimore, Maryland USA, June 26–27, 2014.

Table 1: Examples of sentences removed in preprocessing.

	Example
remove non-ascii symbols	高效的技以抵消影响 . zum Bericht Añoveros Trías de Bes
remove wrong languages from target	Honni soit qui mal y pense ! as you yourself have said : travailler plus pour gagner plus
remove wrong languages from source	je déclare interrompue la session du Parlement européen . Quelle der Tabelle : " what Does the European Union do ? "

sentence pair from our training data if more than 70 percent of the words had a higher count in a different language then the one we expected. In Table 1 some example sentences, which were removed, are illustrated.

In Table 2 the amount of sentences and the corresponding vocabulary sizes of partial and totally cleaned data sets are given. Further we provide the number of out-of-vocabulary words (OOVs) for *newstest2012*. The vocabulary size could be reduced by ~130k words for both source and target side of our bilingual training data while the OOV rate kept the same. Our experiments showed, that the translation quality is the same with or without removing wrong sentences. Nevertheless, we reduced the training data size and also the vocabulary size without any degradation in terms of translation quality.

2.3 Morpho-syntactic Analysis

In order to reduce the source vocabulary size for the German→English translation further, the German text is preprocessed by splitting German compound words with the frequency-based method described in (Koehn and Knight, 2003). To reduce translation complexity, we employ the long-range part-of-speech based reordering rules proposed by Popović and Ney (2006).

3 Translation Systems

In this evaluation, we employ phrase-based translation and hierarchical phrase-based translation. Both approaches are implemented in *Jane* (Vilar et al., 2012; Wuebker et al., 2012), a statistical machine translation toolkit which has been developed at RWTH Aachen University and is freely available for non-commercial use.[2] In the newest internal version, we use the KenLM Language Model Interface provided by (Heafield, 2011) for both decoders.

[2] `http://www.hltpr.rwth-aachen.de/jane/`

3.1 Phrase-based System

In the phrase-based decoder (source cardinality synchronous search, *SCSS*, Wuebker et al. (2012)), we use the standard set of models with phrase translation probabilities and lexical smoothing in both directions, word and phrase penalty, distance-based distortion model, an n-gram target language model and three binary count features. Additional models used in this evaluation are the hierarchical reordering model (*HRM*) (Galley and Manning, 2008) and a word class language model (*wcLM*) (Wuebker et al., 2013). The parameter weights are optimized with minimum error rate training (MERT) (Och, 2003). The optimization criterion is BLEU (Papineni et al., 2002).

3.2 Hierarchical Phrase-based System

In hierarchical phrase-based translation (Chiang, 2007), a weighted synchronous context-free grammar is induced from parallel text. In addition to contiguous *lexical* phrases, *hierarchical* phrases with up to two gaps are extracted. The search is carried out with a parsing-based procedure. The standard models integrated into our Jane hierarchical systems (Vilar et al., 2010; Huck et al., 2012) are: Phrase translation probabilities and lexical smoothing probabilities in both translation directions, word and phrase penalty, binary features marking hierarchical phrases, glue rule, and rules with non-terminals at the boundaries, three binary count features, and an n-gram language model. We utilize the cube pruning algorithm for decoding (Huck et al., 2013a) and optimize the model weights with MERT. The optimization criterion is BLEU.

3.3 Other Tools and Techniques

We employ GIZA++ (Och and Ney, 2003) to train word alignments. The two trained alignments are heuristically merged to obtain a symmetrized word alignment for phrase extraction. All lan-

Table 2: Corpus statistics after each filtering step and compound splitting.

		Vocabulary		OOVs
	Sentences	German	English	newstest2012
Preprocessing 2013	4.19M	1.43M	784K	1019
Preprocessing 2014	4.19M	1.42M	773K	1018
+ remove non-ascii symbols	4.17M	1.36M	713K	1021
+ remove wrong languages from target	4.15M	1.34M	675K	1027
+ remove wrong languages from source	4.08M	1.30M	655K	1039
+ compound splitting	4.08M	652K	655K	441

guage models (*LMs*) are created with the SRILM toolkit (Stolcke, 2002) or with the KenLM language model toolkit (Heafield et al., 2013) and are standard 4-gram LMs with interpolated modified Kneser-Ney smoothing (Kneser and Ney, 1995; Chen and Goodman, 1998). We evaluate in truecase with BLEU and TER (Snover et al., 2006).

3.4 Discriminative Phrase Training

In our baseline translation systems the phrase tables are created by a heuristic extraction from word alignments and the probabilities are estimated as relative frequencies, which is still the state-of-the-art for many standard SMT systems. Here, we applied a more sophisticated discriminative phrase training method for the WMT 2014 German→English task. Similar to (He and Deng, 2012), a gradient-based method is used to optimize a maximum expected BLEU objective, for which we define BLEU on the sentence level with smoothed 3-gram and 4-gram precisions. To that end, the training data is decoded to generate 100-best lists. We apply a leave-one-out heuristic (Wuebker et al., 2010) to make better use of the training data. Using these n-best lists, we iteratively perform updates on the phrasal translation scores of the phrase table. After each iteration, we run MERT, evaluate on the development set and select the best performing iteration. In this work, we perform two rounds of discriminative training on two separate data sets. In the first round, training is performed on the concatenation of newstest2008 through newstest2010 and an automatic selection from the News-commentary, Europarl and Common Crawl corpora. The selection is based on cross-entropy difference of language models and IBM-1 models as described by Mansour et al. (2011) and contains 258K sentence pairs. The training took 4.5 hours for 30 iterations. On top of the final phrase-based systems, a second round of discriminative training is run on the full news-commentary corpus concatenated with newstest2008 through newstest2010.

3.5 A Phrase Orientation Model for Hierarchical Machine Translation

In Huck et al. (2013b) a lexicalized reordering model for hierarchical phrase-based machine translation was introduced. The model scores *monotone*, *swap*, and *discontinuous* phrase orientations in the manner of the one presented by (Tillmann, 2004). Since improvements were reported on a Chinese→English translation task, we investigate the impact of this model on a European language pair. As in German the word order is more flexible compared with the target language English, we expect that an additional reordering model could improve the translation quality. In our experiments we use the same settings which worked best in (Huck et al., 2013b).

4 Setup

We trained the phrase-based and the hierarchical translation system on all available bilingual training data. Corpus statistics can be found in the last row of Table 2. The language model are 4-grams trained on the respective target side of the bilingual data, $\frac{1}{2}$ of the Shuffled News Crawl corpus, $\frac{1}{4}$ of the 10^9 French-English corpus and $\frac{1}{2}$ of the LDC Gigaword Fifth Edition corpus. The monolingual data selection is based on cross-entropy difference as described in (Moore and Lewis, 2010). For the baseline language model, we trained separate models for each corpus, which were then interpolated. For our final experiments, we also trained a single unpruned language model on the concatenation of all monolingual data with KenLM.

Table 3: Results (truecase) for the German→English translation task. BLEU and TER are given in percentage. All HPBT setups are tuned on the concatenation of newstest2012 and newstest2013. The very first SCSS setups are optimized on newstest2012 only.

	newstest2011		**newstest2012**		**newstest2013**	
	BLEU	TER	BLEU	TER	BLEU	TER
SCSS +HRM	22.4	60.1	23.7	59.0	25.9	55.7
+wcLM	22.8	59.6	24.0	58.6	26.3	55.4
+1st round discr.	23.0	59.5	24.2	58.2	26.8	55.1
+tune11+12.	23.4	59.5	24.2	58.6	26.8	55.2
+unprunedLM	23.6	59.5	24.2	58.6	27.1	55.0
+2nd round discr.	23.7	59.5	24.4	58.5	27.2	55.0
HPBT baseline	23.3	59.9	24.2	58.9	26.7	55.6
+wcLM	23.4	59.8	24.1	58.9	26.8	55.6
+HRM	23.3	60.0	24.2	58.9	26.9	55.5
+HRM +wcLM	23.3	59.9	24.1	59.1	26.7	55.9

4.1 Experimental Results

The results of the phrase-based system (SCSS) as well as the hierarchical phrase-based system (HPBT) are summarized in Table 3.

The phrase-based baseline system, which includes the hierarchical reordering model by (Galley and Manning, 2008) and is tuned on newstest2012, reaches a performance of 25.9% BLEU on newstest2013. Adding the word class language model improves performance by 0.4% BLEU absolute and the first round of discriminative phrase training by 0.5% BLEU absolute. Next, we switched to tuning on a concatenation of newstest2011 and newstest2012, which we expect to be more reliable with respect to unseen data. Although the BLEU score does not improve and TER goes up slightly, we kept this tuning set in the subsequent setups, as it yielded longer translations, which in our experience will usually be preferred by human evaluators. Switching from the interpolated language model to the unpruned language model trained with KenLM on the full concatenated monolingual training data in a single pass gained us another 0.3% BLEU. For the final system, we ran a second round of discriminative training on different training data (cf. Section 3.4), which increased performance by 0.1% BLEU to the final score 27.2.

For the phrase-based system, we also experimented with weighted phrase extraction (Mansour and Ney, 2012), but did not observe improvements.

The hierarchical phrase-based baseline without any additional model is on the same level as the phrase-based system including the word class language model, hierarchical reordering model and discriminative phrase training in terms of BLEU. However, extending the system with a word class language model or the additional reordering models does not seem to help. Even the combination of both models does not improve the translation quality. Note, that the hierarchical system was tuned on the concatenation newstest2011 and newstest2012. The final system employs both word class language model and hierarchical reordering model.

Both phrase-based and hierarchical phrase-based final systems are used in the EU-Bridge system combination (Freitag et al., 2014).

5 Conclusion

For the participation in the WMT 2014 shared translation task, RWTH experimented with both phrase-based and hierarchical translation systems. For both approaches, we applied a hierarchical phrase reordering model and a word class language model. For the phrase-based system we employed discriminative phrase training. Additionally, improvements of our preprocessing pipeline compared to our WMT 2013 setup were described. New introduced categories lead to a lower amount of out-of-vocabulary words. Filtering the corpus for wrong languages gives us lower vocabulary sizes for source and target without loosing any performance.

Acknowledgments

The research leading to these results has partially received funding from the European Union Seventh Framework Programme (FP7/2007-2013) under grant agreement n° 287658.

Furthermore, this material is partially based upon work supported by the DARPA BOLT project under Contract No. HR0011- 12-C-0015. Any opinions, findings and conclusions or recommendations expressed in this material are those of the authors and do not necessarily reflect the views of DARPA.

References

Stanley F. Chen and Joshua Goodman. 1998. An Empirical Study of Smoothing Techniques for Language Modeling. Technical Report TR-10-98, Computer Science Group, Harvard University, Cambridge, Massachusetts, USA, August.

David Chiang. 2007. Hierarchical Phrase-Based Translation. *Computational Linguistics*, 33(2):201–228.

Markus Freitag, Stephan Peitz, Joern Wuebker, Hermann Ney, Matthias Huck, Rico Sennrich, Nadir Durrani, Maria Nadejde, Philip Williams, Philipp Koehn, Teresa Herrmann, Eunah Cho, and Alex Waibel. 2014. EU-BRIDGE MT: Combined Machine Translation. In *Proceedings of the ACL 2014 Ninth Workshop on Statistical Machine Translation*, Baltimore, MD, USA, June.

Michel Galley and Christopher D. Manning. 2008. A Simple and Effective Hierarchical Phrase Reordering Model. In *Proceedings of the 2008 Conference on Empirical Methods in Natural Language Processing*, pages 847–855, Honolulu, Hawaii, USA, October.

Xiaodong He and Li Deng. 2012. Maximum Expected BLEU Training of Phrase and Lexicon Translation Models. In *Proceedings of the 50th Annual Meeting of the Association for Computational Linguistics (ACL)*, pages 292–301, Jeju, Republic of Korea, Jul.

Kenneth Heafield, Ivan Pouzyrevsky, Jonathan H. Clark, and Philipp Koehn. 2013. Scalable modified Kneser-Ney language model estimation. In *Proceedings of the 51st Annual Meeting of the Association for Computational Linguistics*, pages 690–696, Sofia, Bulgaria, August.

Kenneth Heafield. 2011. KenLM: faster and smaller language model queries. In *Proceedings of the EMNLP 2011 Sixth Workshop on Statistical Machine Translation*, pages 187–197, Edinburgh, Scotland, United Kingdom, July.

Matthias Huck, Jan-Thorsten Peter, Markus Freitag, Stephan Peitz, and Hermann Ney. 2012. Hierarchical Phrase-Based Translation with Jane 2. *The Prague Bulletin of Mathematical Linguistics*, 98:37–50, October.

Matthias Huck, David Vilar, Markus Freitag, and Hermann Ney. 2013a. A Performance Study of Cube Pruning for Large-Scale Hierarchical Machine Translation. In *Proceedings of the NAACL 7th Workshop on Syntax, Semantics and Structure in Statistical Translation*, pages 29–38, Atlanta, Georgia, USA, June.

Matthias Huck, Joern Wuebker, Felix Rietig, and Hermann Ney. 2013b. A phrase orientation model for hierarchical machine translation. In *ACL 2013 Eighth Workshop on Statistical Machine Translation*, pages 452–463, Sofia, Bulgaria, August.

Reinhard Kneser and Hermann Ney. 1995. Improved Backing-Off for M-gram Language Modeling. In *Proceedings of the International Conference on Acoustics, Speech, and Signal Processing*, volume 1, pages 181–184, May.

Philipp Koehn and Kevin Knight. 2003. Empirical Methods for Compound Splitting. In *Proceedings of European Chapter of the ACL (EACL 2009)*, pages 187–194.

Saab Mansour and Hermann Ney. 2012. A Simple and Effective Weighted Phrase Extraction for Machine Translation Adaptation. In *Proceedings of the International Workshop on Spoken Language Translation (IWSLT)*, pages 193–200, Hong Kong, December.

Saab Mansour, Joern Wuebker, and Hermann Ney. 2011. Combining Translation and Language Model Scoring for Domain-Specific Data Filtering. In *Proceedings of the International Workshop on Spoken Language Translation (IWSLT)*, pages 222–229, San Francisco, California, USA, December.

Robert C. Moore and William Lewis. 2010. Intelligent Selection of Language Model Training Data. In *ACL (Short Papers)*, pages 220–224, Uppsala, Sweden, July.

Franz Josef Och and Hermann Ney. 2003. A Systematic Comparison of Various Statistical Alignment Models. *Computational Linguistics*, 29(1):19–51, March.

Franz Josef Och. 2003. Minimum Error Rate Training in Statistical Machine Translation. In *Proc. of the 41th Annual Meeting of the Association for Computational Linguistics (ACL)*, pages 160–167, Sapporo, Japan, July.

Kishore Papineni, Salim Roukos, Todd Ward, and Wei-Jing Zhu. 2002. Bleu: a Method for Automatic Evaluation of Machine Translation. In *Proceedings of the 41st Annual Meeting of the Association for Computational Linguistics*, pages 311–318, Philadelphia, Pennsylvania, USA, July.

Maja Popović and Hermann Ney. 2006. POS-based Word Reorderings for Statistical Machine Translation. In *International Conference on Language Resources and Evaluation*, pages 1278–1283, Genoa, Italy, May.

Matthew Snover, Bonnie Dorr, Richard Schwartz, Linnea Micciulla, and John Makhoul. 2006. A Study of Translation Edit Rate with Targeted Human Annotation. In *Proceedings of the 7th Conference of the Association for Machine Translation in the Americas*, pages 223–231, Cambridge, Massachusetts, USA, August.

Andreas Stolcke. 2002. SRILM – An Extensible Language Modeling Toolkit. In *Proc. of the Int. Conf. on Speech and Language Processing (ICSLP)*, volume 2, pages 901–904, Denver, Colorado, USA, September.

Christoph Tillmann. 2004. A Unigram Orientation Model for Statistical Machine Translation. In *Proceedings of HLT-NAACL 2004: Short Papers*, HLT-NAACL-Short '04, pages 101–104, Boston, MA, USA.

David Vilar, Daniel Stein, Matthias Huck, and Hermann Ney. 2010. Jane: Open Source Hierarchical Translation, Extended with Reordering and Lexicon Models. In *ACL 2010 Joint Fifth Workshop on Statistical Machine Translation and Metrics MATR*, pages 262–270, Uppsala, Sweden, July.

David Vilar, Daniel Stein, Matthias Huck, and Hermann Ney. 2012. Jane: an advanced freely available hierarchical machine translation toolkit. *Machine Translation*, 26(3):197–216, September.

Joern Wuebker, Arne Mauser, and Hermann Ney. 2010. Training phrase translation models with leaving-one-out. In *Proceedings of the 48th Annual Meeting of the Assoc. for Computational Linguistics*, pages 475–484, Uppsala, Sweden, July.

Joern Wuebker, Matthias Huck, Stephan Peitz, Malte Nuhn, Markus Freitag, Jan-Thorsten Peter, Saab Mansour, and Hermann Ney. 2012. Jane 2: Open Source Phrase-based and Hierarchical Statistical Machine Translation. In *International Conference on Computational Linguistics*, pages 483–491, Mumbai, India, December.

Joern Wuebker, Stephan Peitz, Felix Rietig, and Hermann Ney. 2013. Improving statistical machine translation with word class models. In *Conference on Empirical Methods in Natural Language Processing*, pages 1377–1381, Seattle, USA, October.

Large-scale Exact Decoding: The IMS-TTT submission to WMT14*

Daniel Quernheim
IMS
University of Stuttgart
daniel@ims.uni-stuttgart.de

Fabienne Cap
CIS
Ludwig-Maximilian University of Munich
cap@cis.uni-muenchen.de

Abstract

We present the IMS-TTT submission to WMT14, an experimental statistical tree-to-tree machine translation system based on the multi-bottom up tree transducer including rule extraction, tuning and decoding. Thanks to input parse forests and a "no pruning" strategy during decoding, the obtained translations are competitive. The drawbacks are a restricted coverage of 70% on test data, in part due to exact input parse tree matching, and a relatively high runtime. Advantages include easy redecoding with a different weight vector, since the full translation forests can be stored after the first decoding pass.

1 Introduction

In this contribution, we present an implementation of a translation model that is based on ℓMBOT (the multi bottom-up tree transducer of Arnold and Dauchet (1982) and Lilin (1978)). Intuitively, an MBOT is a synchronous tree sequence substitution grammar (STSSG, Zhang et al. (2008a); Zhang et al. (2008b); Sun et al. (2009)) that has discontiguities only on the target side (Maletti, 2011). From an algorithmic point of view, this makes the MBOT more appealing than STSSG as demonstrated by Maletti (2010). Formally, MBOT is expressive enough to express all sensible translations (Maletti, 2012)[1]. Figure 2 displays sample rules of the MBOT variant, called ℓMBOT, that we use (in a graphical representation of the trees and the alignment). Recently, a shallow version of MBOT has been integrated into the popular Moses toolkit (Braune et al., 2013). Our implementation is exact in the sense that it does absolutely no pruning during decoding and thus preserves all translation candidates, while having no mechanism to handle unknown structures. (We added dummy rules that leave unseen lexical material untranslated.) The coverage is thus limited, but still considerably high. Source-side and target-side syntax restrict the search space so that decoding stays tractable. Only the language model scoring is implemented as a separate reranker[2]. This has several advantages: (1) We can use input parse forests (Liu et al., 2009). (2) Not only is the output optimal with regard to the theoretical model, also the space of translation candidates can be efficiently stored as a weighted regular tree grammar. The best translations can then be extracted using the k-best algorithm by Huang and Chiang (2005). Rule weights can be changed without the need for explicit redecoding, the parameters of the log-linear model can be changed, and even new features can be added. These properties are especially helpful in tuning, where only the k-best algorithm has to be re-run in each iteration. A model in similar spirit has been described by Huang et al. (2006); however, it used target syntax only (using a top-down tree-to-string transducer backwards), and was restricted to sentences of length at most 25. We do not make such restrictions.

The theoretical aspects of ℓMBOT and their use in our translation model are presented in Section 2. Based on this, we implemented a machine translation system that we are going to make available to

*This work was supported by Deutsche Forschungsgemeinschaft grants Models of Morphosyntax for Statistical Machine Translation (Phase 2) and MA/4959/1–1.

[1] A translation is sensible if it is of linear size increase and can be computed by some (potentially copying) top-down tree transducer.

[2] Strictly speaking, this does introduce pruning into the pipeline.

Proceedings of the Ninth Workshop on Statistical Machine Translation, pages 163–170,
Baltimore, Maryland USA, June 26–27, 2014. ©2014 Association for Computational Linguistics

the public. Section 4 presents the most important components of our ℓMBOT implementation, and Section 5 presents our submission to the WMT14 shared translation task.

2 Theoretical Model

In this section, we present the theoretical generative model that is used in our approach to syntax-based machine translation: the multi bottom-up tree transducer (Maletti, 2011). We omit the technical details and give graphical examples only to illustrate how the device works, but refer to the literature for the theoretical background. Roughly speaking, a local multi bottom-up tree transducer (ℓMBOT) has rules that replace one nonterminal symbol N on the source side by a tree, and a sequence of nonterminal symbols on the target side linked to N by one tree each. These trees again have linked nonterminals, thus allowing further rule applications.

Our ℓMBOT rules are obtained automatically from data like that in Figure 1. Thus, we (word) align the bilingual text and parse it in both the source and the target language. In this manner we obtain sentence pairs like the one shown in Figure 1. To these sentence pairs we apply the rule extraction method of Maletti (2011). The rules extracted from the sentence pair of Figure 1 are shown in Figure 2. Note the discontiguous alignment of *went* to *ist* and *gegangen*, resulting in discontiguous rules.

The application of those rules is illustrated in Figure 3 (a *pre-translation* is a pair consisting of a source tree and a sequence of target trees). While it shows a synchronous derivation, our main use case of ℓMBOT rules is *forward application* or *input restriction*, that is the calculation of all target trees that can be derived given a source tree. For a given synchronous derivation d, the source tree generated by d is $s(d)$, and the target tree is $t(d)$. The yield of a tree is the string obtained by concatenating its leaves.

Apart from ℓMBOT application to input trees, we can even apply ℓMBOT to *parse forests* and even *weighted regular tree grammars* (RTGs) (Fülöp and Vogler, 2009). RTGs offer an efficient representation of weighted forests, which are sets of trees such that each individual tree is equipped with a weight. This representation is even more efficient than packed forests (Mi et al., 2008) and moreover can represent an infinite number of weighted trees. The most important property that we utilize is that the output tree language is regular, so we can represent it by an RTG (cf. preservation of regularity (Maletti, 2011)). Indeed, every input tree can only be transformed into finitely many output trees by our model, so for a given finite input forest (which the output of the parser is) the computed output forest will also be finite and thus regular.

3 Translation Model

Given a source language sentence e and corresponding weighted parse forest $F(e)$, our translation model aims to find the best corresponding target language translation $\hat{g}$;[3] i.e.,

$$\hat{g} = \arg\max_g p(g|e) \ .$$

We estimate the probability $p(g|e)$ through a log-linear combination of component models with parameters λ_m scored on the derivations d such that the source tree of d is in the parse forest of e and the yield of the target tree reads g. With

$$D(e,g) = \{d \mid s(d) \in F(e) \text{ and } \mathrm{yield}(t(d)) = g\},$$

we thus have: [4]

$$p(g|e) \propto \sum_{d \in D(e,g)} \prod_{m=1}^{11} h_m(d)^{\lambda_m}$$

Our model uses the following features $h_m(\cdot)$ for a derivation:

(1) Translation weight normalized by source root symbol
(2) Translation weight normalized by all root symbols
(3) Translation weight normalized by leaves on the source side
(4) Lexical translation weight source $\rightarrow$ target
(5) Lexical translation weight target $\rightarrow$ source
(6) Target side language model: $p(g)$
(7) Number of words in g
(8) Number of rules used in the derivation
(9) Number of gaps in the target side sequences
(10) Penalty for rules that have more lexical material on the source side than on the target side or vice versa (absolute value)

[3] Our main translation direction is English to German.

[4] While this is the clean theoretical formulation, we make two approximations to $D(e,g)$: (1) The parser we use returns a pruned parse forest. (2) We only sum over derivations with the same target sentence that actually appear in the k-best list.

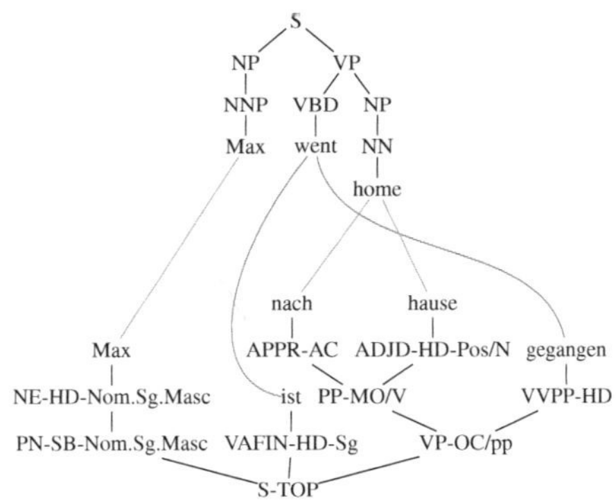

Figure 1: Aligned parsed sentences.

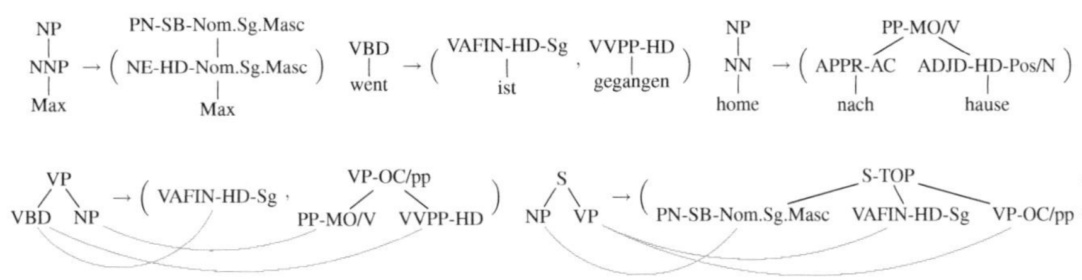

Figure 2: Extracted rules.

(11) Input parse tree probability assigned to $s(t)$ by the parser of e

The rule weights required for (1) are relative frequencies normalized over all extracted rules with the same root symbol on the left-hand side. In the same fashion the rule weights required for (2) are relative frequencies normalized over all rules with the same root symbols on both sides. The lexical weights for (4) and (5) are obtained by multiplying the word translations $w(g_i|e_j)$ [respectively, $w(e_j|g_i)$] of lexically aligned words (g_i, e_j) across (possibly discontiguous) target side sequences.[5] Whenever a source word e_j is aligned to multiple target words, we average over the word translations:[6]

$$h_4(d) = \prod_{\substack{\text{lexical item} \\ e \text{ occurs in } s(d)}} \text{average}\,\{w(g|e) \mid g \text{ aligned to } e\}$$

4 Implementation

Our implementation is very close to the theoretical model and consists of several independent components, most of which are implemented in Python. The system does not have any dependencies other than the need for parsers for the source and target language, a word alignment tool and optionally an implementation of some tuning algorithm. A schematic depiction of the training and decoding pipeline can be seen in Figure 4.

Rule extraction From a parallel corpus of which both halves have been parsed and word aligned, multi bottom-up tree transducer rules are extracted according to the procedure laid out in (Maletti, 2011). In order to handle unknown words, we add dummy identity translation rules for lexical material that was not present in the training data.

Translation model building Given a set of rules, translation weights (see above) are computed for each unique rule. The translation model is then converted into a source, a weight and a target model. The source model (an RTG represented in an efficient binary format) is used for decoding and maps input trees to trees over rule identifiers representing derivations. The weight model and the target model can be used to reconstruct the weight and the target realization of a given derivation.

[5]The lexical alignments are different from the links used to link nonterminals.

[6]If the word e_j has no alignment to a target word, then it is assumed to be aligned to a special NULL word and this alignment is scored.

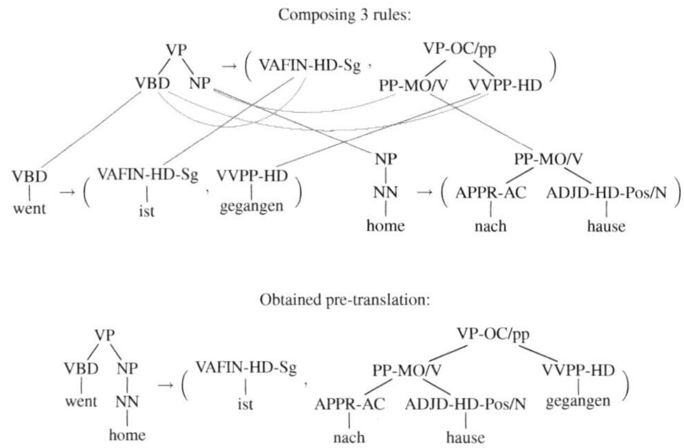

Figure 3: Synchronous rule application.

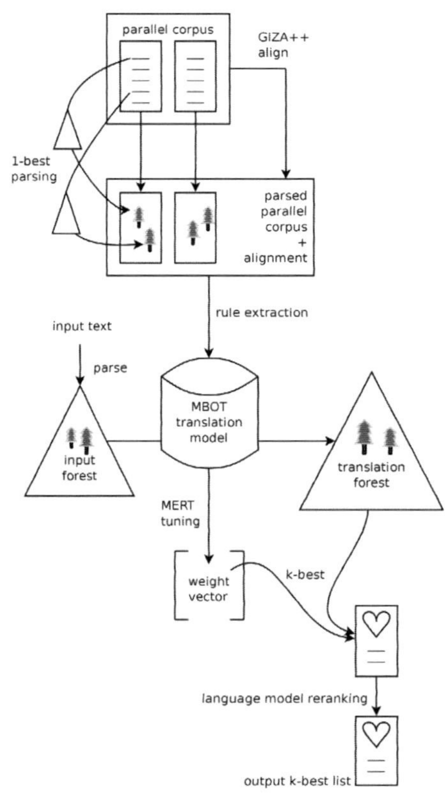

Figure 4: Our machine translation system.

Decoder The decoder transforms a forest of input sentence parse trees to a forest of translation derivations by means of forward application. These derivations are trees over the set of rules (represented by rule identifiers). One of the most useful aspects of our model is the fact that decoding is completely independent of the weights, as no pruning is performed and all translation candidates are preserved in the translation forest. Thus, even after decoding, the weight model can be changed, augmented by new features, etc.; even the target model can be changed, e.g. to support parse tree output instead of string output. In all of our experiments, we used string output, but it is conceivable to use other realizations. For instance, a syntactic language model could be used for output tree scoring. Also, recasing is extremely easy when we have part-of-speech tags to base our decision on (proper names are typically uppercase, as are all nouns in German).

Another benefit of having a packed representation of all candidates is that we can easily check whether the reference translation is included in the candidate set ("force decoding"). The freedom to allow arbitrary target models that rewrite derivations is related to current work on interpreted regular tree grammars (Koller and Kuhlmann, 2011), where arbitrary algebras can be used to compute a realization of the output tree.

k-best extractor From the translation derivation RTGs, a k-best list of derivations can be extracted (Huang and Chiang, 2005) very efficiently. This is the only step that has to be repeated if the rule weights or the parameters of the log-linear model change. The derivations are then mapped to target language sentences (if several derivations realize the same target sentence, their weights are summed) and reranked according to a language model (as was done in Huang et al. (2006)). This is the only part of the pipeline where we deviate from the theoretical log-linear model, and this is where we might make search errors. In principle, one could integrate the language model by intersection with the translation model (as the stateful MBOT model is closed under intersection with finite automata), but this is (currently) not computationally feasible due to the size of models.

Tuning Minimum error rate training (Och, 2003) is implemented using Z-MERT[7] (Zaidan, 2009). A set of source sentences has to be (forest-)parsed and decoded; the translation forests are stored on disk. Then, in each iteration of Z-MERT, it suffices to extract k-best lists from the translation forests according to the current weight vector.

5 WMT14 Experimental setup

We used the training data that was made available for the WMT14 shared translation task on English–German[8]. It consists of three parallel corpora (1.9M sentences of European parliament proceedings, 201K sentences of newswire text, and 2M sentences of web text) and additional monolingual news data for language model training.

The English half of the parallel data was parsed using Egret[9] which is a re-implementation of the Berkeley parser (Petrov et al., 2006). For the German parse, we used the BitPar parser (Schmid, 2004; Schmid, 2006). The BitPar German grammar is highly detailed, which makes the syntactic information contained in the parses extremely useful. Part-of-speech tags and category label are augmented by case, number and gender information, as can be seen in the German parse tree in Figure 1. We only kept the best parse for each sentence during training. After parsing, we prepared three versions of the German corpus: a) RAW, with no morphological post-processing; b) UNSPLIT, using SMOR, a rule-based morphological analyser (Schmid et al., 2004), to reduce words to their base form; c) SPLIT, using SMOR to reduce words to their base form and split compound nouns. After translation, compounds were merged again, and words were re-inflected. Previous experiments using SMOR to lemmatise and split compounds in phrase-based SMT showed improved translation performances, see (Cap et al., 2014a) for details.

We then trained three 5-gram language models on monolingual data using KenLM[10] (Heafield, 2011; Heafield et al., 2013 to appear) for the three setups. For SPLIT and UNSPLIT, we were only able to use the German side of the parallel data, since parsing is a prerequisite for our morphological post-processing and we did not have the resources to parse more data. For RAW, we additionally used the monolingual German data

[7]http://cs.jhu.edu/~ozaidan/zmert/

[8]http://www.statmt.org/wmt14/translation-task.html

[9]https://sites.google.com/site/zhanghl982/egret

[10]http://kheafield.com/code/kenlm/

system	BLEU	BLEU-cased	TER
RAW	17.0	16.4	.770
UNSPLIT	16.4	15.8	.773
SPLIT	16.3	15.7	.773

Table 1: BLEU and TER scores of the submitted systems.

that was distributed for the shared task. Word alignment for all three setups was achieved using GIZA++[11]. As usual, we discarded sentence pairs where one sentence was significantly longer than the other, as well as those that were too long or too short.

For tuning, we chose the WMT12 test set (3,003 sentences of newswire text), available as part of the development data for the WMT13 shared translation task. Since our system had limited coverage on this tuning set, we limited ourselves to the first a subset of sentences we could translate.

When translating the test set, our models used parse trees delivered by the Egret parser. After translation, recasing was done by examining the output syntax tree, using a simple heuristics looking for nouns and sentence boundaries. Since coverage on the test set was also limited, we used the systems as described in (Cap et al., 2014b)[12] as a fallback to translate sentences that our system was not able to translate.

6 Results

We report the overall translation quality, as listed on `http://matrix.statmt.org/`, measured using BLEU (Papineni et al., 2002) and TER (Snover et al., 2006), in Table 1.

We assume that the poor performance of UNSPLIT and SPLIT compared to RAW is due to the fact that we use a significantly smaller language model (as explained above) for these two settings. A detailed analysis will follow after the end of the manual evaluation period.

7 Conclusion and further work

We presented our submission to the WMT14 shared translation task based on a novel, promising "full syntax, no pruning" tree-to-tree approach to statistical machine translation, inspired by Huang et al. (2006). There are, however, still major drawbacks and open problems associated with our approach. Firstly, the coverage can still be significantly improved. In these experiments, our model was able to translate only 70% of the test sentences. To some extent, this number can be improved by providing more training data. Also, more rules can be extracted if we not only use the best parse for rule extraction, but multiple parse trees, or even switch to forest-based rule extraction (Mi and Huang, 2008). Finally, the size of the input parse forest plays a role. For instance, if we only supply the best parse to our model, translation will fail for approximately half of the input.

However, there are inherent coverage limits. Since our model is extremely strict, it will never be able to translate sentences whose parse trees contain structures it has never seen before, since it has to match at least one input parse tree exactly. While we implemented a simple solution to handle unknown words, the issue with unknown structures is not so easy to solve without breaking the otherwise theoretically sound approach. Possibly, glue rules can help.

The second drawback is runtime. We were able to translate about 15 sentences per hour on one processor. Distributing the translation task on different machines, we were able to translate the WMT14 test set (10k sentences) in roughly four days. Given that the trend goes towards parallel programming, and considering the fact that our decoder is written in the rather slow language Python, we are confident that this is not a major problem. We were able to run the whole pipeline of training, tuning and evaluation on the WMT14 shared task data in less than one week. We are currently investigating whether A* k-best algorithms (Pauls and Klein, 2009; Pauls et al., 2010) can help to guide the translation process while maintaining optimality.

Thirdly, currently the language model is not integrated, but implemented as a separate reranking component. We are aware that this might introduce search errors, and that an integrated language model might improve translation quality (see e.g. Chiang (2007) where 3–4 BLEU points are gained by LM integration). Some research on this topic already exists, e.g. (Rush and Collins, 2011) who use dual decomposition, and (Aziz et al., 2013) who replace intersection with an upper bound which is easier to compute.

[11] `https://code.google.com/p/giza-pp/`

[12] We use raw as described in (Cap et al., 2014b) as a fallback for RAW, RI for UNSPLIT and CoRI for SPLIT.

References

André Arnold and Max Dauchet. 1982. Morphismes et bimorphismes d'arbres. *Theoret. Comput. Sci.*, 20(1):33–93.

Wilker Aziz, Marc Dymetman, and Sriram Venkatapathy. 2013. Investigations in exact inference for hierarchical translation. In *Proc. 8th WMT*, pages 472–483.

Fabienne Braune, Nina Seemann, Daniel Quernheim, and Andreas Maletti. 2013. Shallow local multi-bottom-up tree transducers in statistical machine translation. In *Proc. 51th ACL*, pages 811–821.

Fabienne Cap, Alexander Fraser, Marion Weller, and Aoife Cahill. 2014a. How to Produce Unseen Teddy Bears: Improved Morphological Processing of Compounds in SMT. In *Proc. 14th EACL*.

Fabienne Cap, Marion Weller, Anita Ramm, and Alexander Fraser. 2014b. CimS – The CIS and IMS joint submission to WMT 2014 translating from English into German. In *Proc. 9th WMT*.

David Chiang. 2007. Hierarchical phrase-based translation. *Computat. Linguist.*, 33(2):201–228.

Zoltán Fülöp and Heiko Vogler. 2009. Weighted tree automata and tree transducers. In Manfred Droste, Werner Kuich, and Heiko Vogler, editors, *Handbook of Weighted Automata*, EATCS Monographs on Theoret. Comput. Sci., chapter 9, pages 313–403. Springer.

Kenneth Heafield, Ivan Pouzyrevsky, Jonathan H. Clark, and Philipp Koehn. 2013 (to appear). Scalable modified Kneser-Ney language model estimation. In *Proc. 51st ACL*.

Kenneth Heafield. 2011. KenLM: faster and smaller language model queries. In *Proc. 6th WMT*, pages 187–197.

Liang Huang and David Chiang. 2005. Better k-best parsing. In *Proc. IWPT*, pages 53–64.

Liang Huang, Kevin Knight, and Aravind Joshi. 2006. Statistical syntax-directed translation with extended domain of locality. In *Proc. 7th Conf. AMTA*, pages 66–73.

Alexander Koller and Marco Kuhlmann. 2011. A generalized view on parsing and translation. In *Proc. IWPT*, pages 2–13.

Eric Lilin. 1978. *Une généralisation des transducteurs d'états finis d'arbres: les S-transducteurs*. Thèse 3ème cycle, Université de Lille.

Yang Liu, Yajuan Lü, and Qun Liu. 2009. Improving tree-to-tree translation with packed forests. In *Proc. 47th ACL*, pages 558–566.

Andreas Maletti. 2010. Why synchronous tree substitution grammars? In *Proc. HLT-NAACL*, pages 876–884.

Andreas Maletti. 2011. How to train your multi bottom-up tree transducer. In *Proc. 49th ACL*, pages 825–834.

Andreas Maletti. 2012. Every sensible extended top-down tree transducer is a multi bottom-up tree transducer. In *Proc. HLT-NAACL*, pages 263–273.

Haitao Mi and Liang Huang. 2008. Forest-based translation rule extraction. In *Proc. EMNLP*, pages 206–214.

Haitao Mi, Liang Huang, and Qun Liu. 2008. Forest-based translation. In *Proc. 46th ACL*, pages 192–199. ACL.

Franz Josef Och. 2003. Minimum error rate training in statistical machine translation. In *Proc. 41st ACL*, pages 160–167.

Kishore Papineni, Salim Roukos, Todd Ward, and Wei jing Zhu. 2002. BLEU: a method for automatic evaluation of machine translation. In *Proc. 40th ACL*, pages 311–318.

Adam Pauls and Dan Klein. 2009. K-best A* parsing. In *Proc. 47th ACL*, pages 958–966.

Adam Pauls, Dan Klein, and Chris Quirk. 2010. Top-down k-best A* parsing. In *Proc. 48th ACL*, pages 200–204.

Slav Petrov, Leon Barrett, Romain Thibaux, and Dan Klein. 2006. Learning accurate, compact, and interpretable tree annotation. In *Proc. COLING-ACL*, pages 433–440.

Alexander M. Rush and Michael Collins. 2011. Exact decoding of syntactic translation models through lagrangian relaxation. In *Proc. 49th ACL*, pages 72–82.

Helmut Schmid, Arne Fitschen, and Ulrich Heid. 2004. SMOR: A German Computational Morphology Covering Derivation, Composition and Inflection. In *Proc. 4th LREC*.

Helmut Schmid. 2004. Efficient parsing of highly ambiguous context-free grammars with bit vectors. In *Proc. 20th COLING*, pages 162–168.

Helmut Schmid. 2006. Trace prediction and recovery with unlexicalized PCFGs and slash features. In *Proc. 44th ACL*.

Matthew Snover, Bonnie Dorr, Richard Schwartz, Linnea Micciulla, and John Makhoul. 2006. A study of translation edit rate with targeted human annotation. In *Proc. AMTA*.

Jun Sun, Min Zhang, and Chew Lim Tan. 2009. A non-contiguous tree sequence alignment-based model for statistical machine translation. In *Proc. 47th ACL*, pages 914–922.

Omar F. Zaidan. 2009. Z-MERT: A fully configurable open source tool for minimum error rate training of machine translation systems. *The Prague Bulletin of Mathematical Linguistics*, 91:79–88.

Min Zhang, Hongfei Jiang, Aiti Aw, Haizhou Li, Chew Lim Tan, and Sheng Li. 2008a. A tree sequence alignment-based tree-to-tree translation model. In *Proc. 46th ACL*, pages 559–567.

Min Zhang, Hongfei Jiang, Haizhou Li, Aiti Aw, and Sheng Li. 2008b. Grammar comparison study for translational equivalence modeling and statistical machine translation. In *Proc. 22nd COLING*, pages 1097–1104.

Abu-MaTran at WMT 2014 Translation Task: Two-step Data Selection and RBMT-Style Synthetic Rules

Raphael Rubino[⋆], **Antonio Toral**[†], **Victor M. Sánchez-Cartagena**[⋆‡], **Jorge Ferrández-Tordera**[⋆], **Sergio Ortiz-Rojas**[⋆], **Gema Ramírez-Sánchez**[⋆], **Felipe Sánchez-Martínez**[‡], **Andy Way**[†]

[⋆] Prompsit Language Engineering, S.L., Elche, Spain
{rrubino,vmsanchez,jferrandez,sortiz,gramirez}@prompsit.com
[†] NCLT, School of Computing, Dublin City University, Ireland
{atoral,away}@computing.dcu.ie
[‡] Dep. Llenguatges i Sistemes Informàtics, Universitat d'Alacant, Spain
fsanchez@dlsi.ua.es

Abstract

This paper presents the machine translation systems submitted by the Abu-MaTran project to the WMT 2014 translation task. The language pair concerned is English–French with a focus on French as the target language. The French to English translation direction is also considered, based on the word alignment computed in the other direction. Large language and translation models are built using all the datasets provided by the shared task organisers, as well as the monolingual data from LDC. To build the translation models, we apply a two-step data selection method based on bilingual cross-entropy difference and vocabulary saturation, considering each parallel corpus individually. Synthetic translation rules are extracted from the development sets and used to train another translation model. We then interpolate the translation models, minimising the perplexity on the development sets, to obtain our final SMT system. Our submission for the English to French translation task was ranked second amongst nine teams and a total of twenty submissions.

1 Introduction

This paper presents the systems submitted by the Abu-MaTran project (runs named *DCU-Prompsit-UA*) to the WMT 2014 translation task for the English–French language pair. Phrase-based statistical machine translation (SMT) systems were submitted, considering the two translation directions, with the focus on the English to French direction. Language models (LMs) and translation models (TMs) are trained using all the data provided by the shared task organisers, as well as the *Gigaword* monolingual corpora distributed by LDC.

To train the LMs, monolingual corpora and the target side of the parallel corpora are first used individually to train models. Then the individual models are interpolated according to perplexity minimisation on the development sets.

To train the TMs, first a baseline is built using the *News Commentary* parallel corpus. Second, each remaining parallel corpus is processed individually using bilingual cross-entropy difference (Axelrod et al., 2011) in order to separate *pseudo* in-domain and out-of-domain sentence pairs, and filtering the *pseudo* out-of-domain instances with the vocabulary saturation approach (Lewis and Eetemadi, 2013). Third, synthetic translation rules are automatically extracted from the development set and used to train another translation model following a novel approach (Sánchez-Cartagena et al., 2014). Finally, we interpolate the four translation models (baseline, in-domain, filtered out-of-domain and rules) by minimising the perplexity obtained on the development sets and investigate the best tuning and decoding parameters.

The reminder of this paper is organised as follows: the datasets and tools used in our experiments are described in Section 2. Then, details about the LMs and TMs are given in Section 3 and Section 4 respectively. Finally, we evaluate the performance of the final SMT system according to different tuning and decoding parameters in Section 5 before presenting conclusions in Section 6.

Proceedings of the Ninth Workshop on Statistical Machine Translation, pages 171–177,
Baltimore, Maryland USA, June 26–27, 2014.

2 Datasets and Tools

We use all the monolingual and parallel datasets in English and French provided by the shared task organisers, as well as the LDC *Gigaword* for the same languages[1]. For each language, a true-case model is trained using all the data, using the *train-truecaser.perl* script included in the MOSES tool-kit (Koehn et al., 2007).

Punctuation marks of all the monolingual and parallel corpora are then normalised using the script *normalize-punctuation.perl* provided by the organisers, before being tokenised and true-cased using the scripts distributed with the MOSES tool-kit. The same pre-processing steps are applied to the development and test sets. As development sets, we used all the test sets from previous years of WMT, from 2008 to 2013 (*newstest2008-2013*).

Finally, the training parallel corpora are cleaned using the script *clean-corpus-n.perl*, keeping the sentences longer than 1 word, shorter than 80 words, and with a length ratio between sentence pairs lower than 4.[2] The statistics about the corpora used in our experiments after pre-processing are presented in Table 1.

For training LMs we use KENLM (Heafield et al., 2013) and the SRILM tool-kit (Stolcke et al., 2011). For training TMs, we use MOSES (Koehn et al., 2007) version 2.1 with MGIZA++ (Och and Ney, 2003; Gao and Vogel, 2008). These tools are used with default parameters for our experiments except when explicitly said.

The decoder used to generate translations is MOSES using features weights optimised with MERT (Och, 2003). As our approach relies on training individual TMs, one for each parallel corpus, our final TM is obtained by linearly interpolating the individual ones. The interpolation of TMs is performed using the script *tmcombine.py*, minimising the cross-entropy between the TM and the concatenated development sets from 2008 to 2012 (noted *newstest2008-2012*), as described in Sennrich (2012). Finally, we make use of the findings from WMT 2013 brought by the winning team (Durrani et al., 2013) and decide to use the Operation Sequence Model (OSM), based on minimal translation units and Markov chains over sequences of operations, implemented in MOSES and introduced by Durrani et al. (2011).

[1]LDC2011T07 English *Gigaword Fifth Edition*, LDC2011T10 French *Gigaword Third Edition*

[2]This ratio was empirically chosen based on words fertility between English and French.

Corpus	Sentences (k)	Words (M)
Monolingual Data – English		
Europarl v7	2,218.2	59.9
News Commentary v8	304.2	7.4
News Shuffled 2007	3,782.5	90.2
News Shuffled 2008	12,954.5	308.1
News Shuffled 2009	14,680.0	347.0
News Shuffled 2010	6,797.2	157.8
News Shuffled 2011	15,437.7	358.1
News Shuffled 2012	14,869.7	345.5
News Shuffled 2013	21,688.4	495.2
LDC afp	7,184.9	869.5
LDC apw	8,829.4	1,426.7
LDC cna	618.4	45.7
LDC ltw	986.9	321.1
LDC nyt	5,327.7	1,723.9
LDC wpb	108.8	20.8
LDC xin	5,121.9	423.7
Monolingual Data – French		
Europarl v7	2,190.6	63.5
News Commentary v8	227.0	6.5
News Shuffled 2007	119.0	2.7
News Shuffled 2008	4,718.8	110.3
News Shuffled 2009	4,366.7	105.3
News Shuffled 2010	1,846.5	44.8
News Shuffled 2011	6,030.1	146.1
News Shuffled 2012	4,114.4	100.8
News Shuffled 2013	9,256.3	220.2
LDC afp	6,793.5	784.5
LDC apw	2,525.1	271.3
Parallel Data		
10^9 Corpus	21,327.1	549.0 (EN) 642.5 (FR)
Common Crawl	3,168.5	76.0 (EN) 82.7 (FR)
Europarl v7	1,965.5	52.5 (EN) 56.7 (FR)
News Commentary v9	181.3	4.5 (EN) 5.3 (FR)
UN	12,354.7	313.4 (EN) 356.5 (FR)

Table 1: Data statistics after pre-processing of the monolingual and parallel corpora used in our experiments.

3 Language Models

The LMs are trained in the same way for both languages. First, each monolingual and parallel corpus is considered individually (except the parallel version of Europarl and News Commentary) and used to train a 5-gram LM with the modified Kneser-Ney smoothing method. We then interpolate the individual LMs using the script *compute-best-mix* available with the SRILM tool-kit (Stolcke et al., 2011), based on their perplexity scores on the concatenation of the development sets from 2008 to 2012 (the 2013 version is held-out for the tuning of the TMs).

The final LM for French contains all the word sequences from 1 to 5-grams contained in the training corpora without any pruning. However, with the computing resources at our disposal, the English LMs could not be interpolated without pruning non-frequent n-grams. Thus, n-grams with $n \in [3;5]$ with a frequency lower than 2 were removed. Details about the final LMs are given in Table 2.

	1-gram	2-gram	3-gram	4-gram	5-gram
English	13.4	198.6	381.2	776.3	1,068.7
French	6.0	75.5	353.2	850.8	1,354.0

Table 2: Statistics, in millions of n-grams, of the interpolated LMs.

4 Translation Models

In this Section, we describe the TMs trained for the shared task. First, we present the two-step data selection process which aims to (i) separate in and out-of-domain parallel sentences and (ii) reduce the total amount of out-of-domain data. Second, a novel approach for the automatic extraction of translation rules and their use to enrich the phrase table is detailed.

4.1 Parallel Data Filtering and Vocabulary Saturation

Amongst the parallel corpora provided by the shared task organisers, only *News Commentary* can be considered as in-domain regarding the development and test sets. We use this training corpus to build our baseline SMT system. The other parallel corpora are individually filtered using bilingual cross-entropy difference (Moore and Lewis, 2010; Axelrod et al., 2011). This data filtering method relies on four LMs, two in the source and two in the target language, which aim to model particular features of in and out-of-domain sentences.

We build the in-domain LMs using the source and target sides of the *News Commentary* parallel corpus. Out-of-domain LMs are trained on a vocabulary-constrained subset of each remaining parallel corpus individually using the SRILM toolkit, which leads to eight models (four in the source language and four in the target language).[3]

[3]The subsets contain the same number of sentences and the same vocabulary as *News Commentary*.

Then, for each out-of-domain parallel corpus, we compute the bilingual cross-entropy difference of each sentence pair as:

$$[H_{\text{in}}(S_{\text{src}}) - H_{\text{out}}(S_{\text{src}})] + [H_{\text{in}}(S_{\text{trg}}) - H_{\text{out}}(S_{\text{trg}})] \quad (1)$$

where S_{src} and S_{trg} are the source and the target sides of a sentence pair, H_{in} and H_{out} are the cross-entropies of the in and out-of-domain LMs given a sentence pair. The sentence pairs are then ranked and the lowest-scoring ones are taken to train the *pseudo* in-domain TMs. However, the cross-entropy difference threshold required to split a corpus in two parts (*pseudo* in and out-of-domain) is usually set empirically by testing several subset sizes of the top-ranked sentence pairs. This method is costly in our setup as it would lead to training and evaluating multiple SMT systems for each of the *pseudo* in-domain parallel corpora.

In order to save time and computing power, we consider only *pseudo* in-domain sentence pairs those with a bilingual cross-entropy difference below 0, i.e. those deemed more similar to the in-domain LMs than to the out-of-domain LMs ($H_{\text{in}} < H_{\text{out}}$). A sample of the distribution of scores for the out-of-domain corpora is shown in Figure 1. The resulting *pseudo* in-domain corpora are used to train individual TMs, as detailed in Table 3.

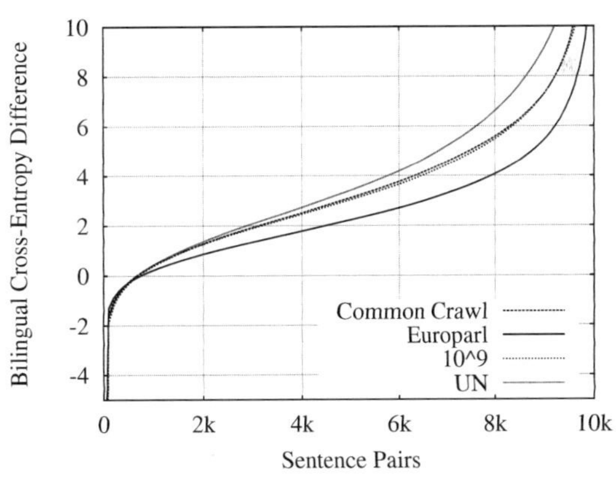

Figure 1: Sample of ranked sentence-pairs (10k) of each of the out-of-domain parallel corpora with bilingual cross-entropy difference

The results obtained using the *pseudo* in-domain data show BLEU (Papineni et al., 2002) scores superior or equal to the baseline score. Only the *Europarl* subset is slightly lower than the baseline, while the subset taken from the 10^9 corpus reaches the highest BLEU compared to the other systems (30.29). This is mainly due to the size of this subset which is ten times larger than the one taken from *Europarl*. The last row of Table 3 shows the BLEU score obtained after interpolating the four *pseudo* in-domain translation models. This system outperforms the best *pseudo* in-domain one by 0.5 absolute points.

Corpus	Sentences (k)	BLEU_{dev}
Baseline	181.3	27.76
Common Crawl	208.3	27.73
Europarl	142.0	27.63
10^9 Corpus	1,442.4	30.29
UN	642.4	28.91
Interpolation	-	30.78

Table 3: Number of sentence pairs and BLEU scores reported by MERT on English–French *newstest2013* for the *pseudo* in-domain corpora obtained by filtering the out-of-domain corpora with bilingual cross-entropy difference. The interpolation of *pseudo* in-domain models is evaluated in the last row.

After evaluating the *pseudo* in-domain parallel data, the remaining sentence pairs for each corpora are considered out-of-domain according to our filtering approach. However, they may still contain useful information, thus we make use of these corpora by building individual TMs for each corpus (in a similar way we built the *pseudo* in-domain models). The total amount of remaining data (more than 33 million sentence pairs) makes the training process costly in terms of time and computing power. In order to reduce these costs, sentence pairs with a bilingual cross-entropy difference higher than 10 were filtered out, as we noticed that most of the sentences above this threshold contain noise (non-alphanumeric characters, foreign languages, etc.).

We also limit the size of the remaining data by applying the vocabulary saturation method (Lewis and Eetemadi, 2013). For the out-of-domain subset of each corpus, we traverse the sentence pairs in the order they are ranked by perplexity difference and filter out those sentence pairs for which we have seen already each 1-gram at least 10 times. Each out-of-domain subset from each parallel corpus is then used to train a TM before interpolating them to create the *pseudo* out-of-domain TM. The results reported by MERT obtained on the *newstest2013* development set are detailed in Table 4.

Mainly due to the sizes of the *pseudo* out-of-domain subsets, the reported BLEU scores are higher than the baseline for the four individual SMT systems and the interpolated one. This latter system outperforms the baseline by 3.61 absolute points. Compared to the results obtained with the *pseudo* in-domain data, we observe a slight improvement of the BLEU scores using the *pseudo* out-of-domain data. However, despite the comparatively larger sizes of the latter datasets, the BLEU scores reached are not that higher. For instance with the 10^9 corpus, the *pseudo* in and out-of-domain subsets contain 1.4 and 5.1 million sentence pairs respectively, and the two systems reach 30.3 and 30.5 BLEU. These scores indicate that the *pseudo* in-domain SMT systems are more efficient on the English–French *newstest2013* development set.

Corpus	Sentences (k)	BLEU_{dev}
Baseline	181.3	27.76
Common Crawl	1,598.7	29.84
Europarl	461.9	28.87
10^9 Corpus	5,153.0	30.50
UN	1,707.3	29.03
Interpolation	-	31.37

Table 4: Number of sentence pairs and BLEU scores reported by MERT on English–French *newstest2013* for the *pseudo* out-of-domain corpora obtained by filtering the out-of-domain corpora with bilingual cross-entropy difference, keeping sentence pairs below an entropy score of 10 and applying vocabulary saturation. The interpolation of *pseudo* out-of-domain models is evaluated in the last row.

4.2 Extraction of Translation Rules

A synthetic phrase-table based on shallow-transfer MT rules and dictionaries is built as follows. First, a set of shallow-transfer rules is inferred from the concatenation of the *newstest2008-2012* development corpora exactly in the same way as in the UA-Prompsit submission to this translation shared task (Sánchez-Cartagena et al., 2014). In summary, rules are obtained from a set of bilingual phrases extracted from the parallel corpus after its morphological analysis and part-of-speech disambiguation with the tools in the Apertium rule-based MT platform (Forcada et al., 2011).

The extraction algorithm commonly used in phrase-based SMT is followed with some added heuristics which ensure that the bilingual phrases extracted are compatible with the bilingual dictionary. Then, many different rules are generated from each bilingual phrase; each of them encodes a different degree of generalisation over the particular example it has been extracted from. Finally, the minimum set of rules which correctly reproduces all the bilingual phrases is found based on integer linear programming search (Garfinkel and Nemhauser, 1972).

Once the rules have been inferred, the phrase table is built from them and the original rule-based MT dictionaries, following the method by Sánchez-Cartagena et al. (2011), which was one of winning systems[4] (together with two online SMT systems) in the pairwise manual evaluation of the WMT11 English–Spanish translation task (Callison-Burch et al., 2011). This phrase-table is then interpolated with the baseline TM and the results are presented in Table 5. A slight improvement over the baseline is observed, which motivates the use of synthetic rules in our final MT system. This small improvement may be related to the small coverage of the Apertium dictionaries: the English–French bilingual dictionary has a low number of entries compared to more mature language pairs in Apertium which have around 20 times more bilingual entries.

System	BLEU_{dev}
Baseline	27.76
Baseline+Rules	28.06

Table 5: BLEU scores reported by MERT on English–French *newstest2013* for the baseline SMT system standalone and with automatically extracted translation rules.

5 Tuning and Decoding

We present in this Section a short selection of our experiments, amongst 15+ different configurations, conducted on the interpolation of TMs, tuning and decoding parameters. We first interpolate the four TMs: the baseline, the *pseudo* in and out-of-domain, and the translation rules, minimising the perplexity obtained on the concatenated development sets from 2008 to 2012 (*newstest2008-2012*). We investigate the use of OSM trained on *pseudo* in-domain data only or using all the parallel data available. Finally, we make variations of the number of n-bests used by MERT.

Results obtained on the development set *newstest2013* are reported in Table 6. These scores show that adding OSM to the interpolated translation models slightly degrades BLEU. However, by increasing the number of n-bests considered by MERT to 200-bests, the SMT system with OSM outperforms the systems evaluated previously in our experiments. Adding the synthetic translation rules degrades BLEU (as indicated by the last row in the Table), thus we decide to submit two systems to the shared task: one without and one with synthetic rules. By submitting a system without synthetic rules, we also ensure that our SMT system is constrained according to the shared task guidelines.

System	BLEU_{dev}
Baseline	27.76
+ *pseudo* in + *pseudo* out	31.93
+ OSM	31.90
+ MERT 200-best	32.21
+ Rules	32.10

Table 6: BLEU scores reported by MERT on English–French *newstest2013* development set.

As MERT is not suitable when a large number of features are used (our system uses 19 fetures), we switch to the Margin Infused Relaxed Algorithm (MIRA) for our submitted systems (Watanabe et al., 2007). The development set used is *newstest2012*, as we aim to select the best decoding parameters according to the scores obtained when decoding the *newstest2013* corpus, after detruecasing and de-tokenising using the scripts distributed with MOSES. This setup allowed us to compare our results with the participants of the translation shared task last year. We pick the decoding parameters leading to the best results in terms of BLEU and decode the official test set of WMT14 *newstest2014*. The results are reported in Table 7. Results on *newstest2013* show that the decoding parameters investigation leads to an overall improvement of 0.1 BLEU absolute. The results on *newstest2014* show that adding synthetic rules did not help improving BLEU and degraded slightly TER (Snover et al., 2006) scores.

In addition to our English→French submission, we submitted a French→English translation. Our French→English MT system is built on the alignments obtained from the English→French direction. The training processes between the two sys-

[4]No other system was found statistically significantly better using the sign test at $p \leq 0.1$.

System	BLEU13A	TER
newstest2013		
Best tuning	31.02	60.77
cube-pruning (pop-limit 10000)	31.04	60.71
increased table-limit (100)	31.06	60.77
monotonic reordering	31.07	60.69
Best decoding	31.14	60.66
newstest2014		
Best decoding	34.90	54.70
Best decoding + Rules	34.90	54.80

Table 7: Case sensitive results obtained with our final English–French SMT system on *newstest2013* when experimenting with different decoding parameters. The best parameters are kept to translate the WMT14 test set (*newstest2014*) and official results are reported in the last two rows.

tems are identical, except for the synthetic rules which are not extracted for the French→English direction. Tuning and decoding parameters for this latter translation direction are the best ones obtained in our previous experiments on this shared task. The case-sensitive scores obtained for French→English on *newstest2014* are 35.0 BLEU13A and 53.1 TER, which ranks us at the fifth position for this translation direction.

6 Conclusion

We have presented the MT systems developed by the Abu-MaTran project for the WMT14 translation shared task. We focused on the French–English language pair and particularly on the English→French direction. We have used a two-step data selection process based on bilingual cross-entropy difference and vocabulary saturation, as well as a novel approach for the extraction of synthetic translation rules and their use to enrich the phrase table. For the LMs and the TMs, we rely on training individual models per corpus before interpolating them by minimising perplexity according to the development set. Finally, we made use of the findings of WMT13 by including an OSM model.

Our English→French translation system was ranked second amongst nine teams and a total of twenty submissions, while our French→English submission was ranked fifth. As future work, we plan to investigate the effect of adding to the phrase table synthetic translation rules based on larger dictionaries. We also would like to study the link between OSM and the different decoding parameters implemented in MOSES, as we observed inconsistent results in our experiments.

Acknowledgments

The research leading to these results has received funding from the European Union Seventh Framework Programme FP7/2007-2013 under grant agreement PIAP-GA-2012-324414 (Abu-MaTran).

References

Amittai Axelrod, Xiaodong He, and Jianfeng Gao. 2011. Domain Adaptation Via Pseudo In-domain Data Selection. In *Proceedings of EMNLP*, pages 355–362.

Chris Callison-Burch, Philipp Koehn, Christof Monz, and Omar Zaidan. 2011. Findings of the 2011 workshop on statistical machine translation. In *Proceedings of WMT*, pages 22–64.

Nadir Durrani, Helmut Schmid, and Alexander Fraser. 2011. A Joint Sequence Translation Model with Integrated Reordering. In *Proceedings of ACL/HLT*, pages 1045–1054.

Nadir Durrani, Barry Haddow, Kenneth Heafield, and Philipp Koehn. 2013. Edinburgh's Machine Translation Systems for European Language Pairs. In *Proceedings of WMT*, pages 112–119.

Mikel L Forcada, Mireia Ginestí-Rosell, Jacob Nordfalk, Jim O'Regan, Sergio Ortiz-Rojas, Juan Antonio Pérez-Ortiz, Felipe Sánchez-Martínez, Gema Ramírez-Sánchez, and Francis M Tyers. 2011. Apertium: A Free/Open-source Platform for Rule-based Machine Translation. *Machine Translation*, 25(2):127–144.

Qin Gao and Stephan Vogel. 2008. Parallel Implementations of Word Alignment Tool. In *Software Engineering, Testing, and Quality Assurance for Natural Language Processing*, pages 49–57.

Robert S Garfinkel and George L Nemhauser. 1972. *Integer Programming*, volume 4. Wiley New York.

Kenneth Heafield, Ivan Pouzyrevsky, Jonathan H. Clark, and Philipp Koehn. 2013. Scalable Modified Kneser-Ney Language Model Estimation. In *Proceedings of ACL*, pages 690–696.

Philipp Koehn, Hieu Hoang, Alexandra Birch, Chris Callison-Burch, Marcello Federico, Nicola Bertoldi, Brooke Cowan, Wade Shen, Christine Moran, Richard Zens, et al. 2007. Moses: Open Source Toolkit for Statistical Machine Translation. In *Proceedings of ACL, Interactive Poster and Demonstration Sessions*, pages 177–180.

William D. Lewis and Sauleh Eetemadi. 2013. Dramatically Reducing Training Data Size Through Vocabulary Saturation. In *Proceedings of WMT*, pages 281–291.

Robert C. Moore and William Lewis. 2010. Intelligent Selection of Language Model Training Data. In *Proceedings of ACL*, pages 220–224.

Franz Josef Och and Hermann Ney. 2003. A Systematic Comparison of Various Statistical Alignment Models. *Computational Linguistics*, 29:19–51.

Franz Josef Och. 2003. Minimum Error Rate Training in Statistical Machine Translation. In *Proceedings of ACL*, volume 1, pages 160–167.

Kishore Papineni, Salim Roukos, Todd Ward, and Wei-Jing Zhu. 2002. BLEU: A Method for Automatic Evaluation of Machine Translation. In *Proceedings of ACL*, pages 311–318.

Víctor M. Sánchez-Cartagena, Felipe Sánchez-Martínez, and Juan Antonio Pérez-Ortiz. 2011. Integrating Shallow-transfer Rules into Phrase-based Statistical Machine Translation. In *Proceedings of MT Summit XIII*, pages 562–569.

Víctor M. Sánchez-Cartagena, Juan Antonio Pérez-Ortiz, and Felipe Sánchez-Martínez. 2014. The UA-Prompsit Hybrid Machine Translation System for the 2014 Workshop on Statistical Machine Translation. In *Proceedings of WMT*.

Rico Sennrich. 2012. Perplexity Minimization for Translation Model Domain Adaptation in Statistical Machine Translation. In *Proceedings of EACL*, pages 539–549.

Matthew Snover, Bonnie Dorr, Richard Schwartz, Linnea Micciulla, and John Makhoul. 2006. A Study of Translation Edit Rate with Targeted Human Annotation. In *Proceedings of AMTA*, pages 223–231.

Andreas Stolcke, Jing Zheng, Wen Wang, and Victor Abrash. 2011. SRILM at Sixteen: Update and Outlook. In *Proceedings of ASRU*.

Taro Watanabe, Jun Suzuki, Hajime Tsukada, and Hideki Isozaki. 2007. Online Large-margin Training for Statistical Machine Translation. In *Proceedings of EMNLP*.

The UA-Prompsit hybrid machine translation system for the 2014 Workshop on Statistical Machine Translation

Víctor M. Sánchez-Cartagena,[*‡] **Juan Antonio Pérez-Ortiz,**[*] **Felipe Sánchez-Martínez**[*]

[*]Dep. de Llenguatges i Sistemes Informàtics,
Universitat d'Alacant, E-03071, Alacant, Spain

[‡]Prompsit Language Engineering,
Av. Universitat, s/n. Edifici Quorum III, E-03202, Elx, Spain

{vmsanchez,japerez,fsanchez}@dlsi.ua.es

Abstract

This paper describes the system jointly developed by members of the Departament de Llenguatges i Sistemes Informàtics at Universitat d'Alacant and the Prompsit Language Engineering company for the shared translation task of the 2014 Workshop on Statistical Machine Translation. We present a phrase-based statistical machine translation system whose phrase table is enriched with information obtained from dictionaries and shallow-transfer rules like those used in rule-based machine translation. The novelty of our approach lies in the fact that the transfer rules used were not written by humans, but automatically inferred from a parallel corpus.

1 Introduction

This paper describes the system jointly submitted by the Departament de Llenguatges i Sistemes Informàtics at Universitat d'Alacant and the Prompsit Language Engineering company to the shared translation task of the ACL 2014 Ninth Workshop on Statistical Machine Translation (WMT 2014). We participated in the English–French translation task with a hybrid system that combines, in a phrase-based statistical machine translation (PBSMT) system, bilingual phrases obtained from parallel corpora in the usual way (Koehn, 2010, ch. 5), and also bilingual phrases obtained from the existing dictionaries in the Apertium rule-based machine translation (RBMT) platform (Forcada et al., 2011) and a number of shallow-transfer machine translation rules automatically inferred from a small subset of the training corpus.

Among the different approaches for adding linguistic information to SMT systems (Costa-Jussà and Farrús, 2014), we followed the path we started with our submission to the Spanish–English WMT 2011 shared translation task (Sánchez-Cartagena et al., 2011b) which consisted of enriching the phrase table of a PBSMT system with phrase pairs generated using the dictionaries and rules in the Apertium (Forcada et al., 2011) Spanish–English RBMT system; our approach was one of the winners[1] (together with two online SMT systems that were not submitted for the task but were included in the evaluation by the organisers and a system by Systran) in the pairwise manual evaluation of the English–Spanish translation task (Callison-Burch et al., 2011). In this submission, however, we only borrow the dictionaries from the Apertium English–French RBMT system and use them to automatically infer the rules from a parallel corpus. We therefore avoid the need for human-written rules, which are usually written by trained experts, and explore a novel way to add morphological information to PBSMT. The rules inferred from corpora and used to enlarge the phrase table are shallow-transfer rules that build their output with the help of the bilingual dictionary and work on flat intermediate representations (see section 3.1); no syntactic parsing is consequently required.

The rest of the paper is organised as follows. The following section outlines related hybrid approaches. Section 3 formally defines the RBMT paradigm and summarises the method followed to automatically infer the shallow-transfer rules, whereas the enrichment of the phrase table is described in section 4. Sections 5 and 6 describe, respectively, the resources we used to build our submission and the results achieved for the English–French language pair. The paper ends with some concluding remarks.

2 Related work

Linguistic data from RBMT systems have already been used to enrich SMT systems (Tyers, 2009; Schwenk et al., 2009; Eisele et al., 2008; Sánchez-Cartagena et al., 2011a). We have already proved

[1]No other system was found statistically significantly better using the sign test at $p \leq 0.10$.

Proceedings of the Ninth Workshop on Statistical Machine Translation, pages 178–185,
Baltimore, Maryland USA, June 26–27, 2014.

that using hand-written rules and dictionaries from RBMT yields better results than using only dictionaries (Sánchez-Cartagena et al., 2011a).

However, in the approach we present in this paper, rules are automatically inferred from a parallel corpus after converting it into the intermediate representation used by the Apertium RBMT platform (see section 3.3). It can be therefore seen as a novel method to add morphological information to SMT, as factored translation models do (Koehn and Hoang, 2007; Graham and van Genabith, 2010). Unlike factored models, we do not estimate independent statistical models for the translation of the different factors (lemmas, lexical categories, morphological inflection attributes, etc.) and for the generation of the final surface forms. Instead, we first infer a set of rules that deal with the grammatical divergences between the languages involved by performing operations such as reorderings, gender and number agreements, etc. Afterwards, we add synthetic phrase pairs generated from these rules and the Apertium dictionaries to the data from which the well-known, classical PBSMT models (Koehn, 2010) are estimated. The rules in our approach operate on the source-language (SL) morphological attributes of the input words and on the target-language (TL) morphological attributes of their translation according to a bilingual dictionary. In addition, they do no contain probabilities or scores, thus they increase the predictability of the output and can be easily corrected by humans. This fact also represents a significant difference with the probabilistic rules used by certain approaches that aim at improving the grammaticality of the SMT output (Riezler and Maxwell III, 2006; Bojar and Hajič, 2008).

With respect to the rule inference approach, other approaches such as those by Sánchez-Martínez and Forcada (2009) and Caseli et al. (2006) can be found in literature; however, our approach is the first strategy for shallow-transfer rule inference which generalises to unseen combinations of morphological inflection attributes in the training corpus (Sánchez-Cartagena et al., 2014).

3 Inferring shallow-transfer rules from parallel corpora

3.1 Shallow-transfer rule-based machine translation

The RBMT process can be split into three different steps (Hutchins and Somers, 1992): (i) analysis of the SL text to build an SL intermediate representation; (ii) transfer from that SL intermediate representation into a TL intermediate representation; and (iii) generation of the final translation from the TL intermediate representation.

Shallow-transfer RBMT systems use relatively simple intermediate representations, which are based on lexical forms consisting of lemma, part of speech and morphological inflection information of the words, and apply simple shallow-transfer rules that operate on sequences of lexical forms: this kind of systems do not perform full parsing. For instance, for translating the English sentence *I like Pierre's house* into French with the Apertium shallow-transfer RBMT platform we have used to build our submission, the following steps are carried out. First, the sentence is analysed as the following sequence of lexical forms:

I `PRN-p:1.num:sg`
like `VB-t:pres.p:`ϵ`:num:`ϵ
Pierre `PN`
's `POS`
house `N-gen:`ϵ`.num:sg`

This sequence is made up of a personal pronoun (`PRN`) in first person (`p:1`) singular (`num:sg`) with lemma *I*, the verb (`VB`) *like* in present tense (`t:pres`), a proper noun (`PN`) with lemma *Pierre*, the possessive ending (`POS`), and a noun (`N`) in singular with lemma *house*. Some morphological inflection attributes have an empty value ϵ because they do not apply to the corresponding language.

Then, structural transfer rules are applied to obtain the TL intermediate representation with the help of the bilingual dictionary, which provides the individual translation of each SL lexical form (including its morphological information). In this case, two rules are applied: the first one makes the verb to agree with the personal pronoun, while the second one translates the English possessive construction into French. The resulting sequence of TL lexical forms is:

Je `PRN-p:1.num:sg`
aime `VB-t:pres.p:1:num:sg`
le `DT-gen:f.num:sg`
maison `N-gen:f.num:sg`
de `PR`
Pierre `PN`

Note that a preposition (`PR`) with lemma *de* and a determiner (`DT`) with lemma *le* and the same gender and number as the common noun have been added by the rule. Finally, the translation into TL is generated from the TL lexical forms: *J'aime la maison de Pierre*.

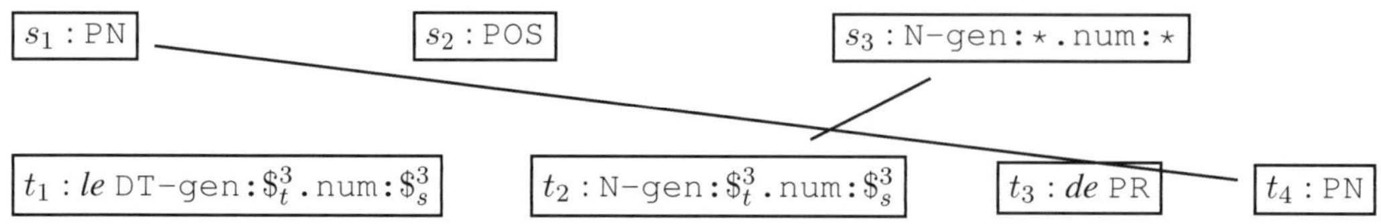

Figure 1: Shallow-transfer rule for the translation of the English Saxon genitive construction into French.

3.2 A rule formalism suitable for rule inference

Figure 1 shows the second rule applied in the example from the previous section encoded with the formalism we have defined for rule inference (Sánchez-Cartagena et al., 2014). Each rule contains a sequence of SL word classes (depicted as the sequence of boxes at the top of the figure) and TL word classes (the sequence of boxes below them). The sequence of SL word classes defines the set of sequences of lexical forms which will match the rule. Each SL word class s_i defines the conditions that must be met by the i-th lexical form matching the rule and contains an optional lemma (no lemma means that any SL lemma is allowed), a lexical category and a set of morphological inflection attributes and their expected values. A wildcard (asterisk) as the value of a morphological inflection attribute means that it matches any possible value. Thus, the rule from the example matches any proper noun followed by a possessive ending and a noun, regardless of its gender and number.

As regards the TL word classes, they contain the same elements as the SL word classes and define the output of the rule. An empty lemma in a TL word class means that it is obtained by looking up in the bilingual dictionary the SL lexical form matching the aligned SL word class (alignments are represented as lines connecting SL and TL word classes). The reference value $\$_s^i$ means that the value of a morphological inflection attribute is copied from the SL lexical form matching the i-th SL word class, while the reference value $\$_t^i$ means that the value is taken from the TL lexical form obtained after looking up in the bilingual dictionary the aforementioned SL lexical form. The rule depicted in Figure 1 generates a sequence of four TL lexical forms. The first one is a determiner whose lemma is *le*, its gender is obtained from the gender of the TL lexical form resulting after looking up in the bilingual dictionary the third matching SL lexical form ($\$_t^3$), that is, the common noun, while its number is directly obtained from the same SL lexical form before dictionary look-up ($\$_s^3$). Although they have not been used in this example, explicit values can be used in the morphological inflection attributes of the SL and TL word classes, thus restricting the SL lexical forms to which the rule can be applied to those having the values in the corresponding SL word classes,[2] and explicitly stating the value that the TL lexical forms produced by the rule will have, respectively.

3.3 Rule inference algorithm

The set of rules that will be used to generate the phrase pairs that will be integrated into the PB-SMT system's phrase table, encoded with the formalism presented in the previous section, are obtained from the parallel corpus by applying the steps described in this section. They are a subset of the steps followed by Sánchez-Cartagena et al. (2014) to infer shallow-transfer rules to be used in Apertium from small parallel corpora.

First, both sides of the parallel corpus are morphologically analysed and converted into the intermediate representations used by Apertium. Word alignments are then obtained by symmetrising (using the refined intersection method proposed by Och and Ney (2003)) the set of alignments provided by GIZA++ (Och and Ney, 2003) when it is run on both translations directions. Afterwards, the bilingual phrase pairs compatible with the alignments are extracted as it is usually done in SMT (Koehn, 2010, Sec. 5.2.3), and those that are not compatible with the bilingual dictionary of the Apertium English–French RBMT system[3] or

[2] In addition to that criterion, our formalism also permits restricting the application of a rule to the SL lexical forms that, after being looked up in the bilingual dictionary, the TL lexical forms obtained from them have specific morphological inflection attribute values (Sánchez-Cartagena et al., 2014) although no restrictions of this type are imposed in the rule depicted in Figure 1.

[3] If the words that belong to open lexical categories (those that carry the meaning of the sentence: nouns, verbs, adjectives, etc.) are aligned with other words that do not match the translation present in the bilingual dictionary, the rule in-

contain punctuation marks or unknown words are discarded. Finally, from each bilingual phrase pair, all the possible rules which correctly reproduce it —when the rule is applied to the SL side of the phrase pair, its TL side is obtained— are generated as follows. First, a very specific rule, which matches only the SL phrase in the bilingual phrase pair is generated; more general rules are then created by modifying this initial rule. The modifications to the initial rule consist of removing lemmas from the SL and TL word classes, introducing wildcard values in the morphological inflection attributes of the SL word classes and adding reference values in the morphological inflection attributes of the TL word classes. The result of this process is a huge set of rules with different levels of generalisation. Obviously, not all the rules in this set will be used: the best ones are automatically selected by considering all the rules obtained from the different bilingual phrase pairs extracted from the corpus and finding the minimum set of rules that meets the following two conditions:

1. Each bilingual phrase pair is correctly reproduced by at least one rule.

2. If a rule matches the SL side of bilingual phrase pair but does not correctly reproduce its TL side, there is another rule that is more specific (i.e. less general) than it, and correctly reproduces its TL side.

This minimisation problem is formulated as an integer linear programming[4] problem (Garfinkel and Nemhauser, 1972) and solved using the *branch and cut* algorithm (Xu et al., 2009).

From the small subset of the huge initial rules obtained by solving the minimisation problem, the rules whose effect can be achieved by combining shorter rules or by translating all or some of the words in isolation (i.e. word for word) are removed. In this way, the number of rules is further reduced and long rules, which are more prone to overgeneralisation because they are inferred from fewer bilingual phrase pairs, are discarded.[5]

ference algorithm is likely to infer many very specific rules that try to correct that lexical mismatch. Since the aim of our approach is learning general rules that deal with the grammatical divergences between languages, the bilingual phrases that contain the aforementioned alignments are discarded. Words from closed lexical categories, that usually suffer deeper changes when the sentence is translated to a different language, are not subject to this restriction.

[4] An integer linear programming problem involves the optimisation (maximisation or minimisation) of a linear objective function subject to linear inequality constraints.

[5] Although longer rules contain more context information, for our rule inferring algorithm there are fewer bilingual phrases from which to infer them, and consequently fewer evidence from which to extract the right reference attributes.

4 Enhancing phrase-based SMT with shallow-transfer linguistic resources

The set of shallow-transfer rules inferred from the parallel corpus are integrated in the PBSMT system, together with the RBMT dictionaries, using the same method we used for our WMT 2011 shared translation task subsmission (Sánchez-Cartagena et al., 2011b). However, it is important to stress that, until now, this strategy had only been tested when the rules to be integrated were hand-written and not automatically obtained from corpora.

Our strategy involves adding to the phrase table of the PBSMT system all the bilingual phrase pairs which either match a shallow-transfer rule or an entry in the bilingual dictionary. Generating the set of bilingual phrase pairs which match bilingual dictionary entries is straightforward. First, all the SL surface forms that are recognised by Apertium and their corresponding lexical forms are generated. Then, these SL lexical forms are translated using the bilingual dictionary, and finally their TL surface forms are generated.

Bilingual phrase pairs which match structural transfer rules are generated in a similar way. First, the SL sentences to be translated are analysed with Apertium to get their SL lexical forms, and then the sequences of lexical forms that match a structural transfer rule are translated with that rule and passed through the rest of the Apertium pipeline in order to get their translations. If a sequence of SL lexical forms is matched by more than one structural transfer rule, it will be used to generate as many bilingual phrase pairs as different rules it matches. This differs from the way in which Apertium translates, as it only applies the longest rule. Note also that the test set is used to guide the phrase extraction in order to avoid the generation of an unmanageable set of phrase pairs.

We add these bilingual phrase pairs directly to the phrase table, rather than adding them to the training corpus and relying on the phrase extraction algorithm (Koehn, 2010, sec. 5.2.3), in order to avoid splitting the multi-word expressions provided by Apertium into smaller phrases (Schwenk et al., 2009, sec. 2). The bilingual phrase pairs are added only once to the list of corpus-extracted phrase pairs, and then the phrase translation probabilities are computed by relative frequency as usual (Koehn, 2010, sec. 5.2.5). A boolean feature function to flag bilingual phrase pairs obtained from the RBMT resources is added to the phrase table in order to conveniently weight the synthetic RBMT phrase pairs.

5 System training

We built a baseline PBSMT Moses (Koehn et al., 2007) system[6] from a subset of the parallel corpora distributed as part of the WMT 2014 shared translation task, namely Europarl (Koehn, 2005), News Commentary and Common Crawl, and a subset of the French monolingual corpora, namely Common Crawl, Europarl, News Commentary and News Crawl. The language model was built with the KenLM language modelling toolkit (Heafield et al., 2013), which was used to train a 5-gram language model using interpolated Kneser-Ney discounting (Goodman and Chen, 1998). Word alignments were computed by means of GIZA++ (Och and Ney, 2003). The weights of the different feature functions were optimised by means of minimum error rate training (Och, 2003) on the 2013 WMT test set.[7]

The phrase table of this baseline system was then enriched with phrase pairs generated from rules automatically inferred from the concatenation of the test corpora distributed for the WMT 2008–2012 shared translation tasks, and from the English–French bilingual dictionary in the Apertium platform.[8] Since the minimisation problem which needs to be solved in order to obtain the rules is very time-consuming, we chose a small rule inference corpus similar to this year's test set. The bilingual dictionary, which contains mappings between SL and TL lemmas, consists of 13 088 entries and is quite small compared to the Spanish–English bilingual dictionary we used in our submission to WMT 2011 (Sánchez-Cartagena et al., 2011b), which consisted of 326 228 bilingual entries. This is because the English–French Apertium linguistic resources were automatically built by crossing data from other existing language pairs.

Table 1 summarises the data about the corpora used to build our submission, both for the PBSMT baseline system and for the rules used to enrich its phrase table.

The corpus used to automatically infer the rules was split into two parts: the larger one (4/5 of the corpus) was used for actual rule inference as described in section 3.3; the remaining corpus was used as a development corpus as explained next. For each rule z, first the proportion $r(z)$ of bilingual phrase pairs correctly reproduced by the rule divided by the number of bilingual phrases it matches is computed. Rules whose proportion $r(z)$ is lower than a threshold value δ are then discarded before solving the minimisation problem. The value of δ is chosen so that it maximises, on the development corpus, the BLEU score (Papineni et al., 2002) obtained by an Apertium-based system which uses the inferred rules; in our submission $\delta = 0.15$. In addition, rules that do not correctly reproduce at least 100 bilingual phrase pairs were also discarded in order to make the minimisation problem computationally feasible.

Task	Corpus	Sentences
Translation model	Europarl	2 007 723
	News Commentary	183 251
	Common Crawl	3 244 152
	Total	5 435 126
	Total clean	4 196 987
Language model	Common Crawl	3 244 152
	Europarl	2 190 579
	News Commentary	227 013
	News Crawl	30 451 749
	Total	36 113 493
Rule inference	newstest 2008–2012	13 071
Tuning	newstest2013	3 000
Test	newstest2014	3 003

Table 1: Size of the corpora used in the experiments. The bilingual training corpora was cleaned up to remove empty parallel sentences and those containing more than 40 tokens.

6 Results and discussion

Table 2 reports the translation performance as measured by BLEU (Papineni et al., 2002), TER (Snover et al., 2006) and METEOR (Banerjee and Lavie, 2005) achieved by the baseline PBSMT, our submission (*UA-Prompsit*), Apertium when it uses the set of inferred rules, and Apertium when it uses no rules at all (word-for-word translation). The size of the phrase table and the amount of unknown words in the test set are also reported when applicable.

According to the three evaluation metrics, the translation performance of our submission is very close to that of the PBSMT baseline (slightly better according to BLEU and TER, and slightly worse according to METEOR). The difference between both systems computed by paired bootstrap

[6]No factored models were used.

[7]The corpora can be downloaded from http://www.statmt.org/wmt14/translation-task.html.

[8]https://svn.code.sf.net/p/apertium/svn/incubator/apertium-en-fr

system	BLEU	TER	METEOR	# of unknown words	phrase table size
baseline	0.3232	0.5807	0.5441	870	100 530 734
UA-Prompsit	0.3258	0.5781	0.5432	861	100 585 182
Apertium-rules	0.0995	0.7767	0.3168	4 743	-
Apertium-word-for-word	0.0631	0.8368	0.2617	4 743	-

Table 2: Case-insensitive BLEU, TER, and METEOR scores obtained, on the *newstest2014* test set, by the baseline PBSMT system (*baseline*), the hybrid system submitted to the WMT 2014 shared translation task (*UA-Prompsit*), Apertium when it uses the set of inferred rules (*Apertium-rules*), and Apertium when it uses no rules at all (*Apertium-word-for-word*). The number of unknown words and the size of the phrase table are also reported when applicable.

resampling (Koehn, 2004) is not statistically significant for any of the three evaluation metrics (1 000 iterations, $p = 0.05$).

An inspection of the 86 rules inferred shows that they encode some of the transformations that one would expect from a set of English–French rules, such as gender and number agreements between nouns, determiners and adjectives, preposition changes, and the introduction of the auxiliary verb *avoir* for the past tense. In addition, the improvement over word-for-word translation achieved when they are used by Apertium is statistically significant for the three evaluation metrics.

One of the reasons for not improving the baseline PBMT system might be the small coverage of the Apertium dictionaries. As already mentioned in the previous section, the English–French bilingual dictionary has a low number of entries compared to more mature language pairs in Apertium which have around 20 times more bilingual entries. Table 1 shows some effects of such a small dictionary: the number of unknown words for the Apertium-based system is really high, and with regards to *UA-Prompsit*, its coverage barely increases when compared to the PBSMT baseline. We plan to test the approach presented in this paper with language pairs for which more mature dictionaries are available in the Apertium project.

In addition to this, due to the tight schedule, we had to remove the rules not reproducing at least 100 bilingual phrase pairs in order to solve the minimisation problem in a short amount of time. This has clearly reduced the amount of rules inferred and prevented some useful information present in the parallel corpus from being incorporated in the form of rules. For instance, no rule matching a sequence longer than 3 lexical forms has been extracted (long bilingual phrases are less frequent than short ones). Future research directions for alleviating this problem include setting the minimum number of reproduced bilingual phrases independently for each sequence of SL lexical categories (Sánchez-Cartagena et al., 2014).

7 Concluding remarks

We have presented the MT system submitted jointly by the Departament de Llenguatges i Sistemes Informàtics at Universitat d'Alacant and Prompsit Language Engineering to the WMT 2014 shared translation task. We developed a hybrid system for the English–French language pair which enriches the phrase table of a standard PBSMT system with phrase pairs generated from the Apertium RBMT dictionaries and a set of shallow-transfer rules automatically inferred from a parallel corpus, also with the help of the dictionaries. This submission aims at solving one strong limitation of a previous submission of our team (Sánchez-Cartagena et al., 2011b): the need for a hand-crafted set of shallow-transfer rules, which can only be written by people with a deep knowledge of the languages involved. Our approach outperforms a standard PBSMT system built from the same data by a small, non statistically significant margin, according to two of the three evaluation metrics used. The low coverage of the dictionaries used and the aggressive pruning carried out when solving the minimisation problem needed to infer the rules are probably the reasons behind such a small improvement over the baseline.

Acknowledgements

Work funded by Universitat d'Alacant through project GRE11-20, by the Spanish Ministry of Economy and Competitiveness through projects TIN2009-14009-C02-01 and TIN2012-32615, by Generalitat Valenciana through grant ACIF/2010/174 (VALi+d programme), and by the European Union Seventh Framework Programme FP7/2007-2013 under grant agreement PIAP-GA-2012-324414 (Abu-MaTran).

References

S. Banerjee and A. Lavie. 2005. Meteor: An automatic metric for mt evaluation with improved correlation with human judgments. In *Proceedings of the ACL Workshop on Intrinsic and Extrinsic Evaluation Measures for Machine Translation and/or Summarization*, pages 65–72.

O. Bojar and J. Hajič. 2008. Phrase-based and deep syntactic English-to-Czech statistical machine translation. In *Proceedings of the third Workshop on Statistical Machine translation*, pages 143–146. Association for Computational Linguistics.

C. Callison-Burch, P. Koehn, C. Monz, and O. Zaidan. 2011. Findings of the 2011 workshop on statistical machine translation. In *Proceedings of the Sixth Workshop on Statistical Machine Translation*, pages 22–64, Edinburgh, Scotland, July. Association for Computational Linguistics.

H. M. Caseli, M. G. V. Nunes, and M. L. Forcada. 2006. Automatic induction of bilingual resources from aligned parallel corpora: application to shallow-transfer machine translation. *Machine Translation*, 20(4):227–245. Published in 2008.

M. R. Costa-Jussà and M. Farrús. 2014. Statistical machine translation enhancements through linguistic levels: A survey. *ACM Comput. Surv.*, 46(3).

A. Eisele, C. Federmann, H. Saint-Amand, M. Jellinghaus, T. Herrmann, and Y. Chen. 2008. Using Moses to integrate multiple rule-based machine translation engines into a hybrid system. In *Proceedings of the Third Workshop on Statistical Machine Translation*, pages 179–182, Columbus, Ohio.

M. L. Forcada, M. Ginestí-Rosell, J. Nordfalk, J. O'Regan, S. Ortiz-Rojas, J. A. Pérez-Ortiz, G. Ramírez-Sánchez F. Sánchez-Martínez, and F. M. Tyers. 2011. Apertium: a free/open-source platform for rule-based machine translation. *Machine Translation*, 25(2):127–144. Special Issue: Free/Open-Source Machine Translation.

R. S. Garfinkel and G. L. Nemhauser. 1972. *Integer programming*, volume 4. Wiley New York.

J. Goodman and S. F. Chen. 1998. An empirical study of smoothing techniques for language modeling. Technical Report TR-10-98, Harvard University, August.

Y. Graham and J. van Genabith. 2010. Factor templates for factored machine translation models. In *IWSLT 2010 : 7th International Workshop on Spoken Language Translation*, pages 275–283.

K. Heafield, I. Pouzyrevsky, J. H. Clark, and P. Koehn. 2013. Scalable modified Kneser-Ney language model estimation. In *Proceedings of the 51st Annual Meeting of the Association for Computational Linguistics*, pages 690–696, Sofia, Bulgaria, August.

W. J. Hutchins and H. L. Somers. 1992. *An introduction to machine translation*, volume 362. Academic Press New York.

P. Koehn and Hieu Hoang. 2007. Factored translation models. In *Proceedings of the 2007 Joint Conference on Empirical Methods in Natural Language Processing and Computational Natural Language Learning (EMNLP-CoNLL)*, pages 868–876, Prague.

P. Koehn, H. Hoang, A. Birch, C. Callison-Burch, M. Federico, N. Bertoldi, B. Cowan, W. Shen, C. Moran, R. Zens, et al. 2007. Moses: Open Source Toolkit for Statistical Machine Translation. In *Annual Meeting of the Association for Computational Linguistics (ACL), demonstration session.*

P. Koehn. 2004. Statistical significance tests for machine translation evaluation. In *Proceedings of the Conference on Empirical Methods in Natural Language Processing*, volume 4, pages 388–395.

P. Koehn. 2005. Europarl: A parallel corpus for statistical machine translation. In *Proceedings of the Tenth Machine Translation Summit*, pages 12–16, Phuket, Thailand, September.

P. Koehn. 2010. *Statistical Machine Translation*. Cambridge University Press.

F. J. Och and H. Ney. 2003. A systematic comparison of various statistical alignment models. *Computational Linguistics*, 29:19–51, March.

F. J. Och. 2003. Minimum error rate training in statistical machine translation. In *Proceedings of the 41st Annual Meeting on Association for Computational Linguistics*, pages 160–167, Sapporo, Japan.

K. Papineni, S. Roukos, T. Ward, and W. Zhu. 2002. Bleu: a method for automatic evaluation of machine translation. In *Proceedings of the 40th Annual Meeting of the ACL*, pages 311–318.

S. Riezler and J. T. Maxwell III. 2006. Grammatical machine translation. In *Proceedings of the main conference on Human Language Technology Conference of the North American Chapter of the Association of Computational Linguistics*, pages 248–255. Association for Computational Linguistics.

V. M. Sánchez-Cartagena, F. Sánchez-Martínez, and J. A. Pérez-Ortiz. 2011a. Integrating shallow-transfer rules into phrase-based statistical machine translation. In *Proceedings of the XIII Machine Translation Summit*, pages 562–569, Xiamen, China, September.

V. M. Sánchez-Cartagena, F. Sánchez-Martínez, and J. A. Pérez-Ortiz. 2011b. The Universitat d'Alacant hybrid machine translation system for wmt 2011. In *Proceedings of the Sixth Workshop on Statistical Machine Translation*, pages 457–463, Edinburgh, Scotland, July. Association for Computational Linguistics.

V. M. Sánchez-Cartagena, J. A. Pérez-Ortiz, and F. Sánchez-Martínez. 2014. A generalised alignment template formalism and its application to the inference of shallow-transfer machine translation rules from scarce bilingual corpora. *Computer Speech and Language*. Submitted to the Special Issue on Hybrid Machine Translation.

F. Sánchez-Martínez and M. L. Forcada. 2009. Inferring shallow-transfer machine translation rules from small parallel corpora. *Journal of Artificial Intelligence Research*, 34(1):605–635.

H. Schwenk, S. Abdul-Rauf, L. Barrault, and J. Senellart. 2009. SMT and SPE Machine Translation Systems for WMT'09. In *Proceedings of the Fourth Workshop on Statistical Machine Translation*, StatMT '09, pages 130–134, Stroudsburg, PA, USA. Association for Computational Linguistics.

M. Snover, B. Dorr, R. Schwartz, L. Micciulla, and J. Makhoul. 2006. A study of translation edit rate with targeted human annotation. In *In Proceedings of Association for Machine Translation in the Americas*, pages 223–231.

F. M. Tyers. 2009. Rule-based augmentation of training data in Breton–French statistical machine translation. In *Proceedings of the 13th Annual Conference of the European Association of Machine Translation*, pages 213–217.

Y. Xu, T. K. Ralphs, L. Ladányi, and M. J. Saltzman. 2009. Computational experience with a software framework for parallel integer programming. *INFORMS Journal on Computing*, 21(3):383–397.

Machine Translation and Monolingual Postediting: The AFRL WMT-14 System

Lane O.B. Schwartz
Air Force Research Laboratory
lane.schwartz@us.af.mil

Timothy Anderson
Air Force Research Laboratory
timothy.anderson.20@us.af.mil

Jeremy Gwinnup
SRA International†
jeremy.gwinnup.ctr@us.af.mil

Katherine M. Young
N-Space Analysis LLC†
katherine.young.1.ctr@us.af.mil

Abstract

This paper describes the AFRL statistical MT system and the improvements that were developed during the WMT14 evaluation campaign. As part of these efforts we experimented with a number of extensions to the standard phrase-based model that improve performance on Russian to English and Hindi to English translation tasks. In addition, we describe our efforts to make use of monolingual English speakers to correct the output of machine translation, and present the results of monolingual postediting of the entire 3003 sentences of the WMT14 Russian-English test set.

1 Introduction

As part of the 2014 Workshop on Machine Translation (WMT14) shared translation task, the human language technology team at the Air Force Research Laboratory participated in two language pairs: Russian-English and Hindi-English. Our machine translation system represents enhancements to our system from IWSLT 2013 (Kazi et al., 2013). In this paper, we focus on enhancements to our procedures with regard to data processing and the handling of unknown words.

In addition, we describe our efforts to make use of monolingual English speakers to correct the output of machine translation, and present the results of monolingual postediting of the entire 3003 sentences of the WMT14 Russian-English test set. Using a binary adequacy classification, we evaluate the entire postedited test set for correctness against the reference translations. Using bilingual judges, we further evaluate a substantial subset of the postedited test set using a more fine-grained adequacy metric; using this metric, we show that monolingual posteditors can successfully produce postedited translations that convey all or most of the meaning of the original source sentence in up to 87.8% of sentences.

2 System Description

We submitted systems for the Russian-to-English and Hindi-to-English MT shared tasks. In all submitted systems, we use the phrase-based `moses` decoder (Koehn et al., 2007). We used only the constrained data supplied by the evaluation for each language pair for training our systems.

2.1 Data Preparation

Before training our systems, a cleaning pass was performed on all data. Unicode characters in the unallocated and private use ranges were all removed, along with C0 and C1 control characters, zero-width and non-breaking spaces and joiners, directionality and paragraph markers.

2.1.1 Hindi Processing

The HindEnCorp corpus (Bojar et al., 2014) is distributed in tokenized form; in order to ensure a uniform tokenization standard across all of our data, we began by detokenized this data using the Moses detokenization scripts. In addition to normalizing various extended Latin punctuation marks to their Basic Latin equivalents, following Bojar et al. (2010) we normalized Devanagari Danda (U+0964), Double Danda (U+0965), and Abbreviation Sign (U+0970) punctuation marks to Latin Full Stop (U+002E), any Devana-

†This work is sponsored by the Air Force Research Laboratory under Air Force contract FA-8650-09-D-6939-029.

Proceedings of the Ninth Workshop on Statistical Machine Translation, pages 186–194,
Baltimore, Maryland USA, June 26–27, 2014. ©2014 Association for Computational Linguistics

GARI DIGIT to the equivalent ASCII DIGIT, and decomposed all Hindi data into Unicode Normalization Form D (Davis and Whistler, 2013) using `charlint`.[1] In addition, we performed Hindi diacritic and vowel normalization, following Larkey et al. (2003).

Since no Hindi-English development test set was provided in WMT14, we randomly sampled 1500 sentence pairs from the Hindi-English parallel training data to serve this purpose. Upon discovering duplicate sentences in the corpus, 552 sentences that overlapped with the training portion were removed from the sample, leaving a development test set of 948 sentences.

2.1.2 Russian Processing

The Russian sentences contained many examples of mixed-character spelling, in which both Latin and Cyrillic characters are used in a single word, relying on the visual similarity of the characters. For example, although the first letter and last letter in the word сейчас appear visually indistinguishable, we find that the former is U+0063 LATIN SMALL LETTER C and the latter is U+0441 CYRILLIC SMALL LETTER ES. We created a spelling normalization program to convert these words to all Cyrillic or all Latin characters, with a preference for all-Cyrillic conversion if possible. Normalization also removes U+0301 COMBINING ACUTE ACCENT (◌́) and converts U+00F2 LATIN SMALL LETTER O WITH GRAVE (ò) and U+00F3 LATIN SMALL LETTER O WITH ACUTE (ó) to the unaccented U+043E CYRILLIC SMALL LETTER O (о).

The Russian-English Common Crawl parallel corpus (Smith et al., 2013) is relatively noisy. A number of Russian source sentences are incorrectly encoded using characters in the Latin-1 supplement block; we correct these sentences by shifting these characters ahead by 350_{hex} code points into the correct Cyrillic character range.[2]

We examine the Common Crawl parallel sentences and mark for removal any non-Russian source sentences and non-English target sentences. Target sentences were marked as non-English if more than half of the characters in the sentence were non-Latin, or if more than half of the words were unknown to the `aspell` English spelling correction program, not counting short words, which frequently occur as (possibly false) cognates across languages (English *die* vs. German *die*, English *on* vs. French *on*, for example). Because `aspell` does not recognize some proper names, brand names, and borrowed words as known English words, this method incorrectly flags for removal some English sentences which have a high proportion of these types of words.

Source sentences were marked as non-Russian if less than one-third of the characters were within the Russian Cyrillic range, or if non-Russian characters equal or outnumber Russian characters and the sentence contains no contiguous sequence of at least three Russian characters. Some portions of the Cyrillic character set are not used in typical Russian text; source sentences were therefore marked for removal if they contained Cyrillic extension characters UKRAINIAN I (і І), YI(ї Ї), GHE WITH UPTURN (ґ Ґ) or IE (є Є) in either upper- or lowercase, with exceptions for U+0406 UKRAINIAN I (І) in Roman numerals and for U+0491 GHE WITH UPTURN (ґ) when it occurred as an encoding error artifact.[3]

Sentence pairs where the source was identified as non-Russian or the target was identified as non-English were removed from the parallel corpus. Overall, 12% of the parallel sentences were excluded based on a non-Russian source sentence (94k instances) or a non-English target sentence (11.8k instances).

Our Russian-English parallel training data includes a parallel corpus extracted from Wikipedia headlines (Ammar et al., 2013), provided as part of the WMT14 shared translation task. Two files in this parallel corpus (`wiki.ru-en` and `guessed-names.ru-en`) contained some overlapping data. We removed 6415 duplicate lines within `wiki.ru-en` (about 1.4%), and removed 94 lines of `guessed-names.ru-en` that were already present in wiki.ru-en (about 0.17%).

[1] `http://www.w3.org/International/charlint`

[2] For example: "Ñïðàâêà ïî ãîðîäàì Ðîññèè è ìèðà." becomes "Справка по городам России и мира."

[3] Specifically, we allowed lines containing ґ where it appears as an encoding error in place of an apostrophe within English words. For example: "Песня The Kelly Family Iґm So Happy представлена вам LyricsKeeper."

2.2 Machine Translation

Our baseline system is a variant of the MIT-LL/AFRL IWSLT 2013 system (Kazi et al., 2013) with some modifications to the training and decoding processes.

2.2.1 Phrase Table Training

For our Russian-English system, we trained a phrase table using the Moses Experiment Management System (Koehn, 2010b), with `mgiza` (Gao and Vogel, 2008) as the word aligner; this phrase table was trained using the Russian-English Common Crawl, News Commentary, Yandex (Bojar et al., 2013), and Wikipedia headlines parallel corpora.

The phrase table for our Hindi-English system was trained using a similar in-house training pipeline, making use of the HindEnCorp and Wikipedia headlines parallel corpora.

2.2.2 Language Model Training

During the training process we built n-gram language models (LMs) for use in decoding and rescoring using the KenLM language modelling toolkit (Heafield et al., 2013). Class-based language models (Brown et al., 1992) were also trained, for later use in n-best list rescoring, using the SRILM language modelling toolkit (Stolcke, 2002).We trained a 6-gram language model from the LDC English Gigaword Fifth Edition, for use in both the Hindi-English and Russian-English systems. All language models were binarized in order to reduce model disk usage and loading time.

For the Russian-to-English task, we concatenated the English portion of the parallel training data for the WMT 2014 shared translation task (Common Crawl, News Commentary, Wiki Headlines and Yandex corpora) in addition to the shared task English monolingual training data (Europarl, News Commentary and News Crawl corpora) into a training set for a large 6-gram language model using KenLM. We denote this model as "BigLM". Individual 6-gram models were also constructed from each respective corpus.

For the Hindi-to-English task, individual 6-gram models were constructed from the respective English portions of the HindEnCorp and Wikipedia headlines parallel corpora, and from the monolingual English sections of the Europarl and News Crawl corpora.

Decoding Features
$\mathsf{P}(\mathbf{f} \mid \mathbf{e})$
$\mathsf{P}(\mathbf{e} \mid \mathbf{f})$
$\mathsf{P}_w(\mathbf{f} \mid \mathbf{e})$
$\mathsf{P}_w(\mathbf{e} \mid \mathbf{f})$
Phrase Penalty
Lexical Backoff
Word Penalty
Distortion Model
Unknown Word Penalty
Lexicalized Reordering Model
Operation Sequence Model
Rescoring Features
$\mathsf{P}_{class}(\mathbf{E})$ – 7-gram class-based LM
$\mathsf{P}_{lex}(\mathbf{F} \mid \mathbf{E})$ – sentence-level averaged lexical translation score

Table 1: Models used in log-linear combination

2.2.3 Decoding, n-best List Rescoring, and Optimization

We decode using the phrase-based `moses` decoder (Koehn et al., 2007), choosing the best translation for each source sentence according to a linear combination of decoding features:

$$\hat{\mathbf{E}} = \arg\max_{\mathbf{E}} \sum_{\forall r} \lambda_r h_r(\mathbf{E}, \mathbf{F}) \tag{1}$$

We make use of a standard set of decoding features, listed in Table 1. In contrast to our IWSLT 2013 system, all experiments submitted to this year's WMT evaluation made use of version 2.1 of `moses`, and incorporated additional decoding features, namely the Operation Sequence Model (Durrani et al., 2011) and Lexicalized Reordering Model (Tillman, 2004; Galley and Manning, 2008).

Following Shen et al. (2006), we use the word-level lexical translation probabilities $\mathsf{P}_w(f_j \mid e_i)$ to obtain a sentence-level averaged lexical translation score (Eq. 2), which is added as an additional feature to each n-best list entry.

$$\mathsf{P}_{lex}(\mathbf{F} \mid \mathbf{E}) = \prod_{j \in 1 \ldots J} \frac{1}{I+1} \sum_{i \in 1 \ldots I} \mathsf{P}_w(f_j \mid e_i) \tag{2}$$

Shen et al. (2006) use the term "IBM model 1 score" to describe the value calculated in Eq. 2. While the lexical probability distribution from IBM Model 1 (Brown et al., 1993) could in fact be used as the $\mathsf{P}_w(f_j \mid e_i)$ in Eq. 2, in practice we use a variant of $\mathsf{P}_w(f_j \mid e_i)$ defined by Koehn et al. (2003).

We also add a 7-gram class language model score $\mathsf{P}_{class}(\mathbf{E})$ (Brown et al., 1992) as an additional feature of each n-best list entry. After adding these features to each translation in an n-best list, Eq. 1 is applied, rescoring the entries to extract new 1-best translations.

To optimize system performance we train scaling factors, λ_r, for both decoding and rescoring features so as to minimize an objective error criterion. In our systems we use DREM (Kazi et al., 2013) or PRO (Hopkins and May, 2011) to perform this optimization. For development data during optimization, we used `newstest2013` for the Russian-to-English task and `newsdev2014` for the Hindi-to-English task supplied by WMT14.

2.2.4 Unknown Words

For the Hindi-to-English task, unknown words were marked during the decoding process and were transliterated by the icu4j Devanagari-to-Latin transliterator.[4]

For the Russian-to-English task, we selectively stemmed and inflected input words not found in the phrase table. Each input sentence was examined to identify any source words which did not occur as a phrase of length 1 in the phrase table. For each such unknown word, we used `treetagger` (Schmid, 1994; Schmid, 1995) to identify the part of speech, and then we removed inflectional endings to derive a stem. We applied all possible Russian inflectional endings for the given part of speech; if an inflected form of the unknown word could be found as a stand-alone phrase in the phrase table, that form was used to replace the unknown word in the original Russian file. If multiple candidates were found, we used the one with the highest frequency of occurrence in the training data. This process replaces words that we know we cannot translate with semantically similar words that we can translate, replacing unknown words like фотоном "photon" (instrumental case) with a known morphological variant фотон "photon" (nominative case) that is found in the phrase table. Selective stemming of just the unknown words allows us to retain information that would be lost if we applied stemming to all the data.

Any remaining unknown words were transliterated as a post-process, using a simple letter-mapping from Cyrillic characters to Latin characters representing their typical sounds.

[4] `http://site.icu-project.org`

	#	Pair	BLEU	BLEU-cased
System	1	hi-en	13.1	12.1
	2	ru-en	32.0	30.8
	3	ru-en	32.2	31.0
	4	ru-en	31.5	30.3
	5	ru-en	33.0	31.1

Table 2: Translation results, as measured by BLEU (Papineni et al., 2002).

2.3 MT Results

Our best Hindi-English system for `newstest2014` is listed in Table 2 as System 1. This system uses a combination of 6-gram language models built from HindEnCorp, News Commentary, Europarl, and News Crawl corpora. Transliteration of unknown words was performed after decoding but before n-best list rescoring.

System 2 is Russian-English, and handles unknown words following §2.2.4. We used as independent decoder features separate 6-gram LMs trained respectively on Common Crawl, Europarl, News Crawl, Wiki headlines and Yandex corpora. This system was optimized with DREM. No rescoring was performed. We also tested a variant of System 2 which did perform rescoring. That variant (not listed in Table 2) performed worse than System 2, with scores of 31.2 BLEU and 30.1 BLEU-cased.

System 3, our best Russian-English system for `newstest2014`, used the BigLM and Gigaword language models (see §2.2.2) as independent decoder features and was optimized with DREM. Rescoring was performed after decoding. Instead of following §2.2.4, unknown words were dropped to maximize BLEU score. We note that the optimizer assigned weights of 0.314 and 0.003 to the BigLM and Gigaword models, respectively, suggesting that the optimizer found the BigLM to be much more use-

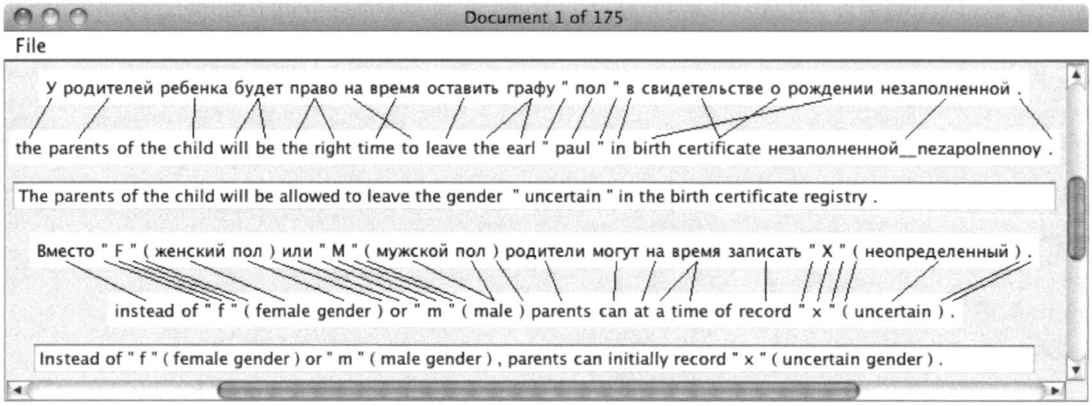

Figure 1: Posteditor user interface

		Documents	Sentences	Words
Posteditor	1	44	950	20086
	2	21	280	6031
	3	25	476	10194
	4	25	298	6164
	5	20	301	5809
	6	15	210	4433
	7	10	140	2650
	8	15	348	6743
	All	175	3003	62110

Table 3: Number of documents within the Russian-English test set processed by each monolingual human posteditor. Number of machine translated sentences processed by each posteditor is also listed, along with the total number of words in the corresponding Russian source sentences.

		# ✓	# ✗	% ✓
Posteditor	1	684	266	72.0%
	2	190	90	67.9%
	3	308	168	64.7%
	4	162	136	54.4%
	5	194	107	64.5%
	6	94	116	44.8%
	7	88	52	62.9%
	8	196	152	56.3%
	All	1916	1087	63.8%

Table 4: For each monolingual posteditor, the number and percentage of sentences judged to be correct (✓) versus incorrect (✗) according to a monolingual human judge.[6]

12	The postedited translation is superior to the reference translation
10	The meaning of the Russian source sentence is fully conveyed in the postedited translation
8	Most of the meaning is conveyed
6	Misunderstands the sentence in a major way; or has many small mistakes
4	Very little meaning is conveyed
2	The translation makes no sense at all

Table 5: Evaluation guidelines for bilingual human judges, adapted from Albrecht et al. (2009).

Evaluation Category					
2	4	6	8	10	12
0.2%	2.2%	9.8%	24.7%	60.2%	2.8%

Table 6: Percentage of evaluated sentences judged to be in each category by a bilingual judge. Category labels are defined in Table 5.

	Evaluation Category					
	2	4	6	8	10	12
# ✗	2	20	72	89	79	4
# ✓	0	1	21	146	493	23
% ✓	0%	5%	23%	62%	86%	85%

Table 7: Number of sentences in each evaluation category (see Table 5) that were judged as correct (✓) or incorrect (✗) according to a monolingual human judge.

ful than the Gigaword LM. This intuition was confirmed by an experimental variation of System 3 (not listed in Table 2) where we omitted the BigLM; that variant performed substantially worse, with scores of 25.3 BLEU and 24.2 BLEU-cased. We also tested a variant of System 3 which did not perform rescoring; that variant (also not listed in Table 2) performed worse, with scores of 31.7 BLEU and 30.6 BLEU-cased.

The results of monolingual postediting (see §3) of System 4 (a variant of System 2 tuned using PRO) uncased output is System 5. Due to time constraints, the monolingual postediting experiments in §3 were conducted (using the machine translation results from System 4) before the results of Systems 2 and 3 were available. The Moses recaser was applied in all experiments except for System 5.

3 Monolingual Postediting

Postediting is the process whereby a human user corrects the output of a machine translation system. The use of basic postediting tools by bilingual human translators has been shown to yield substantial increases in terms of productivity (Plitt and Masselot, 2010) as well as improvements in translation quality (Green et al., 2013) when compared to bilingual human translators working without assistance from machine translation and postediting tools. More sophisticated interactive interfaces (Langlais et al., 2000; Barrachina et al., 2009; Koehn, 2009b; Denkowski and Lavie, 2012) may also provide benefit (Koehn, 2009a).

We hypothesize that for at least some language pairs, monolingual posteditors with no knowledge of the source language can successfully translate a substantial fraction of test sentences. We expect this to be the case especially when the monolingual humans are domain experts with regard to the documents to be translated. If this hypothesis is confirmed, this could allow for multi-stage translation workflows, where less highly skilled monolingual posteditors triage the translation process, postediting many of the sentences, while forwarding on the most difficult sentences to more highly skilled bilingual translators.

Small-scale studies have suggested that monolingual human posteditors, working without knowledge of the source language, can also improve the quality of machine translation output (Callison-Burch, 2005; Koehn, 2010a; Mitchell et al., 2013), especially if well-designed tools provide automated linguistic analysis of source sentences (Albrecht et al., 2009).

In this study, we designed a simple user interface for postediting that presents the user with the source sentence, machine translation, and word alignments for each sentence in a test document (Figure 1). While it may seem counter-intuitive to present monolingual posteditors with the source sentence, we found that the presence of alignment links between source words and target words can in fact aid a monolingual posteditor, especially with regard to correcting word order. For example, in our experiments posteditors encountered some sentences where a word or phrase was enclosed within bracketing punctuation marks (such as quotation marks, commas, or parentheses) in the source sentence, and the machine translation system incorrectly reordered the word or phrase outside the enclosing punctuation; by examining the alignment links the posteditors were able to correct such reordering mistakes.

The Russian-English test set comprises 175 documents in the news domain, totaling 3003 sentences. We assigned each test document to one of 8 monolingual[5] posteditors (Table 3). The postediting tool did not record timing information. However, several posteditors informally reported that they were able to process on average approximately four documents per hour; if accurate, this would indicate a processing speed of around one sentence per minute.

Following Koehn (2010a), we evaluated postedited translation quality according to a binary adequacy metric, as judged by a monolingual English speaker[6] against the En-

[5] All posteditors are native English speakers. Posteditors 2 and 3 know Chinese and Arabic, respectively, but not Russian. Posteditor 8 understands the Cyrillic character set and has a minimal Russian vocabulary from two undergraduate semesters of Russian taken several years ago.

[6] All monolingual adequacy judgements were performed by Posteditor 1. Additional analysis of Posteditor 1's 950 postedited translations were independently judged by bilingual judges against the reference and the source sentence (Table 7).

glish references. In this metric, incorrect spellings of transliterated proper names were not grounds to judge as incorrect an otherwise adequate postedited translation. Binary adequacy results are shown in Table 4; we observe that correctness varied widely between posteditors (44.8–72.0%), and between documents.

Interestingly, several posteditors self-reported that they could tell which documents were originally written in English and were subsequently translated into Russian, and which were originally written in Russian, based on observations that sentences from the latter were substantially more difficult to postedit. Once per-document source language data is released by WMT14 organizers, we intend to examine translation quality on a per-document basis and test whether posteditors did indeed perform worse on documents which originated in Russian.

Using bilingual judges, we further evaluate a substantial subset of the postedited test set using a more fine-grained adequacy metric (Table 5). Because of time constraints, only the first 950 postedited sentences of the test set[6] were evaluated in this manner. Each sentence was evaluated by one of two bilingual human judges. In addition to the 2-10 point scale of Albrecht et al. (2009), judges were instructed to indicate (with a score of 12) any sentences where the postedited machine translation was superior to the reference translation. Using this metric, we show in Table 6 that monolingual posteditors can successfully produce postedited translations that convey all or most of the meaning of the original source sentence in up to 87.8% of sentences; this includes 2.8% which were superior to the reference.

Finally, as part of WMT14, the results of our Systems 1 (hi-en), 3 (ru-en), and 5 (postedited ru-en) were ranked by monolingual human judges against the machine translation output of other WMT14 participants. These judgements are reported in WMT (2014).

Due to time constraints, the machine translations (from System 4) presented to posteditors were not evaluated by human judges, neither using our 12-point evaluation scale nor as part of the WMT human evaluation rankings. However, to enable such evaluation by future researchers, and to enable replication of our experimental evaluation, the System 4 machine translations, the postedited translations, and the monolingual and bilingual evaluation results are released as supplementary data to accompany this paper.

4 Conclusion

In this paper, we present data preparation and language-specific processing techniques for our Hindi-English and Russian-English submissions to the 2014 Workshop on Machine Translation (WMT14) shared translation task. Our submissions examine the effectiveness of handling various monolingual target language corpora as individual component language models (System 2) or alternatively, concatenated together into a single big language model (System 3). We also examine the utility of n-best list rescoring using class language model and lexicalized translation model rescoring features.

In addition, we present the results of monolingual postediting of the entire 3003 sentences of the WMT14 Russian-English test set. Postediting was performed by monolingual English speakers, who corrected the output of machine translation without access to external resources, such as bilingual dictionaries or online search engines. This system scored highest according to BLEU of all Russian-English submissions to WMT14.

Using a binary adequacy classification, we evaluate the entire postedited test set for correctness against the reference translations. Using bilingual judges, we further evaluate a substantial subset of the postedited test set using a more fine-grained adequacy metric; using this metric, we show that monolingual posteditors can successfully produce postedited translations that convey all or most of the meaning of the original source sentence in up to 87.8% of sentences.

Acknowledgements

We would like to thank the members of the SCREAM group at Wright-Patterson AFB.

Opinions, interpretations, conclusions and recommendations are those of the authors and are not necessarily endorsed by the United States Government. Cleared for public release on 1 Apr 2014. Originator reference number RH-14-112150. Case number 88ABW-2014-1328.

References

Joshua S. Albrecht, Rebecca Hwa, and G. Elisabeta Marai. 2009. Correcting automatic translations through collaborations between MT and monolingual target-language users. In *Proceedings of the 12th Conference of the European Chapter of the Association for Computational Linguistics (EACL '12)*, pages 60–68, Athens, Greece, March–April.

Waleed Ammar, Victor Chahuneau, Michael Denkowski, Greg Hanneman, Wang Ling, Austin Matthews, Kenton Murray, Nicola Segall, Yulia Tsvetkov, Alon Lavie, and Chris Dyer. 2013. The CMU machine translation systems at WMT 2013: Syntax, synthetic translation options, and pseudo-references. In *Proceedings of the Eighth Workshop on Statistical Machine Translation (WMT '13)*, pages 70–77, Sofia, Bulgaria, August.

Sergio Barrachina, Oliver Bender, Francisco Casacuberta, Jorge Civera, Elsa Cubel, Shahram Khadivi, Antonio Lagarda, Hermann Ney, Jesús Tom´as, Enrique Vidal, and Juan-Miguel Vilar. 2009. Statistical approaches to computer-assisted translation. *Computational Linguistics*, 35(1):3–28, March.

Ondřej Bojar, Pavel Straň´ak, and Daniel Zeman. 2010. Data issues in English-to-Hindi machine translation. In *Proceedings of the Seventh International Conference on Language Resources and Evaluation (LREC '10)*, pages 1771–1777, Valletta, Malta, May.

Ondřej Bojar, Christian Buck, Chris Callison-Burch, Christian Federmann, Barry Haddow, Philipp Koehn, Christof Monz, Matt Post, Radu Soricut, and Lucia Specia. 2013. Findings of the 2013 Workshop on Statistical Machine Translation. In *Proceedings of the Eighth Workshop on Statistical Machine Translation (WMT '13)*, pages 1–44, Sofia, Bulgaria, August.

Ondřej Bojar, Vojtěch Diatka, Pavel Rychlý, Pavel Straňák, Aleš Tamchyna, and Dan Zeman. 2014. Hindi-English and Hindi-only corpus for machine translation. In *Proceedings of the Ninth International Language Resources and Evaluation Conference (LREC '14)*, Reykjavik, Iceland, May. ELRA, European Language Resources Association.

Peter Brown, Vincent Della Pietra, Peter deSouza, Jenifer Lai, and Robert Mercer. 1992. Class-based n-gram models of natural language. *Computational Linguistics*, 18(4):467–479, December.

Peter Brown, Vincent Della Pietra, Stephen Della Pietra, and Robert Mercer. 1993. The mathematics of statistical machine translation: parameter estimation. *Computational Linguistics*, 19(2):263–311, June.

Chris Callison-Burch. 2005. Linear B system description for the 2005 NIST MT evaluation exercise. In *Proceedings of the NIST 2005 Machine Translation Evaluation Workshop.*

Mark Davis and Ken Whistler. 2013. Unicode normalization forms. Technical Report UAX #15, The Unicode Consortium, September. Rev. 39.

Michael Denkowski and Alon Lavie. 2012. Trans-Center: Web-based translation research suite. In *Proceedings of the AMTA 2012 Workshop on Post-Editing Technology and Practice Demo Session*, November.

Nadir Durrani, Helmut Schmid, and Alexander Fraser. 2011. A joint sequence translation model with integrated reordering. In *Proceedings of the 49th Annual Meeting of the Association for Computational Linguistics (ACL '11)*, pages 1045–1054, Portland, Oregon, June.

Michel Galley and Christopher D. Manning. 2008. A simple and effective hierarchical phrase reordering model. In *Proceedings of the 2008 Conference on Empirical Methods in Natural Language Processing (EMNLP '08)*, pages 848–856, Honolulu, Hawai'i, October.

Qin Gao and Stephan Vogel. 2008. Parallel implementations of word alignment tool. In *Software Engineering, Testing and Quality Assurance for Natural Language Processing*, pages 49–57, Columbus, Ohio, June.

Spence Green, Jeffrey Heer, and Christopher D. Manning. 2013. The efficacy of human post-editing for language translation. In *Proceedings of the ACM SIGCHI Conference on Human Factors in Computing Systems (CHI '13)*, pages 439–448, Paris, France, April–May.

Kenneth Heafield, Ivan Pouzyrevsky, Jonathan H. Clark, and Philipp Koehn. 2013. Scalable modified Kneser-Ney language model estimation. In *Proceedings of the 51st Annual Meeting of the Association for Computational Linguistics (ACL '13)*, pages 690–696, Sofia, Bulgaria, August.

Mark Hopkins and Jonathan May. 2011. Tuning as ranking. In *Proceedings of the 2011 Conference on Empirical Methods in Natural Language Processing (EMNLP '11)*, pages 1352–1362, Edinburgh, Scotland, U.K.

Michaeel Kazi, Michael Coury, Elizabeth Salesky, Jessica Ray, Wade Shen, Terry Gleason, Tim Anderson, Grant Erdmann, Lane Schwartz, Brian Ore, Raymond Slyh, Jeremy Gwinnup, Katherine Young, and Michael Hutt. 2013. The MIT-LL/AFRL IWSLT-2013 MT system. In *The 10th International Workshop on Spoken Language Translation (IWSLT '13)*, pages 136–143, Heidelberg, Germany, December.

Philipp Koehn, Franz Joseph Och, and Daniel Marcu. 2003. Statistical phrase-based translation. In *Proceedings of the 2003 Human Language Technology Conference of the North American Chapter of the Association for Computational Linguistics (HLT-NAACL '13)*, pages 48–54, Edmonton, Canada, May–June.

Philipp Koehn, Hieu Hoang, Alexandra Birch, Chris Callison-Burch, Marcello Federico, Nicola Bertoldi, Brooke Cowan, Wade Shen, Christine Moran, Richard Zens, Chris Dyer, Ondřej Bojar, Alexandra Constantin, and Evan Herbst. 2007. Moses: Open source toolkit for statistical machine translation. In *Proceedings of the 45th Annual Meeting of the Association for Computational Linguistics (ACL '07) Demo and Poster Sessions*, pages 177–180, Prague, Czech Republic, June.

Philipp Koehn. 2009a. A process study of computer aided translation. *Machine Translation*, 23(4):241–263, November.

Philipp Koehn. 2009b. A web-based interactive computer aided translation tool. In *Proceedings of the ACL-IJCNLP 2009 Software Demonstrations*, pages 17–20, Suntec, Singapore, August.

Philipp Koehn. 2010a. Enabling monolingual translators: Post-editing vs. options. In *Human Language Technologies: The 2010 Annual Conference of the North American Chapter of the Association for Computational Linguistics (HLT-NAACL '10)*, pages 537–545, Los Angeles, California, June.

Philipp Koehn. 2010b. An experimental management system. *The Prague Bulletin of Mathematical Linguistics*, 94:87–96, December.

Philippe Langlais, George Foster, and Guy Lapalme. 2000. TransType: A computer-aided translation typing system. In *Proceedings of the ANLP/NAACL 2000 Workshop on Embedded Machine Translation Systems*, pages 46–51, Seattle, Washington, May.

Leah S. Larkey, Margaret E. Connell, and Nasreen Abduljaleel. 2003. Hindi CLIR in thirty days. *ACM Transactions on Asian Language Information Processing (TALIP)*, 2(2):130–142, June.

Linda Mitchell, Johann Roturier, and Sharon O'Brien. 2013. Community-based post-editing of machine translation content: monolingual vs. bilingual. In *Proceedings of the 2nd Workshop on Post-editing Technology and Practice (WPTP-2)*, pages 35–43, Nice, France, September. EAMT.

Kishore Papineni, Salim Roukos, Todd Ward, and Wei-Jing Zhu. 2002. BLEU: A method for automatic evaluation of machine translation. In *Proceedings of the 40th Annual Meeting of the Association for Computational Linguistics (ACL '02)*, pages 311–318, Philadelphia, Pennsylvania, July.

Mirko Plitt and François Masselot. 2010. A productivity test of statistical machine translation post-editing in a typical localisation context. *The Prague Bulletin of Mathematical Linguistics*, 93:7–16, January.

Helmut Schmid. 1994. Probabilistic part-of-speech tagging using decision trees. In *Proceedings of the International Conference on New Methods in Language Processing*, Manchester, England, September.

Helmut Schmid. 1995. Improvements in part-of-speech tagging with an application to German. In *Proceedings of the EACL SIGDAT Workshop*, Dublin, Ireland, March.

Wade Shen, Brian Delaney, and Tim Anderson. 2006. The MIT-LL/AFRL IWSLT-2006 MT system. In *The 3rd International Workshop on Spoken Language Translation (IWSLT '06)*, Kyoto, Japan.

Jason R. Smith, Herve Saint-Amand, Magdalena Plamada, Philipp Koehn, Chris Callison-Burch, and Adam Lopez. 2013. Dirt cheap web-scale parallel text from the common crawl. In *Proceedings of the 51st Annual Meeting of the Association for Computational Linguistics (ACL '13)*, pages 1374–1383, Sofia, Bulgaria, August.

Andreas Stolcke. 2002. SRILM — an extensible language modeling toolkit. In *Proceedings of the 7th International Conference on Spoken Language Processing (ICSLP '02)*, pages 901–904, Denver, Colorado, September.

Christoph Tillman. 2004. A unigram orientation model for statistical machine translation. In *Proceedings of the Human Language Technology Conference of the North American Chapter of the Association for Computational Linguistics (HLT-NAACL '04), Companion Volume*, pages 101–104, Boston, Massachusetts, May.

WMT. 2014. Findings of the 2014 Workshop on Statistical Machine Translation. In *Proceedings of the Ninth Workshop on Statistical Machine Translation (WMT '14)*, Baltimore, Maryland, June.

CUNI in WMT14: Chimera Still Awaits Bellerophon

Aleš Tamchyna, Martin Popel, Rudolf Rosa, Ondřej Bojar
Charles University in Prague, Faculty of Mathematics and Physics
Institute of Formal and Applied Linguistics
Malostranské náměstí 25, Prague, Czech Republic
surname@ufal.mff.cuni.cz

Abstract

We present our English→Czech and English→Hindi submissions for this year's WMT translation task. For English→Czech, we build upon last year's CHIMERA and evaluate several setups. English→Hindi is a new language pair for this year. We experimented with reverse self-training to acquire more (synthetic) parallel data and with modeling target-side morphology.

1 Introduction

In this paper, we describe translation systems submitted by Charles University (CU or CUNI) to the Translation task of the Ninth Workshop on Statistical Machine Translation (WMT) 2014.

In §2, we present our English→Czech systems, CU-TECTOMT, CU-BOJAR, CU-DEPFIX and CU-FUNKY. The systems are very similar to our submissions (Bojar et al., 2013) from last year, the main novelty being our experiments with domain-specific and document-specific language models.

In §3, we describe our experiments with English→Hindi translation, which is a translation pair new both to us and to WMT. We unsuccessfully experimented with reverse self-training and a morphological-tags-based language model, and so our final submission, CU-MOSES, is only a basic instance of Moses.

2 English→Czech

Our submissions for English→Czech build upon last year's successful CHIMERA system (Bojar et al., 2013). We combine several different approaches:

- factored phrase-based Moses model (§2.1),
- domain-adapted language model (§2.2),
- document-specific language models (§2.3),
- deep-syntactic MT system TectoMT (§2.4),
- automatic post-editing system Depfix (§2.5).

We combined the approaches in several ways into our four submissions, as made clear by Table 1. CU-TECTOMT is the stand-alone TectoMT translation system, while the other submissions are Moses-based, using TectoMT indirectly to provide an additional phrase-table. CU-BOJAR uses a factored model and a domain-adapted language model; in CU-DEPFIX, Depfix post-processing is added; and CU-FUNKY also employs document-specific language models.

	CU-TECTOMT	CU-BOJAR	CU-DEPFIX	CU-FUNKY
TectoMT (§2.4)	✓	✓	✓	✓
Factored Moses (§2.1)		✓	✓	✓
Adapted LM (§2.2)		✓	✓	✓
Document-specific LMs (§2.3)				✓
Depfix (§2.5)			✓	✓

Table 1: EN→CS systems submitted to WMT.

2.1 Our Baseline Factored Moses System

Our baseline translation system (denoted "Baseline" in the following) is similar to last year – we trained a factored Moses model on the concatenation of CzEng (Bojar et al., 2012) and Europarl (Koehn, 2005), see Table 2. We use two factors: tag, which is the part-of-speech tag, and stc, which is "supervised truecasing", i.e. the surface form with letter case set according to the lemma; see (Bojar et al., 2013). Our factored Moses system translates from English stc to Czech stc | tag in one translation step.

Our basic language models are identical to last year's submission. We added an adapted language

Proceedings of the Ninth Workshop on Statistical Machine Translation, pages 195–200,
Baltimore, Maryland USA, June 26–27, 2014.

		Tokens [M]	
Corpus	Sents [M]	English	Czech
CzEng 1.0	14.83	235.67	205.17
Europarl	0.65	17.61	15.00

Table 2: English→Czech parallel data.

Corpus	Sents [M]	Tokens [M]
CzEng 1.0	14.83	205.17
CWC Articles	36.72	626.86
CNC News	28.08	483.88
CNA	47.00	830.32
Newspapers	64.39	1040.80
News Crawl	24.91	444.84
Total	215.93	3631.87

Table 3: Czech monolingual data.

model which we describe in the following section. Tables 3 and 4 show basic data about the language models. Aside from modeling surface forms, our language models also capture morphological coherence to some degree.

2.2 Adapted Language Model

We used the 2013 News Crawl to create a language model adapted to the domain of the test set (i.e. news domain) using data selection based on information retrieval (Tamchyna et al., 2012). We use the Baseline system to translate the source sides of WMT test sets 2012–2014. The translations then constitute a "query corpus" for Lucene.[1] For each sentence in the query corpus, we use Lucene to retrieve 20 most similar sentences from the 2013 News Crawl. After de-duplication, we obtained a monolingual corpus of roughly 250 thousand sentences and trained an additional 6-gram language model on this data.

Domain	Factor	Order	Sents [M]	Tokens [M]	ARPA.gz [GB]	Trie [GB]
General	stc	4	201.31	3430.92	28.2	11.8
General	stc	7	24.91	444.84	13.1	8.1
General	tag	10	14.83	205.17	7.2	3.0
News	stc	6	0.25	4.73	0.2	–

Table 4: Czech LMs used in CU-BOJAR. The last small model is described in §2.2.

[1] http://lucene.apache.org

2.3 Document-Specific Language Models

CU-FUNKY further extends the idea described in §2.2. Taking advantage of document IDs which are included in WMT development and test data, we split our dev- (WMT 13) and test-set (WMT 14) into documents. We translate each document with the Baseline system and use Lucene to retrieve 10,000 most similar target-side sentences from News Crawl 2013 for each document sentence.

Using this procedure, we obtain a corpus for each document. On average, the corpora contain roughly 208 thousand sentences after deduplication. Each corpus then serves as the training data for the document-specific language model.

We implemented an alternative to `moses-parallel.perl` which splits the input corpus based on document IDs and runs a separate Moses instance/job for each document. Moreover, it allows to modify the Moses configuration file according to document ID. We use this feature to plant the correct document-specific language model to each job.

In tuning, our technique only adds one weight. In each split, the weight corresponds to a different language model. The optimizer then hopefully averages the utility of this document-specific LM across all documents. The same weight is applied also in the test set translation, exchanging the document-specific LM file.

2.4 TectoMT Deep-Syntactic MT System

TectoMT[2] was one of the three key components in last year's CHIMERA. It is a linguistically-motivated tree-to-tree deep-syntactic translation system with transfer based on Maximum Entropy context-sensitive translation models (Mareček et al., 2010) and Hidden Tree Markov Models (Žabokrtský and Popel, 2009). It is trained on the WMT-provided data: CzEng 1.0 (parallel data) and News Crawl (2007–2012 Czech monolingual sets).

We maintain the same approach to combining TectoMT with Moses as last year – we translate WMT test sets from years 2007–2014 and use them as additional *synthetic* parallel training data – a corpus consisting of the test set source side (English) and TectoMT output (synthetic Czech). We then use the standard extraction pipeline to create

[2] http://ufal.mff.cuni.cz/tectomt/

an additional phrase table from this corpus. The translated data overlap completely both with our development and test data for Moses so that tuning can assign an appropriate weight to the synthetic phrase table.

2.5 Depfix Automatic Post-Editing

As in the previous years, we used Depfix (Rosa, 2013) to post-process the translations. Depfix is an automatic post-editing system which is mainly rule-based and uses various linguistic tools (taggers, parsers, morphological generators, etc.) to detect and correct errors, especially grammatical ones. The system was slightly improved since last year, and a new fixing rule was added for correcting word order in noun clusters translated as genitive constructions.

In English, a noun can behave as an adjective, as in "according to the *house* owners", while in Czech, this is not possible, and a genitive construction has to be used instead, similarly to "according to the owners *of the house*" – the modifier is in the genitive morphological case and follows the noun. However, SMT systems translating into Czech do not usually focus much on word reordering, which leads to non-fluent or incomprehensible constructions, such as "podle domu$_{gen}$ vlastníků$_{gen}$" (according to-the-house of-the-owners). Fortunately, such cases are easy to distinguish with the help of a dependency parser and a morphological tagger – genitive modifiers usually do not precede the head but follow it (unless they are parts of named entities), so we can safely switch the word order to the correct one: "podle vlastníků$_{gen}$ domu$_{gen}$" (according to-the-owners of-the-house).

2.6 Results

We report scores of automatic metrics as shown in the submission system,[3] namely (case-sensitive) BLEU (Papineni et al., 2002) and TER (Snover et al., 2006). The results, summarized in Table 5, show that CU-FUNKY is the most successful of our systems according to BLEU, while the simpler CU-DEPFIX wins in TER. The results of manual evaluation suggest that CU-DEPFIX (dubbed CHIMERA) remains the best performing English→Czech system.

In comparison to other English→Czech systems submitted to WMT 2014, CU-FUNKY ranked as the second in BLEU, and CU-DEPFIX ranked as the second in TER; the winning system, according to both of these metrics, was UEDIN-UNCONSTRAINED.

System	BLEU	TER	Manual
CU-DEPFIX	21.1	0.670	**0.373**
UEDIN-UNCONSTRAINED	**21.6**	**0.667**	0.357
CU-BOJAR	20.9	0.674	0.333
CU-FUNKY	21.2	0.675	0.287
GOOGLE TRANSLATE	20.2	0.687	0.168
CU-TECTOMT	15.2	0.716	-0.177
CU-BOJAR +full 2013 news	20.7	0.677	–

Table 5: Scores of automatic metrics and results of manual evaluation for our systems. The table also lists the best system according to automatic metrics and Google Translate as the best-performing commercial system.

Our analysis of CU-FUNKY suggests that it is not the best performing system on average (despite achieving the highest BLEU scores from our submissions), but that it is rather the most volatile system. Some sentences were obviously improved compared to CU-BOJAR but most got degraded especially in adequacy. We are well aware of the many shortcomings our current implementation has, the most severe of which lie in the sentence selection by Lucene. For instance, we do not use any stopwords or keyword detection methods, and also pretending that each sentence in our monolingual corpus is a "document" for the information retrieval system is far from ideal.

We also evaluated a version of CU-BOJAR which uses not only the adapted LM but also an additional LM trained on the full 2013 News Crawl data (see "CU-BOJAR +full 2013 news" in Table 5) but found no improvement compared to using just the adapted model (trained on a subset of the data).

3 English→Hindi

English-Hindi is a new language pair this year. We submitted an unconstrained system for English→Hindi translation.

We used HindEnCorp (Bojar et al., 2014) as the sole source of parallel data (nearly 276 thousand sentence pairs, around 3.95 million English tokens and 4.09 million Hindi tokens).

Given that no test set from previous years was available and that the size of the development set provided by WMT organizers was only 500 sentence pairs, we held out the first 5000 sentence pairs of HindEnCorp for this purpose. Our development set then consisted of the 500 provided

[3] http://matrix.statmt.org/

Corpus	Sents [M]	Tokens [M]
NewsCrawl	1.27	27.27
HindEnCorp	0.28	4.09
HindMonoCorp	43.38	945.43
Total	44.93	976.80

Table 6: Hindi monolingual data.

English	Hindi	BLEU
stem4	stem4	**22.96±1.17**
lemma	lemma4	22.59±1.17
lemma	lemma	22.41±1.20

Table 7: Comparison of different factor combinations for word alignment.

sentences plus 1500 sentence pairs from HindEnCorp. The remaining 3500 sentence pairs taken from HindEnCorp constituted our test set.

As for monolingual data, we used the News Crawl corpora provided for the task and the new monolingual HindMonoCorp, which makes our submission unconstrained. Table 6 shows statistics of our monolingual data.

We tagged and lemmatized the English data using Morče (Spoustová et al., 2007) and the Hindi data using Siva Reddy's POS tagger.[4]

3.1 Baseline System

The baseline system was eventually our best-performing one. Its design is completely straightforward – it uses one phrase table trained on all parallel data (we translate from "supervised-truecased" English into Hindi forms) and one 5-gram language model trained on all monolingual data. We used KenLM (Heafield et al., 2013) for estimating the model as the data was rather large (see Table 6).

We used GIZA++ (Och and Ney, 2000) as our word alignment tool. We experimented with several coarser representations to make the final alignment more reliable. Table 7 shows the results. The factor "stem4" refers to simply taking the first four characters of each word. For lemmas, we used the outputs of the tools mentioned above. However, lemmas as output by the Hindi tagger were not much coarser than surface forms – the ratio between the number of types is merely 1.11 – so we also tried "stemming" the lemmas (lemma4). Of these variants, stem4-stem4 alignment worked best and we used it for the rest of our experiments.

3.2 Reverse Self-Training

Bojar and Tamchyna (2011) showed a simple technique for improving translation quality in situations where there is only a small amount of parallel data available but where there is a sufficient quantity of target-side monolingual texts. The so-called "reverse self-training" uses a factored system trained in the opposite direction to translate the large monolingual data into the source language. The translation (in the source language, i.e. English in our case) and the original target-side data (Hindi) can be used as additional synthetic parallel data. The authors recommend creating a separate phrase table from it and combining the two translation models as alternatives in the log-linear model (letting tuning weigh their importance).

The factored setup of the reverse system (Hindi→English) is essential – alternative decoding paths with a back-off to a coarser representation (e.g. stems) on the source side (Hindi) give the system the ability to generalize beyond surface forms observed in the training data. The main aim of this technique is to learn new forms of *known* words.

The technique is thus aimed at translating into a morphologically richer language than the source. Indeed, the authors showed that if the target language has considerably more word types than the source, the gains achieved by reverse self-training are higher. In this respect, English→Hindi is not an ideal candidate given that the ratio we observed is only 1.2.

The choice of back-off representation is important. We measure the vocabulary reduction of several options and summarize the results in Table 8. E.g. for stem4, the vocabulary size is roughly 30% compared to the number of surface word forms.

Bojar and Tamchyna (2011) achieved the best results using "nosuf3" ("suffix trimming", i.e. cutting of the last 3 characters of each word); however, they experimented with European languages and the highest reduction of vocabulary reported in the paper is to roughly one half. In our case, the vocabulary is reduced much more, so we opted for a more conservative back-off, namely "nosuf2".

[4] `http://sivareddy.in/downloads#hindi_tools`

Back-off	% of vocab. size
stem4	30.21
lemma4	32.36
nosuf3	36.36
nosuf2	50.76
stem5	53.48
lemma5	57.47
lemma	90.09

Table 8: Options for back-off factors in reverse self-training and the percentage of their vocabulary size compared to surface forms.

We translated roughly 2 million sentences from the Hindi monolingual data, focusing on news to maintain a domain match with the WMT test set. However, adding the synthetic phrase table did not bring any improvement and in fact, the BLEU score dropped to 22.37±1.17 (baseline is 22.96±1.17).

We can attribute the failure of reverse self-training to the nature of the language pair at hand. While Hindi has some synthetic properties (e.g. future tense of verbs or inflection of adjectives are marked by suffixes), its inflectional morphemes are realized mainly by post-positions which are separated from their head-words. Overlooking this essential property, we attempted to use reverse self-training but our technique could contribute only very little.

3.3 Target-Side Morphology

We also experimented with a setup that traditionally works very well for English→Czech translation: using a high-order language model on morphological tags to explicitly model target-side morphological coherence in translation. We used the same monolingual data as for the baseline language model; however, the order of our morphological language model was set to 10.

This setup also brought no improvement over the baseline – in fact, the BLEU score dropped even further to 22.27±1.14.

4 Conclusion

We presented our contributions to the Translation task of WMT 2014.

As we have focused on English→Czech translation for many years, we have developed several complex and well-performing systems for it – an adaptation of the phrase-based Moses system, a linguistically-motivated syntax-based TectoMT system, and an automatic post-editing Depfix system. We combine the individual systems using a very simple yet effective method and the combined system called CHIMERA confirmed its state-of-the-art performance.

For English→Hindi translation, which was a new task for us, we managed to get competitive results by using a baseline Moses setup, but were unable to improve upon those by employing advanced techniques that had proven to be effective for other translation directions.

Acknowledgments

This research was supported by the grants FP7-ICT-2013-10-610516 (QTLeap), FP7-ICT-2011-7-288487 (MosesCore), SVV 260 104. and GAUK 1572314. This work has been using language resources developed, stored and distributed by the LINDAT/CLARIN project of the Ministry of Education, Youth and Sports of the Czech Republic (project LM2010013).

References

Ondřej Bojar and Aleš Tamchyna. 2011. Improving Translation Model by Monolingual Data. In *Proc. of WMT*, pages 330–336. ACL.

Ondřej Bojar, Zdeněk Žabokrtský, Ondřej Dušek, Petra Galuščáková, Martin Majliš, David Mareček, Jiří Maršík, Michal Novák, Martin Popel, and Aleš Tamchyna. 2012. The Joy of Parallelism with CzEng 1.0. In *Proc. of LREC*, pages 3921–3928. ELRA.

Ondrej Bojar, Rudolf Rosa, and Aleš Tamchyna. 2013. Chimera – Three Heads for English-to-Czech Translation. In *Proceedings of the Eighth Workshop on Statistical Machine Translation*, pages 90–96.

Ondřej Bojar, Vojtěch Diatka, Pavel Rychlý, Pavel Straňák, Vít Suchomel, Aleš Tamchyna, and Daniel Zeman. 2014. HindEnCorp – Hindi-English and Hindi-only Corpus for Machine Translation. Reykjavík, Iceland. European Language Resources Association.

Kenneth Heafield, Ivan Pouzyrevsky, Jonathan H. Clark, and Philipp Koehn. 2013. Scalable Modified Kneser-Ney Language Model Estimation. In *Proc. of ACL*.

Philipp Koehn. 2005. Europarl: A Parallel Corpus for Statistical Machine Translation. In *Machine Translation Summit X*, pages 79–86.

David Mareček, Martin Popel, and Zdeněk Žabokrtský. 2010. Maximum entropy translation model in dependency-based MT framework. In *Proc. of WMT and MetricsMATR*, pages 201–206. ACL.

Franz Josef Och and Hermann Ney. 2000. Improved Statistical Alignment Models. In *Proc. of ACL*, pages 440–447, Hong Kong. ACL.

Kishore Papineni, Salim Roukos, Todd Ward, and Wei-Jing Zhu. 2002. BLEU: a method for automatic evaluation of machine translation. In *Proc. of ACL*, pages 311–318, Stroudsburg, PA, USA. ACL.

Rudolf Rosa. 2013. Automatic post-editing of phrase-based machine translation outputs. Master's thesis, Charles University in Prague, Faculty of Mathematics and Physics, Praha, Czechia.

Matthew Snover, Bonnie Dorr, Richard Schwartz, Linnea Micciulla, and John Makhoul. 2006. A study of translation edit rate with targeted human annotation. In *In Proceedings of Association for Machine Translation in the Americas*, pages 223–231.

Drahomíra Spoustová, Jan Hajič, Jan Votrubec, Pavel Krbec, and Pavel Květoň. 2007. The best of two worlds: Cooperation of statistical and rule-based taggers for Czech. In *Proceedings of the Workshop on Balto-Slavonic Natural Language Processing, ACL 2007*, pages 67–74, Praha.

Aleš Tamchyna, Petra Galuščáková, Amir Kamran, Miloš Stanojević, and Ondřej Bojar. 2012. Selecting Data for English-to-Czech Machine Translation. In *Proceedings of the Seventh Workshop on Statistical Machine Translation*, WMT '12, pages 374–381, Stroudsburg, PA, USA. Association for Computational Linguistics.

Zdeněk Žabokrtský and Martin Popel. 2009. Hidden Markov Tree Model in Dependency-based Machine Translation. In *Proc. of ACL-IJCNLP Short Papers*, pages 145–148.

Manawi: Using Multi-Word Expressions and Named Entities to Improve Machine Translation

Liling Tan and Santanu Pal
Applied Linguistics, Translation and Interpretation Department
Universität des Saarlandes
liling.tan@uni-saarland.de
santanu.pal@uni-saarland.de

Abstract

We describe the Manawi[1] (मानवि) system submitted to the 2014 WMT translation shared task. We participated in the English-Hindi (EN-HI) and Hindi-English (HI-EN) language pair and achieved 0.792 for the Translation Error Rate (TER) score[2] for EN-HI, the lowest among the competing systems. Our main innovations are (i) the usage of outputs from NLP tools, viz. billingual multi-word expression extractor and named-entity recognizer to improve SMT quality and (ii) the introduction of a novel filter method based on sentence-alignment features. The Manawi system showed the potential of improving translation quality by incorporating multiple NLP tools within the MT pipeline.

1 Introduction

In this paper, we present Saarland University (USAAR) submission to Workshop for Machine Translation 2014 (WMT 2014) using the Manawi MT system. We participated in the generic translation shared task for the English-Hindi (EN-HI) and Hindi-English (HI-EN) language pairs.

Our Manawi system showcased the incorporation of NLP tools output within the MT pipeline; a bilingual MWE extractor and a bilingual NE recognizer for English and Hindi were implemented. The output from these NLP tools was appended to the training corpus prior to the SMT model training with the MOSES toolkit (Koehn et al., 2007). The resulting system achieves the lowest Translation Error Rate (TER) among competing systems for the English-Hindi language pair.

The rest of the paper is structured as follow: Section 2 describes the implementation of the NLP tools; Section 3 outlines the corpus pre-processing before the MT training process; Section 4 describes the MT system setup; Section 5 describes a simple post-processing component to handle Out-Of-Vocabulary words; Section 6 presents the WMT shared task results for the Manawi system and Section 6 concludes the paper.

2 NLP Tools Implementation

2.1 Bilingual MWE in MT

Multi-Word Expressions (MWE) are defined as "idiosyncratic interpretations that cross word boundaries" (Sag et al., 2002). MWE can be made up of collocations (e.g. *seem ridiculous : behuda dikhai*), frozen expressions (e.g. *exception handling : apavada sancalaka*) or name entities (e.g. *Johnny Cash : Johni Kesh*). Jackendoff (1997) claims that the frequency of MWE and the frequency of single words in a speaker's lexicon are almost equivalent.

Bilingual MWE has shown to be useful for a variety of NLP applications such as multilingual information retrieval (Vechtomova, 2005) and Crosslingual/Multilingual Word Sense Disambiguation (Tan and Bond, 2013; Finlayson and Kulkarni, 2011). For machine translation, various studies had introduced bilingual MWE to improve MT system performance. Lambert (2005) introduced bilingual MWE by grouping them as a single token before training alignment models and they showed that it improved alignment and translation quality. Ren et al. (2009) integrated an in-domain bilingual MWE using log likelihood ratio based hierarchical reducing algorithm and gained +0.61 BLEU score. Similarly, Santanu et al. (2010) single tokenized MWE before training a phrase-based SMT model and achieved 50% improvement in BLEU score.

[1] Multi-word expression And Named-entity And Wikipedia titles (Manawi)

[2] Lower TER often results in better translation

Proceedings of the Ninth Workshop on Statistical Machine Translation, pages 201–206,
Baltimore, Maryland USA, June 26–27, 2014.

In order to improve the word alignment quality, Venkatapathy and Joshi (2006) reported a discriminative approach to use the compositionality information of verb-based multi-word expressions. Pal et al. (2011) discussed the effects of incorporating prior alignment of MWE and NEs directly or indirectly into Phrase-based SMT systems.

2.2 Bilingual MWE Extraction

Monolingual MWE extraction revolves around three approaches (i) rule-based methods relying on morphosyntactic patterns, (ii) statistical methods which use association/frequency measures to determine ngrams as MWE and (iii) hybrid approaches that combine the rule-based and statistical methods.

However, where bilingual MWE extraction techniques are concerned, they operate around two main modus operandi (i) extracting monolingual MWE separately and aligning them at word/phrasal level afterwards or (ii) aligning parallel text at word/phrasal level and then extracting MWE.

We implemented a *language independent bilingual MWE extractor*, (`Muwee`), that produces a parallel dictionary of MWE *without the need for any word/phrasal-level alignment*. `Muwee` makes use of the fact that the number of highly collocated MWE should be the same for each sentences pair.

`Muwee` first extracts MWE separately from the source and target sentences; the MWE are extracted based on bigrams that reports a Pointwise Mutual Information (PMI) score of above 10. Then for each parallel sentence, if the number of MWE are equivalent for the source and target, the bigrams are joint together as a string and contiguous duplicate words are deleted. The removal of contiguous duplicate words is grounded on the fact that linguistically motivated MWE that forms grammatical phrases had shown to improve SMT performances (Pal et al., 2013). Figure 1 presents an example of the MWE extraction process.

MWE with PMI > 10:	['Mahendra Sanskritic', 'Sanskritic University'] ['महेन्द्र संस्कृत', 'संस्कृत बनायागाया']
Concatenated MWE:	'Mahendra Sanskritic Sanskritic University' 'महेन्द्र संस्कृत संस्कृत बनायागाया'
Remove duplicate:	'Mahendra Sanskritic University' 'महेन्द्र संस्कृत बनायागाया'

Figure 1: `Muwee` Extraction Process

2.3 Named-entity Recognition

Named-Entity (NE) recognition is the task of identifying entities such as names of people, organizations and locations. Given a perfect MWE extraction system, NEs would have been captured by MWE extraction. However, the state-of-art MWE extractors have yet been perfected.

To compliment the MWE extracted by `Muwee`, we implemented a bilingual NE extractor by combining outputs from the (i) Stanford English NE Recognizer (NER)[3] and (ii) a Do-It-Yourself (DIY) Hindi NER using CRF++ toolkit[4] with annotated data from NER-SSEA 2008 shared task (Rajeev Sangal and Singh, 2008). We trained a Conditional Random Field classifier for the Hindi NER using unigram features, bigram features and a context window of two words to the left and to the right. And we used the DIY Hindi NER and Stanford NER tool to monolingually annotate the NEs from training corpus for the EN-HI / HI-EN language pair.

Similar to the `Muwee` bilingual extraction criteria, if the number of NEs are the same on the source and target language, the NEs were joint together as a string. We note that sometimes the bilingual NER output contains more than one NE per sentence. For example, our bilingual NER extractor outputs "*Kalpna Chawla Gurdeep Pandher*", which contains two NEs '*Kalpna Chawla*' and '*Gurdeep Pandher*'. Although the resulting bilingual NE does not provide a perfect NE dictionary, it filters out NEs from the sentence and improves word alignments at the start of the MT pipeline.

3 Corpus Preprocessing

The performance of any data driven SMT depends on the quality of training data. Previous studies had shown that filtering out low quality sentence pairs improves the quality of machine translation. For instance, the Moore-Lewis filter removes sentence pairs based on source-side cross-entropy differences (Moore and Lewis, 2010) and the Edinburgh's MT system used the Modified Moore-Lewis filtering (Axelrod et al., 2011) in WMT 2013 shared task (Durrani et al., 2013). CNGL-DCU system extended the Moore-Lewis filter by incorporating lemmas and named enti-

[3] http://nlp.stanford.edu/software/CRF-NER.shtml
[4] http://crfpp.googlecode.com

ties in their definition of perplexity[5] (Rubino et al., 2013; Toral, 2013).

The RWTH Aachen system filtered the Common Crawl Corpus by keeping only sentence pairs that contains at least 70% of the word from a known vocabulary dataset extracted from the other corpora in the WMT 2013 shared task (Peitz et al., 2013). The Docent system from Uppsala University also performed data cleaning on the Common Crawl dataset prior to SMT but they were using more aggressive conditions by (i) removing documents that were identified correctly using a language identification module and (ii) removing documents that falls below a threshold value of alignment points and sentence length ratio (Stymne et al., 2013). Our approach to data cleaning is similar to the Uppsala's system but instead of capitalizing on word-alignments features, we were cleaning the data based on sentence alignment features.

3.1 `GaCha` Filtering: Filter by Character Mean Ratio

Stymne et al. (2013) improved translation quality by cleaning the Common Crawl corpus during the WMT 2013 shared task. They filtered out documents exceeding 60 words and cleaned the remainder of the corpus by exploiting the number of alignment points in word alignments between sentence pairs. Their hypothesis was that sentence pairs with very few alignment points in the intersection would mostly likely not be parallel. This is based on the fact that when using GIZA++ (Och and Ney, 2003), the intersection of alignments is more sparse than the standard SMT symmetrization heuristics like grow-diag-final-and (Koehn, 2005).

Different from Stymne et al., our hypothesis for non-parallelness adheres to sentence level alignment criteria as defined in the Gale-Church algorithm (Gale and Church, 1993). If a sentence pair is parallel, the ratio of the number of characters in the source and target sentence should be coherent to the global ratio of the number of source-target characters in a fully parallel corpus. The Gale-Church algorithm had its parameters tuned to suit European languages and Tan (2013) had demonstrated that sentence-level alignments can be improved by using corpus specific parameters. When using variable parameters to the Gale-Church algorithm, Tan showed that instead of the default parameters set in the original Gale-Church algorithm, using mean ratio of the noisy corpus can also improve sentence level alignments although the ratio from a clean corpus would achieve even better alignments.

Given the premises of the sentence level alignment hypothesis, we clean the training corpus by first calculating the global mean ratio of the number of characters of source sentence to target sentence and then filter out sentence pairs that exceeds or fall below 20% of the global ratio. We call this method, `GaCha` filtering; this cleaning method is more aggressive than cleaning methods described by Stymne et al. but it filters out noisy sentence level alignments created by non-language specific parameters used by sentence aligners such as Gale-Church algorithm.

3.2 Filtering Noise in HindEnCorp

After manual inspection 100 random sentence pairs from the HindEnCorp (Bojar et al., 2014), we found that documents were often misaligned at sentence level or contains HTML special characters. To further reduce the noise in the HindEnCorp, the `Manawi` system was only trained a subset of the HindEnCorp from the following sources (i) DanielPipes, (ii) TIDES and (iii) EILMT. Lastly, we filtered the training data on allowing a maximum of 100 tokens per language per sentence.

Finally, the cleaned data contained 87,692 sentences, only ~36% of the original HindEnCorp training data.

4 System Setup

Data: To train the baseline translation model, we have used the cleaned subset of the data as described in Section 3. For the `Manawi` model, we added the NLP outputs from the MWE and NE extractors presented in Section 2. To train the monolingual language model, we used the Hindi sentences from the HindEnCorp.

System: We used the standard log-linear Phrase based SMT model provided from the MOSES toolkit.

Configuration: We experimented with various maximum phrase length for the translation and n-

[5] The exponent of cross-entropy may be regarded as perplexity

Manawi Submissions (EN-HI)	**BLEU**	**BLEU** (cased)	**TER**
PB-SMT + MWE + NE	**9.9**	7.1	0.869
PB-SMT + MWE + NE + Wiki (Manawi)	7.7	7.6	0.864
Manawi + GaCha Filter	8.9	**8.9**	0.818
Manawi + GaCha Filter + Handle OOV	8.8	8.8	0.800
Manawi + GaCha Filter + Remove OOV	8,9	8.8	**0.792**

Table 1: Manawi System Submissions @ WMT 2014 Translation Shared Task for English-Hindi

Manawi Submissions (HI-EN)	**BLEU**	**BLEU** (cased)	**TER**
PB-SMT + MWE + NE + Wiki (Manawi)	7.7	7.6	0.864
Manawi + GaCha Filter	**8.9**	**8.9**	**0.818**

Table 2: Manawi System Submissions @ WMT 2014 Translation Shared Task for Hindi-English

gram settings for the language model. And we found that using a *maximum phrase length of 5* and *4-gram language model* produced best result in terms of BLEU and TER for our baseline model (i.e. without the incorporation of outputs from the NLP tools). The other experimental settings were:

- *GIZA++* implementation of IBM word alignment model 4 with grow-diagonal-final-and heuristics for performing word alignment and phrase-extraction (Koehn et al., 2003)

- *Minimum Error Rate Training (MERT)* (Och, 2003) on a held-out development set, target language model with Kneser-Ney smoothing (Kneser and Ney, 1995) using language models trained with SRILM (Stolcke, 2002)

- Reordering model[6] was trained on bidirectional (i.e. using both forward and backward models) and conditioned on both source and target language. The reordering model is built by calculating the probabilities of the phrase pair being associated with the given orientation.

Innovation: We demonstrated the incorporation of multiple NLP tools outputs in the SMT pipline by simply using automatically extracted bilingual MWE and NEs as additional parallel data to the cleaned data and ran the translation and statistical model as per the baseline configurations.

[6]For reordering we used lexicalized reordering model, which consists of three different types of reordering by conditioning the orientation of previous and next phrases-monotone (m), swap (s) and discontinuous (d).

5 Post-processing

The MOSES decoder produces translations with Out-Of-Vocabulary (OOV) words that were not translated from the source language. The Manawi system post-processed the decoder output by (i) *handling OOV words* by replacing each OOV word with the most probable translation using the lexical files generated by GIZA++ and (ii) *removing OOV words* from the decoded outputs.

6 Results

Table 1 summarizes the Manawi system submissions for the English-Hindi language pair for WMT 2014 generic translation shared task. The basic Manawi system is a Phrase-based SMT (PB-SMT) setup using extracted MWE and NEs and Wikipedia titles as additional parallel data (i.e. PB-SMT+MWE+NE+Wiki in Table 1). The basic Manawi system achieved 7.7 BLEU score and 0.864 TER.

After filtering the data before training the translation model, the Manawi system performed better at 8.9 BLEU and 0.818 TER. By adding the post-processing component, we achieved the lowest TER score among competing team at 0.792.

7 Conclusion

The Manawi system showed how simple yet effective pre-processing and integration of output from NLP tools improves the performance of MT systems. Using GaCha filtering to remove noisy data and using automatically extracted MWE and NEs as additional parallel data improve word and phrasal alignments at the start of the MT pipeline which eventually improves the quality of machine translation. The best setup for the `Manawi` system achieved the best TER score among the competing system.

Also, the incremental improvements made by step-wise implementation of (i) filtering, (ii) incorporating outputs from NLP tools and (iii) post-processing showed that individual components of the `Manawi` can be integrated into other MT systems without detrimental effects.

Acknowledgments

The research leading to these results has received funding from the People Programme (Marie Curie Actions) of the European Union's Seventh Framework Programme FP7/2007-2013/ under REA grant agreement n ° 317471.

The authors of this paper also thank our colleagues Jörg Knappen and José M.M. Martínez for their help in setting up the server that made the `Manawi` system possible.

References

Amittai Axelrod, Xiaodong He, and Jianfeng Gao. 2011. Domain adaptation via pseudo in-domain data selection. In *Proceedings of the Conference on Empirical Methods in Natural Language Processing*, pages 355–362. Association for Computational Linguistics.

Ondřej Bojar, Vojtěch Diatka, Pavel Rychlý, Pavel Straňák, Aleš Tamchyna, and Dan Zeman. 2014. Hindi-English and Hindi-only Corpus for Machine Translation. In *Proceedings of the Ninth International Language Resources and Evaluation Conference (LREC'14)*, Reykjavik, Iceland, may. ELRA, European Language Resources Association. in prep.

Nadir Durrani, Barry Haddow, Kenneth Heafield, and Philipp Koehn. 2013. Edinburghs machine translation systems for european language pairs. In *Proceedings of the Eighth Workshop on Statistical Machine Translation*, pages 112–119.

Mark Alan Finlayson and Nidhi Kulkarni. 2011. Detecting multi-word expressions improves word sense disambiguation. In *Proceedings of the Workshop on Multiword Expressions: From Parsing and Generation to the Real World*, MWE '11, pages 20–24, Stroudsburg, PA, USA. Association for Computational Linguistics.

William A Gale and Kenneth W Church. 1993. A program for aligning sentences in bilingual corpora. *Computational linguistics*, 19(1):75–102.

Philipp Koehn, Hieu Hoang, Alexandra Birch, Chris Callison-Burch, Marcello Federico, Nicola Bertoldi, Brooke Cowan, Wade Shen, Christine Moran, Richard Zens, et al. 2007. Moses: Open source toolkit for statistical machine translation. In *Proceedings of the 45th Annual Meeting of the ACL on Interactive Poster and Demonstration Sessions*, pages 177–180. Association for Computational Linguistics.

Philipp Koehn. 2005. Europarl: A parallel corpus for statistical machine translation. *MT summit*, 5:79–86.

Patrik Lambert. 2005. Data inferred multi-word expressions for statistical machine translation. In *In MT Summit X*.

Robert C Moore and William Lewis. 2010. Intelligent selection of language model training data. In *Proceedings of the ACL 2010 Conference Short Papers*, pages 220–224. Association for Computational Linguistics.

Franz Josef Och and Hermann Ney. 2003. A systematic comparison of various statistical alignment models. *Computational linguistics*, 29(1):19–51.

Santanu Pal, Tanmoy Chakraborty, and Sivaji Bandyopadhyay. 2011. Handling multiword expressions in phrase-based statistical machine translation. In *In Proceedings of the 13th Machine Translation Summit*, pages 215–224. MT Summit 2011.

Santanu Pal, Mahammed Hasanuzzaman, Sudip Kumar Naskar, and Sivaji Bandyopadhyay. 2013. Impact of linguistically motivated shallow phrases in pb-smt. In *ICON 2013 http://sivajibandyopadhyay.com/publications/Icon-v1.3-camera.pdf*. ICON 2013.

Stephan Peitz, Jan-Thorsten Peter Saab Mansour, Christoph Schmidt, Joern Wuebker, Matthias Huck, Markus Freitag, and Hermann Ney. 2013. The rwth aachen machine translation system for wmt 2013. In *Proceedings of the Eighth Workshop on Statistical Machine Translation*, pages 191–197.

Dipti Misra Sharma Rajeev Sangal and Anil Kumar Singh, editors. 2008. *Proceedings of the IJCNLP-08 Workshop on Named Entity Recognition for South and South East Asian Languages*. Asian Federation of Natural Language Processing, Hyderabad, India, January.

Zhixiang Ren, Yajuan Lü, Jie Cao, Qun Liu, and Yun Huang. 2009. Improving statistical machine translation using domain bilingual multiword expressions. In *Proceedings of the Workshop on Multiword Expressions: Identification, Interpretation, Disambiguation and Applications*, MWE '09, pages 47–54, Stroudsburg, PA, USA. Association for Computational Linguistics.

Raphael Rubino, Antonio Toral, S Cortés Vaıllo, Jun Xie, Xiaofeng Wu, Stephen Doherty, and Qun Liu. 2013. The cngl-dcu-prompsit translation systems for wmt13. In *Proceedings of the Eighth Workshop on Statistical Machine Translation*, pages 211–216.

Ivan A Sag, Timothy Baldwin, Francis Bond, Ann Copestake, and Dan Flickinger. 2002. Multiword expressions: A pain in the neck for nlp. In *Computational Linguistics and Intelligent Text Processing*, pages 1–15. Springer Berlin Heidelberg.

Pal Santanu, Sudip Kumar Naskar, Pavel Pecina, Sivaji Bandyopadhyay, and Andy Way. 2010. Handling named entities and compound verbs in phrase-based statistical machine translation. In *23rd International Conference of Computational Linguistics (Coling 2010), Beijing, Chaina*, pages 46–54.

Sara Stymne, Christian Hardmeier, Jörg Tiedemann, and Joakim Nivre. 2013. Tunable distortion limits and corpus cleaning for smt. In *Proceedings of the Eighth Workshop on Statistical Machine Translation*, pages 225–231.

Liling Tan and Francis Bond. 2013. Xling: Matching query sentences to a parallel corpus using topic models for word sense disambiguation.

Liling Tan. 2013. Gachalign: Gale-church sentence-level alignments with variable parameters [software]. Retrieved from https://db.tt/LLrul4zP and https://code.google.com/p/gachalign/.

Antonio Toral. 2013. Hybrid selection of language model training data using linguistic information and perplexity. *ACL 2013*, page 8.

Olga Vechtomova. 2005. The role of multi-word units in interactive information retrieval. In *ECIR*, pages 403–420.

Sriram Venkatapathy and Aravind K Joshi. 2006. Using information about multi-word expressions for the word-alignment task. In *Proceedings of the Workshop on Multiword Expressions: Identifying and Exploiting Underlying Properties*, pages 20–27. Association for Computational Linguistics.

Edinburgh's Syntax-Based Systems at WMT 2014

Philip Williams[1], Rico Sennrich[1], Maria Nadejde[1],
Matthias Huck[1], Eva Hasler[1], Philipp Koehn[1,2]
[1]School of Informatics, University of Edinburgh
[2]Center for Speech and Language Processing, The Johns Hopkins University

Abstract

This paper describes the string-to-tree systems built at the University of Edinburgh for the WMT 2014 shared translation task. We developed systems for English-German, Czech-English, French-English, German-English, Hindi-English, and Russian-English. This year we improved our English-German system through target-side compound splitting, morphosyntactic constraints, and refinements to parse tree annotation; we addressed the out-of-vocabulary problem using transliteration for Hindi and Russian and using morphological reduction for Russian; we improved our German-English system through tree binarization; and we reduced system development time by filtering the tuning sets.

1 Introduction

For this year's WMT shared translation task we built syntax-based systems for six language pairs:

- English-German
- Czech-English
- French-English
- German-English
- Hindi-English
- Russian-English

As last year (Nadejde et al., 2013), our systems are based on the string-to-tree pipeline implemented in the Moses toolkit (Koehn et al., 2007).

We paid particular attention to the production of grammatical German, trying various parsers and incorporating target-side compound splitting and morphosyntactic constraints; for Hindi and Russian, we employed the new Moses transliteration model to handle out-of-vocabulary words; and for German to English, we experimented with tree binarization, obtaining good results from right binarization.

We also present our first syntax-based results for French-English, the scale of which defeated us last year. This year we were able to train a system using all available training data, a task that was made considerably easier through principled filtering of the tuning set. Although our system was not ready in time for human evaluation, we present BLEU scores in this paper.

In addition to the five single-system submissions described here, we also contributed our English-German and German-English systems for use in the collaborative EU-BRIDGE system combination effort (Freitag et al., 2014).

This paper is organised as follows. In Section 2 we describe the core setup that is common to all systems. In subsequent sections we describe language-pair specific variations and extensions. For each language pair, we present results for both the development test set (newstest2013 in most cases) and for the filtered test set (newstest2014) that was provided after the system submission deadline. We refer to these as 'devtest' and 'test', respectively.

2 System Overview

2.1 Pre-processing

The training data was normalized using the WMT `normalize-punctuation.perl` script then tokenized and truecased. Where the target language was English, we used the Moses tokenizer's `-penn` option, which uses a tokenization scheme that more closely matches that of the parser. For the English-German system we used the default Moses tokenization scheme, which is similar to that of the German parsers.

For the systems that translate into English, we used the Berkeley parser (Petrov et al., 2006; Petrov and Klein, 2007) to parse the target-side of the training corpus. As we will describe in Section 3, we tried a variety of parsers for German.

We did not perform any corpus filtering other than the standard Moses method, which removes

Proceedings of the Ninth Workshop on Statistical Machine Translation, pages 207–214,
Baltimore, Maryland USA, June 26–27, 2014.

sentence pairs with dubious length ratios and sentence pairs where parsing fails for the target-side sentence.

2.2 Translation Model

Our translation grammar is a synchronous context-free grammar (SCFG) with phrase-structure labels on the target side and the generic non-terminal label X on the source side.

The grammar was extracted from the word-aligned parallel data using the Moses implementation (Williams and Koehn, 2012) of the GHKM algorithm (Galley et al., 2004; Galley et al., 2006). For word alignment we used MGIZA++ (Gao and Vogel, 2008), a multi-threaded implementation of GIZA++ (Och and Ney, 2003).

Minimal GHKM rules were composed into larger rules subject to parameterized restrictions on size defined in terms of the resulting target tree fragment. A good choice of parameter settings depends on the annotation style of the target-side parse trees. We used the settings shown in Table 1, which were chosen empirically during the development of last years' systems:

Parameter	Value
Rule depth	5
Node count	20
Rule size	5

Table 1: Parameter settings for rule composition.

Further to the restrictions on rule composition, fully non-lexical unary rules were eliminated using the method described in Chung et al. (2011) and rules with scope greater than 3 (Hopkins and Langmead, 2010) were pruned from the translation grammar. Scope pruning makes parsing tractable without the need for grammar binarization.

2.3 Language Model

We used all available monolingual data to train 5-gram language models. Language models for each monolingual corpus were trained using the SRILM toolkit (Stolcke, 2002) with modified Kneser-Ney smoothing (Chen and Goodman, 1998) and then interpolated using weights tuned to minimize perplexity on the development set.

2.4 Feature Functions

Our feature functions are unchanged from the previous two years. They include the n-gram language model probability of the derivation's target yield, its word count, and various scores for the synchronous derivation.

Each grammar rule has a number of pre-computed scores. For a grammar rule r of the form

$$C \rightarrow \langle \alpha, \beta, \sim \rangle$$

where C is a target-side non-terminal label, α is a string of source terminals and non-terminals, β is a string of target terminals and non-terminals, and $\sim$ is a one-to-one correspondence between source and target non-terminals, we score the rule according to the following functions:

- $p\left(C, \beta \mid \alpha, \sim\right)$ and $p\left(\alpha \mid C, \beta, \sim\right)$, the direct and indirect translation probabilities.
- $p_{lex}\left(\beta \mid \alpha\right)$ and $p_{lex}\left(\alpha \mid \beta\right)$, the direct and indirect lexical weights (Koehn et al., 2003).
- $p_{pcfg}\left(\pi\right)$, the monolingual PCFG probability of the tree fragment π from which the rule was extracted.
- $\exp(-1/count(r))$, a rule rareness penalty.
- $\exp(1)$, a rule penalty. The main grammar and glue grammars have distinct penalty features.

2.5 Tuning

The feature weights were tuned using the Moses implementation of MERT (Och, 2003) for all systems except English-to-German, for which we used k-best MIRA (Cherry and Foster, 2012) due to the larger number of features.

We used tuning sentences drawn from all of the previous years' test sets (except newstest2013, which was used as the development test set). In order to speed up the tuning process, we used subsets of the full tuning sets with sentence pairs up to length 30 (Max-30) and further applied a filtering technique to reduce the tuning set size to 2,000 sentence pairs for the language pairs involving German, French and Czech[1]. We also experimented with random subsets of size 2,000.

For the filtering technique, we make the assumption that finding suitable weights for all the feature functions requires the optimizer to see a range of feature values and to see hypotheses that can partially match the reference translations in order to rank the hypotheses. For example, if a

[1]For Russian and Hindi, the development sets are smaller and no filtering was applied.

tuning example contains many out-of-vocabulary words or is difficult to translate for other reasons, this will result in low quality translation hypotheses and provide the system with little evidence for which features are useful to produce good translations. Therefore, we select high quality examples using a smooth version of sentence-BLEU computed on the 1-best output of a single decoder run on the development set. Standard sentence-BLEU tends to select short examples because they are more likely to have perfect n-gram matches with the reference translation. Very short sentence pairs are less informative for tuning but also tend to have more extreme source-target length ratios which can affect the weight of the word penalty. Thus, we penalize short examples by padding the decoder output with a fixed number of non-matching tokens[2] to the left and right before computing sentence-BLEU. This has the effect of reducing the precision of short sentences against the reference translation while affecting longer sentences proportionally less. Experiments on phrase-based systems have shown that the resulting tuning sets are of comparable diversity as randomly selected sets in terms of their feature vectors and maintain BLEU scores in comparison with tuning on the entire development set.

Table 2 shows the size of the full tuning sets and the size of the subsets with up to length 30, Table 3 shows the results of tuning with different sets. Reducing the tuning sets to Max-30 results in a speed-up in tuning time but affects the performance on some of the devtest/test sets (mostly for Czech-English). However, tuning on the full set took more than 18 days using 12 cores for German-English which is not feasible when trying out several model variations. Further filtering these subsets to a size of 2,000 sentence pairs as described above maintains the BLEU scores in most cases and even improves the scores in some cases. This indicates that the quality of the selected examples is more important than the total number of tuning examples. However, the experiments with random subsets from Max-30 show that random selection also yields results which improve over the results with Max-30 in most cases, though are not always as good as with the filtered sets.[3] The filtered tuning sets yield reasonable performance compared to the full tuning sets except for the German-English devtest set where performance drops by 0.5 BLEU[4].

Tuning set	Cs-En	En-De	De-En
Full	13,055	13,071	13,071
Max-30	10,392	9,151	10,610

Table 2: Size of full tuning sets and with sentence length up to 30.

	devtest		
Tuning set	Cs-En	En-De	De-En
Full	25.1	19.9	26.7
Max-30	24.7	19.8	26.2
Filtered	24.9	19.8	26.2
Random	24.8	19.7	26.4

	test		
Tuning set	Cs-En	En-De	De-En
Full	27.5	19.2	26.9
Max-30	27.2	19.2	27.0
Filtered	27.5	19.1	27.2
Random	27.3	19.4	27.0

Table 3: BLEU results on devtest and test sets with different tuning sets: Full, Max-30, filtered subsets of Max-30 and average of three random subsets of Max-30 (size of filtered/random subsets: 2,000).

3 English to German

We use the projective output of the dependency parser ParZu (Sennrich et al., 2013) for the syntactic annotation of our primary submission. Contrastive systems were built with other parsers: BitPar (Schmid, 2004), the German Stanford Parser (Rafferty and Manning, 2008), and the German Berkeley Parser (Petrov and Klein, 2007; Petrov and Klein, 2008).

The set of syntactic labels provided by ParZu has been refined to reduce overgeneralization phenomena. Specifically, we disambiguate the labels ROOT (used for the root of a sentence, but also commas, punctuation marks, and sentence fragments), KON and CJ (coordinations of different constituents), and GMOD (pre- or postmodifying genitive modifier).

[2]These can be arbitrary tokens that do not match any reference token.

[3]For random subsets from the full tuning set the performance was similar but resulted in standard deviations of up to 0.36 across three random sets.

[4]Note however that due to the long tuning times, we are reporting single tuning runs.

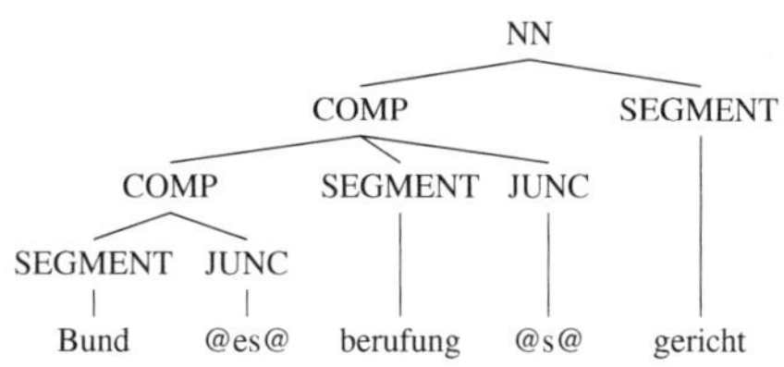

Figure 1: Syntactic representation of split compound *Bundesberufungsgericht* (Engl: *federal appeals court*).

We discriminatively learn non-terminal labels for unknown words using sparse features, rather than estimating a probability distribution of non-terminal labels from singleton statistics in the training corpus.

We perform target-side compound splitting, using a hybrid method described by Fritzinger and Fraser (2010) that combines a finite-state morphology and corpus statistics. As finite-state morphology analyzer, we use Zmorge (Sennrich and Kunz, 2014). An original contribution of our experiments is a syntactic representation of split compounds which eliminates typical problems with target-side compound splitting, namely erroneous reorderings and compound merging. We represent split compounds as a syntactic tree with the last segment as head, preceded by a modifier. A modifier consists of an optional modifier, a segment and a (possibly empty) joining element. An example is shown in Figure 1. This hierarchical representation ensures that compounds can be easily merged in post-processing (by removing the spaces and special characters around joining elements), and that no segments are placed outside of a compound in the translation.

We use unification-based constraints to model morphological agreement within German noun phrases, and between subjects and verbs (Williams and Koehn, 2011). Additionally, we add constraints that operate on the internal tree structure of the translation hypotheses, to enforce several syntactic constraints that were frequently violated in the baseline system:

- correct subcategorization of auxiliary/modal verbs in regards to the inflection of the full verb.
- passive clauses are not allowed to have accusative objects.

system	BLEU devtest	BLEU test
Stanford Parser	19.0	18.3
Berkeley Parser	19.3	18.6
BitPar	19.5	18.6
ParZu	19.6	19.1
+ modified label set	19.8	19.1
+ discriminative UNK weights	19.9	19.2
+ German compound splitting	20.0	19.8
+ grammatical constraints	20.2	20.1

Table 4: English to German translation results on devtest (newstest2013) and test (newstest2014) sets.

- relative clauses must contain a relative (or interrogative) pronoun in their first constituent.

Table 4 shows BLEU scores with systems trained with different parsers, and for our extensions of the baseline system.

4 Czech to English

For Czech to English we used the core setup described in Section 2 without modification. Table 5 shows the BLEU scores.

system	BLEU devtest	BLEU test
baseline	24.8	27.0

Table 5: Czech to English results on the devtest (newstest2013) and test (newstest2014) sets.

5 French to English

For French to English, alignment of the parallel corpus was performed using *fast_align* (Dyer et al., 2013) instead of MGIZA++ due to the large volume of parallel data.

Table 6 shows BLEU scores for the system and Table 7 shows the resulting grammar sizes after filtering for the evaluation sets.

system	BLEU devtest	BLEU test
baseline	29.4	32.3

Table 6: French to English results on the devtest (newsdev2013) and test (newstest2014) sets.

system	devtest	test
baseline	86,341,766	88,657,327

Table 7: Grammar sizes of the French to English system after filtering for the devtest (newstest2013) and test (newstest2014) sets.

6 German to English

German compounds were split using the script provided with Moses.

For training the primary system, the target parse trees were restructured before rule extraction by *right binarization*. Since binarization strategies increase the tree depth and number of nodes by adding virtual non-terminals, we increased the extraction parameters to: *Rule Depth = 7, Node Count = 100, Rule Size = 7*. A thorough investigation of binarization methods for restructuring Penn Treebank style trees was carried out by Wang et al. (2007).

Table 8 shows BLEU scores for the baseline system and two systems employing different binarization strategies. Table 9 shows the resulting grammar sizes after filtering for the evaluation sets. Results on the development set showed no improvement when *left binarization* was used for restructuring the trees, although the grammar size increased significantly.

	BLEU	
system	devtest	test
baseline	26.2	27.2
+ right binarization (primary)	26.8	28.2
+ left binarization	26.3	-

Table 8: German to English results on the devtest (newsdev2013) and test (newstest2014) sets.

system	devtest	test
baseline	11,462,976	13,811,304
+ right binarization	24,851,982	29,133,910
+ left binarization	21,387,976	-

Table 9: Grammar sizes of the German to English systems after filtering for the devtest (newstest2013) and test (newstest2014) sets.

7 Hindi to English

English-Hindi has the least parallel training data of this year's language pairs. Out-of-vocabulary (OOV) input words are therefore a comparatively large source of translation error: in the devtest set (newsdev2014) and filtered test set (newstest2014) the average OOV rates are 1.08 and 1.16 unknown words per sentence, respectively.

Assuming a significant fraction of OOV words to be named entities and thus amenable to transliteration, we applied the post-processing transliteration method described in Durrani et al. (2014) and implemented in Moses. In brief, this is an unsupervised method that i) uses EM to induce a corpus of transliteration examples from the parallel training data; ii) learns a monotone character-level phrase-based SMT model from the transliteration corpus; and iii) substitutes transliterations for OOVs in the system output by using the monolingual language model and other features to select between transliteration candidates.[5]

Table 10 shows BLEU scores with and without transliteration on the devtest and filtered test sets. Due to a bug in the submitted system, the language model trained on the HindEnCorp corpus was used for transliteration candidate selection rather than the full interpolated language model. This was fixed subsequent to submission.

	BLEU	
system	devtest	test
baseline	12.9	14.7
+ transliteration (submission)	13.3	15.1
+ transliteration (fixed)	13.6	15.5

Table 10: Hindi to English results with and without transliteration on the devtest (newsdev2014) and test (newstest2014) sets.

Transliteration increased 1-gram precision from 48.1% to 49.4% for devtest and from 49.1% to 50.6% for test. Of the 2,913 OOV words in test, 938 (32.2%) of transliterations exactly match the reference. Manual inspection reveals that there are also many near matches. For instance, transliteration produces *Bernat Jackie* where the reference is *Jacqui Barnat*.

8 Russian to English

Compared to Hindi-English, the Russian-English language pair has over six times as much parallel data. Nonetheless, OOVs remain a problem: the average OOV rates are approximately half those

[5] This is the variant referred to as Method 2 in Durrani et al. (2014).

of Hindi-English, at 0.47 and 0.51 unknown words per sentence for the devtest (newstest2013) and filtered test (newstest2014) sets, respectively. We address this in part using the same transliteration method as for Hindi-English.

Data sparsity issues for this language pair are exacerbated by the rich inflectional morphology of Russian. Many Russian word forms express grammatical distinctions that are either absent from English translations (like grammatical gender) or are expressed by different means (like grammatical function being expressed through syntactic configuration rather than case). We adopt the widely-used approach of simplifying morphologically-complex source forms to remove distinctions that we believe to be redundant. Our method is similar to that of Weller et al. (2013) except that ours is much more conservative (in their experiments, Weller et al. (2013) found morphological reduction to harm translation indicating that useful information was likely to have been discarded).

We used TreeTagger (Schmid, 1994) to obtain a lemma-tag pair for each Russian word. The tag specifies the word class and various morphosyntactic feature values. For example, the adjective республиканская ('republican') gets the lemma-tag pair республиканский + `Afpfsnf`, where the code A indicates the word class and the remaining codes indicate values for the type, degree, gender, number, case, and definiteness features.

Like Weller et al. (2013), we selectively replaced surface forms with their lemmas and reduced tags, reducing tags through feature deletion. We restricted morphological reduction to adjectives and verbs, leaving all other word forms unchanged. Table 11 shows the features that were deleted. We focused on contextual inflection, making the assumption that inflectional distinctions required by agreement alone were the least likely to be useful for translation (since the same information was marked elsewhere in the sentence) and also the most likely to be the source of 'spurious' variation.

Table 12 shows the BLEU scores for Russian-English with transliteration and morphological reduction. The effect of transliteration was smaller than for Hindi-English, as might be expected from the lower baseline OOV rate. 1-gram precision increased from 57.1% to 57.6% for devtest and from 62.9% to 63.6% for test. Morphological reduction decreased the initial OOV rates by 3.5% and 4.1% on the devtest and filtered test sets. After both morphological and transliteration the 1-gram precisions for devtest and test were 57.7% and 63.8%.

Adjective		Verb	
Type	✗	Type	✗
Degree	✓	VForm	✓
Gender	✗	Tense	✓
Number	✗	Person	✓
Case	✗	Number	✓
Definiteness	✗	Gender	✗
		Voice	✓
		Definiteness	✗
		Aspect	✓
		Case	✓

Table 11: Feature values that are retained (✓) or deleted (✗) during morphological reduction of Russian.

	BLEU	
system	devtest	test
baseline	23.3	29.7
+ transliteration	23.7	30.3
+ morphological reduction	23.8	30.3

Table 12: Russian to English results on the devtest (newstest2013) and test (newstest2014) sets.

9 Conclusion

We have described Edinburgh's syntax-based systems in the WMT 2014 shared translation task. Building upon the already-strong string-to-tree systems developed for previous years' shared translation tasks, we have achieved substantial improvements over our baseline setup: we improved translation into German through target-side compound splitting, morphosyntactic constraints, and refinements to parse tree annotation; we have addressed unknown words using transliteration (for Hindi and Russian) and morphological reduction (for Russian); and we have improved our German-English system through tree binarization.

Acknowledgements

The research leading to these results has received funding from the European Union Seventh Framework Programme (FP7/2007-2013) under grant agreement n° 287658 (EU-BRIDGE).

Rico Sennrich has received funding from the Swiss National Science Foundation under grant P2ZHP1_148717.

References

Stanley F. Chen and Joshua Goodman. 1998. An empirical study of smoothing techniques for language modeling. Technical report, Harvard University.

Colin Cherry and George Foster. 2012. Batch tuning strategies for statistical machine translation. In *Proceedings of the 2012 Conference of the North American Chapter of the Association for Computational Linguistics: Human Language Technologies*, pages 427–436, Montréal, Canada, June. Association for Computational Linguistics.

Tagyoung Chung, Licheng Fang, and Daniel Gildea. 2011. Issues concerning decoding with synchronous context-free grammar. In *Proceedings of the 49th Annual Meeting of the Association for Computational Linguistics: Human Language Technologies*, pages 413–417, Portland, Oregon, USA, June.

Nadir Durrani, Hassan Sajjad, Hieu Hoang, and Philipp Koehn. 2014. Integrating an Unsupervised Transliteration Model into Statistical Machine Translation. In *Proceedings of the 15th Conference of the European Chapter of the ACL (EACL 2014)*, Gothenburg, Sweden, April. To appear.

Chris Dyer, Victor Chahuneau, and Noah A. Smith. 2013. A simple, fast, and effective reparameterization of ibm model 2. In *In Proc. NAACL/HLT 2013*, pages 644–648.

Markus Freitag, Stephan Peitz, Joern Wuebker, Hermann Ney, Matthias Huck, Rico Sennrich, Nadir Durrani, Maria Nadejde, Philip Williams, Philipp Koehn, Teresa Herrmann, Eunah Cho, and Alex Waibel. 2014. EU-BRIDGE MT: Combined Machine Translation. In *Proceedings of the ACL 2014 Ninth Workshop on Statistical Machine Translation*, Baltimore, MD, USA, June.

Fabienne Fritzinger and Alexander Fraser. 2010. How to Avoid Burning Ducks: Combining Linguistic Analysis and Corpus Statistics for German Compound Processing. In *Proceedings of the Joint Fifth Workshop on Statistical Machine Translation and MetricsMATR*, WMT '10, pages 224–234, Uppsala, Sweden.

Michel Galley, Mark Hopkins, Kevin Knight, and Daniel Marcu. 2004. What's in a Translation Rule? In *HLT-NAACL '04*.

Michel Galley, Jonathan Graehl, Kevin Knight, Daniel Marcu, Steve DeNeefe, Wei Wang, and Ignacio Thayer. 2006. Scalable inference and training of context-rich syntactic translation models. In *ACL-44: Proceedings of the 21st International Conference on Computational Linguistics and the 44th annual meeting of the Association for Computational Linguistics*, pages 961–968, Morristown, NJ, USA.

Qin Gao and Stephan Vogel. 2008. Parallel implementations of word alignment tool. In *Software Engineering, Testing, and Quality Assurance for Natural Language Processing*, SETQA-NLP '08, pages 49–57, Stroudsburg, PA, USA.

Mark Hopkins and Greg Langmead. 2010. SCFG decoding without binarization. In *Proceedings of the 2010 Conference on Empirical Methods in Natural Language Processing*, pages 646–655, Cambridge, MA, October.

Philipp Koehn, Franz Josef Och, and Daniel Marcu. 2003. Statistical phrase-based translation. In *NAACL '03: Proceedings of the 2003 Conference of the North American Chapter of the Association for Computational Linguistics on Human Language Technology*, pages 48–54, Morristown, NJ, USA.

Philipp Koehn, Hieu Hoang, Alexandra Birch, Chris Callison-Burch, Marcello Federico, Nicola Bertoldi, Brooke Cowan, Wade Shen, Christine Moran, Richard Zens, Chris Dyer, Ondřej Bojar, Alexandra Constantin, and Evan Herbst. 2007. Moses: open source toolkit for statistical machine translation. In *Proceedings of the 45th Annual Meeting of the ACL on Interactive Poster and Demonstration Sessions*, ACL '07, pages 177–180, Morristown, NJ, USA. Association for Computational Linguistics.

Maria Nadejde, Philip Williams, and Philipp Koehn. 2013. Edinburgh's Syntax-Based Machine Translation Systems. In *Proceedings of the Eighth Workshop on Statistical Machine Translation*, pages 170–176, Sofia, Bulgaria, August.

Franz Josef Och and Hermann Ney. 2003. A systematic comparison of various statistical alignment models. *Comput. Linguist.*, 29(1):19–51, March.

Franz Josef Och. 2003. Minimum error rate training in statistical machine translation. In *Proceedings of the 41st Annual Meeting on Association for Computational Linguistics - Volume 1*, ACL '03, pages 160–167, Morristown, NJ, USA.

Slav Petrov and Dan Klein. 2007. Improved Inference for Unlexicalized Parsing. In *Human Language Technologies 2007: The Conference of the North American Chapter of the Association for Computational Linguistics; Proceedings of the Main Conference*, pages 404–411, Rochester, New York, April.

Slav Petrov and Dan Klein. 2008. Parsing German with Latent Variable Grammars. In *Proceedings of the Workshop on Parsing German at ACL '08*, pages 33–39, Columbus, OH, USA, June.

Slav Petrov, Leon Barrett, Romain Thibaux, and Dan Klein. 2006. Learning accurate, compact, and interpretable tree annotation. In *Proceedings of the 21st International Conference on Computational Linguistics and the 44th annual meeting of the Association for Computational Linguistics*, ACL-44, pages 433–440.

Anna N. Rafferty and Christopher D. Manning. 2008. Parsing Three German Treebanks: Lexicalized and Unlexicalized Baselines. In *Proceedings of the*

Workshop on Parsing German at ACL '08, pages 40–46, Columbus, OH, USA, June.

Helmut Schmid. 1994. Probabilistic part-of-speech tagging using decision trees. In *International Conference on New Methods in Language Processing*, pages 44–49, Manchester, UK.

Helmut Schmid. 2004. Efficient Parsing of Highly Ambiguous Context-Free Grammars with Bit Vectors. In *Proc. of the Int. Conf. on Computational Linguistics (COLING)*, Geneva, Switzerland, August.

Rico Sennrich and Beat Kunz. 2014. Zmorge: A German Morphological Lexicon Extracted from Wiktionary. In *Proceedings of the 9th International Conference on Language Resources and Evaluation (LREC 2014)*, Reykjavik, Iceland, May.

Rico Sennrich, Martin Volk, and Gerold Schneider. 2013. Exploiting Synergies Between Open Resources for German Dependency Parsing, POS-tagging, and Morphological Analysis. In *Proceedings of the International Conference Recent Advances in Natural Language Processing 2013*, pages 601–609, Hissar, Bulgaria.

Andreas Stolcke. 2002. SRILM - an extensible language modeling toolkit. In *Intl. Conf. Spoken Language Processing, Denver, Colorado, September 2002*.

Wei Wang, Kevin Knight, Daniel Marcu, and Marina Rey. 2007. Binarizing Syntax Trees to Improve Syntax-Based Machine Translation Accuracy. In *Joint Conference on Empirical Methods in Natural Language Processing and Computational Natural Language Learning*, pages 746–754.

Marion Weller, Max Kisselew, Svetlana Smekalova, Alexander Fraser, Helmut Schmid, Nadir Durrani, Hassan Sajjad, and Richárd Farkas. 2013. Munich-Edinburgh-Stuttgart submissions at WMT13: Morphological and syntactic processing for SMT. In *Proceedings of the Eighth Workshop on Statistical Machine Translation*, pages 232–239, Sofia, Bulgaria, August.

Philip Williams and Philipp Koehn. 2011. Agreement Constraints for Statistical Machine Translation into German. In *Proceedings of the Sixth Workshop on Statistical Machine Translation*, pages 217–226, Edinburgh, Scotland, July.

Philip Williams and Philipp Koehn. 2012. GHKM Rule Extraction and Scope-3 Parsing in Moses. In *Proceedings of the Seventh Workshop on Statistical Machine Translation*, pages 388–394, Montréal, Canada, June.

DCU-Lingo24 Participation in WMT 2014 Hindi-English Translation task

Xiaofeng Wu, Rejwanul Haque*, Tsuyoshi Okita
Piyush Arora, Andy Way, Qun Liu
CNGL, Centre for Global Intelligent Content
School of Computing, Dublin City University
Dublin 9, Ireland
{xf.wu,tokita,parora,away,qliu}@computing.dcu.ie
*Lingo24, Edinburgh, UK
rejwanul.haque@lingo24.com

Abstract

This paper describes the DCU-Lingo24 submission to WMT 2014 for the Hindi-English translation task. We exploit miscellaneous methods in our system, including: Context-Informed PB-SMT, OOV Word Conversion (OWC), Multi-Alignment Combination (MAC), Operation Sequence Model (OSM), Stemming Align and Normal Phrase Extraction (SANPE), and Language Model Interpolation (LMI). We also describe various pre-processing steps we tried for Hindi in this task.

1 Introduction

This paper describes the DCU-Lingo24 submission to WMT 2014 for the Hindi-English translation task.

All our experiments on WMT 2014 are built upon the Moses phrase-based model (PB-SMT) (Koehn et al., 2007) and tuned with MERT (Och, 2003). Starting from this baseline system, we exploit various methods including Context-Informed PB-SMT (CIPBSMT), zero-shot learning (Palatucci et al., 2009) using neural network-based language modelling (Bengio et al., 2000; Mikolov et al., 2013) for OOV word conversion, various lexical reordering models (Axelrod et al., 2005; Galley and Manning, 2008), various Multiple Alignment Combination (MAC) (Tu et al., 2012), Operation Sequence Model (OSM) (Durrani et al., 2011) and Language Model Interpolation(LMI).

In the next section, the preprocessing steps are explained. In Section 3 a detailed explanation of the technique we exploit is provided. Then in Section 4, we provide our experimental results and resultant discussion.

2 Pre-processing Steps

We use all the training data provided for Hindi–English translation. Following Bojar et al. (2010), we apply a number of normalisation methods on the Hindi corpus. The HindEnCorp parallel corpus compiles several sources of parallel data. We observe that the source-side (Hindi) of the TIDES data source contains font-related noise, i.e. many Hindi sentences are a mixture of two different encodings: UTF-8[1] and WX[2] notations. We prepared a WX-to-UTF-8 font conversion script for Hindi which converts all WX encoded characters into UTF-8, thus removing all WX encoding appearing in the TIDES data.

We also observe that a portion of the English training corpus contained the following bracket-like sequences of characters: -LRB-, -LSB-, -LCB-, -RRB-, -RSB-, and -RCB-.[3] For consistency, those character sequences in the training data were replaced by the corresponding brackets.

For English – both monolingual and the target side of the bilingual data – we perform tokenization, normalization of punctuation, and truecasing. For parallel training data, we filter sentences pairs containing more than 80 tokens on either side and

[1] http://en.wikipedia.org/wiki/UTF-8
[2] http://en.wikipedia.org/wiki/WX_notation
[3] The acronyms stand for (Left | Right) (Round | Square | Curly) Bracket.

Proceedings of the Ninth Workshop on Statistical Machine Translation, pages 215–220,
Baltimore, Maryland USA, June 26–27, 2014.

sentence pairs with length difference larger than 3 times.

3 Techniques Deployed

3.1 Combination of Various Lexical Reordering Model (LRM)

Clearly, Hindi and English have quite different word orders, so we adopt three lexical reordering models to address this problem. They are word-based LRM and phrase-based LRM, which mainly focus on local reordering phenomena, and hierarchical phrase-based LRM, which mainly focuses on longer distance reordering (Galley and Manning, 2008).

3.2 Operation Sequence Model

The Operation Sequence Model (OSM) of Durrani et al. (2011) defines four translation operations: Generate(X,Y), Continue Source Concept, Generate Source Only (X) and Generate Identical, as well as three reordering operations: Insert Gap, Jump Back(W) and Jump Forward.

The probability of an operation sequence $O = (o_1 o_2 \cdots o_J)$ is calculated as in (1):

$$p(O) = \prod_{j=1}^{J} p(o_j | o_{j-n+1} \cdots o_{j-1}) \quad (1)$$

where n indicates the number of previous operations used.

We employ a 9-order OSM in our framework.

3.3 Language Model Interpolation (LMI)

We build a large language model by including data from the English Gigaword fifth edition, the English side of the UN corpus, the English side of the 10^9 French–English corpus and the English side of the Hindi–English parallel data provided by the organisers. We interpolate language models trained using each dataset, with the monolingual data provided split into three parts (news 2007-2013, Europarl (**?**) and news commentary) and the weights tuned to minimize perplexity on the target side of the devset.

The language models in our systems are trained with SRILM (Stolcke, 2002). We train a 5-gram model with Kneser-Ney discounting (Chen and Goodman, 1996).

3.4 Context-informed PB-SMT

Haque et al. (2011) express a context-dependent phrase translation as a multi-class classification problem, where a source phrase with given additional context information is classified into a distribution over possible target phrases. The size of this distribution needs to be limited, and would ideally omit irrelevant target phrase translations that the standard PB-SMT (Koehn et al., 2003) approach would normally include. Following Haque et al. (2011), we derive a context-informed feature $\hat{h}_{\text{mbl}}$ that is expressed as the conditional probability of the target phrase $\hat{e}_k$ given the source phrase $\hat{f}_k$ and its context information (CI), as in (2):

$$\hat{h}_{\text{mbl}} = \log \text{P}(\hat{e}_k | \hat{f}_k, \text{CI}(\hat{f}_k)) \quad (2)$$

Here, CI may include any feature that can provide useful information to disambiguate the given source phrase. In our experiment, we use CCG supertag (Steedman, 2000) as a contextual features. CCG supertag expresses the specific syntactic behaviour of a word in terms of the arguments it takes, and more generally the syntactic environment in which it appears.

We consider the CCG supertags of the context words, as well as of the focus phrase itself. In our model, the supertag of a multi-word focus phrase is the concatenation of the supertags of the words composing that phrase. We generate a window of size $2l + 1$ features (we set l:=2), including the concatenated complex supertag of the focus phrase. Accordingly, the supertag-based contextual information (CI_{st}) is described as in (3):

$$\begin{aligned}\text{CI}_{\text{st}}(\hat{f}_k) = \{&\text{st}(f_{i_k-l}), ..., \text{st}(f_{i_k-1}), \text{st}(\hat{f}_k), \\ &\text{st}(f_{j_k+1}), ..., \text{st}(f_{j_k+l})\}\end{aligned} \quad (3)$$

For the Hindi-to-English translation task, we use part-of-speech (PoS) tags[4] of the source phrase and the neighbouring words as the contextual feature, owing to the fact that supertaggers are readily available only for English.

We use a memory-based machine learning (MBL) classifier (TRIBL: (Daelemans, 2005))[5] that is able to estimate $\text{P}(\hat{e}_k | \hat{f}_k, \text{CI}(\hat{f}_k))$ by similarity-based reasoning over memorized nearest-neighbour examples of source–target phrase translations. Thus, we derive the feature $\hat{h}_{\text{mbl}}$ defined in Equation (2). In addition to $\hat{h}_{\text{mbl}}$,

[4] In order to obtain PoS tags of Hindi words, we used the LTRC shallow parser for Hindi from http://ltrc.iiit.ac.in/analyzer/hindi/shallow-parser-hin-4.0.fc8.tar.gz.

[5] An implementation of TRIBL is freely available as part of the TiMBL software package, which can be downloaded from http://ilk.uvt.nl/timbl.

we derive a simple two-valued feature $\hat{h}_{\text{best}}$, defined in Equation (4):

$$\hat{h}_{\text{best}} = \begin{cases} 1 & \text{if } \hat{e}_k \text{ maximizes } \mathrm{P}(\hat{e}_k | \hat{f}_k, \mathrm{CI}(\hat{f}_k)) \\ \approxeq 0 & \text{otherwise} \end{cases} \tag{4}$$

where $\hat{h}_{\text{best}}$ is set to 1 when $\hat{e}_k$ is one of the target phrases with highest probability according to $\mathrm{P}(\hat{e}_k | \hat{f}_k, \mathrm{CI}(\hat{f}_k))$ for each source phrase $\hat{f}_k$; otherwise $\hat{h}_{\text{best}}$ is set to 0.000001. We performed experiments by integrating these two features $\hat{h}_{\text{mbl}}$ and $\hat{h}_{\text{best}}$ directly into the log-linear model of Moses. Their weights are optimized using minimum error-rate training (MERT)(Och, 2003) on a held-out development set for each of the experiments.

3.5 Morphological Segmentation

Haque et al. (2012) applied a morphological suffix separation process in a Bengali-to-English translation task and showed that suffix separation significantly reduces data sparseness in the Bengali corpus. They also showed an SMT model trained on the suffix-stripped training data significantly outperforms the state-of-the-art PB-SMT baseline. Like Bengali, Hindi is a morphologically very rich and highly inflected Indian language. As done previously for Bengali-to-English (Haque et al., 2012), we employ a suffix-stripping method for lemmatizing inflected Hindi words in the WMT Hindi-to-English translation task. Following Dasgupta and Ng (2006), we developed an unsupervised morphological segmentation method for Hindi. We also used a Hindi lightweight stemmer (Ramanathan and Rao, 2003) in order to prepare a training corpus with only Hindi stems. We prepared Hindi-to-English SMT systems on the both types of training data (i.e. suffix-stripped and stemmed).[6]

3.6 Multi-Alignment Combination (MAC)

Word alignment is a critical component of MT systems. Various methods for word alignment have been proposed, and different models can produce signicantly different outputs. For example, Tu et al. (2012) demonstrates that the alignment agreement between the two best-known alignment tools, namely Giza++(Och and Ney, 2003) and the Berkeley aligner[7] (Liang et al., 2006), is below 70%. Taking into consideration the small size of the the corpus, in order to extract more effective phrase tables, we concatenate three alignments: Giza++ with grow-diag-final-and, Giza++ with intersection, and that derived from the Berkeley aligner.

3.7 Stemming Alignment and Normal Phrase Extraction (SANPE)

The rich morphology of Hindi will cause word alignment sparsity, which results in poor alignment quality. Furthermore, word stemming on the Hindi side usually results in too many English words being aligned to one stemmed Hindi word, i.e. we encounter the problem of phrase over-extraction. Therefore, we conduct word alignment with the stemmed version of Hindi, and then at the phrase extraction step, we replace the stemmed form with the original Hindi form.

3.8 OOV Word Conversion Method

Our algorithm for OOV word conversion uses the recently developed zero-shot learning (Palatucci et al., 2009) using neural network language modelling (Bengio et al., 2000; Mikolov et al., 2013). The same technique is used in (Okita et al., 2014). This method requires neither parallel nor comparable corpora, but rather two monolingual corpora. In our context, we prepare two monolingual corpora on both sides, which are neither parallel nor comparable, and a small amount of already known correspondences between words on the source and target sides (henceforth, we refer to this as the 'dictionary'). Then, we train both sides with the neural network language model, and use a continuous space representation to project words to each other on the basis of a small amount of correspondences in the dictionary. The following algorithm shows the steps involved:

1. Prepare the monolingual source and target sentences.
2. Prepare the dictionary which consists of U entries of source and target sentences comprising non-stop-words.
3. Train the neural network language model on the source side and obtain the real vectors of X dimensions for each word.

[6] Suffixes were separated and completely removed from the training data.

[7] http://code.google.com/p/berkeleyaligner/

4. Train the neural network language model on the target side and obtain the real vectors of X dimensions for each word.

5. Using the real vectors obtained in the above steps, obtain the linear mapping between the dictionary items in two continuous spaces using canonical component analysis (CCA).

In our experiments we use U the same as the entries of Wiki corpus, which is provided among WMT14 corpora, and X as 50. The resulted projection by this algorithm can be used as the OOV word conversion which projects from the source language which among OOV words into the target language. The overall algorithm which uses the projection which we build in the above step is shown in the following.

1. Collect unknown words in the translation outputs.

2. Do Hindi named-entity recognition (NER) to detect noun phrases.

3. If they are noun phrases, do the projection from each unknown word in the source side into the target words (We use the projection prepared in the above steps). If they are not noun phrases, run the transliteration to convert each of them.

We perform Hindi NER by training CRF++ (Kudo et al., 2004) using the Hindi named entity corpus, and use the Hindi shallow parser (Begum et al., 2008) for preprocessing of the inputs.

4 Results and Discussion

4.1 Data

We conduct our experiments on the standard datasets released in the WMT14 shared translation task. We use HindEnCorp[8] (Bojar et al., 2014) parallel corpus for MT system building. We also used the CommonCrawl Hindi monolingual corpus (Bojar et al., 2014) in order to build an additional language model for Hindi.

For the Hindi-to-English direction, we also employed monolingual English data used in the other translation tasks for building the English language model.

[8] http://ufallab.ms.mff.cuni.cz/ bojar/hindencorp/

4.2 Moses Baseline

We employ a standard Moses PB-SMT model as our baseline. The Hindi side is preprocessed but unstemmed. We use Giza++ to perform word alignment, the phrase table is extracted via the grow-diag-final-and heuristic and the max-phrase-length is set to 7.

4.3 Automatic Evaluation

Experiments	BLEU
Moses Baseline	8.7
Context-Based	9.4
Context-Based + CommonCrawl LM	11.4

Table 1: BLEU scores of the English-to-Hindi MT Systems on the WMT test set.

Experiments	BLEU
Moses Baseline	10.1
Context-Based	10.1
Suffix-Stripped	10.0
OWC	11.2
OSM	10.3
Three LRMs	10.5
MAC	10.7
SANPE	10.6
LMI	10.9
LMI+SANPE+MAC+ThreeLRMs+OSM	11.7

Table 2: BLEU scores of the Hindi-to-English MT Systems on the WMT test set.

We prepared a number of MT systems for both English-to-Hindi and Hindi-to-English, and submitted their runs in the WMT 2014 Evaluation Matrix. The BLEU scores of the different English-to-Hindi MT systems (Moses Baseline, Context-Based (CCG) MT system, and Context-Based (CCG) MT system with an additional LM built on the CommonCrawl Hindi monolingual corpus (Bojar et al., 2014)) on the WMT 2014 English-to-Hindi test set are reported in Table 1. As can be seen from Table 1, Context-Based (CCG) MT system produces 0.7 BLEU points improvement (8.04% relative) over the Moses Baseline. When we add an additional large LM built on the CommonCrawl data to the Context-Based (CCG) MT system, we achieved a 2 BLEU-point improvement (21.3% relative) (cf. last row in Table 1) over the Context-Based (CCG) MT system.[9]

The BLEU scores of the different Hindi-to-English MT systems on the WMT 2014 Hindi-to-English test set are reported in Table 2. The first row of Table 2 shows the BLEU score for the Baseline MT system. We note that the performance of the Context-Based (PoS) MT system obtains identical performance to the Moses baseline (10.1 BLEU points) on the WMT 2014 Hindi-to-English test set.

We employed a source language (Hindi) normalisation technique, namely suffix separation, but unfortunately this did not bring about any improvement for the Hindi-to-English translation task. The improvement gained by individually employing OSM, three lexical reordering models, Multi-alignment Combination, Stem-align and normal Phrase Extraction and Language Model Interpolation can be seen in Table 2. Our best system is achieved by combining OSM, Three LMR, MAC, SANPE and LMI, which results in a 1.6 BLEU point improvement over the Baseline.

5 Acknowledgments

This research is supported by the Science Foundation Ireland (Grant 12/CE/I2267) as part of the CNGL Centre for Global Intelligent Content (www.cngl.ie) at Dublin City University.

References

Amittai Axelrod, Ra Birch Mayne, Chris Callison-burch, Miles Osborne, and David Talbot. 2005. Edinburgh system description for the 2005 iwslt speech translation evaluation. In *Proceedings of the International Workshop on Spoken Language Translation (IWSLT)*.

Rafiya Begum, Samar Husain, Arun Dhwaj, Dipti Misra Sharma, Lakshmi Bai, and Rajeev Sangal. 2008. Dependency annotation scheme for indian languages. *In Proceedings of The Third International Joint Conference on Natural Language Processing (IJCNLP)*.

Yoshua Bengio, Rejean Ducharme, and Pascal Vincent. 2000. A neural probabilistic language model. *In Proceedings of Neural Information Systems*.

Ond Bojar, Pavel Stranak, and Daniel Zeman. 2010. Data issues in english-to-hindi machine translation. In *LREC*.

[9]Please note that this is an unconstrained submission.

Ondrej Bojar, V. Diatka, Rychly P., Pavel Stranak, A. Tamchyna, and Daniel Zeman. 2014. Hindi-english and hindi-only corpus for machine translation. In *LREC*.

Stanley F. Chen and Joshua Goodman. 1996. An empirical study of smoothing techniques for language modeling. In *Proceedings of the 34th Annual Meeting on Association for Computational Linguistics*, ACL '96, pages 310–318, Stroudsburg, PA, USA. Association for Computational Linguistics.

Walter Daelemans. 2005. *Memory-based language processing*. Cambridge University Press.

Sajib Dasgupta and Vincent Ng. 2006. Unsupervised morphological parsing of bengali. *Language Resources and Evaluation*, 40(3-4):311–330.

Nadir Durrani, Helmut Schmid, and Alexander Fraser. 2011. A joint sequence translation model with integrated reordering. In *Proceedings of the 49th Annual Meeting of the Association for Computational Linguistics: Human Language Technologies - Volume 1*, HLT '11, pages 1045–1054, Stroudsburg, PA, USA. Association for Computational Linguistics.

Michel Galley and Christopher D. Manning. 2008. A simple and effective hierarchical phrase reordering model. In *Proceedings of the 2008 Conference on Empirical Methods in Natural Language Processing*, pages 848–856, Honolulu, Hawaii, October. Association for Computational Linguistics.

Rejwanul Haque, Sudip Kumar Naskar, Antal van den Bosch, and Andy Way. 2011. Integrating source-language context into phrase-based statistical machine translation. *Machine translation*, 25(3):239–285.

Rejwanul Haque, Sergio Penkale, Jie Jiang, and Andy Way. 2012. Source-side suffix stripping for bengali-to-english smt. In *Asian Language Processing (IALP), 2012 International Conference on*, pages 193–196. IEEE.

Philipp Koehn, Franz Josef Och, and Daniel Marcu. 2003. Statistical phrase-based translation. In *Proceedings of the 2003 Conference of the North American Chapter of the Association for Computational Linguistics on Human Language Technology-Volume 1*, pages 48–54. Association for Computational Linguistics.

Philipp Koehn, Hieu Hoang, Alexandra Birch, Chris Callison-Burch, Marcello Federico, Nicola Bertoldi, Brooke Cowan, Wade Shen, Christine Moran, Richard Zens, Chris Dyer, Ondřej Bojar, Alexandra Constantin, and Evan Herbst. 2007. Moses: Open source toolkit for statistical machine translation. In *Proceedings of the 45th Annual Meeting of the ACL on Interactive Poster and Demonstration Sessions*, ACL '07, pages 177–180, Stroudsburg, PA, USA. Association for Computational Linguistics.

Taku Kudo, Kaoru Yamamoto, and Yuji Matsumoto. 2004. Appliying conditional random fields to japanese morphological analysis. *In Proceedings of EMNLP*.

Percy Liang, Ben Taskar, and Dan Klein. 2006. Alignment by agreement. In *Proceedings of the main conference on Human Language Technology Conference of the North American Chapter of the Association of Computational Linguistics*, pages 104–111. Association for Computational Linguistics.

Tomas Mikolov, Quoc V. Le, and Ilya Sutskever. 2013. Exploiting similarities among languages for machine translation. *ArXiv*.

Franz Josef Och and Hermann Ney. 2003. A systematic comparison of various statistical alignment models. *Computational linguistics*, 29(1):19–51.

Franz Josef Och. 2003. Minimum error rate training in statistical machine translation. In *Proceedings of the 41st Annual Meeting on Association for Computational Linguistics - Volume 1*, ACL '03, pages 160–167, Stroudsburg, PA, USA. Association for Computational Linguistics.

Tsuyoshi Okita, Ali Hosseinzadeh Vahid, Andy Way, and Qun Liu. 2014. Dcu terminology translation system for medical query subtask at wmt14.

Mark Palatucci, Dean Pomerleau, Geoffrey Hinton, and Tom Mitchell. 2009. Zero-shot learning with semantic output codes. In *Neural Information Processing Systems (NIPS)*, December.

Ananthakrishnan Ramanathan and Durgesh D Rao. 2003. A lightweight stemmer for hindi. In *the Proceedings of EACL*.

Mark Steedman. 2000. *The syntactic process*, volume 35. MIT Press.

Andreas Stolcke. 2002. Srilm – an extensible language modeling toolkit. In *Proceedings of the International Conference Spoken Language Processing*, pages 901–904, Denver, CO.

Zhaopeng Tu, Yang Liu, Yifan He, Josef van Genabith, Qun Liu, and Shouxun Lin. 2012. Combining multiple alignments to improve machine translation. In *COLING (Posters)*, pages 1249–1260.

Machine Translation of Medical Texts in the Khresmoi Project

Ondřej Dušek, Jan Hajič, Jaroslava Hlaváčová, Michal Novák, Pavel Pecina, Rudolf Rosa, Aleš Tamchyna, Zdeňka Urešová, Daniel Zeman
Charles University in Prague, Faculty of Mathematics and Physics
Institute of Formal and Applied Linguistics
Malostranské náměstí 25, 11800 Prague, Czech Republic
{odusek,hajic,hlavacova,mnovak,pecina,rosa,tamchyna,uresova,zeman}@ufal.mff.cuni.cz

Abstract

This paper presents the participation of the Charles University team in the WMT 2014 Medical Translation Task. Our systems are developed within the Khresmoi project, a large integrated project aiming to deliver a multi-lingual multi-modal search and access system for biomedical information and documents. Being involved in the organization of the Medical Translation Task, our primary goal is to set up a baseline for both its subtasks (summary translation and query translation) and for all translation directions. Our systems are based on the phrase-based Moses system and standard methods for domain adaptation. The constrained/unconstrained systems differ in the training data only.

1 Introduction

The WMT 2014 Medical Translation Task poses an interesting challenge for Machine Translation (MT). In the "standard" translation task, the end application is the translation itself. In the Medical Translation Task, the MT system is considered a part of a larger system for Cross-Lingual Information Retrieval (CLIR) and is used to solve two different problems: (i) translation of user search queries, and (ii) translation of summaries of retrieved documents.

In query translation, the end user does not even necessarily see the MT output as their queries are translated and search is performed on documents in the target language. In summary translation, the sentences to be translated come from document summaries (snippets) displayed to provide information on each of the documents retrieved by the search. Therefore, translation quality may not be the most important measure in this task – the performance of the CLIR system as a whole is the final criterion. Another fundamental difference from the standard task is the nature of the translated texts. While we can consider document summaries to be ordinary texts (despite their higher information density in terms of terminology from a narrow domain), search queries in the medical domain are an extremely specific type of data, and traditional techniques for system development and domain adaptation are truly put to a test here.

This work is a part of the of the large integrated EU-funded Khresmoi project.[1] Among other goals, such as joint text and image retrieval of radiodiagnostic records, Khresmoi aims to develop technology for transparent cross-lingual search of medical sources for both professionals and laypeople, with the emphasis primarily on publicly available web sources.

In this paper, we describe the Khresmoi systems submitted to the WMT 2014 Medical Translation Task. We participate in both subtasks (summary translation and query translation) for all language pairs (Czech–English, German–English, and French–English) in both directions (to English and from English). Our systems are based on the Moses phrase-based translation toolkit and standard methods for domain adaptation. We submit one constrained and one unconstrained system for each subtask and translation direction. The constrained and unconstrained systems differ in training data only: The former use all allowed training data, the latter take advantage of additional web-crawled data.

We first summarize previous works in MT domain adaptation in Section 2, then describe the data we used for our systems in Section 3. Sec-

[1] http://www.khresmoi.eu/

Proceedings of the Ninth Workshop on Statistical Machine Translation, pages 221–228,
Baltimore, Maryland USA, June 26–27, 2014.

tion 4 contains an account of the submitted systems and their performance in translation of search queries and document summaries. Section 5 concludes the paper.

2 Related work

To put our work in the context of other approaches, we first describe previous work on domain adaptation in Statistical Machine Translation (SMT), then focus specifically on SMT in the medical domain.

2.1 Domain adaptation of Statistical machine translation

Many works on domain adaptation examine the usage of available in-domain data to directly improve in-domain performance of SMT. Some authors attempt to combine the predictions of two separate (in-domain and general-domain) translation models (Langlais, 2002; Sanchis-Trilles and Casacuberta, 2010; Bisazza et al., 2011; Nakov, 2008) or language models (Koehn and Schroeder, 2007). Wu and Wang (2004) use in-domain data to improve word alignment in the training phase. Carpuat et al. (2012) explore the possibility of using word sense disambiguation to discriminate between domains.

Other approaches concentrate on the acquisition of larger in-domain corpora. Some of them exploit existing general-domain corpora by selecting data that resemble the properties of in-domain data (e.g., using cross-entropy), thus building a larger *pseudo-in-domain* training corpus. This technique is used to adapt language models (Eck et al., 2004b; Moore and Lewis, 2010) as well as translation models (Hildebrand et al., 2005; Axelrod et al., 2011) or their combination (Mansour et al., 2011). Similar approaches to domain adaptation are also applied in other tasks, e.g., automatic speech recognition (Byrne et al., 2004).

2.2 Statistical machine translation in the medical domain

Eck et al. (2004a) employ an SMT system for the translation of dialogues between doctors and patients and show that according to automatic metrics, a dictionary extracted from the Unified Medical Language System (UMLS) Metathesaurus and its semantic type classification (U.S. National Library of Medicine, 2009) significantly improves translation quality from Spanish to English when applied to generalize the training data.

Wu et al. (2011) analyze the quality of MT on PubMed[2] titles and whether it is sufficient for patients. The conclusions are very positive especially for languages with large training resources (English, Spanish, German) – the average fluency and content scores (based on human evaluation) are above four on a five-point scale. In automatic evaluation, their systems substantially outperform Google Translate. However, the SMT systems are specifically trained, tuned, and tested on the domain of PubMed titles, and it is not evident how they would perform on other medical texts.

Costa-jussà et al. (2012) are less optimistic regarding SMT quality in the medical domain. They analyze and evaluate the quality of public web-based MT systems (such as Google Translate) and conclude that in both automatic and manual evaluation (on 7 language pairs), the performance of these systems is still not good enough to be used in daily routines of medical doctors in hospitals.

Jimeno Yepes et al. (2013) propose a method for obtaining in-domain parallel corpora from titles and abstracts of publications in the MEDLINE[3] database. The acquired corpora contain from 30,000 to 130,000 sentence pairs (depending on the language pair) and are reported to improve translation quality when used for SMT training, compared to a baseline trained on out-of-domain data. However, the authors use only one source of in-domain parallel data to adapt the translation model, and do not use any in-domain monolingual data to adapt the language model.

In this work, we investigate methods combining the different kinds of data – general-domain, in-domain, and pseudo-in-domain – to find the optimal approach to this problem.

3 Data description

This section includes an overview of the parallel and monolingual data sources used to train our systems. Following the task specification, they are split into constrained and unconstrained sections. The constrained section includes medical-domain data provided for this task (extracted by the provided scripts), and general-domain texts provided as constrained data for the standard task ("general domain" here is used to denote data

[2] http://www.ncbi.nlm.nih.gov/pubmed/

[3] http://www.nlm.nih.gov/pubs/factsheets/medline.html

		Czech–English			German–English			French–English		
dom	set	pairs	source	target	pairs	source	target	pairs	source	target
med	con	2,498	18,126	19,964	4,998	123,686	130,598	6,139	202,245	171,928
gen	con	15,788	226,711	260,505	4,520	112,818	119,404	40,842	1,470,016	1,211,516
gen	unc	–	–	–	9,320	525,782	574,373	13,809	961,991	808,222

Table 1: Number of sentence pairs and tokens (source/target) in parallel training data (in thousands).

dom	set	English	Czech	German	French
med	con	172,991	1,848	63,499	63,022
gen	con	6,132,107	627,493	1,728,065	1,837,457
med	unc	3,275,272	36,348	361,881	908,911
gen	unc	618,084	–	339,595	204,025

Table 2: Number of tokens in monolingual training data (in thousands).

which comes from a mixture of various different domains, mostly news, parliament proceedings, web-crawls, etc.). The unconstrained section contains automatically crawled data from medical and health websites and non-medical data from patent collections.

3.1 Parallel data

The parallel data summary is presented in Table 1.

The main sources of the medical-domain data for all the language pairs include the EMEA corpus (Tiedemann, 2009), the UMLS metathesaurus of health and biomedical vocabularies and standards (U.S. National Library of Medicine, 2009), and bilingual titles of Wikipedia articles belonging to the categories identified to be medical domain. Additional medical-domain data comes from the MAREC patent collection: PatTR (Wäschle and Riezler, 2012) available for DE–EN and FR–EN, and COPPA (Pouliquen and Mazenc, 2011) for FR–EN (only patents from the medical categories A61, C12N, and C12P are allowed in the constrained systems).

The constrained general-domain data include three parallel corpora for all the language pairs: CommonCrawl (Smith et al., 2013), Europarl version 6 (Koehn, 2005), the News Commentary corpus (Callison-Burch et al., 2012). Further, the constrained data include CzEng (Bojar et al., 2012) for CS–EN and the UN corpus for FR–EN.

For our unconstrained experiments, we also employ parallel data from the non-medical patents from the PatTR and COPPA collections (other categories than A61, C12N, and C12P).

3.2 Monolingual data

The monolingual data is summarized in Table 2.

The main sources of the medical-domain monolingual data for all languages involve Wikipedia pages, UMLS concept descriptions, and non-parallel texts extracted from the medical patents of the PatTR collections. For English, the main source is the AACT collection of texts from ClinicalTrials.gov. Smaller resources include: DrugBank (Knox et al., 2011), GENIA (Kim et al., 2003), FMA (Rosse and Mejino Jr., 2008), GREC (Thompson et al., 2009), and PIL (Bouayad-Agha et al., 2000).

In the unconstrained systems, we use additional monolingual data from web pages crawled within the Khresmoi project: a collection of about one million HON-certified[4] webpages in English released as the test collection for the CLEF 2013 eHealth Task 3 evaluation campaign,[5] additional web-crawled HON-certified pages (not publicly available), and other webcrawled medical-domain related webpages.

The constrained general-domain resources include: the News corpus for CS, DE, EN, and FR collected for the purpose of the WMT 2014 Standard Task, monolingual parts of the Europarl and News-Commentary corpora, and the Gigaword for EN and FR.

For the FR–EN and DE–EN unconstrained systems, the additional general domain monolingual data is taken from monolingual texts of non-medical patents in the PatTR collection.

[4] https://www.hon.ch/

[5] https://sites.google.com/site/shareclefehealth/

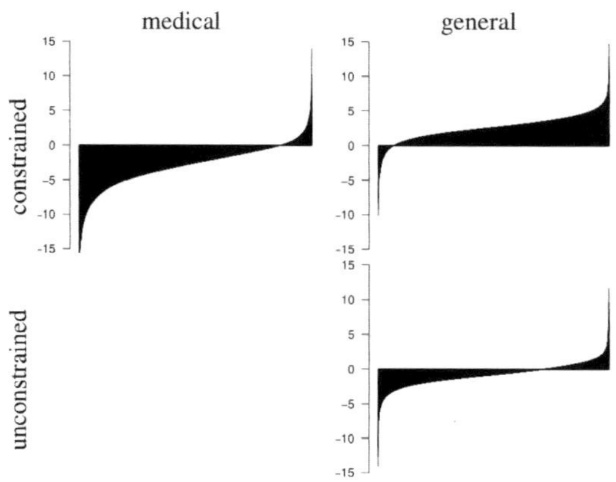

Figure 1: Distribution of the domain-specificity scores in the English–French parallel data sets.

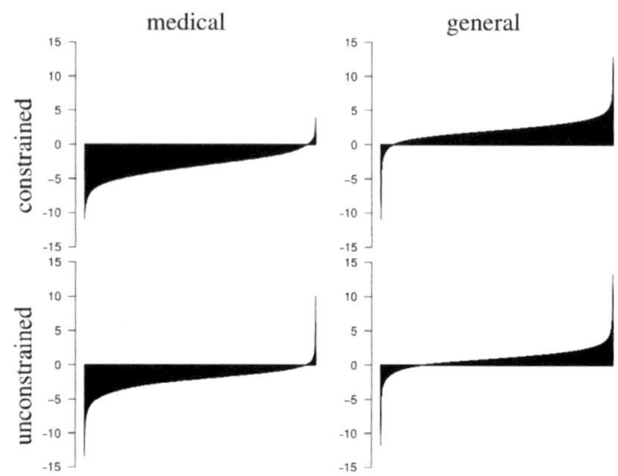

Figure 2: Distribution of the domain-specificity scores in the French monolingual data sets.

3.3 Data preprocessing

The data consisting of crawled web pages, namely CLEF, HON, and non-HON, needed to be cleaned and transformed into a set of sentences. The Boilerpipe (Kohlschütter et al., 2010) and Justext (Pomikálek, 2011) tools were used to remove boilerplate texts and extract just the main content from the web pages. The YALI language detection tool (Majliš, 2012) trained on both in-domain and general domain data then filtered out those cleaned pages which were not identified as written in one of the concerned languages.

The rest of the preprocessing procedure was applied to all the datasets mentioned above, both parallel and monolingual. The data were tokenized and normalized by converting or omitting some (mostly punctuation) characters. A set of language-dependent heuristics was applied in an attempt to restore and normalize the opening/closing quotation marks, i.e. convert "*quoted*" to “*quoted*” (Zeman, 2012). The motivation here is twofold: First, we hope that paired quotation marks could occasionally work as brackets and better denote parallel phrases for Moses; second, if Moses learns to output directed quotation marks, the subsequent detokenization will be easier. For all systems which translate *from* German, decompounding is employed to reduce source-side data sparsity. We used BananaSplit for this task (Müller and Gurevych, 2006).

We perform all training and internal evaluation on lowercased data; we trained recasers to post-process the final submissions.

4 Submitted systems

We first describe our technique of psedo-in-domain data selection in Section 4.1, then compare two methods of combining the selected data in Section 4.2. This, along with using constrained and unconstrained data sets to train the systems (see Section 3), amounts to a total of four system variants submitted for each task. A description of the system settings used is given in Section 4.3.

4.1 Data selection

We follow an approach originally proposed for selection of monolingual sentences for language modeling (Moore and Lewis, 2010) and its modification applied to selection of parallel sentences (Axelrod et al., 2011). This technique assumes two language models for sentence scoring, one trained on (true) in-domain text and one trained on (any) general-domain text in the same language (e.g., English). For both data domains (general and medical), we score each sentence by the difference of its cross-perplexity given the in-domain language model and cross-perplexity given the general-domain language model (in this order). We only keep sentences with a *negative score* in our data, assuming that these are the most “medical-like”. Visualisation of the domain-specificity scores (cross-perplexity difference) in the FR–EN parallel data and FR monolingual data is illustrated in Figures 1 and 2, respectively.[6] The scores (Y axis) are presented for each sentence in increasing order from left to right (X axis).

[6]For the medical domain, constrained and unconstrained parallel data are identical.

		cs→en	de→en	en→cs	en→de	en→fr	fr→en
con	concat	33.64±1.14	32.84±1.24	18.10±0.94	18.29±0.92	33.39±1.11	36.71±1.17
con	interpol	32.94±1.11	32.31±1.20	18.96±0.93	18.41±0.93	34.06±1.11	37.42±1.21
unc	concat	34.10±1.11	34.52±1.20	21.12±1.03	19.76±0.92	36.23±1.03	**38.15±1.16**
unc	interpol	**34.48±1.16**	**34.92±1.17**	**22.15±1.06**	**20.81±0.95**	**36.26±1.13**	37.91±1.13

Table 3: BLEU scores of summary translations.

		cs→en	de→en	en→cs	en→de	en→fr	fr→en
con	concat	30.87±4.70	33.21±5.03	23.25±4.85	17.72±4.75	28.64±3.77	35.56±4.94
con	interpol	32.46±5.05	33.74±4.97	21.56±4.80	16.90±4.39	29.34±3.73	35.28±5.26
unc	concat	**34.88±5.04**	31.24±5.59	22.61±4.91	**19.13±5.66**	**33.08±3.80**	36.73±4.88
unc	interpol	33.82±5.16	**34.19±5.27**	**23.93±5.16**	15.87±11.31	31.19±3.73	**40.25±5.14**

Table 4: BLEU scores of query translations.

The two language models for sentence scoring are trained with a restricted vocabulary extracted from the in-domain training data as words occurring at least twice (singletons and other words are treated as out-of-vocabulary). In our experiments, we apply this technique to select both monolingual data for language models and parallel data for translation models. Selection of parallel data is based on the English side only. The in-domain models are trained on the monolingual data in the target language (constrained or unconstrained, depending on the setting). The general-domain models are trained on the WMT News data.

Compared to the approach of Moore and Lewis (2010) and Axelrod et al. (2011), we prune the model vocabulary more aggressively – we discard not only the singletons, but also all words with non-Latin characters, which helps clean the models from noise introduced by the automatic process of data acquisition by web crawling.

4.2 Data combination

For both parallel and monolingual data, we obtain two data sets after applying the data selection:

- "medical-like" data from the medical domain
- "medical-like" data from the general domain.

For each language pair and for each system type (constrained/unconstrained), we submitted two system variants which differ in how the selected data are combined. The first variant uses a simple concatenation of the two datasets both for parallel data and for language model data. In the second variant, we train separate models for each section and use *linear interpolation* to combine them into a single model. For language models, we use the SRILM linear interpolation feature (Stolcke, 2002). We interpolate phrase tables using Tmcombine (Sennrich, 2012). In both cases, the held-out set for minimizing the perplexity is the system development set.

4.3 System details

We compute word alignment on lowercase 4-character stems using fast_align (Dyer et al., 2013). We create phrase tables using the Moses toolkit (Koehn et al., 2007) with standard settings. We train 5-gram language models on the target-side lowercase forms using SRILM. We use MERT (Och, 2003) to tune model weights in our systems on the development data provided for the task.

The only difference between the system variants for query and summary translation is the tuning set. In both cases, we use the respective sets provided offcially for the shared task.

4.4 Results

Tables 3 and 4 show case-insensitive BLEU scores of our systems.[7] As expected, the unconstrained systems outperform the constrained ones. Linear interpolation outperforms data concatenation quite reliably across language pairs for summary translation. While the picture for query translation is similar, there is more variance in the results, so we cannot state that interpolation definitely works

[7] As we use the same recasers for both summary and query translation, our systems are heavily penalized for wrong letter case in query translation. However, letter case is not taken into account in most CLIR systems. All BLEU scores reported in this paper will be case-insensitive for this reason.

better in this case. This is due to the sizes of the development and test sets and most importantly due to sentence lengths – queries are very short, making BLEU unreliable, MERT unstable, and bootstrap resampling intervals wide.

If we compare our score to the other competitors, we are clearly worse than the best systems for summary translation. From this perspective, our data filtering seems overly eager (i.e., discarding all sentence pairs with a positive perplexity difference). An experiment which we leave for future work is doing one more round of interpolation to combine a model trained on the data with negative perplexity with models trained on the remainder.

5 Conclusions

We described the Charles University MT system used in the Shared Medical Translation Task of WMT 2014. Our primary goal was to set up a baseline for both the subtasks and all translation directions. The systems are based on the Moses toolkit, pseudo-in-domain data selection based on perplexity difference and two different methods of in-domain and out-of-domain data combination: simple data concatenation and linear model interpolation.

We report results of constrained and unconstrained systems which differ in the training data only. In most experiments, using additional data improved the results compared to the constrained systems and using linear model interpolation outperformed data concatenation. While our systems are on par with best results for case-insensitive BLEU score in query translation, our overly eager data selection techniques caused lower scores in summary translation. In future work, we plan to include a special out-of-domain model in our setup to compensate for this problem.

Acknowledgments

This work was supported by the EU FP7 project Khresmoi (contract no. 257528), the Czech Science Foundation (grant no. P103/12/G084), and SVV project number 260 104. This work has been using language resources developed, stored, and distributed by the LINDAT/CLARIN project of the Ministry of Education, Youth and Sports of the Czech Republic (project LM2010013).

References

A. Axelrod, X. He, and J. Gao. 2011. Domain adaptation via pseudo in-domain data selection. In *Proceedings of the 2011 Conference on Empirical Methods in Natural Language Processing*, pages 355–362, Edinburgh, United Kingdom. ACL.

A. Bisazza, N. Ruiz, and M. Federico. 2011. Fill-up versus interpolation methods for phrase-based SMT adaptation. In *Proceedings of the International Workshop on Spoken Language Translation*, pages 136–143, San Francisco, CA, USA. International Speech Communication Association.

O. Bojar, Z. Žabokrtský, O. Dušek, P. Galuščáková, M. Majliš, D. Mareček, J. Maršík, M. Novák, M. Popel, and A. Tamchyna. 2012. The joy of parallelism with CzEng 1.0. In *Proceedings of the Eighth International Conference on Language Resources and Evaluation*, pages 3921–3928, Istanbul, Turkey. European Language Resources Association.

N. Bouayad-Agha, D. R. Scott, and R. Power. 2000. Integrating content and style in documents: A case study of patient information leaflets. *Information Design Journal*, 9(2–3):161–176.

W. Byrne, D. S. Doermann, M. Franz, S. Gustman, J. Hajič, D. W. Oard, et al. 2004. Automatic recognition of spontaneous speech for access to multilingual oral history archives. *Speech and Audio Processing, IEEE Transactions on*, 12(4):420–435.

C. Callison-Burch, P. Koehn, C. Monz, M. Post, R. Soricut, and L. Specia. 2012. Findings of the 2012 Workshop on Statistical Machine Translation. In *Proceedings of the Seventh Workshop on Statistical Machine Translation*, pages 10–51, Montréal, Canada. ACL.

M. Carpuat, H. Daumé III, A. Fraser, C. Quirk, F. Braune, A. Clifton, et al. 2012. Domain adaptation in machine translation: Final report. In *2012 Johns Hopkins Summer Workshop Final Report*, pages 61–72. Johns Hopkins University.

M. R. Costa-jussà, M. Farrús, and J. Serrano Pons. 2012. Machine translation in medicine. A quality analysis of statistical machine translation in the medical domain. In *Proceedings of the 1st Virtual International Conference on Advanced Research in Scientific Areas*, pages 1995–1998, Žilina, Slovakia. Žilinská univerzita.

C. Dyer, V. Chahuneau, and N. A. Smith. 2013. A simple, fast, and effective reparameterization of IBM model 2. In *Proceedings of NAACL-HLT*, pages 644–648.

M. Eck, S. Vogel, and A. Waibel. 2004a. Improving statistical machine translation in the medical domain using the Unified Medical Language System. In *COLING 2004: Proceedings of the 20th International Conference on Computational Linguistics*, pages 792–798, Geneva, Switzerland. ACL.

M. Eck, S. Vogel, and A. Waibel. 2004b. Language model adaptation for statistical machine translation based on information retrieval. In Maria Teresa Lino, Maria Francisca Xavier, Fátima Ferreira, Rute Costa, and Raquel Silva, editors, *Proceedings of the International Conference on Language Resources and Evaluation*, pages 327–330, Lisbon, Portugal. European Language Resources Association.

A. S. Hildebrand, M. Eck, S. Vogel, and A. Waibel. 2005. Adaptation of the translation model for statistical machine translation based on information retrieval. In *Proceedings of the 10th Annual Conference of the European Association for Machine Translation*, pages 133–142, Budapest, Hungary. European Association for Machine Translation.

A. Jimeno Yepes, É. Prieur-Gaston, and A. Névéol. 2013. Combining MEDLINE and publisher data to create parallel corpora for the automatic translation of biomedical text. *BMC Bioinformatics*, 14(1):1–10.

J.-D Kim, T. Ohta, Y. Tateisi, and J. Tsujii. 2003. GENIA corpus – a semantically annotated corpus for bio-textmining. *Bioinformatics*, 19(suppl 1):i180–i182.

C. Knox, V. Law, T. Jewison, P. Liu, Son Ly, A. Frolkis, A. Pon, K. Banco, C. Mak, V. Neveu, Y. Djoumbou, R. Eisner, A. C. Guo, and D. S. Wishart. 2011. DrugBank 3.0: a comprehensive resource for 'Omics' research on drugs. *Nucleic acids research*, 39(suppl 1):D1035–D1041.

P. Koehn and J. Schroeder. 2007. Experiments in domain adaptation for statistical machine translation. In *Proceedings of the Second Workshop on Statistical Machine Translation*, pages 224–227, Prague, Czech Republic. ACL.

P. Koehn, H. Hoang, A. Birch, C. Callison-Burch, M. Federico, N. Bertoldi, B. Cowan, W. Shen, C. Moran, R. Zens, C. Dyer, O. Bojar, A. Constantin, and E. Herbst. 2007. Moses: Open Source Toolkit for Statistical Machine Translation. In *Proceedings of the 45th Annual Meeting of the Association for Computational Linguistics Companion Volume Proceedings of the Demo and Poster Sessions*, pages 177–180, Praha, Czechia, June. ACL.

P. Koehn. 2005. Europarl: a parallel corpus for statistical machine translation. In *Conference Proceedings: the tenth Machine Translation Summit*, pages 79–86, Phuket, Thailand. Asia-Pacific Association for Machine Translation.

C. Kohlschütter, P. Fankhauser, and W. Nejdl. 2010. Boilerplate detection using shallow text features. In *Proceedings of the Third ACM International Conference on Web Search and Data Mining*, WSDM '10, pages 441–450, New York, NY, USA. ACM.

P. Langlais. 2002. Improving a general-purpose statistical translation engine by terminological lexicons. In *COLING-02 on COMPUTERM 2002: second international workshop on computational terminology*, volume 14, pages 1–7, Taipei, Taiwan. ACL.

M. Majliš. 2012. Yet another language identifier. In *Proceedings of the Student Research Workshop at the 13th Conference of the European Chapter of the Association for Computational Linguistics*, pages 46–54, Avignon, France. ACL.

S. Mansour, J. Wuebker, and H. Ney. 2011. Combining translation and language model scoring for domain-specific data filtering. In *International Workshop on Spoken Language Translation*, pages 222–229, San Francisco, CA, USA. ISCA.

R. C. Moore and W. Lewis. 2010. Intelligent selection of language model training data. In *Proceedings of the ACL 2010 Conference Short Papers*, pages 220–224, Uppsala, Sweden. ACL.

C. Müller and I. Gurevych. 2006. Exploring the potential of semantic relatedness in information retrieval. In *LWA 2006 Lernen – Wissensentdeckung – Adaptivität, 9.-11.10.2006, Hildesheimer Informatikberichte*, pages 126–131, Hildesheim, Germany. Universität Hildesheim.

P. Nakov. 2008. Improving English–Spanish statistical machine translation: Experiments in domain adaptation, sentence paraphrasing, tokenization, and recasing. In *Proceedings of the Third Workshop on Statistical Machine Translation*, pages 147–150, Columbus, OH, USA. ACL.

F. J. Och. 2003. Minimum error rate training in statistical machine translation. In *ACL '03: Proceedings of the 41st Annual Meeting on Association for Computational Linguistics*, pages 160–167, Morristown, NJ, USA. ACL.

J. Pomikálek. 2011. *Removing Boilerplate and Duplicate Content from Web Corpora.* PhD thesis, Masaryk University, Faculty of Informatics, Brno.

B. Pouliquen and C. Mazenc. 2011. COPPA, CLIR and TAPTA: three tools to assist in overcoming the patent barrier at WIPO. In *Proceedings of the Thirteenth Machine Translation Summit*, pages 24–30, Xiamen, China. Asia-Pacific Association for Machine Translation.

C. Rosse and José L. V. Mejino Jr. 2008. The foundational model of anatomy ontology. In A. Burger, D. Davidson, and R. Baldock, editors, *Anatomy Ontologies for Bioinformatics*, volume 6 of *Computational Biology*, pages 59–117. Springer London.

G. Sanchis-Trilles and F. Casacuberta. 2010. Log-linear weight optimisation via Bayesian adaptation in statistical machine translation. In *Proceedings of the 23rd International Conference on Computational Linguistics: Posters*, pages 1077–1085, Beijing, China. ACL.

R. Sennrich. 2012. Perplexity minimization for translation model domain adaptation in statistical machine translation. In *Proceedings of the 13th Conference of the European Chapter of the Association for Computational Linguistics*, pages 539–549. ACL.

J. R. Smith, H. Saint-Amand, M. Plamada, P. Koehn, C. Callison-Burch, and A. Lopez. 2013. Dirt cheap web-scale parallel text from the common crawl. In *Proceedings of the 51st Annual Meeting of the Association for Computational Linguistics (Volume 1: Long Papers)*, pages 1374–1383, Sofia, Bulgaria. ACL.

A. Stolcke. 2002. SRILM – an extensible language modeling toolkit. In *Proceedings of International Conference on Spoken Language Processing*, Denver, Colorado, USA.

P. Thompson, S. Iqbal, J. McNaught, and Sophia Ananiadou. 2009. Construction of an annotated corpus to support biomedical information extraction. *BMC bioinformatics*, 10(1):349.

J. Tiedemann. 2009. News from OPUS – a collection of multilingual parallel corpora with tools and interfaces. In *Recent Advances in Natural Language Processing*, volume 5, pages 237–248, Borovets, Bulgaria. John Benjamins.

U.S. National Library of Medicine. 2009. UMLS reference manual. Metathesaurus. Bethesda, MD, USA.

K. Wäschle and S. Riezler. 2012. Analyzing parallelism and domain similarities in the MAREC patent corpus. In M. Salampasis and B. Larsen, editors, *Multidisciplinary Information Retrieval*, volume 7356 of *Lecture Notes in Computer Science*, pages 12–27. Springer Berlin Heidelberg.

H. Wu and H. Wang. 2004. Improving domain-specific word alignment with a general bilingual corpus. In Robert E. Frederking and Kathryn B. Taylor, editors, *Machine Translation: From Real Users to Research*, volume 3265 of *Lecture Notes in Computer Science*, pages 262–271. Springer Berlin Heidelberg.

C. Wu, F. Xia, L. Deleger, and I. Solti. 2011. Statistical machine translation for biomedical text: are we there yet? *AMIA Annual Symposium proceedings*, pages 1290–1299.

D. Zeman. 2012. Data issues of the multilingual translation matrix. In *Proceedings of the Seventh Workshop on Statistical Machine Translation*, pages 395–400, Montréal, Canada. ACL.

Postech's System Description for Medical Text Translation Task

Jianri Li **Se-Jong Kim** **Hwidong Na** **Jong-Hyeok Lee**
Department of Computer Science and Engineering
Pohang University of Science and Technology, Pohang, Republic of Korea
{skywalker, sejong, leona, jhlee}@postech.ac.kr

Abstract

This short paper presents a system description for intrinsic evaluation of the WMT 14's medical text translation task. Our systems consist of phrase-based statistical machine translation system and query translation system between German-English language pairs. Our work focuses on the query translation task and we achieved the highest BLEU score among the all submitted systems for the English-German intrinsic query translation evaluation.

1 Overview

The goal of WMT14's medical text translation task is investigation of capability of machine translation (MT) technologies when it is applied to translating texts and query terms in medical domain. In our work, we focus on its application on cross-lingual information retrieval (CLIR) and evaluation of query translation task.

CLIR techniques aim to increase the accessibility of web documents written by foreign language. One of the key techniques of cross-lingual IR is query translation, which aims to translate the input query into relevant terms in target language.

One way to translate queries is dictionary-based query translation. However, an input query usually consists of multiple terms, which cause low coverage of bilingual dictionary. Alternative way is translating queries using statistical machine translation (SMT) system. However, translation model could contain some noise that is meaningless translation. The goal of our method is to overcome the shortcomings of these approaches by a heuristic hybrid approach.

As a baseline, we use phrase-based statistical machine translation (PBSMT) (Koehn, Och, & Marcu, 2003) techniques to handle queries that consist of multiple terms. To identify multiple terms in a query, we analyze three cases of the formation of queries and generate query translation candidates using term-to-term dictionaries and PBSMT system, and then score these candidates using *co-occurrence word frequency measure* to select the best candidate.

We have done experiment on two language pairs

- English-German
- German-English

The rest of parts in this paper are organized as following: section 2 describes the techniques and system settings used in our experiment, section 3 presents used corpus and experiment result, and section 4 shows a brief conclusion of our work.

2 Method

2.1 Phrase-based machine translation system

The phrase-based statistical machine translation system is implemented using MOSE'S toolkits (Koehn et al., 2007). Bidirectional word alignments were built by MGIZA[1], a multi-thread version of GIZA++ (Och & Ney, 2003), run on a 24 threads machine. The alignment symmetrization method is *grow-diag-final-and* (Koehn et al., 2003), and lexicalized-reordering method is *msd-bidirectional-fe* (Koehn et al., 2007).

For each monolingual corpus, we used a five-gram language model, which was built by IRSTLM toolkit[2] (Federico, Bertoldi, & Cettolo, 2008) with improved Kneser Ney smoothing (Chen & Goodman, 1996; Kneser & Ney, 1995). The language model was integrated as a log-linear feature to decoder.

All the sentences in the training, development and test corpus were tokenized by inserting spaces between words and punctuations, and then converted to most probable cases by truecaseing. Both tokenization and truecasing were done by embedded tools in the MOSE'S toolkits. Finally, all the sentences in the train corpus were cleaned with maximum length 80.

[1] http://www.kyloo.net/software
[2] http://sourceforge.net/projects/irstlm

Proceedings of the Ninth Workshop on Statistical Machine Translation, pages 229–232,
Baltimore, Maryland USA, June 26–27, 2014. ©2014 Association for Computational Linguistics

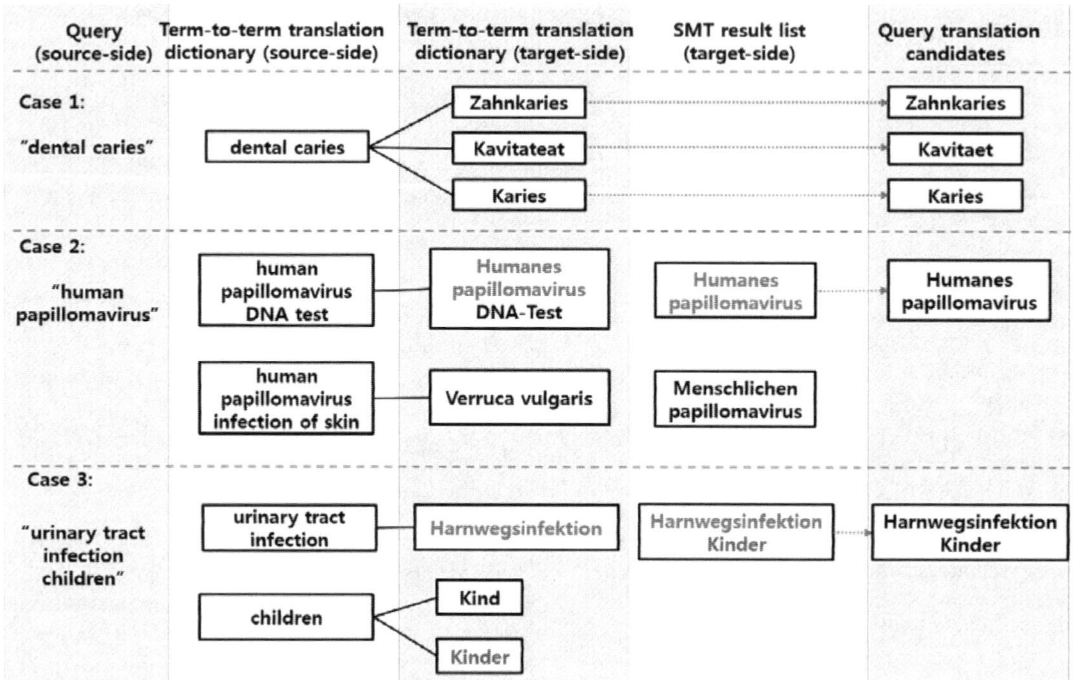

Figure 1. Flow from queries to query translation candidates for each case.

2.2 Query translation system

In general, an input query is not a full sentence. Instead, most of queries contain one or more phrases that consist of several keywords. Furthermore, in the medical domain, many keywords are unfamiliar terminologies for general users. Therefore, term-to-term translation dictionaries in medical domain could be useful resources to translate the queries. In our experiment, we used the parallel terms from Unified Medical Language System (UMLS) and titles of Wikipedia in medical domain, as the term-to-term translation dictionary.

First of all, if a given query is a combination of two or more phrases that concatenated by terms like comma, coordinate conjunction, then the given query is divided into several single phrases, and each of them is translated by our SMT system as a new single query. If the new query satisfies one of cases shown in Figure 1, then its query translation candidates are selected according to the corresponding case, and select the best one of them using proposed measures. Otherwise, if the new query does not satisfy any case, the top 1 result by our PBSMT system is selected as the best query translation candidate. Our method combines the translation results of single queries by following rules: 1) if the original query consists of multiple phrases concatenated by functional words like coordinate conjunctions, then the translation results are combined by translated functional words, 2) if the original query is concatenated by punctuation, then the results are combined by the original punctuation. Finally, the final result is selected by comparing the result from QT system and PBSMT system using the co-occurrence word frequency measure (see Section 2.2.4). The following three subsections describe how we select translation candidate case by case.

2.2.1 Case 1: Full matching

If a single query exactly matches one instance in the dictionary, query translation candidates are the target-side entries in the translation dictionary (Case 1 in Figure 1). If a query translation candidate *qt* is a sequence of words (w_1 to w_n), it is ranked by the co-occurrence word frequency measure (*CF*) using the provided articles of Wikipedia in the medical domain:

$$CF(qt) = \frac{freq(w_1)}{N_{uni}} \prod_{i=2}^{n} \frac{\frac{freq(w_i, w_{i-1})}{N_{bi}}}{\frac{freq(w_{i-1})}{N_{uni}}}, \qquad (1)$$

where $freq(w_1)$ is the frequency of a unigram w_1 in the articles; $freq(w_i, w_{i-1})$ is the frequency of a bigram "w_i w_{i-1}" in the articles; and N_{uni} and N_{bi} is the sum of frequency of all unigram and bigram, respectively.

2.2.2 Case 2: Full inclusion

If a source-side entry of the term-to-term translation dictionary exactly includes a query, its query translation candidate is its SMT result whose all words appear in the target-side entry of the translation dictionary (Case 2 in Figure 1). Among the top 10 results by our PBSMT system, we select the results satisfying this case, and rank them using *CF* and our PBSMT result score (*Score*$_{SMT}$):

$$Score_{QT}(qt) = \lambda \frac{CF(qt)}{\sum_{qt' \in QT} CF(qt')} + (1-\lambda) \frac{Scores_{MT}(qt)}{\sum_{qt' \in QT} Scores_{MT}(qt')} , \quad (2)$$

where λ is the weight by the provided development set; and *QT* is the set of query translation candidates for a query.

2.2.3 Case 1: Full matching

If the left phrase t_{left} or right phrase t_{right} of a query exactly matches one instance in the dictionary, its query translation candidate is its SMT result that includes all words in the target-side entry of the translation dictionary (Case 3 in Figure 1). To rank our SMT results satisfying this case, if the total number of words in t_{left} and t_{right} is same or larger than that in a query, *Score*$_{QT}$ is used, and the other case uses the weighted *Score*$_{QT}$ (*WScore*$_{QT}$):

$$WScore_{QT}(qt) = \frac{N(t_{left}) + N(t_{right})}{N(q)} Score_{QT}(qt) , \quad (3)$$

where $N(t_{left})$ is the number of words in t_{left}; and q is a given query.

2.2.4 Select final result

If a query satisfies any case above, and the candidate with highest score is selected, then we compare the candidate with translation of original query directly obtained from PBSMT system using equation (1). The final result would be the result with higher score between them.

3 Experiment

3.1 Corpus

We only use constrained data provided by WMT 2014 medical translation task.

To train PBSMT system, we use parallel corpora

- EMEA
- MuchMore
- Wikipedia-titles
- Patent-abstract, claim, title
- UMLS

We simply mixed up all available parallel corpora to train a unique translation model.

And for English-German language pair we use monolingual corpora

- Wikipedia-articles
- Patent-descriptions
- UMLS descriptions

And for German-English language pair we use monolingual corpora

- Wikipedia-articles
- Patent-descriptions
- UMLS descriptions
- AACT
- GENIA
- GREC
- FMA
- PIL

We also use target side of parallel corpora as additional monolingual resource to train language model. We separately train a 5-gram language model for each monolingual corpus and integrate them as features to log-linear model in the PBSMT system.

For the query translation (QT) system, we use parallel corpus *Wikipedia-titles* and *UMLS dictionary*, and use monolingual corpus *Wikipedia-articles*.

3.2 Experiment Setting

For the tuning of PBSMT system, we use development set provided by WMT 14 medical task (*khresmoi-summary-dev*). And we use query translation development set (*khresmoi-query-dev*) for the tuning of QT system.

We test our systems on two test set provided by WMT 14 medical task.

- khresmoi-summary-test (for PBSMT)
- khresmoi-query-test (for QT)

For comparison with result from QT system, we translate the test set of query translation task (*khresmoi-query-test*) using PBSMT system without any post-processing.

In our experiment, the performance of translation system is measured by BLEU (%) and translation error rate - TER (%). All these results are evaluated from the evaluation website[3].

3.3 Experiment Result

Table 1 shows the results for the task of translation of sentences from summaries of medical articles.

Table 2 shows the results for the task of translation of queries entered by users of medical information search engines. The performance of QT system is relatively higher than PBSMT system. Especially, the BLEU score of QT system on English-German language pair is the highest score among the all submitted systems.

Language Pair	BLEU	TER
English-German	15.8	0.746
German-English	26.9	0.618

Table 1: BLEU scores of result from PBSMT system for summary translation task.

Language Pair		BLEU	TER
PBSMT	English-German	15.1	0.748
	German-English	22.1	0.638
QT	English-German	**15.3**	**0.746**
	German-English	**24.5**	**0.586**

Table 2: BLEU scores of result for query translation task.

4 Conclusion

We describe the PBSMT system and QT system that are developed for summary translation and query translation of WMT 14 medical translation task. We focus on intrinsic query translation evaluation and propose a hybrid approach by combining dictionary-based approach and SMT based approach using heuristics. The result of query translation experiment shows that our method obtained higher translation accuracy than the baseline (PBSMT) system.

Acknowledgments

This work was supported in part by the National Korea Science and Engineering Foundation (KOSEF) (NRF-2010-0012662), in part by the Brain Korea 21+ Project, and in part by the Korea Ministry of Knowledge Economy (MKE) under Grant No.10041807.

[3] http://matrix.statmt.org

References

Chen, S. F., & Goodman, J. (1996). *An empirical study of smoothing techniques for language modeling*. Paper presented at the Proceedings of the 34th annual meeting on Association for Computational Linguistics.

Federico, M., Bertoldi, N., & Cettolo, M. (2008). *IRSTLM: an open source toolkit for handling large scale language models*. Paper presented at the Interspeech.

Kneser, R., & Ney, H. (1995). *Improved backing-off for m-gram language modeling*. Paper presented at the Acoustics, Speech, and Signal Processing, 1995. ICASSP-95., 1995 International Conference on.

Koehn, P., Hoang, H., Birch, A., Callison-Burch, C., Federico, M., Bertoldi, N., . . . Herbst, E. (2007). *Moses: open source toolkit for statistical machine translation*. Paper presented at the Proceedings of the 45th Annual Meeting of the ACL on Interactive Poster and Demonstration Sessions, Prague, Czech Republic.

Koehn, P., Och, F. J., & Marcu, D. (2003). *Statistical phrase-based translation*. Paper presented at the Proceedings of the 2003 Conference of the North American Chapter of the Association for Computational Linguistics on Human Language Technology-Volume 1.

Och, F. J., & Ney, H. (2003). A systematic comparison of various statistical alignment models. *Comput. Linguist., 29*(1), 19-51. doi: 10.1162/089120103321337421

Domain Adaptation for Medical Text Translation Using Web Resources

Yi Lu, Longyue Wang, Derek F. Wong, Lidia S. Chao, Yiming Wang, Francisco Oliveira
Natural Language Processing & Portuguese-Chinese Machine Translation Laboratory,
Department of Computer and Information Science,
University of Macau, Macau, China
takamachi660@gmail.com, vincentwang0229@hotmail.com,
derekfw@umac.mo, lidiasc@umac.mo, wang2008499@gmail.com,
olifran@umac.mo

Abstract

This paper describes adapting statistical machine translation (SMT) systems to medical domain using in-domain and general-domain data as well as web-crawled in-domain resources. In order to complement the limited in-domain corpora, we apply domain focused web-crawling approaches to acquire in-domain monolingual data and bilingual lexicon from the Internet. The collected data is used for adapting the language model and translation model to boost the overall translation quality. Besides, we propose an alternative filtering approach to clean the crawled data and to further optimize the domain-specific SMT system. We attend the medical summary sentence unconstrained translation task of the Ninth Workshop on Statistical Machine Translation (WMT2014). Our systems achieve the second best BLEU scores for Czech-English, fourth for French-English, English-French language pairs and the third best results for reminding pairs.

1 Introduction

In this paper, we report the experiments carried out by the NLP²CT Laboratory at University of Macau for WMT2014 medical sentence translation task on six language pairs: Czech-English (cs-en), French-English (fr-en), German-English (de-en) and the reverse direction pairs (i.e., en-cs, en-fr and en-de).

As data in specific domain are usually relatively scarce, the use of web resources to complement the training resources provides an effective way to enhance the SMT systems (Resnik and smith, 2003; Esplà-Gomis and Forcada, 2010; Pecina et al., 2011; Pecina et al., 2012; Pecina et al., 2014). In our experiments, we not only use all available training data provided by the WMT2014 standard translation task[1] (general-domain data) and medical translation task[2] (in-domain data), but also acquire addition in-domain bilingual translations (i.e. dictionary) and monolingual data from online sources.

First of all, we collect the medical terminologies from the web. This tiny but significant parallel data are helpful to reduce the out-of-vocabulary words (OOVs) in translation models. In addition, the use of larger language models during decoding is aided by more efficient storage and inference (Heafield, 2011). Thus, we crawl more in-domain monolingual data from the Internet based on domain focused web-crawling approach. In order to detect and remove out-domain data from the crawled data, we not only explore text-to-topic classifier, but also propose an alternative filtering approach combined the existing one (text-to-topic classifier) with perplexity. After carefully pre-processing all the available training data, we apply language model adaptation and translation model adaptation using various kinds of training corpora. Experimental results show that the presented approaches are helpful to further boost the baseline system.

The reminder of this paper is organized as follows. In Section 2, we detail the workflow of web resources acquisition. Section 3 describes the pre-processing steps for the corpora. Section 5 presents the baseline system. Section 6 reports the experimental results and discussions. Finally,

[1] http://www.statmt.org/wmt14/translation-task.html.
[2] http://www.statmt.org/wmt14/medical-task/.

Proceedings of the Ninth Workshop on Statistical Machine Translation, pages 233–238,
Baltimore, Maryland USA, June 26–27, 2014.

the submitted systems and the official results are reported in Section 7.

2 Domain Focused Web-Crawling

In this section, we introduce our domain focused web-crawling approaches on acquisition of in-domain translation terminologies and monolingual sentences.

2.1 Bilingual Dictionary

Terminology is a system of words used to name things in a particular discipline. The in-domain vocabulary size directly affects the performance of domain-specific SMT systems. Small size of in-domain vocabulary may result in serious OOVs problem in a translation system. Therefore, we crawl medical terminologies from some online sources such as dict.cc[3], where the vocabularies are divided into different subjects. We obtain the related bilingual entries in medicine subject by using Scala build-in XML parser and XPath. After cleaning, we collected 28,600, 37,407, and 37,600 entries in total for cs-en, de-en, and fr-en respectively.

2.2 Monolingual Data

The workflow for acquiring in-domain resources consists of a number of steps such as domain identification, text normalization, language identification, noise filtering, and post-processing as well as parallel sentence identification.

Firstly we use an open-source crawler, Combine[4], to crawl webpages from the Internet. In order to classify these webpages as relevant to the medical domain, we use a list of triplets <*term, relevance weight, topic class*> as the basic entries to define the topic. *Term* is a word or phrase. We select terms for each language from the following sources:

- The Wikipedia title corpus, a WMT2014 official data set consisting of titles of medical articles.
- The dict.cc dictionary, as is described in Section 2.1.
- The DrugBank corpus, which is a WMT2014 official data set on bioinformatics and cheminformatics.

For the parallel data, i.e. Wikipedia and dict.cc dictionary, we separate the source and target text into individual text and use either side of them for constructing the term list for different languages. Regarding the DrugBank corpus, we directly extract the terms from the "*name*" field. The vocabulary size of collected text for each language is shown in Table 1.

	EN	CS	DE	FR
Wikipedia Titles	12,684	3,404	10,396	8,436
dict.cc	29,294	16,564	29,963	22,513
DrugBank	2,788			
Total	44,766	19,968	40,359	30,949

Table 1: Size of terms used for topic definition.

Relevance weight is the score for each occurrence of the term, which is assigned by its length, i.e., number of tokens. The *topic class* indicates the topics. In this study, we are interested in medical domain, the topic class is always marked with "MED" in our topic definition.

The topic relevance of each document is calculated[5] as follows:

$$s = \sum_{i=1}^{N} \sum_{j=1}^{4} n_{ij} w_i^t w_j^l \qquad (1)$$

where N is the amount of terms in the topic definition; w_i^t is the weight of term i; w_j^l is the weight of term at location j. n_{ij} is the number of occurrences of term i at j position. In implementation, we use the default values for setting and parameters. Another input required by the crawler is a list of seed URLs, which are web sites that related to medical topic. We limit the crawler from getting the pages within the http domain guided by the seed links. We acquired the list from the Open Directory Project[6], which is a repository maintained by volunteer editors. Totally, we collected 12,849 URLs from the medicine category.

Text normalization is to convert the text of each HTML page into UTF-8 encoding according to the content_charset of the header. In addition, HTML pages often consist of a number of irrelevant contents such as the navigation links, advertisements disclaimers, etc., which may negatively affect the performance of SMT system. Therefore, we use the Boilerpipe tool (Kohlschütter et al., 2010) to filter these noisy data and preserve the useful content that is marked by the tag, <canonicalDocument>. The resulting text is saved in an XML file, which will be further processed by the subsequent tasks. For language identification, we use the language-detection[7] toolkit to determine the possible lan-

[3] http://www.dict.cc/.

[4] http://combine.it.lth.se/.

[5] http://combine.it.lth.se/documentation/DocMain/node6.html.

[6] http://www.dmoz.org/Health/Medicine/.

[7] https://code.google.com/p/language-detection/.

guage of the text, and discard the articles which are in the right language we are interested.

2.3 Data Filtering

The web-crawled documents (described in Section 2.2) may consist a number of out-domain data, which would harm the domain-specific language and translation models. We explore and propose two filtering approaches for this task. The first one is to filter the documents based on their relative score, Eq. (1). We rank all the documents according to their relative scores and select top *K* percentage of entire collection for further processing.

Second, we use a combination method, which takes both the perplexity and relative score into account for the selection. Perplexity-based data selection has shown to be a powerful mean on SMT domain adaptation (Wang et al., 2013; Wang et al., 2014; Toral, 2013; Rubino et al., 2013; Duh et al., 2013). The combination method is carried out as follows: we first retrieve the documents based on their relative scores. The documents are then split into sentences, and ranked according to their perplexity using Eq. (2) (Stolcke et al., 2002). The used language model is trained on the official in-domain data. Finally, top *N* percentage of ranked sentences are considered as additional relevant in-domain data.

$$ppl1(s) = 10^{-\log\frac{P(T)}{Word}} \quad (2)$$

where s is a input sentence or document, $P(T)$ is the probability of n-gram segments estimated from the training set. $Word$ is the number of tokens of an input string.

3 Pre-processing

Both official training data and web-crawled resources are processed using the Moses scripts[8], this includes the text tokenization, truecasing and length cleaning. For trusecasing, we use both the target side of parallel corpora and monolingual data to train the trucase models. We consider the target system is intended for summary translation, the sentences tend to be short in length. We remove sentence pairs which are more than 80 words at length in either sides of the parallel text.

In addition to these general data filtering steps, we introduce some extra steps to pre-process the training data. The first step is to remove the duplicate sentences. In data-driven methods, the more frequent a term occurs, the higher probability it biases. Duplicate data may lead to unpredicted behavior during the decoding. Therefore, we keep only the distinct sentences in monolingual corpus. By taking into account multiple translations in parallel corpus, we remove the duplicate sentence pairs. We also use a biomedical sentence splitter[9] (Rune et al., 2007) to split sentences in monolingual corpora. The statistics of the data are provided in Table 2.

4 Baseline System

We built our baseline system on an optimized level. It is trained on all official in-domain training corpora and a portion of general-domain data. We apply the Moore-Lewis method (Moore and Lewis, 2010) and modified Moore-Lewis method (Axelrod et al., 2011) for selecting in-domain data from the general-domain monolingual and parallel corpora, respectively. The top *M* percentages of ranked sentences are selected as a pseudo in-domain data to train an additional LM and TM. For LM, we linearly interpolate the additional LM with in-domain LM. For TM, the additional model is log-linearly interpolated with the in-domain model using the multi-decoding method described in (Koehn and Schroeder, 2007). Finally, LM adaptation and TM adaptation are combined to further improve the translation quality of baseline system.

5 Experiments and Results

The official medical summary development sets (dev) are used for tuning and evaluating the comparative systems. The official medical summary test sets (test) are only used in our final submitted systems.

The experiments were carried out with the Moses 1.0[10] (Koehn et al., 2007). The translation and the re-ordering model utilizes the "*grow-diag-final*" symmetrized word-to-word alignments created with MGIZA++[11] (Och and Ney, 2003; Gao and Vogel, 2008) and the training scripts from Moses. A 5-gram LM was trained using the SRILM toolkit[12] (Stolcke et al., 2002), exploiting improved modified Kneser-Ney smoothing, and quantizing both probabilities and back-off weights. For the log-linear model training, we take the minimum-error-rate training (MERT) method as described in (Och, 2003).

[8] http://www.statmt.org/moses/?n=Moses.Baseline.

[9] http://www.nactem.ac.uk/y-matsu/geniass/.

[10] http://www.statmt.org/moses/.

[11] http://www.kyloo.net/software/doku.php/mgiza:overview.

[12] http://www.speech.sri.com/projects/srilm/.

Data Set	Lang.	Sent.	Words	Vocab.	Ave. Len.	Sites	Docs
In-domain Parallel Data	cs/en	1,770,421	9,373,482/ 10,605,222	134,998/ 156,402	5.29/ 5.99		
	de/en	3,894,099	52,211,730/ 58,544,608	1,146,262/ 487,850	13.41/ 15.03		
	fr/en	4,579,533	77,866,237/ 68,429,649	495,856/ 556,587	17.00/ 14.94		
General-domain Parallel Data	cs/en	12,426,374	180,349,215/ 183,841,805	1,614,023/ 1,661,830	14.51/ 14.79		
	de/en	4,421,961	106,001,775/ 112,294,414	1,912,953/ 919,046	23.97/ 25.39		
	fr/en	36,342,530	1,131,027,766/ 953,644,980	3,149,336/ 3,324,481	31.12/ 26.24		
In-domain Mono. Data	cs	106,548	1,779,677	150,672	16.70		
	fr	1,424,539	53,839,928	644,484	37.79		
	de	2,222,502	53,840,304	1,415,202	24.23		
	en	7,802,610	199430649	1,709,594	25.56		
General-domain Mono. Data	cs	33,408,340	567,174,266	3,431,946	16.98		
	fr	30,850,165	780,965,861	2,142,470	25.31		
	de	84,633,641	1,548,187,668	10,726,992	18.29		
	en	85,254,788	2,033,096,800	4,488,816	23.85		
Web-crawled In-domain Mono. Data	en	8,448,566	280,211,580	3,047,758	33.16	26	1,601
	cs	44,198	1,280,326	137,179	28.96	4	388
	de	473,171	14,087,687	728,652	29.77	17	968
	fr	852,036	35,339,445	718,141	41.47	10	683

Table 2: Statistics summary of corpora after pre-processing.

In the following sub-sections, we describe the results of **baseline systems**, which are trained on the official corpora. We also present the **enhanced systems** that make use of the web-crawled bilingual dictionary and monolingual data as the additional training resources. Two variants of enhanced system are constructed based on different filtering criteria.

5.1 Baseline System

The baseline systems is constructed based on the combination of TM adaptation and LM adaptation, where the corresponding selection thresholds (M) are manually tuned. Table 3 shows the BLEU scores of baseline systems as well as the threshold values of M for general-domain monolingual corpora and parallel corpora selection, respectively.

By looking into the results, we find that en-cs system performs poorly, because of the limited in-domain parallel and monolingual corpora (shown in Table 2). While the fr-en and en-fr systems achieve the best scores, due the availability of the high volume training data. We experiment with different values of M={0, 25, 50, 75, 100} that indicates the percentages of sentences out of the general corpus used for constructing the LM adaptation and TM adaptation. After tuning the parameter M, we find that BLEU scores of different systems peak at different values of M. LM adaptation can achieve the best translation results for cs-en, en-fr and de-en pairs when M=25, en-cs and en-de pairs when M=50, and fr-en pair when M=75. While TM adaptation yields the best scores for en-fr and en-de pairs at M=25 and cs-en and fr-en pairs at M=50, de-en pair when M=75 and en-cs pair at M=100.

Lang. Pair	BLEU	Mono. (M%)	Parallel (M%)
en-cs	17.57	50%	100%
cs-en	31.29	25%	50%
en-fr	38.36	25%	25%
fr-en	44.36	75%	50%
en-de	18.01	50%	25%
de-en	32.50	25%	75%

Table 3: BLEU scores of baseline systems for different language pairs.

5.2 Based on Relevance Score Filtering

As described in Section 2.3, we use the relevance score to filter out the non-in-domain documents. Once again, we evaluate different values of

K={0, 25, 50, 75, 100} that represents the percentages of crawled documents we used for training the LMs. In Table 4, we show the absolute BLEU scores of the evaluated systems, listed with the optimized thresholds, and the relative improvements (Δ %) in compared to the baseline system. The size of additional training data (for LM) is displayed at the last column.

Lang. Pair	Docs (K%)	BLEU	Δ (%)	Sent.
en-cs	50	17.59	0.11	31,065
en-de	75	18.52	2.83	435,547
en-fr	50	39.08	1.88	743,735
cs-en	75	32.22	2.97	7,943,931
de-en	25	33.50	3.08	4,951,189
fr-en	100	45.45	2.46	8,448,566

Table 4: Evaluation results for systems that trained on relevance-score-filtered documents.

The relevance score filtering approach yields an improvement of 3.08% of BLEU score for de-en pair that is the best result among the language pairs. On the other hand, en-cs pair obtains a marginal gain. The reason is very obvious that the training data is very insufficient. Empirical results of all language pairs expect fr-en indicate that data filtering is the necessity to improve the system performance.

5.3 Based on Moore-Lewis Filtering

In this approach, we need to determine the values of two parameters, top K documents and top N sentences, where K={100, 75, 50} and N={75, 50, 25}, $N < K$. When K=100, it is a conventional perplexity-based data selection method, i.e. no document will be filtered. Table 5 shows the combination of different K and N that gives the best translation score for each language pair. We provide the absolute BLEU for each system, together with relative improvements (Δ%) that compared to the baseline system.

Lang. Pair	Docs (K%)	Target Size (N%)	BLEU	Δ (%)
en-cs	50	25	17.69	0.68
en-de	100	50	18.03	0.11
en-fr	100	50	38.73	0.96
cs-en	100	25	32.20	2.91
de-en	100	25	33.10	1.85
fr-en	100	25	45.22	1.94

Table 5: Evaluation results for systems that trained on combination filtering approach.

In this shared task, we have a quality and quantity in-domain monolingual training data for English. All the systems that take English as the target translation always outperform the other reverse pairs. Besides, we found the systems based on the perplexity data selection method tend to achieve a better scores in BLEU.

6 Official Results and Conclusions

We described our study on developing unconstrained systems in the medical translation task of 2014 Workshop on Statistical Machine Translation. In this work, we adopt the web crawling strategy for acquiring the in-domain monolingual data. In detection the domain data, we exploited Moore-Lewis data selection method to filter the collected data in addition to the build-in scoring model provided by the crawler toolkit. However, after investigation, we found that the two methods are very competitive to each other.

The systems we submitted to the shared task were built using the language models and translation models that yield the best results in the individual testing. The official test set is converted into the *recased* and *detokenized* SGML format. Table 9 presents the official results of our submissions for every language pair.

Lang. Pair	BLEU of Combined systems	Official BLEU
en-cs	23.16 (+5.59)	22.10
cs-en	36.8 (+5.51)	37.40
en-fr	40.34 (+1.98)	40.80
fr-en	45.79 (+1.43)	43.80
en-de	19.36 (+1.35)	18.80
de-en	34.17 (+1.67)	32.70

Table 6: BLEU scores of the submitted systems for the medical translation task in six language pairs.

Acknowledgments

The authors are grateful to the Science and Technology Development Fund of Macau and the Research Committee of the University of Macau for the funding support for their research, under the Reference nos. MYRG076 (Y1-L2)-FST13-WF and MYRG070 (Y1-L2)-FST12-CS.

References

Amittai Axelrod, Xiaodong He, and Jianfeng Gao. 2011. Domain adaptation via pseudo in-domain data selection. In *Proceedings of EMNLP*, pages 355-362.

K. Duh, G. Neubig, K. Sudoh, H. Tsukada. 2013. Adaptation data selection using neural language models: Experiments in machine translation. In *Proceedings of the Annual Meeting of the Association for Computational Linguistics*, pages, 678–683.

M. Esplà-Gomis and M. L. Forcada. 2010. Combining Content-Based and URL-Based Heuristics toHarvest Aligned Bitexts from Multilingual Sites with Bitextor. *The Prague Bulletin of Mathemathical Lingustics*, 93:77–86.

Qin Gao and Stephan Vogel. 2008. Parallel Implementations of Word Alignment Tool. *Software Engineering, Testing, and Quality Assurance for Natural Language Processing*, pp. 49-57.

Kenneth Heafield. 2011. KenLM: Faster and smaller language model queries. In *Proceedings of the Sixth Workshop on Statistical Machine Translation*, pages 187-197.

Papineni, Kishore, Salim Roukos, ToddWard, and-Wei-Jing Zhu. 2002. BLEU: a method for automatic evaluation of machine translation. In *40th Annual Meeting on Association for Computational Linguistics*, ACL '02, pages 311–318, Philadelphia, USA.

Philipp Koehn, Hieu Hoang, Alexandra Birch, Chris Callison-Burch, Marcello Federico, Nicola Bertoldi, Brooke Cowan, Wade Shen, Christine Moran et al. 2007. Moses: Open source toolkit for statistical machine translation. In *Proceedings of ACL*, pages 177-180.

Philipp Koehn and Josh Schroeder. 2007. Experiments in domain adaptation for statistical machine translation. In *Proceedings of the 2nd ACL Workshop on Statistical Machine Translation*, pages 224-227.

Christian Kohlschütter, Peter Fankhauser, and Wolfgang Nejdl. 2010. Boilerplate detection using shallow text features. In *Proceedings of the 3rd ACM International Conference on Web Search and Data Mining*, pages 441-450.

Robert C. Moore and William Lewis. 2010. Intelligent selection of language model training data. In *Proceedings of ACL*: Short Papers, pages 220-224.

Franz Josef Och. 2003. Minimum error rate training in statistical machine translation. *Proceedings of ACL*, pp. 160-167.

Franz Josef Och and Hermann Ney. 2003. A systematic comparison of various statistical alignment models. *Computational Linguistics*, 29:19-51.

P. Pecina, A. Toral, A. Way, V. Papavassiliou, P. Prokopidis, and M. Giagkou. 2011. Towards Using WebCrawled Data for Domain Adaptation in Statistical Machine Translation. In *Proceedings of the 15th Annual Conference of the European Associtation for Machine Translation*, pages 297-304.

P. Pecina, A. Toral, V. Papavassiliou, P. Prokopidis, J. van Genabith, and R. I. C. Athena. 2012. Domain adaptation of statistical machine translation using web-crawled resources: a case study. In *Proceedings of the 16th Annual Conference of the European Association for Machine Translation*, pp. 145-152.

P. Pecina, O. Dušek, L. Goeuriot, J. Hajič, J. Hlaváčová, G. J. Jones, and Z. Urešová. 2014. Adaptation of machine translation for multilingual information retrieval in the medical domain. *Artificial intelligence in medicine*, pages 1-25.

Philip Resnik and Noah A. Smith. 2003. The Web as a parallel corpus. Computational Linguistics, 29:349–380

Raphael Rubino, Antonio Toral, Santiago Cortés Vaíllo, Jun Xie, Xiaofeng Wu, Stephen Doherty, and Qun Liu. 2013. The CNGL-DCU-Prompsit translation systems for WMT13. In *Proceedings of the Eighth Workshop on Statistical Machine Translation*, pages 213-218.

Sætre Rune, Kazuhiro Yoshida, Akane Yakushiji, Yusuke Miyao, Yuichiro Matsubayashi and Tomoko Ohta. 2007. AKANE System: Protein-Protein Interaction Pairs in BioCreAtIvE2 Challenge, PPI-IPS subtask. In *Proceedings of the Second BioCreative Challenge Evaluation Workshop*, pp. 209-212.

Andreas Stolcke. 2002. SRILM-an extensible language modeling toolkit. *Proceedings of the International Conference on Spoken Language Processing*, pp. 901-904.

Antonio Toral. 2013. Hybrid selection of language model training data using linguistic information and perplexity. In *ACL Workshop on Hybrid Machine Approaches to Translation*.

Longyue Wang, Derek F. Wong, Lidia S. Chao, Yi Lu, and Junwen Xing. 2014. A Systematic Comparison of Data Selection Criteria for SMT Domain Adaptation. *The Scientific World Journal*, vol. 2014, Article ID 745485, 10 pages.

Longyue Wang, Derek F. Wong, Lidia S. Chao, Yi Lu, Junwen Xing. 2013. *i*CPE: A Hybrid Data Selection Model for SMT Domain Adaptation. *Chinese Computational Linguistics and Natural Language Processing Based on Naturally Annotated Big Data.* Springer Berlin Heidelberg. pages, 280-290

The DCU Terminology Translation System for the Medical Query Subtask at WMT14

Tsuyoshi Okita, Ali Hosseinzadeh Vahid, Andy Way, Qun Liu
Dublin City University, School of Computing
Glasnevin, Dublin 9
Ireland
{tokita,avahid,away,qliu}@computing.dcu.ie

Abstract

This paper describes the Dublin City University terminology translation system used for our participation in the query translation subtask in the medical translation task in the Workshop on Statistical Machine Translation (WMT14). We deployed six different kinds of terminology extraction methods, and participated in three different tasks: FR–EN and EN–FR query tasks, and the CLIR task. We obtained 36.2 BLEU points absolute for FR–EN and 28.8 BLEU points absolute for EN–FR tasks where we obtained the first place in both tasks. We obtained 51.8 BLEU points absolute for the CLIR task.

1 Introduction

This paper describes the terminology translation system developed at Dublin City University for our participation in the query translation subtask at the Workshop on Statistical Machine Translation (WMT14). We developed six kinds of terminology extraction methods for the problem of medical terminology translation, especially where rare and new words are considered. We have several motivations which we address before providing a description of the actual algorithms undeprinning our work.

First, terminology translation cannot be seen just as a simple extension of the translation process if we use an analogy from human translation. Terminology translation can be considered as more important and a quite different task than translation *per se*, so we need a considerably different way of solving this particular problem. Bilingual terminology selection has been claimed to be the touchstone in human translation, especially where scientific and legal translation are concerned. Terminology selection is often the hardest and most time-consuming process in the translation workflow. Depending on the particular requirements of the use-case (Way, 2013), users may not object to disfluent translations, but will invariably be very sensitive to the wrong selection of terminology, even if the meaning of the chosen terms is correct. This is especially true if this selected terminology does not match with that preferred by the users themselves, in which case users are likely to express some kind of complaint; it may even be that the entire translation is rejected as sub-standard or inappropriate on such grounds.

Second, we look at how to handle new and rare words. If we inspect the process of human translation more closely, it is easy to identify several differences compared to the methods used in statistical MT (SMT). Unless stipulated by the client, the selection of bilingual terminology can be a highly subjective process. Accordingly, it is not necessarily the bilingual term-pair with the highest probability that is chosen by the human translator. It is often the case that statistical methods often forget about or delete less frequent n-grams, but rely on more frequent n-grams using maximum likelihood or Maximum A Priori (MAP) methods. If some terminology is highly suitable, a human translator can use it quite freely. Furthermore, there are a lot of new words in reality for which new target equivalents have to be created by the translators themselves, so the question arises as to how human translators actually select appropriate new terminology. Transliteration, which is often supported by many Asian languages including Hindi, Japanese, and Chinese, is perhaps the easiest things to do under such circumstances. Slight modifications of alphabets/accented characters can sometimes successfully create a valid new term, even for European languages.

The remainder of this paper is organized as follows. Section 2 describes our algorithms. Our decoding strategy in Section 3. Our experimen-

Proceedings of the Ninth Workshop on Statistical Machine Translation, pages 239–245,
Baltimore, Maryland USA, June 26–27, 2014.

tal settings and results are presented in Section 4, and we conclude in Section 5.

2 Our Methods

Apart from the conventional statistical approach to extract bilingual terminology, this medical query task reminds us of two frequently occurring problems which are often ignored: (i) "Can we forget about terminology which occurs only once in a corpus?", and (ii) "What can we do if the terminology does not occur in a corpus?" These two problems require computationally quite different approaches than what is usually done in the standard statistical approach. Furthermore, the medical query task in WMT14 provides a wide range of corpora: parallel and monolingual corpora, as well as dictionaries. These two interesting aspects motivate our extraction methods which we present in this section, including one relatively new Machine Learning algorithm of zero-shot learning arising from recent developments in the neural network community (Bengio et al., 2000; Mikolov et al., 2013b).

2.1 Translation Model

Word alignment (Brown et al., 1993) and phrase extraction (Koehn et al., 2003) can capture bilingual word- and phrase-pairs with a good deal of accuracy. We omit further details of these standard methods which are freely available elsewhere in the SMT literature (e.g. (Koehn, 2010)).

2.2 Extraction from Parallel Corpora

(Okita et al., 2010) addressed the problem of capturing bilingual term-pairs from parallel data which might otherwise not be detected by the translation model. Hence, the requirement in Okita et al. is not to use SMT/GIZA++ (Och and Ney, 2003) to extract term-pairs, which are the common focus in this medical query translation task.

The classical algorithm of (Kupiec, 1993) used in (Okita et al., 2010) counts the statistics of terminology $c(e_{term_i}, f_{term_j}|s_t)$ on the source and the target sides which jointly occur in a sentence s_t after detecting candidate terms via POS tagging, which are then summed up over the entire corpus $\sum_{t=1}^{N} c(e_{term_i}, f_{term_j}|s_t)$. Then, the algorithm adjusts the length of e_{term_i} and f_{term_j}. It can be said that this algorithm captures term-pairs which occur rather frequently. However, this apparent strength can also be seen in disadvantageous terms since the search for terminology occurs densely in each of the sentences which increases the computational complexity of this algorithm, and causes the method to take a considerable time to run. Furthermore, if we suppose that most frequent term-pairs are to be extracted via a standard translation model (as described briefly in the previous section), our efforts to search among frequent pairs is not likely to bring about further gain.

It is possible to approach this in a reverse manner: "less frequent pairs can be outstanding term candidates". Accordingly, if our aim changes to capture only those less frequent pairs, the situation changes dramatically. The number of terms we need to capture is considerably decreased. Many sentences do not include any terminology at all, and only a relatively small subset of sentences includes a few terms, such that term-pairs become sparse with regard to sentences. Term-pairs can be found rather easily if a candidate term-pair co-occurs on the source and the target sides *and* on the condition that the items in the term-pair actually correspond with one another.

This condition can be easily checked in various ways. One way is to translate the source side of the targeted pairs with the alignment option in the Moses decoder (Koehn et al., 2007), which we did in this evaluation campaign. Another way is to use asupervised aligner, such as the Berkeley aligner (Haghighi et al., 2009), to align the targeted pairs and check whether they are actually aligned or not.

We assume two predefined sets of terms at the outset, $E_{term} = \{e_{term_1}, \ldots, e_{term_n}\}$ and $F_{term} = \{f_{term_1}, \ldots, f_{term_n}\}$. We search for possible alignment links between the term-pair only when they co-occur in the same sentence. One obvious advantage of this approach is the computational complexity which is fairly low.

Note that the result of (Okita et al., 2010) shows that the frequency-based approach of (Kupiec, 1993) worked well for NTCIR patent terminology (Fujii et al., 2010), which otherwise would have been difficult to capture via the traditional SMT/GIZA++ method. In contrast, however, this did not work well on the Europarl corpus (Koehn, 2005).

2.3 Terminology Dictionaries

Terminology dictionaries themselves are obviously among the most important resources for bilingual term-pairs. In this medical query translation subtask, two corpora are provided for this purpose: (i) Unified Medical Language System corpus (UMLS corpus),[1] and (ii) Wiki entries.[2]

2.4 Extraction from Terminology Dictionaries: lower-order *n*-grams

Terminology dictionaries provide reliable higher-order *n*-gram pairs. However, they do not often provide the correspondences between the lower-order *n*-grams contained therein. For example, the UMLS corpus provides a term-pair of "abdominal compartment syndrome ||| *syndrome du compartiment abdominal*" (EN|||FR). However, such terminology dictionaries often do not explicitly provide the correspondent pairs "abdominal ||| *abdominal*" (EN|||FR) or "syndrome ||| *syndrome*" (EN|||FR). Clearly, these terminology dictionaries implicitly provide the correspondent pairs. Note that UMLS and Wiki entries provide terminology dictionaries. Hence, it is possible to obtain some suggestion by higher order *n*-gram models if we know their alignments between words on the source and target sides. Algorithm 1 shows the overall procedure.

Algorithm 1 Lower-order *n*-gram extraction algorithm

1: Perform monolingual word alignment for higher-order *n*-gram pairs.
2: Collect only the reliable alignment pairs (i.e. discard unreliable alignment pairs).
3: Extract the lower-order word pairs of our interest.

2.5 Extraction from Monolingual Corpora: Transliteration and Abbreviation

Monolingual corpora can be used in various ways, including:

1. *Transliteration*: Many languages support the fundamental mechanism of between European and Asian languages. Japanese even supports a special alphabet – katakana – for this purpose. Chinese and Hindi also permit transliteration using their own alphabets. However, even among European languages, this mechanism makes it possible to find possible translation counterparts for a given term. In this query task, we did this only for the French-to-English direction and only for words containing accented characters (by rule-based conversion).

2. *Abbreviation*: It is often the case that abbreviations should be resolved in the same language. If the translation includes some abbreviation, such as "C. difficile", this needs to be investigated exhaustively in the same language. However, in the specific domain of medical terminology, it is quite likely that possible phrase matches will be successfully identified.

[1] http://www.nlm.nih.gov/research/umls/.

[2] http://www.wikipedia.org.

2.6 Extraction from Monolingual Corpora: Zero-Shot Learning

Algorithm 2 Algorithm to connect two word embedding space

1: Prepare the monolingual source and target sentences.
2: Prepare the dictionary which consists of U entries of source and target sentences among non-stop-words.
3: Train the neural network language model on the source side and obtain the continuous space real vectors of X dimensions for each word.
4: Train the neural network language model on the target side and obtain the continuous space real vectors of X dimensions for each word.
5: Using the real vectors obtained in the above steps, obtain the linear mapping between the dictionary in two continuous spaces using canonical component analysis (CCA).

Another interesting terminology extraction method requires neither parallel nor comparable corpora, but rather just monolingual corpora on both sides (possibly unrelated to each other) together with a small amount of dictionary entries which provide already known correspondences between words on the source and target sides (henceforth, we refer to this as the 'dictionary'). This method uses the recently developed zero-shot learning (Palatucci et al., 2009) using neural network language modelling (Bengio et al., 2000; Mikolov et al., 2013b). Then, we train both sides with the neural network language model, and use a continuous space representation to project words to each other on the basis of a small amount of correspondences in the dictionary. If we assume that each continuous space is linear (Mikolov et al., 2013c), we can connect them via linear projection (Mikolov et al., 2013b). Algorithm 2 shows this situation.

In our experiments we use U the same as the entries of Wiki and X as 50. Algorithm 3 shows the algorithm to extract the counterpart of OOV words.

Algorithm 3 Algorithm to extract the counterpart of OOV words.

1: Prepare the projection by Algorithm 2.
2: Detect unknown words in the translation outputs.
3: Do the projection of it (the source word) into the target word using the trained linear mappings in the training step.

3 Decoding Strategy

We deploy six kinds of extraction methods: (1) translation model, (2) extraction from parallel corpora, (3) terminology dictionaries, (4) lower-order n-grams, (5) transliteration and abbreviation, and (6) zero-shot learning. Among these we deploy four of them – (2), (4), (5) and (6) – in a limited context, while the remaining two are used without any context, mainly owing to time constraints; only when we did not find the correspondent pairs via (1) and (3), did we complement this by the other methods.

The detected bilingual term-pairs using (1) and (3) can be combined using various methods. One way is to employ a method similar to (confusion network-based) system combination (Okita and van Genabith, 2011; Okita and van Genabith, 2012). First we make a lattice: if we regard one candidate of (1) and two candidates in (3) as translation outputs where the words of two candidates in (3) are connected using an underscore (i.e. one word), we can make a lattice. Then, we can deploy monotonic decoding over them. If we do this for the devset and then apply it to the test set, we can incorporate a possible preference learnt from the development set, i.e. whether the query translator prefers method (1) or UMLS/Wiki translation. MERT process and language model are applied in a similar manner with (confusion network-based) system combination (cf. (Okita and van Genabith, 2011)).

We note also that a lattice structure is useful for handling grammatical coordination. Since queries are formed by real users, reserved words for database query such as "AND" (or "*ET*" (FR)) and "OR" (or "*OU*" (FR)) are frequently observed in the test set. Furthermore, there is repeated use of "and" more than twice, for example "*douleur abnominal et Helicobacter pylori et cancer*", which makes it very difficult to detect the correct coordination boundaries. The lattice on the input side can express such ambiguity at the cost of splitting the source-side sentence in a different manner.

4 Experimental Results

The baseline is obtained in the following way. The GIZA++ implementation (Och and Ney, 2003) of IBM Model 4 is used as the baseline for word alignment: Model 4 is incrementally trained by performing 5 iterations of Model 1, 5 iterations of HMM, 3 iterations of Model 3, and 3 iterations of Model 4. For phrase extraction the grow-diag-final heuristics described in (Koehn et al., 2003) is used to derive the refined alignment from bidirectional alignments. We then perform MERT (Och, 2003) which optimizes parameter settings using the BLEU metric (Papineni et al., 2002), while a 5-gram language model is derived with Kneser-Ney smoothing (Kneser and Ney, 1995) trained using SRILM (Stolcke, 2002). We use the whole training corpora including the WMT14 translation task corpora as well as medical domain data. UMLS and Wikipedia are used just as training corpora for the baseline.

For the extraction from parallel corpora (cf. Section 2.2), we used Genia tagger (Tsuruoka and Tsujii, 2005) and the Berkeley parser (Petrov and Klein, 2007). For the zero-shot learning (cf. Section 2.6) we used scikit learn (Pedregosa et al., 2011), word2vec (Mikolov et al., 2013a), and a recurrent neural network (Mikolov, 2012). Other tools used are in-house software.

Table 2 shows the results for the FR–EN query task. We obtained 36.2 BLEU points absolute, which is an improvement of 6.3 BLEU point absolute (21.1% relative) over the baseline. Table 3 shows the results for the EN–FR query task. We obtained 28.8 BLEU points absolute, which is an improvement of 8.7 BLEU points absolute (43% relative) over the baseline. Our system was the best system for both of these tasks. These improvements over the baseline were statistically significant by a paired bootstrap test (Koehn, 2004).

	Query task FR–EN	
	Our method	baseline
BLEU	36.2	29.9
BLEU cased	30.9	26.5
TER	0.340	0.443

Table 1: Results for FR–EN query task.

extraction	LM	MERT	BLEU (cased)
(1) - (6)	all	Y	30.9
(1), (2), (3)	all	Y	30.3
(1), (3), (6)	all	Y	30.1
(1), (3), (4)	all	Y	29.1
(1), (3), (5)	all	Y	29.0
(1) and (3)	all	Y	29.0
(1) and (3)	medical	Y	27.5
(1) and (3)	WMT	Y	27.0
(1) and (3)	medical	N	25.1
(1) and (3)	WMT	N	24.3
(1)	medical	Y	25.9
(1)	WMT	Y	25.0

Table 2: Table shows the effects of extraction methods, language model and MERT process. All the measurements are by BLEU (cased). In this table, "medical" indicates a language model built on all the medical corpora while "WMT" indicates a language model built on all the non-medical corpora. Note that some sentence in testset can be considered as non-medical domain. Extraction methods (1) - (6) correspond to those described in Section 2.1 - 2.6.

Table 4 shows the results for CLIR task. We obtained 51.8 BLEU points absolute, which is an improvement of 9.4 BLEU point absolute (22.2% relative) over the baseline. Although CLIR task allowed 10-best lists, our submission included only 1-best list. This resulted in the score of P@5 of 0.348 and P@10 of 0.346 which correspond to the second place, despite a good result in terms of BLEU. This is since unlike BLEU score P@5 and P@10 measure whether the whole elements in reference and hypothesis are matched or not. We noticed that our submission included a lot of

	Query task EN–FR	
	Our method	baseline
BLEU	28.8	20.1
BLEU cased	27.7	18.7
TER	0.483	0.582

Table 3: Results for EN–FR query task.

near miss sentences only in terms of capitalization: "abnominal pain and Helicobacter pylori and cancer" (reference) and "abnominal pain and helicobacter pylori and cancer" (submission). These are counted as incorrect in terms of P@5 and P@10.[3] Noted that after submission we obtained the revised score of P@5 of 0.560 and P@10 of 0.560 with the same method but with 2-best lists which handles the capitalization varieties.

	CLIR task FR–EN	
	Our method	baseline
BLEU	51.8	42.2
BLEU cased	46.0	38.3
TER	0.364	0.398
P@5	0.348 (0.560*)	–
P@10	0.346 (0.560*)	–
NDCG@5	0.306	–
NDCG@10	0.307	–
MAP	0.2252	–
Rprec	0.2358	–
bpref	0.3659	–
relRet	1524	–

Table 4: Results for CLIR task.

5 Conclusion

This paper provides a description of the Dublin City University terminology translation system for our participation in the query translation subtask in the medical translation task in the Workshop on Statistical Machine Translation (WMT14). We deployed six different kinds of terminology extraction methods. We obtained 36.2 BLEU points absolute for FR–EN, and 28.8 BLEU points absolute for EN–FR tasks, obtaining first place on both tasks. We obtained 51.8 BLEU points absolute for the CLIR task.

[3] The method which incorporates variation in capitalization in its n-best lists outperforms the best result in terms of P@5 and P@10.

Acknowledgments

This research is supported by the Science Foundation Ireland (Grant 07/CE/I1142) as part of CNGL at Dublin City University.

References

Yoshua Bengio, Rejean Ducharme, and Pascal Vincent. 2000. A neural probabilistic language model. *In Proceedings of Neural Information Systems*, pages 1137–1155.

Peter F. Brown, Vincent J.D Pietra, Stephen A.D.Pietra, and Robert L. Mercer. 1993. The mathematics of statistical machine translation: Parameter estimation. *Computational Linguistics, Vol.19, Issue 2*, pages 263–311.

Atsushi Fujii, Masao Utiyama, Mikio Yamamoto, Takehito Utsuro, Terumasa Ehara, Hiroshi Echizenya, and Sayori Shimohata. 2010. Overview of the patent translation task at the NTCIR-8 workshop. *In Proceedings of the 8th NTCIR Workshop Meeting on Evaluation of Information Access Technologies: Information Retrieval, Question Answering and Cross-lingual Information Access*, pages 293–302.

Aria Haghighi, John Blitzer, John DeNero, and Dan Klein. 2009. Better word alignments with supervised itg models. In *In Proceedings of the Conference of Association for Computational Linguistics*, pages 923–931.

Reinhard Kneser and Hermann Ney. 1995. Improved backing-off for n-gram language modeling. *In Proceedings of the IEEE International Conference on Acoustics, Speech and Signal Processing*, pages 181–184.

Philipp Koehn, Franz Och, and Daniel Marcu. 2003. Statistical phrase-based translation. *In Proceedings of the Human Language Technology Conference of the North American Chapter of the Association for Computationa Linguistics (HLT / NAACL 2003)*, pages 115–124.

Philipp Koehn, H. Hoang, A. Birch, C. Callison-Burch, M. Federico, N. Bertoldi, B. Cowan, W. Shen, C. Moran, R. Zens, C. Dyer, O. Bojar, A. Constantin, and E. Herbst. 2007. Moses: Open source toolkit for Statistical Machine Translation. *In Proceedings of the 45th Annual Meeting of the Association for Computational Linguistics Companion Volume Proceedings of the Demo and Poster Sessions*, pages 177–180.

Philipp Koehn. 2004. Statistical significance tests for machine translation evaluation. *In Proceedings of Conference on Empirical Methods in Natural Language Processing (EMNLP 2004)*, pages 388–395.

Philipp Koehn. 2005. Europarl: A parallel corpus for statistical machine translation. *In Proceedings of the Machine Translation Summit*, pages 79–86.

Philipp Koehn. 2010. Statistical machine translation. *Cambridge University Press.*

Julian. Kupiec. 1993. An algorithm for finding Noun phrase correspondences in bilingual corpora. *In Proceedings of the 31st Annual Meeting of the Association for Computational Linguistics*, pages 17–22.

Tomas Mikolov, Kai Chen, Greg Corrado, and Jeffrey Dean. 2013a. Efficient estimation of word representations in vector space. *In Proceedings of Workshop at International Conference on Learning Representations.*

Tomas Mikolov, Quoc V. Le, and Ilya Sutskever. 2013b. Exploiting similarities among languages for machine translation. *ArXiv:1309.4168.*

Tomas Mikolov, Wen tau Yih, and Geoffrey Zweig. 2013c. Linguistic regularities in continuous space word representations. *In Proceedings of the Conference of the North American Chapter of the Association for Computational Linguistics / Human Language Technology (NAACL/HLT 2005)*, pages 746–751.

Tomas Mikolov. 2012. Statistical language models based on neural networks. *PhD thesis at Brno University of Technology.*

Franz Och and Hermann Ney. 2003. A systematic comparison of various statistical alignment models. *Computational Linguistics*, 29(1):19–51.

Franz Och. 2003. Minimum Error Rate Training in Statistical Machine Translation. *In Proceedings of the 41st Annual Meeting of the Association for Computational Linguistics*, pages 160–167.

Tsuyoshi Okita and Josef van Genabith. 2011. DCU Confusion Network-based System Combination for ML4HMT. *Shared Task on Applying Machine Learning techniques to optimising the division of labour in Hybrid MT (ML4HMT-2011, collocated with LIHMT-2011)*, pages 93–98.

Tsuyoshi Okita and Josef van Genabith. 2012. Minimum Bayes Risk Decoding with Enlarged Hypothesis Space in System Combination. *In Proceedings of 13th International Conference on Intelligent Text Processing and Computational Linguistics (CICLING 2012)*, pages 40–51.

Tsuyoshi Okita, Alfredo Maldonado Guerra, Yvette Graham, and Andy Way. 2010. Multi-word expression-sensitive word alignment. *In Proceedings of the Fourth International Workshop On Cross Ling ual Information Access (CLIA2010, collocated with COLING2010)*, pages 26–34.

Mark Palatucci, Dean Pomerleau, Geoffrey Hinton, and Tom Mitchell. 2009. Zero-shot learning with semantic output codes. In *Neural Information Processing Systems (NIPS)*, pages 1410–1418.

K. Papineni, S. Roukos, T. Ward, and W.J. Zhu. 2002. BLEU: A Method For Automatic Evaluation of Machine Translation. *In Proceedings of the 40th Annual Meeting of the Association for Computational Linguistics (ACL-02).*

F. Pedregosa, G. Varoquaux, A. Gramfort, V. Michel, B. Thirion, O. Grisel, M. Blondel, P. Prettenhofer, R. Weiss, V. Dubourg, J. Vanderplas, A. Passos, D. Cournapeau, M. Brucher, M. Perrot, and E. Duchesnay. 2011. Scikit-learn: Machine learning in Python. *Journal of Machine Learning Research*, 12:2825–2830.

Slav Petrov and Dan Klein. 2007. Learning and inference for hierarchically split PCFGs. In *Proceedings of AAAI (Nectar Track)*, pages 1663–1666.

Andreas Stolcke. 2002. SRILM – An extensible language modeling toolkit. *In Proceedings of the International Conference on Spoken Language Processing*, pages 901–904.

Yoshimasa Tsuruoka and Jun'ichi Tsujii. 2005. Bidirectional inference with the easiest-first strategy for tagging sequence data. *In Proceedings of the Conference on Human Language Technology / Empirical Methods on Natural Language Processing (HLT/EMNLP 2005)*, pages 467–474.

Andy Way. 2013. Traditional and emerging use-cases for machine translation. *In Proceedings of Translating and the Computer 35.*

LIMSI @ WMT'14 Medical Translation Task

Nicolas Pécheux[1,2], **Li Gong**[1,2], **Quoc Khanh Do**[1,2], **Benjamin Marie**[2,3],
Yulia Ivanishcheva[2,4], **Alexandre Allauzen**[1,2], **Thomas Lavergne**[1,2],
Jan Niehues[2], **Aurélien Max**[1,2], **François Yvon**[2]
Univ. Paris-Sud[1], LIMSI-CNRS[2]
B.P. 133, 91403 Orsay, France
Lingua et Machina[3], Centre Cochrane français[4]
{firstname.lastname}@limsi.fr

Abstract

This paper describes LIMSI's submission to the first medical translation task at WMT'14. We report results for English-French on the subtask of sentence translation from summaries of medical articles. Our main submission uses a combination of NCODE (n-gram-based) and MOSES (phrase-based) output and continuous-space language models used in a post-processing step for each system. Other characteristics of our submission include: the use of sampling for building MOSES' phrase table; the implementation of the vector space model proposed by Chen et al. (2013); adaptation of the POS-tagger used by NCODE to the medical domain; and a report of error analysis based on the typology of Vilar et al. (2006).

1 Introduction

This paper describes LIMSI's submission to the first medical translation task at WMT'14. This task is characterized by high-quality input text and the availability of large amounts of training data from the same domain, yielding unusually high translation performance. This prompted us to experiment with two systems exploring different translation spaces, the n-gram-based NCODE (§2.1) and an on-the-fly variant of the phrase-based MOSES (§2.2), and to later combine their output. Further attempts at improving translation quality were made by resorting to continuous language model rescoring (§2.4), vector space subcorpus adaptation (§2.3), and POS-tagging adaptation to the medical domain (§3.3). We also performed a small-scale error analysis of the outputs of some of our systems (§5).

2 System Overview

2.1 NCODE

NCODE implements the bilingual n-gram approach to SMT (Casacuberta and Vidal, 2004; Mariño et al., 2006; Crego and Mariño, 2006) that is closely related to the standard phrase-based approach (Zens et al., 2002). In this framework, the translation is divided into two steps. To translate a source sentence $\mathbf{f}$ into a target sentence $\mathbf{e}$, the source sentence is first reordered according to a set of rewriting rules so as to reproduce the target word order. This generates a word lattice containing the most promising source permutations, which is then translated. Since the translation step is monotonic, the peculiarity of this approach is to rely on the n-gram assumption to decompose the joint probability of a sentence pair in a sequence of *bilingual* units called *tuples*.

The best translation is selected by maximizing a linear combination of feature functions using the following inference rule:

$$\mathbf{e}^* = \operatorname*{argmax}_{\mathbf{e},\mathbf{a}} \sum_{k=1}^{K} \lambda_k f_k(\mathbf{f}, \mathbf{e}, \mathbf{a}) \qquad (1)$$

where K feature functions (f_k) are weighted by a set of coefficients (λ_k) and $\mathbf{a}$ denotes the set of hidden variables corresponding to the reordering and segmentation of the source sentence. Along with the n-gram translation models and target n-gram language models, 13 conventional features are combined: 4 *lexicon models* similar to the ones used in standard phrase-based systems; 6 *lexicalized reordering models* (Tillmann, 2004; Crego et al., 2011) aimed at predicting the orientation of the next translation unit; a "weak" distance-based *distortion model*; and finally a *word-bonus model* and a *tuple-bonus model* which compensate for the system preference for short translations. Features are estimated during the training phase. Training source sentences are first reordered so as to match

Proceedings of the Ninth Workshop on Statistical Machine Translation, pages 246–253,
Baltimore, Maryland USA, June 26–27, 2014.

the target word order by unfolding the word alignments (Crego and Mariño, 2006). Tuples are then extracted in such a way that a unique segmentation of the bilingual corpus is achieved (Mariño et al., 2006) and n-gram translation models are then estimated over the training corpus composed of tuple sequences made of surface forms or POS tags. Reordering rules are automatically learned during the unfolding procedure and are built using part-of-speech (POS), rather than surface word forms, to increase their generalization power (Crego and Mariño, 2006).

2.2 On-the-fly System (OTF)

We develop an alternative approach implementing an on-the-fly estimation of the parameter of a standard phrase-based model as in (Le et al., 2012b), also adding an inverse translation model. Given an input source file, it is possible to compute only those statistics which are required to translate the phrases it contains. As in previous works on on-the-fly model estimation for SMT (Callison-Burch et al., 2005; Lopez, 2008), we first build a suffix array for the source corpus. Only a limited number of translation examples, selected by deterministic random sampling, are then used by traversing the suffix array appropriately. A coherent translation probability (Lopez, 2008) (which also takes into account examples where translation extraction failed) is then estimated. As we cannot compute exactly an inverse translation probability (because sampling is performed independently for each source phrase), we resort to the following approximation:

$$p(\bar{f}|\bar{e}) = \min\left(1.0, \frac{p(\bar{e}|\bar{f}) \times freq(\bar{f})}{freq(\bar{e})}\right) \quad (2)$$

where the $freq(\cdot)$ is the number of occurrences of the given phrase in the whole corpus, and the numerator $p(\bar{e}|\bar{f}) \times freq(\bar{f})$ represents the predicted joint count of $\bar{f}$ and $\bar{e}$. The other models in this system are the same as in the default configuration of MOSES.

2.3 Vector Space Model (VSM)

We used the vector space model (VSM) of Chen et al. (2013) to perform domain adaptation. In this approach, each phrase pair $(\bar{f}, \bar{e})$ present in the phrase table is represented by a C-dimensional vector of TF-IDF scores, one for each sub-corpus, where C represents the number of sub-corpora (see Table 1). Each component $w_c(\bar{f}, \bar{e})$ is a standard TF-IDF weight of each phrase pair for the cth sub-corpus. TF$(\bar{f}, \bar{e})$ is the raw joint count of $(\bar{f}, \bar{e})$ in the sub-corpus; the IDF$(\bar{f}, \bar{e})$ is the inverse document frequency across all sub-corpora.

A similar C-dimensional representation of the development set is computed as follows: we first perform word alignment and phrase pairs extraction. For each extracted phrase pair, we compute its TF-IDF vector and finally combine all vectors to obtain the vector for the develompent set:

$$w_c^{dev} = \sum_{j=0}^{J} \sum_{k=0}^{K} count_{dev}(\bar{f}_j, \bar{e}_k) w_c(\bar{f}_j, \bar{e}_k) \quad (3)$$

where J and K are the total numbers of source and target phrases extracted from the development data, respectively, and $count_{dev}(\bar{f}_j, \bar{e}_k)$ is the joint count of phrase pairs $(\bar{f}_j, \bar{e}_k)$ found in the development set. The similarity score between each phrase pair's vector and the development set vector is added into the phrase table as a VSM feature. We also replace the joint count with the marginal count of the source/target phrase to compute an alternative average representation for the development set, thus adding two VSM additional features.

2.4 SOUL

Neural networks, working on top of conventional n-gram back-off language models, have been introduced in (Bengio et al., 2003; Schwenk et al., 2006) as a potential means to improve discrete language models. As for our submitted translation systems to WMT'12 and WMT'13 (Le et al., 2012b; Allauzen et al., 2013), we take advantage of the recent proposal of (Le et al., 2011). Using a specific neural network architecture, the *Structured OUtput Layer* (SOUL), it becomes possible to estimate n-gram models that use large vocabulary, thereby making the training of large neural network language models feasible both for target language models and translation models (Le et al., 2012a). Moreover, the peculiar parameterization of continuous models allows us to consider longer dependencies than the one used by conventional n-gram models (e.g. $n = 10$ instead of $n = 4$).

Additionally, continuous models can also be easily and efficiently adapted as in (Lavergne et al., 2011). Starting from a previously trained SOUL model, only a few more training epochs are

	Corpus	Sentences	Tokens (en-fr)	Description	wrd-lm	pos-lm
in-domain	COPPA	454 246	10-12M		-3	-15
	EMEA	324 189	6-7M		26	-1
	PATTR-ABSTRACTS	634 616	20-24M		22	21
	PATTR-CLAIMS	888 725	32-36M		6	2
	PATTR-TITLES	385 829	3-4M		4	-17
	UMLS	2 166 612	8-8M	term dictionary	-7	-22
	WIKIPEDIA	8 421	17-18k	short titles	-5	-13
out-of-domain	NEWSCOMMENTARY	171 277	4-5M		6	16
	EUROPARL	1 982 937	54-60M		-7	-33
	GIGA	9 625 480	260-319M		27	52
all parallel	all	17M	397-475M	concatenation	33	69
target-lm	medical-data		-146M		69	-
	wmt13-data		-2 536M		49	-
devel/test	DEVEL	500	10-12k	*khresmoi-summary*		
	LMTEST	3 000	61-69k	see Section 3.4		
	NEWSTEST12	3 003	73-82k	from WMT'12		
	TEST	1 000	21-26k	*khresmoi-summary*		

Table 1: Parallel corpora used in this work, along with the number of sentences and the number of English and French tokens, respectively. Weights (λ_k) from our best NCODE configuration are indicated for each sub-corpora's bilingual word language model (wrd-lm) and POS factor language model (pos-lm).

needed on a new corpus in order to adapt the parameters to the new domain.

3 Data and Systems Preparation

3.1 Corpora

We use all the available (constrained) medical data extracted using the scripts provided by the organizers. This resulted in 7 sub-corpora from the medical domain with distinctive features. As out-of-domain data, we reuse the data processed for WMT'13 (Allauzen et al., 2013).

For pre-processing of medical data, we closely followed (Allauzen et al., 2013) so as to be able to directly integrate existing translation and language models, using in-house text processing tools for tokenization and detokenization steps (Déchelotte et al., 2008). All systems are built using a "true case" scheme, but sentences fully capitalized (plentiful especially in PATTR-TITLES) are previously lowercased. Duplicate sentence pairs are removed, yielding a sentence reduction up to 70% for EMEA. Table 1 summarizes the data used along with some statistics after the cleaning and pre-processing steps.

3.2 Language Models

A medical-domain 4-gram language model is built by concatenating the target side of the parallel data and all the available monolingual data[1], with modified Kneser-Ney smoothing (Kneser and Ney, 1995; Chen and Goodman, 1996), using the SRILM (Stolcke, 2002) and KENLM (Heafield, 2011) toolkits. Although more similar to term-to-term dictionaries, UMLS and WIKIPEDIA proved better to be included in the language model. The large out-of-domain language model used for WMT'13 (Allauzen et al., 2013) is additionaly used (see Table 1).

3.3 Part-of-Speech Tagging

Medical data exhibit many peculiarities, including different syntactic constructions and a specific vocabulary. As standard POS-taggers are known not to perform very well for this type of texts, we use a specific model trained on the Penn Treebank and on medical data from the MedPost project (Smith et al., 2004). We use Wapiti (Lavergne et al., 2010), a state-of-the-art CRF implementation, with a standard feature set. Adaptation is performed as in (Chelba and Acero, 2004) using the out-of-domain model as a prior when training the in-domain model on medical data. On a medical test set, this adaptation leads to a 8 point reduction of the error rate. A standard model is used for WMT'13 data. For the French side, due to the lack of annotaded data for the medical domain, corpora are tagged using the TreeTagger (Schmid, 1994).

[1] Attempting include one language model per sub-corpora yielded a significant drop in performance.

3.4 Proxy Test Set

For this first edition of a Medical Translation Task, only a very small development set was made available (DEVEL in Table 1). This made both system design and tuning challenging. In fact, with such a small development set, conventional tuning methods are known to be very unstable and prone to overfitting, and it would be suboptimal to select a configuration based on results on the development set only.[2] To circumvent this, we artificially created our own internal test set by randomly selecting 3 000 sentences out from the 30 000 sentences from PATTR-ABSTRACTS having the lowest perplexity according to 3-gram language models trained on both sides of the DEVEL set. This test set, denoted by LMTEST, is however highly biaised, especially because of the high redundancy in PATTR-ABSTRACTS, and should be used with great care when tuning or comparing systems.

3.5 Systems

NCODE We use NCODE with default settings, 3-gram bilingual translation models on words and 4-gram bilingual translation factor models on POS, for each included corpora (see Table 1) and for the concatenation of them all.

OTF When using our OTF system, all in-domain and out-of-domain data are concatenated, respectively. For both corpora, we use a maximum random sampling size of 1 000 examples and a maximum phrase length of 15. However, all sub-corpora but GIGA[3] are used to compute the vectors for VSM features. Decoding is done with MOSES[4] (Koehn et al., 2007).

SOUL Given the computational cost of computing n-gram probabilities with neural network models, we resort to a reranking approach. In the following experiments, we use 10-gram SOUL models to rescore 1 000-best lists. SOUL models provide *five* new features: a target language model score and four translation scores (Le et al., 2012a).

We reused the SOUL models trained for our participation to WMT'12 (Le et al., 2012b). Moreover, target language models are adapted by running 6 more epochs on the new medical data.

[2]This issue is traditionally solved in Machine Learning by folded cross-validation, an approach that would be too prohibitive to use here.

[3]The GIGA corpus is actually very varied in content.

[4]`http://www.statmt.org/moses/`

System Combination As NCODE and OTF differ in many aspects and make different errors, we use system combination techniques to take advantage of their complementarity. This is done by reranking the concatenation of the 1 000-best lists of both systems. For each hypothesis within this list, we use two global features, corresponding either to the score computed by the corresponding system or 0 otherwise. We then learn reranking weights using Minimum Error Rate Training (MERT) (Och, 2003) on the development set for this combined list, using only these two features (SysComb-2). In an alternative configuration, we use the two systems without the SOUL rescoring, and add instead the five SOUL scores as features in the system combination reranking (SysComb-7).

Evaluation Metrics All BLEU scores (Papineni et al., 2002) are computed using cased `multi-bleu` with our internal tokenization. Reported results correspond to the average and standard deviation across 3 optimization runs to better account for the optimizer variance (Clark et al., 2011).

4 Experiments

4.1 Tuning Optimization Method

MERT is usually used to optimize Equation 1. However, with up to 42 features when using SOUL, this method is known to become very sensitive to local minima. Table 2 compares MERT, a batch variant of the Margin Infused Relaxation Algorithm (MIRA) (Cherry and Foster, 2012) and PRO (Hopkins and May, 2011) when tuning an NCODE system. MIRA slightly outperforms PRO on DEVEL, but seems prone to overfitting. However this was not possible to detect before the release of the test set (TEST), and so we use MIRA in all our experiments.

	DEVEL	TEST
MERT	$47.0_{\pm 0.4}$	$44.1_{\pm 0.8}$
MIRA	$47.9_{\pm 0.0}$	$44.8_{\pm 0.1}$
PRO	$47.1_{\pm 0.1}$	$45.1_{\pm 0.1}$

Table 2: Impact of the optimization method during the tuning process on BLEU score, for a baseline NCODE system.

4.2 Importance of the Data Sources

Table 3 shows that using the out-of-domain data from WMT'13 yields better scores than only using the provided medical data only. Moreover, combining both data sources drastically boosts performance. Table 1 displays the weights (λ_k) given by NCODE to the different sub-corpora bilingual language models. Three corpora seems particulary useful: EMEA, PATTR-ABSTRACTS and GIGA. Note that several models are given a negative weight, but removing them from the model surprisingly results in a drop of performance.

	DEVEL	TEST
medical	42.2± 0.1	39.6± 0.1
WMT'13	43.0± 0.1	41.0± 0.0
both	48.3± 0.1	45.4± 0.0

Table 3: BLEU scores obtained by NCODE trained on medical data only, WMT'13 data only, or both.

4.3 Part-of-Speech Tagging

Using the specialized POS-tagging models for medical data described in Section 3.3 instead of a standart POS-tagger, a 0.5 BLEU points increase is observed. Table 4 suggests that a better POS tagging quality is mainly beneficial to the reordering mechanism in NCODE, in contrast with the POS-POS factor models included as features.

Reordering	Factor model	DEVEL	TEST
std	std	47.9± 0.0	44.8± 0.1
std	spec	47.9± 0.1	45.0± 0.1
spec	std	48.4± 0.1	45.3± 0.1
spec	spec	48.3± 0.1	45.4± 0.0

Table 4: BLEU results when using a standard POS tagging (std) or our medical adapted specialized method (spec), either for the reordering rule mechanism (Reordering) or for the POS-POS bilingual language models features (Factor model).

4.4 Development and Proxy Test Sets

In Table 5, we assess the importance of domain adaptation via tuning on the development set used and investigate the benefits of our internal test set.

Best scores are obtained when using the provided development set in the tuning process. Using NEWSTEST12 as development set unsurprisingly leads to poor results, as no domain adaptation is carried out. However, using LMTEST does not result in much better TEST score. We also note a positive correlation between DEVEL and TEST. From the first three columns, we decided to use the DEVEL data set as development set for our submission, which is *a posteriori* the right choice.

DEVEL	LMTEST	NEWSTEST12	TEST
[48.3± 0.1]	46.8± 0.1	26.2± 0.1	45.4± 0.0
41.8± 0.2	**[48.9± 0.1]**	18.5± 0.1	40.1± 0.1
39.8± 0.1	37.4± 0.2	**[29.0± 0.1]**	39.0± 0.3

Table 5: Influence of the choice of the development set when using our baseline NCODE system. Each row corresponds to the choice of a development set used in the tuning process, indicated by a surrounded BLEU score.

Table 6: Contrast of our two main systems and their combination, when adding SOUL language (LM) and translation (TM) models. Stars indicate an adapted LM. BLEU results for the best run on the development set are reported.

	DEVEL	TEST
NCODE	48.5	45.2
+ SOUL LM	49.4	45.7
+ SOUL LM*	49.8	45.9
+ SOUL LM + TM	50.1	47.0
+ SOUL LM*+ TM	50.1	47.0
OTF	46.6	42.5
+ VSM	46.9	42.8
+ SOUL LM	48.6	44.0
+ SOUL LM*	48.4	44.2
+ SOUL LM + TM	49.6	44.8
+ SOUL LM*+ TM	49.7	44.9
SysComb-2	50.5	46.6
SysComb-7	50.7	46.5

4.5 NCODE vs. OTF

Table 6 contrasts our different approaches. Preliminary experiments suggest that OTF is a comparable but cheaper alternative to a full MOSES system.[5] We find a large difference in performance,

[5]A control experiment for a full MOSES system (using a single phrase table) yielded a BLEU score of 45.9 on DEVEL and 43.2 on TEST, and took 3 more days to complete.

	extra	*missing*		*incorrect*					*unknown*		
	word	content	filler	disamb.	form	style	term	order	word	term	**all**
syscomb	4	13	20	47	62	8	18	21	1	11	**205**
OTF+VSM+SOUL	4	4	31	44	82	6	20	42	3	12	**248**

Table 7: Results for manual error analysis following (Vilar et al., 2006) for the first 100 test sentences.

NCODE outperforming OTF by 2.8 BLEU points on the TEST set. VSM does not yield any significant improvement, contrarily to the work of Chen et al. (2013); it may be the case all individual sub-corpus are equally good (or bad) at approximating the stylistic preferences of the TEST set.

4.6 Integrating SOUL

Table 6 shows the substantial impact of adding SOUL models for both baseline systems. With only the SOUL LM, improvements on the test set range from 0.5 BLEU points for NCODE system to 1.2 points for the OTF system. The adaptation of SOUL LM with the medical data brings an additional improvement of about 0.2 BLEU points.

Adding all SOUL translation models yield an improvement of 1.8 BLEU points for NCODE and of 2.4 BLEU points with the OTF system using VSM models. However, the SOUL adaptation step has then only a modest impact. In future work, we plan to also adapt the translation models in order to increase the benefit of using in-domain data.

4.7 System Combination

Table 6 shows that performing the system combination allows a gain up to 0.6 BLEU points on the DEVEL set. However this gain does not transfer to the TEST set, where instead a drop of 0.5 BLEU is observed. The system combination using SOUL scores showed the best result over all of our other systems on the DEVEL set, so we chose this (*a posteriori* sub-obtimal) configuration as our main system submission.

Our system combination strategy chose for DEVEL about 50% hypotheses among those produced by NCODE and 25% hypotheses from OTF, the remainder been common to both systems. As expected, the system combination prefers hypotheses coming from the best system. We can observe nearly the same distribution for TEST.

5 Error Analysis

The high level of scores for automatic metrics encouraged us to perform a detailed, small-scale analysis of our system output, using the error types proposed by Vilar et al. (2006). A single annotator analyzed the output of our main submission, as well as our OTF variant. Results are in Table 7.

Looking at the most important types of errors, assuming the translation hypotheses were to be used for rapid assimilation of the text content, we find a moderate number of unknown terms and incorrectly translated terms. The most frequent error types include missing fillers, incorrect disambiguation, form and order, which all have some significant impact on automatic metrics. Comparing more specifically the two systems used in this small-scale study, we find that our combination (which reused more than 70% of hypotheses from NCODE) mostly improves over the OTF variant on the choice of correct word form and word order. We may attribute this in part to a more efficient reordering strategy that better exploits POS tags.

6 Conclusion

In this paper, we have demonstrated a successful approach that makes use of two flexible translation systems, an n-gram system and an on-the-fly phrase-based model, in a new medical translation task, through various approaches to perform domain adaptation. When combined with continuous language models, which yield additional gains of up to 2 BLEU points, moderate to high-quality translations are obtained, as confirmed by a fine-grained error analysis. The most challenging part of the task was undoubtedly the lack on an internal test to guide system development. Another interesting negative result lies in the absence of success for our configuration of the vector space model of Chen et al. (2013) for adaptation. Lastly, a more careful integration of medical terminology, as provided by the UMLS, proved necessary.

7 Acknowledgements

We would like to thank Guillaume Wisniewski and the anonymous reviewers for their helpful comments and suggestions.

References

Alexandre Allauzen, Nicolas Pécheux, Quoc Khanh Do, Marco Dinarelli, Thomas Lavergne, Aurélien Max, Hai-son Le, and François Yvon. 2013. LIMSI @ WMT13. In *Proceedings of the Workshkop on Statistical Machine Translation*, pages 62–69, Sofia, Bulgaria.

Yoshua Bengio, Réjean Ducharme, Pascal Vincent, and Christian Jauvin. 2003. A neural probabilistic language model. *Journal of Machine Learning Research*, 3(6):1137–1155.

Chris Callison-Burch, Colin Bannard, and Josh Schroeder. 2005. Scaling phrase-based statistical machine translation to larger corpora and longer phrases. In *Proceedings of ACL*, Ann Arbor, USA.

Francesco Casacuberta and Enrique Vidal. 2004. Machine translation with inferred stochastic finite-state transducers. *Computational Linguistics*, 30(3):205–225.

Ciprian Chelba and Alex Acero. 2004. Adaptation of maximum entropy classifier: Little data can help a lot. In *Proceedings of the Conference on Empirical Methods in Natural Language Processing (EMNLP)*, Barcelona, Spain.

Stanley F. Chen and Joshua T. Goodman. 1996. An empirical study of smoothing techniques for language modeling. In *Proceedings of the 34th Annual Meeting of the Association for Computational Linguistics (ACL)*, pages 310–318, Santa Cruz, NM.

Boxing Chen, Roland Kuhn, and George Foster. 2013. Vector space model for adaptation in statistical machine translation. In *Proceedings of ACL*, Sofia, Bulgaria.

Colin Cherry and George Foster. 2012. Batch tuning strategies for statistical machine translation. In *Proceedings of the 2012 Conference of the North American Chapter of the Association for Computational Linguistics: Human Language Technologies*, pages 427–436. Association for Computational Linguistics.

Jonathan H Clark, Chris Dyer, Alon Lavie, and Noah A Smith. 2011. Better Hypothesis Testing for Statistical Machine Translation : Controlling for Optimizer Instability. In *Better Hypothesis Testing for Statistical Machine Translation : Controlling for Optimizer Instability*, pages 176–181, Portland, Oregon.

Josep M. Crego and José B. Mariño. 2006. Improving statistical MT by coupling reordering and decoding. *Machine Translation*, 20(3):199–215.

Josep M. Crego, François Yvon, and José B. Mariño. 2011. N-code: an open-source bilingual N-gram SMT toolkit. *Prague Bulletin of Mathematical Linguistics*, 96:49–58.

Daniel Déchelotte, Gilles Adda, Alexandre Allauzen, Olivier Galibert, Jean-Luc Gauvain, Hélène Maynard, and François Yvon. 2008. LIMSI's statistical translation systems for WMT'08. In *Proc. of the NAACL-HTL Statistical Machine Translation Workshop*, Columbus, Ohio.

Kenneth Heafield. 2011. KenLM: Faster and Smaller Language Model Queries. In *Proceedings of the Sixth Workshop on Statistical Machine Translation*, pages 187–197, Edinburgh, Scotland, July. Association for Computational Linguistics.

Mark Hopkins and Jonathan May. 2011. Tuning as ranking. In *Proceedings of the Conference on Empirical Methods in Natural Language Processing*, EMNLP '11, pages 1352–1362, Stroudsburg, PA, USA. Association for Computational Linguistics.

Reinhard Kneser and Herman Ney. 1995. Improved backing-off for m-gram language modeling. In *Proceedings of the International Conference on Acoustics, Speech, and Signal Processing, ICASSP'95*, pages 181–184, Detroit, MI.

Philipp Koehn, Hieu Hoang, Alexandra Birch, Chris Callison-Burch, Marcello Federico, Nicola Bertoldi, Brooke Cowan, Wade Shen, Christine Moran, Richard Zens, Chris Dyer, Ondrej Bojar, Alexandra Constantin, and Evan Herbst. 2007. Moses: Open source toolkit for statistical machine translation. In *Proceedings of the 45th Annual Meeting of the Association for Computational Linguistics Companion Volume Proceedings of the Demo and Poster Sessions*, pages 177–180, Prague, Czech Republic, June. Association for Computational Linguistics.

Thomas Lavergne, Olivier Cappé, and François Yvon. 2010. Practical very large scale CRFs. In *Proceedings the 48th Annual Meeting of the Association for Computational Linguistics (ACL)*, pages 504–513. Association for Computational Linguistics, July.

Thomas Lavergne, Hai-Son Le, Alexandre Allauzen, and François Yvon. 2011. LIMSI's experiments in domain adaptation for IWSLT11. In Mei-Yuh Hwang and Sebastian Stüker, editors, *Proceedings of the heigth International Workshop on Spoken Language Translation (IWSLT)*, San Francisco, CA.

Hai-Son Le, Ilya Oparin, Alexandre Allauzen, Jean-Luc Gauvain, and François Yvon. 2011. Structured output layer neural network language model. In *Proceedings of ICASSP*, pages 5524–5527.

Hai-Son Le, Alexandre Allauzen, and François Yvon. 2012a. Continuous space translation models with neural networks. In *Proceedings of the 2012 conference of the north american chapter of the association for computational linguistics: Human language technologies*, pages 39–48, Montréal, Canada, June. Association for Computational Linguistics.

Hai-Son Le, Thomas Lavergne, Alexandre Allauzen, Marianna Apidianaki, Li Gong, Aurélien

Max, Artem Sokolov, Guillaume Wisniewski, and François Yvon. 2012b. LIMSI @ WMT12. In *Proceedings of the Seventh Workshop on Statistical Machine Translation*, pages 330–337, Montréal, Canada.

Adam Lopez. 2008. Tera-Scale Translation Models via Pattern Matching. In *Proceedings of COLING*, Manchester, UK.

José B. Mariño, Rafael E. Banchs, Josep M. Crego, Adrià de Gispert, Patrick Lambert, José A.R. Fonollosa, and Marta R. Costa-Jussà. 2006. N-gram-based machine translation. *Computational Linguistics*, 32(4):527–549.

Franz Josef Och. 2003. Minimum error rate training in statistical machine translation. In *Proceedings of the 41st Annual Meeting on Association for Computational Linguistics*, pages 160–167, Stroudsburg, PA, USA. Association for Computational Linguistics.

Kishore Papineni, Salim Roukos, Todd Ward, and Wei-Jing Zhu. 2002. Bleu: a Method for Automatic Evaluation of Machine Translation. In *Proceedings of 40th Annual Meeting of the Association for Computational Linguistics*, pages 311–318, Philadelphia, USA, July. Association for Computational Linguistics.

Helmut Schmid. 1994. Probabilistic part-of-speech tagging using decision trees. In *Proceedings of International Conference on New Methods in Language Processing*, September.

Holger Schwenk, Daniel Dchelotte, and Jean-Luc Gauvain. 2006. Continuous space language models for statistical machine translation. In *Proceedings of the COLING/ACL on Main conference poster sessions*, pages 723–730, Morristown, NJ, USA. Association for Computational Linguistics.

L. Smith, T. Rindflesch, and W. J. Wilbur. 2004. Medpost: a part of speech tagger for biomedical text. *Bioinformatics*, 20(14):2320–2321.

A. Stolcke. 2002. SRILM - an extensible language modeling toolkit. In *Proceedings of the International Conference on Spoken Language Processing (ICSLP)*, pages 901–904, Denver, Colorado, September.

Christoph Tillmann. 2004. A unigram orientation model for statistical machine translation. In *Proceedings of HLT-NAACL*, pages 101–104.

David Vilar, Jia Xu, Luis Fernando D'Haro, and Hermann Ney. 2006. Error Analysis of Statistical Machine Translation Output. In *LREC*, Genoa, Italy.

Richard Zens, Franz Joseph Och, and Herman Ney. 2002. Phrase-based statistical machine translation. In M. Jarke, J. Koehler, and G. Lakemeyer, editors, *KI-2002: Advances in artificial intelligence*, volume 2479 of *LNAI*, pages 18–32. Springer Verlag.

Combining Domain Adaptation Approaches for Medical Text Translation

Longyue Wang, Yi Lu, Derek F. Wong, Lidia S. Chao, Yiming Wang, Francisco Oliveira
Natural Language Processing & Portuguese-Chinese Machine Translation Laboratory,
Department of Computer and Information Science,
University of Macau, Macau, China
vincentwang0229@hotmail.com,
{mb25435, derekfw, lidiasc, mb25433, olifran}@umac.mo

Abstract

This paper explores a number of simple and effective techniques to adapt statistical machine translation (SMT) systems in the medical domain. Comparative experiments are conducted on large corpora for six language pairs. We not only compare each adapted system with the baseline, but also combine them to further improve the domain-specific systems. Finally, we attend the WMT2014 medical summary sentence translation constrained task and our systems achieve the best BLEU scores for Czech-English, English-German, French-English language pairs and the second best BLEU scores for reminding pairs.

1. Introduction

This paper presents the experiments conducted by the NLP[2]CT Laboratory at the University of Macau for WMT2014 medical sentence translation task on six language pairs: Czech-English (cs-en), French-English (fr-en), German-English (de-en) and the reverse direction pairs, i.e., en-cs, en-fr and en-de.

By comparing the medical text with common text, we discovered some interesting phenomena in medical genre. We apply domain-specific techniques in data pre-processing, language model adaptation, translation model adaptation, numeric and hyphenated words translation. Compared to the baseline systems (detailed in Section 2 & 3), the results of each method show reasonable gains. We combine individual approach to further improve the performance of our systems. To validate the robustness and language-independency of individual and combined systems, we conduct experiments on the official training data (detailed in Section 3) in all six language pairs. We anticipate the numeric comparison (BLEU scores) on these individual and combined domain adaptation approaches that could be valuable for others on building a real-life domain-specific system.

The reminder of this paper is organized as follows. In Section 2, we detail the configurations of our experiments as well as the baseline systems. Section 3 presents the specific pre-processing for medical data. In Section 4 and 5, we describe the language model (LM) and translation model (TM) adaptation, respectively. Besides, the techniques for numeric and hyphenated words translation are reported in Section 6 and 7. Finally, the performance of design systems and the official results are reported in Section 8.

2. Experimental Setup

All available training data from both WMT2014 standard translation task[1] (general-domain data) and medical translation task[2] (in-domain data) are used in this study. The official medical summary development sets (dev) are used for tuning and evaluating all the comparative systems. The official medical summary test sets (test) are only used in our final submitted systems.

The experiments were carried out with the Moses 1.0[3] (Koehn et al., 2007). The translation and the re-ordering model utilizes the "*grow-diag-final*" symmetrized word-to-word alignments created with MGIZA++[4] (Och and Ney,

[1] http://www.statmt.org/wmt14/translation-task.html.
[2] http://www.statmt.org/wmt14/medical-task/.
[3] http://www.statmt.org/moses/.
[4] http://www.kyloo.net/software/doku.php/mgiza:overview.

Proceedings of the Ninth Workshop on Statistical Machine Translation, pages 254–259,
Baltimore, Maryland USA, June 26–27, 2014.

2003; Gao and Vogel, 2008) and the training scripts from Moses. A 5-gram LM was trained using the SRILM toolkit[5] (Stolcke et al., 2002), exploiting improved modified Kneser-Ney smoothing, and quantizing both probabilities and back-off weights. For the log-linear model training, we take the minimum-error-rate training (MERT) method as described in (Och, 2003).

3. Task Oriented Pre-processing

A careful pre-processing on training data is significant for building a real-life SMT system. In addition to the general data preparing steps used for constructing the baseline system, we introduce some extra steps to pre-process the training data.

The first step is to remove the duplicate sentences. In data-driven methods, the more frequent a term occurs, the higher probability it biases. Duplicate data may lead to unpredicted behavior during the decoding. Therefore, we keep only the distinct sentences in monolingual corpus. By taking into account multiple translations in parallel corpus, we remove the duplicate sentence pairs. The second concern in pre-processing is symbol normalization. Due to the nature of medical genre, symbols such as numbers and punctuations are commonly-used to present chemical formula, measuring unit, terminology and expression. Fig. 1 shows the examples of this case. These symbols are more frequent in medical article than that in the common texts. Besides, the punctuations of *apostrophe* and *single quotation* are interchangeably used in French text, e.g. "*l'effet de l'inhibition*". We unify it by replacing with the *apostrophe*. In addition, we observe that some monolingual training subsets (e.g., Gene Regulation Event Corpus) contain sentences of more than 3,000 words in length. To avoid the long sentences from harming the true-case model, we split them into sentences with a sentence splitter[6] (Rune et al., 2007) that is optimized for biomedical texts. On the other hand, we consider the target system is intended for summary translation, the sentences tend to be short in length. For instance, the average sentence lengths in development sets of cs, fr, de and en are around 15, 21, 17 and 18, respectively. We remove sentence pairs which are more than 80 words at length. In order to that our experiments are reproducible, we give the detailed statistics of task oriented pre-processed training data in Table 2.

1,25-OH
47 to **80%**
10-20 ml/kg
A**&**E department
Infective endocarditis **(**IE**)**

Figure 1. Examples of the segments with symbols in medical texts.

To validate the effectiveness of the pre-processing, we compare the SMT systems trained on original data[7] (*Baseline*1) and task-oriented-processed data (*Baseline*2), respectively. Table 1 shows the results of the baseline systems. We found all the *Baseline*2 systems outperform the *Baseline*1 models, showing that the systems can benefit from using the processed data. For cs-en and en-cs pairs, the BLEU scores improve quite a lot. For other language pairs, the translation quality improves slightly.

By analyzing the *Baseline*2 results (in Table 1) and the statistics of training corpora (in Table 2), we can further elaborate and explain the results. The en-cs system performs poorly, because of the short average length of training sentences, as well as the limited size of in-domain parallel and monolingual corpora. On the other hand, the fr-en system achieves the best translation score, as we have sufficient training data. The translation quality of cs-en, en-fr, fr-en and de-en pairs is much higher than those in the other pairs. Hence, *Baseline*2 will be used in the subsequent comparisons with the proposed systems described in Section 4, 5, 6 and 7.

Lang. Pair	*Baseline*1	*Baseline*2	Diff.
en-cs	12.92	**17.57**	+4.65
cs-en	20.85	**31.29**	+10.44
en-fr	38.31	**38.36**	+0.05
fr-en	44.27	**44.36**	+0.09
en-de	17.81	**18.01**	+0.20
de-en	32.34	**32.50**	+0.16

Table 1: BLEU scores of two baseline systems trained on original and processed corpora for different language pairs.

4. Language Model Adaptation

The use of LMs (trained on large data) during decoding is aided by more efficient storage and inference (Heafield, 2011). Therefore, we not

[5] http://www.speech.sri.com/projects/srilm/.

[6] http://www.nactem.ac.uk/y-matsu/geniass/.

[7] Data are processed according to Moses baseline tutorial: http://www.statmt.org/moses/?n=Moses.Baseline.

Data Set	Lang.	Sent.	Words	Vocab.	Ave. Len.
In-domain Parallel Data	cs/en	**1,770,421**	9,373,482/ 10,605,222	134,998/ 156,402	**5.29/ 5.99**
	de/en	3,894,099	52,211,730/ 58,544,608	1,146,262/ 487,850	13.41/ 15.03
	fr/en	**4,579,533**	77,866,237/ 68,429,649	495,856/ 556,587	17.00/ 14.94
General-domain Parallel Data	cs/en	12,426,374	180,349,215/ 183,841,805	1,614,023/ 1,661,830	14.51/ 14.79
	de/en	4,421,961	106,001,775/ 112,294,414	1,912,953/ 919,046	23.97/ 25.39
	fr/en	36,342,530	1,131,027,766/ 953,644,980	3,149,336/ 3,324,481	31.12/ 26.24
In-domain Mono. Data	cs	**106,548**	1,779,677	150,672	16.70
	fr	1,424,539	53,839,928	644,484	37.79
	de	2,222,502	53,840,304	1,415,202	24.23
	en	**7,802,610**	199430649	1,709,594	25.56
General-domain Mono. Data	cs	33,408,340	567,174,266	3,431,946	16.98
	fr	30,850,165	780,965,861	2,142,470	25.31
	de	84,633,641	1,548,187,668	10,726,992	18.29
	en	85,254,788	2,033,096,800	4,488,816	23.85

Table 2: Statistics summary of corpora after pre-processing.

only use the in-domain training data, but also the selected pseudo in-domain data[8] from general-domain corpus to enhance the LMs (Toral, 2013; Rubino et al., 2013; Duh et al., 2013). Firstly, each sentence *s* in general-domain monolingual corpus is scored using the cross-entropy difference method in (Moore and Lewis, 2010), which is calculated as follows:

$$score(s) = H_I(s) - H_G(s) \quad (1)$$

where *H*(*s*) is the length-normalized cross-entropy. *I* and *G* are the in-domain and general-domain corpora, respectively. *G* is a random subset (same size as the *I*) of the general-domain corpus. Then top *N* percentages of ranked data sentences are selected as a pseudo in-domain subset to train an additional LM. Finally, we linearly interpolate the additional LM with in-domain LM.

We use the top *N*% of ranked results, where *N*={0, 25, 50, 75, 100} percentages of sentences out of the general corpus. Table 3 shows the absolute BLEU points for *Baseline*2 (*N*=0), while the LM adapted systems are listed with values relative to the *Baseline*2. The results indicate that LM adaptation can gain a reasonable improvement if the LMs are trained on more relevant data for each pair, instead of using the whole training data. For different systems, their BLEU scores peak at different values of *N*. It gives the best results for cs-en, en-fr and de-en pairs when *N*=25, en-cs and en-de pairs when *N*=50, and fr-en pair when *N*=75. Among them, en-cs and en-fr achieve the highest BLEU scores. The reason is that their original monolingual (in-domain) data for training the LMs are not sufficient. When introducing the extra pseudo in-domain data, the systems improve the translation quality by around 2 BLEU points. While for cs-en, fr-en and de-en pairs, the gains are small. However, it can still achieve a significant improvement of 0.60 up to 1.12 BLEU points.

Lang.	*N*=0	*N*=25	*N*=50	*N*=75	*N*=100
en-cs	17.57	+1.66	**+2.08**	+1.72	+2.04
cs-en	31.29	**+0.94**	+0.60	+0.66	+0.47
en-fr	38.36	**+1.82**	+1.66	+1.60	+0.08
fr-en	44.36	+0.91	+1.09	**+1.12**	+0.92
en-de	18.01	+0.57	**+1.02**	-4.48	-4.54
de-en	32.50	**+0.60**	+0.50	+0.56	+0.38

Table 3: BLEU scores of LM adapted systems.

5. Translation Model Adaptation

As shown in Table 2, general-domain parallel corpora are around 1 to 7 times larger than the in-domain ones. We suspect if general-domain corpus is broad enough to cover some in-domain sentences. To observe the domain-specificity of general-domain corpus, we firstly evaluate systems trained on general-domain corpora. In Ta-

[8] Axelrod et al. (2011) names the selected data as *pseudo in-domain data*. We adopt both terminologies in this paper.

ble 4, we show the BLEU scores of general-domain systems[9] on translating the medical sentences. The BLEU scores of the compared systems are relative to the *Baseline*2 and the size of the used general-domain corpus is relative to the corresponding in-domain one. For en-cs, cs-en, en-fr and fr-en pairs, the general-domain parallel corpora we used are 6 times larger than the original ones and we obtain the improved BLEU scores by 1.72 up to 3.96 points. While for en-de and de-en pairs, the performance drops sharply due to the limited training corpus we used. Hence we can draw a conclusion: the general-domain corpus is able to aid the domain-specific translation task if the general-domain data is large and broad enough in content.

Lang. Pair	BLEU	Diff.	Corpus
en-cs	21.53	+3.96	+601.89%
cs-en	33.01	+1.72	
en-fr	41.57	+3.21	+693.59%
fr-en	47.33	+2.97	
en-de	16.54	-1.47	+13.63%
de-en	27.35	-5.15	

Table 4: The BLEU scores of systems trained on general-domain corpora.

Taking into account the performance of general-domain system, we explore various data selection methods to derive the pseudo in-domain sentence pairs from general-domain parallel corpus for enhancing the TMs (Wang et al., 2013; Wang et al., 2014). Firstly, sentence pair in corresponding general-domain corpora is scored by the modified Moore-Lewis (Axelrod et al., 2011), which is calculated as follows:

$$score(s) = \left[H_{I-src}(s) - H_{G-src}(s)\right] + \left[H_{I-tgt}(s) - H_{G-tgt}(s)\right] \quad (2)$$

which is similar to Eq. (1) and the only difference is that it considers the both the source (*src*) and target (*tgt*) sides of parallel corpora. Then top *N* percentage of ranked sentence pairs are selected as a pseudo in-domain subset to train an individual translation model. The additional model is log-linearly interpolated with the in-domain model (*Baseline*2) using the multi-decoding method described in (Koehn and Schroeder, 2007).

Similar to LM adaptation, we use the top *N*% of ranked results, where *N*={0, 25, 50, 75, 100} percentages of sentences out of the general corpus. Table 5 shows the absolute BLEU points for *Baseline*2 (*N*=0), while for the TM adapted systems we show the values relative to the *Baseline*2. For different systems, their BLEU peak at different *N*. For en-fr and en-de pairs, it gives the best translation results at *N*=25. Regarding cs-en and fr-en pairs, the optimal performance is peaked at *N*=50. While the best results for de-en and en-cs pairs are *N*=75 and *N*=100 respectively. Besides, performance of TM adapted system heavily depends on the size and (domain) broadness of the general-domain data. For example, the improvements of en-de and de-en systems are slight due to the small general-domain corpora. While the quality of other systems improve about 3 BLEU points, because of their large and broad general-domain corpora.

Lang.	*N*=0	*N*=25	*N*=50	*N*=75	*N*=100
en-cs	17.57	+0.84	+1.53	+1.74	**+2.55**
cs-en	31.29	+2.03	**+3.12**	+3.12	+2.24
en-fr	38.36	**+3.87**	+3.66	+3.53	+2.88
fr-en	44.36	+1.29	**+3.36**	+1.84	+1.65
en-de	18.01	**+0.02**	-0.13	-0.07	0
de-en	32.50	-0.12	+0.06	**+0.31**	+0.24

Table 5: BLEU scores of TM adapted systems.

6. Numeric Adaptation

As stated in Section 3, *numeric* occurs frequently in medical texts. However, numeric expression in dates, time, measuring unit, chemical formula are often sparse, which may lead to OOV problems in phrasal translation and reordering. Replacing the sparse numbers with placeholders may produce more reliable statistics for the MT models.

Moses has support using placeholders in training and decoding. Firstly, we replace all the numbers in monolingual and parallel training corpus with a common symbol (a sample phrase is illustrated in Fig. 2). Models are then trained on these processed data. We use the XML markup translation method for decoding.

Original:	Vitamin D 1,25-OH
Replaced:	Vitamin D @num@, @num@-OH

Figure 2. Examples of placeholders.

Table 6 shows the results on this number adaptation approach as well as the improvements compared to the *Baseline*2. The method improves the *Baseline*2 systems by 0.23 to 0.40 BLEU scores. Although the scores increase slightly, we still believe this adaptation method is significant for medical domain. The WMT2014 medical task only focuses on the summary of

[9] General-domain systems are trained only on genera-domain training corpora (i.e., parallel, monolingual).

medical text, which may contain fewer chemical expression in compared with the full article. As the used of numerical instances increases, placeholder may play a more important role in domain adaptation.

Lang. Pair	BLEU (Dev)	Diff.
en-cs	17.80	+0.23
cs-en	31.52	+0.23
en-fr	38.72	+0.36
fr-en	44.69	+0.33
en-de	18.41	+0.40
de-en	32.88	+0.38

Table 6: BLEU scores of numeric adapted systems.

7. Hyphenated Word Adaptation

Medical texts prefer a kind of compound words, hyphenated words, which is composed of more than one word. For instance, "*slow-growing*" and "*easy-to-use*" are composed of words and linked with hyphens. These hyphenated words occur quite frequently in medical texts. We analyze the development sets of cs, fr, en and de respectively, and observe that there are approximately 3.2%, 11.6%, 12.4% and 19.2% of sentences that contain one or more hyphenated words. The high ratio of such compound words results in Out-Of-Vocabulary words (OOV) [10], and harms the phrasal translation and reordering. However, a number of those hyphenated words still have chance to be translated, although it is not precisely, when they are tokenized into individual words.

Algorithm: Alternative-translation Method

Input:

1. A sentence, s, with M hyphenated words
2. Translation lexicon

Run:

1. **For** $i = 1, 2, \ldots, M$
2. Split the ith hyphenated word (C_i) into P_i
3. Translate P_i into T_i
4. **If** (T_i are not OOVs):
5. Put alternative translation T_i in XML
6. **Else**: keep C_i unchanged

Output:

Sentence, s', embedded with alternative translations for all T_i.

End

Table 7: Alternative-translation algorithm.

[10] Default tokenizer does not handle the hyphenated words.

To resolve this problem, we present an *alternative-translation* method in decoding. Table 7 shows the proposed algorithm.

In the implementation, we apply XML markup to record the translation (terminology) for each compound word. During the decoding, a hyphenated word delimited with markup will be replaced with its corresponding translation. Table 8 shows the BLEU scores of adapted systems applied to hyphenated translation. This method is effective for most language pairs. While the translation systems for en-cs and cs-en do not benefit from this adaptation, because the hyphenated words ratio in the en and cs dev are asymmetric. Thus, we only apply this method for en-fr, fr-en, de-en and en-de pairs.

Lang. Pair	BLEU (Dev)	Diff.
en-cs	16.84	-0.73
cs-en	31.23	-0.06
en-fr	39.12	+0.76
fr-en	45.02	+0.66
en-de	18.64	+0.63
de-en	33.01	+0.51

Table 8: BLEU scores of hyphenated word adapted systems.

3. Final Results and Conclusions

According to the performance of each individual domain adaptation approach, we combined the corresponding models for each language pair. In Table 10, we show the BLEU scores and its increments (compared to the *Baseline*2) of combined systems in the second column. The official test set is converted into the *recased* and *detokenized* SGML format. The official results of our submissions are given in the last column of Table 9.

Lang. Pair	BLEU of Combined systems	Official BLEU
en-cs	23.66 (+6.09)	22.60
cs-en	38.05 (+6.76)	37.60
en-fr	42.30 (+3.94)	41.20
fr-en	48.25 (+3.89)	47.10
en-de	21.14 (+3.13)	20.90
de-en	36.03 (+3.53)	35.70

Table 9: BLEU scores of the submitted systems for the medical translation task.

This paper presents a set of experiments conducted on all available training data for six language pairs. We explored various domain adaptation approaches for adapting medical translation systems. Compared with other methods, language model adaptation and translation model adaptation are more effective. Other adapted techniques are still necessary and important for building a real-life system. Although all individual methods are not fully additive, combining them together can further boost the performance of the overall domain-specific system. We believe these empirical approaches could be valuable for SMT development.

Acknowledgments

The authors are grateful to the Science and Technology Development Fund of Macau and the Research Committee of the University of Macau for the funding support for their research, under the Reference nos. MYRG076 (Y1-L2)-FST13-WF and MYRG070 (Y1-L2)-FST12-CS. The authors also wish to thank the colleagues in CNGL, Dublin City University (DCU) for their helpful suggestion and guidance on related work.

Reference

Amittai Axelrod, Xiaodong He, and Jianfeng Gao. 2011. Domain adaptation via pseudo in-domain data selection. In *Proceedings of EMNLP*, pages 355-362.

K. Duh, G. Neubig, K. Sudoh, H. Tsukada. 2013. Adaptation data selection using neural language models: Experiments in machine translation. In *Proceedings of the Annual Meeting of the Association for Computational Linguistics*, pages, 678–683.

Qin Gao and Stephan Vogel. 2008. Parallel implementations of word alignment tool. *Software Engineering, Testing, and Quality Assurance for Natural Language Processing*, pages 49-57.

Kenneth Heafield. 2011. KenLM: Faster and smaller language model queries. In *Proceedings of the Sixth Workshop on Statistical Machine Translation*, pages 187-197.

Philipp Koehn and Josh Schroeder. 2007. Experiments in domain adaptation for statistical machine translation. In *Proceedings of the 2nd ACL Workshop on Statistical Machine Translation*, pages 224-227.

Philipp Koehn, Hieu Hoang, Alexandra Birch, Chris Callison-Burch, Marcello Federico, Nicola Bertoldi, Brooke Cowan, Wade Shen, Christine Moran et al. 2007. Moses: open source toolkit for statistical machine translation. In *Proceedings of ACL*, pages 177-180.

Robert C. Moore and William Lewis. 2010. Intelligent selection of language model training data. In *Proceedings of ACL*: Short Papers, pages 220-224.

Sætre Rune, Kazuhiro Yoshida, Akane Yakushiji, Yusuke Miyao, Yuichiro Matsubayashi and Tomoko Ohta. 2007. AKANE system: protein-protein interaction pairs in BioCreAtIvE2 challenge, PPI-IPS subtask. In *Proceedings of the Second BioCreative Challenge Evaluation Workshop*, pages 209-212.

Raphael Rubino, Antonio Toral, Santiago Cortés Vaíllo, Jun Xie, Xiaofeng Wu, Stephen Doherty, and Qun Liu. 2013. The CNGL-DCU-Prompsit translation systems for WMT13. In *Proceedings of the Eighth Workshop on Statistical Machine Translation*, pages 213-218.

Andreas Stolcke and others. 2002. SRILM-An extensible language modeling toolkit. In *Proceedings of the International Conference on Spoken Language Processing*, pages 901-904.

Antonio Toral. 2013. Hybrid selection of language model training data using linguistic information and perplexity. In *ACL Workshop on Hybrid Machine Approaches to Translation*.

Franz Josef Och and Hermann Ney. 2003. A systematic comparison of various statistical alignment models. *Computational Linguistics*, 29:19-51.

Franz Josef Och. 2003. Minimum error rate training in statistical machine translation. In *Proceedings of the 41st Annual Meeting on Association for Computational Linguistics*, pages 160-167.

Longyue Wang, Derek F. Wong, Lidia S. Chao, Yi Lu, and Junwen Xing. 2014 "A Systematic Comparison of Data Selection Criteria for SMT Domain Adaptation," *The Scientific World Journal*, vol. 2014, Article ID 745485, 10 pages.

Longyue Wang, Derek F. Wong, Lidia S. Chao, Yi Lu, Junwen Xing. 2013. *i*CPE: A Hybrid Data Selection Model for SMT Domain Adaptation. *Chinese Computational Linguistics and Natural Language Processing Based on Naturally Annotated Big Data*. Springer Berlin Heidelberg. pages, 280-290.

Experiments in Medical Translation Shared Task at WMT 2014

Jian Zhang, Xiaofeng Wu,
Iacer Calixto, Ali Hosseinzadeh Vahid, Xiaojun Zhang,
Andy Way, Qun Liu

The CNGL Centre for Global Intelligent Content
School of Computing
Dublin City University, Ireland
{zhangj,xiaofengwu,
icalixto,avahid,xzhang,
away,qliu}@computing.dcu.ie

Abstract

This paper describes Dublin City University's (DCU) submission to the WMT 2014 Medical Summary task. We report our results on the test data set in the French to English translation direction. We also report statistics collected from the corpora used to train our translation system. We conducted our experiment on the Moses 1.0 phrase-based translation system framework. We performed a variety of experiments on translation models, reordering models, operation sequence model and language model. We also experimented with data selection and removal the length constraint for phrase-pair extraction.

1 System Description

1.1 Training Data Statistics and Preparation

The training corpora provided to the medical translation shared task can be divided into 3 categories:

Medical in-domain corpora: these corpora contain documents, patents, articles, terminology lists, and titles that are representative of the same medical domain as the development and test data sets (Table 1, second column).

Medical out-of-domain corpora: these corpora also contain medical documents, patents, articles, terminologies lists and titles, but describe a different domain from the development and test data sets (Table 1, third column).

General domain corpora: these corpora consist of general-domain text (WMT 2014 general translation subtask corpora), and encompass various domains. (We did not use these corpora in our system).

Corpus	In-domain parallel sentence number	Out-of-domain parallel sentence number
EMEA	1,092,568	0
COPPA	664,658	2,841,849
PatTR-title	408,502	2,096,270
PatTR-abstract	688,147	3,009,523
PatTR-claims	1,105,230	5,861,621
UMLS	85,705	0
Wikipedia	8,448	0
TOTAL	4,053,258	13,809,263

Table 1: WMT 2014 Medical Translation shared task parallel training data before preprocessing.

Within all the provided training corpora from WMT 2014, 70.72% of the medical in domain bilingual sentences, and 100% of the medical out-of-domain bilingual sentences were obtained from patent document collections. Motivated by these percentages, we view the WMT 2014 medical translation shared task as similar to training a patent-specific translation system. The monolingual corpora are taken from 9 different corpora collections, and there is no clear demarcation of the in/out-of-domain boundaries (except the PatTR collection). Our method of differentiating between the in/out-of-domain monolingual corpora is that only English sentences from the third column of Table 1, and the patent description documents from PatTR collection, are out-of-domain monolingual corpora. All other English

Proceedings of the Ninth Workshop on Statistical Machine Translation, pages 260–265,
Baltimore, Maryland USA, June 26–27, 2014. ©2014 Association for Computational Linguistics

sentences are treated as an in-domain monolingual resource.

A patent document usually comprises title, abstract, claims and description fields. The documents often use its unique formatting and contain linguistic idiosyncrasies, which distinguish patent-specific translation systems from general translation systems, in both training and translation phases (Ceauşu et al., 2011). We have also found that some common writing styles are constantly used, especially for long sentences. For example, a typical patent claim begins with

```
Method of [X], which comprising:
```

followed by a numbered list. The abstract field normally contains one paragraph only, but with multiple sentences. Those long sentences are necessarily filtered out to facilitate efficient word alignment, using a tool such as GIZA++ (Och, 2003) word aligner with the default parameter settings. However, because statistical machine translation depends on the training data to estimate translation probability, more high quality training data often leads a better translation result. One possible method of including long sentences into the training cycle is to change the word aligner's parameter settings to handle longer sentences; however, aligning long sentences is time consuming. Our solution is to capture the styled long sentences and attempt to split them on both source and target side simultaneously according to the numbered list or sentence boundary indications. If the sentence number after splitting are matching in both source and target sides, and each sentence pair is within the token length ratio of 3, we assume the split attempt is successful, otherwise the sentences are kept unchanged and will be filtered out eventually. We applied our splitting attempt approach on the patent documents at the data preparation step which consequently results in 19.35% and 7.1% increase in the number of sentence pairs compared with the original medical in-domain (from 4053258 to 4837382) and overall medical (from 17862521 to 19124142) datasets respectively.

Another finding from the training corpora is that the titles of the patent documents are often capitalized in the training corpora. Since we are training a true-cased translation system, and the translation inputs contain non-title sentences, capitalized training sentences will contribute biased weights to our true-case model. We addressed this issue by creating a lowercase version of the title corpora, then we trained our true-case model with the lowercased titles corpora and other non-title corpora. We also included the lowercased title corpora in the translation system training.

We tokenized the training corpora using the tokenizer script distributed in the Moses 1.0 framework with additional patent document non-breaking preferences observed during data preparation, such as Figs and FIGS etc., and a modified aggressive setting (split hyphen character in all cases). Other data preparation steps included character normalization, character/token based foreign language detection, HTML/XML tag removal, case insensitive duplication removal, longer sentence removal (2-80, length ratio 9), resulting in the preprocessed data shown in Table 2.

Corpus	In-domain parallel sentence number	Out-of-domain parallel sentence number
EMEA	273,532	0
COPPA	1,374,371	6,075,599
PatTR-title	63,856	3,457,164
PatTR-abstract	599,435	2,595,515
PatTR-claims	876,603	4,244,324
UMLS	85,683	0
Wikipedia	8,438	0
TOTAL	3,956,478	16,372,602

Table 2: WMT 2014 Medical Translation shared task parallel training data after preprocessing steps.

1.2 Training Data Selection

It is an open secret that high quality and large quantity of the parallel corpus are the two most important factors for a high-quality SMT system. These factors assist the word aligner in producing a precise alignment model, which in turn brings benefits to the other SMT training steps.

The quantity factor also helps the SMT system to cover more translation input variations. In order to efficiently use the training corpora listed in Table 2, we explored some data selection methodologies. We used the feature decay algorithm (Bicici et al., 2014) to select the training instances transductively, using the source side of the test set. We built systems with the pre-defined selection proportions in token number, 1/64, 1/32, 1/16, 1/8, 1/2, 3/4 and 1 of all the in-domain medical training data, then searched for the best performing system using the test data set as our baseline (Table 3). For the purpose of making the potential baseline systems comparable, instance selection was employed after word alignment using word aligner MGIZA++ (Gao and Vogel, 2008) on all the available data. The transductive learning uses features extracted from the source data of the development set with the default feature decay algorithm weight settings. All of systems were trained using the default phrase-based training parameter settings of Moses 1.0 framework, with additional msd-bidirectional-fe reordering model (Koehn et al., 2005). We extract phrase pairs based on grow-diag-final-and (Koehn et al., 2003) heuristics. The language model was created with open source IRSTLM toolkit (Federico et al., 2008) using all the English in-domain data (monolingual and parallel). We used 5-gram with modied Kneser-Ney smoothing (Kneser and Ney, 1995). The tuning step used minimum error rate training (MERT) (Och, 2003). The performance was measured by the test data set in case insensitive BLEU score.

Proportions	Test set case insensitive BLEU
1/64	0.4374
1/32	0.4409
1/16	0.4370
1/8	**0.4419**
1/4	0.4390
1/2	0.4399
3/4	0.4397
1	0.4260

Table 3: Feature decay algorithm transductive learning selection on all in-domain data using extracted features from the source side of the test data set. We choose system uses 1/8 proportions of the in-domain data as our baseline system.

Our results show that the system trained with 1/8 proportion of the in-domain medical training data (398,098 sentence pairs) selected by FDA outperformed the others. We chose this system as our baseline system.

2 Experiments

2.1 Maximum Phrase Length

While extracting phrase pairs, collecting longer phrases is not guaranteed to produce a better quality phrase table than the shorter settings, even setting the maximum phrase length to three can achieve top performance (Koehn et al., 2003). We take this WMT 2014 opportunity to study the capability of long phrase lengths (>=10). We trained translation models with phrase length setting from 10 to 15, employed them to our baseline system and compared the performance with the default setting (length = 7).

Phrase Length	Phrase Table Entries	Test set case insensitive BLEU
7 (Baseline)	19.31	0.4419
10	29.67	0.4400
11	32.87	0.4416
12	35.95	0.4444*
13	38.91	**0.4448***
14	41.75	0.4444*
15	44.47	0.4362

Table 4: -max-phrase-length setting experiment, where phrase table entries is in millions. * indiactes statistically significant improvement at the p = 0.05 level.[1]

As stated in (Koehn et al., 2003) and expected, the size of the phrase table is linear with respect to the maximum phrase length restriction. Surprisingly, we also found the performance can still improve after the default length setting, until a peak point (Table 4).

It is also interesting to see the effect for each sentence in the test set when the default phrase length setting in Moses framework is changed. We first evaluated the sentence level BLEU scores for the systems listed in Table 4, then compared them with our baseline system sentence level BLEU scores and categorised the compared results into increased, decreased or unaffected groups (Figure 1). We found that system with -max-phrase-length set to 12 is influenced the least (158, 118 and 724 sentences have BLEU score increased, decreased and unaffected respectively) and with -max-phrase-length sets to 10 is influenced the most (261, 257 and 482 sentences have BLEU score increased, decreased and unaffected respectively).

We then looked into the decoding phase and tried to discover the actual phrase length that was used to generate the translation outputs. We exposed the translation segmentations by triggering the -report-segmentation decoding parameter

[1]The same notation is used for the rest of the tables in this paper

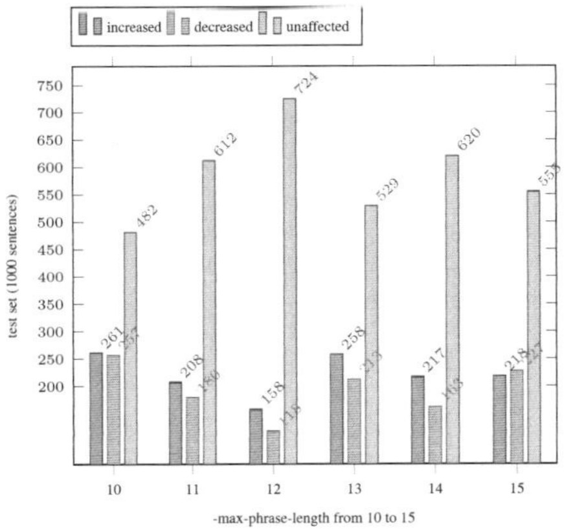

Figure 1: Sentence level BLEU score affects when enlarge -max-phrase-length

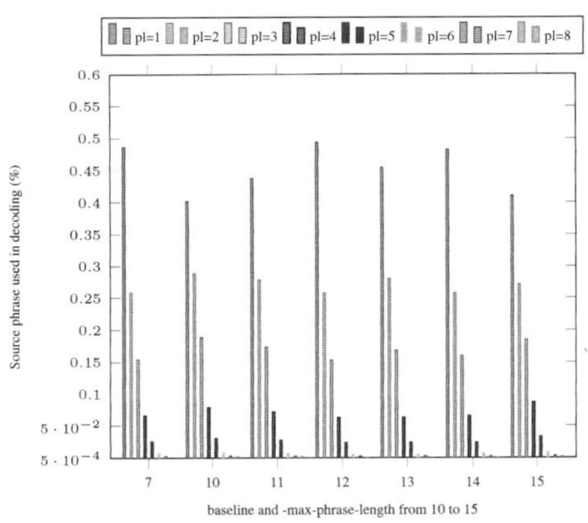

Figure 2: Phrase length (pl) distribution used in decoding

in the Moses framework and computed the percentage of different phrases used according to the phrase token number (Figure 2). The translation is mostly generated from short source phrases (length<4) in all the systems during decoding, which we think is the reason that setting phrase extraction to length 3 can achieve top performance.

We did not carry out more experiments in this case, as we think there is no absolute maximum phrase length setting which can fit into all experiments and such experiments depend on many factors, such as the similarity between the training corpus and then testing data. The choice to set -max-phrase-length to 13 is purely directed by the BLEU score shown in Table 4.

2.2 Reordering Models

Ceauşu et al. (2011) also found that long-range reordering is one of the characteristics of patent documents; however, long-range reordering increases the difficulty of SMT training and decoding. We experimented two approaches to address this challenge. Apart from the msd-bidirectional-fe lexical reordering model (Koehn et al., 2005) in our baseline system, the phrase-based orientation and hierarchical orientation reordering models (Galley and Manning, 2008) can capture long distance dependencies. The phrase-based orientation reordering model is similar to the lexical reordering approach, the only difference between these two models is the phrase-based reordering model performs reordering only on the phrase level, but the hierarchical reordering model does not have such constraint - it does not require phrases to be adjacent. OSM (Durrani, 2011) (Durrani, 2013b) is a sequence model integrating the N-gram-based translation model and reordering model. It defines three operations for reordering and considers all reordering possibilities within a fixed window while searching. We experimented with both reordering models, and found that the system defined with three reordering models performs better (Table 5) than OSM. We then tried to use both OSM and the reordering models together, which produced the best system at this point.

Systems	**Test set case insensitive BLEU**
Baseline + 13	0.4448
+ OSM	0.4472
+ pho-ho	0.4551*
+ pho-ho + OSM	**0.4561***

Table 5: Reordering Model or/and OSM results

2.3 Two Translation Models

The back-off model aims to produce translations for the unknown words or unknown phrases in the primary translation table by yielding the phrase table translation probability from primary translation table to the back-off table, as in (Koehn et al., 2012a)

$$p_{BO}(e|f) = \begin{cases} p_1(e|f) & if\ count_1(f) > 0 \\ p_2(e|f) & otherwise \end{cases}$$

Moreover, we look at using the back off model

as a domain adaptation approach, which is to constrain the translation options within the target domain unless no options can be found, in which case the translation will be selected from the back-off model.

Phrase table fill-up (Bisazza et al., 2011) is a very similar approach with back-off models, it collects and uses the phrase pairs from the out-of-domain phrase table only when the input is unavailable at the in-domain phrase table. It merges the in-domain and out-of-domain translation models into one, where the scores are taken from more reliable source. To distinguish the source of a phrase pair entry, fill-up assigns a binary value as an additional feature at the merged phrase table.

We trained our out-of-domain translation model separately using all of the out-of-domain medical data listed at Table 2 with the same parameter settings as our baseline system, then employed Moses's back-off model feature to pass the primary and back-off translation models to the decoder at tuning and translation time. The fill-up tool was sourced from (Bisazza et al., 2011) at Moses's distribution. Our experiment results (Table 6) show that the fill-up approach performed better than the back-off model approach.

Systems	Test set case insensitive BLEU
Baseline + 13 + pho-ho + OSM	0.4561
Back-off	0.4573
Fill-up	**0.4599***

Table 6: Back-off and fill-up experiment results

2.4 Language Model

Until now, we have reported our results using a language model trained with all in-domain medical data only. We also took the similar approach to (Koehn et al., 2007) and carried out language model experiments. We trained our out-of-domain language model with all the out-of-domain English sentences mentioned in section 1.1, then interpolated the in-domain and out-of-domain language model by optimizing the perplexity to the development data set. We received a similar picture to (Koehn et al., 2007), where the language model trained with only in-domain data performed the best (Table 7).

Our final submission for WMT 2014 Medical Translation shared task is the * system at Table 7.

Systems	Test set case insensitive BLEU
Baseline + 13 + pho-ho + OSM + Fill-up*	**0.4599**
out-of-domain LM	0.4461
interpolated LM	0.4592

Table 7: Language model experiment results

3 Conclusion

In this paper, we report our results on the WMT 2014 in the French to English translation direction. We shared our statistics for the bilingual corpora used to train our translation system. All systems were trained using the open source Moses 1.0 translation framework. Based on the feature set of Moses phrased-based translation system, we carried out our experiments on translation models, reordering models, operation sequence model and language model. We also experimented on data selection and releasing the length restriction while extracting phrase pairs.

4 Acknowledgements

This research is supported by the Science Foundation Ireland (Grant 12/CE/I2267) as part of the Centre for Next Generation Localisation (www.cngl.ie) at Dublin City University. We would also like to acknowledge Ergun Bicici who gives suggestions at the data selection approach.

References

Alexandru Ceauşu, John Tinsley, Jian Zhang and Andy Way. 2011. *Experiments on domain adaptation for patent machine translation in the PLuTO project*, The 15th conference of the European Association for Machine Translation, Leuven, Belgium.

Arianna Bisazza, Nick Ruiz, and Marcello Federico. 2011. *Fill-up versus Interpolation Methods for Phrase-based SMT Adaptation.*, In International Workshop on Spoken Language Translation (IWSLT), San Francisco, CA.

Durrani, N., Schmid, H., and Fraser, A. 2011. *A Joint Sequence Translation Model with Integrated Reordering.*, The 49th Annual Meeting of the Association for Computational Linguistics, Portland, Oregon, USA.

Durrani, N., Fraser, A., Schmid, H., Hoang, H., and Koehn, P. 2013b. *Can Markov Models Over Minimal Translation Units Help Phrase-Based SMT*, The 51th Annual Meeting of the Association for Computational Linguistics, Sofia, Bulgaria.

Ergun Bicici and Deniz Yuret. 2014. *Optimizing Instance Selection for Statistical Machine Translation with Feature Decay Algorithms*, IEEE/ACM Transactions On Audio, Speech, and Language Processing (TASLP).

Franz J. Och and Hermann Ney. 2003. *A systematic comparison of various statistical alignment models*, Computational Linguistics, 29(1):1951.

Franz Josef Och. 2003. *Minimum error rate training in statistical machine translation*, The 41th Annual Meeting of the Association for Computational Linguistics, Sapporo, Japan.

Marcello Federico, Nicola Bertoldi, and Mauro Cettolo. 2008. *IRSTLM: an open source toolkit for handling large scale language models*, Interspeech, Brisbane, Australia.

Michel Galley and Christopher D. Manning. 2008. *A simple and effective hierarchical phrase reordering model.* , The 2008 Conference on Empirical Methods in Natural Language Processing,pages 848856, Honolulu, Hawaii, October. Association for Computational Linguistics.

Qin Gao and Stephan Vogel. 2008. *Parallel implementations of word alignment tool*, In Software Engineering, Testing, and Quality Assurance for Natural Language Processing, SETQA-NLP 2008, pages 49-57, Stroudsburg, PA, USA. Association for Computational Linguistics.

Philipp Koehn, Amittai Axelrod, Alexandra Birch Mayne, Chris Callison-Burch, Miles Osborne and David Talbot. 2005. *Edinburgh System Description for the 2005 IWSLT Speech Translation Evaluation*, International Workshop on Spoken Language Translation.

Philipp Koehn and Josh Schroeder. 2007. *Experiments in Domain Adaptation for Statistical Machine Translation*, The Second Workshop on Statistical Machine Translation, pages 224227, Prague.

Philipp Koehn, Amittai Axelrod, Alexandra Birch Mayne, Chris Callison-Burch, Miles Osborne and David Talbot. 2003. *Statistical phrase-based translation*, 2003 Conference of the North American Chapter of the Association for Computational Linguistics on Human Language Technology, pages 4854, Edmonton, Canada.

Philipp Koehn, and Barry Haddow. 2012. *Interpolated backoff for factored translation models.*, The 10th Conference of the Association for Machine Translation in the Americas (AMTA).

Reinhard Kneser and Hermann Ney 1995. *Improved backing-off for m-gram language modeling.*, IEEE International Conference on Acoustics, Speech and Signal Processing, pages 181184.

Randomized Significance Tests in Machine Translation

Yvette Graham **Nitika Mathur** **Timothy Baldwin**
Department of Computing and Information Systems
The University of Melbourne
ygraham@unimelb.edu.au, nmathur@student.unimelb.edu.au, tb@ldwin.net

Abstract

Randomized methods of significance testing enable estimation of the probability that an increase in score has occurred simply by chance. In this paper, we examine the accuracy of three randomized methods of significance testing in the context of machine translation: paired bootstrap resampling, bootstrap resampling and approximate randomization. We carry out a large-scale human evaluation of shared task systems for two language pairs to provide a gold standard for tests. Results show very little difference in accuracy across the three methods of significance testing. Notably, accuracy of all test/metric combinations for evaluation of English-to-Spanish are so low that there is not enough evidence to conclude they are any better than a random coin toss.

1 Introduction

Automatic metrics, such as BLEU (Papineni et al., 2002), are widely used in machine translation (MT) as a substitute for human evaluation. Such metrics commonly take the form of an automatic comparison of MT output text with one or more human reference translations. Small differences in automatic metric scores can be difficult to interpret, however, and statistical significance testing provides a way of estimating the likelihood that a score difference has occurred simply by chance. For several metrics, such as BLEU, standard significance tests cannot be applied due to scores not comprising the mean of individual sentence scores, justifying the use of randomized methods.

Bootstrap resampling was one of the early randomized methods proposed for statistical significance testing of MT (Germann, 2003; Och, 2003; Kumar and Byrne, 2004; Koehn, 2004), to assess for a pair of systems how likely a difference in BLEU scores occurred by chance. Empirical tests detailed in Koehn (2004) show that even for test sets as small as 300 translations, BLEU confidence intervals can be computed as accurately as if they had been computed on a test set 100 times as large.

Approximate randomization was subsequently proposed as an alternate to bootstrap resampling (Riezler and Maxwell, 2005). Theoretically speaking, approximate randomization has an advantage over bootstrap resampling, in that it does not make the assumption that samples are representative of the populations from which they are drawn. Both methods require some adaptation in order to be used for the purpose of MT evaluation, such as combination with an automatic metric, and therefore it cannot be taken for granted that approximate randomization will be more accurate in practice. Within MT, approximate randomization for the purpose of statistical testing is also less common.

Riezler and Maxwell (2005) provide a comparison of approximate randomization with bootstrap resampling (distinct from *paired* bootstrap resampling), and conclude that since approximate randomization produces higher p-values for a set of apparently equally-performing systems, it more conservatively concludes statistically significant differences, and recommend preference of approximate randomization over bootstrap resampling for MT evaluation. Conclusions drawn from experiments provided in Riezler and Maxwell (2005) are oft-cited, with experiments interpreted as evidence that bootstrap resampling is overly optimistic in reporting significant differences (Riezler and Maxwell, 2006; Koehn and Monz, 2006; Galley and Manning, 2008; Green et al., 2010; Monz, 2011; Clark et al., 2011).

Our contribution in this paper is to revisit statistical significance tests in MT — namely, bootstrap resampling, paired bootstrap resampling and

Proceedings of the Ninth Workshop on Statistical Machine Translation, pages 266–274,
Baltimore, Maryland USA, June 26–27, 2014.

approximate randomization — and find problems with the published formulations. We redress these issues, and apply the tests in statistical testing of two language pairs. Using human judgments of translation quality, we find only very minor differences in significance levels across the three tests, challenging claims made in the literature about relative merits of tests.

2 Revisiting Statistical Significance Tests for MT Evaluation

First, we revisit the formulations of bootstrap resampling and approximate randomization algorithms as presented in Riezler and Maxwell (2005). At first glance, both methods appear to be two-tailed tests, with the null hypothesis that the two systems perform equally well. To facilitate a two-tailed test, absolute values of pseudo-statistics are computed before locating the absolute value of the actual statistic (original difference in scores). Using absolute values of pseudo-statistics is not problematic in the approximate randomization algorithm, and results in a reasonable two-tailed significance test. However, the bootstrap algorithm they provide uses an additional shift-to-zero method of simulating the null hypothesis. The way in which this shift-to-zero and absolute values of pseudo-statistics are applied is non-standard. Combining shift-to-zero and absolute values of pseudo-statistics results in all pseudo-statistics that fall below the mean pseudo-statistic to be omitted from computation of counts later used to compute p-values. The version of the bootstrap algorithm, as provided in the pseudo-code, is effectively a one-tailed test, and since this does not happen in the approximate randomization algorithm, experiments appear to compare p-values from a one-tailed bootstrap test directly with those of a two-tailed approximate randomization test. This inconsistency is not recognized, however, and p-values are compared as if both tests are two-tailed.

A better comparison of p-values would first require doubling the values of the one-sided bootstrap, leaving those of the two-sided approximate randomization algorithm as-is. The results of the two tests on this basis are extremely close, and in fact, in two out of the five comparisons, those of the bootstrap would have marginally *higher* p-values than those of approximate randomization. As such, it is conceivable to conclude that the experiments actually show no substantial difference in Type I error between the two tests, which is consistent with results published in other fields of research (Smucker et al., 2007). We also note that the pseudo-code contains an unconventional computation of mean pseudo-statistics, τ_B, for shift-to-zero.

Rather than speculate over whether these issues with the original paper were simply presentational glitches or the actual basis of the experiments reported on in the paper, we present a normalized version of the two-sided bootstrap algorithm in Figure 1, and report on the results of our own experiments in Section 4. We compare this method with approximate randomization and also *paired* bootstrap resampling (Koehn, 2004), which is widely used in MT evaluation. We carry out evaluation over a range of MT systems, not only including pairs of systems that perform equally well, but also pairs of systems for which one system performs marginally better than the other. This enables evaluation of not only Type I error, but the overall accuracy of the tests. We carry out a large-scale human evaluation of all WMT 2012 shared task participating systems for two language pairs, and collect sufficient human judgments to facilitate statistical significance tests. This human evaluation data then provides a gold-standard against which to compare randomized tests. Since all randomized tests only function in combination with an automatic MT evaluation metric, we present results of each randomized test across four different MT metrics.

3 Randomized Significance Tests

3.1 Bootstrap Resampling

Bootstrap resampling provides a way of estimating the population distribution by sampling with replacement from a representative sample (Efron and Tibshirani, 1993). The test statistic is taken as the difference in scores of the two systems, $S_X - S_Y$, which has an expected value of 0 under the null hypothesis that the two systems perform equally well. A bootstrap pseudo-sample consists of the translations by the two systems (X_b, Y_b) of a bootstrapped test set (Koehn, 2004), constructed by sampling with replacement from the original test set translations. The bootstrap distribution S_{boot} of the test statistic is estimated by calculating the value of the pseudo-statistic $S_{X_b} - S_{Y_b}$ for each pseudo-sample.

Set $c = 0$

Compute actual statistic of score differences $S_X - S_Y$ on test data

Calculate sample mean $\tau_B = \frac{1}{B}\sum_{b=1}^{B} S_{X_b} - S_{Y_b}$ over bootstrap samples $b = 1, ..., B$

For bootstrap samples $b = 1, ..., B$

  Sample with replacement from variable tuples test sentences for systems X and Y

  Compute pseudo-statistic $S_{X_b} - S_{Y_b}$ on bootstrap data

  If $|S_{X_b} - S_{Y_b} - \tau_B| \geq |S_X - S_Y|$

    $c = c + 1$

If $c/B \leq \alpha$

  Reject the null hypothesis

Figure 1: Two-sided bootstrap resampling statistical significance test for automatic MT evaluation

Set $c = 0$

Compute actual statistic of score differences $S_X - S_Y$ on test data

For random shuffles $r = 1, ..., R$

  For sentences in test set

    Shuffle variable tuples between systems X and Y with probability 0.5

  Compute pseudo-statistic $S_{X_r} - S_{Y_r}$ on shuffled data

  If $S_{X_r} - S_{Y_r} \geq S_X - S_Y$

    $c = c + 1$

If $c/R \leq \alpha$

  Reject the null hypothesis

Figure 2: Approximate randomization statistical significance test for automatic MT evaluation

The null hypothesis distribution S_{H_0} can be estimated from S_{boot} by applying the shift method (Noreen, 1989), which assumes that S_{H_0} has the same shape but a different mean than S_{boot}. Thus, S_{boot} is transformed into S_{H_0} by subtracting the mean bootstrap statistic from every value in S_{boot}.

Once this shift-to-zero has taken place, the null hypothesis is rejected if the probability of observing a more extreme value than the actual statistic is lower than a predetermined p-value α, which is typically set to 0.05. In other words, the score difference is significant at level $1 - \alpha$.

Figure 3 provides a one-sided implementation of bootstrap resampling, where H_0 is that the score of System X is less than or equal to the score of

Set $c = 0$

Compute actual statistic of score differences $S_X - S_Y$ on test data

Calculate sample mean $\tau_B = \frac{1}{B}\sum_{b=1}^{B} S_{X_b} - S_{Y_b}$ over bootstrap samples $b = 1, ..., B$

For bootstrap samples $b = 1, ..., B$

  Sample with replacement from variable tuples test sentences for systems X and Y

  Compute pseudo-statistic $S_{X_b} - S_{Y_b}$ on bootstrap data

  If $S_{X_b} - S_{Y_b} - \tau_B \geq S_X - S_Y$

    $c = c + 1$

If $c/B \leq \alpha$

  Reject the null hypothesis

Figure 3: One-sided Bootstrap resampling statistical significance test for automatic MT evaluation

Set $c = 0$

For bootstrap samples $b = 1, ..., B$

  If $S_{X_b} < S_{Y_b}$

    $c = c + 1$

If $c/B \leq \alpha$

  Reject the null hypothesis

Figure 4: Paired bootstrap resampling randomized significance test

System Y. Figure 5 includes a typical example of bootstrap resampling applied to BLEU, for a pair of systems for which differences in scores are significant, while Figure 6 shows the same for METEOR but for a pair of systems with no significant difference in scores.

3.2 Approximate Randomization

Unlike bootstrap, approximate randomization does not make any assumptions about the population distribution. To simulate a distribution for the null hypothesis that the scores of the two systems are the same, translations are shuffled between the two systems so that 50% of each pseudo-sample is drawn from each system. In the context of machine translation, this can be interpreted as each translation being equally likely to have been produced by one system as the other (Riezler and Maxwell, 2005).

The test statistic is taken as the difference in scores of the two systems, $S_X - S_Y$. If there is

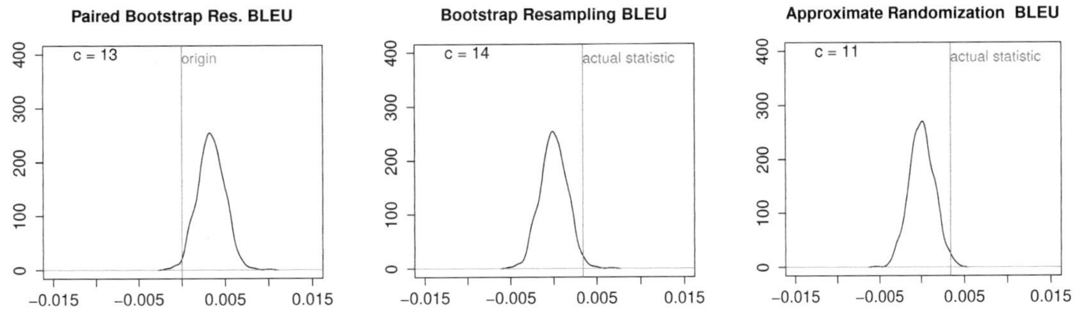

Figure 5: Pseudo-statistic distributions for a typical pair of systems with close BLEU scores for each randomized test (System F vs. System G).

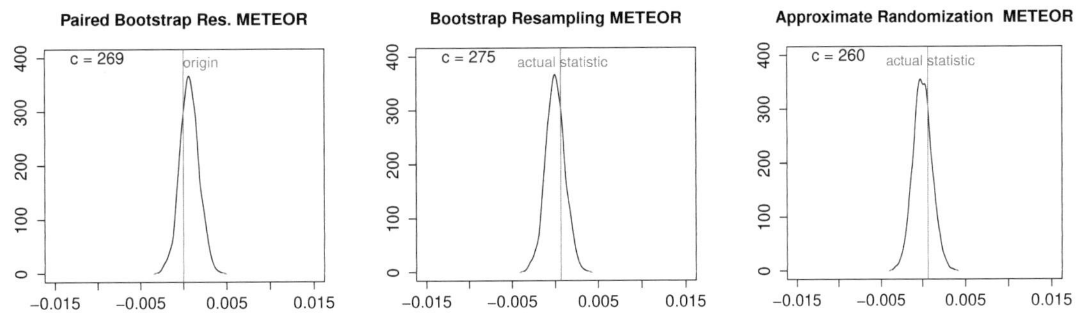

Figure 6: Pseudo-statistic distributions of METEOR with randomized tests (System D vs. System A).

a total of S sentences, then a total of 2^S shuffles is possible. If S is large, instead of generating all 2^S possible combinations, we instead generate samples by randomly permuting translations between the two systems with equal probability. The distribution of the test statistic under the null hypothesis is approximated by calculating the pseudo-statistic, $S_{X_r} - S_{Y_r}$, for each sample. As before, the null hypothesis is rejected if the probability of observing a more extreme value than the actual test statistic is lower than α.

Figure 2 provides a one-sided implementation of approximate randomization for MT evaluation, where the null hypothesis is that the score of System X is less than or equal to the score of System Y. Figure 5 shows a typical example of pseudo-statistic distributions for approximate randomization for a pair of systems with a small but significant score difference according to BLEU, and Figure 6 shows the same for METEOR applied to a pair of systems where no significant difference is concluded.

3.3 Paired Bootstrap Resampling

Paired bootstrap resampling (Koehn, 2004) is shown in Figure 4. Unlike the other two randomized tests, this method makes no attempt to simulate the null hypothesis distribution. Instead, bootstrap samples are used to estimate confidence intervals of score differences, with confidence intervals not containing 0 implying a statistically significant difference.

We compare what takes place with the two other tests, by plotting differences in scores for bootstrapped samples, $S_{X_b} - S_{Y_b}$, as shown in Figure 5 for BLEU and Figure 6 for METEOR. Instead of computing counts with reference to the actual statistic, the line through the origin provides the cut-off for counts.

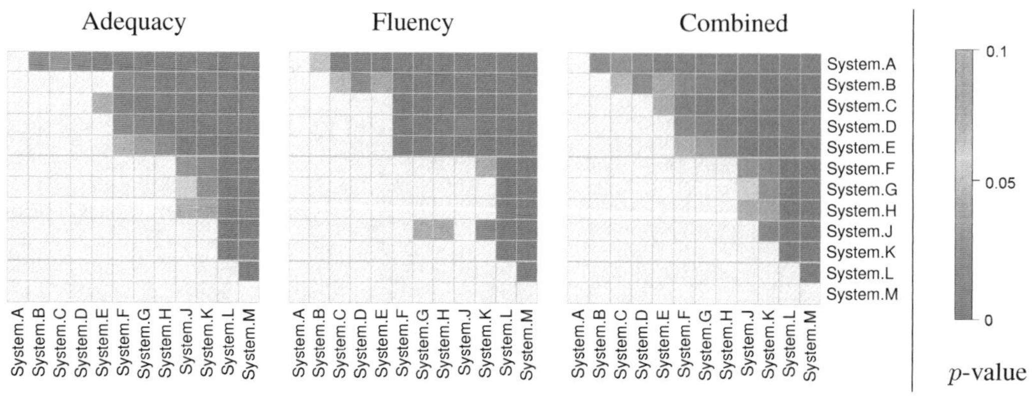

Figure 7: Human evaluation pairwise significance tests for Spanish-to-English systems (colored cells denote scores for System *row* being significantly greater than System *column*.

4 Evaluation

In order to evaluate the accuracy of the three randomized significance significance tests, we compare conclusions reached in a human evaluation of shared task participant systems. We carry out a large-scale human evaluation of all participating systems from WMT 2012 (Callison-Burch et al., 2012) for the Spanish-to-English and English-to-Spanish translation tasks. Large numbers of human assessments of translations were collected using Amazon's Mechanical Turk, with strict quality control filtering (Graham et al., 2013). A total of 82,100 human adequacy assessments and 62,400 human fluency assessments were collected. After the removal of quality control items and filtering of judgments from low-quality workers, this resulted in an average of 1,280 adequacy and 1,013 fluency assessments per system for Spanish-to-English (12 systems), and 1,483 adequacy and 1,534 fluency assessments per system for English-to-Spanish (11 systems). To remove bias with respect to individual human judge preference scoring severity/leniency, scores provided by each human assessor were standardized according to the mean and standard deviation of all scores provided by that individual.

Significance tests were carried out over the scores for each pair of systems separately for adequacy and fluency assessments using the Wilcoxon rank-sum test. Figure 7 shows pairwise significance test results for fluency, adequacy and the combination of the two tests, for all pairs of Spanish-to-English systems. Combined fluency and adequacy significance test results are constructed as follows: if a system's adequacy score is significantly greater than that of another, the combined conclusion is that it is significantly better, at that significance level. Only when a tie in adequacy scores occurs are fluency judgments used to break the tie. In this case, p-values from significance tests applied to fluency scores of that system pair are used. For example, in Figure 7, adequacy scores of System B are not significantly greater than those of Systems C, D and E, while fluency scores for System B are significantly greater than those of the three other systems. The combined result for each pair of systems is therefore taken as the p-value from the corresponding fluency significance test.

We use the combined human evaluation pairwise significant tests as a gold standard against which to evaluate the randomized methods of statistical significance testing. We evaluate paired bootstrap resampling (Koehn, 2004) and bootstrap resampling as shown in Figure 3 and approximate randomization as shown in Figure 2, each in combination with four automatic MT metrics: BLEU (Papineni et al., 2002), NIST (NIST, 2002), METEOR (Banerjee and Lavie, 2005) and TER (Snover et al., 2006).

4.1 Results and Discussion

Figure 8 shows the outcome of pairwise randomized significance tests for each metric for Spanish-to-English systems, and Table 1 shows numbers of correct conclusions and accuracy of each test.

When we compare conclusions made by the three randomized tests for Spanish-to-English systems, there is very little difference in p-values for all pairs of systems. For both BLEU and NIST,

		Paired Bootst. Resamp.		Bootst. Resamp.		Approx. Rand.	
α		Conc.	Acc.(%)	Conc.	Acc. (%)	Conc.	Acc. (%)
0.05	BLEU	53	80.3 [68.7, 89.1]	53	80.3 [68.7, 89.1]	53	80.3 [68.7, 89.1]
	NIST	**54**	**81.8** [70.4, 90.2]	**54**	**81.8** [70.4, 90.2]	**54**	**81.8** [70.4, 90.2]
	METEOR	52	78.8 [67.0, 87.9]	52	78.8 [67.0, 87.9]	52	78.8 [67.0, 87.9]
	TER	52	78.8 [67.0, 87.9]	52	78.8 [67.0, 87.9]	52	78.8 [67.0, 87.9]
0.01	BLEU	51	77.3 [65.3, 86.7]	51	77.3 [65.3, 86.7]	51	77.3 [65.3, 86.7]
	NIST	51	77.3 [65.3, 86.7]	51	77.3 [65.3, 86.7]	51	77.3 [65.3, 86.7]
	METEOR	53	80.3 [68.7, 89.1]	53	80.3 [68.7, 89.1]	53	80.3 [68.7, 89.1]
	TER	51	77.3 [65.3, 86.7]	51	77.3 [65.3, 86.7]	51	77.3 [65.3, 86.7]
0.001	BLEU	48	72.7 [60.4, 83.0]	48	72.7 [60.4, 83.0]	48	72.7 [60.4, 83.0]
	NIST	48	72.7 [60.4, 83.0]	48	72.7 [60.4, 83.0]	48	72.7 [60.4, 83.0]
	METEOR	53	80.3 [68.7, 89.1]	53	80.3 [68.7, 89.1]	52	78.8 [67.0, 87.9]
	TER	50	75.8 [63.6, 85.5]	51	77.3 [65.3, 86.7]	52	78.8 [67.0, 87.9]

Table 1: Accuracy of randomized significance tests for Spanish-to-English MT with four automatic metrics, based on the WMT 2012 participant systems.

		Paired Bootst. Resamp.		Bootst. Resamp.		Approx. Rand.	
α		Conc.	Acc.(%)	Conc.	Acc. (%)	Conc.	Acc. (%)
0.05	BLEU	**34**	**61.8** [47.7, 74.6]	**34**	**61.8** [47.7, 74.6]	**34**	**61.8** [47.7, 74.6]
	NIST	32	58.2 [44.1, 71.3]	32	58.2 [44.1, 71.3]	32	58.2 [44.1, 71.3]
	METEOR	31	56.4 [42.3, 69.7]	31	56.4 [42.3, 69.7]	31	56.4 [42.3, 69.7]
	TER	32	58.2 [44.1, 71.3]	32	58.2 [44.1, 71.3]	32	58.2 [44.1, 71.3]
0.01	BLEU	33	60.0 [45.9, 73.0]	33	60.0 [45.9, 73.0]	33	60.0 [45.9, 73.0]
	NIST	32	58.2 [44.1, 71.3]	32	58.2 [44.1, 71.3]	32	58.2 [44.1, 71.3]
	METEOR	31	56.4 [42.3, 69.7]	32	58.2 [44.1, 71.3]	32	58.2 [44.1, 71.3]
	TER	30	54.5 [40.6, 68.0]	30	54.5 [40.6, 68.0]	30	54.5 [40.6, 68.0]
0.001	BLEU	33	60.0 [45.9, 73.0]	33	60.0 [45.9, 73.0]	33	60.0 [45.9, 73.0]
	NIST	33	60.0 [45.9, 73.0]	32	58.2 [44.1, 71.3]	32	58.2 [44.1, 71.3]
	METEOR	32	58.2 [44.1, 71.3]	32	58.2 [44.1, 71.3]	32	58.2 [44.1, 71.3]
	TER	30	54.5 [40.6, 68.0]	30	54.5 [40.6, 68.0]	31	56.4 [42.3, 69.7]

Table 2: Accuracy of randomized significance tests for English-to-Spanish MT with four automatic metrics, based on the WMT 2012 participant systems.

all three randomized methods produce p-values so similar that when α thresholds are applied, all three tests produce precisely the same set of pairwise conclusions for each metric. When tests are combined with METEOR and TER, similar results are observed: at the α thresholds of 0.05 and 0.01, precisely the same conclusions are drawn for both metrics combined with each of the three tests, and at most a difference of two conclusions at the lowest α level.

Table 2 shows the accuracy of each test on the English-to-Spanish data, showing much the same set of conclusions at all α levels. For BLEU and NIST, all three tests again produce precisely the same conclusions, at $p < 0.01$ there is at most a single different conclusion for METEOR, and only at the lowest p-value level is there a single difference for TER.

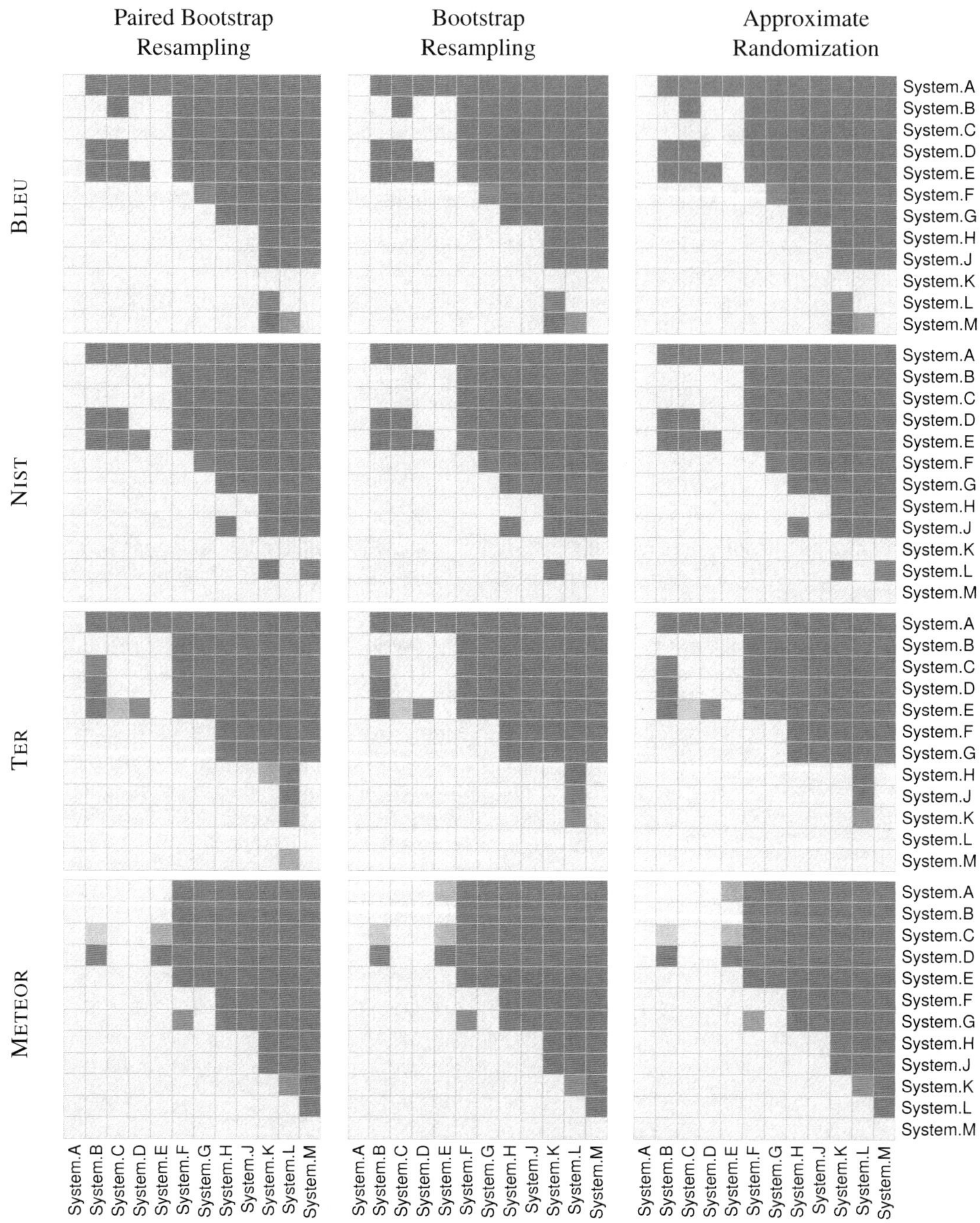

Figure 8: Automatic metric pairwise randomized significance test results for Spanish-to-English systems (colored cells denote scores for System *row* significantly greater than System *column*).

Finally, we examine which combination of metric and test is most accurate for each language pair at the conventional significance level of $p < 0.05$. For Spanish-to-English evaluation, NIST combined with any of the three randomized tests is most accurate, making 54 out of 66 (82%) correct conclusions. For English-to-Spanish, BLEU in combination with any of the three randomized tests, is most accurate at 62%. For both language pairs, however, differences in accuracy for metrics are not significant (Chi-square test).

For English-to-Spanish evaluation, an accuracy as low as 62% should be a concern. This level of accuracy for significance testing – only making the correct conclusion in 6 out of 10 tests – acts as a reminder that no matter how sophisticated the significance test, it will never make up for flaws in an underlying metric. When we take into account the fact that lower confidence limits all fall below 50%, significance tests based on these metrics for English-to-Spanish are effectively no better than a random coin toss.

5 Conclusions

We provided a comparison of bootstrap resampling and approximate randomization significance tests for a range of automatic machine translation evaluation metrics. To provide a gold-standard against which to evaluate randomized tests, we carried out a large-scale human evaluation of all shared task participating systems for the Spanish-to-English and English-to-Spanish translation tasks from WMT 2012. Results showed for many metrics and significance levels that all three tests produce precisely the same set of conclusions, and when conclusions do differ, it is commonly only by a single contrasting conclusion, which is not significant. For English-to-Spanish MT, the results of the different MT evaluation metric/significance test combinations are not significantly higher than a random baseline.

Acknowledgements

We wish to thank the anonymous reviewers for their valuable comments. This research was supported by funding from the Australian Research Council.

References

S. Banerjee and A. Lavie. 2005. METEOR: An automatic metric for mt evaluation with improved correlation with human judgements. In *Proc. Wkshp. Intrinsic and Extrinsic Evaluation Measures for Machine Translation and/or Summarization*, pages 65–73, Ann Arbor, MI. ACL.

C. Callison-Burch, P. Koehn, C. Monz, M. Post, R. Soricut, and L. Specia. 2012. Findings of the 2012 Workshop on Statistical Machine Translation. In *Proc. 7th Wkshp. Statistical Machine Translation*, pages 10–51, Montreal, Canada. ACL.

J. H. Clark, C. Dyer, A. Lavie, and N. A. Smith. 2011. Better hypothesis testing for statistical machine translation: Controlling for optimizer instability. In *Proc. of the 49th Annual Meeting of the Assoc. Computational Linguistics: Human Language Technologies: short papers-Volume 2*, pages 176–181, Portland, OR. ACL.

B. Efron and R. J. Tibshirani. 1993. *An Introduction to the Bootstrap*. Chapman & Hall, New York City, NY.

M. Galley and C. D. Manning. 2008. A simple and effective hierarchical phrase reordering model. In *Proc. of the Conference on Empirical Methods in Natural Language Processing*, pages 848–856, Edinburgh, Scotland. ACL.

U. Germann. 2003. Greedy decoding for statistical machine translation in almost linear time. In *Proc. of the 2003 Conference of the North American Chapter of the Assoc. Computational Linguistics on Human Language Technology-Volume 1*, pages 1–8, Edmonton, Canada. ACL.

Y. Graham, T. Baldwin, A. Moffat, and J. Zobel. 2013. Continuous measurement scales in human evaluation of machine translation. In *Proc. 7th Linguistic Annotation Wkshp. & Interoperability with Discourse*, pages 33–41, Sofia, Bulgaria. ACL.

S. Green, M. Galley, and C. D. Manning. 2010. Improved models of distortion cost for statistical machine translation. In *Human Language Technologies: The 2010 Annual Conference of the North American Chapter of the Assoc. Computational Linguistics*, pages 867–875, Los Angeles, CA. ACL.

P. Koehn and C. Monz. 2006. Manual and automatic evaluation of machine translation between European languages. In *Proceedings of the Workshop on Statistical Machine Translation*, pages 102–121, New York City, NY. ACL.

P. Koehn. 2004. Statistical significance tests for machine translation evaluation. In *Proc. of Empirical Methods in Natural Language Processing*, pages 388–395, Barcelona, Spain. ACL.

S. Kumar and W. J. Byrne. 2004. Minimum Bayes-risk decoding for statistical machine translation. In *HLT-NAACL*, pages 169–176, Boston, MA. ACL.

C. Monz. 2011. Statistical machine translation with local language models. In *Proc. of the Conference on Empirical Methods in Natural Language Processing*, pages 869–879, Edniburgh, Scotland. ACL.

NIST. 2002. Automatic Evaluation of Machine Translation Quality Using N-gram Co-Occurrence Statistics. Technical report.

E. W. Noreen. 1989. *Computer intensive methods for testing hypotheses*. Wiley, New York City, NY.

F. J. Och. 2003. Minimum error rate training in statistical machine translation. In *Proc. 41st Ann. Meeting of the Assoc. Computational Linguistics*, pages 160–167, Sapporo, Japan. ACL.

K. Papineni, S. Roukos, T. Ward, and W. J. Zhu. 2002. A method for automatic evaluation of machine translation. In *Proc. 40th Ann. Meeting of the Assoc. Computational Linguistics*, pages 311–318, Philadelphia, PA. ACL.

S. Riezler and J. T. Maxwell. 2005. On some pitfalls in automatic evaluation and significance testing for mt. In *Proc. of the ACL Workshop on Intrinsic and Extrinsic Evaluation Measures for Machine Translation and/or Summarization*, pages 57–64, Ann Arbor, MI. ACL.

S. Riezler and J. T. Maxwell. 2006. Grammatical machine translation. In *Proc. of the Main Conference on Human Language Technology Conference of the North American Chapter of the Assoc. Computational Linguistics*, pages 248–255, New York City, NY. ACL.

M. Smucker, J. Allan, and B. Carterette. 2007. A comparison of statistical significance tests for information retrieval evaluation. In *Proc. of the Sixteenth ACM Conference on Information and Knowledge Management (CIKM 2007)*, pages 623–632, Lisbon, Portugal. ACM.

M. Snover, B. Dorr, R. Scwartz, J. Makhoul, and L. Micciula. 2006. A study of translation error rate with targeted human annotation. In *Proc. 7th Biennial Conf. of the Assoc. Machine Translaiton in the Americas*, pages 223–231, Boston, MA. ACL.

Estimating Word Alignment Quality for SMT Reordering Tasks

Sara Stymne Jörg Tiedemann Joakim Nivre
Uppsala University
Department of Linguistics and Philology
firstname.lastname@lingfil.uu.se

Abstract

Previous studies of the effect of word alignment on translation quality in SMT generally explore link level metrics only and mostly do not show any clear connections between alignment and SMT quality. In this paper, we specifically investigate the impact of word alignment on two pre-reordering tasks in translation, using a wider range of quality indicators than previously done. Experiments on German–English translation show that reordering may require alignment models different from those used by the core translation system. Sparse alignments with high precision on the link level, for translation units, and on the subset of crossing links, like intersected HMM models, are preferred. Unlike SMT performance the desired alignment characteristics are similar for small and large training data for the pre-reordering tasks. Moreover, we confirm previous research showing that the fuzzy reordering score is a useful and cheap proxy for performance on SMT reordering tasks.

1 Introduction

Word alignment is a key component in all state-of-the-art statistical machine translation (SMT) systems, and there has been some work exploring the connection between word alignment quality and translation quality (Och and Ney, 2003; Fraser and Marcu, 2007; Lambert et al., 2012). The standard way to evaluate word alignments in this context is by using metrics like alignment error rate (AER) and F-measure on the link level, and the general conclusion appears to be that translation quality benefits from alignments with high recall (rather than precision), at least for large training data. Although many other ways of measuring alignment quality have been proposed, such as working on translation units (Ahrenberg et al., 2000; Ayan and Dorr, 2006; Søgaard and Kuhn, 2009) or using link degree and related measures (Ahrenberg, 2010), these methods have not been used to study the relation between alignment and translation quality, with the exception of Lambert et al. (2012).

Word alignment is also used for many other tasks besides translation, including term bank creation (Merkel and Foo, 2007), cross-lingual annotation projection for part-of-speech tagging (Yarowsky et al., 2001), semantic roles (Pado and Lapata, 2005), pronoun anaphora (Postolache et al., 2006), and cross-lingual clustering (Täckström et al., 2012). Even within SMT itself, there are tasks such as reordering that often make crucial use of word alignments. For instance, source language reordering commonly relies on rules learnt automatically from word-aligned data (e.g., Xia and McCord (2004)). As far as we know, no one has studied the impact of alignment quality on these additional tasks, and it seems to be tacitly assumed that alignments that are good for translation are also good for other tasks.

In this paper we set out to explore the impact of alignment quality on two pre-reordering tasks for SMT. In doing so, we employ a wider range of quality indicators than is customary, and for reference these indicators are used also to assess overall translation quality. To allow an in-depth exploration of the connections between several aspects of word alignment and reordering, we limit our study to one language pair, German–English. We think this is a suitable language pair for studying reordering since it has both short range and long range reorderings. Our main focus is on using relatively large training data, 2M sentences, but we also report results with small training data, 170K sentences. The main conclusion of our study is that alignments that are optimal for translation are not necessarily optimal for reordering, where pre-

Proceedings of the Ninth Workshop on Statistical Machine Translation, pages 275–286,
Baltimore, Maryland USA, June 26–27, 2014.

cision is of greater importance than recall. For SMT the best alignments are different depending on corpus size, but for the reordering tasks results are stable across training data size.

In section 2 we discuss previous work related to word alignment and SMT. In section 3, we introduce the word alignment quality indicators we use, and show experimental results for a number of alignment systems on an SMT task. In section 4, we turn to reordering for SMT and use the same quality indicators to study the impact of alignment quality on reordering quality. In section 5 we briefly describe results using small training data. In section 6, we conclude and suggest directions for future work.

2 Word Alignment and SMT

Word alignment is the task of relating words in one language to words in the translation in another language, see an example in Figure 1. Word alignment models can be learnt automatically from large corpora of sentence aligned data. Brown et al. (1993) proposed the so-called IBM models, which are still widely used. These five models estimate alignments from corpora using the expectation-maximization algorithm, and each model adds some complexity. Model 4 is commonly used in SMT systems. There have been many later suggestions of alternatives to these models. These are often alternatives to model 2, such as the HMM model (Vogel et al., 1996) and fast_align (Dyer et al., 2013).

All these generative models produce directional alignments where one word in the source can be linked to many target words (1–m links) but not vice versa. It is generally desirable to also allow n–1 and n–m links, and to achieve this it is common practice to perform word alignment in both directions and to symmetrize them using some heuristic. A number of common symmetrization strategies are described in Table 1 (Koehn et al., 2005). There are also other alternatives, such as the refined method (Och and Ney, 2003), or link deletion from the union (Fossum et al., 2008).

There is also a wide range of alternative approaches to word alignment. For example, various discriminative models have been proposed in the literature (Liu et al., 2005; Moore, 2005; Taskar et al., 2005). Their advantage is that they may integrate a wide range of features that may lead to improved alignment quality. However, most of these models require external tools (for creating linguistic features) and manually aligned training data, which we do not have for our data sets (besides the data we need for evaluation). Investigating these types of models are outside the scope of our current work.

Symmetrization	Description
int: intersection	$A_{TS} \cap A_{ST}$
uni: union	$A_{TS} \cup A_{ST}$
gd: grow-diag	intersection plus adjacent links from the union if both linked words are unaligned
gdf: grow-diag-final	gd with links from the union added in a final step if either linked word is unaligned
gdfa: grow-diag-final-and	gd with links from the union added in a final step if both linked words are unaligned

Table 1: Symmetrization strategies for word alignments A_{TS} and A_{ST} in two directions

Word alignments are used as an important knowledge source for training SMT systems. In word-based SMT, the parameters of the generative word alignment models are essentially the translation model of the system. In phrase-based SMT (PBSMT) (Koehn et al., 2003), which is among the state-of-the-art systems today, word alignments are used as a basis for extracting phrases and estimating phrase alignment probabilities. Similarly, word alignments are also used for estimating rule probabilities in various kinds of hierarchical and syntactic SMT (Chiang, 2007; Yamada and Knight, 2002; Galley et al., 2004).

Intrinsic evaluation of word alignment is generally based on a comparison to a gold standard of human alignments. Based on the gold standard, metrics like precision, recall and F-measure can be calculated for each alignment link, see Eqs. 1–2, where A are hypothesized alignment links and G are gold standard links. Another common metric is alignment error rate (AER) (Och and Ney, 2000), which is based on a distinction between sure, S, and possible, P, links in the gold standard. $1-$AER is identical to balanced F-measure when the gold standard does not make a distinction between S and P.

$$\text{Precision}(A, G) = \frac{|G \cap A|}{|A|} \quad (1)$$

$$\text{Recall}(A, G) = \frac{|G \cap A|}{|G|} \quad (2)$$

$$\text{AER} = 1 - \frac{|P \cap A| + |S \cap A|}{|S| + |A|} \quad (3)$$

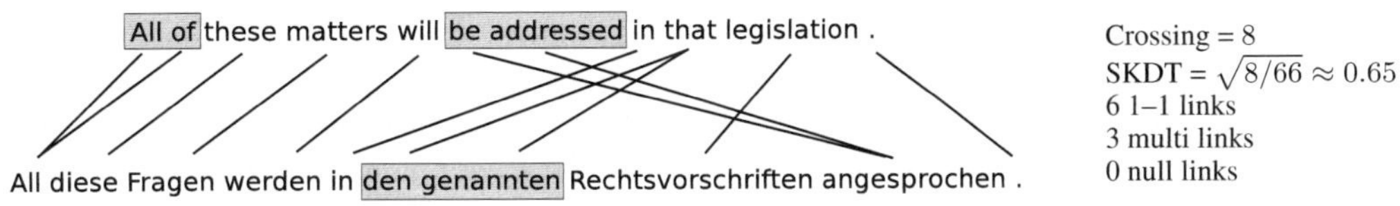

Figure 1: An example alignment illustrating n–1, 1–m and crossing links.

The relation between word alignment quality and PBSMT has been studied by some researchers. Och and Ney (2000) looked at the impact of IBM and HMM models on the alignment template approach (Och et al., 1999) in terms of AER. They found that AER correlates with human evaluation of sentence level quality, but not with word error rate. Fraser and Marcu (2007) found that there is no correlation between AER and Bleu (Papineni et al., 2002), especially not when the P-set is large. They found that a balanced F-measure is a better indicator of Bleu, but that a weighted F-measure is even better (see Eq. 4) mostly with a higher weight for recall than for precision. This weight, however, needs to be optimized for each data set, language pair, and gold standard alignment separately.

$$\mathrm{F}(A, G, \alpha) = \left(\frac{\alpha}{\text{Precision(A,G)}} + \frac{1-\alpha}{\text{Recall(A,G)}} \right)^{-1} \quad (4)$$

Ayan and Dorr (2006) on the other hand found some evidence for the importance of precision over recall. However, they used much smaller training data than Fraser and Marcu (2007). They also suggested using a measure called consistent phrase error-rate (CPER), but found that it was hard to assess the impact of alignment on MT, both with AER and CPER. Lambert et al. (2012) performed a study where they investigated the effect of word alignment on MT using a large number of word alignment indicators. They found that there was a difference between large and small datasets in that alignment precision was more important with small data sets, and recall more important with large data sets. Overall they did not find any indicator that was significant over two language pairs and different corpus sizes. There were more significant indicators for large datasets, however.

Most researchers who propose new alignment models perform both a gold standard evaluation and an SMT evaluation (Liang et al., 2006; Ganchev et al., 2008; Junczys-Dowmunt and Szał, 2012; Dyer et al., 2013). The relation between the two types of evaluation is often quite weak. Several of these studies only show AER on their gold standard, despite its well-known shortcomings.

Even though many studies have shown some relation between translation quality and AER or weighted F-measure, it has rarely been investigated thoroughly in its own right, and, as far as we are aware, not for other tasks than SMT. Furthermore, most of these studies considers nothing else but link level agreement. In this paper we take a broader view on alignment quality and explore the effect of other types of quality indicators as well.

3 Word Alignment Quality Indicators

We investigate four groups of quality indicators. The first group is the classic group where metrics are calculated on the alignment link level, which has been used in several studies. In our experiments we use a gold standard that does not make use of distinctions between sure and possible links, as suggested by Fraser and Marcu (2007). With this, we can calculate the standard metrics P(recision) R(ecall) and F(-measure). We will mainly use balanced F-measure, but occasionally also report weighted F-measure. As noted before, 1−AER is equivalent to balanced F when only sure links are used, and will thus not be reported separately.

Søgaard and Kuhn (2009) and Søgaard and Wu (2009) suggested working on the translation unit (TU) level, instead of the link level. A translation unit, or cept (Goutte et al., 2004), is defined as a maximally connected subgraph of an alignment. In Figure 1, the twelve links form nine translation units. Søgaard and Wu (2009) suggest the metric TUER, translation unit error rate, shown in Eq. 5, where A_U are hypothesized translation units, and G_U are gold standard translation units.[1] They use TUER to establish lower bounds for the coverage of alignments from different formalisms, not to evaluate SMT. While they only use TUER, it

[1] TUER is similar to CPER (Ayan and Dorr, 2006), which measures the error rate of extracted phrases. Due to how phrase extraction handle null links, there are differences, however.

is also possible to define Precision, Recall and F-measure over translation units in the same way as for alignment links. We will use these three measures to get a broader picture of TUs in alignment evaluation. Also in this case, 1−TUER is equivalent to F-measure.

$$\text{TUER}(A, G) = 1 - \frac{2|A_U \cap G_U|}{|A_U| + |G_U|} \quad (5)$$

The TU metrics are quite strict, since they require exact matching of TUs. Tiedemann (2005) suggested the MWU metrics for word alignment evaluation, which also consider partial matches of annotated multi-word units, which is a similar concept to TUs. In those metrics, precision and recall grow proportionally to the number of correctly aligned words within translation units. Proposed links are in this way scored according to their overlap with translation units in the gold standard. Precision and recall are defined in Eqs. 6–7, where $overlap(X_U, Y)$ is the number of source and target words in X_U that overlap with translation units in Y normalized by the size of X_U (in terms of source and target words). Note, that TUs need to overlap in source and target. Otherwise, their overlap will be counted as zero.

$$P_{MWU} = \sum_{A_U \in A} \frac{overlap(A_U, G)}{|A|} \quad (6)$$

$$R_{MWU} = \sum_{G_U \in G} \frac{overlap(G_U, A)}{|G|} \quad (7)$$

There have also been attempts at classifying alignments in other ways, not related to a gold standard. Ahrenberg (2010) proposed several ways to categorize human alignments, including link degree, reordering of links, and structural correspondence. He used these indicators to profile hand-aligned corpora from different domains. We will not use structural correspondence, which requires a dependency parser, and which we believe is error prone when performed automatically. We will use what we call *link degree*, i.e., how many alignment links each word obtains. Ahrenberg (2010) used a fine-grained scheme of the percentage for different degrees, including isomorphism 1–1, deletion 0–1, reduction m–1, and paraphrase m–n. Similar link degree classes were used by Lambert et al. (2012). In this work we will reduce these classes into three: 1–1 links, null links, which combine the 0–1 and 1–0 cases, and multi links where there are many words on at least one side.

Ahrenberg (2010) also proposed to measure reorderings. He does this by calculating the percentage of links with crossings of different lengths. To define this he only considers adjacent links in the source using the distance between corresponding target words, which means that his metric becomes a directional measure. Reorderings of alignments was also used by Genzel (2010), who used *crossing score*, the number of crossing links, to rank reordering rules. This is non-directional and simpler to calculate than Ahrenberg (2010)'s metrics, and implicitly covers length since a long distance reordering leads to a higher number of pairwise crossing links. Birch and Osborne (2011) suggest using squared Kendall τ distance (SKTD), see Eq. 8, where n is the number of links, as a basis of LR-score, an MT metric that takes reordering into account. They found that squaring τ better explained reordering, than using only τ. In this study we will use both, crossing score and SKTD. Figure 1 shows these scores for an example sentence. These two measures only tell us how much reordering there is. To quantify this relative to the gold standard we also report the absolute difference between the number of gold standard crossings and system crossings, which we call *Crossdiff*. To account for the quality of crossings, to some extent, we will also report precision, recall, and F-measure for the subset of translation units that are involved in a crossing.

$$\text{SKTD} = \sqrt{\frac{|\text{crossing link pairs}|}{(n^2 - n)/2}} \quad (8)$$

3.1 Alignment Experiments

We perform all our experiments for German–English. The alignment indicators are calculated on a corpus of 987 hand aligned sentences (Pado and Lapata, 2005). The gold standard contains explicit null links, which the symmetrized automatic alignments do not. To allow a straightforward comparison we consistently remove all null links when comparing system alignments to the gold standard.

For creating the automatic alignments we used GIZA++ (Och and Ney, 2003) to compute directional alignments for model 2–4 and the HMM model, and fast_align (fa) (Dyer et al., 2013) as newer alternatives to model 2. These models require large amounts of data to be estimated reliably. To achieve this we concatenated the gold standard with the large SMT training data (see

	Alignment links				Translation units				MWU			Link degree			Link crossings					
	Total	P	R	F	Total	P	R	F	P	R	F	1-1	null	multi	Total	SKTD	P	R	F	Crossdiff
gold	22629	–	–	–	17068	–	–	–	–	–	–	.542	.328	.130	30163	.292	–	–	–	0
2-int	15362	.850	.577	.687	15362	.701	.631	.664	.849	.712	.774	.500	.500	.000	10064	.267	.551	.463	.503	20099
3-int	16573	.860	.630	.727	16573	.707	.686	.697	.857	.776	.814	.561	.439	.000	12682	.274	.553	.521	.537	17481
4-int	16529	.903	.660	.763	16529	.743	.720	.731	.901	.813	.855	.559	.441	.000	11229	.251	.663	.522	.584	18934
HMM-int	14871	.922	.606	.731	14871	.768	.669	.715	.920	.750	.827	.476	.524	.000	8077	.221	.709	.417	.525	22086
fa-int	15997	.857	.606	.710	15997	.696	.652	.673	.854	.742	.794	.531	.469	.000	9724	.246	.568	.471	.515	20439
2-gd	22882	.702	.710	.706	16511	.599	.579	.589	.806	.827	.816	.524	.289	.186	21823	.270	.446	.444	.445	8340
3-gd	21961	.757	.734	.745	17644	.650	.672	.661	.817	.855	.836	.608	.270	.122	21886	.278	.492	.523	.507	8277
4-gd	22754	.768	.772	.770	17611	.670	.692	.681	.839	.886	.862	.605	.247	.148	21966	.259	.583	.517	.548	8197
HMM-gd	19430	.812	.698	.751	15831	.709	.658	.682	.878	.820	.848	.499	.407	.094	14334	.231	.621	.411	.495	15829
fa-gd	23148	.702	.719	.710	17043	.589	.588	.588	.802	.839	.820	.548	.258	.194	18578	.242	.454	.447	.450	11585
2-gdfa	23840	.687	.724	.705	17469	.575	.588	.582	.780	.841	.809	.590	.216	.194	25616	.279	.419	.473	.444	6718
3-gdfa	23049	.736	.749	.742	18732	.621	.681	.650	.786	.870	.826	.684	.188	.128	27119	.294	.451	.561	.500	4547
4-gdfa	23704	.751	.787	.769	18561	.645	.701	.672	.813	.901	.855	.673	.172	.154	26977	.275	.529	.562	.545	3044
HMM-gdfa	20554	.799	.726	.761	16955	.685	.681	.683	.857	.851	.854	.565	.337	.098	17399	.246	.584	.475	.524	12764
fa-gdfa	23717	.693	.726	.710	17612	.575	.594	.584	.785	.846	.815	.587	.214	.199	20384	.247	.439	.465	.452	9779
2-gdf	29050	.591	.758	.664	17089	.511	.512	.512	.761	.876	.814	.625	.002	.373	59592	.338	.321	.438	.370	29429
3-gdf	26575	.660	.775	.713	18354	.588	.632	.609	.778	.891	.831	.712	.064	.225	50834	.344	.387	.552	.455	20671
4-gdf	26529	.693	.812	.748	18269	.628	.673	.650	.810	.922	.862	.706	.070	.223	47216	.322	.459	.585	.514	17053
HMM-gdf	23886	.725	.765	.744	16660	.651	.635	.643	.851	.887	.869	.579	.251	.169	36881	.309	.473	.499	.486	6718
fa-gdf	26724	.633	.748	.686	17454	.524	.536	.530	.769	.865	.814	.589	.101	.310	34309	.379	.351	.445	.392	4146
2-uni	30712	.566	.769	.652	15864	.503	.468	.485	.774	.869	.818	.584	.002	.413	71223	.349	.305	.396	.345	41060
3-uni	28093	.636	.789	.704	17391	.592	.603	.597	.791	.889	.837	.684	.067	.249	61823	.355	.381	.523	.441	31660
4-uni	27920	.670	.827	.740	17411	.636	.649	.642	.826	.921	.871	.682	.074	.244	57408	.333	.456	.564	.504	27245
HMM-uni	24712	.707	.772	.738	15980	.649	.608	.628	.857	.881	.869	.561	.260	.180	42264	.319	.459	.475	.467	12101
fa-uni	27951	.612	.756	.676	16385	.512	.491	.504	.781	.867	.822	.548	.111	.346	38285	.396	.336	.407	.368	8122

Table 2: Values for alignment quality indicators for the different alignments, where 2–4, HMM, and fa are alignment models, and symmetrization strategies refer to Table 1

Section 3.2) of 2M sentences during alignment. For symmetrization we used all methods in Table 1, as implemented in the Moses toolkit (Koehn et al., 2007) and in fast_align (Dyer et al., 2013).

Based on the automatically aligned gold standard, we calculated all alignment indicators for all settings. The complete results can be found in Table 2, where we have ordered the symmetrization methods with the most sparse, intersection, on top. Overall we can see that while several of the alignment methods create a much higher number of alignment links than the gold standard, they do not produce many more translation units. This is very interesting and indicates why link level statistics may not be accurate enough to predict the performance of certain downstream applications. As expected, the metric scores for translation units are lower than for link level metrics. This is partly due to the fact that these measures do not count any partially correct links; the MWU metrics which considers partial matches often have higher scores than link level metrics. Another finding is that the number of crossings vary a lot with more than twice as many as the reference for model2+union, and less than three times as many for HMM+intersection. The HMM and fa models have fewer reorderings than the IBM models.

We are now interested in the relation between alignment evaluation on the link level and on the translation unit level, which has not been thoroughly investigated before. Table 3 shows the correlations between the various metrics. Both precision and F-measure at the link level have significant correlations to all TU metrics. Link level recall, on the other hand, is significantly negatively correlated with TU precision, but not significantly correlated to any other TU metric, not even TU recall. Link level precision is thus highly important for matching translation units. We can also note here that while there is a trade-off between precision and recall on link level, this is not the case for translation units, which can have both high precision and high recall. The same is not true for MWU, that allows partial matching, where we also see at least some precision/recall trade-off.

3.2 SMT Experiments

For reference, we first study the impact of alignment on SMT performance. Our SMT system is a standard PBSMT system trained on WMT13

	Translation unit		
Link level ↓	P	R	F
P	**.95**	**.77**	**.90**
R	**−.57**	−.22	−.42
F	**.70**	**.90**	**.83**

Table 3: Pearson correlations between gold standard word alignment evaluation on the link level and on translation unit level. Significant correlations are marked with bold (< 0.01).

data.[2] We trained a German–English system on 2M sentences from Europarl and News Commentary. We used the target side of the parallel corpus and the SRILM toolkit (Stolcke, 2002) to train a 5-gram language model. For training the translation model and for decoding we used the Moses toolkit (Koehn et al., 2007). We applied a standard feature set consisting of a language model feature, four translation model features, word penalty, phrase penalty, and distortion cost. For tuning we used minimum error-rate training (Och, 2003). In order to minimize the risk of tuning influencing the results, we used a fixed set of weights for each experiment, tuned on a model 4+gdfa alignment.[3] For tuning we used newstest2009 with 2525 sentences, and for testing we used newstest2013 with 3000 sentences. Evaluation was performed using the Bleu metric (Papineni et al., 2002). The same system setup was used for the SMT systems with reordering.

Table 4 shows the results on the SMT task. Model 3 and 4 with gd/gdfa symmetrization yield the highest scores. There is a larger difference between systems with different symmetrization than between systems with different alignment models. The sparse intersection symmetrization gives the poorest results. The top row in Table 5 shows correlations between Bleu and all word alignment quality indicators. There are significant correlations with link level recall. A weighted link level F-measure with $\alpha = 0.3$ gives a significant correlation of .72, which confirms the results of Fraser and Marcu (2007). There are no significant correlations with the TU metrics but a positive correlation with the number of TUs. For the MWU metrics the correlations are similar to the link level,

[2] `http://www.statmt.org/wmt13/translation-task.html`

[3] This could have disfavored the other alignments, so we also performed control experiments where we ran separate tunings for each alignment. While the absolute results varied somewhat, the correlations with alignment indicators were stable.

	m2	m3	m4	HMM	fa
inter	18.1	19.1	19.3	18.8	18.9
gd	20.4	20.9	20.9	20.5	20.6
gdfa	20.4	20.7	20.8	20.5	20.5
gdf	19.4	19.7	20.1	19.9	20.0
union	19.2	19.6	19.8	19.7	20.0

Table 4: Baseline Bleu scores for different symmetrization heuristics

suggesting that they measure similar things. Intuitively it seems important for SMT to match full translation units, but it might be the case that the phrase extraction strategy is robust as long as there are partial matches. There are no significant correlations with link degree or link crossings, except a negative correlation with Crossdiff, which means that it is good to have a similar number of crossings as the baseline. These results confirm results from previous studies that link level measures, especially recall and weighted F-measure show some correlation with SMT quality whereas precision does not.

4 Reordering Tasks for SMT

Reordering is an important part of any SMT system. One way to address it is to add reordering models to standard PBSMT systems, for instance lexicalized reordering models (Koehn et al., 2005), or to directly model reordering in hierarchical (Chiang, 2007) or syntactic translation models (Yamada and Knight, 2002). Another type of approach is preordering, where the source side is reordered to mimic the target side before translation. There have also been approaches where reordering is modeled as part of the evaluation of MT systems (Birch and Osborne, 2011).

We can distinguish two main types of approaches to preordering in SMT, either by using hand-written rules, which often operate on syntactic trees (Collins et al., 2005), or by reordering rules that are learnt automatically based on a word aligned corpus (Xia and McCord, 2004). The latter approach is of interest to us, since it is based on word alignments.

There has been much work on automatic learning of reordering rules, which can be based on different levels of annotation, such as part-of-speech tags (Rottmann and Vogel, 2007; Niehues and Kolss, 2009; Genzel, 2010), chunks (Zhang et al., 2007) or parse trees (Xia and McCord, 2004). In general, all these approaches lead to improvements of translation quality. The reordering is always applied on the translation input. It can also be applied on the source side of the training corpora, which sometimes improves the results (Rottmann and Vogel, 2007), but sometimes does not make a difference (Stymne, 2012). When preordering is performed on the translation input, it can be presented to the decoder as a 1-best reordering (Xia and McCord, 2004), as an n-best list (Li et al., 2007), or as a lattice of possible reorderings (Rottmann and Vogel, 2007; Zhang et al., 2007).

In the preordering studies cited above it is often not even stated which alignment model was used. A few authors mention the alignment tool that has been applied but no comparison between different alignment models is performed in any of the papers we are aware of. Li et al. (2007), for example, simply state that they used GIZA++ and gdf symmetrization and that they removed less probable multi links. Lerner and Petrov (2013) use the intersection of HMM alignments and claims that model 4 did not add much value. Genzel (2010) did mention that using a standard model 4 was not successful for his rule learning approach. Instead he used filtered model-1-alignments, which he claims was more successful. However, there are no further analyses or comparisons between the alignments reported in any of these papers.

Another type of approach to reordering is to only reorder the data in order to improve word alignments, and to restore the original word order before training the SMT system. This type of approach has the advantage that no modifications are needed for the translation input. This approach has also been used both with hand-written rules (Carpuat et al., 2010; Stymne et al., 2010) and with rules based on initial word alignments on non-reordered texts (Holmqvist et al., 2009). For the latter approach a small study of the effect of gd and gdfa symmetrizations was presented, which only showed small variations in quality scores (Holmqvist et al., 2012).

Below we present the two tasks that we study in this paper: part-of-speech-based reordering for creating input lattices for SMT and alignment-based reordering for improving phrase-tables. We evaluate the performance of these tasks in relation to the use of different alignment models and symmetrization heuristics. For these tasks we are mainly interested in the full translation task, for which we report Bleu scores. In addition we also show fuzzy reordering score (FRS), which focuses

	Alignment links				Translation units				MWU		
	Total	P	R	F	Total	P	R	F	P	R	F
SMT, Bleu	.33	−.25	**.56**	.46	**.65**	−.20	.16	−.02	−.29	**.59**	.44
POSReo, FRS	**−.80**	**.87**	−.49	**.75**	−.23	**.90**	**.81**	**.89**	**.82**	−.45	.22
POSReo, Bleu	**−.64**	**.74**	−.27	**.85**	.05	**.80**	**.80**	**.86**	**.67**	−.23	.35
AlignReo, FRS	**−.77**	**.88**	−.43	**.84**	−.11	**.90**	**.88**	**.92**	**.81**	−.37	.31
AlignReo, Bleu	**−.81**	**.83**	**−.58**	**.61**	−.24	**.75**	**.64**	**.72**	**.71**	**−.53**	.04

	Link degree			Link crossings					
	1-1	null	multi	Total	SKTD	P	R	F	Crossdiff
SMT, Bleu	.33	−.30	.21	−.05	−.14	−.09	.25	.07	**−.63**
POSReo, FRS	−.41	**.84**	**−.89**	**−.81**	**−.70**	**.90**	.21	**.86**	−.41
POSReo, Bleu	−.17	**.66**	**−.80**	**−.71**	**−.60**	**.79**	.42	**.89**	−.49
AlignReo, FRS	−.32	**.77**	**−.86**	**−.80**	**−.73**	**.94**	.27	**.92**	−.38
AlignReo, Bleu	**−.57**	**.83**	**−.79**	**−.93**	**−.91**	**.86**	−.07	**.69**	**−.52**

Table 5: Pearson correlations between different alignment characteristics and scores for the translation and reordering tasks. Significant correlations are marked with bold (< 0.01).

only on the reordering component (Talbot et al., 2011). It compares a system reordering to a reference reordering, by measuring how many chunks that have to be moved to get an identical word order, see Eq. 9, where C is the number of contiguously aligned chunks, and M the number of words. To find the reference ordering we apply the method of Holmqvist et al. (2009), described in Section 4.2, to the gold standard alignment.

$$\text{FRS} = 1 - \frac{C - 1}{M - 1} \tag{9}$$

4.1 Part-of-Speech-Based Reordering

Our first reordering task is a part-of-speech-based preordering method described by Rottmann and Vogel (2007) and Niehues and Kolss (2009), which was successfully used for German–English translation. Rules are learnt from a word aligned POS-tagged corpus. Based on the alignments, tag patterns are identified that give rise to specific reorderings. These patterns are then scored based on relative frequency.[4] The rules are then applied to the translation input to create a reordering lattice, with normalized edge scores based on rule scores. In our experiments we only use rules with a score higher than 0.2, to limit the size of the lattices. For calculating FRS, we pick the highest scoring 1-best word order from the lattices.

We learn rules from our entire SMT training corpus varying alignment models and symmetrization. To investigate only the effect of word alignment for creating reordering rules, we do not change the SMT system, which is trained based on model 4+gdfa alignments. The only thing that varies for the translation task is thus the input lattice given to this SMT system.

The results are shown in Tables 6 and 7. Most Bleu scores are better than using the same SMT system without preordering, with a Bleu score of 20.8. The results on FRS and Bleu are highly correlated at .94, despite the fact that we use a lattice as SMT input, and the 1-best order for FRS. For both metrics sparse symmetrization like intersection and gd performs best. Model 4 and HMM perform best with similar Bleu scores, but FRS is better for the HMM model.

Table 5 shows the correlations with the word alignment indicators, in the rows labeled *POSReo*. There are strong correlations with all TU metrics, contrary to the SMT task. There are also significant correlations with link level precision and bal-

	m2	m3	m4	HMM	fa
inter	.577	.575	.581	.596	.567
gd	.555	.559	.570	.589	.546
gdfa	.540	.540	.559	.579	.539
gdf	.439	.499	.542	.560	.495
union	.442	.492	.544	.563	.486

Table 6: Fuzzy reordering scores for part-of-speech-based reordering for different alignments

	m2	m3	m4	HMM	fa
inter	21.4	21.6	21.8	21.6	21.6
gd	21.5	21.6	21.6	21.7	21.5
gdfa	21.4	21.5	21.7	21.7	21.4
gdf	20.3	21.0	21.4	21.5	21.0
union	20.3	21.5	21.6	21.5	20.8

Table 7: Bleu scores for part-of-speech-based reordering for different alignments

[4]Note that we do not use words (Rottmann and Vogel, 2007) or wild cards (Niehues and Kolss, 2009) in our rules.

anced F-measure. The correlation with weighted link level F-measure is even higher, .91 for $\alpha = 0.6$. This is an indication that this algorithm is more sensitive to precision than the SMT task. As for the SMT task, the correlation patterns are similar for the MWU metrics as for link level. For link degree, null alignments are correlated, but there is a negative correlation for multi links. The correlations with the number of crossings and SKTD are negative, which means that it is better to have a low number of crossings. This may seem counter-intuitive, but note in Table 1 that many alignments have a much higher number of crossings than the baseline. The precision of the crossing links is highly correlated with performance on this task, while the recall is not. This tells us that it is important that the crossings we find in the alignment are good, but that it is less important that we find all crossings. This makes sense since the rule learner can then learn at least a subset of all existing crossings well.

4.2 Reordering for Alignment

In our second reordering task we investigate alignment-based reordering for improving phrase-tables (Holmqvist et al., 2009; Holmqvist et al., 2012). This strategy first performs a word alignment, based on which the source text is reordered to remove all crossings. A second alignment is trained on the reordered data, which is then restored to the original order before training the full SMT system. In Holmqvist et al. (2012) it was shown that this strategy leads to improvements in link level recall and F-measure as well as small translation improvements for English–Swedish. It also led to small improvements for German–English translation.

Similar to the previous experiments, we now vary alignment models and symmetrization that are used for reordering during the first step. The second step is kept the same using model 4+gdfa in order to focus on the reordering step in our comparisons. Tables 8 and 9 show the results of these experiments. In this case the reordering strategy was not successful, always producing lower Bleu scores than the baseline of 20.8. However, there are some interesting differences in these outcomes. On this task as well, FRS and Bleu scores are highly correlated at .89, which was expected, since this method directly uses the reordered data to train phrase tables. For the best systems, the FRS scores are higher than for the previous task, see Table 6, which shows that reordering directly based on alignments is easier than learning and applying rules based on them, given suitable alignments. On this task, again, the sparser alignments are the most successful on both tasks. Here, however, the HMM model gives the best Bleu scores, and similar FRS scores to model 4.

	m2	m3	m4	HMM	fa
inter	.583	.604	.669	.654	.598
gd	.548	.583	.646	.642	.561
gdfa	.532	.564	.633	.645	.553
gdf	.422	.482	.571	.574	.474
union	.395	.455	.552	.545	.452

Table 8: Fuzzy reordering scores for alignment-based reordering for different alignments

	m2	m3	m4	HMM	fa
inter	19.5	19.5	19.9	20.2	19.4
gd	19.3	19.5	19.8	20.2	19.3
gdfa	19.1	19.2	19.6	20.0	19.2
gdf	18.3	18.2	18.6	19.0	18.9
union	17.4	17.8	18.4	18.8	18.8

Table 9: Bleu scores for alignment-based reordering for different alignments

Table 5 shows the correlations with the word alignment indicators, in the rows labeled *Align-Reo*. The correlation patterns are very similar to the previous task. A few more indicators are significantly negatively correlated with alignment-based reordering than with the other reordering tasks and metrics. The performance on our two reordering tasks are significantly correlated at .76. Again alignments with good scores on TU metrics, link level precision and crossing link precision are preferable. For this task, the best correlation with weighted link level F-measure is .86 for $\alpha = 0.8$. Again, we thus see that sparse alignments with high precision on all measures including the crossing subset, are important.

5 Small Training Data

Since previous work has suggested that training data size influences the relation between alignment and SMT quality for small and large training data (Lambert et al., 2012), we investigated this issue also for our reordering tasks. We repeated all our experiments on a small dataset, only the News Commentary data from WMT13, with 170K sentences. Due to space constraints we cannot show all results in the paper, but the main findings are summarized in this section.

To acquire alignment results we realigned the gold standard concatenated with the smaller data, to reflect the actual quality of alignment with a small dataset. As expected the quality scores tend to be lower with less data. Overall the same systems tend to perform good on each metric with the small and large data, even though there is some variation in the ranking between systems. On the SMT task as well, the Bleu scores are lower, as expected. In this case fast_align is doing best followed by model 4 and 3. The best symmetrization is again gd and gdfa. There are also some differences in the correlation profile. Link recall and number of translation units are no longer significantly correlated, whereas the number of crossings and SKTD are. The highest correlation for link level F-measure is .60 for balanced F-measure, showing that precision is equally important to recall with less data.

For the reordering tasks the scores are again lower. The POS-based reorderings again help over the baseline SMT, whereas the alignment-based reordering leads to slightly lower scores. The correlation profile look exactly the same for Bleu for POS-based reordering. FRS for both tasks and Bleu for alignment-based reordering have the same correlation profiles as Bleu for alignment-based reordering on large data. There are thus very small differences in the word alignment quality indicators that are relevant with large and small training data, while there are some differences on the SMT task. For weighted link level F-measure, the highest correlations are found with $\alpha = 0.6$–0.7 on the different metrics, again showing that precision is more important than recall. For FRS on both tasks and Bleu for alignment-based reordering, model4 and HMM with intersection and gd still perform best. For Bleu for POS-based reordering, gdfa and model 3 also give good results.

6 Conclusion and Future Work

We have shown that the best combination of alignment and symmetrization models for SMT are not the best models for reordering tasks in our experimental setting. For SMT, high recall is more important than precision with large training data, while precision and recall are of equal importance with small training data. This finding supports previous research (Fraser and Marcu, 2007; Lambert et al., 2012). Translation unit metrics are not predictive of SMT performance. For the large data condition model 3 and 4 with gd and gdfa symmetrization gave the best results, whereas fast_align with gd and gdfa was best with small training data.

For the two preordering tasks we investigated, however, link level weighted F-measure that gave more weight to precision was important, as well as all TU metrics. It was also important to have high precision for the crossing subset of TUs. Hence, it is more important to reliably find some crossings than to find all crossings. This make sense since the extracted rules or performed reorderings are likely good in such cases, even if we are not able to find all possible reorderings. In conclusion, based on this study, we recommend intersection symmetrization with model 4 and HMM for SMT reordering tasks.

We have studied two relatively different reordering tasks with two training data sizes, but found that they to a large extent prefer the same types of alignments. Moreover, the results on these two reordering tasks correlates strongly with FRS, which is much cheaper to calculate than SMT metrics that may even require retraining of full SMT systems. This is consistent with Talbot et al. (2011) who suggested FRS for preordering tasks. We thus would encourage developers of alignment methods to not only give results for SMT, but also for FRS, as a proxy for reordering tasks. Furthermore, it is also useful to give results on TU metrics in addition to link level metrics to complement the evaluation.

In this paper, we have looked at existing generative alignment and symmetrization models. In future work, we would also like to investigate other models, including the removal of low-confidence links, which has previously been proposed for prereordering (Li et al., 2007; Genzel, 2010). Given the results, it also seems motivated to develop or adapt the existing models in general, to better fit the properties of specific auxiliary tasks. Furthermore, we need to validate our findings on other language pairs, especially for non-related languages with even more diverse word order.

Acknowledgments

This work was supported by the Swedish strategic research programme eSSENCE.

References

Lars Ahrenberg, Magnus Merkel, Anna Sågvall Hein, and Jörg Tiedemann. 2000. Evaluation of word alignment systems. In *Proceedings of LREC*, volume III, pages 1255–1261, Athens, Greece.

Lars Ahrenberg. 2010. Alignment-based profiling of Europarl data in an English-Swedish parallel corpus. In *Proceedings of LREC*, pages 3398–3404, Valetta, Malta.

Necip Fazil Ayan and Bonnie J. Dorr. 2006. Going beyond AER: An extensive analysis of word alignments and their impact on MT. In *Proceedings of Coling and ACL*, pages 9–16, Sydney, Australia.

Alexandra Birch and Miles Osborne. 2011. Reordering metrics for MT. In *Proceedings of ACL*, pages 1027–1035, Portland, Oregon, USA.

Peter F. Brown, Stephen Della Pietra, Vincent J. Della Pietra, and Robert L. Mercer. 1993. The mathematics of statistical machine translation: Parameter estimation. *Computational Linguistics*, 19(2):263–311.

Marine Carpuat, Yuval Marton, and Nizar Habash. 2010. Improving Arabic-to-English statistical machine translation by reordering post-verbal subjects for alignment. In *Proceedings of ACL, Short Papers*, pages 178–183, Uppsala, Sweden.

David Chiang. 2007. Hierarchical phrase-based translation. *Computational Linguistics*, 33(2):202–228.

Michael Collins, Philipp Koehn, and Ivona Kučerová. 2005. Clause restructuring for statistical machine translation. In *Proceedings of ACL*, pages 531–540, Ann Arbor, Michigan, USA.

Chris Dyer, Victor Chahuneau, and Noah A. Smith. 2013. A simple, fast, and effective reparameterization of IBM model 2. In *Proceedings of NAACL*, pages 644–648, Atlanta, Georgia, USA.

Victoria Fossum, Kevin Knight, and Steven Abney. 2008. Using syntax to improve word alignment precision for syntax-based machine translation. In *Proceedings of WMT*, pages 44–52, Columbus, Ohio.

Alexander Fraser and Daniel Marcu. 2007. Measuring word alignment quality for statistical machine translation. *Computational Linguistics*, 33(3):293–303.

Michel Galley, Mark Hopkins, Kevin Knight, and Daniel Marcu. 2004. What's in a translation rule? In *Proceedings of NAACL*, pages 273–280, Boston, Massachusetts, USA.

Kuzman Ganchev, João V. Graça, and Ben Taskar. 2008. Better alignments = better translations? In *Proceedings of ACL*, pages 986–993, Columbus, Ohio, USA.

Dmitriy Genzel. 2010. Automatically learning source-side reordering rules for large scale machine translation. In *Proceedings of Coling*, pages 376–384, Beijing, China.

Cyril Goutte, Kenji Yamada, and Eric Gaussier. 2004. Aligning words using matrix factorisation. In *Proceedings of ACL*, pages 502–509, Barcelona, Spain.

Maria Holmqvist, Sara Stymne, Jody Foo, and Lars Ahrenberg. 2009. Improving alignment for SMT by reordering and augmenting the training corpus. In *Proceedings of WMT*, pages 120–124, Athens, Greece.

Maria Holmqvist, Sara Stymne, Lars Ahrenberg, and Magnus Merkel. 2012. Alignment-based reordering for SMT. In *Proceedings of LREC*, Istanbul, Turkey.

Marcin Junczys-Dowmunt and Arkadiusz Szał. 2012. SyMGiza++: Symmetrized word alignment models for statistical machine translation. In *International Joint Conference of Security and Intelligent Information Systems*, pages 379–390, Warsaw, Poland.

Philipp Koehn, Franz Josef Och, and Daniel Marcu. 2003. Statistical phrase-based translation. In *Proceedings of NAACL*, pages 48–54, Edmonton, Alberta, Canada.

Philipp Koehn, Amittai Axelrod, Alexandra Birch Mayne, Chris Callison-Burch, Miles Osborne, and David Talbot. 2005. Edinburgh system description for the 2005 IWSLT speech translation evaluation. In *Proceedings of the International Workshop on Spoken Language Translation*, Pittsburgh, Pennsylvania, USA.

Philipp Koehn, Hieu Hoang, Alexandra Birch, Chris Callison-Burch, Marcello Federico, Nicola Bertoldi, Brooke Cowan, Wade Shen, Christine Moran, Richard Zens, Chris Dyer, Ondrej Bojar, Alexandra Constantin, and Evan Herbst. 2007. Moses: Open source toolkit for statistical machine translation. In *Proceedings of ACL, Demonstration Session*, pages 177–180, Prague, Czech Republic.

Patrik Lambert, Simon Petitrenaud, Yanjun Ma, and Andy Way. 2012. What types of word alignment improve statistical machine translation? *Machine Translation*, 26(4):289–323.

Uri Lerner and Slav Petrov. 2013. Source-side classifier preordering for machine translation. In *Proceedings of EMNLP*, pages 513–523, Seattle, Washington, USA.

Chi-Ho Li, Minghui Li, Dongdong Zhang, Mu Li, Ming Zhou, and Yi Guan. 2007. A probabilistic approach to syntax-based reordering for statistical machine translation. In *Proceedings of the 45th Annual Meeting of the ACL*, pages 720–727, Prague, Czech Republic.

Percy Liang, Ben Taskar, and Dan Klein. 2006. Alignment by agreement. In *Proceedings of NAACL*, pages 104–111, New York City, New York, USA.

Yang Liu, Qun Liu, and Shouxun Lin. 2005. Log-linear models for word alignment. In *Proceedings of ACL*, pages 459–466, Ann Arbor, Michigan, USA.

Magnus Merkel and Jody Foo. 2007. Terminology extraction and term ranking for standardizing term banks. In *Proceedings of the 16th Nordic Conference on Computational Linguistics*, pages 349–354, Tartu, Estonia.

Robert C. Moore. 2005. A discriminative framework for bilingual word alignment. In *Proceedings of HLT and EMNLP*, pages 81–88, Vancouver, British Columbia, Canada.

Jan Niehues and Muntsin Kolss. 2009. A POS-based model for long-range reorderings in SMT. In *Proceedings of WMT*, pages 206–214, Athens, Greece.

Franz Josef Och and Hermann Ney. 2000. A comparison of alignment models for statistical machine translation. In *Proceedings of Coling*, pages 1086–1090, Saarbrücken, Germany.

Franz Josef Och and Hermann Ney. 2003. A systematic comparison of various statistical alignment models. *Computational Linguistics*, 29(1):19–51.

Franz Josef Och, Christoph Tillmann, and Hermann Ney. 1999. Improved alignment models for statistical machine translation. In *Proceedings of the Joint Conference of EMNLP and Very Large Corpora*, pages 20–28, College Park, Maryland, USA.

Franz Josef Och. 2003. Minimum error rate training in statistical machine translation. In *Proceedings of ACL*, pages 160–167, Sapporo, Japan.

Sebastian Pado and Mirella Lapata. 2005. Cross-linguistic projection of role-semantic information. In *Proceedings of HLT and EMNLP*, pages 859–866, Vancouver, British Columbia, Canada.

Kishore Papineni, Salim Roukos, Todd Ward, and Wei-Jing Zhu. 2002. BLEU: A method for automatic evaluation of machine translation. In *Proceedings of ACL*, pages 311–318, Philadelphia, Pennsylvania, USA.

Oana Postolache, Dan Cristea, and Constantin Orăsan. a. 2006. Transferring coreference chains through word alignment. In *Proceedings of LREC*, pages 889–892, Genoa, Italy.

Kay Rottmann and Stephan Vogel. 2007. Word reordering in statistical machine translation with a POS-based distortion model. In *Proceedings of the 11th International Conference on Theoretical and Methodological Issues in Machine Translation*, pages 171–180, Skövde, Sweden.

Anders Søgaard and Jonas Kuhn. 2009. Empirical lower bounds on alignment error rates in syntax-based machine translation. In *Proceedings of the Third Workshop on Syntax and Structure in Statistical Translation*, pages 19–27, Boulder, Colorado, USA.

Anders Søgaard and Dekai Wu. 2009. Empirical lower bounds on translation unit error rate for the full class of inversion transduction grammars. In *Proceedings of 11th International Conference on Parsing Technologies*, pages 33–36, Paris, France.

Andreas Stolcke. 2002. SRILM – an extensible language modeling toolkit. In *Proceedings of ICSLP*, pages 901–904, Denver, Colorado, USA.

Sara Stymne, Maria Holmqvist, and Lars Ahrenberg. 2010. Vs and OOVs: Two problems for translation between German and English. In *Proceedings of WMT and MetricsMATR*, pages 183–188, Uppsala, Sweden.

Sara Stymne. 2012. Clustered word classes for preordering in statistical machine translation. In *Proceedings of ROBUS-UNSUP 2012: Joint Workshop on Unsupervised and Semi-Supervised Learning in NLP*, pages 28–34, Avignon, France.

Oscar Täckström, Ryan McDonald, and Jakob Uszkoreit. 2012. Cross-lingual word clusters for direct transfer of linguistic structure. In *Proceedings of NAACL*, pages 477–487, Montréal, Quebec, Canada.

David Talbot, Hideto Kazawa, Hiroshi Ichikawa, Jason Katz-Brown, Masakazu Seno, and Franz Och. 2011. A lightweight evaluation framework for machine translation reordering. In *Proceedings of WMT*, pages 12–21, Edinburgh, Scotland.

Ben Taskar, Lacoste-Julien Simon, and Dan Klein. 2005. A discriminative matching approach to word alignment. In *Proceedings of HLT and EMNLP*, pages 73–80, Vancouver, British Columbia, Canada.

Jörg Tiedemann. 2005. Optimisation of word alignment clues. *Natural Language Engineering*, 11(03):279–293. Special Issue on Parallel Texts.

Stephan Vogel, Hermann Ney, and Christoph Tillman. 1996. HMM-based word alignment in statistical translation. In *Proceedings of Coling*, pages 836–841, Copenhagen, Denmark.

Fei Xia and Michael McCord. 2004. Improving a statistical MT system with automatically learned rewrite patterns. In *Proceedings of Coling*, pages 508–514, Geneva, Switzerland.

Kenji Yamada and Kevin Knight. 2002. A decoder for syntax-based statistical MT. In *Proceedings of ACL*, pages 303–310, Philadelphia, Pennsylvania, USA.

David Yarowsky, Grace Ngai, and Richard Wicentowski. 2001. Inducing multilingual text analysis tools via robust projection across aligned corpora. In *Proceedings of the First International Conference on Human Language Technology*, pages 1–8, San Diego, California, USA.

Yuqi Zhang, Richard Zens, and Hermann Ney. 2007. Improved chunk-level reordering for statistical machine translation. In *Proceedings of the International Workshop on Spoken Language Translation*, pages 21–28, Trento, Italy.

Dependency-based Automatic Enumeration of Semantically Equivalent Word Orders for Evaluating Japanese Translations

Hideki Isozaki, Natsume Kouchi
Okayama Prefectural University
111 Kuboki, Soja-shi, Okayama, 719-1197, Japan
isozaki@cse.oka-pu.ac.jp

Tsutomu Hirao
NTT Communication Science Laboratories
2-4, Hikaridai, Seika-cho, Sorakugun, Kyoto, 619-0237, Japan
hirao.tsutomu@lab.ntt.co.jp

Abstract

Scrambling is acceptable reordering of verb arguments in languages such as Japanese and German. In automatic evaluation of translation quality, BLEU is the de facto standard method, but BLEU has only very weak correlation with human judgements in case of Japanese-to-English/English-to-Japanese translations. Therefore, alternative methods, IMPACT and RIBES, were proposed and they have shown much stronger correlation than BLEU. Now, RIBES is widely used in recent papers on Japanese-related translations. RIBES compares word order of MT output with manually translated reference sentences but it does not regard scrambling at all. In this paper, we present a method to enumerate scrambled sentences from dependency trees of reference sentences. Our experiments based on NTCIR Patent MT data show that the method improves sentence-level correlation between RIBES and human-judged adequacy.

1 Introduction

Statistical Machine Translation has grown with an automatic evaluation method BLEU (Papineni et al., 2002). BLEU measures local word order by n-grams and does not care about global word order. In JE/EJ translations, this insensitivity degrades BLEU's correlation with human judgements.

Therefore, alternative automatic evaluation methods are proposed. Echizen-ya and Araki (2007) proposed IMPACT. Isozaki et al. (2010) presented the idea of RIBES. Hirao et al. (2011) named this method "RIBES" (Rank-based Intuitive Bilingual Evaluation Score). This version of RIBES was defined as follows:

$$\text{RIBES} = \text{NKT} \times P^{\alpha}$$

Table 1: Meta-evaluation of NTCIR-7 JE task data (Spearman's ρ, System-level correlation)

BLEU	METEOR	ROUGE-L	IMPACT	**RIBES**
0.515	0.490	0.903	0.826	**0.947**

where NKT (Normalized Kendall's τ) is defined by $(\tau + 1)/2$. This NKT is used for measuring word order similarity between a reference sentence and an MT output sentence. Thus, RIBES penalizes difference of global word order. P is precision of unigrams. RIBES is defined for each test sentence and averaged RIBES is used for evaluating the entire test corpus.

Table 1 is a table in an IWSLT-2012 invited talk (http://hltc.cs.ust.hk/iwslt/slides/Isozaki2012_slides.pdf). METEOR was proposed by Banerjee and Lavie (2005). ROUGE-L was proposed by Lin and Och (2004). According to this table, RIBES with $\alpha = 0.2$ has a very strong correlation (Spearman's ρ = 0.947) with human-judged adequacy. For each sentence, we use the average of adequacy scores of three judges. Here, we call this average "Adequacy". We focus on Adequacy because current SMT systems tend to output inadequate sentences. Note that only single reference translations are available for this task although use of multiple references is common for BLEU.

RIBES is publicly available from http://www.kecl.ntt.co.jp/icl/lirg/ribes/ and was used as a standard quality measure in recent NTCIR PatentMT tasks (Goto et al., 2011; Goto et al., 2013). Table 2 shows the result of meta-evaluation at NICTR-9/10 PatentMT. The table shows that RIBES is more reliable than BLEU and NIST.

Current RIBES has the following improvements.

- BLEU's Brevity Penalty (BP) was introduced

Proceedings of the Ninth Workshop on Statistical Machine Translation, pages 287–292,
Baltimore, Maryland USA, June 26–27, 2014.

Table 2: Meta-evaluation at NTCIR-9/10 PatentMT (Spearman's ρ, Goto et al. 2011, 2013)

	BLEU	NIST	**RIBES**
NTCIR-9 JE	−0.042	−0.114	**0.632**
NTCIR-9 EJ	−0.029	−0.074	**0.716**
NTCIR-10 JE	0.31	0.36	**0.88**
NTCIR-10 EJ	0.36	0.22	**0.79**

in order to penalize too short sentences.

$$\text{RIBES} = \text{NKT} \times P^{\alpha} \times \text{BP}^{\beta}$$

where $\alpha = 0.25$ and $\beta = 0.10$. BLEU uses BP for the entire test corpus, but RIBES uses it for each sentence.

- The word alignment algorithm in the original RIBES used only bigrams for disambiguation when the same word appears twice or more in one sentence. This restriction is now removed, and longer n-grams are used to get a better alignment.

RIBES is widely used in recent Annual Meeings of the (Japanese) Association for NLP. International conference papers on Japanese-related translations also use RIBES. (Wu et al., 2012; Neubig et al., 2012; Goto et al., 2012; Hayashi et al., 2013). Dan et al. (2012) uses RIBES for Chinese-to-Japanese translation.

However, we have to take "*scrambling*" into account when we think of Japanese word order. Scrambling is also observed in other languages such as German. Current RIBES does not regard this fact.

2 Methodology

For instance, a Japanese sentence S1

jon **ga** sushi-ya **de** o-sushi **wo** tabe-ta .
(John ate sushi at a sushi restaurant.)

has the following acceptable word orders.

1. jon **ga** sushi-ya **de** o-sushi **wo** tabe-ta .
2. jon **ga** o-sushi **wo** sushi-ya **de** tabe-ta .
3. sushi-ya **de** jon **ga** o-sushi **wo** tabe-ta .
4. sushi-ya **de** o-sushi **wo** jon **ga** tabe-ta .
5. o-sushi **wo** jon **ga** sushi-ya **de** tabe-ta .
6. o-sushi **wo** sushi-ya **de** jon **ga** tabe-ta .

The boldface short words "**ga**", "**de**", and "**wo**", are *case markers* ("*Kaku joshi*" in Japanese).

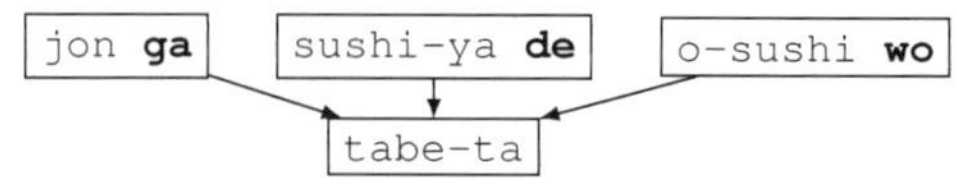

Figure 1: Dependency Tree of S1

- "**ga**" is a nominative case marker that means the noun phrase before it is the subject of a following verb/adjective.
- "**de**" is a locative case marker that means the noun phrase before it is the location of a following verb/adjective.
- "**wo**" is an accusative case marker that means the noun phrase before it is the direct object of a following verb.

The term "*scrambling*" stands for these acceptable permutations. These case markers explicitly show grammatical cases and reordering of them does not hurt interpretation of these sentences. Almost all other permutations of words are not acceptable ($*$).

$*$ jon **ga de** sushi-ya o-sushi tabe-ta **wo** .
$*$ jon **de** sushi-ya **ga** o-sushi **wo** tabe-ta .
$*$ jon tabe-ta **ga** o-sushi **wo** sushi-ya **de** .
$*$ sushi-ya **ga** jon tabe-ta **de** o-sushi **wo** .

Most readers unfamiliar with Japanese will not understand which word order is acceptable.

2.1 Scrambling as Post-Order Traversal of Depenedncy Trees

Here, we describe this "*scrambling*" from the viewpoint of Computer Science. Figure 1 shows S1's dependency tree. Each box indicates a "*bunsetsu*" or a grammatical chunk of words. Each arrow starts from a modifier (dependent) to its head.

The root of S1 is "tabe-ta" (ate). This verb has three modifiers:

- "jon **ga**" (John is its subject)
- "sushi-ya **de**" (A sushi restaurant is its location)
- "o-sushi **wo**" (Sushi is its object)

It is well known that Japanese is a typical head-final language. In order to generate a head-final word order from this dependency tree, we should output tree nodes in **post-order**. That is, we have to output all children of a node N before the node N itself.

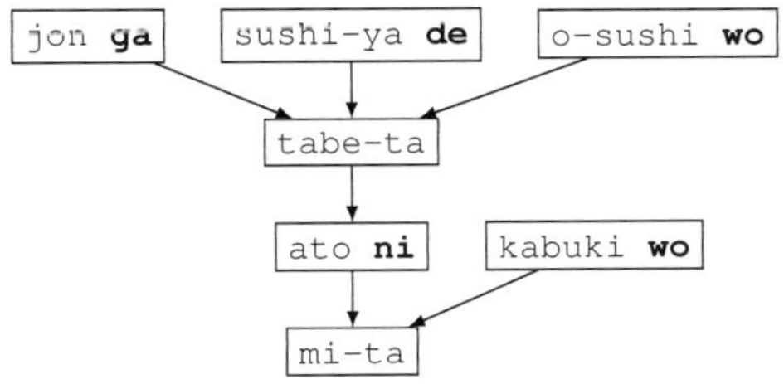

Figure 2: Dependency Tree of S2

All of the above acceptable word orders follows this post-order. Even in post-order traverse, precedence among children is not determined and this fact leads to different permutations of children. In the above example, the root "tabe-ta" has three children, and its permutation is 3! = 6.

2.2 Simple Case Marker Constraint

Figure 2 shows the dependency tree of a more complicated sentence S2:

> jon **ga** sushi-ya **de** o-sushi **wo** tabe-ta ato **ni** kabuki **wo** mi-ta .
> (John watched kabuki after eating sushi at a shushi restaurant)

Kabuki is a traditional Japanese drama performed in a theatre. In this case, the root "mi-ta" (watched) has two children: "ato **ni**" (after it) and "kabuki **wo**" (kabuki is its object).

- "**ni**" is a dative/locative case marker that means the noun phrase before it is an indirect object or a location/time of a following verb/adjective.

In this case, we obtain $3! \times 2! = 12$ permutations:

1. *S1P* ato **ni** kabuki **wo** mi-ta .
2. kabuki **wo** *S1P* ato **ni** mi-ta .

Here, *S1P* is any of the above 3! permutations of S1. If we use S1's 3 as *S1P* in S2's 1, we get

> sushi-ya **de** jon **ga** o-sushi **wo** tabe-ta ato **ni** kabuki **wo** mi-ta .

However, we cannot accept all of these permutations equally. For instance,

> kabuki **wo** o-sushi **wo** sushi-ya **de** jon **ga** tabe-ta ato **ni** mi-ta .

is comprehensible but strange. This strangeness comes from the two objective markers "wo" before the first verb "tabe-ta." Which did John eat, kabuki or sushi? Semantically, we cannot eat kabuki (drama), and we can understand this sentence. But syntactic ambiguity causes this strangeness. Without semantic knowledge about kabuki and sushi, we cannot disambiguate this case.

For readers/listeners, we should avoid such syntactically ambiguous sentences. Modifiers (here, "kabuki **wo**") of a verb (here, "mi-ta", watched) should not be placed before another verb (here, "tabe-ta", ate).

In Japanese, verbs and adjectives are used similarly. In general, adjectives are not modified by "**wo**" case markers. Therefore, we can place "**wo**" case markers before adjectives. In the following sentences, "atarashii" (new) is an adjective and placing "inu **wo**" (A dog is the direct object) before "atarashii" does not make the sentence ambiguous.

- *atarashii* ie **ni** inu **wo** ture te itta .

((Someone) took the dog to the new house.)

- inu **wo** *atarashii* ie **ni** ture te itta .

This idea leads to the following Simple Case Marker Constraint:

Definition 1 (Simple Case Marker Constraint) *If a reordered sentence has a case marker phrase of a verb that precedes another verb before the verb, the sentence is rejected. "**wo**" case markers can precede adjectives before the verb.*

This is a primitive heuristic constraint and there must be better ways to make it more flexible. If we use Nihongo Goi Taikei (Ikehara et al., 1997), we will be able to implement such a flexible constraint. For example, some verbs such as "sai-ta" (bloomed) are never modified by "**wo**" case marker phrases. Therefore, the following sentence is not ambiguous at all although the **wo** phrase precedes "sai-ta".

- hana **ga** sai-ta ato **ni** sono ki **wo** mi-ta .

((Someone) saw the tree after it bloomed.)

- sono ki **wo** hana **ga** sai-ta ato **ni** mi-ta .

2.3 Evaluation with scrambled sentences

As we mentioned before, RIBES measures global word order similarity between machine-translated sentences and reference sentences. It does not regard scrambling at all. When the target language allows scrambling just like Japanese, RIBES should consider scrambling.

Once we have a correct dependency tree of the reference sentence, we enumerate scrambled sentences by reordering children of each node. The number of the reordered sentences depend on the structure of the dependency tree.

Current RIBES code (RIBES-1.02.4) assumes that every sentence has a fixed number of references, but here the number of automatically generated reference sentences depends on the dependency structure of the original reference sentence. Therefore, we modified the code for variable numbers of reference sentences. RIBES-1.02.4 simply uses the maximum value of the scores for different reference sentences, and we followed it.

Here, we compare the following four methods.

- single: We use only single reference translations provided by the NTCIR organizers.

- postOrder: We generate all permutations of the given reference sentence generated by post-order traversals of its dependency tree. This can be achieved by the following two steps. First, we enumerate all permutations of child nodes at each node. Then, we combine these permutations. This is implemented by cartesian products of the permutation sets.

- caseMarkers: We reorder only "case marker (*kaku joshi*) phrases". Here, a "case marker phrase" is post-order traversal of a subtree rooted at a case marker *bunsetsu*. For instance, the root of the following sentence S3 has a non-case marker child "`kaburi ,`" (wear) between case marker children, "`jon` **`ga`**" and "`zubon` **`wo`**" (Trousers are the object). Figure 3 shows its dependency tree.

  `jon` **`ga`** `shiroi boushi` **`wo`** `kaburi ,`
  `kuroi zubon` **`wo`** `hai te iru.`
  (John wears a white hat and wears black trousers.)

  This is implemented by removing non-case marker nodes from the set of child nodes to be reordered in the above "postOrder" method. For simplicity, we do not reorder other markers such as the topic marker "**`wa`**" here. This is future work.

- proposed: We reorder only *contiguous* case marker children of a node, and we accept sentences that satisfy the aforementioned Simple Case Marker Constraint. S3's root node has two case marker children, but they are not contiguous. Therefore, we do not reorder them. We expect that the constraint inhibit generation of incomprehensible or misleading sentences.

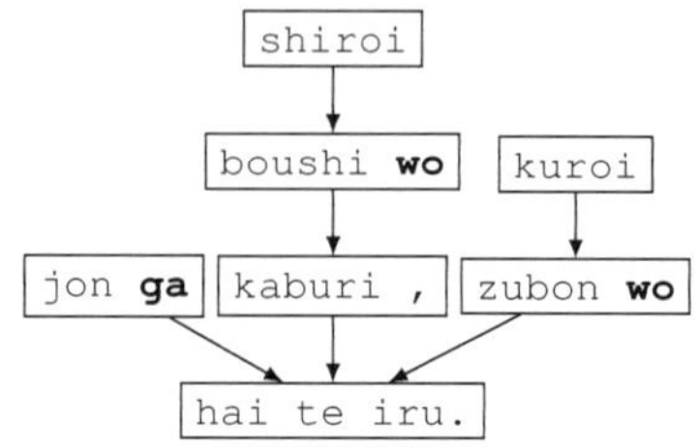

Figure 3: Dependency Tree of S3

Table 3: Distribution of the number of generated permutations

#permutations	1	2	4	6	8	12	16	24	>24
single	100	0	0	0	0	0	0	0	0
proposed	70	20	7	3	0	0	0	0	0
caseMarkers	64	23	4	6	2	2	0	2	0
postOrder	1	17	9	11	4	12	1	12	33

3 Results

We applied the above four methods to the reference sentences of human-judged 100 sentences of NTCIR-7 Patent MT EJ task. (Fujii et al., 2008) We applied CaboCha (Kudo and Matsumoto, 2002) to the reference sentences, and manually corrected the dependency trees because Japanese dependency parsers are not satisfactory in terms of sentence accuracy (Tamura et al., 2007).

To support this manual correction, CaboCha's XML output was automatically converted to dependency tree pictures by using `cabochatrees` package for LaTeX. `http://softcream.oka-pu.ac.jp/wp/wp-content/uploads/cabochatrees.pdf`. Then, it is easy to find mistakes of the dependency trees. In addition, CaboCha's dependency accuracy is very high (89–90%) (Kudo and Matsumoto, 2002). Therefore, it took only one day to fix dependency trees of one hundred reference sentences.

Table 3 shows distribution of the number of word orders generated by the above methods. PostOrder sometimes generates tens of thousands of permutations.

Figure 4 shows a sentence-level scatter plot between Adequacy and RIBES for the baseline Moses system. Each × indicates a sentence.

Arrows indicate significant improvements of RIBES scores by the proposed method. For instance, the × mark at (5.0, 0.53) corresponds to an MT output:

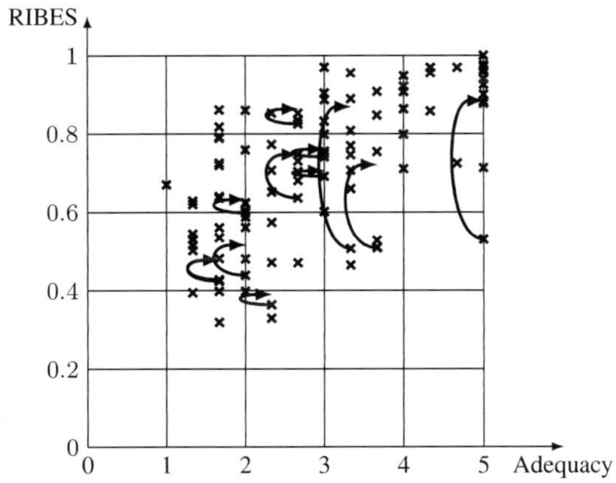

Average of RIBES: 0.706 → 0.719
Pearson's r: 0.607 → 0.663
Spearman's ρ: 0.607 → 0.670

Figure 4: Scatter plot between Adequacy and RIBES for 100 human-judged sentences in the output of NTCIR-7's baseline Moses system and the effects of the proposed method

```
indekkusu kohna wo zu 25 ni shimesu .
```

which is a Japanese translation of "FIG.25 shows the index corner." The reference sentence for this sentence is

```
zu 25 ni indekkusu kohna wo shimeshi
te iru .
```

In this case, RIBES is 0.53, but all of the three judges evaluated this as 5 of 5-point scale. That is, RIBES disagrees with human judges. The proposed method reorders this reference sentence as follows:

```
indekkusu kohna wo zu 25 ni shimeshi
te iru .
```

This is very close to the above MT output and RIBES is 0.884 for this automatically reordered reference sentence. This shows that automatic reordering reduces the gap between single-reference RIBES and Adequacy.

Although RIBES strongly correlates with adequacy at the system level (Table 1), it has only mediocre correlation with adequacy at the sentence level: Spearman's ρ is 0.607 for the baseline Moses system. The "proposed" method improves it to 0.670.

We can draw similar scatter plots for each system. **Table 4** summarises such improvement of correlations. And this is the main result of this paper. The "**proposed**" method consistently improves sentence-level correlation between Adequacy and RIBES.

Table 4: Improvement of sentence-level correlation between Adequacy and RIBES for human-judged NTCIR-7 EJ systems (MAIN RESULT)

	Pearson's r	Spearman's ρ
	single → **proposed**	single → **proposed**
tsbmt	0.466 → 0.472	0.439 → 0.452
Moses	0.607 → 0.663	0.607 → 0.670
NTT	0.709 → 0.735	0.692 → 0.727
NICT-ATR	0.620 → 0.631	0.582 → 0.608
kuro	0.555 → 0.608	0.515 → 0.550

Table 5: Increase of averaged RIBES scores

	Adeq.	RIBES			
system		single	**proposed**	caseMarkers	postOrder
tsbmt	3.527	0.715	0.718$_8$	0.719	0.756$_9$
moses	2.897	0.706	0.719$_2$	0.722	0.781
NTT	2.740	0.671	0.683	0.686	0.756$_5$
NICT-ATR	2.587	0.655	0.664	0.670	0.749
kuro	2.420	0.629	0.638	0.647	0.752

Table 5 shows increase of averaged RIBES, but this increase is not always an improvement. We expected that "PostOrder" generates not only acceptable sentences but also incomprehensible or misleading sentences. This must be harmful to the automatic evaluation by RIBES. Accoding to this table, PostOrder gave higher RIBES scores to all systems and correlation between RIBES and Adequacy is lost as expected.

The ranking by RIBES-1.02.4 with "single" reference sentences completely agrees with Adequacy, but the weakest constraint, "postOrder", disagrees. Spearman's ρ of the two ranks is 0.800 but Pearson's r is as low as 0.256. It generates too many incomprehensible/misleading word orders, and they also raise RIBES scores of bad translations. On the other hand, "*proposed*" and "*caseMarkers*" agree with Adequacy except the ranks of tsbmt and the baseline Moses.

4 Concluding Remarks

RIBES is now widely used in Japanese-related translation evaluation. But RIBES sometimes penalizes good sentences because it does not regard scrambling. Once we have correct dependency trees of reference sentences, we can automatically enumerate semantically equivalent word orders. Less constrained reordering tend to generate syntactically ambiguous sentences. They become incomprehensible or misleading sentences. In order to avoid them, we introduced Simple Case Marker Constraint and restricted permutations to contiguous case marker children of verbs/adjectives. Then, sentence-level correlation coefficients were improved.

The proposed enumeration method is also applicable to other automatic evaluation methods such as BLEU, IMPACT, and ROUGE-L, but we have to modify their codes for variable numbers of multi-reference sentences. We will examine them in the full paper.

We hope our method is also useful for other languages that have scrambling.

Acknowledgement

This research was supported by NTT Communication Science Laboratories.

References

Satanjeev Banerjee and Alon Lavie. 2005. Meteor: An automatic metric for MT evaluation with improved correlation with human judgements. In *Proc. of ACL Workshop on Intrinsic and Extrinsic Evaluation Measures for MT and Summarization*, pages 65–72.

Han Dan, Katsuhito Sudoh, Xianchao Wu, Kevin Duh, Hajime Tsukada, and Masaaki Nagata. 2012. Head finalization reordering for Chinese-to-Japanese machine translation. In *Proceedings of SSST-6, Sixth Workshop on Syntax, Semantics and Structure in Statistical Translation*, pages 57–66.

Hiroshi Echizen-ya and Kenji Araki. 2007. Automatic evaluation of machine translation based on recursive acquisition of an intuitive common parts continuum. In *MT Summit XI*, pages 151–158.

Atsushi Fujii, Masao Uchimura, Mikio Yamamoto, and Takehito Usturo. 2008. Overview of the patent machine translation task at the NTCIR-7 workshop. In *Working Notes of the NTCIR Workshop Meeting (NTCIR)*.

Isao Goto, Bin Lu, Ka Po Chow, Eiichiro Sumita, and Benjamin K. Tsou. 2011. Overview of the patent machine translation task at the NTCIR-9 workshop. In *Working Notes of the NTCIR Workshop Meeting (NTCIR)*.

Isao Goto, Masao Utiyama, and Eiichiro Sumita. 2012. Post-ordering by parsing for japanese-english statistical machine translation. In *Proc. of the Annual Meeting of the Association of Computational Linguistics (ACL)*, pages 311–316.

Isao Goto, Ka Po Chow, Bin Lu, Eiichiro Sumita, and Benjamin K. Tsou. 2013. Overview of the patent machine translation task at the NTCIR-10 workshop. In *Working Notes of the NTCIR Workshop Meeting (NTCIR)*.

Katsuhiko Hayashi, Katsuhito Sudoh, Hajime Tsukada, Jun Suzuki, and Masaaki Nagata. 2013. Shift-reduce word reordering for machine translation. In *Proc. of the Conference on Empirical Methods in Natural Language Processing (EMNLP)*, pages 1382–1386.

Tsutomu Hirao, Hideki Isozaki, Kevin Duh, Katsuhito Sudoh, Hajime Tsukada, and Masaaki Nagao. 2011. RIBES: An automatic evaluation method of translation based on rank correlation (in Japanese). In *Proc. of the Annual Meeting of the Association for Natural Language Processing*, pages 1115–1118.

Satoru Ikehara, Masahiro Miyazaki, Satoshi Shirai, Akio Yokoo, Hiromi Nakaiwa, Kentaro Ogura, Yoshifumi Ooyama, and Yoshihiko Hayashi. 1997. *Goi-Taikei — A Japanese Lexicon (in Japanese)*. Iwanami Shoten.

Hideki Isozaki, Tsutomu Hirao, Kevin Duh, Katsuhito Sudoh, Hajime Tsukada, and Masaaki Nagata. 2010. Automatic evaluation of translation quality for distant language pairs. In *Proc. of the Conference on Empirical Methods in Natural Language Processing (EMNLP)*, pages 944–952.

Taku Kudo and Yuji Matsumoto. 2002. Japanese dependency analysis using cascaded chunking. In *Proc. of the Conference on Computational Natural Language Learning (CoNLL)*.

Chin-Yew Lin and Franz Josef Och. 2004. Automatic evaluation of translation quality using longest common subsequences and skip-bigram statistics. In *Proc. of the Annual Meeting of the Association of Computational Linguistics (ACL)*, pages 605–612.

Graham Neubig, Taro Watanabe, and Shinsuke Mori. 2012. Inducing a discriminative parser to optimize machine translation reordering. In *Proc. of the Conference on Empirical Methods in Natural Language Processing (EMNLP)*, pages 843–853.

Kishore Papineni, Salim Roukos, Todd Ward, and Wei-Jing Zhu. 2002. BLEU: a method for automatic evaluation of machine translation. In *Proc. of the Annual Meeting of the Association of Computational Linguistics (ACL)*, pages 311–318.

Akihiro Tamura, Hiroya Takamura, and Manabu Okumura. 2007. Japanese dependency analysis using the ancestor-descendant relation. In *Proc. of the Conference on Empirical Methods in Natural Language Processing (EMNLP)*, pages 600–609.

Xianchao Wu, Takuya Matsuzaki, and Jun'ichi Tsujii. 2012. Akamon: An open source toolkit for tree/forest-based statistical machine translation. In *Proc. of the Annual Meeting of the Association of Computational Linguistics (ACL)*, pages 127–132.

Results of the WMT14 Metrics Shared Task

Matouš Macháček and **Ondřej Bojar**
Charles University in Prague, Faculty of Mathematics and Physics
Institute of Formal and Applied Linguistics
machacekmatous@gmail.com and bojar@ufal.mff.cuni.cz

Abstract

This paper presents the results of the WMT14 Metrics Shared Task. We asked participants of this task to score the outputs of the MT systems involved in WMT14 Shared Translation Task. We collected scores of 23 metrics from 12 research groups. In addition to that we computed scores of 6 standard metrics (BLEU, NIST, WER, PER, TER and CDER) as baselines. The collected scores were evaluated in terms of system level correlation (how well each metric's scores correlate with WMT14 official manual ranking of systems) and in terms of segment level correlation (how often a metric agrees with humans in comparing two translations of a particular sentence).

1 Introduction

Automatic machine translation metrics play a very important role in the development of MT systems and their evaluation. There are many different metrics of diverse nature and one would like to assess their quality. For this reason, the Metrics Shared Task is held annually at the Workshop of Statistical Machine Translation[1], starting with Koehn and Monz (2006) and following up to Bojar et al. (2014).

In this task, we asked metrics developers to score the outputs of WMT14 Shared Translation Task (Bojar et al., 2014). We have collected the computed metrics' scores and use them to evaluate quality of the metrics.

The systems' outputs, human judgements and evaluated metrics are described in Section 2. The quality of the metrics in terms of system level correlation is reported in Section 3. Segment level correlation with a detailed discussion and a slight change in the calculation compared to the previous year is reported in Section 4.

2 Data

We used the translations of MT systems involved in WMT14 Shared Translation Task together with reference translations as the test set for the Metrics Task. This dataset consists of 110 systems' outputs and 10 reference translations in 10 translation directions (English from and into Czech, French, German, Hindi and Russian). For most of the translation directions each system's output and the reference translation contain 3003 sentences. For more details please see the WMT14 overview paper (Bojar et al., 2014).

2.1 Manual MT Quality Judgements

During the WMT14 Translation Task, a large scale manual annotation was conducted to compare the systems. We used these collected human judgements for the evalution of the automatic metrics.

The participants in the manual annotation were asked to evaluate system outputs by ranking translated sentences relative to each other. For each source segment that was included in the procedure, the annotator was shown the outputs of five systems to which he or she was supposed to assign ranks. Ties were allowed.

These collected rank labels for each five-tuple of systems were then interpreted as 10 pairwise comparisons of systems and used to assign each system a score that reflects how high that system was usually ranked by the annotators. Please see the WMT14 overview paper for details on how this score is computed. You can also find inter- and intra-annotator agreement estimates there.

2.2 Participants of the Metrics Shared Task

Table 1 lists the participants of WMT14 Shared Metrics Task, along with their metrics. We have

[1] http://www.statmt.org/wmt13

Proceedings of the Ninth Workshop on Statistical Machine Translation, pages 293–301,
Baltimore, Maryland USA, June 26–27, 2014.

Metric	Participant
APAC	Hokkai-Gakuen University (Echizen'ya, 2014)
BEER	ILLC – University of Amsterdam (Stanojevic and Sima'an, 2014)
RED-*	Dublin City University (Wu and Yu, 2014)
DISCOTK-*	Qatar Computing Research Institute (Guzman et al., 2014)
ELEXR	University of Tehran (Mahmoudi et al., 2013)
LAYERED	Indian Institute of Technology, Bombay (Gautam and Bhattacharyya, 2014)
METEOR	Carnegie Mellon University (Denkowski and Lavie, 2014)
AMBER, BLEU-NRC	National Research Council of Canada (Chen and Cherry, 2014)
PARMESAN	Charles University in Prague (Barančíková, 2014)
TBLEU	Charles University in Prague (Libovický and Pecina, 2014)
UPC-IPA, UPC-STOUT	Technical University of Catalunya (Gonzàlez et al., 2014)
VERTA-W, VERTA-EQ	University of Barcelona (Comelles and Atserias, 2014)

Table 1: Participants of WMT14 Metrics Shared Task

collected 23 metrics from a total of 12 research groups.

In addition to that we have computed the following two groups of standard metrics as baselines:

- **Mteval.** The metrics BLEU (Papineni et al., 2002) and NIST (Doddington, 2002) were computed using the script `mteval-v13a.pl`[2] which is used in the OpenMT Evaluation Campaign and includes its own tokenization. We run `mteval` with the flag `--international-tokenization` since it performs slightly better (Macháček and Bojar, 2013).
- **Moses Scorer.** The metrics TER (Snover et al., 2006), WER, PER and CDER (Leusch et al., 2006) were computed using the Moses scorer which is used in Moses model optimization. To tokenize the sentences we used the standard tokenizer script as available in Moses toolkit.

We have normalized all metrics' scores such that better translations get higher scores.

3 System-Level Metric Analysis

While the Spearman's ρ correlation coefficient was used as the main measure of system-level metrics' quality in the past, we have decided to use Pearson correlation coefficient as the main measure this year. At the end of this section we give reasons for this change.

We use the following formula to compute the Pearson's r for each metric and translation direction:

[2] `http://www.itl.nist.gov/iad/mig//tools/`

$$r = \frac{\sum_{i=1}^{n}(H_i - \bar{H})(M_i - \bar{M})}{\sqrt{\sum_{i=1}^{n}(H_i - \bar{H})^2}\sqrt{\sum_{i=1}^{n}(M_i - \bar{M})^2}} \tag{1}$$

where H is the vector of human scores of all systems translating in the given direction, M is the vector of the corresponding scores as predicted by the given metric. $\bar{H}$ and $\bar{M}$ are their means respectively.

Since we have normalized all metrics such that better translations get higher score, we consider metrics with values of Pearson's r closer to 1 as better.

You can find the system-level correlations for translations into English in Table 2 and for translations out of English in Table 3. Each row in the tables contains correlations of a metric in each of the examined translation directions. The metrics are sorted by average Pearson correlation coefficient across translation directions. The best results in each direction are in bold.

The reported empirical confidence intervals of system level correlations were obtained through bootstrap resampling of 1000 samples (confidence level of 95 %).

As in previous years, a lot of metrics outperformed BLEU in system level correlation. In into-English directions, metric DISCOTK-PARTY-TUNED has the highest correlation in two language directions and it is also the best correlated metric on average according to both Pearson and Spearman's coefficients. The second best correlated metric on average (according to Pearson) is LAYERED which is also the single best metric in Hindi-to-English direction. Metrics REDSYS and REDSYSSENT are quite unstable, they win in French-to-English and Czech-to-English directions respectively but they perform very poorly in other directions.

Except METEOR, none of the participants took part in the last year metrics task. We can therefore compare current and last year results only for METEOR and baseline metrics. METEOR, the last year winner, performs generally well in some directions but it horribly suffers when evaluating translations from non-Latin script (Russian and especially Hindi). For the baseline metrics the results are quite similar across the years. In both years BLEU performs best among baseline metrics, closely followed by CDER. NIST is in the middle of the list in both years. The remaining baseline metrics TER, WER and PER perform much worse.

The results into German are markedly lower and have broader confidence intervals than the results in other directions. This could be explained by a very high number (18) of participating systems of similar quality. Both human judgements and automatic metrics are negatively affected by these circumstances. To preserve the reliability of overall metrics' performance across languages, we decided to exclude English-to-German direction from the average Pearson and Spearman's correlation coefficients.

In other out-of-English directions, the best correlated metric on average according to Pearson coefficient is NIST, even though it does not win in any single direction. CDER is the second best according to Pearson and the best metric according to Spearman's. Again it does not win in any single direction. The metrics PER and WER are quite unstable. Each of them wins in two directions but performs very badly in others.

Compared to the last year results, the order of metrics participating in both years is quite similar: NIST and CDER performed very well both years, followed by BLEU. The metrics TER and WER are again at the end of the list. An interesting change is that PER perform much better this year.

3.1 Reasons for Pearson correlation coefficient

In the translation task, there are often similar systems with human scores very close to each other. It can therefore easily happen that even a good metric compares two similar systems differently from humans. We believe that the penalty incurred by the metric for such a swap should somehow reflect that the systems were hard to separate.

Since the Spearman's ρ converts both human and metric scores to ranks and therefore disregards the absolute differences in the scores, it does exactly what we feel is not fair. The Pearson correlation coefficient does not suffer from this problem. We are aware of the fact that Pearson correlation coefficient also reflects whether the relation between manual and automatic scores is linear (as opposed to e.g. quadratic). We don't think this would be negatively affecting any of the metrics since overall, the systems are of a comparable quality and the metrics are likely to behave linearly in this small range of scores.

Moreover, the general agreement to adopt Pearson instead of Spearman's correlation coefficient was already apparent during the WMT12 workshop. This change just did not get through for WMT13.

4 Segment-Level Metric Analysis

We measure the quality of metrics' segment-level scores using Kendall's τ rank correlation coefficient. In this type of evaluation, a metric is expected to predict the result of the manual pairwise comparison of two systems. Note that the golden truth is obtained from a compact annotation of five systems at once, while an experiment with text-to-speech evaluation techniques by Vazquez-Alvarez and Huckvale (2002) suggests that a genuine pairwise comparison is likely to lead to more stable results.

In the past, slightly different variations of Kendall's τ computation were used in the Metrics Tasks. Also some of the participants have noticed a problem with ties in the WMT13 method. Therefore, we discuss several possible variants in detail in this paper.

4.1 Notation for Kendall's τ computation

The basic formula for Kendall's τ is:

$$\tau = \frac{|Concordant| - |Discordant|}{|Concordant| + |Discordant|} \quad (2)$$

where $Concordant$ is the set of all human comparisons for which a given metric suggests the same order and $Discordant$ is the set of all human comparisons for which a given metric disagrees. In the original Kendall's τ, comparisons with human or metric ties are considered neither concordant nor discordant. However in the past, Metrics

Correlation coefficient	Pearson Correlation Coefficient						Spearman's
Direction	fr-en	de-en	hi-en	cs-en	ru-en	Average	Average
Considered Systems	8	13	9	5	13		
DISCOTK-PARTY-TUNED	.977 ± .009	**.943 ± .020**	.956 ± .007	.975 ± .031	**.870 ± .022**	**.944 ± .018**	**.912 ± .043**
LAYERED	.973 ± .009	.893 ± .026	**.976 ± .006**	.941 ± .045	.854 ± .023	.927 ± .022	.894 ± .047
DISCOTK-PARTY	.970 ± .010	.921 ± .024	.862 ± .015	.983 ± .025	.856 ± .023	.918 ± .019	.856 ± .046
UPC-STOUT	.968 ± .010	.915 ± .025	.898 ± .013	.948 ± .040	.837 ± .024	.913 ± .022	≀ .901 ± .045
VERTA-W	.959 ± .011	.867 ± .029	.920 ± .011	.934 ± .050	.848 ± .024	.906 ± .025	.868 ± .045
VERTA-EQ	.959 ± .011	.854 ± .031	.927 ± .010	.938 ± .048	.842 ± .024	.904 ± .025	.857 ± .046
TBLEU	.952 ± .012	.832 ± .034	.954 ± .007	.957 ± .040	.803 ± .027	.900 ± .024	.841 ± .056
BLEU_NRC	.953 ± .012	.823 ± .035	.959 ± .007	.946 ± .044	.787 ± .028	.894 ± .025	≀ .855 ± .056
BLEU	.952 ± .012	.832 ± .034	.956 ± .007	.909 ± .054	.789 ± .027	.888 ± .027	.833 ± .058
UPC-IPA	.966 ± .010	.895 ± .027	.914 ± .010	.824 ± .073	.812 ± .026	.882 ± .029	≀ .858 ± .044
CDER	.954 ± .012	.823 ± .034	.826 ± .016	.965 ± .035	.802 ± .027	.874 ± .025	.807 ± .050
APAC	.963 ± .010	.817 ± .034	.790 ± .016	.982 ± .026	.816 ± .026	.874 ± .022	.807 ± .049
REDSYS	**.981 ± .008**	.898 ± .026	.676 ± .022	.989 ± .021	.814 ± .026	.872 ± .021	.786 ± .047
REDSYSSENT	.980 ± .008	.910 ± .024	.644 ± .023	**.993 ± .018**	.807 ± .027	.867 ± .020	.771 ± .043
NIST	.955 ± .011	.811 ± .035	.784 ± .016	.983 ± .025	.800 ± .027	.867 ± .023	≀ .824 ± .055
DISCOTK-LIGHT	.965 ± .011	.935 ± .022	.557 ± .025	.954 ± .038	.791 ± .027	.840 ± .024	.774 ± .046
METEOR	.975 ± .009	.927 ± .022	.457 ± .027	.980 ± .029	.805 ± .026	.829 ± .023	≀ .788 ± .046
TER	.952 ± .012	.775 ± .038	.618 ± .021	.976 ± .031	.809 ± .027	.826 ± .026	.746 ± .057
WER	.952 ± .012	.762 ± .038	.610 ± .021	.974 ± .033	.809 ± .027	.821 ± .026	.736 ± .058
AMBER	.948 ± .012	.910 ± .026	.506 ± .026	.744 ± .095	.797 ± .027	.781 ± .037	.728 ± .051
PER	.946 ± .013	.867 ± .031	.411 ± .025	.883 ± .063	.799 ± .028	.781 ± .032	.698 ± .047
ELEXR	.971 ± .009	.857 ± .031	.535 ± .026	.945 ± .044	−.404 ± .045	.581 ± .031	.652 ± .046

Table 2: System-level correlations of automatic evaluation metrics and the official WMT human scores when translating into English. The symbol "≀" indicates where the Spearman's ρ average is out of sequence compared to the main Pearson average.

Correlation coefficient	Pearson Correlation Coefficient						Spearman's
Direction	en-fr	en-hi	en-cs	en-ru	Average	en-de	Average
Considered Systems	13	12	10	9		18	(excl. en-de)
NIST	.941 ± .022	.981 ± .006	.985 ± .006	.927 ± .012	**.959 ± .012**	.200 ± .046	**.850 ± .030**
CDER	.949 ± .020	.949 ± .010	.982 ± .006	.938 ± .011	.955 ± .012	.278 ± .045	.840 ± .036
AMBER	.928 ± .023	**.990 ± .004**	.972 ± .008	.926 ± .012	.954 ± .012	.241 ± .045	.817 ± .041
METEOR	.941 ± .021	.975 ± .007	.976 ± .007	.923 ± .013	.954 ± .012	.263 ± .045	.806 ± .039
BLEU	.937 ± .022	.973 ± .007	.976 ± .007	.915 ± .013	.950 ± .012	.216 ± .046	≀ .809 ± .036
PER	.936 ± .023	.931 ± .011	**.988 ± .005**	**.941 ± .011**	.949 ± .013	.190 ± .047	≀ .823 ± .037
APAC	.950 ± .020	.940 ± .011	.973 ± .008	.929 ± .012	.948 ± .013	.346 ± .044	.799 ± .041
TBLEU	.932 ± .023	.968 ± .008	.973 ± .008	.912 ± .013	.946 ± .013	.239 ± .046	≀ .805 ± .039
BLEU_NRC	.933 ± .022	.971 ± .007	.974 ± .008	.901 ± .014	.945 ± .013	.205 ± .046	≀ .809 ± .039
ELEXR	.885 ± .029	.962 ± .009	.979 ± .007	.938 ± .011	.941 ± .014	.260 ± .044	.768 ± .036
TER	.954 ± .019	.829 ± .017	.978 ± .007	.931 ± .012	.923 ± .014	.324 ± .045	.745 ± .035
WER	**.960 ± .018**	.516 ± .026	.976 ± .007	.932 ± .011	.846 ± .016	**.357 ± .045**	.696 ± .037
PARMESAN	n/a	n/a	.962 ± .009	n/a	.962 ± .009	n/a	.915 ± .048
UPC-IPA	.940 ± .021	n/a	.969 ± .008	.921 ± .013	.943 ± .014	.285 ± .045	.785 ± .050
REDSYSSENT	.941 ± .021	n/a	n/a	n/a	.941 ± .021	.208 ± .045	≀ .962 ± .038
REDSYS	.940 ± .021	n/a	n/a	n/a	.940 ± .021	.208 ± .045	.962 ± .038
UPC-STOUT	.940 ± .021	n/a	.938 ± .011	.919 ± .013	.933 ± .015	.301 ± .044	.713 ± .040

Table 3: System-level correlations of automatic evaluation metrics and the official WMT human scores when translating out of English. The symbol "≀" indicates where the Spearman's ρ average is out of sequence compared to the main Pearson average.

Tasks (Callison-Burch et al. (2012) and earlier), comparisons with human ties were considered as discordant.

To easily see which pairs are counted as concordant and which as discordant, we have developed the following tabular notation. This is for example the WMT12 method:

		Metric		
WMT12		$<$	$=$	$>$
Human	$<$	1	-1	-1
	$=$	X	X	X
	$>$	-1	-1	1

Given such a matrix $C_{h,m}$ where $h, m \in \{<, =, >\}$[3] and a metric we compute the Kendall's τ the following way:

We insert each extracted human pairwise comparison into exactly one of the nine sets $S_{h,m}$ according to human and metric ranks. For example the set $S_{<,>}$ contains all comparisons where the left-hand system was ranked better than right-hand system by humans and it was ranked the other way round by the metric in question.

To compute the numerator of Kendall's τ, we take the coefficients from the matrix $C_{h,m}$, use them to multiply the sizes of the corresponding sets $S_{h,m}$ and then sum them up. We do not include sets for which the value of $C_{h,m}$ is X. To compute the denominator of Kendall's τ, we simply sum the sizes of all the sets $S_{h,m}$ except those where $C_{h,m} = \text{X}$. To define it formally:

$$\tau = \frac{\sum\limits_{\substack{h,m \in \{<,=,>\} \\ C_{h,m} \neq \text{X}}} C_{h,m} |S_{h,m}|}{\sum\limits_{\substack{h,m \in \{<,=,>\} \\ C_{h,m} \neq \text{X}}} |S_{h,m}|} \qquad (3)$$

4.2 Discussion on Kendall's τ computation

In 2013, we thought that metric ties should not be penalized and we decided to excluded them like the human ties. We will denote this method as WMT13:

		Metric		
WMT13		$<$	$=$	$>$
Human	$<$	1	X	-1
	$=$	X	X	X
	$>$	-1	X	1

It turned out, however, that it was not a good idea: metrics could game the scoring by avoiding hard cases and assigning lots of ties. A natural solution is to count the metrics ties also in denominator to avoid the problem. We will denote this variant as WMT14:

		Metric		
WMT14		$<$	$=$	$>$
Human	$<$	1	0	-1
	$=$	X	X	X
	$>$	-1	0	1

The WMT14 variant does not allow for gaming the scoring like the WMT13 variant does. Compared to WMT12 method, WMT14 does not penalize ties.

We were also considering to get human ties involved. The most natural variant would be the following variant denoted as HTIES:

		Metric		
HTIES		$<$	$=$	$>$
Human	$<$	1	0	-1
	$=$	0	1	0
	$>$	-1	0	1

Unfortunately this method allows for gaming the scoring as well. The least risky choice for metrics in hard cases would be to assign a tie because it cannot worsen the Kendall's τ and there is quite a high chance that the human rank is also a tie. Metrics could be therefore tuned to predict ties often but such metrics are not very useful. For example, the simplistic metric which assigns the same score to all candidates (and therefore all pairs would be tied by the metric) would get the score equal to the proportion of ties in all human comparisons. It would become one of the best performing metrics in WMT13 even though it is not informative at all.

We have decided to use WMT14 variant as the main evaluation measure this year, however, we are also reporting average scores computed by other variants.

4.3 Kendall's τ results

The final Kendall's τ results are shown in Table 4 for directions into English and in Table 5 for directions out of English. Each row in the tables contains correlations of a metric in given directions. The metrics are sorted by average correlation across translation directions. The highest correlation in each column is in bold. The tables also contain average Kendall's τ computed by other variants including the variant WMT13 used last year. Metrics which did not compute scores in all directions are at the bottom of the tables. The

[3] Here the relation $<$ always means "is better than" even for metrics where the better system receives a higher score.

Direction	fr-en	de-en	hi-en	cs-en	ru-en	Avg	Averages of other variants of Kendall's τ		
Extracted-pairs	26090	25260	20900	21130	34460		WMT12	WMT13	HTIES
DiscoTK-party-tuned	**.433 ± .012**	**.380 ± .013**	.434 ± .013	**.328 ± .015**	**.355 ± .011**	**.386 ± .013**	**.386 ± .013**	.386 ± .013	.306 ± .010
BEER	.417 ± .013	.337 ± .014	**.438 ± .013**	.284 ± .016	.333 ± .011	.362 ± .013	.358 ± .013	.363 ± .013	≀ **.318 ± .011**
REDcombSent	.406 ± .012	.338 ± .014	.417 ± .013	.284 ± .015	.336 ± .011	.356 ± .013	.346 ± .013	.360 ± .013	.317 ± .011
REDcombSysSent	.408 ± .012	.338 ± .014	.416 ± .013	.282 ± .014	.336 ± .011	.356 ± .013	.346 ± .013	.359 ± .013	.316 ± .010
Meteor	.406 ± .012	.334 ± .014	.420 ± .013	.282 ± .015	.329 ± .010	.354 ± .013	.341 ± .013	.359 ± .013	≀ .317 ± .010
REDSysSent	.404 ± .012	.338 ± .014	.386 ± .014	.283 ± .015	.321 ± .010	.346 ± .013	.335 ± .013	.350 ± .013	.309 ± .010
REDSent	.403 ± .012	.336 ± .014	.383 ± .014	.283 ± .015	.323 ± .011	.345 ± .013	.334 ± .013	.349 ± .013	.308 ± .010
UPC-IPA	.412 ± .012	.340 ± .014	.368 ± .014	.274 ± .015	.316 ± .011	.342 ± .013	≀ .340 ± .014	.343 ± .014	.300 ± .011
UPC-STOUT	.403 ± .012	.345 ± .014	.352 ± .014	.275 ± .015	.317 ± .011	.338 ± .013	.336 ± .013	.339 ± .013	.294 ± .011
VERTa-W	.399 ± .013	.321 ± .015	.386 ± .014	.263 ± .015	.315 ± .011	.337 ± .014	.320 ± .014	≀ .342 ± .014	≀ .304 ± .011
VERTa-EQ	.407 ± .013	.315 ± .014	.384 ± .013	.263 ± .015	.312 ± .011	.336 ± .013	≀ .323 ± .013	.341 ± .013	.302 ± .011
DiscoTK-party	.395 ± .013	.334 ± .014	.362 ± .013	.264 ± .016	.305 ± .011	.332 ± .013	≀ .332 ± .013	.332 ± .013	.263 ± .011
AMBER	.367 ± .013	.313 ± .014	.362 ± .013	.246 ± .016	.294 ± .011	.316 ± .013	.302 ± .013	.321 ± .014	≀ .286 ± .011
BLEU_NRC	.382 ± .013	.272 ± .014	.322 ± .014	.226 ± .016	.269 ± .011	.294 ± .013	.267 ± .014	.303 ± .014	.271 ± .011
sentBLEU	.378 ± .013	.271 ± .014	.300 ± .013	.213 ± .016	.263 ± .011	.285 ± .013	.258 ± .014	.293 ± .014	.264 ± .011
APAC	.364 ± .012	.271 ± .014	.288 ± .014	.198 ± .016	.276 ± .011	.279 ± .013	.243 ± .014	.290 ± .014	.261 ± .011
DiscoTK-light	.311 ± .014	.224 ± .015	.238 ± .013	.187 ± .016	.209 ± .011	.234 ± .014	.234 ± .014	.234 ± .014	.184 ± .011
DiscoTK-light-kool	.005 ± .001	.001 ± .000	.000 ± .000	.002 ± .001	.001 ± .000	.002 ± .001	−.996 ± .001	≀ **.676 ± .256**	≀ .211 ± .005

Table 4: Segment-level Kendall's τ correlations of automatic evaluation metrics and the official WMT human judgements when translating into English. The last three columns contain average Kendall's τ computed by other variants. The symbol "≀" indicates where the averages of other variants are out of sequence compared to the WMT14 variant.

Direction	en-fr	en-de	en-hi	en-cs	en-ru	Avg	Averages of other variants of Kendall's τ		
Extracted-pairs	33350	54660	28120	55900	28960		WMT12	WMT13	HTIES
BEER	.292 ± .012	**.268 ± .009**	.250 ± .013	**.344 ± .009**	**.440 ± .013**	**.319 ± .011**	**.314 ± .011**	**.320 ± .011**	.272 ± .009
Meteor	.280 ± .012	.238 ± .009	.264 ± .012	.318 ± .009	.427 ± .012	.306 ± .011	.283 ± .011	.313 ± .011	≀ **.273 ± .008**
AMBER	.264 ± .012	.227 ± .009	**.286 ± .012**	.302 ± .009	.397 ± .013	.295 ± .011	.269 ± .011	.303 ± .011	.266 ± .009
BLEU_NRC	.261 ± .012	.202 ± .009	.234 ± .013	.297 ± .009	.391 ± .012	.277 ± .011	.235 ± .011	.289 ± .011	.256 ± .009
APAC	.253 ± .012	.210 ± .008	.203 ± .012	.292 ± .009	.388 ± .013	.269 ± .011	.217 ± .011	.285 ± .011	.252 ± .008
sentBLEU	.256 ± .012	.191 ± .009	.227 ± .012	.290 ± .009	.381 ± .013	.269 ± .011	≀ .232 ± .011	.280 ± .011	.246 ± .009
UPC-STOUT	.279 ± .011	.234 ± .008	n/a	.282 ± .009	.425 ± .013	.305 ± .011	.300 ± .010	.306 ± .011	.256 ± .008
UPC-IPA	.264 ± .012	.227 ± .009	n/a	.298 ± .009	.426 ± .013	.304 ± .011	.292 ± .011	≀ .308 ± .011	≀ .259 ± .008
REDSent	**.293 ± .012**	.242 ± .009	n/a	n/a	n/a	.267 ± .010	.246 ± .010	.273 ± .011	.257 ± .008
REDcombSysSent	.291 ± .012	.244 ± .009	n/a	n/a	n/a	.267 ± .010	≀ .249 ± .010	.272 ± .010	.256 ± .008
REDcombSent	.290 ± .012	.242 ± .009	n/a	n/a	n/a	.266 ± .010	.248 ± .010	.271 ± .011	.256 ± .008
REDSysSent	.290 ± .012	.239 ± .008	n/a	n/a	n/a	.264 ± .010	.235 ± .010	≀ .273 ± .010	≀ .257 ± .008

Table 5: Segment-level Kendall's τ correlations of automatic evaluation metrics and the official WMT human judgements when translating out of English. The last three columns contain average Kendall's τ computed by other variants. The symbol "≀" indicates where the averages of other variants are out of sequence compared to the WMT14 variant.

possible values of τ range between -1 (a metric always predicted a different order than humans did) and 1 (a metric always predicted the same order as humans). Metrics with a higher τ are better.

We also computed empirical confidence intervals of Kendall's τ using bootstrap resampling. We varied the "golden truth" by sampling from human judgments. We have generated 1000 new sets and report the average of the upper and lower 2.5 % empirical bound, which corresponds to the 95 % confidence interval.

In directions into English (Table 4), the strongest correlated segment-level metric on average is DISCOTK-PARTY-TUNED followed by BEER. Unlike the system level correlation, the results are much more stable here. DISCOTK-PARTY-TUNED has the highest correlation in 4 of 5 language directions. Generally, the ranking of metrics is almost the same in each direction.

The only two metrics which also participated in last year metrics task are METEOR and SENTBLEU. In both years, METEOR performed quite well unlike SENTBLEU which was outperformed by most of the metrics.

The metric DISCOTK-LIGHT-KOOL is worth mentioning. It is deliberately designed to assign the same score for all systems for most of the segments. It obtained scores very close to zero (i.e. totally uninformative) in WMT14 variant. In WMT13 thought it reached the highest score.

In directions out of English (Table 5), the metric with highest correlation on average across all directions is BEER, followed by METEOR.

5 Conclusion

In this paper, we summarized the results of the WMT14 Metrics Shared Task, which assesses the quality of various automatic machine translation metrics. As in previous years, human judgements collected in WMT14 serve as the golden truth and we check how well the metrics predict the judgements at the level of individual sentences as well as at the level of the whole test set (system-level).

This year, neither the system-level nor the segment-level scores are directly comparable to the previous years. The system-level scores are affected by the change of the underlying interpretation of the collected judgements in the main translation task evaluation as well as our choice of Pearson coefficient instead of Spearman's rank correlation. The segment-level scores are affected by the different handling of ties this year. Despite somewhat sacrificing the year-to-year comparability, we believe all changes are towards a fairer evaluation and thus better in the long term.

As in previous years, segment-level correlations are much lower than system-level ones, reaching at most Kendall's τ of 0.45 for the best performing metric in its best language pair. So there is quite some research work to be done. We are happy to see that many new metrics emerged this year, which also underlines the importance of the Metrics Shared Task.

Acknowledgements

This work was supported by the grant FP7-ICT-2011-7-288487 (MosesCore) of the European Union. We are grateful to Jacob Devlin and also Preslav Nakov for pointing out the issue of rewarding ties and for further discussion.

References

Barančíková, P. (2014). Parmesan: Improving Meteor by More Fine-grained Paraphrasing. In *Proceedings of the Ninth Workshop on Statistical Machine Translation*, Baltimore, USA. Association for Computational Linguistics.

Bojar, O., Buck, C., Federmann, C., Haddow, B., Koehn, P., Leveling, J., Monz, C., Pecina, P., Post, M., Saint-Amand, H., Soricut, R., Specia, L., and Tamchyna, A. (2014). Findings of the 2014 workshop on statistical machine translation. In *Proceedings of the Ninth Workshop on Statistical Machine Translation*.

Callison-Burch, C., Koehn, P., Monz, C., Post, M., Soricut, R., and Specia, L. (2012). Findings of the 2012 workshop on statistical machine translation. In *Proceedings of the Seventh Workshop on Statistical Machine Translation*, pages 10–51, Montréal, Canada. Association for Computational Linguistics.

Chen, B. and Cherry, C. (2014). A Systematic Comparison of Smoothing Techniques for Sentence-Level BLEU. In *Proceedings of the Ninth Workshop on Statistical Machine Translation*, Baltimore, USA. Association for Computational Linguistics.

Comelles, E. and Atserias, J. (2014). VERTa participation in the WMT14 Metrics Task. In *Proceedings of the Ninth Workshop on Statistical*

Machine Translation, Baltimore, USA. Association for Computational Linguistics.

Denkowski, M. and Lavie, A. (2014). Meteor Universal: Language Specific Translation Evaluation for Any Target Language. In *Proceedings of the Ninth Workshop on Statistical Machine Translation*, Baltimore, USA. Association for Computational Linguistics.

Doddington, G. (2002). Automatic evaluation of machine translation quality using n-gram co-occurrence statistics. In *Proceedings of the second international conference on Human Language Technology Research*, HLT '02, pages 138–145, San Francisco, CA, USA. Morgan Kaufmann Publishers Inc.

Echizen'ya, H. (2014). Application of Prize based on Sentence Length in Chunk-based Automatic Evaluation of Machine Translation. In *Proceedings of the Ninth Workshop on Statistical Machine Translation*, Baltimore, USA. Association for Computational Linguistics.

Gautam, S. and Bhattacharyya, P. (2014). LAYERED: Description of Metric for Machine Translation Evaluation in WMT14 Metrics Task. In *Proceedings of the Ninth Workshop on Statistical Machine Translation*, Baltimore, USA. Association for Computational Linguistics.

Gonzàlez, M., Barrón-Cedeño, A., and Màrquez, L. (2014). IPA and STOUT: Leveraging Linguistic and Source-based Features for Machine Translation Evaluation. In *Proceedings of the Ninth Workshop on Statistical Machine Translation*, Baltimore, USA. Association for Computational Linguistics.

Guzman, F., Joty, S., Màrquez, L., and Nakov, P. (2014). DiscoTK: Using Discourse Structure for Machine Translation Evaluation. In *Proceedings of the Ninth Workshop on Statistical Machine Translation*, Baltimore, USA. Association for Computational Linguistics.

Koehn, P. and Monz, C. (2006). Manual and automatic evaluation of machine translation between european languages. In *Proceedings on the Workshop on Statistical Machine Translation*, pages 102–121, New York City. Association for Computational Linguistics.

Leusch, G., Ueffing, N., and Ney, H. (2006). CDER: Efficient MT Evaluation Using Block Movements. In *In Proceedings of EACL*, pages 241–248.

Libovický, J. and Pecina, P. (2014). Tolerant BLEU: a Submission to the WMT14 Metrics Task. In *Proceedings of the Ninth Workshop on Statistical Machine Translation*, Baltimore, USA. Association for Computational Linguistics.

Macháček, M. and Bojar, O. (2013). Results of the WMT13 Metrics Shared Task. In *Proceedings of the Eighth Workshop on Statistical Machine Translation*, pages 45–51, Sofia, Bulgaria. Association for Computational Linguistics.

Mahmoudi, A., Faili, H., Dehghan, M., and Maleki, J. (2013). ELEXR: Automatic Evaluation of Machine Translation Using Lexical Relationships. In Castro, F., Gelbukh, A., and González, M., editors, *Advances in Artificial Intelligence and Its Applications*, volume 8265 of *Lecture Notes in Computer Science*, pages 394–405. Springer Berlin Heidelberg.

Papineni, K., Roukos, S., Ward, T., and jing Zhu, W. (2002). BLEU: a method for automatic evaluation of machine translation. pages 311–318.

Snover, M., Dorr, B., Schwartz, R., Micciulla, L., and Makhoul, J. (2006). A study of translation edit rate with targeted human annotation. In *In Proceedings of Association for Machine Translation in the Americas*, pages 223–231.

Stanojevic, M. and Sima'an, K. (2014). BEER: A Smooth Sentence Level Evaluation Metric with Rich Ingredients. In *Proceedings of the Ninth Workshop on Statistical Machine Translation*, Baltimore, USA. Association for Computational Linguistics.

Vazquez-Alvarez, Y. and Huckvale, M. (2002). The reliability of the itu-t p.85 standard for the evaluation of text-to-speech systems. In Hansen, J. H. L. and Pellom, B. L., editors, *INTERSPEECH*. ISCA.

Wu, X. and Yu, H. (2014). RED, The DCU Submission of Metrics Tasks. In *Proceedings of the Ninth Workshop on Statistical Machine Translation*, Baltimore, USA. Association for Computational Linguistics.

Efforts on Machine Learning over Human-mediated Translation Edit Rate

Eleftherios Avramidis
German Research Center for Artificial Intelligence (DFKI)
Language Technology Lab
Alt Moabit 91c, 10559 Berlin, Germany
eleftherios.avramidis@dfki.de

Abstract

In this paper we describe experiments on predicting HTER, as part of our submission in the Shared Task on Quality Estimation, in the frame of the 9th Workshop on Statistical Machine Translation. In our experiment we check whether it is possible to achieve better HTER prediction by training four individual regression models for each one of the edit types (deletions, insertions, substitutions, shifts), however no improvements were yielded. We also had no improvements when investigating the possibility of adding more data from other non-minimally post-edited and freely translated datasets. Best HTER prediction was achieved by adding deduplicated WMT13 data and additional features such as (a) rule-based language corrections (language tool) (b) PCFG parsing statistics and count of tree labels (c) position statistics of parsing labels (d) position statistics of tri-grams with low probability.

1 Introduction

As Machine Translation (MT) gets integrated into regular translation workflows, its use as base for post-editing is radically increased. As a result, there is a great demand for methods that can automatically assess the MT outcome and ensure that it is useful for the translator and can lead to more productive translation work.

Although many agree that the quality of the MT output itself is not adequate for the professional standards, there has not yet been a widely-accepted way to measure its quality on par with human translations. One such metric, the Human Translation Edit Rate (HTER) (Snover et al., 2006), is the focus of the current submission. HTER is highly relevant to the need of adapting MT to the needs of translators, as it aims to measure how far it is from an acceptable equivalent translation done by humans.

HTER is used here in the frame of Quality Estimation, i.e. having the goal of being able to predict the post-editing effort in a real case environment, right before the translation is given to the user, without real access to the correct translation. For this purpose the text of the source and the produced translation is analyzed by automatic tools in order to infer indications (numerical features) that may be relevant to the quality of the translation. These features are used in a statistical model whose parameters are estimated with common supervised Machine Learning techniques.

This work presents an extensive search over various set-ups and parameters for such techniques, aiming to build a model that better predicts HTER over the data of the Shared Task of the 9th Workshop on Statistical Machine Translation.

2 New approaches being tested

2.1 Break HTER apart

HTER is a complex metric, in the sense that it is calculated as a linear function over specific types of *edit distance*. The official algorithm performs a comparison between the MT output and the corrected version of this output by a human translator, who performed the minimum number of changes. The comparison results in counting the number of insertions, deletions, substitutions and shifts (e.g. reordering). The final HTER score is the total number of edits divided by the number of reference words.

$$\text{HTER} = \frac{\#\text{insertions} + \#\text{dels} + \#\text{subs} + \#\text{shifts}}{\#\text{reference words}}$$

We notice that the metric is clearly based on four edit types that are seemingly independent of each other. This poses the question whether the existing

Proceedings of the Ninth Workshop on Statistical Machine Translation, pages 302–306,
Baltimore, Maryland USA, June 26–27, 2014.

approach of learning the entire metric altogether introduces way too much complexity in the machine learning process. Instead, we test the hypothesis that it is more effective to build a separate model for each error type and then put the output of each model on the overall HTER fraction shown above.

Following this idea, we score the given translations again in order to produce all four HTER factors (insertions, deletions, substitutions and shifts) and we train four regression models accordingly. This way, each model can be optimized separately, in order to better fit the particular error type, unaffected by the noise that other error types may infer.

2.2 Rounding of individual edit type predictions

Due to the separate model per error type, it is possible to perform corrections on the predicted error count for each error type, before the calculation of the entire HTER score. This may be helpful, given the observation that continuous statistical models may produce a real number as prediction for the count of edits, whereas the actual requirement is an integer.

Here, we take this opportunity and test the hypothesis that prediction of the overall HTER is better, if the output of the four individual models is rounded to the closest integer, before entered in the HTER ratio.

2.3 More data by approximating minimal post-edits

We investigate whether prediction performance can be improved by adding further data. This rises from the fact that the original number of sentences is relatively small, given the amount of usable features. Unfortunately, the amount of openly available resources of minimally post-edited translations are few, given the fact that this relies on a costly manual process usually done by professionals.

Consequently, we add more training samples, using reference translations of the source which are not post-edited. In order to ensure that the additional data still resemble minimally post-edited translations as required for HTER, we include those additional sentences only if they match specific similarity criteria. In particular, the translations are filtered, based on the amount of edits between the MT output and the reference translation; sentences with an amount of edits above the threshold are omitted.

3 Methods

3.1 Machine Learning on a regression problem

Fitting a statistical model in order to predict continuous values is clearly a regression problem. The task takes place on a sentence level, given a set of features describing the source and translation text, and the respective edit score for the particular sentence.

For this purpose we use Support Vector Regression - SVR (Basak et al., 2007), which uses linear learning machines in order to map a non-linear function into a feature space induce by a high-dimensional kernel. Similar to the baseline, the RBF kernel was used, whose parameters where adjusted via a grid search, cross-validated (10 folds) on all data that was available for each variation of the training.

3.2 Features

As explained, the statistical model predicts the edit counts based on a set of features. Our analysis focuses on "black-box" features, which only look superficially on the given text and the produced translation, without further knowledge on how this translation was produced. These features depend on several automatic extraction mechanisms, mostly based on existing language processing tools.

3.2.1 Baseline features

A big set of features is adopted from the baseline of the Shared Task description:

Language models: provide the smoothed n-gram probability and the n-gram perplexity of the sentence.

Source frequency: A set of eight features includes the percentage of uni-grams, bi-grams and tri-grams of the processed sentence in frequency quartiles 1 (lower frequency words) and 4 (higher frequency words) in the source side of a parallel corpus (Callison-Burch et al., 2012).

Count-based features include count and percentage of tokens, unknown words, punctuation marks, numbers, tokens which do or do not contain characters "a-z"; the absolute difference between number of tokens in source and target normalized by source length, number of occurrences of the target word within the target hypothesis averaged for all words in the hypothesis (type/token ratio).

3.2.2 Additional features

Additionally to the baseline features, the following feature groups are considered:

Rule-based language correction is a result of hand-written controlled language rules, that indicate mistakes on several pre-defined error categories (Naber, 2003). We include the number of errors of each category as a feature.

Parsing Features: We parse the text with a PCFG grammar (Petrov et al., 2006) and we derive the counts of all node labels (e.g. count of verb phrases, noun phrases etc.), the parse log-likelihood and the number of the n-best parse trees generated (Avramidis et al., 2011). In order to reduce unnecessary noise, in some experiments we separate a group of "basic" parsing labels, which include only verb phrases, noun phrases, adjectives and subordinate clauses.

Position statistics: This are derivatives of the previous feature categories and focus on the position of unknown words, or node tree tags. For each of them, we calculate the average position index over the sentence and the standard deviation of these indices.

3.3 Evaluation

All specific model parameters were tested with cross validation with 10 equal folds on the training data. Cross validation is useful as it reduces the possibility of overfitting, yet using the entire amount of data.

The regression task is evaluated in terms of Mean Average Error (MAE).

4 Experiment setup

4.1 Implementation

The open source *language tool*[1] is used to annotate source and target sentences with automatically detected monolingual error tags. Language model features are computed with the SRILM toolkit (Stolcke, 2002) with an order of 5, based on monolingual training material from Europarl v7.0 (Koehn, 2005) and News Commentary (Callison-Burch et al., 2011). For the parsing parsing features we used the Berkeley Parser (Petrov and Klein, 2007) trained over an English and a Spanish treebank (Taulé et al., 2008).[2] Baseline features are extracted using Quest and HTER edits and scores are recalculated by modifying the original TERp code. The annotation process is organised with the Ruffus library (Goodstadt, 2010) and the learning algorithms are executed using the Scikit Learn toolkit (Pedregosa et al., 2011).

[1]Open source at http://languagetool.org

datasets	feature set	MAE
wmt14	baseline	0.142
wmt14	all features	0.143
wmt14,wmt13	baseline	0.140
wmt14,wmt13	all features	0.138

Table 1: Better scores are achieved when training with both WMT14 and deduplicated WMT13 data

4.2 Data

In our effort to reproduce HTER in a higher granularity, we noticed that HTER scoring on the official data was reversed: the calculation was performed by using the MT output as reference and the human post-edition as hypothesis. Therefore, the denominator on the "official" scores is the number of tokens on the MT output. This makes the prediction even easier, as this number of tokens is always known.

Apart from the data provided by the WMT14, we include additional minimally post-edited data from WMT13. It was observed that about 30% of the WMT13 data already occurred in the WMT14 set. Since this would negatively affect the credibility of the cross-fold evaluation (section 3.3) and also create duplicates, we filtered out incoming sentences with a string match higher than 85% to the existing ones.

The rest of the additional data (section 2.3) was extracted from the test-sets of shared tasks WMT2008-2011.

5 Results

5.1 Adding data from previous year

Adding deduplicated data from the HTER prediction task of WMT13 (Section 4.2) leads to an improvement of about 0.004 of MAE for the best feature-set, as it can be seen by comparing the respective entries of the two horizontal blocks of Table 1.

[2]although the Spanish grammar performed purely in this case and was eliminated as a feature

feature set	MAE
baseline (b)	0.140
b + language tool	0.141
b + source parse	0.141
b + parse pos	0.142
b + basic parse pos	0.139
b + parse count	0.139
b + low prob trigram pos	0.139
all without char count	0.139
all without lang. tool	0.139
all features	**0.138**

Table 2: Comparing models built with several different feature sets, including various combinations of the features described in section 3.2. All models trained on combination of WMT14 and WMT13 data

5.2 Feature sets

We tested separately several feature sets, additionally to the baseline feature set and the feature set containing all features. The feature sets tested are based on the feature categories explained in Section 3.2.2 and the results are seen in Table 2. One can see that there is little improvement on the MAE score, which is achieved best by using all features.

Adding individual categories of features on the baseline has little effect. Namely, the language tool annotation, the source parse features and the source and target parse positional features deteriorate the MAE score, when added to the baseline features.

On the contrary, there is a small positive contribution by using the position statistics of only the "basic" parsing nodes (i.e. noun phrases, verb phrases, adjectives and subordinate clauses). Similarly positive is the effect of the count of parsed node labels for source and target and the features indicating the position of tri-grams with low probability (lower than the deviation of the mean). Although language tool features deteriorate the score of the baseline model when added, their absense has a negative effect when compared to the full feature set.

5.3 Separate vs. single HTER predictor

Table 3 includes comparisons of models that test the hypothesis mentioned in Section 2.1. For both models trained over the baseline or with additional features, the MAE score is higher (worse), when

features	mode		MAE	std +/-
baseline	single		0.140	0.012
baseline	combined		0.148	0.018
baseline	combined	round	0.152	0.018
all	single		0.138	0.009
all	combined		0.160	0.019
all	combined	round	0.162	0.020

Table 3: The combination of 4 different estimators (combined) does not bring any improvement, when compared to the single HTER estimator. Models trained on both WMT14 and WMT13 data

separate models are trained. This indicates that our hypothesis does not hold, at least for the current setting of learning method and feature sets. Rounding up individual edit type predictions to the closes integer, before the calculation of the HTER ratio, deteriorates the scores even more.

5.4 Effect of adding non-postedited sentences

In Table 4 we can see that adding more data, which are not minimally post-edited (but normal references), does not contribute to a better model, even if we limit the number of edits. The lowest MAE is 0.176, when compared to the one of our best model which is 0.138.

The best score when additional sentences are imported, is achieved by allowing sentences that have between up to edits, and particularly up to 3 substitutions and up to 1 deletion. Increasing the number of edits on more than 4, leads to a further deterioration of the model. One can also see that adding training instances where MT outputs did not require any edit, also yields scores worse than the baseline.

6 Conclusion and further work

In our submission, we process the test set with the model using all features (Table 2). We additionally submit the model trained with additional filtered sentences, as indicated in the second row of Table 4.

One of the basic hypothesis of this experiment, that each edit type can better be learned individually, was not confirmed given these data and settings. Further work could include more focus on the individual models and more elaborating on features that may be specific for each error type.

del	ins	sub	shifts	total	add. sentences	MAE	std+/-
0	0	0	0	0	275	0.177	0.049
1	**0**	**3**	**0**	**4**	**480**	**0.176**	**0.040**
1	0	2	0	3	433	0.177	0.040
0	0	4	0	4	432	0.177	0.040
2	1	0	0	3	296	0.177	0.048
2	0	3	0	5	530	0.178	0.038
4	0	2	0	6	485	0.178	0.041
4	4	0	0	8	310	0.178	0.046
2	1	0	1	4	309	0.178	0.047
1	0	5	0	6	558	0.179	0.039
1	4	5	0	10	1019	0.200	0.031

Table 4: Indicative MAE scores achieved by adding filtered not minimally post-edited WMT translation

References

Eleftherios Avramidis, Maja Popović, David Vilar, and Aljoscha Burchardt. 2011. Evaluate with Confidence Estimation : Machine ranking of translation outputs using grammatical features. In *Proceedings of the Sixth Workshop on Statistical Machine Translation*, pages 65–70, Edinburgh, Scotland, July. Association for Computational Linguistics.

Debasish Basak, Srimanta Pal, and Dipak Chandra Patranabis. 2007. Support vector regression. *Neural Information Processing-Letters and Reviews*, 11(10):203–224.

Chris Callison-Burch, Philipp Koehn, Christof Monz, and Omar Zaidan. 2011. Findings of the 2011 Workshop on Statistical Machine Translation. In *Proceedings of the Sixth Workshop on Statistical Machine Translation*, pages 22–64, Edinburgh, Scotland, July. Association for Computational Linguistics.

Chris Callison-Burch, Philipp Koehn, Christof Monz, Matt Post, Radu Soricut, and Lucia Specia. 2012. Findings of the 2012 Workshop on Statistical Machine Translation. In *Proceedings of the Seventh Workshop on Statistical Machine Translation*, pages 10–51, Montréal, Canada, June. Association for Computational Linguistics.

Leo Goodstadt. 2010. Ruffus: a lightweight Python library for computational pipelines. *Bioinformatics*, 26(21):2778–2779.

Philipp Koehn. 2005. Europarl: A parallel corpus for statistical machine translation. *Proceedings of the tenth Machine Translation Summit*, 5:79–86.

Daniel Naber. 2003. A rule-based style and grammar checker. Technical report, Bielefeld University, Bielefeld, Germany.

Fabian Pedregosa, Gaël Varoquaux, Alexandre Gramfort, Vincent Michel, Bertrand Thirion, Olivier Grisel, Mathieu Blondel, Peter Prettenhofer, Ron Weiss, Vincent Dubourg, Jake Vanderplas, Alexandre Passos, David Cournapeau, Matthieu Brucher, Matthieu Perrot, and Édouard Duchesnay. 2011. Scikit-learn: Machine learning in python. *Journal of Machine Learning Research*, 12:2825–2830.

Slav Petrov and Dan Klein. 2007. Improved inference for unlexicalized parsing. In *Proceedings of the 2007 Annual Conference of the North American Chapter of the Association for Computational Linguistics*, Rochester, New York. Association for Computational Linguistics.

Slav Petrov, Leon Barrett, Romain Thibaux, and Dan Klein. 2006. Learning Accurate, Compact, and Interpretable Tree Annotation. In *Proceedings of the 21st International Conference on Computational Linguistics and 44th Annual Meeting of the Association for Computational Linguistics*, pages 433–440, Sydney, Australia, July. Association for Computational Linguistics.

Matthew Snover, B Dorr, Richard Schwartz, L Micciulla, and John Makhoul. 2006. A study of translation edit rate with targeted human annotation. In *Proceedings of Association for Machine Translation in the Americas*, pages 223–231.

Andreas Stolcke. 2002. SRILM – An Extensible Language Modeling Toolkit. In *Proceedings of the Seventh International Conference on Spoken Language Processing*, pages 901–904. ISCA, September.

Mariona Taulé, Antònia Martí, and Marta Recasens. 2008. AnCora: Multilevel Annotated Corpora for Catalan and Spanish. In *Proceedings of the Sixth International Conference on Language Resources and Evaluation (LREC'08)*, Marrakech, Morocco, May. European Language Resources Association (ELRA).

SHEF-Lite 2.0: Sparse Multi-task Gaussian Processes for Translation Quality Estimation

Daniel Beck and **Kashif Shah** and **Lucia Specia**
Department of Computer Science
University of Sheffield
Sheffield, United Kingdom
{debeck1,kashif.shah,l.specia}@sheffield.ac.uk

Abstract

We describe our systems for the WMT14 Shared Task on Quality Estimation (subtasks 1.1, 1.2 and 1.3). Our submissions use the framework of Multi-task Gaussian Processes, where we combine multiple datasets in a multi-task setting. Due to the large size of our datasets we also experiment with Sparse Gaussian Processes, which aim to speed up training and prediction by providing sensible sparse approximations.

1 Introduction

The purpose of machine translation (MT) quality estimation (QE) is to provide a quality prediction for new, unseen machine translated texts, without relying on reference translations (Blatz et al., 2004; Specia et al., 2009; Bojar et al., 2013). A common use of quality predictions is the decision between post-editing a given machine translated sentence and translating its source from scratch, based on whether its post-editing effort is estimated to be lower than the effort of translating the source sentence.

The WMT 2014 QE shared task defined a group of tasks related to QE. In this paper, we describe our submissions for subtasks 1.1, 1.2 and 1.3. Our models are based on Gaussian Processes (GPs) (Rasmussen and Williams, 2006), a non-parametric kernelised probabilistic framework. We propose to combine multiple datasets to improve our QE models by applying GPs in a multi-task setting. Our hypothesis is that using sensible multi-task learning settings gives improvements over simply pooling all datasets together.

Task 1.1 focuses on predicting post-editing effort for four language pairs: English-Spanish (**en-es**), Spanish-English (**es-en**), English-German (**en-de**), and German-English (**de-en**). Each contains a different number of source sentences and their human translations, as well as 2-3 versions of machine translations: by a statistical (SMT) system, a rule-based system (RBMT) system and, for en-es/de only, a hybrid system. Source sentences were extracted from tests sets of WMT13 and WMT12, and the translations were produced by top MT systems of each type and a human translator. Labels range from 1 to 3, with 1 indicating a perfect translation and 3, a low quality translation.

The purpose of task 1.2 is to predict HTER scores (Human Translation Error Rate) (Snover et al., 2006) using a dataset composed of 896 English-Spanish sentences translated by a MT system and post-edited by a professional translator. Finally, task 1.3 aims at predicting post-editing time, using a subset of 650 sentences from the Task 1.2 dataset.

For each task, participants can submit two types of results: scoring and ranking. For scoring, evaluation is made in terms of Mean Absolute Error (MAE) and Root Mean Square Error (RMSE). For ranking, DeltaAvg and Spearman's rank correlation were used as evaluation metrics.

2 Model

Gaussian Processes are a Bayesian non-parametric machine learning framework considered the state-of-the-art for regression. They assume the presence of a latent function $f : \mathbb{R}^F \rightarrow \mathbb{R}$, which maps a vector $\mathbf{x}$ from feature space F to a scalar value. Formally, this function is drawn from a GP prior:

$$f(\mathbf{x}) \sim \mathcal{GP}(\mathbf{0}, k(\mathbf{x}, \mathbf{x}')),$$

which is parameterised by a mean function (here, $\mathbf{0}$) and a covariance kernel function $k(\mathbf{x}, \mathbf{x}')$. Each response value is then generated from the function evaluated at the corresponding input, $y_i = f(\mathbf{x}_i) + \eta$, where $\eta \sim \mathcal{N}(0, \sigma_n^2)$ is added white-noise.

Proceedings of the Ninth Workshop on Statistical Machine Translation, pages 307–312,
Baltimore, Maryland USA, June 26–27, 2014. ©2014 Association for Computational Linguistics

Prediction is formulated as a Bayesian inference under the posterior:

$$p(y_*|\mathbf{x}_*, \mathcal{D}) = \int_f p(y_*|\mathbf{x}_*, f)p(f|\mathcal{D}),$$

where $\mathbf{x}_*$ is a test input, y_* is the test response value and $\mathcal{D}$ is the training set. The predictive posterior can be solved analitically, resulting in:

$$y_* \sim \mathcal{N}(\mathbf{k}_*^T(\mathbf{K} + \sigma_n^2 I)^{-1}\mathbf{y}, \\ k(x_*, x_*) - \mathbf{k}_*^T(\mathbf{K} + \sigma_n^2 I)^{-1}\mathbf{k}_*),$$

where $\mathbf{k}_* = [k(\mathbf{x}_*, \mathbf{x}_1)k(\mathbf{x}_*, \mathbf{x}_2)\dots k(\mathbf{x}_*, \mathbf{x}_n)]^T$ is the vector of kernel evaluations between the training set and the test input and $\mathbf{K}$ is the kernel matrix over the training inputs (the Gram matrix).

The kernel function encodes the covariance (similarity) between each input pair. While a variety of kernel functions are available, here we followed previous work in QE using GP (Cohn and Specia, 2013; Shah et al., 2013) and employed a squared exponential (SE) kernel with automatic relevance determination (ARD):

$$k(\mathbf{x}, \mathbf{x}') = \sigma_f^2 \exp\left(-\frac{1}{2}\sum_{i=1}^{F}\frac{x_i - x_i'}{l_i}\right),$$

where F is the number of features, σ_f^2 is the covariance *magnitude* and $l_i > 0$ are the feature *lengthscales*.

The resulting model hyperparameters (SE variance σ_f^2, noise variance σ_n^2 and SE lengthscales l_i) were learned from data by maximising the model likelihood. All our models were trained using the GPy[1] toolkit, an open source implementation of GPs written in Python.

2.1 Multi-task learning

The GP regression framework can be extended to multiple outputs by assuming $f(\mathbf{x})$ to be a vector valued function. These models are commonly referred as *coregionalization* models in the GP literature (Álvarez et al., 2012). Here we refer to them as *multi-task* kernels, to emphasize our application.

In this work, we employ a separable multi-task kernel, similar to the one used by Bonilla et al. (2008) and Cohn and Specia (2013). Considering a set of D tasks, we define the corresponding multi-task kernel as:

$$k((\mathbf{x}, d), (\mathbf{x}', d')) = k_{\text{data}}(\mathbf{x}, \mathbf{x}') \times \mathbf{B}_{d,d'}, \quad (1)$$

[1] http://sheffieldml.github.io/GPy/

where k_{data} is a kernel on the input points, d and d' are task or metadata information for each input and $\mathbf{B} \in \mathbb{R}^{D \times D}$ is the multi-task matrix, which encodes task covariances. For task 1.1, we consider each language pair as a different task, while for tasks 1.2 and 1.3 we use additional datasets for the same language pair (en-es), treating each dataset as a different task.

To perform the learning procedure the multi-task matrix should be parameterised in a sensible way. We follow the parameterisations proposed by Cohn and Specia (2013), which we briefly describe here:

Independent: $\mathbf{B} = \mathbf{I}$. In this setting each task is modelled independently. This is not strictly equivalent to independent model training because the tasks share the same data kernel (and the same hyperparameters);

Pooled: $\mathbf{B} = \mathbf{1}$. Here the task identity is ignored. This is equivalent to pooling all datasets in a single task model;

Combined: $\mathbf{B} = \mathbf{1} + \alpha\mathbf{I}$. This setting leverages between independent and pooled models. Here, $\alpha > 0$ is treated as an hyperparameter;

Combined+: $\mathbf{B} = \mathbf{1} + \text{diag}(\boldsymbol{\alpha})$. Same as "combined", but allowing one different α value per task.

2.2 Sparse Gaussian Processes

The performance bottleneck for GP models is the Gram matrix inversion, which is $O(n^3)$ for standard GPs, with n being the number of training instances. For multi-task settings this can be a potential issue because these models replicate the instances for each task and the resulting Gram matrix has dimensionality $nd \times nd$, where d is the number of tasks.

Sparse GPs tackle this problem by approximating the Gram matrix using only a subset of m *inducing inputs*. Without loss of generalisation, consider these m points as the first instances in the training data. We can then expand the Gram matrix in the following way:

$$\mathbf{K} = \begin{bmatrix} \mathbf{K}_{mm} & \mathbf{K}_{m(n-m)} \\ \mathbf{K}_{(n-m)m} & \mathbf{K}_{(n-m)(n-m)} \end{bmatrix}.$$

Following the notation in (Rasmussen and Williams, 2006), we refer $\mathbf{K}_{m(n-m)}$ as $\mathbf{K}_{mn}$ and its transpose as $\mathbf{K}_{nm}$. The block structure of $\mathbf{K}$ forms the basis of the so-called Nyström approximation:

$$\tilde{\mathbf{K}} = \mathbf{K}_{nm}\mathbf{K}_{mm}^{-1}\mathbf{K}_{mn}, \quad (2)$$

which results in the following predictive posterior:

$$\begin{aligned} y_* \sim \mathcal{N}(&\mathbf{k}_{m*}^T\tilde{\mathbf{G}}^{-1}\mathbf{K}_{mn}\mathbf{y}, \quad (3)\\ &k(\mathbf{x}_*, \mathbf{x}_*) - \mathbf{k}_{m*}^T\mathbf{K}_{mm}^{-1}\mathbf{k}_{m*} + \\ &\sigma_n^2\mathbf{k}_{m*}^T\tilde{\mathbf{G}}^{-1}\mathbf{k}_{m*}), \end{aligned}$$

where $\tilde{\mathbf{G}} = \sigma_n^2\mathbf{K}_{mm} + \mathbf{K}_{mn}\mathbf{K}_{nm}$ and $\mathbf{k}_{m*}$ is the vector of kernel evaluations between test input $\mathbf{x}_*$ and the m inducing inputs. The resulting training complexity is $O(m^2n)$.

The remaining question is how to choose the inducing inputs. We follow the approach of Snelson and Ghahramani (2006), which note that these inducing inputs do not need to be a subset of the training data. Their method considers each input as a hyperparameter, which is then optimised jointly with the kernel hyperparameters.

2.3 Features

For all tasks we used the QuEst framework (Specia et al., 2013) to extract a set of 80 black-box features as in Shah et al. (2013), for which we had all the necessary resources available. Examples of the features extracted include:

- N-gram-based features:
  - Number of tokens in source and target segments;
  - Language model (LM) probability of source and target segments;
  - Percentage of source 1–3-grams observed in different frequency quartiles of a large corpus of the source language;
  - Average number of translations per source word in the segment as given by IBM 1 model from a large parallel corpus of the language, with probabilities thresholded in different ways.
- POS-based features:
  - Ratio of percentage of nouns/verbs/etc in the source and target segments;
  - Ratio of punctuation symbols in source and target segments;
  - Percentage of direct object personal or possessive pronouns incorrectly translated.

For the full set of features we refer readers to QuEst website.[2]

To perform feature selection, we followed the approach used in Shah et al. (2013) and ranked the features according to their learned lengthscales (from the lowest to the highest). The lengthscale of a feature can be interpreted as the relevance of such feature for the model. Therefore, the outcome of a GP model using an ARD kernel can be viewed as a list of features ranked by relevance, and this information can be used for feature selection by discarding the lowest ranked (least useful) ones.

3 Preliminary Experiments

Our submissions are based on multi-task settings. For task 1.1, we consider each language pair as a different task, training one model for all pairs. For tasks 1.2 and 1.3, we used additional datasets and encoded each one as a different task (totalling 3 tasks):

WMT13: these are the datasets provided in last year's QE shared task (Bojar et al., 2013). We combined training and test sets, totalling $2,754$ sentences for HTER prediction and $1,003$ sentences for post-editing time prediction, both for English-Spanish.

EAMT11: this dataset is provided by Specia (2011) and is composed of $1,000$ English-Spanish sentences annotated in terms of HTER and post-editing time.

For each task we prepared two submissions: one trained on a standard GP with the full 80 features set and another one trained on a sparse GP with a subset of 40 features. The features were chosen by training a smaller model on a subset of 400 instances and following the procedure explained in Section 2.3 for feature selection, with a pre-define cutoff point on the number of features (40), based on previous experiments. The sparse models were trained using 400 inducing inputs.

To select an appropriate multi-task setting for our submissions we performed preliminary experiments using a 90%/10% split on the corresponding training set for each task. The resulting MAE scores are shown in Tables 1 and 2, for standard and sparse GPs, respectively. The boldface figures correspond to the settings we choose for the

[2] http://www.quest.dcs.shef.ac.uk/quest_files/features_blackbox

	Task 1.1				Task 1.2	Task 1.3
	en-es	es-en	en-de	de-en	en-es	en-es
Independent	**0.4905**	0.5325	**0.5962**	**0.5452**	0.2047	0.4486
Pooled	0.4957	0.5171	0.6012	0.5612	**0.2036**	0.8599
Combined	0.4939	**0.5162**	0.6007	0.5550	0.2321	0.7489
Combined+	0.4932	0.5182	0.5990	0.5514	0.2296	**0.4472**

Table 1: MAE results for preliminary experiments on standard GPs. Post-editing time scores for task 1.3 are shown on log time per word.

	Task 1.1				Task 1.2	Task 1.3
	en-es	es-en	en-de	de-en	en-es	en-es
Independent	0.5036	0.5274	0.6002	0.5532	0.3432	**0.3906**
Pooled	0.4890	**0.5131**	0.5927	0.5532	**0.1597**	0.6410
Combined	**0.4872**	0.5183	0.5871	**0.5451**	0.2871	0.6449
Combined+	0.4935	0.5255	**0.5864**	0.5458	0.1659	0.4040

Table 2: MAE results for preliminary experiments on sparse GPs. Post-editing time scores for task 1.3 are shown on log time per word.

official submissions, after re-training on the corresponding full training sets.

To check the speed-ups obtained from using sparse GPs, we measured wall clock times for training and prediction in Task 1.1 using the "Independent" multi-task setting. Table 3 shows the resulting times and the corresponding speed-ups when comparing to the standard GP. For comparison, we also trained a model using 200 inducing inputs, although we did not use the results of this model in our submissions.

	Time (secs)	Speed-up
Standard GP	12122	–
Sparse GP (m=400)	3376	3.59x
Sparse GP (m=200)	978	12.39x

Table 3: Wall clock times and speed-ups for GPs training and prediction: full versus sparse GPs.

4 Official Results and Discussion

Table 4 shows the results for Task 1.1. Using standard GPs we obtained improved results over the baseline for English-Spanish and English-German only, with particularly substantial improvements for English-Spanish, which also happens for sparse GPs. This may be related to the larger size of this dataset when compared to the others. Our results here are mostly inconclusive though and we plan to investigate this setting more in depth in the future. Specifically, due to the coarse behaviour of the labels, ordinal regression GP models (like the one proposed in (Chu et al., 2005)) could be useful for this task.

Results for Task 1.2 are shown in Table 5. The standard GP model performed unusually poorly when compared to the baseline or the sparse GP model. To investigate this, we inspected the resulting model hyperparameters. We found out that the noise σ_n^2 was optimised to a very low value, close to zero, which characterises overfitting. The same behaviour was not observed with the sparse model, even though it had a much higher number of hyperparameters to optimise, and was therefore more prone to overfitting. We plan to investigate this issue further but a possible cause could be bad starting values for the hyperparameters.

Table 6 shows results for Task 1.3. In this task, the standard GP model outperformed the baseline, with the sparse GP model following very closely. These figures represent significant improvements compared to our submission to the same task in last year's shared task (Beck et al., 2013), where we were not able to beat the baseline. The main differences between last year's and this year's models are the use of additional datasets and a higher number of features (25 vs. 40). The competitive results for the sparse GP models are very promising because they show we can combine multiple datasets to improve post-editing time prediction while employing a sparse model to cope with speed issues.

	en-es		es-en		en-de		de-en	
	Δ	ρ	Δ	ρ	Δ	ρ	Δ	ρ
Standard GP	**0.21**	**-0.33**	0.11	-0.15	**0.26**	**-0.36**	0.24	**-0.27**
Sparse GP	**0.17**	**0.27**	0.12	-0.17	0.23	-0.33	0.14	-0.17
Baseline	0.14	-0.22	0.12	-0.21	0.23	-0.34	0.21	-0.25

	en-es		es-en		en-de		de-en	
	MAE	RMSE	MAE	RMSE	MAE	RMSE	MAE	RMSE
Standard GP	**0.49**	**0.63**	0.62	0.77	**0.63**	**0.74**	0.65	**0.77**
Sparse GP	0.54	0.69	0.54	0.69	0.64	**0.75**	0.66	0.79
Baseline	0.52	0.66	0.57	0.68	0.64	0.76	0.65	0.78

Table 4: Official results for task 1.1. The top table shows results for the ranking subtask (Δ: DeltaAvg; ρ: Spearman's correlation). The bottom table shows results for the scoring subtask.

	Ranking		Scoring	
	Δ	ρ	MAE	RMSE
Standard GP	0.72	0.09	18.15	23.41
Sparse GP	**7.69**	**0.43**	**15.04**	**18.38**
Baseline	5.08	0.31	15.23	19.48

Table 5: Official results for task 1.2.

	Ranking		Scoring	
	Δ	ρ	MAE	RMSE
Standard GP	**16.08**	**0.64**	**17.13**	**27.33**
Sparse GP	**16.33**	**0.63**	**17.42**	**27.35**
Baseline	14.71	0.57	21.49	34.28

Table 6: Official results for task 1.3.

5 Conclusions

We proposed a new setting for training QE models based on Multi-task Gaussian Processes. Our settings combined different datasets in a sensible way, by considering each dataset as a different task and learning task covariances. We also proposed to speed-up training and prediction times by employing sparse GPs, which becomes crucial in multi-task settings. The results obtained are specially promising in the post-editing time task, where we obtained the same results as with standard GPs and improved over our models from the last evaluation campaign.

In the future, we plan to employ our multi-task models in large-scale settings, like datasets annotated through crowdsourcing platforms. These datasets are usually labelled by dozens of annotators and multi-task GPs have proved an interesting framework for learning the annotation noise (Cohn and Specia, 2013). However, multiple tasks can easily make training and prediction times prohibitive, and thus another direction if work is to use recent advances in sparse GPs, like the one proposed by Hensman et al. (2013). We believe that the combination of these approaches could further improve the state-of-the-art performance in these tasks.

Acknowledgments

This work was supported by funding from CNPq/Brazil (No. 237999/2012-9, Daniel Beck) and from European Union's Seventh Framework Programme for research, technological development and demonstration under grant agreement no. 296347 (QTLaunchPad).

References

Mauricio A. Álvarez, Lorenzo Rosasco, and Neil D. Lawrence. 2012. Kernels for Vector-Valued Functions: a Review. *Foundations and Trends in Machine Learning*, pages 1–37.

Daniel Beck, Kashif Shah, Trevor Cohn, and Lucia Specia. 2013. SHEF-Lite : When Less is More for Translation Quality Estimation. In *Proceedings of WMT13*, pages 337–342.

John Blatz, Erin Fitzgerald, and George Foster. 2004. Confidence estimation for machine translation. In *Proceedings of the 20th Conference on Computational Linguistics*, pages 315–321.

Ondej Bojar, Christian Buck, Chris Callison-Burch, Christian Federmann, Barry Haddow, Philipp Koehn, Christof Monz, Matt Post, Radu Soricut, and Lucia Specia. 2013. Findings of the 2013 Workshop on Statistical Machine Translation. In *Proceedings of WMT13*, pages 1–44.

Edwin V. Bonilla, Kian Ming A. Chai, and Christopher K. I. Williams. 2008. Multi-task Gaussian Process Prediction. *Advances in Neural Information Processing Systems.*

Wei Chu, Zoubin Ghahramani, Francesco Falciani, and David L Wild. 2005. Biomarker discovery in microarray gene expression data with Gaussian processes. *Bioinformatics*, 21(16):3385–93, August.

Trevor Cohn and Lucia Specia. 2013. Modelling Annotator Bias with Multi-task Gaussian Processes: An Application to Machine Translation Quality Estimation. In *Proceedings of ACL.*

James Hensman, Nicolò Fusi, and Neil D. Lawrence. 2013. Gaussian Processes for Big Data. In *Proceedings of UAI.*

Carl Edward Rasmussen and Christopher K. I. Williams. 2006. *Gaussian processes for machine learning*, volume 1. MIT Press Cambridge.

Kashif Shah, Trevor Cohn, and Lucia Specia. 2013. An Investigation on the Effectiveness of Features for Translation Quality Estimation. In *Proceedings of MT Summit XIV.*

Edward Snelson and Zoubin Ghahramani. 2006. Sparse Gaussian Processes using Pseudo-inputs. In *Proceedings of NIPS.*

Matthew Snover, Bonnie Dorr, Richard Schwartz, Linnea Micciulla, and John Makhoul. 2006. A study of translation edit rate with targeted human annotation. In *Proceedings of Association for Machine Translation in the Americas.*

Lucia Specia, Craig Saunders, Marco Turchi, Zhuoran Wang, and John Shawe-Taylor. 2009. Improving the confidence of machine translation quality estimates. In *Proceedings of MT Summit XII.*

Lucia Specia, Kashif Shah, José G. C. De Souza, and Trevor Cohn. 2013. QuEst - A translation quality estimation framework. In *Proceedings of ACL Demo Session.*

Lucia Specia. 2011. Exploiting objective annotations for measuring translation post-editing effort. In *Proceedings of EAMT.*

Referential Translation Machines for Predicting Translation Quality

Ergun Biçici
Centre for Next Generation Localisation
School of Computing
Dublin City University, Dublin, Ireland.
ergun.bicici@computing.dcu.ie

Andy Way
Centre for Next Generation Localisation
School of Computing
Dublin City University, Dublin, Ireland.
away@computing.dcu.ie

Abstract

We use referential translation machines (RTM) for quality estimation of translation outputs. RTMs are a computational model for identifying the translation acts between any two data sets with respect to interpretants selected in the same domain, which are effective when making monolingual and bilingual similarity judgments. RTMs achieve top performance in automatic, accurate, and language independent prediction of sentence-level and word-level statistical machine translation (SMT) quality. RTMs remove the need to access any SMT system specific information or prior knowledge of the training data or models used when generating the translations and achieve the top performance in WMT13 quality estimation task (QET13). We improve our RTM models with the Parallel FDA5 instance selection model, with additional features for predicting the translation performance, and with improved learning models. We develop RTM models for each WMT14 QET (QET14) subtask, obtain improvements over QET13 results, and rank 1st in all of the tasks and subtasks of QET14.

1 Introduction

We use referential translation machines (RTM) for quality estimation of translation outputs, which is a computational model for identifying the acts of translation for translating between any given two data sets with respect to a reference corpus selected in the same domain. RTMs reduce our dependence on any task dependent resource. Prediction of translation quality is important because the expected translation performance can help in estimating the effort required for correcting the translations during post-editing by human translators.

Bicici et al. (2013) develop the Machine Translation Performance Predictor (MTPP), a state-of-the-art, language independent, and SMT system extrinsic machine translation performance predictor, which can predict translation quality by looking at the test source sentences and becomes the 2nd overall after also looking at the translation outputs as well in QET12 (Callison-Burch et al., 2012). RTMs achieve the top performance in QET13 (Bojar et al., 2013), ranking 1st or 2nd in all of the subtasks. RTMs rank 1st in all of the tasks and subtasks of QET14 (Bojar et al., 2014).

Referential translation models (Section 2) present an accurate and language independent solution for predicting the performance of natural language tasks such as the quality estimation of translation. We improve our RTM models (Biçici, 2013) by:

- using a parameterized, fast implementation of FDA, FDA5, and our Parallel FDA5 instance selection model (Biçici et al., 2014),
- better modeling of the language in which similarity judgments are made with improved optimization and selection of the LM data,
- increased feature set for also modeling the structural properties of sentences,
- extended learning models.

2 Referential Translation Machine (RTM)

Referential translation machines provide a computational model for quality and semantic similarity judgments in monolingual and bilingual settings using retrieval of relevant training data (Biçici, 2011; Biçici and Yuret, 2014) as interpretants for reaching shared semantics (Biçici, 2008). RTMs achieve top performance when predicting the quality of translations in QET14 and QET13 (Biçici,

Proceedings of the Ninth Workshop on Statistical Machine Translation, pages 313–321,
Baltimore, Maryland USA, June 26–27, 2014.

2013), top performance when predicting monolingual cross-level semantic similarity (Jurgens et al., 2014), good performance when evaluating the semantic relatedness of sentences and their entailment (Marelli et al., 2014), and a language independent solution and good performance when judging the semantic similarity of sentences (Agirre et al., 2014; Biçici and Way, 2014).

RTM is a computational model for identifying the acts of translation for translating between any given two data sets with respect to a reference corpus selected in the same domain. An RTM model is based on the selection of interpretants, data close to both the training set and the test set, which allow shared semantics by providing context for similarity judgments. In semiotics, an interpretant I interprets the signs used to refer to the real objects (Biçici, 2008). Each RTM model is a data translation model between the instances in the training set and the test set. We use the Parallel FDA5 (Feature Decay Algorithms) instance selection model for selecting the interpretants (Biçici et al., 2014; Biçici and Yuret, 2014) this year, which allows efficient parameterization, optimization, and implementation of FDA, and build an MTPP model (Section 2.1). We view that acts of translation are ubiquitously used during communication:

> *Every act of communication is an act of translation* (Bliss, 2012).

Given a training set $\texttt{train}$, a test set $\texttt{test}$, and some corpus $\mathcal{C}$, preferably in the same domain as the training and test sets, the RTM steps are:

1. FDA5$(\texttt{train}, \texttt{test}, \mathcal{C}) \rightarrow \mathcal{I}$
2. MTPP$(\mathcal{I}, \texttt{train}) \rightarrow \mathcal{F}_{\texttt{train}}$
3. MTPP$(\mathcal{I}, \texttt{test}) \rightarrow \mathcal{F}_{\texttt{test}}$
4. learn$(M, \mathcal{F}_{\texttt{train}}) \rightarrow \mathcal{M}$
5. predict$(\mathcal{M}, \mathcal{F}_{\texttt{test}}) \rightarrow \hat{q}$

Step 1 selects the interpretants, $\mathcal{I}$, relevant to both the training and test data. Steps 2 and 3 use $\mathcal{I}$ to map $\texttt{train}$ and $\texttt{test}$ to a new space where similarities between translation acts can be derived more easily. Step 4 trains a learning model M over the training features, $\mathcal{F}_{\texttt{train}}$, and Step 5 obtains the predictions. RTM relies on the representativeness of $\mathcal{I}$ as a medium for building data translation models between $\texttt{train}$ and $\texttt{test}$.

Our encouraging results in QET provides a greater understanding of the acts of translation we ubiquitously use and how they can be used to predict the performance of translation and judging the semantic similarity between text. RTM and MTPP models are not data or language specific and their modeling power and good performance are applicable in different domains and tasks.

2.1 The Machine Translation Performance Predictor (MTPP)

MTPP (Biçici et al., 2013) is a state-of-the-art and top performing machine translation performance predictor, which uses machine learning models over features measuring how well the test set matches the training set to predict the quality of a translation without using a reference translation.

2.2 MTPP Features for Translation Acts

MTPP measures the coverage of individual test sentence features found in the training set and derives indicators of the closeness of test sentences to the available training data, the difficulty of translating the sentence, and the presence of acts of translation for data transformation. Feature functions use statistics involving the training set and the test sentences to determine their closeness. Since they are language independent, MTPP allows quality estimation to be performed extrinsically. MTPP uses n-gram features defined over text or common cover link (CCL) (Seginer, 2007) structures as the basic units of information over which similarity calculations are made. Unsupervised parsing with CCL extracts links from base words to head words, representing the grammatical information instantiated in the training and test data.

We extend the MTPP model we used last year (Biçici, 2013) in its learning module and the features included. Categories for the features (S for source, T for target) used are listed below where the number of features are given in brackets for S and T, {#S, #T}, and the detailed descriptions for some of the features are presented in (Biçici et al., 2013). The number of features for each task differs since we perform an initial feature selection step on the tree structural features (Section 2.3). The number of features are in the range $337-437$.

- *Coverage* $\{56, 54\}$: Measures the degree to which the test features are found in the training set for both S ($\{56\}$) and T ($\{54\}$).
- *Perplexity* $\{45, 45\}$: Measures the fluency of the sentences according to language models

(LM). We use both forward ({30}) and backward ({15}) LM features for S and T.

- *TreeF* {*0, 10-110*}: 10 base features and up to 100 selected features of T among parse tree structures (Section 2.3).
- *Retrieval Closeness* {*16, 12*}: Measures the degree to which sentences close to the test set are found in the selected training set, $\mathcal{I}$, using FDA (Biçici and Yuret, 2011a) and BLEU, F_1 (Biçici, 2011), *dice*, and tf-idf cosine similarity metrics.
- *IBM2 Alignment Features* {*0, 22*}: Calculates the sum of the entropy of the distribution of alignment probabilities for S ($\sum_{s \in S} -p \log p$ for $p = p(t|s)$ where s and t are tokens) and T, their average for S and T, the number of entries with $p \geq 0.2$ and $p \geq 0.01$, the entropy of the word alignment between S and T and its average, and word alignment log probability and its value in terms of bits per word. We also compute word alignment percentage as in (Camargo de Souza et al., 2013) and potential BLEU, F_1, WER, PER scores for S and T.
- *IBM1 Translation Probability* {*4, 12*}: Calculates the translation probability of test sentences using the selected training set, $\mathcal{I}$ (Brown et al., 1993).
- *Feature Vector Similarity* {*8, 8*}: Calculates similarities between vector representations.
- *Entropy* {*2, 8*}: Calculates the distributional similarity of test sentences to the training set over top N retrieved sentences (Biçici et al., 2013).
- *Length* {*6, 3*}: Calculates the number of words and characters for S and T and their average token lengths and their ratios.
- *Diversity* {*3, 3*}: Measures the diversity of co-occurring features in the training set.
- *Synthetic Translation Performance* {*3, 3*}: Calculates translation scores achievable according to the n-gram coverage.
- *Character* n*-grams* {*5*}: Calculates cosine between character n-grams (for n=2,3,4,5,6) obtained for S and T (Bär et al., 2012).
- *Minimum Bayes Retrieval Risk* {*0, 4*}: Calculates the translation probability for the translation having the minimum Bayes risk among the retrieved training instances.
- *Sentence Translation Performance* {*0, 3*}: Calculates translation scores obtained according to $q(T, R)$ using BLEU (Papineni et al., 2002), NIST (Doddington, 2002), or F_1 (Biçici and Yuret, 2011b) for q.
- *LIX* {*1, 1*}: Calculates the LIX readability score (Wikipedia, 2013; Björnsson, 1968) for S and T. [1]

For Task 1.1, we have additionally used comparative BLEU, NIST, and F_1 scores as additional features, which are obtained by comparing the translations with each other and averaging the result (Biçici, 2011).

2.3 Bracketing Tree Structural Features

We use the parse tree outputs obtained by CCL to derive features based on the bracketing structure. We derive 5 statistics based on the geometric properties of the parse trees: number of brackets used (numB), depth (depthB), average depth (avg depthB), number of brackets on the right branches over the number of brackets on the left (R/L) [2], average right to left branching over all internal tree nodes (avg R/L). The ratio of the number of right to left branches shows the degree to which the sentence is right branching or not. Additionally, we capture the different types of branching present in a given parse tree identified by the number of nodes in each of its children.

Table 1 depicts the parsing output obtained by CCL for the following sentence from WSJ23 [3]:

Many fund managers argue that now 's the time to buy .

We use Tregex (Levy and Andrew, 2006) for visualizing the output parse trees presented on the left. The bracketing structure statistics and features are given on the right hand side. The root node of each tree structural feature represents the number of times that feature is present in the parsing output of a document.

3 RTM in the Quality Estimation Task

We participate in all of the four challenges of the quality estimation task (QET) (Bojar et al., 2014), which include English to Spanish (en-es), Spanish to English (es-en), English to German (en-de), and German to English (de-en) translation directions. There are two main categories of challenges: sentence-level prediction (Task 1.*) and

[1] LIX=$\frac{A}{B} + C\frac{100}{A}$, where A is the number of words, C is words longer than 6 characters, B is words that start or end with any of ".", ":", "!", "?" similar to (Hagström, 2012).

[2] For nodes with uneven number of children, the nodes in the odd child contribute to the right branches.

[3] Wall Street Journal (WSJ) corpus section 23, distributed with Penn Treebank version 3 (Marcus et al., 1993).

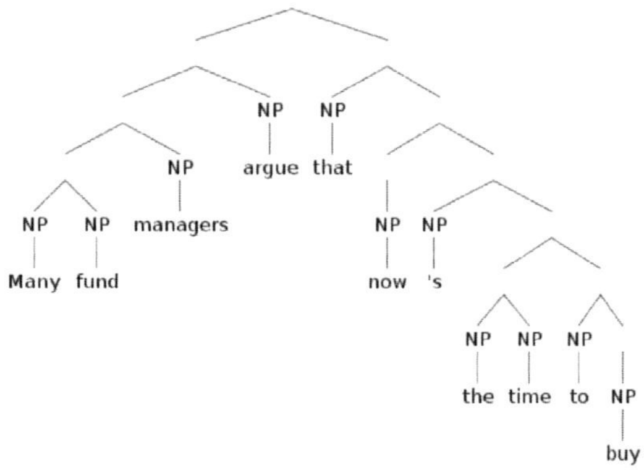

		CCL		
numB	depthB	avg depthB	R/L	avg R/L
24.0	9.0	0.375	2.1429	3.401

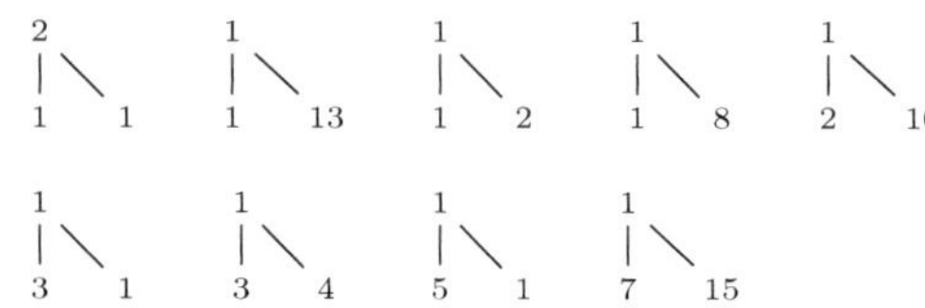

Table 1: Tree features for a parsing output by CCL (immediate non-terminals replaced with NP).

word-level prediction (Task 2). Task 1.1 is about predicting post-editing effort (PEE), Task 1.2 is about predicting HTER (human-targeted translation edit rate) (Snover et al., 2006) scores of translations, Task 1.3 is about predicting post-editing time (PET), and Task 2 is about binary, ternary, or multi-class classification of word-level quality.

For each task, we develop individual RTM models using the parallel corpora and the LM corpora distributed by the translation task (WMT14) (Bojar et al., 2014) and the LM corpora provided by LDC for English (Parker et al., 2011) and Spanish (Ângelo Mendonça, 2011) [4]. The parallel corpora contain 4.5M sentences for de-en with 110M words for de and 116M words for en and 15.1M sentences for en-es with 412M words for en and 462M words for es. We do not use any resources provided by QET including data, software, or baseline features. Instance selection for the training set and the language model (LM) corpus is handled by parallel FDA5 (Biçici et al., 2014), whose parameters are optimized for each translation task. LM are trained using SRILM (Stolcke, 2002). We tokenize and true-case all of the corpora. The true-caser is trained on all of the available training corpus using Moses (Koehn et al., 2007). Table 2 lists the number of sentences in the training and test sets for each task.

Task	Train	Test
Task 1.1 (en-es)	3816	600
Task 1.1 (es-en)	1050	450
Task 1.1 (en-de)	1400	600
Task 1.1 (de-en)	1050	450
Task 1.2 (en-es)	896	208
Task 1.3 (en-es)	650	208
Task 2 (en-es)	1957	382
Task 2 (es-en)	900	150
Task 2 (en-de)	715	150
Task 2 (de-en)	350	100

Table 2: Number of sentences in different tasks.

For each task or subtask, we select 375 thousand (K) training instances from the available parallel training corpora as interpretants for the individual RTM models using parallel FDA5. We add the selected training set to the 3 million (M) sentences selected from the available monolingual corpora for each LM corpus. The statistics of the training data selected by and used as interpretants in the RTM models is given in Table 3. The details of instance selection with parallel FDA5 are provided in (Biçici et al., 2014).

Task	S	T
Task 1.1 (en-es)	6.2	6.9
Task 1.1 (es-en)	7.9	7.4
Task 1.1 (en-de)	6.1	6
Task 1.1 (de-en)	6.9	6.4
Task 1.2 (en-es)	6.1	6.7
Task 1.3 (en-es)	6.2	6.8
Task 2 (en-es)	6.2	6.8
Task 2 (es-en)	7.5	7
Task 2 (en-de)	5.9	5.9
Task 2 (de-en)	6.3	6.8

Table 3: Number of words in $\mathcal{I}$ (in millions) selected for each task (S for source, T for target).

3.1 Learning Models and Optimization:

We use ridge regression (RR), support vector regression (SVR) with RBF (radial basis functions) kernel (Smola and Schölkopf, 2004), and ex-

[4] English Gigaword 5th, Spanish Gigaword 3rd edition.

Task	Translation	Model	r	RMSE	MAE	RAE
Task1.1	es-en	FS-RR	0.3512	0.6394	0.5319	0.9114
	es-en	PLS-RR	0.3579	0.6746	0.5488	0.9405
	en-de	PLS-TREE	0.2922	0.7496	0.6223	0.9404
	en-de	TREE	0.2845	0.7485	0.6241	0.9431
	en-es	TREE	0.4485	0.619	0.45	0.9271
	en-es	PLS-TREE	0.4354	0.6213	0.4723	0.973
	de-en	RR	0.3415	0.7475	0.6245	0.9653
	de-en	PLS-RR	0.3561	0.7711	0.6236	0.9639
Task1.2	en-es	SVR	0.4769	0.203	0.1378	0.8443
	en-es	TREE	0.4708	0.2031	0.1372	0.8407
Task1.3	en-es	SVR	0.6974	21543	14866	0.6613
	en-es	RR	0.6991	21226	15325	0.6817

Table 4: Training performance of the top 2 individual RTM models prepared for different tasks.

tremely randomized trees (TREE) (Geurts et al., 2006) as the learning models. TREE is an ensemble learning method over randomized decision trees. These models learn a regression function using the features to estimate a numerical target value. We also use these learning models after a feature subset selection with recursive feature elimination (RFE) (Guyon et al., 2002) or a dimensionality reduction and mapping step using partial least squares (PLS) (Specia et al., 2009), both of which are described in (Biçici et al., 2013). We optimize the learning parameters, the number of features to select, the number of dimensions used for PLS, and the parameters for parallel FDA5. More detailed descriptions of the optimization processes are given in (Biçici et al., 2013; Biçici et al., 2014). We optimize the learning parameters by selecting ε close to the standard deviation of the noise in the training set (Biçici, 2013) since the optimal value for ε is shown to have linear dependence to the noise level for different noise models (Smola et al., 1998). We select the top 2 systems according to their performance on the training set. For Task 2, we use both Global Linear Models (GLM) (Collins, 2002) and GLM with dynamic learning (GLMd) we developed last year (Biçici, 2013). GLM relies on Viterbi decoding, perceptron learning, and flexible feature definitions. GLMd extends the GLM framework by parallel perceptron training (McDonald et al., 2010) and dynamic learning with adaptive weight updates in the perceptron learning algorithm:

$$\mathbf{w} = \mathbf{w} + \alpha \left(\Phi(\mathbf{x}_i, \mathbf{y}_i) - \Phi(\mathbf{x}_i, \hat{\mathbf{y}}) \right), \quad (1)$$

where Φ returns a global representation for instance i and the weights are updated by α, which dynamically decays the amount of the change during weight updates at later stages and prevents large fluctuations with updates.

3.2 Training Results

We use mean absolute error (MAE), relative absolute error (RAE), root mean squared error (RMSE), and correlation (r) to evaluate (Biçici, 2013). DeltaAvg (Callison-Burch et al., 2012) calculates the average quality difference between the top $n-1$ quartiles and the overall quality for the test set. Table 4 provides the training results.

3.3 Test Results

Task 1.1: Predicting the Post-Editing Effort for Sentence Translations: Task 1.1 is about predicting post-editing effort (PEE) and their ranking. The results on the test set are given in Table 5 where QuEst (Shah et al., 2013) SVR lists the baseline system results. Rank lists the overall ranking in the task out of about 10 submissions. We obtain the rankings by sorting according to the predicted scores and randomly assigning ranks in case of ties. RTMs with SVR PLS learning is able to achieve the top rank in this task.

Task 1.2: Predicting HTER of Sentence Translations Task 1.2 is about predicting HTER (human-targeted translation edit rate) (Snover et al., 2006), where case insensitive translation edit rate (TER) scores obtained by TERp (Snover et al., 2009) and their ranking. We derive features over sentences that are true-cased. The results on the test set are given in Table 6 where the ranks are out of about 11 submissions. We are also able to achieve the top ranking in this task.

Ranking Translations		DeltaAvg	r	Rank
en-es	TREE	0.26	-0.41	1
	PLS-TREE	0.26	-0.38	2
	QuEst SVR	0.14	-0.22	
es-en	PLS-RR	0.20	-0.35	2
	FS-RR	0.19	-0.36	3
	QuEst SVR	0.12	-0.21	
en-de	TREE	0.39	-0.54	1
	PLS-TREE	0.33	-0.42	2
	QuEst SVR	0.23	-0.34	
de-en	RR	0.38	-0.51	1
	PLS-RR	0.35	-0.45	2
	QuEst SVR	0.21	-0.25	
Scoring Translations		**MAE**	**RMSE**	**Rank**
en-es	TREE	0.49	0.61	1
	PLS-TREE	0.49	0.61	2
	QuEst SVR	0.52	0.66	
es-en	FS-RR	0.53	0.64	1
	PLS-RR	0.55	0.71	2
	QuEst SVR	0.57	0.68	
en-de	TREE	0.58	0.68	1
	PLS-TREE	0.60	0.71	2
	QuEst SVR	0.64	0.76	
de-en	RR	0.55	0.67	1
	PLS-RR	0.57	0.74	2
	QuEst SVR	0.65	0.78	

Table 5: RTM-DCU Task1.1 results on the test set and baseline results.

Ranking Translations		DeltaAvg	r	Rank
en-es	SVR	9.31	0.53	1
	TREE	8.57	0.48	2
	QuEst SVR	5.08	0.31	
Scoring Translations		**MAE**	**RMSE**	**Rank**
en-es	SVR	13.40	16.69	2
	TREE	14.03	17.48	4
	QuEst SVR	15.23	19.48	

Table 6: RTM-DCU Task1.2 results on the test set and baseline results.

Task 1.3: Predicting Post-Editing Time for Sentence Translations Task 1.3 involves the prediction of the post-editing time (PET) for a translator to post-edit the MT output. The results on the test set are given in Table 7 where the ranks are out of about 10 submissions. RTMs become the top in all metrics with RR and SVR learning models.

Task 2: Prediction of Word-level Translation Quality Task 2 is about binary, ternary, or multi-class classification of word-level quality. We develop individual RTM models for each subtask and use the GLM and GLMd learning models (Biçici, 2013), for predicting the quality at the word-level. The features used are similar to last year's (Biçici, 2013) and broadly categorized as CCL links, word context based on surrounding words, word alignments, word lengths, word locations, word prefixes and suffixes, and word forms (i.e. capital, contains digit or punctuation).

Ranking Translations		DeltaAvg	r	Rank
en-es	RR	17.02	0.68	1
	SVR	16.60	0.67	2
	QuEst SVR	14.71	0.57	
Scoring Translations		**MAE**	**RMSE**	**Rank**
en-es	SVR	16.77	26.17	1
	RR	17.50	25.97	7
	QuEst SVR	21.49	34.28	

Table 7: RTM-DCU Task1.3 results on the test set and baseline results.

The results on the test set are given in Table 8 where the ranks are out of about 8 submissions. RTMs with GLM or GLMd learning becomes the top this task as well.

	Model	Binary		Ternary		Multi-class	
		wF_1	Rank	wF_1	Rank	wF_1	Rank
en-es	GLM	0.351	6	0.299	5	0.268	1
	GLMd	0.329	7	0.266	6	0.032	7
es-en	GLM	0.269	2	0.220	2	0.087	1
	GLMd	0.291	1	0.239	1	0.082	2
en-de	GLM	0.453	1	0.211	2	0.150	1
	GLMd	0.369	2	0.219	1	0.125	2
en-es	GLM	0.261	1	0.083	2	0.024	2
	GLMd	0.230	2	0.086	1	0.031	1

Table 8: RTM-DCU Task 2 results on the test set. wF_1 is the average weighted F_1 score.

3.4 RTMs Across Tasks and Years

We compare the difficulty of tasks according to the RAE levels achieved. RAE measures the error relative to the error when predicting the actual mean. A high RAE is an indicator that the task is hard. In Table 9, we list the test results including the RAE obtained for different tasks and subtasks including RTM results at QET13 (Biçici, 2013). The best results are obtained for Task 1.3, which shows that we can only reduce the error with respect to knowing and predicting the mean by about 28%.

4 Conclusion

Referential translation machines achieve top performance in automatic, accurate, and language independent prediction of sentence-level and word-level statistical machine translation (SMT) quality. RTMs remove the need to access any SMT system specific information or prior knowledge of the training data or models used when generating the translations.

Task	Translation	Model	r	RMSE	MAE	RAE
Task1.1	es-en	FS-RR	0.3285	0.6373	0.5308	0.9
	es-en	PLS-RR	0.3105	0.7124	0.5549	0.9409
	en-de	PLS-TREE	0.4427	0.7091	0.6028	0.8883
	en-de	TREE	0.5256	0.6788	0.5838	0.8602
	en-es	TREE	0.4087	0.6114	0.4938	1.0983
	en-es	PLS-TREE	0.4163	0.6084	0.4852	1.0794
	de-en	RR	0.5399	0.6735	0.5513	0.8204
	de-en	PLS-RR	0.4878	0.737	0.567	0.8437
Task1.2	en-es	SVR	0.5499	0.1669	0.134	0.8532
	en-es	TREE	0.5175	0.1748	0.1403	0.8931
Task1.3	en-es	SVR	0.6336	26174	16770	0.7223
	en-es	RR	0.6359	25966	17496	0.7536
QET13 Task1.1	en-es	PLS-SVR	0.5596	0.1683	0.1326	0.8849
		SVR	0.5082	0.1728	0.1385	0.924
QET13 Task1.3	en-es	PLS-SVR	0.6752	86.62	49.62	0.6919
		SVR	0.6682	90.36	49.21	0.6862

Table 9: Test performance of the top 2 individual RTM models prepared for different tasks and RTM results from QET13 on similar tasks (Biçici, 2013).

Acknowledgments

This work is supported in part by SFI (07/CE/I1142) as part of the CNGL Centre for Global Intelligent Content (www.cngl.org) at Dublin City University and in part by the European Commission through the QTLaunchPad FP7 project (No: 296347). We also thank the SFI/HEA Irish Centre for High-End Computing (ICHEC) for the provision of computational facilities and support.

References

Eneko Agirre, Carmen Banea, Claire Cardie, Daniel Cer, Mona Diab, Aitor Gonzalez-Agirre, Weiwei Guo, Rada Mihalcea, German Rigau, and Janyce Wiebe. 2014. SemEval-2014 Task 10: Multilingual semantic textual similarity. In *Proceedings of the 8th International Workshop on Semantic Evaluation (SemEval-2014)*, Dublin, Ireland, August.

Daniel Bär, Chris Biemann, Iryna Gurevych, and Torsten Zesch. 2012. Ukp: Computing semantic textual similarity by combining multiple content similarity measures. In **SEM 2012: The First Joint Conference on Lexical and Computational Semantics – Volume 1: Proceedings of the main conference and the shared task, and Volume 2: Proceedings of the Sixth International Workshop on Semantic Evaluation (SemEval 2012)*, pages 435–440, Montréal, Canada, 7-8 June. Association for Computational Linguistics.

Ergun Biçici and Andy Way. 2014. RTM-DCU: Referential translation machines for semantic similarity. In *SemEval-2014: Semantic Evaluation Exercises - International Workshop on Semantic Evaluation*, Dublin, Ireland, 23-24 August.

Ergun Biçici and Deniz Yuret. 2011a. Instance selection for machine translation using feature decay algorithms. In *Proceedings of the Sixth Workshop on Statistical Machine Translation*, pages 272–283, Edinburgh, Scotland, July. Association for Computational Linguistics.

Ergun Biçici and Deniz Yuret. 2011b. RegMT system for machine translation, system combination, and evaluation. In *Proceedings of the Sixth Workshop on Statistical Machine Translation*, pages 323–329, Edinburgh, Scotland, July. Association for Computational Linguistics.

Ergun Biçici and Deniz Yuret. 2014. Optimizing instance selection for statistical machine translation with feature decay algorithms. *IEEE/ACM Transactions On Audio, Speech, and Language Processing (TASLP)*.

Ergun Biçici, Declan Groves, and Josef van Genabith. 2013. Predicting sentence translation quality using extrinsic and language independent features. *Machine Translation*, 27:171–192, December.

Ergun Biçici, Qun Liu, and Andy Way. 2014. Parallel FDA5 for fast deployment of accurate statistical machine translation systems. In *Proceedings of the Ninth Workshop on Statistical Machine Translation*, Baltimore, USA, June. Association for Computational Linguistics.

Ergun Biçici. 2011. *The Regression Model of Machine Translation*. Ph.D. thesis, Koç University. Supervisor: Deniz Yuret.

Ergun Biçici. 2013. Referential translation machines for quality estimation. In *Proceedings of the Eighth Workshop on Statistical Machine Translation*, Sofia, Bulgaria, August. Association for Computational Linguistics.

Ergun Biçici. 2008. Consensus ontologies in socially interacting multiagent systems. *Journal of Multiagent and Grid Systems*.

Carl Hugo Björnsson. 1968. *Läsbarhet*. Liber.

Chris Bliss. 2012. Comedy is translation, February. http://www.ted.com/talks/chris_bliss_comedy_is_translation.html.

Ondřej Bojar, Christian Buck, Chris Callison-Burch, Christian Federmann, Barry Haddow, Philipp Koehn, Christof Monz, Matt Post, Radu Soricut, and Lucia Specia. 2013. Findings of the 2013 Workshop on Statistical Machine Translation. In *Proc. of the Eighth Workshop on Statistical Machine Translation*, pages 1–44, Sofia, Bulgaria, August. Association for Computational Linguistics.

Ondřej Bojar, Christian Buck, Christian Federmann, Barry Haddow, Philipp Koehn, Matouš Macháček, Christof Monz, Pavel Pecina, Matt Post, Herve Saint-Amand, Radu Soricut, and Lucia Specia. 2014. Findings of the 2014 workshop on statistical machine translation. In *Proc. of the Ninth Workshop on Statistical Machine Translation*, Balrimore, USA, June. Association for Computational Linguistics.

Peter F. Brown, Stephen A. Della Pietra, Vincent J. Della Pietra, and Robert L. Mercer. 1993. The mathematics of statistical machine translation: Parameter estimation. *Computational Linguistics*, 19(2):263–311, June.

Chris Callison-Burch, Philipp Koehn, Christof Monz, Matt Post, Radu Soricut, and Lucia Specia. 2012. Findings of the 2012 workshop on statistical machine translation. In *Proc. of the Seventh Workshop on Statistical Machine Translation*, pages 10–51, Montréal, Canada, June. Association for Computational Linguistics.

José Guilherme Camargo de Souza, Christian Buck, Marco Turchi, and Matteo Negri. 2013. FBK-UEdin participation to the WMT13 quality estimation shared task. In *Proceedings of the Eighth Workshop on Statistical Machine Translation*, pages 352–358, Sofia, Bulgaria, August. Association for Computational Linguistics.

Michael Collins. 2002. Discriminative training methods for hidden markov models: theory and experiments with perceptron algorithms. In *Proceedings of the ACL-02 conference on Empirical methods in natural language processing - Volume 10*, EMNLP '02, pages 1–8, Stroudsburg, PA, USA. Association for Computational Linguistics.

George Doddington. 2002. Automatic evaluation of machine translation quality using n-gram co-occurrence statistics. In *Proceedings of the second international conference on Human Language Technology Research*, pages 138–145, San Francisco, CA, USA. Morgan Kaufmann Publishers Inc.

Pierre Geurts, Damien Ernst, and Louis Wehenkel. 2006. Extremely randomized trees. *Machine Learning*, 63(1):3–42.

Isabelle Guyon, Jason Weston, Stephen Barnhill, and Vladimir Vapnik. 2002. Gene selection for cancer classification using support vector machines. *Machine Learning*, 46(1-3):389–422.

Kenth Hagström. 2012. Swedish readability calculator. https://github.com/keha76/Swedish-Readability-Calculator.

David Jurgens, Mohammad Taher Pilehvar, and Roberto Navigli. 2014. SemEval-2014 Task 3: Cross-level semantic similarity. In *Proceedings of the 8th International Workshop on Semantic Evaluation (SemEval-2014)*, Dublin, Ireland, August.

Philipp Koehn, Hieu Hoang, Alexandra Birch, Chris Callison-Burch, Marcello Federico, Nicola Bertoldi, Brooke Cowan, Wade Shen, Christine Moran, Richard Zens, Chris Dyer, Ondrej Bojar, Alexandra Constantin, and Evan Herbst. 2007. Moses: Open source toolkit for statistical machine translation. In *ACL*, pages 177–180, Prague, Czech Republic, June.

Roger Levy and Galen Andrew. 2006. Tregex and Tsurgeon: tools for querying and manipulating tree data structures. In *Proceedings of the fifth international conference on Language Resources and Evaluation*.

Mitchell P. Marcus, Mary Ann Marcinkiewicz, and Beatrice Santorini. 1993. Building a large annotated corpus of english: the penn treebank. *Comput. Linguist.*, 19(2):313–330, June.

Marco Marelli, Stefano Menini, Marco Baroni, Luisa Bentivogli, Raffaella Bernardi, and Roberto Zamparelli. 2014. SemEval-2014 Task 1: Evaluation of compositional distributional semantic models on full sentences through semantic relatedness and textual entailment. In *Proceedings of the 8th International Workshop on Semantic Evaluation (SemEval-2014)*, Dublin, Ireland, August.

Ryan McDonald, Keith Hall, and Gideon Mann. 2010. Distributed training strategies for the structured perceptron. In *Human Language Technologies: The 2010 Annual Conference of the North American Chapter of the Association for Computational Linguistics*, pages 456–464, Los Angeles, California, June. Association for Computational Linguistics.

Kishore Papineni, Salim Roukos, Todd Ward, and Wei-Jing Zhu. 2002. BLEU: a method for automatic evaluation of machine translation. In *Proc. of 40th Annual Meeting of the Association for Computational Linguistics*, pages 311–318, Philadelphia, Pennsylvania, USA, July. Association for Computational Linguistics.

Robert Parker, David Graff, Junbo Kong, Ke Chen, and Kazuaki Maeda. 2011. English Gigaword fifth edition, Linguistic Data Consortium.

Yoav Seginer. 2007. *Learning Syntactic Structure*. Ph.D. thesis, Universiteit van Amsterdam.

Kashif Shah, Eleftherios Avramidis, Ergun Biçici, and Lucia Specia. 2013. Quest - design, implementation and extensions of a framework for machine translation quality estimation. *Prague Bull. Math. Linguistics*, 100:19–30.

Alex J. Smola and Bernhard Schölkopf. 2004. A tutorial on support vector regression. *Statistics and Computing*, 14(3):199–222, August.

A. J. Smola, N. Murata, B. Schölkopf, and K.-R. Müller. 1998. Asymptotically optimal choice of ε-loss for support vector machines. In L. Niklasson, M. Boden, and T. Ziemke, editors, *Proceedings of the International Conference on Artificial Neural Networks*, Perspectives in Neural Computing, pages 105–110, Berlin. Springer.

Matthew Snover, Bonnie Dorr, Richard Schwartz, Linnea Micciulla, and John Makhoul. 2006. A Study of Translation Edit Rate with Targeted Human Annotation. In *Proceedings of Association for Machine Translation in the Americas,*.

Matthew Snover, Nitin Madnani, Bonnie J. Dorr, and Richard Schwartz. 2009. Fluency, adequacy, or hter?: exploring different human judgments with a tunable mt metric. In *Proceedings of the Fourth Workshop on Statistical Machine Translation*, StatMT '09, pages 259–268, Stroudsburg, PA, USA. Association for Computational Linguistics.

Lucia Specia, Nicola Cancedda, Marc Dymetman, Marco Turchi, and Nello Cristianini. 2009. Estimating the sentence-level quality of machine translation systems. In *Proceedings of the 13th Annual Conference of the European Association for Machine Translation (EAMT)*, pages 28–35, Barcelona, May. EAMT.

Andreas Stolcke. 2002. Srilm - an extensible language modeling toolkit. In *Proc. Intl. Conf. on Spoken Language Processing*, pages 901–904.

Wikipedia. 2013. Lix. http://en.wikipedia.org/wiki/LIX.

David Graff Denise DiPersio Ângelo Mendonça, Daniel Jaquette. 2011. Spanish Gigaword third edition, Linguistic Data Consortium.

FBK-UPV-UEdin participation in the WMT14 Quality Estimation shared-task

José G. C. de Souza* University of Trento Fondazione Bruno Kessler Trento, Italy desouza@fbk.eu

Jesús González-Rubio* PRHLT Group U. Politècnica de València Valencia, Spain jegonzalez@prhlt.upv.es

Christian Buck* University of Edinburgh School of Informatics Edinburgh, Scotland, UK cbuck@lantis.de

Marco Turchi, Matteo Negri Fondazione Bruno Kessler turchi,negri@fbk.eu

Abstract

This paper describes the joint submission of Fondazione Bruno Kessler, Universitat Politècnica de València and University of Edinburgh to the Quality Estimation tasks of the Workshop on Statistical Machine Translation 2014. We present our submissions for Task 1.2, 1.3 and 2. Our systems ranked first for Task 1.2 and for the Binary and Level1 settings in Task 2.

1 Introduction

Quality Estimation (QE) for Machine Translation (MT) is the task of evaluating the quality of the output of an MT system without reference translations. Within the WMT 2014 QE Shared Task four evaluation tasks were proposed, covering both word and sentence level QE. In this work we describe the Fondazione Bruno Kessler (FBK), Universitat Politècnica de València (UPV) and University of Edinburgh (UEdin) approach and system setup for the shared task.

We developed models for two sentence-level tasks: Task 1.2, scoring for post-editing effort, and Task 1.3, predicting post-editing time, and for all word-level variants of Task 2, binary and multiclass classification. As opposed to previous editions of the shared task, this year the participants were not supplied with the MT system that was used to produce the translation. Furthermore no system-internal features were provided. Thus, while the trained models are tuned to detect the errors of a specific system the features have to be generated independently (black-box).

2 Sentence Level QE

We submitted runs to two sentence-level tasks: Task 1.2 and Task 1.3. The first task aims at predicting the Human mediated Translation Edit Rate (HTER) (Snover et al., 2006) between a suggestion generated by a machine translation system and its manually post-edited version. The data set contains 1,104 English-Spanish sentence pairs post-edited by one translator (896 for training and 208 for test). The second task requires to predict the time, in milliseconds, that was required to post edit a translation given by a machine translation system. Participants are provided with 858 English-Spanish sentence pairs, source and suggestion, along with their respective post-edited sentence and post-editing time in seconds (650 data points for training and 208 for test). We participated in the scoring mode of both tasks.

2.1 Features

For our sentence-level submissions we compute features using different resources that do not use the MT system internals. We use the same set of features for both Task 1.2 and 1.3.

QuEst Black-box features (quest79). We extract 79 black-box features that capture the complexity, fluency and adequacy aspects of the QE problem. These features are extracted using the implementation provided by the QuEst framework (Specia et al., 2013). Among them are the 17 baseline features provided by the task organizers.

The **complexity** features are computed on the source sentence and indicate the complexity of translating the segment. Examples of these features are the language model (LM) probabilities of the source sentence computed in a corpus of the source language, different surface counts like the number of punctuation marks and the number of tokens in the source sentence, among others.

The **fluency** features are computed over the translation generated by the MT system and indicate how fluent the translation is in the target

*Contributed equally to this work.

Proceedings of the Ninth Workshop on Statistical Machine Translation, pages 322–328, Baltimore, Maryland USA, June 26–27, 2014.

language. One example would again be the LM probability of the translation given by a LM model trained on a corpus of the target language. Another example is the average number of occurrences of the target word within the target segment.

The third aspect covered by the QuEst features is the **adequacy** of the translation with respect to the source sentence, i.e., how the meaning of the source is preserved in the translation. Examples of features are the ratio of nouns, verbs and adjectives in the source and in the translation. For a more detailed description of the features in this group please refer to (Specia et al., 2013).

Word alignment (wla). Following our last year's submission (de Souza et al., 2013a) we explore information about word alignments to extract quantitative (amount and distribution of the alignments) and qualitative features (importance of the aligned terms). Our assumption is that features that explore what is aligned can bring improvements to tasks where sentence-level semantic relations need to be identified. We train the word alignment models with the MGIZA++ toolkit (Gao and Vogel, 2008) implementation of the IBM models (Brown et al., 1993). The models are built on the concatenation of Europarl, News Commentary, and MultiUN parallel corpora made available in the QE shared task of 2013, comprising about 12.8 million sentence pairs. A more detailed description of the 89 features extracted can be found in (de Souza et al., 2013a; de Souza et al., 2013b).

Word Posterior Probabilities (wpp). Using an external SMT system we produce 100k-best lists from which we derive Word Posterior Probabilities as detailed in Subsection 3.1.

We use the geometric mean of these probabilities to derive a sentence-level score.

Because the system that we use to produce the N-best list is not the same that generated the suggestions some suggested words never appear in the N-best list and thus receive zero probability. To overcome this issue we first clip the WPPs to a minimum probability. Using a small sample of the data to estimate this number we arrive at:

$$\log(p)_{min} = -2.$$

N-best diversity (div). Using the same 100k-best list as above we extract a number of measures that grasp the spatial distribution of hypotheses in the search space as described in (de Souza et al., 2013a).

Word Prediction (wpred). We introduce the use of the predictions provided by the word-level QE system described in Section 3 to leverage information for the sentence-level tasks. We combine the **binary** word-level predictions in different ways, with the objective of measuring the fluency of the translation in a more fine-grained way. We target a quantitative aspect of the words by computing ratios of `OK` or `BAD` predictions. Furthermore, we also explore a qualitative aspect by calculating ratios of different classes of words given by their part-of-speech tags, indicating the quality of distinct meaningful regions that compose the translation sentence. In total, we compute 18 features:

- number of `OK` predictions divided by the no. of words in the translation sentence (1 feature);
- number of `OK` function/content words predictions divided by the no. of function/content words in the translation (2 features);
- number of `OK` nouns, verbs, proper-nouns, adjective, pronouns predictions divided by the total nouns, verbs, proper-nouns, adjective, pronouns (5 features);
- size of the longest sequence of `OK`/`BAD` word predictions divided by the total number of `OK`/`BAD` predictions in the translation (2 features);
- number of `OK` predicted n-grams divided by the total number of n-grams in the translation. We vary n from 2 to 5 (4 features);
- number of words predicted as `OK` in the first/second half of the translation divided by the total number of words in the first/second half of the translation (2 features).
- number of words predicted as `OK` in the first/second quarter of the translation divided by the total number of words in the first/second quarter of the translation (2 features).

For some instances of the sentence-level tasks we were not able to produce word-level predictions due to an incomplete overlap between the word-level and sentence-level tasks datasets. For such data points we use the median of the feature column for Task 1.2 and the mean for Task 1.3.

Method	Features	Train T1.2	Train T1.3	Test T1.2	Test T1.3
SVR	baseline	16.90	16864	15.23	21490
ET	baseline	16.25	17888	17.73	19400
ET	quest79 + wla + wpp	15.62	17474	14.44	18658
ET	quest79 + wla + wpp + div[2]	15.57	17471	14.38	18693
ET	quest79 + wla + wpp + div + wpred[1]	15.05	16392	12.89	17477

Table 1: Training and test results for Task 1.2 and 1.3. Scores are the MAE on a development set randomly sampled from the training data (20%). Baseline features were provided by the shared task organizers. We used Support Vector Machines (SVM) regression to train the baseline models (first row). Submissions are marked with [1] and [2] for primary and secondary, respectively.

2.2 Experimental Setup

We build the sentence-level models for both tasks (T1.2 and T1.3) with the features described in Section 2.1 using one learning algorithm: extremely randomized trees (ET) (Geurts et al., 2006). ET is an ensemble of randomized trees in which each decision tree can be parameterized differently. When a tree is built, the node splitting step is done at random by picking the best split among a random subset of the input features. All the trees are grown on the whole training set and the results of the individual trees are combined by averaging their predictions. The models produced by this method demonstrated to be robust to a large number of input features. For our experiments and submissions we used the ET implementation included in the Scikit-learn library (Pedregosa et al., 2011).

During training we evaluate the models on a development set. The development set was obtained by randomly sampling 20% of the training data. The remaining 80% were used for training. The training process was carried out by optimizing the ET hyper-parameters with 100 iterations of random search optimization (Bergstra and Bengio, 2012) set to minimize the mean absolute error (MAE)[1] on 10-fold cross-validation over the training data. The ET hyper-parameters optimized are: the number of decision trees in the ensemble, the maximum number of features to consider when looking for the best split, the maximum depth of the trees used in the ensembles, the minimal number of samples required to split a node of the tree, and the minimum number of samples in newly created leaves. For the final submissions we run the random search with 1000 iterations over the whole training dataset.

2.3 Results

We train models on different combinations of feature groups (described in Section 2.1). Experiments results are summarized in Table 1. We have results with baseline features for both SVR and the ET models. For Task 1.2, adding features from different groups leads to increasing improvements. The combination of the *quest79*, *wla* and *wpp* groups outperforms the SVR baseline for Task 1.2 but not for Task 1.3. However, when compared to the ET model trained with the baseline features, it is possible to observe improvements with this group of features. In addition, adding the *div* group on top of the previous three leads to marginal improvements for both tasks. The best feature combination is given when adding the features based on the word-level predictions, configuring the combination of all the feature groups together (a total of 221 features). For both tasks this is our primary submission. The contrastive run for both tasks is the best feature group combination without the word-prediction-based features, *quest79*, *wla*, *wpp* and *div* for Task 1.2 and *quest79*, *wla*, *wpp* for Task 1.3.

Results on the test set can be found in the two last columns of Table 1 and are in line with what we found in the training phase. The rows that do not correspond to the official submissions and that are reported on the test set are experiments done after the evaluation phase. For both tasks the improvements increase as we add features on top of the baseline feature set and the best performance is reached when using the word prediction features with all the other features. The SVR baselines performance are the official numbers provided by the organizers. For Task 1.2 our primary submission achieves a MAE score lower than the score achieved during the training phase, showing that the model is robust. For Task 1.3, however, we do not observe such trend. Even though

[1]Given by $MAE = \frac{\sum_{i=1}^{N} |H(s_i) - V(s_i)|}{N}$, where $H(s_i)$ is the hypothesis score for the entry s_i and $V(s_i)$ is the gold standard value for s_i in a dataset with N entries.

the primary submission for this task consistently improves over the other feature combinations, it does not outperform the score obtained during the training phase. This might be explained due to the difference in the distribution between training and test labels. In Task 1.2 the two distributions are more similar than in Task 1.3, which presents slightly different distributions between training and test data.

3 Word-Level QE

Task 2 is the word-level quality estimation of automatically translated news sentences without given reference translations. Participants are required to produce a label for each word in one or more of the following settings:

Binary classification: a `OK/BAD` label, where `BAD` indicates the need for editing the word.

Level1 classification: `OK`, `Accuracy`, or `Fluency` label specifying a coarser level of errors for each word, or `OK` for words with no error.

Multi-Class classification: one of the 20 error labels described in the shared-task description or `OK` for words with no error.

We submit word-level quality estimations for the English-Spanish translation direction. The corpus contains 1957 training sentences for a total of 47411 Spanish words, and 382 test sentences for a total of 9613 words.

3.1 Features

Word Posterior Probabilities (WPP) In order to generate an approximation of the decoder's search space as well as an N-best list of possible translations we re-translate the source using the system that is available for the 2013 WMT QE Shared Task (Bojar et al., 2013).

Certainly, there is a mismatch between the original system and the one that we used but, since our system was trained using the same news domain as the QE data, we assume that both face similar ambiguous words or possible reorderings. Using this system we generate a 100k-best list which is the foundation of several features.

We extract a set of word-level features based on posterior probabilities computed over N-best lists as proposed by previous works (Blatz et al., 2004; Ueffing and Ney, 2007; Sanchis et al., 2007).

Consider a target word e_i belonging to a translation $\mathbf{e} = e_1 \ldots e_i \ldots e_{|\mathbf{e}|}$ generated from a source sentence $\mathbf{f}$. Let $\mathcal{N}(\mathbf{f})$ be the list of N-best translations for $\mathbf{f}$. We compute features as the normalized sum of probabilities of those translations $\mathcal{S}(e_i) \subseteq \mathcal{N}(\mathbf{f})$ that "contain" word e_i:

$$\frac{1}{\sum_{\mathbf{e}'' \in \mathcal{N}(\mathbf{f})} \mathrm{P}(\mathbf{e}'' \mid \mathbf{f})} \sum_{\mathbf{e}' \in \mathcal{S}(e_i)} \mathrm{P}(\mathbf{e}' \mid \mathbf{f}) \quad (1)$$

where $\mathrm{P}(\mathbf{e} \mid \mathbf{f})$ is the probability translation $\mathbf{e}$ given source sentence $\mathbf{f}$ according to the SMT model.

We follow (Zens and Ney, 2006) and extract three different WPP features depending on the criteria chosen to compute $\mathcal{S}(e_i)$:

$\mathcal{S}(e_i) = \{\mathbf{e}' \in \mathcal{N}(\mathbf{f}) \mid \mathbf{a} = \mathrm{Le}(\mathbf{e}', \mathbf{e}) \wedge e'_{a_i} = e_i\}$

$\mathcal{S}(e_i)$ contain those translations $\mathbf{e}'$ for which the word Levenshtein-aligned (Levenshtein, 1966) to position i in $\mathbf{e}$ is equal to e_i.

$\mathcal{S}(e_i) = \{\mathbf{e}' \in \mathcal{N}(\mathbf{f}) \mid e'_i = e_i\}$

A second option is to select those translations $\mathbf{e}'$ that contain the word $\mathbf{e}_i$ at position i.

$\mathcal{S}(e_i) = \{\mathbf{e}' \in \mathcal{N}(\mathbf{f}) \mid \exists i' : e'_{i'} = e_i\}$

As third option, we select those translations $\mathbf{e}'$ that contain the word e_i, disregarding its position.

Confusion Networks (CN) We use the same N-best list used to compute the WPP features in the previous section to compute features based on the graph topology of confusion networks (Luong et al., 2014). First, we Levenshtein-align all translations in the N-best list using $\mathbf{e}$ as skeleton, and merge all of them into a confusion network. In this network, each word-edge is labelled with the posterior probability of the word. The output edges of each node define different *confusion sets* of words, each word belonging to one single confusion set. Each complete path passing through all nodes in the network represents one sentence in the N-best list, and must contain exactly one link from each confusion set. Looking to the confusion set which the hypothesis word belongs to, we extract four different features: maximum and minimum probability in the set (2 features), number of alternatives in the set (1 feature) and entropy of the alternatives in the set (1 feature).

Language Models (LM) As language model features we produced n-gram length/backoff behaviour and conditional probabilities for every word in the sentence. We employed both an interpolated LM taken from the MT system discussed in Section 3 as well as a very large LM which we built on 62 billion tokens of monolingual data extracted from Common Crawl, a public web crawl. While generally following the procedure of Buck et al. (2014) we apply an additional lowercasing step before training the model.

Word Lexicons (WL) We compute two different features based on statistical word lexicons (Blatz et al., 2004):

Avg. probability: $\frac{1}{|\mathbf{f}|+1}\sum_{j=0}^{|\mathbf{f}|}\mathrm{P}(e_i \mid f_j)$

Max. probability: $\max_{0\leq j\leq|\mathbf{f}|}\mathrm{P}(e_i \mid f_j)$

where $\mathrm{P}(e \mid f)$ is a probabilistic lexicon, and f_0 is the source "NULL" word (Brown et al., 1993).

POS tags (POS) We extract the part-of-speech (POS) tags for both source and translation sentences using TreeTagger (Schmid, 1994). We use the actual POS tag of the target word as a feature. Specifically, we represent it as a *one-hot* indicator vector where all values are equal to zero except the one representing the current tag of the word, which is set to one. Regarding the source POS tags, we first compute the lexical probability of each target word given each source word. Then, we compute two different feature vectors for each target word. On the one hand, we use an indicator vector to represent the POS tag of the maximum probability source word. On the other hand, we sum up the indicator vectors for all the source words each one weighted by the lexical probability of the corresponding word. As a result, we obtain a vector that represents the probability distribution of source POS tags for each target word. Additionally, we extract a binary feature that indicates whether the word is a *stop word* or not.[2]

Stacking (S) Finally, we also exploit the diverse granularity of the word labels. The word classes for the Level1 and Multi-class conditions are fine grained versions of the Binary annotation, i.e. the `OK` examples are the same for all cases.

We re-use our binary predictions as an additional feature for the finer-grained classes. However, due to time constrains, we were not able to run the proper nested cross-validation but used a model trained on all available data, which therefore over-fits on the training data. Cross-validation results using the stacking approach are thus very optimistic.

[2] https://code.google.com/p/stop-words/

3.2 Classifiers

We use bidirectional long short-term memory recurrent neural networks (BLSTM-RNNs) as implemented in the RNNLib package (Graves, 2008). Recurrent neural networks are a connectionist model containing a self-connected hidden layer. The recurrent connection provides information of previous inputs, hence, the network can benefit from past contextual information. Long short-term memory is an advanced RNN architecture that allows context information over long periods of time. Finally, BLSTM-RNNs combine bidirectional recurrent neural networks and the long short-term memory architecture allowing forward and backward context information. Using such context modelling classifier we can avoid the use of context-based features that have been shown to lead to only slight improvements in QE accuracy (González-Rubio et al., 2013).

As a secondary binary model we train a CRF. Our choice of implementation is Pocket CRF[3] which, while currently unmaintained, implements continuous valued features. We use a history of size 2 for all features and perform 10-fold cross-validation, training on 9 folds each time.

3.3 Experimental Setup

The free parameters of the BLSTM-RNNs are optimized by 10-fold cross-validation on the training set. Each cross-validation experiment consider eight folds for training, one held-out fold for development, and a final held-out fold for testing. We estimate the neural network with the eight training folds using the prediction performance in the validation fold as stopping criterion. The result of each complete cross-validation experiment is the average of the results for the predictions of the ten held-out test folds. Additionally, to avoid noise due to the random initialization of the network, we repeat each cross-validation experiment ten times and average the results. Once the optimal values of the free parameters are established, we estimate a new BLSTM-RNN using the full training corpus and we use it as the final model to predict the class labels of the test words.

Since our objective is to detect words that need to be edited, we use the weighted averaged F_1 score over the different class labels that denote an error as our main performance metric ($\mathrm{wF1_{err}}$). We also report the weighted averaged F_1 scores

[3] http://pocket-crf-1.sourceforge.net/

Method	Features	Binary		Level1		MultiClass	
		$wF1_{err}$	$wF1_{all}$	$wF1_{err}$	$wF1_{all}$	$wF1_{err}$	$wF1_{all}$
BLSTM-RNNs	LM+WPP+CN+WL	35.9	63.0	23.7	59.4	10.7	55.5
	+POS	**38.5**[1]	62.7	26.7[1]	59.5	12.7[1]	55.5
	+Stacking	—	—	**82.9**[2]	93.9	**64.7**[2]	88.0
CRF	LM+WPP+CN+WL+POS	39.5[2]	62.4 0	—	—	—	—

Table 2: Cross-validation results for the different setups tested for Task 2. Our two submissions are marked as ([1]) and ([2]) respectively.

over all the classes ($wF1_{all}$).

3.4 Results

Table 2 presents the $wF1_{err}$ and $wF1_{all}$ scores for different sets of features. Our initial experiment includes language model (LM), word posterior probability (WPP), confusion network (CN), and word lexicon (WL) features for a total of 11 features. We extend this basic feature set with the indicator features based on POS tags for a total of 163 features. We further extend the feature vectors by adding the stacking feature in a total of 164 features.

Analyzing the results we observe that prediction accuracy is quite low. Our hypothesis is that this is due to the skewed class distribution. Even for the binary classification scenario (the most balanced of the three conditions), `OK` labels account for two thirds of the samples. This effect worsens with increasing number of error classes and the resulting sparsity of observations. As a result, the system tends to classify all samples as `OK` which leads to the low F_1 scores presented in Table 2.

We can observe that the use of POS tags indicator features clearly improved the prediction accuracy of the systems in the three conditions. This setup is our primary submission for the three conditions of task 2.

In addition, we observe that the use of the stacking feature provides a considerable improvement in prediction accuracy for Level1 and MultiClass. As discussed above the cross-validation results for the stacking features are very optimistic. Test predictions using this setup are our contrastive submission for Level1 and MultiClass conditions.

Results achieved on the official test set can be found in Table 3. Much in line with our cross-validation results the stacking-features prove helpful, albeit by a much lower margin. For the binary task the RNN model strongly outperforms the CRF.

Setup	Binary	Level1	MultiClass
BLSTM-RNN	**48.7**	37.2	17.1
+ Stacking	—	**38.5**	**23.1**
CRF	42.6	—	—

Table 3: Test results for Task 2. Numbers are weighted averaged F_1 scores (%) for all but the OK class.

4 Conclusion

This paper describes the approaches and system setups of FBK, UPV and UEdin in the WMT14 Quality Estimation shared-task. In the sentence-level QE tasks 1.2 (predicting post-edition effort) and 1.3 (predicting post-editing time, in ms) we explored different features and predicted with a supervised tree-based ensemble learning method. We were able to improve our results by exploring features based on the word-level predictions made by the system developed for Task 2. Our best system for Task 1.2 ranked first among all participants.

In the word-level QE task (Task 2), we explored different sets of features using a BLSTM-RNN as our classification model. Cross-validation results show that POS indicator features, despite sparse, were able to improve the results of the baseline features. Also, the use of the stacking feature provided a big leap in prediction accuracy. With this model, we ranked first in the Binary and Level1 settings of Task 2 in the evaluation campaign.

Acknowledgments

This work was supported by the MateCat and Casmacat projects, which are funded by the EC under the 7th Framework Programme. The authors would like to thank Francisco Álvaro Muñoz for providing the RNN classification software.

References

James Bergstra and Yoshua Bengio. 2012. Random Search for Hyper-Parameter Optimization. *Journal of Machine Learning Research*, 13:281–305.

John Blatz, Erin Fitzgerald, George Foster, Simona Gandrabur, Cyril Goutte, Alex Kulesza, Alberto Sanchis, and Nicola Ueffing. 2004. Confidence estimation for machine translation. In *Proceedings of the international conference on Computational Linguistics*, pages 315–321.

Ondřej Bojar, Christian Buck, Chris Callison-Burch, Christian Federmann, Barry Haddow, Philipp Koehn, Christof Monz, Matt Post, Radu Soricut, and Lucia Specia. 2013. Findings of the 2013 Workshop on Statistical Machine Translation. In *Proceedings of the Eighth Workshop on Statistical Machine Translation*, pages 1–44.

Peter F. Brown, Vincent J. Della Pietra, Stephen A. Della Pietra, and Robert L. Mercer. 1993. The mathematics of statistical machine translation: parameter estimation. *Computational Linguistics*, 19:263–311.

Christian Buck, Kenneth Heafield, and Bas van Ooyen. 2014. N-gram Counts and Language Models from the Common Crawl. In *Proceedings of the Language Resources and Evaluation Conference*.

José G. C. de Souza, Christian Buck, Marco Turchi, and Matteo Negri. 2013a. FBK-UEdin participation to the WMT13 Quality Estimation shared-task. In *Proceedings of the Eighth Workshop on Statistical Machine Translation*, pages 352–358.

José G. C. de Souza, Miquel Esplá-Gomis, Marco Turchi, and Matteo Negri. 2013b. Exploiting qualitative information from automatic word alignment for cross-lingual nlp tasks. In *Proceedings of the 51st Annual Meeting of the Association for Computational Linguistics*, pages 771–776.

Qin Gao and Stephan Vogel. 2008. Parallel implementations of word alignment tool. In *Software Engineering, Testing, and Quality Assurance for Natural Language Processing*, pages 49–57.

Pierre Geurts, Damien Ernst, and Louis Wehenkel. 2006. Extremely randomized trees. *Machine Learning*, 63(1):3–42.

Jesús González-Rubio, José R. Navarro-Cerdan, and Francisco Casacuberta. 2013. Partial least squares for word confidence estimation in machine translation. In *6th Iberian Conference on Pattern Recognition and Image Analysis, (IbPRIA) LNCS 7887*, pages 500–508. Springer.

Alex Graves. 2008. Rnnlib: A recurrent neural network library for sequence learning problems. `http://sourceforge.net/projects/rnnl/`.

Vladimir Levenshtein. 1966. Binary codes capable of correcting deletions, insertions and reversals. *Soviet Physics Doklady*, 10(8):707–710.

Ngoc-Quang Luong, Laurent Besacier, and Benjamin Lecouteux. 2014. Word confidence estimation and its integration in sentence quality estimation for machine translation. In *Knowledge and Systems Engineering*, volume 244, pages 85–98. Springer.

F. Pedregosa, G. Varoquaux, A. Gramfort, V. Michel, B. Thirion, O. Grisel, M. Blondel, P. Prettenhofer, R. Weiss, V. Dubourg, J. Vanderplas, A. Passos, D. Cournapeau, M. Brucher, M. Perrot, and E. Duchesnay. 2011. Scikit-learn : Machine Learning in Python. *Journal of Machine Learning Research*, 12:2825–2830.

Alberto Sanchis, Alfons Juan, and Enrique Vidal. 2007. Estimation of confidence measures for machine translation. In *Proceedings of the Machine Translation Summit XI*, pages 407–412.

Helmut Schmid. 1994. Probabilistic part-of-speech tagging using decision trees. In *Proceedings of International Conference on New Methods in Language Processing*, volume 12, pages 44–49.

Matthew Snover, Bonnie Dorr, Richard Schwartz, Linnea Micciulla, and John Makhoul. 2006. A Study of Translation Edit Rate with Targeted Human Annotation. In *Association for Machine Translation in the Americas*.

Lucia Specia, Kashif Shah, José G. C. de Souza, and Trevor Cohn. 2013. QuEst–a translation quality estimation framework. In *Proceedings of the 51st Annual Meeting of the Association for Computational Linguistics*, pages 79–84.

Nicola Ueffing and Hermann Ney. 2007. Word-level confidence estimation for machine translation. *Computational Linguistics*, 33:9–40.

Richard Zens and Hermann Ney. 2006. N-gram posterior probabilities for statistical machine translation. In *Proceedings of the Workshop on Statistical Machine Translation*, pages 72–77.

Target-Centric Features for Translation Quality Estimation

Chris Hokamp and **Iacer Calixto** and **Joachim Wagner** and **Jian Zhang**
CNGL Centre for Global Intelligent Content
Dublin City University
School of Computing
Dublin, Ireland
{chokamp|icalixto|jwagner|zhangj}@computing.dcu.ie

Abstract

We describe the DCU-MIXED and DCU-SVR submissions to the WMT-14 Quality Estimation task 1.1, predicting sentence-level perceived post-editing effort. Feature design focuses on target-side features as we hypothesise that the source side has little effect on the quality of human translations, which are included in task 1.1 of this year's WMT Quality Estimation shared task. We experiment with features of the QuEst framework, features of our past work, and three novel feature sets. Despite these efforts, our two systems perform poorly in the competition. Follow up experiments indicate that the poor performance is due to improperly optimised parameters.

1 Introduction

Translation quality estimation tries to predict the quality of a translation given the source and target text but no reference translations. Different from previous years (Callison-Burch et al., 2012; Bojar et al., 2013), the WMT 2014 Quality Estimation shared task is MT system-independent, i. e. no glass-box features are available and translations in the training and test sets are produced by different MT systems and also by human translators.

This paper describes the CNGL@DCU team submission to task 1.1 of the WMT 2014 Quality Estimation shared task.[1] The task is to predict the **perceived** post-editing effort given a source sentence and its raw translation. Due to the inclusion of human translation in the task, we focus our efforts on target-side features as we expect that the quality of a translation produced by a human translator is much less affected by features of the source than by extrinsic factors such as time pressure and familiarity with the domain.

To build our quality estimation system, we use and extend the QuEst framework for translation quality estimation[2] (Shah et al., 2013; Specia et al., 2013). QuEst provides modules for feature extraction and machine learning. We modify both the feature extraction framework and the machine learning components to add functionality to QuEst.

The novel features we add to our systems are *(a)* a language model on a combination of stop words and POS tags, *(b)* inverse glass-box features for translating the translation, and *(c)* random indexing (Sahlgren, 2005) for measuring the semantic similarity of source and target side across languages. Furthermore, we integrated *(d)* source-side pseudo-reference features (Soricut and Echihabi, 2010) and *(e)* error grammar features (Wagner, 2012), which were used first in MT quality estimation by (Rubino et al., 2012; Rubino et al., 2013).

The remaining sections are organised as follows. Section 2 gives details on the features we use. Section 3 describes how we set up our experiments. Results are presented in Section 4 and conclusions are drawn in Section 5 together with pointers to future work.

2 Features

This section describes the features we extract from source and target sentences in order to train prediction models and to make predictions in addition to the baseline features provided for the task.

We focus on the target side as we assume that the quality of the source side has little predictive power for human translations, which are included in task 1.1.

[1] A CNGL system based on referential translation machines is submitted separately (Biçici and Way, 2014).

[2] http://www.quest.dcs.shef.ac.uk/

Proceedings of the Ninth Workshop on Statistical Machine Translation, pages 329–334,
Baltimore, Maryland USA, June 26–27, 2014.

2.1 QuEst Black-Box Features and Baseline Features

We use the QuEst framework to extract 47 basic black-box features from both source and target side, such as the ratio of the number of tokens, punctuation statistics, number if mismatched brackets and quotes, language model perplexity, n-gram frequency quartile statistics ($n = 1, 2, 3$), and coarse-grained POS frequency ratios. 17 of the 47 features are identical to the baseline features from the shared task website, i. e. 30 features are new. To train the language models and to extract frequency information, we use the News Commentary corpus (Bojar et al., 2013).

2.2 POS and Stop Word Language Model Features

For all languages, we extract probability and perplexity features from language models trained on POS tagged corpora. POS tagging is performed using the IMS Tree Tagger (Schmid, 1994).

We also experiment with language models built from a combination of stop words[3] and POS tags. Starting with a tokenised corpus, and its POS-tagged counterpart, we create a new representation of the corpus by replacing POS tags for stop words with the literal stop word that occurred in the original corpus, leaving non-stop word tags intact.[4] The intuition behind the approach is that the combined POS and stop word model should encode the distributional tendencies of the most common words in the language.

The log-probability and the perplexity of the target side are used as features. The development of these features was motivated by manual examination of the common error types in the training data. We noted that stop word errors (omission, mistranslation, mis-translation of idiom), are prevalent in all language pairs, indicating that features which focus on stop word usage could be useful for predicting the quality of machine translation. We implement POS and stop word language models inside the QuEst framework.

2.3 Source-Side Pseudo-Reference Features

We extract source-side pseudo-reference features (Albrecht and Hwa, 2008; Soricut and Echihabi, 2010; Rubino et al., 2012), for English to German quality prediction using a highly-tuned German to English translation system (Li et al., 2014) working in the reverse direction. The MT system translates the German target side, the quality of which is to be predicted, back into English, and we extract pseudo-reference features on the source side:

- BLEU score (Papineni et al., 2002) between back-translation and original source sentence, and
- TER score (Snover et al., 2006).

For the 5th English to German test set item, for example, the translation

(1) *Und belasse sie dort eine Woche.*

is translated back to English as

(2) *and leave it there for a week .*

and compared to the original source sentence

(3) *Leave for a week.*

producing a BLEU score of 0.077 using the Python interface to the cdec toolkit (Chahuneau et al., 2012).

2.4 Inverse Glass-Box Features for Translating the Translation

In the absence of direct glass-box features, we obtain glass-box features from translating the raw translation back to the source language using the same MT system that we use for the source-side pseudo-reference features. We extract features from the following components of the Moses decoder: distortion model, language model, lexical reordering, lexical translation probability, operational sequence model (Durrani et al., 2013), phrase translation probability, and the decoder score.

The intuition for this set of features is that back-translating an incorrect translation will give low system-internal scores, e. g. a low phrase translation score, and produce poor output with low language model scores (garbage in, garbage out).

We are not aware of any previous work using inverse glass-box features of translating the target side to another language for quality estimation.

[3] We use the stop word lists from Apache Lucene (McCandless et al., 2010).

[4] The News Commentary corpus from WMT13 was used to build these models, same as for the black-box features (Section 2.1).

2.5 Semantic Similarity Using Random Indexing

These features try to measure the semantic similarity of source and target side of a translation unit for quality estimation using random indexing (Sahlgren, 2005). We experiment with adding the similarity score of the source and target random vectors.

For each source and target pair in the English-Spanish portion of the Europarl corpus (Koehn, 2005), we initialize a sparse random vector. We then create token vectors for each source and target token by summing the vectors for all of the segments where the token occurs. To extract the similarity feature for new source and target pairs, we map them into the vector space by taking the centroid of the token vectors for the source side and the target side, and computing their cosine similarity.

2.6 Error Grammar Parsing

We obtain features from monolingual parsing with three grammars:

1. the vanilla grammar shipped with the Blipp parser (Charniak, 2000; Charniak and Johnson, 2005) induced from the Penn-Treebank (Marcus et al., 1994),
2. an error grammar induced from Penn-Treebank trees distorted according to an error model (Foster, 2007), and
3. a grammar induced from the union of the above two treebanks.

Features include the log-ratios between the probability of the best parse obtained with each grammar and structural differences measured with Parseval (Black et al., 1991) and leaf-ancestor (Sampson and Babarczy, 2003) metrics. These features have been shown to be useful for judging the grammaticality of sentences (Wagner et al., 2009; Wagner, 2012) and have been used in MT quality estimation before (Rubino et al., 2012; Rubino et al., 2013).

3 Experimental Setup

This section describes how we set up our experiments.

3.1 Cross-Validation

Decisions about parameters are made in 10-fold cross-validation on the training data provided for the task. As the datasets for task 1.1 include three to four translations for each source segment, we group segments by their source side and split the data for cross-validation between segments to ensure that a source segment does not occur in both training and test data for any of the cross-validation runs.

We implement these modifications to cross-validation and randomisation in the QuEst framework.

3.2 Training

We use the QuEst framework to train our models. Support vector regression (SVR) meta-parameters are optimised using QuEst's default settings, exploring RBF kernels with two possible values for each of the three meta-parameters C, γ and ϵ.[5]

The two final models are trained on the full training set with the meta-parameters that achieved the best average cross-validation score.

3.3 Classifier Combination

We experiment with combining logistic regression (LR) and support vector regression (SVR) by first choosing the instances where LR classification is confident and using the LR class label (1, 2, or 3) as predicted perceived post-editing effort, and falling back to SVR for all other instances.

We employ several heuristics to decide whether to use the output of LR or SVR. As the LR classifier learns a decision function for each of the three classes, we can exploit the scores of the classes to measure the confidence of the LR classifier about its decision. If the LR classifier is confident, we use its prediction directly, otherwise we use the SVR prediction.

For the cases where one of the three decision functions for the LR classifier is positive, we select the prediction directly, falling back to SVR when the classifier is not confident about any of the three classes. We implement the LR+SVR classifier combination inside the QuEst framework.

4 Results

Table 1 shows cross-validation results for the 17 baseline features, the combination of all features and target-side features only. We do not show combinations of individual feature sets and baseline features that do not improve over the base-

[5] We only discovered this limitation of the default configuration after the system submission, see Sections 4 and 5.

Features	Classifier	RMSE	MAE
Basel.17	LR+SVR	0.75	0.62
ALL	LR+SVR	0.74	0.59
ALL	LR>0.5+SVR	0.75	0.58
Target	LR+SVR	0.75	0.59
ALL	LR>0.5+SVR-r	0.78	**0.55**

Table 1: Cross-validation results for English to German. LR > 0.5 indicates that we require the LR decision function to be > 0.5. SVR-r rounds the output to the nearest natural number.

line. Several experiments, including those with the semantic similarity feature sets, are thus omitted. Furthermore, we only exemplify one language pair (English to German), as the other language pairs show similar patterns. The feature set *target* contains the subset of the QuEst black-box features (Section 2.1) which only examine the target side.

Our best results for English to German in the cross-validation experiments are achieved by combining a logistic regression (LR) classifier with support vector regression (SVR). Furthermore, performance on the cross-validation is slightly improved for the mean absolute error (MAE) by rounding SVR scores to the nearest integer. For the root-mean-square error (RMSE), rounding has the opposite effect.

Performing a more fine-grained grid search for the meta-parameters C, γ and ϵ after system submission, we were able to match the scores for the baseline features published on the shared task website.

4.1 Parameters for the Final Models

The final two models for system submission are trained on the full data set. We submit our best system according to MAE in cross-validation combining LR, SVR and rounding with all features (ALL) as DCU-MIXED. For our second submission, we choose SVR on its own (system DCU-SVR). For English-Spanish, we only submit DCU-SVR.

5 Conclusions and Future Work

We identified improperly optimised parameters of the SVR component as the cause, or at least as a contributing factor, for the placement of our systems below the official baseline system. Other potential factors may be an error in our experimental setup or over-fitting. Therefore, we plan to repeat the experiments with a more fine-grained grid search for optimal parameters and/or will try another machine learning toolkit.

Unfortunately, due to the above problems with our system so far, we cannot draw conclusions about the effectiveness of our novel feature sets.

A substantial gain is achieved on the MAE metric with the rounding method, indicating that the majority of prediction errors are below 0.5.[6] Future work should account for this effect. Two ideas are: *(a)* round all predictions before evaluation and *(b)* use more fine-grained gold values, e. g. the (weighted) average over multiple annotations as in the WMT 2012 quality estimation task (Callison-Burch et al., 2012).

For the error grammar method, the next step will be to adjust the error model to errors found in translations. It may be possible to do this without a time-consuming analysis of errors: Wagner (2012) suggests to use parallel data of authentic errors and corrections to build the error grammar, first parsing the corrections and then guiding the error creation procedure with the edit operations inverse to the corrections. Post-editing corpora can play this role and have recently become available (Potet et al., 2012).

Furthermore, future work should explore the inverse glass-box feature idea with arbitrary target languages for the MT system. (There is no requirement that the glass-box system translates back to the original source language).

Finally, we would like to integrate referential translation machines (Biçici, 2013; Biçici and Way, 2014) into our system as they performed well in the WMT quality estimation tasks this and last year.

Acknowledgments

This research is supported by the European Commission under the 7th Framework Programme, specifically its Marie Curie Programme 317471, and by the Science Foundation Ireland (Grant 12/CE/I2267) as part of CNGL (www.cngl.ie) at Dublin City University. We thank the anonymous reviewers and Jennifer Foster for their comments on earlier versions of this paper.

[6]The simultaneous increase on RMSE can be explained if there is a sufficient number of errors above 0.5: After squaring, these errors are still quite small, e. g. 0.36 for an error of 0.6, but after rounding, the square error becomes 1.0 or 4.0.

References

Joshua Albrecht and Rebecca Hwa. 2008. The role of pseudo references in MT evaluation. In *Proceedings of the Third Workshop on Statistical Machine Translation*, pages 187–190, Columbus, Ohio, June. Association for Computational Linguistics.

Ergun Biçici and Andy Way. 2014. Referential translation machines for predicting translation quality. In *Proceedings of the Nineth Workshop on Statistical Machine Translation*, Baltimore, USA, June. Association for Computational Linguistics.

Ergun Biçici. 2013. Referential translation machines for quality estimation. In *Proceedings of the Eighth Workshop on Statistical Machine Translation*, pages 343–351, Sofia, Bulgaria, August. Association for Computational Linguistics.

Ezra Black, Steve Abney, Dan Flickinger, Claudia Gdaniec, Robert Grishman, Philip Harrison, Donald Hindle, Robert Ingria, Fred Jelinek, Judith Klavans, Mark Liberman, Mitchell Marcus, Salim Roukos, Beatrice Santorini, and Tomek Strzalkowski. 1991. A procedure for quantitatively comparing the syntactic coverage of English grammars. In E. Black, editor, *Proceedings of the HLT Workshop on Speech and Natural Language*, pages 306–311, Morristown, NJ, USA. Association for Computational Linguistics.

Ondřej Bojar, Christian Buck, Chris Callison-Burch, Christian Federmann, Barry Haddow, Philipp Koehn, Christof Monz, Matt Post, Radu Soricut, and Lucia Specia. 2013. Findings of the 2013 Workshop on Statistical Machine Translation. In *Proceedings of the Eighth Workshop on Statistical Machine Translation*, pages 1–44, Sofia, Bulgaria, August. Association for Computational Linguistics.

Chris Callison-Burch, Philipp Koehn, Christof Monz, Matt Post, Radu Soricut, and Lucia Specia. 2012. Findings of the 2012 Workshop on Statistical Machine Translation. In *Proceedings of the Seventh Workshop on Statistical Machine Translation*, pages 10–51, Montréal, Canada, June. Association for Computational Linguistics.

Victor Chahuneau, Noah A. Smith, and Chris Dyer. 2012. pycdec: A python interface to cdec. *Prague Bull. Math. Linguistics*, 98:51–62.

Eugene Charniak and Mark Johnson. 2005. Course-to-fine n-best-parsing and maxent discriminative reranking. In *Proceedings of the 43rd Annual Meeting of the ACL (ACL-05)*, pages 173–180, Ann Arbor, Michigan, June. Association for Computational Linguistics.

Eugene Charniak. 2000. A maximum entropy inspired parser. In *Proceedings of the First Annual Meeting of the North American Chapter of the Association for Computational Linguistics (NAACL-00)*, pages 132–139, Seattle, WA.

Nadir Durrani, Barry Haddow, Kenneth Heafield, and Philipp Koehn. 2013. Edinburgh's machine translation systems for European language pairs. In *Proceedings of the Eighth Workshop on Statistical Machine Translation*, pages 114–121, Sofia, Bulgaria, August. Association for Computational Linguistics.

Jennifer Foster. 2007. Treebanks gone bad: Parser evaluation and retraining using a treebank of ungrammatical sentences. *International Journal on Document Analysis and Recognition*, 10(3-4):129–145.

Philipp Koehn. 2005. Europarl: A parallel corpus for statistical machine translation. In *MT summit*, volume 5, pages 79–86.

Liangyou Li, Xiaofeng Wu, Santiago Cortés Vaíllo, Jun Xie, Jia Xu, Andy Way, and Qun Liu. 2014. The DCU-ICTCAS-Tsinghua MT system at WMT 2014 on German-English translation task. In *Proceedings of the Nineth Workshop on Statistical Machine Translation*, Baltimore, USA, June. Association for Computational Linguistics.

Mitchell Marcus, Grace Kim, Mary Ann Marcinkiewicz, Robert MacIntyre, Ann Bies, Mark Ferguson, Karen Katz, and Britta Schasberger. 1994. The Penn Treebank: Annotating predicate argument structure. In *Proceedings of the 1994 ARPA Speech and Natural Language Workshop*, pages 114–119.

Michael McCandless, Erik Hatcher, and Otis Gospodnetic. 2010. *Lucene in Action, Second Edition: Covers Apache Lucene 3.0*. Manning Publications Co., Greenwich, CT, USA.

Kishore Papineni, Salim Roukos, Todd Ward, and Wei-Jing Zhu. 2002. BLEU: a method for automatic evaluation of machine translation. In *Proceedings of the 40th Annual Meeting on Association for Computational Linguistics (ACL02)*, pages 311–318, Morristown, NJ, USA. Association for Computational Linguistics.

Marion Potet, Emmanuelle Esperança-Rodier, Laurent Besacier, and Hervé Blanchon. 2012. Collection of a large database of French-English SMT output corrections. In *Proceedings of the 8th International Conference on Language Resources and Evaluation (LREC)*.

Raphael Rubino, Jennifer Foster, Joachim Wagner, Johann Roturier, Rasul Samad Zadeh Kaljahi, and Fred Hollowood. 2012. Dcu-symantec submission for the wmt 2012 quality estimation task. In *Proceedings of the Seventh Workshop on Statistical Machine Translation*, pages 138–144, Montréal, Canada, June. Association for Computational Linguistics.

Raphael Rubino, Joachim Wagner, Jennifer Foster, Johann Roturier, Rasoul Samad Zadeh Kaljahi, and Fred Hollowood. 2013. DCU-Symantec at the

WMT 2013 quality estimation shared task. In *Proceedings of the Eighth Workshop on Statistical Machine Translation*, pages 392–397, Sofia, Bulgaria, August. Association for Computational Linguistics.

Magnus Sahlgren. 2005. An introduction to random indexing. In *Methods and Applications of Semantic Indexing Workshop at the 7th International Conference on Terminology and Knowledge Engineering (TKE)*, volume 5, Copenhagen, Denmark.

Geoffrey Sampson and Anna Babarczy. 2003. A test of the leaf-ancestor metric for parse accuracy. *Natural Language Engineering*, 9(4):365–380.

Helmut Schmid. 1994. Probabilistic part-of-speech tagging using decision trees. In *Proceedings of the International Conference on New Methods in Language Processing*, Manchester, United Kingdom.

Kashif Shah, Eleftherios Avramidis, Ergun Biçici, and Lucia Specia. 2013. QuEst - design, implementation and extensions of a framework for machine translation quality estimation. *The Prague Bulletin of Mathematical Linguistics*, 100.

Matthew Snover, Bonnie Dorr, Richard Schwartz, Linnea Micciulla, and John Makhoul. 2006. A study of translation edit rate with targeted human annotation. In *Proceedings of association for machine translation in the Americas*, pages 223–231.

Radu Soricut and Abdessamad Echihabi. 2010. Trustrank: Inducing trust in automatic translations via ranking. In *Proceedings of the 48th Annual Meeting of the Association for Computational Linguistics*, pages 612–621, Uppsala, Sweden, July. Association for Computational Linguistics.

Lucia Specia, Kashif Shah, Jose G.C. de Souza, and Trevor Cohn. 2013. QuEst - a translation quality estimation framework. In *Proceedings of the 51st Annual Meeting of the Association for Computational Linguistics: System Demonstrations*, pages 79–84, Sofia, Bulgaria, August. Association for Computational Linguistics.

Joachim Wagner, Jennifer Foster, and Josef van Genabith. 2009. Judging grammaticality: Experiments in sentence classification. *CALICO Journal (Special Issue of the 2008 CALICO Workshop on Automatic Analysis of Learner Language)*, 26(3):474–490.

Joachim Wagner. 2012. *Detecting grammatical errors with treebank-induced, probabilistic parsers*. Ph.D. thesis, Dublin City University, Dublin, Ireland.

LIG System for Word Level QE task at WMT14

Ngoc-Quang Luong **Laurent Besacier** **Benjamin Lecouteux**
LIG, Campus de Grenoble
41, Rue des Mathématiques,
UJF - BP53, F-38041 Grenoble Cedex 9, France
{ngoc-quang.luong,laurent.besacier,benjamin.lecouteux}@imag.fr

Abstract

This paper describes our Word-level QE system for WMT 2014 shared task on Spanish - English pair. Compared to WMT 2013, this year's task is different due to the lack of SMT setting information and additional resources. We report how we overcome this challenge to retain most of the important features which performed well last year in our system. Novel features related to the availability of multiple systems output (new point of this year) are also proposed and experimented along with baseline set. The system is optimized by several ways: tuning the classification threshold, combining with WMT 2013 data, and refining using *Feature Selection* strategy on our development set, before dealing with the test set for submission.

1 Introduction

1.1 Overview of task 2 in WMT14

This year WMT calls for methods which predict the MT output quality at run-time, on both levels: sentence (Task 1) and word (Task 2). Towards a SMT system-independent and widely-applied estimation, MT outputs are collected from multiple translation means (machine and human), therefore all SMT specific settings (and the associated features that could have been extracted from it) become unavailable. This initiative puts more challenges on participants, yet motivates number of SMT-unconventional approaches and inspires the endeavors aiming at an "Evaluation For All".

We focus our effort on Task 2 (Word-level QE), where, unlike in WMT2013, participants are requested to generate prediction labels for words in three variants:

- Binary: words are judged as *Good* (no translation error), or *Bad* (need for editing).
- Level 1: the *Good* class is kept intact, whereas *Bad* one is further divided into subcategories: *Accuracy* issue (the word does not accurately reflect the source text) and *Fluency* issue (the word does not relate to the form or content of the target text).
- Multi-class: more detailed judgement, where the translation errors are further decomposed into 16 labels based on MQM[1] metric.

1.2 Related work

WMT 2013 witnessed several attempts dealing with this evaluation type in its first launch. Han et al. (2013); Luong et al. (2013) employed the Conditional Random Fields (CRF) (Lafferty et al., 2001) model as their Machine Learning method to address the problem as a sequence labeling task. Meanwhile, Bicici (2013) extended the global learning model by dynamic training with adaptive weight updates in the perceptron training algorithm. As far as prediction indicators are concerned, Bicici (2013) proposed seven word feature types and found among them the "common cover links" (the links that point from the leaf node containing this word to other leaf nodes in the same subtree of the syntactic tree) the most outstanding. Han et al. (2013) focused only on various n-gram combinations of target words. Inheriting most of previously-recognized features, Luong et al. (2013) integrated a number of new indicators relying on graph topology, pseudo reference, syntactic behavior (constituent label, distance to the semantic tree root) and polysemy characteristic. Optimization endeavors were also made to enhance the baseline, including classification threshold tuning, feature selection and boosting technique (Luong et al., 2013).

[1] http://www.qt21.eu/launchpad/content/training

Proceedings of the Ninth Workshop on Statistical Machine Translation, pages 335–341,
Baltimore, Maryland USA, June 26–27, 2014.

1.3 Paper outline

The rest of our paper is structured as follows: in the next section, we describe 2014 provided data for Task 2, and the additional data used to train the system. Section 3 lists the entire feature set, involving WMT 2013 set as well as a new feature proposed for this year. Baseline system experiments and methods for optimizing it are furthered discussed in Section 4 and Section 5 respectively. Section 6 selects the most outstanding system for submission. The last section summarizes the approach and opens new outlook.

2 Data and Supporting Resources

For English - Spanish language pair in Task 2, the organizers released two bilingual data sets: the training and the test ones. The training set contains 1.957 MT outputs, in which each token is annotated with one appropriate label. In the binary variant, the words are classified into *"OK"* (no translation error) or *"BAD"* (edit operators needed) label. Meanwhile, in the level 1 variant, they belong to *"OK"*, *"Accuracy"* or *"Fluency"* (two latter ones are divided from *"BAD"* label of the first subtask). In the last variant, multi-class, beside *"Accuracy"* and *"Fluency"* we have further 15 labels based on MQM metric: *Terminology, Mistranslation, Omission, Addition, Untranslated, Style/register, Capitalization, Spelling, Punctuation, Typography, Morphology_(word_form), Part_of_speech, Agreement, Word_order, Function_words, Tense/aspect/mood, Grammar* and *Unintelligible*. The test set consists of 382 sentences where all the labels accompanying words are hidden. For optimizing parameters of the classifier, we extract last 200 sentences from the training set to form a development (dev) set. Besides, the Spanish - English corpus provided in WMT 2013 (total of 1087 tuples) is also exploited to enrich our WMT 2014 system. Unfortunately, 2013 data can only help us in the binary variant, due to the discrepancy in training labels. Some statistics about each set can be found in Table 1.

In addition, additional (MT-independent) resources are used for the feature extraction, including:

- Spanish and English Word Language Models (LM)
- Spanish and English POS Language Models
- Spanish - English 2013 MT system

On the contrary, no specific MT setting is provided (e.g. the code to re-run Moses system like WMT 2013), leading to the unavailability of some crucial resources, such as the *N*-best list and alignment information. Coping with this, we firstly thought of using the Moses "Constrained Decoding" option as a method to tie our (already available) decoder's output to the given target translations (this feature is supported by the latest version of Moses (Koehn et al., 2007) in 2013). Our hope was that, by doing so, both *N*-best list and alignment information would be generated during decoding. But the decoder failed to output all translations (only $1/4$ was obtained) when the number of allowed unknown words (*-max-unknowns*) was set as 0. Switching to non zero value for this option did not help either since, even if more outputs were generated, alignment information was biased in that case due to additional/missing words in the obtained MT output. Ultimately, we decided to employ GIZA++ toolkit (Och and Ney, 2003) to obtain at least the alignment information (and associated features) between source text and target MT output. However, no *N*-best list were extracted nor available as in last year system. Nevertheless, we tried to extract some features equivalent to last year N-best features (details can be found in Section 3.2).

3 Feature Extraction

In this section, we briefly list out all the features used in WMT 2013 (Luong et al., 2013) that were kept for this year, followed by some proposed features taking advantage of the provided resources and multiple translation system outputs (for a same source sentence).

3.1 WMT13 features

- Source word features: all the source words that align to the target one, represented in BIO[2] format.
- Source alignment context features: the combinations of the target word and one word before (left source context) or after (right source context) the source word aligned to it.

[2] http://www-tsujii.is.s.u-tokyo.ac.jp/GENIA/tagger/

Statistics	WMT2014			WMT2013		
	train	dev	test	train	dev	test
#segments	1757	200	382	753	50	284
#words	40975	6436	9613	18435	1306	7827
%G (OK) : %B (BAD)	67 : 33	58 : 42	-	70 : 30	77 : 23	75 : 25

Table 1: Statistics of corpora used in LIG's system. We use the notion name+year to indicate the dataset. For instance, **train14** stands for the training set of WMT14

- Target alignment context features: the combinations of the source word and each word in the window ± 2 (two before, two after) of the target word.
- Backoff Behaviour: a score assigned to the word according to how many times the target Language Model has to back-off in order to assign a probability to the word sequence, as described in (Raybaud et al., 2011).
- Part-Of-Speech (POS) features (using TreeTagger[3] toolkit): The target word's POS; the source POS (POS of all source words aligned to it); bigram and trigram sequences between its POS and the POS of previous and following words.
- Binary lexical features that indicate whether the word is a: *stop word* (based on the stop word list for target language), *punctuation* symbol, *proper name* or *numerical*.
- Language Model (LM) features: the *"longest target n-gram length"* and *"longest source n-gram length"*(length of the longest sequence created by the current target (source aligned) word and its previous ones in the target (source) LM). For example, with the target word w_i: if the sequence $w_{i-2}w_{i-1}w_i$ appears in the target LM but the sequence $w_{i-3}w_{i-2}w_{i-1}w_i$ does not, the n-gram value for w_i will be 3.
- The *word's constituent label* and *its depth in the tree* (or the distance between it and the tree root) obtained from the constituent tree as an output of the Berkeley parser (Petrov and Klein, 2007) (trained over a Spanish treebank: AnCora[4]).
- Occurrence in Google Translate hypothesis: we check whether this target word appears in the sentence generated by Google Translate engine for the same source.
- Polysemy Count: the *number of senses* of each word given its POS can be a reliable indicator for judging if it is the translation of a particular source word. Here, we investigate the polysemy characteristic in both target word and its aligned source word. For source word (English), the number of senses can be counted by applying a Perl extension named Lingua::WordNet[5], which provides functions for manipulating the WordNet database. For target word (Spanish), we employ BabelNet[6] - a multilingual semantic network that works similarly to WordNet but covers more European languages, including Spanish.

3.2 WMT14 additional features

- POS's LM based features: we exploit the Spanish and English LMs of POS tag (provided as additional resources for this year's QE tasks) for calculating the maximum length of the sequences created by the current target token's POS and those of previous ones. The same score for POS of aligned source word(s) is also computed. Besides, the back-off score for word's POS tag is also taken into consideration. Actually, these feature types are listed in Section 3.1 for target word, and we proposed the similar ones for POS tags. In summary, three POS LM's new features are built, including: *"longest target n-gram length"*, *"longest source n-gram length"* and *back-off score* for POS tag.
- Word Occurrence in multiple translations: one novel point in this year's shared task is that the targets come from multiple MT

[3] http://www.ims.uni-stuttgart.de/projekte/corplex/TreeTagger/
[4] http://clic.ub.edu/corpus/en/ancora
[5] http://search.cpan.org/dist/Lingua-Wordnet/Wordnet.pm
[6] http://babelnet.org

outputs (from systems or from humans) for the same source sentences. Obviously, one would have a "natural" intuition that: the occurrence of a word in all (or almost) systems implies a higher likelihood of being a correct translation. Relying on this observation, we add a new binary-value feature, telling whether the current token can be found in more than **N%** (in our experiments, we choose $N = 50$) out of all translations generated for the same source sentence. Here, in order to make the judgments more accurate, we propose several additional references besides those provided in the corpora, coming from: (1) Google Translate system, (2) The baseline SMT engine provided for WMT2013 English - Spanish QE task. These two MT outputs are added to the already available MT outputs of a given source sentence, before calculating the (above described) binary feature.

4 Baseline Experiments and Optimization Strategies

4.1 Machine Learning Method

Motivated by the idea of addressing Word Confidence Estimation (WCE) problem as a sequence labeling process, we employ the Conditional Random Fields (CRFs) for our model training, with WAPITI toolkit (Lavergne et al., 2010). Let $X = (x_1, x_2, \ldots, x_N)$ be the random variable over data sequence to be labeled, $Y = (y_1, y_2, \ldots, y_N)$ be the output sequence obtained after the labeling task. Basically, CRF computes the probability of the output sequence Y given the input sequence X by:

$$p_\theta(Y|X) = \frac{1}{Z_\theta(X)} exp \left\{ \sum_{k=1}^{K} \theta_k F_k(X,Y) \right\} \quad (1)$$

where $F_k(X,Y) = \sum_{t=1}^{T} f_k(y_{t-1}, y_t, x_t)$; $\{f_k\}$ $(k = \overline{1,K})$ is a set of feature functions; $\{\theta_k\}$ $(k = \overline{1,K})$ are the associated parameter values; and $Z_\theta(x)$ is the normalization function. In the training phase, we set the maximum number of iterations, the stop window size, and stop epsilon value at $200; 6$ and 0.00005 respectively.

System	Label	Pr(%)	Rc(%)	F(%)
BL(bin)	OK	66.67	81.92	73.51
	Bad	60.69	41.92	49.58
BL(L1)	OK	63.86	82.83	72.12
	Accuracy	22.14	14.89	17.80
	Fluency	50.40	27.98	35.98
BL(mult)	OK	63.32	87.56	73.49
	Fluency	14.44	10.10	11.88
	Mistranslation	9.95	5.69	7.24
	Terminology	3.62	3.89	3.75
	Unintelligible	52.97	16.56	25.23
	Agreement	5.93	11.76	7.88
	Untranslated	5.65	7.76	6.53
	Punctuation	56.97	25.82	35.53
BL+WMT 13(bin)	OK	68.62	82.69	75.01
	Bad	64.38	45.73	53.47

Table 2: Average Pr, Rc and F for labels of all-feature binary and multi-class systems, obtained on our WMT 2014 dev set (200 sentences). In **BL(multi)**, classes with zero value for Pr or Rc will not be reported

4.2 Experimental Classifiers

We experiment with the following classifiers:

- **BL(bin)**: all features (WMT14+WMT13) trained on **train14** only, using binary labels (*"OK"* and *"BAD"*)
- **BL(L1)**: all features trained on **train14** only, using level 1 labels (*"OK"*, *"Accuracy"*, and *"Fluency"*)
- **BL(mult)**: all features trained on **train14** only, using 16 labels
- **BL+WMT13(bin)**: all features trained on **train14 + {train+dev+test}13**, using binary labels.

System quality in Precision (Pr), Recall (Rc) and F score (F) are shown in Table 2. It can be observed that promising results are found in binary variant where both **BL(bin)** and **BL+WMT(bin)** are able to reach at least 50% F score in detecting errors (*BAD* class), meanwhile the performances in *"OK"* class go far beyond (73.51% and 75.01% respectively). Interestingly, the combination with WMT13 data boosts the baseline prediction capability in both labels: **BL+WMT13(bin)** outperforms **BL(bin)** in 1.10% (3.89%) for *OK* (*BAD*) label. Nevertheless, level 1 and multi-class systems maintain only good score for *"OK"* class. In addition, **BL(mult)** seems suffer seriously from its class imbalance, as well as the lack of training data for each, resulting in the inability of prediction for several among them (not all are reported in Table 2).

4.3 Decision threshold tuning for binary task

In binary systems **BL(bin)** and **BL+WMT13(bin)**, we run the classification task multiple times, corresponding to a decision threshold increase from 0.300 to 0.975 (step = 0.025). The values of Precision (Pr), Recall (Rc) and F-score (F) for *OK* and *BAD* label are tracked along this threshold variation, allowing us to select the optimal threshold that yields the highest $F_{avg} = \frac{F(OK)+F(BAD)}{2}$. Figure 1 shows that **BL(bin)** reaches the best performance at the threshold value of **0.95**, meanwhile the one for **BL+WMT13(bin)** is **0.75**. The latter threshold (0.75) has been used for the primary system submitted.

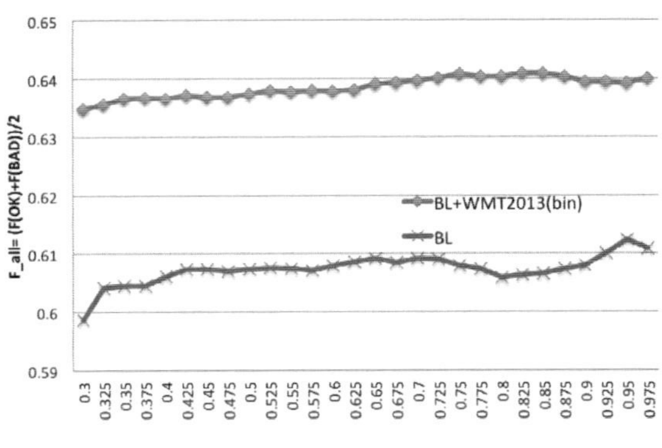

Figure 1: Decision threshold tuning on **BL(bin)** and **BL+WMT2013(bin)**

4.4 Feature Selection

In order to improve the preliminary scores of all-feature systems, we conduct a feature selection which is based on the hypothesis that some features may convey "noise" rather than "information" and might be the obstacles weakening the other ones. In order to prevent this drawback, we propose a method to filter the best features based on the "Sequential Backward Selection" algorithm[7]. We start from the full set of N features, and in each step sequentially remove the most useless one. To do that, all subsets of (N-1) features are considered and the subset that leads to the best performance gives us the weakest feature (not involved in the considered set). This procedure is also called "leave one out" in the literature. Obviously, the discarded feature is not considered in the following steps. We iterate the process until there is only one remaining feature in the set, and use the following score for comparing systems: $F_{avg}(all) = \frac{F_{avg}(OK)+F_{avg}(BAD)}{2}$, where $F_{avg}(OK)$ and $F_{avg}(BAD)$ are the averaged F scores for *OK* and *BAD* label, respectively, when threshold varies from 0.300 to 0.975. This strategy enables us to sort the features in descending order of importance, as displayed in Table 3. Figure 2 shows the evolution of the performance as more and more features are removed. The feature selection is done from the **BL+WMT2013(bin)** system.

We observe in Table 3 four valuable features which appear in top 10 in both WMT13 and WMT14 systems: *Source POS*, *Occur in Google Translate*, *Left source context* and *Right target context*. Among our proposed features, *"Occurrence in multiple systems"* is the most outstanding one with rank 3, *"longest target POS gram length"* plays an average role with rank 12, whereas *"longest source POS gram length"* is much less beneficial with the last position in the list. Figure 2 reveals that the optimal subset of features is the top 18 in Table 3, after discarding 6 weakest ones. This set will be used to train again the classifiers in all subtasks and compare to the baseline ones.

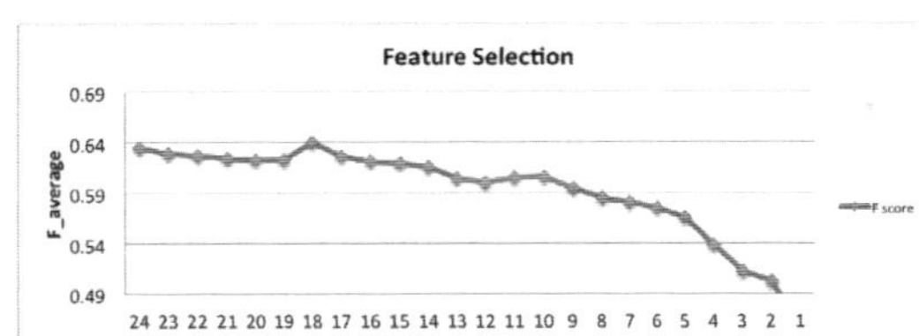

Figure 2: The evolution of the performance as more and more features are removed (from **BL+WMT2013(bin)** system)

5 Submissions

After finishing the optimization process and comparing systems, we select two most out-standing ones (of each subtask) for the submission of this year's shared task. They are the following:

- Binary variant: **BL+WMT13(bin)** and **FS(bin)** (feature selection from the same corresponding system)
- Level 1 variant: **BL(L1)** and **FS(L1)** (feature selection from the same corresponding system)

[7] http://research.cs.tamu.edu/prism/lectures/pr/pr_l11.pdf

Rank	WMT2014	WMT2013
1	Target POS	**Source POS**
2	Longest target gram length	**Occur in Google Translate**
3	Occurrence in multiple systems	Nodes
4	Target word	Target POS
5	**Occur in Google Translate**	WPP any
6	**Source POS**	**Left source context**
7	Numeric	**Right target context**
8	Polysemy count (target)	Numeric
9	**Left source context**	Polysemy count(target)
10	**Right Target context**	Punctuation
11	Constituent label	**Stop word**
12	Longest target POS gram length	Right source context
13	Punctuation	**Target word**
14	Stop word	Distance to root
15	Number of occurrences	Backoff behaviour
16	Left target context	Constituent label
17	Backoff behaviour	Proper name
18	Polysemy count (source)	Number of occurrences
19	Source Word	Min
20	Proper Name	Max
21	Distance to root	Left target context
22	Longest source gram length	Polysemy count (source)
23	Right source context	Longest target gram length
24	Longest source POS gram length	Longest source gram length
25		Source Word

Table 3: The rank of each feature (in term of usefulness) in **WMT2014** and **WMT2013** systems. The bold ones perform well in both cases. Note that feature sets are not exactly the same for 2013 and 2014 (see explanations in section 3).

- Multi-class variant: **BL(mult)** and **FS(mult)** (feature selection from the same corresponding system)

The official results can be seen in Table 4. This year, in order to appreciate the translation error detection capability of WCE systems, the **official** evaluation metric used for systems ranking is the **average F score** for all but the *"OK"* class. For the non-binary variant, this average is weighted by the frequency of the class in the test data. Nevertheless, we find the F scores for *"OK"* class are also informative, since they reflect how good our systems are in identifying correct translations. Therefore, both scores are reported in Table 4.

System	F("OK") (%)	Average F(%)
FS(bin) (primary)	74.0961	0.444735
FS(L1)	73.9856	0.317814
FS(mult)	76.6645	0.204953
BL+WMT2013(bin)	74.6503	0.441074
BL(L1)	74.0045	0.317894
BL(mult)	76.6645	0.204953

Table 4: The F scores for "OK" class and the average F scores for the remaining classes (official WMT14 metric) , obtained on test set.

6 Conclusion and perspectives

We presented our preparation for this year's shared task on QE at word level, for the English - Spanish language pair. The lack of some information on MT system internals was a challenge. We made efforts to maintain most of well-performing 2013 features, especially the source side ones, and propose some novel features based on this year's corpus specificities, as well as combine them with those of last year. Generally, our results are not able to beat those in WMT13 for the same language pair, yet still promising under these constraints. As future work, we are thinking of using more efficiently the existing references (coming from provided translations and other reliable systems) to obtain stronger indicators, as well as examine other ML methods besides CRF.

References

Ergun Bicici. Referential translation machines for quality estimation. In *Proceedings of the Eighth Workshop on Statistical Machine Translation*, pages 343–351, Sofia, Bulgaria, August 2013. Association for Computational Linguistics. URL http://www.aclweb.org/anthology/W13-2242.

Aaron Li-Feng Han, Yi Lu, Derek F. Wong, Lidia S. Chao, Liangye He, and Junwen Xing. Quality estimation for machine translation using the joint method of evaluation criteria and statistical modeling. In *Proceedings of the Eighth Workshop on Statistical Machine Translation*, pages 365–372, Sofia, Bulgaria, August 2013. Association for Computational Linguistics. URL http://www.aclweb.org/anthology/W13-2245.

Philipp Koehn, Hieu Hoang, Alexandra Birch, Chris Callison-Burch, Marcello Federico, Nicola Bertoldi, Brooke Cowan, Wade Shen, Christine Moran, Richard Zens, Chris Dyer, Ondrej Bojar, Alexandra Constantin, and Evan Herbst. Moses: Open source toolkit for statistical machine translation. In *Proceedings of the 45th Annual Meeting of the Association for Computational Linguistics*, pages 177–180, Prague, Czech Republic, June 2007.

John Lafferty, Andrew McCallum, and Fernando Pereira. Conditional random fields: Probabilistic models for segmenting et labeling sequence data. In *Proceedings of ICML-01*, pages 282–289, 2001.

Thomas Lavergne, Olivier Cappé, and François Yvon. Practical very large scale crfs. In *Proceedings of the 48th Annual Meeting of the Association for Computational Linguistics*, pages 504–513, 2010.

Ngoc Quang Luong, Laurent Besacier, and Benjamin Lecouteux. Word confidence estimation and its integration in sentence quality estimation for machine translation. In *Proceedings of the fifth international conference on knowledge and systems engineering (KSE)*, Hanoi, Vietnam, October 2013.

Franz Josef Och and Hermann Ney. A systematic comparison of various statistical alignment models. *Computational Linguistics*, 29(1): 19–51, 2003.

Slav Petrov and Dan Klein. Improved inference for unlexicalized parsing. In *Proceedings of NAACL HLT 2007*, pages 404–411, Rochester, NY, April 2007.

S. Raybaud, D. Langlois, and K. Smaï li. "this sentence is wrong." detecting errors in machine - translated sentences. In *Machine Translation*, pages 1–34, 2011.

Matthew Snover, Nitin Madnani, Bonnie Dorr, and Richard Schwartz. Terp system description. In *MetricsMATR workshop at AMTA*, 2008.

Exploring Consensus in Machine Translation for Quality Estimation

Carolina Scarton and **Lucia Specia**
Department of Computer Science, University of Sheffield
Regent Court, 211 Portobello, Sheffield, S1 4DP, UK
{c.scarton,l.specia}@sheffield.ac.uk

Abstract

This paper presents the use of consensus among Machine Translation (MT) systems for the WMT14 Quality Estimation shared task. Consensus is explored here by comparing the MT system output against several alternative machine translations using standard evaluation metrics. Figures extracted from such metrics are used as features to complement baseline prediction models. The hypothesis is that knowing whether the translation of interest is similar or dissimilar to translations from multiple different MT systems can provide useful information regarding the quality of such a translation.

1 Introduction

While Machine Translation (MT) evaluation metrics can rely on the similarity of the MT system output to reference (human) translations as a proxy to quality assessment, this is not possible for MT systems in use, translating unseen texts. Quality Estimation (QE) metrics are used in such settings as a way of predicting translation quality. While reference translations are not available for QE, previous work has explored the so called *pseudo-references* (Soricut and Echihabi, 2010; Soricut et al., 2012; Soricut and Narsale, 2012; Shah et al., 2013). Pseudo-references are alternative translations produced by MT systems different from the system that we intend to predict quality for (Albrecht and Hwa, 2008). These can be used to provide additional features to train QE models. Such features are normally figures resulting from automatic metrics (such as BLEU, Papineni et al. (2002)) computed between pseudo-references and the output of the given MT system.

Soricut and Echihabi (2010) explore pseudo-references for document-level QE prediction to rank outputs from an MT system. The pseudo-references-based features are BLEU scores extracted by comparing the output of the MT system under investigation and the output of an off-the-shelf MT system, for both the target and the source texts. The statistical MT system training data is also used as pseudo-references to compute training data-based features. The use of pseudo-references has been shown to outperform strong baseline results. Soricut and Narsale (2012) propose a method that uses sentence-level prediction models for document-level QE. They also use a pseudo-references-based feature (based in BLEU) and claim that this feature is one of the most powerful in the framework.

For QE at sentence-level, Soricut et al. (2012) use BLEU based on pseudo-references combined with other features to build the best QE system of the WMT12 QE shared task.[1] Shah et al. (2013) use pseudo-references in the same way to extract a BLEU feature for sentence-level prediction. Feature analysis on a number of datasets showed that this feature contributed the most across all datasets.

Louis and Nenkova (2013) apply pseudo-references for summary evaluation. They use six systems classified as "best systems", "mediocre systems" or "worst systems" to make the comparison, with ROUGE (Lin and Och, 2004) as quality score. They also experiment with a combination of the "best systems" and the "worst systems". The use of only "best systems" led to the best results. Examples of "bad summaries" are said not to be very useful because a summary close to the worst systems outputs can mean that either it is bad or it is too different from the best systems outputs in terms of content. Albrecht and Hwa (2008) use pseudo-references to improve MT evaluation by combining them with a single human reference. They show that the use of pseudo-references im-

[1] http://www.statmt.org/wmt12/

Proceedings of the Ninth Workshop on Statistical Machine Translation, pages 342–347,
Baltimore, Maryland USA, June 26–27, 2014.

proves the correlation with human judgements.

Soricut and Echihabi (2010) claim that pseudo-references should be produced by systems as different as possible from the MT system of interest. This ensures that the similarities found among the systems' translations are not related to the similarities of the systems themselves. Therefore, the assumption that a translation from system X shares some characteristics with a translation from system Y is not a mere coincidence. Another way to make the most of pseudo-references is to use an MT system known as generally better (or worse) than the MT system of interest. In that case, the comparison will lead to whether the MT system of interest is similar to a good (or bad) MT system.

However, in most scenarios it is difficult to rely on the average translation quality of a given system as an absolute indicator of its quality. This is particularly true for sentence-level QE, where the quality of a given system can vary significantly across sentences. Finding translations from MT systems that are considerably different can also be a challenge. In this paper we exploit pseudo-references in a different way: measuring the consensus among different MT systems in the translations they produce. As sources of pseudo-references, we use translations given in a multi-translation dataset or those produced by the participants in the WMT translation task for the same data. While some MT systems can be similar to each other, for some language pairs, such as English-Spanish, a wide range of MT systems with different average qualities are available. Our hypothesis is that by using translations from several MT systems we can find **consensual information** (even if some of the systems are similar to the one of interest). The use of more than one MT system is expected to smooth out the effect of "coincidences" in the similarities between systems' translations.

This paper describes the use of consensual information for the WMT14 QE shared task (USHEFF-consensus system), simulating a scenario where we do not know the quality of the pseudo-references, nor the characteristics of any MT systems (the system of interest or the systems which generated the pseudo-references). We participated in all variants of Task 1, sentence-level QE, for both for scoring and ranking. Section 2 explains how we extracted consensual information for all tasks. Section 3 shows our official results compared to the baselines provided. Section 4 presents some conclusions.

2 Consensual information extraction

The consensual information is exploited in two different ways in Task 1. Task 1.1 used"perceived" post-editing effort labels as quality scores for scoring and ranking in four languages pairs. These labels vary within [1-3], where:

- 1 = perfect translation
- 2 = near miss translation (sentences with 2-3 errors that are easy to fix)
- 3 = very low quality sentence.

The training and test sets for each language pair in Task 1.1 contain 3-4 translations of the same source sentences. The language pairs are German-English (DE-EN) with 150 source sentences for test and 350 source sentences for training, English-German (EN-DE) with 150 source sentences for test and 350 source sentences for training, English-Spanish (EN-ES) with 150 source sentences for test and 954 source sentences for training, and Spanish-English (ES-EN) with 150 source sentences for test and 350 source sentences for training. The translations for each language pair include a human translation and translations produced by a statistical MT (SMT) system, a rule-based MT (RBMT) system, and a hybrid system (for the EN-DE and EN-ES language pairs only).

By inspecting the source side of the training set, we noticed that the translations were ordered per systems, since the source file had sentences repeated in batches. For example, the EN-ES language pair had 954 English sentences and 3,816 Spanish sentences. In the source file, the English sentences were repeated in batches of 954 sentences. Based on that, we assumed that in the target file each set of 954 translations in sequence corresponded to a given MT system (or human).

For each system (human translation is considered as a system, since we do not know the order of the translations), we calculate the consensual information considering the other 2-3 systems available as pseudo-references.

The quality scores for Task 1.2 and Task 1.3 were computed as HTER (Human Translation Error Rate (Snover et al., 2006)) and post-editing time, respectively, for both scoring and ranking.

The datasets were a mixture of test sets from the WMT13 and WMT12 translation shared tasks for the EN-ES language pair only. In this case, the consensual information was extracted by using systems submitted to the WMT translation shared tasks of both years. Therefore, for each source sentence in the WMT12/13 data, all translations produced by the participating MT systems of that year were used as pseudo-references. The *uedin* system outputs for both WMT13 and WMT12 were not considered, since the datasets in Tasks 1.2 and 1.3 were created from translations generated by this system.[2]

The Asyia Toolkit[3] (Giménez and Màrquez, 2010) was used to extract the automatic metrics considered as features. BLEU, TER (Snover et al., 2006), METEOR (Banerjee and Lavie, 2005) and ROUGE (Lin and Och, 2004) are used in all task variants. For Tasks 1.2 and 1.3 we also use metrics based on syntactic similarities from shallow and dependency parser information (metrics SPOc(*) and DPmHWCM_c1, respectively, in Asyia). BLEU is a precision-oriented metric that compares n-grams (n=1-4 in our case) from reference documents against n-grams of the MT output, measuring how close the output of a system is to one or more references. TER (Translation Error Rate) measures the minimum number of edits required to transform the MT output into the closest reference document. METEOR (Metric for Evaluation of Translation with Explicit ORdering) scores MT outputs by aligning them with given references. This alignment can be done by exact, stem, synonym and paraphrases matching (here, exact matching was used). ROUGE is a recall-oriented metric that measures similarity between sentences by considering the longest common n-gram statistics between a translation sentence and the corresponding reference sentence. SPOc(*) measures the lexical overlap according to the chunk types of the syntactic realisation. The '*' means that an average of all chunk types is computed. DPmHWCM_c1 is based on the matching of head-word chains. We considered the match of grammatical categories of only one head-word.

These consensual features are combined with the 17 QuEst baseline features provided by the shared task organisers.

[2]WMT14 QE shared task organisers, personal communication, March 2014.

[3]http://asiya.lsi.upc.edu/

3 Experiments and Results

The results reported herein are the official shared task results, that is, they were computed using the true scores of the test set made available by the organisers after our submission.

For training the QE models, we used Support Vector Machines (SVM) regression algorithm with a radial basis function (RBF) kernel with the hyperparameters optimised via grid search. The scikit-learn algorithm available in the QuEst Framework[4] (Specia et al., 2013) was used for that.

We compared the results obtained against using only the QuEst baseline (**BL**) features, which is the same system used as the official baseline for the shared task. For the scoring variant we also compare our results against a baseline that "predicts" the average of the true scores of the training set as scores for each sentence of the test set (**Mean** – each sentence has the same predicted score).

For all language pairs in Task 1.1, Table 1 shows the average results for the scoring variant using MAE (Mean Absolute Error) as evaluation metric, while Table 2 shows the results for the ranking variant using DeltaAvg.

The results for scoring improved over the baselines with the use of consensual information for language pairs DE-EN and EN-ES. For EN-DE and ES-EN the consensual features achieved similar results to BL. The best result for consensual information features was achieved with EN-ES (0.03 of MAE difference from BL).

For the ranking variant, the consensual information improved the results for all language pairs. The largest improvement from consensual-based features was achieved for ES-EN, with a difference of 0.11 from the baseline. It is worth mentioning that for ES-EN our system achieved the best ranking result in Task 1.1.

Since the results varied for different languages pairs, we further inspected them for each language pair. First, we looked at the true scores distribution and realised that the first batch of translations for each language pair was probably the human reference since the percentage of 1s – the best quality score – was much higher for this system (see Figure 1 for EN-DE as an example). By using this human translation as a reference for the other MT systems, we computed BLEU for each sentence

[4]http://www.quest.dcs.shef.ac.uk/

	DE-EN	EN-DE	EN-ES	ES-EN
Mean	0.67	0.68	0.46	0.58
BL	0.65	0.64	0.52	0.57
BL+Consensus	**0.63**	0.64	**0.49**	0.57

Table 1: Scoring results for Task 1.1 in terms of MAE

	DE-EN	EN-DE	EN-ES	ES-EN
BL	0.21	0.23	0.14	0.12
BL+Consensus	**0.28**	**0.26**	**0.21**	**0.23**

Table 2: Ranking results for Task 1.1 in terms of DeltaAvg

and averaged these values. The results are shown in Table 3.

For DE-EN, EN-DE and EN-ES, the various systems appeared to be less dissimilar in terms of BLEU, when compared to ES-EN. For ES-EN, the difference between the two MT systems was higher than for other language pairs (0.12 for the test set and 0.11 for the training set). Moreover, for DE-EN, EN-DE and EN-ES, the difference between the averaged BLEU score of the training set and the average BLEU score of the test set is very small (smaller than 0.01). For ES-EN, however, the difference between the scores for the training and test sets was also higher (0.04 for System1 and 0.03 for System2). This can be one reason why the consensual features did not show improvements for this language pair. Since the systems are considerably different and also there is a considerable difference between training and test sets, the data can be too noisy to be used as pseudo-references.

For EN-DE, the reasons for the bad performance of consensual features are not clear. This language pair showed the worst average quality scores for all systems. Reasons for this can include characteristics of German language, such as compound words which are not well treated in MT, and complex grammar. One hypothesis is that these low BLEU scores (as Table 3 shows) introduce noise instead of useful information for QE. Another difference that appeared only in EN-DE was the distributions of the scores across the different systems. As Figure 1 shows, System1 has a distribution considerably different from the other two systems. For the other language pairs, the distributions across different systems were more uniform. This difference can be another factor influencing the results for this language pair.

Table 4 shows the results for scoring (MAE) and Table 5 shows the results for ranking (DeltaAvg) for Tasks 1.2 and 1.3.

	Task 1.2	Task 1.3
Mean	16.93	23.34
BL	15.23	21.49
BL+Consensus	**13.61**	**21.48**

Table 4: Scoring results of Tasks 1.2 and 1.3 in terms of MAE

	Task 1.2	Task 1.3
BL	5.08	14.71
BL+Consensus	**7.93**	**14.98**

Table 5: Ranking results of Tasks 1.2 and 1.3 in terms of DeltaAvg

For Tasks 1.2 and 1.3 the use of consensual information only slightly improved the baseline results for scoring. For the ranking variant, BL+Consensus achieved better results, but only significantly so for Task 1.2. Therefore, consensual information seems useful to rank sentences according to predicted HTER, its contribution to predicting actual HTER is not noticeable. For post-editing time as quality labels, the improvement achieved with the use of consensual information was marginal.

4 Conclusions

The use of consensual information of MT systems can be useful to improve state-of-the-art results for QE. For some scenarios, it is possible to acquire several translations for a given source segment, but with no additional information on the quality or type of MT systems used to produce them. Therefore, these translations could not be used as pseudo-references in the same way as in (Soricut and Echihabi, 2010).

	DE-EN		EN-DE			EN-ES			ES-EN	
	Sys1	Sys2	Sys1	Sys2	Sys3	Sys1	Sys2	Sys3	Sys1	Sys2
Average BLEU (test)	0.31	0.25	0.20	0.19	0.21	0.36	0.29	0.32	**0.44**	**0.32**
Average BLEU (training)	0.31	0.26	0.21	0.18	0.22	0.35	0.29	0.31	**0.40**	**0.29**

Table 3: Average BLEU of systems in Task 1.1

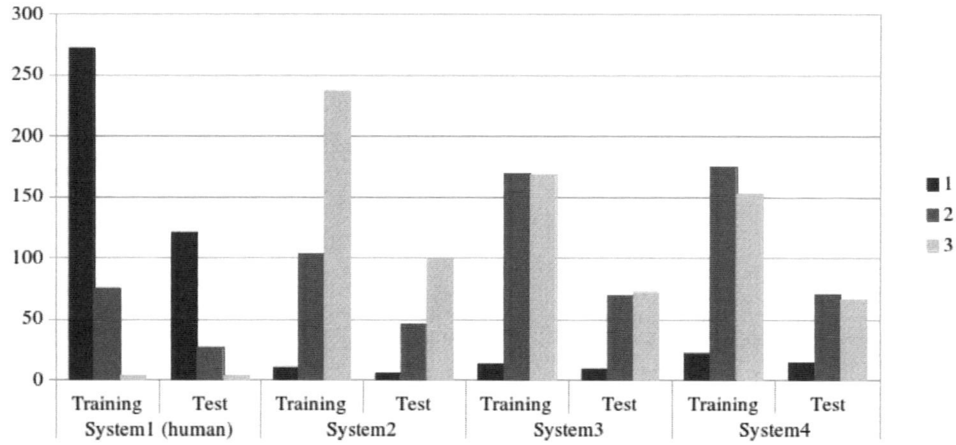

Figure 1: Distribution of true quality scores for the EN-DE language pair

The use of several references with the hypothesis that they share consensual information has been shown useful in some settings, particularly in Task 1.1. In others, the results were inconclusive. In particular, the approach does not seem appropriate for scenarios where the MT systems are considerably different (as shown in Table 3). In those cases, better ways to exploit consensual information need to be investigated further.

Acknowledgements: This work was supported by the EXPERT (EU Marie Curie ITN No. 317471) project.

References

Joshua S. Albrecht and Rebecca Hwa. 2008. The role of pseudo references in mt evaluation. In *Proceedings of WMT 2008*, pages 187–190, Columbus, Ohio, USA.

Satanjeev Banerjee and Alon Lavie. 2005. Meteor: An automatic metric for mt evaluation with improved correlation with human judgments. In *Proceedings of the ACL 2005 Workshop on Intrinsic and Extrinsic Evaluation Measures for MT and/or Summarization.*

Jesús Giménez and Lluís Màrquez. 2010. Asiya: An Open Toolkit for Automatic Machine Translation (Meta-)Evaluation. *The Prague Bulletin of Mathematical Linguistics*, (94):77–86.

Chin-Yew Lin and Franz J. Och. 2004. Automatic Evaluation of Machine Translation Quality Using Longest Common Subsequence and Skip-Bigram Statics. In *Proceedings of ACL 2004*, Barcelona, Spain.

Annie Louis and Ani Nenkova. 2013. Automatically assessing machine summary content without a gold standard. *Computational Linguistics*, 39(2):267–300, June.

Kishore Papineni, Salim Roukos, Todd Ward, and Wei jing Zhu. 2002. Bleu: a method for automatic evaluation of machine translation. In *Proceedings of ACL 2002*, pages 311–318, Philadelphia, USA.

Kashif Shah, Trevor Cohn, and Lucia Specia. 2013. An Investigation on the Effectiveness of Features for Translation Quality Estimation. In *Proceedings of the XIV MT Summit*, pages 167–174, Nice, France.

Matthew Snover, Bonnie Dorr, Richard Schwartz, Linnea Micciulla, and John Makhoul. 2006. A study of translation edit rate with targeted human annotation. In *Proceedings of AMTA 2006*, pages 223–231.

Radu Soricut and Abdessamad Echihabi. 2010. TrustRank: Inducing Trust in Automatic Translations via Ranking. In *Proceedings of the ACL 2010*, pages 612–621, Uppsala, Sweden.

Radu Soricut and Sushant Narsale. 2012. Combining Quality Prediction and System Selection for Improved Automatic Translation Output. In *Proceedings of WMT 2012*, Montreal, Canada.

Radu Soricut, Nguyen Bach, and Ziyuan Wang. 2012. The SDL Language Weaver Systems in the WMT12 Quality Estimation Shared Task. In *Proceedings of WMT 2012*, Montreal, Canada.

Lucia Specia, Kashif Shah, Jose G.C. de Souza, and Trevor Cohn. 2013. Quest - a translation quality estimation framework. In *Proceedings of WMT 2013: System Demonstrations*, ACL-2013, pages 79–84, Sofia, Bulgaria.

LIMSI Submission for WMT'14 QE Task

Guillaume Wisniewski and **Nicolas Pécheux** and **Alexandre Allauzen** and **François Yvon**
Université Paris Sud and LIMSI-CNRS
91 403 ORSAY CEDEX, France
{wisniews, pecheux, allauzen, yvon}@limsi.fr

Abstract

This paper describes LIMSI participation to the WMT'14 Shared Task on Quality Estimation; we took part to the word-level quality estimation task for English to Spanish translations. Our system relies on a random forest classifier, an ensemble method that has been shown to be very competitive for this kind of task, when only a few dense and continuous features are used. Notably, only 16 features are used in our experiments. These features describe, on the one hand, the quality of the association between the source sentence and each target word and, on the other hand, the fluency of the hypothesis. Since the evaluation criterion is the f_1 measure, a specific tuning strategy is proposed to select the optimal values for the hyper-parameters. Overall, our system achieves a 0.67 f_1 score on a randomly extracted test set.

1 Introduction

This paper describes LIMSI submission to the WMT'14 Shared Task on Quality Estimation. We participated in the word-level quality estimation task (Task 2) for the English to Spanish direction. This task consists in predicting, for each word in a translation hypothesis, whether this word should be post-edited or should rather be kept unchanged.

Predicting translation quality *at the word level* raises several interesting challenges. First, this is a (relatively) new task and the best way to formulate and evaluate it has still to be established. Second, as most works on quality estimation have only considered prediction at the sentence level, it is not clear yet which features are really effective to predict quality at the word and a set of baseline features has still to be found. Finally, several characteristic of the task (the limited number of training examples, the unbalanced classes, etc.) makes the use of 'traditional' machine learning algorithms difficult. This papers describes how we addressed this different issues for our participation to the WMT'14 Shared Task.

The rest of this paper is organized as follows. Section 2 gives an overview of the shared task data that will justify some of the design decisions we made. Section 3 describes the different features we have considered and Section 4, the learning methods used to estimate the classifiers parameters. Finally the results of our models are presented and analyzed in Section 5.

2 World-Level Quality Estimation

WMT'14 shared task on quality estimation number 2 consists in predicting, for each word of a translation hypothesis, whether this word should be post-edited (denoted by the BAD label) or should be kept unchanged (denoted by the OK label). The shared task organizers provide a bilingual dataset from English to Spanish[1] made of translations produced by three different MT systems and by one human translator; these translations have then been annotated with word-level labels by professional translators. No additional information about the systems used, the derivation of the translation (such as the lattices or the alignment between the source and the best translation hypothesis) or the tokenization applied to identify words is provided.

The distributions of the two labels for the different systems is displayed in Table 1. As it could be expected, the class are, overall, unbalanced and the systems are of very different quality: the proportion of BAD and OK labels highly depends on the system used to produce the translation hypotheses. However, as our preliminary experiments have shown, the number of examples is

[1] We did not consider the other language pairs.

Proceedings of the Ninth Workshop on Statistical Machine Translation, pages 348–354,
Baltimore, Maryland USA, June 26–27, 2014. ©2014 Association for Computational Linguistics

too small to train a different confidence estimation system for each system.

The distribution of the number of BAD labels per sentence is very skewed: on average, one word out of three (precisely 35.04%) in a sentence is labeled as BAD but the median of the distribution of the ratio of word labeled BAD in a sentence is 20% and its standard deviation is pretty high (34.75%). Several sentences have all their words labeled as either OK or BAD, which is quite surprising as the sentences of the corpus for Task 2 have been selected because there were 'near miss translations' that is to say translations that should have contained no more that 2 or 3 errors.

Another interesting finding is that the proportion of word to post-edit is the same across the different parts-of-speech (see Table 2).[2]

Table 1: Number of examples and distribution of labels for the different systems on the training set

System	#sent.	#words	% OK	% BAD
1	791	19,456	75.48	24.52
2	621	14,620	59.11	40.89
3	454	11,012	59.76	40.24
4	90	2,296	36.85	63.15
Total	1,956	47,384	64.90	35.10

Table 2: Distribution of labels according to the POS on the training set

POS	% in train	% BAD
NOUN	23.81	35.02
ADP	15.06	35.48
DET	14.90	32.88
VERB	14.64	41.26
PUNCT	10.92	27.26
ADJ	6.61	35.68
CONJ	5.04	30.77
PRON	4.58	43.15
ADV	4.39	36.56

As the classes are unbalanced, prediction performance will be evaluated in terms of precision, recall and f_1 score computed on the BAD label. More precisely, if the number of true positive (i.e. BAD word predicted as BAD), false positive (OK word predicted as BAD) and false negative (BAD word predicted as OK) are denoted tp_{BAD}, fp_{BAD} and fn_{BAD}, respectively, the quality of a confidence estimation system is evaluated by the three following metrics:

$$p_{\text{BAD}} = \frac{\text{tp}_{\text{BAD}}}{\text{tp}_{\text{BAD}} + \text{fp}_{\text{BAD}}} \quad (1)$$

$$r_{\text{BAD}} = \frac{\text{tp}_{\text{BAD}}}{\text{tp}_{\text{BAD}} + \text{fn}_{\text{BAD}}} \quad (2)$$

$$f_1 = \frac{2 \cdot p_{\text{BAD}} \cdot r_{\text{BAD}}}{p_{\text{BAD}} + r_{\text{BAD}}} \quad (3)$$

3 Features

In our experiments, we used 16 features to describe a given target word t_i in a translation hypothesis $\mathbf{t} = (t_j)_{j=1}^m$. To avoid sparsity issues we decided not to include any lexicalized information such as the word or the previous word identities. As the translation hypotheses were generated by different MT systems, no white-box features (such as word alignment or model scores) are considered. Our features can be organized in two broad categories:

Association Features These features measure the quality of the 'association' between the source sentence and a target word: they characterize the probability for a target word to appear in a translation of the source sentence. Two kinds of association features can be distinguished.

The first one is derived from the lexicalized probabilities $p(t|s)$ that estimate the probability that a source word s is translated by the target word t_j. These probabilities are aggregated using an arithmetic mean:

$$p(t_j|\mathbf{s}) = \frac{1}{n}\sum_{i=1}^{n} p(t_j|s_i) \quad (4)$$

where $\mathbf{s} = (s_i)_{i=1}^n$ is the source sentence (with an extra NULL token). We assume that $p(t_j|s_i) = 0$ if the words t_j and s_i have never been aligned in the train set and also consider the geometric mean of the lexicalized probabilities, their maximum value (i.e. $\max_{s \in \mathbf{s}} p(t_j|s)$) as well as a binary feature that fires when the target word t_j is not in the lexicalized probabilities table.

The second kind of association features relies on pseudo-references, that is to say, translations of the source sentence produced by an independent MT system. Many works have considered

[2]We used FreeLing (http:nlp.lsi.upc.edu/freeling/) to predict the POS tags of the translation hypotheses and, for the sake of clarity, mapped the 71 tags used by FreeLing to the 11 universal POS tags of Petrov et al. (2012).

pseudo-references to design new MT metrics (Albrecht and Hwa, 2007; Albrecht and Hwa, 2008) or for confidence estimation (Soricut and Echihabi, 2010; Soricut and Narsale, 2012) but, to the best of our knowledge, this is the first time that they are used to predict confidence at the word level.

Pseudo-references are used to define 3 binary features which fire if the target word is in the pseudo-reference, in a 2-gram shared between the pseudo-reference and the translation hypothesis or in a common 3-gram, respectively. The lattices representing the search space considered to generate these pseudo-references also allow us to estimate the *posterior probability* of a target word that quantifies the probability that it is part of the system output (Gispert et al., 2013). Posteriors aggregate two pieces of information for each word in the final hypothesis: first, all the paths in the lattice (i.e. the number of translation hypotheses in the search space) where the word appears in are considered; second, the decoder scores of these paths are accumulated in order to derive a confidence measure at the word level. In our experiments, we considered pseudo-references and lattices produced by the n-gram based system developed by our team for last year WMT evaluation campaign (Allauzen et al., 2013), that has achieved very good performance.

Fluency Features These features measure the 'fluency' of the target sentence and are based on different language models: a 'traditional' 4-gram language model estimated on WMT monolingual and bilingual data (the language model used by our system to generate the pseudo-references); a continuous-space 10-gram language model estimated with SOUL (Le et al., 2011) (also used by our MT system) and a 4-gram language model based on Part-of-Speech sequences. The latter model was estimated on the Spanish side of the bilingual data provided in the translation shared task in 2013. These data were POS-tagged with FreeLing (Padró and Stanilovsky, 2012).

All these language models have been used to define two different features :

- the probability of the word of interest $p(t_j|h)$ where $h = t_{j-1}, ..., t_{j-n+1}$ is the history made of the $n-1$ previous words or POS
- the ratio between the probability of the sentence and the 'best' probability that can be achieved if the target word is replaced by any other word (i.e. $\max_{v \in \mathcal{V}} p(t_1, ..., t_{j-1}, v, t_{j+1}, ..., t_m)$ where the max runs over all the words of the vocabulary).

There is also a feature that describes the back-off behavior of the conventional language model: its value is the size of the largest n-gram of the translation hypothesis that can be estimated by the language model without relying on back-off probabilities.

Finally, there is a feature describing, for each word that appears more than once in the train set, the probability that this word is labeled BAD. This probability is simply estimated by the ratio between the number of times this word is labeled BAD and the number of occurrences of this word.

It must be noted that most of the features we consider rely on models that are part of a 'classic' MT system. However their use for predicting translation quality at the word-level is not straightforward, as they need to be applied to sentences with a given unknown tokenization. Matching the tokenization used to estimate the model to the one used for collecting the annotations is a tedious and error-prone process and some of the prediction errors most probably result from mismatches in tokenization.

4 Learning Methods

4.1 Classifiers

Predicting whether a word in a translation hypothesis should be post-edited or not can naturally be framed as a binary classification task. Based on our experiments in previous campaigns (Singh et al., 2013; Zhuang et al., 2012), we considered random forest in all our experiments.[3]

Random forest (Breiman, 2001) is an ensemble method that learns many classification trees and predicts an aggregation of their result (for instance by majority voting). In contrast with standard decision trees, in which each node is split using the best split among all features, in a random forest the split is chosen randomly. In spite of this simple and counter-intuitive learning strategy, random forests have proven to be very good 'out-of-the-box' learners. Random forests have achieved very good performance in many similar

[3]we have used the implementation provided by `scikit-learn` (Pedregosa et al., 2011).

tasks (Chapelle and Chang, 2011), in which only a few dense and continuous features are available, possibly because of their ability to take into account complex interactions between features and to automatically partition the continuous features value into a discrete set of intervals that achieves the best classification performance.

As a baseline, we consider logistic regression (Hastie et al., 2003), a simple linear model where the parameters are estimated by maximizing the likelihood of the training set.

These two classifiers do not produce only a class decision but yield an instance probability that represents the degree to which an instance is a member of a class. As detailed in the next section, thresholding this probability will allow us to directly optimize the f_1 score used to evaluate prediction performance.

4.2 Optimizing the f_1 Score

As explained in Section 2, quality prediction will be evaluated in terms of f_1 score. The learning methods we consider can not, as most learning method, directly optimize the f_1 measure during training, since this metric does not decompose over the examples. It is however possible to take advantage of the fact that they actually estimate a probability to find the largest f_1 score on the training set.

Indeed these probabilities are used with a threshold (usually 0.5) to produce a discrete (binary) decision: if the probability is above the threshold, the classifier produces a positive output, and otherwise, a negative one. Each threshold value produces a different trade-off between true positives and false positives and consequently between recall and precision: as the the threshold becomes lower and lower, more and more example are assigned to the positive class and recall increase at the expense of precision.

Based on these observations, we propose the following three-step method to optimize the f_1 score on the training set:

1. the classifier is first trained using the 'standard' learning procedure that optimizes either the 0/1 loss (for random forest) or the likelihood (for the logistic regression);

2. all the possible trade-offs between recall and precision are enumerated by varying the threshold; exploiting the monotonicity of thresholded classifications,[4] this enumeration can be efficiently done in $\mathcal{O}(n \cdot \log n)$ and results in at most n threshold values, where n is the size of the training set (Fawcett, 2003);

3. all the f_1 scores achieved for the different thresholds found in the previous step are evaluated; there are strong theoretical guarantees that the optimal f_1 score that can be achieved on the training set is one of these values (Boyd and Vandenberghe, 2004).

Figure 1 shows how f_1 score varies with the decision threshold and allows to assess the difference between the optimal value of the threshold and its default value (0.5).

Figure 1: Evolution of the f_1 score with respect to the threshold used to transform probabilities into binary decisions

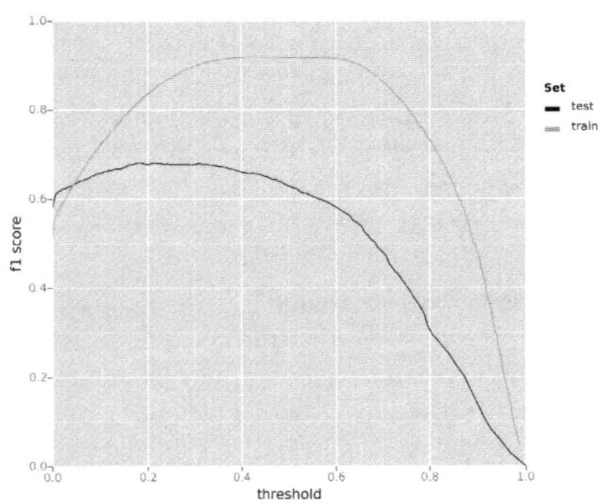

5 Experiments

The features and learning strategies described in the two previous sections were evaluated on the English to Spanish datasets. As no official development set was provided by the shared task organizers, we randomly sampled 200 sentences from the training set and use them as a test set throughout the rest of this article. Preliminary experiments show that the choice of this test has a very low impact on the classification performance. The different hyper-parameters of the training algorithm

[4]Any instance that is classified positive with respect to a given threshold will be classified positive for all lower thresholds as well.

Table 3: Prediction performance for the two learning strategies considered

Classifier	thres.	r_{BAD}	p_{BAD}	f_1
Random forest	0.43	0.64	0.69	0.67
Logistic regression	0.27	0.51	0.72	0.59

were chosen by maximizing classification performance (as evaluated by the f_1 score) estimated on 150 sentences of the training set kept apart as a validation set.

Results for the different learning algorithms considered are presented in Table 3. Random forest clearly outperforms a simple logistic regression, which shows the importance of using non-linear decision functions, a conclusion at pair with our previous results (Zhuang et al., 2012; Singh et al., 2013).

The overall performance, with a f_1 measure of 0.67, is pretty low and in our opinion, not good enough to consider using such a quality estimation system in a computer-assisted post-edition context. However, as shown in Table 4, the prediction performance highly depends on the POS category of the words: it is quite good for 'plain' words (like verb and nouns) but much worse for other categories.

There are two possible explanations for this observation: predicting the correctness of some morpho-syntaxic categories may be intrinsically harder (e.g. for punctuation the choice of which can be highly controversial) or depend on information that is not currently available to our system. In particular, we do not consider any information about the structure of the sentence and about the labels of the context, which may explain why our system does not perform well in predicting the labels of determiners and conjunctions. In both cases, this result brings us to moderate our previous conclusions: as a wrong punctuation sign has not the same impact on translation quality as a wrong verb, our system might, regardless of its f_1 score, be able to provide useful information about the quality of a translation. This also suggests that we should look for a more 'task-oriented' metric.

Finally, Figure 2 displays the *importance* of the different features used in our system. Random forests deliver a quantification of the importance of a feature with respect to the predictability of the target variable. This quantification is derived from the position of a feature in a decision tree: features used in the top nodes of the trees, which contribute to the final prediction decision of a larger fraction of the input samples, play a more important role than features used near the leaves of the tree. It appears that, as for our previous experiments (Wisniewski et al., 2013), the most relevant feature for predicting translation quality is the feature derived from the SOUL language model, even if other fluency features seem to also play an important role. Surprisingly enough, features related to the pseudo-reference do not seem to be useful. Further experiments are needed to explain the reasons of this observation.

Table 4: Prediction performance for each POS tag

System	f_1
VERB	0.73
PRON	0.72
ADJ	0.70
NOUN	0.69
ADV	0.69
overall	0.67
DET	0.62
ADP	0.61
CONJ	0.57
PUNCT	0.56

6 Conclusion

In this paper we described the system submitted for Task 2 of WMT'14 Shared Task on Quality Estimation. Our system relies on a binary classifier and consider only a few dense and continuous features. While the overall performance is pretty low, a fine-grained analysis of the errors of our system shows that it can predict the quality of plain words pretty accurately which indicates that a more 'task-oriented' evaluation may be needed.

Acknowledgments

This work was partly supported by ANR project Transread (ANR-12-CORD-0015). Warm thanks to Quoc Khanh Do for his help for training a SOUL model for Spanish.

References

Joshua Albrecht and Rebecca Hwa. 2007. Regression for sentence-level mt evaluation with pseudo refer-

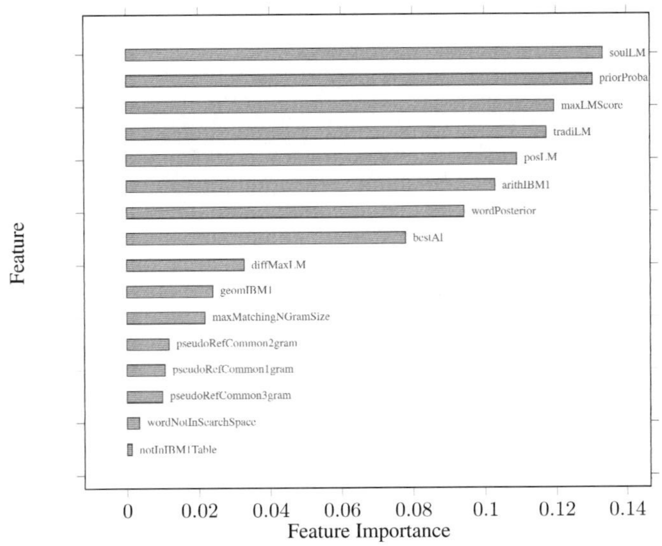

Figure 2: Features considered by our system sorted by their relevance for predicting translation errors

ences. In *Proceedings of the 45th Annual Meeting of the Association of Computational Linguistics*, pages 296–303, Prague, Czech Republic, June. ACL.

Joshua Albrecht and Rebecca Hwa. 2008. The role of pseudo references in MT evaluation. In *Proceedings of the Third Workshop on Statistical Machine Translation*, pages 187–190, Columbus, Ohio, June. ACL.

Alexandre Allauzen, Nicolas Pécheux, Quoc Khanh Do, Marco Dinarelli, Thomas Lavergne, Aurélien Max, Hai-Son Le, and François Yvon. 2013. LIMSI @ WMT13. In *Proceedings of the Eighth Workshop on Statistical Machine Translation*, pages 62–69, Sofia, Bulgaria, August. ACL.

Stephen Boyd and Lieven Vandenberghe. 2004. *Convex Optimization*. Cambridge University Press, New York, NY, USA.

Leo Breiman. 2001. Random forests. *Mach. Learn.*, 45(1):5–32, October.

Olivier Chapelle and Yi Chang. 2011. Yahoo! learning to rank challenge overview. In Olivier Chapelle, Yi Chang, and Tie-Yan Liu, editors, *Yahoo! Learning to Rank Challenge*, volume 14 of *JMLR Proceedings*, pages 1–24. JMLR.org.

Tom Fawcett. 2003. ROC Graphs: Notes and Practical Considerations for Researchers. Technical Report HPL-2003-4, HP Laboratories, Palo Alto.

Adrià Gispert, Graeme Blackwood, Gonzalo Iglesias, and William Byrne. 2013. N-gram posterior probability confidence measures for statistical machine translation: an empirical study. *Machine Translation*, 27(2):85–114.

Trevor Hastie, Robert Tibshirani, and Jerome H. Friedman. 2003. *The Elements of Statistical Learning*. Springer, July.

Hai-Son Le, Ilya Oparin, Alexandre Allauzen, Jean-Luc Gauvain, and François Yvon. 2011. Structured output layer neural network language model. In *Acoustics, Speech and Signal Processing (ICASSP), 2011 IEEE International Conference on*, pages 5524–5527. IEEE.

Lluís Padró and Evgeny Stanilovsky. 2012. Freeling 3.0: Towards wider multilinguality. In *Proceedings of the Language Resources and Evaluation Conference (LREC 2012)*, Istanbul, Turkey, May. ELRA.

F. Pedregosa, G. Varoquaux, A. Gramfort, V. Michel, B. Thirion, O. Grisel, M. Blondel, P. Prettenhofer, R. Weiss, V. Dubourg, J. Vanderplas, A. Passos, D. Cournapeau, M. Brucher, M. Perrot, and E. Duchesnay. 2011. Scikit-learn: Machine learning in Python. *Journal of Machine Learning Research*, 12:2825–2830.

Slav Petrov, Dipanjan Das, and Ryan McDonald. 2012. A universal part-of-speech tagset. In *Proceedings of the Eight International Conference on Language Resources and Evaluation (LREC'12)*, Istanbul, Turkey, may. European Language Resources Association (ELRA).

Anil Kumar Singh, Guillaume Wisniewski, and François Yvon. 2013. LIMSI submission for the WMT'13 quality estimation task: an experiment with n-gram posteriors. In *Proceedings of the Eighth Workshop on Statistical Machine Translation*, pages 398–404, Sofia, Bulgaria, August. ACL.

Radu Soricut and Abdessamad Echihabi. 2010. Trustrank: Inducing trust in automatic translations via ranking. In *Proceedings of the 48th Annual Meeting of the Association for Computational Linguistics*, pages 612–621, Uppsala, Sweden, July. ACL.

Radu Soricut and Sushant Narsale. 2012. Combining quality prediction and system selection for improved automatic translation output. In *Proceedings of the Seventh Workshop on Statistical Machine Translation*, pages 163–170, Montréal, Canada, June. ACL.

Guillaume Wisniewski, Anil Kumar Singh, and François Yvon. 2013. Quality estimation for machine translation: Some lessons learned. *Machine Translation*, 27(3).

Yong Zhuang, Guillaume Wisniewski, and François Yvon. 2012. Non-linear models for confidence estimation. In *Proceedings of the Seventh Workshop on Statistical Machine Translation*, pages 157–162, Montréal, Canada, June. ACL.

Parmesan: Meteor without Paraphrases with Paraphrased References

Petra Barančíková
Institute of Formal and Applied Linguistics
Charles University in Prague, Faculty of Mathematics and Physics
Malostranské náměstí 25, Prague, Czech Republic
barancikova@ufal.mff.cuni.cz

Abstract

This paper describes Parmesan, our submission to the 2014 Workshop on Statistical Machine Translation (WMT) metrics task for evaluation English-to-Czech translation. We show that the Czech Meteor Paraphrase tables are so noisy that they actually can harm the performance of the metric. However, they can be very useful after extensive filtering in targeted paraphrasing of Czech reference sentences prior to the evaluation. Parmesan first performs targeted paraphrasing of reference sentences, then it computes the Meteor score using only the exact match on these new reference sentences. It shows significantly higher correlation with human judgment than Meteor on the WMT12 and WMT13 data.

1 Introduction

The metric for automatic evaluation of machine translation (MT) Meteor[1] (Denkowski and Lavie, 2011) has shown high correlation with human judgment since its appearance. It outperforms traditional metrics like BLEU (Papineni et al., 2002) or NIST (Doddington, 2002) as it explicitly addresses their weaknesses – it takes into account recall, distinguishes between functional and content words, allows language-specific tuning of parameters and many others.

Another important advantage of Meteor is that it supports not only exact word matches between a hypothesis and its corresponding reference sentence, but also matches on the level of stems, synonyms and paraphrases. The Meteor Paraphrase tables (Denkowski and Lavie, 2010) were created automatically using the *pivot* method (Bannard and Callison-Burch, 2005) for six languages.

The basic setting of Meteor for evaluation of Czech sentences offers two levels of matches - exact and paraphrase. In this paper, we show the impact of the quality of paraphrases on the performance of Meteor. We demonstrate that the Czech Meteor Paraphrase tables are full of noise and their addition to the metric worsens its correlation with human judgment. However, they can be very useful (after extensive filtering) in creating new reference sentences by targeted paraphrasing.

Parmesan[2] starts with a simple greedy algorithm for substitution of synonymous words from a hypothesis in its corresponding reference sentence. Further, we apply Depfix (Rosa et al., 2012) to fix grammar errors that might arise by the substitutions.

Our method is independent of the evaluation metric used. In this paper, we use Meteor for its consistently high correlation with human judgment and we attempt to tune it further by modifying its paraphrase tables. We show that reducing the size of the Meteor Paraphrase tables is very beneficial. On the WMT12 and WMT13 data, the Meteor scores computed using only the exact match on our new references significantly outperform Meteor with both exact and paraphrase match on original references. However, this result was not confirmed by this year's data.

We perform our experiments on English-to-Czech translations, but the method is largely language independent.

2 Related Work

Our paraphrasing work is inspired by Kauchak and Barzilay (2006). They are trying to improve the accuracy of MT evaluation of Chinese-to-English translation by targeted paraphrasing, i.e. making a reference closer in wording to a hypothesis (MT output) while keeping its meaning and correctness.

[1] We use the the version 1.4., which was recently outdated as the new version 1.5. was released for WMT14

[2] PARaphrasing for MEteor SANs paraphrases

Proceedings of the Ninth Workshop on Statistical Machine Translation, pages 355–361,
Baltimore, Maryland USA, June 26–27, 2014.

Having a hypothesis $H = h_1, ..., h_n$ and its corresponding reference translation $R = r_1, ..., r_m$, they select a set of candidates $C = \{\langle r_i, h_j \rangle | r_i \in R \setminus H, h_j \in H \setminus R\}$. C is reduced to pairs of words appearing in the same WordNet (Miller, 1995) synset only. For every pair $\langle r_i, h_j \rangle \in C$, h_j is evaluated in the context $r_1, ..., r_{i-1}, \Box, r_{i+1}, ..., r_m$ and if confirmed, the new reference sentence $r_1, ..., r_{i-1}, h_j, r_{i+1}, ..., r_m$ is created. This way, several reference sentences might be created, all with a single changed word with respect to the original one.

In Barančíková et al. (2014), we experiment with several methods of paraphrasing of Czech sentences and filtering the Czech Meteor tables. We show that the amount of noise in the multi-word paraphrases is very high and no automatic filtering method we used outperforms omitting them completely. We present an error analysis based method of filtering paraphrases consisting of pairs of single words, which is used in subsection 3.1. From several methods of paraphrasing, we achieved the best results a with simple greedy method, which is presented in section 4.

3 Data

We perform our experiments on data sets from the English-to-Czech translation task of WMT12 (Callison-Burch et al., 2012), WMT13 (Bojar et al., 2013) and WMT14 (Bojar et al., 2014). The data sets contain 13/14[3]/10 files with Czech outputs of MT systems. In addition, each data set contains one file with corresponding reference sentences and one with original English source sentences. We perform morphological analysis and tagging of the hypotheses and the reference sentences using Morče (Spoustová et al., 2007).

The human judgment of hypotheses is available as a relative ranking of performance of five systems for a sentence. We calculated the score for every system by the "> others" method (Bojar et al., 2011), which was the WMT12 official system score. It is computed as $\frac{wins}{wins+loses}$. We refer to this interpretation of human judgment as *silver standard* to distinguish it from the official system scores, which were computed differently each year (here referred to as *gold standard*).

[3]We use only 12 of them because two of them (FDA.2878 and online-G) have no human judgments.

	WMT12	WMT13	WMT14
WordNet	0.26	0.22	0.24
filtered Meteor	1.53	1.29	1.39
together	1.59	1.34	1.44

Table 1: Average number of one-word paraphrases per sentence found in WordNet, filtered Meteor tables and their union over all systems.

3.1 Sources of Paraphrases

We use two available sources of Czech paraphrases – the Czech WordNet 1.9 PDT (Pala and Smrž, 2004) and the Meteor Paraphrase Tables (Denkowski and Lavie, 2010).

The Czech WordNet 1.9 PDT contains paraphrases of high quality, however, their amount is insufficient for our purposes. It contains 13k pairs of synonymous lemmas and only one paraphrase per four sentences on average is found in the data (see Table 1). For that reason, we employ the Czech Meteor Paraphrase tables, too. They are quite the opposite of Czech WordNet – they are large in size, but contain a lot of noise.

We attempt to reduce the noise in the Czech Meteor Paraphrase tables in the following way. We keep only pairs consisting of single words since we were not successful in reducing the noise effectively for the multi-word paraphrases (**?**).

Using Morče, we first perform morphological analysis of all one-word pairs and replace the word forms with their lemmas. We keep only pairs of different lemmas. Further, we dispose of pairs of words that differ in their parts of speech (POS) or contain an unknown word (typically a foreign word).

In this way we have reduced 684k paraphrases in the original Czech Meteor Paraphrase tables to only 32k pairs of lemmas. We refer to this table as filtered Meteor.

4 Creating New References

We create new references similarly to Kauchak and Barzilay (2006). Let H_L, R_L be sets of lemmas from a hypothesis and a corresponding reference sentence, respectively. Then we select candidates for paraphrasing in the following way: $C_L = \{(r, h) | r \in R_L \setminus H_L, h \in H_L \setminus R_L, r_{POS} = h_{POS}\}$, where r_{POS} and h_{POS} denote the part of speech of the respective lemma.

Further, we restrict the set C_L to pairs appearing in our paraphrase tables only. If a word has several

Source	*The location alone is classic.*				
Hypothesis	*Samotné*	*místo*	*je*	*klasické*	.
	Actual	place$_{neut}$	is	classic$_{neut}$	.
	The place alone is classic.				
Reference	*Už*	*poloha*	*je*	*klasická*	.
	Already	position$_{fem}$	is	classic$_{fem}$	.
	The position itself is classic.				
Before Depfix	*Už*	*místo*	*je*	*klasická*	.
	Already	place$_{neut}$	is	classic$_{fem}$	.
	*The place itself is classic.				
New reference	*Už*	*místo*	*je*	*klasické*	.
	Already	place$_{neut}$	is	classic$_{neut}$	.
	The place itself is classic.				

Figure 1: Example of the targeted paraphrasing. The hypothesis is grammatically correct and has very similar meaning as the reference sentence. The new reference is closer in wording to the hypothesis, but the agreement between the noun and the adjective is broken. Depfix resolves the error and the final reference is correct. Number of overlapping unigrams increased from 2 to 4.

metric	reference	WMT12	WMT13
BLEU	original	0.751	0.835
	new	0.834	**0.891**
METEOR	original	0.833	0.817
	new	**0.927**	**0.891**
1 - TER	original	0.274	0.760
	new	0.283	0.781

Table 2: Pearson's correlation of different metrics with the silver standard.

paraphrases in C_L, we give preference to those found in WordNet or even better in both WordNet and filtered Meteor.

We proceed word by word from the beginning of the reference sentence to its end. If a lemma of a word appears as the first member of a pair in restricted C_L, it is replaced by the word form from hypothesis that has its lemma as the second element of that pair, i.e., by the paraphrase from the hypothesis. Otherwise, the original word the reference sentence is kept.

When integrating paraphrases to the reference sentence, it may happen that the sentence becomes ungrammatical, e.g., due to a broken agreement (see Figure 1). Therefore, we apply Depfix (Rosa et al., 2012) – a system for automatic correction of grammatical errors that appear often in English-to-Czech MT outputs.

Depfix analyses the input sentences using a range of natural language processing tools. It fixes errors using a set of linguistically-motivated rules and a statistical component it contains.

5 Choosing a metric

Our next step is choosing a metric that correlates well with human judgment. We experiment with three common metrics – BLEU, Meteor and TER. Based on the results (see Table 2), we decided to employ Meteor in WMT14 as our metric because it shows consistently highest correlations.

6 Meteor settings

Based on the positive impact of filtering Meteor Paraphrase Tables for targeted lexical paraphrasing of reference sentences (see the column **Basic** in Table 4), we experiment with the filtering them yet again, but this time as an inner part of the Meteor evaluation metric (i.e. for the paraphrase match).

We experiment with seven different settings that are presented in Table 3. All of them are created by reducing the original Meteor Paraphrase tables, except for the setting referred to as **WordNet** in the table. In this case, the paraphrase table is generated from one-word paraphrases in Czech WordNet to all their possible word forms found in CzEng (Bojar et al., 2012).

Prior paraphrasing reference sentences and using Meteor with the **No paraphr.** setting for computing scores constitutes Parmesan – our submission to the WMT14 for evaluation English-to-Czech translation. In the tables with results,

setting	size	description of the paraphrase table
Basic	684k	The original Meteor Paraphrase Tables
One-word	181k	**Basic** without multi-word pairs
Same POS	122k	**One-word** + only same part-of-speech pairs
Diff. Lemma	71k	**Same POS** + only forms of different lemma
Same Lemma	51k	**Same POS** + only forms of same lemma
No paraphr.	0	No paraphrase tables, i.e., exact match only
WordNet	202k	Paraphrase tables generated from Czech WordNet

Table 3: Different paraphrase tables for Meteor and their size (number of paraphrase pairs).

WMT12

reference	Basic	One-word	Same POS	Same Lemma	Diff. Lemma	No paraphr.	WordNet
Original	0.833	0.836	0.840	0.838	0.863	0.861	0.863
Before Depfix	0.905	0.908	0.911	0.911	0.931	0.931	0.931
New	0.927	0.930	0.931	0.932	0.950	**0.951**	**0.951**

WMT13

references	Basic	One-word	Same POS	Same Lemma	Diff. Lemma	No paraphr.	WordNet
Original	0.817	0.820	0.823	0.821	0.850	0.848	0.850
Before Depfix	0.865	0.867	0.869	0.868	0.895	0.895	0.894
New	0.891	0.892	0.893	0.892	**0.915**	**0.915**	**0.915**

Table 4: Pearson's correlation of Meteor and the silver standard.

Parmesan scores are highlighted by the box and the best scores are in bold.

7 Results

7.1 WMT12 and WMT13

The results of our experiments are presented in Table 4[4] as Pearson's correlation coefficient of the Meteor scores and the human judgment. The results in both tables are very consistent. There is a clear positive impact of the prior paraphrasing of the reference sentences and of applying Depfix. The results also show that independently of a reference sentence used, reducing the Meteor paraphrase tables in evaluation is always beneficial.

We use a freely available implementation[5] of Meng et al. (1992) to determine whether the difference in correlation coefficients is statistically significant. The tests show that Parmesan performs better than original Meteor with 99% certainty on the data from WMT12 and WMT13.

Diff. Lemma and **WordNet** settings give the best results on the original reference sentences. That is because they are basically a limited version of the paraphrase tables we use for creating our new references, which contain both all different lemmas of the same part of speech from Meteor Paraphrase tables and all lemmas from the WordNet.

The main reason of the worse performance of the metric when employing the Meteor Paraphrase tables is the noise. It is especially apparent for multi-word paraphrases (Barančíková et al., 2014); however, there are problems among one-word paraphrases as well. Significant amount of them are pairs of different word forms of a single lemma, which may award even completely non-grammatical sentences. This is reflected in the low correlation of the **Same Lemma** setting.

Even worse is the fact that the metric may award even parts of the hypothesis left untranslated, as the original Meteor Paraphrase tables contain English words and their Czech translations as paraphrases. There are for example pairs: *pšenice - wheat*[6], *vůdce - leader*, *vařit - cook*, *poloostrov - peninsula*. For these reasons, the differences among the systems are more blurred and the metric performs worse than without using the paraphrases.

[4]The results of WMT13 using the gold standard are in Table 5.

[5]http://www.cnts.ua.ac.be/~vincent/scripts/rtest.py

[6]In all examples the Czech word is the correct translation of the English side.

WMT13

references	Basic	One-word	Same POS	Same Lemma	Diff. Lemma	No paraphr.	WordNet
Original	0.856	0.859	0.862	0.860	0.885	0.883	0.884
Before Depfix	0.894	0.896	0.898	0.897	0.918	0.917	0.917
New	0.918	0.918	0.919	0.919	**0.933**	**0.933**	**0.933**

Table 5: Pearson's correlation of Meteor and the gold standard – *Expected Wins* (Bojar et al., 2013). The results corresponds very well with the silver standard in Table 4.

	frequency	Basic	No paraphr.
WMT12	0.75	0.837	0.869
WMT13	0.61	0.818	0.852

Table 6: The *frequency* column shows average number of substitution per sentence using the original Meteor Paraphrase tables only. The rest shows Pearson's correlation with the silver standard using these paraphrases.

We also experimented with paraphrasing using the original Meteor Paraphrase tables for a comparison. We used the same pipeline as it is described in Section 4, but used only original one-word paraphrases from the Meteor Paraphrase tables. Even though the paraphrase tables are much larger than our filtered Meteor tables, the amount of substituted words is much smaller (see Table 6) due to not being lemmatized. The **Basic** setting in Table 6 corresponds well with the setting **One-word** in Table 4 on original reference sentences. The results for **No paraphr.** setting in Table 6 outperforms all correlations with original references but cannot compete with our new reference sentences created by the filtered Meteor and WordNet.

7.2 WMT14

The WMT14 data did not follow similar patterns as data from two previous years. The results are presented in Table 7 (the silver standard) and in Table 8 (the gold standard).

While reducing the Meteor tables during the evaluation is still beneficial, this is not entirely valid about the prior paraphrasing of reference sentences. The baseline correlation of Meteor is rather high and paraphrasing sometimes helps and sometimes harms the performance of the metric. Nevertheless, the differences in correlation between the original references and the new ones are very small (0.012 at most).

In contrast to WMT12 and WMT13, the first phase of paraphrasing before applying Depfix causes a drop in correlation. On the other hand, applying Depfix is again always beneficial.

With both standards, the best result is achieved on the original reference with the **No paraphr.** and the **WordNet** setting. Parmesan outperforms Meteor by a marginal difference (0.005) on the silver standard, whereas using the gold standard, Meteor is better by exactly the same margin. However, the correlation of the two standards is 0.997.

There is a distinctive difference between the data from previous years and this one. In the WMT14, the English source data for translating to Czech are sentences originally English or professionally translated from Czech to English. In the previous years, on the other hand, the source data were equally composed from all competing languages, i.e., only fifth/sixth of data is originally English.

One more language involved in the translation seems as a possible ground for the beneficial effect of prior paraphrasing of reference sentences. Therefore, we experiment with limiting the WMT12 and WMT13 data to only sentences that are originally Czech or English. However, Parmesan on this limited translations again significantly outperforms Meteor and the results (see Table 9) follow similar patterns as on the whole data sets.

8 Conclusion and Future Work

We have demonstrated a negative effect of noise in the Czech Meteor Paraphrase tables to the performance of Meteor. We have shown that large-scale reduction of the paraphrase tables can be very beneficial for targeted paraphrasing of reference sentences. The Meteor scores computed without the Czech Meteor Paraphrase tables on these new reference sentences correlates significantly better with the human judgment than original Meteor on the WMT12 and WMT13 data. However, the WMT14 data has not confirmed

WMT14

reference	Basic	One-word	Same POS	Same Lemma	Diff. Lemma	No paraphr.	WordNet
Original	0.963	0.967	0.965	0.968	0.970	**0.973**	0.973
Before Depfix	0.957	0.958	0.959	0.959	0.965	0.965	0.965
New	0.968	0.965	0.969	0.969	0.968	0.968	0.968

Table 7: Pearson's correlation of Meteor and the silver standard.

WMT14

reference	Basic	One-word	Same POS	Same Lemma	Diff. Lemma	No paraphr.	WordNet
Original	0.967	0.968	0.969	0.972	0.972	**0.974**	**0.974**
Before Depfix	0.958	0.959	0.959	0.960	0.963	0.963	0.963
New	0.966	0.966	0.966	0.967	0.962	0.962	0.962

Table 8: Pearson's correlation of Meteor and the gold standard – *TrueSkill* (Bojar et al., 2014). Note that as opposed to official WMT14 results, the version 1.4 of Meteor is still used in this table.

WMT12

reference	Basic	One-word	Same POS	Same Lemma	Diff. Lemma	No paraphr.	WordNet
Original	0.781	0.779	0.782	0.772	0.807	0.798	0.801
Before Depfix	0.872	0.872	0.874	0.874	0.898	0.899	0.899
New	0.897	0.897	0.897	0.897	**0.923**	**0.923**	**0.923**

WMT13

reference	Basic	One-word	Same POS	Same Lemma	Diff. Lemma	No paraphr.	WordNet
Original	0.805	0.810	0.813	0.813	0.842	0.840	0.844
Before Depfix	0.843	0.846	0.849	0.848	0.879	0.877	0.877
New	0.874	0.877	0.878	0.877	0.877	**0.902**	**0.902**

Table 9: Pearson's correlation of Meteor and the silver standard on sentences originally Czech or English only. In this case, the interpretation of human judgment was computed only on those sentences as well.

this result and the improvement was very small. Furthermore, Parmesan performs even worse than Meteor on the gold standard.

In the future, we plan to thoroughly examine the reason for the different performance on WMT14 data. We also intend to make more sophisticated paraphrases including word order changes and other transformation that cannot be expressed by simple substitution of two words. We are also considering extending Parmesan to more languages.

Acknowledgment

I would like to thank Ondřej Bojar for his helpful suggestions. This research was partially supported by the grants SVV project number 260 104 and FP7-ICT-2011-7-288487 (MosesCore). This work has been using language resources developed and/or stored and/or distributed by the LINDAT/CLARIN project of the Ministry of Education, Youth and Sports of the Czech Republic (project LM2010013).

References

Colin Bannard and Chris Callison-Burch. 2005. Paraphrasing with Bilingual Parallel Corpora. In *Proceedings of the 43rd Annual Meeting on Association for Computational Linguistics*, ACL '05, pages 597–604, Stroudsburg, PA, USA. Association for Computational Linguistics.

Petra Barančíková, Rudolf Rosa, and Aleš Tamchyna. 2014. Improving Evaluation of English-Czech MT through Paraphrasing. In *Proceedings of the 9th International Conference on Language Resources and Evaluation (LREC 2014)*, Reykjavík, Iceland. European Language Resources Association.

Ondřej Bojar, Miloš Ercegovčević, Martin Popel, and Omar F. Zaidan. 2011. A Grain of Salt for the WMT Manual Evaluation. In *Proceedings of the Sixth Workshop on Statistical Machine Translation*, WMT '11, pages 1–11, Stroudsburg, PA, USA. Association for Computational Linguistics.

Ondřej Bojar, Zdeněk Žabokrtský, Ondřej Dušek, Petra Galuščáková, Martin Majliš, David Mareček, Jiří Maršík, Michal Novák, Martin Popel, and Aleš Tamchyna. 2012. The Joy of Parallelism with CzEng 1.0. In *Proc. of LREC*, pages 3921–3928. ELRA.

Ondřej Bojar, Christian Buck, Chris Callison-Burch, Christian Federmann, Barry Haddow, Philipp Koehn, Christof Monz, Matt Post, Radu Soricut, and Lucia Specia. 2013. Findings of the 2013 Workshop on Statistical Machine Translation. In *Proceedings of the Eighth Workshop on Statistical Machine Translation*, pages 1–44, Sofia, Bulgaria, August. Association for Computational Linguistics.

Ondřej Bojar, Christian Buck, Christian Federmann, Barry Haddow, Philipp Koehn, Matouš Macháček, Christof Monz, Pavel Pecina, Matt Post, Herve Saint-Amand, Radu Soricut, and Lucia Specia. 2014. Findings of the 2014 Workshop on Statistical Machine Translation. In *Proceedings of the Ninth Workshop on Statistical Machine Translation*, Baltimore, USA, June. Association for Computational Linguistics.

Chris Callison-Burch, Philipp Koehn, Christof Monz, Matt Post, Radu Soricut, and Lucia Specia. 2012. Findings of the 2012 Workshop on Statistical Machine Translation. In *Seventh Workshop on Statistical Machine Translation*, pages 10–51, Montréal, Canada.

Michael Denkowski and Alon Lavie. 2010. METEOR-NEXT and the METEOR Paraphrase Tables: Improved Evaluation Support For Five Target Languages. In *Proceedings of the ACL 2010 Joint Workshop on Statistical Machine Translation and Metrics MATR*.

Michael Denkowski and Alon Lavie. 2011. Meteor 1.3: Automatic Metric for Reliable Optimization and Evaluation of Machine Translation Systems. In *Proceedings of the EMNLP 2011 Workshop on Statistical Machine Translation*.

George Doddington. 2002. Automatic Evaluation of Machine Translation Quality Using N-gram Cooccurrence Statistics. In *Proceedings of the Second International Conference on Human Language Technology Research*, HLT '02, pages 138–145, San Francisco, CA, USA. Morgan Kaufmann Publishers Inc.

David Kauchak and Regina Barzilay. 2006. Paraphrasing for Automatic Evaluation. In *Proceedings of the main conference on Human Language Technology Conference of the North American Chapter of the Association of Computational Linguistics*, HLT-NAACL '06, pages 455–462, Stroudsburg, PA, USA. Association for Computational Linguistics.

Xiao-Li Meng, Robert Rosenthal, and Donald B Rubin. 1992. Comparing correlated correlation coefficients. *Psychological bulletin*, 111(1):172.

George A. Miller. 1995. WordNet: A Lexical Database for English. *COMMUNICATIONS OF THE ACM*, 38:39–41.

Karel Pala and Pavel Smrž. 2004. Building Czech WordNet. *In Romanian Journal of Information Science and Technology*, 7:79–88.

Kishore Papineni, Salim Roukos, Todd Ward, and Wei-Jing Zhu. 2002. BLEU: A Method for Automatic Evaluation of Machine Translation. In *Proceedings of the 40th Annual Meeting on Association for Computational Linguistics*, ACL '02, pages 311–318, Stroudsburg, PA, USA. Association for Computational Linguistics.

Rudolf Rosa, David Mareček, and Ondřej Dušek. 2012. DEPFIX: A System for Automatic Correction of Czech MT Outputs. In *Proceedings of the Seventh Workshop on Statistical Machine Translation*, WMT '12, pages 362–368, Stroudsburg, PA, USA. Association for Computational Linguistics.

Drahomíra Spoustová, Jan Hajič, Jan Votrubec, Pavel Krbec, and Pavel Květoň. 2007. The Best of Two Worlds: Cooperation of Statistical and Rule-Based Taggers for Czech. In *Proceedings of the Workshop on Balto-Slavonic Natural Language Processing, ACL 2007*, pages 67–74, Praha.

A Systematic Comparison of Smoothing Techniques for Sentence-Level BLEU

Boxing Chen and Colin Cherry
National Research Council Canada
first.last@nrc-cnrc.gc.ca

Abstract

BLEU is the *de facto* standard machine translation (MT) evaluation metric. However, because BLEU computes a geometric mean of n-gram precisions, it often correlates poorly with human judgment on the sentence-level. Therefore, several smoothing techniques have been proposed. This paper systematically compares 7 smoothing techniques for sentence-level BLEU. Three of them are first proposed in this paper, and they correlate better with human judgments on the sentence-level than other smoothing techniques. Moreover, we also compare the performance of using the 7 smoothing techniques in statistical machine translation tuning.

1 Introduction

Since its invention, BLEU (Papineni et al., 2002) has been the most widely used metric for both machine translation (MT) evaluation and tuning. Many other metrics correlate better with human judgments of translation quality than BLEU, as shown in recent WMT Evaluation Task reports (Callison-Burch et al., 2011; Callison-Burch et al., 2012). However, BLEU remains the *de facto* standard evaluation and tuning metric. This is probably due to the following facts:

1. BLEU is language independent (except for word segmentation decisions).

2. BLEU can be computed quickly. This is important when choosing a tuning metric.

3. BLEU seems to be the best tuning metric from a quality point of view - i.e., models trained using BLEU obtain the highest scores from humans and even from other metrics (Cer et al., 2010).

One of the main criticisms of BLEU is that it has a poor correlation with human judgments on the sentence-level. Because it computes a geometric mean of n-gram precisions, if a higher order n-gram precision (eg. $n = 4$) of a sentence is 0, then the BLEU score of the entire sentence is 0, no matter how many 1-grams or 2-grams are matched. Therefore, several smoothing techniques for sentence-level BLEU have been proposed (Lin and Och, 2004; Gao and He, 2013).

In this paper, we systematically compare 7 smoothing techniques for sentence-level BLEU. Three of them are first proposed in this paper, and they correlate better with human judgments on the sentence-level than other smoothing techniques on the WMT metrics task. Moreover, we compare the performance of using the 7 smoothing techniques in statistical machine translation tuning on NIST Chinese-to-English and Arabic-to-English tasks. We show that when tuning optimizes the expected sum of these sentence-level metrics (as advocated by Cherry and Foster (2012) and Gao and He (2013) among others), all of these metrics perform similarly in terms of their ability to produce strong BLEU scores on a held-out test set.

2 BLEU and smoothing

2.1 BLEU

Suppose we have a translation T and its reference R, BLEU is computed with precision $P(N,T,R)$ and brevity penalty BP(T,R):

$$\text{BLEU}(N,T,R) = P(N,T,R) \times \text{BP}(T,R) \quad (1)$$

where $P(N,T,R)$ is the geometric mean of n-gram precisions:

$$P(N,T,R) = \left(\prod_{n=1}^{N} p_n \right)^{\frac{1}{N}} \quad (2)$$

Proceedings of the Ninth Workshop on Statistical Machine Translation, pages 362–367,
Baltimore, Maryland USA, June 26–27, 2014.

and where:

$$p_n = \frac{m_n}{l_n} \tag{3}$$

m_n is the number of matched n-grams between translation T and its reference R, and l_n is the total number of n-grams in the translation T. BLEU's brevity penalty punishes the score if the translation length $\text{len}(T)$ is shorter than the reference length $\text{len}(R)$, using this equation:

$$\text{BP}(T, R) = \min\left(1.0, \exp\left(1 - \frac{\text{len}(R)}{\text{len}(T)}\right)\right) \tag{4}$$

2.2 Smoothing techniques

The original BLEU was designed for the document-level; as such, it required no smoothing, as some sentence would have at least one 4-gram match. We now describe 7 smoothing techniques that work better for sentence-level evaluation. Suppose we consider matching n-grams for $n = 1 \ldots N$ (typically, $N = 4$). Let m_n be the original match count, and m'_n be the modified n-gram match count.

Smoothing 1: if the number of matched n-grams is 0, we use a small positive value ϵ to replace the 0 for n ranging from 1 to N. The number ϵ is set empirically.

$$m'_n = \epsilon, \text{ if } m_n = 0. \tag{5}$$

Smoothing 2: this smoothing technique was proposed in (Lin and Och, 2004). It adds 1 to the matched n-gram count and the total n-gram count for n ranging from 2 to N.

$$m'_n = m_n + 1, \text{ for } n \text{ in } 2 \ldots N, \tag{6}$$

$$l'_n = l_n + 1, \text{ for } n \text{ in } 2 \ldots N. \tag{7}$$

Smoothing 3: this smoothing technique is implemented in the NIST official BLEU toolkit *mteval-v13a.pl*.[1] The algorithm is given below. It assigns a geometric sequence starting from $1/2$ to the n-grams with 0 matches.

```
1. invcnt = 1
2. for n in 1 to N
3.     if m_n = 0
4.         invcnt = invcnt × 2
5.         m'_n = 1/invcnt
6.     endif
7. endfor
```

[1] available at http://www.itl.nist.gov/iad/mig/tests/mt/2009/

Smoothing 4: this smoothing technique is novel to this paper. We modify Smoothing 3 to address the concern that shorter translations may have inflated precision values due to having smaller denominators; therefore, we give them proportionally smaller smoothed counts. Instead of scaling *invcnt* with a fixed value of 2, we replace line 4 in Smoothing 3's algorithm with Equation 8 below.

$$\textit{invcnt} = \textit{invcnt} \times \frac{K}{\ln(\text{len}(T))} \tag{8}$$

It assigns larger values to *invcnt* for shorter sentences, resulting in a smaller smoothed count. K is set empirically.

Smoothing 5: this smoothing technique is also novel to this paper. It is inspired by the intuition that matched counts for similar values of n should be similar. To a calculate the n-gram matched count, it averages the $n-1$, n and $n+1$ –gram matched counts. We define $m'_0 = m_1 + 1$, and calculate m'_n for $n > 0$ as follows:

$$m'_n = \frac{m'_{n-1} + m_n + m_{n+1}}{3} \tag{9}$$

Smoothing 6: this smoothing technique was proposed in (Gao and He, 2013). It interpolates the maximum likelihood estimate of the precision p_n with a prior estimate p_n^0. The prior is estimated by assuming that the ratio between p_n and p_{n-1} will be the same as that between p_{n-1} and p_{n-2}. Formally, the precisions of lower order n-grams, i.e., p_1 and p_2, are not smoothed, while the precisions of higher order n-grams, i.e. $n > 2$, are smoothed as follows:

$$p_n = \frac{m_n + \alpha p_n^0}{l_n + \alpha} \tag{10}$$

where α is set empirically, and p_n^0 is computed as

$$p_n^0 = p_{n-1} \times \frac{p_{n-1}}{p_{n-2}} \tag{11}$$

Smoothing 7: this novel smoothing technique combines smoothing 4 and smoothing 5. That is, we first compute a smoothed count for those 0 matched n-gram counts using Smoothing 4, and then take the average of three counts to set the final matched n-gram count as in Equation 9.

3 Experiments

We carried out two series of experiments. The 7 smoothing techniques were first compared in

set	year	lang.	#system	#seg. pair
dev	2008	xx-en	43	7,804
test1	2012	xx-en	49	34,909
test2	2013	xx-en	94	281,666
test3	2012	en-xx	54	47,875
test4	2013	en-xx	95	220,808

Table 1: Statistics of the WMT dev and test sets.

the metric task as evaluation metrics, then they were compared as metrics for tuning SMT systems to maximize the sum of expected sentence-level BLEU scores.

3.1 Evaluation task

We first compare the correlations with human judgment for the 7 smoothing techniques on WMT data; the development set (dev) is the WMT 2008 all-to-English data; the test sets are the WMT 2012 and WMT 2013 all-to-English, and English-to-all submissions. The languages "all" ("xx" in Table 1) include French, Spanish, German, Czech and Russian. Table 1 summarizes the dev/test set statistics.

Following WMT 2013's metric task (Macháček and Bojar, 2013), for the segment level, we use Kendall's rank correlation coefficient τ to measure the correlation with human judgment:

$$\tau = \frac{\#\text{concordant-pairs} - \#\text{discordant-pairs}}{\#\text{concordant-pairs} + \#\text{discordant-pairs}} \tag{12}$$

We extract all pairwise comparisons where one system's translation of a particular segment was judged to be better than the other system's translation, i.e., we removed all tied human judgments for a particular segment. If two translations for a particular segment are assigned the same BLEU score, then the #concordant-pairs and #discordant-pairs both get a half count. In this way, we can keep the number of total pairs consistent for all different smoothing techniques.

For the system-level, we used Spearman's rank correlation coefficient ρ and Pearson's correlation coefficient γ to measure the correlation of the metric with human judgments of translation. If we compute document-level BLEU as usual, all 7 smoothing techniques actually get the same result, as document-level BLEU does not need smoothing. We therefore compute the document-level BLEU as the weighted average of sentence-level BLEU, with the weights being the reference lengths:

	Into-English		
smooth	seg τ	sys γ	sys ρ
crp	–	0.720	0.887
0	0.165	0.759	0.887
1	0.224	0.760	0.887
2	0.226	0.757	0.887
3	0.224	0.760	0.887
4	0.228	0.763	0.887
5	0.234	0.765	0.887
6	0.230	0.754	0.887
7	**0.236**	**0.766**	0.887

Table 2: Correlations with human judgment on WMT data for Into-English task. Results are averaged on 4 test sets. "crp" is the origianl IBM corpus-level BLEU.

$$\text{BLEU}_d = \frac{\sum_{i=1}^{D} \text{len}(R_i)\text{BLEU}_i}{\sum_{i=1}^{D} \text{len}(R_i)} \tag{13}$$

where BLEU_i is the BLEU score of sentence i, and D is the size of the document in sentences.

We first set the free parameters of each smoothing method by grid search to optimize the sentence-level score on the dev set. We set ϵ to 0.1 for Smoothing 1; $K = 5$ for Smoothing 4; $\alpha = 5$ for Smoothing 6.

Tables 2 and 3 report our results on the metrics task. We compared the 7 smoothing techniques described in Section 2.2 to a baseline with no smoothing (Smoothing 0). All scores match n-grams $n = 1$ to 4. Smoothing 3 is implemented in the standard official NIST evaluation toolkit (*mteval-v13a.pl*). Results are averaged across the 4 test sets.

All smoothing techniques improved sentence-level correlations (τ) over no smoothing. Smoothing method 7 got the best sentence-level results on both the Into-English and Out-of-English tasks.

On the system-level, our weighted average of sentence-level BLEU scores (see Equation 13) achieved a better correlation with human judgement than the original IBM corpus-level BLEU. However, the choice of which smoothing technique is used in the average did not make a very big difference; in particular, the system-level rank correlation ρ did not change for 13 out of 14 cases. These methods help when comparing one hypothesis to another, but taken as a part of a larger average, all seven methods assign relatively low scores

	Out-of-English		
smooth	seg τ	sys γ	sys ρ
crp	–	0.712	0.744
0	0.119	0.715	0.744
1	0.178	0.722	**0.748**
2	0.180	0.725	0.744
3	0.178	0.724	0.744
4	0.181	0.727	0.744
5	0.184	0.731	0.744
6	0.182	0.725	0.744
7	**0.187**	**0.734**	0.744

Table 3: Correlations with human judgment on WMT data for Out-of-English task. Results are averaged on 4 test sets. "crp" is the origianl IBM corpus-level BLEU.

to the cases that require smoothing, resulting in similar system-level rankings.

3.2 Tuning task

In this section, we explore the various BLEU smoothing methods in the context of SMT parameter tuning, which is used to set the decoder's linear model weights w. In particular, we use a tuning method that maximizes the sum of expected sentence-level BLEU scores, which has been shown to be a simple and effective method for tuning with large feature sets by both Cherry and Foster (2012) and Gao and He (2013), but which requires a smoothed sentence-level BLEU approximation. For a source sentence f_i, the probability of the kth translation hypothesis e_i^k is its exponentiated and normalized model score:

$$P_w(e_i^k|f_i) = \frac{\exp(score_w(e_i^k, f_i))}{\sum_{k'} \exp(score_w(e_i^{k'}, f_i))}$$

where k' ranges over all hypotheses in a K-best list.[2] We then use stochastic gradient descent (SGD) to minimize:

$$\lambda||w||^2 - \sum_i \Big[\text{len}(R_i) \times E_{P_w}\Big(\text{BLEU}(e_i^k, f_i)\Big)\Big]$$

Note that we scale the expectation by reference length to place more emphasis on longer sentences. We set the regularization parameter λ, which determines the trade-off between a high expected BLEU and a small norm, to $\lambda = 10$.

Following Cherry and Foster (2012), we tune with a MERT-like batch architecture: fixing a set of K-best lists, optimizing, and then re-decoding the entire dev set to K-best and aggregating with previous lists to create a better K-best approximation. We repeat this outer loop 15 times.

[2]We use $K = 100$ in our experiments.

corpus	# segs	# en tok
	Chinese-English	
train	10.1M	283M
tune	1,506	161K
MT06	1,664	189K
MT08	1,357	164K
	Arabic-English	
train	1,512K	47.8M
tune	1,664	202K
MT08	1,360	205K
MT09	1,313	187K

Table 4: Statistics of the NIST Chinese-English and Arabic-English data.

We carried out experiments in two different settings, both involving data from NIST Open MT 2012.[3] The first setting is based on data from the Chinese-to-English constrained track, comprising about 283 million English running words. The second setting uses NIST 2012 Arabic-to-English data, but excludes the UN data. There are about 47.8 million English running words in these training data. The dev set (*tune*) for the Chinese-to-English task was taken from the NIST 2005 evaluation set, augmented with some web-genre material reserved from other NIST corpora. We test on the evaluation sets from NIST 2006 and 2008. For the Arabic-to-English task, we use the evaluation sets from NIST 2006, 2008, and 2009 as our dev set and two test sets, respectively. Table 4 summarizes the training, dev and test sets.

Experiments were carried out with an in-house, state-of-the-art phrase-based system. Each corpus was word-aligned using IBM2, HMM, and IBM4 models, and the phrase table was the union of phrase pairs extracted from these separate alignments, with a length limit of 7. The translation model (TM) was smoothed in both directions with Kneser-Ney smoothing (Chen et al., 2011). We use the hierarchical lexicalized reordering model (RM) (Galley and Manning, 2008), with a distortion limit of 7. Other features include lexical weighting in both directions, word count, a distance-based RM, a 4-gram LM trained on the target side of the parallel data, and a 6-gram En-

[3]http://www.nist.gov/itl/iad/mig/openmt12.cfm

	Tune	std	MT06	std	MT08	std
0	27.6	0.1	35.6	0.1	29.0	0.2
1	27.6	0.0	35.7	0.1	29.1	0.1
2	27.5	0.1	35.8	0.1	29.1	0.1
3	27.6	0.1	35.8	0.1	29.1	0.1
4	27.6	0.1	35.7	0.2	29.1	0.2
5	27.6	0.1	35.5	0.1	28.9	0.2
6	27.5	0.1	35.7	0.1	29.0	0.2
7	27.6	0.1	35.6	0.1	29.0	0.1

Table 5: Chinese-to-English Results for the small feature set tuning task. Results are averaged across 5 replications; *std* is the standard deviation.

glish *Gigaword* LM.

We also conducted a set of experiments with a much larger feature set. This system used only GIZA++ for word alignment, increased the distortion limit from 7 to 9, and is trained on a high-quality subset of the parallel corpora used earlier. Most importantly, it includes the full set of sparse phrase-pair features used by both Hopkins and May (2011) and Cherry and Foster (2012), which results in nearly 7,000 features.

Our evaluation metric is the original IBM BLEU, which performs case-insensitive matching of n-grams up to $n = 4$. We perform random replications of parameter tuning, as suggested by Clark et al. (2011). Each replication uses a different random seed to determine the order in which SGD visits tuning sentences. We test for significance using the MultEval tool,[4] which uses a stratified approximate randomization test to account for multiple replications. We report results averaged across replications as well as standard deviations, which indicate optimizer stability.

Results for the small feature set are shown in Tables 5 and 6. All 7 smoothing techniques, as well as the no smoothing baseline, all yield very similar results on both Chinese and Arabic tasks. We did not find any two results to be significantly different. This is somewhat surprising, as other groups have suggested that choosing an appropriate BLEU approximation is very important. Instead, our experiments indicate that the selected BLEU smoothing method is not very important.

The large-feature experiments were only conducted with the most promising methods according to correlation with human judgments:

[4] available at https://github.com/jhclark/multeval

	Tune	std	MT08	std	MT09	std
0	46.9	0.1	46.5	0.1	49.1	0.1
1	46.9	0.0	46.4	0.1	49.1	0.1
2	46.9	0.0	46.4	0.1	49.0	0.1
3	47.0	0.0	46.5	0.1	49.2	0.1
4	47.0	0.0	46.5	0.1	49.2	0.1
5	46.9	0.0	46.4	0.1	49.1	0.1
6	47.0	0.0	46.4	0.1	49.1	0.1
7	47.0	0.0	46.4	0.1	49.0	0.1

Table 6: Arabic-to-English Results for the small feature set tuning task. Results are averaged across 5 replications; *std* is the standard deviation.

	Tune	std	MT06	std	MT08	std
mira	29.9	0.1	38.0	0.1	31.0	0.1
0	29.5	0.1	37.9	0.1	31.4	0.3
2	29.6	0.3	38.0	0.2	31.1	0.2
4	29.9	0.2	38.1	0.1	31.2	0.2
6	29.7	0.1	37.9	0.2	31.0	0.2
7	29.7	0.2	**38.0**	0.2	31.2	0.1

Table 7: Chinese-to-English Results for the large feature set tuning task. Results are averaged across 5 replications; *std* is the standard deviation. Significant improvements over the no-smoothing baseline ($p \leq 0.05$) are marked in bold.

0: No smoothing (baseline)
2: Add 1 smoothing (Lin and Och, 2004)
4: Length-scaled pseudo-counts (this paper)
6: Interpolation with a precision prior (Gao and He, 2013)
7: Combining Smoothing 4 with the match interpolation of Smoothing 5 (this paper)

The results of the large feature set experiments are shown in Table 7 for Chinese-to-English and Table 8 for Arabic-to-English. For a sanity check, we compared these results to tuning with our very stable Batch k-best MIRA implementation (Cherry and Foster, 2012), listed as *mira*, which shows that all of our expected BLEU tuners are behaving reasonably, if not better than expected.

Comparing the various smoothing methods in the large feature scenario, we are able to see significant improvements over the no-smoothing baseline. Notably, Method 7 achieves a significant improvement over the no-smoothing baseline in 3 out of 4 scenarios, more than any other method. Unfortunately, in the Chinese-English MT08 scenario, the no-smoothing baseline significantly out-

	Tune	std	MT08	std	MT09	std
mira	47.9	0.1	47.3	0.0	49.3	0.1
0	48.1	0.1	47.2	0.1	49.5	0.1
2	48.0	0.1	**47.4**	0.1	**49.7**	0.1
4	48.1	0.2	**47.4**	0.1	49.6	0.1
6	48.2	0.0	47.3	0.1	**49.7**	0.1
7	48.1	0.1	**47.3**	0.1	**49.7**	0.1

Table 8: Arabic-to-English Results for the large feature set tuning task. Results are averaged across 5 replications; *std* is the standard deviation. Significant improvements over the no-smoothing baseline ($p \leq 0.05$) are marked in bold.

performs all smoothed BLEU methods, making it difficult to draw any conclusions at all from these experiments. We had hoped to see at least a clear improvement in the tuning set, and one does see a nice progression as smoothing improves in the Chinese-to-English scenario, but no corresponding pattern emerges for Arabic-to-English.

4 Conclusions

In this paper, we compared seven smoothing techniques for sentence-level BLEU. Three of them are newly proposed in this paper. The new smoothing techniques got better sentence-level correlations with human judgment than other smoothing techniques. On the other hand, when we compare the techniques in the context of tuning, using a method that requires sentence-level BLEU approximations, they all have similar performance.

References

Chris Callison-Burch, Philipp Koehn, Christof Monz, and Omar Zaidan. 2011. Findings of the 2011 workshop on statistical machine translation. In *Proceedings of the Sixth Workshop on Statistical Machine Translation*, pages 22–64, Edinburgh, Scotland, July. Association for Computational Linguistics.

Chris Callison-Burch, Philipp Koehn, Christof Monz, Matt Post, Radu Soricut, and Lucia Specia. 2012. Findings of the 2012 workshop on statistical machine translation. In *Proceedings of the Seventh Workshop on Statistical Machine Translation*, pages 10–51, Montréal, Canada, June. Association for Computational Linguistics.

Daniel Cer, Christopher D. Manning, and Daniel Jurafsky. 2010. The best lexical metric for phrase-based statistical mt system optimization. In *Human Language Technologies: The 2010 Annual Conference of the North American Chapter of the Association for Computational Linguistics*, pages 555–563, Los Angeles, California, June. Association for Computational Linguistics.

Boxing Chen, Roland Kuhn, George Foster, and Howard Johnson. 2011. Unpacking and transforming feature functions: New ways to smooth phrase tables. In *MT Summit 2011*.

Colin Cherry and George Foster. 2012. Batch tuning strategies for statistical machine translation. In *NAACL 2012*.

Jonathan H. Clark, Chris Dyer, Alon Lavie, and Noah A. Smith. 2011. Better hypothesis testing for statistical machine translation: Controlling for optimizer instability. In *ACL 2011*.

Michel Galley and C. D. Manning. 2008. A simple and effective hierarchical phrase reordering model. In *EMNLP 2008*, pages 848–856, Hawaii, October.

Jianfeng Gao and Xiaodong He. 2013. Training mrf-based phrase translation models using gradient ascent. In *Proceedings of the 2013 Conference of the North American Chapter of the Association for Computational Linguistics: Human Language Technologies*, pages 450–459, Atlanta, Georgia, June. Association for Computational Linguistics.

Mark Hopkins and Jonathan May. 2011. Tuning as ranking. In *EMNLP 2011*.

Chin-Yew Lin and Franz Josef Och. 2004. Automatic evaluation of machine translation quality using longest common subsequence and skip-bigram statistics. In *Proceedings of the 42nd Meeting of the Association for Computational Linguistics (ACL'04), Main Volume*, pages 605–612, Barcelona, Spain, July.

Matouš Macháček and Ondřej Bojar. 2013. Results of the WMT13 metrics shared task. In *Proceedings of the Eighth Workshop on Statistical Machine Translation*, pages 45–51, Sofia, Bulgaria, August. Association for Computational Linguistics.

Kishore Papineni, Salim Roukos, Todd Ward, and Wei-Jing Zhu. 2002. BLEU: A method for automatic evaluation of Machine Translation. In *Proceedings of the 40th Annual Meeting of the Association for Computational Linguistics (ACL)*, pages 311–318, Philadelphia, July. ACL.

VERTa participation in the WMT14 Metrics Task

Elisabet Comelles
Universitat de Barcelona
Barcelona, Spain
elicomelles@ub.edu

Jordi Atserias
Yahoo! Labs
Barcelona, Spain
jordi@yahoo-inc.com

Abstract

In this paper we present VERTa, a linguistically-motivated metric that combines linguistic features at different levels. We provide the linguistic motivation on which the metric is based, as well as describe the different modules in VERTa and how they are combined. Finally, we describe the two versions of VERTa, VERTa-EQ and VERTa-W, sent to WMT14 and report results obtained in the experiments conducted with the WMT12 and WMT13 data into English.

1 Introduction

In the Machine Translation (MT) process, the evaluation of MT systems plays a key role both in their development and improvement. From the MT metrics that have been developed during the last decades, BLEU (Papineni et al., 2002) is one of the most well-known and widely used, since it is fast and easy to use. Nonetheless, researchers such as (Callison-Burch et al., 2006) and (Lavie and Dekowski, 2009) have claimed its weaknesses regarding translation quality and its tendency to favour statistically-based MT systems. As a consequence, other more complex metrics that use linguistic information have been developed. Some use linguistic information at lexical level, such as METEOR (Denkowski and Lavie, 2011); others rely on syntactic information, either using constituent (Liu and Hildea, 2005) or dependency analysis (Owczarzack et al., 2007a and 2007b; He et al., 2010); others use more complex information such as semantic roles (Giménez and Márquez, 2007 and 2008a; Lo et al., 2012). All these metrics focus on partial aspects of language; however, other researchers have tried to combine information at different linguistic levels in order to follow a more holistic approach. Some of these metrics follow a machine-learning approach (Leusch and Ney, 2009; Albrecht and Hwa, 2007a and 2007b), others combine a wide variety of metrics in a simple and straightforward way (Giménez, 2008b; Giménez and Márquez, 2010; Specia and Giménez, 2010). However, very little research has been performed on the impact of the linguistic features used and how to combine this information from a linguistic point of view. Hence, our proposal is a linguistically-based metric, VERTa (Comelles et al., 2012), which uses a wide variety of linguistic features at different levels, and aims at combining them in order to provide a wider and more accurate coverage than those metrics working at a specific linguistic level. In this paper we provide a description of the linguistic information used in VERTa, the different modules that form VERTa and how they are combined according to the language evaluated and the type of evaluation performed. Moreover, the two versions of VERTa participating in WMT14, VERTa-EQ and VERTa-W are described. Finally, for the sake of comparison, we use the data available in WMT12 and WMT13 to compare both versions to the metrics participating in those shared tasks.

2 Linguistic Motivation

Before developing VERTa, we analysed those linguistic phenomena that an MT metric should cover. From this analysis, we decided to organise the information into the following groups:

- **Lexical information**. The use of lexical semantics plays a key role when comparing a hypothesis and reference segment, since it allows for identifying relations of synonymy, hypernymy and hyponymy.
- **Morphological information**. This type of information is crucial when dealing with languages with a rich inflectional morphology, such as Spanish, French or Cata-

Proceedings of the Ninth Workshop on Statistical Machine Translation, pages 368–375,
Baltimore, Maryland USA, June 26–27, 2014.

lan because it helps in covering phenomena related to tense, mood, gender, number, aspect or case. In addition, morphology in combination with syntax (morpho-syntax) is also important to identify agreement (i.e. subject-verb agreement). This type of information should be taken into account when evaluating the fluency of a segment.

- **Syntactic information.** This type of information covers syntactic structure, syntactic relations and word order.
- **Semantic information.** Named Entities (NEs), sentence polarity and time expressions are included here.

All this information described above should be taken into account when developing a metric that aims at covering linguistic phenomena at different levels and evaluate both adequacy and fluency.

3 Metric Description

In order to cover the above linguistic features, VERTa is organised into different modules: *Lexical similarity module*, *Morphological similarity module*, *Dependency similarity module* and *Semantic similarity module*. Likewise, an *Ngram similarity module* has also been added in order to account for similarity between chunks in the hypothesis and reference segments. Each metric works first individually and the final score is the Fmean of the weighted combination of the Precision and Recall of each metric in order to get the results which best correlate with human assessment. This way, the different modules can be weighted depending on their importance regarding the type of evaluation (fluency or adequacy) and language evaluated. In addition, the modular design of this metric makes it suitable for all languages. Even those languages that do not have a wide range of NLP tools available could be evaluated, since each module can be used isolated or in combination.

All metrics use a weighted precision and recall over the number of matches of the particular element of each level (words, dependency triples, ngrams, etc) as shown below.

$$P = \frac{\sum_{\partial \in D} W_\partial * nmatch_\partial(\nabla(h))}{|\nabla(h)|}$$

$$R = \frac{\sum_{\partial \in D} W_\partial * nmatch_\partial(\nabla(r))}{|\nabla(r)|}$$

Where r is the reference, h is the hypothesis and ∇ is a function that given a segment will return the elements of each level (e.g. words at lexical level and triples at dependency level). D is the set of different functions to project the level element into the features associated to each level, such as word-form, lemma or partial-lemma at lexical level. $nmatch_\partial()$ is a function that returns the number of matches according to the feature ∂ (i.e. the number of lexical matches at the lexical level or the number of dependency triples that match at the dependency level). Finally, W is the set of weights]0 1] associated to each of the different features in a particular level in order to combine the different kinds of matches considered in that level.

All modules forming VERTa and the linguistic features used are described in detail in the following subsections.

3.1 Lexical module

Inspired by METEOR, the lexical module matches lexical items in the hypothesis segment to those in the reference segment taking into account several linguistic features. However, while METEOR uses word-form, synonymy, stemming and paraphrasing, VERTa relies on word-form, synonymy[1], lemma, partial lemma[2], hypernyms and hyponyms. In addition, a set of weights is assigned to each type of match depending on their importance as regards semantics (see Table 1).

	W	Match	Examples	
			HYP	**REF**
1	1	Word-form	*east*	*east*
2	1	Synonym	*believed*	*considered*
3	1	Hypernym	*barrel*	*keg*
4	1	Hyponym	*keg*	*barrel*
5	.8	Lemma	*is_BE*	*are_BE*
6	.6	Part-lemma	*danger*	*dangerous*

Table 1. Lexical matches and examples.

3.2 Morphological similarity module

The morphological similarity module is based on the matches established in the lexical module (except for the partial-lemma match) in combination with Part-of-Speech (PoS) tags from the annotated corpus[3]. The aim of this module is to

[1] Information on synonyms, lemmas, hypernyms and hyponyms is obtained from WordNet 3.0.

[2] Lemmas that share the first four letters.

[3] The corpus has been PoS tagged using the Stanford Parser (de Marneffe et al. 2006).

compensate the broader coverage of the lexical module, preventing matches such as *invites* and *invite*, which although similar in terms of meaning, do not coincide as for their morphological information. Therefore, this module turns more appropriate to assess the fluency of a segment rather than its adequacy. In addition, this module will be particularly useful when evaluating languages with a richer inflectional morphology (i.e. Romance languages).

In line with the lexical similarity metric, the morphological similarity metric establishes matches between items in the hypothesis and the reference sentence and a set of weights (W) is applied. However, instead of comparing single lexical items as in the previous module, in this module we compare pairs of features in the order established in Table 2.

W	Match	Examples	
		HYP	REF
1	(Word-form, PoS)	(he, PRP)	(he, PRP)
1	(Synonym, PoS)	(VIEW, NNS)	(OPINON, NNS)
1	(Hypern., PoS)	(PUBLICA-TION, NN)	(MAGA-ZINE, NN)
1	(Hypon., PoS)	(MAGA-ZINE, NN)	(PUBLI-CATION, NN)
.8	(LEMMA, PoS)	can_(CAN, MD)	Could_(CAN, MD)

Table 2. Morphological module matches.

3.3 Dependency similarity module

The dependency similarity metric helps in capturing similarities between semantically comparable expressions that show a different syntactic structure (see Example 1), as well as changes in word order (see Example 2).

Example 1:

HYP: *...the interior minister...*

REF: *...the minister of interior...*

In example 1 both hypothesis and reference chunks convey the same meaning but their syntactic constructions are different.

Example 2:

HYP: ***After a meeting Monday night with the head of Egyptian intelligence chief Omar Suleiman*** *Haniya said....*

REF: *Haniya said,* ***after a meeting on Monday evening with the head of Egyptian Intelligence General Omar Suleiman...***

In example 2, the adjunct realised by the PP *After a meeting Monday night with the head of Egyptian intelligence chief Omar Suleiman* occupies different positions in the hypothesis and reference strings. In the hypothesis it is located at the beginning of the sentence, preceding the subject *Haniya*, whereas in the reference, it is placed after the verb. By means of dependencies, we can state that although located differently inside the sentence, both subject and adjunct depend on the verb.

This module works at sentence level and follows the approach used by (Owczarzack et al., 2007a and 2007b) and (He et al., 2010) with some linguistic additions in order to adapt it to our metric combination. Similar to the morphological module, the dependency similarity metric also relies first on those matches established at lexical level – word-form, synonymy, hypernymy, hyponymy and lemma – in order to capture lexical variation across dependencies and avoid relying only on surface word-form. Then, by means of flat triples with the form Label(Head, Mod) obtained from the parser[4], four different types of dependency matches have been designed (see Table 3) and weights have been assigned to each type of match.

W	Match Type	Match Descr.
1	Complete	Label1=Label2 Head1=Head2 Mod1=Mod2
1	Partial_no_label	Label1≠Label2 Head1=Head2 Mod1=Mod2
.9	Partial_no_mod	Label1=Label2 Head1=Head2 Mod1≠Mod2
.7	Partial_no_head	Label1=Label2 Head1≠Head2 Mod1=Mod2

Table 3. Dependency matches.

In addition, dependency categories also receive a different weight depending on how informative they are: *dep*, *det* and _[5] which receive 0.5, whereas the rest of categories are assigned the maximum weight (1).

Finally, a set of language-dependent rules has been added with two goals: 1) capturing similarities between different syntactic structures con-

[4] Both hypothesis and reference strings are annotated with dependency relations by means of the Stanford parser (de Marneffe et al. 2006).

[5] _ stands for no_dep_label

veying the same meaning; and 2) restricting certain dependency relations (i.e. subject word order when translating from Arabic to English).

3.4 Ngram similarity module

The ngram similarity metric matches chunks in the hypothesis and reference segments and relies on the matches set by the lexical similarity metric, which allows us to work not only with word-forms but also with synonyms, lemmas, partial-lemmas, hypernyms and hyponyms as shown in Example 3, where the chunks [*the situation in the area*] and [*the situation in the region*] do match, even though *area* and *region* do not share the same word-form but a relation of synonymy.

Example 3:
HYP: … *the situation in the* ***area***…
REF: … *the situation in the* ***region***…

3.5 Semantics similarity module

As confirmed by the lexical module, semantics plays an important role in the evaluation of adequacy. This has also been claimed by (Lo and Wu, 2010) who report that their metric based on semantic roles outperforms other well-known metrics when adequacy is assessed. With this aim in mind the semantic similarity module uses other semantic features at sentence level: NEs, time expressions and polarity.

Regarding NEs, we use Named-Entity recognition (NER) and Named-Entity linking (NEL). Following previous NE-based metrics (Reeder et al., 2011 and Giménez, 2008) the NER metric[6] aims at capturing similarities between NEs in the hypothesis and reference segments. On the other hand NEL[7] focuses only on those NEs that appear on Wikipedia, which allows for linking NEs regardless of their external form. Thus, *EU* and *European Union* will be captured as the same NE, since both of them are considered as the same organisation in Wikipedia.

As regards time expressions, the TIMEX metric matches temporal expressions in the hypothesis and reference segments regardless of their form. The tool used is the Stanford Temporal Tagger (Chang and Manning, 2012) which recognizes not only points in time but also duration. By means of this metric, different syntactic structures conveying the same time expression can be matched, such as *on February 3rd* and *on the third of February*.

Finally, it has been reported that negation might pose a problem to SMT systems (Wetzel and Bond, 2012). In order to answer such need, a module that checks the polarity of the sentence has been added using the dictionary strategy described (Atserias et al., 2012):

- Adding 0.5 for each weak positive word.
- Adding 1.0 for each strong positive word.
- Subtracting 0.5 for each weak negative word.
- Subtracting 1.0 for each strong negative word.

For each query term score, the value is propagated to the query term positions by reducing its strength in a factor of 1/n, where n is the distance between the query term and the polar term.

According to the experiments performed, this module shows a low correlation with human judgements on adequacy, since only partial aspects of translation are considered, whereas human judges assess whole segments. However, regardless of how well/bad the module correlates with human judgements, it proves useful to check partial aspects of the segments translated, such as the correct translation of NEs or the correct translation of negation.

3.6 Metrics combination

The modular design of VERTa allows for providing different weights to each module depending on the type of evaluation and the language evaluated. Thus following linguistic criteria when evaluating adequacy, those modules which must play a key role are the lexical and dependency module, since they are more related to semantics; whereas, when evaluating fluency those related to morphology, morphosyntax and constituent word order will be the most important. Moreover, metrics can also be combined depending on the type of language evaluated. If a language with a rich inflectional morphology is assessed, the morphology module should be given a higher weight; whereas if the language evaluated does not show such a rich inflectional morphology, the weight of the morphology module should be lower.

4 Experiments and results

Experiments were carried out on WMT data, specifically on WMT12 and WMT13 data, all languages into English. Languages "all" include French, German, Spanish and Czech for WMT12

[6] In order to identify NEs we use the Supersense Tagger (Ciaramita and Altun, 2006).
[7] The NEL module uses a graph-based NEL tool (Hachey, Radford and Curran, 2010) which links NEs in a text with those in Wikipedia pages.

and French, German, Spanish, Czech and Russian for WMT13. Both segment and system level evaluations were performed. Evaluation sets provided by WMT organizers were used to calculate both segment and system level correlations.

Since VERTa has been mainly designed to assess either adequacy or fluency separately, our goal for WMT14 was to find the best combination in order to evaluate whole translation quality. Firstly we decided to explore the influence of each module separately. To this aim, all modules described above, except for the semantics one were used and tested separately. Secondly, all modules were assigned the same weight and tested in combination (VERTa-EQ). The reason why the semantics module was disregarded is that it does not usually correlate well with human judgements, as stated above. Each module was set as follows:

- Lexical module. As described above, except for the use of hypernyms/hyponyms matches that were disregarded.
- Morphological module. As described above, except for the lemma-PoS match and the hypernyms/hyponyms-PoS match.
- Dependency module. As described above.
- Ngram module. As described above, using a 2-gram length.

Finally, we used the module combination aimed at evaluating adequacy, which is mainly based on the dependency and lexical modules, but with a stronger influence of the ngram module in order to control word order (VERTa-W). Weights were manually assigned, based on results obtained in previous experiments conducted for adequacy and fluency (Comelles et al., 2012), as follows:

- Lexical module: 0.41
- Morphological module: 0
- Dependency module: 0.40
- Ngram module: 0.19

Experiments aimed at evaluating the influence of each module (see Table 4 and Table 5) show that the dependency module, in the case of WMT12 data, and the lexical module in the case of WMT13 data, are the most effective ones. However, the influence of the ngram module and the morphological module varies depending on the source language. The fact that the dependency module correlates better with human judgements than others might be due to its flexibility to capture different syntactic constructions that convey the same meaning. In addition, the good performance of the lexical module is due to the use of lexical semantic relations. On the other hand, in general the morphological module shows a better performance than the ngram one, which might be due to the type of source languages and the possible translation mistakes. All source languages are highly-inflected languages and this might cause problems when translating into English, since its inflectional morphology is not as rich as theirs. As for the low performance of the ngram module in the cs-en (especially, in WMT12 data), it might be due to the fact that Czech word order is unrestricted, whereas English shows a stricter word order and this might cause translation issues. A longer ngram distance might have been more appropriate to control word order in this case.

Module	fr-en	de-en	es-en	cs-en
Lexical	.16	.20	.18	.14
Morph.	.17	.19	.18	.12
Depend.	**.18**	**.24**	**.20**	**.17**
Ngram	.16	.17	.15	.08

Table 4. Segment-level Kendall's tau correlation per module with WMT12 data.

Module	fr-en	de-en	es-en	cs-en	ru-en
Lexical	**.239**	**.254**	**.294**	**.227**	**.220**
Morph.	.236	.243	.295	.214	.191
Depend.	.232	.247	.275	.220	.199
Ngram	.237	.245	.283	.213	.189

Table 5. Segment-level Kendall's tau correlation per module with WMT13 data.

Finally, two versions of VERTa were compared: the unweighted combination (VERTa-EQ) and the weighted one (VERTa-W). These two versions were also compared to some of the best performing metrics in WMT12 (see Table 6 and Table 7) and WMT13 (see Table 8 and Table 9): Spede07-pP, METEOR, SEMPOR and AMBER (Callison-Burch et al., 2012); SIMPBLEU-RECALL, METEOR and DEPREF-ALIGN[8]). As regards WMT12 data at segment level, the unweighted version achieves similar results to those obtained by the best performing metrics. On the other hand, VERTa-W's results are slightly worse, especially for fr-en and es-en pairs, which is due to the fact that the morphological module has been disregarded in this ver-

[8] http://www.statmt.org/wmt13/papers.html

sion. Regarding system level correlation, neither VERTa-EQ nor VERTa-W achieves a high correlation with human judgements.

Metric	fr-en	de-en	es-en	cs-en
Spede07-pP	**.26**	**.28**	**.26**	**.21**
METEOR	.25	.27	.24	.21
VERTa-EQ	**.26**	**.28**	**.26**	.20
VERTa-W	.24	.28	.25	.20

Table 6. Segment-level Kendall's tau correlation WMT12.

Metric	fr-en	de-en	es-en	cs-en
SEMPOR	.80	**.92**	.94	**.94**
AMBER	**.85**	.79	**.97**	.83
VERTa-EQ	.83	.71	.89	.66
VERTa-W	.79	.73	.91	.66

Table 7. System-level Spearman's rho correlation WMT12.

As for segment level WMT13 results (see Table 8), although both VERTa-EQ and VERTa-W's performance is worse than that of the two best-performing metrics, both versions achieve a third and fourth position for all language pairs, except for fr-en. As regards system level correlations (see Table 9), both versions of VERTa show the best performance for de-en and ru-en pairs, as well as for the average score.

5 Conclusions and Future Work

In this paper we have presented VERTa, a linguistically-based MT metric. VERTa allows for modular combination depending on the language and type of evaluation conducted. Although VERTa has been designed to evaluate adequacy and fluency separately, in order to evaluate whole MT quality, a couple of versions have been used: VERTa-EQ, an unweighted version that uses all modules, and VERTa-W a weighted version that uses the lexical, dependency and ngram modules.
Experiments have shown that the modules that best correlate with human judgements are the dependency and lexical modules. In addition, both VERTa-EQ and VERTa-W have been compared to the best performing metrics in WMT12 and WMT13 shared tasks. VERTa-EQ has proved to be in line with results obtained by Spede07-pP and METEOR in WMT12 at segment level, while in WMT13, both VERTa and VERTa-W occupy the third and fourth position after METEOR and DEPREF-ALIGN as regards segment level and the first position at system level.

In the future, we plan to continue working on the improvement of VERTa and use automatic tuning of module's weight in order to achieve the final version that best correlates with human judgements on ranking. Likewise, we would like to explore the use of VERTa to evaluate other languages but English and how NLP tool errors may influence the performance of the metric.

6 Acknowledgements

We would like to acknowledge Victoria Arranz and Irene Castellón for their valuable comments and sharing their knowledge.
This work has been partially funded by the Spanish Government (projects SKATeR, TIN2012-38584-C06-06 and Holopedia, TIN2010-21128-C02-02).

Metric	fr-en	de-en	es-en	cs-en	ru-en	Average
SIMPBLEU-RECALL	**.303**	**.318**	**.388**	**.260**	**.234**	**.301**
METEOR	.264	.293	.324	.265	.239	.277
VERTa-EQ	.252	.280	.318	.239	.215	.261
VERTa-W	.253	.278	.314	.238	.222	.261
DEPREF-ALIGN	.257	.267	.312	.228	.200	.253

Table 8. Segment-level Kendall's tau correlation WMT13.

Metric	fr-en	de-en	es-en	cs-en	ru-en	Average
METEOR	.984	.961	**.979**	**.964**	.789	.935
DEPREF-ALIGN	**.995**	.966	.965	**.964**	.768	.931
VERTa-EQ	.989	**.970**	.972	.936	**.814**	**.936**
VERTa-W	.989	**.980**	.972	.945	**.868**	**.951**

Table 9. System-level Spearman's rho correlation WMT13.

Reference

J. S. Albrecth and R. Hwa. 2007. A Re-examination of Machine Learning Approaches for Sentence-Level MT Evaluation. In *The Proceedings of the 45th Annual Meeting of the ACL*, Prague, Czech Republic.

J. S. Albrecth and R. Hwa. 2007. Regression for Sentence-Level MT Evaluation with Pseudo References. In *The Proceedings of the 45th Annual Meeting of the ACL*, Prague, Czech Republic.

J. Atserias, R. Blanco, J. M. Chenlo and C. Rodriquez. 2012. FBM-Yahoo at RepLab 2012, *CLEF (Online Working Notes/Labs/Workshop) 2012*, September 20, 2012.

C. Callison-Burch, M. Osborne and P. Koehn. 2006. Re-evaluating the role of BLEU in machine translation research. In *Proceedings of the EACL 2006.*

C. Callison-Burch, P. Kohen, Ch. Monz, M. Post, R. Soricut and L. Specia. 2012. Findings of the 2012 Workshop on Statistical Machine Translation. In *Proceedings of the 7th Workshop on Statistical Machine Translation*. Montréal. Canada.

A. X. Chang and Ch. D. Manning. 2012. SUTIME: A Library for Recognizing and Normalizing Time Expressions. *8th International Conference on Language Resources and Evaluation (LREC 2012).*

M. Ciaramita and Y. Altun. 2006. Broad-coverage sense disambiguation and information extraction with a supersense sequence tagger. Empirical Methods in *Natural Language Processing (EMNLP).*

E. Comelles, J. Atserias, V. Arranz and I. Castellón. 2012. VERTa: Linguistic features in MT evaluation. *Proceedings of the Eighth International Conference on Language Resources and Evaluation (LREC'12),* Istanbul, Turkey.

M.C. de Marneffe, B. MacCartney and Ch. D. Manning. 2006. Generating Typed Dependency Parses from Phrase Structure Parses in *Proceedings of the 5th Edition of the International Conference on Language Resources and Evaluation (LREC-2006).* Genoa, Italy.

M. J. Denkowski and A. Lavie. 2011. METEOR 1.3: Automatic Metric for Reliable Optimization and Evaluation of Machine Translation Systems in *Proceedings of the 6th Workshop on Statistical Machine Translation (ACL-2011).* Edinburgh, Scotland, UK.

J. Giménez and Ll. Màrquez. 2007. Linguistic features for automatic evaluation of heterogeneous MT systems in *Proceedings of the 2nd Workshop on Statistical Machine Translation (ACL),* Prague, Czech Repubilc.

J. Giménez and Ll. Màrquez. 2008. A smorgasbord of features for automatic MT evaluation in *Proceedings of the 3rd Workshop on Statistical Machine Translation (ACL).* Columbus. OH.

J. Gimenez. 2008. *Empirical Machine Translation and its Evaluation*. Doctoral Dissertation. UPC.

J. Giménez and Ll. Márquez. 2010. Linguistic Measures for Automatic Machine Translation Evaluation. *Machine Translation*, 24(3–4),77–86. Springer.

B. Hachey, W. Radford and J. R. Curran. 2011. Graph-based named entity linking with Wikipedia in *Proceedings of the 12th International conference on Web information system engineering*, pages 213-226, Springer-Verlag, Berlin, Heidelberg.

Y. He, J. Du, A. Way and J. van Genabith. 2010. The DCU Dependency-based Metric in WMT-Metrics MATR 2010. *In Proceedings of the Joint Fifth Workshop on Statistical Machine Translation and Metrics MATR (WMT 2010),* Uppsala, Sweden.

A. Lavie and M. J. Denkowski. 2009. The METEOR Metric for Automatic Evaluation of Machine Translation. *Machine Translation, 23.*

G. Leusch and H. Ney. 2008. BLEUSP, INVWER, CDER: Three improved MT evaluation measures. In *NIST Metrics for Machine Translation 2008 Evaluation (MericsMATR08),* Waikiki, Honolulu, Hawaii, October 2008.

D. Liu and D. Hildea. 2005. Syntactic Features for Evaluation of Machine Translation in *Proceedings of the ACL Workshop on Intrinsic and Extrinsic Evaluation Measures for Machine Translation and/or Summarization*, Ann Arbor

Ch.Lo and D. Wu. 2010. Semantic vs. Syntactic vs. Ngram Structure for Machine Translation Evaluation. In *Proceedings of the 4th Workshop on Syntax Semantics and Structure in Statistical Translation.* Beijing. China.

Ch. Lo, A. K. Tumurulu and D. Wu. 2012. Fully Automatic Semantic MT Evaluation. *Proceedings of the 7th Wrokshop on Statistical Machine Translation*, Montréal, Canada, June 7-8.

K. Owczarzak, J. van Genabith and A. Way. 2007. Dependency-Based Automatic Evaluation for Machine Translation in *Proceedings of SSST, NAACL-HLT/AMTA Workshop on Syntax and Structure I Statistical Translation,* Rochester, New York.

K. Owczarzak, J. van Genabith and A. Way. 2007. Labelled Dependencies in Machine Translation Evaluation in *Proceedings of the ACL Workshop on Statistical Machine Translation,* Prague, Czech Republic.

K. Papineni, S. Roukos, T. Ward and W. Zhu. 2002. BLEU: A Method for Automatic Evaluation of Machine Translation. In *Proceedings of the 40th Annual Meeting of the Association for Computational Linguistics* (ACL02). Philadelphia. PA.

F. Reeder, K. Miller, J. Doyon and J. White. 2001. The Naming of Things and the Confusion of Tongues: an MT Metric. *Proceedings of the Workshop on MT Evaluation "Who did what to whom?" at Machine Translation Summit VIII.*

L. Specia and J. Giménez. 2010. Combining Confidence Estimation and Reference-based Metrics for Segment-level MT Evaluation. *The Ninth Conference of the Association for Machine Translation in the Americas* (AMTA 2010), Denver, Colorado.

D. Wetzel and F. Bond. 2012. Enriching Parallel Corpora for Statistical Machine Translation with Semantic Negation Rephrasing. *Proceedings of SSST-6, Sixth Workshop on Syntax, Semantics and Structure in Statistical Translation*, Jeju, Republic of Korea.

Meteor Universal: Language Specific Translation Evaluation for Any Target Language

Michael Denkowski **Alon Lavie**
Language Technologies Institute
Carnegie Mellon University
Pittsburgh, PA 15213 USA
{mdenkows,alavie}@cs.cmu.edu

Abstract

This paper describes Meteor Universal, released for the 2014 ACL Workshop on Statistical Machine Translation. Meteor Universal brings language specific evaluation to previously unsupported target languages by (1) automatically extracting linguistic resources (paraphrase tables and function word lists) from the bitext used to train MT systems and (2) using a universal parameter set learned from pooling human judgments of translation quality from several language directions. Meteor Universal is shown to significantly outperform baseline BLEU on two new languages, Russian (WMT13) and Hindi (WMT14).

1 Introduction

Recent WMT evaluations have seen a variety of metrics employ language specific resources to replicate human translation rankings far better than simple baselines (Callison-Burch et al., 2011; Callison-Burch et al., 2012; Macháček and Bojar, 2013; Snover et al., 2009; Denkowski and Lavie, 2011; Dahlmeier et al., 2011; Chen et al., 2012; Wang and Manning, 2012, *inter alia*). While the wealth of linguistic resources for the WMT languages allows the development of sophisticated metrics, most of the world's 7,000+ languages lack the prerequisites for building advanced metrics. Researchers working on low resource languages are usually limited to baseline BLEU (Papineni et al., 2002) for evaluating translation quality.

Meteor Universal brings language specific evaluation to any target language by combining linguistic resources automatically learned from MT system training data with a universal metric parameter set that generalizes across languages. Given only the bitext used to build a standard phrase-based translation system, Meteor Universal learns a paraphrase table and function word list, two of the most consistently beneficial language specific resources employed in versions of Meteor. Whereas previous versions of Meteor require human ranking judgments in the target language to learn parameters, Meteor Universal uses a single parameter set learned from pooling judgments from several languages. This universal parameter set captures general preferences shown by human evaluators across languages. We show this approach to significantly outperform baseline BLEU for two new languages, Russian and Hindi. The following sections review Meteor's scoring function (§2), describe the automatic extraction of language specific resources (§3), discuss training of the universal parameter set (§4), report experimental results (§5), describe released software (§6), and conclude (§7).

2 Meteor Scoring

Meteor evaluates translation hypotheses by aligning them to reference translations and calculating sentence-level similarity scores. For a hypothesis-reference pair, the space of possible alignments is constructed by exhaustively identifying all possible matches between the sentences according to the following matchers:

Exact: Match words if their surface forms are identical.

Stem: Stem words using a language appropriate Snowball Stemmer (Porter, 2001) and match if the stems are identical.

Synonym: Match words if they share membership in any synonym set according to the WordNet database (Miller and Fellbaum, 2007).

Paraphrase: Match phrases if they are listed as

Proceedings of the Ninth Workshop on Statistical Machine Translation, pages 376–380,
Baltimore, Maryland USA, June 26–27, 2014.

paraphrases in a language appropriate paraphrase table (described in §3.2).

All matches are generalized to phrase matches with a span in each sentence. Any word occurring within the span is considered covered by the match. The final alignment is then resolved as the largest subset of all matches meeting the following criteria in order of importance:

1. Require each word in each sentence to be covered by zero or one matches.

2. Maximize the number of covered words across both sentences.

3. Minimize the number of *chunks*, where a *chunk* is defined as a series of matches that is contiguous and identically ordered in both sentences.

4. Minimize the sum of absolute distances between match start indices in the two sentences. (Break ties by preferring to align phrases that occur at similar positions in both sentences.)

Alignment resolution is conducted as a beam search using a heuristic based on the above criteria.

The Meteor score for an aligned sentence pair is calculated as follows. Content and function words are identified in the hypothesis (h_c, h_f) and reference (r_c, r_f) according to a function word list (described in §3.1). For each of the matchers (m_i), count the number of content and function words covered by matches of this type in the hypothesis ($m_i(h_c)$, $m_i(h_f)$) and reference ($m_i(r_c)$, $m_i(r_f)$). Calculate weighted precision and recall using matcher weights ($w_i...w_n$) and content-function word weight (δ):

$$P = \frac{\sum_i w_i \cdot (\delta \cdot m_i(h_c) + (1-\delta) \cdot m_i(h_f))}{\delta \cdot |h_c| + (1-\delta) \cdot |h_f|}$$

$$R = \frac{\sum_i w_i \cdot (\delta \cdot m_i(r_c) + (1-\delta) \cdot m_i(r_f))}{\delta \cdot |r_c| + (1-\delta) \cdot |r_f|}$$

The parameterized harmonic mean of P and R (van Rijsbergen, 1979) is then calculated:

$$F_{mean} = \frac{P \cdot R}{\alpha \cdot P + (1-\alpha) \cdot R}$$

To account for gaps and differences in word order, a fragmentation penalty is calculated using the total number of matched words (m, averaged over hypothesis and reference) and number of chunks (ch):

$$Pen = \gamma \cdot \left(\frac{ch}{m}\right)^{\beta}$$

The Meteor score is then calculated:

$$Score = (1 - Pen) \cdot F_{mean}$$

The parameters α, β, γ, δ, and $w_i...w_n$ are tuned to maximize correlation with human judgments.

3 Language Specific Resources

Meteor uses language specific resources to dramatically improve evaluation accuracy. While some resources such as WordNet and the Snowball stemmers are limited to one or a few languages, other resources can be learned from data for any language. Meteor Universal uses the same bitext used to build statistical translation systems to learn function words and paraphrases. Used in conjunction with the universal parameter set, these resources bring language specific evaluation to new target languages.

3.1 Function Word Lists

The function word list is used to discriminate between content and function words in the target language. Meteor Universal counts words in the target side of the training bitext and considers any word with relative frequency above 10^{-3} to be a function word. This list is used only during the scoring stage of evaluation, where the tunable δ parameter controls the relative weight of content versus function words. When tuned to match human judgments, this parameter usually reflects a greater importance for content words.

3.2 Paraphrase Tables

Paraphrase tables allow many-to-many matches that can encapsulate any local language phenomena, including morphology, synonymy, and true paraphrasing. Identifying these matches allows far more sophisticated evaluation than is possible with simple surface form matches. In Meteor Universal, paraphrases act as the catch-all for non-exact matches. Paraphrases are automatically extracted from the training bitext using the translation pivot approach (Bannard and Callison-Burch, 2005). First, a standard phrase table is learned from the bitext (Koehn et al., 2003). Paraphrase extraction then proceeds as follows. For each target language phrase (e_1) in the table, find each source phrase f that e_1 translates. Each alternate phrase ($e_2 \neq e_1$) that translates f is considered a paraphrase with probability $P(f|e_1) \cdot P(e_2|f)$. The total probability of e_2 being a paraphrase of e_1 is the sum over all possible pivot phrases f:

$$P(e_2|e_1) = \sum_f P(f|e_1) \cdot P(e_2|f)$$

To improve paraphrase precision, we apply several language independent pruning techniques. The following are applied to each paraphrase instance (e_1, f, e_2):

- Discard instances with very low probability ($P(f|e_1) \cdot P(e_2|f) < 0.001$).
- Discard instances where e_1, f, or e_2 contain punctuation characters.
- Discard instances where e_1, f, or e_2 contain only function words (relative frequency above 10^{-3} in the bitext).

The following are applied to each final paraphrase (e_1, e_2) after summing over all instances:

- Discard paraphrases with very low probability ($P(e_2|e_1) < 0.01$).
- Discard paraphrases where e_2 is a sub-phrase of e_1.

This constitutes the full Meteor paraphrasing pipeline that has been used to build tables for fully supported languages (Denkowski and Lavie, 2011). Paraphrases for new languages have the added advantage of being extracted from the same bitext that MT systems use for phrase extraction, resulting in ideal paraphrase coverage for evaluated systems.

4 Universal Parameter Set

Traditionally, building a version of Meteor for a new target language has required a set of human-scored machine translations, most frequently in the form of WMT rankings. The general lack of availability of these judgments has severely limited the number of languages for which Meteor versions could be trained. Meteor Universal addresses this problem with the introduction of a "universal" parameter set that captures general human preferences that apply to all languages for which judgment data does exist. We learn this parameter set by pooling over 100,000 binary ranking judgments from WMT12 (Callison-Burch et al., 2012) that cover 8 language directions (details in Table 1). Data for each language is scored using the same resources (function word list and paraphrase table only) and scoring parameters are tuned to maximize agreement (Kendall's τ) over all judgments from all languages, leading to a single parameter set. The universal parameter set encodes the following general human preferences:

Direction	Judgments
cs-en	11,021
de-en	11,934
es-en	9,796
fr-en	11,594
en-cs	18,805
en-de	14,553
en-es	11,834
en-fr	11,562
Total	101,099

Table 1: Binary ranking judgments per language direction used to learn parameters for Meteor Universal

- Prefer recall over precision.
- Prefer word choice over word order.
- Prefer correct translations of content words over function words.
- Prefer exact matches over paraphrase matches, while still giving significant credit to paraphrases.

Table 2 compares the universal parameters to those learned for specific languages in previous versions of Meteor. Notably, the universal parameter set is more balanced, showing a normalizing effect from generalizing across several language directions.

5 Experiments

We evaluate the Universal version of Meteor against full language dedicated versions of Meteor and baseline BLEU on the WMT13 rankings. Results for English, Czech, German, Spanish, and French are biased in favor of Meteor Universal since rankings for these target languages are included in the training data while Russian constitutes a true held out test. We also report the results of the WMT14 Hindi evaluation task. Shown

Language	α	β	γ	δ	w_{exact}	w_{stem}	w_{syn}	w_{par}
English	0.85	0.20	0.60	0.75	1.00	0.60	0.80	0.60
Czech	0.95	0.20	0.60	0.80	1.00	–	–	0.40
German	0.95	1.00	0.55	0.55	1.00	0.80	–	0.20
Spanish	0.65	1.30	0.50	0.80	1.00	0.80	–	0.60
French	0.90	1.40	0.60	0.65	1.00	0.20	–	0.40
Universal	0.70	1.40	0.30	0.70	1.00	–	–	0.60

Table 2: Comparison of parameters for language specific and universal versions of Meteor.

WMT13 τ	M-Full	M-Universal	BLEU
English	0.214	0.206	0.124
Czech	0.092	0.085	0.044
German	0.163	0.157	0.097
Spanish	0.106	0.101	0.068
French	0.150	0.137	0.099
Russian	–	0.128	0.068

WMT14 τ	M-Full	M-Universal	BLEU
Hindi	–	0.264	0.227

Table 3: Sentence-level correlation with human rankings (Kendall's τ) for Meteor (language specific versions), Meteor Universal, and BLEU

in Table 3, Meteor Universal significantly outperforms baseline BLEU in all cases while suffering only slight degradation compared to versions of Meteor tuned for individual languages. For Russian, correlation is nearly double that of BLEU. This provides substantial evidence that Meteor Universal will further generalize, bringing improved evaluation accuracy to new target languages currently limited to baseline language independent metrics.

For the WMT14 evaluation, we use the traditional language specific versions of Meteor for all language directions except Hindi. This includes Russian, for which additional language specific resources (a Snowball word stemmer) help significantly. For Hindi, we use the release version of Meteor Universal to extract linguistic resources from the constrained training bitext provided for the shared translation task. These resources are used with the universal parameter set to score all system outputs for the English–Hindi direction.

6 Software

Meteor Universal is included in Meteor version 1.5 which is publicly released for WMT14. Meteor 1.5 can be downloaded from the official webpage[1] and a full tutorial for Meteor Universal is available online.[2] Building a version of Meteor for a new language requires a training bitext (*corpus.f*, *corpus.e*) and a standard Moses format phrase table (*phrase-table.gz*) (Koehn et al., 2007). To extract linguistic resources for Meteor, run the new language script:

```
$ python scripts/new_language.py out \
corpus.f corpus.e phrase-table.gz
```

To use the resulting files to score translations with Meteor, use the new language option:

```
$ java -jar meteor-*.jar test ref -new \
out/meteor-files
```

Meteor 1.5, including Meteor Universal, is free software released under the terms of the GNU Lesser General Public License.

7 Conclusion

This paper describes Meteor Universal, a version of the Meteor metric that brings language specific evaluation to any target language using the same resources used to build statistical translation systems. Held out tests show Meteor Universal to significantly outperform baseline BLEU on WMT13 Russian and WMT14 Hindi. Meteor version 1.5 is freely available open source software.

Acknowledgements

This work is supported in part by the National Science Foundation under grant IIS-0915327, by the Qatar National Research Fund (a member of the Qatar Foundation) under grant NPRP 09-1140-1-177, and by the NSF-sponsored XSEDE program under grant TG-CCR110017.

[1] http://www.cs.cmu.edu/~alavie/METEOR/

[2] http://www.cs.cmu.edu/~mdenkows/meteor-universal.html

References

Colin Bannard and Chris Callison-Burch. 2005. Paraphrasing with bilingual parallel corpora. In *Proceedings of the 43rd Annual Meeting of the Association for Computational Linguistics (ACL'05)*, pages 597–604, Ann Arbor, Michigan, June. Association for Computational Linguistics.

Chris Callison-Burch, Philipp Koehn, Christof Monz, and Omar Zaidan. 2011. Findings of the 2011 workshop on statistical machine translation. In *Proceedings of the Sixth Workshop on Statistical Machine Translation*, pages 22–64, Edinburgh, Scotland, July. Association for Computational Linguistics.

Chris Callison-Burch, Philipp Koehn, Christof Monz, Matt Post, Radu Soricut, and Lucia Specia. 2012. Findings of the 2012 workshop on statistical machine translation. In *Proceedings of the Seventh Workshop on Statistical Machine Translation*, pages 10–51, Montréal, Canada, June. Association for Computational Linguistics.

Boxing Chen, Roland Kuhn, and George Foster. 2012. Improving amber, an mt evaluation metric. In *Proceedings of the Seventh Workshop on Statistical Machine Translation*, pages 59–63, Montréal, Canada, June. Association for Computational Linguistics.

Daniel Dahlmeier, Chang Liu, and Hwee Tou Ng. 2011. Tesla at wmt 2011: Translation evaluation and tunable metric. In *Proceedings of the Sixth Workshop on Statistical Machine Translation*, pages 78–84, Edinburgh, Scotland, July. Association for Computational Linguistics.

Michael Denkowski and Alon Lavie. 2011. Meteor 1.3: Automatic metric for reliable optimization and evaluation of machine translation systems. In *Proceedings of the Sixth Workshop on Statistical Machine Translation*, pages 85–91, Edinburgh, Scotland, July. Association for Computational Linguistics.

Philipp Koehn, Franz Josef Och, and Daniel Marcu. 2003. Statistical phrase-based translation. In *Proc. of NAACL/HLT 2003*.

Philipp Koehn, Hieu Hoang, Alexandra Birch, Chris Callison-Burch, Marcello Federico, Nicola Bertoldi, Brooke Cowan, Wade Shen, Christine Moran, Richard Zens, Chris Dyer, Ondrej Bojar, Alexandra Constantin, and Evan Herbst. 2007. Moses: Open source toolkit for statistical machine translation. In *Proceedings of the 45th Annual Meeting of the Association for Computational Linguistics Companion Volume Proceedings of the Demo and Poster Sessions*, pages 177–180, Prague, Czech Republic, June. Association for Computational Linguistics.

Matouš Macháček and Ondřej Bojar. 2013. Results of the WMT13 metrics shared task. In *Proceedings of the Eighth Workshop on Statistical Machine Translation*, pages 45–51, Sofia, Bulgaria, August. Association for Computational Linguistics.

George Miller and Christiane Fellbaum. 2007. WordNet. http://wordnet.princeton.edu/.

Kishore Papineni, Salim Roukos, Todd Ward, and Wei-Jing Zhu. 2002. BLEU: A method for automatic evalution of machine translation. In *Proceedings of the 40th Annual Meeting of the Association for Computational Linguistics*, pages 311–318, Philadelphia, Pennsylvania, USA, July.

Martin Porter. 2001. Snowball: A language for stemming algorithms. http://snowball.tartarus.org/texts/.

Matthew Snover, Nitin Madnani, Bonnie Dorr, and Richard Schwartz. 2009. Fluency, adequacy, or HTER? Exploring different human judgments with a tunable MT metric. In *Proceedings of the Fourth Workshop on Statistical Machine Translation*, pages 259–268, Athens, Greece, March. Association for Computational Linguistics.

C. J. van Rijsbergen, 1979. *Information Retrieval*, chapter 7. Butterworths, London, UK, 2nd edition.

Mengqiu Wang and Christopher Manning. 2012. Spede: Probabilistic edit distance metrics for mt evaluation. In *Proceedings of the Seventh Workshop on Statistical Machine Translation*, pages 76–83, Montréal, Canada, June. Association for Computational Linguistics.

Application of Prize based on Sentence Length in Chunk-based Automatic Evaluation of Machine Translation

Hiroshi Echizen'ya
Hokkai-Gakuen University
S26-Jo, W11-Chome, Chuo-ku,
Sapporo 064-0926 Japan
echi@lst.hokkai-s-u.ac.jp

Kenji Araki
Hokkaido University
N 14-Jo, W 9-Chome, Kita-ku,
Sapporo 060-0814 Japan
araki@ist.hokudai.ac.jp

Eduard Hovy
Carnegie Mellon University
5000 Forbes Avenue
Pittsburgh, PA 15213 USA
hovy@cmu.edu

Abstract

As described in this paper, we propose a new automatic evaluation metric for machine translation. Our metric is based on chunking between the reference and candidate translation. Moreover, we apply a prize based on sentence-length to the metric, dissimilar from penalties in BLEU or NIST. We designate this metric as **A**utomatic Evaluation of Machine Translation in which the **P**rize is **A**pplied to a **C**hunk-based metric (APAC). Through meta-evaluation experiments and comparison with several metrics, we confirmed that our metric shows stable correlation with human judgment.

1 Introduction

In the field of machine translation, various automatic evaluation metrics have been proposed. Among them, chunk-based metrics such as METEOR(A. Lavie and A. Agarwal, 2007), ROUGE-L(Lin and Och, 2004), and IMPACT(H. Echizen-ya and K. Araki, 2007) are effective. In general, BLEU(K. Papineni et al., 2002), NIST(NIST, 2002), and RIBES(H. Isozaki et al., 2010) use a penalty for calculation of scores because the high score is often given extremely when the candidate translation is short. Therefore, the penalty is effective to obtain high correlation with human judgment. On the other hand, almost all chunk-based metrics use the F-measure based on a precision by candidate translation and a recall by reference. Moreover, they assign a penalty for the difference of chunk order between the candidate translation and the reference, not the penalty for the difference of sentence length. Nevertheless, it is also important for chunk-based metrics to examine the sentence length. In chunk-based metrics, each word's weight depends on the sentence length. For example, the weight of each word is 0.2 (=1/5) when the number of words in a sentence is 5; it is 0.1 (=1/10) when the number of words in a sentence is 10. Therefore, the weight of the non-matched word in the short sentence is large.

To resolve this problem, it is effective for short sentences to give a prize based on the sentence length in the chunk-based metrics. Therefore, we propose a new metric using a prize based on the sentence length. We designate this metric as **A**utomatic Evaluation of Machine Translation in which the **P**rize is **A**pplied to a **C**hunk-based metric (APAC). In our metric, the weight of a non-matched word becomes small for the short sentence by awarding of the prize. It is almost identical to that for a long sentence by awarding of the prize. Therefore, our metric does not depend heavily on sentence length because the weight of non-matched words is constantly small. We confirmed the effectiveness of APAC using meta-evaluation experiments.

2 Score calculation in APAC

The APAC score is calculated in two phases. In the first phase, the chunk sequence is determined between a candidate translation and the reference. The chunk sequence

Proceedings of the Ninth Workshop on Statistical Machine Translation, pages 381–386,
Baltimore, Maryland USA, June 26–27, 2014. ©2014 Association for Computational Linguistics

is determined using the **L**ongest **C**ommon **S**ubsequence (LCS). Generally, several chunk sequences are obtained using LCS. In that case, APAC determines only one chunk sequence using the number of words in each chunk and the position of each chunk.

For example, in between the candidate translation "In this case, the system power supply is accessory battery 86." and "In this case, the system power supply is the accessory power supply battery 86.", the chunk sequence is "in this case, the system power supply is", "accessory" and "battery 86.", and the chunk sequence is ony one in these sentences. Only one chunk sequence is determined using the number of words in each chunk and the position of each chunk when several chunk sequences are obtained.

The second phase is calculation of the score based on the determined chunk sequence. The Ch_score in Eq. (3) is calculated using the determined chunk sequence. In Eq. (3), ch denotes each chunk and ch_num represents the number of chunks. Moreover, $length(ch)$ is the word number of each chunk. β is the weight parameter for the length of each chunk. For example, in between the candidate translation "In this case, the system power supply is accessory battery 86." and "In this case, the system power supply is the accessory power supply battery 86.", ch_num is 3 ("in this case, the system power supply is", "accessory" and "battery 86."). Therefore, Ch_score is 91 ($=9^{2.0}+1^{2.0}+3^{2.0}$) when β is 2.0.

$$P=\left\{\left(\frac{\sum_{i=0}^{RN-1}(\alpha^i\times Ch\_score)}{m^\beta}\right)^{\frac{1}{\beta}} +0.5\times Prize\_m\right\}/2.0 \quad (1)$$

$$R=\left\{\left(\frac{\sum_{i=0}^{RN-1}(\alpha^i\times Ch\_score)}{n^\beta}\right)^{\frac{1}{\beta}} +0.5\times Prize\_n\right\}/2.0 \quad (2)$$

$$Ch\_score=\sum_{ch\in ch\_num} length(ch)^\beta \quad (3)$$

$$Prize\_m=\frac{1}{log(m)+1} \quad (4)$$

$$Prize\_n=\frac{1}{log(n)+1} \quad (5)$$

$$APAC\ \ score=\frac{(1+\gamma^2)RP}{R+\gamma^2 P} \quad (6)$$

The P and R in Eqs. (1) and (2) respectively denote precision by candidate translation and recall by reference. These are calculated using the Ch_score obtained using Eq. (3). Therein, m and n respectively represent the word numbers of the candidate translation and the reference. Moreover, the chunk sequence determination process is repeated recursively to all common words. The number of determination processes of the chunk sequence is high when the word order of the candidate translation differs from that of the reference. The RN is the number of determination processes of the chunk sequence. Here, α is the parameter for the chunk order. It is less than 1.0. The value of the Ch_score is small when the chunk order between the candidate translation and references differs because the value of $length(ch)$ in each chunk becomes small. For example, in between the candidate translation "In this case, the system power supply is accessory battery 86." and "In this case, the system power supply is the accessory power supply battery 86.", $\left(\frac{\sum_{i=0}^{RN-1}(\alpha^i\times Ch\_score)}{m^\beta}\right)^{\frac{1}{\beta}}$ is 0.773 ($=\sqrt{\frac{91}{169}}=\sqrt{\frac{\sum_{i=0}^{1-1}(0.1^0\times 91)}{13^{2.0}}}$) and $\left(\frac{\sum_{i=0}^{RN-1}(\alpha^i\times Ch\_score)}{n^\beta}\right)^{\frac{1}{\beta}}$ is 0.596 ($=\sqrt{\frac{91}{256}}=\sqrt{\frac{\sum_{i=0}^{1-1}(0.1^0\times 91)}{16^{2.0}}}$) when α and β respectively stand for 0.1 and 2.0. The value of RN is 1 because there is no more matching words after the determined chunks ("in this case, the system power supply is", "accessory" and "battery 86.") are removed from the candidate translation "In this case, the system power supply is accessory battery 86." and "In this case, the system power supply is the accessory power supply battery 86.".

Moreover, $Prize\_m$ and $Prize\_n$ in Eqs. (1) and (2) are calculated respectively using Eqs.

(4) and (5). Each is less than 1.0. For example, in the candidate translation "In this case, the system power supply is accessory battery 86." and "In this case, the system power supply is the accessory power supply battery 86.", $Prize\_m$ and $Prize\_n$ respectively stand for 0.473 ($=\frac{1}{1.114+1}=\frac{1}{log(13)+1}$) and 0.454 ($=\frac{1}{1.204+1}=\frac{1}{log(16)+1}$). These values become large in the short sentences. They become small in the long sentences. Therefore, the weight of each non-matched word is small in the short sentences. It is kept small in the long sentences. Finally, the score is calculated using Eq. (6). This equation shows the f-measure based on P and R. In Eq. (6), γ is determined as P/R(C. J. V. Rijsbergen, 1979). The $APAC$ $score$ is between 0.0 and 1.0. For example, in the candidate translation "In this case, the system power supply is accessory battery 86." and "In this case, the system power supply is the accessory power supply battery 86.", P and R respectively stand for 0.505 ($=\frac{0.773+0.5\times0.473}{2.0}$) and 0.412 ($=\frac{0.596+0.5\times0.454}{2.0}$). Therefore, $APAC$ $score$ is 0.445 ($=\frac{0.521}{1.171}=\frac{(1+1.503)\times0.412\times0.505}{0.412+1.503\times0.505}$) and γ is 1.226 ($=\frac{0.505}{0.412}$)

3 Experiments

3.1 Experimental Procedure

Meta-evaluation experiments are performed using WMT2012(C. Callison-Burch et al., 2012) data and WMT2013(O. Bojar et al., 2013) data, and NTCIR-7(A. Fujii et al., 2008) data and NTCIR-9(A. Goto et al., 2011) data. All sentences by NTCIR data are English patent sentences obtained through Japanese-to-English translation. The number of references is 1. In NTICR-7 data, the average value in the evaluation results of three human judgments is used as the scores of 1–5 from the perspective of adequacy and fluency. In NTCIR-9 data, the evaluation results of one human judgment is used as the scores of 1–5 from the view of adequacy and acceptance. For this meta-evaluation, we used only English and Japanese candidate translations because we can evaluate them in comparison with other languages correctly.

We calculated the correlation between the scores by automatic evaluation and the scores by human judgments at the system level and the segment level, respectively. Spearman's rank correlation coefficient is used at the system level. The Kendall tau rank correlation coefficient is used in the segment level.

Moreover, we used BLEU (ver. 13a), NIST (ver. 13a), METEOR (ver. 1.4), and APAC with no prize (APAC_no_p) as the automatic evaluation metrics for comparison with APAC as shown in Eqs. (4) and (5). In APAC_no_p, $\left(\frac{\sum_{i=0}^{RN-1}(\alpha^i \times Ch\_score)}{m^\beta}\right)^{\frac{1}{\beta}}$ as P and $\left(\frac{\sum_{i=0}^{RN-1}(\alpha^i \times Ch\_score)}{m^\beta}\right)^{\frac{1}{\beta}}$ as R are used respectively in Eqs. (1) and (2).

3.2 Experimental Results

Tables 1 and 2 respectively present Spearman's rank correlation coefficients of system-level and Kendall tau rank correlation coefficients of segment-level in WMT2012 data. Tables 3 and 4 respectively show Spearman's rank correlation coefficients of the system-level and Kendall tau rank correlation coefficients of segment-level in WMT2013 data. Moreover, Tables 5 and 6 respectively present Spearman's rank correlation coefficients of system-level and Kendall tau rank correlation coefficients of segment-level in NTCIR-7 data. Tables 7 and 8 respectively show Spearman's rank correlation coefficients of system-level and Kendall tau rank correlation coefficients of the segment level in NTCIR-9 data.

In APAC, 0.1 and 1.2 were used as the values of parameters α and β by the preliminarily experimentally obtained results. In Tables 1–8, "Rank" denotes the ranking based on "Avg." The value of "()" denotes the number of MT systems in Tables 1, 3, 5, and 7. The value of "()" represents the number of sentence pairs in Tables 2, 4, 6, and 8. These values depend on the data.

3.3 Discussion

The results presented in Tables 1–8 indicate that APAC can obtain the most stable correlation coefficients among some metrics. The ranking of APAC is No. 1 through NTCIR data in Tables 5–8. In WMT data of Tables 1–4, the ranking of APAC is the lowest except for Table 3. However, the difference

	cs-en(6)	de-en(16)	es-en(12)	fr-en(15)	Avg.	Rank
APAC	0.886	0.650	0.958	0.811	0.826	5
APAC_no_p	0.886	0.676	0.958	0.807	0.832	3
METEOR	0.943	0.841	0.979	0.818	0.895	1
BLEU	0.886	0.674	0.958	0.796	0.828	4
NIST	0.943	0.700	0.944	0.779	0.841	2

Table 1: Spearman's rank correlation coefficient of system-level in WMT2012 data.

	cs-en(11,155)	de-en(12,042)	es-en(9,880)	fr-en(11,682)	Avg.	Rank
APAC	0.185	0.204	0.209	0.226	0.206	3
APAC_no_p	0.189	0.207	0.208	0.226	0.207	2
METEOR	0.223	0.279	0.248	0.243	0.248	1

Table 2: Kendall tau rank correlation coefficient of the segment level in WMT2012 data.

between the ranking of METEOR, which is the highest, and that of APAC is not larger in WMT data. The correlation coefficients of APAC in NTCIR data of Tables 5–8 are higher than those of METEOR. In Tables 5 and 6, underlining in APAC signifies that the differences between correlation coefficients obtained using APAC and METEOR are statistically significant at the 5% significance level. In Table 7, the correlation coefficients of METEOR, BLEU, and NIST are extremely low. Only one human judgment was used in NTCIR-9 data. As a result, APAC is fundamentally effective for various languages independent of the differences in the grammatical structures between languages: these experimentally obtained results indicate that APAC is the most stable metric.

Moreover, in APAC, the correlation coefficients of the segment level in NTCIR data were increased using the prize of Eqs. (4) and (5). In WMT data, the correlation coefficients are almost identical using the prize. Therefore, use of the prize was fundamentally effective at the segment level. The evaluation quality of segment level is generally very low in the automatic evaluation metrics. Therefore, it is extremely important to improve the correlation coefficient of segment level. Application of the prize is effective to improve the evaluation quality of the segment level.

4 Conclusion

As described in this paper, we proposed a new chunk-based automatic evaluation metric using the prize based on the sentence length. The experimentally obtained results indicate that APAC is the most stable metric.

We will improve APAC to obtain higher correlation coefficients in future studies. Particularly, we will strive to improve the correlation coefficients at the segment level. The APAC software will be released by `http://www.lst.hokkai-s-u.ac.jp/~echi/automatic_evaluation_mt.html`.

Acknowledgments

This work was done as research under the AAMT/JAPIO Special Interest Group on Patent Translation. The Japan Patent Information Organization (JAPIO) and the National Institute of Information (NII) provided corpora used in this work. The author gratefully acknowledges support from JAPIO and NII.

References

O. Bojar, C. Buck, C. Callison-Burch, C. Federmann, B. Haddow, P. Koehn, C. Monz, M. Post, R. Sortcut and L. Specia. 2013. Findings of the 2013 Workshop on Statistical Machine Translation. Proceedings of the Eighth Workshop on Statistical Machine Translation. pp.1–44.

C. Callison-Burch, P. Koehn, C. Monz, M. Post, R. Sortcut and L. Specia. 2012. Findings of the 2012 Workshop on Statistical Machine Translation. Proceedings of the Seventh Workshop on Statistical Machine Translation. pp.10–51.

H. Echizen-ya and K. Araki. 2007. Automatic Evaluation of Machine Translation based on

	cs-en(11)	de-en(17)	es-en(12)	fr-en(13)	ru-en(19)	Avg.	Rank
APAC	0.900	0.904	0.916	0.934	0.709	0.873	3
APAC_no_p	0.909	0.909	0.937	0.934	0.721	0.882	2
METEOR	0.982	0.946	0.923	0.967	0.889	0.941	1
BLEU	0.945	0.897	0.853	0.951	0.614	0.852	4
NIST	0.900	0.828	0.804	0.786	0.465	0.757	5

Table 3: Spearman's rank correlation coefficient of the system level in WMT2013 data.

Metrics	cs-en (85,469)	de-en (128,668)	es-en (67,832)	fr-en (80,741)	ru-en (151,422)	Avg.	Rank
APAC	0.144	0.163	0.169	0.139	0.121	0.147	3
APAC_no_p	0.148	0.167	0.176	0.142	0.123	0.151	2
METEOR	0.222	0.236	0.241	0.194	0.226	0.224	1

Table 4: Kendall tau rank correlation coefficient of the segment level in WMT2013 data.

Recursive Acquisition of an Intuitive Common Parts Continuum. Proceedings of the Eleventh Machine Translation Summit. pp.151–158.

A. Fujii, M. Utiyama, M. Yamamoto and T. Utsuro. 2008. Overview of the Patent Translation Task at the NTCIR-7 Workshop. Proceedings of the Seventh NTCIR Workshop Meeting on Evaluation of Information Access Technologies: Information Retrieval, Question Answering and Cross-lingual Information Access. pp.389–400.

I. Goto, B. Lu, K. P. Chow, E. Sumita and B. K. Tsou. 2011. Overview of the Patent Translation Task at the NTCIR-9 Workshop. Proceedings of the Ninth NTCIR Workshop Meeting. pp.559–578.

H. Isozaki, T. Hirao, K. Duh, K. Sudoh and H. Tsukada. 2010. Automatic Evaluation of Translation Quality for Distant Language Pairs. Proceedings of the 2010 Conference on Empirical Methods in Natural Language Processing. pp.944–952.

A. Lavie and A. Agarwal. 2007. Meteor: An Automatic Metric for MT Evaluation with High Levels of Correlation with Human Judgments. Proceedings of the Second Workshop on Statistical Machine Translation.

Chin-Yew Lin and F. J. Och. 2004. Automatic Evaluation of Machine Translation Quality Using the Longest Common Subsequence and Skip-Bigram Statistics. *In Proc. of ACL'04*, 606–613.

NIST. 2002. Automatic Evaluation of Machine Translation Quality Using N-gram Co-Occurrence Statistics. *http://www.nist.gov/speech/tests/mt/doc/ngram-study.pdf*.

K. Papineni, S. Roukos, T. Ward, and Wei-Jing Zhu. 2002. BLEU: a Method for Automatic Evaluation of Machine Translation. Proceedings of the 40th Annual Meeting of the Association for Computational Linguistics (ACL). pp.311–318.

C. J. Van Rijsbergen. 1979. *Information Retrieval (2nd ed.)*, Butterworths.

	Adequacy(15)	Fluency(15)	Avg.	Rank
APAC	0.872	0.805	0.839	1
APAC_no_p	0.872	0.805	0.839	1
METEOR	0.424	0.380	0.402	5
BLEU	0.582	0.586	0.584	3
NIST	0.578	0.568	0.573	4

Table 5: Spearman's rank correlation coefficient of the system level in NTCIR-7 data.

	Adequacy (1,500)	Fluency (1,500)	Avg.	Rank
APAC	0.494	0.489	0.491	1
APAC_no_p	0.482	0.476	0.479	2
METEOR	0.366	0.383	0.375	3

Table 6: Kendall tau rank correlation coefficient of the segment level in NTCIR-7 data.

	Adequacy (19)	Acceptance (14)	Avg.	Rank
APAC	0.182	0.298	0.240	1
APAC_no_p	0.182	0.298	0.240	1
METEOR	-0.081	0.015	-0.033	4
BLEU	-0.123	0.059	-0.032	3
NIST	-0.344	-0.275	-0.309	5

Table 7: Spearman's rank correlation coefficient of the system level in NTCIR-9 data.

	Adequacy (5,700)	Acceptance (5,700)	Avg.	Rank
APAC	0.250	0.261	0.256	1
APAC_no_p	0.242	0.250	0.246	2
METEOR	0.167	0.217	0.192	3

Table 8: Kendall tau rank correlation coefficient of segment-level in NTCIR-9 data.

LAYERED: Metric for Machine Translation Evaluation

Shubham Gautam
Computer Science & Engineering,
IIT Bombay
shubhamg@cse.iitb.ac.in

Pushpak Bhattacharyya
Computer Science & Engineering,
IIT Bombay
pb@cse.iitb.ac.in

Abstract

This paper describes the LAYERED metric which is used for the shared WMT'14 metrics task. Various metrics exist for MT evaluation: BLEU (Papineni, 2002), METEOR (Alon Lavie, 2007), TER (Snover, 2006) etc., but are found inadequate in quite a few language settings like, for example, in case of free word order languages. In this paper, we propose an MT evaluation scheme that is based on the NLP layers: lexical, syntactic and semantic. We contend that higher layer metrics are after all needed. Results are presented on the corpora of ACL-WMT, 2013 and 2014. We end with a metric which is composed of weighted metrics at individual layers, which correlates very well with human judgment.

1 Introduction

Evaluation is an integral component of machine translation (MT). Human evaluation is difficult and time consuming so there is a need for a metric which can give the better evaluation in correlation to human judgement. There are several existing metrics such as: BLEU, METEOR *etc.* but these only deal with the lexical layer combining *bag of words* and *n-gram* based approach.

We present an analysis of BLEU and the higher layer metrics on the ACL WMT 2013 corpora with 3 language pairs: French-English, Spanish-English and German-English. For syntactic layer, we considered three metrics: Hamming score, Kendall's Tau distance score and the spearman rank score. Syntactic layer metrics take care of reordering within the words of the sentences so these may play an important role when there is a decision to be made between two MT output sentences of two different systems when both the sentences have same number of n-gram matches *wrt* the reference sentence but there is a difference in the ordering of the sentence. We will discuss these metrics in detail in the following sections. The next NLP layer in consideration is the semantic layer which deals with the meaning of the sentences. For semantic layer, we considered two metrics: Shallow semantic score and Deep semantic score. On semantic layer, we considered entailment based measures to get the score.

Ananthkrishnan et al. (2007) mentioned some issues in automatic evaluation using BLEU. There are some disadvantages of the existing metrics also such as: *BLEU* does not take care of reordering of the words in the sentence. *BLEU*-like metrics can give same score by permuting word order. These metrics can be unreliable at the level of individual sentences because there can be small number of n-grams involved. We would see in this paper that the correlation of BLEU is lower compared to the semantic layer metrics.

Section 2 presents the study of related work in MT evaluation. Section 3 presents the importance of each NLP layer in evaluation of MT output. It discusses the metrics that each layer contributes to the achievement of the final result. In section 4, various experiments are presented with each metric on the top 10 ranking systems of WMT 13 corpora which are ranked on the basis of the human ranking. Each metric is discussed with the graphical representation so that it would become clear to analyze the effect of each metric. In section 5, spearman correlation of the metrics is calculated with human judgement and comparisons are shown. In section 6, we discuss the need of a metric which should be a combination of the metrics presented in the above sections and present a weighted metric which is the amalgamation of the metrics at individual layers. Section 7 presents the results of the proposed metric on WMT 14 data and compares it with other existing metrics.

Proceedings of the Ninth Workshop on Statistical Machine Translation, pages 387–393,
Baltimore, Maryland USA, June 26–27, 2014.

2 Related Work

Machine translation evaluation has always remained as the most popular measure to judge the quality of a system output compared to the reference translation. Papineni (2002) proposed BLEU as an automatic MT evaluation metric which is based on the n-gram matching of the reference and candidate sentences. This is still considered as the most reliable metric and used widely in the MT community for the determination of the translation quality. BLEU averages the precision for unigram, bigram and up to 4-gram and applies a length penalty if the generated sentence is shorter than the best matching (in length) reference translation. Alternative approaches have been designed to address problems with BLEU. Doddington and George (2003) proposed NIST metric which is derived from the BLEU evaluation criterion but differs in one fundamental aspect: instead of n-gram precision, the information gain from each n-gram is taken into account. TER (Snover, 2006) tries to improve the hypothesis/reference matching process based on the edit-distance and METEOR (Alon Lavie, 2007) considered linguistic evidence, mostly lexical similarity, for more intelligent matching. Liu and Gildea (2005), Owczarzak et al. (2007), and Zhang et al. (2004) use syntactic overlap to calculate the similarity between the hypothesis and the reference. Padó and Galley (2009) proposed a metric that evaluates MT output based on a rich set of textual entailment features. There are different works that have been done at various NLP layers. Giménez tl al. (2010) provided various linguistic measures for MT evaluation at different NLP layers. Ding Liu and Daniel Gildea (2005) focussed the study on the syntactic features that can be helpful while evaluation.

3 Significance of NLP Layers in MT Evaluation

In this section, we discuss the different NLP layers and how these are important for evalution of MT output. We discuss here the significance of three NLP layers: Lexical, Syntactic and Semantic layers.

3.1 Lexical Layer

Lexical layer emphasizes on the comparison of the words in its original form irrespective of any lexical corpora or any other resource. There are some metrics in MT evaluation which considers only these features. Most popular of them is *BLEU*, this is based on the n-gram approach and considers the matching upto 4-grams in the reference and the candidate translation. BLEU is designed to approximate human judgement at a corpus level, and performs badly if used to evaluate the quality of individual sentences. Another important metric at this layer is TER (Translation Edit Rate) which measures the number of edits required to change a system output into one of the references. For our experiments, we would consider BLEU as the baseline metric on lexical layer.

3.2 Syntactic Layer

Syntactic layer takes care of the syntax of the sentence. It mainly focusses on the reordering of the words within a sentence. Birch and Osborne (2011) has mentioned some metrics on this layer: Hamming score and Kendall's Tau Distance (KTD) score. We additionally calculated the spearman rank score on this layer. Scores are calculated first by giving ranking of words in the reference sentence and then putting the rank number of the word in the candidate sentence. Now, we have the relative ranking of the words of both the sentences, so final score is calculated.

3.3 Semantic Layer

Semantic layer goes into the meaning of the sentence, so we need to compare the dependency tree of the sentences. At this layer, we used *entailment* based metrics for the comparison of dependencies. Padó and Galley (2009) illustrated the use of text entailment based features for MT evaluation. We introduced two metrics at this layer: *first* is *Shallow semantic score*, which is based on the dependencies generated by a shallow parser and then the dependency comparison is carried out. *Second* is *Deep semantic score*, which goes more deep into the semantic of the sentence. For *shallow semantic score*, we used stanford dependency parser (Marie-Catherine et al., 2006) while for *deep semantic score*, we used UNL (Universal Networking Language)[1] dependency generator.

Semantic layer may play an important role when there are different words in two sentences but they are synonym of each other or are related to each other in some manner. In this case, lexical and syntactic layers can't identify the similarity of

[1]http://www.undl.org/unlsys/unl/unl2005/UW.htm

the sentences because there exist a need of some semantic background knowledge which occurs at the semantic layer. Another important role of semantic layer is that there can be cases when there is reordering of the phrases in the sentences, *e.g.*, active-passive voice sentences. In these cases, dependencies between the words remain intact and this can be captured through dependency tree generated by the parser.

4 Experiments

We conducted the experiments on WMT 13 corpora for French-English, Spanish-English and German-English language pairs. We calculated the score of each metric for the top 10 ranking system (wmt, 2013) (as per human judgement) for each language pair.

Note:

1. In the graphs, metric score is multiplied by 100 so that a better view can be captured.

2. In each graph, the scores of French-English (fr-en), Spanish-English (es-en) and German-English (de-en) language pairs are represented by red, black and blue lines respectively.

4.1 BLEU Score

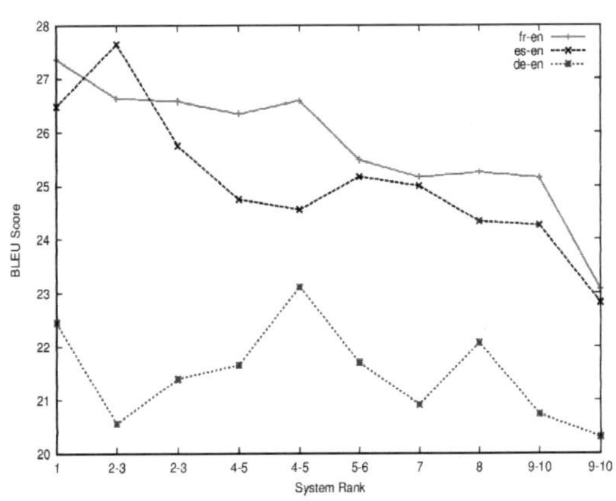

Figure 1: BLEU Score

We can see from the graph of fig. 1 that for de-en and es-en language pair, BLEU is not able to capture the phenomenon appropriately. In fact, it is worse in de-en pair. Because the graph should be of decreasing manner *i.e.*, as the rank of the system increases (system gets lower rank compared to the previous one), the score should also decrease.

4.2 Syntactic Layer

Because the BLEU score was not able to capture the idealistic curve in the last section so we considered the syntactic layer metrics. This layer is considered because it takes care of the reordering of the words within the sentence pair. The idea here is that if one candidate translation has lower reordering of words *w.r.t.* reference translation then it has higher chances of matching to the reference sentence.

4.2.1 Hamming Score

The hamming distance measures the number of disagreements between two permutations. First we calculate the hamming distance and then calculate the fraction of words placed in the same position in both sentences, finally we calculate the *hamming score* by subtracting the fraction from 1. It is formulated as follows:

$$d_h(\pi, \sigma) = 1 - \frac{\sum_{i=1}^{n} x_i}{n}, x_i = \begin{cases} 0; \ if \ \pi(i) = \sigma(i) \\ 1; \ otherwise \end{cases}$$

where, n is the length of the permutation.

Hamming scores for all three language pairs mentioned above are shown in fig. 2. As we can see from the graph that initially its not good for the top ranking systems but it follows the ideal curve for the discrimination of lower ranking systems for the language pairs fr-en and es-en.

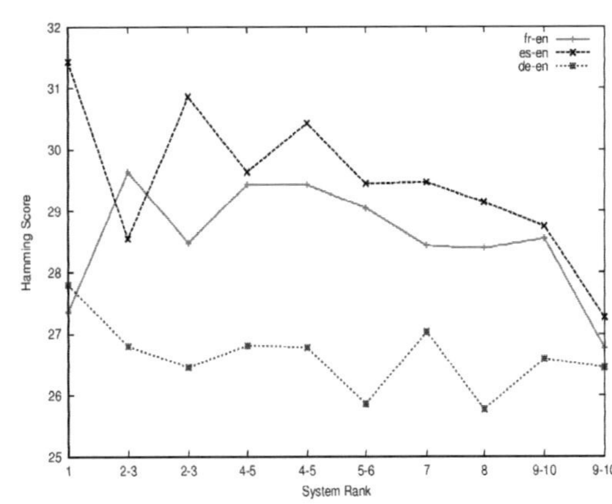

Figure 2: Hamming Score

4.2.2 Kendall's Tau Distance (KTD)

Kendall's tau distance is the minimum number of transpositions of two adjacent symbols necessary to transform one permutation into another. It represents the percentage of pairs of elements which share the same order between two permutations. It is defined as follows:

$$d_k(\pi,\sigma) = 1 - \sqrt{\frac{\sum_{i=1}^{n}\sum_{j=1}^{n} z_{ij}}{Z}}$$

$$where,\ z_{ij} = \begin{cases} 0;\ if\ \pi(i) < \pi(j)\ and\ \sigma(i) < \sigma(j) \\ 1;\ otherwise \end{cases}$$

This can be used for measuring word order differences as the relative ordering of words has been taken into account. KTD scores are shown in fig. 3. It also follows the same phenomenon as the hamming score for fr-en and es-en pair but for de-en pair, it gives the worst results.

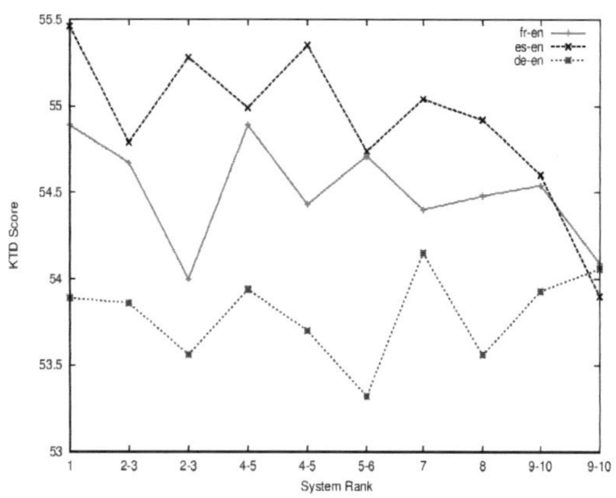

Figure 3: KTD Score

4.2.3 Spearman Score

Spearman rank correlation coefficient is basically used for assessing how well the relationship between two variables can be described using a monotonic function. Because we are using syntactic layer metrics to keep track of the reordering between two sentences, so this can be used by ranking the words of the first sentence (ranging from 1 to n, where n is the length of the sentence) and then checking where the particular word (with index i) is present in the second sentence in terms of ranking. Finally, we calculated the spearman score as follows:

$$\rho = 1 - \frac{6\sum d_i^2}{n(n^2-1)}$$

where, $d_i = x_i - y_i$ is the difference between the ranks of words of two sentences.

Spearman score lies between -1 to +1 so we convert it to the range of 0 to +1 so that all the metrics would lie in the same range.

4.3 Semantic Layer

We can see from the last two sections that there were some loopholes on the metrics of both the layers as can be seen in the graphical representations. So, there arises a need to go higher in the hierarchy. The next one in the queue is semantic layer which takes care of the meaning of the sentences. At this layer, we considered two metrics. Both metrics are based on the concept of *text entailment*. First we should understand, what is it?

Text Entailment

According to wikipedia[2], "Textual entailment (TE) in natural language processing is a directional relation between text fragments. The relation holds whenever the truth of one text fragment follows from another text. In the TE framework, the entailing and entailed texts are termed *text* (t) and *hypothesis* (h), respectively."

First, the dependencies for both reference (R) as well as candidate (C) translation are generated using the parser that is used (will vary in both the following metrics). Then, the entailment phenomenon is applied from R to C *i.e.,* dependencies of C are searched in the dependency graph of R. Matching number of dependencies are calculated, then a score is obtained as follows:

$$Score_{R-C} = \frac{No.\ of\ matched\ dependencies\ of\ C\ in\ R}{Total\ no.\ of\ dependencies\ of\ C} \quad (1)$$

Similarly, another score is also obtained by applying the entailment phenomenon in the reversed direction *i.e. from C to R* as follows:

$$Score_{C-R} = \frac{No.\ of\ matched\ dependencies\ of\ R\ in\ C}{Total\ no.\ of\ dependencies\ of\ R} \quad (2)$$

Final score is obtained by taking the average of the above two scores as follows:

$$Score_{final} = \frac{Score_{R-C} + Score_{C-R}}{2} \quad (3)$$

Now, we discuss how can we use this concept in the metrics at semantic layer:

4.3.1 Shallow Semantic Score

This metric uses the stanford dependency parser (Marie-Catherine et al., 2006) to generate the dependencies. After getting the dependencies for both reference (R) as well as candidate (C) translation, entailment phenomenon is applied and the final score is obtained using eq. (3).

[2]http://wikipedia.org/

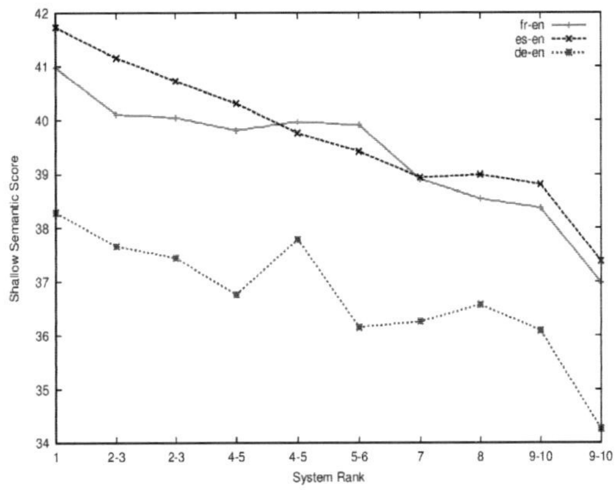

Figure 4: Shallow Semantic Score

We can see from fig. 4 that for French-English and Spanish-English pairs, the graph is very good compared to the other metrics at the lower layers. In fact, there is only one score in es-en pair that a lower ranking system gets better score than the higher ranking system.

4.3.2 Deep Semantic Score

This metric uses the UNL dependency graph generator for taking care of the semantic of the sentence that shallow dependency generator is not able to capture. Similar to the shallow semantic score, after getting the dependencies from the UNL, entailment score is calculated in both directions *i.e.* $R \rightarrow C$ *and* $C \rightarrow R$.

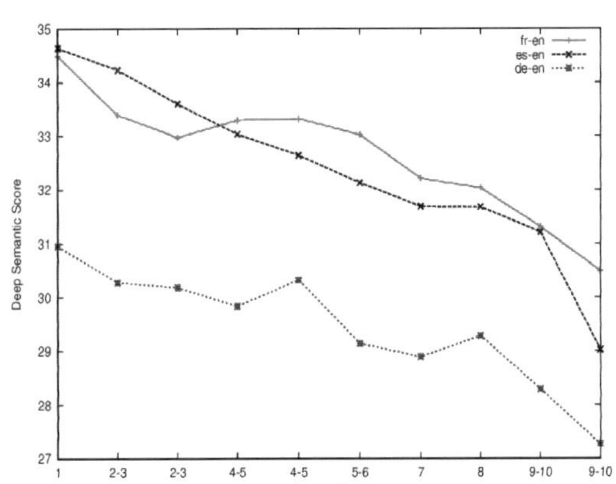

Figure 5: Deep Semantic Score

Fig. 5 shows that deep semantic score curve also follows the same path as shallow semantic score. In fact, for Spanish-English pair, the path is ideal *i.e., the score is decreasing as the system rank is increasing.*

5 Correlation with Human Judgement

We calculated spearman rank correlation coefficient for the different scores calculated in the last section. This score ranges from -1 to +1. Form table 1, we can see that the correlation score is better with semantic layer metrics compared to the BLEU score (lower layer metrics). In comparison to the WMT 13 results (wmt-result, 2013), $\rho_{Shallow}$ score for French-English pair is intermediate between the highest and lowest correlation system. ρ_{Deep} score for Spanish-English is highest among all the systems presented at WMT 13. So, it arises a need to take into account the semantic of the sentence while evaluating the MT output.

Language Pair	ρ_{BLEU}	$\rho_{Shallow}$	ρ_{Deep}
French-English	0.95	**0.96**	0.92
Spanish-English	0.89	0.98	**1.00**
German-English	0.36	0.88	0.89

Table 1: Correlation with BLEU Score, Shallow Semantic Score and Deep Semantic Score

6 Hybrid Approach

We reached to a situation where we can't ignore the score of any layer's metric because each metric helps to capture some of the phenomenon which other may not capture. So, we used a hybrid approach where the final score of our proposed metric depends on the layered metrics. As already said, we performed our experiments on ACL-WMT 2013 corpora, but it provided only the rank of the systems. Due to availability of ranking of the systems, we used SVM-rank to learn the parameters.

Our final metric looks as follows:

Final-Score = a*BLEU + b*Hamming + c*KTD + d*Spearman + e*Shallow-Semantic-Score + f*Deep-Semantic-Score

where, a,b,c,d,e,f are parameters

6.1 SVM-rank

SVM-rank learns the parameters from the training data and builds a model which contains the learned parameters. These parameters (model) can be used for ranking of a new set of data.

Parameters

We made the training data of the French-English, Spanish-English and German-English language

Metric	Pearson Correlation					
	fr-en	de-en	hi-en	cs-en	ru-en	Average
LAYERED	.973	.893	.976	.940	.843	.925
BLEU	.952	.831	.956	.908	.774	.884
METEOR	.975	.926	.457	.980	.792	.826
NIST	.955	.810	.783	.983	.785	.863
TER	.952	.774	.618	.977	.796	.823

Table 2: Correlation with different metrics in WMT 14 Results

pairs. Then we ran SVM-rank and obtained the scores for the parameters.

So, our final proposed metric looks like:
Final-Score = 0.26*BLEU + 0.13*Hamming + 0.03*KTD + 0.04*Spearman + 0.28*Shallow-Semantic-Score + 0.26* Deep-Semantic-Score

7 Performance in WMT 2014

Table 2 shows the performance of our metric on WMT 2014 data (wmt-result, 2014). It performed very well in almost all language pairs and it gave the highest correlation with human in Hindi-English language pair. On an average, our correlation was 0.925 with human considering all the language pairs. This way, we stood out on second position considering the average score while the first ranking system obtained the correlation of 0.942. Its clear from table 2 that the proposed metric gives the correlation better than the standard metrics in most of the cases. If we look at the average score of the metrics in table 2 then we can see that LAYERED obtains much higher score than the other metrics.

8 Conclusion

Machine Translation Evaluation is an exciting field that is attracting the researchers from the past few years and the work in this field is enormous. We started with the need of using higher layer metrics while evaluating the MT output. We understand that it might be a little time consuming but its efficient and correlation with human judgement is better with semantic layer metric compared to the lexical layer metric. Because, each layer captures some linguistic phenomenon so we can't completely ignore the metrics at individual layers. It gives rise to a hybrid approach which gives the weightage for each metric for the calculation of final score. We can see from the results of WMT 2014 that the correlation with LAYERED metric is better than the standard existing metrics in most of the language pairs.

References

Alexandra Birch, School of Informatics, University of Edinburgh *Reordering Metrics for Statistical Machine Translation.* Phd Thesis, 2011.

Alexandra Birch and Miles Osborne *Reordering Metrics for MT.* Proceedings of the 49th Annual Meeting of the Association for Computational Linguistics: Human Language Technologies - Volume 1, series = HLT 2011.

Alon Lavie and Abhaya Agarwal. *METEOR: An Automatic Metric for MT Evaluation with High Levels of Correlation with Human Judgments,* Proceedings of the Second Workshop on Statistical Machine Translation, StatMT 2007.

Ananthakrishnan R and Pushpak Bhattacharyya and M Sasikumar and Ritesh M Shah *Some Issues in Automatic Evaluation of English-Hindi MT: More Blues for BLEU.* ICON, 2007.

Doddington and George *Automatic evaluation of machine translation quality using N-gram co-occurrence statistics, NIST.* Proceedings of the 2nd International Conference on Human Language Technology Research HLT 2002.

Ding Liu and Daniel Gildea *Syntactic Features for Evaluation of Machine Translation.* Workshop On Intrinsic And Extrinsic Evaluation Measures For Machine Translation And/or Summarization, 2005.

Findings of the 2013 Workshop on Statistical Machine Translation. ACL-WMT 2013.

Giménez, Jesús and Màrquez, Lluís *Linguistic Measures for Automatic Machine Translation Evaluation.* Machine Translation, December, 2010.

Liu D, Gildea D *Syntactic features for evaluation of machine translation.* ACL 2005 workshop on intrinsic and extrinsic evaluation measures for machine translation and/or summarization.

Owczarzak K, Genabith J, Way A *Evaluating machine translation with LFG dependencies.* Machine Translation 21(2):95119.

Marie-Catherine de Marneffe, Bill MacCartney and Christopher D. Manning. *Generating Typed Dependency Parses from Phrase Structure Parses*. LREC 2006.

Matthew Snover and Bonnie Dorr and Richard Schwartz and Linnea Micciulla and John Makhoul. *A Study of Translation Edit Rate with Targeted Human Annotation*, In Proceedings of Association for Machine Translation in the Americas, 2006.

Papineni, Kishore and Roukos, Salim and Ward, Todd and Zhu, Wei-Jing. *BLEU: A Method for Automatic Evaluation of Machine Translation*. Proceedings of the 40th Annual Meeting on Association for Computational Linguistics, ACL 2002.

Results of the WMT13 Metrics Shared Task. ACL-WMT 2013.

Results of the WMT14 Metrics Shared Task. ACL-WMT 2014.

Sebastian Padó and Michel Galley and Dan Jurafsky and Chris Manning *Robust Machine Translation Evaluation with Entailment Features*. Proceedings of ACL-IJCNLP 2009, ACL 2009.

Zhang Y, Vogel S, Waibel A *Interpreting Bleu/NIST scores: how much improvement do we need to have a better system?*. In: Proceedings of the 4th international conference on language resources and evaluation. Lisbon, Portugal.

IPA and STOUT: Leveraging Linguistic and Source-based Features for Machine Translation Evaluation

Meritxell Gonzàlez, Alberto Barrón-Cedeño
TALP Research Center,
Technical University of Catalonia
{mgonzalez,albarron}@lsi.upc.edu

Lluís Màrquez
Qatar Computing Research Institute
Qatar Foundation
lmarquez@qf.org.qa

Abstract

This paper describes the UPC submissions to the *WMT14 Metrics Shared Task*: UPC-IPA and UPC-STOUT. These metrics use a collection of evaluation measures integrated in ASIYA, a toolkit for machine translation evaluation. In addition to some standard metrics, the two submissions take advantage of novel metrics that consider linguistic structures, lexical relationships, and semantics to compare both source and reference translation against the candidate translation. The new metrics are available for several target languages other than English. In the the official WMT14 evaluation, UPC-IPA and UPC-STOUT scored above the average in 7 out of 9 language pairs at the system level and 8 out of 9 at the segment level.

1 Introduction

Evaluating Machine Translation (MT) quality is a difficult task, in which even human experts may fail to achieve a high degree of agreement when assessing translations. Conducting manual evaluations is impractical during the development cycle of MT systems or for transation applications addressed to general users, such as online translation portals. Automatic evaluation measures bring valuable benefits in such situations. Compared to manual evaluation, automatic measures are cheap, more objective, and reusable across different test sets and domains.

Nonetheless, automatic metrics are far from perfection: when used in isolation, they tend to stress specific aspects of the translation quality and neglect others (particularly during tuning); they are often unable to capture little system improvements (enhancements in very specific aspects of the translation process); and they may make unfair comparisons when they are not able to reflect real differences among the quality of different MT systems (Giménez, 2008).

ASIYA, the core of our approach, is an open-source suite for automatic machine translation evaluation and output analysis.[1] It provides a rich set of heterogeneous metrics and tools to evaluate and analyse the quality of automatic translations. The ASIYA core toolkit was first released in 2009 (Giménez and Màrquez, 2010a) and has been continuously improved and extended since then (Gonzàlez et al., 2012; Gonzàlez et al., 2013).

In this paper we first describe the most recent enhancements to ASIYA: (*i*) linguistic-based metrics for French and German; (*ii*) an extended set of source-based metrics for English, Spanish, German, French, Russian, and Czech; and (*iii*) the integration of mechanisms to exploit the alignments between sources and translations. These enhancements are all available in ASIYA since version 3.0. We have used them to prepare the UPC submissions to the *WMT14 Metrics Task*: UPC-IPA and UPC-STOUT, which serve the purpose of testing their usefulness in a real comparative setting.

The rest of the paper is structured as follows. Section 2 describes the new reference-based metrics developed, including syntactic parsers for languages other than English. Section 3 gives the details of novel source-based metrics, developed for almost all the language pairs in this challenge. Section 4 explains our simple metrics combination strategy and analyses the results obtained with both approaches, UPC-IPA and UPC-STOUT, when applied to the WMT13 dataset. Finally, Section 5 summarises our main contributions.

2 Reference-based Metrics

We recently added a new set of metrics to ASIYA, which estimate the similarity between reference (*ref*) and candidate (*cand*) translations. The met-

[1] http://asiya.lsi.upc.edu

Proceedings of the Ninth Workshop on Statistical Machine Translation, pages 394–401,
Baltimore, Maryland USA, June 26–27, 2014.

rics rely either on structural linguistic information (Section 2.1), on a semantic mapping (Section 2.2), or on word n-grams (Section 2.3).

2.1 Parsing-based Metrics

Our initial set of parsing-based metrics is a follow-up of the proposal by Giménez and Màrquez (2010b): it leverages the structural information provided by linguistic processors to compute several similarity cues between two analyzed sentences. ASIYA includes plenty of metrics that capture syntactic and semantic aspects of a translation. New metrics based on linguistic structural information for French and German and upgraded versions of the parsers for English and Spanish are available since version 3.0.[2]

In the WMT14 evaluation, we opt for metrics based on shallow parsing (SP), constituency parsing (CP), and dependency parsing (DPm)[3]. Measures based on named entities (NE) and semantic roles (SR) were used to analyse translations into English as well. The nomenclature used below follows the same patterns as in the ASIYA's manual (Gonzàlez and Giménez, 2014). The manual describes every family of metrics in detail. Next, we briefly depict the concrete metrics involved in our submissions to the *WMT14 Shared Task*.

The set of SP metrics is available for English, German, French, Spanish and Catalan. They measure the lexical overlapping between parts-of-speech elements in the candidate and reference translations. For instance, SP-Op(VB) measures the proportion of correctly translated verbs; and the coarser SP-Op(*) averages the overlapping between the words for each part of speech. We also use NIST (Doddington, 2002) to compute accumulated scores over sequences of $n = 1..5$ parts of speech (SP-pNIST).

Similarly, CP metrics analyse similarities between constituent parse trees associated to candidate and reference translations. For instance, CP-STMi5 and CP-STM4 compute, respectively, the proportion of (individual) length-5 and accumulated up to length-4 matching sub-paths of the syntactic tree (Liu and Gildea, 2005). CP-Oc(*) computes the lexical overlap averaged over all the phrase constituents. Constituent trees are obtained using the parsers of Charniak and Johnson (2005), Bonsai v3.2 (Candito et al., 2010b), and Berkeley Parser (Petrov et al., 2006; Petrov and Klein, 2007) for English, French, and German, respectively.

Measures based on dependency parsing (DPm) — available for English and French thanks to the MALT parser (Nivre et al., 2007)— capture the similarities between dependency tree items (i.e., heads and modifiers). The pre-trained models for French were obtained from the French Treebank (Candito et al., 2010a) and used to train the Bonsai parser, which in turn uses the MALT parser. For instance, DPm-HWCM_w-3 retrieves average accumulated proportion of matching *word*-chains (Liu and Gildea, 2005) up to length 3; and DPm-HWCMi_c-3 computes the proportion of matching *category*-chains of length 3.

2.2 Explicit-Semantics Metric

Additionally, we borrowed a metric originally proposed in the field of Information Retrieval: explicit semantic analysis (ESA) (Gabrilovich and Markovitch, 2007). ESA is a similarity metric that relies on a large corpus of general knowledge to represent texts. Our knowledge corpora are composed of $\sim 100K$ Wikipedia articles from 2010 for the following target languages: English, French and German. In this case, *ref* and *cand* translations are both mapped onto the Wikipedia collection W. The similarities between each text and every article $a \in W$ are computed on the basis of the cosine measure in order to compose a similarities vector that represents the text. That is:

$$\vec{ref} = \{sim(ref, a)\, \forall a \in W\} \ , \quad (1)$$
$$\vec{cand} = \{sim(cand, a)\, \forall a \in W\} \ . \quad (2)$$

As the i-th elements in both $\vec{ref}$ and $\vec{cand}$ represent the similarity of *ref* and *cand* sentences to a common article, the similarity between *ref* and *cand* can be estimated by computing $sim(\vec{ref}, \vec{cand})$.

2.3 Language-Independent Resource-Free Metric

We consider a simple characterisation based on *word n-grams*. Texts are broken down into overlapping word sequences of length n, with 1-word shifting. The similarity between *cand* and *ref* is computed on the basis of the Jaccard coefficient (Jaccard, 1901). We used this metric for the pairs English–Russian and Russian-English, considering $n = 2$ (NGRAM-jacTok2ngram). For the

[2] Equivalent resources were previously available for English, Catalan, and Spanish.

[3] ASIYA includes two dependency parsers; the *m* identifies the metrics calculated using the MALT parser.

rest of the pairs we opt for the character-n-gram metrics described in Section 3.1, but they showed no positive results in the English–Russian pair during our tuning experiments.

3 Source-based Metrics

We enhance our evaluation module by including a set of new metrics that compare the source text against the translations. The metrics can be divided into two subsets: those that do not require any external resources (Section 3.1) and those that depend on a parallel corpus (Section 3.2).

3.1 Language-Independent Resource-Free Metrics

We opted for two characterisations that allow for the comparison of texts across languages without external resources nor language-related knowledge —as far as the languages use the same writing system.[4]

The first characterisation is *character n-grams*; proposed by McNamee and Mayfield (2004) for cross-language information retrieval between European languages. Texts are broken down into overlapping character sequences of length n, with 1-character shifting. We opt for case-folded bigrams (NGRAM-cosChar2ngrams), as they allowed for the best performance across all the pairs (except for *From/To* Russian pairs) during tuning.

The second characterisation (NGRAM-jacCognates) is based on the concept of *cognateness*; originally proposed for bitexts alignment (Simard et al., 1992). A word is a pseudo-cognate candidate if (*i*) it has only letters and $|w| \geq 4$, (*ii*) it contains at least one digit, or (*iii*) it is a single punctuation mark. *src* and *cand* sentences are then represented as word vectors, containing only those words fulfilling one of the previous conditions. In the case of (*i*) the word is cut down to its leading four characters only.

In both cases (*character n-grams* and *cognateness*) *cand* translations are compared against *src* sentences on the basis of the cosine similarity measure.

3.2 Parallel-Corpus Metrics

We consider two metrics that make use of parallel corpora: *length factor* and *alignment*.

[4]Previous research showed that transliteration is a good short-cut when dealing with different writing systems (Barrón-Cedeño et al., 2014).

Table 1: Length factor parameters as estimated on the WMT13 parallel corpora.

pair	μ	σ	pair	μ	σ
en–cs	0.972	0.245	*cs–en*	1.085	0.273
en–de	1.176	0.926	*de–en*	0.961	0.463
en–fr	1.158	0.411	*fr–en*	0.914	0.313
en–ru	1.157	0.678	*ru–en*	1.069	0.668

The length factor (LeM) is rooted in the fact that the length of a text and its translation tend to preserve a certain length correlation. For instance, translations from English into Spanish or French tend to be longer than their source. Similar measures were proposed during the statistical machine translation early days, both considering character- and word-level lengths (Gale and Church, 1993; Brown et al., 1991). Pouliquen et al. (2003) defines the length factor as:

$$\varrho(d') = e^{-0.5\left(\frac{\frac{|d'|}{|d_q|}-\mu}{\sigma}\right)^2}, \quad (3)$$

where μ and σ represent the mean and standard deviation of the character lengths between translations of texts from L into L'. This is a stochastic normal distribution that results in higher values as the length of the target text approaches the expected value given the source. Table 1 includes the values for each language pair, as estimated on the WMT13 parallel corpora. Note that this metric was not applied to Hindi–English since this language pair was not present in the WMT13 challenge.

The last of our newly-added measures relies on the word alignments calculated between the sentence pairs *src–cand* and *src–ref*. We trained alignment models for each language pair using the Berkeley Aligner[5], and devised three variants of an ALGN metric, which compute: (*i*) the proportion of aligned words between *src* and *cand* (ALGNs); (*ii*) the proportion of aligned words between *cand* and *ref*, calculated as the combination of the alignments *src–cand* and *src–ref* (ALGNr); and (*iii*) the ratio of shared alignments between *src–cand* and *src–ref* (ALGNp).

4 Experimental Results

The tuning and selection of the different metrics to build UPC-IPA and UPC-STOUT was

[5]https://code.google.com/p/berkeleyaligner

conducted considering the *WMT13 Metrics Task* dataset (Macháček and Bojar, 2013), and the resources distributed for the *WMT13 Translation Task* (Bojar et al., 2013). Table 2 gives a complete list of these metrics grouped by families. First, we calculated the Pearson's correlation with the human judgements for all the metrics in the current version of the ASIYA repository, including standard MT evaluation metrics, such as METEOR (Denkowski and Lavie, 2011), GTM (Melamed et al., 2003), -TERp-A (Snover et al., 2009) (a variant of TER tuned towards adequacy), WER (Nießen et al., 2000) and PER (Tillmann et al., 1997). We selected the best performing metrics (i.e., those resulting in high Pearson coefficients) in each family across all the *From/To* English translation language pairs, including the newly developed measures —even if they performed poorly compared to others (see This is how the UPC-STOUT metrics sets for both *from* English and *To* English translation pairs were composed[6] (see Table 3).

Table 2: Metrics considered in the experiments separated by families according to the type of grammatical items they use.

1. -WER	17. DPm-HWCM_r-1
2. -PER	18. DPm-Or(*)
3. -TERp-A	19. SR-Or(*)
4. METEOR-ex	20. SR-Or
5. METEOR-pa	21. SR-Orv(*)
6. GTM-3	22. SR-Orv
7. SP-Op(*)	23. NE-Oe(*)
8. SP-pNIST	24. NE-Oe(**)
9. CP-STMi-5	25. ESA
10. CP-STMi-2	26. NGRAM-jacTok2ngrams
11. CP-STMi-3	27. NGRAM-jacCognates
12. CP-STM-4	28. NGRAM-cosChar2ngrams
13. CP-Oc(*)	29. LeM
14. DPm-HWCM_w-3	30. ALGNp
15. DPm-HWCM_c-3	31. ALGNs
16. DPm-HWCMi_c-3	32. ALGNr

Table 3: Metrics considered in each system.[7]

BAS: 1–6	SYN: 7–18
SEM: 19–25	SRC: 26–32
IPA: 1–9, 25–31	STOUT: 1–32

[6]Parser-based measures are not present in Czech nor Russian as target languages, ALGN is not available for French pairs, and ESA is not applied to Russian as target.

The metric sets included in UPC-IPA are light versions of the UPC-STOUT ones. They were composed following different criteria, depending on the translation direction. Parsing-based measures were already available in the previous version of ASIYA when translating into English — they are known to be robust across domains and are usually good indicators of translation quality (Giménez and Màrquez, 2007). So, in order to assess the gain achieved with these measures with respect the new ones, UPC-IPA neglects the measures based on structural information obtained from parsers. In contrast, this distinction was not suitable for the *From* English pairs since the number of resources and measures varies for each language. Hence, in this latter case, UPC-IPA used only the subset of measures from UPC-STOUT that required no or little resources.

In summary, when English is the *target* language, UPC-IPA uses the baseline evaluation metrics along with the length factor, alignments-based metrics, character n-grams, and ESA. In addition to the above metrics, UPC-STOUT uses the linguistic-based metrics over parsing trees, named entities, and semantic roles. When English is the *source* language, UPC-IPA relies on the basic collection of metrics and character n-grams only. UPC-STOUT includes the alignment-based metrics, length factor, ESA, and the syntactic parsers applied to both German and French.

In all cases (metric sets and language pairs), the translation quality score is computed as the uniformly-averaged linear combination (ULC) of all the individual metrics for each sentence in the testset. Its calculation implies the normalization of heterogeneous scores (some of them are negative or unbounded), into the range $[0, 1]$. As a consequence, the scores of UPC-IPA and UPC-STOUT constitute a natural way of ranking different translations, rather than an overall quality estimation measure. We opt for this linear combination for simplicity. The discussion below suggests that a more sophisticated method for weight tuning (e.g., relying on machine learning methods) would be required for each language pair, domain and/or task since different metric families perform notably different for each subtask.

We complete our experimentation by evaluating more configurations: BAS, a baseline

[7]These are the full sets of measures for each configuration. However, each specific subset for *From/To* English can vary slightly depending on the available resources.

Table 4: System-level Pearson correlation for automatic metrics over translations *From/To* English.

WMT13	*en–fr*	*en–de*	*en–es*	*en–cs*	*en–ru*	*fr–en*	*de–en*	*es–en*	*cs–en*	*ru–en*
UPC-IPA	93.079	85.147	88.702	85.259	70.345	96.755	94.660	95.065	94.316	72.083
UPC-STOUT	94.274	**90.193**	73.314	84.743	**70.544**	**96.916**	96.208	96.704	96.666	74.050
BAS	92.502	84.251	90.051	86.584	67.655	95.777	96.506	95.98	96.539	71.536
SYN	95.68	87.297	**96.965**	n/a	n/a	96.291	96.592	96.052	95.238	73.083
BAS+SYN	**94.584**	87.786	95.162	n/a	n/a	96.684	97.057	96.101	96.402	72.800
SEM	89.735	83.647	35.694	**95.067**	n/a	95.629	96.601	**98.021**	96.595	**76.158**
BAS+SEM	92.254	87.005	47.321	89.107	n/a	96.337	**97.534**	97.568	**97.371**	74.804
SRC	14.465	-16.796	-22.466	-49.981	39.527	13.405	-51.371	71.64	-73.254	68.766
BAS+SRC	93.637	76.401	83.754	64.742	54.128	95.395	90.889	93.299	89.216	71.882
WMT13-Best	94.745	93.813	96.446	86.036	81.194	98.379	97.789	99.171	83.734	94.768
WMT13-Worst	78.787	-45.461	87.677	69.151	61.075	95.118	92.239	79.957	60.918	82.058

Table 5: Segment-level Kendall's τ correlation for automatic metrics over translations *From/To* English.

WMT13	*en–fr*	*en–de*	*en–es*	*en–cs*	*en–ru*	*fr–en*	*de–en*	*es–en*	*cs–en*	*ru–en*
UPC-IPA	18.625	14.901	17.057	7.805	15.132	22.832	25.769	26.907	21.207	19.904
UPC-STOUT	**19.488**	15.012	17.166	**8.545**	15.279	23.090	27.117	26.848	21.332	19.100
BAS	19.477	13.589	16.975	8.449	**15.599**	**24.060**	**28.259**	**28.381**	**23.346**	**20.983**
SYN	16.554	14.970	16.444	n/a	n/a	22.365	24.289	23.889	20.232	17.679
BAS+SYN	19.112	**16.016**	**18.122**	n/a	n/a	23.940	28.068	27.988	23.180	19.659
SEM	12.184	9.249	10.871	3.808	n/a	17.282	19.083	20.859	15.186	14.971
BAS+SEM	19.167	13.291	15.857	7.732	n/a	22.024	25.788	26.360	21.427	19.117
SRC	2.745	2.481	1.152	1.992	5.247	2.181	1.154	8.700	-4.023	16.267
BAS+SRC	18.32	13.017	15.698	7.666	13.619	22.292	24.948	26.780	17.603	20.707
WMT13-Best	21.897	19.459	20.699	11.283	18.899	26.836	29.565	24.271	21.665	25.584
WMT13-Worst	16.753	13.910	3.024	4.431	13.166	14.008	14.542	14.494	9.667	13.178

with standard and commonly used MT metrics; SYN, the reference-based syntactic metrics; SEM, the reference-based semantic metrics; SRC, the source-based metrics; and the combination of BAS with every other configuration: BAS+SYN, BAS+SEM, and BAS+SRC. Their purpose is to evaluate the contribution of the newly developed sets of metrics with respect to the baseline. The composition of the different configurations is summarised in Tables 2 and 3.

Evaluation results are shown in Tables 4 and 5. For each configuration and language pair, we show the correlation coefficients obtained at the *system-* and the *segment-level*, respectively. As customary with the WMT13 dataset, Pearson correlation was computed at the system-level, whereas Kendall's τ was used to estimate segment-level rank correlations. Additionally to the two submitted and seven extra configurations, we include the coefficients obtained with the *Best* and *Worst* systems reported in the official WMT13 evaluation for each language pair.

Although the results of our two submitted systems are not radically different to each other, UPC-STOUT consistently outperforms UPC-IPA. The currently available version of ASIYA, including the new metrics, allows for a performance close to the top-performing evaluation measures in last year's challenge, even with our naïve combination strategy.

It is worth noting that no configuration behaves the same way throughout the different languages. In some cases (e.g., with the SRC configuration), the bad performance can be explained by the weaknesses of the necessary resources when computing certain metrics. When analysed in detail, the cause can be ascribed to different metric families in each case. As a result, it is clear that specific configurations are necessary for evaluating different languages and domains. We plan to approach these issues as part of our future work.

When looking at the system-level figures, one can observe that the SEM set allows for a considerable improvement over the baseline system. The further inclusion of the SYN set —when available—, tends to increase the quality of the estimations, mainly when English is the source language. These properties impact on some of the UPC-STOUT configurations. In contrast, when looking at the segment-level scores, while

Table 6: System-level Pearson correlation results in the WMT14 Metrics shared task

	en–fr	*en–de*		*en–cs*	*en–ru*
UPC-IPA	93.7	13.0		96.8	92.2
UPC-STOUT	93.8	14.8		93.8	92.1
WMT14-Best	95.9	19.8		98.8	94.2
WMT14-Worst	88.8	1.1		93.8	90.3
	fr–en	*de–en*	*hi–en*	*cs–en*	*ru–en*
UPC-IPA	96.6	89.4	91.5	82.4	80.0
UPC-STOUT	96.8	91.4	89.8	94.7	82.5
WMT14-Best	98.1	94.2	97.6	99.3	86.1
WMT14-Worst	94.5	76.0	41.1	74.1	-41.7

Table 7: Segment-level Kendall's τ correlation results in the WMT14 Metrics shared task

	en–fr	*en–de*		*en–cs*	*en–ru*
UPC-IPA	26.3	21.7		29.7	42.6
UPC-STOUT	27.8	22.4		28.1	42.5
WMT14-Best	29.7	25.8		34.4	44.0
WMT14-Worst	25.4	18.5		28.1	38.1
	fr–en	*de–en*	*hi–en*	*cs–en*	*ru–en*
UPC-IPA	41.2	34.1	36.7	27.4	32.4
UPC-STOUT	40.3	34.5	35.1	27.5	32.4
WMT14-Best	43.3	38.1	43.8	32.8	36.4
WMT14-Worst	31.1	22.5	23.7	18.7	21.2

the SYN measures still tend to provide some gain over the baseline, the SEM ones do not. Finally, it merits some attention the good results achieved by the baseline for translations into English. We may remark here that our baseline included also the best performing state-of-the-art metrics, including all the variants of METEOR, that reported good results in the WMT13 challenge.

Tables 6 and 7 show the official results obtained by UPC-IPA and UPC-STOUT in WMT14.[8] The best and worst figures for each language pair are included for comparison —the worst performing submission at segment level is neglected as it seems to be a dummy (Macháček and Bojar, 2014 to appear). Both UPC-IPA and UPC-STOUT configurations resulted in different performances depending on the language pair. UPC-STOUT scored above the average for all the language pairs except for *en–cs* at both system and segment level, and *en–ru* at system level. Although the evaluation results are not directly comparable to the WMT13 ones, one can note that the results were notably better for pairs that involved Czech and Russian, and worse for those that involved French and German at system level. Analysing the impact of the evaluation methods and building comparable results in order to address a study on configurations for different languages is part of our future work.

5 Conclusions

This paper describes the UPC submission to the WMT14 metrics for automatic machine translation evaluation task. The core of our evaluation system is ASIYA, a toolkit for MT evaluation. Besides the formerly available metrics in ASIYA, we experimented with new metrics for machine translation evaluation, with especial focus on translation from English into other languages.

As previous work on English as target language has proven, syntactic and semantic analysis can contribute positively to the evaluation of automatic translations. For this reason, we integrated a set of new metrics for different languages, aimed at evaluating a translation from different perspectives. Among the novelties, (*i*) new shallow metrics, borrowed from Information Retrieval, were included to compare the candidate translation against both the reference translation (monolingual comparison) and the source sentence (cross-language comparison), including explicit semantic analysis and the lexical-based characterisations character n-grams and pseudo-cognates; (*ii*) new parsers for other languages than English were applied to compare automatic and reference translation at the syntactic level; (*iii*) an experimental metric based on alignments; and (*iv*) a metric based on the correlation of the translations' expected lengths was included as well. Our preliminary experiments showed that the combination of these and standard MT evaluation metrics allows for a performance close to the best in last year's competition for some language pairs.

The new set of metrics is already available in the current version of the toolkit ASIYA v3.0 (Gonzàlez and Giménez, 2014). Our current efforts are focused on the exploitation of more sophisticated methods to combine the contributions of each metric, and the extension of the list of supported languages.

Acknowledgements

This work was funded by the Spanish Ministry of Education and Science (TACARDI project, TIN2012-38523-C02-00).

[8]At the time of submitting this paper, the evaluation results for WMT14 Metrics Task were provisional.

References

Alberto Barrón-Cedeño, Monica Lestari Paramita, Paul Clough, and Paolo Rosso. 2014. A Comparison of Approaches for Measuring Cross-Lingual Similarity of Wikipedia Articles. *Advances in Information Retrieval. Proceedings of the 36th European Conference on IR Research*, LNCS (8416):424–429. Springer-Verlag.

Ondřej Bojar, Christian Buck, Chris Callison-Burch, Christian Federmann, Barry Haddow, Philipp Koehn, Christof Monz, Matt Post, Radu Soricut, and Lucia Specia. 2013. Findings of the 2013 Workshop on Statistical Machine Translation. In *Proceedings of the Eighth Workshop on Statistical Machine Translation*, pages 1–44, Sofia, Bulgaria, August. Association for Computational Linguistics.

Peter F. Brown, Jennifer C. Lai, and Robert L. Mercer. 1991. Aligning Sentences in Parallel Corpora. In Douglas E. Appelt, editor, *Proceedings of the 29th Annual Meeting of the Association for Computational Linguistics (ACL 1991)*, pages 169–176, Berkeley, CA, USA. Association for Computational Linguistics.

Marie Candito, Benot Crabb, and Pascal Denis. 2010a. Statistical French dependency parsing: treebank conversion and first results. In *The seventh international conference on Language Resources and Evaluation (LREC)*, Valletta, Malta.

Marie Candito, Joakim Nivre, Pascal Denis, and Enrique Henestroza Anguiano. 2010b. Benchmarking of Statistical Dependency Parsers for French. In *Proc. 23rd Intl. COLING Conference on Computational Linguistics: Poster Volume*, pages 108–116, Beijing, China.

Eugene Charniak and Mark Johnson. 2005. Coarse-to-Fine N-best Parsing and MaxEnt Discriminative Reranking. In *Proc. 43rd Annual Meeting of the Association for Computational Linguistics (ACL)*, pages 173–180, Stroudsburg, PA, USA. Association for Computational Linguistics.

Michael Denkowski and Alon Lavie. 2011. Meteor 1.3: Automatic Metric for Reliable Optimization and Evaluation of Machine Translation Systems. In *Proceedings of the 6th Workshop on Statistical Machine Translation*, pages 85–91, Stroudsburg, PA, USA. Association for Computational Linguistics.

George Doddington. 2002. Automatic Evaluation of Machine Translation Quality Using N-gram Co-Occurrence Statistics. In *Proceedings of the 2nd International Conference on Human Language Technology*, pages 138–145, San Francisco, CA, USA. Morgan Kaufmann Publishers Inc.

E. Gabrilovich and S. Markovitch. 2007. Computing Semantic Relatedness Using Wikipedia-based Explicit Semantic Analysis. In *20th International Joint Conference on Artificial Intelligence*, pages 1606–1611, San Francisco, CA, USA.

William A. Gale and Kenneth, W. Church. 1993. A Program for Aligning Sentences in Bilingual Corpora. *Computational Linguistics*, 19:75–102.

Jesús Giménez and Lluís Màrquez. 2007. Linguistic Features for Automatic Evaluation of Heterogeneous MT Systems. In *Proc. of 2nd Workshop on statistical Machine Translation (WMT07), ACL'07, Prague, Czech Republic*.

Jesús Giménez and Lluís Màrquez. 2010a. Asiya: An Open Toolkit for Automatic Machine Translation (Meta-)Evaluation. *The Prague Bulletin of Mathematical Linguistics*, 94:77–86.

Jesús Giménez and Lluís Màrquez. 2010b. Linguistic Measures for Automatic Machine Translation Evaluation. *Machine Translation*, 24(3–4):77–86.

Jesús Giménez. 2008. *Empirical Machine Translation and its Evaluation*. Ph.D. thesis, Universitat Politcnica de Catalunya, July.

Meritxell Gonzàlez and Jesús Giménez. 2014. Asiya: An Open Toolkit for Automatic Machine Translation (Meta-)Evaluation, v3.0, February. http://asiya.lsi.upc.edu.

Meritxell Gonzàlez, Jesús Giménez, and Lluís Màrquez. 2012. A Graphical Interface for MT Evaluation and Error Analysis. In *Proc. Annual Meeting of the Association for Computational Linguistics (ACL). System Demonstration*, pages 139–144, Jeju, South Korea, July. Association for Computational Linguistics.

Meritxell Gonzàlez, Laura Mascarell, and Lluís Màrquez. 2013. tSearch: Flexible and Fast Search over Automatic translation for Improved Quality/Error Analysis. In *Proc. 51st Annual Meeting of the Association for Computational Linguistics (ACL). System Demonstration*, pages 181–186, Sofia, Bulgaria, August.

Paul Jaccard. 1901. Étude comparative de la distribution florale dans une portion des Alpes et des Jura. *Bulletin del la Société Vaudoise des Sciences Naturelles*, 37:547–579.

Ding Liu and Daniel Gildea. 2005. Syntactic Features for Evaluation of Machine Translation. In *Proceedings of ACL Workshop on Intrinsic and Extrinsic Evaluation Measures for MT and/or Summarization*, pages 25–32, Stroudsburg, PA, USA. Association for Computational Linguistics.

Matouš Macháček and Ondřej Bojar. 2013. Results of the WMT13 metrics shared task. In *Proceedings of the Eighth Workshop on Statistical Machine Translation*, pages 45–51, Sofia, Bulgaria, August. Association for Computational Linguistics.

Matouš Macháček and Ondřej Bojar. 2014 (to appear). Results of the WMT14 metrics shared task. In *Proceedings of the Ninth Workshop on Statistical Machine Translation*, Baltimare, US, June. Association for Computational Linguistics.

Paul McNamee and James Mayfield. 2004. Character N-Gram Tokenization for European Language Text Retrieval. *Information Retrieval*, 7(1-2):73–97.

I. Dan Melamed, Ryan Green, and Joseph P. Turian. 2003. Precision and Recall of Machine Translation. In *Proceedings of the Joint Conference on Human Language Technology and the North American Chapter of the Association for Computational Linguistics (HLT-NAACL)*, pages 61–63, Stroudsburg, PA, USA. Association for Computational Linguistics.

Sonja Nießen, Franz Josef Och, Gregor Leusch, and Hermann Ney. 2000. An Evaluation Tool for Machine Translation: Fast Evaluation for MT Research. In *Proceedings of the 2nd International Conference on Language Resources and Evaluation (LREC)*.

Joakim Nivre, Johan Hall, Jens Nilsson, Atanas Chanev, Gülsen Eryigit, Sandra Kübler, Svetoslav Marinov, and Erwin Marsi. 2007. MaltParser: A language-independent system for data-driven dependency parsing. *Natural Language Engineering*, 13(2):95–135.

Slav Petrov and Dan Klein. 2007. Improved Inference for Unlexicalized Parsing. In *Proc. Human Language Technologies (HLT)*, pages 404–411. Association for Computational Linguistics, April.

Slav Petrov, Leon Barrett, Romain Thibaux, and Dan Klein. 2006. Learning accurate, compact, and interpretable tree annotation. In *21st International Conference on Computational Linguistics and the 44th annual meeting of the Association for Computational Linguistics*, ACL-44, pages 433–440, Stroudsburg, PA, USA. Association for Computational Linguistics.

Bruno Pouliquen, Ralf Steinberger, and Camelia Ignat. 2003. Automatic Identification of Document Translations in Large Multilingual Document Collections. In *Proceedings of the International Conference on Recent Advances in Natural Language Processing (RANLP-2003)*, pages 401–408, Borovets, Bulgaria.

Michel Simard, George F. Foster, and Pierre Isabelle. 1992. Using Cognates to Align Sentences in Bilingual Corpora. In *Proceedings of the Fourth International Conference on Theoretical and Methodological Issues in Machine Translation*.

Matthew Snover, Nitin Madnani, Bonnie Dorr, and Richard Schwartz. 2009. Fluency, adequacy, or HTER? Exploring different human judgments with a tunable MT metric. In *Proceedings of the 4th Workshop on Statistical Machine Translation*, pages 259–268, Stroudsburg, PA, USA. Association for Computational Linguistics.

Christoph Tillmann, Stefan Vogel, Hermann Ney, A. Zubiaga, and H. Sawaf. 1997. Accelerated DP based Search for Statistical Translation. In *Proceedings of European Conference on Speech Communication and Technology*, pages 2667–2670.

DiscoTK: Using Discourse Structure for Machine Translation Evaluation

Shafiq Joty Francisco Guzmán Lluís Màrquez and **Preslav Nakov**
ALT Research Group
Qatar Computing Research Institute — Qatar Foundation
{sjoty,fguzman,lmarquez,pnakov}@qf.org.qa

Abstract

We present novel automatic metrics for machine translation evaluation that use discourse structure and convolution kernels to compare the discourse tree of an automatic translation with that of the human reference. We experiment with five transformations and augmentations of a base discourse tree representation based on the rhetorical structure theory, and we combine the kernel scores for each of them into a single score. Finally, we add other metrics from the ASIYA MT evaluation toolkit, and we tune the weights of the combination on actual human judgments. Experiments on the WMT12 and WMT13 metrics shared task datasets show correlation with human judgments that outperforms what the best systems that participated in these years achieved, both at the segment and at the system level.

1 Introduction

The rapid development of statistical machine translation (SMT) that we have seen in recent years would not have been possible without automatic metrics for measuring SMT quality. In particular, the development of BLEU (Papineni et al., 2002) revolutionized the SMT field, allowing not only to compare two systems in a way that strongly correlates with human judgments, but it also enabled the rise of discriminative log-linear models, which use optimizers such as MERT (Och, 2003), and later MIRA (Watanabe et al., 2007; Chiang et al., 2008) and PRO (Hopkins and May, 2011), to optimize BLEU, or an approximation thereof, directly. While over the years other strong metrics such as TER (Snover et al., 2006) and Meteor (Lavie and Denkowski, 2009) have emerged, BLEU remains the de-facto standard, despite its simplicity.

Recently, there has been steady increase in BLEU scores for well-resourced language pairs such as Spanish-English and Arabic-English. However, it was also observed that BLEU-like n-gram matching metrics are unreliable for high-quality translation output (Doddington, 2002; Lavie and Agarwal, 2007). In fact, researchers already worry that BLEU will soon be unable to distinguish automatic from human translations.[1] This is a problem for most present-day metrics, which cannot tell apart raw machine translation output from a fully fluent professionally post-edited version thereof (Denkowski and Lavie, 2012).

Another concern is that BLEU-like n-gram matching metrics tend to favor phrase-based SMT systems over rule-based systems and other SMT paradigms. In particular, they are unable to capture the syntactic and semantic structure of sentences, and are thus insensitive to improvement in these aspects. Furthermore, it has been shown that lexical similarity is both insufficient and not strictly necessary for two sentences to convey the same meaning (Culy and Riehemann, 2003; Coughlin, 2003; Callison-Burch et al., 2006).

The above issues have motivated a large amount of work dedicated to design better evaluation metrics. The Metrics task at the Workshop on Machine Translation (WMT) has been instrumental in this quest. Below we present QCRI's submission to the Metrics task of WMT14, which consists of the DiscoTK family of discourse-based metrics.

In particular, we experiment with five different transformations and augmentations of a discourse tree representation, and we combine the kernel scores for each of them into a single score which we call DISCOTK$_{light}$. Next, we add to the combination other metrics from the ASIYA MT evaluation toolkit (Giménez and Màrquez, 2010), to produce the DISCOTK$_{party}$ metric.

[1]This would not mean that computers have achieved human proficiency; it would rather show BLEU's inadequacy.

Proceedings of the Ninth Workshop on Statistical Machine Translation, pages 402–408,
Baltimore, Maryland USA, June 26–27, 2014.

Finally, we tune the relative weights of the metrics in the combination using human judgments in a learning-to-rank framework. This proved to be quite beneficial: the tuned version of the DISCOTK$_{party}$ metric was the best performing metric in the WMT14 Metrics shared task.

The rest of the paper is organized as follows: Section 2 introduces our basic discourse metrics and the tree representations they are based on. Section 3 describes our metric combinations. Section 4 presents our experiments and results on datasets from previous years. Finally, Section 5 concludes and suggests directions for future work.

2 Discourse-Based Metrics

In our recent work (Guzmán et al., 2014), we used the information embedded in the discourse-trees (DTs) to compare the output of an MT system to a human reference. More specifically, we used a state-of-the-art sentence-level discourse parser (Joty et al., 2012) to generate discourse trees for the sentences in accordance with the Rhetorical Structure Theory (RST) of discourse (Mann and Thompson, 1988). Then, we computed the similarity between DTs of the human references and the system translations using a convolution tree kernel (Collins and Duffy, 2001), which efficiently computes the number of common subtrees. Note that this kernel was originally designed for syntactic parsing, and the subtrees are subject to the constraint that their nodes are taken with all or none of their children, i.e., if we take a direct descendant of a given node, we must also take all siblings of that descendant. This imposes some limitations on the type of substructures that can be compared, and motivates the enriched tree representations explained in subsections 2.1–2.4.

The motivation to compare discourse trees, is that translations should preserve the coherence relations. For example, consider the three discourse trees (DTs) shown in Figure 1. Notice that the *Attribution* relation in the reference translation is also realized in the system translation in (b) but not in (c), which makes (b) a better translation compared to (c), according to our hypothesis.

In (Guzmán et al., 2014), we have shown that discourse structure provides additional information for MT evaluation, which is not captured by existing metrics that use lexical, syntactic and semantic information; thus, discourse should be considered when developing new rich metrics.

Here, we extend our previous work by developing metrics that are based on new representations of the DTs. In the remainder of this section, we will focus on the individual DT representations that we will experiment with; then, the following section will describe the metric combinations and tuning used to produce the DiscoTK metrics.

2.1 DR-LEX$_1$

Figure 2a shows our first representation of the DT. The lexical items, i.e., words, constitute the leaves of the tree. The words in an Elementary Discourse Unit (EDU) are grouped under a predefined tag **EDU**, to which the nuclearity status of the EDU is attached: *nucleus* vs. *satellite*. Coherence relations, such as *Attribution*, *Elaboration*, and *Enablement*, between adjacent text spans constitute the internal nodes of the tree. Like the EDUs, the nuclearity statuses of the larger discourse units are attached to the relation labels. Notice that with this representation the tree kernel can easily be extended to find subtree matches at the word level, i.e., by including an additional layer of *dummy* leaves as was done in (Moschitti et al., 2007). We applied the same solution in our representations.

2.2 DR-NOLEX

Our second representation DR-NOLEX (Figure 2b) is a simple variation of DR-LEX$_1$, where we exclude the lexical items. This allows us to measure the similarity between two translations in terms of their discourse structures alone.

2.3 DR-LEX$_2$

One limitation of DR-LEX$_1$ and DR-NOLEX is that they do not separate the structure, i.e., the skeleton, of the tree from its labels. Therefore, when measuring the similarity between two DTs, they do not allow the tree kernel to give partial credit to subtrees that differ in labels but match in their structures. DR-LEX$_2$, a variation of DR-LEX$_1$, addresses this limitation as shown in Figure 2c. It uses predefined tags **SPAN** and **EDU** to build the skeleton of the tree, and considers the nuclearity and/or relation labels as properties (added as children) of these tags. For example, a **SPAN** has two properties, namely its nuclearity and its relation, and an **EDU** has one property, namely its nuclearity. The words of an EDU are placed under the predefined tag **NGRAM**.

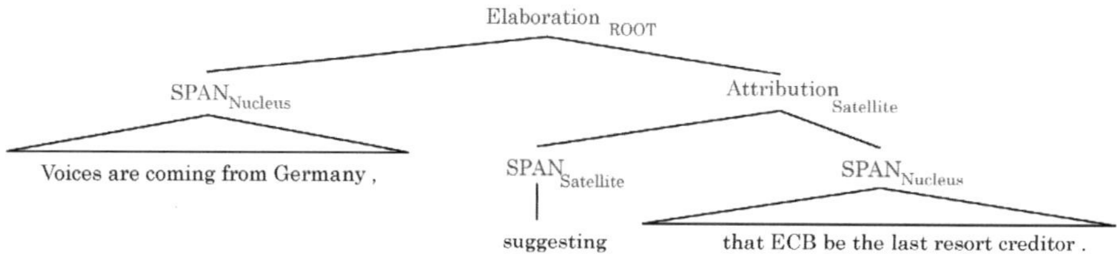

(a) A reference (human-written) translation.

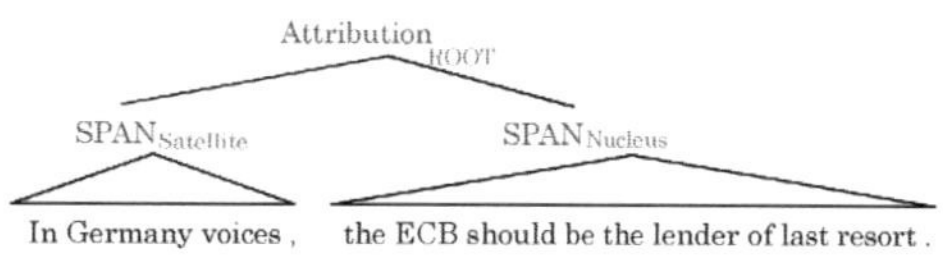

(b) A higher quality (system-generated) translation.

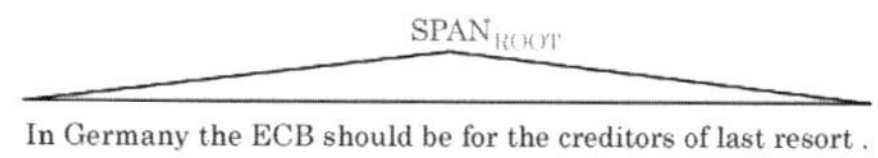

(c) A lower quality (system-generated) translation.

Figure 1: Three discourse trees for the translations of a source sentence: (a) the reference, (b) a higher quality automatic translation, and (c) a lower quality automatic translation.

2.4 DR-LEX$_{1.1}$ and DR-LEX$_{2.1}$

Although both DR-LEX$_1$ and DR-LEX$_2$ allow the tree kernel to find matches at the word level, the words are compared in a bag-of-words fashion, i.e., if the trees share a common word, the kernel will find a match regardless of its position in the tree. Therefore, a word that has occurred in an EDU with status *Nucleus* in one tree could be matched with the same word under a *Satellite* in the other tree. In other words, the kernel based on these representations is insensitive to the nuclearity status and the relation labels under which the words are matched. DR-LEX$_{1.1}$, an extension of DR-LEX$_1$, and DR-LEX$_{2.1}$, an extension of DR-LEX$_2$, are sensitive to these variations at the lexical level. DR-LEX$_{1.1}$ (Figure 2d) and DR-LEX$_{2.1}$ (Figure 2e) propagate the nuclearity statuses and/or the relation labels to the lexical items by including three more subtrees at the EDU level.

3 Metric Combination and Tuning

In this section, we describe our Discourse Tree Kernel (DiscoTK) metrics. We have two main versions: DISCOTK$_{light}$, which combines the five DR-based metrics, and DISCOTK$_{party}$, which further adds the Asiya metrics.

3.1 DISCOTK$_{light}$

In the previous section, we have presented several discourse tree representations that can be used to compare the output of a machine translation system to a human reference. Each representation stresses a different aspect of the discourse tree.

In order to make our estimations more robust, we propose DISCOTK$_{light}$, a metric that takes advantage of all the previous discourse representations by linearly interpolating their scores. Here are the processing steps needed to compute this metric:

(*i*) Parsing: We parsed each sentence in order to produce discourse trees for the human references and for the outputs of the systems.

(*ii*) Tree enrichment/simplification: For each sentence-level discourse tree, we generated the five different tree representations: DR-NOLEX, DR-LEX$_1$, DR-LEX$_{1.1}$, DR-LEX$_2$, DR-LEX$_{2.1}$.

(*iii*) Estimation: We calculated the per-sentence similarity scores between tree representations of the system hypothesis and the human reference using the extended convolution tree kernel as described in the previous section. To compute the system-level similarity scores, we calculated the average sentence-level similarity; note that this ensures that our metric is "the same" at the system and at the segment level.

(*iv*) Normalization: In order to make the scores of the different representations comparable, we performed a min–max normalization[2] for each metric and for each language pair.

(*v*) Combination: Finally, for each sentence, we computed DISCOTK$_{light}$ as the average of the normalized similarity scores of the different representations. For system-level experiments, we performed linear interpolation of system-level scores.

[2]Where $x' = (x - \min)/(\max - \min)$.

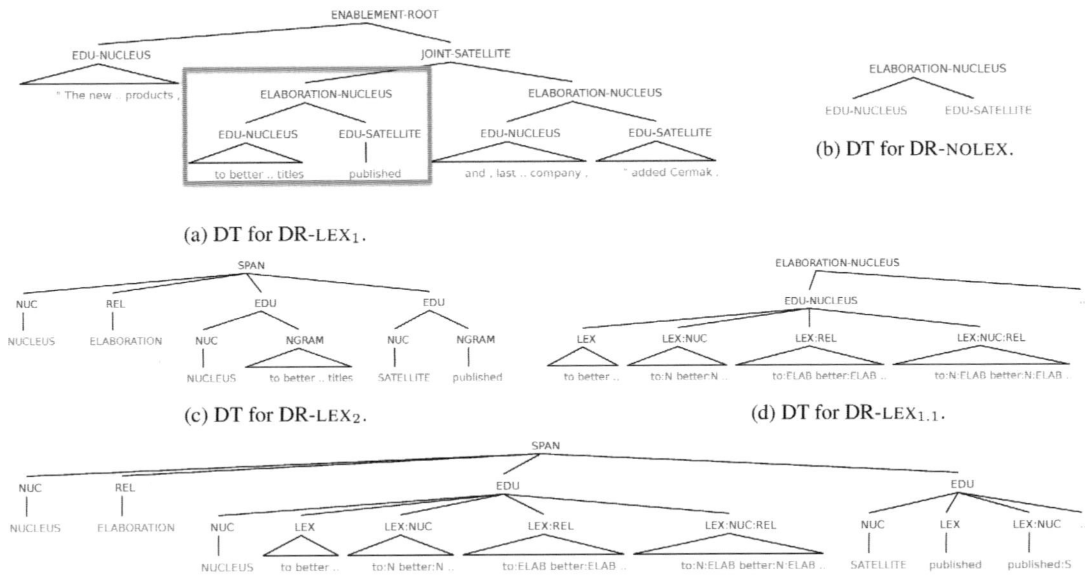

(a) DT for DR-LEX$_1$.

(b) DT for DR-NOLEX.

(c) DT for DR-LEX$_2$.

(d) DT for DR-LEX$_{1.1}$.

(e) DT for DR-LEX$_{2.1}$.

Figure 2: Five different representations of the discourse tree (DT) for the sentence *"The new organisational structure will also allow us to enter the market with a joint offer of advertising products, to better link the creation of content for all the titles published and, last but not least, to continue to streamline significantly the business management of the company," added Cermak.* Note that to avoid visual clutter, (b)–(e) show alternative representations only for the highlighted subtree in (a).

3.2 DISCOTK$_{party}$

One of the weaknesses of the above discourse-based metrics is that they use unigram lexical information, which does not capture reordering. Thus, in order to make more informed and robust estimations, we extended DISCOTK$_{light}$ with the composing metrics of the ASIYA's ULC metric (Giménez and Màrquez, 2010), which is a uniform linear combination of twelve individual metrics and was the best-performing metric at the system and at the segment levels at the WMT08 and WMT09 metrics tasks.

In order to compute the individual metrics from ULC, we used the ASIYA toolkit,[3] but we departed from ASIYA's ULC by replacing TER and Meteor with newer versions thereof that take into account synonymy lookup and paraphrasing ('TERp-A' and 'Meteor-pa' in ASIYA's terminology). We then combined the five components in DISCOTK$_{light}$ and the twelve individual metrics from ULC; we call this combination DISCOTK$_{party}$.

[3]http://nlp.lsi.upc.edu/asiya/

We combined the scores using linear interpolation in two different ways:

(i) Uniform combination of min-max normalized scores at the segment level. We obtained system-level scores by computing the average over the segment scores.

(ii) Trained interpolation at the sentence level. We determined the interpolation weights for the above-described combination of 5+12 = 17 metrics using a pairwise learning-to-rank framework and classification with logistic regression, as we had done in (Guzmán et al., 2014). We obtained the final test-time sentence-level scores by passing the interpolated raw scores through a sigmoid function. In contrast, for the final system-level scores, we averaged the per-sentence interpolated raw scores.

We also tried to learn the interpolation weights at the system level, experimenting with both regression and classification. However, the amount of data available for this type of training was small, and the learned weights did not perform significantly better than the uniform combination.

3.3 Post-processing

Discourse-based metrics, especially DR-NOLEX, tend to produce many ties when there is not enough information to do complete discourse analysis. This contributes to lower τ scores for DiscoTK$_{light}$. To alleviate this issue, we used a simple tie-breaking strategy, in which ties between segment scores for different systems are resolved by using perturbations proportional to the global system-level scores produced by the same metric, i.e., $x'^{seg}_{sys} = x^{seg}_{sys} + \epsilon * \sum_s x^s_{sys}$. Here, ϵ is automatically chosen to avoid collisions with scores not involved in the tie. This post-processing is not part of the metric; it is only applied to our segment-level submission to the WMT'14 metrics task.

4 Experimental Evaluation

In this section, we present some of our experiments to decide on the best DiscoTK metric variant and tuning set. For tuning, testing and comparison, we worked with some of the datasets available from previous WMT metrics shared tasks, i.e., 2011, 2012 and 2013. From previous experiments (Guzmán et al., 2014), we know that the tuned metrics perform very well on cross-validation for the same-year dataset. We further know that tuning can be performed by concatenating data from all the into-English language pairs, which yields better results than training separately by language pair. For the WMT14 metrics task, we investigated in more depth whether the tuned metrics generalize well to new datasets. Additionally, we tested the effect of concatenating datasets from different years.

Table 1 shows the main results of our experiments with the DiscoTK metrics. We evaluated the performance of the metrics on the WMT12 and WMT13 datasets both at the segment and the system level, and we used WMT11 as an additional tuning dataset. We measured the performance of the metrics in terms of correlation with human judgements. At the segment level, we evaluated using Kendall's Tau (τ), recalculated following the WMT14 official Kendall's Tau implementation. At the system level, we used Spearman's rank correlation (ρ) and Pearson's correlation coefficient (r). In all cases, we averaged the results over all into-English language pairs. The symbol '$\varnothing$' represents the untuned versions of our metrics, i.e., applying a uniform linear combination of the individual metrics.

We trained the tuned versions of the DiscoTK measures using different datasets (WMT11, WMT12 and WMT13) in order to study across-corpora generalization and the effect of training dataset size. The symbol '+' stands for concatenation of datasets. We trained the tuned versions at the segment level using Maximum Entropy classifiers for pairwise ranking (cf. Section 3). For the sake of comparison, the first group of rows contains the results of the best-performing metrics at the WMT12 and WMT13 metrics shared tasks and the last group of rows contains the results of the ASIYA combination of metrics, i.e., DiscoTK$_{party}$ without the discourse components.

Several conclusions can be drawn from Table 1. First, DiscoTK$_{party}$ is better than DiscoTK$_{light}$ in all settings, indicating that the discourse-based metrics are very well complemented by the heterogeneous metric set from ASIYA. DiscoTK$_{light}$ achieves competitive scores at the system level (which would put the metric among the best participants in WMT12 and WMT13); however, as expected, it is not robust enough at the segment level. On the other hand, the tuned versions of DiscoTK$_{party}$ are very competitive and improve over the already strong ASIYA in each configuration both at the segment- and the system-level. The improvements are small but consistent, showing that using discourse increases the correlation with human judgments.

Focusing on the results at the segment level, it is clear that the tuned versions offer an advantage over the simple uniform linear combinations. Interestingly, for the tuned variants, given a test set, the results are consistent across tuning sets, ruling out over-fitting; this shows that the generalization is very good. This result aligns well with what we observed in our previous studies (Guzmán et al., 2014). Learning with more data (WMT11+12 or WMT12+13) does not seem to help much, but it does not hurt performance either. Overall, the τ correlation results obtained with the tuned DiscoTK$_{party}$ metric are much better than the best results of any participant metrics at WMT12 and WMT13 (20.1% and 9.5% relative improvement, respectively).

At the system level, we observe that tuning over the DiscoTK$_{light}$ metric is not helpful (results are actually slightly lower), while tuning the more complex DiscoTK$_{party}$ metric yields slightly better results.

		Segment Level		System Level			
		WMT12	WMT13	WMT12		WMT13	
Metric	Tuning	τ	τ	ρ	r	ρ	r
SEMPOS	na	–	–	0.902	0.922	–	–
SPEDE07PP	na	0.254	–	–	–	–	–
METEOR-WMT13	na	–	0.264	–	–	0.935	**0.950**
	∅	0.171	0.162	0.884	0.922	0.880	0.911
	WMT11	0.207	0.201	0.860	0.872	0.890	0.909
DISCOTK$_{light}$	WMT12	–	0.200	–	–	0.889	0.910
	WMT13	0.206	–	0.865	0.871	–	–
	WMT11+12	–	0.197	–	–	0.890	0.910
	WMT11+13	0.207	–	0.865	0.871	–	–
	∅	0.257	0.231	0.907	0.915	**0.941**	0.928
	WMT11	0.302	0.282	**0.915**	**0.940**	0.934	0.946
DISCOTK$_{party}$	WMT12	–	0.284	–	–	0.936	0.940
	WMT13	**0.305**	–	0.912	0.935	–	–
	WMT11+12	–	**0.289**	–	–	0.936	0.943
	WMT11+13	0.304	–	0.912	0.934	–	–
	∅	0.273	0.252	0.899	0.909	0.932	0.922
	WMT11	0.301	0.279	0.913	0.935	0.934	0.944
ASIYA	WMT12	–	0.277	–	–	0.932	0.938
	WMT13	0.303	–	0.908	0.932	–	–
	WMT11+12	–	0.277	–	–	0.934	0.940
	WMT11+13	0.303	–	0.908	0.933	–	–

Table 1: Evaluation results on WMT12 and WMT13 datasets at segment and system level for the main combined DiscoTK measures proposed in this paper.

The scores of our best metric are higher than those of the best participants in WMT12 and WMT13, according to Spearman's ρ, which was the official metric in those years. Overall, our metrics are comparable to the state-of-the-art at the system level. The differences between Spearman's ρ and Pearson's r coefficients are not dramatic, with r values being always higher than ρ.

Given the above results, we submitted the following runs to the WMT14 Metrics shared task: *(i)* DISCOTK$_{party}$ tuned on the concatenation of datasets WMT11+12+13, as our primary run; *(ii)* Untuned DISCOTK$_{party}$, to verify that we are not over-fitting the training set; and *(iii)* Untuned DISCOTK$_{light}$, to see the performance of a metric using discourse structures and word unigrams.

The results for the WMT14 Metrics shared task have shown that our primary run, DISCOTK$_{party}$ tuned, was the *best-performing* metric both at the segment- and at the system-level (Macháček and Bojar, 2014). This metric yielded significantly better results than its untuned counterpart, confirming the importance of weight tuning and the absence of over-fitting during tuning. Finally, the untuned DISCOTK$_{light}$ achieved relatively competitive, albeit slightly worse results for all language pairs, except for Hindi-English, where system translations resembled a "word salad", and were very hard to discourse-parse accurately.

5 Conclusion

We have presented experiments with novel automatic metrics for machine translation evaluation that take discourse structure into account. In particular, we used RST-style discourse parse trees, which we compared using convolution kernels. We further combined these kernels with metrics from ASIYA, also tuning the weights. The resulting DISCOTK$_{party}$ tuned metric was the best-performing at the segment- and system-level at the WMT14 metrics task.

In an internal evaluation on the WMT12 and WMT13 metrics datasets, this tuned combination showed correlation with human judgments that outperforms the best systems that participated in these shared tasks. The discourse-only metric ranked near the top at the system-level for WMT12 and WMT13; however, it is weak at the segment-level since it is sensitive to parsing errors, and most sentences have very little internal discourse structure.

In the future, we plan to work on an integrated representation of syntactic, semantic and discourse-based tree structures, which would allow us to design evaluation metrics based on more fine-grained features, and would also allow us to train such metrics using kernel methods. Furthermore, we want to make use of discourse parse information beyond the sentence level.

References

Chris Callison-Burch, Miles Osborne, and Philipp Koehn. 2006. Re-evaluating the role of BLEU in machine translation research. In *Proceedings of the Eleventh Conference of the European Chapter of the Association for Computational Linguistics*, EACL'06, pages 249–256, Trento, Italy.

David Chiang, Yuval Marton, and Philip Resnik. 2008. Online large-margin training of syntactic and structural translation features. In *Proceedings of the Conference on Empirical Methods in Natural Language Processing*, EMNLP'08, pages 224–233, Honolulu, Hawaii.

Michael Collins and Nigel Duffy. 2001. Convolution Kernels for Natural Language. In *Neural Information Processing Systems*, NIPS'01, pages 625–632, Vancouver, Canada.

Deborah Coughlin. 2003. Correlating automated and human assessments of machine translation quality. In *Proceedings of the Machine Translation Summit IX*, MT Summit'03, pages 23–27, New Orleans, LA, USA.

Christopher Culy and Susanne Riehemann. 2003. The limits of n-gram translation evaluation metrics. In *Proceedings of the Machine Translation Summit IX*, MT Summit'03, pages 1–8, New Orleans, LA, USA.

Michael Denkowski and Alon Lavie. 2012. Challenges in predicting machine translation utility for human post-editors. In *Proceedings of the Tenth Conference of the Association for Machine Translation in the Americas*, AMTA'12, pages 40–49, San Diego, CA, USA.

George Doddington. 2002. Automatic evaluation of machine translation quality using n-gram co-occurrence statistics. In *Proceedings of the Second International Conference on Human Language Technology Research*, HLT'02, pages 138–145, San Francisco, CA, USA.

Jesús Giménez and Lluís Màrquez. 2010. Linguistic Measures for Automatic Machine Translation Evaluation. *Machine Translation*, 24(3–4):77–86.

Francisco Guzmán, Shafiq Joty, Lluís Màrquez, and Preslav Nakov. 2014. Using discourse structure improves machine translation evaluation. In *Proceedings of 52nd Annual Meeting of the Association for Computational Linguistics*, ACL'14, Baltimore, MD, USA.

Mark Hopkins and Jonathan May. 2011. Tuning as ranking. In *Proceedings of the Conference on Empirical Methods in Natural Language Processing*, EMNLP'11, pages 1352–1362, Edinburgh, Scotland, UK.

Shafiq Joty, Giuseppe Carenini, and Raymond Ng. 2012. A Novel Discriminative Framework for Sentence-Level Discourse Analysis. In *Proceedings of the Joint Conference on Empirical Methods in Natural Language Processing and Computational Natural Language Learning*, EMNLP-CoNLL'12, pages 904–915, Jeju Island, Korea.

Alon Lavie and Abhaya Agarwal. 2007. METEOR: An automatic metric for MT evaluation with high levels of correlation with human judgments. In *Proceedings of the Second Workshop on Statistical Machine Translation*, WMT'07, pages 228–231, Prague, Czech Republic.

Alon Lavie and Michael Denkowski. 2009. The METEOR metric for automatic evaluation of machine translation. *Machine Translation*, 23(2-3):105–115.

Matouš Macháček and Ondřej Bojar. 2014. Results of the WMT14 Metrics Shared Task. In *Proceedings of the Ninth Workshop on Statistical Machine Translation*, WMT'14, Baltimore, MD, USA.

William Mann and Sandra Thompson. 1988. Rhetorical Structure Theory: Toward a Functional Theory of Text Organization. *Text*, 8(3):243–281.

Alessandro Moschitti, Silvia Quarteroni, Roberto Basili, and Suresh Manandhar. 2007. Exploiting syntactic and shallow semantic kernels for question answer classification. In *Proceedings of the 45th Annual Meeting of the Association of Computational Linguistics*, ACL'07, pages 776–783, Prague, Czech Republic.

Franz Josef Och. 2003. Minimum error rate training in statistical machine translation. In *Proceedings of the 41st Annual Meeting of the Association for Computational Linguistics*, ACL'03, pages 160–167, Sapporo, Japan.

Kishore Papineni, Salim Roukos, Todd Ward, and Wei-Jing Zhu. 2002. BLEU: a method for automatic evaluation of machine translation. In *Proceedings of 40th Annual Meeting of the Association for Computational Linguistics*, ACL'02, pages 311–318, Philadelphia, PA, USA.

Matthew Snover, Bonnie Dorr, Richard Schwartz, Linnea Micciulla, and John Makhoul. 2006. A study of translation edit rate with targeted human annotation. In *Proceedings of the Seventh Biennial Conference of the Association for Machine Translation in the Americas*, AMTA'06, pages 223–231, Cambridge, MA, USA.

Taro Watanabe, Jun Suzuki, Hajime Tsukada, and Hideki Isozaki. 2007. Online large-margin training for statistical machine translation. In *Proceedings of the Joint Conference on Empirical Methods in Natural Language Processing and Computational Natural Language Learning*, EMNLP-CoNLL'07, pages 764–773, Prague, Czech Republic.

Tolerant BLEU: a Submission to the WMT14 Metrics Task

Jindřich Libovický and **Pavel Pecina**
Charles University in Prague, Faculty of Mathematics and Physics
Institute of Formal ad Applied Linguistics
{libovicky, pecina}@ufal.mff.cuni.cz

Abstract

This paper describes a machine translation metric submitted to the WMT14 Metrics Task. It is a simple modification of the standard BLEU metric using a monolingual alignment of reference and test sentences. The alignment is computed as a minimum weighted maximum bipartite matching of the translated and the reference sentence words with respect to the relative edit distance of the word prefixes and suffixes. The aligned words are included in the n-gram precision computation with a penalty proportional to the matching distance. The proposed tBLEU metric is designed to be more tolerant to errors in inflection, which usually does not effect the understandability of a sentence, and therefore be more suitable for measuring quality of translation into morphologically richer languages.

1 Introduction

Automatic evaluation of machine translation (MT) quality is an important part of the machine translation pipeline. The possibility to run an evaluation algorithm many times while training a system enables the system to be optimized with respect to such a metric (e.g., by Minimum Error Rate Training (Och, 2003)). By achieving a high correlation of the metric with human judgment, we expect the system performance to be optimized also with respect to the human perception of translation quality.

In this paper, we propose an MT metric called tBLEU (tolerant BLEU) that is based on the standard BLEU (Papineni et al., 2002) and designed to suit better when translation into morphologically richer languages. We aim to have a simple language independent metric that correlates with human judgment better than the standard BLEU.

Several metrics try to address this problem as well and usually succeed to gain a higher correlation with human judgment (e.g. METEOR (Denkowski and Lavie, 2011), TerrorCat (Fishel et al., 2012)). However, they usually use some language-dependent tools and resources (METEOR uses stemmer and parahprasing tables, TerrorCat uses lemmatization and needs training data for each language pair) which prevent them from being widely adopted.

In the next section, the previous work is briefly summarized. Section 3 describes the metric in detail. The experiments with the metric are described in Section 4 and their results are summarized in Section 5.

2 Previous Work

BLEU (Papineni et al., 2002) is an established and the most widely used automatic metric for evaluation of MT quality. It is computed as a harmonic mean of the n-gram precisions multiplied by the brevity penalty coefficient which ensures also high recall. Formally:

$$\text{BLEU} = \text{BP} \cdot \exp\left(\sum_{n=1}^{4} \frac{1}{4} \log p_n\right),$$

where BP is the brevity penaly defined as follows:

$$\text{BP} = \begin{cases} 1 & \text{if } c > r \\ e^{1-\frac{r}{c}} & \text{otherwise} \end{cases},$$

c is the length of the test sentence (number of tokens), r is the length of the reference sentence, and p_n is the proportion of n-grams from the test sentence found in the reference translations.

The original experiments with the English to Chinese translation (Papineni et al., 2002) reported very high correlation of BLEU with human judgments. However, these scores were computed using multiple reference translations (to capture translation variability) but in practice, only one

Proceedings of the Ninth Workshop on Statistical Machine Translation, pages 409–413,
Baltimore, Maryland USA, June 26–27, 2014.

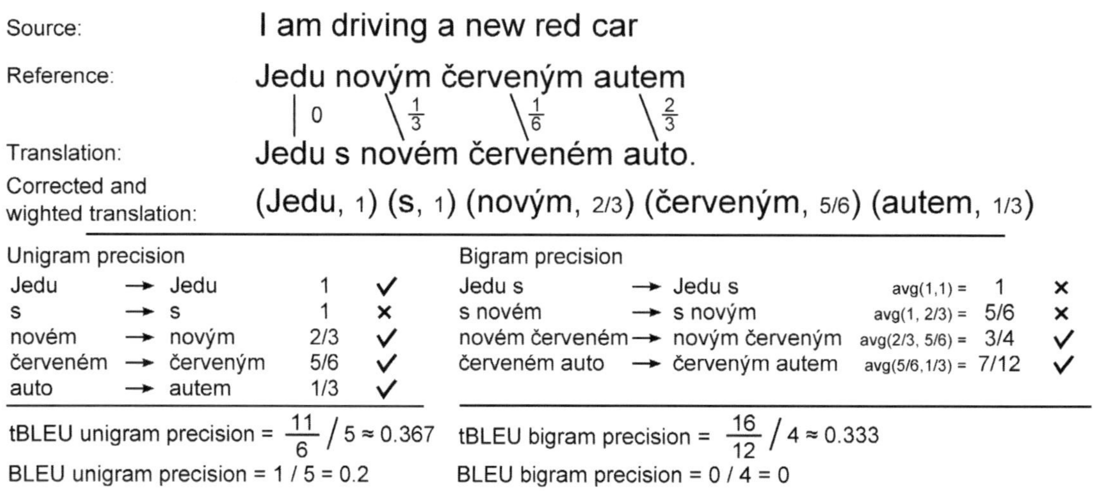

Figure 1: An example of the unigram and bigram precision computation for translation from English to Czech with the test sentence having minor inflection errors and an additional preposition. The first two lines contain the source sentence in English and a correct reference translation in Czech. On the third line, there is an incorrectly translated sentence with errors in inflection. Between the second and the third line, the matching with respect to the affix distance is shown. The fourth line contains the corrected test sentence with the words weights. The bottom part of the figure shows computation of the unigram and bigram precisions. The first column contains the original translation n-grams, the second one the corrected n-grams, the third one the n-gram weights and the last one indicates whether a matching n-gram is contained in the reference sentence.

reference translation is usually available and therefore the BLEU scores are often underestimated.

The main disadvantage of BLEU is the fact that it treats words as atomic units and does not allow any partial matches. Therefore, words which are inflectional variants of each other are treated as completely different words although their meaning is similar (e.g. *work*, *works*, *worked*, *working*). Further, the n-gram precision for $n > 1$ penalizes difference in word order between the reference and the test sentences even though in languages with free word order both sentences can be correct (Bojar et al., 2010; Condon et al., 2009).

There are also other widely recognized MT evaluation metrics: The NIST score (Doddington, 2002) is also an n-gram based metric, but in addition it reflects how informative particular n-grams are. A metric that achieves a very high correlation with human judgment is METEOR (Denkowski and Lavie, 2011). It creates a monolingual alignment using language dependent tools as stemmers and synonyms dictionaries and computes weighted harmonic mean of precision and recall based on the matching.

Some metrics are based on measuring the edit distance between the reference and test sentences. The Position-Independent Error Rate (PER) (Leusch et al., 2003) is computed as a length-normalized edit distance of sentences treated as bags of words. The Translation Edit Rate (TER) (Snover et al., 2006) is a number of edit operation needed to change the test sentence to the most similar reference sentence. In this case, the allowed editing operations are insertions, deletions and substitutions and also shifting words within a sentence.

A different approach is used in TerrorCat (Fishel et al., 2012). It uses frequencies of automatically obtained translation error categories as base for machine-learned pairwise comparison of translation hypotheses.

In the Workshop of Machine Translation (WMT) Metrics Task, several new MT metrics compete annually (Macháček and Bojar, 2013). In the comptetition, METEOR and TerrorCat scored better that the other mentioned metrics.

3 Metric Description

tBLEU is computed in in two steps. Similarly to the METEOR score, we first make a monolingual alignment between the reference and the test sentences and then apply an algorithm similar to the standard BLEU but with modified n-gram precisions.

The monolingual alignment is computed as a minimum weighted maximum bipartite matching between words in a reference sentence and a translation sentence[1] using the Munkres assignment algorithm (Munkres, 1957).

We define a weight of an alignment link as the *affix distance* of the test sentence word w_i^t and the reference sentence word w_j^r: Let S be the longest common substring of w_i^t and w_i^r. We can rewrite the strings as a concatenation of a prefix, the common substring and a suffix:

$$w^t = w_{i,p}^t S w_{i,s}^t$$
$$w^r = w_{j,p}^r S w_{j,s}^r$$

Further, we define the affix distance as:

$$\mathrm{AD}(w^r, w^t) = \max\left\{1, \frac{L(w_{j,p}^r, w_{i,p}^t) + L(w_{s,j}^r, w_{s,i}^t)}{|S|}\right\}$$

if $|S| > 0$ and $\mathrm{AD}(w^r, w^t) = 1$ otherwise. L is the Levensthein distance between two strings.

For example the affix distance of two Czech words *vzpomenou* and *zapomenout* (different forms of verbs remember and forget) is computed in the following way: The longest common substring is *pomenou* which has a length of 7. The prefixes are *vz* and *za* and their edit distance is 2. The suffixes are an empty string and *t* which with the edit distance 1. The total edit distance of prefixes and suffixes is 3. By dividing the total edit distance by the length of the longest common substring, we get the affix distance $\frac{3}{7} \approx 0.43$.

We denote the resulting set of matching pairs of words as $M = \{(w_i^r, w_i^t)\}_{i=1}^m$ and for each test sentence $S^t = (w_1^t, ..., w_m^t)$ we create a corrected sentence $\hat{S}^t = (\hat{w}_1^t, ..., \hat{w}_m^t)$ such that

$$\hat{w}_i^t = \begin{cases} w^r & \text{if } \exists w^t: (w^r, w^t) \in M \ \&\ \mathrm{AD}(w^r, w^t) \le \epsilon \\ w_i^t & \text{otherwise.} \end{cases}$$

This means that the words from the test sentence which were matched with the affix distance smaller than ϵ are "corrected" by substituting them by the matching words from the reference sentence. The threshold ϵ is a free parameter of the metric. When the threshold is set to zero, no corrections are made and therefore the metric is equivalent to the standard BLEU.

[1]The matching is always one-to-one which means that some words remain unmatched if the sentences have different number of words.

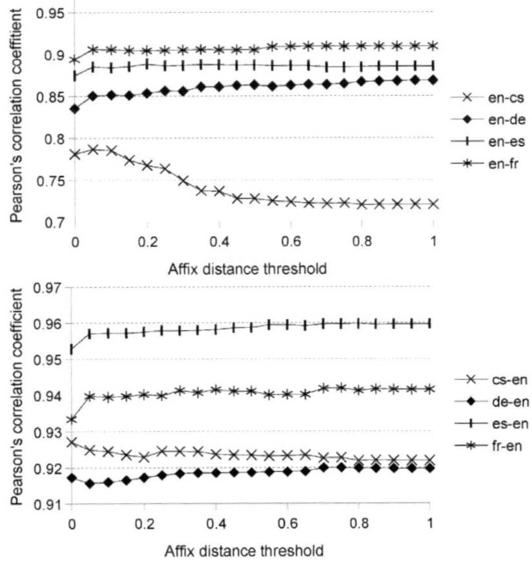

Figure 2: Dependence of the Pearson's correlation of tBLEU with the WMT13 human judgments on the affix distance threshold for translations from English and to English.

The words in the corrected sentence are assigned the weights as follows:

$$v(\hat{w}_i^t) = \begin{cases} 1 - \mathrm{AD}(\hat{w}_i^t, w_i^t) & \text{if } \hat{w}_i^t \ne w_i^t \\ 1 & \text{otherwise.} \end{cases}$$

In other words, the weights penalize the corrected words proportionally to the affix distance from the original words.

While computing the n-gram precision, two matching n-grams $(\hat{w}_1^t, \dots \hat{w}_n^t)$ and $(w_1^r, \dots w_n^r)$ contribute to the n-gram precision with a score of

$$s(w_1^t, \dots, w_n^t) = \sum_{i=1}^{n} v(\hat{w}_i^t) \ / \ n$$

instead of one as it is in the standard BLEU. The rest of the BLEU score computation remains unchanged. While using multiple reference translation, the matching is done for each of the reference sentence, and while computing the n-gram precision, the reference sentences with the highest weight is chosen. The computation of the n-gram precision is illustrated in Figure 1.

direction	BLEU	METEOR	tBLEU
en-cs	.781	.860	.787
en-de	.835	.868	.850
en-es	.875	.878	.884
en-fr	.887	.906	.906
from English	.844	.878	.857

Table 1: System level Pearson's correlation with the human judgment for systems translating from English computed on the WMT13 dataset.

direction	BLEU	METEOR	tBLEU
cs-en	.925	.985	.927
de-en	.916	.962	.917
es-en	.957	.968	.953
fr-en	.940	.983	.933
to English	.923	.974	.935

Table 2: System level Pearson's correlation with the human judgment for systems translating to English computed on the WMT13 dataset.

4 Evaluation

We evaluated the proposed metric on the dataset used for the WMT13 Metrics Task (Macháček and Bojar, 2013). The dataset consists of 135 systems' outputs in 10 directions (5 into English 5 out of English). Each system's output and the reference translation contain 3000 sentences. According to the WMT14 guidelines, we report the the Pearson's correlation coefficient instead of the Spearman's coefficient that was used in the last years.

Twenty values of the affix distance threshold were tested in order to estimate what is the most suitable threshold setting. We report only the system level correlation because the metric is designed to compare only the whole system outputs.

5 Results

The tBLEU metric generally improves the correlation with human judgment over the standard BLEU metric for directions from English to languages with richer inflection.

Examining the various threshold values showed that dependence between the affix distance threshold and the correlation with the human judgment varies for different language pairs (Figure 2). For translation from English to morphologically richer languages than English – Czech, German, Spanish and French – using the tBLEU metric increased the correlation over the standard BLEU. For Czech the correlation quickly decreases for threshold values bigger than 0.1, whereas for the other languages it still grows. We hypothesize this because the big morphological changes in Czech can entirely change the meaning.

For translation to English, the correlation slightly increases with the increasing threshold value for translation from French and Spanish, but decreases for Czech and German.

There are different optimal affix distance thresholds for different language pairs. However, the threshold of 0.05 was used for our WMT14 submission because it had the best average correlation on the WMT13 data set. Tables 1 and 2 show the results of the tBLEU for the particular language pairs for threshold 0.05. While compared to the BLEU score, the correlation is slightly higher for translation from English and approximately the same for translation to English.

The results on the WMT14 dataset did not show any improvement over the BLEU metric. The reason of the results will be further examined.

6 Conclusion and Future Work

We presented tBLEU, a language-independent MT metric based on the standard BLEU metric. It introduced the affix distance – relative edit distances of prefixes and suffixes of two string after removing their longest common substring. Finding a matching between translation and reference sentences with respect to this matching allows a penalized substitution of words which has been most likely wrongly inflected and therefore less penalizes errors in inflection.

This metric achieves a higher correlation with the human judgment than the standard BLEU score for translation to morphological richer languages without the necessity to employ any language specific tools.

In future work, we would like to improve word alignment between test and reference translations by introducing word position and potentially other features, and implement tBLEU in MERT to examine its impact on system tuning.

7 Acknowledgements

This research has been funded by the Czech Science Foundation (grant n. P103/12/G084) and the EU FP7 project Khresmoi (contract no. 257528).

References

Ondřej Bojar, Kamil Kos, and David Mareček. 2010. Tackling sparse data issue in machine translation evaluation. In *Proceedings of the ACL 2010 Conference Short Papers*, pages 86–91. Association for Computational Linguistics.

Sherri Condon, Gregory A Sanders, Dan Parvaz, Alan Rubenstein, Christy Doran, John Aberdeen, and Beatrice Oshika. 2009. Normalization for automated metrics: English and arabic speech translation. *Proceedings of MT Summit XII. Association for Machine Translation in the Americas, Ottawa, ON, Canada.*

Michael Denkowski and Alon Lavie. 2011. Meteor 1.3: Automatic metric for reliable optimization and evaluation of machine translation systems. In *Proceedings of the Sixth Workshop on Statistical Machine Translation*, WMT '11, pages 85–91, Stroudsburg, PA, USA. Association for Computational Linguistics.

George Doddington. 2002. Automatic evaluation of machine translation quality using n-gram co-occurrence statistics. In *Proceedings of the Second International Conference on Human Language Technology Research*, HLT '02, pages 138–145, San Francisco, CA, USA. Morgan Kaufmann Publishers Inc.

Mark Fishel, Rico Sennrich, Maja Popović, and Ondřej Bojar. 2012. Terrorcat: a translation error categorization-based mt quality metric. In *Proceedings of the Seventh Workshop on Statistical Machine Translation*, pages 64–70. Association for Computational Linguistics.

Gregor Leusch, Nicola Ueffing, Hermann Ney, et al. 2003. A novel string-to-string distance measure with applications to machine translation evaluation. In *Proceedings of MT Summit IX*, pages 240–247. Citeseer.

Matouš Macháček and Ondřej Bojar. 2013. Results of the WMT13 metrics shared task. In *Proceedings of the Eighth Workshop on Statistical Machine Translation*, pages 45–51, Sofia, Bulgaria, August. Association for Computational Linguistics.

James Munkres. 1957. Algorithms for the assignment and transportation problems. *Journal of the Society for Industrial & Applied Mathematics*, 5(1):32–38.

Franz Josef Och. 2003. Minimum error rate training in statistical machine translation. In *Proceedings of the 41st Annual Meeting on Association for Computational Linguistics*, pages 160–167, Sapporo, Japan.

Kishore Papineni, Salim Roukos, Todd Ward, and Wei-Jing Zhu. 2002. Bleu: a method for automatic evaluation of machine translation. In *Proceedings of the 40th annual meeting on association for computational linguistics*, pages 311–318. Association for Computational Linguistics.

Matthew Snover, Bonnie Dorr, Richard Schwartz, Linnea Micciulla, and John Makhoul. 2006. A study of translation edit rate with targeted human annotation. In *Proceedings of association for machine translation in the Americas*, pages 223–231.

BEER: BEtter Evaluation as Ranking

Miloš Stanojević
ILLC
University of Amsterdam
mstanojevic@uva.nl

Khalil Sima'an
ILLC
University of Amsterdam
k.simaan@uva.nl

Abstract

We present the UvA-ILLC submission of the BEER metric to WMT 14 metrics task. BEER is a sentence level metric that can incorporate a large number of features combined in a linear model. Novel contributions are (1) efficient tuning of a large number of features for maximizing correlation with *human system ranking*, and (2) novel features that give smoother sentence level scores.

1 Introduction

The quality of sentence level (also called segment level) evaluation metrics in machine translation is often considered inferior to the quality of corpus (or system) level metrics. Yet, a sentence level metrics has important advantages as it:

1. provides an informative score to individual translations
2. is assumed by MT tuning algorithms (Hopkins and May, 2011).
3. facilitates easier statistical testing using sign test or t-test (Collins et al., 2005)

We think that the root cause for most of the difficulty in creating a good sentence level metric is the sparseness of the features often used. Consider the n-gram counting metrics (BLEU (Papineni et al., 2002)): counts of higher order n-grams are usually rather small, if not zero, when counted at the individual sentence level. Metrics based on such counts are brittle at the sentence level even when they might be good at the corpus level. Ideally we should have features of varying granularity that we can optimize on the actual evaluation task: relative ranking of system outputs.

Therefore, in this paper we explore two kinds of less sparse features:

Character n-grams are features at the sub-word level that provide evidence for translation adequacy - for example whether the stem is correctly translated,

Abstract ordering patterns found in tree factorizations of permutations into Permutation Trees (PETs) (Zhang and Gildea, 2007), including non-lexical alignment patterns.

The BEER metric combines features of both kinds (presented in Section 2).

With the growing number of adequacy and ordering features we need a model that facilitates efficient training. We would like to train for optimal Kendall τ correlation with rankings by human evaluators. The models in the literature tackle this problem by

1. training for another similar objective – e.g., tuning for absolute adequacy and fluency scores instead on rankings, or
2. training for rankings directly but with metaheuristic approaches like hill-climbing, or
3. training for pairwise rankings using learning-to-rank techniques

Approach (1) has two disadvantages. One is the inconsistency between the training and the testing objectives. The other, is that absolute rankings are not reliable enough because humans are better at giving relative than absolute judgments (see WMT manual evaluations (Callison-Burch et al., 2007)).

Approach (2) does not allow integrating a large number of features which makes it less attractive.

Approach (3) allows integration of a large number of features whose weights could be determined in an elegant machine learning framework. The output of learning in this approach can be either a function that ranks all hypotheses directly (global ranking model) or a function that assigns a score

Proceedings of the Ninth Workshop on Statistical Machine Translation, pages 414–419,
Baltimore, Maryland USA, June 26–27, 2014.

to each hypothesis individually which can be used for ranking (local ranking model) (Li, 2011). Local ranking models are preferable because they provide absolute distance between hypotheses like most existing evaluation metrics.

In this paper we follow the learning-to-rank approach which produces a local ranking model in a similar way to PRO MT systems tuning (Hopkins and May, 2011).

2 Model

Our model is a fairly simple linear interpolation of feature functions, which is easy to train and simple to interpret. The model determines the *similarity* of the hypothesis h to the reference translation r by assigning a weight w_i to each feature $\phi_i(h, r)$. The linear scoring function is given by:

$$score(h, r) = \sum_i w_i \times \phi_i(h, r) = \vec{w} \cdot \vec{\phi}$$

2.1 Adequacy features

The features used are precision P, recall R and F1-score F for different counts:

$P_{function}$, $R_{function}$, $F_{function}$ on matched function words

$P_{content}$, $R_{content}$, $F_{content}$ on matched content words (all non-function words)

P_{all}, R_{all}, F_{all} on matched words of any type

$P_{char\ n-gram}$, $R_{char\ n-gram}$, $F_{char\ n-gram}$ matching of the character n-grams

By differentiating function and non-function words we might have a better estimate of which words are more important and which are less. The last, but as we will see later the most important, adequacy feature is matching character n-grams, originally proposed in (Yang et al., 2013). This can reward some translations even if they did not get the morphology completely right. Many metrics solve this problem by using stemmers, but using features based on character n-grams is more robust since it does not depend on the quality of the stemmer. For character level n-grams we can afford higher-order n-grams with less risk of sparse counts as on word n-grams. In our experiments we used character n-grams for size up to 6 which makes the total number of all adequacy features 27.

2.2 Ordering features

To evaluate word order we follow (Isozaki et al., 2010; Birch and Osborne, 2010) in representing reordering as a permutation and then measuring the distance to the ideal monotone permutation. Here we take one feature from previous work – Kendall τ distance from the monotone permutation. This metrics on the permutation level has been shown to have high correlation with human judgment on language pairs with very different word order.

Additionally, we add novel features with an even less sparse view of word order by exploiting hierarchical structure that exists in permutations (Zhang and Gildea, 2007). The trees that represent this structure are called PETs (PErmutation Trees – see the next subsection). Metrics defined over PETs usually have a better estimate of long distance reorderings (Stanojević and Sima'an, 2013). Here we use simple versions of these metrics:

Δ_{count} the ratio between the number of different permutation trees (PETs) (Zhang and Gildea, 2007) that could be built for the given permutation over the number of trees that could be built if permutation was completely monotone (there is a perfect word order).

$\Delta_{[\,]}$ ratio of the number of monotone nodes in a PET to the maximum possible number of nodes – the lenght of the sentence n.

$\Delta_{<>}$ ratio of the number of inverted nodes to n

$\Delta_{=4}$ ratio of the number of nodes with branching factor 4 to n

$\Delta_{>4}$ ratio of the number of nodes with branching factor bigger than 4 to n

2.3 Why features based on PETs?

PETs are recursive factorizations of permutations into their minimal units. We refer the reader to (Zhang and Gildea, 2007) for formal treatment of PETs and efficient algorithms for their construction. Here we present them informally to exploit them for presenting novel ordering metrics.

A PET is a tree structure with the nodes decorated with operators (like in ITG) that are themselves permutations that cannot be factorized any further into contiguous sub-parts (called operators). As an example, see the PET in Figure 1a. This PET has one 4-branching node, one inverted

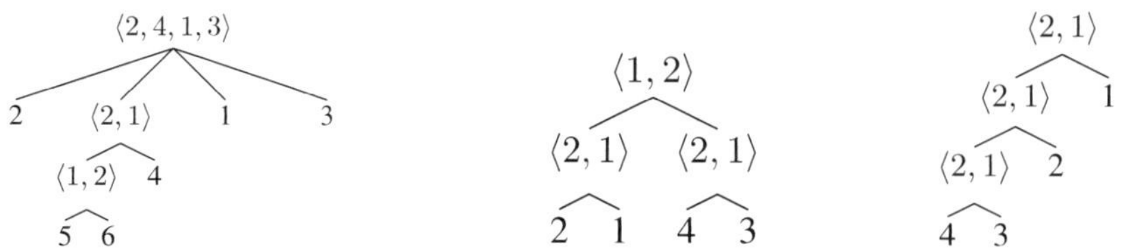

(a) Complex PET (b) PET with inversions (c) Fully inverted PET

Figure 1: Examples of PETs

node and one monotone. The nodes are decorated by *operators* that stand for a permutation of the direct children of the node.

PETs have two important properties that make them attractive for observing ordering: firstly, the PET operators show the minimal units of ordering that constitute the permutation itself, and secondly the higher level operators capture hidden patterns of ordering that cannot be observed without factorization. Statistics over patterns of ordering using PETs are non-lexical and hence far less sparse than word or character n-gram statistics.

In PETs, the minimal operators on the node stand for ordering that cannot be broken down any further. The binary monotone operator is the simplest, binary inverted is the second in line, followed by operators of length four like $\langle 2, 4, 1, 3\rangle$ (Wu, 1997), and then operators longer than four. The larger the branching factor under a PET node (the length of the operator on that node) the more complex the ordering. Hence, we devise possible branching feature functions over the operator length for the nodes in PETs:

- factor 2 - with two features: $\Delta_{[\,]}$ and $\Delta_{<>}$ (there are no nodes with factor 3 (Wu, 1997))
- factor 4 - feature $\Delta_{=4}$
- factor bigger than 4 - feature $\Delta_{>4}$

All of the mentioned PETs node features, except $\Delta_{[\,]}$ and Δ_{count}, signify the wrong word order but of different magnitude. Ideally all nodes in a PET would be binary monotone, but when that is not the case we are able to quantify how far we are from that ideal binary monotone PET.

In contrast with word n-grams used in other metrics, counts over PET operators are far less sparse on the sentence level and could be more reliable. Consider permutations 2143 and 4321 and their corresponding PETs in Figure 1b and 1c. None of them has any exact n-gram matched (we ignore unigrams now). But, it is clear that 2143 is somewhat better since it has at least some words in more or less the right order. These "abstract n-grams" pertaining to correct ordering of full phrases could be counted using $\Delta_{[\,]}$ which would recognize that on top of the PET in 1b there is the monotone node unlike the PET in 1c which has no monotone nodes at all.

3 Tuning for human judgment

The task of correlation with human judgment on the sentence level is usually posed in the following way (Macháček and Bojar, 2013):

- Translate all source sentences using the available machine translation systems
- Let human evaluators rank them by quality compared to the reference translation
- Each evaluation metric should do the same task of ranking the hypothesis translations
- The metric with higher Kendall τ correlation with human judgment is considered better

Let us take any pair of hypotheses that have the same reference r where one is better (h_{good}) than the other one (h_{bad}) as judged by human evaluator. In order for our metric to give the same ranking as human judges do, it needs to give the higher score to the h_{good} hypothesis. Given that our model is linear we can derive:

$$\begin{aligned} score(h_{good}, r) > score(h_{bad}, r) &\Leftrightarrow \\ \vec{w} \cdot \vec{\phi}_{good} > \vec{w} \cdot \vec{\phi}_{bad} &\Leftrightarrow \\ \vec{w} \cdot \vec{\phi}_{good} - \vec{w} \cdot \vec{\phi}_{bad} > 0 &\Leftrightarrow \\ \vec{w} \cdot (\vec{\phi}_{good} - \vec{\phi}_{bad}) > 0 & \\ \vec{w} \cdot (\vec{\phi}_{bad} - \vec{\phi}_{good}) < 0 & \end{aligned}$$

The most important part here are the last two equations. Using them we formulate ranking problem as a problem of binary classification: the positive training instance would have feature values

$\vec{\phi}_{good} - \vec{\phi}_{bad}$ and the negative training instance would have feature values $\vec{\phi}_{bad} - \vec{\phi}_{good}$. This trick was used in PRO (Hopkins and May, 2011) but for the different task:

- tuning the model of the SMT system
- objective function was an evaluation metric

Given this formulation of the training instances we can train the classifier using pairs of hypotheses. Note that even though it uses pairs of hypotheses for training in the evaluation time it uses only one hypothesis – it does not require the pair of hypotheses to compare them. The score of the classifier is interpreted as confidence that the hypothesis is a good translation. This differs from the majority of earlier work which we explain in Section 6.

4 Experiments on WMT12 data

We conducted experiments for the metric which in total has 33 features (27 for adequacy and 6 for word order). Some of the features in the metric depend on external sources of information. For function words we use listings that are created for many languages and are distributed with METEOR toolkit (Denkowski and Lavie, 2011). The permutations are extracted using METEOR aligner which does fuzzy matching using resources such as WordNet, paraphrase tables and stemmers. METEOR is not used for any scoring, but only for aligning hypothesis and reference.

For training we used the data from WMT13 human evaluation of the systems (Macháček and Bojar, 2013). Before evaluation, all data was lowercased and tokenized. After preprocessing, we extract training examples for our binary classifier. The number of non-tied human judgments per language pair are shown in Table 1. Each human judgment produces two training instances : one positive and one negative. For learning we use regression implementation in the Vowpal Wabbit toolkit [1].

Tuned metric is tested on the human evaluated data from WMT12 (Callison-Burch et al., 2012) for correlation with the human judgment. As baseline we used one of the best ranked metrics on the sentence level evaluations from previous WMT tasks – METEOR (Denkowski and Lavie, 2011). The results are presented in the Table 2. The presented results are computed using definition of Kendall τ from the WMT12 (Callison-Burch et al., 2012) so the scores could be compared with other metrics on the same dataset that were reported in the proceedings of that year (Callison-Burch et al., 2012).

[1] https://github.com/JohnLangford/vowpal_wabbit

language pair	#comparisons
cs-en	85469
de-en	128668
es-en	67832
fr-en	80741
ru-en	151422
en-cs	102842
en-de	77286
en-es	60464
en-fr	100783
en-ru	87323

Table 1: Number of human judgments in WMT13

language pair	BEER with paraphrases	BEER without paraphrases	METEOR
en-cs	**0.194**	0.190	0.152
en-fr	0.257	0.250	**0.262**
en-de	**0.228**	0.217	0.180
en-es	0.227	**0.235**	0.201
cs-en	**0.215**	0.213	0.205
fr-en	**0.270**	0.254	0.249
de-en	**0.290**	0.271	0.273
es-en	**0.267**	0.249	0.247

Table 2: Kendall τ correleation on WMT12 data

The results show that BEER with and without paraphrase support outperforms METEOR (and almost all other metrics on WMT12 metrics task) on the majority of language pairs. Paraphrase support matters mostly when the target language is English, but even in language pairs where it does not help significantly it can be useful.

5 WMT14 evaluation task results

In Table 4 and Table 3 you can see the results of top 5 ranked metrics on the segment level evaluation task of WMT14. In 5 out of 10 language pairs BEER was ranked the first, on 4 the second best and on one third best metric. The cases where it failed to win the first place are:

- against DISCOTK-PARTY-TUNED on * - English except Hindi-English. DISCOTK-PARTY-TUNED participated only in evaluation of English which suggests that it uses some language specific components which is not the case with the current version of BEER
- against METEOR and AMBER on English-Hindi. The reason for this is simply that we

Direction	en-fr	en-de	en-hi	en-cs	en-ru
BEER	**.295**	**.258**	.250	**.344**	**.440**
METEOR	.278	.233	.264	.318	.427
AMBER	.261	.224	**.286**	.302	.397
BLEU-NRC	.257	.193	.234	.297	.391
APAC	.255	.201	.203	.292	.388

Table 3: Kendall τ correlations on the WMT14 human judgements when translating out of English.

Direction	fr-en	de-en	hi-en	cs-en	ru-en
DISCOTK-PARTY-TUNED	**.433**	**.381**	.434	**.328**	**.364**
BEER	.417	.337	**.438**	.284	.337
REDCOMBSENT	.406	.338	.417	.284	.343
REDCOMBSYSSENT	.408	.338	.416	.282	.343
METEOR	.406	.334	.420	.282	.337

Table 4: Kendall τ correlations on the WMT14 human judgements when translating into English.

did not have the data to tune our metric for Hindi. Even by treating Hindi as English we manage to get high in the rankings for this language.

From metrics that participated in all language pairs on the sentence level on average BEER has the best correlation with the human judgment.

6 Related work

The main contribution of our metric is a linear combination of features with far less sparse statistics than earlier work. In particular, we employ novel ordering features over PETs, a range of character n-gram features for adequancy, and direct tuning for human ranking.

There are in the literature three main approaches for tuning the machine translation metrics.

Approach 1 SPEDE (Wang and Manning, 2012), metric of (Specia and Giménez, 2010), ROSE-reg (Song and Cohn, 2011), ABS metric of (Padó et al., 2009) and many others train their regression models on the data that has absolute scores for adequacy, fluency or post-editing and then test on the ranking problem. This is sometimes called pointwise approach to learning-to-rank. In contrast our metric is trained for ranking and tested on ranking.

Approach 2 METEOR is tuned for the ranking and tested on the ranking like our metric but the tuning method is different. METEOR has a non-linear model which is hard to tune with gradient based methods so instead they tune their parameters by hill-climbing (Lavie and Agarwal, 2008). This not only reduces the number of features that could be used but also restricts the fine tuning of the existing small number of parameters.

Approach 3 Some methods, like ours, allow training of a large number of parameters for ranking. Global ranking models that directly rank hypotheses are used in ROSE-rank (Song and Cohn, 2011) and PAIR metric of (Padó et al., 2009). Our work is more similar to the training method for local ranking models that give score directly (as it is usually expected from an evaluation metric) which was originally proposed in (Ye et al., 2007) and later applied in (Duh, 2008) and (Yang et al., 2013).

7 Conclusion and future plans

We have shown the advantages of combining many simple features in a tunable linear model of MT evaluation metric. Unlike majority of the previous work we create a framework for training large number of features on human rankings and at the same time as a result of tuning produce a score based metric which does not require two (or more) hypotheses for comparison. The features that we used are selected for reducing sparseness on the sentence level. Together the smooth features and the learning algorithm produce the metric that has a very high correlation with human judgment.

For future research we plan to investigate some more linguistically inspired features and also explore how this metric could be tuned for better tuning of statistical machine translation systems.

Acknowledgments

This work is supported by STW grant nr. 12271 and NWO VICI grant nr. 277-89-002.

References

Alexandra Birch and Miles Osborne. 2010. LRscore for Evaluating Lexical and Reordering Quality in MT. In *Proceedings of the Joint Fifth Workshop on Statistical Machine Translation and MetricsMATR*, pages 327–332, Uppsala, Sweden, July. Association for Computational Linguistics.

Chris Callison-Burch, Cameron Fordyce, Philipp Koehn, Christof Monz, and Josh Schroeder. 2007.

(Meta-) Evaluation of Machine Translation. In *Proceedings of the Second Workshop on Statistical Machine Translation*, StatMT '07, pages 136–158, Stroudsburg, PA, USA. Association for Computational Linguistics.

Chris Callison-Burch, Philipp Koehn, Christof Monz, Matt Post, Radu Soricut, and Lucia Specia. 2012. Findings of the 2012 Workshop on Statistical Machine Translation. In *Proceedings of the Seventh Workshop on Statistical Machine Translation*, pages 10–51, Montréal, Canada, June. Association for Computational Linguistics.

Michael Collins, Philipp Koehn, and Ivona Kučerová. 2005. Clause Restructuring for Statistical Machine Translation. In *Proceedings of the 43rd Annual Meeting on Association for Computational Linguistics*, ACL '05, pages 531–540, Stroudsburg, PA, USA. Association for Computational Linguistics.

Michael Denkowski and Alon Lavie. 2011. Meteor 1.3: Automatic Metric for Reliable Optimization and Evaluation of Machine Translation Systems. In *Proceedings of the EMNLP 2011 Workshop on Statistical Machine Translation.*

Kevin Duh. 2008. Ranking vs. Regression in Machine Translation Evaluation. In *Proceedings of the Third Workshop on Statistical Machine Translation*, StatMT '08, pages 191–194, Stroudsburg, PA, USA. Association for Computational Linguistics.

Mark Hopkins and Jonathan May. 2011. Tuning as Ranking. In *Proceedings of the 2011 Conference on Empirical Methods in Natural Language Processing*, pages 1352–1362, Edinburgh, Scotland, UK., July. Association for Computational Linguistics.

Hideki Isozaki, Tsutomu Hirao, Kevin Duh, Katsuhito Sudoh, and Hajime Tsukada. 2010. Automatic Evaluation of Translation Quality for Distant Language Pairs. In *Proceedings of the 2010 Conference on Empirical Methods in Natural Language Processing*, EMNLP '10, pages 944–952, Stroudsburg, PA, USA. Association for Computational Linguistics.

Alon Lavie and Abhaya Agarwal. 2008. METEOR: An Automatic Metric for MT Evaluation with High Levels of Correlation with Human Judgments. In *Proceedings of the ACL 2008 Workshop on Statistical Machine Translation.*

Hang Li. 2011. *Learning to Rank for Information Retrieval and Natural Language Processing*. Synthesis Lectures on Human Language Technologies. Morgan & Claypool Publishers.

Matouš Macháček and Ondřej Bojar. 2013. Results of the WMT13 Metrics Shared Task. In *Proceedings of the Eighth Workshop on Statistical Machine Translation*, pages 45–51, Sofia, Bulgaria, August. Association for Computational Linguistics.

Sebastian Padó, Michel Galley, Dan Jurafsky, and Christopher D. Manning. 2009. Textual Entailment Features for Machine Translation Evaluation. In *Proceedings of the Fourth Workshop on Statistical Machine Translation*, StatMT '09, pages 37–41, Stroudsburg, PA, USA. Association for Computational Linguistics.

Kishore Papineni, Salim Roukos, Todd Ward, and Wei-Jing Zhu. 2002. BLEU: A Method for Automatic Evaluation of Machine Translation. In *Proceedings of the 40th Annual Meeting on Association for Computational Linguistics*, ACL '02, pages 311–318, Stroudsburg, PA, USA. Association for Computational Linguistics.

Xingyi Song and Trevor Cohn. 2011. Regression and Ranking based Optimisation for Sentence Level MT Evaluation. In *Proceedings of the Sixth Workshop on Statistical Machine Translation*, pages 123–129, Edinburgh, Scotland, July. Association for Computational Linguistics.

Lucia Specia and Jesús Giménez. 2010. Combining Confidence Estimation and Reference-based Metrics for Segment-level MT Evaluation. In *Ninth Conference of the Association for Machine Translation in the Americas*, AMTA-2010, Denver, Colorado.

Miloš Stanojević and Khalil Sima'an. 2013. Evaluating Long Range Reordering with Permutation-Forests. In *ILLC Prepublication Series, PP-2013-14*. University of Amsterdam.

Mengqiu Wang and Christopher D. Manning. 2012. SPEDE: Probabilistic Edit Distance Metrics for MT Evaluation. In *Proceedings of the Seventh Workshop on Statistical Machine Translation*, WMT '12, pages 76–83, Stroudsburg, PA, USA. Association for Computational Linguistics.

Dekai Wu. 1997. Stochastic inversion transduction grammars and bilingual parsing of parallel corpora. *Computational linguistics*, 23(3):377–403.

Muyun Yang, Junguo Zhu, Sheng Li, and Tiejun Zhao. 2013. Fusion of Word and Letter Based Metrics for Automatic MT Evaluation. In *Proceedings of the Twenty-Third International Joint Conference on Artificial Intelligence*, IJCAI'13, pages 2204–2210. AAAI Press.

Yang Ye, Ming Zhou, and Chin-Yew Lin. 2007. Sentence Level Machine Translation Evaluation As a Ranking Problem: One Step Aside from BLEU. In *Proceedings of the Second Workshop on Statistical Machine Translation*, StatMT '07, pages 240–247, Stroudsburg, PA, USA. Association for Computational Linguistics.

Hao Zhang and Daniel Gildea. 2007. Factorization of synchronous context-free grammars in linear time. In *In NAACL Workshop on Syntax and Structure in Statistical Translation (SSST.*

RED: DCU-CASICT Participation in WMT2014 Metrics Task

Xiaofeng Wu[†], Hui Yu[*], Qun Liu[†*]
[†]CNGL Centre for Global Intelligent Content
School of Computing, Dublin City University
Dublin 9, Ireland
[*]Key Laboratory of Intelligent Information Processing
Institute of Computing Technology, Chinese Academy of Sciences
Beijing, China
{xiaofengwu,qliu}@computing.dcu.ie, yuhui@ict.ac.cn

Abstract

Based on the last year's DCU-CASIST participation on WMT metrics task, we further improve our model in the following ways: 1) parameter tuning 2) support languages other than English. We tuned our system on all the data of WMT 2010, 2012 and 2013. The tuning results as well as the WMT 2014 test results are reported.

1 Introduction

Automatic evaluation plays a more and more important role in the evolution of machine translation. There are roughly two categories can be seen: namely lexical information based and structural information based.

1) Lexical information based approaches, among which, BLEU (?), Translation Error Rate (TER) (?) and METEOR (?) are the most popular ones and, with simplicity as their merits, cannot adequately reflect the structural level similarity.

2) A lot of structural level based methods have been exploited to overcome the weakness of the lexical based methods, including Syntactic Tree Model(STM)(?), a constituent tree based approach, and Head Word Chain Model(HWCM)(?), a dependency tree based approach. Both of the methods compute the similarity between the sub-trees of the hypothesis and the reference. Owczarzak et al (?; ?; ?) presented a method using the Lexical-Functional Grammar (LFG) dependency tree. MAXSIM (?) and the method proposed by Zhu et al (?) also employed the syntactic information in association with lexical information. As we know that the hypothesis is potentially noisy, and these errors are enlarged through the parsing process. Thus the power of syntactic information could be considerably weakened.

In this paper, based on our attempt on WMT metrics task 2013 (?), we propose a metrics named RED (REference Dependency based automatic evaluation method). Our metrics employs only the reference dependency tree which contains both the lexical and syntactic information, leaving the hypothesis side unparsed to avoid error propagation.

2 Parameter Tuning

In RED, we use $F\text{-}score$ as our final score. $F\text{-}score$ is calculated by Formula (1), where α is a value between 0 and 1.

$$F\text{-}score = \frac{precision \cdot recall}{\alpha \cdot precision + (1-\alpha) \cdot recall} \quad (1)$$

The dependency tree of the reference and the string of the translation are used to calculate the precision and recall. In order to calculate precision, the number of the dep-ngrams (the ngrams obtained from dependency tree[1]) should be given, but there is no dependency tree for the translation in our method. We know that the number of dep-ngrams has an approximate linear relationship with the length of the sentence, so we use the length of the translation to replace the number of the dep-ngrams in the translation dependency tree. Recall can be calculated directly since we know the number of the dep-ngrams in the reference. The precision and recall are computed as follows.

$$precision_n = \frac{\sum_{d \in D_n} p_{(d,hyp)}}{len_h}$$

$$recall_n = \frac{\sum_{d \in D_n} p_{(d,hyp)}}{count_{n(ref)}}$$

D_n is the set of dep-ngrams with the length of n. len_h is the length of the translation. $count_{n(ref)}$ is the number of the dep-ngrams with the length of n in the reference. $p_{(d,hpy)}$ is 0 if there is no match and a positive number between 0 and 1 otherwise(?).

[1]We define two types of dep-ngrams: 1) the head word chain(?); 2) fix-floating(?))

Proceedings of the Ninth Workshop on Statistical Machine Translation, pages 420–425,
Baltimore, Maryland USA, June 26–27, 2014.

The final score of RED is achieved using Formula (2), in which a weighted sum of the dep-ngrams' $F\text{-}score$ is calculated. w_{ngram} ($0 \leq w_{ngram} \leq 1$) is the weight of dep-ngram with the length of n. $F\text{-}score_n$ is the $F\text{-}score$ for the dep-ngrams with the length of n.

$$RED = \sum_{n=1}^{N}(w_{ngram} \times F\text{-}score_n) \quad (2)$$

Other parameters to be tuned includes:

- Stem and Synonym

  Stem(?) and synonym (WordNet[2]) are introduced with the following three steps. First, we obtain the alignment with METEOR Aligner (?) in which not only exact match but also stem and synonym are considered. We use stem, synonym and exact match as the three match modules. Second, the alignment is used to match for a dep-ngram. We think the dep-ngram can match with the translation if the following conditions are satisfied. 1) Each of the words in the dep-ngram has a matched word in the translation according to the alignment; 2) The words in dep-ngram and the matched words in translation appear in the same order; 3) The matched words in translation must be continuous if the dep-ngram is a fixed-floating ngram. At last, the match module score of a dep-ngram is calculated according to Formula (3). Different match modules have different effects, so we give them different weights.

$$s_{mod} = \frac{\sum_{i=1}^{n} w_{m_i}}{n}, \quad 0 \leq w_{m_i} \leq 1 \quad (3)$$

  m_i is the match module (exact, stem or synonym) of the ith word in a dep-ngram. w_{m_i} is the match module weight of the ith word in a dep-ngram. n is the number of words in a dep-ngram.

- Paraphrase

  When introducing paraphrase, we don't consider the dependency tree of the reference, because paraphrases may not be contained in the head word chain and fixed-floating structures. Therefore we first obtain the alignment with METEOR Aligner, only considering paraphrase; Then, the matched paraphrases are extracted from the alignment and defined as paraphrase-ngram. The score of a paraphrase is $1 \times w_{par}$, where w_{par} is the weight of paraphrase-ngram.

- Function word

  We introduce a parameter w_{fun} ($0 \leq w_{fun} \leq 1$) to distinguish function words and content words. w_{fun} is the weight of function words. The function word score of a dep-ngram or paraphrase-ngram is computed according to Formula (4).

$$s_{fun} = \frac{C_{fun} \times w_{fun} + C_{con} \times (1 - w_{fun})}{C_{fun} + C_{con}} \quad (4)$$

  C_{fun} is the number of function words in the dep-ngram or paraphrase-ngram. C_{con} is the number of content words in the dep-ngram or paraphrase-ngram.

$$REDp = \sum_{n=1}^{N}(w_{ngram} \times F\text{-}score_{pn}) \quad (5)$$

$$F\text{-}score_p = \frac{precision_p \cdot recall_p}{\alpha \cdot precision_p + (1-\alpha) \cdot recall_p} \quad (6)$$

$precision_p$ and $recall_P$ in Formula (6) are calculated as follows.

$$precision_p = \frac{score_{par_n} + score_{dep_n}}{len_h}$$

$$recall_p = \frac{score_{par_n} + score_{dep_n}}{count_n(ref) + count_n(par)}$$

len_h is the length of the translation. $count_{n(ref)}$ is the number of the dep-ngrams with the length of n in the reference. $count_n(par)$ is the number of paraphrases with length of n in reference. $score_{par_n}$ is the match score of paraphrase-ngrams with the length of n. $score_{dep_n}$ is the match score of dep-ngrams with the length of n. $score_{par_n}$ and $score_{dep_n}$ are calculated as follows.

$$score_{par_n} = \sum_{par \in P_n} (1 \times w_{par} \times s_{fum})$$

$$score_{dep_n} = \sum_{d \in D_n} (p_{(d,hyp)} \times s_{mod} \times s_{fun})$$

[2]http://wordnet.princeton.edu/

Metrics		BLEU	TER	HWCM	METEOR	RED	RED-sent	RED-syssent
WMT 2010	cs-en	0.255	0.253	0.245	0.319	0.328	**0.342**	**0.342**
	de-en	0.275	0.291	0.267	0.348	0.361	0.371	**0.375**
	es-en	0.280	0.263	0.259	0.326	0.333	0.344	**0.347**
	fr-en	0.220	0.211	0.244	0.275	0.283	**0.329**	0.328
	ave	0.257	0.254	0.253	0.317	0.326	0.346	**0.348**
WMT 2012	cs-en	0.157	-	0.158	0.212	0.165	0.218	0.212
	de-en	0.191	-	0.207	0.275	0.218	**0.283**	0.279
	es-en	0.189	-	0.203	0.249	0.203	0.255	**0.256**
	fr-en	0.210	-	0.204	0.251	0.221	0.250	**0.253**
	ave	0.186	-	0.193	0.246	0.201	**0.251**	0.250
WMT 2013	cs-en	0.199	-	0.153	**0.265**	0.228	0.260	0.256
	de-en	0.220	-	0.182	0.293	0.267	**0.298**	0.297
	es-en	0.259	-	0.220	0.324	0.312	**0.330**	0.326
	fr-en	0.224	-	0.194	0.264	0.257	**0.267**	0.266
	ru-en	0.162	-	0.136	0.239	0.200	**0.262**	0.225
	ave	0.212	-	0.177	0.277	0.252	**0.283**	0.274
WMT 2014	hi-en	-	-	-	**0.420**	-	0.383	0.386
	de-en	-	-	-	0.334	-	0.336	**0.338**
	cs-en	-	-	-	0.282	-	**0.283**	**0.283**
	fr-en	-	-	-	**0.406**	-	0.403	0.404
	ru-en	-	-	-	**0.337**	-	0.328	0.329
	ave	-	-	-	**0.355**	-	0.347	0.348

Table 1: Sentence level correlations tuned on WMT 2010, 2012 and 2013; tested on WMT 2014. The value in bold is the best result in each raw. *ave* stands for the average result of the language pairs on each year. RED stands for our untuned system, RED-sent is G.sent.2, RED-syssent is G.sent.1

P_n is the set of paraphrase-ngrams with the length of n. D_n is the set of dep-ngrams with the length of n.

There are totally nine parameters in RED. We tried two parameter tuning strategies: Genetic search algorithm (**?**) and a Grid search over two subsets of parameters. The results of Grid search is more stable, therefore our final submission is based upon Grid search. We separate the 9 parameters into two subsets. When searching Subset 1, the parameters in Subset 2 are fixed, and vice versa. Several iterations are executed to finish the parameter tuning process. For system level coefficient score, we set two optimization goals: G.sys.1) to maximize the sum of Spearman's ρ rank correlation coefficient on system level and Kendall's τ correlation coefficient on sentence level or G.sys.2) only the former; For sentence level coefficient score, we also set two optimization goals: G.sent.1) the same as G.sys.1, G.sent.2) only the latter part of G.sys.1.

3 Experiments

In this section we report the experimental results of RED on the tuning set, which is the combination of WMT2010, WMT2012 and WMT2013 data set, as well as the test results on the WMT2014. Both the sentence level evaluation and the system level evaluation are conducted to assess the performance of our automatic metrics. At the sentence level evaluation, Kendall's rank correlation coefficient τ is used. At the system level evaluation, the Spearman's rank correlation coefficient ρ is used.

3.1 Data

There are four language pairs in WMT2010 and WMT2012 including German-English, Czech-English, French-English and Spanish-English. For WMT2013, except these 4 language pairs, there is also Russian-English. As the test set, WMT 2014 has also five language pairs, but the organizer removed Spanish-English and replace it with Hindi-English. For into-English tasks, we parsed the En-

Metrics		BLEU	TER	HWCM	METEOR	RED	RED-sys	RED-syssent
WMT 2010	cs-en	0.840	0.783	0.881	0.839	0.839	**0.937**	0.881
	de-en	0.881	0.892	0.905	0.927	0.933	**0.95**	0.948
	es-en	0.868	0.903	0.824	0.952	**0.969**	0.965	**0.969**
	fr-en	0.839	0.833	0.815	0.865	0.873	0.875	**0.905**
	ave	0.857	0.852	0.856	0.895	0.903	**0.931**	0.925
WMT 2012	cs-en	0.886	0.886	0.943	0.657	**1**	**1**	**1**
	de-en	0.671	0.624	0.762	0.885	0.759	0.935	**0.956**
	es-en	0.874	0.916	0.937	0.951	0.951	**0.965**	0.958
	fr-en	0.811	0.821	0.818	0.843	0.818	**0.871**	0.853
	ave	0.810	0.811	0.865	0.834	0.882	**0.942**	0.941
WMT 2013	cs-en	0.936	0.800	0.818	0.964	0.964	**0.982**	0.972
	de-en	0.895	0.833	0.816	0.961	0.951	0.958	**0.978**
	es-en	0.888	0.825	0.755	0.979	0.930	**0.979**	0.965
	fr-en	0.989	0.951	0.940	0.984	0.989	**0.995**	0.984
	ru-en	0.670	0.581	0.360	0.789	0.725	**0.847**	0.821
	ave	0.875	0.798	0.737	0.834	0.935	**0.952**	0.944
WMT 2014	hi-en	**0.956**	0.618	-	0.457	-	0.676	0.644
	de-en	0.831	0.774	-	0.926	-	0.897	**0.909**
	cs-en	0.908	0.977	-	0.980	-	0.989	**0.993**
	fr-en	0.952	0.952	-	0.975	-	**0.981**	0.980
	ru-en	0.774	0.796	-	0.792	-	**0.803**	0.797
	ave	**0.826**	0.740	-	0.784	-	0.784	0.770

Table 2: System level correlations tuned on WMT 2010, 2012 and 2013, tested on 2014. The value in bold is the best result in each raw. *ave* stands for the average result of the language pairs on each year. RED stands for our untuned system, RED-sys is G.sys.2, RED-syssent is G.sys.1

Metrics		BLEU	TER	METEOR	RED	RED-sent	RED-syssent
WMT 2010	en-fr	0.33	0.31	0.369	0.338	**0.390**	0.369
	en-de	0.15	0.08	0.166	0.141	**0.214**	0.185
WMT 2012	en-fr	-	-	0.26	0.171	**0.273**	0.266
	en-de	-	-	0.180	0.129	**0.200**	0.196
WMT 2013	en-fr	-	-	0.236	0.220	0.237	**0.239**
	en-de	-	-	0.203	0.185	0.215	**0.219**
WMT 2014	en-fr	-	-	0.278	-	**0.297**	0.293
	en-de	-	-	0.233	-	**0.236**	0.229

Table 3: Sentence level correlations tuned on WMT 2010, 2012 and 2013, and tested on 2014. The value in bold is the best result in each raw. RED stands for our untuned system, RED-sent is G.sent.2, RED-syssent is G.sent.1

glish reference into constituent tree by Berkeley parser and then converted the constituent tree into dependency tree by Penn2Malt [3]. We also conducted English-to-French and English-to-German experiments. The German and French dependency parser we used is Mate-Tool [4].

[3]http://w3.msi.vxu.se/ nivre/research/Penn2Malt.html
[4]https://code.google.com/p/mate-tools/

In the experiments, we compare the performance of our metric with the widely used lexical based metrics BLEU, TER, METEOR and a dependency based metrics HWCM. The results of RED are provided with exactly the same external resources like METEOR. The results of BLEU, TER and METOER are obtained from official report of WMT 2010, 2012, 2013 and 2014 (if they

Metrics		BLEU	TER	METEOR	RED	RED-sys	RED-syssent
WMT 2010	en-fr	0.89	0.89	0.912	0.881	**0.932**	0.928
	en-de	0.66	0.65	0.688	0.657	**0.734**	**0.734**
WMT 2012	en-fr	0.80	0.69	0.82	0.639	**0.914**	**0.914**
	en-de	0.22	**0.41**	0.180	0.143	0.243	0.243
WMT 2013	en-fr	0.897	0.912	0.924	0.914	0.931	**0.936**
	en-de	0.786	0.854	**0.879**	0.85	0.8	0.8
WMT 2014	en-fr	0.934	**0.953**	0.940	-	0.942	0.943
	en-de	0.065	**0.163**	0.128	-	0.047	0.047

Table 4: System level correlations for English to Franch and German, tuned on WMT 2010, 2012 and 2013; tested on WMT 2014. The value in bold is the best result in each raw. RED stands for our untuned system, RED-sys is G.sys.2, RED-syssent is G.sys.1

are available). The experiments of HWCM is performed by us.

3.2 Sentence-level Evaluation

Kendall's rank correlation coefficient τ is employed to evaluate the correlation of all the MT evaluation metrics and human judgements at the sentence level. A higher value of τ means a better ranking similarity with the human judges. The correlation scores of are shown in Table 1. Our method performs best when maximum length of dep-n-gram is set to 3, so we present only the results when the maximum length of dep-n-gram equals 3. From Table 1, we can see that: firstly, parameter tuning improve performance significantly on all the three tuning sets; secondly, although the best scores in the column RED-sent are much more than RED-syssent, but the outperform is very small, so by setting these two optimization goals, RED can achieve comparable performance; thirdly, without parameter tuning, RED does not perform well on WMT 2012 and 2013, and even with parameter tuning, RED does not outperform METEOR as much as WMT 2010; lastly, on the test set, RED does not outperform METEOR.

3.3 System-level Evaluation

We also evaluated the RED scores with the human rankings at the system level to further investigate the effectiveness of our metrics. The matching of the words in RED is correlated with the position of the words, so the traditional way of computing system level score, like what BLEU does, is not feasible for RED. Therefore, we resort to the way of adding the sentence level scores together to obtain the system level score. At system level evaluation, we employ Spearman's rank correlation coefficient ρ. The correlations and the average scores are shown in Table 2.

From Table 2, we can see similar trends as in Table 1 with the following difference: firstly, without parameter tuning, RED perform comparably with METEOR on all the three tuning sets; secondly, on test set, RED also perform comparably with METEOR. thirdly, RED perform very bad on Hindi-English, which is a newly introduced task this year.

3.4 Evaluation of English to Other Languages

We evaluate both sentence level and system level score of RED on English to French and German. The reason we only conduct these two languages are that the dependency parsers are more reliable in these two languages. The results are shown in Table 3 and 4.

From Table 3 and 4 we can see that the tuned version of RED still perform slightly better than METEOR with the only exception of system level en-de.

4 Conclusion

In this paper, based on the last year's DCU-CASICT submission, we further improved our method, namely RED. The experiments are carried out at both sentence-level and system-level using to-English and from-English corpus. The experiment results indicate that although RED achieves better correlation than BLEU, HWCM, TER and comparably performance with METEOR at both sentence level and system level, the performance is not stable on all language pairs, such as the sentence level correlation score of Hindi to

English and the system level score of English to German. To further study the sudden diving of the performance is our future work.

Acknowledgments

This research is supported by the Science Foundation Ireland (Grant 12/CE/I2267) as part of the CNGL Centre for Global Intelligent Content (www.cngl.ie) at Dublin City University and National Natural Science Foundation of China (Grant 61379086).

References

Ergun Biçici and Deniz Yuret. 2011. Instance selection for machine translation using feature decay algorithms. In *Proceedings of the Sixth Workshop on Statistical Machine Translation*, pages 272–283. Association for Computational Linguistics.

Yee Seng Chan and Hwee Tou Ng. 2008. Maxsim: A maximum similarity metric for machine translation evaluation. In *Proceedings of ACL-08: HLT*, pages 55–62.

Michael Denkowski and Alon Lavie. 2011. Meteor 1.3: automatic metric for reliable optimization and evaluation of machine translation systems. In *Proceedings of the Sixth Workshop on Statistical Machine Translation*, WMT '11, pages 85–91, Stroudsburg, PA, USA. Association for Computational Linguistics.

Alon Lavie and Abhaya Agarwal. 2007. Meteor: an automatic metric for mt evaluation with high levels of correlation with human judgments. In *Proceedings of the Second Workshop on Statistical Machine Translation*, StatMT '07, pages 228–231, Stroudsburg, PA, USA. Association for Computational Linguistics.

Ding Liu and Daniel Gildea. 2005. Syntactic features for evaluation of machine translation. In *Proceedings of the ACL Workshop on Intrinsic and Extrinsic Evaluation Measures for Machine Translation and/or Summarization*, pages 25–32.

Karolina Owczarzak, Josef van Genabith, and Andy Way. 2007a. Dependency-based automatic evaluation for machine translation. In *Proceedings of the NAACL-HLT 2007/AMTA Workshop on Syntax and Structure in Statistical Translation*, SSST '07, pages 80–87, Stroudsburg, PA, USA. Association for Computational Linguistics.

Karolina Owczarzak, Josef van Genabith, and Andy Way. 2007b. Evaluating machine translation with lfg dependencies. *Machine Translation*, 21(2):95–119, June.

Karolina Owczarzak, Josef van Genabith, and Andy Way. 2007c. Labelled dependencies in machine translation evaluation. In *Proceedings of the Second Workshop on Statistical Machine Translation*, StatMT '07, pages 104–111, Stroudsburg, PA, USA. Association for Computational Linguistics.

K. Papineni, S. Roukos, T. Ward, and W.J. Zhu. 2002. BLEU: a method for automatic evaluation of machine translation. In *Proceedings of the 40th annual meeting on association for computational linguistics*, pages 311–318. Association for Computational Linguistics.

Martin F Porter. 2001. Snowball: A language for stemming algorithms.

Libin Shen, Jinxi Xu, and Ralph Weischedel. 2010. String-to-dependency statistical machine translation. *Computational Linguistics*, 36(4):649–671.

Matthew Snover, Bonnie Dorr, Richard Schwartz, Linnea Micciulla, and John Makhoul. 2006. A study of translation edit rate with targeted human annotation. In *Proceedings of Association for Machine Translation in the Americas*, pages 223–231.

Xiaofeng Wu, Hui Yu, and Qun Liu. 2013. Dcu participation in wmt2013 metrics task. In *Proceedings of the Eighth Workshop on Statistical Machine Translation*. Association for Computational Linguistics.

H. Yu, X. Wu, Q. Liu, and S. Lin. 2014. RED: A Reference Dependency Based MT Evaluation Metric. In *To be published*.

Junguo Zhu, Muyun Yang, Bo Wang, Sheng Li, and Tiejun Zhao. 2010. All in strings: a powerful string-based automatic mt evaluation metric with multiple granularities. In *Proceedings of the 23rd International Conference on Computational Linguistics: Posters*, COLING '10, pages 1533–1540, Stroudsburg, PA, USA. Association for Computational Linguistics.

Crowdsourcing High-Quality Parallel Data Extraction from Twitter*

Wang Ling[123] **Luís Marujo**[123] **Chris Dyer**[2] **Alan Black**[2] **Isabel Trancoso**[13]
(1)L^{2}F Spoken Systems Lab, INESC-ID, Lisbon, Portugal
(2)Language Technologies Institute, Carnegie Mellon University, Pittsburgh, PA, USA
(3)Instituto Superior Técnico, Lisbon, Portugal
{lingwang,lmarujo,cdyer,awb}@cs.cmu.edu
isabel.trancoso@inesc-id.pt

Abstract

High-quality parallel data is crucial for a range of multilingual applications, from tuning and evaluating machine translation systems to cross-lingual annotation projection. Unfortunately, automatically obtained parallel data (which is available in relative abundance) tends to be quite noisy. To obtain high-quality parallel data, we introduce a crowdsourcing paradigm in which workers with only basic bilingual proficiency identify translations from an automatically extracted corpus of parallel microblog messages. For less than $350, we obtained over 5000 parallel segments in five language pairs. Evaluated against expert annotations, the quality of the crowdsourced corpus is significantly better than existing automatic methods: it obtains an performance comparable to expert annotations when used in MERT tuning of a microblog MT system; and training a parallel sentence classifier with it leads also to improved results. The crowdsourced corpora will be made available in `http://www.cs.cmu.edu/~lingwang/microtopia/`.

1 Introduction

High-quality parallel data is essential for tuning and evaluating statistical MT systems, and it plays a role in a wide range of multilingual NLP applications, such as word sense disambiguation (Gale et al., 1992; Ng et al., 2003; Specia et al., 2005), paraphrasing (Bannard and Callison-burch, 2005; Ganitkevitch et al., 2012), annotation projection (Das and Petrov, 2011), and other language-specific applications (Schwarck et al., 2010; Liu et al., 2011). While large amounts of parallel data can be easily obtained by mining the web (Resnik and Smith, 2003), comparable corpora (Munteanu and Marcu, 2005), and even social media sites (Ling et al., 2013), automatically extracted parallel tends to be noisy, and, as a result, "evaluation-quality" parallel corpora have generally been produced at considerable expense by targeted translation efforts (Bojar et al., 2013, *inter alia*). Unfortunately, in some domains such as microblogs, the *only* corpora that are available are automatically extracted and noisy.

While phrase-based translation models can effectively learn translation rules from noisy parallel data (Goutte et al., 2012), having a subset of high-quality parallel segments is nevertheless crucial. Firstly, the automatic parallel data extraction system's parameters can be tuned by optimizing on the gold standard data. Secondly, even though the parallel data used to train MT systems can contain a considerable amount of noise, it is conventional to use human annotated parallel data to tune and evaluate the system. Finally, other NLP applications may not be as noise-robust as MT.

We introduce a new crowdsourcing protocol for obtaining high-quality parallel data from noisy, automatically extracted parallel data (§3), focusing on the challenging case of identifying parallel data in microblog messages (Ling et al., 2013). In contrast to previous attempts to use crowdsourcing to obtain parallel data, in which workers performed translation (Ambati and Vogel, 2010; Zaidan and Callison-Burch, 2011; Post et al., 2012; Ambati et al., 2012), our approach only requires that they identify whether a candidate message contains a translation, and if so, what the spans of the translated segments are. This is a much simpler task than translation, and one that can often be completed by workers with only a basic proficiency in the source and target languages.

For evaluation (§4), we use our protocol to build

* A sample of the crowdsourced corpora and the interfaces used are available as supplementary material.

Proceedings of the Ninth Workshop on Statistical Machine Translation, pages 426–436,
Baltimore, Maryland USA, June 26–27, 2014.

parallel datasets on a Chinese-English corpus originally extracted from Sina Weibo and for which we have expert annotations. This lets us quantify the effectiveness of our method under different task variations. We also show that the crowdsourced corpus performs as well as expert annotation (and better than the automatically extracted corpus) for tuning an MT system with MERT. We next apply our method on a corpus of five language pairs (en-ar, en-ja, en-ko, en-ru, en-zh) extracted from Twitter (§5), for which we have no gold-standard data. Using this data in a cross-validation setup, we train and evaluate a maxent classifier for detecting parallel data (§6), and then we conclude (§7).

2 Related Work

Our work crosses crowdsourcing techniques and automatic parallel data extraction from microblogs. In this section, we shall provide background information and analysis of the work performed in these two fields.

2.1 Parallel Data Extraction from Microblogs

Many sources of parallel data exist on the web. The most popular choice are parallel web pages (Resnik and Smith, 2003), while other work have looked at specific domains with large amounts of data, such as Wikipedia (Smith et al., 2010). Microblogs, such as Twitter and Sina Weibo, represent a subdomain of the Web. Some of its characteristics is the informal language used and the short nature of the messages that are posted. Due to its large size and growing popularity, work has been done on parallel data extraction from this domain. Ling et al. (2013) attempt to find naturally occurring parallel data from Sina Weibo and Twitter. Some examples of what is found are illustrated in Figure 1. The extraction process starts by finding the parallel segments within the same message and the word alignments between those segments that maximize a hand-tuned model score.

Another method (Jehl et al., 2012) leverages CLIR (Cross Lingual Information Retrieval) techniques to find pairs of tweets that are translations. The main challenge in this approach is the large amount of pairs of tweets that must be considered, which raises some scalability issues when processing billions of tweets.

Our crowdsourcing method can be applied to annotate data from any naturally occurring source. In this paper, we will use the corpus developed by Ling et al. (2013), since it is publicly available and has parallel data for 6 languages from Twitter, and for 10 languages from Sina Weibo.

2.2 Parallel Data using Crowdsourcing

Most of the work done in building parallel data using crowdsourcing (Ambati and Vogel, 2010; Zaidan and Callison-Burch, 2011; Post et al., 2012; Ambati et al., 2012) relies on using crowdsourcing workers to translate. These methods must address the fact that workers may produce poor and sometimes incorrect translations. Thus, in order to find good translations, subsequent postediting and/or ranking is generally necessary.

In contrast, in our work, crowdsourcing is used for data extraction rather than translation, a substantially simpler task than translation (in particular, translation of informal text) that requires less expertise in the language pair (basic proficiency in the two languages is generally sufficient to successfully complete the task). Furthermore, assessing whether a worker performed the task correctly and combining the outputs of different workers is simpler. The time spent per item is also reduced: our annotation interface only requires the worker to make a few clicks on the tweet to complete each annotation, meaning that tasks are completed faster and with less effort, allowing us to obtain translations at lower cost. On the other hand, the main drawback of our method is that it can only obtain parallel data from translations that exist, which corresponds to the amount of posts that have been translated and posted. This limits the potential coverage of our method. Furthermore, the resulting datasets may not be fully representative of the Twitter domain, since not all types of content are translated and follow the same distribution as the data in Twitter.

3 Proposed Crowdsourcing Protocol

As discussed above, automatically extracted parallel is often noisy. The sources of error range from language detection errors, to errors determining if material is actually translation, and errors in extracting the appropriate spans of the translated material. Consider the fragment of the microblog parallel corpus mined by Ling et al. (2013), which is shown in Figure 1. In the Korean-English message, the system may incorrectly added the untranslated word *Hahah* in the English segment, and missed the translated word *Weather*. At a high level, the task faced by annotators will be to identify and resolve such errors.

3.1 Overview

We separate the tasks of identifying the parallel posts, which we shall denote by **identification**, and of locating the parallel segments, which we will call **location**. The justification for this is that the majority of the tweets are not parallel, as reported by Ling et al. (2013), and the location of the parallel data is only applicable if the tweet actually contains parallel data. This is also desirable because the identification task is simpler than the location task. Firstly, identifying whether a tweet contains translations requires much less proficiency in the respective languages than locating the parallel segments, since it only requires the worker to understand parts of the message. This means we can have more potential workers capable of performing this task. Secondly, the first task is a binary decision, and each annotation can be completed with only one action, which means that the average required time for this task is much lower than the second task and the payment required for each hit will naturally be lower as well. Finally, combining worker results for a binary decision is simpler than combining translations, since the space of possible answers is several orders of magnitude lower.

As crowdsourcing platform, we use Amazon's Mechanical Turk. In this platform, the requesters can submit **tasks**, where one can define the number of workers n that will complete each task and what is the payment p for each task submission, henceforth denoted as **job**. In our work, we had to consider the following components:

- **Interface** - To submit a task, an interface must be provided, which workers will be using to complete the job.
- **Worker Quality Prediction** - After submitting a job, the requester can accept and pay the agreed fee or reject the task. It is crucial to have a method to automatically predict whether workers have performed the job properly, and reject them otherwise.
- **Result Combination** - It is common for multiple workers to complete the same task with different results. Thus, a method must be implemented to combine multiple responses for correctly predicting the desired response.

We structured each of our tasks as a series of q questions, which include a small number of references r, for which we know the answers. Thus, the amount of answers we obtain for each dollar is given by $\frac{q-r}{np}$, where n is the number of workers per task and p is the payment for each task. In order to maximize this quotient, we can either reduce the number of reference question r, the number of workers per task n, or the payment p. However, reducing r will also limit our capability of estimating the quality of the worker results, since we will have less data to make such prediction. For the same reason, reducing n will limit our ability to combine results properly. As for the payment p, while there is no direct effect on our task, it has been noted that workers will perform the task faster for higher payments (Post et al., 2012). In our work, we will propose methods to predict quality and combine results that will minimize the requirements for n and r, while maximizing the quality of the final results.

3.2 Parallel Post Identification

In the identification task, for each question, we will show a post, and solicit the worker to detect if it contains translations in a given language pair.

Interface The interface for this task is straightforward. We present to the worker each tweet individually, together with a checkbox to be checked in case the tweet contains parallel data. The navigation between tweets is done by adding next and previous buttons, allowing the user to go back and review previous answers. Finally, the worker can only submit the HIT after traversing all 25 questions. Unlike the work in crowdsourcing translation (Zaidan and Callison-Burch, 2011), where automatic translation systems are discouraged, since it produces poor output, we allow its usage as long as this leads to correct annotations. In fact, we add a button to automatically translate the tweet into English from the non-English language.

Worker Quality Prediction We accept the job if it answers enough reference questions correctly. We consider two different approaches to select references. A random sampler that selects tweets randomly and a balanced sampler that selects the same number of positive and negative samples. As notation, we will denote as acceptor

؟ .. من عنده نفس مشكلتي في التويتر Who has the same of my problem .. ? http://t.co/hlrJdKOt
オーバーヘッドプロジェクタと共に使われる透明画 - a transparency for use with an overhead projector
날씨 너무 좋아! 누군가랑 손잡고 공원 산책하고 싶다!! 내가 좋아하는 파아란 하늘^^*Weather is so nice! I wanna go for a walk w/ someone. Hahah
http://t.co/Yz6qmhHV меня никто не спрашивает, он просто ДОЛЖЕН стать моим любимым оппой <3 | He MUST to be my lovely oppa! <3
奥巴马公开宣称支持同性恋婚姻 Barack Obama speaks out and declares support for same-sex marriage http://t.co/gle6PKJG 副总统拜登道歉拖奥黑下水 http://t.co/tPVmaFWW

Figure 1: Parallel microblog posts in 5 language pairs. Shaded backgrounds mark the parallel segments (annotated manually), non shaded parts do not have translations.

$accept(rand, c, r)$ a setup where the worker's job is accepted if c out of r randomly sampled references are correctly answered. Likewise, acceptor $accept(bal, c, r)$ denotes the same setup using balanced reference questions.

Result Combination Given n jobs with answers for a question that can be either positive or negative, we calculate the weighted ratio of positive answers, given by $\frac{\sum_{i=1..n} \delta_p(i)w(i)}{\sum_{i=1..n} w(i)}$, where δ_p is one if answer i is positive and 0 otherwise, and $w(i)$ is the weight of the worker. $w(i)$ is defined as the ratio of correct answers from job i in the reference set. If the weighted ratio is higher than 0.5, we label the tweet as positive and otherwise as negative.

3.3 Parallel Data Location

In the location task, we also present one tweet per question, where the worker will be asked to identify the parallel segments. The worker can also define that there are no translations in the tweet.

Interface The interface for this task presents the user with one tweet at a time, and allows the user to break the tweet into segments, by clicking between characters. Each segment can then be classified as English, the non-English language (Ex: Mandarin), or non-parallel, which is the default option. To understand the concept of non-parallel segments, notice that when we are locating parallel data in tweets, we are essentially breaking the tweet into the structure "N_{left} P_{left} N_{middle} P_{right} N_{right}", where P_{left} and P_{right} are the parallel segments and N_{left}, N_{middle} and N_{right} are textual segments that are non-parallel. These may not exist, for instance, the Arabic tweet in Figure 1 (line 1) does not contain any non-parallel text and does not require any non-parallel segments to delineate the parallel data. The Korean tweet (line 2), on the other hand, has an N_{middle} corresponding to 내가ㅈ아핳ㄴ퍄안ㄹ 하늘^^* and an N_{right} corresponding to *Hahah* and requires two non-parallel segments to locate the parallel data.

Thus, if the worker does not commit any errors, each question can be answered with at most four clicks, when all five segments exist, and two option choices for identifying the parallel segments. In the easiest case, when only the parallel segments exist, only one click and two option choices are needed. If there are no translations, the button *no translations* can be clicked.

For instance, to annotate the Korean tweet in Figure 1, the worker must click immediately before 내가, then before *Weather* and finally before *Hahah*. Then on the drop-down box of the first and and third segments, the worker must choose Korean and English, respectively. The interface after these operations is show in Figure 2.

Work Quality Prediction To score the worker's jobs, we use the scoring function devised in (Ling et al., 2013), which measures the word overlap between the reference parallel segments segments and the predicted segments. However, setting the score threshold to accept a job is a challenge, since scores are bound to change for different language-pairs and domains. Moreover, some tweets are harder to annotate than others. Learning this threshold automatically requires annotated data, which we do not have for all language pairs and domains. Thus, we propose a method to generate thresholds specifically for each sample.

We consider a "smart but lazy" pseudo worker, who will complete the same jobs automatically and generate scores that the real worker's jobs must beat to be accepted. We say he is "smart",

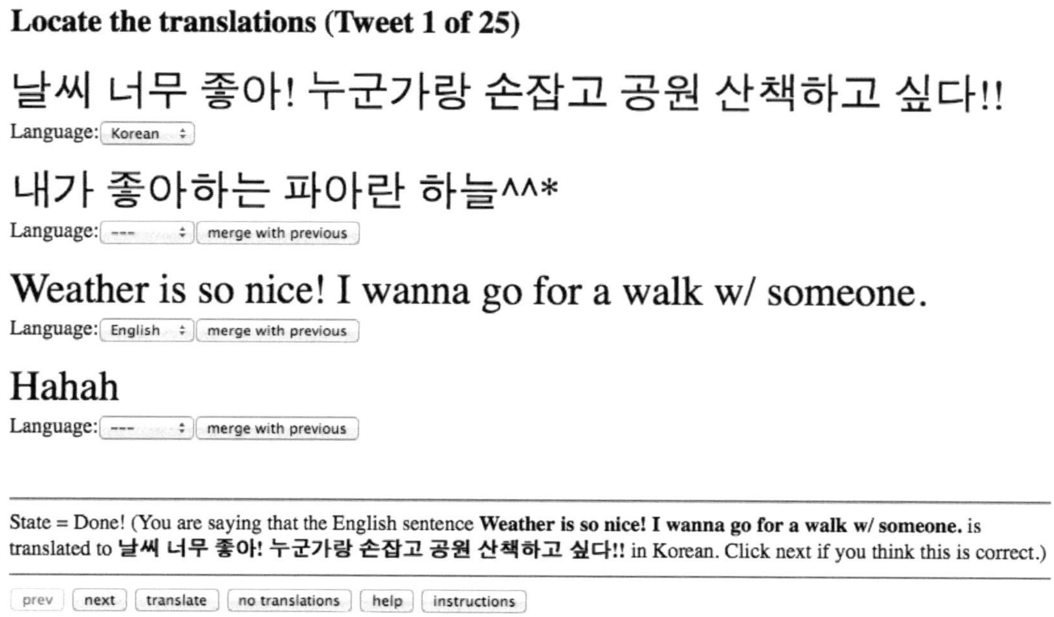

Figure 2: Location Interface (After the annotation is performed)

since he knows the reference annotation, and "lazy" because he will only define a new non-parallel segment if it is significant, otherwise it will just be left in the parallel segments. By significant, we will define whether it is at least 20% larger (in number of characters) than the parallel segments. For instance, in the Korean example in Figure 1, *Hahah* would be left in the English parallel segment, while 내가 좋아하는 파아란 하늘 ^^* would not be in the Korean segment. We will accept a job if the average of the scores in the reference set is higher or equal than the pseudo worker's scores. This acceptor shall be denoted as $accept(lazy, a)$, where a is the number of references used.

Another option is to use the automatic system's output as a baseline that workers must improve to be accepted. We will also test this option and call this acceptor $accept(auto, a)$.

Result Combination Unlike the identification task, where the result is binary and combining multiple decisions is straightforward, the range of results from this task is larger and combining them is a challenge. Thus, we score each job based on the WER on the reference set and use annotations of the highest scoring job.

4 Experiments

To obtain results on the effectiveness of the methods described in Section 3, we will first perform experiments using pre-annotated data. We use the annotated dataset with tweets in Mandarin-English from Sina Weibo created in (Ling et al., 2013). It consists of approximately 4000 tweets crawled from Sina Weibo that were annotated on whether they contained parallel data and the location of the parallel segments. In our experiment, we sample 1000 tweets from this dataset, where 602 tweets were parallel and 398 were not.[1]

We will not submit the same tasks using different setups, since we would have to pay the cost of the tasks multiple times. Furthermore, we know the answers for all the questions in this controlled experiment, the quality of a job can be evaluated precisely by using all questions as references. Thus, we will perform the task once, with a larger number of workers and accepting and rejecting jobs based on their real quality. Then, we will use the resulting datasets and simulate the conditions using different setups.

Acceptor	$avg(a)$	$avg(r)$	d
$accept(rand, 2, 2)$	0.44	0.00	0.44
$accept(rand, 3, 4)$	0.44	0.00	0.44
$accept(rand, 4, 4)$	0.55	0.04	0.51
$accept(bal, 2, 2)$	0.69	0.09	0.60
$accept(bal, 3, 4)$	0.64	**0.03**	**0.61**
$accept(bal, 4, 4)$	**0.76**	0.15	**0.61**

Table 1: Agreement with the expert annotations for different acceptors.

Acceptor	prec	recall	F1	acc	κ
Automatic	0.87	0.69	0.77	0.75	0.51
All jobs	0.75	0.84	0.8	0.74	0.44
$accept(rand, 2, 2)$	0.85	0.92	0.88	0.86	0.69
$accept(rand, 3, 4)$	0.84	0.93	0.88	0.85	0.68
$accept(rand, 4, 4)$	0.91	0.95	0.93	0.92	0.82
$accept(bal, 2, 2)$	0.94	0.94	**0.94**	0.92	0.84
$accept(bal, 3, 4)$	0.93	0.95	**0.94**	**0.93**	**0.85**
$accept(bal, 4, 4)$	0.94	0.93	0.93	0.92	0.84

Table 2: Parallel post prediction scores using different acceptors.

4.1 Identification Task

The 1000 tweets were distributed into 40 tasks with 25 questions each ($q = 25$). Each task is to be performed by 5 workers ($n = 5$) and upon acceptance, a worker would be rewarded with 6 cents ($p = 0.06$). As we know the answers for all the questions in this case, we will calculate the Cohen's Kappa between the responses of each job and the expert annotator, and accept a job if it is higher than 0.5. We decided to use Cohen's kappa to evaluate a job, rather than accuracy, since each set of 25 questions does not contain the same number of positive and negative samples. For instance, in a set of 20 negative samples, a worker would achieve an accuracy of 80% if he simply answers negatively to all questions, which is not an adequate assessment of the job's quality. On the other hand, the Cohen's Kappa balances the positive and negative question in each task by using their prior probabilities. In total, there were 566 jobs, where 200 where accepted and 366 were rejected.

Next, we pretended that we only have access to 4 references, which will be used for quality estimation and simulate the acceptances and rejections for each strategy. Table 1 shows the averages of the real Kappa values of accepted (column $avg(a)$) and rejected jobs (column $avg(r)$) using different acceptors. Our goal is to maximize the number of acceptances with high Kappa values and minimize those that have low Kappa values. Thus, we define d as the difference between $avg(a)$ and $avg(r)$. From the results, we observe that using a balanced reference yields a much better estimation of the jobs quality using our metric d. Similar conclusions can be reached by comparing $accept(rand, 3, 4)$ with $accept(bal, 3, 4)$ and $accept(rand, 4, 4)$ with $accept(bal, 4, 4)$. Quality predictors that use balanced reference sets achieve approximately the same results for d. However, the setup $accept(bal, 3, 4)$ has a lower Kappas for both $avg(a)$ and $avg(r)$, which means that it is less likely to reject good jobs at the cost of accepting more bad jobs. This is desirable from an ethical perspective, since workers are not responsible for errors in our quality prediction. Furthermore, rejecting good jobs has a negative impact on the progress of the task, since good workers may be discouraged to perform more tasks.

Results on the identification task, obtained for $n = 3$, are shown in Table 2. Naturally, using a balanced reference set yields better results, since these have a higher d value. We can also see the importance of quality prediction, since not performing quality estimation (row *All jobs*) will yield worse results than the automatic system.

Next, we will compare results using different numbers of workers. We fix the quality prediction methodology to $accept(bal, 3, 4)$ and results are shown in Table 3. We observe that in general, using more workers will generate better results, but score gains from adding another worker becomes lower as n increases. One problem for $n = 2$ is the fact that there are many cases where two workers with the same weight chose a positive and a negative answer, in which case, no decision can be made, and we simply choose false by default. This explains the high recall and low precision values. However, this problem seems to occur much less with higher values of n.

4.2 Location Task

For the location task, we used the predicted parallel posts the identification task with the setup $accept(bal, 3, 4)$ and $n = 5$. We preferred to use this rather than using the expert annotations, since it would not contain false positives, which does not simulate a real situation. Then, we used 500 out of

[1]We wished to annotate a sample where the number of parallel posts is high, so that we would have enough samples to perform the location task.

# workers	prec	recall	F1	acc	κ
Automatic	0.87	0.69	0.77	0.75	0.51
1	0.86	0.85	0.85	0.82	0.64
2	0.85	0.95	0.90	0.87	0.72
3	0.93	0.95	0.94	0.93	0.85
4	0.94	0.96	0.95	0.94	0.87
5	0.96	0.96	**0.96**	**0.95**	**0.90**

Table 3: Identification scores for different n.

Number of jobs	1	2	3	4	5
Automatic	0.16	0.16	0.16	0.16	0.16
All Jobs	0.23	0.21	0.07	**0.06**	**0.06**
$accept(auto, 4)$	0.09	0.06	**0.06**	**0.06**	**0.06**
$accept(lazy, 4)$	**0.06**	**0.05**	**0.06**	**0.06**	**0.06**

Table 4: Parallel data location scores for different acceptors (rows) and different numbers of workers. Each cell denotes the WER for that setup.

	Auto (Pos)	Crowd	Expert	Auto (All)
Size	483	479	483	*908*
EN-ZH	10.21	10.49	**10.51**	10.71
ZH-EN	7.59	**7.87**	7.82	8.02

Table 5: BLEU score comparison using different corpora for MERT tuning. The *Size* row denotes the number of sentences of each corpus, and the *EN-ZH* and *ZH-EN* rows denote the BLEU scores of the respective language pair and tuning dataset.

the 607 identified positive samples. This makes 20 tasks in total, with 25 questions ($q = 25$), and each task would be run until 5 jobs are accepted ($n = 5$). For this task, we set a payment of 30 cents ($p = 0.3$), since it is a more complex task. Again, since we have the expert annotations for all questions, we calculated the average WER on all answers and rejected jobs scoring less than 0.6[2].

This task is mainly focused on the quality prediction of the workers, as the result combination is done by finding the job with the highest score in the reference set. This means, for an arbitrary large n, all quality estimation methods will produce the same result, since we will find the best job on the references eventually. However, better quality estimation will allow us to find the best jobs with lower n, which makes the task less expensive. Table 4 shows results using different setups. In these results, we set aside 4 questions to be used as references. We can see that for low n (1 or 2), if we simply accept all jobs, the quality of the results will be lower than the automatic system. For $n = 4$, this approach can achieve a WER score of 0.06. However, if we use the automatic system as a baseline that jobs must surpass, we can achieve this WER score with only two jobs, which reduces the cost of this task by half. Yet, this is strongly dependent on the automatic system, as a worse system will be easier to match for the workers. On the other hand, using the smart but lazy pseudo worker, where we degrade the reference annotations slightly, we can see that we can obtain the 0.06 WER score using only the first worker. At $n = 2$, we can see that the WER improves to 0.05, which is lost for $n = 3$. This is because the prediction of the quality of the job using the workers is not always precise.

4.3 Machine Translation Results

Finally, we will perform an extrinsic test to see how the improvements obtained by using crowdsourcing map to Machine Translations. We will build an out of domain MT system using the FBIS dataset (LDC2003E14), a corpus of 300K sentence pairs from the news domain in the Chinese-English pair using the Moses (Koehn et al., 2007) pipeline. Due to the small size of our crowdsourced corpus, we will use it in the MERT tuning (Och, 2003), and test its effects compared to automatically extracted parallel data and the experts judgements. As the test set, we will use 1,500 sentence pairs from the Weibo gold standard from Ling et al. (2013), that were not used in our crowdsourcing experiment to prevent data overlap. For reordering, we use the MSD reordering model (Axelrod et al., 2005) and as the language model, we use a 5-gram model with Kneser-Ney smoothing (Heafield, 2011). Finally, results are presented with BLEU-4 (Papineni et al., 2002).

We build 3 tuning corpora, the automatically extracted corpus (denoted *Auto*), the crowdsourced corpus (denoted *Crowd*) and the corpus annotated by the expert (denoted *Expert*). This is done by taking the 1000 tweets used in this experiment, select those that were identified as parallel according to each criteria. For the automatic extraction, the authors in (Ling et al., 2013) simply use all tweets as parallel, which may influence the tuning results. Thus, we test two versions of this corpus, one where we take all samples as parallel (denoted *Auto (All)*), and one where we use the expert's decision for the identification task only (de-

[2]Determined empirically

Pair	Parallel	Avg(en)	cost(I)	cost(L)	total
en-ar	1512	8.3	\$35.7	\$43.2	\$76.2
en-zh	1302	8.7	\$35.7	\$37.2	\$70.2
en-ja	1155	7.9	\$35.7	\$33.0	\$68.7
en-ko	1008	7.1	\$35.7	\$28.8	\$64.5
en-ru	798	6.3	\$35.7	\$22.8	\$58.5
all	5775	–	\$178.5	\$165.0	\$343.5

Table 7: AMT costs for crowdsourced corpora from Twitter.

noted *Auto (Pos)*). In the crowdsourcing case, we use the $accept(bal, 3, 4)$ setup, with $n = 5$, for the identification task and the $accept(lazy, 4)$ setup, with $n = 2$, for the location task. From the resulting parallel tweets, we also remove all tweets that were used as reference in the $accept(lazy, 4)$ quality estimator, as this would give an unfair advantage to the crowdsourced corpora.

Results are shown in Table 5, where each cell contains the average BLEU score in 5 MERT runs, using a different tuning dataset. Surprisingly, using the whole set of automatically extracted corpora actually achieves better results than using carefully selected data that are parallel. We believe that is because many non-parallel segments actually contain comparable information that can be used to improve the weights during MERT tuning. However, this does not mean that the quality of the automatically crawled corpus is better than the crowdsourced and expert annotated corpus. When using a similar number of parallel sentences, we observe that using the crowdsourced corpus yields better scores than the automatically extracted corpora, comparable to experts annotations. While results are not significantly better than automatically extracted corpora, this suggests that the crowdsourced corpora has a better overall quality than automatically extracted corpora.

5 Five Language Twitter Parallel Corpus

Now that we have established the effectiveness of our technique for extracting high-quality parallel data in a scenario where we have gold standard annotations, we apply it to creating parallel corpora in five languages on Twitter, for which we have no gold-standard parallel data: Arabic, Mandarin, Japanese, Korean and Russian. Once again, we use the extracted automatically Twitter corpus from Ling et al. (2013) and deploy the task in Mechanical Turk. We use the setup that obtained the best results in Section 4. For the identification task, we used the $accept(bal, 3, 4)$ setup, with $n = 5$. The payment for each task was 0.06 dollars. Thus, for this task, each dollar spent yields 70 annotated tweets. For the location task, we used the $accept(lazy, 4)$ setup, with $n = 2$ and each task was rewarded with 0.3 dollars. To obtain the tweet sample, we filtered the corpora in Ling et al. (2013) for tweets with alignment scores higher than 0.1. Then, we uniformly extracted 2500 tweets for each language. To generate gold standard references, the authors manually annotated 40 samples for each pair.

Table 7 contains information about the resulting corpora. The number of parallel sentences extracted from the 2500 tweets in each language pair is shown in column *Parallel* and we can see that this differs given the language pair. We can also see in column *Avg(en)* that the average number of English words is much smaller than what is seen in more formal domains. Finally, Arabic parallel data seems more predominant from our samples followed by Mandarin, while Russian parallel data seem scarcer.

6 Discriminative Parallel Data Detection

While the work in (Ling et al., 2013) used a linear combination of three models, the alignment, language and segment features, these weights were determined manually. However, using the crowdsourced corpus (in Section 5), we will apply previously proposed methods that learn a classifier with machine learning techniques as in related work on finding parallel data (Resnik and Smith, 2003; Munteanu and Marcu, 2005). In our work, we use a max entropy classifier model, similar to that presented by Munteanu and Marcu (2005) to detect parallel data in tweets. Our features are:

- **Alignment feature** - The baseline feature is the alignment score from the work in (Ling et al., 2013), and measures how well the parallel segments align, which is derived from the content-based matching methods for detecting parallel data (Resnik and Smith, 2003).

- **User features** - An observation in (Ling et al., 2013) is that a user that frequently posts in parallel is likely to post more parallel messages. Based on this, we added the average alignment score from all messages of the same user and the ratio of messages that are predicted to be parallel as features.

	Weibo (en-zh)	Twitter (en-zh)	Twitter (en-ar)	Twitter (en-ru)	Twitter (en-ko)	Twitter (en-ja)
Alignment	0.781	0.599	0.721	0.692	0.635	0.570
+User	0.814	0.598	0.721	0.705	0.650	0.566
+Length	0.839	0.603	0.725	0.706	0.650	0.569
+Repetition	**0.849**	0.652	0.763	0.729	0.655	0.579
+Language	**0.849**	**0.668**	**0.782**	**0.737**	**0.747**	**0.584**

Table 6: Classification Results using a 10-fold cross validation over different datasets. Each cell contains the F-measure using a given dataset and an incremental set of features.

- **Repetition features** - There are many words that are not translated, such as hashtags, at mentions, numbers and named entities. So, if we see these repeated twice in the same post, it can be used as a strong cue that this was the result of a translation. Hence, we define features for each of these cases, that trigger if either of these occur in multiples of two times in the same post. Named Entities were identified using a naive approach by considering words with capital letters.

- **Length feature** - It is known that the length differences between parallel sentences can be modelled by a normal distribution (Gale and Church, 1991). Hence, we used parallel data in the respective language to determine $(\tilde{\mu}, \tilde{\sigma}^2)$, which lets us calculate the likelihood of two hypothesized segments being parallel. Since we did not have annotated parallel data for this domain, we used the top 2000 scoring parallel sentences from the respective Twitter dataset in (Ling et al., 2013).

- **Language feature** - It is common for non-English words to be found in English segments, such as names of foreign celebrities, numbers and hashtags. However, when this happens to the majority of the words in a segment that is supposed to be English, it may indicated that there was an error in the language detection. The same happens with non-English segments. We used the same naive approach to detect languages as in (Ling et al., 2013), where we calculate the ratio of number of words in the English segment and the total number of words from the segment detected as English and the ratio of the number of Foreign words and the total number of words in the Foreign segment ,detected by their unicode ranges. This was also included in the work in (Ling et al., 2013).

Results using a 10 fold cross-validation are shown in Table 6. In general, we can see that the classifier performs worse in Twitter datasets compared to the Weibo dataset. We believe that this is because parallel sentences extracted from Twitter are smaller, due to the 140 character limit, which does not hold in Sina Weibo. Each parallel English segment from the Sina Weibo parallel data contains 15.4 words on average. On other hand, we see in Table 7 that this number is smaller in the parallel data from Twitter. This means that the aligner will have a much smaller range of words to align when detecting parallel data, which makes it more difficult to find parallel segments.

As for the features, we observe that by defining these simple features, we can get a significant improvement over previous baselines. For the **User** feature, we see that the improvements in the Weibo dataset are much larger than in the Twitter datasets. This is because the Twitter dataset was crawled uniformly, whereas the Weibo dataset was focused on users that post parallel data frequently. Thus, in the Weibo dataset there more posts that were posted by the same user, which does not happen as frequently in the Twitter dataset. As for the **Length** feature, we can see that it yields a small but consistent improvement over all datasets. **Repetition** based features also lead to improvements across all datasets, and produces a 5% improvement in the English-Mandarin Twitter dataset. Finally, **language** based features also add another improvement over previous results.

7 Conclusions

We presented a crowdsourcing approach to extract parallel data from tweets. As opposed to methods to crowdsource translations, our tasks do not require workers to translate sentences, but to find them in tweets. Our method is divided into two tasks. First, we identify which tweets contain translations, and we show that multiple worker's jobs can be combined to obtain results comparable to those of expert annotators. Secondly, tweets that are found to contain translations are given to other workers to locate the parallel segments, where we can also obtain high quality results. Then, we use our method to extract high quality parallel data from Twitter in 5 language pairs. Finally, we improve the automatic identification of tweets with translations by using a max entropy classifier trained on the crowdsourced data.

We are currently extracting more data and the crowdsourced parallel data from Twitter will made be available to the public.

References

[Ambati and Vogel2010] Vamshi Ambati and Stephan Vogel. 2010. Can crowds build parallel corpora for machine translation systems? In *Proceedings of the NAACL HLT 2010 Workshop on Creating Speech and Language Data with Amazon's Mechanical Turk*, Stroudsburg, PA, USA. Association for Computational Linguistics.

[Ambati et al.2012] Vamshi Ambati, Stephan Vogel, and Jaime Carbonell. 2012. Collaborative workflow for crowdsourcing translation. In *Proceedings of the ACM 2012 Conference on Computer Supported Cooperative Work*, CSCW '12, pages 1191–1194, New York, NY, USA. ACM.

[Axelrod et al.2005] Amittai Axelrod, Ra Birch Mayne, Chris Callison-burch, Miles Osborne, and David Talbot. 2005. Edinburgh system description for the 2005 iwslt speech translation evaluation. In *Proceedings International Workshop on Spoken Language Translation (IWSLT*.

[Bannard and Callison-burch2005] Colin Bannard and Chris Callison-burch. 2005. Paraphrasing with bilingual parallel corpora. In *In ACL-2005*, pages 597–604.

[Bojar et al.2013] Ondřej Bojar, Christian Buck, Chris Callison-Burch, Christian Federmann, Barry Haddow, Philipp Koehn, Christof Monz, Matt Post, Radu Soricut, and Lucia Specia. 2013. Findings of the 2013 Workshop on Statistical Machine Translation. In *Proceedings of the Eighth Workshop on Statistical Machine Translation*, pages 1–44, Sofia, Bulgaria, August. Association for Computational Linguistics.

[Das and Petrov2011] Dipanjan Das and Slav Petrov. 2011. Unsupervised part-of-speech tagging with bilingual graph-based projections. In *Proceedings of the 49th Annual Meeting of the Association for Computational Linguistics: Human Language Technologies - Volume 1*, HLT '11, pages 600–609, Stroudsburg, PA, USA. Association for Computational Linguistics.

[Gale and Church1991] William A. Gale and Kenneth W. Church. 1991. A program for aligning sentences in bilingual corpora. In *Proceedings of the 29th Annual Meeting on Association for Computational Linguistics*, ACL '91, pages 177–184, Stroudsburg, PA, USA. Association for Computational Linguistics.

[Gale et al.1992] William A. Gale, Kenneth W. Church, and David Yarowsky. 1992. Using bilingual materials to develop word sense disambiguation methods.

[Ganitkevitch et al.2012] Juri Ganitkevitch, Yuan Cao, Jonathan Weese, Matt Post, and Chris Callison-Burch. 2012. Joshua 4.0: Packing, PRO, and paraphrases. In *Proceedings of the Seventh Workshop on Statistical Machine Translation*, pages 283–291, Montréal, Canada, June. Association for Computational Linguistics.

[Goutte et al.2012] Cyril Goutte, Marine Carpuat, and George Foster. 2012. The impact of sentence alignment errors on phrase-based machine translation performance. In *Proc. of AMTA*.

[Heafield2011] Kenneth Heafield. 2011. KenLM: faster and smaller language model queries. In *Proceedings of the Sixth Workshop on Statistical Machine Translation*, pages 187–197, Edinburgh, Scotland, United Kingdom, July.

[Jehl et al.2012] Laura Jehl, Felix Hieber, and Stefan Riezler. 2012. Twitter translation using translation-based cross-lingual retrieval. In *Proceedings of the Seventh Workshop on Statistical Machine Translation*, pages 410–421, Montréal, Canada, June. Association for Computational Linguistics.

[Koehn et al.2007] Philipp Koehn, Hieu Hoang, Alexandra Birch, Chris Callison-burch, Richard Zens, Rwth Aachen, Alexandra Constantin, Marcello Federico, Nicola Bertoldi, Chris Dyer, Brooke Cowan, Wade Shen, Christine Moran, and Ondrej Bojar. 2007. Moses: Open source toolkit for statistical machine translation. In *Proceedings of the 45th Annual Meeting of the Association for Computational Linguistics Companion Volume Proceedings of the Demo and Poster Sessions*, pages 177–180, Prague, Czech Republic, June. Association for Computational Linguistics.

[Ling et al.2013] Wang Ling, Guang Xiang, Chris Dyer, Alan Black, and Isabel Trancoso. 2013. Microblogs as parallel corpora. In *Proceedings of the 51st Annual Meeting on Association for Computational Linguistics*, ACL '13. Association for Computational Linguistics.

[Liu et al.2011] Feifan Liu, Fei Liu, and Yang Liu. 2011. Learning from chinese-english parallel data for chinese tense prediction. In *IJCNLP*, pages 1116–1124.

[Munteanu and Marcu2005] Dragos Munteanu and Daniel Marcu. 2005. Improving machine translation performance by exploiting comparable corpora. *Computational Linguistics*, 31(4):477–504.

[Ng et al.2003] Hwee Tou Ng, Bin Wang, and Yee Seng Chan. 2003. Exploiting parallel texts for word sense disambiguation: An empirical study. In *Proceedings of ACL03*, pages 455–462.

[Och2003] Franz Josef Och. 2003. Minimum error rate training in statistical machine translation. In *Proceedings of the 41st Annual Meeting on Association for Computational Linguistics - Volume 1*, ACL '03, pages 160–167, Stroudsburg, PA, USA. Association for Computational Linguistics.

[Papineni et al.2002] Kishore Papineni, Salim Roukos, Todd Ward, and Wei-Jing Zhu. 2002. Bleu: a method for automatic evaluation of machine translation. In *Proceedings of the 40th Annual Meeting on Association for Computational Linguistics*, ACL '02, pages 311–318, Stroudsburg, PA, USA. Association for Computational Linguistics.

[Post et al.2012] Matt Post, Chris Callison-Burch, and Miles Osborne. 2012. Constructing parallel corpora for six indian languages via crowdsourcing. In *Proceedings of the Seventh Workshop on Statistical Machine Translation*, pages 401–409, Montréal, Canada, June. Association for Computational Linguistics.

[Resnik and Smith2003] Philip Resnik and Noah A. Smith. 2003. The web as a parallel corpus. *Computational Linguistics*, 29:349–380.

[Schwarck et al.2010] Florian Schwarck, Alexander Fraser, and Hinrich Schütze. 2010. Bitext-based resolution of german subject-object ambiguities. In *Human Language Technologies: The 2010 Annual Conference of the North American Chapter of the Association for Computational Linguistics*, HLT '10, pages 737–740, Stroudsburg, PA, USA. Association for Computational Linguistics.

[Smith et al.2010] Jason R. Smith, Chris Quirk, and Kristina Toutanova. 2010. Extracting parallel sentences from comparable corpora using document level alignment. In *Human Language Technologies: The 2010 Annual Conference of the North American Chapter of the Association for Computational Linguistics*, HLT '10, pages 403–411, Stroudsburg, PA, USA. Association for Computational Linguistics.

[Specia et al.2005] Lucia Specia, Maria Das Graças, Volpe Nunes, and Mark Stevenson. 2005. Exploiting parallel texts to produce a multilingual sense tagged corpus for word sense disambiguation. In *Proceedings of RANLP-05, Borovets*, pages 525–531.

[Zaidan and Callison-Burch2011] Omar F. Zaidan and Chris Callison-Burch. 2011. Crowdsourcing translation: professional quality from non-professionals. In *Proceedings of the 49th Annual Meeting of the Association for Computational Linguistics: Human Language Technologies - Volume 1*, HLT '11, pages 1220–1229, Stroudsburg, PA, USA. Association for Computational Linguistics.

Using Comparable Corpora to Adapt MT Models to New Domains

Ann Irvine
Center for Language and Speech Processing
Johns Hopkins University

Chris Callison-Burch
Computer and Information Science Dept.
University of Pennsylvania

Abstract

In previous work we showed that when using an SMT model trained on old-domain data to translate text in a new-domain, most errors are due to unseen source words, unseen target translations, and inaccurate translation model scores (Irvine et al., 2013a). In this work, we target errors due to inaccurate translation model scores using new-domain comparable corpora, which we mine from Wikipedia. We assume that we have access to a large old-domain parallel training corpus but only enough new-domain parallel data to tune model parameters and do evaluation. We use the new-domain comparable corpora to estimate additional feature scores over the phrase pairs in our baseline models. Augmenting models with the new features improves the quality of machine translations in the medical and science domains by up to 1.3 BLEU points over very strong baselines trained on the 150 million word Canadian Hansard dataset.

1 Introduction

Domain adaptation for machine translation is known to be a challenging research problem that has substantial real-world application. In this setting, we have access to training data in some old-domain of text but very little or no training data in the domain of the text that we wish to translate. For example, we may have a large corpus of parallel newswire training data but no training data in the medical domain, resulting in low quality translations at test time due to the mismatch.

In Irvine et al. (2013a), we introduced a taxonomy for classifying machine translation errors related to lexical choice. Our 'S4' taxonomy includes seen, sense, score, and search errors. Seen errors result when a source language word or phrase in the test set was not observed at all during training. Sense errors occur when the source language word or phrase was observed during training but not with the correct target language translation. If the source language word or phrase was observed with its correct translation during training, but an incorrect alternative outweighs the correct translation, then a score error has occurred. Search errors are due to pruning in beam search decoding. We measured the impact of each error type in a domain adaptation setting and concluded that seen and sense errors are the most frequent but that there is also room for improving errors due to inaccurate translation model scores (Irvine et al., 2013a). In this work, we target *score* errors, using comparable corpora to reduce their frequency in a domain adaptation setting.

We assume the setting where we have an old-domain parallel training corpus but no new domain training corpus.[1] We do, however, have access to a mixed-domain comparable corpus. We identify new-domain text within our comparable corpus and use that data to estimate new translation features on the translation models extracted from old-domain training data. Specifically, we focus on the French-English language pair because carefully curated datasets exist in several domains for tuning and evaluation. Following our prior work, we use the Canadian Hansard parliamentary proceedings as our old-domain and adapt models to both the medical and the science domains (Irvine et al., 2013a). At over 8 million sentence pairs,

[1] Some prior work has referred to old-domain and new-domain corpora as out-of-domain and in-domain, respectively.

Proceedings of the Ninth Workshop on Statistical Machine Translation, pages 437–444,
Baltimore, Maryland USA, June 26–27, 2014.

the Canadian Hansard dataset is one of the largest publicly available parallel corpora and provides a very strong baseline. We give details about each dataset in Section 4.1.

We use comparable corpora to estimate several signals of translation equivalence. In particular, we estimate the contextual, topic, and orthographic similarity of each phrase pair in our baseline old-domain translation model. In Section 3, we describe each feature in detail. Using just 5 thousand comparable new-domain document pairs, which we mine from Wikipedia, and five new phrase table features, we observe performance gains of up to 1.3 BLEU points on the science and medical translation tasks over very strong baselines.

2 Related Work

Recent work on machine translation domain adaptation has focused on either the language modeling component or the translation modeling component of an SMT model. Language modeling research has explored methods for subselecting new-domain data from a large monolingual target language corpus for use as language model training data (Lin et al., 1997; Klakow, 2000; Gao et al., 2002; Moore and Lewis, 2010; Mansour et al., 2011). Translation modeling research has typically assumed that either (1) two parallel datasets are available, one in the old domain and one in the new, or (2) a large, mixed-domain parallel training corpus is available. In the first setting, the goal is to effectively make use of both the old-domain and the new-domain parallel training corpora (Civera and Juan, 2007; Koehn and Schroeder, 2007; Foster and Kuhn, 2007; Foster et al., 2010; Haddow and Koehn, 2012; Haddow, 2013). In the second setting, it has been shown that, in some cases, training a translation model on a subset of new-domain parallel training data within a larger training corpus can be more effective than using the complete dataset (Mansour et al., 2011; Axelrod et al., 2011; Sennrich, 2012; Gascó et al., 2012).

For many language pairs and domains, *no* new-domain parallel training data is available. Wu et al. (2008) machine translate new-domain source language monolingual corpora and use the synthetic parallel corpus as additional training data. Daumé and Jagarlamudi (2011), Zhang and Zong (2013), and Irvine et al. (2013b) use new-domain comparable corpora to mine translations for unseen words. That work follows a long line of research on bilingual lexicon induction (e.g. Rapp (1995), Schafer and Yarowsky (2002), Koehn and Knight (2002), Haghighi et al. (2008), Irvine and Callison-Burch (2013), Razmara et al. (2013)). These efforts improve S4 *seen*, and, in some instances, *sense* error types. To our knowledge, no prior work has focused on fixing errors due to inaccurate translation model *scores* in the setting where no new-domain parallel training data is available.

In Klementiev et al. (2012), we used comparable corpora to estimate several features for a given phrase pair that indicate translation equivalence, including contextual, temporal, and topical similarity. The definitions of phrasal and lexical contextual and topic similarity that we use here are taken from our prior work, where we replaced bilingually estimated phrase table features with the new features and cited applications to low resource SMT. In this work we also focus on *scoring* a phrase table using comparable corpora. However, here we work in a domain adaptation setting and seek to augment, not replace, an existing set of bilingually estimated phrase table features.

3 Phrase Table Scoring

We begin with a scored phrase table estimated using our old-domain parallel training corpus. The phrase table contains about 201 million unique source phrases up to length seven and about 479 million total phrase pairs. We use Wikipedia as a source for comparable document pairs (details are given in Section 4.1). We augment the bilingually estimated features with the following: (1) lexical and phrasal contextual similarity estimated over a comparable corpus, (2) lexical and phrasal topical similarity estimated over a comparable corpus, and (3) lexical orthographic similarity.

Contextual Similarity We estimate contextual similarity[2] by first computing a context vector for each source and target word and phrase in our phrase table using the source and target sides of our comparable corpus, respectively. We begin by collecting vectors of counts of words that appear in the context of each source and target phrase, p_s and p_t. We use a bag-of-words context consisting of the two words to the left and two words to

[2]Similar to *distributional similarity*, which is typically defined monolingually.

the right of each occurrence of each phrase. Various means of computing the component values of context vectors from raw context frequency counts have been proposed (e.g. Rapp (1999), Fung and Yee (1998)). Following Fung and Yee (1998), we compute the value of the k-th component of p_s's contextual vector, C_{p_s}, as follows:

$$C_{p_{s_k}} = n_{p_s,k} * (log(n/n_k) + 1)$$

where $n_{p_s,k}$ and n_k are the number of times the k-th source word, s_k, appears in the context of p_s and in the entire corpus, and n is the maximum number of occurrences of any word in the data. Intuitively, the more frequently s_k appears with p_s and the less common it is in the corpus in general, the higher its component value. The context vector for p_s, C_{p_s}, is M-dimensional, where M is the size of the source language vocabulary. Similarly, we compute N-dimensional context vectors for all target language words and phrases, where N is the size of the target language vocabulary.

We identify the most probable translation t for each of the M source language words, s, as the target word with the highest $p(t|s)$ under our word aligned old-domain training corpus. Given this dictionary of unigram translations, we then *project* each M-dimensional source language context vector into the N-dimensional target language context vector space. To compare a given pair of source and target context vectors, C_{p_s} and C_{p_t}, respectively, we compute their cosine similarity, or their dot product divided by the product of their magnitudes:

$$sim_{contextual}(p_s, p_t) = \frac{C_{p_s} \cdot C_{p_t}}{||C_{p_s}||||C_{p_t}||}$$

For a given phrase pair in our phrase table, we estimate *phrasal* contextual similarity by directly comparing the context vectors of the two phrases themselves. Because context vectors for phrases, which tend to be less frequent than words, can be sparse, we also compute lexical contextual similarity over phrase pairs. We define lexical contextual similarity as the average of the contextual similarity between all word pairs within the phrase pair.

Topic Similarity Phrases and their translations are likely to appear in articles written about the same topic in two languages. We estimate topic similarity using the distribution of words and phrases across Wikipedia pages, for which we have interlingual French-English links. Specifically, we compute topical vectors by counting the number of occurrences of each word and phrase across Wikipedia pages. That is, for each source and target phrase, p_s and p_t, we collect M-dimensional topic vectors, where M is the number of Wikipedia page pairs used (in our experiments, M is typically $5,000$). We use Wikipedia's interlingual links to align the French and English topic vectors and normalize each topic vector by the total count. As with contextual similarity, we compare a pair of source and target topic vectors, T_{p_s} and T_{p_t}, respectively, using cosine similarity:

$$sim_{topic}(p_s, p_t) = \frac{T_{p_s} \cdot T_{p_t}}{||T_{p_s}||||T_{p_t}||}$$

We estimate both phrasal and lexical topic similarity for each phrase pair. As before, lexical topic similarity is estimated by taking an average topic similarity across all word pairs in a given phrase pair.

Orthographic Similarity We make use of one additional signal of translation equivalence: orthographic similarity. In this case, we do not reference comparable corpora but simply compute the edit distance between a given pair of phrases. This signal is often useful for identifying translations of technical terms, which appear frequently in our medical and science domain corpora. However, because of word order variation, we do not measure edit distance on phrase pairs directly. For example, French *embryon humain* translates as English *human embryo*; *embryon* translates as *embryo* and *humain* translates as *human*. Although both word pairs are cognates, the words appear in opposite orders in the two phrases. Therefore, directly measuring string edit distance across the phrase pair would not effectively capture the relatedness of the words. Hence, we only measure lexical orthographic similarity, not phrasal. We compute lexical orthographic similarity by first computing the edit distance between each word pair, w_s and w_t, within a given phrase pair, normalized by the lengths of the two words:

$$sim_{orth}(w_s, w_t) = \frac{ed(w_s, w_t)}{\frac{|w_s||w_t|}{2}}$$

We then compute the average normalized edit distance across all word pairs.

The above similarity metrics all allow for scores of zero, which can be problematic for our log-

Corpus	Source Words	Target Words
Training		
Canadian Hansard	161.7 m	144.5 m
Tune-1 / Tune-2 / Test		
Medical	53k / 43k / 35k	46k / 38k / 30k
Science	92k / 120k / 120k	75k / 101k / 101k
Language Modeling and Comparable Corpus Selection		
Medical	-	5.9 m
Science	-	3.6 m

Table 1: Summary of the size of each corpus of text used in this work in terms of the number of source and target word tokens.

linear translation models. We describe our experiments with different minimum score cutoffs in Section 4.2.

4 Experimental Setup

4.1 Data

We assume that the following data is available in our translation setting:

- Large old-domain parallel corpus for training
- Small new-domain parallel corpora for tuning and testing
- Large new-domain English monolingual corpus for language modeling and identifying new-domain-like comparable corpora
- Large mixed-domain comparable corpus, which includes some text from the new-domain

These data conditions are typical for many real-world uses of machine translation. A summary of the size of each corpus is given in Table 1.

Our old-domain training data is taken from the Canadian Hansard parliamentary proceedings dataset, which consists of manual transcriptions and translations of meetings of the Canadian parliament. The dataset is substantially larger than the commonly used Europarl corpus, containing over 8 million sentence pairs and about 150 million word tokens of French and English.

For tuning and evaluation, we use new-domain medical and science parallel datasets released by Irvine et al. (2013a). The medical texts consist of documents from the European Medical Agency (EMEA), originally released by Tiedemann (2009). This data is primarily taken from prescription drug label text. The science data is made up of translated scientific abstracts from the fields of physics, biology, and computer science. For both the medical and science domains, we use three held-out parallel datasets of about 40 and 100 thousand words,[3] respectively, released by Irvine et al. (2013a). We do tuning on *dev1*, additional parameter selection on *test2*, and blind testing on *test1*.

We use large new-domain monolingual English corpora for language modeling and for selecting new-domain-like comparable corpora from our mixed domain comparable corpus. Specifically, we use the English side of the medical and science training datasets released by Irvine et al. (2013a). We do not use the parallel French side of the training data at all; our data setting assumes that no new-domain parallel data is available for training.

We use Wikipedia as a source of comparable corpora. There are over half a million pairs of inter-lingually linked French and English Wikipedia documents.[4] We assume that we have enough monolingual new-domain data in one language to rank Wikipedia pages according to how *new-domain-like* they are. In particular, we use our new-domain English language modeling data to measure new-domain-likeness. We could have targeted our learning even more by using our new-domain French test sets to select comparable corpora. Doing so may increase the similarity between our test data and comparable corpora. However, to avoid overfitting any particular test set, we use our large English new-domain language modeling corpus instead.

For each inter-lingually linked pair of French and English Wikipedia documents, we compute the percent of English phrases up to length four that are observed in the English monolingual new-domain corpus and rank document pairs by the geometric mean of the four overlap measures. More sophisticated ways to identify new-domain-like Wikipedia pages (e.g. (Moore and Lewis, 2010)) may yield additional performance gains, but, qualitatively, the ranked Wikipedia pages seem reasonable for the purposes of generating a large set of top-k new-domain document pairs. The top-10 ranked pages for each domain are listed in Table 2. The top ranked science domain pages are primarily related to concepts from the field of physics but also include computer science and chemistry

[3] Or about 4 thousand lines each. The sentences in the medical domain text are much shorter than those in the science domain.

[4] As of January 2014.

Science	Medical
Diagnosis (artificial intelligence)	Pregabalin
Absorption spectroscopy	Cetuximab
Spectral line	Fluconazole
Chemical kinetics	Calcitonin
Mahalanobis distance	Pregnancy category
Dynamic light scattering	Trazodone
Amorphous solid	Rivaroxaban
Magnetic hyperthermia	Spironolactone
Photoelasticity	Anakinra
Galaxy rotation curve	Cladribine

Table 2: Top 10 Wikipedia articles ranked by their similarity to large new-domain English monolingual corpora.

topics. The top ranked medical domain pages are nearly all prescription drugs, which makes sense given the content of the EMEA medical corpus.

4.2 Phrase-based Machine Translation

We word align our old-domain training corpus using GIZA++ and use the Moses SMT toolkit (Koehn et al., 2007) to extract a translation grammar. In this work, we focus on phrase-based SMT models, however our approach to using new-domain comparable corpora to estimate translation scores is theoretically applicable to any type of translation grammar.

Our baseline models use a phrase limit of seven and the standard phrase-based SMT feature set, including forward and backward phrase and lexical translation probabilities. Additionally, we use the standard lexicalized reordering model. We experiment with two 5-gram language models trained using SRILM with Kneser-Ney smoothing on (1) the English side of the Hansard training corpus, and (2) the relevant new-domain monolingual English corpus. We experiment with using, first, only the old-domain language model and, then, both the old-domain and the new-domain language models.

Our first comparison system augments the standard feature set with the orthographic similarity feature, which is not based on comparable corpora. Our second comparison system uses both the orthographic feature and the contextual and topic similarity features estimated over a *random* set of comparable document pairs. The third system estimates contextual and topic similarity using new-domain-like comparable corpora. We tune our phrase table feature weights for each model separately using batch MIRA (Cherry and Foster, 2012) and new-domain tuning data. Results are averaged over three tuning runs, and we use the implementation of approximate randomization released by Clark et al. (2011) to measure the statistical significance of each feature-augmented model compared with the baseline model that uses the same language model(s).

As noted in Section 3, the features that we estimate from comparable corpora may be zero-valued. We use our second tuning sets[5] to tune a minimum threshold parameter for our new features. We measure performance in terms of BLEU score on the second tuning set as we vary the new feature threshold between $1e-07$ and 0.5 for each domain. A threshold of 0.01, for example, means that we replace all feature with values less than 0.01 with 0.01. For both new-domains, performance drops when we use thresholds lower than 0.01 and higher than 0.25. We use a minimum threshold of 0.1 for all experiments presented below for both domains.

5 Results

Table 3 presents a summary of our results on the test set in each domain. Using only the old-domain language model, our baselines yield BLEU scores of 22.70 and 21.29 on the medical and science test sets, respectively. When we add the orthographic similarity feature, BLEU scores increase significantly, by about 0.4 on the medical data and 0.6 on science. Adding the contextual and topic features estimated over a random selection of comparable document pairs improves BLEU scores slightly in both domains. Finally, using the most new-domain like document pairs to estimate the contextual and topic features yields a 1.3 BLEU score improvement over the baseline in both domains. For both domains, this result is a statistically significant improvement[6] over each of the first three systems.

In both domains, the new-domain language models contribute substantially to translation quality. Baseline BLEU scores increase by about 6 and 5 BLEU score points in the medical and science domains, respectively, when we add the new-domain language models. In the medical domain, neither the orthographic feature nor the orthographic feature in combination with contextual and topic features estimated over random document pairs results in a significant BLEU score improvement. However, using the orthographic feature and the contextual and topic features estimated over new-domain document pairs yields a

[5] *test2* datasets released by Irvine et al. (2013a)

[6] p-value < 0.01

Language Model(s)	System	Medical	Science
Old	Baseline	22.70	21.29
	+ Orthographic Feature	23.09* (+0.4)	21.86* (+0.6)
	+ Orthographic & Random CC Features	23.22* (+0.5)	21.88* (+0.6)
	+ Orthographic & New-domain CC Features	23.98* (+1.3)	22.55* (+1.3)
Old+New	Baseline	28.82	26.18
	+ Orthographic Feature	29.02 (+0.2)	26.40* (+0.2)
	+ Orthographic & Random CC Features	28.86 (+0.0)	26.52* (+0.3)
	+ Orthographic & New-domain CC Features	29.16* (+0.3)	26.50* (+0.3)

Table 3: Comparison between the performance of baseline old-domain translation models and domain-adapted models in translating science and medical domain text. We experiment with two language models: *old*, trained on the English side of our Hansard old-domain training corpus and *new*, trained on the English side of the parallel training data in each new domain. We use comparable corpora of $5,000$ (1) random, and (2) the most new-domain-like document pairs to score phrase tables. All results are averaged over three tuning runs, and we perform statistical significance testing comparing each system augmented with additional features with the baseline system that uses the same language model(s). * indicates that the BLEU scores are statistically significant with $p < 0.01$.

small but significant improvement of 0.3 BLEU. In the science domain, in contrast, all three augmented models perform statistically significantly better than the baseline. Contextual and topic features yield only a slight improvement above the model that uses only the orthographic feature, but the difference is statistically significant. For the science domain, when we use the new domain language model, there is no difference between estimating the contextual and topic features over random comparable document pairs and those chosen for their similarity with new-domain data.

Differences across domains may be due to the fact that the medical domain corpora are much more homogenous, containing the often boilerplate text of prescription drug labels, than the science domain corpora. The science domain corpora, in contrast, contain abstracts from several different scientific fields; because that data is more diverse, a randomly chosen mixed-domain set of comparable corpora may still be relevant and useful for adapting a translation model.

We experimented with varying the number of comparable document pairs used for estimating contextual and topic similarity but saw no significant gains from using more than $5,000$ in either domain. In fact, performance dropped in the medical domain when we used more than a few thousand document pairs. Our proposed approach orders comparable document pairs by how new-domain-like they are and augments models with new features estimated over the top-k. As a result, using more comparable document pairs means that there is more data from which to estimate signals, but it also means that the data is less new-domain like overall. Using a domain similarity threshold to choose a subset of comparable document pairs may prove useful in future work, as the ideal amount of comparable data will depend on the type and size of the initial mixed-domain comparable corpus as well as the homogeneity of the text domain of interest.

We also experimented with using a third language model estimated over the English side of our comparable corpora. However, we did not see any significant improvements in translation quality when we used this language model in combination with the old and new domain language models.

6 Conclusion

In this work, we targeted SMT errors due to translation model *scores* using new-domain comparable corpora. Our old-domain French-English baseline model was trained on the Canadian Hansard parliamentary proceedings dataset, which, at 8 million sentence pairs, is one of the largest publicly available parallel datasets. Our task was to adapt this baseline to the medical and scientific text domains using comparable corpora. We used new-domain parallel data only to tune model parameters and do evaluation. We mined Wikipedia for new-domain-like comparable document pairs, over which we estimated several additional features scores: contextual, temporal, and orthographic similarity. Augmenting the strong baseline with our new feature set improved the quality of machine translations in the medical and science domains by up to 1.3 BLEU points.

7 Acknowledgements

This material is based on research sponsored by DARPA under contract HR0011-09-1-0044 and by the Johns Hopkins University Human Language Technology Center of Excellence. The views and conclusions contained in this publication are those of the authors and should not be interpreted as representing official policies or endorsements of DARPA or the U.S. Government.

References

Amittai Axelrod, Xiaodong He, and Jianfeng Gao. 2011. Domain adaptation via pseudo in-domain data selection. In *Proceedings of the Conference on Empirical Methods in Natural Language Processing (EMNLP)*.

Colin Cherry and George Foster. 2012. Batch tuning strategies for statistical machine translation. In *Proceedings of the Conference of the North American Chapter of the Association for Computational Linguistics (NAACL)*.

Jorge Civera and Alfons Juan. 2007. Domain adaptation in statistical machine translation with mixture modelling. In *Proceedings of the Workshop on Statistical Machine Translation (WMT)*.

Jonathan H. Clark, Chris Dyer, Alon Lavie, and Noah A. Smith. 2011. Better hypothesis testing for statistical machine translation: controlling for optimizer instability. In *Proceedings of the Conference of the Association for Computational Linguistics (ACL)*.

Hal Daumé, III and Jagadeesh Jagarlamudi. 2011. Domain adaptation for machine translation by mining unseen words. In *Proceedings of the Conference of the Association for Computational Linguistics (ACL)*.

George Foster and Roland Kuhn. 2007. Mixture-model adaptation for SMT. In *Proceedings of the Workshop on Statistical Machine Translation (WMT)*.

G. Foster, C. Goutte, and R. Kuhn. 2010. Discriminative instance weighting for domain adaptation in SMT. In *Proceedings of the Conference on Empirical Methods in Natural Language Processing (EMNLP)*.

Pascale Fung and Lo Yuen Yee. 1998. An IR approach for translating new words from nonparallel, comparable texts. In *Proceedings of the Conference of the Association for Computational Linguistics (ACL)*.

Jianfeng Gao, Joshua Goodman, Mingjing Li, and Kai-Fu Lee. 2002. Toward a unified approach to statistical language modeling for chinese. *ACM Transactions on Asian Language Information Processing (TALIP)*.

Guillem Gascó, Martha-Alicia Rocha, Germán Sanchis-Trilles, Jesús Andrés-Ferrer, and Francisco Casacuberta. 2012. Does more data always yield better translations? In *Proceedings of the Conference of the European Association for Computational Linguistics (EACL)*.

Barry Haddow and Philipp Koehn. 2012. Analysing the effect of out-of-domain data on SMT systems. In *Proceedings of the Workshop on Statistical Machine Translation (WMT)*.

Barry Haddow. 2013. Applying pairwise ranked optimisation to improve the interpolation of translation models. In *Proceedings of the Conference of the North American Chapter of the Association for Computational Linguistics (NAACL)*.

Aria Haghighi, Percy Liang, Taylor Berg-Kirkpatrick, and Dan Klein. 2008. Learning bilingual lexicons from monolingual corpora. In *Proceedings of the Conference of the Association for Computational Linguistics (ACL)*.

Ann Irvine and Chris Callison-Burch. 2013. Supervised bilingual lexicon induction with multiple monolingual signals. In *Proceedings of the Conference of the North American Chapter of the Association for Computational Linguistics (NAACL)*.

Ann Irvine, John Morgan, Marine Carpuat, Hal Daumé III, and Dragos Munteanu. 2013a. Measuring machine translation errors in new domains. *Transactions of the Association for Computational Linguistics*, 1(October).

Ann Irvine, Chris Quirk, and Hal Daume III. 2013b. Monolingual marginal matching for translation model adaptation. In *Proceedings of the Conference on Empirical Methods in Natural Language Processing (EMNLP)*.

Dietrich Klakow. 2000. Selecting articles from the language model training corpus. In *Proceedings of the IEEE International Conference on Acoustics, Speech, and Signal Processing (ICASSP)*.

Alex Klementiev, Ann Irvine, Chris Callison-Burch, and David Yarowsky. 2012. Toward statistical machine translation without parallel corpora. In *Proceedings of the Conference of the European Association for Computational Linguistics (EACL)*.

Philipp Koehn and Kevin Knight. 2002. Learning a translation lexicon from monolingual corpora. In *ACL Workshop on Unsupervised Lexical Acquisition*.

Philipp Koehn and Josh Schroeder. 2007. Experiments in domain adaptation for statistical machine translation. In *Proceedings of the Workshop on Statistical Machine Translation (WMT)*.

Philipp Koehn, Hieu Hoang, Alexandra Birch, Chris Callison-Burch, Marcello Federico, Nicola Bertoldi, Brooke Cowan, Wade Shen, Christine Moran,

Richard Zens, Chris Dyer, Ondrej Bojar, Alexandra Constantin, and Evan Herbst. 2007. Moses: Open source toolkit for statistical machine translation. In *Proceedings of the Conference of the Association for Computational Linguistics (ACL)*.

Sung-Chien Lin, Chi-Lung Tsai, Lee-Feng Chien, Ker-Jiann Chen, and Lin-Shan Lee. 1997. Chinese language model adaptation based on document classification and multiple domain-specific language models. In *Fifth European Conference on Speech Communication and Technology*.

Saab Mansour, Joern Wuebker, and Hermann Ney. 2011. Combining translation and language model scoring for domain-specific data filtering. In *Proceedings of the International Workshop on Spoken Language Translation (IWSLT)*.

Robert C. Moore and William Lewis. 2010. Intelligent selection of language model training data. In *Proceedings of the Conference of the Association for Computational Linguistics (ACL)*.

Reinhard Rapp. 1995. Identifying word translations in non-parallel texts. In *Proceedings of the Conference of the Association for Computational Linguistics (ACL)*.

Reinhard Rapp. 1999. Automatic identification of word translations from unrelated English and German corpora. In *Proceedings of the Conference of the Association for Computational Linguistics (ACL)*.

Majid Razmara, Maryam Siahbani, Reza Haffari, and Anoop Sarkar. 2013. Graph propagation for paraphrasing out-of-vocabulary words in statistical machine translation. In *Proceedings of the Conference of the Association for Computational Linguistics (ACL)*.

Charles Schafer and David Yarowsky. 2002. Inducing translation lexicons via diverse similarity measures and bridge languages. In *Proceedings of the Conference on Natural Language Learning (CoNLL)*.

Rico Sennrich. 2012. Perplexity minimization for translation model domain adaptation in statistical machine translation. In *Proceedings of the Conference of the European Association for Computational Linguistics (EACL)*.

Jörg Tiedemann. 2009. News from OPUS - A collection of multilingual parallel corpora with tools and interfaces. In N. Nicolov, K. Bontcheva, G. Angelova, and R. Mitkov, editors, *Recent Advances in Natural Language Processing (RANLP)*.

Hua Wu, Haifeng Wang, and Chengqing Zong. 2008. Domain adaptation for statistical machine translation with domain dictionary and monolingual corpora. In *Proceedings of the International Conference on Computational Linguistics (COLING)*.

Jiajun Zhang and Chengqing Zong. 2013. Learning a phrase-based translation model from monolingual data with application to domain adaptation. In *Proceedings of the Conference of the Association for Computational Linguistics (ACL)*.

Dynamic Topic Adaptation for SMT using Distributional Profiles

Eva Hasler[1] **Barry Haddow**[1] **Philipp Koehn**[1,2]
[1]School of Informatics, University of Edinburgh
[2]Center for Language and Speech Processing, Johns Hopkins University
e.hasler@ed.ac.uk, {bhaddow,pkoehn}@inf.ed.ac.uk

Abstract

Despite its potential to improve lexical selection, most state-of-the-art machine translation systems take only minimal contextual information into account. We capture context with a topic model over distributional profiles built from the context words of each translation unit. Topic distributions are inferred for each translation unit and used to adapt the translation model dynamically to a given test context by measuring their similarity. We show that combining information from both local and global test contexts helps to improve lexical selection and outperforms a baseline system by up to 1.15 BLEU. We test our topic-adapted model on a diverse data set containing documents from three different domains and achieve competitive performance in comparison with two supervised domain-adapted systems.

1 Introduction

The task of lexical selection plays an important role in statistical machine translation (SMT). It strongly depends on context and is particularly difficult when the domain of a test document is unknown, for example when translating web documents from diverse sources. Selecting translations of words or phrases that preserve the sense of the source words is closely related to the field of *word sense disambiguation* (WSD), which has been studied extensively in the past.

Most approaches to WSD model context at the sentence level and do not take the wider context of a word into account. Some of the ideas from the field of WSD have been adapted for machine translation (Carpuat and Wu, 2007b; Carpuat and Wu, 2007a; Chan et al., 2007). For example, Carpuat and Wu (2007a) extend word sense disambiguation to phrase sense disambiguation and show improved performance due to the better fit with multiple possible segmentations in a phrase-based system. Carpuat (2009) test the "one sense per discourse" hypothesis (Gale et al., 1992) for MT and find that enforcing it as a constraint at the document level could potentially improve translation quality. Our goal is to make correct lexical choices in a given context without explicitly enforcing translation consistency.

More recent work in SMT uses latent representations of the document context to dynamically adapt the translation model with either monolingual topic models (Eidelman et al., 2012; Hewavitharana et al., 2013) or bilingual topic models (Hasler et al., 2014), thereby allowing the translation system to disambiguate source phrases using document context. Eidelman et al. (2012) also apply a topic model to each test sentence and find that sentence context is sufficient for picking good translations, but they do not attempt to combine sentence and document level information. Sentence-level topic adaptation for SMT has also been employed by Hasler et al. (2012). Other approaches to topic adaptation for SMT include Zhao and Xing (2007) and Tam et al. (2008), both of which use adapted lexical weights.

In this paper, we present a topic model that learns latent distributional representations of the context of a phrase pair which can be applied to both local and global contexts at test time. We introduce similarity features that compare latent representations of phrase pair types to test contexts to disambiguate senses for improved lexical selection. We also propose different strategies for combining local and global topical context and show that using clues from both levels of contexts is beneficial for translation model adaptation. We evaluate our model on a dynamic adaptation task where the domain of a test document is unknown and hence the problem of lexical selection is harder.

Proceedings of the Ninth Workshop on Statistical Machine Translation, pages 445–456,
Baltimore, Maryland USA, June 26–27, 2014.

2 Related work

Most work in the WSD literature has modelled disambiguation using a limited window of context around the word to disambiguate. Cai et al. (2007), Boyd-graber and Blei (2007) and Li et al. (2010) further tried to integrate the notion of latent topics to address the sparsity problem of the lexicalised features typically used in WSD classifiers. The most closely related work in the area of sense disambiguation is by Dinu and Lapata (2010) who propose a disambiguation method for solving lexical similarity and substitution tasks. They measure word similarity in context by learning distributions over senses for each target word in the form of lower-dimensional distributional representations. Before computing word similarities, they contextualise the global sense distribution of a word using the sense distribution of words in the test context, thereby shifting the sense distribution towards the test context. We adopt a similar distributional representation, but argue that our representation does not need this disambiguation step because at the level of phrase pairs the ambiguity is already much reduced.

Our model performs adaptation using similarity features which is similar to the approach of Costa-jussà and Banchs (2010) who learn a vector space model that captures the source context of every training sentence. In Banchs and Costa-jussà (2011), the vector space model is replaced with representations inferred by Latent Semantic Indexing. However, because their latent representations are learned over training sentences, they have to compare the current test sentence to the latent vector of every training instance associated with a translation unit. The highest similarity value is then used as a feature value. Instead, our model learns latent distributional representations of phrase pairs that can be directly compared to test contexts and are likely to be more robust. Because context words of a phrase pair are tied together in the distributional representations, we can use sparse priors to cluster context words associated with the same phrase pair into few topics.

Recently, Chen et al. (2013) have proposed a vector space model for domain adaptation where phrase pairs are assigned vectors that are defined in terms of the training corpora. A similar vector is built for an in-domain development set and the similarity to the development set is used as a feature during translation. While their vector representations are similar to our latent topic representations, their model has no notion of structure beyond corpus boundaries and is adapted towards a single target domain (*cross-domain*). Instead, our model learns the latent topical structure automatically and the translation model is adapted *dynamically* to each test instance.

We are not aware of prior work in the field of MT that investigates combinations of local and global context. In their recent work on neural language models, Huang et al. (2012) combine the scores of two neural networks modelling the word embeddings of previous words in a sequence as well as those of words from the surrounding document by averaging over all word embeddings occurring in the same document. The score of the next word in a sequence is computed as the sum of the scores of both networks, but they do not consider alternative ways of combining contextual information.

3 Phrase pair topic model (PPT)

Our proposed model aims to capture the relationship between *phrase pairs* and *source words* that frequently occur in the local context of a phrase pair, that is, context words occurring in the same sentence. It therefore follows the *distributional hypothesis* (Harris, 1954) which states that words that occur in the same contexts tend to have similar meanings. For a phrase pair, the idea is that words that occur frequently in its context are indicative of the sense that is captured by the target phrase translating the source phrase.

We assume that all phrase pairs share a global set of topics and during topic inference the distribution over topics for each phrase pair is induced from the latent topic of its context words in the training data. In order to learn topic distributions for each phrase pair, we represent phrase pairs as documents containing all context words from the source sentence context in the training data. These distributional profiles of phrase pairs are the input to the topic modelling algorithm which learns topic clusters over context words.

Figure 1a shows a graphical representation of the following generative process for training. For each of P phrase pairs pp_i in the collection

1. Draw a topic distribution from an asymmetric Dirichlet prior, $\theta_p \sim \text{Dirichlet}(\alpha_0, \alpha \dots \alpha)$.
2. For each position c in the distributional profile of pp_i, draw a topic from that distribution, $z_{p,c} \sim \text{Multinomial}(\theta_p)$.

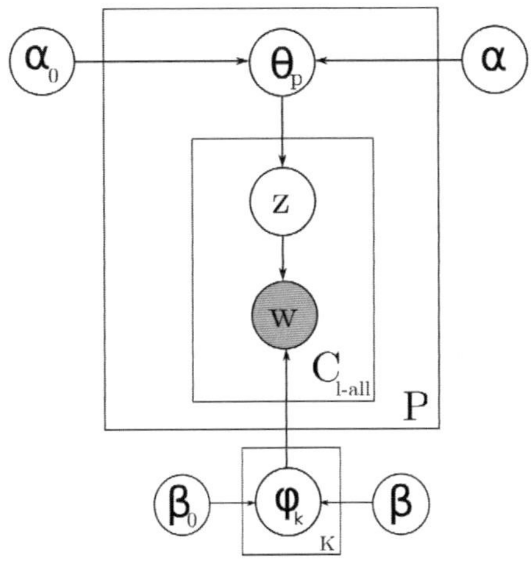

(a) Inference on phrase pair documents (training).

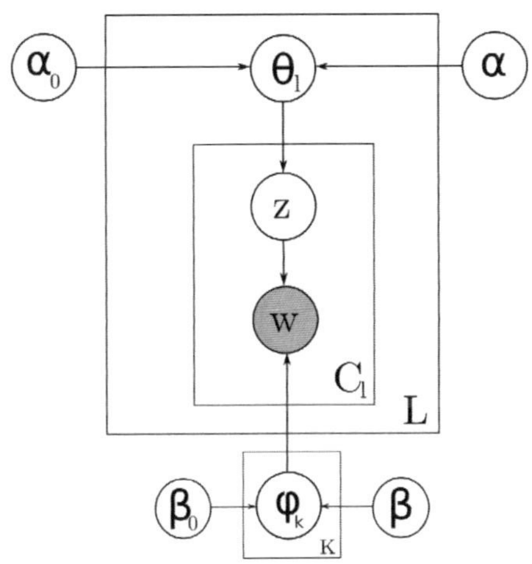

(b) Inference on local test contexts (test).

Figure 1: Graphical representation of the phrase pair topic (PPT) model.

3. Conditioned on topic $z_{p,c}$, choose a context word $w_{p,c} \sim$ Multinomial($\psi_{z_{p,c}}$).

α and β are parameters of the Dirichlet distributions and ϕ_k denotes topic-dependent vocabularies over context words. Test contexts are generated similarly by drawing topic mixtures θ_l for each test context[1] as shown in Figure 1b, drawing topics z for each context position and then drawing context words w for each z. The asymmetric prior on topic distributions (α_0 for topic 0 and α for all other topics) encodes the intuition that there are words occurring in the context of many phrase pairs which can be grouped under a topic with higher a priori probability than the other topics. Figure 1a shows the model for training inference on the distributional representations for each phrase pair, where C_{l-all} denotes the number of context words in all sentence contexts that the phrase pair was seen in the training data, P denotes the number of phrase pairs and K denotes the number of latent topics. The model in Figure 1b has the same structure but shows inference on test contexts, where C_l denotes the number of context words in the test sentence context and L denotes the number of test instances. θ_p and θ_l denote the topic distribution for a phrase pair and a test context, respectively.

3.1 Inference for PPT model

We use collapsed variational Bayes (Teh et al., 2006) to infer the parameters of the PPT model. The posterior distribution over topics is computed as shown below

$$P(z_{p,c} = k|\mathbf{z}^{-(p,c)}, \mathbf{w_c}, p, \alpha, \beta) \propto \frac{(\mathbb{E}_{\hat{q}}[n^{-(p,c)}_{.,k,w_c}] + \beta)}{(\mathbb{E}_{\hat{q}}[n^{-(p,c)}_{.,k,.}] + W_c \cdot \beta)} \cdot (\mathbb{E}_{\hat{q}}[n^{-(p,c)}_{d,k,.}] + \alpha) \quad (1)$$

where $z_{p,c}$ denotes the topic at position c in the distributional profile p, $\mathbf{w_c}$ denotes all context word tokens in the collection, W_c is the total number of context words and $\mathbb{E}_{\hat{q}}$ is the expectation under the variational posterior. $n^{-(p,c)}_{.,k,w_c}$ and $n^{-(p,c)}_{p,k,.}$ are counts of topics occurring with context words and distributional profiles, respectively, and $n^{-(p,c)}_{.,k,.}$ is a topic occurrence count.

Before training the topic model, we remove stop words from all documents. When inferring topics for test contexts, we ignore unseen words because they do not contribute information for topic inference. In order to speed up training inference, we limit the documents in the collection to those corresponding to phrase pairs that are needed to translate the test set[2]. Inference was run for 50 iterations on the distributional profiles for training and for 10 iterations on the test contexts. The output of the training inference step is a model file with all the necessary statistics to compute posterior topic distributions (which are loaded before running test inference), and the set of topic vectors for all phrase pairs. The output of test inference is

[1]A local test context is defined as all words in the test sentence excluding stop words, while contexts of phrase pairs in training do not include the words belonging to the source phrase. The naming in the figure refers to local test contexts L, but global test contexts will be defined similarly.

[2]Reducing the training contexts by scaling or sampling would be expected to speed up inference considerably.

the set of induced topic vectors for all test contexts.

3.2 Modelling local and global context

At training time, our model has access to context words only from the local contexts of each phrase pair in their distributional profiles, that is, other words in the same source sentence as the phrase pair. This is useful for reducing noise and constraining the semantic space that the model considers for each phrase pair during training. At test time, however, we are not limited to applying the model only to the immediate surroundings of a source phrase to disambiguate its meaning. We can potentially take any size of test context into account to disambiguate the possible senses of a source phrase, but for simplicity we consider two sizes of context here which we refer to as local and global context.

Local context Words appearing in the sentence around a test source phrase, excluding stop words.

Global context Words appearing in the document around a test source phrase, excluding stop words.

4 Similarity features

We define similarity features that compare the topic vector θ_p assigned to a phrase pair[3] to the topic vector assigned to a test context, The feature is defined for each source phrase and all its possible translations in the phrase table, as shown below

$$sim(pp_i, test\ context) = cosine(\theta_{p_i}, \theta_c), \quad \forall pp_i \in \{pp_i | \bar{s} \rightarrow \bar{t_i}\} \quad (2)$$

Unlike Banchs and Costa-jussà (2011), we do not learn topic vectors for every training sentence which results in a topic vector per phrase pair token, but instead we learn topic vectors for each phrase pair type. This is more efficient but also more appealing from a modelling point of view, as the topic distributions associated with phrase pairs can be thought of as expected latent contexts. The application of the similarity feature is visualised in Figure 2. On the left, there are two applicable phrase pairs for the source phrase *noyau*, *noyau → kernel* and *noyau → nucleus*, with their distributional representations (words belonging to the *IT* topic versus the *scientific* topic) and assigned topic vectors θ_p. The local and global test contexts are similarly represented by a document containing the context words and a resulting topic vector θ_l or θ_g. The test context vector θ_c can be one of θ_l and θ_g or a combination of both. In this example, the distributional representation of *noyau → kernel* has a larger topical overlap with the test context and will more likely be selected during decoding.

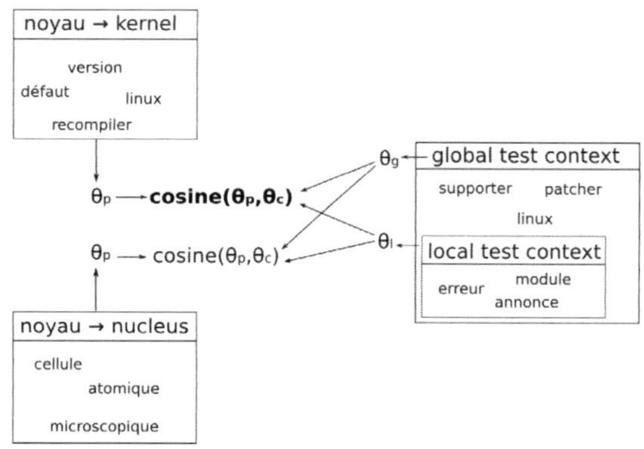

Figure 2: Similarity between topic vectors of two applicable phrase pairs θ_p and the topic vectors θ_l and θ_g from the local and global test context during test time.

While this work focuses on exploring vector space similarity for adaptation, mostly for computational ease, it may be possible to derive probabilistic translation features from the PPT model. This could be a useful addition to the model and we leave this as an avenue for future work.

Types of similarity features
We experiment with local and global phrase similarity features, *phrSim-local* and *phrSim-global*, to perform dynamic topic adaptation. These two similarity features can be combined by adding them both to the log-linear SMT model, in which case each receive separate feature weights. Whenever we use the + symbol in our results tables, the additional features were combined with existing features log-linearly. However, we also experimented with an alternative combination of local and global information where we combine the local and global topic vectors for each test context before computing similarity features.[4] We were

[3]The mass of topic 0 is removed from the vectors and the vectors are renormalised before computing similarity features.

[4]The combined topic vectors were renormalised before computing their similarities with each candidate phrase pair.

motivated by the observation that there are cases where the local and global features have an opposite preference for one translation over another, but the log-linear combination can only learn a global preference for one of the features. Combining the topic vectors allows us to potentially encode a preference for one of the contexts that depends on each test instance.

For similarity features derived from combined topic vectors, $\oplus$ denotes the additive combination of topic vectors, $\otimes$ denotes the multiplicative combination of topic vectors and $\circledast$ denotes a combination that favours the local context for longer sentences and backs off incrementally to the global context for shorter sentences.[5] The intuition behind this combination is that if there is already sufficient evidence in the local context, the local topic mixture may be more reliable than the global mixture.

We also experiment with a combination of the phrase pair similarity features derived from the PPT model with a document similarity feature from the pLDA model described in Hasler et al. (2014). The motivation is that their model learns topic mixtures for documents and uses phrases instead of words to infer the topical context. Therefore, it might provide additional information to our similarity features.

5 Data and experimental setup

Our experiments were carried out on a mixed French-English data set containing the TED corpus (Cettolo et al., 2012), parts of the News Commentary corpus (NC) and parts of the Commoncrawl corpus (CC) from the WMT13 shared task (Bojar et al., 2013) as described in Table 1. To ensure that the baseline model does not have an implicit preference for any particular domain, we selected subsets of the NC and CC corpora such that the training data contains 2.7M English words per domain. We were guided by two constraints in chosing our data set in order to simulate an environment where very diverse documents have to be translated, which is a typical scenario for web translation engines: 1) the data has document boundaries and the content of each document is assumed to be topically related, 2) there is some degree of topical variation within each data set. This setup allows us to evaluate our dynamic topic adaptation approach because the test documents are from different domains and also differ within each domain, which makes lexical selection a much harder problem. The topic adaptation approach does not make use of the domain labels in training or test, because it infers topic mixtures in an unsupervised way. However, we compare the performance of our dynamic approach to domain adaptation methods by providing them the domain labels for each document in training and test.

In order to abstract away from adaptation effects that concern tuning of length penalties and language models, we use a mixed tuning set containing data from all three domains and train one language model on the concatenation of the target sides of the training data. Word alignments are trained on the concatenation of all training data and fixed for all models. Table 2 shows the average length of a document for each domain. While a CC document contains 29.1 sentences on average, documents from NC and TED are on average more than twice as long. The length of a document could have an influence on how reliable global topic information is but also on how important it is to have information from both local and global test contexts.

Data	Mixed	CC	NC	TED
Train	354K (6450)	110K	103K	140K
Dev	2453 (39)	818	817	818
Test	5664 (112)	1892	1878	1894

Table 1: Number of sentence pairs and documents (in brackets) in the data sets.

Data	CC	NC	TED
Test documents	65	31	24
Avg sentences/doc	29.1	60.6	78.9

Table 2: Average number of sentences per document in the test set (per domain).

5.1 Unadapted baseline system

Our baseline is a phrase-based French-English system trained on the concatenation of all parallel data. It was built with the Moses toolkit (Koehn et al., 2007) using the 14 standard core features including a 5-gram language model. Translation quality is evaluated on a large test set, using the average feature weights of three optimisation runs with PRO (Hopkins and May, 2011). We use the

[5]The interpolation weights between local and global topic vectors were set proportional to sentence lengths between 1 and 30. The length of longer sentences was clipped to 30.

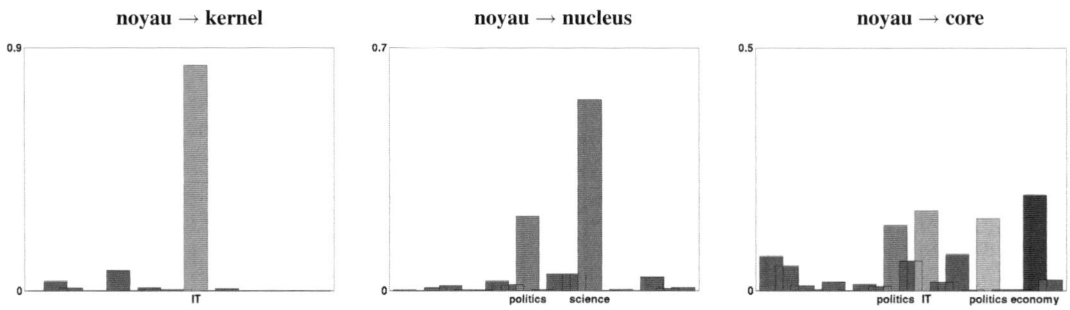

Figure 3: Topic distributions for source phrase *noyau* and three of its translations (20 topics without topic 0). Colored bars correspond to topics *IT*, *politics*, *science*, *economy* with topic proportions $\geq$10%.

mteval-v13a.pl script to compute case-insensitive BLEU scores.

5.2 Domain-adapted benchmark systems

As domain-aware benchmark systems, we use the linear mixture model (DOMAIN1) of Sennrich (2012) and the phrase table fill-up method (DOMAIN2) of Bisazza et al. (2011) (both available in the Moses toolkit). For both systems, the domain labels of the documents are used to group documents of the same domain together. We build adapted tables for each domain by treating the remaining documents as out-of-domain data and combining in-domain with out-of-domain tables. For development and test, the domain labels are used to select the respective domain-adapted model for decoding. Both systems have an advantage over our model because of their knowledge of domain boundaries in the data. This allows for much more confident lexical choices than using an unadapted system but is not possible without prior knowledge about each document.

5.3 Implementation of similarity features

After all topic vectors have been computed, a feature generation step precomputes the similarity features for all pairs of test contexts and applicable phrase pairs for translating source phrases in a test instance. The phrase table of the baseline model is filtered for every test instance (a sentence or document, depending on the context setting) and each entry is augmented with features that express its semantic similarity to the test context. We use a wrapper around the Moses decoder to reload the phrase table for each test instance, which enables us to run parameter optimisation (PRO) in the usual way to get one set of tuned weights for all test sentences. It would be conceivable to use topic-specific weights instead of one set of global weights, but this is not the focus of this work.

6 Qualitative evaluation of phrase pair topic distributions

In order to verify that the topic model is learning useful topic representations for phrase pairs, we inspect the inferred topic distributions for three phrase pairs where the translation of the same source word differs depending on the topical context: *noyau* → *kernel*, *noyau* → *nucleus* and *noyau* → *core*. Figure 3 shows the topic distributions for a PPT model with 20 topics (with topic 0 removed) and highlights the most prominent topics with labels describing their content (politics, IT, science, economy)[6]. The most peaked topic distribution was learned for the phrase pair *noyau* → *kernel* which would be expected to occur mostly in an IT context and the topic with the largest probability mass is in fact related to IT. The most prominent topic for the phrase pair *noyau* → *nucleus* is the science topic, though it seems to be occurring in with the political topic as well. The phrase pair *noyau* → *core* was assigned the most ambiguous topic distribution with peaks at the politics, economy and IT topics. Note also that its topic distribution overlaps with those of the other translations, for example, like the phrase pair *noyau* → *kernel*, it can occur in IT contexts. This shows that the model captures the fact that even within a given topic there can still be ambiguity about the correct translation (both target phrases *kernel* and *core* are plausible translations in an IT context).

[6]Topic labels were assigned by inspecting the most probable context words for each topic according to the model.

Ambiguity of phrase pair topic vectors

The examples in the previous section show that the level of ambiguity differs between phrase pairs that constitute translations of the same source phrase. It is worth noting that introducing bilingual information into topic modelling reduces the sense ambiguity present in monolingual text by preserving only the intersection of the senses of source and target phrases. For example, the distributional profiles of the source phrase *noyau* would contain words that belong to the senses *IT*, *politics*, *science* and *economy*, while the words in the context of the target phrase *kernel* can belong to the senses *IT* and *food* (with source context words such as *grain*, *protéines*, *produire*). Thus, the monolingual representations would still contain a relatively high level of ambiguity while the distributional profile of the phrase pair *noyau* $\rightarrow$ *kernel* preserves only the *IT* sense.

7 Results and discussion

In this section we present experimental results of our model with different context settings and against different baselines. We used bootstrap resampling (Koehn, 2004) to measure significance on the mixed test set and marked all statistically significant results compared to the respective baselines with asterisk (*: $p \leq 0.01$).

7.1 Local context

In Table 3 we compare the results of the concatenation baseline and a model containing the *phrSim-local* feature in addition to the baseline features, for different numbers of latent topics. We show results for the mixed test set containing documents from all three domains as well as the individual results on the documents from each domain. While all topic settings yield improvements over the baseline, the largest improvement on the mixed test set (+0.48 BLEU) is achieved with 50 topics. Topic adaptation is most effective on the TED portion of the test set where the increase in BLEU is 0.59.

Model	Mixed	CC	NC	TED
Baseline	26.86	19.61	29.42	31.88
10 topics	*27.15	19.87	29.63	32.36
20 topics	*27.19	19.92	**29.76**	32.31
50 topics	***27.34**	**20.13**	29.70	**32.47**
100 topics	*27.26	20.02	29.75	32.40
>Baseline	+0.48	+0.52	+0.34	+0.59

Table 3: BLEU scores of baseline system + *phrSim-local* feature for different numbers of topics.

7.2 Global context

Table 4 shows the results of the baseline plus the *phrSim-global* feature that takes into account the whole document context of a test sentence. While the largest overall improvement on the mixed test set is equal to the improvement of the local feature, there are differences in performance for the individual domains. For Commoncrawl documents, the results vary slightly but the largest improvement is still achieved with 50 topics and is almost the same for both. For News Commentary, the scores with the local feature are consistently higher than the scores with the global feature (0.20 and 0.22 BLEU higher for 20 and 50 topics). For TED, the trend is opposite with the global feature performing better than the local feature for all topics (0.28 and 0.40 BLEU higher for 10 and 20 topics). The best improvement over the baseline for TED is 0.83 BLEU, which is higher than the improvement with the local feature.

Model	Mixed	CC	NC	TED
Baseline	26.86	19.61	29.42	31.88
10 topics	*27.30	20.01	29.61	32.64
20 topics	***27.34**	20.07	29.56	**32.71**
50 topics	*27.27	**20.12**	29.48	32.55
100 topics	*27.24	19.95	**29.66**	32.52
>Baseline	+0.48	+0.51	+0.24	+0.83

Table 4: BLEU scores of baseline system + *phrSim-global* feature for different numbers of topics.

7.3 Relation to properties of test documents

To make these results more interpretable, Table 5 lists some of the properties of the test documents per domain. Of the three domains, CC has the shortest documents on average and TED the longest. To understand how this affects topic inference, we measure topical drift as the average divergence (cosine distance) of the local topic distributions for each test sentence to the global topic distribution of their surrounding document. There seems to be a correlation between document length and topical drift, with CC documents showing the least topical drift and TED documents showing the most. This makes sense intuitively because the longer a document is, the more likely it is that the content of a given sentence diverges from the overall topical structure of the document. While this can explain why for CC documents using local or global context results in similar performance, it does not explain the better performance of the local feature for NC documents. The last row of Table 5 shows that sentences in the NC documents are on average the longest and longer sentences would be expected to yield more reliable topic estimates than shorter sentences. Thus, we assume that local context yields better performance for NC because on average the sentences are long enough to yield reliable topic estimates. When local context provides reliable information, it may be more informative than global context because it can be more specific.

For TED, we see the largest topical drift per document, which could lead us to believe that the document topic mixtures do not reflect the topical content of the sentences too well. But considering that the sentences are on average shorter than for the other two domains, it is more likely that the local context in TED documents can be unreliable when the sentences are too short. TED documents contain transcribed speech and are probably less dense in terms of information content than News commentary documents. Therefore, the global context may be more informative for TED which could explain why relying on the global topic mixtures yields better results.

Property	**CC**	**NC**	**TED**
Per document			
Avg number of sentences	29.1	60.6	78.9
Avg topical divergence	0.35	0.43	0.49
Avg sentence length	26.2	31.5	21.7

Table 5: Properties of test documents per domain. Average topical divergence is defined as the average cosine distance of local to global topic distributions in a document.

7.4 Combinations of local and global context

In Table 6 we compare a system that already contains the global feature from a model with 50 topics to the combinations of local and global similarity features described in Section 4.

Of the four combinations, the additive combination of topic vectors ($\oplus$) yields the largest improvement over the baseline with +0.63 BLEU on the mixed test set and +0.88 BLEU on TED. The improvements of the combined model are larger than the improvements for each context on its own, with the only exception being the NC portion of the test set where the improvement is not larger than using just the local context. A possible reason is that when one feature is consistently better for one of the domains (local context for NC), the log-linear combination of both features (tuned on data from all domains) would result in a weaker overall model for that domain. However, if both features encode similar information, as we assume to be the case for CC documents, the presence of both features would reinforce the preference of each and result in equal or better performance. For the additive combination, we expect a similar effect because adding together two topics vectors that have peaks at different topics would make the resulting topic vector less peaked than either of the original vectors.

Model	**Mixed**	**CC**	**NC**	**TED**
Baseline	26.86	19.61	29.42	31.88
+ global	27.27	20.12	29.48	32.55
+ local	*27.43	20.18	29.65	**32.79**
$\oplus$ local	***27.49**	**20.30**	**29.66**	32.76
$\otimes$ local	27.34	20.24	29.61	32.50
$\circledast$ local	*27.45	20.22	29.51	**32.79**
$\oplus$ >BL	+0.63	+0.69	+0.24	+0.88

Table 6: BLEU scores of baseline and combinations of phrase pair similarity features with local and global context (significance compared to baseline+global). All models were trained with 50 topics.

The additive topic vector combination is slightly better than the log-linear feature combination, though the difference is small. Nevertheless, it shows that combining topic vectors before computing similarity features is a viable alternative to log-linear combination, with the potential to design more expressive combination functions. The multiplicative combination performs slightly worse than the additive combination, which suggests that the information provided by the two contexts is not always in agreement. In some cases, the global context may be more reliable while in other cases the local context may have more accurate topic estimates and a voting approach does not take advantage of complementary information. The combination of topic vectors

Source: Le **noyau** contient de nombreux pilotes, afin de fonctionner chez la plupart des utilisateurs.
Reference: The precompiled **kernel** includes a lot of drivers, in order to work for most users.

Source: Il est prudent de consulter les pages de manuel ou les faq spécifiques à votre **os**.
Reference: It's best to consult the man pages or faqs for your **os**.

Source: Nous fournissons nano (un petit éditeur), vim (vi amélioré), qemacs (clone de emacs), **elvis**, joe .
Reference: Nano (a lightweight editor), vim (vi improved), qemacs (emacs clone), **elvis** and joe.

Source: Elle a introduit des politiques [..] à coté des **relations** de gouvernement à gouvernement traditionnelles.
Reference: She has introduced policies [..] alongside traditional government-to-government **relations**.

Figure 4: Examples of test sentences and reference translations with the ambiguous source words and their translations in bold.

depending on sentence length (⊛) performs well for Cc and TED but less well for Nc where we would expect that it helps to prefer the local information. This indicates that the rather ad-hoc way in which we encoded dependency on the sentence length may need further refinement to make better use of the local context information.

Model	noyau →	os →
Baseline	nucleus	bones
global	kernel*	os*
local	nucleus	bones
global⊕local	kernel*	os*

Table 7: Translations of ambiguous source words where global context yields the correct translation (* denotes the correct translation).

Model	elvis →	relations →
Baseline	elvis*	relations*
global	the king	relationship
local	elvis*	relations*
global⊕local	the king	relations*

Table 8: Translations of ambiguous source words where local context yields the correct translation (* denotes the correct translation).

7.5 Effect of contexts on translation

To give an intuition of how lexical selection is affected by contextual information, Figure 4 shows four test sentences with an ambiguous source word and its translation in bold. The corresponding translations with the baseline, the global and local similarity features and the additive combination are shown in Table 7 for the first two examples where the global context yields the correct translation (as indicated by *) and in Table 8 for the last two examples where the local context yields the correct translation.[7] In Table 7, the additive combination preserves the choice of the global model and yields the correct translations, while in Table 8 only the second example is translated correctly by the combined model. A possible explanation is that the topical signal from the global context is stronger and results in more discriminative similarity values. In that case, the preference of the global context would be likely to have a larger influence on the similarity values in the combined model. A useful extension could be to try to detect for a given test instance which context provides more reliable information (beyond encoding sentence length) and boost the topic distribution from that context in the combination.

7.6 Comparison with domain adaptation

Table 9 compares the additive model (⊕) to the two domain-adapted systems that know the domain label of each document during training and test. Our topic-adapted model yields overall competitive performance with improvements of +0.37 and +0.25 BLEU on the mixed test set, respectively. While it yields slightly lower performance on the Nc documents, it achieves equal performance on TED documents and improves by up to +0.94 BLEU on Commoncrawl documents. This can be explained by the fact that Commoncrawl is the most diverse of the three domains with documents crawled from all over web, thus we expect topic adaptation to be most effective in comparison to domain adaptation in this scenario. Our dynamic approach allows us to adapt the similarity features to each test sentence and test document individually and is therefore more flexible than

[7]For these examples, the local model happens to yield the same translations as the baseline model.

Type of adaptation	Model	Mixed	Cc	Nc	TED
Domain-adapted	DOMAIN1	27.24	19.61	29.87	32.73
	DOMAIN2	27.12	19.36	29.78	32.71
Topic-adapted	global $\oplus$ local	***27.49**	**20.30**	29.66	**32.76**
	>DOMAIN1	+0.25	+0.69	-0.21	+0.03
	>DOMAIN2	+0.37	+0.94	-0.12	+0.05

Table 9: BLEU scores of translation model using similarity features derived from PPT model (50 topics) in comparison with two (supervised) domain-adapted systems.

Model	Mixed	Cc	Nc	TED
Baseline	26.86	19.61	29.42	31.88
+ docSim	27.22	20.11	29.63	32.40
+ phrSim-global $\oplus$ phrSim-local	*27.58	20.34	**29.71**	32.96
+ phrSim-global $\circledast$ phrSim-local	***27.60**	**20.35**	29.70	**33.03**
global$\circledast$local>BL	+0.74	+0.74	+0.38	+1.15

Table 10: BLEU scores of baseline, baseline + document similarity feature and additional phrase pair similarity features (significance compared to baseline+docSim). All models were trained with 50 topics.

cross-domain adaptation approaches while requiring no information about the domain of a test instance.

7.7 Combination with an additional document similarity feature

To find out whether similarity features derived from different types of topic models can provide complementary information, we add the *phrSim* features to a system that already includes a document similarity feature (*docSim*) derived from the pLDA model (Hasler et al., 2014) which learns topic distributions at the document level and uses phrases instead of words as the minimal units. The results are shown in Table 10. Adding the two best combinations of local and global context from Table 6 yields the best results on TED documents with an increase of 0.63 BLEU over the baseline + *docSim* model and 1.15 BLEU over the baseline. On the mixed test set, the improvement is 0.38 BLEU over the baseline + *docSim* model and 0.74 BLEU over the baseline. Thus, we show that combining different scopes and granularities of similarity features consistently improves translation results and yields larger gains than using each of the similarity features alone.

8 Conclusion

We have presented a new topic model for dynamic adaptation of machine translation systems that learns topic distributions for phrase pairs. These latent topic representations can be compared to latent representations of local or global test contexts and integrated into the translation model via similarity features.

Our experimental results show that it is beneficial for adaptation to use contextual information from both local and global contexts, with BLEU improvements of up to 1.15 over the baseline system on TED documents and 0.74 on a large mixed test set with documents from three domains. Among four different combinations of local and global information, we found that the additive combination of topic vectors performs best. We conclude that information from both contexts should be combined to correct potential topic detection errors in either of the two contexts. We also show that our dynamic adaptation approach performs competitively in comparison with two supervised domain-adapted systems and that the largest improvement is achieved for the most diverse portion of the test set.

In future work, we would like to experiment with more compact distributional profiles to speed up inference and explore the possibilities of deriving probabilistic translation features from the PPT model as an extension to the current model. Another avenue for future work could be to combine contextual information that captures different types of information, for example, to distinguish between semantic and syntactic aspects in the local context.

Acknowledgements

This work was supported by funding from the Scottish Informatics and Computer Science Alliance (Eva Hasler) and funding from the European Union Seventh Framework Programme (FP7/2007-2013) under grant agreement 287658 (EU BRIDGE) and grant agreement 288769 (ACCEPT). Thanks to Annie Louis for helpful comments on a draft of this paper and thanks to the anonymous reviewers for their useful feedback.

References

Rafael E Banchs and Marta R Costa-jussà. 2011. A Semantic Feature for Statistical Machine Translation. In *SSST-5 Proceedings of the Fifth Workshop on Syntax, Semantics and Structure in Statistical Translation*, pages 126–134.

Arianna Bisazza, Nick Ruiz, and Marcello Federico. 2011. Fill-up versus Interpolation Methods for Phrase-based SMT Adaptation. In *Proceedings of IWSLT*.

Ondrej Bojar, Christian Buck, Chris Callison-Burch, Christian Federmann, Barry Haddow, Philipp Koehn, Christof Monz, Matt Post, Radu Soricut, and Lucia Specia. 2013. Findings of the 2013 workshop on statistical machine translation. In *Proceedings of WMT 2013*.

Jordan Boyd-graber and David Blei. 2007. A Topic Model for Word Sense Disambiguation. In *Proceedings of EMNLP-CoNLL*, pages 1024–1033.

Jun Fu Cai, Wee Sun Lee, and Yee Whye Teh. 2007. Improving Word Sense Disambiguation Using Topic Features. In *Proceedings of EMNLP*, pages 1015–1023.

Marine Carpuat and Dekai Wu. 2007a. How Phrase Sense Disambiguation outperforms Word Sense Disambiguation for Statistical Machine Translation. In *International Conference on Theoretical and Methodological Issues in MT*.

Marine Carpuat and Dekai Wu. 2007b. Improving Statistical Machine Translation using Word Sense Disambiguation. In *Proceedings of EMNLP*, pages 61–72.

Marine Carpuat. 2009. One Translation per Discourse. In *Proceedings of the NAACL HLT Workshop on Semantic Evaluations: Recent Achievements and Future Directions*, pages 19–27.

Mauro Cettolo, Christian Girardi, and Marcello Federico. 2012. WIT3: Web Inventory of Transcribed and Translated Talks. In *Proceedings of EAMT*.

Yee Seng Chan, Hwee Tou Ng, and David Chiang. 2007. Word Sense Disambiguation Improves Statistical Machine Translation. In *Proceedings of ACL*.

Boxing Chen, Roland Kuhn, and George Foster. 2013. Vector Space Model for Adaptation in Statistical Machine Translation. In *Proceedings of ACL*, pages 1285–1293.

Marta R. Costa-jussà and Rafael E. Banchs. 2010. A vector-space dynamic feature for phrase-based statistical machine translation. *Journal of Intelligent Information Systems*, 37(2):139–154, August.

Georgiana Dinu and Mirella Lapata. 2010. Measuring Distributional Similarity in Context. In *Proceedings of EMNLP*, pages 1162–1172.

Vladimir Eidelman, Jordan Boyd-Graber, and Philip Resnik. 2012. Topic Models for Dynamic Translation Model Adaptation. In *Proceedings of ACL*.

William A Gale, Kenneth W Church, and David Yarowsky. 1992. One Sense Per Discourse. In *Proceedings of the workshop on Speech and Natural Language*.

Zellig Harris. 1954. Distributional structure. *Word*, 10(23):146–162.

Eva Hasler, Barry Haddow, and Philipp Koehn. 2012. Sparse Lexicalised Features and Topic Adaptation for SMT. In *Proceedings of IWSLT*.

Eva Hasler, Phil Blunsom, Philipp Koehn, and Barry Haddow. 2014. Dynamic Topic Adaptation for Phrase-based MT. In *Proceedings of the 14th Conference of the European Chapter of the Association for Computational Linguistics*, Gothenburg, Sweden.

Sanjika Hewavitharana, Dennis N Mehay, and Sankaranarayanan Ananthakrishnan. 2013. Incremental Topic-Based Translation Model Adaptation for Conversational Spoken Language Translation. In *Proceedings of ACL*, pages 697–701.

Mark Hopkins and Jonathan May. 2011. Tuning as ranking. In *Proceedings of the Conference on Empirical Methods in Natural Language Processing*, Edinburgh, United Kingdom.

Eric H Huang, Richard Socher, Christopher D Manning, and Andrew Y Ng. 2012. Improving Word Representations via Global Context and Multiple Word Prototypes. In *Proceedings of ACL*, pages 873–882.

Philipp Koehn, Hieu Hoang, Alexandra Birch, Chris Callison-Burch, Marcello Federico, Nicola Bertoldi, Brooke Cowan, Wade Shen, Christine Moran, Richard Zens, Chris Dyer, Ondrej Bojar, Alexandra Constantin, and Evan Herbst. 2007. Moses: Open source toolkit for SMT. In *Proceedings of ACL: Demo and poster sessions*.

Philipp Koehn. 2004. Statistical Significance Tests for Machine Translation Evaluation. In *Proc. of EMNLP*.

Linlin Li, Benjamin Roth, and Caroline Sporleder. 2010. Topic Models for Word Sense Disambiguation and Token-based Idiom Detection. In *Proceedings of ACL*, pages 1138–1147.

Rico Sennrich. 2012. Perplexity Minimization for Translation Model Domain Adaptation in Statistical Machine Translation. In *Proceedings of EACL*.

Yik-Cheung Tam, Ian Lane, and Tanja Schultz. 2008. Bilingual LSA-based adaptation for statistical machine translation. *Machine Translation*, 21(4):187–207, November.

Yee Whye Teh, David Newman, and Max Welling. 2006. A collapsed variational Bayesian inference algorithm for LDA. In *Proceedings of NIPS*.

B Zhao and E P Xing. 2007. HM-BiTAM: Bilingual topic exploration, word alignment, and translation. *Neural Information Processing*.

Unsupervised Adaptation for Statistical Machine Translation

Saab Mansour and **Hermann Ney**
Human Language Technology and Pattern Recognition
Computer Science Department
RWTH Aachen University
Aachen, Germany
{mansour,ney}@cs.rwth-aachen.de

Abstract

In this work, we tackle the problem of language and translation models domain-adaptation without explicit bilingual in-domain training data. In such a scenario, the only information about the domain can be induced from the source-language test corpus. We explore unsupervised adaptation, where the source-language test corpus is combined with the corresponding hypotheses generated by the translation system to perform adaptation. We compare unsupervised adaptation to supervised and pseudo supervised adaptation. Our results show that the choice of the adaptation (target) set is crucial for successful application of adaptation methods. Evaluation is conducted over the German-to-English WMT newswire translation task. The experiments show that the unsupervised adaptation method generates the best translation quality as well as generalizes well to unseen test sets.

1 Introduction

Over the last few years, large amounts of statistical machine translation (SMT) monolingual and bilingual corpora were collected. Early years focused on structured data translation such as newswire. Nowadays, due to the relative success of SMT, new domains of translation are being explored, such as lecture and patent translation (Cettolo et al., 2012; Goto et al., 2013).

The task of domain adaptation tackles the problem of utilizing existing resources mainly drawn from one domain (e.g. parliamentary discussion) to maximize the performance on the target (test) domain (e.g. newswire).

To be able to perform adaptation, a *target set* representing the test domain is used to manipulate the general-domain models. Previous work on SMT adaptation focused on the scenario where (small) bilingual in-domain or pseudo in-domain training data are available. Furthermore, small attention was given to the choice of the target set for adaptation. In this work, we explore the problem of adaptation where no explicit bilingual data from the test domain is available for training, and the only resource encapsulating information about the domain is the source-language test corpus itself.

We explore how to utilize the source-language test corpus for adapting the language model (LM) and the translation model (TM). A combination of source and automatically translated target of the test set is compared to using the source side only for TM adaptation. Furthermore, we compare using the test set to using in-domain data and a pseudo in-domain data (e.g. news-commentary as opposed to newswire).

Experiments are done on the WMT 2013 German-to-English newswire translation task. Our best adaptation method shows competitive results to the best submissions of the evaluation.

This paper is structured as follows. We review related work in Section 2 and introduce the basic adaptation methods in Section 3. The experimental setup is described in Section 4, results are discussed in Section 5 and we conclude in Section 6.

2 Related Work

A broad range of methods and techniques have been suggested in the past for domain adaptation for both SMT and automatic speech recognition (ASR).

For ASR, (Bellegarda, 2004) gives an overview of LM adaptation methods. He differentiates between two cases regarding the availability of in-domain adaptation data: *(i)* the data is available and can be directly used to manipulate a background (general domain) corpus, and *(ii)* the data is not available or too small, and then it can be gathered or automatically generated during the

Proceedings of the Ninth Workshop on Statistical Machine Translation, pages 457–465,
Baltimore, Maryland USA, June 26–27, 2014.

recognition process. (Bacchiani and Roark, 2003) compare supervised against unsupervised (using automatic transcriptions) in-domain data for LM training for the task of ASR. They show that augmenting the supervised in-domain to the training of the LM performs better than the unsupervised in-domain. In addition, they perform "self-training", where the test set is automatically transcribed and added to the LM. When using a strong baseline, no improvements in recognition quality are achieved. We differ from their work by using the unsupervised test data to adapt a general-domain bilingual corpus. We also performed initial experiments of "self-training" for language modeling, where (artificial) perplexity improvement was achieved but without an impact on the machine translation (MT) quality.

(Zhao et al., 2004) tackle LM adaptation for SMT. Similarly to our work, they use automatically generated hypotheses to perform adaptation. We extend their work by using the hypotheses also for TM adaptation. (Hildebrand et al., 2005) perform LM and TM adaptation based on information retrieval methods. They use the source-language test corpus to filter the bilingual data, and then use the target side of the filtered bilingual data to perform LM adaptation. We differ from their work by using both the in-domain source-language corpus and its corresponding automatic translation for adaptation, which is shown in our experiments to achieve superior results than when using the source-side information only. (Foster and Kuhn, 2007) perform LM and TM adaptation using mixture modeling. In their setting, the mixture weights are modified to express adaptation. They compare cross-domain (in-domain available) against dynamic adaptation. In the dynamic adaptation scenario, they utilize the source side of the development set to adapt the mixture weights (LM adaptation is possible as they only use parallel training data, which enables filtering based on the source side and then keeping the corresponding target side of the data). For an in-domain test set, the cross-domain setup performs better than the dynamic adaptation method. (Ueffing et al., 2007) use the test set translations as additional data to train the TM. One important aspect in their work is confidence measurement to remove noisy translation. In our approach, we use the automatic test set translations to adapt the SMT models rather than augmenting it as additional TM data. We also compare different adaptation sets. Furthermore, we do not use confidence measures to filter the automatic translations as they are only used to adapt the general-domain system and are not augmented to the TM.

In this work, we apply cross-entropy scoring for adaptation as done by (Moore and Lewis, 2010). Moore and Lewis (2010) apply adaptation by using an LM-based cross-entropy filtering for LM training. Axelrod et al. (2011) generalized the method for TM adaptation by interpolating the source and target LMs. These two works focused on a scenario where in-domain training data are available for adaptation. In this work, we focus on a scenario where in-domain training data is not labeled, and the main resource for adaptation is the source-language test data.

In recent WMT evaluations, the method of (Moore and Lewis, 2010) was utilized by several translation systems (Koehn and Haddow, 2012; Rubino et al., 2013). These systems use pseudo in-domain corpus, i.e., news-commentary, as the target domain (while the test domain is newswire). The contribution of this work is two fold: we show that the choice of the target set is crucial for adaptation, in addition, we show that an unsupervised target set performs best in terms of translation quality as well as generalization performance to unseen test sets (in comparison to using pseudo in-domain data or the references as target sets).

3 Cross-Entropy Adaptation

In this work, we use sample scoring for the purpose of adaptation. We start by introducing the scoring framework and then show how we utilize it to perform filtering based adaptation and weighted phrase extraction based adaptation.

LM cross-entropy scores can be used for both monolingual data weighting for LM training as done by (Moore and Lewis, 2010), or bilingual weighting for TM training as done by (Axelrod et al., 2011).

We differentiate between two types of data sets: the *adaptation set* (target) representative of the test-domain which we refer to also as in-domain (IN), and the general-domain (GD) set which we want to adapt.

The scores for each sentence in the general-domain corpus are based on the cross-entropy difference of the IN and GD models. Denoting $H_M(x)$ as the cross entropy of sentence x according to model M, then the cross entropy difference $DH_M(x)$ can be written as:

$$DH_M(x) = H_{M_{IN}}(x) - H_{M_{GD}}(x) \quad (1)$$

The intuition behind eq. (1) is that we are interested in sentences as close as possible to the in-domain, but also as far as possible from the general corpus. Moore and Lewis (2010) show that using eq. (1) for LM filtering performs better in terms of perplexity than using in-domain cross-entropy only ($H_{M_{IN}}(x)$). For more details about the reasoning behind eq. (1) we refer the reader to (Moore and Lewis, 2010).

Axelrod et al. (2011) adapted eq. (1) for bilingual data filtering for the purpose of TM training. The bilingual LM cross entropy difference for a sentence pair (f_r, e_r) in the GD corpus is then defined by:

$$DH_{LM}(f_r, e_r) = DH_{LM_{src}}(f_r) + DH_{LM_{trg}}(e_r) \quad (2)$$

For IBM Model 1 (M1), the cross-entropy $H_{M1}(f_r|e_r)$ is defined similarly to the LM cross-entropy, and the resulting bilingual cross-entropy difference will be of the form:

$$DH_{M1}(f_r, e_r) = DH_{M1}(f_r|e_r) + DH_{M1}(e_r|f_r)$$

The combined LM+M1 score is obtained by summing the LM and M1 bilingual cross-entropy difference scores:

$$d_r = DH_{LM}(f_r, e_r) + DH_{M1}(f_r, e_r) \quad (3)$$

3.1 Filtering

A common framework to perform sample filtering is to score each sample according to a model, and then assigning a threshold on the score which filters out unwanted samples. If the score we generate is related to the probability that the sample was drawn from the same distribution as the in-domain data, we are selecting the samples most relevant to our domain. In this way we can achieve adaptation of the general-domain data.

We use the LM cross-entropy difference from eq. (1) for LM filtering and a combined LM+M1 score (eq. (3) for TM filtering. We sort the sentences in the general-domain according to the score and select the best 50%,25%,...,6.25% training instances. Our models are then trained on the selected portions of the training data, and the best performing portion (according to perplexity for LM training and BLEU for TM training) on the development set is chosen as the adapted corpus.

3.2 Weighted Phrase Extraction

The classical phrase model is trained using a "simple" maximum likelihood estimation, resulting in phrase translation probabilities being defined by relative frequency:

$$p(\tilde{f}|\tilde{e}) = \frac{\sum_r c_r(\tilde{f}, \tilde{e})}{\sum_{\tilde{f}'} \sum_r c_r(\tilde{f}', \tilde{e})} \quad (4)$$

Here, $\tilde{f}, \tilde{e}$ are contiguous phrases, $c_r(\tilde{f}, \tilde{e})$ denotes the count of $(\tilde{f}, \tilde{e})$ being a translation of each other (usually according to word alignment and heuristics) in sentence pair (f_r, e_r). One method to introduce weights to eq. (4) is by weighting each sentence pair by a weight w_r. Eq. (4) will now have the extended form:

$$p(\tilde{f}|\tilde{e}) = \frac{\sum_r w_r \cdot c_r(\tilde{f}, \tilde{e})}{\sum_{\tilde{f}'} \sum_r w_r \cdot c_r(\tilde{f}', \tilde{e})} \quad (5)$$

It is easy to see that setting $\{w_r = 1\}$ will result in eq. (4) (or any non-zero equal weights). Increasing the weight w_r of the corresponding sentence pair will result in an increase of the probabilities of the phrase pairs extracted. Thus, by increasing the weight of in-domain sentence pairs, the probability of in-domain phrase translations could also increase.

We utilize d_r from eq. (3) using a combined LM+M1 scores for our suggested weighted phrase extraction. d_r can be assigned negative values, and lower d_r indicates sentence pairs which are more relevant to the in-domain. Therefore, we negate the term d_r to get the notion of higher is closer to the in-domain, and use an exponent to ensure positive values. The final weight is of the form:

$$w_r = e^{-d_r} \quad (6)$$

This term is proportional to perplexities, as the exponent of entropy is perplexity by definition.

One could also use filtering for TM adaptation, but, as shown in (Mansour and Ney, 2012), filtering for TM could only reduce the size and weighting performs better than filtering.

4 Experimental Setup

4.1 Training Data

The experiments are done on the recent German-to-English WMT 2013 translation task [1]. For

[1] The translation task resources of WMT 2013 are available under: http://www.statmt.org/wmt13/

Corpus	Sent	De	En
Training data			
news-commentary	177K	4.8M	4.5M
europarl	1 888K	51.5M	51.9M
common-crawl	2 030K	47.8M	47.7M
total	4 095K	104.1M	104M
Test data			
newstest08	2051	52446	49749
newstest09	2525	68512	65648
newstest10	2489	68232	62024
newstest11	3003	80181	74856
newstest12	3003	79912	73089
newstest13	3000	69066	64900

Table 1: German-English bilingual training and test data statistics: the number of sentence pairs (Sent), German (De) and English (En) words are given.

Corpus	Tokens [M]	ppl	
		dev	test
bi.en	88	216.5	192.7
giun	775	229.0	198.9
ns	1 479	144.1	122.7

Table 2: German-English monolingual corpora statistics: the number of tokens is given in millions [M], *ppl* is the perplexity of the corresponding corpus.

German-English WMT 2013, the common-crawl bilingual corpus was introduced, enabling more impact for TM adaptation on the SMT system quality. Monolingual English data exists with more than 1 billion words, making LM adaptation and size reduction a wanted feature. We use *newstest08* throughout *newstest13* to evaluate the SMT systems. The baseline systems are built using all (unfiltered) available monolingual and bilingual training data. The bilingual corpora and the test data statistics are summarized in Table 1.

In Table 2, we summarize the size and LM perplexity of the different monolingual corpora for the German-English task over the LM development set *newstest09* and test set *newstest13*. The corpora are split into three parts, the English side of the bilingual side (*bi.en*), the giga-fren joined with undoc (*giun*) and the news-shuffle (*ns*) corpus. To keep the perplexity results comparable, we use the intersection vocabulary of the different corpora as a reference vocabulary. From the table, we notice that as expected, the in-domain corpus *news-shuffle* generate the best perplexity values.

4.2 SMT System

The baseline system is built using the open-source SMT toolkit Jane[2], which provides state-of-the-art phrase-based SMT system (Wuebker et al., 2012). We use the standard set of models with phrase translation probabilities for source-to-target and target-to-source directions, smoothing with lexical weights, a word and phrase penalty, distance-based reordering, hierarchical reordering model (Galley and Manning, 2008) and a 4-gram target language model. The baseline system is competitive and using adaptation we will show comparable results to the best systems of WMT 2013. The SMT system was tuned on the development set *newstest10* with minimum error rate training (MERT) (Och, 2003) using the BLEU (Papineni et al., 2002) error rate measure as the optimization criterion. We test the performance of our system on the *newstest08...newstest13* sets using the BLEU and translation edit rate (TER) (Snover et al., 2006) measures. We use TER as an additional measure to verify the consistency of our improvements and avoid over-tuning. All results are based on true-case evaluation. We perform bootstrap resampling with bounds estimation as described by (Koehn, 2004). We use the 90% and 95% (denoted by † and ‡ correspondingly in the tables) confidence thresholds to draw significance conclusions.

5 Results

To perform adaptation, an adaptation set representing the in-domain needs to be specified to be plugged in eq. (1) as IN. The choice of the adaptation corpus is crucial for the successful application of the cross-entropy based scoring, as the closer the corpus is to our test domain, the better adaptation we get. For the WMT task, the choice of the adaptation corpus is not an easy task. The genre of the test sets is newswire, while the bilingual training data is composed of news-commentary, parliamentary records (europarl) and common-crawl noisy data. On the other hand, the monolingual data includes large amounts of in-domain newswire data (news-shuffle).

For LM training, the task of adaptation might be unprofitable in terms of performance, as the

[2] www.hltpr.rwth-aachen.de/jane

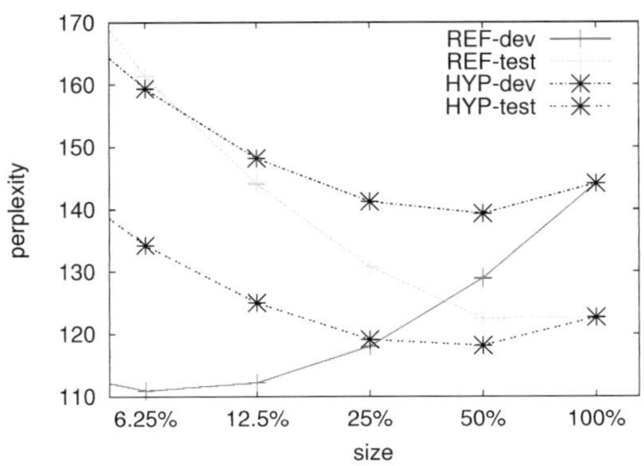

Figure 1: Size (fraction of *news-shuffle* data) against the resulting LM perplexity on *dev* and *test*, using different filtering sets.

majority of the training is in-domain. Still, one might hope that by using adaptation, a more compact and comparable LM can be generated. Another point is that LM training is less demanding than TM training, and a comparison of the results of LM and TM adaptation might prove fruitful and convey additional information.

Next, we start with LM adaptation experiments where we mainly compare different adaptation sets for filtering over the final translation quality. A comparison to the full (unfiltered LM) is also produced. For TM adaptation, we repeat the adaptation sets choice experiment and analyze the difference between the sets.

5.1 LM Adaptation

To evaluate our methods experimentally, we use the German-English translation task to compare different adaptation sets for filtering and then analyze the full versus the filtered LM SMT system results. We recall that *newstest09* is used as a development set and *newstest13* as a test set in the LM experiments.

The different adaptation sets for filtering that we explore are: *(i)* unsupervised: an automatic translation of the test sets (*newstest08...newstest13*), where the baseline system (without adaptation) is used to generate the hypotheses which then define the adaptation corpus for filtering (*HYP*), *(ii)* supervised: the references of the test sets *newstest08...newstest12* concatenated, *newstest13* is kept as a blind set, which will also help us determine if overfitting occurs (*REF*), and *(iii)* pseudo supervised: a pseudo in-domain corpus, *news-commentary*, where the domain is similar to the test set domain, but the style might differ (*NC*). Next, we filter the *news-shuffle* (*ns*) and *giga-fren+undoc* (*giun*) according to the three suggested adaptations sets, where we plug each adaptation set in eq. (1) as IN and compare their performance.

Corpus	**Adapt set**	**Optimal size**	**ppl dev**	**ppl test**
ns	none	100%	144	123
	NC	100%	144	123
	REF	6.25%	111	161
	HYP	50%	139	118
giun	none	100%	229	199
	NC	50%	215	185
	REF	6.25%	161	171
	HYP	12.5%	187	159

Table 3: Optimal size portion and resulting perplexities, across adaptation sets (**NC**, **REF** and **HYP**) and monolingual LM training corpora.

5.1.1 Perplexity Results

In Figure 1, we draw the size portion versus the dev and test perplexities for the *REF* and *HYP* adaptation sets over the *news-shuffle* corpus. *REF* performs best for filtering the dev set, where an optimum is achieved when using only 6.25% of the news-shuffle data, with a perplexity of 111 in comparison to 144 perplexity of the full LM. Measuring perplexities over newstest08-12, *REF* based filtering achieves 109 while the full LM achieves 140. The good performance on the seen sets comes with the cost of severe overfitting, where the test set perplexity using 6.25% of the data is 161, much higher than 123 generated by the full LM. On the other hand, *HYP* achieves an optimum for both sets when using 50% of the data. A summary of the best results across monolingual corpora and adaptation sets is given in Table 3. Filtering the *giun* monolingual corpus shows similar results to *ns* filtering, where overfitting occurs on the blind test set when using *REF* as the target domain. *HYP*-based adaptation achieves the best LM perplexity on the blind test set. *NC*-based adaptation retains the biggest amount of data, 50% for the *giun* corpus and 100% (no filtering) for the *ns* corpus. *REF*-based adaptation shows overfitting on the seen dev set, and the worst results on the blind test set when filtering the *ns* corpus.

LM data	Adapt. set	ppl	newstest10		newstest11		newstest12		newstest13	
			BLEU	TER	BLEU	TER	BLEU	TER	BLEU	TER
bi.en+giun	none	162	23.2	59.6	21.2	61.0	21.8	60.9	24.6	57.2
	NC	160	23.2	59.3	21.5	61.0	21.9	60.7	24.6	57.0
	REF	158	23.7	59.2	21.9	60.5	22.2	60.5	24.5	57.3
	HYP	151	23.6	59.2	21.5	60.9	22.2	60.4	25.1	56.7
+ns	none	111	24.5	59.1	22.1	61.3	23.3	60.1	25.9	56.7
	NC	111	24.4	58.7	22.1	60.5	23.4	59.7	25.5	56.6
	REF	143	25.7	57.8	23.0	59.9	24.2	59.4	24.1	57.8
	HYP	109	25.0	58.2	22.1	60.6	23.5	59.6	25.9	56.3

Table 4: German-English LM filtering results using different adaptation sets. The LM perplexity over the blind test set *nestest13*, as well as BLEU and TER percentages are presented.

5.1.2 Translation Results

Next, we measure whether the improvements of the single adapted corpora carry over to the mixture LM both in perplexity and translation quality. The mixture LM is created by linear interpolation (of *bi.en*, *giun* and *ns*) with perplexity minimization on the dev set using the SRILM toolkit[3]. We carry out two experiments, in the first we interpolate the English side of the bilingual data with a *giun* LM, then we add the *ns* LM. This way we measure whether the effects of adaptation carry over to a stronger baseline.

The SMT systems built using the full and filtered LMs are compared in Table 4. The table includes the data used for LM training, the adaptation set used to filter the data, the perplexity of the resulting LM on the test set (*newstest13*) and the resulting SMT system quality over *newstest10...newstest13*.

Starting with the first block of experiments using LM data composed from the English side of the bilingual corpora and the *giun* corpus (bi.en+giun), the unfiltered LM performs worse, both in terms of perplexity and translation quality. The *NC* based adaptation improves the results slightly, with gains upto +0.3% BLEU on *newstest11* and -0.3% TER on *newstest10*. The overfitting behavior of *REF* adapted LMs carries over to the mixture LM, mainly on the translation quality. The *REF* adapted LM system translation results are better on the test sets used to perform the adaptation, but worse on the blind test set (*newstest13*). The *HYP* system performs best in terms of perplexity. *REF* is better than *HYP* over the non-blind test sets, but *HYP* outperforms *REF* on *newstest13* with an improvement of +0.6% BLEU and -0.6% TER.

The second block of experiments where newsshuffle (*ns*) is added to the mixture shows even stronger overfitting for *REF*. The *REF* based adaptation is performing worse in terms of perplexity, 143 in comparison to 111 for the full LM. On the blind set *newstest13*, *REF* is hindering the results with a loss of -1.8% BLEU in comparison to the full system, and a loss of -0.4% BLEU in comparison to the corresponding system without *ns*. On the non-blind sets, *REF* is performing best, showing typical overfitting. Comparing the full LM system to the *HYP* adapted LM, big improvements are mainly observed on TER, with significance at the 95% level for *newstest10*.

We conclude that using the references as adaptation set causes overfitting, using a pseudo in-domain set as the news-commentary does not improve the results, and the best choice is using the automatic translations (*HYP*).

As already mentioned in Section 2, we experimented with adding the automatic translations of the test sets (*HYP*) to the LM. Doing so resulted in 8 points perplexity reduction, but no impact on the MT quality was observed. Therefore, we deem these perplexity improvements by adding *HYP* as artificial.

5.2 TM Adaptation

In the LM adaptation experiments, we found that using the test sets automatic translation as the adaptation set (*HYP* system) for filtering performed best, in terms of LM quality (perplexity) and translation quality, when compared to the other suggested adaptation sets, especially on the blind test set.

[3]http://www.speech.sri.com/projects/srilm/

LM	TM	newstest10		newstest11		newstest12		newstest13	
		BLEU	TER	BLEU	TER	BLEU	TER	BLEU	TER
full	full	24.5	59.1	22.1	61.3	23.3	60.1	25.9	56.7
HYP	full	25.0	58.2‡	22.1	60.6	23.5	59.6	25.9	56.3
	TM Filtering								
	REF-25%	25.1	57.9‡	22.4	60.2‡	24.0‡	59.1‡	25.5	56.7
	HYP-50%	25.2	58.0‡	22.2	60.5†	23.8†	59.4‡	26.0	56.4
	TM Weighting								
	ppl.NC	25.0	58.1‡	22.5	60.2‡	23.6	59.5†	26.1	56.2
	ppl.TST	24.8	58.8	22.3	60.7	23.6	59.7	26.0	56.3
	ppl.REF	24.8	58.2‡	22.2	60.3†	23.7	59.5†	25.5	56.4
	ppl.HYP	25.4‡	57.8‡	22.5	60.1‡	23.9‡	59.3‡	26.4†	55.9‡

Table 5: German-English TM filtering and weighting results using different adaptation sets. The results are given in BLEU and TER percentages. Significance is measured over the full system (first row).

For TM adaptation, we experiment with filtering and weighting based adaptation. By using weighting, we expect further improvements over the baseline and better differentiation between the competing adaptation sets.

To perform filtering, we concatenate all the bilingual corpora in Table 1 and sort them according to the combined LM+M1 cross-entropy score. We then extract the top 50%,25%,... bilingual sentence from the sorted corpus, generate the phrase table for each setup and reoptimize the system using MERT on the development set.

Weighted phrase extraction is based on the same LM+M1 combined cross entropy score as filtering, but instead of discarding whole sentences we weight them according to their relevance to the adaptation set being used.

In this section, we compare the three adaptation sets suggested for LM filtering for the TM component. In addition, one might argue that for the bilingual case, the source side of the test set might be sufficient to perform adaptation, or even it might perform better for TM adaptation as the automatically generated translation might not be as reliable. We perform an experiment using the source side of the test sets as an adaptation set to score the source side of the bilingual corpora (denoted *TST* in the experiments). To summarize, we collect 4 corpora as adaptation sets to be used for adapting the TM: *(i) NC*, *HYP*, and *REF* as defined for LM but using both source and target (automatically generated for *HYP*) sides, and *(ii) TST* using only the source side of the test sets.

The results comparing the 4 suggested adaptation sets for filtering and weighting are given in Table 5. In this table, we use *newstest10* as before for MERT optimization and display results for *newstest10...newstest13*. Note that for TM filtering and weighting we use the *HYP* adapted LM as it achieves the best results in the previous section.

For filtering, the *NC* and *TST* adaptation sets could not improve the dev results over the full system therefore they are omitted. *REF* based adaptation achieves the best dev results when using 25% of the bilingual data while *HYP* based adaptation uses 50% of the data. For TM filtering, only slight overfitting is observed, where the *REF* system is slightly better than *HYP* on the non blind sets and is worse on the blind test set. We hypothesize that no severe overfitting is observed for TM filtering as we use a strong LM adapted with the *HYP* set, therefore degradation is lessened.

Next, we focus on weighted phrase extraction for adaptation using the various adaptation sets. Comparing filtering to weighting, weighting improves for the *ppl.HYP* based adaptation but a slight loss is observed for the *ppl.REF* system except on the blind test set. We conclude that due to the usage of more data in the weighting scenario, overfitting is lessened. Using the source side of the test sets for weighting (*ppl.TST*) achieves good results, with improvements over the *ppl.REF* system on *newstest13*.

The *ppl.HYP* system achieves the best results among the weighted systems. Comparing the full unadapted system with the LM+TM adapted *ppl.HYP* system, we achieve significant BLEU improvements on most sets, TER improvements are significant in all cases with 95% significance level. The highest gains are on the development set with

+0.9% BLEU and -1.3% TER improvements, on the test sets, *newstest12* improves with +0.6% BLEU and -0.8% TER and *newstest13* improves with +0.5% BLEU and -0.8% TER. The *ppl.HYP* system is comparable to the best single system of WMT 2013 [4] (26.4% BLEU vs 26.8% BLEU for Edinburgh submission, RWTH submission is a system combination). Note that we are not using the LDC GigaWord corpus.

We conclude that using in-domain automatic translations (*HYP*) for TM weighting performs best, better than using source side only in-domain (*TST*) and better than using the references (*REF*) especially on the blind test set. TM adaptation shows further improvements on top of LM adaptation and achieves significant gains.

6 Conclusion

In this work, we tackle the problem of adaptation without labeled bilingual in-domain training data. The only information about the test domain is encapsulated in the test sets themselves. We experiment with unsupervised adaptation for SMT, using automatic translations of the test sets, focusing on adaptation for the LM and the TM components. We use cross-entropy based scoring for the task of adaptation, as this method proved successful in previous work. We utilize filtering for LM adaptation, while we compare filtering and weighting for TM adaptation.

For LM adaptation, the setup we devise already contains a majority of in-domain data, still we could report improvements over the unadapted baseline. We compose three different adaptation sets for filtering using automatic translation of the test data (*HYP*), a pseudo in-domain set (*NC*) and the references (*REF*) of the test sets (keeping one blind test set). The *NC* based filtering is not able to perform good selection, for *news-shuffle* the whole corpus is retained and for *giun* 50% of the data is retained. The perplexity results and the translation quality are virtually unchanged in comparison to the full system. Using *REF* as the target set causes overfitting, where the results are better on the seen test sets but worse on the blind test set. The best performing target set in our experiments is the unsupervised *HYP* adaptation set, achieving the best perplexity as well as the best translation quality on the blind test set. Therefore, we conclude that for developing a successful SMT system that can generalize to new data the *HYP* based adaptation is preferred.

Next, we perform TM adaptation, where we repeat the comparison between the different adaptation sets for filtering as well as weighting. We also compare to adaptation based only on the source side of the test sets (*TST*). The LM adaptation results hold for TM adaptation, where using the automatic translations method shows the best results for the blind test set. Our experiments show that using the source side only of the test set for adaptation performs worse than the unsupervised method, reminiscent to results reported in previous work comparing supervised source side against bilingual filtering (Axelrod et al., 2011). For filtering, the *REF* system suffers from overfitting, while when using weighting for adaptation, overfitting is lessened. Comparing the unadapted baseline to the adapted LM and TM system using the *HYP* set, improvements of +1.0% BLEU and -1.3% TER are reported on the development set while +0.5% BLEU and -0.8% TER improvements are reported on the blind test set.

[4] http://matrix.statmt.org/matrix/systems_list/1712

Acknowledgments

This material is based upon work supported by the DARPA BOLT project under Contract No. HR0011-12-C-0015. Any opinions, findings and conclusions or recommendations expressed in this material are those of the authors and do not necessarily reflect the views of DARPA.

References

Amittai Axelrod, Xiaodong He, and Jianfeng Gao. 2011. Domain adaptation via pseudo in-domain data selection. In *Proceedings of the 2011 Conference on Empirical Methods in Natural Language Processing*, pages 355–362, Edinburgh, Scotland, UK., July. Association for Computational Linguistics.

M. Bacchiani and B. Roark. 2003. Unsupervised language model adaptation. In *Acoustics, Speech, and Signal Processing, 2003. Proceedings. (ICASSP '03). 2003 IEEE International Conference on*, volume 1, pages I–224 – I–227 vol.1, april.

Jerome R Bellegarda. 2004. Statistical language model adaptation: review and perspectives. *Speech Communication*, 42(1):93 – 108. Adaptation Methods for Speech Recognition.

M Federico M Cettolo, L Bentivogli, M Paul, and S Stüker. 2012. Overview of the iwslt 2012 evaluation campaign. In *International Workshop on*

Spoken Language Translation, pages 12–33, Hong Kong, December.

George Foster and Roland Kuhn. 2007. Mixture-model adaptation for SMT. In *Proceedings of the Second Workshop on Statistical Machine Translation*, pages 128–135, Prague, Czech Republic, June. Association for Computational Linguistics.

Michel Galley and Christopher D. Manning. 2008. A Simple and Effective Hierarchical Phrase Reordering Model. In *Proceedings of the 2008 Conference on Empirical Methods in Natural Language Processing*, pages 847–855, Honolulu, Hawaii, USA, October.

Isao Goto, Bin Lu, Ka Po Chow, Eiichiro Sumita, and Benjamin K Tsou. 2013. Overview of the patent machine translation task at the ntcir-10 workshop. In *Proceedings of the 10th NTCIR Conference*, volume 10, pages 260–286, Tokyo, Japan, June.

Almut Silja Hildebrand, Matthias Eck, Stephan Vogel, and Alex Waibel. 2005. Adaptation of the translation model for statistical machine translation based on information retrieval. In *Proceedings of the 10th EAMT conference on "Practical applications of machine translation"*, pages 133–1142, May.

Philipp Koehn and Barry Haddow. 2012. Towards effective use of training data in statistical machine translation. In *Proceedings of the Seventh Workshop on Statistical Machine Translation*, pages 317–321, Montréal, Canada, June. Association for Computational Linguistics.

Philipp Koehn. 2004. Statistical Significance Tests for Machine Translation Evaluation. In *Proc. of the Conf. on Empirical Methods for Natural Language Processing (EMNLP)*, pages 388–395, Barcelona, Spain, July.

Saab Mansour and Hermann Ney. 2012. A simple and effective weighted phrase extraction for machine translation adaptation. In *International Workshop on Spoken Language Translation*, pages 193–200, Hong Kong, December.

Robert C. Moore and William Lewis. 2010. Intelligent selection of language model training data. In *Proceedings of the ACL 2010 Conference Short Papers*, pages 220–224, Uppsala, Sweden, July. Association for Computational Linguistics.

Franz J. Och. 2003. Minimum Error Rate Training in Statistical Machine Translation. In *Proceedings of the 41th Annual Meeting of the Association for Computational Linguistics*, pages 160–167, Sapporo, Japan, July.

Kishore Papineni, Salim Roukos, Todd Ward, and Wei-Jing Zhu. 2002. Bleu: a Method for Automatic Evaluation of Machine Translation. In *Proceedings of the 41st Annual Meeting of the Association for Computational Linguistics*, pages 311–318, Philadelphia, Pennsylvania, USA, July.

Raphael Rubino, Antonio Toral, Santiago Cortés Vaíllo, Jun Xie, Xiaofeng Wu, Stephen Doherty, and Qun Liu. 2013. The CNGL-DCU-Prompsit translation systems for WMT13. In *Proceedings of the Eighth Workshop on Statistical Machine Translation*, pages 213–218, Sofia, Bulgaria, August. Association for Computational Linguistics.

Matthew Snover, Bonnie Dorr, Richard Schwartz, Linnea Micciulla, and John Makhoul. 2006. A Study of Translation Edit Rate with Targeted Human Annotation. In *Proceedings of the 7th Conference of the Association for Machine Translation in the Americas*, pages 223–231, Cambridge, Massachusetts, USA, August.

Nicola Ueffing, Gholamreza Haffari, and Anoop Sarkar. 2007. Transductive learning for statistical machine translation. In *Proceedings of the 45th Annual Meeting of the Association of Computational Linguistics*, pages 25–32, Prague, Czech Republic, June. Association for Computational Linguistics.

Joern Wuebker, Matthias Huck, Stephan Peitz, Malte Nuhn, Markus Freitag, Jan-Thorsten Peter, Saab Mansour, and Hermann Ney. 2012. Jane 2: Open source phrase-based and hierarchical statistical machine translation. In *International Conference on Computational Linguistics*, Mumbai, India, December.

Bing Zhao, Matthias Eck, and Stephan Vogel. 2004. Language model adaptation for statistical machine translation with structured query models. In *Proceedings of the 20th international conference on Computational Linguistics*, COLING '04, Stroudsburg, PA, USA. Association for Computational Linguistics.

An Empirical Comparison of Features and Tuning for Phrase-based Machine Translation

Spence Green, Daniel Cer, and **Christopher D. Manning**
Computer Science Department, Stanford University
{spenceg,danielcer,manning}@stanford.edu

Abstract

Scalable discriminative training methods are now broadly available for estimating phrase-based, feature-rich translation models. However, the sparse feature sets typically appearing in research evaluations are less attractive than standard dense features such as language and translation model probabilities: they often overfit, do not generalize, or require complex and slow feature extractors. This paper introduces *extended features*, which are more specific than dense features yet more general than lexicalized sparse features. Large-scale experiments show that extended features yield robust BLEU gains for both Arabic-English (+1.05) and Chinese-English (+0.67) relative to a strong feature-rich baseline. We also specialize the feature set to specific data domains, identify an objective function that is less prone to overfitting, and release fast, scalable, and language-independent tools for implementing the features.

1 Introduction

Scalable discriminative algorithm design for machine translation (MT) has lately been a booming enterprise. There are now algorithms for every taste: probabilistic and distribution-free, online and batch, regularized and unregularized. Technical differences aside, the papers that apply these algorithms to phrase-based translation often share a curious empirical characteristic: the algorithms support extra features, but the features do not significantly improve translation. For example, Hopkins and May (2011) showed that PRO with some simple ad hoc features only exceeds the baseline on one of three language pairs. Gimpel and Smith (2012b) observed a similar result for both PRO and their ramp-loss algorithm. Cherry and Foster (2012) found that, at least in the batch case, many algorithms produce similar results, and features only significantly increased quality for one of three language pairs. Only recently did Cherry (2013) and Green et al. (2013b) identify certain features that consistently reduce error.

These empirical results suggest that feature design and model fitting, the subjects of this paper, warrant a closer look. We introduce an effective *extended feature* set for phrase-based MT and identify a loss function that is less prone to overfitting. Extended features share three attractive characteristics with the standard Moses *dense features* (Koehn et al., 2007): ease of implementation, language independence, and independence from ancillary corpora like treebanks. In our experiments, they do not overfit and can be extracted efficiently during decoding. Because all feature weights are tuned on the development set, the new feature templates are amenable to feature augmentation (Daumé III, 2007), a simple domain adaptation technique that we show works surprisingly well for MT.

Extended features are designed according to a principle rather than a rule: they should fire less than standard dense features, which are general, but more than so-called *sparse features*, which are very specific—they are usually lexicalized—and thus prone to overfitting. This principle is motivated by analysis, which shows how expressive models can be a mixed blessing in the translation setting. It is obvious that features allow the model to fit the tuning data more tightly. For example, sparse lexicalized features could reduce tuning error by learning that the references prefer *U.S.* over *United States*, a minor lexical distinction. Reference choice should matter more than in the dense case, an issue that we quantify. We also show that frequency cutoffs, which are a crude but common form of feature selection, are unnecessary and even detrimental when features follow this principle.

We report large-scale translation quality experiments relative to both dense and feature-rich baselines. Our best feature set, which includes domain adaptation features, yields an average +1.05 BLEU improvement for Arabic-English and +0.67 for

Proceedings of the Ninth Workshop on Statistical Machine Translation, pages 466–476,
Baltimore, Maryland USA, June 26–27, 2014. ©2014 Association for Computational Linguistics

Chinese-English. In addition to the extended feature set, we show that an online variant of expected error (Och, 2003) is significantly faster to compute, less prone to overfitting, and nearly as effective as a pairwise loss. We release all software—feature extractors, and fast word clustering and data selection packages—used in our experiments.[1]

2 Phrase-based Models and Learning

The log-linear approach to phrase-based translation (Och and Ney, 2004) directly models the predictive translation distribution

$$p(e|f;w) = \frac{1}{Z(f)} \exp\left[w^\top \phi(e,f)\right] \quad (1)$$

where e is the target string, f is the source string, $w \in \mathbb{R}^d$ is the vector of model parameters, $\phi(\cdot) \in \mathbb{R}^d$ is a feature map, and $Z(f)$ is an appropriate normalizing constant. Assume that there is also a function $\rho(e,f) \in \mathbb{R}^d$ that produces a recombination map for the features. That is, each coordinate in ρ represents the state of the corresponding coordinate in ϕ. For example, suppose that ϕ_j is the log probability produced by the n-gram language model (LM). Then ρ_j would be the appropriate LM history. Recall that recombination collapses derivations with equivalent recombination maps during search and thus affects learning. This issue significantly influences feature design.

To learn w, we follow the online procedure of Green et al. (2013b), who calculate gradient steps with AdaGrad (Duchi et al., 2011) and perform feature selection via L_1 regularization in the FOBOS (Duchi and Singer, 2009) framework. This procedure accommodates any loss function for which a subgradient can be computed. Green et al. (2013b) used a PRO objective (Hopkins and May, 2011) with a logistic (surrogate) loss function. However, later results showed overfitting (Green et al., 2013a), and we found that their online variant of PRO tends to produce short translations like its batch counterpart (Nakov et al., 2013). Moreover, PRO requires sampling, making it slow to compute.

To address these shortcomings, we explore an online variant of expected error (Och, 2003, Eq.7). Let $\mathbf{E}_t = \{e_i\}_{i=1}^n$ be a scored n-best list of translations at time step t for source input f_t. Let $G(e)$ be a gold error metric that evaluates each candidate translation with respect to a set of one or more references. The smooth loss function is

$$\begin{aligned}\ell_t(w_{t-1}) &= E_{p(e|f_t;w_{t-1})}[G(e)] \\ &= \frac{1}{Z} \sum_{e' \in \mathbf{E}_t} \exp\left(w^\top \phi(e',f)\right) \cdot G(e')\end{aligned} \quad (2)$$

with normalization constant $Z = \sum_{e' \in \mathbf{E}_t} \exp\left(w^\top \phi(e',f)\right)$. The gradient g_t for coordinate j is:

$$\begin{aligned}g_t = E[G(e)\phi_j(e,f_t)] - \\ E[G(e)]E[\phi_j(e,f_t)]\end{aligned} \quad (3)$$

To our knowledge, we are the first to experiment with the online version of this loss.[2] When $G(e)$ is sentence-level BLEU+1 (Lin and Och, 2004)—the setting in our experiments—this loss is also known as expected BLEU (Cherry and Foster, 2012). However, other metrics are possible.

3 Extended Phrase-based Features

We divide our feature templates into five categories, which are well-known sources of error in phrase-based translation. The features are defined over derivations $d = \{r_i\}_{i=1}^D$, which are ordered sequences of rules r from the translation model. Define functions $f(\cdot)$ to be the source string of a rule or derivation and $e(\cdot)$ to be the target string. *Local features* can be extracted from individual rules and do not declare any state in the recombination map, thus for all local features i we have $\rho_i = 0$. *Non-local features* are defined over partial derivations and declare some state, either a real-valued parameter or an index indicating a categorical value like an n-gram context.

For each language, the extended feature templates require unigram counts and a word-to-class mapping $\varphi : w \mapsto c$ for word $w \in V$ and class $c \in C$. These can be extracted from any monolingual data; our experiments simply use both sides of the unaligned parallel training data.

The features are language-independent, but we will use Arabic-English as a running example.

3.1 Lexical Choice

Lexical choice features make more specific distinctions between target words than the dense translation model features (Koehn et al., 2003).

[1] http://nlp.stanford.edu/software/phrasal

[2] Gao and He (2013) used stochastic gradient descent and expected BLEU to learn phrase table feature weights, but not the full translation model w.

Lexicalized rule indicator (Liang et al., 2006a) Some rules occur frequently enough that we can learn rule-specific weights that augment the dense translation model features. For example, our model learns the following rule indicator features and weights:

أسباب $\Rightarrow$ reasons	-0.022
أسباب $\Rightarrow$ reasons for	0.002
أسباب $\Rightarrow$ the reasons for	0.016

These translations are all correct depending on context. When the plural noun أسباب 'reasons' appears in a construct state (*iDafa*) the preposition *for* is unrealized. Moreover, depending on the context, the English translation might also require the determiner *the*, which is also unrealized. The weights reflect that أسباب 'reasons' often appears in construct and boost insertion of necessary target terms. To prevent overfitting, this template only fires an indicator for rules that occur more than 50 times in the parallel training data (this is different from frequency filtering on the tuning data; see section 6.1). The feature is local.

Class-based rule indicator Word classes abstract over lexical items. For each rule r, a *prototype* that abstracts over many rules can be built by concatenating $\{\varphi(w) : w \in f(r)\}$ with $\{\varphi(w) : w \in e(r)\}$. For example, suppose that Arabic class 492 consists primarily of Arabic present tense verbs and class 59 contains English auxiliaries. Then the model might penalize a rule prototype like `492>59_59`, which drops the verb. This template fires an indicator for each rule prototype and is local.

Target unigram class (Ammar et al., 2013) Target lexical items with similar syntactic and semantic properties may have very different frequencies in the training data. These frequencies will influence the dense features. For example, in one of our English class mappings the following words map to the same class:

word	**class**	**freq.**
surface-to-surface	0	269
air-to-air	0	98
ground-to-air	0	63

The classes capture common linguistic attributes of these words, which is the motivation for a full class-based LM. Learning unigram weights directly is surprisingly effective and does not require building another LM. This template fires a separate indicator for each class $\{\varphi(w) : w \in e(r)\}$ and is local.

3.2 Word Alignments

Word alignment features allow the model to recognize fine-grained phrase-internal information that is largely opaque in the dense model.

Lexicalized alignments (Liang et al., 2006a) Consider the internal alignments of the rule:

	sunday	,
يوم		1
الاحد	2	

Alignment 1 $\langle$يوم 'day' $\Rightarrow$,$\rangle$ is incorrect and alignment 2 is correct. The dense translation model features might assign this rule high probability if alignment 1 is a common alignment error. Lexicalized alignment features allow the model to compensate for these events. This feature fires an indicator for each alignment in a rule—including multiword cliques—and is local.

Class-based alignments Like the class-based rule indicator, this feature template replaces each lexical item with its word class, resulting in an alignment prototype. This feature fires an indicator for each alignment in a rule after mapping lexical items to classes. It is local.

Source class deletion Phrase extraction algorithms often use a "grow" symmetrization step (Och and Ney, 2003) to add alignment points. Sometimes this procedure can produce a rule that deletes important source content words. This feature template allows the model to penalize these rules by firing an indicator for the class of each unaligned source word. The feature is local.

Punctuation ratio Languages use different types and ratios of punctuation (Salton, 1958). For example, quotation marks are not commonly used in Arabic, but they are conventional in English. Furthermore, spurious alignments often contain punctuation. To control these two phenomena, this feature template returns the ratio of target punctuation tokens to source punctuation tokens for each derivation. Since the denominator is constant, this feature can be computed incrementally as a derivation is constructed. It is local.

Function word ratio Words can also be spuriously aligned to non-punctuation, non-digit function words such as determiners and particles. Furthermore, linguistic differences may account for differences in function word occurrences. For example, English has a broad array of modal verbs and auxiliaries not found in Arabic. This feature template takes the 25 most frequent words in each language (according to the unigram counts), and computes the ratio between target and source function words for each derivation. As before the denominator is constant, so the feature can be computed efficiently. It is local.

3.3 Phrase Boundaries

The LM and hierarchical reordering model are the only dense features that cross phrase boundaries.

Target-class bigram boundary We have already added target class unigrams. We find that both lexicalized and class-based bigrams cause overfitting, therefore we restrict to bigrams that straddle phrase boundaries. The feature template fires an indicator for the concatenation of the word classes on either side of each boundary. This feature is non-local and its recombination state ρ is the word class at the right edge of the partial derivation.

3.4 Derivation Quality

To satisfy strong features like the LM, or hard constraints like the distortion limit, the phrase-based model can build derivations from poor translation rules. For example, a derivation consisting mostly of unigram rules may miss idiomatic usage that larger rules can capture. All of these feature templates are local.

Source dimension (Hopkins and May, 2011) An indicator feature for the source dimension of the rule: $|f(r)|$.

Target dimension (Hopkins and May, 2011) An indicator for the target dimension: $|e(r)|$.

Rule shape (Hopkins and May, 2011) The conjunction of source and target dimension: $|f(r)|\_|e(r)|$.

3.5 Reordering

Lexicalized reordering models score the orientation of a rule in an alignment grid. We use the same baseline feature extractor as Moses, which has three classes: monotone, swap, and discontinuous. We also add the non-monotone class, which is a conjunction of swap and discontinuous, for a total of eight orientations.[3]

[3]Each class has "with-previous" and "with-next" specializations.

Algorithm (implementation)	#threads	Time
Brown (wcluster)	1	1023.39
Clark (cluster_neyessen)	1	890.11
Och (mkcls)	1	199.04
PredictiveFull (this paper)	8	3.27
Predictive (this paper)	8	2.42

Table 1: Wallclock time (min.sec) to generate a mapping from a vocabulary of 63k English words (3.7M tokens) to 512 classes. All experiments were run on the same server, which had eight physical cores. Our Java implementation is multi-threaded; the C++ baselines are single-threaded.

Lexicalized rule orientation (Liang et al., 2006a) For each rule, the template fires an indicator for the concatenation of the orientation class, each element in $f(r)$, and each element in $e(r)$. To prevent overfitting, this template only fires for rules that occur more than 50 times in the training data. The feature is non-local and its recombination state ρ is the rule orientation.

Class-based rule orientation For each rule, the template fires an indicator for the concatenation of the orientation class, each element in $\{\varphi(w) : w \in f(r)\}$, and each element in $\{\varphi(w) : w \in e(r)\}$. The feature is non-local and its recombination state ρ is the rule orientation.

Signed linear distortion The dense feature set includes a simple reordering cost model. Assume that $[r]$ returns the index of the leftmost source index in $f(d)$ and $[[r]]$ returns the rightmost index. Then the linear distortion is:

$$\delta = [r_1] + \sum_{i=2}^{D} |[[r_{i-1}]] + 1 - [r_i]| \quad (4)$$

This score does not distinguish between left and right distortion. To correct this issue, this feature template fires an indicator for each signed component in the sum, for each positive and negative component. The feature is non-local and its recombination state ρ is the signed distortion.

3.6 Feature Dependencies

While unigram counts are trivial to compute, the same is not necessarily true of the word-to-class mapping φ. Standard algorithms run in $O(n^2)$, where $n = |V|$. Table 1 shows an evaluation of standard implementations of several popular algorithms: **Brown** et al. (1992) implemented by Liang

(2005); **Clark** (2003) without the morphological prior, which increases training time dramatically; and the implementation of **Och** (1999) that comes with the GIZA++ word aligner. The latter has been used recently for MT features (Ammar et al., 2013; Cherry, 2013; Yu et al., 2013). In a broad survey, Christodoulopoulos et al. (2010) found that for several downstream tasks, most word clustering algorithms—including Brown and Clark—result in similar task accuracy. For our large-scale setting, the primary issue is then the time to estimate φ.

For large corpora the existing implementations may require days or weeks, making our feature set less practical than the traditional dense MT features. Consequently, we re-implemented the predictive one-sided class model of Whittaker and Woodland (2001) with the parallelized clustering algorithm of Uszkoreit and Brants (2008) (**Predictive**), which was originally developed for very large scale language modeling. Our implementation uses multiple threads on a single processor instead of MapReduce. We also added two extensions that are useful for translation features. First, we map all digits to 0. This reduces sparsity while retaining useful patterns such as *0000* (e.g., years) and *0th* (e.g., ordinals). Second, we mapped all words occurring fewer than τ times to an `<unk>` token. In our experiment, these two changes reduce the vocabulary size by 71.1%. They also make the mapping φ more robust to unseen events during translation decoding. For a conservative comparison to the other three algorithms, we include results without these two extensions (**PredictiveFull**).[4]

4 Domain Adaptation Features

Feature augmentation is a simple yet effective domain adaptation technique (Daumé III, 2007). Suppose that the source data comes from M domains. Then for each original feature ϕ_i, we add M additional features, one for each domain. The original feature ϕ_i can be interpreted as a prior over the M domains (Finkel and Manning, 2009, fn.2).

Most of the extended features are defined over rules, so the critical issue is how to identify in-domain rules. The trick is to know which training sentence pairs are in-domain. Then we can annotate all rules extracted from these instances with domain labels. The in-domain rule sets need not be disjoint since some rules might be useful across domains.

This paper explores the following approach: we choose one of the M domains as the default. Next, we collect some source sentences for each of the $M - 1$ remaining domains. Using these examples we then identify in-domain sentence pairs in the bitext via data selection, in our case the feature decay algorithm (Biçici and Yuret, 2011). Finally, our rule extractor adds domain labels to all rules extracted from each selected sentence pair. Crucially, these labels do not influence which rules are extracted or how they are scored. The resulting phrase table contains the same rules, but with a few additional annotations.

Our method assumes domain labels for each source input to be decoded. Our experiments utilize gold, document-level labels, but accurate sentence-level domain classifiers exist (Wang et al., 2012).

4.1 Augmentation of Extended Features

Irvine et al. (2013) showed that lexical selection is the most quantifiable and perhaps most common source of error in phrase-based domain adaptation. Our development experiments seemed to confirm this hypothesis as augmentation of the class-based and non-lexical (e.g., Rule shape) features did not reduce error. Therefore, we only augment the lexicalized features: rule indicators and orientations, and word alignments.

4.2 Domain-Specific Feature Templates

In-domain Rule Indicator (Durrani et al., 2013) An indicator for each rule that matches the input domain. This template fires a generic in-domain indicator and a domain-specific indicator (e.g., the features might be `indomain` and `indomain-nw`). The feature is local.

Adjacent Rule Indicator Indicators for adjacent in-domain rules. This template also fires both generic and domain-specific features. The feature is non-local and the state is a boolean indicating if the last rule in a partial derivation is in-domain.

5 Experiments

We evaluate and analyze our feature set under a variety of large-scale experimental conditions including multiple domains and references. To our knowledge, the only language pairs with sufficient research resources to support this protocol are Arabic-English (Ar-En) and Chinese-English (Zh-En). The

[4]For the baselines the training settings are the suggested defaults: Brown, default; Clark, 10 iterations, frequency cutoff $\tau = 5$; Och, 10 iterations. Our implementation: PredictiveFull, 30 iterations, $\tau = 0$; Predictive, 30 iterations, $\tau = 5$.

	Bilingual		Monolingual
	#Seg.	*#Tok.*	*#Tok.*
Ar-En	6.6M	375M	990M
Zh-En	9.3M	538M	

Table 2: Bilingual and monolingual training corpora. The monolingual English data comes from the AFP and Xinhua sections of English Gigaword 4 (LDC2009T13).

	#Seg.		#Ref.	Domains
	Ar-En	Zh-En		
tune	5,604	5,900	4	nw,wb,bn
dev	1,075	1,597	4	nw
dev-dom	2,203	2,317	1	nw,wb,bn
test1	1,313	820	4	nw,wb
test2	1,378	1,370	4	nw,wb
test3	628	613	1	nw,wb,bn

Table 3: Development, test, and tuning data. Domain abbreviations: broadcast news (**bn**), newswire (**nw**), and web (**wb**).

training corpora[5] come from several Linguistic Data Consortium (LDC) sources from 2012 and earlier (Table 2). The test, development, and tuning corpora[6] come from the NIST OpenMT and MetricsMATR evaluations (Table 3). Extended features benefit from more tuning data, so we concatenated five NIST data sets to build one large tuning set. Observe that all test data come from later epochs than the tuning and development data.

From these data we built phrase-based MT systems with Phrasal (Green et al., 2014).[7] We aligned the parallel corpora with the Berkeley aligner (Liang et al., 2006b) with standard settings and symmetrized via the grow-diag heuristic. We created separate English LMs for each language pair by concatenating the monolingual Gigaword data with the target-side of the respective bitexts. For each corpus we estimated unfiltered 5-gram language models with lmplz (Heafield et al., 2013).

For each condition we ran the learning algorithm for 25 epochs[8] and selected the model according to the maximum uncased, corpus-level BLEU-4 (Papineni et al., 2002) score on the dev set.

5.1 Results

We evaluate the new feature set relative to two baselines. **Dense** is the same baseline as Green et al. (2013b); these dense features are included in all of the models that follow. **Sparse** is their best feature-rich model, which adds lexicalized rule indicators, alignments, orientations, and source deletions without bitext frequency filtering.

We do not perform a full ablation study. Both the approximate search and the randomization of the order of tuning instances make the contributions of each individual template differ from run to run. Resource constraints prohibit multiple large-scale runs for each incremental feature. Instead, we divide the extended feature set into two parts, and report large-scale results. **Ext** includes all extended features except for the the filtered lexicalized feature templates. **Ext+Filt** adds those filtered lexicalized templates: rule indicators and orientations, and word alignments (section 3).

Table 4 shows translation quality results. The new feature set significantly exceeds the baseline Dense model for both language pairs. An interesting result is that the new extended features alone match the strong Sparse baseline. The class-based features, which are more general, should clearly be preferred to the sparse features when decoding out-of-domain data (so long as word mappings are trained for that data). The increased runtime per iteration comes not from feature extraction but from larger inner products as the model size increases.

Next, we add the domain features from section 4.2. We marked in-domain sentence pairs by concatenating the tuning data with additional bn and wb monolingual in-domain data from several LDC sources.[9] The FDA selection size was set to 20 times the number of in-domain examples for each genre. Newswire was selected as the default domain since most of the bitext comes from that domain.

The bottom rows of Tables 4a and 4b compare

[5]We tokenized the English with Stanford CoreNLP according to the Penn Treebank standard (Marcus et al., 1993), the Arabic with the Stanford Arabic segmenter (Monroe et al., 2014) according to the Penn Arabic Treebank standard (Maamouri et al., 2008), and the Chinese with the Stanford Chinese segmenter (Chang et al., 2008) according to the Penn Chinese Treebank standard (Xue et al., 2005).

[6]Data sources: tune, MT023568; dev, MT04; dev-dom, domain adaptation dev set is MT04 and all wb and bn data from LDC2007E61; test1, MT09 (Ar-En) and MT12 (Zh-En); test2, Progress0809 which was revealed in the OpenMT 2012 evaluation; test3, MetricsMATR08-10.

[7]System settings: distortion limit of 5, cube pruning beam size of 1200, maximum phrase length of 7.

[8]Other learning settings: 16 threads, mini-batch size of 20; L_1 regularization strength $\lambda = 0.001$; learning rate $\eta_0 = 0.02$; initialization of LM to 0.5, word penalty to -1.0, and all other dense features to 0.2; initialization of extended features to 0.0.

[9]Catalog: LDC2007T24, LDC2008T08, LDC2008T18, LDC2012T16, LDC2013T01, LDC2013T05, LDC2013T14.

Model	#features	Epochs	Min. / Epoch	tune	dev	test1	test2	test3
DENSE (D)	18	24	3	49.52	50.25	47.98	43.41	27.56
D+SPARSE	48,597	24	8	56.51	52.98	49.55	45.40	29.02
D+EXT	62,931	16	11	57.83	54.33	49.66	45.66	29.15
D+EXT+FILT	94,606	17	14	59.13	55.35	50.02	46.24	29.59
D+EXT+FILT+DOM	123,353	22	18	59.97	29.20†	**50.45**	**46.24**	**30.84**

(a) Ar-En.

Model	#features	Epochs	Min. / Epoch	tune	dev	test1	test2	test3
DENSE (D)	18	17	3	32.82	34.96	26.61	26.72	10.19
D+SPARSE	55,024	17	8	38.91	36.68	27.86	28.41	10.98
D+EXT	67,936	16	13	40.96	37.19	28.27	28.40	10.72
D+EXT+FILT	100,275	17	14	41.38	37.36	28.68	28.90	11.24
D+EXT+FILT+DOM	126,014	17	14	41.70	17.20†	***28.71***	***28.96***	***11.67***

(b) Zh-En.

Table 4: Translation quality results (uncased BLEU-4 %). Per-epoch times are in minutes (Min.). Statistical significance relative to D+SPARSE, the strongest baseline: **bold** ($p < 0.001$) and ***bold-italic*** ($p < 0.05$). Significance is computed by the permutation test of Riezler and Maxwell (2005). †The dev score of EXT+FILT+DOM is the dev-dom data set from Table 3, so it is not comparable with the other rows.

EXT+FILT+DOM to the baselines and other feature sets. The gains relative to SPARSE are statistically significant for all six test sets.

A crucial result is that with domain features accuracy relative to EXT+FILT never decreases: a single domain-adapted system is effective across domains. Irvine et al. (2013) showed that when models from multiple domains are interpolated, scoring errors affecting lexical selection—the model could have generated the correct target lexical item but did not—increase significantly. We do not observe that behavior, at least from the perspective of BLEU.

Table 5 separates out per-domain results. The web data appears to be the hardest domain. That is sensible given that broadcast news transcripts are more similar to newswire, the default domain, than web data. Moreover, inspection of the bitext sources revealed very little web data, so our automatic data selection is probably less effective. Accuracy on newswire actually increases slightly.

Ar-En	test1		test2		test3		
	nw	wb	nw	wb	bn	nw	wb
EF	59.78	39.55	51.69	**38.80**	30.39	37.59	20.58
EFD	**60.21**	**40.38**	**51.76**	38.77	**31.63**	**38.18**	**22.37**
Zh-En							
EF	34.56	**21.94**	17.38	12.07	**3.04**	17.42	12.83
EFD	**34.87**	21.82	**17.96**	**12.66**	3.01	**17.74**	**13.80**

Table 5: Per-domain results (uncased BLEU-4 %). Here **bold** simply indicates the maximum in each column. Model abbreviations: EF is EXT+FILT and EFD is EXT+FILT+DOM.

6 Analysis

6.1 Learning

Loss Function In a now classic empirical comparison of batch tuning algorithms, Cherry and Foster (2012) showed that PRO and expected BLEU yielded similar translation quality results. In contrast, Table 6a shows significant differences between these loss functions. First, expected BLEU can be computed faster since it is linear in the n-best list size, whereas exact computation of the PRO objective is $O(n^2)$ (thus sampling is often used). It also converges faster. Second, PRO tends to select larger models.[10] Finally, PRO seems to overfit on the tuning set, since there are no gains on test1.

Feature Selection A common yet crude method of feature selection is frequency cutoffs on the

[10]PRO L_1 regularization strength of $\lambda = 0.01$, above which model size decreases but translation quality degrades.

Loss	#epochs	Min./Epoch	#feat.	tune	test1
EB	17	14	94,606	59.13	50.02
PRO	14	25	181,542	61.20	50.09

(a) PRO vs. expected BLEU (EB) for EXT+FILT.

Feature Selection	#features	tune	test1
L_1	94,606	59.13	50.02
Freq. cutoffs	23,617	56.84	49.79

(b) Feature selection for EXT+FILT.

Model	#refs	tune	test1
DENSE	4	49.52	47.98
DENSE	1	49.34	47.78
EXT+FILT	4	59.13	50.02
EXT+FILT	1	55.39	48.88

(c) Single- vs. multiple-reference tuning.

Table 6: Ar-En learning comparisons.

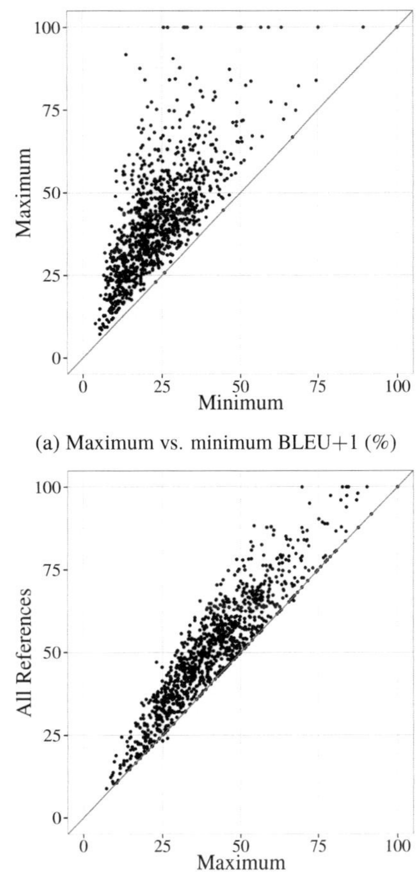

(a) Maximum vs. minimum BLEU+1 (%)

(b) BLEU+1 (%) according to all four references vs. maximum

Figure 1: Reference choice analysis for Ar-En DENSE output on the dev set.

tuning data. Only features that fire more than some threshold are admitted into the feature set. Table 6b shows that for our new feature set, L_1 regularization—which simply requires setting a regularization strength parameter—is more effective than frequency cutoffs.

References Few MT data sets supply multiple references. Even when they do, those references are but a sample from a larger pool of possible translations. This observation has motivated attempts at generating lattices of translations for evaluation (Dreyer and Marcu, 2012; Bojar et al., 2013). But evaluation is only part of the problem. Table 6c shows that the DENSE model, which has only a few features to describe the data, is little affected by the elimination of references. In contrast, the feature-rich model degrades significantly. This may account for the underperformance of features in single-reference settings like WMT (Durrani et al., 2013; Green et al., 2013a). The next section explores the impact of references further.

6.2 Reference Variance

We took the DENSE Ar-En output for the dev data, which has four references, and computed the sentence-level BLEU+1 with respect to each reference. Figure 1a shows a point for each of the 1,075 translations. The horizontal axis is the minimum score with respect to any reference and the vertical axis is the maximum (BLEU has a maximum value of 1.0). Ideally, from the perspective of learning, the scores should cluster around the diagonal: the references should yield similar scores. This is hardly the case. The mean difference is $M = 18.1$ BLEU, with a standard deviation $SD = 11.5$.

Figure 1b shows the same data set, but with the maximum on the horizontal axis and the multiple-reference score on the vertical axis. Assuming a constant brevity penalty, the maximum lower-bounds the multiple-reference score since BLEU aggregates n-grams across references. The multiple-reference score is an "easier" target since the model has more opportunities to match n-grams.

Consider again the single-reference condition and one of the pathological cases at the top of Figure 1a. Suppose that the low-scoring reference is observed in the single-reference condition. The more expressive feature-rich model has a greater capacity to fit that reference when, under another reference, it would have matched the translation exactly and incurred a low loss.

Nakov et al. (2012) suggested extensions to BLEU+1 that were subsequently found to improve accuracy in the single-reference condition (Gimpel and Smith, 2012a). Repeating the min/max calculations with the most effective extensions (according to Gimpel and Smith (2012a)) we observe lower variance (M = 17.32, SD = 10.68). These extensions are very simple, so a more sophisticated noise model is a promising future direction.

7 Related Work

We review work on phrase-based discriminative feature sets that influence decoder search, and domain adaptation with features.[11]

7.1 Feature Sets

Variants of some extended features are scattered throughout previous work: unfiltered lexicalized rule indicators and alignments (Liang et al., 2006a); rule shape (Hopkins and May, 2011); rule orientation (Liang et al., 2006b; Cherry, 2013); target unigram class (Ammar et al., 2013). We found that other prior features did not improve translation: higher-order target lexical n-grams (Liang et al., 2006a; Watanabe et al., 2007; Gimpel and Smith, 2012b), higher-order target class n-grams (Ammar et al., 2013), target word insertion (Watanabe et al., 2007; Chiang et al., 2009), and many other unpublished ideas transmitted through received wisdom.

To our knowledge, Yu et al. (2013) were the first to experiment with non-local (derivation) features for phrase-based MT. They added discriminative rule features conditioned on target context. This is a good idea that we plan to explore. However, they do not mention if their non-local features declare recombination state. Our empirical experience is that non-local features are less effective when they do not influence recombination.

Liang et al. (2006a) proposed replacing lexical items with supervised part-of-speech (POS) tags to reduce sparsity. This is a natural idea that lay dormant until recently. Ammar et al. (2013) incorporated unigram and bigram target class features. Yu et al. (2013) used word classes as backoff features to reduce overfitting. Wuebker et al. (2013) replaced all lexical items in the bitext and monolingual data with classes, and estimated the dense feature set. Then they added these dense class-based features to the baseline lexicalized system. Finally, Cherry (2013) experimented with class-based hierarchical reordering features. However, his features used a bespoke representation rather than the simple full rule string that we use.

7.2 Domain Adaptation with Features

Both Clark et al. (2012) and Wang et al. (2012) augmented the baseline dense feature set with domain labels. They each showed modest improvements for several language pairs. However, neither incorporated a notion of a default prior domain.

Liu et al. (2012) investigated local adaption of the log-linear scores by selecting comparable bitext examples for a given source input. After selecting a small local corpus, their algorithm then performs several online update steps—starting from a globally tuned weight vector—prior to decoding the input. The resulting model is effectively a locally weighted, domain-adapted classifier.

Su et al. (2012) proposed domain adaptation via monolingual source resources much as we use in-domain monolingual corpora for data selection. They labeled each bitext sentence with a topic using a Hidden Topic Markov Model (HTMM) Gruber et al. (2007). Source topic information was then mixed into the translation model dense feature calculations. This work follows Chiang et al. (2011), who present a similar technique but using the same gold NIST labels that we use. Hasler et al. (2012) extended these ideas to a discriminative sparse feature set by augmenting both rule and unigram alignment features with HTMM topic information.

8 Conclusion

This paper makes four major contributions. First, we introduced *extended features* for phrase-based MT that exceeded both dense and feature-rich baselines. Second, we specialized the features to source domains, further extending the gains. Third, we showed that online expected BLEU is faster and more stable than online PRO for extended features. Finally, we released fast, scalable, language-independent tools for implementing the feature set. Our work should help practitioners quickly establish higher baselines on the way to more targeted linguistic features. However, our analysis showed that reference choice may restrain otherwise justifiable enthusiasm for feature-rich MT.

[11] Space limitations preclude discussion of re-ranking features.

Acknowledgments We thank John DeNero for comments on an earlier version of this work. The first author is supported by a National Science Foundation Graduate Research Fellowship. This work was supported by the Defense Advanced Research Projects Agency (DARPA) Broad Operational Language Translation (BOLT) program through IBM. Any opinions, findings, and conclusions or recommendations expressed in this material are those of the author(s) and do not necessarily reflect the view of DARPA or the US government.

References

W. Ammar, V. Chahuneau, M. Denkowski, G. Hanneman, W. Ling, A. Matthews, et al. 2013. The CMU machine translation systems at WMT 2013: Syntax, synthetic translation options, and pseudo-references. In *WMT*.

E. Biçici and D. Yuret. 2011. Instance selection for machine translation using feature decay algorithms. In *WMT*.

O. Bojar, M. Macháček, A. Tamchyna, and D. Zeman. 2013. Scratching the surface of possible translations. In I. Habernal and V. Matoušek, editors, *Text, Speech, and Dialogue*, volume 8082 of *Lecture Notes in Computer Science*, pages 465–474. Springer Berlin Heidelberg.

P-C. Chang, M. Galley, and C. D. Manning. 2008. Optimizing Chinese word segmentation for machine translation performance. In *WMT*.

C. Cherry and G. Foster. 2012. Batch tuning strategies for statistical machine translation. In *HLT-NAACL*.

C. Cherry. 2013. Improved reordering for phrase-based translation using sparse features. In *HLT-NAACL*.

D. Chiang, K. Knight, and W. Wang. 2009. 11,001 new features for statistical machine translation. In *HLT-NAACL*.

D. Chiang, S. DeNeefe, and M. Pust. 2011. Two easy improvements to lexical weighting. In *ACL*.

C. Christodoulopoulos, S. Goldwater, and M. Steedman. 2010. Two decades of unsupervised POS induction: How far have we come? In *EMNLP*.

J. H. Clark, A. Lavie, and C. Dyer. 2012. One system, many domains: Open-domain statistical machine translation via feature augmentation. In *AMTA*.

H. Daumé III. 2007. Frustratingly easy domain adaptation. In *ACL*.

M. Dreyer and D. Marcu. 2012. HyTER: Meaning-equivalent semantics for translation evaluation. In *NAACL*.

J. Duchi and Y. Singer. 2009. Efficient online and batch learning using forward backward splitting. *JMLR*, 10:2899–2934.

J. Duchi, E. Hazan, and Y. Singer. 2011. Adaptive subgradient methods for online learning and stochastic optimization. *JMLR*, 12:2121–2159.

N. Durrani, B. Haddow, K. Heafield, and P. Koehn. 2013. Edinburgh's machine translation systems for European language pairs. In *WMT*.

J. R. Finkel and C. D. Manning. 2009. Hierarchical bayesian domain adaptation. In *HLT-NAACL*.

J. Gao and X. He. 2013. Training MRF-based phrase translation models using gradient ascent. In *NAACL*.

K. Gimpel and N. A. Smith. 2012a. Addendum to structured ramp loss minimization for machine translation. Technical report, Language Technologies Institute, Carnegie Mellon University.

K. Gimpel and N. A. Smith. 2012b. Structured ramp loss minimization for machine translation. In *HLT-NAACL*.

S. Green, D. Cer, K. Reschke, R. Voigt, J. Bauer, S. Wang, and others. 2013a. Feature-rich phrase-based translation: Stanford University's submission to the WMT 2013 translation task. In *WMT*.

S. Green, S. Wang, D. Cer, and C. D. Manning. 2013b. Fast and adaptive online training of feature-rich translation models. In *ACL*.

S. Green, D. Cer, and C. D. Manning. 2014. Phrasal: A toolkit for new directions in statistical machine translation. In *WMT*.

A. Gruber, Y. Weiss, and M. Rosen-Zvi. 2007. Hidden topic markov models. In *AISTATS*.

E. Hasler, B. Haddow, and P. Koehn. 2012. Sparse lexicalised features and topic adaptation for SMT. In *IWSLT*.

K. Heafield, I. Pouzyrevsky, J. H. Clark, and P. Koehn. 2013. Scalable modified Kneser-Ney language model estimation. In *ACL, Short Papers*.

M. Hopkins and J. May. 2011. Tuning as ranking. In *EMNLP*.

A. Irvine, J. Morgan, M. Carpuat, H. Daumé III, and D. Munteanu. 2013. Measuring machine translation errors in new domains. *TACL*, 1.

P. Koehn, F. J. Och, and D. Marcu. 2003. Statistical phrase-based translation. In *NAACL*.

P. Koehn, H. Hoang, A. Birch, C. Callison-Burch, M. Federico, N. Bertoldi, et al. 2007. Moses: Open source toolkit for statistical machine translation. In *ACL, Demonstration Session*.

P. Liang, A. Bouchard-Côté, D. Klein, and B. Taskar. 2006a. An end-to-end discriminative approach to machine translation. In *ACL*.

P. Liang, B. Taskar, and D. Klein. 2006b. Alignment by agreement. In *NAACL*.

P. Liang. 2005. Semi-supervised learning for natural language. Master's thesis, Massachusetts Institute of Technology.

C.-Y. Lin and F. J. Och. 2004. ORANGE: a method for evaluating automatic evaluation metrics for machine translation. In *COLING*.

L. Liu, H. Cao, T. Watanabe, T. Zhao, M. Yu, and C. Zhu. 2012. Locally training the log-linear model for SMT. In *EMNLP-CoNLL*.

M. Maamouri, A. Bies, and S. Kulick. 2008. Enhancing the Arabic Treebank: A collaborative effort toward new annotation guidelines. In *LREC*.

M. Marcus, M. A. Marcinkiewicz, and B. Santorini. 1993. Building a large annotated corpus of English: The Penn Treebank. *Computational Linguistics*, 19:313–330.

W. Monroe, S. Green, and C. D. Manning. 2014. Word segmentation of informal Arabic with domain adaptation. In *ACL, Short Papers*.

P. Nakov, F. Guzman, and S. Vogel. 2012. Optimizing for sentence-level BLEU+1 yields short translations. In *COLING*.

P. Nakov, F. Guzmán, and S. Vogel. 2013. A tale about PRO and monsters. In *ACL, Short Papers*.

F. J. Och and H. Ney. 2003. A systematic comparison of various statistical alignment models. *Computational Linguistics*, 29(1):19–51.

F. J. Och and H. Ney. 2004. The alignment template approach to statistical machine translation. *Computational Linguistics*, 30(4):417–449.

F. J. Och. 2003. Minimum error rate training for statistical machine translation. In *ACL*.

K. Papineni, S. Roukos, T. Ward, and W. Zhu. 2002. BLEU: a method for automatic evaluation of machine translation. In *ACL*.

S. Riezler and J. T. Maxwell. 2005. On some pitfalls in automatic evaluation and significance testing in MT. In *ACL Workshop on Intrinsic and Extrinsic Evaluation Measures for Machine Translation and/or Summarization*.

G. Salton. 1958. The use of punctuation patterns in machine translation. *Mechanical Translation*, 5(1):16–24, July.

J. Su, H. Wu, H. Wang, Y. Chen, X. Shi, H. Dong, and Q. Liu. 2012. Translation model adaptation for statistical machine translation with monolingual topic information. In *ACL*.

J. Uszkoreit and T. Brants. 2008. Distributed word clustering for large scale class-based language modeling in machine translation. In *ACL-HLT*.

W. Wang, K. Macherey, W. Macherey, F. J. Och, and P. Xu. 2012. Improved domain adaptation for statistical machine translation. In *AMTA*.

T. Watanabe, J. Suzuki, H. Tsukada, and H. Isozaki. 2007. Online large-margin training for statistical machine translation. In *EMNLP-CoNLL*.

E. W. D. Whittaker and P. C. Woodland. 2001. Efficient class-based language modelling for very large vocabularies. In *ICASSP*.

J. Wuebker, S. Peitz, F. Rietig, and H. Ney. 2013. Improving statistical machine translation with word class models. In *EMNLP*.

N. Xue, F. Xia, F. Chiou, and M. Palmer. 2005. The Penn Chinese Treebank: Phrase structure annotation of a large corpus. *Natural Language Engineering*, 11(2):207–238.

H. Yu, L. Huang, H. Mi, and K. Zhao. 2013. Max-violation perceptron and forced decoding for scalable MT training. In *EMNLP*.

Bayesian Reordering Model with Feature Selection

Abdullah Alrajeh[ab] **and Mahesan Niranjan**[b]
[a]Computer Research Institute, King Abdulaziz City for Science and Technology (KACST)
Riyadh, Saudi Arabia, asrajeh@kacst.edu.sa
[b]School of Electronics and Computer Science, University of Southampton
Southampton, United Kingdom, {asar1a10, mn}@ecs.soton.ac.uk

Abstract

In phrase-based statistical machine translation systems, variation in grammatical structures between source and target languages can cause large movements of phrases. Modeling such movements is crucial in achieving translations of long sentences that appear natural in the target language. We explore generative learning approach to phrase reordering in Arabic to English. Formulating the reordering problem as a classification problem and using naive Bayes with feature selection, we achieve an improvement in the BLEU score over a lexicalized reordering model. The proposed model is compact, fast and scalable to a large corpus.

1 Introduction

Currently, the dominant approach to machine translation is statistical, starting from the mathematical formulations and algorithms for parameter estimation (Brown et al., 1988), further extended in (Brown et al., 1993). These early models, widely known as the IBM models, were word-based. Recent extensions note that a better approach is to group collections of words, or phrases, for translation together, resulting in a significant focus these days on phrase-based statistical machine translation systems.

To deal with the alignment problem of one-to-many word alignments in the IBM model formulation, whereas phrase-based models may have many-to-many translation relationships, IBM models are trained in both directions, source to target and target to source, and their word alignments are combined (Och and Ney, 2004).

While phrase-based systems are a significant improvement over word-based approaches, a particular issue that emerges is long-range reorderings at the phrase level (Galley and Manning, 2008). Analogous to speech recognition systems, translation systems relied on language models to produce more fluent translation. While early work penalized phrase movements without considering reorderings arising from vastly differing grammatical structures across language pairs like Arabic-English, many researchers considered lexical reordering models that attempted to learn orientation based on content (Tillmann, 2004; Kumar and Byrne, 2005; Koehn et al., 2005). These approaches may suffer from the data sparseness problem since many phrase pairs occur only once (Nguyen et al., 2009).

As an alternative way of exploiting function approximation capabilities offered by machine learning methods, there is recent interest in formulating a learning problem that aims to predict reordering from linguistic features that capture their context. An example of this is the maximum entropy method used by (Xiang et al., 2011; Nguyen et al., 2009; Zens and Ney, 2006; Xiong et al., 2006).

In this work we apply a naive Bayes classifier, combined with feature selection to address the reordering problem. To the best of our knowledge, this simple model of classification has not been used in this context previously. We present empirical results comparing our work and previously proposed lexicalized reordering model. We show that our model is scalable to large corpora.

The remainder of this paper is organized as follows. Section 2 discusses previous work in the field and how that is related to our paper. Section 3 gives an overview of the baseline translation system. Section 4 introduces the Bayesian reordering model and gives details of different inference methods, while, Section 5 describes feature selection method. Section 6 presents the experiments and reports the results evaluated as classification and translation problems. Finally, we end the paper with a summary of our conclusions and perspectives.

Proceedings of the Ninth Workshop on Statistical Machine Translation, pages 477–485,
Baltimore, Maryland USA, June 26–27, 2014.

Symbol	Notation
f/e	a source / target sentence (string)
$\bar{\mathbf{f}}/\bar{\mathbf{e}}$	a source / target phrase sequence
N	the number of examples
K	the number of classes
$(\bar{f}_n, \bar{e}_n)$	the n-th phrase pair in $(\bar{\mathbf{f}}, \bar{\mathbf{e}})$
o_n	the orientation of $(\bar{f}_n, \bar{e}_n)$
$\phi(\bar{f}_n, \bar{e}_n)$	the feature vector of $(\bar{f}_n, \bar{e}_n)$

Table 1: Notation used in this paper.

2 Related Work

The phrase reordering model is a crucial component of any translation system, particularly between language pairs with different grammatical structures (e.g. Arabic-English). Adding a lexicalized reordering model consistently improved the translation quality for several language pairs (Koehn et al., 2005). The model tries to predict the orientation of a phrase pair with respect to the previous adjacent target words. Ideally, the reordering model would predict the right position in the target sentence given a source phrase, which is difficult to achieve. Therefore, positions are grouped into limited orientations or classes.The orientation probability for a phrase pair is simply based on the relative occurrences in the training corpus.

The lexicalized reordering model has been extended to tackle long-distance reorderings (Galley and Manning, 2008). This takes into account the hierarchical structure of the sentence when considering such an orientation. Certain examples are often used to motivate syntax-based systems were handled by this hierarchical model, and this approach is shown to improve translation performance for several translation tasks with small computational cost.

Despite the fact that the lexicalized reordering model is always biased towards the most frequent orientation for such a phrase pair, it may suffer from a data sparseness problem since many phrase pairs occur only once. Moreover, the context of a phrase might affect its orientation, which is not considered as well.

Adopting the idea of predicting orientation based on content, it has been proposed to represent each phrase pair by linguistic features as reordering evidence, and then train a classifier for prediction. The maximum entropy classifier is a popular choice among many researchers (Zens and Ney, 2006; Xiong et al., 2006; Nguyen et al., 2009; Xiang et al., 2011). Max-margin structure classifiers were also proposed (Ni et al., 2011). Recently, Cherry (2013) proposed using sparse features optimize BLEU with the decoder instead of training a classifier independently.

We distinguish our work from the previous ones in the following. We propose a fast reordering model using a naive Bayes classifier with feature selection. In this study, we undertake a comparison between our work and lexicalized reordering model.

3 Baseline System

In statistical machine translation, the most likely translation $\mathbf{e}_{\text{best}}$ of an input sentence $\mathbf{f}$ can be found by maximizing the probability $p(\mathbf{e}|\mathbf{f})$, as follows:

$$\mathbf{e}_{\text{best}} = \arg\max_{\mathbf{e}} p(\mathbf{e}|\mathbf{f}). \tag{1}$$

A log-linear combination of different models (features) is used for direct modeling of the posterior probability $p(\mathbf{e}|\mathbf{f})$ (Papineni et al., 1998; Och and Ney, 2002):

$$\mathbf{e}_{\text{best}} = \arg\max_{\mathbf{e}} \sum_{i=1}^{n} \lambda_i h_i(\mathbf{f}, \mathbf{e}) \tag{2}$$

where the feature $h_i(\mathbf{f}, \mathbf{e})$ is a score function over sentence pairs. The translation model and the language model are the main features in any system although additional features $h(.)$ can be integrated easily (such as word penalty). State-of-the-art systems usually have around ten features (i.e. $n = 10$).

In phrase-based systems, the translation model can capture the local meaning for each source phrase. However, to capture the whole meaning of a sentence, its translated phrases need to be in the correct order. The language model, which ensures fluent translation, plays an important role in reordering; however, it prefers sentences that are grammatically correct without considering their actual meaning. Besides that, it has a bias towards short translations (Koehn, 2010). Therefore, developing a reordering model will improve the accuracy particularly when translating between two grammatically different languages.

3.1 Lexicalized Reordering Model

Phrase reordering modeling involves formulating phrase movements as a classification problem where each phrase position considered as a class (Tillmann, 2004). Some researchers classified phrase movements into three categories (monotone, swap, and discontinuous) but the classes can be extended to any arbitrary number (Koehn and Monz, 2005). In general, the distribution of phrase orientation is:

$$p(o_k|\bar{f}_n, \bar{e}_n) = \frac{1}{Z} h(\bar{f}_n, \bar{e}_n, o_k) \,. \quad (3)$$

This lexicalized reordering model is estimated by relative frequency where each phrase pair $(\bar{f}_n, \bar{e}_n)$ with such an orientation (o_k) is counted and then normalized to yield the probability as follows:

$$p(o_k|\bar{f}_n, \bar{e}_n) = \frac{\text{count}(\bar{f}_n, \bar{e}_n, o_k)}{\sum_o \text{count}(\bar{f}_n, \bar{e}_n, o)}. \quad (4)$$

The orientation class of a current phrase pair is defined with respect to the previous target word or phrase (i.e. word-based classes or phrase-based classes). In the case of three categories (monotone, swap, and discontinuous): monotone is the previous source phrase (or word) that is previously adjacent to the current source phrase, swap is the previous source phrase (or word) that is next-adjacent to the current source phrase, and discontinuous is not monotone or swap.

Galley and Manning (2008) extended the lexicalized reordering mode to tackle long-distance phrase reorderings. Their hierarchical model enables phrase movements that are more complex than swaps between adjacent phrases.

4 Bayesian Reordering Model

Many feature-based reordering models have been proposed to replace the lexicalized reordering model. The reported results showed consistent improvement in terms of various translation metrics.

Naive Bayes method has been a popular classification model of choice in many natural language processing problems (e.g. text classification). Naive Bayes is a simple classifier that ignores correlation between features, but has the appeal of computational simplicity. It is a generative probabilistic model based on Bayes' theorem as below:

$$p(o_k|\bar{f}_n, \bar{e}_n) = \frac{p(\bar{f}_n, \bar{e}_n|o_k)p(o_k)}{\sum_o p(\bar{f}_n, \bar{e}_n|o)p(o)}. \quad (5)$$

The class prior can be estimated easily as a relative frequency (i.e. $p(o_k) = \frac{N_k}{N}$). The likelihood distribution $p(\bar{f}_n, \bar{e}_n|o_k)$ is defined based on the type of data. The classifier will be naive if we assume that feature variables are conditionally independent. The naive assumption simplifies our distribution and hence reduces the parameters that have to be estimated. In text processing, multinomial is used as a class-conditional distribution (Rogers and Girolami, 2011). The distribution is defined as:

$$p(\bar{f}_n, \bar{e}_n|\mathbf{q}) = C \prod_m q_m^{\phi_m(\bar{f}_n, \bar{e}_n)} \quad (6)$$

where C is a multinomial coefficient,

$$C = \frac{(\sum_m \phi_m(\bar{f}_n, \bar{e}_n))!}{\prod_m \phi_m(\bar{f}_n, \bar{e}_n)!}, \quad (7)$$

and $\mathbf{q}$ are a set of parameters, each of which is a probability. Estimating these parameters for each class by maximum likelihood,

$$\arg\max_{\mathbf{q}_k} \prod_n^{N_k} p(\bar{f}_n, \bar{e}_n|\mathbf{q}_k), \quad (8)$$

will result in (Rogers and Girolami, 2011):

$$q_{km} = \frac{\sum_n^{N_k} \phi_m(\bar{f}_n, \bar{e}_n)}{\sum_{m'}^{M} \sum_n^{N_k} \phi_{m'}(\bar{f}_n, \bar{e}_n)}. \quad (9)$$

MAP estimate It is clear that q_{km} might be zero which means the probability of a new phrase pair with nonzero feature $\phi_m(\bar{f}_n, \bar{e}_n)$ is always zero because of the product in (6). Putting a prior over $\mathbf{q}$ is one smoothing technique. A conjugate prior for the multinomial likelihood is the Dirichlet distribution and the MAP estimate for q_{km} is (Rogers and Girolami, 2011):

$$q_{km} = \frac{\alpha - 1 + \sum_n^{N_k} \phi_m(\bar{f}_n, \bar{e}_n)}{M(\alpha - 1) + \sum_{m'}^{M} \sum_n^{N_k} \phi_{m'}(\bar{f}_n, \bar{e}_n)} \quad (10)$$

where M is the feature vector's length or the feature dictionary size and α is a Dirichlet parameter with a value greater than one. The derivation is in Appendix A.

Bayesian inference Instead of using a point estimate of $\mathbf{q}$ as shown previously in equation (10), Bayesian inference is based on the whole parameter space in order to incorporate uncertainty into our multinomial model. This requires a posterior probability distribution over $\mathbf{q}$ as follows:

$$p(\bar{f}_n, \bar{e}_n|o_k) = \int p(\bar{f}_n, \bar{e}_n|\mathbf{q}_k)p(\mathbf{q}_k|\boldsymbol{\alpha}_k)\, \mathrm{d}\mathbf{q}_k$$
$$= C \frac{\Gamma\left(\sum_m \alpha_{km}\right) \prod_m \Gamma(\alpha_{km} + \phi_m(\bar{f}_n, \bar{e}_n))}{\prod_m \Gamma(\alpha_{km})\, \Gamma\left(\sum_m \alpha_{km} + \phi_m(\bar{f}_n, \bar{e}_n)\right)}. \quad (11)$$

Here $\boldsymbol{\alpha}_k$ are new hyperparameters of the posterior derived by means of Bayes theorem as follows:

$$p(\mathbf{q}_k|\boldsymbol{\alpha}_k) = \frac{p(\mathbf{q}_k|\boldsymbol{\alpha}) \prod_n^{N_k} p(\bar{f}_n, \bar{e}_n|\mathbf{q}_k)}{\int p(\mathbf{q}_k|\boldsymbol{\alpha}) \prod_n^{N_k} p(\bar{f}_n, \bar{e}_n|\mathbf{q}_k) \mathrm{d}\mathbf{q}_k}. \quad (12)$$

The solution of (11) will result in:

$$\boldsymbol{\alpha}_k = \boldsymbol{\alpha} + \sum_n^{N_k} \Phi(\bar{f}_n, \bar{e}_n). \quad (13)$$

For completeness we give a summary of derivations of equations (11) and (13) in Appendix B, more detailed discussions can be found in (Barber, 2012).

5 Feature Selection

In several high dimensional pattern classification problems, there is increasing evidence that the discriminant information may be in small subspaces, motivating feature selection (Li and Niranjan, 2013). Having irrelevant or redundant features could affect the classification performance (Liu and Motoda, 1998). They might mislead the learning algorithms or overfit them to the data and thus have less accuracy.

The aim of feature selection is to find the optimal subset features which maximize the ability of prediction, which is the main concern, or simplify the learned results to be more understandable. There are many ways to measure the goodness of a feature or a subset of features; however the criterion will be discussed is mutual information.

5.1 Mutual Information

Information criteria are based on the concept of entropy which is the amount of randomness. The distribution of a fair coin, for example, is completely random so the entropy of the coin is very high. The following equation calculates the entropy of a variable X (MacKay, 2002):

$$H(X) = -\sum_x p(x) \log p(x). \quad (14)$$

The mutual information of a feature X can be measured by calculating the difference between the prior uncertainty of the class variable Y and the posterior uncertainty after using the feature as follows (MacKay, 2002):

$$I(X;Y) = H(Y) - H(Y|X) \quad (15)$$
$$= \sum_{x,y} p(x,y) \log \frac{p(x,y)}{p(x)p(y)}.$$

The advantage of mutual Information over other criteria is the ability to detect nonlinear patterns. The disadvantage is its bias towards higher arbitrary features; however this problem can be solved by normalizing the information as follows (Estévez et al., 2009):

$$I_{norm}(X;Y) = \frac{I(X;Y)}{\min(H(X), H(Y))}. \quad (16)$$

6 Experiments

The corpus used in our experiments is MultiUN which is a large-scale parallel corpus extracted from the United Nations website[1] (Eisele and Chen, 2010). We have used Arabic and English portion of MultiUN. Table 2 shows the general statistics.

Statistics	Arabic	English
Sentence Pairs	9.7 M	
Running Words	255.5 M	285.7 M
Word/Line	22	25
Vocabulary Size	677 K	410 K

Table 2: General statistics of Arabic-English MultiUN (M: million, K: thousand).

We simplify the problem by classifying phrase movements into three categories (monotone, swap, discontinuous). To train the reordering models, we used GIZA++ to produce word alignments (Och and Ney, 2000). Then, we used the `extract` tool that comes with the Moses [2] toolkit (Koehn et al., 2007) in order to extract phrase pairs along with their orientation classes.

Each extracted phrase pair is represented by linguistic features as follows:

- Aligned source and target words in a phrase pair. Each word alignment is a feature.

[1] http://www.ods.un.org/ods/

[2] Moses is an open source toolkit for statistical machine translation (www.statmt.org/moses/).

- Words within a window around the source phrase to capture the context. We choose adjacent words of the phrase boundary.

Most researchers build one reordering model for the whole training set (Zens and Ney, 2006; Xiong et al., 2006; Nguyen et al., 2009; Xiang et al., 2011). Ni et al. (Ni et al., 2011) simplified the learning problem to have as many sub-models as source phrases. Training data were divided into small independent sets where samples having the same source phrase are considered a training set. In our experiments, we have chosen the first method.

We compare lexicalized and Bayesian reordering models in two phases. In the classification phase, we see the performance of the models as a classification problem. In the translation phase, we test the actual impact of these reordering models in a translation system.

6.1 Classification

We built naive Bayes classifier with both MAP estimate and Bayesian inference. We also used mutual Information in order to select the most informative features for our classification task.

Table 3 reports the error rate of the reordering models compared to the lexicalized reordering model. All experiments reported here were repeated three times to evaluate the uncertainties in our results. The results shows that there is no advantage to using Bayesian inference instead of MAP estimate.

Classifier	Error Rate
Lexicalized model	25.2%
Bayes-MAP estimate	19.53%
Bayes-Bayesian inference	20.13%

Table 3: Classification error rate of both lexicalized and Bayesian models.

The feature selection process reveals that many features have low mutual information. Hence they are not related to the classification task and can be excluded from the model. Figure 1 shows the normalized mutual information for all extracted features.

A ranking threshold for selecting features based on their mutual information is specified experimentally. In Figure 2, we tried different thresholds ranging from 0.001 to 0.05 and measure the error rate after each reduction. Although there is no much gain in terms of performance but the Bayesian model maintains low error rate when the proportion of selected features is low. The model with almost half of the feature space is as good as the one with full feature space.

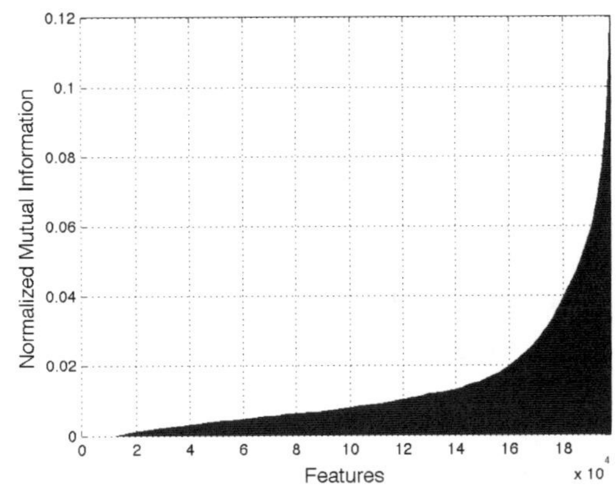

Figure 1: Normalized mutual information for all extracted features (ranked from lowest to highest).

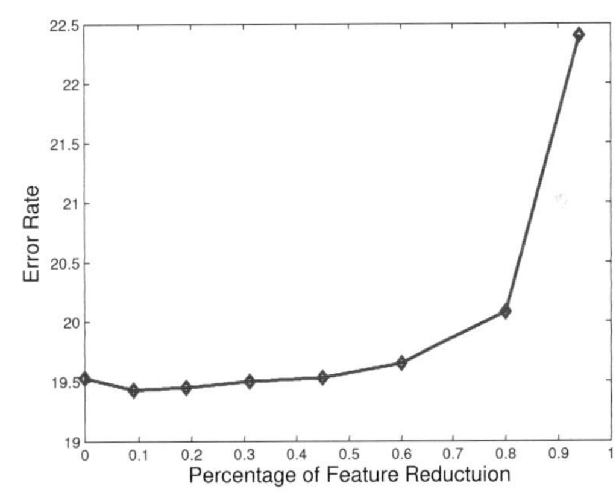

Figure 2: Classification error rate of the Baysien model with different levels of feature reduction.

6.2 Translation

6.2.1 Experimental Design

We used the Moses toolkit (Koehn et al., 2007) with its default settings. The language model is a 5-gram with interpolation and Kneser-Ney smoothing (Kneser and Ney, 1995). We tuned the system by using MERT technique (Och, 2003).

We built four Arabic-English translation systems. Three systems differ in how their reordering models were estimated and the fourth system is a baseline system without reordering model. In all cases, orientation extraction is hierarchical-based since it is the best approach while orientations are monotone, swap and discontinuous. The model is trained in Moses by specifying the configuration string `hier-msd-backward-fe`.

As commonly used in statistical machine translation, we evaluated the translation performance by BLEU score (Papineni et al., 2002). The test sets are NIST MT06 and NIST MT08. Table 4 shows statistics of development and test sets. We also computed statistical significance for the proposed models using the *paired bootstrap resampling* method (Koehn, 2004).

Evaluation Set		Arabic	English
Development	sentences	696	696
	words	19 K	21 K
NIST MT06	sentences	1797	7188
	words	49 K	223 K
NIST MT08	sentences	813	3252
	words	25 K	117 K

Table 4: Statistics of development and test sets. The English side in NIST is larger because there are four translations for each Arabic sentence.

6.2.2 Results

We first demonstrate in Table 5 a general comparison of the proposed model and the lexicalized model in terms of disc size and average speed in a translation system. The size of Bayesian model is far smaller. The lexicalized model is slightly faster than the Bayesian model because we have overhead computational cost to extract features and compute the orientation probabilities. However, the disc size of our model is much smaller which makes it more efficient practically for large-scale tasks.

Model	Size (MB)	Speed (s/sent)
Lexicalized model	604	2.2
Bayesian model	18	2.6

Table 5: Disc size and average speed of the reordering models in a translation system.

Table 6 shows the BLEU scores for the translation systems according to two test sets. The baseline system has no reordering model. In the two test sets, our Bayesian reordering model is better than the lexicalized one with at least 95% statistical significance. As we have seen in the classification section, Bayes classifier with Bayesian inference has no advantage over MAP estimate.

Translation System	MT06	MT08
Baseline	28.92	32.13
BL+ Lexicalized model	30.86	34.22
BL+ Bayes-MAP estimate	**31.21***	**34.72***
BL+ Bayes-Baysien inference	31.20	34.69

Table 6: BLEU scores for Arabic-English translation systems (*: better than the baseline with at least 95% statistical significance).

7 Conclusion

In this paper, we have presented generative modeling approach to phrase reordering in machine translation. We have experimented with translation from Arabic to English and shown improvements over the lexicalized model of estimating probabilities as relative frequencies of phrase movements. Our proposed Bayesian model with feature selection is shown to be superior. The training time of the model is as fast as the lexicalized model. Its storage requirement is many times smaller which makes it more efficient practically for large-scale tasks.

The feature selection process reveals that many features have low mutual information. Hence they are not related to the classification task and can be excluded from the model. The model with almost half of the feature space is as good as the one with full feature space.

Previously proposed discriminative models might achieve higher score than the reported results. However, our model is scalable to large-scale systems since parameter estimation require only one pass over the data with limited memory (i.e. no iterative learning). This is a critical advantage over discriminative models.

Our current work focuses on three issues. The first is improving the translation speed of the proposed model. The lexicalized model is slightly faster. The second is using more informative features. We plan to explore part-of-speech information, which is more accurate in capturing content. Finally, we will explore different feature selection methods. In our experiments, feature reduction is based on univariate ranking which is riskier than multivariate ranking. This is because useless feature can be useful with others.

References

D. Barber. 2012. *Bayesian Reasoning and Machine Learning*. Cambridge University Press.

P. Brown, J. Cocke, S. Della Pietra, V. Della Pietra, F. Jelinek, R. Mercer, and P. Roossin. 1988. A statistical approach to language translation. In *12th International Conference on Computational Linguistics (COLING)*, pages 71–76.

P. Brown, V. Pietra, S. Pietra, and R. Mercer. 1993. The mathematics of statistical machine translation: Parameter estimation. *Computational Linguistics*, 19(2):263–311.

C. Cherry. 2013. Improved reordering for phrase-based translation using sparse features. In *Proceedings of the 2013 Conference of the North American Chapter of the Association for Computational Linguistics: Human Language Technologies*, pages 22–31, Atlanta, Georgia, June. Association for Computational Linguistics.

A. Eisele and Y. Chen. 2010. Multiun: A multilingual corpus from united nation documents. In Daniel Tapias, Mike Rosner, Stelios Piperidis, Jan Odjik, Joseph Mariani, Bente Maegaard, Khalid Choukri, and Nicoletta Calzolari (Conference Chair), editors, *Proceedings of the Seventh conference on International Language Resources and Evaluation*, pages 2868–2872. European Language Resources Association (ELRA), 5.

P. Estévez, M. Tesmer, C. Perez, and J. Zurada. 2009. Normalized mutual information feature selection. *Trans. Neur. Netw.*, 20(2):189–201, February.

M. Galley and C. Manning. 2008. A simple and effective hierarchical phrase reordering model. In *Proceedings of the 2008 Conference on Empirical Methods in Natural Language Processing*, pages 848–856, Hawaii, October. Association for Computational Linguistics.

R. Kneser and H. Ney. 1995. Improved backing-off for m-gram language modeling. *IEEE International Conference on Acoustics, Speech and Signal Processing*, pages 181–184.

P. Koehn and C. Monz. 2005. Shared task: Statistical machine translation between european languages. In *Proceedings of ACL Workshop on Building and Using Parallel Texts*, pages 119–124. Association for Computational Linguistics.

P. Koehn, A. Axelrod, A. Mayne, C. Callison-Burch, M. Osborne, and D. Talbot. 2005. Edinburgh system description for the 2005 IWSLT speech translation evaluation. In *Proceedings of International Workshop on Spoken Language Translation*, Pittsburgh, PA.

P. Koehn, H. Hoang, A. Birch, C. Callison-Burch, M. Federico, N. Bertoldi, B. Cowan, W. Shen, C. Moran, R. Zens, C. Dyer, O. Bojar, A. Constantin, and E. Herbst. 2007. Moses: Open source toolkit for statistical machine translation. In *Proceedings of the ACL 2007 Demo and Poster Sessions*, pages 177–180.

P. Koehn. 2004. Statistical significance tests for machine translation evaluation. In Dekang Lin and Dekai Wu, editors, *Proceedings of EMNLP 2004*, pages 388–395, Barcelona, Spain, July. Association for Computational Linguistics.

P. Koehn. 2010. *Statistical Machine Translation*. Cambridge University Press.

S. Kumar and W. Byrne. 2005. Local phrase reordering models for statistical machine translation. In *Proceedings of Human Language Technology Conference and Conference on Empirical Methods in Natural Language Processing*, pages 161–168, Vancouver, British Columbia, Canada, October. Association for Computational Linguistics.

Hongyu Li and M. Niranjan. 2013. Discriminant subspaces of some high dimensional pattern classification problems. In *IEEE International Workshop on Machine Learning for Signal Processing (MLSP)*, pages 27–32.

H. Liu and H. Motoda. 1998. *Feature Selection for Knowledge Discovery and Data Mining*. Kluwer Academic Publishers, Norwell, MA, USA.

D. MacKay. 2002. *Information Theory, Inference & Learning Algorithms*. Cambridge University Press, New York, NY, USA.

V. Nguyen, A. Shimazu, M. Nguyen, and T. Nguyen. 2009. Improving a lexicalized hierarchical reordering model using maximum entropy. In *Proceedings of the Twelfth Machine Translation Summit (MT Summit XII)*. International Association for Machine Translation.

Y. Ni, C. Saunders, S. Szedmak, and M. Niranjan. 2011. Exploitation of machine learning techniques in modelling phrase movements for machine translation. *Journal of Machine Learning Research*, 12:1–30, February.

F. Och and H. Ney. 2000. Improved statistical alignment models. In *Proceedings of the 38th Annual Meeting of the Association of Computational Linguistics (ACL)*.

F. Och and H. Ney. 2002. Discriminative training and maximum entropy models for statistical machine translation. In *Proceedings of the 40th Annual Meeting of the Association for Computational Linguistics (ACL)*.

F. Och and H. Ney. 2004. The alignment template approach to statistical machine translation. *Computational Linguistics*, 30(4):417–449.

F. Och. 2003. Minimum error rate training in statistical machine translation. In *Proceedings of the 41st Annual Meeting on Association for Computational Linguistics - Volume 1*, ACL '03, pages 160–167, Stroudsburg, PA, USA. Association for Computational Linguistics.

K. Papineni, S. Roukos, and T. Ward. 1998. Maximum likelihood and discriminative training of direct translation models. In *Proceedings of ICASSP*, pages 189–192.

K. Papineni, S. Roukos, T. Ward, and W. Zhu. 2002. Bleu: a method for automatic evaluation of machine translation. In *Proceedings of the 40th Annual Meeting on Association for Computational Linguistics*, pages 311–318, Stroudsburg, PA, USA. Association for Computational Linguistics.

S. Rogers and M. Girolami. 2011. *A First Course in Machine Learning*. Chapman & Hall/CRC, 1st edition.

C. Tillmann. 2004. A unigram orientation model for statistical machine translation. In *Proceedings of HLT-NAACL: Short Papers*, pages 101–104.

B. Xiang, N. Ge, and A. Ittycheriah. 2011. Improving reordering for statistical machine translation with smoothed priors and syntactic features. In *Proceedings of SSST-5, Fifth Workshop on Syntax, Semantics and Structure in Statistical Translation*, pages 61–69, Portland, Oregon, USA. Association for Computational Linguistics.

D. Xiong, Q. Liu, and S. Lin. 2006. Maximum entropy based phrase reordering model for statistical machine translation. In *Proceedings of the 21st International Conference on Computational Linguistics and 44th Annual Meeting of the ACL*, pages 521–528, Sydney, July. Association for Computational Linguistics.

R. Zens and H. Ney. 2006. Discriminative reordering models for statistical machine translation. In *Proceedings on the Workshop on Statistical Machine Translation*, pages 55–63, New York City, June. Association for Computational Linguistics.

A MAP Estimate Derivation

Multinomial distribution is defined as:

$$p(\mathbf{x}|\mathbf{q}) = C \prod_m q_m^{x_m} \tag{17}$$

where C is a multinomial coefficient,

$$C = \frac{(\sum_m x_m)!}{\prod_m x_m!}, \tag{18}$$

and q_m is an event probability ($\sum_m q_m = 1$).

A maximum a posteriori probability (MAP) estimate requires a prior over $\mathbf{q}$. Dirichlet distribution is a conjugate prior and is defined as:

$$p(\mathbf{q}|\boldsymbol{\alpha}) = \frac{\Gamma(\sum_m \alpha_m)}{\prod_m \Gamma(\alpha_m)} \prod_m q_m^{\alpha_m - 1} \tag{19}$$

where α_m is is a parameter with a positive value.

Finding the MAP estimate for $\mathbf{q}$ given a data is as follows:

$$\begin{aligned}
\mathbf{q}^* &= \arg\max_{\mathbf{q}} p(\mathbf{q}|\boldsymbol{\alpha}, \mathbf{X}) \\
&= \arg\max_{\mathbf{q}} \{p(\mathbf{q}|\boldsymbol{\alpha})p(\mathbf{X}|\mathbf{q})\} \\
&= \arg\max_{\mathbf{q}} \left\{ p(\mathbf{q}|\boldsymbol{\alpha}) \prod_n p(\mathbf{x}_n|\mathbf{q}) \right\} \\
&= \arg\max_{\mathbf{q}} \left\{ \prod_m q_m^{\alpha_m - 1} \prod_{n,m} q_m^{x_{nm}} \right\} \\
&= \arg\max_{\mathbf{q}} \left\{ \sum_m \log q_m^{\alpha_m - 1} + \sum_{n,m} \log q_m^{x_{nm}} \right\}.
\end{aligned} \tag{20}$$

Since our function is subject to constraints ($\sum_m q_m = 1$), we introduce Lagrange multiplier as follows:

$$f(\mathbf{q}) = \sum_m \log q_m^{\alpha_m - 1} + \sum_{n,m} \log q_m^{x_{nm}} - \lambda(\sum_m q_m - 1). \tag{21}$$

Now we can find $\mathbf{q}^*$ by taking the partial derivative with respect to one variable q_m:

$$\begin{aligned}
\frac{\partial f(\mathbf{q})}{\partial q_m} &= \frac{\alpha_m - 1 + \sum_n x_{nm}}{q_m} - \lambda \\
q_m &= \frac{\alpha_m - 1 + \sum_n x_{nm}}{\lambda}.
\end{aligned} \tag{22}$$

Finally, we sum both sides over M to find λ :

$$\begin{aligned}
\lambda \sum_m q_m &= \sum_m \left(\alpha_m - 1 + \sum_n x_{nm} \right) \\
\lambda &= \sum_m (\alpha_m - 1) + \sum_{n,m} x_{nm}.
\end{aligned} \tag{23}$$

The solution can be simplified by choosing the same value for each α_m which will result in:

$$q_m = \frac{\alpha - 1 + \sum_n x_{nm}}{M(\alpha - 1) + \sum_{n,m'} x_{nm'}}. \tag{24}$$

B Bayesian Inference Derivation

In Appendix A, the inference is based on a single point estimate of $\mathbf{q}$ that has the highest posterior probability. However, it can be based on the whole parameter space to incorporate uncertainty. The probability of a new data point marginalized over the posterior as follows:

$$p(\mathbf{x}|\boldsymbol{\alpha}, \mathbf{X}) = \int p(\mathbf{x}|\mathbf{q})p(\mathbf{q}|\boldsymbol{\alpha}, \mathbf{X})\, \mathrm{d}\mathbf{q}, \quad (25)$$

$$p(\mathbf{q}|\boldsymbol{\alpha}, \mathbf{X}) = \frac{p(\mathbf{q}|\boldsymbol{\alpha})p(\mathbf{X}|\mathbf{q})}{\int p(\mathbf{q}|\boldsymbol{\alpha})p(\mathbf{X}|\mathbf{q})\mathrm{d}\mathbf{q}}. \quad (26)$$

Since Dirichlet and Multinomial distributions are conjugate pairs, they form the same density as the prior. Therefore the posterior is also Dirichlet. Now we can expand the posterior expression and re-arrange it to look like a Dirichlet as follows:

$$\begin{aligned} p(\mathbf{q}|\boldsymbol{\alpha}, \mathbf{X}) &\propto p(\mathbf{q}|\boldsymbol{\alpha}) \prod_n p(\mathbf{x}_n|\mathbf{q}) \\ &\propto \prod_m q_m^{\alpha_m - 1} \prod_n \prod_m q_m^{x_{nm}} \\ &\propto \prod_m q_m^{(\alpha_m + \sum_n x_{nm}) - 1}. \end{aligned} \quad (27)$$

The new hyperparameters of the posterior is:

$$\alpha_m^* = \alpha_m + \sum_n x_{nm}. \quad (28)$$

Finally, we expand and re-arrange Dirichlet and multinomial distributions inside the integral in (25) as follows:

$$\begin{aligned} &p(\mathbf{x}|\boldsymbol{\alpha}, \mathbf{X}) = \\ &\int C \prod_m q_m^{x_m} \frac{\Gamma\left(\sum_m \alpha_m^*\right)}{\prod_m \Gamma(\alpha_m^*)} \prod_m q_m^{\alpha_m^* - 1} \mathrm{d}\mathbf{q} \\ &= C \frac{\Gamma\left(\sum_m \alpha_m^*\right)}{\prod_m \Gamma(\alpha_m^*)} \int \prod_m q_m^{\alpha_m^* + x_m - 1} \mathrm{d}\mathbf{q}. \end{aligned} \quad (29)$$

Note that inside the integral looks a Dirichlet without a normalizing constant. If we multiply and divide by its normalizing constant (i.e. Beta function), the integral is going to be one because it is a density function, resulting in:

$$\begin{aligned} &p(\mathbf{x}|\boldsymbol{\alpha}, \mathbf{X}) = C \frac{\Gamma\left(\sum_m \alpha_m^*\right)}{\prod_m \Gamma(\alpha_m^*)} \\ &\mathrm{B}(\boldsymbol{\alpha}^* + \mathbf{x}) \int \frac{1}{\mathrm{B}(\boldsymbol{\alpha}^* + \mathbf{x})} \prod_m q_m^{\alpha_m^* + x_m - 1} \mathrm{d}\mathbf{q}_c \\ &= C \frac{\Gamma\left(\sum_m \alpha_m^*\right)}{\prod_m \Gamma(\alpha_m^*)} \mathrm{B}(\boldsymbol{\alpha}^* + \mathbf{x}) \\ &= C \frac{\Gamma\left(\sum_m \alpha_m^*\right)}{\prod_m \Gamma(\alpha_m^*)} \frac{\prod_m \Gamma(\alpha_m^* + x_m)}{\Gamma\left(\sum_m (\alpha_m^* + x_m)\right)}. \end{aligned} \quad (30)$$

Augmenting String-to-Tree and Tree-to-String Translation with Non-Syntactic Phrases

Matthias Huck and **Hieu Hoang** and **Philipp Koehn**
School of Informatics
University of Edinburgh
10 Crichton Street
Edinburgh EH8 9AB, UK
{mhuck,hhoang,pkoehn}@inf.ed.ac.uk

Abstract

We present an effective technique to easily augment GHKM-style syntax-based machine translation systems (Galley et al., 2006) with phrase pairs that do not comply with any syntactic well-formedness constraints. Non-syntactic phrase pairs are distinguished from syntactic ones in order to avoid harming effects. We apply our technique in state-of-the-art string-to-tree and tree-to-string setups. For tree-to-string translation, we furthermore investigate novel approaches for translating with source-syntax GHKM rules in association with input tree constraints and input tree features.

1 Introduction

Syntax-based statistical machine translation systems utilize linguistic information that is obtained by parsing the training data. In *tree-to-string* translation, source-side syntactic tree annotation is employed, while *string-to-tree* translation exploits target-side syntax. The syntactic parse tree annotation constrains phrase extraction to syntactically well-formed phrase pairs: spans of syntactic phrases must match constituents in the parse tree. Standard phrase-based and hierarchical phrase-based statistical machine translation systems, in contrast, allow all phrase pairs that are consistent with the word alignment (Koehn et al., 2003; Chiang, 2005).

A restriction of the phrase inventory to syntactically well-formed phrase pairs entails that possibly valuable information from the training data remains disregarded. While we would expect phrase pairs that are not linguistically motivated to be less reliable, discarding them altogether might be an overly harsh decision. The quality of an inventory of syntactic phrases depends heavily on the tree annotation scheme and the quality of the syntactic parses of the training data. Phrase pairs that do not span constituents in the tree annotation obtained from syntactic parses can provide reasonable alternative segmentations or alternative translation options which prove to be valuable to the decoder.

In this work, we augment the phrase inventories of string-to-tree and tree-to-string translation systems with phrase pairs that are not induced in the syntax-based extraction. We extract continuous phrases that are consistent with the word alignment, without enforcing any constraints with respect to syntactic tree annotation. Non-syntactic phrases are added as rules to the baseline syntactic grammar with a fill-up technique. New rules are only added if their right-hand side does not exist yet. We extend the glue grammar with a special glue rule to allow for application of non-syntactic phrases during decoding. A feature in the log-linear model combination serves to distinguish non-syntactic phrases from syntactic ones. During decoding, the decoder can draw on both syntactic and non-syntactic phrase table entries and produce derivations which resort to both types of phrases. Such derivations yield hypotheses that make use of the alternative segmentations and translation options provided through non-syntactic phrases. The search space is more diverse, and in some cases all hypotheses from purely syntax-based derivations score worse than a translation that applies one or more non-syntactic phrases. We empirically demonstrate that this technique can lead to substantial gains in translation quality.

Our syntactic translation models conform to the GHKM syntax approach as proposed by **G**alley, **H**opkins, **K**night, and **M**arcu (Galley et al., 2004) with composed rules as in (Galley et al., 2006) and (DeNeefe et al., 2007). State-of-the-art GHKM string-to-tree systems have recently shown very competitive performance in public

Proceedings of the Ninth Workshop on Statistical Machine Translation, pages 486–498,
Baltimore, Maryland USA, June 26–27, 2014.

evaluation campaigns (Nadejde et al., 2013; Bojar et al., 2013). We apply the GHKM approach not only in a string-to-tree setting as in previous work, but employ it to build tree-to-string systems as well. We conduct tree-to-string translation with text input and additionally adopt translation with tree input and input tree constraints as suggested for hierarchical translation by Hoang and Koehn (2010). We also implement translation with tree input and feature-driven soft tree matching. The effect of augmenting the systems with non-syntactic phrases is evaluated for all variants.

2 Outline

The remainder of the paper is structured as follows: We review some of the basics of syntax-based translation in the next section (Section 3) and sketch the characteristics of our GHKM string-to-tree and tree-to-string translation frameworks.

In Section 4, we describe our technique to augment GHKM-style syntax-based systems with phrase pairs that do not comply with any syntactic well-formedness constraints.

Section 5 contains the empirical part of the paper. We first describe our experimental setup (5.1), followed by a presentation of the translation results (5.2). We also include a few translation examples (5.3) in order to illustrate the differences between the syntax-based baseline systems and the setups augmented with non-syntactic phrases. The empirical part is concluded with a brief discussion (5.4).

In the final part of the paper (Section 6), we give a survey of previous work that has dealt with problems related to overly restrictive syntactic grammars for statistical machine translation, inadequate syntactic parses, and insufficient coverage of syntactic phrase inventories. A broad spectrum of diverse methods has been proposed in the literature, many of which are quite dissimilar from ours but nevertheless related. We conclude the paper in Section 7.

3 Syntax-based Translation

In syntax-based translation, a probabilistic synchronous context-free grammar (SCFG) is induced from bilingual training corpora. The parallel training data is word-aligned and annotated with syntactic parses on either target side (string-to-tree), source side (tree-to-string), or both (tree-to-tree). A syntactic phrase extraction procedure extracts rules which are consistent with the word-alignment and conform with certain syntactic validity constraints.

Extracted rules are of the form $A, B \rightarrow \langle \alpha, \beta, ^{\sim} \rangle$. The right-hand side of the rule $\langle \alpha, \beta \rangle$ is a bilingual phrase pair that may contain non-terminal symbols, i.e. $\alpha \in (V_F \cup N_F)^+$ and $\beta \in (V_E \cup N_E)^+$, where V_F and V_E denote the source and target terminal vocabulary, and N_F and N_E denote the source and target non-terminal vocabulary, respectively. The non-terminals on the source side and on the target side of rules are linked in a one-to-one correspondence. The $\sim$ relation defines this one-to-one correspondence. The left-hand side of the rule is a pair of source and target non-terminals, $A \in N_F$ and $B \in N_E$.

Decoding is typically carried out with a parsing-based algorithm, in our case a customized version of CYK+ (Chappelier and Rajman, 1998). The parsing algorithm is extended to handle translation candidates and to incorporate language model scores via cube pruning (Chiang, 2007).

3.1 GHKM String-to-Tree Translation

In GHKM string-to-tree translation (Galley et al., 2004; Galley et al., 2006; DeNeefe et al., 2007), rules are extracted from training instances which consist of a source sentence, a target sentence along with its constituent parse tree, and a word alignment matrix. This tuple is interpreted as a directed graph (the *alignment graph*), with edges pointing away from the root of the tree, and word alignment links being edges as well. A set of nodes (the *frontier set*) is determined that contains only nodes with non-overlapping closure of their spans.[1] By computing *frontier graph fragments*—fragments of the alignment graph such that their root and all sinks are in the frontier set—the GHKM extractor is able to induce a minimal set of rules which explain the training instance. The internal tree structure can be discarded to obtain flat SCFG rules. Minimal rules can be assembled to build larger *composed rules*.

Non-terminals on target sides of string-to-tree rules are syntactified. The target non-terminal vocabulary of the SCFG contains the set of labels of the frontier nodes, which is in turn a subset

[1]The *span* of a node in the alignment graph is defined as the set of source-side words that are reachable from this node. The *closure* of a span is the smallest interval of source sentence positions that covers the span.

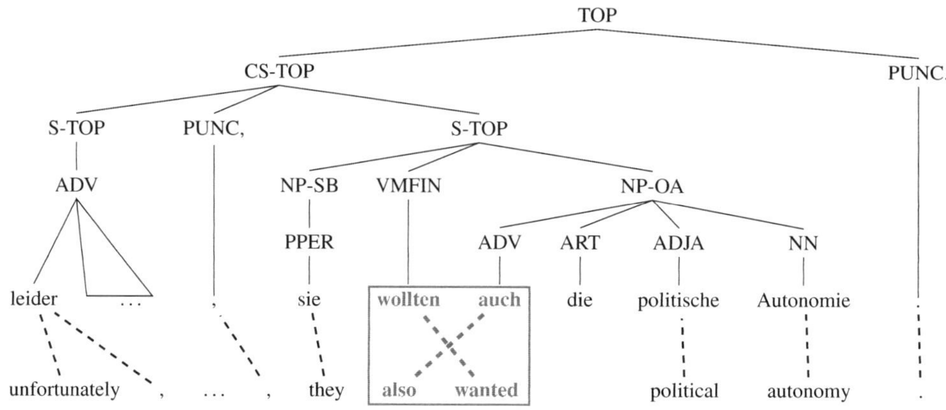

Figure 1: Word-aligned training sentence pair with target-side syntactic annotation.

of (or equal to) the set of constituent labels in the parse tree. It furthermore contains an initial non-terminal symbol Q. Source sides of the rules are not decorated with syntactic annotation. The source non-terminal vocabulary contains a single generic non-terminal symbol X.

In addition to the extracted grammar, the translation system makes use of a special *glue grammar* with an *initial rule*, *glue rules*, a *final rule*, and *top rules*. The glue rules provide a fall back method to just monotonically concatenate partial derivations during decoding. As we add tokens which mark the sentence start ("<s>") and the sentence end ("</s>"), the rules in the glue grammar are of the following form:

Initial rule:

$$X,Q \rightarrow \langle \text{<s>}\ X^{\sim 0}, \text{<s>}\ Q^{\sim 0} \rangle$$

Glue rules:

$$X,Q \rightarrow \langle X^{\sim 0} X^{\sim 1}, Q^{\sim 0} B^{\sim 1} \rangle$$

for all $B \in N_E$

Final rule:

$$X,Q \rightarrow \langle X^{\sim 0}\ \text{</s>}, Q^{\sim 0}\ \text{</s>} \rangle$$

Top rules:

$$X,Q \rightarrow \langle \text{<s>}\ X^{\sim 0}\ \text{</s>}, \text{<s>}\ B^{\sim 0}\ \text{</s>} \rangle$$

for all $B \in N_E$

3.2 GHKM Tree-to-String Translation

The described techniques for GHKM string-to-tree translation can be adjusted for tree-to-string translation in a straightforward manner. Rules are extracted from training instances which consist of a source sentence along with its constituent parse tree, a target sentence, and a word alignment matrix. We omit the details.

For GHKM tree-to-string translation, we investigate three decoding variants:

Tree-to-string translation with text input. The decoder can construct any source-side syntactic analysis that the grammar permits, very similar to string-to-tree translation.

Tree-to-string translation with tree input and input tree constraints. Syntactic annotation over the input data is provided to the decoder. The source-side syntactic non-terminals of a tree-to-string translation rule need to match the constituent span in the input sentence, otherwise the rule cannot be applied. This variant follows the method that was suggested for hierarchical translation by Hoang and Koehn (2010).

Tree-to-string translation with tree input and input tree features. Syntactic annotation over the input data is provided to the decoder. No hard matching constraints are imposed, but the decoder is informed about matches and mismatches of the syntactic annotation in the rules and in the input tree. It takes them into account for the score computation.

4 Non-Syntactic Phrases for GHKM Translation

The syntactic constraints in GHKM extraction can unfortunately prevent useful phrase pairs from being included in the phrase inventory. Consider the example in Figure 1: the highlighted phrase pair $\langle$*also wanted, wollten auch*$\rangle$ cannot be extracted from this training instance for string-to-tree translation.

In the standard phrase-based approach, in contrast, all continuous phrases that are consistent with the word alignment are extracted (Och et al., 1999; Och, 2002). The set of continuous bilingual phrases $\mathscr{BP}(f_1^J, e_1^I, A)$, given a training instance comprising a source sentence f_1^J, a target sentence e_1^I, and a word alignment $A \subseteq \{1,...,I\} \times \{1,...,J\}$, is defined as follows:

$$\mathscr{BP}(f_1^J, e_1^I, A) =$$
$$\Big\{ \langle f_{j_1}^{j_2}, e_{i_1}^{i_2} \rangle : \exists (i,j) \in A : i_1 \leq i \leq i_2 \wedge j_1 \leq j \leq j_2$$
$$\wedge \forall (i,j) \in A : i_1 \leq i \leq i_2 \leftrightarrow j_1 \leq j \leq j_2 \Big\}$$

Consistency for continuous phrases is based upon merely two constraints in this definition: (1.) At least one source and target position within the phrase must be aligned, and (2.) words from inside the source phrase may only be aligned to words from inside the target phrase and vice versa. The highlighted phrase pair from the example does not violate these constraints.

In order to augment our GHKM syntax-based systems with non-syntactic phrases, we obey the following procedure:

- The set $\mathscr{BP}$ is extracted from all training instances, and phrase translation probabilities are computed separately from those in the syntactic phrase inventory.
- Non-syntactic phrases are converted to rules by providing a special left-hand side non-terminal X.
- A phrase table fill-up method is applied to enhance the syntactic phrase inventory with entries from the non-syntactic phrase inventory. Non-syntactic rules are only added to the final grammar if no syntactic rule with the same (source *and* target) right-hand side is present. This method is inspired by previous work in domain adaptation (Bisazza et al., 2011).
- The glue grammar is extended with a new glue rule

  $$X, Q \rightarrow \langle X^{\sim 0} X^{\sim 1}, Q^{\sim 0} X^{\sim 1} \rangle$$

  that enables the system to make use of non-syntactic rules in decoding.
- A binary feature is added to the log-linear model (Och and Ney, 2002) to distinguish non-syntactic rules from syntactic ones, and to be able to assign a tuned weight to the non-syntactic part of the grammar.

5 Empirical Evaluation

We evaluate the effect of augmenting GHKM syntax-based translation systems—both string-to-tree and tree-to-string—with non-syntactic phrase pairs on the English→German language pair using the standard newstest sets of the Workshop on Statistical Machine Translation (WMT) for testing.[2] The experiments are conducted with the open-source *Moses* implementations of GHKM rule extraction (Williams and Koehn, 2012) and decoding with CYK+ parsing and cube pruning (Hoang et al., 2009).

5.1 Experimental Setup

We work with an English–German parallel training corpus of around 4.5 M sentence pairs (after corpus cleaning). The parallel data originates from three different sources which have been eligible for the constrained track of the ACL 2014 Ninth Workshop on Statistical Machine Translation shared translation task: Europarl (Koehn, 2005), News Commentary, and the Common Crawl corpus as provided on the WMT website. Word alignments are created by aligning the data in both directions with MGIZA++ (Gao and Vogel, 2008) and symmetrizing the two trained alignments (Och and Ney, 2003; Koehn et al., 2003). For string-to-tree translation, we parse the German target side with BitPar (Schmid, 2004).[3] For tree-to-string translation, we parse the English source side of the parallel data with the English Berkeley Parser (Petrov et al., 2006).

When extracting syntactic phrases, we impose several restrictions for composed rules, in particular a maximum number of twenty tree nodes per rule, a maximum depth of five, and a maximum size of five. We discard rules with non-terminals on their right-hand side if they are singletons in the training data.

Only the 100 best translation options per distinct source side with respect to the weighted phrase-level model scores are loaded by the decoder. The decoder is configured with a maximum chart span of 25 and a rule limit of 100.

A standard set of models is used in the baselines, comprising phrase translation probabilities and lexical translation probabilities in both direc-

[2] `http://www.statmt.org/wmt14/translation-task.html`

[3] We remove grammatical case and function information from the annotation obtained with BitPar.

system	dev		newstest2013				newstest2014			
	BLEU	TER	BLEU	Δ	TER	Δ	BLEU	Δ	TER	Δ
phrase-based	33.0	48.8	18.8		64.5		18.2		66.9	
+ lexicalized reordering	34.2	48.1	19.2		64.5		18.3		67.1	
string-to-string (syntax-directed extraction)	32.6	49.4	18.2		65.4		17.8		68.0	
+ non-syntactic phrases	33.4	49.0	18.7	+0.5	65.0	−0.4	18.3	+0.5	67.6	−0.4
string-to-tree	33.6	48.7	19.5		63.9		18.6		66.9	
+ non-syntactic phrases	34.3	48.0	19.8	+0.3	63.6	−0.3	19.1	+0.5	66.2	−0.7
tree-to-string	34.0	48.5	19.5		63.8		18.5		67.0	
+ non-syntactic phrases	33.9	48.4	19.3	−0.2	64.0	+0.2	18.7	+0.2	66.6	−0.4
+ input tree constraints	33.7	48.4	19.3		63.9		18.3		67.0	
+ non-syntactic phrases	34.2	48.2	19.7	+0.4	63.6	−0.3	18.7	+0.3	66.5	−0.5
+ input tree features	34.3	48.3	19.6		63.7		18.6		67.0	
+ non-syntactic phrases	34.4	48.1	19.9	+0.3	63.4	−0.3	18.8	+0.2	66.5	−0.5

Table 1: English→German experimental results (truecase). BLEU scores are given in percentage.

tions, word and phrase penalty, an n-gram language model, a rule rareness penalty, and the monolingual PCFG probability of the tree fragment from which the rule was extracted (Williams et al., 2014). Phrase translation probabilities are smoothed via Good-Turing smoothing.

The language model (LM) is a large interpolated 5-gram LM with modified Kneser-Ney smoothing (Kneser and Ney, 1995; Chen and Goodman, 1998). The target side of the parallel corpus and the monolingual German News Crawl corpora are employed as training data. We use the SRILM toolkit (Stolcke, 2002) to train the LM and rely on KenLM (Heafield, 2011) for language model scoring during decoding.

Model weights are optimized to maximize BLEU (Papineni et al., 2002) with batch MIRA (Cherry and Foster, 2012) on 1000-best lists. We selected 2000 sentences from the newstest2008-2012 sets as a development set. The selected sentences obtained high sentence-level BLEU scores when being translated with a baseline phrase-based system, and do each contain less than 30 words for more rapid tuning. newstest2013 and newstest2014 are used as unseen test sets. Translation quality is measured in truecase with BLEU and TER (Snover et al., 2006).[4]

We apply a phrase length limit of five when extracting non-syntactic phrases for the fill-up of syntactic phrase tables.

[4]TER scores are computed with `tercom` version 0.7.25 and parameters `-N -s`.

5.2 Translation Results

Table 1 comprises the results of our empirical evaluation of the translation quality achieved by the different systems.

5.2.1 Phrase-based Baselines

We set up two phrase-based baselines for comparison. Their set of models is the same as for the syntax-based baselines, with the exception of the PCFG probability. One of the phrase-based systems moreover utilizes a lexicalized reordering model (Galley and Manning, 2008). No non-standard advanced features (like an operation sequence model or class-based LMs) are engrafted. The maximum phrase length is five, search is carried out with cube pruning at a k-best limit of 1000. A maximum number of 100 translation options per source side are taken into account.

5.2.2 String-to-String Contrastive System

A further contrastive experiment is done with a string-to-string system. The extraction method for this string-to-string system is GHKM syntax-directed with syntactic target-side annotation from BitPar, as in the string-to-tree setup. We actually extract the same rules but strip off the syntactic labels. The final grammar contains rules with a single generic non-terminal instead of syntactic ones. Note that a side effect of this is that the phrase inventory of the string-to-string system contains a larger amount of hierarchical phrases[5] than the string-to-tree system, though the same rules are extracted. The reason is that we discard singleton hierarchical rules when we normalize the frequencies after extraction. Many rules that are singletons when the syntax decoration is taken into account have in fact been seen multiple times if syntactic labels are not distinguished, due to pooling of counts.

The string-to-string system is on newstest2013 1.0 points BLEU worse than the phrase-based system with lexicalized reordering and on newstest2014 0.5 points BLEU. We gain 0.5 points BLEU on both of the test sets if we augment the string-to-string system with non-syntactic phrases from the standard phrase-based extractor according to our procedure from Section 4.

5.2.3 String-to-Tree System

The translation quality of the string-to-tree system surpasses the translation quality of the better phrase-based baseline slightly (by 0.3 points BLEU on both test sets). The string-to-tree system is clearly superior to the string-to-string system, which verifies that syntactic non-terminals are indeed vital. We get a nice gain of 0.5 points BLEU and 0.7 points TER on newstest2014 if we augment the string-to-tree system with non-syntactic phrases. The phrase-based system is outperformed by 0.8 points BLEU.

5.2.4 Tree-to-String Systems

The tree-to-string baseline with text input performs at the level of the string-to-tree baseline, but augmenting it with non-syntactic phrases yields only a small improvement or even harms a little (on newstest2013).

Decoding with tree input and input tree constraints causes a minor loss in translation quality. We however observed a decoding speed-up. If we employ non-syntactic phrases to augment the tree-to-string setup with input tree constraints, we provide the new non-syntactic rules in the grammar with a particular property: their left-hand side non-terminal X can match any constituent span in the input sentence. The decoder would not be able to utilize non-syntactic phrases without this relaxation. Syntactic phrases amount to an increase of up to 0.4 points BLEU (newstest2013) and 0.5 points TER (newstest2014) in the tree-constrained setup.

Our best tree-to-string setup takes tree input, but involves soft matching features instead of hard input tree constraints. We incorporate two features, one that fires for matches and another one that fires for mismatches. The motivation for not relying on just one feature which would penalize mismatches is that the number of syntactic non-terminals in the derivation can differ between hypotheses. Not all constituent spans need to be matched (or mismatched) by non-terminals, some can be overlaid through larger rules.[6] Tree-to-string translation with input tree features benefits from being augmented with non-syntactic phrases by 0.2 to 0.3 points BLEU. The resulting system is minimally better than the best string-to-tree system on newstest2013, and slightly worse than it on newstest2014.

5.3 Translation Examples

We illustrate the differences between the syntax-based baseline systems and the setups augmented with non-syntactic phrases by means of two translation examples from newstest2014. Both examples are string-to-tree translations.

Figures 2 and 3 depict an example that corresponds well to the word-aligned training sentence pair with target-side syntactic annotation from Figure 1. Figure 2 shows the translation, segmentation, and parse tree derived by the string-to-tree baseline system as single-best output for the preprocessed input sentence: "*the lessees were against this and also wanted longer terms .*" The reference translation is: "*Die Pächter waren dagegen und wollten zudem längere Laufzeiten.*" Figure 3 shows the translation, segmentation, and parse tree derived by the string-to-tree system augmented with non-syntactic phrases. There are two word substitutions with respect to the reference in the latter translation, but they convey the same meaning. The baseline translation fails to convey the meaning, mostly because "*terms*" is translated to the verb "*gesehen*", which is a wrong syntactic analysis in the given context. Interestingly, the segmentation applied by the two systems is rather similar, apart from the interval "*also wanted*" which cannot be translated en bloc by the baseline. All rules in the baseline gram-

[5] We define *hierarchical phrases* as rules with non-terminals on their right-hand side, in contrast to *lexical phrases* which are continuous rules with right-hand sides that contain terminal symbols only.

[6] Also remember that we discarded the internal tree structure to obtain flat SCFG rules.

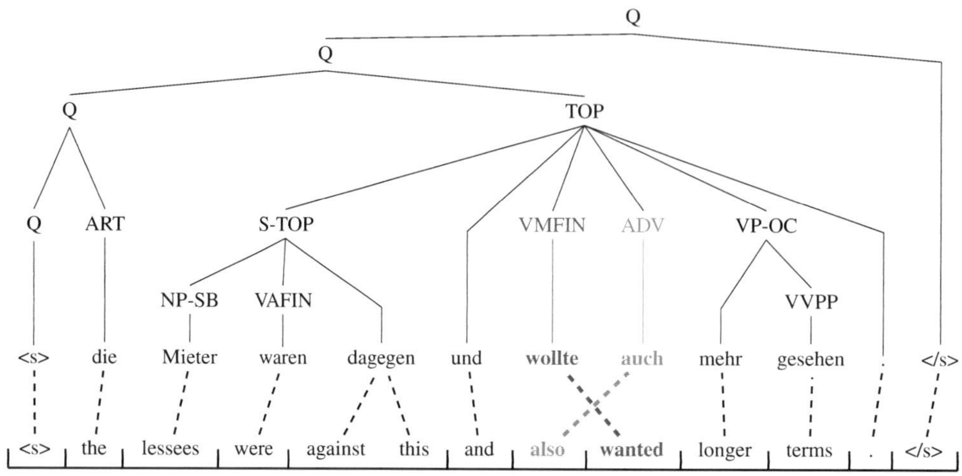

Reference: *Die Pächter waren dagegen und wollten zudem längere Laufzeiten.*

Figure 2: Translation and parse tree from the string-to-tree system.

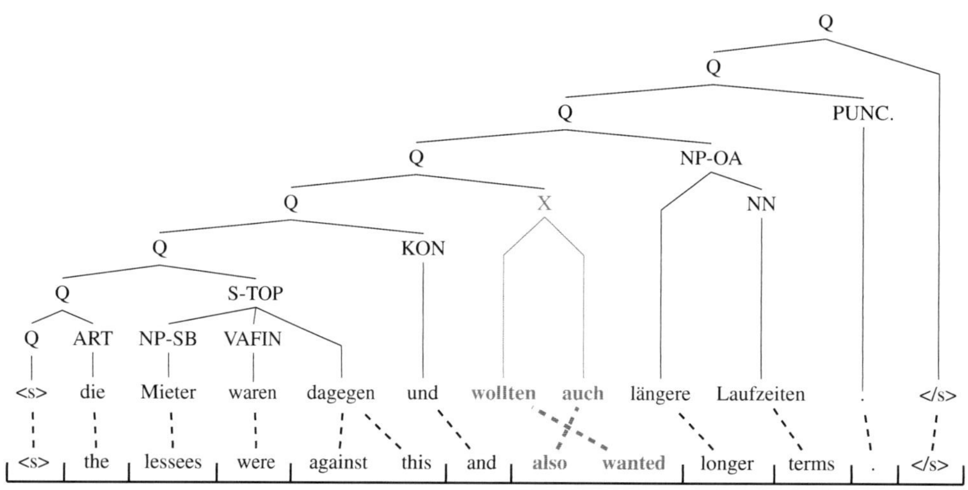

Reference: *Die Pächter waren dagegen und wollten zudem längere Laufzeiten.*

Figure 3: Translation and parse tree from the string-to-tree system augmented with non-syntactic phrases.

mar that contain "*also wanted*" as part of their source side imply a larger source-side lexical context that is not present in the given sentence. None of those rules matches the input. The baseline has to translate "*also*" and "*wanted*" separately and fails to translate the verb to a plural form German verb. The next rule in bottom-up order is already involved in the incorrect choice of a verb for "*terms*". The string-to-tree system augmented with non-syntactic phrases applies more glue rules, but this is beneficial in the present example, as it breaks apart the faulty syntactic derivation.

Figures 4 and 5 depict a second example. Compared to the baseline, filling up the phrase table with non-syntactic phrases had the effect of disassembling the originally nicely built syntactic tree structure over the translation nearly completely. Four non-syntactic phrases are applied, three of them span over target-side punctuation marks. The baseline translation is more literal and conveys the meaning, but the system augmented with non-syntactic phrases produces a more fluent output. Its translation seems more natural and happens to match the reference in this case.

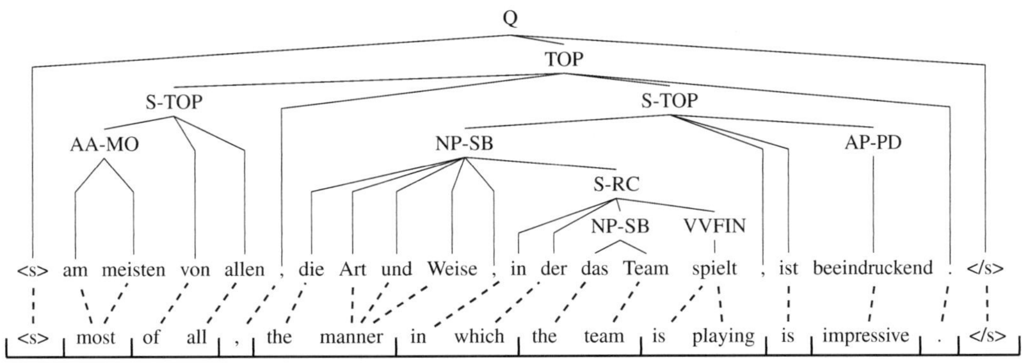

Reference: *Vor allem die Art und Weise, wie die Mannschaft spielt, ist beeindruckend.*

Figure 4: Translation and parse tree from the string-to-tree system.

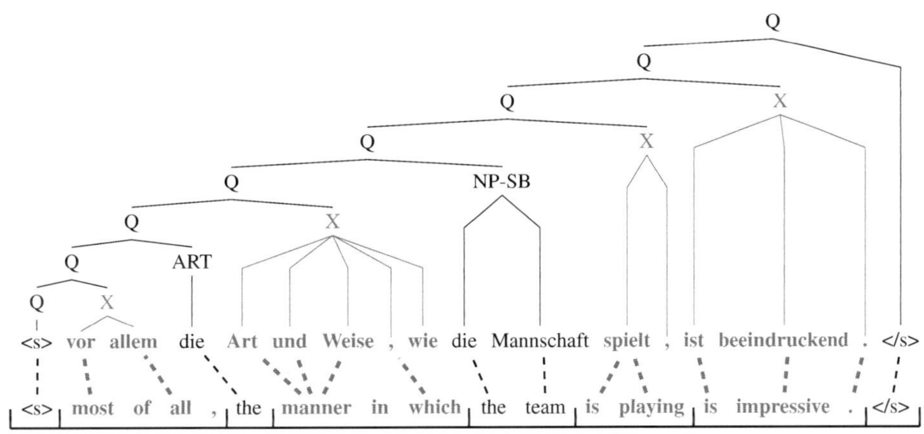

Reference: *Vor allem die Art und Weise, wie die Mannschaft spielt, ist beeindruckend.*

Figure 5: Translation and parse tree from the string-to-tree system augmented with non-syntactic phrases.

phrase table entries	**unfiltered**		**dev**		**newstest2013**		**newstest2014**	
	hier.	lexical	hier.	lexical	hier.	lexical	hier.	lexical
phrase-based	–	184.9 M	–	25.3 M	–	29.0 M	–	28.0 M
string-to-string	58.3 M	19.9 M	4.3 M	2.9 M	5.7 M	3.3 M	5.3 M	3.3 M
+ non-syntactic phrases	58.3 M	191.1 M	4.3. M	25.4 M	5.7 M	29.1 M	5.3 M	28.1 M
string-to-tree	39.7 M	21.2 M	4.9 M	3.4 M	5.7 M	3.8 M	5.5 M	3.7 M
+ non-syntactic phrases	39.7 M	192.4 M	4.9 M	25.8 M	5.7 M	29.6 M	5.5 M	28.6 M
tree-to-string	29.5 M	21.1 M	7.7 M	2.8 M	9.0 M	3.3 M	8.7 M	3.2 M
+ non-syntactic phrases	29.5 M	192.6 M	7.7 M	26.1 M	9.0 M	29.9 M	8.7 M	28.9 M

Table 2: Phrase inventory statistics for the different English→German translation systems. "*hier.*" denotes hierarchical phrases, i.e. rules with non-terminals on their right-hand side, "*lexical*" denotes continuous phrases.

5.4 Discussion

A drawback of our method is that it increases the size of the synchronous context-free grammar massively. Most phrase pairs from standard phrase-based extraction are actually not present in the GHKM rule set, even with composed rules. A large fraction of the extracted non-syntactic phrases is such added to the phrase inventory through phrase table fill-up. Table 2 shows the phrase inventory statistics for the different systems.

Another question relates to the glue rule applications. The application of a non-syntactic rule is always accompanied with a respective glue rule application in our implementation. The string-to-tree baseline utilizes glue rules on average 3.0 times in each single-best translation (measured on newstest2014), the string-to-tree system augmented with non-syntactic phrases utilizes glue rules on average 7.0 times. We considered an implementation that allows for embedding of non-syntactic rules into hierarchical rules (other than the glue rules) but did not see improvements with it as yet. Furthermore, efficiency concerns become more relevant in such an implementation.

6 Related Work

Issues with overly restrictive syntactic grammars for statistical machine translation, inadequate syntactic parses, and insufficient coverage have been tackled from several different directions in the literature.

A proposed approach to attain better syntactic phrase inventories is to restructure the syntactic parse trees in a preprocessing step (Wang et al., 2007; Wang et al., 2010; Burkett and Klein, 2012). This line of research aims at rearranging parse trees in a way that makes them a better fit for the requirements of the bilingual downstream application. Conversely, Fossum et al. (2008) retain the structure of the parse trees and modify the word alignments.

Marcu et al. (2006) relax syntactic phrase extraction constraints in their SPMT Model 2 to allow for phrases that do not match the span of one single constituent in the parse tree. SPMT Model 2 rules are created from spans that are consistent with the word alignment and covered by multiple constituents such that the union of the constituents matches the span. Pseudo non-syntactic non-terminals are introduced for the left-hand sides of SPMT Model 2 rules. Special additional rules allow for combination of those non-syntactic left-hand side non-terminals with genuine syntactic non-terminals on the right-hand sides of other rules during decoding.

Another line of research took the hierarchical phrase-based model (Chiang, 2005; Chiang, 2007) as a starting point and extended it with syntactic enhancements. In their SAMT system, Zollmann and Venugopal (2006) labeled the non-terminals of the hierarchical model with composite symbols derived from the syntactic tree annotation. Similar methods have been applied with CCG labels (Almaghout et al., 2012). Venugopal et al. (2009) and Stein et al. (2010) keep the grammar of the non-terminals of the hierarchical model unlabeled and apply the syntactic information in a separate model. Other authors added features which fire for phrases complying with certain syntactic properties while retaining all phrase pairs of the hierarchical model (Marton and Resnik, 2008; Vilar et al., 2008).

In a tree-to-tree translation setting, Chiang (2010) proposed techniques to soften the syntactic constraints. A fuzzy approach with complex non-terminal symbols as in SAMT is employed to overcome the limitations during phrase extraction. In decoding, substitutions of non-terminals are not restricted to matching ones. Any left-hand side non-terminal can substitute any right-hand side non-terminal. The decoder decides on the best derivation based on the tuned weights of a large number of binary features.

Joining phrase inventories that come from multiple origins is a common method in domain adaptation (Bertoldi and Federico, 2009; Niehues and Waibel, 2012) but has also been applied in the contexts of lightly-supervised training (Schwenk, 2008; Huck et al., 2011) and of forced alignment training (Wuebker et al., 2010). For our purposes, we apply a fill-up method in the manner of the one that has been shown to perform well for domain adaptation in earlier work (Bisazza et al., 2011).

Previous research that resembles our work most has been presented by Liu et al. (2006) and by Hanneman and Lavie (2009).

Liu et al. (2006) allow for application of non-syntactic phrase pairs in their tree-to-string alignment template (TAT) system. The translation probabilities for the non-syntactic phrases are obtained from a standard phrase-based extraction pipeline. A non-syntactic phrase pair can however only be applied if its source side matches a subtree in the parsed input sentence. Syntactic and non-syntactic phrases are not distinguished, and overlap between the syntactic and non-syntactic part of the phrase inventory is not avoided. The decoder picks the entry with the higher phrase translation probability, which means that non-syntactic phrase table entries can supersede syntactic entries. The authors report improvements of 0.6 points BLEU on the 2005 NIST Chinese→English task with four reference translations.

Hanneman and Lavie (2009) examine non-syntactic phrases for tree-to-tree translation with the Stat-XFER framework as developed at Carnegie Mellon University (Lavie, 2008). They combine syntactic and non-syntactic phrase inventories and reestimate the probabilities for both types of phrase pairs by adding up the observed absolute frequencies. Two combination schemes are evaluated: combination with all extractable valid non-syntactic phrases ("direct combination") and combination with only those non-syntactic phrases whose source sides are not equal to the source side of any syntactic phrase ("syntax-prioritized combination"). On a French→English translation task, Hanneman and Lavie (2009) report improvements of around 2.6 points BLEU by adding non-syntactic phrases on top of their Stat-XFER syntactic baselines. Their best setup however does not reach the performance of a standard phrase-based system, which is still 1.6 points BLEU better.

Apart from the differences in the underlying syntax-based translation technology (string-to-tree/tree-to-string GHKM vs. TAT vs. Stat-XFER), our work also constitutes a novel contribution as compared to the previous approaches by Liu et al. (2006) and Hanneman and Lavie (2009) with respect to the following:

- The phrase inventory is augmented with non-syntactic phrases by means of a fill-up technique. Overlap is prevented, whereas not only new source sides, but also new target-side translation options can be added.
- The probabilities of syntactic phrase pairs are the same as in the syntax-based baseline, and the probabilities of the non-syntactic phrase pairs are the same as in a phrase-based system. Counts of syntactic and non-syntactic phrases are not summed up to obtain new estimates.
- Non-syntactic phrase pairs are distinguished from syntactic ones with an additional feature.

7 Conclusions

String-to-tree and tree-to-string translation systems can easily be augmented with non-syntactic phrases by means of phrase table fill-up, a special non-terminal symbol for left-hand sides of non-syntactic rules in the grammar, and an additional glue rule. A binary feature enables the system to distinguish non-syntactic phrases from syntactic ones and—on the basis of the respective feature weight—to favor syntactically motivated phrases during decoding.

Our results on an English→German translation task demonstrate the beneficial effect of augmenting GHKM translation systems with non-syntactic phrase pairs. Empirical gains in translation quality are up to 0.5 points BLEU and 0.7 points TER over the baseline on the recent test set of the shared translation task of the ACL 2014 Ninth Workshop on Statistical Machine Translation.

While GHKM-style syntactic translation has typically been utilized in string-to-tree settings in previous research, we have also adopted it to build tree-to-string systems in this work. Source syntax establishes interesting further directions for GHKM systems. We investigated two of them: input tree constraints and input tree features.

String-to-tree and tree-to-string GHKM systems perform roughly at the same level in terms of translation quality. Our best string-to-tree setup outperforms a phrase-based baseline by up to 0.8 points BLEU and 0.9 points TER (on newstest2014), our best tree-to-string setup outperforms the phrase-based baseline by up to 0.7 points BLEU and 1.1 points TER (on newstest2013).

Acknowledgements

The research leading to these results has received funding from the European Union Seventh Framework Programme (FP7/2007-2013) under grant agreements n° 287658 (EU-BRIDGE) and n° 288487 (MosesCore).

References

Hala Almaghout, Jie Jiang, and Andy Way. 2012. Extending CCG-based Syntactic Constraints in Hierarchical Phrase-Based SMT. In *Proc. of the Annual Conf. of the European Assoc. for Machine Translation (EAMT)*, pages 193–200, Trento, Italy, May.

Nicola Bertoldi and Marcello Federico. 2009. Domain Adaptation for Statistical Machine Translation with Monolingual Resources. In *Proc. of the Workshop on Statistical Machine Translation (WMT)*, pages 182–189, Athens, Greece, March.

Arianna Bisazza, Nick Ruiz, and Marcello Federico. 2011. Fill-up versus Interpolation Methods for Phrase-based SMT Adaptation. In *Proc. of the Int. Workshop on Spoken Language Translation (IWSLT)*, pages 136–143, San Francisco, CA, USA, December.

Ondřej Bojar, Christian Buck, Chris Callison-Burch, Christian Federmann, Barry Haddow, Philipp Koehn, Christof Monz, Matt Post, Radu Soricut, and Lucia Specia. 2013. Findings of the 2013 Workshop on Statistical Machine Translation. In *Proc. of the Workshop on Statistical Machine Translation (WMT)*, pages 1–44, Sofia, Bulgaria, August.

David Burkett and Dan Klein. 2012. Transforming Trees to Improve Syntactic Convergence. In *Proc. of the Conf. on Empirical Methods for Natural Language Processing (EMNLP)*, Jeju Island, South Korea, July.

Jean-Cédric Chappelier and Martin Rajman. 1998. A Generalized CYK Algorithm for Parsing Stochastic CFG. In *Proc. of the First Workshop on Tabulation in Parsing and Deduction*, pages 133–137, Paris, France, April.

Stanley F. Chen and Joshua Goodman. 1998. An Empirical Study of Smoothing Techniques for Language Modeling. Technical Report TR-10-98, Computer Science Group, Harvard University, Cambridge, MA, USA, August.

Colin Cherry and George Foster. 2012. Batch Tuning Strategies for Statistical Machine Translation. In *Proc. of the Human Language Technology Conf. / North American Chapter of the Assoc. for Computational Linguistics (HLT-NAACL)*, pages 427–436, Montréal, Canada, June.

David Chiang. 2005. A Hierarchical Phrase-Based Model for Statistical Machine Translation. In *Proc. of the Annual Meeting of the Assoc. for Computational Linguistics (ACL)*, pages 263–270, Ann Arbor, MI, USA, June.

David Chiang. 2007. Hierarchical Phrase-Based Translation. *Computational Linguistics*, 33(2):201–228, June.

David Chiang. 2010. Learning to Translate with Source and Target Syntax. In *Proc. of the Annual Meeting of the Assoc. for Computational Linguistics (ACL)*, pages 1443–1452, Uppsala, Sweden, July.

Steve DeNeefe, Kevin Knight, Wei Wang, and Daniel Marcu. 2007. What Can Syntax-Based MT Learn from Phrase-Based MT? In *Proc. of the 2007 Joint Conf. on Empirical Methods in Natural Language Processing and Computational Natural Language Learning (EMNLP-CoNLL)*, pages 755–763, Prague, Czech Republic, June.

Victoria Fossum, Kevin Knight, and Steven Abney. 2008. Using Syntax to Improve Word Alignment Precision for Syntax-Based Machine Translation. In *Proc. of the Workshop on Statistical Machine Translation (WMT)*, pages 44–52, Columbus, OH, USA, June.

Michel Galley and Christopher D. Manning. 2008. A Simple and Effective Hierarchical Phrase Reordering Model. In *Proc. of the Conf. on Empirical Methods for Natural Language Processing (EMNLP)*, pages 847–855, Honolulu, HI, USA, October.

Michel Galley, Mark Hopkins, Kevin Knight, and Daniel Marcu. 2004. What's in a translation rule? In *Proc. of the Human Language Technology Conf. / North American Chapter of the Assoc. for Computational Linguistics (HLT-NAACL)*, pages 273–280, Boston, MA, USA, May.

Michel Galley, Jonathan Graehl, Kevin Knight, Daniel Marcu, Steve DeNeefe, Wei Wang, and Ignacio Thayer. 2006. Scalable Inference and Training of Context-Rich Syntactic Translation Models. In *Proc. of the 21st International Conf. on Computational Linguistics and 44th Annual Meeting of the Assoc. for Computational Linguistics*, pages 961–968, Sydney, Australia, July.

Qin Gao and Stephan Vogel. 2008. Parallel Implementations of Word Alignment Tool. In *Software Engineering, Testing, and Quality Assurance for Natural Language Processing*, SETQA-NLP '08, pages 49–57, Columbus, OH, USA, June.

Greg Hanneman and Alon Lavie. 2009. Decoding with Syntactic and Non-syntactic Phrases in a Syntax-based Machine Translation System. In *Proceedings of the Third Workshop on Syntax and Structure in Statistical Translation*, SSST '09, pages 1–9, Boulder, CO, USA, June.

Kenneth Heafield. 2011. KenLM: Faster and Smaller Language Model Queries. In *Proc. of the Workshop on Statistical Machine Translation (WMT)*, pages 187–197, Edinburgh, Scotland, UK, July.

Hieu Hoang and Philipp Koehn. 2010. Improved Translation with Source Syntax Labels. In *Proc. of the Workshop on Statistical Machine Translation (WMT)*, pages 409–417, Uppsala, Sweden, July.

Hieu Hoang, Philipp Koehn, and Adam Lopez. 2009. A Unified Framework for Phrase-Based, Hierarchical, and Syntax-Based Statistical Machine Translation. In *Proc. of the Int. Workshop on Spoken Language Translation (IWSLT)*, pages 152–159, Tokyo, Japan, December.

Matthias Huck, David Vilar, Daniel Stein, and Hermann Ney. 2011. Lightly-Supervised Training for Hierarchical Phrase-Based Machine Translation. In *Proc. of the EMNLP 2011 Workshop on Unsupervised Learning in NLP*, pages 91–96, Edinburgh, Scotland, UK, July.

Reinhard Kneser and Hermann Ney. 1995. Improved Backing-Off for M-gram Language Modeling. In *Proceedings of the International Conference on Acoustics, Speech, and Signal Processing*, volume 1, pages 181–184, Detroit, MI, USA, May.

Philipp Koehn, Franz Joseph Och, and Daniel Marcu. 2003. Statistical Phrase-Based Translation. In *Proc. of the Human Language Technology Conf. / North American Chapter of the Assoc. for Computational Linguistics (HLT-NAACL)*, pages 127–133, Edmonton, Canada, May/June.

Philipp Koehn. 2005. Europarl: A parallel corpus for statistical machine translation. In *Proc. of the MT Summit X*, Phuket, Thailand, September.

Alon Lavie. 2008. Stat-XFER: A General Search-Based Syntax-Driven Framework for Machine Translation. In Alexander Gelbukh, editor, *Computational Linguistics and Intelligent Text Processing*, volume 4919 of *Lecture Notes in Computer Science*, pages 362–375. Springer Berlin Heidelberg.

Yang Liu, Qun Liu, and Shouxun Lin. 2006. Tree-to-string Alignment Template for Statistical Machine Translation. In *Proc. of the 21st International Conf. on Computational Linguistics and the 44th Annual Meeting of the Assoc. for Computational Linguistics (ACL)*, pages 609–616, Sydney, Australia, July.

Daniel Marcu, Wei Wang, Abdessamad Echihabi, and Kevin Knight. 2006. SPMT: Statistical Machine Translation with Syntactified Target Language Phrases. In *Proc. of the Conf. on Empirical Methods for Natural Language Processing (EMNLP)*, pages 44–52, Sydney, Australia.

Yuval Marton and Philip Resnik. 2008. Soft Syntactic Constraints for Hierarchical Phrased-Based Translation. In *Proc. of the Annual Meeting of the Assoc. for Computational Linguistics (ACL)*, pages 1003–1011, Columbus, OH, USA, June.

Maria Nadejde, Philip Williams, and Philipp Koehn. 2013. Edinburgh's Syntax-Based Machine Translation Systems. In *Proc. of the Workshop on Statistical Machine Translation (WMT)*, pages 170–176, Sofia, Bulgaria, August.

Jan Niehues and Alex Waibel. 2012. Detailed Analysis of Different Strategies for Phrase Table Adaptation in SMT. In *Proc. of the Conf. of the Assoc. for Machine Translation in the Americas (AMTA)*, San Diego, CA, USA, October/November.

Franz Josef Och and Hermann Ney. 2002. Discriminative Training and Maximum Entropy Models for Statistical Machine Translation. In *Proc. of the Annual Meeting of the Assoc. for Computational Linguistics (ACL)*, pages 295–302, Philadelphia, PA, USA, July.

Franz Josef Och and Hermann Ney. 2003. A Systematic Comparison of Various Statistical Alignment Models. *Computational Linguistics*, 29(1):19–51, March.

Franz Josef Och, Christoph Tillmann, and Hermann Ney. 1999. Improved Alignment Models for Statistical Machine Translation. In *Proc. of the Joint SIGDAT Conf. on Empirical Methods in Natural Language Processing and Very Large Corpora (EMNLP99)*, pages 20–28, University of Maryland, College Park, MD, USA, June.

Franz Josef Och. 2002. *Statistical Machine Translation: From Single-Word Models to Alignment Templates*. Ph.D. thesis, RWTH Aachen University, Aachen, Germany, October.

Kishore Papineni, Salim Roukos, Todd Ward, and Wei-Jing Zhu. 2002. Bleu: a Method for Automatic Evaluation of Machine Translation. In *Proc. of the Annual Meeting of the Assoc. for Computational Linguistics (ACL)*, pages 311–318, Philadelphia, PA, USA, July.

Slav Petrov, Leon Barrett, Romain Thibaux, and Dan Klein. 2006. Learning Accurate, Compact, and Interpretable Tree Annotation. In *Proc. of the 21st International Conference on Computational Linguistics and 44th Annual Meeting of the Assoc. for Computational Linguistics*, pages 433–440, Sydney, Australia, July.

Helmut Schmid. 2004. Efficient Parsing of Highly Ambiguous Context-Free Grammars with Bit Vectors. In *Proc. of the Int. Conf. on Computational Linguistics (COLING)*, Geneva, Switzerland, August.

Holger Schwenk. 2008. Investigations on Large-Scale Lightly-Supervised Training for Statistical Machine Translation. In *Proc. of the Int. Workshop on Spoken Language Translation (IWSLT)*, pages 182–189, Waikiki, HI, USA, October.

Matthew Snover, Bonnie Dorr, Richard Schwartz, Linnea Micciulla, and John Makhoul. 2006. A Study of Translation Edit Rate with Targeted Human Annotation. In *Proc. of the Conf. of the Assoc. for Machine Translation in the Americas (AMTA)*, pages 223–231, Cambridge, MA, USA, August.

Daniel Stein, Stephan Peitz, David Vilar, and Hermann Ney. 2010. A Cocktail of Deep Syntactic Features for Hierarchical Machine Translation. In *Proc. of the Conf. of the Assoc. for Machine Translation in the Americas (AMTA)*, Denver, CO, USA, October/November.

Andreas Stolcke. 2002. SRILM – an Extensible Language Modeling Toolkit. In *Proc. of the Int. Conf. on Spoken Language Processing (ICSLP)*, volume 3, Denver, CO, USA, September.

Ashish Venugopal, Andreas Zollmann, Noah A. Smith, and Stephan Vogel. 2009. Preference Grammars: Softening Syntactic Constraints to Improve Statistical Machine Translation. In *Proc. of the Human Language Technology Conf. / North American Chapter of the Assoc. for Computational Linguistics (HLT-NAACL)*, pages 236–244, Boulder, CO, USA, June.

David Vilar, Daniel Stein, and Hermann Ney. 2008. Analysing Soft Syntax Features and Heuristics for Hierarchical Phrase Based Machine Translation. In *Proc. of the Int. Workshop on Spoken Language Translation (IWSLT)*, pages 190–197, Waikiki, HI, USA, October.

Wei Wang, Kevin Knight, and Daniel Marcu. 2007. Binarizing Syntax Trees to Improve Syntax-Based Machine Translation Accuracy. In *Proceedings of the 2007 Joint Conference on Empirical Methods in Natural Language Processing and Computational Natural Language Learning (EMNLP-CoNLL)*, pages 746–754, Prague, Czech Republic, June.

Wei Wang, Jonathan May, Kevin Knight, and Daniel Marcu. 2010. Re-structuring, Re-labeling, and Re-aligning for Syntax-based Machine Translation. *Computational Linguistics*, 36(2):247–277, June.

Philip Williams and Philipp Koehn. 2012. GHKM Rule Extraction and Scope-3 Parsing in Moses. In *Proc. of the Workshop on Statistical Machine Translation (WMT)*, pages 388–394, Montréal, Canada, June.

Philip Williams, Rico Sennrich, Maria Nadejde, Matthias Huck, Eva Hasler, and Philipp Koehn. 2014. Edinburgh's Syntax-Based Systems at WMT 2014. In *Proc. of the Workshop on Statistical Machine Translation (WMT)*, Baltimore, MD, USA, June.

Joern Wuebker, Arne Mauser, and Hermann Ney. 2010. Training Phrase Translation Models with Leaving-One-Out. In *Proc. of the Annual Meeting of the Assoc. for Computational Linguistics (ACL)*, pages 475–484, Uppsala, Sweden, July.

Andreas Zollmann and Ashish Venugopal. 2006. Syntax Augmented Machine Translation via Chart Parsing. In *Proc. of the Workshop on Statistical Machine Translation (WMT)*, pages 138–141, New York City, NY, USA, June.

Linear Mixture Models for Robust Machine Translation

Marine Carpuat, Cyril Goutte and **George Foster**
Multilingual Text Processing
National Research Council
Ottawa, ON K1A0R6, Canada
firstname.lastname@nrc.ca

Abstract

As larger and more diverse parallel texts become available, how can we leverage heterogeneous data to train robust machine translation systems that achieve good translation quality on various test domains? This challenge has been addressed so far by repurposing techniques developed for domain adaptation, such as linear mixture models which combine estimates learned on homogeneous subdomains. However, learning from large heterogeneous corpora is quite different from standard adaptation tasks with clear domain distinctions. In this paper, we show that linear mixture models can reliably improve translation quality in very heterogeneous training conditions, even if the mixtures do not use any domain knowledge and attempt to learn generic models rather than adapt them to the target domain. This surprising finding opens new perspectives for using mixture models in machine translation beyond clear cut domain adaptation tasks.

1 Introduction

While machine translation tasks used to be defined by drawing training and test data from a single well-defined domain, current systems have to deal with increasingly heterogeneous data, both at training and at test time. As larger and more diverse parallel texts become available, how can we leverage heterogeneous data to train statistical machine translation (SMT) systems that achieve good translation quality on various test domains?

So far, this challenge has been addressed by repurposing techniques developed for more clear-cut domain adaptation scenarios, such as linear mixture models (Koehn and Schroeder, 2007; Foster and Kuhn, 2007; Sennrich, 2012b). Instead of estimating models on the whole training corpus at once, linear mixture models are built as follows: (1) partition the training corpus into homogeneous domain-based component, (2) train one model per component, (3) linearly mix models using weights learned to adapt to the test domain, (4) replace resulting model in translation system.

In this paper, we aim to gain a better understanding of the benefits of linear mixture models in heterogeneous data conditions, by examining key untested assumptions:

- Should mixture component capture domain information? Previous work assumes that training data should be organized into domains. When manual domain distinctions are not available, previous work uses clustering approaches to approximate manual domain distinctions (Sennrich, 2012a). However, it is unclear whether it is necessary to use or mimic domain distinctions in order to define mixture components.

- Mixture models are usually assumed to improve translation quality by giving more weight to parts of the training corpus that are more relevant to the test domain. Is this intuition still valid in our more complex heterogeneous training conditions? If not, how do mixture models affect translation probability estimates?

In order to answer these questions, we propose to study several variants of linear mixture models that reflect different modeling assumptions and different levels of domain knowledge. We first

Proceedings of the Ninth Workshop on Statistical Machine Translation, pages 499–509,
Baltimore, Maryland USA, June 26–27, 2014.

consider two methods for setting mixture weights: adaptation to the test domain via maximum likelihood, and uniform mixtures that make no assumption about the domain of interest (Section 2). Then, we will describe a wide range of techniques that can be used to define mixture components (Section 3). Again, these techniques reflect opposite modeling assumptions: manually defined domains and automatic clusters attempt to organize heterogeneous training sets into homogeneous groups that represent distinct domains, while random samples capture no domain information and simply provide different views of the training set.

We present an empirical investigation of all the variations outlined above using a strong system trained on large and diverse training corpora, for two language pairs and two distinct test domains. Our results show that linear mixtures reliably and robustly improve the quality of machine translation (Section 5). While they were originally developed for domain adaptation tasks, linear mixtures that have no domain knowledge can perform as well as traditional mixtures meant to perform domain adaptation. This suggests that improvements do not stem from domain modeling per se, but from better generic estimates from the heterogeneous training data. Further analysis shows that the linear mixture estimates are very different from estimates obtained using more explicit smoothing schemes (Section 6).

2 Linear Mixtures for Translation Models

Does domain knowledge yield better translation quality when learning linear mixture weights for the translation model of a phrase-based MT system? We leave the study of linear mixtures for language and reordering models for future work.

2.1 Maximum Likelihood Mixtures

In the standard domain adaptation scenario, the linear mixture combines translation probabilities learned on distinct sub-domains in the training corpus. The conditional translation probability of phrase t given s is defined as:

$$p(t|s) = \sum_{k=1}^{K} \lambda_k p_k(t|s) \quad (1)$$

where $p_k(t|s)$ is a conditional translation probability learned on subset k of the training corpus. Note that for all phrase pairs (s, t) that are not observed in component k of the training corpus, we will have $p_k(t|s) = 0$. As a result, the resulting distributions are not normalized.

The weights λ_k are learned to adapt the translation model to a development set, which represents the domain of interest. First, we extract all phrase pairs from the development set, using the same technique used to extract phrases from the training set as part of standard phrase-based MT training. This yields a joint distribution $\tilde{p}(s, t)$, which can be used to define a maximum likelihood objective:

$$\hat{\lambda} = \text{argmax}_\lambda \sum_{s,t} \tilde{p}(s,t) \log \sum_{k=1}^{K} \lambda_k p_k(s|t). \quad (2)$$

We use the Expectation Maximization algorithm to solve this maximization problem.

2.2 Uniform Mixtures

We will consider uniform mixtures where all components are weighted equally:

$$p(t|s) = \frac{1}{K} \sum_{k=1}^{K} p_k(t|s). \quad (3)$$

In contrast with maximum likelihood mixtures, uniform mixtures are not meant to adapt the translation model to a specific test domain. Instead, they combine estimates learned on various subsets of the data in the hope of obtaining a better estimate of the translation probability distributions from the (possibly heterogeneous) training domain as a whole.

2.3 Why Not Use Loglinear Mixtures?

In current machine translation systems, there are two straightforward ways to combine estimates from heterogneous training data: linear and loglinear mixtures. We argue that linear mixtures are a better model for combining domain-specific probabilities, since they sum translation probabilities, while loglinear mixtures multiply probabilities. In a loglinear mixture, a translation candidate t for a phrase s will only be scored highly if all components agree that it is highly probable. In contrast, in a linear mixture, t can be a top translation candidate overall even if it is not a preferred translation in some of the components. When the training data is very heterogeneous, linear mixtures are therefore preferable.

Previous work provides empirical evidence supporting this. For instance, Foster et al. (2010) found that linear mixtures outperform log linear mixtures when adapting a French-English system to the medical domain, as well as on a Chinese-English NIST translation task.

2.4 Estimating Conditional Translation Probabilities

Within each mixture component, we extract all phrase-pairs, compute relative frequencies, and use Kneser-Ney smoothing (Chen et al., 2011) to produce the final estimate of conditional translation probabilities $p_k(t|s)$. Per-component probabilities are then combined in Eq. 1 and 3. Similarly, baseline translation probabilities are learned using Kneser-Ney smoothed frequencies collected on the entire training set.

3 Defining Mixture Components

We assume that the heterogeneous training corpus can be split into basic elements that will be organized in various ways to define the K mixture components. Basic components could be documents or sets of sentences defined along various criteria. Sennrich (2012a) show that using isolated sentences as basic elements might not provide sufficient information, as smoothing component assignments using neighboring sentences benefits translation quality. In our experiments, basic elements are sets of parallel sentences which share the same provenance, genre and dialect, as we will see in Section 4.

We consider four very different ways of defining mixture components by grouping the basic corpus elements: (1) manual partition of the training corpus into domains, (2) automatically learning homogeneous domains using text clustering algorithms, (3) random partitioning, (4) sampling with replacement.

3.1 Manually Defined Domains

Heterogeneous training data is usually grouped into domains manually using provenance information. In most previous work, such domain distinctions are very clear and easy to define. For instance, Haddow (2013) uses European parliament proceedings to improve translation of text in the movie subtitles and News Commentary domains; Sennrich (2012a) aims to translate Alpine Club reports using components trained on European parliament proceedings and movie subtitles. Foster et al. (2010) work with a slightly different setting when defining mixture components for the NIST Chinese-English translation task: while there is no single obvious "in-domain" component in the NIST training set, homogeneous domains can still be defined in a straightforward fashion based on the provenance of the data (e.g., Hong Kong Hansards vs. Hong Kong Law vs. News articles from FBIS, etc.). We take a similar approach in our experiments. However, we will see that since our training data is very heterogeneous, we take into account other dimensions beyond provenance, such as genre and dialect information (Section 4).

3.2 Induced Domains Using Automatic Clustering Algorithms

We propose to use automatic text clustering techniques to organize basic elements into homogeneous clusters that are seen as sub-domains. In our experiments, we apply clustering algorithms to the target (English) side of the corpus only.

Each corpus element is transformed into a vector-space format by constructing a tf.idf vector representation. After indexing, we filter out stopwords as well as words occuring in a single document. We then weight each word token by the log of its frequency in the document, combined with an inverse document frequency (Salton and McGill, 1983) followed by a normalization to unit length. The cosine similarity between each pair of elements is obtained by simply computing the scalar product, resulting in a $N \times N$ similarity matrix, where N is the number of corpus elements.

For clustering, we used Ward's hierarchical clustering algorithm (Ward, 1963). We start with one cluster per corpus element, i.e. N clusters. From the similarity matrix, we identify the two most similar clusters and merge them into a single one, resulting in $N-1$ clusters. The similarity matrix is updated using Ward's method to form a $(N-1)\times(N-1)$ similarity matrix. The process is repeated on the new set of clusters, until we reach the target number of clusters K.

3.3 Random Partitioning

We consider random partitions of the training corpus. They are generated by using a random number generator to assign each basic element to one of K clusters. Resulting components therefore do not capture any domain information. Each com-

Arabic-English Training Conditions			
	segs	src	en
train	8.5M	262M	207M
Test Domain 1: Webforum			
	segs	src	en
dev (tune)	4.1k	66k	72k
web1 (eval)	2.2k	35k	38k
web2 (eval)	2.4k	37k	40k
Test Domain 2: News			
	segs	src	en
dev (tune)	1664	54k	51k
news (eval)	813	32k	29k

Table 1: Statistics for Arabic-English data: Number of segments (segs), source tokens (src) and English tokens (en) for each corpus. For English dev and test sets, word counts averaged across 2 references.

Chinese-English Training Conditions			
	segs	src	en
train	11M	234M	253M
Test Domain 1: Webforum			
	segs	src	en
dev (tune)	2.7k	61k	77k
web1 (eval)	1.4k	31k	38k
web2 (eval)	1.2k	29k	36k
Test Domain 2: News			
	segs	src	en
dev (tune)	1.7k	39k	24k
news (eval)	0.7k	19k	19k

Table 2: Statistics for Chinese-English data: Number of segments (segs), source tokens (src) and English tokens (en) for each corpus. For English dev and test sets, word counts averaged across 4 references.

ponent can potentially be as heterogeneous as the full training set.

3.4 Random Sampling with Replacement

All previous techniques assume that the training corpus should be partitioned into distinct clusters. We now consider mixture components that break this assumption, and simply represent several, possibly overlapping, views of the training corpus. They are defined by sampling basic corpus elements uniformly with replacement. This approach simply requires defining a number of samples K and the size n of each sample. We set the sample size n to the average size of the manual clusters. We do not fix K in advance: in order to provide a fair comparison with corpus partitioning techniques where components achieve coverage of the entire training set by definition, we keep generating samples until all basic elements have been used, and use all resulting K components.

When using uniform linear mixtures, this approach is similar to bootstrap aggregating (bagging) for regression (Breiman, 1996), where a more stable model is learned by averaging K estimates obtained by sampling the training set uniformly and with replacement.

4 Experiment Settings

We evaluate our linear mixture models on two different language pairs, Arabic-English and Chinese-English, and two different test domains.

4.1 Training Conditions

We use the large-scale heterogeneous training conditions defined in the DARPA BOLT project. Data statistics for both language pairs are given in Tables 1 and 2. Training corpora cover a wide variety of sources, genres, dialects, domains, topics.

For instance, for the Arabic task, the training corpus is originally bundled into 48 files representing different provenance and epochs. The data spans 15 genres (defined based on data provenance, they range from lexicon to newswire, United Nations, and many variants of web data such as webforum, weblog, newsgroup, etc.) and 4 automatically tagged dialects (Egyptian, Levantine, Modern Standard Arabic, and untagged). The distribution along each of these dimensions is very unbalanced, and each corpus file often contains text in more than one genre, epoch or dialect.

As a result, we divide the large training corpus into basic elements, based on the available metadata. We define basic corpus elements as a subset of sentences from the same provenance (i.e. corpus file), dialect and genre. For Arabic, splitting the original 48 files along these dimensions yields 82 basic elements. Similarly, the Chinese data was split into a set of 101 basic elements, using genre, dialects, as well as time span information to split the original files. Figure 1 shows the wide range of component sizes in the Arabic and Chinese collection. For Arabice, notice that several components are very small, from 6 lines and 90 words to 5.3 million lines and 137M words.

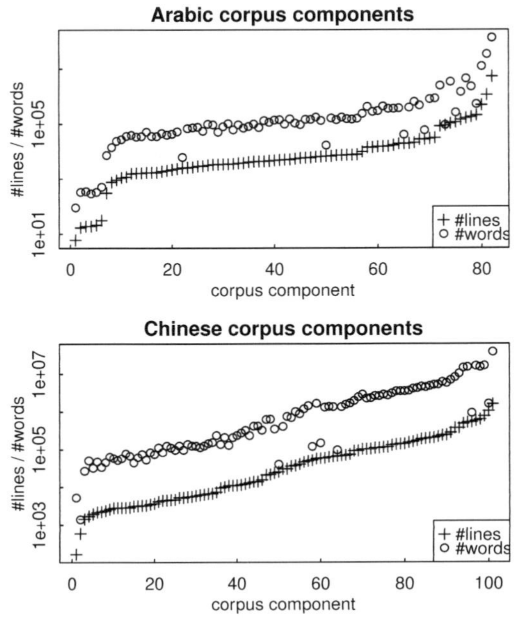

Figure 1: Sizes of the 82 Arabic-English (top) and 101 Chinese-English (bottom) corpus components.

4.2 Definition of Mixture Components

Manual partitions were created first by the system developers, based on intuitions on the nature of the test domain and manual inspection of the training data. The main goal was to group data into components that are large enough to reliably estimate translation probabilities, but small enough to be homogeneous. This resulted in $K_m = 10$ clusters for Arabic, and $K_m = 17$ for Chinese.

Automatic partitions are created as described in Section 3. Preliminary experiments with the hierarchical agglomerative clustering algorithm showed that the number of clusters used did not have a big impact on translation quality,[1] so we will only present results that use the same number of clusters as in the manual partitions (10 for Arabic and 17 for Chinese).

Results for random partitions are averaged across experiments run with four random seeds.

4.3 Test Domains

We consider two test domains, as described in Tables 1 and 2: webforum and news.

The webforum test domain is defined by development test sets made available through BOLT. It contains very informal text drawn from online discussion of various topics. Taking these data sets as the definition of the target domain, there is no single obvious in-domain section of the training corpus. For instance, for Arabic, the dev set sentences are almost exclusively written in the Egyptian dialect. Therefore, Egyptian webforum data is presumably the closest to the test domain, but Egyptian weblogs or mixed-dialect broadcast conversations could potentially be useful as well.

We also test the Arabic and Chinese systems on the news domain. The goal of these experiments is to evaluate the robustness of linear mixtures across different test domains. We use publicly available test sets from the NIST evaluation. The dev set used to learn maximum likelihood mixtures and tune the translation system is the NIST section of the 2006 test set. We evaluate system performance on the newswire section of the NIST 2008 test set.

4.4 Machine Translation System

We use an in-house implementation of a Phrase-based Statistical Machine Translation system (Koehn et al., 2007) to build strong baseline systems for both language pairs. Translation hypotheses are scored according to the following features:

- 4 phrase-table scores: Kneser-Ney smoothed phrasal translation probabilites and lexical weights, in both translation directions (Chen et al., 2011)[2]
- 6 hierarchical lexicalized reordering scores (Galley and Manning, 2008)
- a word penalty, and a word-displacement distortion penalty
- a Good-Turing smoothed 4-gram language model trained on the Gigaword corpus, Kneser-Ney smoothed 5-gram models trained on the English side of the training corpus, and an additional 5-gram model trained on monolingual webforum data.

Weights for these features are learned using a batch version of the MIRA algorithm (Chiang, 2012). Phrase pairs are extracted from several word alignments of the training set: HMM, IBM2, and IBM4. Word alignments are kept constant across all experiments.

We apply our linear mixture models to both translation probability scores, in each direction. The reordering and language models are not

[1]We tried $K = \{2, 4, \ldots, 18, 20\}$ for Arabic and $K = \{12, 14, \ldots, 20\}$ for Chinese, plus all basic components.

[2]The Arabic-English system uses 6 additional binary features which fire if a phrase-pair was generated by one of the 3 word alignment methods in each translation direction.

Test domain	Webforum	
Arabic eval	Forum1	Forum2
Linear mix	**39.67**	**40.60**
Loglinear mix	37.53	38.80
Chinese eval	Forum1	Forum2
Linear mix	**30.17**	**26.86**
Loglinear mix	27.65	23.78

Table 3: Impact of mixture type on translation quality as measured by BLEU.

adapted. Note that systems used to translate the web1 and web2 test sets are always tuned on the webforum tuning set, while systems used to translate data in the news domain are tuned on a news development set. The relevant tuning set is also used for learning maximum likelkihood mixtures when appropriate.

5 Findings: Impact on Translation Quality

5.1 Linear vs. Loglinear Mixtures

Before focusing exclusively on linear mixtures, we confirm that they outperform loglinear mixtures. This comparison was conducted on the webforum domain, using manually defined domains as components. For linear mixtures, we trained the weights using maximum likelihood. Loglinear mixture weights are trained by MIRA. Table 3 shows that linear mixtures yield consistently and significantly higher BLEU scores than loglinear mixtures, which is consistent with existing results (Foster et al., 2010, inter alia).

5.2 Impact of Mixture Components

We now focus on linear mixtures and measure the impact on translation quality of the various component types described in Section 3. In all cases, mixtures weights are estimated by maximum likelihood. Results are summarized in Table 4 for both Arabic and Chinese.

The main result is that all mixture models considered significantly improve on the "no mix" baseline for both languages. Directly using the 101 basic elements for Chinese and the 82 basic elements for Arabic significantly improves on the baseline. Grouping the basic elements into coarser clusters can further improve BLEU. For Arabic, automatic partitioning (randomly or by clustering) yields better BLEU scores than manual partitioning, while the manual and cluster-based domains yield the highest BLEU scores for Chinese.

Test domain	**Webforum**		**News**
Arabic eval	*web1*	*web2*	*news*
Cluster domains	40.11	40.60	**57.95**
Random partition	**40.43**	**40.63**	57.78
Random sample	39.94	40.36	57.85
Manual domains	39.67	40.60	57.63
Basic elements	39.83	40.63	57.57
No mix	38.64	39.21	56.59
Chinese eval	*web1*	*web2*	*news*
Cluster domains	29.82	26.34	**37.22**
Random partition	29.50	26.21	36.83
Random sample	29.47	26.17	36.70
Manual domains	**30.17**	**26.86**	36.90
Basic elements	29.29	26.25	36.17
No mix	28.61	25.63	35.96

Table 4: Impact of mixture component definition on BLEU score: there is no clear benefit to explicitly modeling domains.

5.3 Impact of Mixture Weights

Does domain knowledge yield better translation quality when learning linear mixture weights? We answer this question by comparing the translation quality obtained with maximum likelihood vs. uniform mixtures. The maximum likelihood weights are set once per domain, using the relevant domain development set, while the uniform mixture is the same across all test domains.

Table 5 shows that maximum likelihood weights generally have a slight advantage over uniform weights, especially in the Webforum domain. On "basic elements" in Arabic, the gain is a massive 5 BLEU points, which we attribute to the fact that, as shown in Figure 1, there are many more very small components in Arabic. Those get a disproportionate influence in the uniform mixture, hurting the overall performance. On the other hand, the uniform mixture performs better in the News domain. This might be explained by the fact that the tune and test sets are more distant in News than in Webforum, as suggested by the fact that the tuning BLEU scores are not as good at predicing test BLEU rankings in the news domain as in the webforum domain.

Overall, the difference in performance between the best linear mixture and the "no mix" baseline is 1.4 to 1.6 BLEU on Arabic, and 0.7 to 1.3 BLEU on Chinese. By comparison, the delta between the two weight setting approaches (maximum likelihood vs. uniform), depending on the partitioning technique, is below 0.4 BLEU for Arabic (except for Basic elements, +3.6 BLEU) and below 0.57 BLEU for Chinese. It is therefore clear that the gain from using linear mixtures is much larger than the influence of the mixture weight setting, except in the one specific case discussed above.

Taken together, these results show that linear mixtures can reliably and robustly improve the quality of machine translation. But surprisingly, linear mixtures that have no domain knowledge (random partition + uniform weights) can sometimes perform as well as traditional mixtures meant to perform domain adaptation. This suggests that improvements cannot be only explained by improved domain modeling.

Test domain	**Webforum**		**News**
Arabic eval	*web1*	*web2*	*news*
Cluster domains	**40.11**	**40.60**	57.95
w/ uniform mix	39.63	40.15	**58.21**
Random partition	**40.43**	**40.63**	57.78
w/ uniform mix	40.31	40.15	**58.18**
Random sample	**39.94**	40.36	58.06
w/ uniform mix	39.88	**40.56**	**58.65**
Manual domains	39.67	**40.60**	57.63
w/ uniform mix	**39.93**	40.18	**58.00**
Basic elements	**39.83**	**40.63**	57.57
w/ uniform mix	34.84	35.82	**58.46**
No mix	38.64	39.21	56.59
Chinese eval	*web1*	*web2*	*news*
Cluster domains	**29.82**	**26.34**	37.22
w/ uniform mix	29.44	25.94	**37.47**
Random partition	**29.50**	**26.21**	36.83
w/ uniform mix	29.43	25.89	**36.95**
Random sample	**29.47**	**26.17**	**36.70**
w/ uniform mix	28.47	25.54	36.61
Manual domains	**30.17**	**26.86**	36.90
w/ uniform mix	29.25	26.36	**36.95**
Basic elements	**29.29**	**26.25**	36.17
w/ uniform mix	29.23	25.81	**36.63**
No mix	28.61	25.63	35.96

Table 5: Impact of linear mixture weights on translation quality as measured by BLEU: using domain knowledge when setting weights has an unreliable impact.

6 Findings: Impact on Translation Probability Estimates

Thus far, all our experiments have measured the impact of different types of linear mixtures on overall translation quality. But what is the impact of these various estimations methods on the learned phrasal translation probability distributions themselves? More specifically, how do translation probabilities estimated using linear mixtures differ from global "no mix" estimates? If linear mixtures do not only capture domain knowledge as suggested by Section 5, do they simply perform a form of smoothing? If so, how does this implicit smoothing compare to more explicit smoothing schemes for translation probabilities?

6.1 How do linear mixtures affect translation probabilities?

Let us compare translation probabilities estimated directly on the entire corpus $P_{nomix}(t|s)$, with linear mixtures $p_{mix}(t|s) = \sum_{k=1}^{K} \lambda_k p_k(t|s)$. The difference between $p_{mix}(t|s)$ and $p_{nomix}(t|s)$ is hard to represent analytically in the general case, but studying a few particular cases can help us gain a better understanding.

First, we observe that linear mixtures scale down the contribution of component-specific source phrases. Assume that the phrase s occurs only once in the training corpus, with translation t. By definition, there is a single mixture component k such that $p_{mix}(t|s) = \lambda_k$, which is likely to be smaller than $p_{nomix}(t|s) = 1$. In the slightly more general case where s occurs more than once, but always in the same component k, then $p_{mix}(t|s) = \lambda_k p_{nomix}(t|s)$, which has no impact on the ranking of translation candidates for s, but yields a smaller feature value for the decoder.

Second, let us consider the case of very frequent "general language" phrases. They should have roughly the same translation distributions in all mixture components: If the $p_k(t|s)$ distributions are the same in each component, the λ_k values learned do not matter, they have no impact on $p_{mix}(t|s) = p_{nomix}(t|s)$.

In between these extremes, the impact of linear mixtures depends on the frequency and ambiguity of translation candidates t across mixture components. For instance, let us assume that the mixture components are somehow defined such that they partition the translate candidates t of a phrase s into separate clusters. In that case, for each t, there

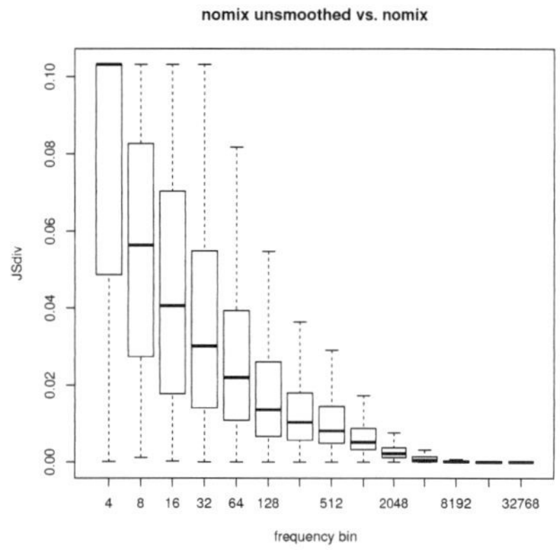

Figure 2: Comparing translation probability distributions with and without Kneser Ney smoothing for Chinese phrase-tables: boxplots of Jensen-Shannon divergences binned by source phrase frequency. For instance, the box and whisker at x = 8 represent the distribution of the values of Jensen-Shannon divergence between the unsmoothed and smoothed translation probability distribution for all Chinese phrases seen between 5 and 8 times during phrase extraction.

is a k such that $p_k(t|s) = p_{nomix}(t|s)$. The ranking of translation candidates t for s according to $p_{mix}(t|s)$ can be very different from $p_{nomix}(t|s)$, as controlled by the λ values used.

6.2 Smoothing Effects

As a basis for comparison, let us analyze the difference between unsmoothed relative frequencies and smoothed translation probabilities using a conventional smoothing scheme. We focus on the Kneser-Ney smoothing scheme (Chen et al., 2011), since it is used to smooth translation probabilities in the 'nomix" baseline as well as in all mixture components.

For seen phrase pairs (with $f(s,t) > 0$), the difference between Kneser-Ney estimates $p_{kn}(t|s)$ and relative frequency estimates $p_{rf}(t|s)$ can be written as:

$$p_{rf}(t|s) - p_{kn}(t|s) = \frac{D}{f(s)} - \frac{D * n(s) * p_b(t)}{f(s)} \quad (4)$$

where D is a discount coefficient, $f(s)$ is the raw frequency for source phrase s, $n(s)$ is the number of translation candidates for s in the phrase-table, $p_b(t)$ is a back-off distribution proportional to $n(t)$. The first term is a discount that increases when s is rare, while the second term adds some probability mass back, based on the frequency and degree of ambiguity of the target phrase t. Therefore, Kneser-Ney smoothing has primarily a discount effect, applied on rare source phrases. In addition, for more frequent and ambiguous phrases, the relative frequency can be adjusted up or down depending on how ambiguous s and t are.

Overall, there are some similarities between the impact of Kneser-Ney smoothing and linear mixtures, since one can expect that the translation distributions will diverge more from global relative frequencies for rare phrases than for frequent phrases. However, the discounting / down-scaling effects are controlled by very different parameters in linear mixtures than in Kneser-New smoothing. In order to better understand these differences in practice, an empirical analysis is required.

6.3 Empirical Comparison

How do linear mixtures and smoothing affect translation probabilities $p(t|s)$ in practice? We use the Jensen-Shannon divergence (Lin, 1991) to quantify the distance between (a) various mixture model estimates and (b) the global smoothed relative frequency estimates used in our baseline "no mix" experiments. In addition, we also compare the Kneser-Ney smoothed translation probabilities with unsmoothed relative frequencies, in order to highlight the difference between standard smoothing techniques and linear mixture models.

Figures 2 and 3 show the distributions of divergence values by source phrase frequencies for Chinese-English phrase-tables. The divergence from the global estimate is the largest for rare phrases in all cases, as expected based on previous Sections. However, the Figures also highlight the different behavior of linear mixtures compared to Kneser-Ney smoothing. The divergence values are much higher overall for the linear mixtures than for smoothing (note that the difference in range on the y axis in Figure 2 vs. Figure 3). In addition, linear mixtures have a large impact on translation probabilities not only on the rarest source phrases but also on relatively frequent phrases: in Figure 3, the median Jensen-Shannon divergence remains high for source phrases extracted up to 128 times from the training set[3], while the median value drops significantly as the frequency range in-

[3]Recall that we use multiple word alignment methods, so extraction counts are summed across all alignment methods.

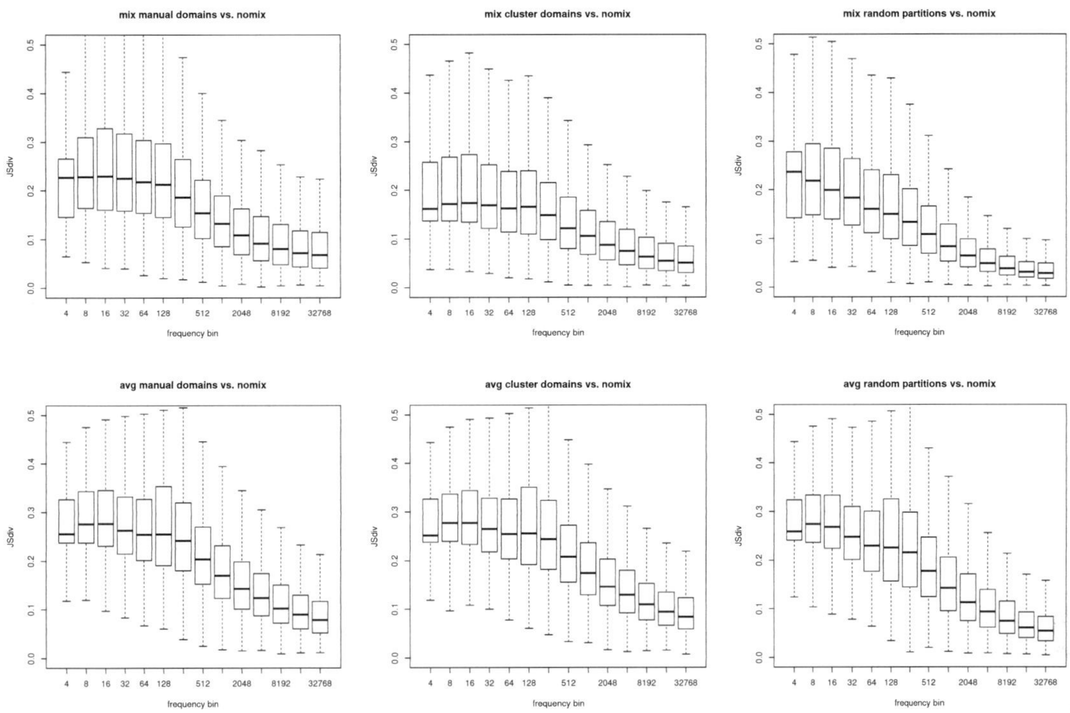

Figure 3: Comparing translation probability distributions of mixtures vs. "nomix" on Chinese webforum data, including EM weights (top row) and uniform weights (bottom row).

creases in Figure 2. In addition, uniform mixtures have an even higher impact on frequent phrases than mixtures based on EM weights.

Furthermore, the nature of mixture components used has a visible impact on the divergence distributions in Figure 3: random partitions yield lower divergences for very frequent source phrases.

Overall, the linear mixtures result in very different translation probability distributions than global estimates, including smoothed estimates. This suggests that standard smoothing techniques can be improved when learning from heterogeneous training data, and that mixture components are beneficial even when they do not explicitly capture domain distinctions.

7 Related work

Most previous work on domain adaptation in machine translation presupposes a clear-cut distinction between in-domain and out-of-domain data (Koehn and Schroeder, 2007; Foster and Kuhn, 2007; Duh et al., 2010; Bisazza et al., 2011; Haddow and Koehn, 2012; Sennrich, 2012b; Haddow and Koehn, 2012; Clark et al., 2012, among many others). We focused instead on a different less-studied question: how can we leverage training data drawn from a wide variety of sources, genres, time periods, to translate a domain represented by a small development set?

Many approaches focus on mapping the test domain to a single subset of the training data. In contrast, we show that the test domain can be flexibly represented by a mixture of many components. Yamamoto and Sumita (2007) cluster the parallel data using bilingual representations, and assign data to a single cluster at test time. Wang et al. (2012) show how to detect a known domain at test time in order to configure a generic translation system with domain-specific feature weights. Others select a subset of training data that is relevant to the test domain, using e.g., IR techniques (Hildebrand et al., 2005) or language model cross-entropy (Axelrod et al., 2011).

Closer to this work, Sennrich (2012a) proposes a sentence-level clustering approach to automatically recover domain distinctions in a heteorogeneous corpus obtained by concatenating data from a small number of very distant domains. The target domain was Alpine Club reports, while out of domain data sets comprised European parliament proceedings and movie subtitles. We address training conditions where the dimensions for organizing the training data are not as clear-cut, and show that partitions that do not attempt to mimick domain distinctions can improve translation quality. It would be interesting to see whether our conclusion holds in these more artificial training settings, and whether sentence-level corpus organization could help translation quality in our settings.

Finally, recent work shows that linear mixture weights can be optimized for BLEU, either directly (Haddow, 2013), or by simulating discriminative training (Foster et al., 2013). In this paper, we limited our studies to maximum likelihood and uniform mixtures, however, the various mixture component definitions proposed here can also be applied when maximizing BLEU.

8 Conclusion

We have presented an extensive study of linear mixtures for training translation models on very heterogeneous data on Arabic-English and Chinese-English translation tasks. In addition, we evaluated the robustness of our models across two distinct domains on the Arabic-English task.

Our results show that linear mixtures reliably and robustly improve the quality of machine translation. Improvements on the mixture-free baseline system range from 0.7 to 1.6 BLEU points depending on the components and weights used. While linear mixture translation models were originally proposed for domain adaptation tasks, we showed that linear mixtures that have no domain knowledge can perform as well or better than traditional mixtures meant to perform domain adaptation. This suggests that improvements with linear mixture models do not only stem from giving more weight to sections of the training data that are relevant to the test domain, as is assumed in a standard domain adaptation task. Improvements also come from averaging better generic estimates from the heterogeneous training data. In other words, in heterogeneous training settings, linear mixture models improve translation quality even though they do not perform domain adaptation. Finally, we show that while linear mixtures can be viewed as a smoothing technique, linear mixture estimates do not diverge from global estimates in the same way as Kneser-Ney smoothed translation probabilities. In particular, while smoothing primarily has a large discounting effect for rare source phrases, linear mixtures yield differences in translation probabilities for phrases with a wider range of frequencies.

These surprising results encourage us to rethink the use of mixture models, and opens up new ways of conceptualizing learning from heterogeneous data beyond domain adaptation. In future work, we will extend this study by varying the granularity of basic elements used to define mixture components, including sentences and phrases, and will explore how they compare with more general smoothing techniques.

Acknowledgments

This research was supported in part by DARPA contract HR0011-12-C-0014 under subcontract to Raytheon BBN Technologies. The authors would like to thank the reviewers and the PORTAGE group at the National Research Council.

References

Amittai Axelrod, Xiaodong He, and Jianfeng Gao. 2011. Domain adaptation via pseudo in-domain data selection. In *Proceedings of the Conference on Empirical Methods in Natural Language Processing*, EMNLP '11, pages 355–362.

Arianna Bisazza, Nick Ruiz, and Marcello Federico. 2011. Fill-up versus interpolation methods for phrase-based SMT adaptation. *International Workshop on Spoken Language Translation (IWSLT)*.

Leo Breiman. 1996. Bagging predictors. *Machine Learning*, 24(2):123–140.

Boxing Chen, Roland Kuhn, George Foster, and Howard Johnson. 2011. Unpacking and transforming feature functions: New ways to smooth phrase tables. In *Proceedings of Machine Translation Summit*.

David Chiang. 2012. Hope and fear for discriminative training of statistical translation models. *Journal of Machine Learning Research*, 13(1):1159–1187, April.

Jonathan H. Clark, Alon Lavie, and Chris Dyer. 2012. One system, many domains: Open-domain statistical machine translation via feature augmentation. In *Proceedings of the Conference of the Association for Machine Translation in the Americas*.

Kevin Duh, Katsuhito Sudoh, and Hajime Tsukada. 2010. Analysis of translation model adaptation in statistical machine translation.

George Foster and Roland Kuhn. 2007. Mixture-model adaptation for SMT. In *Proceedings of the Second Workshop on Statistical Machine Translation*, pages 128–135.

George Foster, Cyril Goutte, and Roland Kuhn. 2010. Discriminative instance weighting for domain adaptation in statistical machine translation. In *Proceedings of the Conference on Empirical Methods in Natural Language Processing*.

George Foster, Boxing Chen, and Roland Kuhn. 2013. Simulating discriminative training for linear mixture adaptation in statistical machine translation. In *Proceedings of the XIV Machine Translation Summit*, pages 183–190.

Michel Galley and Christopher D. Manning. 2008. A simple and effective hierarchical phrase reordering model. In *Proceedings of the Conference on Empirical Methods in Natural Language Processing*, EMNLP '08, pages 848–856.

Barry Haddow and Philipp Koehn. 2012. Analysing the effect of out-of-domain data on SMT systems. In *Proceedings of the Seventh Workshop on Statistical Machine Translation*, pages 422–432.

Barry Haddow. 2013. Applying pairwise ranked optimisation to improve the interpolation of translation models. In *Proceedings of the 2013 Conference of the North American Chapter of the Association for Computational Linguistics: Human Language Technologies*, pages 342–347.

Almut Silja Hildebrand, Matthias Eck, Stephan Vogel, and Alex Waibel. 2005. Adaptation of the translation model for statistical machine translation based on information retrieval. In *European Association for Machine Translation*.

Philipp Koehn and Josh Schroeder. 2007. Experiments in Domain Adaptation for Statistical Machine Translation. In *Workshop on Statistical Machine Translation*.

Philipp Koehn, Hieu Hoang, Alexandra Birch, Chris Callison-Burch, Marcello Federico, Nicola Bertoldi, Brooke Cowan, Wade Shen, Christine Moran, Richard Zens, Chris Dyer, Ondrej Bojar, Alexandra Constantin, and Evan Herbst. 2007. Moses: Open Source Toolkit for Statistical Machine Translation. In *Annual Meeting of the Association for Computational Linguistics (ACL), demonstration session*.

Jianhua Lin. 1991. Divergence measures based on the shannon entropy. *IEEE Trans. Inf. Theor.*, 37(1):145–151, September.

Rico Sennrich. 2012a. Mixture-modeling with unsupervised clusters for domain adaptation in statistical machine translation. In *16th Conference of the European Association for Machine Translation (EAMT)*.

Rico Sennrich. 2012b. Perplexity minimization for translation model adaptation in statistical machine tra. In *Thirteenth Conference of the European Chapter of the Association for Computational Linguistics (EACL)*.

Wei Wang, Klaus Macherey, Wolfgang Macherey, Franz Och, and Peng Xu. 2012. Improved domain adaptation for statistical machine translation. In *10th biennial conference of the Association for Machine Translation in the Americas (AMTA)*.

Hirofumi Yamamoto and Eiichiro Sumita. 2007. Bilingual cluster based models for statistical machine translation. In *Proceedings of the 2007 Joint Conference on Empirical Methods in Natural Language Processing and Computational Natural Language Learning (EMNLP-CoNLL)*, pages 514–523.

Author Index